The Greatest War

THE GREATEST WAR

Americans in Combat
1941–1945

Gerald Astor

PRESIDIO

For the late Donald I. Fine

Copyright © 1999 by Gerald Astor

Published by Presidio Press Inc.
505 B San Marin Drive, Suite 300
Novato, CA 94945-1340

Library of Congress Cataloging-in-Publication Data

Astor, Gerald, 1926–
    The greatest war : Americans in combat, 1941–1945 / Gerald Astor.
        p.   cm.
    Includes bibliographical references and index.
    ISBN 0-89141-695-1
       1. World War, 1939–1945—United States. 2. World War,
1939–1945—Personal narratives, American. 3. United States—Armed
Forces Biography. I. Title.
D769.A85   1999
940.54'1273—dc21   99-43632
                              CIP

Printed in the United States of America

Contents

Preface

When I told Gen. George Ruhlen that I intended to write a book covering the battles fought by Americans during World War II, he wrote to me, "How many pages are you projecting, 5,000 or squeeze it into 3,000?" His comment was well taken, for an encyclopedic account of what happened to Americans in World War II would require many volumes and in fact the historian Samuel Eliot Morison produced something on the nature of twenty books covering just the engagements of the Navy and the Marines.

However, my intention was not to cover the war from objective to objective nor was it to describe the details of strategy and tactics. I freely confess that, even in an oversize manuscript, I have omitted many hard-fought battles, units, and individuals who underwent the same hardships, terror, and sorrow, and who, in spite of their ordeals, overcame. Instead I hope to present a sense of what the American fighting man (women in World War II were restricted to clerical and service positions although as the book indicates, some nurses underwent much of what the men did) experienced in terms of what he thought, felt, saw, heard, and tried to do. Words on a page cannot match those moments under fire but by their own voices the soldiers, sailors, and airmen reveal the nature of that war well beyond anything shown in films or TV, except perhaps for *Saving Private Ryan*. (Even here one might quibble about the premise upon which the story unfolds.)

Having written six books on World War II, I am well aware that eye-witness accounts or oral histories have their weaknesses due to faulty memories, skewed perspectives, and the common human resort to self service. On the other hand, these same deficiencies also afflict official reports. In his letter to me, George Ruhlen remarked that a friend of his named Brewster commanded a task force whose mission was to regain possession of a crossroads during the Battle of the Bulge. "Some 20 accounts were written by 'historians' who were never there, most inaccurate, but only one writer ever contacted Colonel Brewster for his recollection of that action."

I expect there will be some who will dispute an individual's version of some events in this book, but I believe that by relying on as many sources and veterans as I have the essential truth of the experiences is correct. Although many of the sensations and the reactions of those on the scenes seem similar—the most replicated comment was "Suddenly, all hell broke loose—" there were significant differences from year to year, from campaign to campaign from area to area.

It was the biggest of all wars and those who fought the battles deserve to be heard.

Acknowledgments

So many people have shared their memories and experiences with me that I cannot cite them individually. Their words are credited to them in the text and to some extent through Roll Call.

I received special help from Paul Stillwell of the United States Naval Institute in Annapolis; Joseph Caver of the United States Air Force Historical Research Center at Maxwell Field, Alabama; Dr. David Keough at the United States Army History Library at Carlisle Barracks, Pennsylvania; the United States Naval Historical Center; Debbie Pogue at the United States Military Academy Library; Jim Altieri; William Cain; Tracy Derks; Len Lomell; Benjamin Mabry; Jason Poston.

Small portions of this book appeared in some of my previous writings on World War II.

1
"This Is Not a Drill!"

Martin Low, a twenty-two-year-old fighter pilot assigned to the U.S. Army Air Corps' 78th Pursuit Squadron at Wheeler Field on Oahu, recalled, "That night, I had too many as usual, woke up about 7:30, and then retrieved the newspaper that had been delivered to my room. I heard the unique sound of a dive bomber. The Navy would often make passes at Wheeler as part of their practice runs but when I looked up and saw the wheels were down I thought, 'that guy is really in a hurry.' Then I saw a 100-pound bomb leave the belly; they used spotting charges to mark their drops—and it landed right in the middle of a hangar. I thought, 'Oh my God, is that guy in trouble.' There was a tremendous explosion and at that moment I saw the rising sun insignia on the airplane."

John Alicki, a sergeant with the 53d Antiaircraft Brigade, his enlistment time up and ready to sail to the mainland for civilian life, remembered, "On that Sunday morning, they got me up a little early and held me to my promise to go to church. We were entering the church just before 8:00 A.M. when we heard in the distance something like firecrackers. As we went into the church the sound became more audible. When I stepped outside, I saw the red disk emblem on the sides of the planes."

Arthur Price, an aviation metalsmith with the Navy's Patrol Wing 2, had spent Saturday night with friends in an enlisted-housing area at Kaneohe, a newly constructed naval air station on the eastern shore of Oahu. A few days before, his unit had concluded an exercise that involved the Army Air Corps, with blue the designation for the Navy and red for their opposite numbers.

"I was awakened by enemy airplanes buzzing the housing area. There was an observation tower nearby, and to the Japanese it must have looked like an aircraft-control tower, because the first thing they did was strafe the tower. That woke us up.

"My first reaction was, 'I thought those maneuvers were over on Friday. What are they doing today? It must be the damned red army again.' The planes flew by, and then, all of a sudden, one of us said, 'That's not a star. That's a red ball. The only thing that's got that is Japanese. What the hell is he doing here?' At that point we didn't see any bullets flying around or anything, even though the planes were pretty low. Then we heard the rat-a-tat-tat of strafing on the beach and knew this was for real. We got into a car and drove to the squadron hangar arriving just about the time everybody else was showing up from the barracks nearby."

Seaman Adolph Leonard Seton, who had enlisted in 1939, was on deck. "That morning, when I saw a dark olive-drab plane with a 'meatball' insignia passing close aboard, astern of the *St. Louis* (a light cruiser) in the navy yard near Battleship Row, my first reaction was: 'That stupid bastard! He'll be court-martialed for this!' I thought it was a lone, berserk Japanese pilot, who somehow had gotten to Pearl and now would be in trouble with his navy and ours."

Ensign Ted Hechler Jr., a 1940 graduate of the United States Naval Academy, rolled over in his bunk aboard the cruiser USS *Phoenix* at 7:55 A.M., awakened by a loudspeaker that sounded an alert condition for a duty section. "I was not planning to respond. Instead, I grumbled something to my roommate. I complained about yet another damned drill and in Pearl Harbor on a Sunday morning, no less. In probably no more than ten or twenty seconds, this was all changed. I heard the sound of feet running on the deck overhead. Then came the sounds of the Klaxon horn and the announcement, 'All hands, general quarters.' This meant us, and we started to move out of our bunks. The voice on the loudspeaker now became shrill as the message changed to 'All hands, general quarters! Man the antiaircraft batteries. This is *not* a drill! The words 'This is not a drill' were repeated over and over, almost pleadingly." Indeed, earwitnesses cite that five-word declaration as having echoed and reechoed throughout the day.

Officially, the alarm went out between 0757 and 0758. At the Ford Island command center, as a color guard prepared to hoist the flag at 0755, Lt. Cmdr. Logan Ramsey of Patrol Wing 2 with responsibility for aerial reconnaissance of the ocean observed a plane diving over the station. He called upon a subordinate to get the aircraft number for disciplinary action. The latter reported a red band on the offender and moments later a black object dropped, followed by an explosion. Ramsey understood immediately. He charged into the radio room and ordered all operators at the sets to send in English the message, "Air Raid, Pearl Harbor, This is not a drill!"

Aboard the battleship *Oklahoma*, Ens. Paul H. Backus, USNA 1939, heard a slightly different version. "When the attack started, I was in my cabin, in my bunk, half-awake. The general alarm jerked me out of my dozing state. Its clamor was paralleled by an announcement over the general announcing system. 'This is a real Jap air attack and no shit.' I recognized the voice. It was Herb Rommel, a senior reserve ensign, who had grabbed the microphone on his way to his battle station in turret four. Only under the most unusual circumstances would an officer personally make an announcement in those days of formal battleship routine. And the use of obscene language by anyone over the announcing system was just unheard of. So this had to be real; moreover, right after the last word of the announcement, the whole ship shuddered. It was the first torpedo hitting our port side."

At the Marine barracks in the Pearl Harbor installation, the flag-raising ritual, replete with bandsmen and leathernecks was about to begin. Captain Samuel R. Shaw, USNA 1934, commanded A Company. "The old and the new guard marched on and were standing at ease, waiting to begin the ceremony of morning colors. The men were equipped with M1 rifles and each man had three clips of ball ammunition. The men looked idly around as a column of planes apparently guiding on the road from Honolulu passed over the main gate area, flying at a surprisingly low altitude, headed toward the ships moored along the length of Ford Island.

"The sergeant of the old guard, a man who had a lot of time in Shanghai and seen much of the Japanese forces there, did a double take, a long and careful second look. He turned to the officer of the day and said, 'Sir, those are Japanese war planes.'

"The officer in turn took a hard look and said, 'By God, you're right! Music, sound call "Call to arms!"' As the first notes from the bugle sounded, the harbor shook with the explosion of a torpedo in the side of one of our battleships. Without another command, the Marines in guard formation loaded their rifles, took aim and began firing."

Marine lieutenant Cornelius C. Smith Jr. had been drinking coffee in a mess hall when the first blast rocked the building and bounced his oversize coffee cup onto the deck. From the lanai he watched a dry dock erupt in flames and smoke hundreds of feet into the air. ". . . the bombs are falling. They whistle to earth with ear-shattering explosions. You can see the morning sunlight glisten on the bombs as they fall—silvery flashes like trout or mackerel jumping out of the water.

"Who said the Japs were cross-eyed, second-rate pilots who couldn't hit the broad side of a barn door? Maybe so, but I'm standing on our Navy Yard parade ground looking up at them, while they're making a sandpile out of the yard. They're kicking the hell out of Pearl Harbor, and it's enough to turn your stomach.

"Friends back home used to ask about the Japs. 'Hell, we could blow them out of the water in three weeks!' But here we are with our pants down and the striking force of our Pacific fleet is settling on the bottom of East Loch, Pearl Harbor. Who wouldn't be ashamed?"

Captain Brooke Allen, commander of a B-17 squadron based at Hickam Field, Hawaii, burst from his quarters, clad only in a bathrobe that flapped open as he waved his arms at an overhead raider while shouting, "I knew the little sons of bitches would do it on a Sunday! I knew it!" He quickly regained his composure, paused long enough to hastily don clothing, and rushed to the flight line to see if he could get planes airborne.

Immediately after he realized that those overhead were enemy planes, Martin Low said, "I got my best friend from across the hall and told him we're under attack. I started to drive in my car to the hangar and when I was about fifty feet from it, I heard a 'rat-a-tat-tat' against the side of the car. We jumped out, and hid under the theater. We watched in utter consternation. Because they were worried about sabotage, the planes had all been lined up in neat rows where they could be easily guarded. One burst of fire could hit all the ships in a line."

Gordon Austin, the CO for the 47th Pursuit Squadron temporarily housed at Haleiwa Field, a sandy strip ordinarily used for training exercises, had flipped a coin with his operations officer on whether the squadron would fly on 7 December. "It came down 'give the boys a day off.'" Austin and some friends flew to Molokai that Saturday evening and early Sunday went deer hunting. "Somebody rushed up to us and said, 'The Japanese have attacked Pearl Harbor.' We flew back in a B-18 [an obsolete precursor to the B-17] and as we crossed the channel from Molokai to Oahu, they were saying, 'Boy, they sure are making this realistic'—we'd had so many exercises like this. Navy planes used to come in on Sunday morning from off the carriers. They would come over Wheeler Field and when they got there they would run the prop pitch up and make an awful racket and wake everybody up about 7:30 in the morning. But over the radio we could hear, 'This is not a drill.' Still dubious, we decided to stay airborne and when we saw the smoke off Pearl Harbor, again the word was 'realistic.' We were over Diamond Head and suddenly we were in a sea of flak. The U.S. Navy was firing on us. My heart jumped up in my mouth. I never got scared like that the rest of the war. We landed at Wheeler Field. The P-40s' tails were gone. They were sitting nose up; all of them burning."

A flight of eighteen Navy aircraft, from the USS *Enterprise* steaming a course 200 miles due west, encountered similar trouble. Several were shot down by Japanese fighter cover before the Americans even discovered their home base was under attack. Others who had been instructed to land at Ford Island reeled under hails of shrapnel and bullets from friendly forces aiming at anything in the skies.

The same hostile reaction beset a flock of eleven B-17Es, the latest model four-engine Flying Fortresses that had taken off from a California airfield for the 2,400-mile trip to Hickam Field, first stop enroute to bolster the air arm in the Philippines. Their bombsights and machine guns were neatly packed in crates stowed in the fuselages. American sailors on ships and soldiers on the ground cut loose at the big bombers lumping them in as part of the attack.

Even as Brooke Allen struggled to take aloft one of the still airworthy B-17s from his squadron, a few minutes after eight o'clock, the Fortresses from the States approached Oahu. Major Truman H. Landon, the officer in command of the bombers, observed oncoming aircraft and assumed it was the Air Force out to welcome them. But when the "hosts" suddenly fired upon them, Landon realized they were Japanese. To conserve fuel for the 2,400-mile trip, the American planes carried a skeleton crew, not enough men to man their machine guns even if they had been installed. With no ability to defend themselves, the B-17s scattered, ducking into the clouds or opting for a quick touchdown at any open field, including an emergency landing on a golf course.

Richard Carmichael, one of almost a quarter of the 1936 graduates of West Point who elected an Air Corps career, commanded a B-17 bound for Hickam Field. "I had been stationed at Wheeler Field, flying P-12s and P-26s [early-model fighter planes] so as it broke dawn coming in to the Hawaiian Islands, I was pointing out all the various sights. We came around with Diamond Head on our right, Waikiki Beach, the Hawaina Hotel, the Royal Hawaiian, and the harbor. Somebody tapped me on the shoulder and said, 'Look at all those white puffs up there in the air ahead. I looked up and said, 'Well, the Navy must be practicing.' We had heard maybe they were having a maneuver of some sort on Sunday morning. We didn't get very excited about it until we had to get up really close.

"We got close enough to hear the control tower was under fire. By this time we could see airplanes. We alerted and I called in and asked for landing instructions. The answer came back, 'Land from west to east, but use caution, the field is under attack.' We had to fly around the ships and as we started into this pattern on the downwind leg, the navy started shooting at us. At the same time, somebody said, 'We have a pursuit airplane, a Japanese plane on our tail.' Things had gone to hell in a handbasket. Everything was happening. All the battleships, all that smoke there—they had already been hit and were on fire.

"I said, 'to hell with this. I am going up to Wheeler and see if I can get into my old home base.' To get away from the fighter on our tail, I remembered there were always clouds over the Koolau Mountain Range on the eastern side of Oahu. I got up in the base of the clouds before this guy shot us down, or maybe he wasn't even shooting at us.

"We could see the whole hangar line of Wheeler was on fire. I thought about fuel and another place to land. I checked with Sergeant Carter and he said, 'We have about forty-five minutes of fuel left.' That would give me enough time to fly around the north end of the Koolau Mountains and take a look at Waimanalo, our old gunnery camp. In the meantime, someone spotted another field and said 'There are U.S. fighters down there, P-40s at our old officers' swimming beach, Haleiwa,' but I continued on down to Waimanalo. When I got there, there was an airplane on fire on the runway, one of Ted Landon's. There were PT boats in the harbor and some were on fire. The place was under attack and I decided to go back to the fighter squadron at Haleiwa and landed there.

"The field at Haleiwa was now under attack and we taxied over to the trees to get close enough to [hide] our B-17s out of the way. We got out and the sergeants started unloading the guns and mounting them. Jim Twaddell and I looked up and saw a fighter coming right down the runway, firing at us. We decided to take cover in a hell of a hurry. This was right close to the beach and we ran there, saw a big rock with an open space under it.

"I said, 'Come on, Jim, we'll get under the rock.' We didn't know it but the waves were out at that particular time. Just as we got under, here came the waves. They almost drowned us. It ruined our watches and everything. There we were, the brave squadron commander and the weather officer, hiding under the rocks, and all the sergeants were out trying to shoot down the enemy."

Lieutenant General Walter C. Short, commissioned after graduation from the University of Illinois in 1902 and a veteran of the American Expeditionary Force in France during World War I, commanded the Army's Hawaiian Department whose primary responsibility was to protect the bases there and the fleet. Like his opposite number, Adm. Husband E. Kimmel, Short arrived on station in February 1941.

On the evening of 6 December Short and his wife had attended a party at the Schofield Barracks Officers' Club, leaving the festivities an hour or so before midnight. The route home took them by Pearl Harbor, crammed with ships ablaze with lights. Short remarked to an associate, "What a target that would make!" But it was a casual aside rather than a foreboding.

Lieutenant Colonel James A. Mollison, chief of staff for the local Air Corps, who like so many others at first thought the explosions came from Navy or Marine pilots who inadvertently dropped ordnance, had rushed to his headquarters at Hickam Field. From there he telephoned Short's chief of staff, Col. Walter Phillips, still trying to decide the source of the noise. When Mollison informed him the islands and bases were under attack, the incredulous Phillips snorted, "You're out of your mind, Jimmy. What's the matter, are you drunk? Wake up, wake up!"

Exasperated, Mollison held the receiver out to enable Phillips to hear the sounds of bombs and machine guns. Even then Phillips vacillated, until a second staff officer called with the news. The chief of staff scurried next door to Short's quarters.

"I heard the first bombs," said Short, "and my first idea was that the Navy was having some battle practice, either that they hadn't told me about or that I'd forgotten that they had told me about it. When some more dropped I went out on the back porch to take a look at what was going on, and about that time the chief of staff came running over to my quarters around three minutes after eight and said he had just gotten a message . . . that it was the real thing."

Short hurried to his headquarters at Fort Shafter where wounded men already lay on stretchers beside the base hospital and soldiers frantically dug trenches. While the general now knew Pearl Harbor itself was under attack he had no knowledge of events there since the anchorage was not visible from Shafter. A colonel whose home overlooked the harbor arrived to breathlessly inform Short, "I just saw two battleships sunk."

"That's ridiculous!" insisted Short.

When the attack began, Adm. Husband E. Kimmel, a 1904 graduate of the Naval Academy and commander in chief of the United States fleet (Cin-CUS), also was in his residence dressing as he awaited confirmation of a report that one of his destroyers, the USS *Ward* had sunk a submarine trespassing near the islands. He was on the telephone with the duty officer at naval headquarters when a yeoman burst into the latter's office shouting, "There's a message from the signal tower saying the Japanese are attacking Pearl Harbor and this is no drill." The officer relayed the shocking news. Kimmel slammed down the receiver and as he buttoned his white uniform jacket ran outside. From the lawn of the residence of Mrs. John B. Earle, wife of a navy captain next door, Kimmel could clearly see Battleship Row being hammered, bombers circling the hapless vessels, dumping tons of devastating explosives.

Mrs. Earle recalled, "[they] could plainly see the rising suns on the wings and would have seen the pilots' faces had they leaned out." She described the admiral as watching "in utter disbelief and completely stunned," his face "as white as the uniform he wore."

Kimmel would say, "I knew right away that something terrible was going on, that this was not a casual raid by just a few stray planes. The sky was full of the enemy." Horrified, he saw "*Arizona* lift out of the water, then sink back down—way down."

It is unlikely that the appalled admiral actually realized the devastation of what he witnessed. A bomb had struck the *Arizona* close to its No. 2 turret and detonated the forward magazine. The blast wiped out nearly 1,000 men including the skipper Capt. Franklyn Van Valkenburg and RAdm. Isaac Kidd, commander of the First Battleship Division. The explosion showered the adjoining repair vessel, USS *Vestal* with debris—pieces of the battlewagon, whole human bodies, some alive, legs, arms, and heads. The force of the eruption hurled some 100 men from the *Vestal* overboard, including her skipper, Comdr. Cassin B. Young. Dripping oil and seawater he clambered back aboard to cancel an "abandon ship" order. For the hapless *Arizona* the torment continued with more bombs and torpedoes until it settled in the harbor, with fewer than 200 survivors from a complement of 1,400.

Paul Backus, aroused on the *Oklahoma* by the profanity uttered by a fellow ensign over the loudspeaker, had to shake awake his cabinmate, Ens. Lewis Bailey Pride Jr. who slept through both the general alarm and the announcement. "We threw on some clothes. While doing so, we asked each other how in hell the Japs managed to get in without being detected by the PBYs [from Patrol Wing 2]. These were the big seaplanes based at Ford Island. Every morning, these flying boats used to roar down the channel and stagger into the air for their daily surveillance patrol. When the battleships were in port, this very early takeoff was damned annoying. As the large planes applied full power down past Battleship Row, they awakened all the junior officers. (The senior officers didn't mind because they lived ashore.)"

Actually, three PBYs from Arthur Price's squadron had flown the customary search mission. One of them spotted the submarine outside the harbor and dropped a smoke bomb as part of the attack upon the invader by the destroyer *Ward*. However, the PBYs, on patrol since four or five in the morning, did not range to the north, the direction from which the Japanese convoy approached the islands.

Backus made his way topside. Unknown to him, he had been the last to see his friend Bailey Pride. He saw a Marine acquaintance endeavoring to close a hatch. No one who survived the attack would ever again see that man alive either. Hurrying by the gun deck where the 5-inch/25 antiaircraft mounts were located he noticed the sailors were not manning the weapons. "I asked why. It turned out that the boxes containing the ready ammunition were padlocked and there was no compressed air for the rammers. The padlocks were broken and the ammunition hand-rammed into the breeches. Then the gun crews discovered there were no firing locks on the breech blocks. They had been removed and were down in the armory being cleaned for a scheduled admiral's inspection. As a result, not a shot was fired from these guns before the ship rolled over.

"The gunnery officer, Lt. Comdr. Harry H. Henderson, wanted to keep a portion of the antiaircraft battery manned and ready while we were in port. He is reported to have been overruled by the captain. Apparently, Captain Bode believed the threat of an attack was insignificant, and it was more important to get ready for the inspection that was scheduled for Monday. As part of our preparation for the inspection, some of our blisters were open when the attack took place. The manhole covers had been removed in some instances so that the blisters could be aired out for a later cleaning. Obviously our resistance to flooding was minimal when the torpedoes hit. When the blisters dipped under, flooding had to be massive.

"The *Arizona* blew up at about this time. A huge spout of flame and gray-black smoke shot skyward way above her foretop. The explosion sounded like many depth charges going off simultaneously. I found out later that the only *Arizona* officer forward of her stack to survive was Ens. Douglas Hein. A classmate of mine, Doug told me that he was with the admiral and captain on the flag bridge when the explosion occurred. When he regained consciousness, he was in the water, not knowing how he got there. He was badly burned on his back, head, and hands, but otherwise intact. Doug recovered fully, but the tragedy is that he was lost later in an aircraft accident.

"About the same time, the lines securing the *Oklahoma* to the *Maryland* had started to pop as the list on the ship increased rapidly. The executive officer [Comdr. J. W. Kenworthy] watching all of this from his station, gave the word to abandon ship. This word was picked up and passed along topside by shouts. I think by this time power had been lost and the general announcing system was out. In retrospect, fewer lives might have been lost if those of us topside had made more effort to get the word to those below decks to abandon ship.

"I can recollect distinctly only that first torpedo explosion that helped roust me out of my bunk, although there had been at least four or five hits by this time. Ensign Norm Hoffman counted five torpedo hits during the time he was running from the wardroom to his turret via its lower handling room and the climb up the center column to the turret booth. There were two more hits while he was in the booth testing telephones before William F. Greenaway, the leading boatswain's mate in the second division, put his head up the hatch in the overhang and relayed Commander Kenworthy's order to abandon ship." The severe list of the *Oklahoma* indicated the mortally wounded battleship was about to capsize.

"Before going over the side," said Backus, "I remember seeing some of the *Maryland*'s guns firing with *Oklahoma* sailors helping to man them. Avoiding the torpedoes and the possibility of a quick rollover, I went over the high side, which was the starboard side. I can't remember climbing over a bulwark or going through the lifelines, but I do remember sliding down the side of the ship behind some members of the Marine detachment and ending up on the antitorpedo blister. Once on the blister, I ran forward a few frames before going into the water between the ships. I remember thinking that I probably could not make the climb from the water to the *Maryland*'s blister, that there might be a boat tied up under the *Maryland*'s bow into which I could climb and, if not, Ford Island's shore wasn't that far away."

Survivor Backus said, "The water between the ships was covered with fuel oil, but it was not burning as it was in other parts of the harbor. The swim up to and around the bow of the *Maryland* was uneventful. There *was* a *Maryland* motor whaleboat tied directly under her huge starboard anchor. Two

Oklahoma sailors, one a boatswain's mate, second class, were already in the boat. Another joined us soon after I climbed in. I had a look at the engine and found it was a new diesel with which I was unfamiliar. I could not find the starter. All three sailors indicated that they, too, were strangers to the engine, so the four of us sat in the boat until there was a lull. I remember looking up at the gigantic anchor right over our heads and thinking that if a bomb hit the *Maryland*'s forecastle we would have had it. (I was told afterward that a bomb had hit her forecastle but obviously it did not damage the chain stopper.) [During] the lull the boatswain's mate remembered where the starter switch was. I told him to take over as coxswain, I'd be engineer, and the other two would help survivors out of the water.

"We made at least two, possibly three or four, trips between the waters around the *Oklahoma* and the Ford Island fuel dock. A few bigger boats were in the area. There were quite a few people in the water. They were covered with fuel oil. Many were choking and spitting. The *Oklahoma*'s senior medical officer, Comdr. Fred M. Rohow, an older man, was in trouble. Dr. Rohow either had been wounded or had been hurt getting off the ship. We got him and some others aboard for one boatload. At one point while we were retrieving survivors, I realized the guns were roaring again. I looked up and could see what looked like bombers at high altitude. Even more nerve-wracking was the shrapnel from our own guns which was splashing all around us. All of this was associated with the second wave of the Japanese attack."

Backus and his comrades pulled a "Filipino or Chamoro" steward from the water. "He had just come out of the porthole of a second-deck compartment on the starboard side. The porthole was by this time several feet under water, the ship having rolled all the way over to port. He was almost in a state of shock. He had had to fight his way out against the surging flood of water entering through the porthole. There were many others in the compartment for whom he did not have much hope. No others surfaced in the immediate vicinity during the next few minutes.

"On our last run by the overturned hull of the *Oklahoma*, I noticed an officer in dress whites, with spy glass and white gloves standing on the overturned hull near the stern. There were a couple of sailors with him in undress whites. As we swung in close aboard, I realized the officer was Ens. John 'Dapper Dan' Davenport, a good friend and classmate. He was the junior officer of the deck and was manning the quarterdeck. As the ship rolled over, he and the sailors on watch with him just rotated their station to keep up with the roll. At that point there was plenty of room in the boat for the three of them but 'Dapper Dan' refused to ride with us. The boat was filthy with oil and he would have nothing to do with us. He and his watch were taken off a short time later by, presumably, a much cleaner boat.

"There were no more *Oklahoma* survivors evident in the water. We delivered our last load to the fuel dock, my crew left me when I indicated I wanted to go back out to help around the *California*. There seemed to be fires in the water alongside her and some swimmers in the water in the vicinity. Other boats were headed for them and, I believe, pulled them out. We beached the *Maryland* whaleboat by the fuel dock and went ashore." Hundreds of bedraggled men, blackened with oil, burned, wounded, exhausted, staggered ashore, paddling there on their own or else rescued by a small flotilla of boats crisscrossing the harbor to pluck sailors from the water.

Equally beset by the marauding enemy aircraft, the battleship *West Virginia* absorbed a torpedo during the second pass at Battleship Row. Then another pair struck home and the ship listed to port just as flames broke out in a turret, followed by another massive explosion. The *West Virginia*'s skipper Capt. Mervyn Bennion and her navigator Lt. Comdr. T. T. Beattie met on the bridge to determine what action to take. As the pair discussed their options, a half-dozen torpedoes wracked the hull and a pair of bombs exploded topside. A large chunk of shrapnel ripped open Bennion's stomach. As he lay dying, another officer summoned help. A chief pharmacist's mate applied first aid and mess attendant Dorie Miller arrived to help remove the stricken officer from further danger. Bennion died within a few minutes. Miller, an African American and like all blacks restricted to steward ranks, with no training, then helped man a machine gun. Credited with knocking down a pair of enemy aircraft, Miller won a Navy Cross for heroism, but only after pressure from outside the Navy.

As an assistant control officer for antiaircraft aboard the cruiser *Phoenix*, Ted Hechle, while responding to "general quarters," moved into high gear at the sound of the ship's .50-caliber machine guns yammering overhead. He raced up three decks above the main one to his station in "sky forward," an aerie above the bridge to control the four 5-inch/25 guns of the starboard battery. "I was propelled on my journey by the sight of a torpedo plane that flew past the *Phoenix* at deck level. It carried a big red ball on the side. As I reached my station, our battery was already training out. The awnings which were still up from the admiral's inspection had to be taken down so the guns could train out. Locks were chopped off the ammunition boxes.

"Because of the lack of high-level horizontal bombers—the kind of planes I was capable of directing fire at—during the initial stages of the attack—I found myself an unwilling occupant of a front-row seat from which to witness the proceedings. The sky seemed filled with diving planes and the black bursts of exploding antiaircraft shells. Our batteries were among those firing shells in 'local control' which meant the fire originated from the guns themselves. The Japanese planes were too close for us to take advantage of the more sophisticated automatic control which was normally provided by my station. In essence, the guns were laying out a pattern of steel in the hope that the Japanese planes would fly through it and be damaged in the process. I have often described the experience as akin to trying to swat an angry swarm of bees in the confines of a telephone booth. To make matters worse, our shells were set with a minimum peacetime fuse setting which would not permit them to explode until they had reached a safe distance from the ship. In addition, some of the fuses were defective with the result that the exploded projectiles were coming down ashore. Our best weapons under these conditions were the machine guns, which accounted for a number of enemy aircraft.

"By shortly after 8:00 A.M. the harbor was a riot of explosions and gunfire. I looked at the battle line from which huge plumes of black smoke were rising. As I watched, I saw the *Arizona* wracked by a tremendous explosion. Her foremast came crashing down into the inferno. Since I was in the corresponding station in my own ship, I naturally thought about what my own fate might be in the next few minutes.

"Bombs were exploding on the Naval air station at Ford Island and the Army air base at Hickam Field. A Japanese torpedo plane came down our port side. It couldn't have been more than 150 feet above the water and looked as if the pilot had throttled down, having just launched his torpedo at the battle line. He banked to the left as he got opposite us, as if to turn away. I could see .50-caliber tracer slugs going right out to the plane and passing through the fuselage at the wing joint. Suddenly, flames shot out from underneath, and he continued his turn and bank to the left until he had rolled over onto his back. A great cheer went up from our crew, because his demise was apparent. Unfortunately, he crashed onto the deck of the seaplane tender *Curtiss,* inflicting a number of casualties.

"Another plane came in, low over the water, toward our starboard quarter. This time I saw a cross fire of tracers from the *Phoenix* and other ships. There was an explosion on the plane and in the next instant there was nothing left but its debris descending to the water. Moments later, I heard the 'zing' of a bullet whistling by. Later, we discovered a hole in the shield of a range finder below us. The air was so full of flying bullets and shrapnel by that time it was impossible to tell the source, but that bullet constituted the total damage inflicted on the *Phoenix* that day."

At Kaneohe, aviation metalsmith Arthur Price Jr. came upon a scene of ruins. "The first wave of planes had strafed all the PBYs we had sitting out on the beaching ramp, and they were all burned. Our fire trucks were there, but they couldn't do much with burning aluminum. Even the planes out on the water were on fire. One of our boys who had been on watch in a plane out in the bay was strafed, but he had sense enough to crawl onto the ramp. I went over and picked him up, but he was already dead. I put him in the back of the squadron truck and wrapped him in a cloth. There was nothing else I could do for him, so I just left him there.

"Meanwhile, our men were setting up machine guns outside the VP-14 hangar. I went over to try to help out, and then somebody shouted, 'Here comes a group of bombers.' Our skipper said, 'Let's get the hell out of here.' So he and I and another man jumped into the truck and we started heading over toward another hangar. When we got there, we looked up, and there came a formation of eight to twelve bombers, flying in a beautiful Vee formation at about 1,200 feet. As soon as we saw them approaching the hangar, we got out of the truck and dove under some construction material. The planes got right above us and let their bombs go. That was the end of our new hangar.

"About that time, a Zero fighter came down. We thought he was going to strafe us, because his guns were going, but evidently the pilot had been shot already. He just flew straight into the ground right ahead of our truck, shooting the whole way. He hit the ground maybe 500 feet from us, and was thrown out of the plane. He was dead, of course, and all chopped up, so we threw him in the back of the truck. So here we were carrying the dead American from the seaplane ramp and the dead Japanese from the Zero.

"We drove back to our hangar, and there encountered Chief Aviation Ordnanceman John Finn, a man who was later awarded the Medal of Honor for his heroism that day." Finn had mounted a machine gun atop a construction scaffolding to shoot at the enemy planes. Blazing gasoline surrounded him but he kept firing until hit by strafers. "He [Finn] was all shot up—looked as if he'd been peppered with small stuff, .30-caliber machine guns. So it was back into the truck once more to take the chief to sick bay. He and the skipper and I were in the front, and the two corpses were in back.

"When we got to our destination, wounded men were flaked out all through the passageways because there were so many of them that there was no place to put them. I thought the medical people would keep Chief Finn there, he was in such bad shape. But he said, 'No, I just want to get patched up.' He wouldn't stay. Twenty minutes later he was right down at the skeleton of the hangar getting the ordnance things organized.

"By nine o'clock, when things had died down [at Kaneohe but not immediately around Pearl Harbor] our three PBYs came back from patrol and they didn't have a scratch on them. Those were the only planes we had left, because we lost thirty-three of our thirty-six that morning."

Returning from the hunting expedition, Gordon Austin met Lt. George S. Welch, the assistant operations officer of the 47th Pursuit Squadron. "Where have you been?" asked Austin.

"I've been shooting down Japs," Austin quoted Welch. "There's one off the road there." Inspection of the wreckage revealed the bodies of three crewmen from a torpedo bomber. Welch and a fellow pilot, Lt. Kenneth Taylor, had spent the evening carousing, and in an all-night poker game that did not break up until shortly before 8:00 A.M. When Japanese gunners strafed the officers' club, the pilots jumped into their car and sped off to Haleiwa.

The Japanese apparently were unaware of the field for it went untouched. As elsewhere the American aircraft were, in Taylor's words, "lined up in perfect line right down one side of the field. At Haleiwa we had no revetments, and we just parked them there just to look nice and also keep them bunched so we could guard them easier." However, word of the assault had reached the base and by the time Welch and Taylor came to the flight line, crews were already loading the fighters.

The two roared off in their P-40s and headed for Wheeler Field to arm their guns with .50-caliber ammunition. Landing between attacks by the Japanese they stocked their weapons and went in search of the foe. In a scrap with half a dozen or so enemy planes, Welch said, "We took off directly into them and shot down some. I shot down one right on Lieutenant Taylor's tail." Subsequently, the pair landed, rearmed, and headed for the Marines' Ewa Field. "At that time there was a whole string of planes looking like a traffic pattern," said Taylor. "We went down and got in the traffic pattern and shot down several planes there. I know for certain I had shot down two planes or perhaps more."

Adolph Seton, passing out sound-powered phones for antiaircraft stations on the *St. Louis,* was struck by the response of his shipmates. "Our crew acted as though this was another drill except for outbursts of cheering every time a plane was hit within our limited firing bearings. Seton's skipper, Capt. George A Rood recalled that no one issued an order to commence firing. "Our battery people knew what was up, knew what to do and [they] took the initiative and opened fire with everything that would bear." Subsequently, the *St. Louis* claimed six enemy planes shot down but officially received credit for three.

While the gunners blazed away, Rood conned his ship toward the open sea with as much speed as his reduced boiler power could generate. "I knew that if any Jap submarines were present, they would be lying off the entrance ready to torpedo outgoing vessels and so we buckled on speed." As the cruiser headed for the open sea a steel cable from a dredge blocked the way. Captain Rood called for full speed ahead and he says his ship "hit that cable a smashing blow and snapped it like a violin string."

Churning through the water at twenty-two knots in an eight-knot zone, the *St. Louis* cleaved through the narrow channel at the harbor entrance. At flank speed, the cruiser nevertheless made an easy prey since the narrow lane rendered torpedo evasion tactics impossible—Kimmel's predecessor had described the harbor as "a goddamn mousetrap."

Indeed, an enemy midget submarine lurking at the entrance launched a perfectly lined up pair of torpedoes at the oncoming cruiser. The lead missile set to hit on the starboard side apparently ran too deep for it struck a spit of coral and exploded, soaking crewmen with seawater. The second one, possibly knocked off course by that detonation, veered into coral and also blew up. Had either missile found its mark and the *St. Louis* foundered, the hulk would have bottled up the harbor.

Lightened by the release of its tin fish, the midget sub popped to the surface. Gun crews from the cruiser instantly opened fire and claimed a hit on the conning tower of the raider, which disappeared. As the *St. Louis* set its course for the open sea, the 7 December 1941, raid passed into history with a finale of strafing sorties on airfields. Some two hours after the first Japanese planes roared over the anchorage, the last of them vanished to rendezvous with the carriers. They left behind 8 battleships, 3 light cruisers, 3 destroyers, and 4 auxiliary craft that either sank, capsized, were heavily damaged, or less so. The Naval air arm reported 13 fighters, 21 scout bombers, 46 patrol bombers, and a handful of other planes lost. The Hawaiian Air Force wrote off 4 B-17s, 12 B-18s, a pair of A-20s [two-engine bombers], 32 P-40s, 20 P-36s, plus a considerable number of other aircraft including 88 pursuit or fighters and 34 bombers damaged. In addition, installations catering to both Navy and Air Corps needs had been ravaged. Worst of all was the cost in lives, more than 2,400, with 2,000 from the Navy. Another 1,178 required treatment for injuries, horrible burns, and grievous injury to limbs and organs. The raiders escaped with only 29 planes down, 1 full-size submarine, and 5 midget subs destroyed.

Within two hours after the raid began, the Pearl Harbor anchorage was choked with sunken or smashed ships that for days oozed oil whose fires would burn for weeks. Ashore, the Navy docks and maintenance shops lay in ruins. At Wheeler and Hickam Fields, along with lesser airfields, heaps of often barely recognizable scorched metal sat smoldering. Hangars, operations buildings, and barracks showed gaping holes if not reduced to piles of debris. Amid frantic efforts to rescue those trapped on sunken or blazing ships and buildings could be heard the sirens of ambulances, the occasional drone of aircraft, and the sporadic discharge of weapons in the hands of trigger-sensitive defenders who now believed a full-scale invasion might be imminent.

Brooke Allen, the B-17 pilot who first tried to get off the ground with an empty Fort, admitted that in his haste he flooded an engine and rather than try to make it on only three abandoned the effort. On a second attempt, with a bomb load, he went in search of the Japanese carriers. "I found an American one to the south. With a personal feeling that the Japanese had come from the north, I made a maximum range search. The weather was bad and I'd have to get down on the deck at times and up to altitude also to take maximum advantage of visibility. With only one airplane it would have been unusually fortunate if I had stumbled across the task force. I returned with a minimum of fuel and a heart full of disgust that I had been unable to locate them."

Martin Low recalled getting airborne in a P-40 shortly after 10:00 A.M. and scouring the skies for signs of the enemy. "When I got near Pearl Harbor, they opened up on me and I realized they were a little tender. The Japanese were long gone. The rest of the day, we just sat around. We had an alcoholic colonel in command and every five minutes he claimed there were Japanese fighters over the waterworks, the electrical plant, or whatever. We kept busy filling every container with water, moving the remaining planes into revetments, setting up tents.

"At 8:00 P.M. our squadron went to a naval air station on the other side of the island to take over planes that had been at the gunnery camp [Haleiwa]. We traveled in a staff car in a total blackout. We had our .45s pointed out of the windows. Every wave that hit the beach we saw as another landing barge."

Enroute to Pearl Harbor on 7 December was a trio of U.S. submarines. Aboard the *Pompano* sailed a former Naval Academy football star, Slade Cutter, a native of Chicago. "On the morning of the seventh, about five minutes of 8:00 A.M." remembered Cutter "the radioman came up through the conning tower, reached up, and handed the officer of the deck a dispatch, which read, 'Air raid on Pearl Harbor. This is no drill.'" On the *Pompano*, said Cutter, were several officers traveling to take command of other submarines and they along with his own skipper, Lewis Parks, had served in China. "They got to talking about the Japs: 'That's just like those yellow bastards. They'd do something like that.' And they believed it right away."

Because of engine trouble, the *Pompano* had been delayed for repairs. Had the sub arrived on schedule, 6:00 A.M. at Pearl Harbor, *Pompano* would have become another target of opportunity in the anchorage. The vessel, however, still came under fire. "We were about 135 miles northeast of Pearl Harbor on the great circle route from San Francisco to Pearl, when we were attacked by Japanese aircraft." The *Pompano* and its companions, in an attempt to make up for lost time, hastened toward the islands, traveling on the surface. "We had pumped out all of our variable water, to lighten us, to make more speed through the water. As soon as this message came in, Parks said, 'Rig ship for dive and compensate. Get the water back in so we can dive.'

"We weren't done when we got attacked by the first wave coming back [from Pearl Harbor]. And we were strafed. The other submarines went under. We weren't damaged."

By the time the three submarines reached Hawaii, it was night and they were instructed to submerge until the following evening. Escorted by a destroyer they headed into the harbor. "We didn't know anything that had gone on," said Cutter. "We had no idea of the damage. The first thing we saw on the reef was a Navy fighter. It had been crash-landed but it didn't look like it had been damaged very much. A little farther, Hickam Field was just burning. Ford Island, that was burning. Right ahead of us was the *Nevada*, which was beached. Then we turned the corner and saw the battleships, this way and that—the masts—all of them didn't sink on an even keel. We passed the floating dry dock where the *Shaw* had been blown up. When we came closer, there was the *Oklahoma*, upside down. The *Utah*, upside down and the *Arizona* was still burning and it looked like there were six inches of oil on the water. It was a very depressing sight. We got into port to tie up. There were a bunch of people on dock but we couldn't get people to handle our lines. It was like they were all in a daze."

A day after the attack, Gordon Austin and the commander of the 14th Pursuit Air Wing, Brig. Gen. Howard Davidson toured Pearl Harbor in the company of an admiral. Austin remembered Davidson telling the admiral, "Except for the human misery, the human disaster, the human losses in the attack, it is the best thing that ever happened to the U.S. Navy."

"As a young captain I was just gasping for air hearing that comment to a black shoe [seagoing rather than aviator] sailor. Davidson said, 'If the war had started and you people had gone to sea with all your battleships, the Japs would have sunk them all at sea and you would have lost all hands.'" Davidson had a point in that a few weeks later, the British dreadnoughts *Prince of Wales* and *Repulse* were both sunk in the South China Sea by enemy aircraft with heavy loss of life. The enemy was long gone, having successfully achieved its first strategy, neutralization of the U.S. fleet.

2
Preattack Maneuvers

By the mid-1930s, the more aggressive elements of the Japanese industrial complex, responding both to an Imperial tradition and the ravages of a worldwide depression, dominated political policy in the country. In 1931, a bogus incident in the Chinese province of Manchuria provoked a full-scale attack. Japan conquered the unorganized defenders and created a puppet, "independent" state called Manchukuo.

Over the next few years, a series of attempted coups and assassinations shook Japan. Ultimately, the proponents of a greater Japan crushed the opposition. Expansion became the goal. Achievement mandated a substantially larger army and navy. The Nipponese government circumvented the limitations of the naval treaties, secretly building a pair of huge battleships, the *Yamato* and the *Musashi*. These were much bigger than anything launched by the United States. If the United States had matched these dreadnoughts it could not have moved them through the Panama Canal.

To Western diplomats and military strategists the Sino-Japanese War of 1937 and the bellicose pronouncements from Japan ordained a collision course between East and West. Americans sympathized with the Chinese as newsreels showed the ravages of war inflicted upon civilians by the Japanese invaders. In 1937, when Japanese bombers sank the U.S. Navy gunboat *Panay* on the Yangtze River, Americans turned angry and hostility remained even after an apology and indemnity payment. Diplomats, missionaries, business representatives, and service personnel in China perceived a growing arrogance that bordered on contempt from Japanese military whom they encountered.

Satisfaction of Japanese aims could not be accomplished with indigenous resources and the only way to sustain the Empire lay in a southern advance. That route meant bumping heads with the British, Dutch, French, and American interests rather than the Soviet Union, a northern military threat but less of a reservoir of scarce raw materials. The new power in the Far East threatened to slam doors opened to Western trade by gunboats in the nineteenth century. A newspaper reputed to speak for the foreign office in 1940 bluntly asserted, "Japan must remove all elements in East Asia which will interfere with its plans. Britain, the United States, France, and the Netherlands must be forced out of the Far East. Asia is the territory of the Asiatics."

Along with more bites of Chinese territory, a further series of actions by the Japanese affronted the Western democracies. On the heels of Germany's smashing defeat of the French in June 1940, Japanese soldiers moved into northern French Indochina [what would become Vietnam, Laos, and Cambodia] and few doubted that the troops would soon march southward. In retaliation for the invasion of Indochina, President Franklin D. Roosevelt declared an embargo on further shipments of scrap iron and steel. By the end of the year, the sanctions would begin to pinch the Japanese economy and its war-making potential.

On 27 September 1940, Japan signed the Tripartite Pact, a treaty that pledged Germany, Italy, and Japan to "assist one another with all political, economic, and military means when one of the three Contracting Parties is attacked by a power at present not involved in the European War or in the Sino-Japanese conflict." Clearly, the only country that qualified as a target was the United States since the Soviet Union still held a nonaggression pact with Hitler. Germany had lost the Battle of Britain in the skies during the summer of 1940 and as the Nazi legions prepared to chew up the Soviet Union the Third Reich thus tried to enlist Japan in an active role, urging an attack upon Singapore and British possessions in the Far East. To sweeten the proposal, the Hitler government even pledged ". . . if Japan got into a conflict with the United States, Germany on her part would take the necessary steps at once. It made no difference with whom the United States first came into conflict, whether it was with Germany or with Japan."

Harsh rhetoric from both sides generated intense discussions at the top levels of government in Tokyo and Washington. A new ambassador, Adm. Kichisaburo Nomura, presented his credentials in Washington. Nomura seems to have negotiated in good faith but he had little influence at home. Although Washington offered to accommodate the Japanese hunger for Indochina's rice and minerals, the Imperial Army overran the colony toward the end of July 1941. Roosevelt promptly froze the assets of both Japan and China (with the agreement of the Chinese Chiang Kai-shek) and a week later leveled an embargo on high-octane gasoline and crude oil, vital to the military forces.

As the tension with Japan had increased, Army and Navy brass had taken a number of steps to improve their readiness for war. In the Far East, the Asiatic Fleet under Adm. Thomas Hart had grown in size, although hardly enough to match what the Japanese could muster. The Army Air Force beefed up its Philippine arsenal, adding fighter planes and a new group of B-17 Flying Fortress bombers, with more like those destined for the Far East that arrived during the attack on Pearl Harbor.

In July 1941, Douglas MacArthur, formerly the military advisor for the Commonwealth of the Philippines had been recalled to active duty as commander in chief, United States Army Forces in the Far East. He continued to develop an ambitious plan to defend the Philippines with a bulked-up nexus of U.S. soldiers plus the redoubtable Philippine Scouts and an army of indigenous conscripts. Meanwhile, as December approached, Admiral Hart prudently sent many of his vessels to sea rather than pen them up in the vulnerable Manila Bay.

Throughout this period, Washington through the State Department, the secretaries of the army and the navy, and the uniformed heads of the armed forces continually advised their commanders in such major bastions as the Philippines and Hawaii of the tension with Nippon. There was no shortage of messages counseling the likes of MacArthur, Hart, Short, and Kimmel of the need to ready themselves for a possible outbreak of war.

On the other hand there was at least one serious error in the distribution of intelligence. Enemy agents, directed by the Japanese consulate in Honolulu, fed information on military matters to Tokyo. On 24 September the consulate was asked for precise information about the location of warships in the anchorage. Having broken the Japanese diplomatic code, American intelligence deciphered the dispatches that later would become known as the "bomb plot message." Unfortunately, the authorities in Washington failed to advise either Kimmel or Short of the specific request for details about the deployment of the fleet in Pearl Harbor that implied plans for an attack. In their defense the authorities insisted the Japanese, like all nations, routinely sought such material. Whether Kimmel and Short would have acted differently if privy to the "bomb plot" is unknown.

When Short assumed his command he operated under the policies of the Army's chief of staff, George C. Marshall, who stressed, "The risk of sabotage and the risk involved in a surprise raid by Air and by submarine constitutes [*sic*] the real perils of the situation. Frankly, I do not see any landing threat in the Hawaiian Islands [Short commanded 25,000 ground troops to repel an invasion] so long as we have air superiority." Marshall specifically instructed his subordinate, "Please keep clearly in mind in all of your negotiations [with military and civilian authorities in the islands] that our mission is to protect the base and the Naval concentrations."

Short, upon inspection of his fief, perceived obvious weaknesses in his air force, and attempted to disperse and shield his fighters and bombers. He advised the adjutant general in Washington, "The concentration of these airplanes at Wheeler Field and at Hickam Field presents a very serious problem in the protection against hostile aviation." Short asked for $1.5 million worth of bunkers in which to stash 142 single-engine fighters, 121 double-engine pursuit ships, 25 two-engine bombers, and 70 four-engine bombers. It was a fairly modest sum even in 1941 dollars but Washington never acted on his plea.

Half-hearted efforts to open up more air fields to spread out assets had created a few strips like Haleiwa but these were more in the nature of training or emergency sites rather than functioning bases. As an infantry officer, Short may well have been unaware of the quality of his Hawaiian Air Force. By December 1941, the war planners, convinced that the Japanese would hit the outermost Pacific bases including the Philippines, Wake, and Guam, shipped available aircraft toward these points, stripping Hawaii of some of its planes in the process. Short may not have known, indeed many of those more directly concerned with the Air Corps did not realize, just how weak was the U.S. in the skies. The pursuit or fighter-plane force included obviously obsolescent P-36s and P-37s as well as early and inadequate P-40 models. The B-18 bomber, a woefully underpowered ship, at best could barely muster 170 to 180 miles per hour. Only a handful of the new B-17 or two-engine A-20s were available.

The head of the Hawaiian Air Force, Maj. Gen. Frederick L. Martin and RAdm. Patrick N. L. Bellinger, both aviators, in an example of armed-services cooperation, at the instigation of their bosses, Kimmel and Short, produced a plan for a joint action in the event of an attack upon Hawaii and the fleet. On 31 March 1941, the authors noted, "A successful, sudden raid against our ships and Naval installations on Oahu might prevent effective offensive action by our forces in the Western Pacific for a long period . . ." They cautioned a raiding force could come without any advance information from intelligence and it might consist of carriers that steamed within 300 miles.

The Martin-Bellinger Report stated, "The aircraft at present available in Hawaii are inadequate to maintain for any extended period from bases on Oahu, a patrol extensive enough to insure that an air attack from an Orange [the designation of an enemy] carrier cannot arrive over Oahu as a complete surprise."

Daily patrols that covered an arc through 360 degrees seaward were the most effective means to discover intruders, but Martin-Bellinger admitted the Hawaiian command lacked the personnel and planes to carry out such missions. Under an agreement reached between the Army and Navy, long-range reconnaissance was the responsibility of the Navy and its PBYs. The Army would scout only twenty miles offshore, of value perhaps for locating submarines but useless against a surprise air attack.

Another study by an Air Corps officer in the summer of 1941 raised again the specter of carrierborne raids. The investigator noted the routes the enemy must take—either north or south in a westerly direction—to avoid shipping lanes, pinpointed the probable time of an attack—early morning—and what it would require to combat a force composed of half a dozen flattops. The report recommended an allotment to Hawaii of 180 B-17s or similar four-engine bombers and 36 torpedo-bearing medium bombers. The infusion of aircraft would have eased the Navy's patrol-search burden and theoretically deployed a puissant attack force upon the enemy fleet. But at the time, the entire Air Corps owned only 109 B-17s with many of them committed to MacArthur, mainland defense, or Great Britain.

Short was perceptive enough to focus on the need for a system to provide an early warning of air attacks. Early in his tenure he asked his superiors to obtain permission from the secretary of the interior for permission to construct a radar-detection apparatus atop Haleakala, a mountain on Maui and one of the highest elevations in the islands. The National Park Service as a subset of the Department of the Interior governed Haleakala. And while agreeing to allow temporary use of the promontory, the service demanded approval of all plans and structures, giving advance notice that nothing that altered the natural appearance of the reservation or interfered with sightseeing would be permitted. The view from the mountaintop held priority over national defense. That officials of the National Park Services could reject the War Department's petition indicates the degree of confusion and lack of leadership in official Washington.

Frustrated in that direction, Short counted on radars placed elsewhere in the islands but at best the detectors could pick up approaching aircraft at a distance of seventy-five miles, minimal time to scramble interceptors and man antiaircraft batteries. How seriously Short took his aircraft control and warning (ACW) net is problematical. At the inquiry after the disaster of 7 December, he remarked, "At the time we had just gotten in the machines and set up. I thought this was fine training for them. I was trying to get training and doing it for training more than any idea that it would be real."

About an hour before the first Japanese planes commenced the attack, Pvt. George E. Elliott, a trainee working the oscilloscope at the Opana Mobile Radar Station on the northern tip of Oahu, picked up an odd array of blips. His companion, an experienced technician, Pvt. Joseph L. Lockard, decided, "It must be a flight of some sort." The radar indicated some 50 planes coming from the north at a distance of 136 miles. After discussion on whether to report what was probably a Navy operation, Elliott phoned the Fort Shafter Information Center.

Lieutenant Kermit Tyler, a pilot in the 78th Pursuit Squadron, only vaguely familiar with the capabilities of radar and on duty in the information center answered. He knew of scattered reports of aircraft from other radar stations but this was the largest flight sighted. Aware that B-17s were expected from the mainland, Tyler either assumed the incoming traffic was that bunch or else it was some Navy operation. He advised Lockhard, "Well, don't worry about it." The Opana station tracked the images until they were forty-five miles out, and then shut down. Had the radar warning been heeded, the American forces would have had as much as fifty minutes of advance notice of the attack. Possibly Short's dismissal of the ACW's usefulness was transmitted to the lower echelons.

Along with the radar advisory, the destroyer *Ward*'s encounter with a submarine some fifteen minutes or so earlier in the morning was another signal missed by the defenders. The sub, on the surface in restricted waters, first was noticed by a supply ship that notified the *Ward* and then a PBY on morning patrol also spotted it. Having dropped depth charges, both the destroyer and the PBY notified superiors. Admiral Kimmel was still trying to interpret the meaning when he heard the bombs.

The strike on Pearl Harbor was enhanced by an American obsession with the potential for sabotage. Occidentals, both in the States and those in residence in Hawaii focused on a population that included 160,000 of Japanese background, 37,500 of whom were foreign born. Publicity about the successes of "fifth columns" organized by the Germans to ease their conquests skewed decisions on Hawaii. In the final week of November 1941, Short discounted the possibilities of a Japanese attack. His conversations with the Navy indicated the Japanese fleet was either in home ports or else headed south. (Observers had reported a convoy moving in that direction and it eventually moved at other targets in the Pacific.) He zeroed in upon sabotage as the primary threat. As a consequence, aircraft instead of being dispersed with guns loaded, were stripped of their ammunition that was safely under lock and key, lined up in neat, easily guarded formation fit for mass destruction.

On 7 November, at a cabinet meeting Secretary of State Cordell Hull spoke candidly of the international situation. He emphasized, "relations were extremely critical" and that "we should be on the lookout for a military attack anywhere by Japan at any time." On that same date, Saburo Kurusu as a special envoy embarked on the *China Clipper,* ostensibly for another try at resolving differences. After Kurusu reached Washington, representatives of the two countries conferred in search of a rapprochement. Neither side budged from its positions. Japan demanded a free hand in China, the end of all embargoes, refused to commit itself to evacuation of French Indochina, and did not deign to even mention its support of Hitler. The American position, submitted on 26 November was based on principles of respect for the territorial integrity and sovereignty of nations, noninterference in those countries' internal affairs, equal commercial opportunity, and maintenance of the status quo in the Pacific except through alteration by peaceful means. Acceptance by Japan would roll back all of its expansion and limit the future of the empire.

While Hull, Roosevelt, Nomura, and Kurusu negotiated, Japanese ships were already at sea, with one group headed for the British-governed Malaysia, another aimed at a Philippine invasion, and the third bound for the waters off Hawaii.

In Hawaii there was a sense of war in the near future with Japan but while some considered shooting imminent, few believed they were directly in the line of fire. Admiral Kimmel spoke in terms of war at sea. He arranged for all of the capital ships when in the narrow channel to face out to sea rather than have egress blocked by the need for a battlewagon to steam in a circle in order to head for the ocean. But he, as had his predecessor, refused to have antitorpedo nets installed on the grounds they reduced room to maneuver and because the shallow water protected against a submarine attack. The idea of torpedoes delivered from the air seems not to have occurred to Kimmel and his staff. He directed a perfunctory surveillance of the seas, using his carriers *Enterprise* and *Lexington* for reconnaissance in the outlying areas, while a handful of patrol planes based in Hawaii reconnoitered limited sections of the nearer approaches. Left untouched were the northern reaches, where wind directions most favored a carrier-based assault on the American base.

General Short, too, saw no reason to fear a blow at Pearl. He was unaware that the Navy patrols covered only a small portion of the ocean. However, he had specific instructions from the War Department that he use his assets, B-17s and B-18s, to assist the Navy in this responsibility.

While their commanders wrestled with their obligations based on their understanding of the geomilitary situation, the lower echelons saw only modest modifications in their lives. Ted Hechler of the *Phoenix* remembered "the customary prewar ways lasted right up to the time war started." He noted that on the morning of 6 December, the commander of Cruiser Division 9, carried out the traditional inspection. "The men were in their whites, lined up in rows for personnel inspection. When it came to the inspection of the ship herself, RAdm. H. Fairfax Leary had on his white gloves so he could check for dust."

Paul Backus noted, "There was a great feeling of cockiness among those with whom I worked and played. I don't recall anyone ever expressing any concern about potential combat, naval or otherwise, with the Japanese."

In Washington, however, there were grave doubts about the future. The code breakers on 29 November cracked a pair of messages that became known as the "winds" dispatches. In these the foreign ministry advised Ambassador Nomura that in the event of an emergency—severance of diplomatic relations and the cutoff of international communications—the daily short-wave radio news from Tokyo would use Japanese words for "East wind rain" to signify a danger point with the U.S. Other climactic turns covered relations with Great Britain and the Soviet Union. The precaution convinced all but the most optimistic American foreign policy people of an approaching crisis. Military authorities were duly informed of the gravity portended by the "winds" system.

On 6 December, Foreign Minister Shigenori Togo notified Nomura that the ministry would transmit a fourteen-part response to the American proposals. The procedures employed for sending the lengthy message, in retrospect, suggest the foreign ministry was in no hurry to see the contents delivered. At the same time, the Japanese held up an appeal from President Roosevelt to Emperor Hirohito for more than ten hours. Meanwhile, American Navy technicians utilizing decrypting machines labored to unscramble the text. By late evening all but the last part had been handed by the decoders to top Navy and Army brass, the State Department, and the White House. According to Lt. Lester Shulz, who physically brought the document to the president, Roosevelt read through the fifteen pages, a flat-out rejection of all American ideas, and handed them to Harry Hopkins, his close advisor. When Hopkins had gone through the papers, Roosevelt said, "This means war."

The chief executive, however, did not immediately sound a loud alert. He waited until Admiral Stark returned from an evening at the theater before calling him. Stark later claimed nothing Roosevelt said indicated hostilities were any closer, although there was already consensus that Japan was likely to attack at any time. Nor was the Army greatly aroused by the latest news. Brigadier General Sherman, the head of that branch's intelligence, decided the Japanese statement carried "little military significance." As a consequence, Miles saw no reason to disturb Gen. George C. Marshall, the chief of staff.

On 7 December, while the intelligence sections finally delivered a last element of the message at about 8:30 A.M. Washington, D.C., time [2:30 A.M. at Pearl Harbor], which offered no wiggle room, a brief note from Togo to Nomura stunned Col. Rufus S. Bratton, the Army's intelligence expert in the Far Eastern Section. Togo ordered Nomura not to deliver the fourteen-part statement to the American authorities until 1:00 P.M., Washington time. Ordinarily the diplomatic corps took Sundays off. But more significantly, no previous directive from Tokyo ever specified a precise hour. In fact, at that moment, the first of the Japanese planes would be a few minutes from Pearl Harbor to begin unloading their bombs and torpedoes.

Bratton was convinced that the Japanese expected to attack an American installation in the Pacific. However, he later agreed, "Nobody in ONI [Office of Naval Intelligence] nobody in G-2 [Army Intelligence] knew that any major element of the fleet was in Pearl Harbor on Sunday morning the 7th of December. We all thought they had gone to sea . . . because that was part of the war plan, and they had been given a war warning."

The cabinet officials and military leaders in Washington tried to guess what area would be most vulnerable at that appointed hour. Based on their limited knowledge of Japanese naval movement the most likely target appeared to be Kota Baharu, on the coast of Malaysia. It was agreed by Admiral Stark and General Marshall that all outlying possessions should be advised of the imminent threat.

The notices promptly went off to the first addressees, the Caribbean Defense Command, MacArthur in the Philippines, and the Presidio on the California coast. But atmospheric conditions blocked the radio channel for Hawaii. Instead of going to the Navy, which maintained better communications with the islands, the officer from the War Department Signal Center chose to use teletype through Western Union with a relay from San Francisco, via RCA, to Hawaii. Unfortunately, transmission of messages under this system did not instantly put the word out. The message would first need to be put in code, then deciphered by the receiving station for delivery to the likes of Short and Kimmel.

Honolulu recorded Marshall's warning at 7:33 A.M., as the first wave of airplanes droned on, a mere thirty-five miles from Oahu. The message carried no priority stamp and was placed with a batch of other cables scheduled for delivery by a motorcycle-borne delivery boy. The first bomb exploded about 7:55. The caution from Marshall never reached Short or Kimmel.

Somewhere between 1:30 and 2:00 P.M. a naval commander handed a dispatch from Hawaii to John H. Dillon, an assistant to Secretary of the Navy Frank Knox conferring with top aides. Dillon recalled the message, "We are being attacked. This is no drill." Knox gasped, "My God, this can't be true. This must mean the Philippines." Admiral Stark quickly checked and said, "No, sir, this is Pearl."

At 4:00 P.M. eastern standard time, Japanese Imperial Headquarters announced that a state of war existed between Japan and the United States and the British Empire. On the following day, Roosevelt spoke to the American people by radio about "a date which will live in infamy" as he called on Congress for a declaration of war.

3
The Philippine Defenses

The smashing success of the attack on Pearl Harbor resulted from perfectly plotted strategy backed by excellent logistical support. The raid benefitted hugely from American complacency, underestimation of Japanese military power and prowess. The U.S. commanders demonstrated a lack of imagination as they stressed a potential fifth column while blind to the possibility of a much more devastating type of assault. The continuation of a spit-and-polish Navy rather than a combat-prepared one meant that shipboard guns could not operate with requisite swiftness. Luck all fell to the attackers. American planes and ships in their limited reconnaissance did not blunder upon the fleet. At the appointed hour the harbor happened to be crammed with targets; only the two aircraft carriers were out of reach. The weather was perfect. The failure to sound an alarm at the radar sighting in large part resulted from the coincidence of the B-17s enroute. Atmospheric conditions blocked a potentially last-minute warning to the base. Even an hour of grace might have greatly reduced the losses, but from the Japanese standpoint everything that could go right did. From the American side it was a total disaster. Luck would have no role in the next major achievement by the Japanese.

For the United States, the Philippines, which blocked access to the Dutch East Indies, the British South Pacific possessions including Australia, and American outposts at Guam and Wake, were an obvious target for any military moves. The northernmost reaches lie less than 350 miles from mainland Asia. Flight distance from Formosa [Taiwan] the big island wrested away from China by Japan, is perhaps 700 miles to the Philippines' largest city, Manila.

After the U.S. had decisively defeated the Spanish fleet in the Battle of Manila Bay in 1898 and routed the occupying arm, Spain ceded the territory to the U.S. By the 1930s, America had lost its appetite for territory so far from the mainland and for rule so inimical to the tradition of freedom. That these colonial holdings no longer seemed profitable also weighed upon the minds of government officials, particularly as the Great Depression blighted the economy. Responding to needs at home and the agitation within the islands, an agreement between the U.S. and local leaders specified that the Commonwealth of the Philippines, established in 1935, would receive complete independence in 1946. Until that time, the U.S. would control only matters of foreign affairs and defense with participation in these activities by the local government. The citizens elected Manuel Luis Quezon as the first president of the Commonwealth.

Eager as the islands were to escape from American rule, the political powers recognized the threat from Japan. In this, the desires of both the Philippine authorities and the U.S. were the same. Aware of the potential for a conflict with Japan, in 1935, Quezon recruited his old friend Gen. Douglas MacArthur, then outgoing chief of staff for the U.S. Army. The new military adviser to the Philippines was on familiar turf. His father, Gen. Arthur MacArthur, a Civil War veteran, had participated in the campaign to oust the Spanish and then subdue a rebellion against American rule while Douglas studied at West Point.

Immediately after graduation from the U.S. Military Academy as top man in the Class of 1903, Douglas MacArthur worked as an engineer to help map the territory. "The Philippines charmed me. The delightful hospitality, the respect and affection expressed for my father, the amazingly attractive result of a mixture of Spanish culture and American industry, the languorous laze that seemed to glamorize even the most routine chores of life, the fun-loving men, the moonbeam delicacy of its lovely women, fastened me with a grip that has never relaxed." It was not all lush, tropical romance for on one occasion, MacArthur shot it out with a pair of "desperadoes," killing both with his pistol.

By World War I, MacArthur, who had been recommended for but did not receive a Medal of Honor during the altercation with Mexico's bandit-patriot Pancho Villa, had advanced to the rank of colonel, serving as chief of staff for the U.S. 42d Division, part of the American Expeditionary Force that fought in France. MacArthur continually led his men out of the trenches and his personal bravery plus his adept strategy and tactics as a brigade commander added four more Silver Stars and a pair of Distinguished Services Crosses. A brigadier general by the time of the armistice and commander of the 42d, MacArthur achieved a reputation for personal courage under fire and irregular military dress.

Always dapper, younger than most senior officers, MacArthur developed a rapport with the doughboys of that era. His successes and his style also generated a hearty disdain in some colleagues and superiors. During the late 1920s, MacArthur returned to the Philippines for a three-year stint and became friendly with the former rebel and now political leader, Manuel Quezon. Earlier, he did a tour as superintendent at West Point and finally ascended to the post of Army chief of staff in 1930. For a time he adroitly managed to avoid political bear traps during a time of turmoil, ranging from the court-martial of Gen. Billy Mitchell, the early exponent of air power, to the pressure of disarmament forces, and the ever thinner budgets for the military.

He studied the past and thought of the future. He foresaw maneuver and movement as decisive, recognizing that planes, tanks, and mechanization meant the end of World War I–style trench combat with massive, immobile armies confronting one another. He argued in favor of stockpiling the strategic materials that would become so critical for World War II and he reestablished the Order of the Purple Heart, a medal issued to those wounded or killed due to enemy action.

But in 1932, he stumbled. Some 25,000 World War I veterans, accompanied often by their families, had encamped in Washington, D.C., while they sought an appropriation of a federal payment for their service during the war. They dubbed themselves the Bonus Expeditionary Force (BEF) and MacArthur, always hostile to any group that seemed to lack respect for the forces of law and order, imbued with the habits of a lifetime in a military environment, scoffed at what he perceived as a rabble of malcontents: "In the end," said MacArthur, "their frustration combined with careful needling by the Communists, turned them into a sullen, riotous mob."

According to *American Caesar*, William Manchester's biography of MacArthur, he considered 90 percent of the bonus marchers fakes although a Veterans Administration survey found 94 percent had army or navy service records, with more than two-thirds having served overseas. MacArthur mobilized troops to deal with the squatters. After members of the BEF scuffled with soldiers near the Capitol, the general defied orders from President Herbert Hoover and directed his forces to evict the main body of supplicants from a campground across the Anacostia River. In the ensuing melee, tents, shacks, and makeshift shelters were put to the torch, tear gas and bayonets routed the civilians leaving two babies dead and a child lacerated by a bayonet. (In his book, *Reminiscences*, MacArthur insisted no one was killed.)

President Franklin D. Roosevelt, inaugurated little more than six months later, bent on curing the Depression, and suspicious of MacArthur's ambitions, kept him and his army on a short leash and starved for funds. Tarred by a personal scandal involving a mistress, described as a "Eurasian beauty," buffeted by cliques in the military establishment whose animosity dated back to World War I, and resented by veterans for the treatment of the BEF, MacArthur, after Roosevelt refused to extend his tour as chief of staff for more than a matter of months, expected to retire.

Franklin Roosevelt arranged for Congress to fund a U.S. military mission in the Philippines. Commonwealth president Manuel Quezon found MacArthur delighted to accept the post of military advisor, with $33,000 a year added to his salary as a U.S. major general, a considerable stipend for the 1930s. To serve as MacArthur's chief of staff, the War Department assigned Maj. Dwight David Eisenhower, who had been an aide while the general served as the chief of staff for the U.S. Army. (The experience led Eisenhower to respond later to a question of whether he knew MacArthur, "I studied dramatics under him for four years in Washington and five in the Philippines.")

The general had taken up residence in a six-room penthouse atop the Manila Hotel and immersed himself in building the Philippines into a defensive stronghold, "a Pacific Switzerland." Under the strategy created by his predecessors in the War and Navy Departments, MacArthur was expected to operate in accord with War Plan Orange (WPO), modified slightly over the years and coded as WPO-1, WPO-2, and finally WPO-3. The War Plan Orange scenario envisioned meeting a thrust by the Japanese at the Philippines with a retreat of the defenders into the narrow, jungle-like peninsula of Bataan that lay along the western edge of Manila Bay and was backed up by several fortified islands including the redoubt at Corregidor whose big guns could deny any enemy the use of the Manila anchorage. The resistance would be expected to contain the Japanese until the military might of the U.S., convoyed by the Navy, would cross the Pacific and blast the invaders from the archipelago and any other sites temporarily in their hands.

WPO in any shape hardly fitted MacArthur's vision for waging war. While not openly disavowing WPO, he determined to design an organization that need not retreat to Bataan. Instead of a small, elite military capable of holding off a much larger opposition by dint of carefully prepared, well-stocked positions that employed terrain and vegetation for its own advantage, MacArthur sought to develop enough ground, air, and sea strength to make any strike at the Philippines too costly for the Japanese, even after independence in 1946. He planned an army whose active duty and reserve elements added up to forty Filipino divisions, 400,000 soldiers, trained, equipped, and led by a cadre of officers schooled at a local replica of West Point. His navy would be fifty speedy, torpedo-armed boats that would ply the surrounding waters with such swiftness and stealth that they could disrupt the approach of any large ships. For control of the sky he considered 250 aircraft necessary. To go from blueprints to reality, MacArthur estimated a period of ten years and an expenditure of a quarter-billion dollars by the Commonwealth along with subsidies from the U.S. to meet its responsibilities.

For all of the years he had spent in the Philippines previously and his experiences as chief of staff during the first years of the Great Depression, MacArthur's schemes lacked a sense of reality. The belief that American officers and noncoms along with those Filipino graduates of West Point could transform the conscripts into fully qualified soldiers with five and a half months of training was a fantasy. The men, however willing, were not reared in the kind of industrial society that marked the West. They had neither the experience nor the education to adapt quickly to the demands upon modern troops. When they started to arrive at the training camps in 1937, those charged with transforming the draftees into soldiers discovered their recruits spoke eight distinct languages and eighty-seven different dialects. More than one-fifth, including some designated as first sergeants or company clerks were illiterate in any tongue. The sharp schisms and deficiencies in language skills and customs seriously hampered instruction and communication.

Equally defeating, the Commonwealth was no more prepared to provide the kinds of appropriations necessary to field the requisite number of men and equipment each year than was the United States with its own armed forces. The original local budget of $25 million annually was almost instantly pared to less than one-third and in the year preceding Pearl Harbor, appropriations came to a measly $1 million. MacArthur, however, continued to argue that he could and would make the islands impregnable. Both his case and his achievements were hampered by alienation with Washington, D.C. Pacifist elements regarded MacArthur as a warmonger. Few in Congress cared to expend great sums on fortifications or armaments for a place that would soon be free of U.S. control. MacArthur's influence in the States waned further as he was forced to retire from active duty as an American officer when he refused to relinquish his appointment as the Philippine commander with the rank of field marshal.

MacArthur's inability to procure military hardware and money for the defenses of the Commonwealth stirred doubts in Quezon. The Japanese conquests in China persuaded Quezon that a declaration of neutrality might be the one way to avoid turning his country into a battleground. He even contemplated dismissal of MacArthur and shocked his field marshal with a public statement, "It's good to hear men say that the Philippines can repel an invasion, but it's not true and the people should know it isn't." Newspapers in the islands published the conflicting views of the president and his military advisor, causing considerable anxiety among the reading public. Again, MacArthur's memoirs do not indicate any difference of opinion with Quezon.

The bombs and bullets that shattered the peace of Europe in September 1939 emphatically announced that neither negotiations nor appeasement could prevent war. The blitzkrieg juggernaut of Nazi Germany that rolled over Poland, Denmark, Norway, Holland, Belgium, and finally France, the bare escape of British troops from Dunkirk, and the siege of London by Adolf Hitler's *Luftwaffe* cast doubt over the ability of Great Britain to defend its Far East empire.

After the Japanese seized the opportunity to take over French Indochina and pressured Dutch and French colonies to accept Tokyo's concept of a "Greater East Asia Co-Prosperity Sphere," there was little doubt who would be the senior partner and the chief beneficiary. No slouch at exploiting an opportunity either, MacArthur wrote to the current Army chief of staff, Gen. George C. Marshall, and noted that since the Philippine Army soon would be absorbed into that of the U.S.—a leap of the general's imagination, since the War Department had not yet come to that decision—he expected to shut down his office as military advisor. He suggested to Marshall the establishment of a Far East command covering all U.S. Army activities and nominated himself to be in charge.

After dithering over the idea for several months, worsening conditions convinced the policy makers to eventually adopt MacArthur's idea. Along with extra appropriations designed to strengthen the indigenous forces, a cable from Marshall on 27 July 1941 announced creation of the United States Army Forces in the Far East (USAFFE) and recalling him to active duty, designated MacArthur as the commanding general. In his memoirs, MacArthur remarked, "I was given the rank of lieutenant general, although my retired rank was that of a full general."

MacArthur now had the role he coveted and a platform from which to importune ears no longer deaf to the sounds of Japan's marching feet. But America was close to 10,000 miles away, its defense factories slowly gearing up and their prime customers already in a shooting war with the Axis Powers of Germany and Italy; Great Britain and the Soviet Union also demanded the tools to fight.

Short on money, equipment, and trained fighting men in 1941, MacArthur's USAFFE, however, boasted some war assets and with the conviction of President Roosevelt that confrontation with Japan appeared inevitable, there was the promise of a substantial enhancement of resources. On hand, the general could count upon a cadre of 297 graduates of West Point. The most senior were MacArthur and a former football all-America, coast artilleryman Col. Paul Bunker representing the Class of '03. The most junior included several from the Class of '41, infantry lieutenants, like Alexander "Sandy" Nininger and Hector Polla who arrived only ten days before the attack on Pearl Harbor. Mixed in were officers from almost every class in between—former cavalryman, Gen. Jonathan Wainwright '06, infantry specialist Gen. Clifford Bluemel '09, engineer Col. Hugh J. Casey '18, the military law expert Albert Svihra '22, Italian-born infantry leader Floyd Forte '34, and bomber pilot Colin P. Kelly '37. The practice of admitting a few men from the islands to the U.S. institution included nineteen well-schooled Filipino officers like Vincente Lim '14 and Fidel V. Segundo '17, both of whom commanded Philippine Army divisions.

In the delicate minuet to prevent trodding on the sensitive toes of the host people, forty-five of the American West Pointers along with a number of non-Academy, regular army officers, and noncoms were attached to the existing, largely on paper in some instances, twelve Philippine Army divisions. Although they technically served as advisors to the Filipino officers, in practice, the latter almost always deferred to the Americans.

To achieve his goals, MacArthur, on 1 September 1941, began to mobilize the Philippine Army. Elements of the ten reserve divisions, who theoretically had already undergone some training, were to be called up gradually until the total of 75,000 would be on active duty by 15 December. MacArthur, who received his fourth star as a full general shortly after he assumed his new post, simultaneously hectored Washington to satisfy his dire needs and voiced optimism for the future. In October 1941, MacArthur became privy to a plan known as Rainbow Five, the overall Allied strategy for war with Japan and with the other Axis powers—the British, the Dutch in their colonies, and the Free French were already at war with Germany and Italy—which conceded the loss of the U.S. possessions of Wake, Guam, and the Philippines. The scenario assumed that in a two-ocean, worldwide conflict the Philippines could not be held. In that respect, Rainbow went beyond Orange.

MacArthur, while not opposing Rainbow Five, had argued that it was a mistake to write off the Philippines. Instead, he persuaded Marshall and Adm. Thomas Hart, commander of the Asiatic Fleet, that he could stop the Japanese at the water's edge. He believed the enemy would not make his move before April 1942 and by then MacArthur insisted he would field more than 100,000 well-trained and equipped troops backed up by a strong Air Corps while Hart's fleet would deal with the Japanese Navy.

The decision to scrap first the defensive bastion philosophy of WPO and then revise Rainbow Five to include preservation of the Philippine Islands dictated significant changes in operations by the Philippine military commander. Guarding the potential landing sites among the roughly 250 miles of Luzon beaches demanded a considerably larger army than would have been required to retain only Bataan and the fortified positions at the mouth of Manila Bay. MacArthur thus opted not to augment the highly professional Philippine Scouts with a limited number of well-equipped soldiers and pursued quantity rather than quality. The choice of arena also meant a major shift in logistics, deployment of food, ammunition, fuel, and other supplies where these items could be retrieved by the defenders of Luzon's approaches rather than on Bataan. MacArthur's choice of strategy and its fulfillment would have a critical effect on the struggle to defend the Philippines.

As the portents of war gathered in ever-darker clouds, the highest American civilian official on the scene was Francis Sayre, the U.S. high commissioner. In his State Department capacity, after being warned of the crisis with Japan, he met with Hart and MacArthur on 27 November. Both Sayre and Hart feared an imminent thrust by the Japanese. However, recalled Sayre, "Back and forth paced General MacArthur, smoking a black cigar and assuring Admiral Hart and myself in reassuring terms that the existing alignment and movement of Japanese troops convinced him that there would be no Japanese attack before spring."

Although the public perception, aided and abetted by the strength of his personality and oratory, regarded MacArthur as the man in charge of the Far East, in reality he commanded only the U.S. Army. His opposite number for the Navy, RAdm. Thomas Hart, three years older and an 1897 graduate of the Naval Academy, was stiff-necked, peevish, the epitome of the martinet. He zealously guarded his prerogatives and it was inevitable that frost would govern relations between the two military leaders.

Like MacArthur, Hart had received little in the way of reinforcements as 1941 ebbed. The major additions amounted to a dozen submarines and six PT boats as well as the understrength 4th Marine Regiment transferred from duty in China. The U.S. Asiatic Fleet consisted of Hart's flagship, the heavy cruiser *Houston;* a single light cruiser; thirteen World War I, four-stack destroyers; the subs; and the PT boats plus a handful of miscellaneous craft including tenders, gunboats, minesweepers, and tankers. Conspicuous by their absence were any battleships or aircraft carriers. Two dozen PBYs, the slow moving amphibious patrol planes, made up the fleet air arm.

As a young destroyer officer, William Mack said that when he came to the Asiatic Fleet in 1939, there was an underlying feeling of trouble ahead. "It was totally a peacetime system. But I think we all knew, in our hearts, that war was just around the corner—the corner being one or two years. About six months later, the ship was given sonar which meant the ships in the Asiatic Fleet were considered the front line. We suddenly realized that they were being serious back in the States—they were giving us something we were going to have to have. Before that time, we had depth charges in the destroyers and that was it. The doctrine for finding a submarine [before sonar] was simply to sight its periscope, take a bearing on it, estimate the range, and run down toward him to drop some depth charges."

The installation of sonar aboard the destroyers was a tangible sign of the approach of war. In November 1940, said Mack, all dependents began to be evacuated. "The fleet tempo changed considerably. We no longer went to China—we stayed around the Philippines. For the last year before the war started we were roughly on a war footing; we still had awnings [for shade against midday sun] and movie machines but we were expecting something to happen." At the same time Mack continued to wear his formal whites and carry a sword when going ashore until just about a month before the start of the war.

Army nurse Madeline Ullom, who reached the archipelago almost a year before war broke out, noticed in May 1941 a change in ambience as "social activities greatly decreased. Curfews were routine. Alerts were frequent. Field exercises were longer and more intensive. The Army-Navy Game, the event of the year, when reservations at the club were made months in advance, was all but canceled." Still, she remembered, "An American flag moved gently in the breeze above the central entrance to Sternberg [Hospital]. A feeling of security filled the atmosphere. The military corpsmen and Filipino aides were skilled and efficient. A high quality of duty performance was required and obtained. Supervision was meager. Professional dedication at all times was paramount. Inspection days brought no apprehension."

Major Philip Fry, who already had one tour in the Philippines on his record, had returned to the islands in November. Almost immediately upon his arrival, he had noticed a project at the Fort McKinley officers' club. "I started over there with Ted Lilly [an officer acquaintance from a previous tour]. Just outside of the front of the club I saw the entrance to an immense dugout, the shaft down was within twenty feet of the steps of the club. It led down from fifty or more feet. This dugout was beneath the area of the officers' club, the tennis courts, and the commanding general's quarters. It had a series of corridors and compartments and was designed as a divisional command post but it was never completed." The swift passage of events would prevent further work or use.

Another recent immigrant, Sam Grashio, wore the gold bars of a second lieutenant and the wings of silver as a P-40 pilot assigned to the 21st Pursuit Squadron. Two years at Gonzaga University had provided Grashio with enough academic credits to enlist in the Washington Air National Guard and then undergo training in the Air Corps. "I thought of flying only in the narrow sense; taking to the air in the best World War I movie tradition, embellished with goggles and helmet, scarf waving in the breeze. I thought little about *why* I was training and flying so much. Of course I knew that war had been going on in Europe ever since September 1939, but in flying school I thought of it mostly when a fellow cadet of Greek lineage would needle me about what his countrymen were doing to the Italian troops Benito Mussolini had so injudiciously sent to invade Greece.

"My mistaken perception of the world deepened soon after the 21st Pursuit Squadron sailed from San Francisco on 1 November 1941. Our ship was the *President Coolidge*, a former luxury liner then being used as a troop transport. Life was lovely; there were no duties, the food was magnificent, and we did not even know where we were going." Not until the vessel reached Hawaii did Grashio and his colleagues figure out they were bound for Manila.

"Nothing happened that might have suggested, even remotely, that a real war was not far off," said Grashio. "On board the *Coolidge*, there were a number of senior officers who had just graduated from the National War College. Having little to do, I listened to them extensively. To a man they were convinced that there would be no war with Japan because the Japanese would not be so stupid as to start a war they would be certain to lose within a few weeks."

A cold dose of reality should have struck Grashio on 6 December when he heard a speech from Col. Harold George, a senior airman. George warned that war was imminent, that the Japanese had 3,000 planes in Formosa only 600 miles away, and already they had been seen doing aerial reconnaissance over the Philippines. George concluded with remarks indicating he believed Grashio and his fellow fliers were members of a "suicide squadron." Grashio, unconvinced, offered to bet the squadron commander Lt. Ed Dyess five pesos there would be no war with Japan. "Ed took the bet at once and laid another five it would begin within a week."

On that timetable, the members of the 21st had painfully little time to prepare. Their machines were as fresh as the pilots; only eighteen of the twenty-four allotted had been removed from their shipping crates and assembled by 8 December. Four had never even been flown and the others had not yet been adjusted for maximum performance.

At the Navy Department in Washington the experts doubted MacArthur's forces could hold off an onslaught on the beaches and not be forced to retreat along the lines of War Plan Orange. Although Hart wanted to fight it out with the Imperial Navy in Philippine waters, he was instructed to safeguard his vessels by deploying them southward. Furthermore, since his fleet was considered to be part of the overall Rainbow strategy, he had to be prepared to sail to the Dutch East Indies and join with the Allied ships there.

As a young naval officer, Robert Lee Dennison received an assignment from Hart to be a contact with the commander of the USAFFE. "MacArthur had a very elementary understanding of the use of a navy. He, like a good many Army officers of his time, looked on a navy as a seaward extension of the army's flank and that's all. There was no personal contact between Hart's staff, MacArthur's staff, or MacArthur or Hart. MacArthur didn't know what we were up to in terms of ship movements or what our war plans were, nor did we know what his plans were. That was the purpose of my being in this particular capacity."

Those expected to implement MacArthur's strategy on the ground discovered some painful weaknesses. Glen Townsend, as a U.S. Army colonel, assumed command of the 11th Regiment, a component of the Philippine Army's 11th Infantry Division in September 1941. "I found that the regiment was composed of Ilocanos and Igorots in about equal numbers. I found that they spoke eleven different dialects and that Christian and Pagan had little liking for each other. All of the enlisted personnel had taken the prescribed five-and-one-half-months' training. They were proficient only in close-order drill and saluting. The officers, being mainly political appointees had less training than the men they were supposed to lead." To "advise" the regiment, the American aides to Townsend added up to ten other officers and seven enlisted men.

The paucity of personal gear possessed by his men and the unit's equipment appalled Townsend. His Filipino soldiers had no blankets, raincoats, mosquito bars, entrenching tools, or steel helmets. They wore rubber-soled shoes and pith helmets. The standard uniform was one pair of khaki shorts and one shirt. They also owned one set of blue-denim fatigues. The anti-tank company supposed to field 37mm guns had none. The entire regiment depended upon four trucks and eight field telephones. There were 81mm mortars, but no ammunition other than that designed for target practice would be available until three months after the Japanese invaded.

For the basic infantryman's weapon, the U.S. Army had sold the Commonwealth its surplus Lee-Enfield rifles. Unfortunately, the stock of these pieces was too long for the short-statured Filipinos and could not be aimed with the butt in the crotch of the shoulder where the recoil could be comfortably absorbed. Instead, soldiers were forced to brace their Lee Enfields against their upper arms ahead of the shoulder and incurred nasty bruises while lowering their ability to effectively fire the rifles. On the plus side, Townsend says the would-be soldiers struck him as physically fit, eager to learn, and presented no disciplinary problems.

It seems obvious that MacArthur miscalculated what it would take to create an effective local army. Clifford Bluemel, who as a young lieutenant in 1914 had served a tour in the islands, was among those who had returned to the Philippines as the war clouds darkened. "I got there in June 1940 to command the 45th Infantry, Philippine Scouts. It was a good regiment, about sixty men to a company. [In August 1941] I was told that three colonels, Brougher, Jones, and Bluemel would run a school for the training of ten Philippine Army divisions' staff officers. They were all Filipinos, some of them graduates of West Point.

"I ran the school from 8:00 in the morning until 11:30 and from 1:00 to 4:30 in the afternoon. Then we all went out and walked for fifty minutes—everybody. I also ran the school from 7:00 to 9:00 at night. They thought that was terrible, and that I was a rough S.O.B. But I had only six weeks to train them. I even ran it all day Saturday sometimes, and they didn't like that. Sunday they had off. When I threatened to run it on Sunday, I almost had a riot one time."

Around the first of November, MacArthur and his chief of staff Sutherland visited Bluemel at his school. "We had drinks and talked about different things. MacArthur talked about the Tojo Cabinet which had been formed in Japan. He said, 'The Tojo Cabinet is not the war cabinet. The Tojo Cabinet will fall, and there will be another cabinet which will be the war cabinet.'"

MacArthur's conviction that the political process in Japan had not yet reached the war-kindling point indicates his confidence that he still had time to prepare. Bluemel had no intelligence that could contradict his chief but other remarks by MacArthur took him aback. "Before I went to the Philippines, an officer who had been the military attaché in Germany gave a talk on the handling of the three-regiment divisions by the German Army. It was to me an ideal system. We had that four-regiment division, and it took six hours [for an order] to get the division moving. The former attaché said a German general could get a three-regiment division moving in no time with an oral order. He just gave an infantry colonel his mission and boundaries, attached a battalion of light artillery to him, and so on.

"I asked MacArthur what he thought about it. He talked for half an hour. The man, I think, had never read and found that the Germans had a three-regiment division. It began to shake my confidence in him a little. I thought 'That man doesn't even know anything about handling a three-regiment division. Yet the Philippine Army has three-regiment divisions.'"

With the school course completed by mid-November, Bluemel was assigned to command the 31st Division of the Philippine Army, organized and mobilized in Zambales Province. Recalled Bluemel, "I went to see this great Philippine Army that MacArthur had trained. The enlisted men of my command were all Filipinos. Most of them spoke Tagalog and some English. Several spoke other dialects. They [the 31st Division] were supposed to have had five months' training prior to induction in the service. The basic training given them during that five-month period was poor. Most of them had fired five rounds or less with the World War I Enfield. Very few had fired the .30- or .50-caliber machine gun. Apparently the artillerymen had never fired the 75mm gun and in some cases had never seen one fired.

"There was a Colonel Irwin, who had the 31st Infantry Regiment [part of the 31st Division]. Irwin had been a major in the 45th, and I had utmost respect for him. He was a fine officer—a man who would do things. He had the regiment organized." To Bluemel's shock, Irwin informed him the regiment had never been on the target range. Bluemel instructed Irwin, "The principal thing the infantry must know is how to shoot and how to march. That's basic infantry training, because they've got to be able to march and when they get to their destination, they've got to be able to get fire superiority quickly and beat the enemy." He arranged for the troops to use the target range at the Olongapo Naval Base at Subic Bay. One battalion from the 31st Infantry Regiment managed to expend some fifty rounds per man and a second battalion fired half that amount. The arrival of the 4th Marine Regiment from China at Olongapo closed the range to the army and a third battalion from the 31st never got to squeeze off a single bullet. The troops would not have a further opportunity to use their weapons before they met the enemy in actual combat.

According to Bluemel, toward the end of November, "The Army-Navy Game was to be played. I got a table reserved at the Army-Navy Club. Some people were going to sit there with me, and we were going to have some drinks and listen to the game." (Ordinarily the broadcast of the football game was an excuse for a gala, with the two services enthusiastically partying. However, in deference to the Far East crisis, the celebration had been canceled.)

Still Bluemel figured he could at least quietly enjoy the game at the club and he dropped by MacArthur's headquarters to obtain a pass for the day. To his astonishment, the G-3 plans and operations officer told him no passes were to be granted for the weekend. And he was advised to see Sutherland and ask to see a secret report. "I went in and told him the G-3 sent me and that there's a document I should see. It went something like this:'The conference with the Nomura delegation [special envoys from Japan to Washington] has been terminated and will not be renewed.' I said, 'My God! That's war! When the Japanese are ready to attack, they don't declare war; they attack, and then declare war.'" As commander of the 31st Division, Bluemel quickly reported to Jonathan Wainwright, in charge of the northern Luzon defenses. Wainwright knew of the radiogram about the breakdown in negotiations. In fact, he had been looking for Bluemel and now directed him to start organizing beach defenses.

The strongest defensive unit was the Philippine Division. It included the U.S.-manned 31st Infantry Regiment that with only 1,800 GIs added up to little more than half of the normal contingent. However, the remainder of the outfit came from the Philippine Scouts, the one local fighting force that from an effectiveness standpoint matched the best from the States. Although the Philippine Army was almost literally a paper tiger, the Scouts, formed into the 45th and 57th Infantry Regiments, were men who had opted for a lifetime military career. The inception of the Scouts dated back to 1901 when the U.S. Congress authorized recruitment of a force of Filipinos for service in the American Army, and whose appropriations would come directly from its military parent rather than from monies designated for the territory. Equipped and armed on a par with the 31st Infantry Regiment, the Scouts brought pride and élan to their job. While certain tribal customs such as a fealty to kinsmen and elders occasionally annoyed their American compatriots, the Scouts also displayed a sense of discipline that earned admiration even from U.S. officers who ordinarily considered Filipinos inferior. Most of the officers in the Philippines, as the war approached, con-

tinued to be drawn from the U.S. Army, West Pointers, regulars, and reservists called to the colors. Some Filipino graduates of West Point also occupied command positions. Many of the Scouts achieved the status of non-
commissioned officers.

As an elite organization, the Scouts could be selective about admission,
and in the quality of personnel the outfit matched the soldiers from the
States. The Scouts also equalled the GIs in equipment; the infantrymen carried the latest weapon, the M1 Garand rifle. Some of the Scouts at first disdained the M1 that featured faster firepower rather than the accuracy of the
Springfield with which a soldier carefully squeezed off each shot.

Although MacArthur bombarded Washington with requisitions for the
new Garand M1 rifles, the other troops labored with either Springfield '03s
or the highly unreliable Lee-Enfield. Neither weapon could unleash the
number of bullets in a given time as an M1. Ancient machine guns, dud mortar shells, a lack of adequate or big enough artillery, a shortage of vehicles—
whatever a modern army needed the USAFFE could only order and hope
it would arrive in time. Indeed, early in December MacArthur received word
of a covey of cargo and troop ships steaming toward the Philippines under
the guidance of the cruiser *Pensacola*. The holds and decks of the vessels carried the mortar and artillery shells so desperately needed and bore the
crated aircraft of the 27th Light Bombardment Group whose pilots had already resided in the islands.

The defenders had already welcomed the American-crewed 192d and
194th Tank Battalions, with 108 light tanks as well as some additional coast
artillery. In his original prescription for a successful defense of his turf,
MacArthur spoke of a fleet of fifty or sixty torpedo boats. Attached to the
Asiatic Fleet at the time of Pearl Harbor were only the six seventy-seven-foot
craft of Motor Torpedo Boat Squadron 3. Lieutenant John Bulkeley and his
fellow torpedo boat crewmen spent their time investigating the waters
around the archipelago and prudently located caches of fuel and supplies
for future emergencies. "I was damned if I knew what I would be expected
to do in the Philippines. I figured my missions would be determined by the
theater commander."

The addition of the six torpedo boats hardly added up to the seagoing
power that MacArthur envisioned as necessary. The third leg of his planned
buildup, however, more closely approached his blueprint. With 8,100 Air
Corps personnel—flight crews, mechanics, and other ground-service experts—stationed in the Philippines by 7 December 1941, these troops constituted the single largest complement of Americans. What is remarkable
about the Army Air Corps presence in December 1941 is how much had
been accomplished in a short period. The first true effort to build an island-
based air wing began in May 1941, a bare six months before the first bombs

dropped. The War Department dispatched a conservative, old-school officer plagued by poor health, Gen. Henry Clagett to survey the needs. Fortunately, Clagett's chief of staff, a dedicated aviator who flew during World War I, Col. Harold George, compensated for his superior's lack of imagination with vision and energy. His success or failure, however, rested upon forces beyond the scope of either his wisdom or his industry.

The tasks ahead seemed insurmountable. The men from Washington learned that only four airfields with military capacity existed on Luzon, whose major city of Manila lay just 700 miles from bomber bases on Formosa. Furthermore, only Clark Field could be considered a first-class base. Both Nielson Field, the fighter strip near Manila, and Iba, the base along the western coast, lacked facilities for service of planes. Ground access to Nichols, the principal field for fighter planes, six miles south of Manila, depended upon a single narrow road that crossed a river bridge. One well-placed bomb could isolate Nichols from any entry or exit. Furthermore, although it had hard-surfaced runways, improper drainage rendered one section useless during the rainy season.

Under prodding from George, a handful of aviation engineers had started the slow process of carving out additional strips throughout the islands but the pace was so slow none were ever completely finished before the enemy struck. With George sounding the Klaxon, and with the backing of MacArthur, authorities hoped that genuine airpower might be enough to halt a Japanese advance at least long enough for a Philippine rescue operation. The best and latest that America could provide began to arrive in the islands. Some of the first pilots shipped to the Philippines in 1940 had been taken aback to discover that in combat they were expected to fly the same outmoded P-26 in which they had trained. But as the sense of urgency heightened, first came P-35s, and then the latest, the P-40 Warhawk.

To bolster the thin ranks of the Air Corps, the 34th Pursuit Squadron, equipped with P-40s was hastily dispatched overseas. It reached Manila on 20 November 1941, poorly prepared for action. A quartermaster refused to include barrels of antifreeze on the grounds it was not needed in the tropics. The 34th's water-cooled P-40s thus landed in the Philippines lacking a basic fluid for proper operation. The outfit's chief clerk, Sgt. Thomas Gage Jr., a 1940 enlistee from Tulsa, was among those aboard the SS *Coolidge* when it docked after the twenty-day voyage from Hawaii. "When we arrived at Nichols and after we got our P-40s put together," says Gage, "we were ordered to exchange our P-40s for the worn-out P-35s the 24th Group had been flying. The P-35s' engines were completely worn out when we got them. They had [ten months earlier] been on a ship bound for some Swedish colony and when the ship was in Manila they had been commandeered. The instruments were in Swedish." The details of diversion of these Severskymanufactured aircraft from their original destination to the U.S. Air Corps differ slightly in official accounts but the condition of the planes was as Gage described.

Construction at the Del Carmen airfield had hardly started before the 34th moved in. They were supposed to be only the first of several units to be stationed at what was expected to be a field capable of handling B-17s. Even as the 34th moved in, ordnance people scattered 500- and 1,000-pound bombs in the brush for eventual use by the oversize tennants. There was no running water, no latrine, and only a small river available for the basic amenities. The nearest town lay three miles off but the biggest problem was the strip itself. Dust as much as six-inches deep layered the bared ground. Airfield engineers had used molasses to cover the surface as they graded the runways, hoping that would produce a grass resistant to the production of dust but to little avail. Sometimes, after one pilot took off, the next man in line could see nothing for three to five minutes. The grit fouled the tired engines of the P-35s beyond the aid of primitive maintenance.

"We were issued," says Gage, "twelve Springfield rifles and six drum Lewis machine guns for aerodrome defense. The Lewis guns had no sights and the drums were loaded with no tracers. We dug six pits, six-feet deep, and about four in diameter. In the center was placed a steel pole on which a Lewis was mounted. Each pit had a drum, reserve drums were in a central supply, and a runner was to fetch when needed." Antiaircraft defenses at Del Carmen obviously were pitiful.

By the first week of December 1941, the 24th Pursuit Group listed seventy-two P-40s and eighteen P-35s available for combat. However, some planes had just been assembled and delivered; their machinery untested and requiring tuneups. Additional P-40s were still in crates, awaiting assembly. None of the pursuit ships were outfitted with adequate oxygen equipment. The fliers could not handle enemy aircraft at the higher altitudes. The slower P-35s, lightly armored, with worn-out engines and .30-caliber machine guns were hardly suitable for 1941 aerial warfare.

Fighter aircraft had never been the first priority of George and MacArthur. Both of them considered the prime requisite for a defense lay in the bomber and particularly the newest version, the B-17 Flying Fortress. An impressive start in dispatch of the four-engine bombers had landed a total of thirty-five in the Philippines—almost triple the number stationed in Hawaii. Backing up the Fortresses, the Philippine command could call on some aging and obsolescent B-18s and B-10s, useful at best for reconnaissance and ferrying supplies. Aware of the danger of keeping all thirty-five Fortresses in one target basket and expecting reinforcements, the Air Force had begun to construct a field on a former pineapple plantation on Mindinao, well out of range of the Formosa threat. On the eve of the Japanese attack, sixteen of the B-17s had been flown to Del Monte Field, Mindanao. The remainder were to follow and make that their base until suitably protected places could be created on Luzon.

The presence of the B-17s appeared to provide a devastating potential against any invasion fleet. But even these bombers, among the earlier models of the Fort, lacked essential features that later became standard equipment. The first B-17s entered battle without the power turrets, heavy armor, and tail guns that would carry the fight deep into Germany and blast Pacific sites late in the war. On paper, the Philippine Air Force bolstered the Americans. But its sixty aircraft was made up of forty-two P-13s, primary trainers. The planes listed for combat were a dozen P-26s, biplanes successful in knocking King Kong off the Empire State Building but long abandoned as useful for war by the U.S., and three B-10s, equally obsolescent.

Perhaps the worst aspect of the defenses of airfields and other installations was the absence of a functioning early-warning system. The latest radar systems, ones that could detect both heading and altitude of aircraft, key to the summer of 1940 Royal Air Force success against the might of German bombers in the Battle of Britain, and were almost totally absent from the islands. To supplement the inadequate electronic systems, inexperienced watchers, still being schooled in aircraft recognition, equipped with binoculars, were expected to spot incoming traffic—through clouds or at extreme altitudes—and then relay the information over an antiquated telephone network. The system as developed in China earlier worked reasonably well but there the attackers traveled long distances over land where they would be observed while still far from their targets. Against the Philippines, the raiders flew over the water from Formosa or launched from aircraft carriers, invisible to observers on land. The destruction of the U.S. air arm would render the Americans unable to fly effective reconnaissance over the seagoing approaches. Because the shortages of weaponry included proper antiaircraft batteries the defenders could not mount any opposition to the aerial thrusts.

The pace of preparedness had picked up dramatically in the last month or two before December. But the military might on hand was a long way from the ability to stop a better-organized and better-armed Japan. Whether the forces under MacArthur and Hart would have been ready by April, the general's date for an attack, is conjecture. The Japanese, well supplied with intelligence from countrymen living in the Philippines and aided by dissident Filipinos hostile to the existing government and the American presence, were aware of the effort to prevent any capture of the islands. The move to war reflected the desire of the expansionist elements not to gamble on MacArthur's chances of achieving his goal by springtime.

MacArthur, like others in his command, would express astonishment over the attack on Pearl Harbor, believing the Philippines would always be the first objective. But the Japanese may well have been aware of War Plan Orange, predicated upon the ability of the U.S. Navy to bring relief to the Americans and Philippines holding out on Bataan. The war that began at Pearl Harbor, now menaced the Philippines, the closest U.S. stronghold to Japan and an obvious prize if Imperial Japan expected to seize control of the Western Pacific and Southeast Asia.

4
Still Asleep

On Sunday night, 7 December in the Philippine Islands—because of the international date line, it was Saturday, 6 December in Hawaii and Washington D.C. 5,000 miles away—the 27th Bombardment Group tossed a bash at the Manila Hotel in honor of their Army Air Force commander, Gen. Lewis Brereton. Amid a raunchy affair that featured the "best entertainment this side of Minsky's" (a reference to a chain of burlesque houses in the States), General Brereton chatted with RAdm. William R. Purnell, chief of staff for the top Navy officer in the Far East. Others in the group were Adm. Thomas C. Hart and Brig. Gen. Richard K. Sutherland, chief of staff for the supreme commander of all the American and Philippine military, Gen. Douglas MacArthur. Admiral Purnell remarked that it was only a question of days or perhaps hours until the shooting started. Sutherland agreed, adding that the War and Navy Departments in Washington expected hostilities might erupt at any moment. Brereton immediately instructed his chief of staff to place all air units on "combat alert," as of Monday morning, 8 December. The party at the Manila Hotel wound down sometime after midnight. The airmen straggled back to their quarters in the darkest hours of the morning.

Ten minutes after the first explosives rained down upon the hapless Pearl Harbor anchorage, at 2:30 A.M. his time, a startled radio operator at Asiatic Fleet headquarters in Manila intercepted a stunning, unencrypted Morse code message, issued under the aegis of Adm. Husband E. Kimmel the Honolulu-based Pacific Fleet commander, "Air Raid on Pearl Harbor. This is no drill." Almost simultaneously, a typhoon of torpedoes, bombs, bullets, and shells struck other Japanese targets in Malaya, Thailand, Singapore, and Shanghai.

Because he knew the unique technical style of the Hawaii sender, the Manila radioman realized the communiqué was genuine and alerted his duty officer, Lt. Col. William T. Clement, a Marine who in turn contacted Admiral Hart. As a youthful naval officer then, Charles Adair remembered, "He [Clement] then called the various staff officers. I was in the apartment house where I was living when I got a call about 3:15, maybe a little earlier. All he said was, 'Charlie, come on down to the office.' I didn't even ask him what had happened because I knew what had happened. I was sure of it. I didn't keep him on the phone. I got dressed as quickly as I could and walked rapidly or ran part of the way through the park and over to where the headquarters was located [in the Marsman Building, at Pier 7 in Manila]. Once I got into the office, the communicators handed me a tape about six feet long or so, and I started pulling it through my fingers. 'This ship sunk. That ship sunk, et cetera,' with the details of some of the things that had gone on."

Commander S.S. Murray, the recently arrived boss of a submarine division operating out of Manila, after a familiarization cruise in the local waters celebrated with a round of golf on Saturday. He retired for the night on a submarine tender. "A few minutes before 2:00 A.M., I was awakened by Cmdr. James Fife, chief staff officer, commander of submarines, Asiatic, saying that Pearl Harbor had been attacked. After Fife awakened me and we had talked to the squadron commander, in the meantime sending for all the submarine skippers, and the message being sent for all submarines to alert them and to tell them to make immediate preparations to be sent on patrol, we started getting them ready."

As a junior officer on the sub *Seadragon,* Norvell Ward shared an apartment with three colleagues in Manila, and missed any official alarm. "We were having breakfast at the Army-Navy Club in Manila, picked up the *Manila Herald*—JAPANESE ATTACK PEARL HARBOR! We caught the ferry over [to the Cavite Naval Yard] and there we were at war."

Destroyer skipper Edward Parker, after a voyage to the Philippines to collect mail flown in from the States rejoined his division at Tarakan, a port in Borneo. "Early Monday morning, about 3:15, the voice over the tube said, 'Captain, important message coming in from the *Marblehead* [flagship for the destroyer division].' I put on my bathrobe and ran up. 'The Japanese had attacked Pearl Harbor, or something like that. Govern yourself accordingly.' [I thought] What the hell does 'govern yourself accordingly' mean?"

Not until perhaps an hour after the first report received at Manila Navy headquarters did General Sutherland learn of the blow at Pearl Harbor and then only from a commercial newscast. An enlisted army signalman happened to have tuned in to a California radio station. He immediately reported to his duty officer and the word passed up to Sutherland who telephoned the MacArthur penthouse atop the Manila Hotel.

"Pearl Harbor!" the astounded MacArthur supposedly exclaimed. "It should be our strongest point." Within ten minutes, at 3:40 A.M., a call from Washington, D.C., to MacArthur confirmed the news bulletin. According to MacArthur, he asked his wife Jean to fetch his Bible and he read before rushing off to confer with his staff. (Richard Sutherland once claimed, "His dispatches were replete with references to the deity but he has no more religion than a goat.")

Ten years later, Hart explained the failure to inform the Army of Kimmel's urgent message. He insisted Clement had tried to get through to someone at headquarters for the U.S. Army Forces, Far East but could not get a response. He allegedly passed the word to a staff officer at his home. While the news slowly percolated into other military services, it reached naval circles much faster. Lieutenant John D. Bulkeley, head of Motor Torpedo Boat Squadron 3, said, "The night of 8 December we were all asleep in the officers' quarters at Cavite when my telephone rang about three in the morning and I first learned the Japs had struck at Pearl Harbor. I was told, 'We are at war' and that Rear Admiral [Francis] Rockwell wanted to see me immediately."

Mary Rose Harrington, a Navy nurse at the hospital compound beside the Cavite navy base remembered, "I was on night duty. It was a beautiful moonlit night and after I'd made rounds of the sick officers' building I thought I'd walk outdoors. But the assistant master of arms came dashing in to say that Honolulu had been bombed. Then I saw a captain and the war plan officer, talking loudly and we started to wake people up in the middle of the night."

Nor did the Navy advise the Air Force's Brereton of the war's opening salvo. At the main Philippine airbase, Clark Field, sixty miles north of Manila, someone heard a radio news flash about the Japanese bombardment of Pearl Harbor. In the absence of verification from any official sources, however, during a period in which rumor rampaged through military circles, the only action taken was to notify the base commander.

Sam Grashio, P-40 pilot stationed at Nichols Field recalled, "About 2:30 A.M. on 8 December, Lt. L. A. Coleman, the officer of the day, banged on the door of the officers' living quarters and yelled to us to report at once to the operations tent. We dressed in a rush, jumped into a waiting vehicle, and sped away. [Lieutenant Ed] Dyess announced enigmatically that there was an emergency, but ten minutes later he told us to go back to our quarters. It seemed to me I had just fallen asleep when Coleman began banging on doors again. This time he shouted at us to get dressed, that Pearl Harbor had been attacked! It was about 4:45 A.M. We dashed back to Nichols. Dyess confirmed that Pearl Harbor had indeed been bombed by the Japanese. He ordered us into our new P-40E pursuit planes and directed us to start our engines and stand by on the radio."

Other U.S. airfields also sounded alerts and then a series of official and unofficial statements brought word of the attack upon the installations in Hawaii. Meanwhile, MacArthur's staff contacted Brereton and told him what they knew—which was limited. There had been no official declaration of war by the Japanese and the information on what had happened at Honolulu remained sketchy. At 5:00 A.M. the Air Force chief checked in at headquarters.

For most of the military personnel in the Philippines the news reached them haphazardly. Some units received word fairly quickly to mobilize and report to their assignments before dawn. Others became aware almost by pure happenstance. West Pointer Harold K. Johnson, a captain serving as operations officer for the 57th Infantry, a Philippine Scouts regiment, said, "We had heard rumors all over Manila on Sunday, 7 December that an attack had been made on Hawaii but the rumors were not given very much credence because it appeared to be such an illogical action to those of us in the Philippines. We figured we were the prime target and we had mixed viewpoints.

"There was an element of complacency . . . because we listened to and believed the Navy and the boasts that they would drive the Japanese fleet from the sea within a matter of a week or ten days. At the same time we knew we were a long way from the West Coast [of the U.S.] and if the Navy didn't drive the Japanese fleet from the sea, why, we were in trouble.

"It was Monday morning on the 8th before our regiment finally got the word. I was having breakfast in my robe about 6:30 when I got a call from a friend of mine. He said Colonel Clarke wants you to alert the regiment to move out of the barracks. [My friend] was a company commander from a sister regiment, serving in Bataan at the time, doing some survey work and cleaning up trails." Johnson quickly asked for a confirmation of the order from Clarke and with that instantly set to his tasks.

Colonel Clifford Bluemel, USMA '09, commander of the 31st Philippine Division, also swallowed the preliminary facts at breakfast. "On the morning of 8 December I ate with Col. [John] Irwin, Captain Bauer and one other officer. Bauer came into the mess and said, 'Did you hear the radio?'

"I said, 'I don't have any radio. What is it?'

"He said, 'Pearl Harbor, Wheeler Field, and Hickam Field were all bombed! The planes were destroyed on the ground, and a lot of the fleet was damaged!'

"I said, 'Oh my God! Who did it?'

"He said, 'The Japs did it.'

"I said, 'Well, we are at war now.'"

Lieutenant Colonel Irvin Alexander, of the quartermaster corps, a mustang who matriculated at West Point via the University of Indiana and a stint as a machine gun corporal with a federalized national guard during World War I, was at Fort Stotsenburg, some fifty miles north of Manila. "At breakfast on the morning, our radio told us that Pearl Harbor had been attacked with considerable naval damage. The announcement brought our breakfast to a mournful end, for we knew war was inevitable, and that we were on the hottest of war's seats."

Philip Fry, an infantry officer who had arrived in the islands less than three weeks before, recalled being at Fort William McKinley in the 45th Infantry

Regiment's barracks hard by the first golf green and close to the officers' club and the tennis courts. "On the morning of December 8th, just around dawn I was awakened by some officer rushing in and announcing that we were at war. He told of the attack on Pearl Harbor as, dressed in our pajamas, we eagerly crowded around him for the news. I dressed quickly and walked to the club, found the place in an uproar, everyone seeking news. I managed to get a cup of coffee. Left the club and started walking to division headquarters. On the way I saw the 57th and 45th Infantry forming in full field equipment preparatory to taking the field. Decided then to cast my lot with one of these fine old regiments. I had no desire to enter a first class shooting war with untrained troops. I asked for immediate assignment to the 57th Infantry and got it just like that."

Unlike Mary Rose Harrington, Army nurse Madeline Ullom stationed at Sternberg General Hospital in Manila a few miles from Cavite, greeted the morning of 8 December blissfully unaware of what had happened. "A generous slice of luscious papaya with a squeeze of tangy lime was ever a good way to begin breakfast. The lithe Filipino lad with the big armful of newspapers wended his barefoot way among the tables. His big brown eyes were solemn. His wide cheery grin was absent. His soft murmur was barely audible as he handed each, 'Your paper, mom.' Big black headlines across the front page blared the attack on Pearl Harbor."

There was a brief lull for the major Air Corps units while the Japanese opened the assault on the Philippines: First on the radio station at Aparri on the northernmost tip of Luzon; then fighter planes operating from a carrier destroyed two Navy PBYs in Davao Gulf near Mindanao, but missed their tender. Shortly after, the enemy hit at the airfield located near Baguio. Missing from these efforts was any sort of offensive blow by the Americans. Behind the failure to initiate any action lies a murky tale, confusions of command and decision. When General Brereton, air commander for the USAFFE, learned of the raid on Pearl Harbor, he had immediately hurried to MacArthur's headquarters, instructing his subordinates to ready the B-17s for a raid, with Formosa the obvious target. But instead of being able to confer with MacArthur, Brereton could not get beyond Chief of Staff, Sutherland an imperious, zealous officer whose arrogant manner made him the most unpopular man on MacArthur's staff.

Sutherland brusquely informed Brereton that his boss was too busy with Admiral Hart to discuss the immediate role for the Air Corps. That MacArthur and Brereton did not confer is the one undisputable fact about what occurred in the early hours of 8 December, Manila time. According to Sutherland's recollections, the airman announced that he would attack Formosa with his B-17s. The chief of staff claimed that after Brereton declared his intentions, Sutherland inquired, "What is the target? Where are the fields?" He did not know. He had no target data. There were twenty fields on Formosa. General Brereton had no notion of what he would attack and he would almost certainly lose his planes. Brereton later insisted he had proposed hitting the Japanese troopships crowded into Takao Harbor on Formosa.

Accounts from various sources indicate that at the hour Brereton attempted to see his commander in chief and obtain permission for the bombing raid on Formosa, MacArthur was unwilling to make any move against the Japanese. Absent a declaration of war from any party, he spoke of warnings from Washington that he not take any action the Japanese might seize upon as provocative. He later explained to an historian, Louis Morton, "My orders were explicit not to initiate hostilities against the Japanese."

Eugene Eubank, who had joined the Army in 1917, commanded the 19th Bomb Group. He remembered, "General Brereton called me early on Monday morning and his exact words were, 'A hostile act has been committed at Pearl Harbor.' I flew down to Nichols Field and while I was there I heard him, two or three times, on the phone, presumably talking to General Sutherland, urging him to give us authority to mount a mission against the Japanese. The question was whether we would go up to Formosa and bomb the airfields or whether we would go against Japanese ships. That required a different type of bomb. You can't load for a mission until you know the target. We could have moved the planes but we were waiting for a mission, for orders to bomb the Japanese in Formosa or in the sea."

In his memoirs, MacArthur remarked that upon word of a force of enemy bombers over the Lingayen Gulf on course for Manila at 9:30 A.M. he was still, "under the impression that the Japanese had suffered a setback at Pearl Harbor, and their failure to close in on me supported that belief. I therefore contemplated an air reconnaissance to the north, using bombers with fighter protection, to ascertain a true estimate of the situation and to exploit any possible weaknesses that might develop on the enemy's front." Subsequently, he said, having learned that the Japanese had succeeded in their Hawaiian venture, he changed his mind. Although the events at Pearl Harbor signaled about as clearly an act of war as conceivable regardless of what was achieved and had been confirmed by Washington, MacArthur, thus in an altogether uncharacteristic fashion, dithered for five hours. Finally, at 10:10 in the morning, through Sutherland, he agreed to photo reconnaissance flights, the first steps necessary for an attack by the B-17s.

The commander of the USAFFE, in the course of denying that he ever consulted with Brereton or knew of any interview the airman had with Sutherland, added, "As a matter of fact, an attack on Formosa, with its heavy air concentrations by our small bomber force without fighter cover, which because of the great distance involved and the limited range of the fighters was impossible, would have been suicidal. In contrast, the enemy's bombers from Formosa had fighter protection from their air carriers, an entirely different condition from our own."

MacArthur was probably correct in his estimate of the outcome of a B-17 raid on Formosa but his reasoning smacks of hindsight. The American bombers with their thin, unarmored fuselages; the cumbersome, manually operated turrets; and absence of tail guns would have made them easy prey. The range of the P-40s fell well short of the requirements to escort the bombers to Formosa and return. And the lack of oxygen equipment for high altitude flight meant the fighters could not stay with their flock.

Few if any U.S. strategists possessed accurate intelligence on the quality of the Japanese air force and MacArthur was dead wrong when he referred to bombers coming from Formosa as being convoyed by carrier-based fighters. In fact, the Japanese Zero had been modified and its pilots trained in ways that added hundreds of miles to its range. The sorties against Luzon that struck the vital American installations early in war employed land-based Zeros.

As an intelligence officer for the Air Corps in the Philippines, Capt. Allison Ind enthusiastically supported an immediate retaliation on Formosa by the B-17s. "We had no illusions," said Ind. "These folders [descriptions of objectives on Formosa] were not comparable with the exact and elaborate sheets of the RAF and the *Luftwaffe* prepared as they had been over a dozen, a score and more of years. We had none of their beautifully calibrated bomb-target maps, indicating best approaches and even bomb-release lines for given speeds and altitudes. But we had something complete enough to make this bombing mission a very far cry from the blind stab it would have had to be otherwise. Maybe we could deliver a real hurt, if not a staggering blow, to the enemy, at his very point of departure for an invasion action against the Philippines." Others thought quite differently and the Air Corps settled for a three-bomber photoreconnaissance to take off around noon or a bit later. The mission was delayed while technicians located the proper cameras and arranged for them to be flown to Clark Field from Del Monte.

Whatever the discussions at USAFFE headquarters during the morning of 8 December, the airmen throughout the area responded to a pair of warnings. Brereton's Washington boss, Gen. Henry (Hap) Arnold, telephoned the Philippines to caution against a repeat of the Hawaiian experience. Even without the advice from half a world away, when radar at Iba had indicated incoming hostile traffic, the duty officer at Clark Field had ordered the B-17s to get out of harms way. The bombers had placidly cruised the skies in great circles for two hours, staying in radio contact with the nearby communications tower. The first series of strikes from the sky ignited a host of defensive missions. The P-40s started patrols to cover Clark Field. Pilots at airbases not involved in these operations remained by their ships, ready on signal to meet the invaders.

At the northern tip of Luzon, the closest point to the Imperial Japanese forces stationed on Formosa, the Philippine Army's 11th Division guarded the beach approaches around the town of Aparri. Like all Philippine military units, Americans either commanded or "advised" the indigenous soldiers. Information about a state of war reached some units there almost eight hours after the news reached Manila. Colonel Glen R. Townsend served as the commanding officer of the 11th Regiment. "About ten o'clock on the morning of December 8th," recalled Townsend, "one of the Filipino officers came to tell me he had heard over his car radio that Japanese planes had bombed Hawaii. I thought of Orson Welles and the men from Mars." [The radio drama in 1939 panicked thousands who believed outer space beings had invaded the U.S.]

"But Captain Pilar insisted, so I walked with him to his car nearby. When he turned the radio on, the announcer was just telling about the bombing of Baguio [the summer capital of the Philippines and site of some military installations and a resort area]. That convinced me there was a war on, but if more was needed it came an hour or so later. Eighty-four Japanese bombers passed directly over the camp. We later learned that these struck Clark Field."

Word of the Pearl Harbor attack and reports of incoming aircraft had reached operational elements of the 34th Pursuit Squadron at Del Carmen and pilots took off because of the alerts. Tom Gage, working in the squadron offices of the Del Carmen Airfield currently under construction, away from the flight line remained ignorant that the country was at war. "A little before noon, one of the cooks, Shorty Batson, came running down to tell me they had heard on the Manila radio that Pearl Harbor had been bombed. Shortly after I heard what sounded like distant reports of firecrackers exploding. I stepped out and took a look around the sky and over toward the direction of Clark Field [14 miles to the north] the sky was covered by black dots. My first thought was 'My God! Look at the enemy planes—there's thousands of them.' It took a few minutes for me to sort out the antiaircraft bursts and barely visible were two lines of very small black dots, flying in formation, above and beyond the shell smoke. I immediately hotfooted across the area and found Lt. Jack Jennings, the squadron adjutant, in his tent, reading a book! I told him Clark Field was being bombed. His reply was, 'Is that official, Sergeant?' I replied, 'Hell, Lieutenant, look out the back of your tent! Clark Field is going up in smoke!'"

At Clark, an hour before noon, with no imminent attack by Japanese planes in the area, most of the aircraft including P-40s and B-17s, were back on the ground. While ground crews hastily refueled the ships and stocked the prescribed ordnance for the bombers, air crews snatched a few moments of rest or a quick snack. About 11:30, Iba airfield alerted all Air Corps bases of a large formation of planes coming in from the China Sea, apparently vectored on Manila but the heading also meant the enemy would approach Clark Field.

The warning of approaching planes over the China Sea scrambled flights of fighters from other bases. The 3d Squadron at Iba saw nothing in the vicinity of their home field, nor could they spot anything amiss at either Manila or Clark Field. Running low on gas, the P-40s returned to Iba. Just as planes formed up for an orderly landing, Iba literally went up in flash and smoke. Enemy bombers, cruising at 28,000 feet, out of sight and well out of range of the P-40s had unloaded devastating strings of explosives across the base. The place was completely destroyed, the radar station and its operators wiped out, every building reduced to rubble, anyone not in a foxhole died. Five P-40s were lost and the surviving flights scattered to emergency sites, with several crashing from lack of fuel or damage from dogfights.

At Nichols Field, P-40 pilot Grashio said, "After the initial alert, we cut our engines, got out of the cockpits, and sat under the wings, and waited as seemingly endless hours dragged by. Suddenly about 11:30 A.M. we received an urgent call to prepare for action, though just what action was unspecified. Soon, Ed Dyess divided our eighteen P-40s into three groups and led two of them, A and B into the air. I was to lead the remaining six, Flight C, and follow him, but a couple of our planes developed minor engine difficulties that delayed us just long enough that we lost contact with A and B Flights. Only at about 11:50 did my flight actually get into the air. We flew to Laguna de Bay, a huge lake just south of Nichols Field, and for the first time tested our .50-caliber machine guns by firing short bursts into the water. More of the fruits of unreadiness appeared only minutes later. Two pilots in my flight reported that their engines were throwing so much oil on the windshields that they couldn't see. They could only go back to Nichols.

"By now Flights A and B were not only out of sight but, for reasons unknown, out of radio contact as well. Since I had received no orders other than to get into the air and follow the other flights, our isolation was complete. Since I had to do something, I radioed [the others] that we should fly toward Clark Field, sixty miles north. It seemed a logical target for Japanese planes flying in from the north." The fighter squadrons, alerted by Iba, prowled the skies, searching sectors over the China Sea, Bataan, and Corregidor. Clark Field, during the period when its own ships from the 20th Pursuit Squadron required refueling, lay naked.

The bombs that smashed the radar installation at Iba eliminated the most definitive source of intelligence on enemy raids. The native observers, trained to report flights approaching the islands, relayed their information over the lines of the notoriously unreliable Philippine telephone system to air headquarters at Nielson Field. In turn, the word passed over the teletype or by radio to the different squadrons. But by midday of 8 December, the wires that normally carried the messages were dead, victims either of sabotage or the frequent technical problems.

"We arrived over Clark Field about 12:20 P.M." said Grashio. "It was a gorgeous day. The sky was blue and the air smooth as glass. Observing the idyllic look of the area I still could not feel that I might become personally involved in a shooting war at any moment. It may seem incredible that anyone could have been in such an abstracted condition eight hours after Pearl Harbor but I accepted the fact of war only when it hit me in the face, and there were many like me.

"Observing nothing unusual at Clark, C Flight flew westward toward the China Sea. Suddenly I spotted planes at about our altitude (10,000 feet) moving south. We closed in, pulses racing. No sweat! They were only some other P-40s. Before we could get close enough to tell which squadron they belonged to, however, our earphones were suddenly filled with hysterical shouts from the tower operator far below, 'All P-40s return to Clark Field. Enemy bombers overhead.' These ominous words were almost immediately intermixed with the terrifying whoomp of bombs exploding. To my utter astonishment, the formation of P-40s continued serenely on a southerly course, climbing gradually. Obviously they had not heard the frantic order to return to Clark. What happened to their radios? It was the second snafu on a day filled with them."

At 12:30 P.M., about the moment that Grashio recognized a friendly group of P-40s, the 19th Bombardment Group staff continued to plot the assault upon Formosa. The P-40s of the 20th Pursuit Squadron at Clark Field taxied to the runway, ready for the signal to take off. Already, bombs had been loaded into several B-17s, and the aircraft scheduled to collect photo intelligence on Formosan bases rumbled into position for the start of their mission.

Lieutenant Fred T. Crimmins Jr., commander of one plane, started to walk across the field toting a machine gun that required a minor fix. His crew, grabbing lunch, was astonished to hear an unconfirmed radio report that at that very moment Japanese bombers were over Clark Field. Crimmins reached a hangar and passed the weapon to a sergeant for repair when the base Klaxon sounded its urgent alarm. The pilot and the mechanic rushed outside and peered into the sky. In the clear blue above, from over the mountains to the northwest, they saw two precision Vees, one behind the other. Serenely droning toward them at 18,000 feet, the pair heard the engines even as the first of the P-40s roared down the runway, now frantic to get off before the hammer fell.

There had been no warning at all, according to those on the scene, and it was a matter of seconds or perhaps a minute between the sight of the Japanese flights and the fall of the bombs. And when these plummeted to the target the devastation was horrendous. The pattern of the two bomber waves spewed explosives across the field, shattering the officers quarters, the parked P-40s, the headquarters building, the maintenance shops, and hangar areas. Almost every structure took a hit and many blazed flames without restraint; the apparatus to control fires had been destroyed. No means to summon help existed; the blasts obliterated the communications center. The 200th Coast Artillery, responsible for antiaircraft defense, coped with ammunition manufactured a minimum of nine years earlier. Most fuses were badly corroded and an expert guess reported that only one of every six of the three-inch rounds actually fired. Tracers and flaming debris ignited nearby trees and the long grass. A giant pall of dust and a thick black cloud from a burning oil dump rose so high in the air that a pilot near Iba saw the sinister cloud. At ground zero, the fumes reduced visibility well below 100 feet.

Flight C from the 21st Pursuit Squadron, with Sam Grashio in command, started to respond to the control tower appeal for help. "Right at this critical juncture," said Grashio, "Joe Cole radioed his engine was throwing oil so badly that he could not see out of his windshield. Like the two others with the same trouble, he had to return to Nichols Field. This left McGown, Williams, and myself. We turned back toward Clark. In the distance I got my first glimpse of the spectacular destructiveness of war. It was astounding! Where the airfield should have been the whole area was boiling with smoke, dust and flames. In the middle was a huge column of greasy black smoke from the top of which ugly red flames billowed intermittently. Momentarily, I thought how utterly, abysmally wrong the senior officers on the *Coolidge* had been, a reflection almost immediately replaced by pity for those on the ground who must be going through hell. I said a quick prayer, asking God to help them and thanking Him for sparing me, at least for the moment, from being on the receiving end of Japanese bombs.

"About 12:50 P.M., directly over the field, I noticed several enemy dive bombers perhaps 800 feet below us and 2,000 feet above the ground bombing and strafing. All our flight training had been directed toward moments and opportunities like this. I signaled my wingmen to attack. Just then, an enemy dive bomber shot out of the smoke maybe 500 feet below. I looked at once for McGown. He was nowhere in sight. Gus Williams had disappeared, too.

"Instead, about 100 yards behind and above me were two Zeros, closing in. They opened fire. I veered sharply to the left. My plane shuddered as a cannon burst hit the left wing and blew a hole big enough to throw a hat through. For the first time that day I had the hell scared out of me. Momentarily, I was sure I was going to die on the first day of the war. Instinctively, I began to pray again, this time with greater fervor than before. I also remembered what Ed [Dyess] had told me many times; never try to outmaneuver a Zero; go into a steep dive and try to outrace it. I pushed the throttle wide open and roared for the ground. The wind shrieked past me and the earth flashed upward at horrifying speed. Technical manuals specifically warned against a power dive in an untested plane, and I was in a P-40 that had been in the air a grand total of two hours. But with two Zeros on your tail, the admonitions in technical manuals are not the first things you think about. My luck held. When I tried to pull out of the dive at treetop level just west of Clark the plane responded magnificently. Glancing back, I was overjoyed to see the two Zeros falling steadily behind. The superior diving capability of the P-40 had saved my hindquarters."

Grashio said he saw enemy tracers pass increasingly wide of the mark and eventually the pair of Zeros turned away. "I breathed a prayer of thanks only to break out anew in a cold sweat. Would I be able to land with the gaping hole in the wing? I radioed Nichols tower for advice. I was told to climb to 8,000 feet above an uninhabited area and simulate a landing. Wheels and flaps down. I did so. The hole in the wing presented no problems. Nevertheless, many curious and doubtless apprehensive people stood along the runway when I came down about 1:30, the first pilot to make it back to Nichols from combat."

On the ground at Clark Field, however, rather than celebrating the return of a pilot, the airmen and ground crews, not killed or badly wounded, struggled to recover, dispensing what medical aid they could to the injured and seeking to arrange transport for them to the Fort Stotsenburg Hospital. But the respite from the onslaught was pitilessly short as dozens of Japanese fighters roared through the smoke. Machine guns and 20mm cannons hammered away at the parked Fortresses, totally exposed to the strafing runs. Only a few had been ruined by the high-altitude attack of a few minutes earlier, but the fighter runs, at a few feet off the ground, completely wrecked all but two or three and even those absorbed some damage. The three ships scheduled to survey Formosa, having never left the earth, lay in smoldering ruins. Four of the P-40s at Clark managed to get airborne before the bombs rendered the field useless. Five others in the process of taking off and five more lined up to await their turn were turned into junk. The quartet that escaped registered three downed Zeros and a handful of other interceptors that rushed to the scene claimed several other kills. But the costs to the enemy were negligible.

The only Fort to survive was that of John W. Carpenter a 1939 graduate of West Point who had transferred from the field artillery to become a B-17 pilot with the 19th Bomb Group."The airplane I inherited was a dog, and all the way across the Pacific this thing had been blowing generators. Every time you would turn around, you would blow another generator. My squadron had been ordered to disperse down to Del Monte around the fifth of December but as usual my airplane was out for a generator so I stayed on Clark with the ground echelon.

"Word came around to report to group headquarters. They said the Hawaiian Islands had been attacked and Hickam was gone. At that time we didn't have any orders and couldn't do anything. Our commander then, Col. E. L. Eubank then tried to get permission to load up and go bomb the Japs—no way. They said, all right, we are not going to get these airplanes caught on the ground here; everybody get out and go. They assigned reconnaissance sectors for the different airplanes. We all took to the air, all except my aircraft, which was out for generators. There wasn't another airplane on the ground. Everybody got to work and they finally got my airplane fixed.

"We got up in the air and headed out and [I] was just at the far reach of my assigned sector when word came through on radio, a recall for all airplanes. The rest of the B-17s were fairly close in by that time, and they landed. When I finally got back, all the other airplanes were on the ground. We came down through the clouds out over the mountains and one of my crew said, 'Look there, there is a big thunderstorm right over Clark Field,' and sure enough there was this big thunderstorm. Only it wasn't a thunderstorm. All our airplanes on the ground were burning, and this was the smoke going up for all the world like a big thunder-bumper over the airport.

"About that time we began to get word over the radio . . . an officer had climbed up in the control tower and called. My airplane and another were circling east of the field. The other plane—a fellow named Earl Tash—had come up from Mindanao and was going to land for repairs that couldn't be accomplished at Del Monte. The tower said, 'We are under attack. Better go elsewhere to land.' Tash managed to get his gear up when the Jap fighters jumped him. He got away and headed on to Mindanao. He had enough gas but I didn't have enough to make it.

"We had a standard approach procedure where we would come in on a heading from Mount Arayat on the east of Clark. With your gear down, the ack-ack weren't suppose to shoot at you. We had an Army National Guard outfit from Albuquerque just recently transferred over there, and they couldn't tell a four-engine airplane from a single-engine one and would fire on anything that approached the field. We had to be very careful to return in accord with proper approach procedure. Here we were with gear and flaps down headed into Clark below 500 feet. About that time the Jap fighters hit us. We thought all the Jap aircraft were gone but heck no. Their bombers had been over and done all the damage, and then waves of fighters hit the place, one after another. Here we were gear and flaps down, guns stowed—fat, dumb, and happy—between two of the waves. I was worried I didn't have much runway, only about 1,200 feet undamaged, and concentrated on setting it down on the edge of the field and here came these fighters.

"First we thought they must be P-40s out of Nichols Field and then all of a sudden we realized those little red lights that were flashing on the front end of the wings weren't playing. About that time a fighter went by, and I could see the Rising Sun on his wings. We threw everything to the firewall, got the gear and flaps up, and fortunately nobody was hit in my airplane. We took a few bullets and headed back up into the clouds. We knew that Nichols had been bombed and I didn't have fuel to go anywhere else. We hid in the clouds over on the other side of Mount Arayat until I was just about empty and then came in and landed at Clark. Fortunately, the air raid was over for the moment."

With the only airplane that could fly at Clark, Carpenter was ordered to undertake a reconnaissance flight toward Formosa. "My job was to go up and see if we could take pictures of what was going on. About halfway up my generators went out and I had to abort. I would never have made it to Formosa. They would have murdered me, single airplane all by itself. The briefing officer, the group operations officer, said, 'I want you to go up there and take some pictures. You had better stay up around 20,000 feet. I don't think they can get you up there.' Every fighter they had was very active at that altitude and higher," noted Carpenter who remembered that as squadron intelligence officer he agreed with his briefer. "From all the information we had, they had a bunch of old fixed-gear airplanes that could hardly fly above 10,000 feet."

Carpenter said, "We had talked about possibilities and felt something like this was coming. We were convinced with our B-17s we could fly back and forth across the China Sea and sink anything the Japs could send down with just our one group of bombers. Our esprit was high. We knew we could do the job. We were also convinced that immediately after the Japs attacked, the biggest convoy you ever saw in your life was starting out from San Francisco to come over and reinforce the Philippines. We were going to take care of this thing in short order. It was not just a hope. I think it was really a belief on the part of most of our people in the Philippines."

Major Alva Fitch, commander of a battery for the 23d Field Artillery Regiment, a Philippine Scouts outfit, on the morning of 8 December was at his Fort Stotensburg post near Clark Field. Although aware of the news, Fitch and his battery received no orders, but busied themselves with digging in for protection against air raids. "We were just sitting down to luncheon when

Johnny [an aide], hearing a suspicious noise went outside. I looked at my watch. It was 12:48. Johnny called to us. We saw a flight of fifty-three bombers very high. We speculated as to their identity for a very few seconds, and took to the ditch. About one minute later, Clark Field exploded. The entire Clark Field area erupted in a column of smoke and dust and with an awful and impressive roar.

"I ran for the barracks where I found the battery engaged in antiaircraft operations with Springfield rifles, with far more danger to themselves than to the airplanes. The rifles had been recently issued and only a few of the men had ever fired them before. I stopped the rifle fire, and put the men in the trenches we had dug earlier. By this time, attack planes were strafing the airplanes on the ground, and the AA installations in the vicinity. They passed low over the battery and turned back into the smoke. This started the troops firing again. I am still surprised that none of them were killed by their own barrage."

Colonel Irvin Alexander, in charge of supply matters at Fort Stotsenburg, who learned by radio of the war's opening blast, recalled, "As we went about our duties that morning we had little more information but heard a rumor that Baguio had been bombed. At lunch I turned on the radio at 12:30 P.M. to hear the news from Don Bell, our favorite Manila announcer. He reported Baguio had been bombed that morning and there was an unconfirmed rumor that Clark Field had also been initiated. Clark Field being less than a mile from where we were sitting, I laughed, as I started to say, 'Another example of the accuracy of the news.'

"In the middle of the sentence my face froze, for I became aware of the whistling approach of hundreds of bombs. This shrieking was followed by terrific explosions that made our house shake and groan like it was in the midst of a violent earthquake. We rushed out to the parade ground to see columns of smoke and dust rising from the airfield. Searching the sky, I discovered the attackers, a Vee-shaped formation of fifty-four bombers, high up, perhaps 20,000 feet, heading for home. The war had begun for us."

The action at Clark Field lasted only about forty-five minutes but when the Japanese withdrew, almost nothing usable remained of the best of the American air stations in the Philippines. Not a single plane that had been on the ground could fly. Bomb craters pockmarked the strips. Fires raged in the gutted hangars and buildings. Casualties numbered fifty-five dead and more than a hundred men wounded. MacArthur and his people now faced a defense of the Philippines with half of their B-17 arsenal gone, and a similar situation with available fighters. Furthermore, the damage to Clark meant the remainder of the Fortresses would have to operate from Del Monte in Mindanao, 1,000 miles south. Longer flying distances meant additional stress on engines and crews.

What happened to Clark Field was a miniature replica of the disaster at Pearl Harbor. An outraged Gen. Hap Arnold, as chief of the Army Air Forces, and Brereton's boss, chewed out the commander of the Far Eastern Air Force, demanding "how in hell" he could have been caught with his bombers down a full nine hours after hearing of what happened at Pearl Harbor. General George C. Marshall, as MacArthur's superior, soon afterward remarked to a correspondent, "I just don't know how MacArthur happened to let his planes get caught on the ground."

Early in December, Adm. Thomas Hart with tens of thousands of square miles of ocean available for dispersal of his fleet prudently had dispatched much of it out of immediate reach of any attack. Only five destroyers—two of which were under repair—plus the bulk of his submarines cruised the waters in the Manila Bay area. The remainder of Hart's forces hung out well south, and once the news of Pearl Harbor reached Hart, he ordered his vessels even farther beyond harms way, to the neighborhood of the Dutch possession, Borneo. The first and second days of the war thus passed with no significant consequences to the U.S. Asiatic Fleet.

Although Admiral Hart had assigned most of his ships to more southern seas, points well away from the base in Manila Bay, on the day of this attack, two destroyers were in the navy yard undergoing repairs and the *John D. Ford*, the four-stacker with William Mack aboard, hovered nearby, awaiting its annual overhaul. "[When] we received a message from Pearl Harbor," said Mack, "we immediately activated our explosives systems and ripped down the awnings and we were all ready. We knew we weren't going into the yard but we didn't know what to do until somebody told us, so we were lying off Cavite."

The ship remained on station and on the morning of 10 December, the crew saw a few Zeros fly by but nothing happened until noon. "Then," Mack continued, "fifty-four high-level bombers came over at about 10,000 feet and made practice runs on the waterfront of the Philippines and the ships in the harbor and on the Cavite naval yard. They made three dry runs; they were actually unopposed; there were no P-40s anywhere in sight. We were sitting there thinking that was going to be a great show when all our P-40 pilots got away from the country club and went up there and showed them a thing or two. But not one P-40 showed anywhere.

"These fifty-four aircraft were bombing first the Philippine waterfront and then Manila, and they devastated that. Then they went around in a sort of triangular circle and devastated the shipyard where the *Pillsbury* and *Perry* were frantically trying to get themselves back together and get out. They [the planes] came across where the *John D. Ford* was [and merchant ships] and dropped bombs on all of us, but we were not hit."

Also undergoing overhaul at Cavite were a pair of submarines, *Sealion* and *Seadragon*, skippered by Comdr. Dick Voge and Comdr. Pete Ferrall with

Norvell Ward as one of Ferrall's junior officers. Tied up alongside each other the two captains, and some of the crew, like Ward, scanned the skies. Ward remembered, "We watched the Jap bomber formation go over at about 22,000, 25,000 feet, watched them make a practice run from west to east, then turn around and come back and make their first bombing run from east to west. We saw the bombs drop on the pier and other buildings up in the shipyard. We saw them release, we saw them coming down, but we knew on that run that they were going to miss us, just a little bit, and they did." The absence of fighters to interfere or effective ground fire gave the Japanese the leisure to make dry runs before the actual attacks, thereby enabling them to enhance their effectiveness.

"We manned our .50-caliber [machine] guns. We manned our three-inch gun, as did the *Sealion*," said Ward. "Dick Voge turned to Pete Ferrall and said, 'I think we're damn fools staying up here on the bridge.' Pete said, 'I agree with you.' Dick cleared his people off the topside and we cleared ours. Voge had all of his go down below into the control room, whereas on the *Seadragon* some of us stayed up in the conning tower. I stayed there and so did Sam Hunter. Diaz, our chief pharmacist's mate, remained up in the conning tower among two or three others. Pete Ferrall went down to the control room.

"On the next run the *Sealion* received two bomb hits, one right on their conning tower and the other in the after engine room. If anyone had been in the conning tower of the *Sealion* they would have been wiped out. The *Sealion* lost three men, I believe, who were in the after engine room when the bomb hit. Shrapnel from the *Sealion*'s conning tower went through ours. It took off the back of Sam Hunter's head and shattered Diaz's arm. I was standing there with my hand on Sam's shoulder, and I was fortunate in that I got scraped across the belly by some shrapnel. Sam was killed instantly; Diaz was able to walk to the hospital, and I had a superficial wound."

Lieutenant John Bulkeley's Motor Torpedo Boat Squadron 3 responded to the air raid warning and sped out into the comparative safety of Manila Bay. "The admiral sent us a two-hour warning that they were coming—from Formosa, and were headed on down in our direction across northern Luzon. So we hauled our boats out into the bay. They kept beautiful formations . . . and they came in at about 20,000, with their fighters on up above to protect them from ours—only ours didn't show! I kept thinking," said Bulkeley, "wait until those Army pilots leave the officers' club and go after them. We knew we couldn't get appropriations for the Navy; all the money was going into those P-40s. I hadn't heard anything about the destruction of Clark Field and the other airfields." Bulkeley and the rest of his squadron quickly discovered they were among the targets. "They swung over Manila and began to paste the harbor shipping. It was a beautiful clear day, and I remember the sun made rainbows on the waterspouts of their bombs. They were 150 to 200 feet high and it made a mist screen so dense you could hardly tell what was happening to the ships.

"But then that beautiful Vee pivoted slowly and moved over Cavite—began circling it like a flock of well-disciplined buzzards. They were too high for us to see the bomb bay doors open, but we could see the stuff drop slowly, picking up speed; only as we watched we found we had troubles of our own. Because five little dive bombers peeled off that formation, one by one, and started straight down for us. When they were down to about 1,500 feet, they leveled off and began unloading. Of course, we gave our boats full throttle and began circling and twisting, both to dodge the bombs and get a shot at them. Our gunners loved it—it was their first crack at the Japs. . . . They'd picked out one plane and were pouring it up into the sky, when we saw the plane wobble, and pretty soon she took off down the bay, weaving unsteadily, smoking, and all at once, two or three miles away, she just wobbled down into the drink with a big splash."

Bulkeley said of Cavite after the enemy finally ended its two-hour rampage: "They'd flattened it—there isn't any other word. Here was the only American naval base in the Orient beyond Pearl Harbor pounded into bloody rubbish. . . . We began loading in the wounded to take them to Cañacao Hospital . . . There was half an inch of blood on the landing platform at Cañacao—we could hardly keep on our feet, for blood is as slippery as crude oil—and the aprons of the hospital attendants were so blood-spattered they looked like butchers."

After confirmation of the start of hostilities, Lt. Madeline Ullom at Sternberg Hospital read a red-bordered form labeled IMMEDIATE ACTION that directed the staff to "discharge all patients who could possibly go." A very few helpless patients remained on the wards. Foxholes were dug on the lawns of the hospital for protection. When air raid sirens wailed several times that first day, the cries of "Hit the dirt!" showed the disadvantages of white uniforms. A warehouse issued fatigues ordinarily worn by men but quickly tailored to appropriate sizes. Ullom and the others received gas masks and helmets.

"Filipino troops and the constabulary were armed and patrolled the streets," Lieutenant Ullom said. "Manila was in blackout. Heavy curtains hung over the windows. Blue paper covered flashlights. Rumors were abundant. Rumors were believed because we could not comprehend that Americans were not capable of the almost impossible." The impact of war closed in upon the nurses. "Casualties flowed into Sternberg. Huge abdominal gashes, an arm or a leg almost severed, a hunk of buried or protruded shrapnel were common sights. The dead and dying were interspersed among the wounded. Facilities were taxed beyond capacity to adequately and immediately operate and treat the multitude. The waiting section extended to the lawn between the wards and surgery. Patients were lined up side by side, on stretchers and blankets. Big bloody dressings reflected the hues of magnificent poinsettias. Hypodermics were injected to take the edge from severe pain. A colored mark on the forehead provided quick reference to determine time of medication. The Emergency Medical Tag fastened to the top pajama button kept records. Considerate men often implored us to care for a fellow soldier they felt was more critically injured, although they were next in line. Chaplains Oliver and Tiffany along with others moved among the casualties to administer the Last Rites, to console the injured. With religious duties completed, they carried litters, acted as messengers. Many former army nurses, stationed at Sternberg before marriage, hastened to volunteer their services.

"Everyone was on duty, time meant nothing. Many took turns sleeping on the operating tables, on the floor between raids. When the first bombs fell near Sternberg I was so scared I felt petrified. A patient's abdomen had just been opened when an air raid alarm sounded. We continued to operate. The thin galvanized roof above surgery rattled. We were so busy that outside sounds seemed far away. After that session, my fears left me."

Admiral Hart, with an eagle's eye view of the destruction of Cavite from atop the Marsman Building, which housed naval headquarters, lost only one docked submarine, but the raid cost the Navy a major source of maintenance and supply, including more than 200 torpedoes stored at Cavite. Without adequate facilities, with no protection against a Japanese thrust from the air, and badly undergunned in any surface encounters, the Navy wrote off the Philippines. Except for the submarines, the six-boat PT squadron, and a few PBYs, the Asiatic Fleet abandoned the local waters. Within three days, MacArthur had lost not only two potential offensive weapons; he was also bereft of the vital means for any defense of the beaches.

5
Early Engagements

Obedient to the terms of the treaty signed with the Japanese, the Third Reich, on 11 December, declared war on the United States. Some Americans, hostile to Germany for its persecution of Jews, its conquests of neighbors, and out of affection for the Allied opposition, had entered the conflict well before December 1941.

James Goodson, a nineteen-year-old student at the University of Toronto, torpedoed while aboard the steamship *Athenia* a day after war broke out in 1939, and with an English mother, quickly enlisted in the Royal Air Force. Sent to Canada for training, he returned to the United Kingdom as the Battle of Britain was winding down, flying first Hurricanes and then Spitfires. The RAF operated mixed squadrons made up of Canadians, Aussies, New Zealanders, South Africans, East Indians, and Americans. After the fall of the European allies there were also French, Poles, Czechs, and Norwegians. In September 1940, in what was more likely a politico-propaganda move rather than a tactical one, the RAF created the 71 Squadron, an all-American unit under the nominal leadership of a former U.S. Marine pilot, William Taylor. Actually, a Briton ran operations because the top RAF officer, Air Marshal Trafford Leigh-Mallory, objected to a squadron composed of American volunteers whom he believed lacked discipline. Four months passed before the first Eagle Squadron began to function.

Leigh-Mallory's opinion, one shared at the time by Hap Arnold, initially proved correct. In it first sorties, the 71 Squadron performed poorly and an RAF officer replaced Taylor with the assignment to whip the bunch into shape. Subsequently, two more Eagle Squadrons were formed, the 121 and the 133. Among the members of the 71 was Bill Dunn, a refugee in June 1940, from the life of an infantryman trapped with the British Expeditionary Force in France.

The tales of an uncle who flew in World War I and a stepfather who also piloted a plane in that conflict motivated Dunn to join the RAF. Dunn had acquired 150 hours of flying when in 1934 he went to Fort Lincoln [Texas] and told the recruiting officer he wanted to enlist in the Army Air Corps. "Recruiting people will promise you anything to get your name on the dotted line and I found myself in the infantry with a musket. The pay was supposed to be $21 a month but, in 1934 with the Depression on, Roosevelt cut all government employees' wages 20 percent. As a buck private I got $16.85 a month. Every so often some local restaurant would put a sign in the window, NO DOGS OR SOLDIERS ALLOWED.

"I finished my army service and when the war broke out I thought I'd whip up to Canada and join the RAF. I couldn't get into a flying outfit but the Seaforth Highlanders were taking volunteers. A sergeant major asked me where I came from and I said the U.S. He said, 'Sorry, we can't take you, no American citizens. However, if you walk around the block and come back in maybe you can decide you're from some place in Canada.' I went out and came back and said, 'Moose Jaw.' He asked, 'Where is that?' I said, 'How the hell would I know, I just thought of it.' He told me, 'It's in Saskatchewan and don't forget it. You're enlisted.'"

On 10 May 1940, when the German offensive started to roll through Holland and Belgium, Canadian specialists were chosen to assist the British Expeditionary Force. "I was a mortar platoon sergeant," recalled Dunn, "and they needed mortars, Bren gun carrier people, machine gunners. We were taken to France as part of the 61st Highland Division. On 14 or 15 May, when Germans broke through Belgium and were coming toward us, we were ordered to retreat to better positions. We fell back several times and followed the railroad all the way down to Saint-Omer and then back to the coast to Calais until they evacuated about 1,000 of us.

"After the Battle of Britain, the British were very short of pilots. The air ministry sent around a message that anyone with at least 500 hours flying time could transfer to the RAF. I didn't have 500 but when I wrote 130–150, somehow the pencil slipped a little, my ones looked like fives. German Stuka bombers bombed our camp at Borden and I shot two of them down with a Lewis machine gun and I think that helped my being accepted. I was awfully tired of carrying the damned mortar around the countryside. It was good to be out of the infantry.

"I went to flying school and had a total of sixty-five hours before going operational as a Hurricane pilot. The Hurricane was reasonably fast, a good climber and very maneuverable. During the Battle of Britain there were nineteen RAF squadrons equipped with Hurricanes, seven flew Spitfires. The real load fell on the Hurricane pilots. I don't mean to shortchange the Spit boys. They did an excellent job in taking the 109s off the backs of the Hurricanes while they were knocking the bombers about. It annoys me when the Spit gets all the credit and the hard-working Hurricane is forgotten by the historians."

Goodson, Dunn, et al., had been preceded by a trio of accomplished American pilots, Shorty Keough, Gene Tobin, and Andrew Mamedoff, all of whom, frustrated in an effort to form a replica of the Lafayette Escadrille of World War I for the French, reached England in time to serve in the 1940 summer campaign known as the Battle of Britain. When Dunn entered the 71 Squadron, the three were already on hand. "Shorty Keough was killed by a bomb. Red Tobin was shot down and killed. During bad weather, Andy Mamedoff ran into a hill. Another American, Mike Kolendorfski, was shot down by two ME 109s.

"The Eagle Squadrons weren't the greatest outfits in the world," said Dunn. "They were more of a propaganda idea. The 71 did a fair amount of combat work, the 121 did a little bit but the 133 never got into any to speak of. There was a lot of reluctance among the Americans in the RAF squadrons. They were happy where they were in the mixed squadrons. They already had their buddies. The squadron leaders—flight lieutenants—the intelligence, maintenance, and armament officers, and the ground crew were all English. The fighter pilots were Americans, about eighteen of us. We were formed about March or April 1941. The first fighter sweep I ever went on, a German squadron came up to meet us and suddenly our squadron leader said, 'Let's go get them.' First thing I know I'm sitting up there in the sky all by myself. There wasn't a soul around me. I looked below and there was everybody milling around, a big gaggle squirting at one another. I thought I'd better get down there and see what's going on and join the fight.

"When I got down there in that milling mess, a bunch of tracers went flying over my canopy and another bunch of tracers went flying across my nose. I shoved the throttle full forward and headed my aircraft back toward England. I went straight home, flat out. Scared? You bet I was. On the way back I noticed that the fingers on my right hand were numb. I finally realized I was holding the control column so tight that I had cut off all the circulation in my fingers. I kept thinking, 'What the hell am I doing up here? I should be back in the Seaforths with my 3-inch mortar.' I think that if I had landed and somebody asked, 'Do you want to go back to the infantry?' I might have said yes. But luckily there wasn't anybody there to make the offer.

"No one in the squadron seemed to have noticed my sudden departure from the fight. At least nobody said anything about it. I had never fired my guns in anger before and I had less than a hundred flying hours in the RAF, probably about twenty hours in a Hurricane. It suddenly scared the hell out of me because it dawned on me that I wasn't quite ready for that sort of thing. I really went to work learning how to fly my aircraft and when I wasn't on alert duty I did a lot of air-to-air and air-to-ground firing practice. Most important, I had to condition my mental attitude toward aerial warfare. I used to tell myself the other guy was no better than I was and he was probably just as scared. So I calmed down and I decided to use a tactic of strike fast, fire at close range, and get the hell out. My limited skill as a fighter pilot in those days wouldn't permit me to stay and mix it up with some Kraut pilot."

Shortly after he resolved to teach himself how to fight, Dunn put his practice to the test during an encounter with an enemy Messerschmitt. "I dove behind a 109, seventy-five feet behind him. He filled up the whole windscreen. It's hard to miss when you're that close. I started firing at him, chips flew off his aircraft. He caught fire and started down. I watched him go all the way in. He crashed near a crossroads in France. A fellow in our squadron confirmed the victory for me. The feeling was one of elation. Shooting down the first one gives you confidence in yourself. Shooting down an airplane you don't really think of the guy who was in it. You must remember could have been the other way around. You're happy that it was him and not you. My old wing commander Paddy Donaldson used to say, 'Kill the bastard before the bastard kills you.'"

Dunn developed into one of the more accomplished members of his outfit. "I preferred the element of surprise on my side. Give them a bounce; get in a good long squirt, and get the hell out. I saw guys as soon as we lost the element of surprise tangle with the Germans in a dogfight. That was stupid. He might be a much better acrobatic pilot. The only result would be to get your rear end shot off. I [wanted] to close in on him until his aircraft just about filled my windscreen, give him a good blast at short range, 150 to 50 yards, and get out fast. If you missed, no big deal. Come back tomorrow and try again."

As the war continued, Dunn switched to the Spitfire. "It was the best. It had absolutely no bad habits. You couldn't even scare yourself in it. It had a very high rate of climb, great maneuverability, fast, so fast you could almost close the throttle and still feel yourself sliding through the air. It was very light and I flew as high as 32,000 feet and it flew very well. We did convoy duty toward France hoping to get something to come up. Then they started doing fighter sweeps which would get them to scramble for a fight but then the Germans figured out there wasn't any point in going up there and wasting a lot of ammunition on fighters because there was no damage we could do. So we escorted Blenheim and Stirling bombers on what we called 'circus operations.' Then of course the enemy would come up in droves and we'd get in some pretty big fights. The biggest involved 300 aircraft. You spent more time trying not to run into the other guys than shooting at one another.

"After a while we started carrying bombs on our fighters and the Germans didn't know whether our fighters were coming over France as just fighters or fighter-bombers so they'd have to engage us. We carried bombs for selected targets, marshaling yards or airdromes. We'd do things like fly over a seaplane base in Holland, trying to arrive at dawn, shoot up the seaplanes, then turn and cut across a German 109 base and catch the 109s being scrambled. We'd be long gone by the time they were getting off the deck to chase us. We always caught them flatfooted These were all volunteer operations.

A couple of guys would plan something, get group approval and we'd go. We never took more than four aircraft on an intruder operation. After we hit the target it was every man for himself getting home."

As a Spitfire pilot, on 27 August 1941, Dunn flew escort for Blenheims raiding a steel mill at Lille, France. "I shot down two ME 109Fs. I also got shot up by a third ME 109. The front of my right foot was shot off, two machine gun bullets hit my right leg and one creased the back of my head." Dunn told writer Vern Haugland (*The Eagle Squadrons*) "I dived on one of two ME 109Fs, fired from a distance of 150 yards and fired again to within 50 yards. Pieces of the aircraft flew off, and engine oil spattered my windscreen. The plane looked like a blowtorch with a bluish white flame as it went down.

"Tracers from another 109F behind me flashed past my cockpit. I pulled back the throttle, jammed down the flaps, and skidded my plane sharply out of his gunsight. The German overshot me by about ten feet, as he crossed overhead I could see the black cross insignia, unit markings, and a red rooster painted on the side of the cockpit.

"The 109 was now within my range. With a burst of only three seconds I had him out of commission. A wisp of smoke from the engine turned almost immediately into a sheet of flame. The plane rolled over on its back. As it started down, the tail section broke off . . . I fired at another ME 109 and saw smoke coming from it. Just as I started to press the gun button my plane lurched sharply. I heard explosions. A ball of fire streamed through the cockpit, smashing into the instrument panel. There were two heavy blows against my right leg, and as my head snapped forward I began to lose consciousness.

"My mind cleared again, and I realized that the earth was coming up toward me. I tugged back on the control column and pulled back into a gradual dive toward the English Channel, fifty miles away. I checked the plane for damage. The tip of the right wing was gone. The rudder had been badly damaged. The instruments on the right side of my panel were shattered. There was blood on the cockpit floor. When I looked at my right leg I saw that the toe of my boot had been shot off. My trouser leg was drenched with blood. I could feel warm, sticky fluid seeping from under my helmet to my neck and cheek. I gulped oxygen to fight off nausea.

"Releasing my shoulder harness, I started to climb out of the cockpit. For some reason I paused. The engine was still running all right and the plane seemed flyable. I slid back into my seat. I would try to make it home . . . Crossing the Channel, the engine began to lose power. I switched on the radio telephone and called May Day. Within a few moments I had an escort of two Spitfires. They led me across the coastal cliffs to the grass airfield at Hawkinge, near Folkestone. The escorting pilot signaled that my landing gear had extended.

"I dropped smoothly onto the newly mowed turf and taxied to a waiting ambulance. An airman climbed up on the wing and shouted at me that I was in the wrong area and must taxi over to the dispersal hut if I wanted fuel and ammunition. Then he saw my bloody face and helmet and called the medical officer." Dunn spent three months recuperating at RAF medical facilities. By the time he was ready to fly missions again, the U.S. had entered the war. "Both victories are classified as unconfirmed for several days but then the German Air Force released some info about their boys who got shot down the same date, time, and place." With these two 109s, Dunn had now accounted for five enemy planes and became the first American accredited as an ace.

The Eagle Squadrons finally passed into history in September 1942, dropping their RAF designations to become American outfits with appropriate insignia and uniforms. During eighteen months of operations the three units racked up 73 confirmed enemy planes destroyed.

In a different capacity, fighter pilot Johnny Alison, under the Lend-Lease Act in which the United States supplied Great Britain with arms in return for the use of bases, in 1941 traveled to England as an advisor. "Hub [Hubert] Zemke and I took P-40s to England to demonstrate the use of the P-40." Alison, a graduate of the Army flight school in 1937, added, "My job was to visit RAF units, tell them the experiences we had with the P-40, and help them in tactical use of it. The British were not entirely satisfied with the airplane; they said it was a good airplane but that it was lacking in performance characteristics and they didn't want to use it in England. They sent them to Russia and the Middle East.

"At the time there were a great many arguments about the relative merits of British equipment and ours. The British were not satisfied with the armament of the B-17. They said it didn't have enough turrets in it. Our boys insisted they could use it and it would be a mighty good ship because it could run away from the Germans. One of our boys wrote a letter, 'The Godamned British are so turret-minded that if Winston Churchill died, they would fix a tail turret to his ass before they let his soul go to heaven.'" Actually, Alison was more aware than most of the vulnerability of the early models of the Flying Fortress. He remembered, "When they first introduced the B-17, fighter pilots found it easy to get up and stay with it because there was no tailgun. You could get right in the cone and shoot it down without any trouble. But nobody in the Air Corps was going to listen to a second lieutenant pursuit pilot who said, 'I can shoot these things down very easily.'" The British actually had accepted twenty B-17s for use in daylight raids, while the bulk of the RAF bomber force operated during the darkness. The brief experiment ended after poor bombing results and a failure to knock down a single enemy fighter.

The surviving B-17s were returned to their original owner and the P-40s committed to England instead went to the Soviet Union. Alison accompanied them to help acquaint the Red Air Force with the machines. In an account, Alison reported, "We assisted the Russians in putting them together at Archangel, checked out the Russian pilots, and had a turn amongst the Russian squadrons. That was behind the front. The German observation planes were coming over at that time and the Russians had nothing fast enough to intercept the JU-88s. After we had completed putting the P-40s together, they were very reluctant to let us see anything or do anything. I stayed five months, during which I was unable to get in any flying time."

Even earlier than those from the States rallied to the British cause, a handful of American airmen had begun to confront the Japanese in China. The founding father and leader for what stretched into an eight-year campaign was Claire Chennault, a college dropout, onetime factory worker, English teacher, and an old man of twenty-eight when as a reserve officer courtesy of the 1918 version of OCS he pinned on his Army wings. As a fighter pilot and instructor he innovated tactics. Chennault argued against individual dogfights and stressed that maneuvers and attacks in formation made the most effective use of fighter firepower.

Bluntly outspoken, Chennault criticized the hidebound tactics taught in Air Corps schools and argued vociferously for a greater role for fighters. An unwelcome scold to his superiors, Chennault, with his limited formal education, and never having been invited to attend the Command and General Staff School, a prerequisite to advancement by the mid-1930s, reached a dead end in the Air Corps. His treatises on air combat, however, had caught the attention of Chinese leaders desperately seeking help in an escalating struggle with Japan. In 1937, plagued by poor health, as a forty-seven-year-old captain about to be grounded for medical reasons, Chennault retired from the U.S. Air Corps and accepted a three-month contract at $1,000 a month plus expenses from the Chinese government for a study of its Air Force. Instead of ninety days, he would spend eight years in China battling the Japanese through the air.

Only a few months after Chennault set foot in Shanghai, the smoldering conflict with Japan burst into a full fledged war. Chennault volunteered his services, not only because of his sympathy with his hosts but also because, "I wanted to give [his theories on aerial tactics] an acid test in combat." Generalissimo Chiang immediately accepted the offer, commissioning Chennault to oversee training of several squadrons of fighters and bombers. The actual command of the Chinese Air Force belonged to Gen. Peter Mow [Mow Pan-Tzu], a Soviet-trained flier. Chennault discovered his fliers unqualified and worse they viewed practice missions as beneath them. When he set up a raid the pilots dropped their bombs among civilians rather than the targeted enemy naval vessel. A day later the Chinese by error attacked a British cruiser in the Yangtze River.

Nevertheless, he started to achieve some results. Chennault launched his pilots against enemy attacks on Nanking and in five days they knocked down fifty-four planes. Although it was rumored that in these days Chennault himself engaged in the fighting there is no evidence that he ever actually participated and even less confirmation for any planes shot down. Because of the Chennault tactics, the Japanese now tacked on fighters to escort bomber missions.

Madame Chiang persuaded Chennault against his better judgment to create an international squadron. Chinese pilots balked at taking orders from the outsiders, many of whom were undisciplined adventurers, boozers, and devotees of brothels when not in the air. After a few successful sorties, the enterprise literally went up in smoke. Perhaps because of careless talk during their carousing, the enemy got wind of a forthcoming raid. The U.S.-built Vultee bombers were gassed, armed, and all lined up on the airfield when the Japanese hit them at sundown. "What was left of the Chinese bombing force," said Chennault, "vanished in five seconds of flame and dust. With it went the jobs of the International Squadron pilots."

Discouraged, Chennault returned for a brief stay in the States where he sought to rejoin the Air Corps and contribute his considerable knowledge of Japanese tactics, pilots, and aircraft. The authorities showed no interest in him nor in his materials. Rejected at home, Chennault went back to China where all he could do was observe the Japanese take total control of the air. The Soviet squadrons had departed. The planes they sold to China proved no match for the enemy. Frustrated, the American continued to gather data and build his intelligence net. In October 1940, the Generalissimo asked Chennault to meet with T. V. Soong, the official arranging to buy military supplies in the States. Together they were to approach Washington in an effort to beg, borrow, or recruit the elements of an effective air force. Chennault sought to curry favor when he passed along to Army intelligence specifications for the latest Japanese fighter, the Zero. American aeronautical experts poured over the documents and then appraised the fighter described in the documents and its performance as impossible. The Air Corps itself never received a copy of the papers, thus making it understandable why pilots like John Carpenter were so ignorant of the enemy's capability. Henry "Hap" Arnold, head of the Air Corps, had nourished a grudge against Chennault ever since 1932 when he criticized maneuvers directed by Arnold. To others the former airman was an unknown retired captain in the pay of a foreign government.

On the other hand, T. V. Soong had access to top political circles. He deftly influenced movers and shakers already sympathetic to China and, spurred on by increased British anxiety over pressure on crown colonies in the Far East, he found willing audiences. With President Roosevelt's backing, 100 early model P-40s, originally destined for the British who agreed to accept a later version, were shipped to China. There were problems with spare parts, ammunition, gunsights, radios, and other gear, but, more important, the plan included Americans with military aircraft experience. Recruiters circulated through the Marines, Navy, and Army, much to the outrage of local commanders as well as high brass unhappy at the loss of skilled people. Salaries for volunteers to maintain and fly ranged from $250 a month to $750 for a squadron leader, with some extra benefits such as a ration allowance and an unwritten agreement of bonuses for planes shot down. Pilots were guaranteed $600 a month over a one-year contract as employees of the innocent-sounding Central Aircraft Manufacturing Corporation (CAMC), a subsidiary of a Chinese military purchasing operation.

In June and July 1941, the first members of the American Volunteer Group (AVG), a mixed bag of pilots and ground personnel, with P-40s and spare parts, sailed for Rangoon, the Burmese port of entry to the Far East. From there they traveled to Toungoo, a former RAF field, to begin their indoctrination in the P-40 and the science of aerial warfare authored by Claire Chennault. When he finally reached Toungoo on 21 August Chennault's tiny air force seemed about to fall apart. In the midst of jungle and teak plantations the shabby town of Toungoo sweltered under 100-degree days laced with excessively high humidity. Insects gorged themselves on humans living in screenless barracks. Burmese cooks fed the Americans an unappetizing menu of fish and rice. Electricity flowed intermittently and while the men waited for airplanes they stewed in disillusion. Several pilots and ground crewmen handed in their resignations to Chennault on the grounds of misrepresentation by CAMC. Shrewdly, the commander terminated these individuals. Once rid of them, he set hard rules. The contracts provided fines and dishonorable discharges for anyone who quit. He outlined a program of regular flight training, ground classes, and physical-fitness routines. Order was restored and as airplanes arrived, sagging spirits revived.

In March 1941, David Lee "Tex" Hill, son of a missionary in Korea, was a Navy pilot on the carrier *Ranger*. He recalled "We were in Norfolk, Virginia, and we came down from a flight one day and a shipmate grabbed Ed Rector and me, took us to a room, and told a man there, [Retired Navy commander Rutledge Irvine] 'Here's a couple of guys who will go with you.' We didn't know what he was talking about. [Irvine] had a map and it showed Burma and where they were building the Burma Road and said they were looking for pilots to patrol this area. That sounded real good to us, adventurous. It was a fast deal—he explained it real fast. 'You'll get $600 a month and all you'll be doing is patrolling the Burma Road.' I don't think any in our group realized until we got there that our job would be any more than patrol work for the Burma Road.

"I'd always wanted to go to the Orient because I happened to be born in Korea. I'd sought to get an exchange from the carrier to one of the ships in the Far East. The thing that motivated me to go to China was more or less adventure. I knew Chennault was running the show but I knew nothing about him. We signed these contracts. Our skipper flew to Washington to see if he couldn't stop it because our particular squadron on the *Ranger* and the ship itself were operational, ready to go. Bert Christman, Ed Rector, and myself all had key positions. Eddie was in operations, I was assistant gunnery officer, and Christman was on the administrative end. When our skipper came back from Washington, he said, 'I don't know what's going on, fellows, but this is bigger than me.' He gave us all a big party.

"We landed in Rangoon in July 1941. I met Chennault there. I think anyone meeting him for the first time would definitely get the impression that he was a very dynamic, strong person and would get confidence in him. Chennault had wanted to recruit 100 pilots with 500 hours' experience. He went to Hap Arnold and asked for this and Hap said, 'Hell, we give you 100 pilots with that kind of experience, you'd fold up our whole pursuit section.' Chennault said, 'You can't spare me 100 pilots with that kind of experience, you don't have any pursuit section to begin with.' That kind of thing always got him in trouble with people."

In 1937, Jasper Harrington, son of an Alabama farmer, who enrolled in the Air Corps to become an airplane mechanic, saw a priority message from Air Corps headquarters about an opportunity to become part of a flying combat group in China. Harrington and several others signed contracts with CAMC. Harrington recalled arriving in Rangoon where the P-40s were off-loaded and assembled for flight to Toungoo. "The ship with the spare parts was sunk before it reached Rangoon. We received the 100 P-40s but one of them was dropped in the drink so we wound up with 99 and no spare parts." To keep AVG flying meant scrounging from the British, salvaging from the training crackups, with repairs not always as prescribed in manuals.

Hill remembered, "We went immediately up to Toungoo [Burma] which was the base where we were going to have training. I had never seen a P-40. This was the first in-line engine I'd seen. On the takeoff, that nose seemed big and heavy out front but once I got airborne I quickly got acquainted with the airplane. You never forget the basic things. You crawl in an airplane and it takes you an hour or two, you feel at home. You get confidence in your plane, you have complete confidence you can do anything with it you need. The old man made me feel there wasn't anything we couldn't do in it, that we could handle the situation with the equipment we had, if we used it properly. Chennault conducted tactical lectures and then we would go out and practice in the air. He tried to get us around fifty hours in these planes.

"He had blackboard and chalk. He exhibited the type of formation that we would fly and the tactics that we would use against the Japs. It was a two-ship element, the basic formation, and that was the first time I ever heard of it. In the Navy we flew three ships [the Vee] and that was basic in the Air Corps, too. He believed the basic element being two ships, he could build it on up—four, six—always working in pairs. As long as you have two, you have a combat team. I think this was his innovation. Later, everybody went to it. In the Navy they called it the Thacweave. I was on the same ship with Jim Thach when, hell, we were still flying three-ship elements.

"I got the very distinct impression from his lectures that he had actually engaged the Japanese Zero. A man couldn't talk about just exactly how this plane was going to react unless he had encountered it, and how we would use our equipment to the best advantage against it." For the heavy P-40 that amounted to speed while diving rather than maneuvers in tight turns. "That was the secret to the whole thing, as long as we followed [what Chennault taught] we had no problem. Everything he told us in his tactical lectures happened. When we made our first contacts with these enemy Zeros they behaved as he said they would."

Chennault brought to the table more than personal observation. He relied on captured manuals and lectured that the enemy were well trained but lacked initiative and improvisation. "They have been drilled for hundreds of hours in flying precise formations and rehearsing set tactics for each situation they encounter. Japanese pilots fly by the book, and these are the books they use. Study them and you will always be one step ahead of the enemy." He counseled his fliers to make a pass, shoot, and then break off. "You need to sharpen your shooting eye. Nobody ever gets too good at gunnery. The more Japs you get with your first burst, the fewer there are to jump you later. Accurate fire saves ammunition. Your plane carries a limited number of bullets."

On the cusp between training and operations against the Japanese, several pilots thought up the idea of decorating their dull, olive-drab P-40s with nose art. Chennault, aware of the need for boosts in morale, agreed for mechanics to paint a malevolent eye over sharklike teeth. Later he remarked, "How the term Flying Tigers was derived from the shark-nosed P-40s I will never know." Nevertheless the sobriquet soon became popular.

During the first months of the outfit's life, morale dove and soared. Beset by wretched living conditions, substandard equipment, and inadequate supplies, it was not a well-disciplined collection of men. Rather it was a mixture of idealists, soldiers of fortune, and hard-living types like Greg "Pappy" Boyington, who subsequently won renown as a Marine pilot. Over the years, the AVG people developed an élan, a spirit derived from their commander. Bruce Holloway, USMA 1937, who joined the Flying Tigers early in 1943, offered an objective view of Chennault. "As far as being a tactician is concerned, and particularly as being able to practically read the minds of the enemy, the Japanese over there, he was unequaled. He could tell you what they were going to do the next day almost 100 percent. He would back you to the hilt. His two biggest faults were related. He was about the poorest loser that I have ever seen.

"We would play softball and he was the pitcher on my ball team. He was a pretty good pitcher except he would get tired after about the third or fourth inning. We would always be ahead then and we would always lose the game, couldn't get him out of there. He would sort of sulk off. That night, he would want to play badminton. Anyone of us could beat him at badminton. Then he would want to play Ping-Pong. Anyone of us could beat him at Ping-Pong.

"He would get lower and lower and if we had any whiskey, we would drink that. He would sometimes end up wanting to wrestle somebody and he would usually challenge Casey Vincent who was the biggest guy. Casey would stave him off, usually until he went off to bed or we ate dinner. But once in a while he would grab Casey and end up getting thrown over in the corner. He was just a terribly poor loser. The related part is he couldn't get along with anybody above him unless they absolutely agreed with him. He didn't know the meaning of the word compromise . . . He would go out of channels. He made a mission back to the States once because the president wrote him a letter and said he would like to see him. He went all the way back to Washington and saw the president, just bypassed channels. You just don't do things like that."

Cheannault organized the group into three squadrons, "Adam and Eve" led by Robert Sandell, "Panda Bears" under Jack Newkirk, and "Hell's Angels" commanded by Arvid "Oley" Olson. The primary mission of the AVG was to protect both ends of the Burma Road, China's only access to supplies. Chennault stationed Hell's Angels in Rangoon and the other pair at Kunming. As the Flying Tigers entered the final stages of preparation to intercept the almost-daily raids of Kunming by Japanese bombers, a dispatch from RAF headquarters in Rangoon advised Chennault of Pearl Harbor.

The actual baptism of fire for the new air force began on 20 December, as the early-warning system alerted Chennault of ten enemy bombers headed toward Kunming. A total of twenty-four P-40s in three elements scrambled in midmorning. A section of four shark-toothed fighters spotted the twin-engine raiders. Buck fever momentarily slowed reaction.The enemy jettisoned their ordnance and slipped into cloud cover. Chennault, alerted by radio to the situation, quickly calculated the most likely course of retreat and directed the other interceptors accordingly. The overanxious Americans forgot about tactics and fell on the planes haphazardly. Nevertheless, they closed sufficiently to pour .50-caliber bullets into the targets, sending six crashing to the ground with smoke pouring from the badly damaged survivors.

In Rangoon, three days later, Americans and RAF pilots took off with reports of a formation of fifty-four bombers advancing on the city. Oley Olson led the fifteen P-40s and eighteen British Brewster Buffalo fighters circled at 18,000 feet as a reception committee. The enemy approached from the east, at an altitude of 16,000 feet. The hosts dived on the formation of bombers ripping up gas tanks, wings, and fuselages. Even as a number of the enemy smoked, burned, and exploded, others bore down on the Mingaladon Airfield blasting barracks, the operations building, and the radio shack while strafing runs shot up ground crews. Some attacked the docks and shipping, inflicting heavy damage.

One of the Americans, Robert "Duke" Hedman, a former Army flyer, hitherto regarded as a by-the-book aviator who had outrun another Flying Tiger to take off in an available P-40, astonished everyone by achieving ace status with the knockdown of five enemy planes in that one day. In contrast to his reputation, Hedman had been described by an RAF pilot over Rangoon as "a ruddy idiot" when he observed him amidst the swarm of Japanese bombers fleeing toward Thailand. The final count for the day confirmed 25 planes shot out of the sky by the AVG and the British recorded 7 more. Losses to the Americans were 2 pilots and 3 planes, while their allies suffered 5 KIA and 11 Buffalos wrecked.

Two days later, on Christmas Day, a force of nearly 100 Japanese bombers and escorts zeroed in on Rangoon. The outnumbered defenders could muster only a dozen P-40s and sixteen Buffalos. Four enemy attacked Hedman while he busily pursued a Nakajima I-97 fighter and blew off his canopy, forcing him to set down at a satellite airstrip. British ground forces confirmed 28 Japanese downed, with the AVG claiming 17 of the victims. No Americans were lost.

Chennault dispatched the Panda Bears to relieve the battered Hell's Angels in Rangoon. Tex Hill's introduction to combat occurred over Tak, Thailand. "Jack Newkirk was my squadron leader, and there was Jim Howard, Bert Christman, and myself. Newkirk had Christman flying his wing, Howard was leading my element, and I was flying his wing. We took off early one morning and went over to this airdrome. Christman developed engine trouble and had to come back. We went over at an altitude of 10,000 feet, dropped down on this airdrome. When we made this run on the field, the first thing I know when we pulled up—hell, there are more of us in the circle.

"When we pulled up there was a Jap coming toward Newkirk. He just turned into him head-on, just as Newkirk pulled off his first strafing pass.

He just disintegrated. Then I looked around and here was this Jap on Jim Howard's tail, just sitting back there. I hate to say this, but I don't think that Jim even knew that we had been attacked from above on this trip until we got back. I shot the Jap off his tail because I was so nervous. I was so excited, hell, I wasn't even looking through the gunsight. I was just looking through the windshield. Of course, we had tracer bullets. It was just like putting a hose on a man. I just flew right up the guy's tail and brought around on him. I saw it set on fire and it went down.

"In the meantime, a fellow had made a pass on me from overhead that I didn't see. Why I didn't get it, I don't know, because when I got back I had thirty-three holes in my plane. I felt it when it hit and looked back down. I could see the metal on the wings turn back. I don't know whether it was the way his guns were bore-sighted but it was just at the critical point where they intersected and began to spread. The holes were on either side of my wings. I began learning fast from that time on. I think my neck size increased about an inch, keeping my head on a swivel, looking around."

As enemy forces pushed through the Philippines and the Asian mainland, while German armor rolled on in North Africa, U.S. sources, desperate for any good news in the early months of the war, pumped up stories about the AVG in action. Winston Churchill cabled the governor of Burma: "The magnificent victories these Americans have won in the air over the paddy fields of Burma are comparable in character, if not in scope, with those won by the Royal Air Force over the orchards and hop fields of Kent in the Battle of Britain."

The successes of the AVG and that of the RAF notwithstanding, the Japanese Army relentlessly pushed toward Rangoon and all along the coast. Mitsubishi bombers and Zero fighters continued to smash at targets in Burma and China. Fearful his command would become a subsidiary of the British in Burma, and perceiving the imminent loss of the country along with the entire Malay Peninsula, Chennault contrived to withdraw his tiny armada to China. He also started to bill for the $500 bonuses China had verbally agreed to pay per shot-down enemy plane.

While that bolstered his pilots' morale, Chennault coped with his precarious position. Ostensibly on the grounds of efficiency, he pleaded to keep the AVG as an independent duchy under contract to China. The Air Corps, intent upon setting its chain of command in order, began steps to restore him to active duty with the eventual goal of installing more tractable officers over him. The harsh air war in the China-Burma-India (CBI) Theater would be accompanied by nasty strife among those running the show.

6
Retreat

Having successfully ravaged the American fleet at Pearl Harbor, Imperial Japan focused on demolishing the remnants of the first lines of U.S. defenses in the Far East. Guam, a U.S. possession dating back to the Spanish-American War and a lone outpost amid the otherwise Japanese held Marianas, succumbed after a twenty-five minute token defense on 10 December. But when the Japanese, on 11 December, attacked a second chunk of American turf, Wake Island, roughly halfway between Hawaii and Guam, they encountered dogged resistance from a small band of Marines backed by a few airplanes and former naval guns installed as artillery. Not until 23 December did the defenders run up a white flag. In their zeal to boost U.S. morale, the military flacks claimed the Wake Marine commander, Maj. James P. Devereaux, at the onset of the assault responded to a query of what he needed, "Send us more Japs." Undoubtedly aware of the overwhelming forces arrayed against Wake, Devereaux never issued any such statement.

And as these two puny bastions fell, the Imperial ground forces struck at the heart of the U.S. interests in the Philippines. The badly rattled members of Sam Grashio's 21st Pursuit Squadron regrouped at Nichols Field, minus a number of their planes and pilots, early casualties, on the afternoon of 8 December. Under orders, Ed Dyess gathered the remnants of his flock and led them back to Clark Field where, according to Grashio, he guided them safely down to a field pitted with craters and covered with several inches of dust as fine as flour.

"That night we survivors," recalled Grashio, "still half-dazed, slept in the jungle. When we awoke at dawn, somewhat recovered from the shock of the previous day's disaster, it occurred to someone that we might be caught napping again, so we were ordered to take our P-40s up to 15,000 feet and get into position ready to attack. When a plane taxied to takeoff position, the cloud of dust that rose exceeded in size and density anything I had ever seen prior to the clouds caused by the bombing of the day before. Moreover, the field was full of bomb craters. Thus, three-minute intervals were prescribed between takeoffs.

"Even so, there were several accidents. One pilot lost his engine, careened madly into the jungle, and was killed. I got airborne without mishap but Bob

Clark, who followed me, did not allow enough time for the dust to settle, lost his way, and crashed blindly into a parked B-17 bomber. There was a sudden flash of light, a violent explosion, and hail of bullets all over the area as flaming gasoline from the planes ruptured tanks set off the six loaded .50-caliber machine guns it carried. Bob was killed instantly.

"My own promising start was short-lived," Grashio continued, "At about 9,000 feet, my engine started cutting out and losing power. Down I came, trying desperately to identify the problem and to restrain my panic. Soon the engine cut in again, then went out, then cut in once more. Gradually I gained control of the plane in the sense that I felt reasonably sure I could land, though it was clear I could not maintain flying speed. The sticking point was that there was a certain identification procedure for landing that specified entry corridors. This I would have to ignore if I was to get the plane down at all. So I came in from an unexpected direction. Our antiaircraft batteries, understandably trigger happy after the events of the day before, promptly opened fire on me. Fortunately, their marksmanship had not improved overnight. I got down unscathed." Mechanics went to work on Grashio's P-40 and that afternoon, another pilot tried to take the plane up. The engine quit during takeoff, causing a fatal crash.

For Alva Fitch, with a battery of 2.95-inch mountain guns, the commotion caused among his troops by the raid at nearby Clark Field on 8 December remained his only glimpse of the war, as nearly two uneventful days passed. A short distance from Stotsenburg, Fitch had posted sentries at a jungle bivouac. A rumored parachute assault brought a summons for Fitch's unit to protect Stotsenburg. "The Battery looked ridiculous with the guns dug in in front of Post Headquarters, astride the flagpole, shooting toward the hospital. On the morning of the tenth, a flight of twenty-seven bombers raided Stotsenburg without much damage. They bombed the stables and the utilities. Several cavalry horses were killed or wounded. The ice plant was put out of order."

Major Philip Fry had seized an opportunity to volunteer his services to the 57th Infantry, the well established Philippine Scouts regiment. "This decision cost me an immediate promotion to Lt. Colonel but was well worth it. The CO of the 57th, Col. George Clarke, was visibly pleased to have a few senior officers assigned. The 57th had been badly depleted of senior people by the organization of the Philippine Army. All they had left were a bunch of youngsters. My rank entitled me to Ted Lilly's job as executive officer but I wanted my own command of combat troops and asked for a battalion. I was assigned the 3d, Frank Brokaw the 2d Battalion. We were given guides and staff cars and off we went to locate our new commands.

"The 3d Battalion position was located in a draw between officers' row [housing designed for commanders] and Guadaloupe. The units were badly congested and a beautiful target for the bombing attack I expected in a few minutes. I assembled the officers and informed them of my assumption of command. They were all so young, and a bit dazed by the speed of events. We started preparations for a move that night. We had sufficient weapons carriers but needed busses to move the men. I was given thirty-three civilian busses and two Ford sedans for me and my staff. At dusk we started out and it was a terrible nightmare. My orders were changed so many times they had me dizzy. Our convoy of about sixty vehicles was turned around. The roads were jammed; every mile there was a traffic jam. On both sides the rice paddies were flooded. There was absolutely no cover of any kind. All officers were on foot, trying to make our way through. We were in a helluva fix and the Philippine defense could have been given a mortal blow that night, but the Nips were busy working our airfields.

"We broke through and headed for San Fernando. Our position was regimental reserve near Florida Blanca. We were the first battalion to arrive and were completely under cover by daylight. Poor George Clarke was there and frantic about the remainder of the regiment. He kept bothering me about them until I suggested he go look for them because we were busy. Not a nice gesture but I was provoked beyond endurance."

On a map, the island of Luzon has the rough shape of a mitten, with the thumb at the left as it narrows toward its southern end. From the northern tip, about 275 miles from Manila, extend several rugged mountain ranges that peter out into the central plains just above the city. An invasion force striking at the fingertips would have a long, difficult line of march toward Manila, particularly against a well-orchestrated defense. However, the space between the thumb and the rest of the glove approximates the Lingayen Gulf, an indentation from which a network of highways and roads led to Manila and an attractive route for conquest.

General Jonathan Wainwright commanded the forces assigned to wall off all of northern Luzon. Under him served three Philippine Army Divisions, a Philippine Scout cavalry regiment, an infantry battalion, a single battery of field artillery—Alva Fitch's outfit—and a supply unit. On paper it was a formidable number of soldiers but the territory stretched over thousands of square miles including mile upon mile of beach. The steep mountains, thick vegetation, and lack of many suitable roads restricted communication and movement. Wainwright's army was little more than a paper organization. The Filipino divisions expected to halt any enemy incursions were of the ilk described by Glen Townsend and Clifford Bluemel: reservists summoned to duty in September, most of whom had little instruction in the art of war. The problems of supply storage loomed larger in light of limited means of transport. After Rainbow Five supplanted War Plan Orange, ammunition, foodstuffs, and other necessities had been moved to sites spread around Luzon.

The Japanese came ashore at two ports, Aparri, located at the tip of what would be a ring finger in the Luzon mitten, and at Vigan, along the western shore. So thin were Wainwright's forces, he had only a single company of infantry in the vicinity of Aparri and not a man at Vigan. The initial troops splashing ashore at Aparri probably numbered about 2,000. To the eye of the U.S. officer in charge, however, the invaders seemed five times as many. Since he had less than 200 untrained and ill-equipped defenders he ordered a retreat without firing a single shot.

From Del Carmen, Lt. Samuel Marrett led his squadron on a mission. "After takeoff," recalled Tom Gage, "there were conflicting orders to change the destination." Marrett chose to intercept at Vigan rather than Aparri. Deteriorated engines forced nine of the sixteen P-35s to abort and scramble to turn back. P-40s that preceded the 34th to the area had been able to work over the landing forces with fragmentation bombs and strafing runs after Japanese air cover had left.

With only pairs of .30- and .50-caliber machine guns, the remnants of the 34th dove on the beachhead, the barges, and some larger vessels near the shore. Marrett led the attack, picking out for himself a 10,000-ton vessel. He made several passes at it and then bore in at almost masthead height while surrounding cruisers and destroyers threw shells at him. Just as the squadron commander began to pull out of his dive, his target blew up; he apparently had ignited an ammunition cache. The blast ripped away the wing of Marrett's aircraft. Other pilots saw his plane crash into the sea even as debris from his victim started to splash down into the water.

"The squadron came back to Del Carmen just before noon," says Gage. "I remember one of the pilots remarking how machine gunning the troops landing on the beach made him sick at his stomach because of the slaughter." But there was neither time to mourn Marrett nor listen to war stories at Del Carmen. "We had some P-40s there fueling up. As the P-35s came in and landed, some Zeros came right in with them. They proceeded to beat up the base camp and shoot up the line. Myself, my two clerks Robert Reynolds and Dermott Toycen, Lieutenant Jennings, and several pilot officers ran over the hill away from the line and lay down flat. We couldn't see but could sure hear. Spent bullets buzzed around. One clanged off the edge of Reynolds's tin helmet.

"The attack only lasted a few minutes but it seemed like hours. After the enemy left, it was real quiet—then we could hear the flames crackling. We could see a P-40 hooked to a gasoline truck, both on fire. One of our men had been caught in the open and took cover under the gasoline-tank truck.

After tracers set that on fire, he slipped under the P-40. When the fire traveled down the hose and set the plane on fire, he just got up and strolled away, ignoring the strafing completely. On this day all the propaganda rubbish about the inferior Japanese material went down the drain. Those fuel wing tanks dropped by the Zeros were far better than ours."

As the Filipino infantry hastily backed off, the one blow aimed at the incoming troops near Aparri came from the sky. Remnants of the Air Corps in the shape of a pair of B-17s attacked the landing fleet. Captain Colin Kelly piloted one of the two ships. With Clark patched up enough to service B-17s, Kelly, and several others, arrived from Mindanao on the morning of 10 December to carry out missions against an aircraft carrier reported in the neighborhood. In the air, Kelly, toting three 600-pound bombs in his racks, became separated from the others as he headed north. From almost four miles up, the crew gazed down on the enemy ships, some of whom blasted away at the coastline while others ferried in men and supplies. Kelly ignored these targets for the moment and searched for the aircraft carrier but, although the hunt went almost to Formosa, the target was never spotted. Returning toward Luzon, the airman picked out the biggest vessel off the coast, what they believed was a battleship.

Bombardier Meyer Levin, a corporal in an Air Corps–era when the job did not carry a commission, tracked the target and at the appropriate moment released the bombs. To the men in the Fort, it appeared as if they scored two near misses and one direct hit. Kelly headed for home but not before his navigator Lt. Joe Bean noticed far below a half-dozen Japanese fighter planes taking off from the Aparri airfield now possessed by the enemy.

The Americans, descending through the clouds, prepared for touchdown at Clark. Suddenly the navigator's dome exploded into pieces and the instrument panel shattered. A burst of fire beheaded the radio operator stationed at the left waist gun and wounded another gunner. Fighters had tracked them more than 100 miles and closed in for the kill. Bullets ripped into the left wing, fire enveloped the ship; the fuel tanks of the earliest B-17s were not self-sealing.

Kelly consulted the crew on the damage, ordered them to bail out. Levin and Bean frantically worked to pry open the bottom escape hatch whose pins were corroded. Levin went first and then Bean who saw the copilot Lt. Donald Robins moving toward the top escape hatch. The aircraft disintegrated with a mighty blast. Dangling from his parachute, Bean saw four others swinging in the air. Still not finished, the enemy fighters swept by to strafe the men floating down. A bullet chipped Bean's ankle but the others escaped unscathed. Search teams from Clark found the badly burned copilot who had been blasted free of the ship when it exploded. Somehow he managed to yank his ripcord and reach the ground alive. But Kelly's body was discovered amid the wreckage. He was the first graduate of the USMA to die in the defense of the Philippines.

With only defeats to announce, the authorities quickly proclaimed Kelly a hero and awarded him a posthumous Distinguished Service Cross for allegedly sinking the battleship *Haruna*. Post–World War II research revealed no battleship ever was in the area nor did the attack sink any Japanese ship. Samuel Marrett, who probably struck a more effective blow for the cause and with greater disregard for his own survival, received a Distinguished Service Cross, but none of the fame and glory accorded Kelly. Marrett, as a mustang, or former enlisted man elevated to the ranks of the commissioned, struck his chief clerk, Tom Gage, as a "bitter" man. For reasons of personality, background, or misperception of the events, the publicity focused on the West Pointer.

John Carpenter, as a B-17 pilot whose suicidal mission to Formosa fell through only after his generators failed, during the first few days flew missions from the patched runways at Clark. "On the third day of the war, I had been up to Lingayen Gulf and I was briefed for the next mission while my airplane was being serviced. We were just ready to go, walking over to the airplane and a flight of three P-40s was taking off. It was in the dry season and it was a sod field. It was pretty dusty. The third guy in the [P-40] element got disoriented in the dust and got off course on his takeoff and ran right through my B-17. He hit just outboard of the outboard engine, took off the wing, went right through, and broke our back halfway down the fuselage.

"He turned around 180 degrees facing the other way. We ran over. I expected it to burst into flames and we thought we would pull him out. There wasn't anything left of that fighter except the pilot's seat, and he was sitting strapped in it. His right hand was on the stick; his left on the throttle. There wasn't anything else left of that airplane. He looked at us; we looked at him. He reached down and undid his safety belt, got out, and said, 'Goddamn,' walked away. He ruined my airplane and that was serious because that was my means of escape from the Philippines.

"We had moved our ground echelons out from Clark and set up a camp on the Bamban River. The Japs used to come by and strafe us about three times a day. But we all had pretty good slit trenches and we didn't lose many people. But every time an airplane came in to be repaired, serviced, or whatever, my crew and I were on hand saying, 'Aren't you very tired? Don't you want to rest a while and let us take this next mission?' We want to get our hands on an airplane but you can bet your boots they all said, 'Oh, no. I am not tired.' They might have flown five missions that day but they weren't going to get out of their airplane because they knew what was going on."

The Air Corps had succeeded in disrupting the beachhead at Vigan with the early morning raid by five B-17s accompanied by P-40s and then the 34th's P-35s. The attacks damaged and beached a pair of transports, sank a minesweeper, inflicted some damage to a pair of warships, and chewed up a number of soldiers. But it was the last well-choreographed effort by the FEAF (Far East Air Force) as successive waves of enemy planes reduced U.S. Philippine air operations to spasms of little import. The run at Del Carmen had destroyed twelve P-35s, damaged the remaining six so badly, that the 34th to all intents and purposes was grounded. Conditions were almost as bad with other squadrons. At nightfall 10 December, the defenders could count only thirty airworthy fighters.

Americans in Manila began to appreciate the situation. On duty at Sternberg General Hospital, Madeline Ullom recalled, "A large formation of silver planes were silhouetted against the blue sky. The rumor must surely be true. We smiled. Reinforcements had arrived. Bombs suddenly began to drop on the nearby Pasig River. Shell windows fell from the eye-ear-nose-throat clinic. Crystal chandeliers in the officers' ward dining room swayed from the ceiling. The sound of the bombs hurt our eardrums. The feeling pierced our hearts. The truth was apparent. We were soon to remark, 'If you see one plane flying in formation, you know it is ours.'"

The defenders were confused and back on their heels. One American officer with the 21st Philippine Division said that after some dark shapes hovered near the mouth of the Agno River, a field artillery unit opened up. "It was like dropping a match in a warehouse of Fourth of July fireworks," he remarked. "Instantly Lingayen Gulf was ablaze. As far as the eye could see the flashes of artillery, shell-bursts, tracer machine gun bullets, and small arms . . . Thousands of shadows were killed that night." Townsend recalled, "On the night of 10 December, I heard a fusillade of rifle and machine gun fire on a nearby river."

In the morning, the only evidence of anything amiss was a single life preserver which may not even have been Japanese. Neither sunken vessels nor corpses of blasted bodies were found. "Later," said Townsend, "we read in the Manila papers that the Japs had landed at Lingayen but after a terrific battle they had been annihilated." The erroneous report of the victory originated with a Filipino commander who insisted his forces repulsed an enemy landing. Investigation after the war revealed a single enemy motorboat had ventured into the area on a reconnaissance.

Alva Fitch noted, "In general things were fairly quiet. A tremendous amount of false information continued to come by telegraph. This kept the staff in turmoil. Apparently there were a lot of fifth columnists in the telegraph system. It was so bad that all information and even orders received by telegraph were suspect and had to be verified. A few days after the landing at Vigan, we received a telegram from a 'Colonel Jones' of the constabulary saying that a column of 40,000 Japs with some mechanized equipment was marching south from Vigan to Damortis. It was fairly routine to hear of fictitious landings in force, of parachute landings, and of large Jap convoys. The telegraph service became so unreliable that eventually motor or airplane couriers were used for delivery of most important orders."

The confusion created by poor communications, misinformation, and unwillingness to digest bad news affected MacArthur's judgment. Even *after* the war was over he would write in his *Reminiscences:* "On December 10th . . . Twelve transports with naval escorts landed troops at Aparri in the north and Vigan on the west coast. Our air force attacked these transports sinking four and damaging three others. [Actually, the foe lost only three of its troop and cargo carriers.] . . . At the end of the first week of war there had been many widely scattered actions, but the all-out attack had not yet come. The enemy had carried out fourteen major air raids, but paid dearly in the loss of transports, planes, and troops, and at least two major warships damaged. He had attempted a landing in the Lingayen area, but was repulsed with severe loss by a Philippine Army division. At Aparri, Vigan, and Legaspi there had been only local activity."

In fact, the Japanese at Clark Field lost only seven fighters compared with the horrendous damage done to American planes, personnel, and installations. Americans were credited with four kills at Del Carmen but lost an entire squadron. The enemy casualties at other airfields, at Cavite, and other navy bases were similarly negligible when weighed against the damage inflicted. The Lingayen defeat was sheer fantasy and the "local activity" at the three Luzon sites amounted to a firm foothold on the island. Wainwright put it, "The rat was in the house."

What was true was that the main body of MacArthur's army had yet to engage the enemy. The Japanese units, under Lt. Gen. Masaharu Homma, Fourteenth Army commander, rapidly trekked south in a strategy designated to pinch off northern Luzon. The objective of invaders from the west was control of Lingayen Gulf. With that site in hand, large numbers of troops and their supplies could be aimed at Manila. Meanwhile, another unopposed landing on the southeastern coast at Legaspi on 12 December confronted the defenders with an enemy at the backdoor.

The booty for the Japanese included an airstrip near Legaspi. Three B-17s, operating from the Del Monte base, attempted to attack the occupants only to discover themselves overmatched against the now-resident Japanese fighter planes. Only one Fort managed to escape unscathed to the home base; the two others crash-landed. Further operations by the big bombers from Del Monte were in jeopardy. MacArthur agreed with Brereton's decision to move the remainder of the B-17s to Darwin, Australia. They flew off on 15 December, four days before a series of heavy assaults from the air upon Del Monte. Among those left behind was John Carpenter.

Whether MacArthur at the time of the first Japanese landings truly believed he still had a shot at denying the enemy the Philippines, he early on realized the shakiness of such an ambitious strategy. On 12 December he sent word to Quezon, the Philippine president, to ready himself for movement to Corregidor on four hours' notice. "Startled" by the ominous import, Quezon conferred with MacArthur that evening. MacArthur said there was no immediate concern but only that he was "preparing for the worst in case the Japanese should land in great force at different places." Under these circumstances, explained MacArthur, effective strategy would require a concentration of Fil-American units and the site would be Bataan.

And to the horror of Quezon, MacArthur added that the plan would require shift of his headquarters, the high commissioner's office, and the Commonwealth government to the rocky fastness of Corregidor. In this event he would declare Manila an open city. An incredulous Quezon asked, "Do you mean, General, that tomorrow you will declare Manila an open city and that some time during the day we shall have to go to Corregidor?" MacArthur reassured Quezon that this was just contingency strategy and he merely wanted the president to be aware of the possibility.

At the start of hostilities, Wainwright assigned Clifford Bluemel and the 31st Philippine Army Division responsibility for defending the South China Sea coastline near Zambales, perhaps sixty miles south of the Lingayen Gulf landing zones. Nearly a week of war had passed when Bluemel discovered that his latest additions, artillerymen who had undergone basic training, had never fired their 75mm guns. Under his instructions, each battery expended two rounds per gun because that was all he felt he could spare. Bluemel, outraged by the responsibilities thrust upon an "untrained rabble," was equally vehement in his disparagement of the revised Rainbow Five that expected units such as his to repulse the Japanese. "MacArthur and Sutherland were trying to draw up a plan in a few days after discarding the one that had been worked on for twenty-five years, which to me, shows inability to command." He criticized his commander for a strategy that ignored the peculiarities of terrain and roads. "MacArthur practically had no transportation for us. He was too busy thinking about meeting them at the beaches. The artillery was old wooden-wheeled artillery and I had nothing to tow it. We had to portage it. I sent a young officer to a mine and he confiscated some fifty trucks and brought them to me. We pushed the guns up on the trucks to portage them. We couldn't tow them because the wooden wheels would fall off if we went at truck speed. We could not even have run three or four miles an hour with them, the way we moved horse-drawn artillery. It's something MacArthur should have known."

The 31st Division area included the now-destroyed airfield at Iba. According to Bluemel, some of the American enlisted men "took to the hills" after the air raids blasted their base. "A Filipino came to me with a note from them, 'We won't come in unless we get a note that it's all right.' They thought the Japs had landed." A handwritten message from Bluemel convinced the fugitives that Americans still controlled the territory and they returned.

Bluemel had the habit of riding his horse up and down his zone during the night. He said, "I came in from reconnaissance on the morning of the 24th of December. I had a Filipino officer, Pastor Martelino, who was a graduate of West Point and a very intelligent man who said, 'There's a message in code.' But I had no code; we had no code book. I got on the phone and found somebody who had a code book. He sent it out to me, and I translated it: 'You will move your division to Bataan immediately.' I started the movement with buses of the Trytran Bus Company [which I confiscated]. A fellow named [Ramón] Magsaysay was the manager; he later became president of the Philippines. Magsaysay went with me in charge of the buses."

As early as 19 December, signs of a reversion to War Plan Orange—retreat to Bataan in hopes of preserving a presence until relief could arrive—showed up in the deployment of the Fil-American forces. The 26th Cavalry, a Philippine Scout regiment, had traveled north to meet the invaders and Fitch's guns accompanied them. But while in bivouac Fitch received word consigning his battery to Bataan. The artillerymen marched south for three nights where Fitch heard the disquieting news to continue their retreat.

"The Philippine Army was withdrawing into Bataan," Fitch said. "General Bluemel's division from Zambales was coming in the night. Time was of the essence. The only road would be no place for mules [used to pull the pack artillery pieces] with a division of the Philippine Army using it. There was no other course but to go on to Balanga in the daylight. This was no pleasant prospect. To move my mules down a narrow road, entirely flanked by impassable fish ponds, in daylight through heavy traffic, and with Jap planes swarming overhead, would not be pleasant.

"The Battery had marched all night with full war loads and the men and animals were dead tired. We began arriving about dusk. The animals were strung out at long intervals. I rode my horse off the road into a grass plot in the public square to watch them pass. A couple of policemen came rushing out of the municipio to tell me of my outrage and to save their lawn. I hadn't the heart to tell them their damned town would be blown off the map in a few hours. We made bivouac that night in a semiexhausted state. We had marched from Tarlac in three days, and more than thirty-five miles in twenty-four hours."

Fitch said that several nights after he reached Bataan a commotion that included artillery fire awakened him to a possible surprise assault. He and an associate reconnoitered and discovered his fears were groundless. But enroute to his bivouac area he stalled in a traffic jam. "While we were waiting," reported Fitch, "a man stuck his pistol against my ear and told us to get moving or he would kill us. It was General Bluemel. He had been reduced to a state of semi-insanity by the task of moving his division from Zambales to Bataan, and was trying to clear the traffic jam before daylight. We helped him and got home before morning."

Philip Fry, with the 3d Battalion of the 57th Infantry, also initially moved to block the Japanese advance. "On December 19, because of probable landings at Subic Bay near Olongapo, orders came to move there and defend the Zig Zag Trail in that sector. This being a daylight move, I instructed all units to maintain thirty seconds between any vehicles to avoid any tendencies to close up on straight stretches."

The troops reached their designated spot and started to dig in and prepare defenses covering the trails. But as Fry and the others in the outfit readied themselves for battle once again they received new instructions and shifted their location. By the end of December, the 57th had withdrawn to Bataan, to occupy the right flank of defenses from Mabatang on the shore of Manila Bay and behind the Balantay River in a line that extended westward for about three-quarters of a mile.

There were no significant Air Corps resources available to ravage the fleet in the Lingayen Gulf but the U.S. Navy still had one seemingly puissant weapon, its flotilla of submarines. Admiral Hart, dispatched three undersea boats to strike the enemy ships. The USS *Stingray*, USS *Saury*, and USS *Salmon* all slipped in among the covey of troop ships, freighters, landing craft, and warships debarking men. The invasion force was already in the shoal waters near the shore by the time the three subs got into position to make their forays. But they sank only two vessels.

Charles Adair, a member of Admiral Hart's staff, remarked, "These people would fire. They could see the torpedoes and knew where they were going. They could hear them hit, bounce off, and nothing happened. Then they would get a terrific depth-charging, for the Japanese destroyers would chase them, drive them under, and depth-charge them. The Lingayen Gulf is not very deep anyway—in some places about 120 feet or even less. When they came back and Admiral Hart wanted to know what happened they'd tell him they hadn't sunk anything. He would want to know why and they were unable to tell him. General MacArthur would want to know why the submarines hadn't been able to sink any ships with the torpedoes and I'm sure Admiral Hart had no answers to give him. He couldn't believe that such well-trained submarine officers could be so ineffective. That went on until morale was very low so far as the submariners were concerned."

How many of the invaders at Lingayen and elsewhere were framed in the periscopes and had torpedoes unloosed at them is unknown. But the consistently disappointing results underscored a miserable failure in Navy weaponry. In an effort to conserve funds, the standard Mark-14 torpedo, at $10,000 apiece, was considered so expensive that it had never been tested with a live warhead. Instead, during peacetime submarines and destroyers fired missiles armed with water-filled warheads. Once the war began, the Mark-14 more often than not failed to hit the target or to explode when it managed to home in. Not until 1943 would Bureau of Ordnance experts finally correct problems with the depth mechanism and exploders.

The ill-prepared pair of Philippine Army divisions assigned to block entry at Lingayen folded quickly, although an occasional unit fought bravely before being overrun. The Filipino soldiers streamed backward in an ever-deepening rout. The chief resistance to the advance came from Fitch's former associates, the 26th Cavalry, Philippine Scouts, mounted on horses, "a true cavalry delaying action, fit to make a man's heart sing" commented ex-cavalryman Jonathan Wainwright.

But two days after landing, as Christmas Eve approached, the Fourteenth Army under Homma grasped the best roads in the islands, daggers pointed at Manila. Although Homma's forces that came ashore at the Lingayen sites added up to 43,000 men, MacArthur informed Marshall that the invaders numbered from 80,000 to 100,000 and he could only field about 40,000, "in units partially equipped." In fact, MacArthur actually had probably double the number of men in uniform commanded by Homma. The reinforcements aboard the *Pensacola*-led convoy, however, including a light bomber squadron and more P-40s, detoured to Australia. The general himself traveled by Packard automobile into Luzon to confer with Wainwright who now asked permission to retreat. A message from Gen. George Parker, the Southern Luzon commander, reported that 10,000 Japanese from the Lamon Bay landings were advancing on Manila. When all this had been translated onto a map; MacArthur read its import: His Luzon forces were in imminent danger of being trapped in a standard pincers strategy.

Quezon's worst fears took tangible shape. On 23 December, the USAFFE commander advised all his subordinates " WPO is in effect." On the afternoon before Christmas he drafted an announcement, "In order to spare Manila from any possible air or ground attacks, consideration is being given by military authorities to declaring Manila an open city." On 26 December the two big Manila newspapers bore the same headline: MANILA ES CIUDAD ABIERTA.

Until the very last days of the crisis before the shooting war commenced, contact between the Army and the Navy had been tenuous. Robert Lee Dennison, whom Admiral Hart deputized as his liaison with MacArthur, recalled, "There was no personal contact between Hart's staff, MacArthur's staff, or

MacArthur and Hart. MacArthur didn't know what we were up to in terms of ship movements or what our war plans were, nor did we know what his were. That was the purpose of my being in this particular capacity. It wasn't much use until the war did break out."

According to Dennison the lack of coordination and communication was not because MacArthur was unwilling to share matters. "MacArthur was completely open with me. When I first reported to him, he called his staff in and instructed them in my presence that they were to show me all the dispatches that were exchanged between themselves and Washington and he intended to do the same. And this was whether I asked for [the material] or not, because how could I ask for something I didn't know existed. I was appalled to find [Col. Charles] Willougby the G-2, telling the G-2 in the War Department things that were completely different from what MacArthur was telling the chief of staff of the Army. There was no communications intrastaff worth a damn."

According to Dennison he went to MacArthur's headquarters one morning around nine. "He said, 'Before I talk with you, I want you to hear what I'm going to tell my staff.' He called them in and he said, 'Gentlemen, I'm going to declare Manila an open city as of midnight tonight.'" Dennsion claimed, "This was the first anybody had ever heard of it. After he [finished] I said, 'May I go back and talk to Admiral Hart?'—which I did. Hart didn't usually show much emotion but he said, 'What!' Then he got up out of his chair and said, 'Sit down and write that down!' I wrote a simple sentence, 'At 9:10 this morning, General MacArthur told me and so on.'

"Hart read it and still couldn't believe it, because he'd been making preparations to operate out of Manila. They'd moved the submarine tender *Canopus* alongside the seawall in the port district. We'd taken off warheads, torpedo exploders, and distributed them all over that general area so they wouldn't be concentrated in one place, and put camouflage over the tender. She was in shoal water so that if hit she wouldn't submerge. We were planning on continuing submarine operations. We had barges of fuel oil all around the Manila area and all kinds of supplies that we couldn't possibly get out. We needed more than a few hours, which meant we couldn't back up this concept of an open city because we had to have those supplies. It was an example of complete lack of consultation or accord between two senior commanders—MacArthur didn't comprehend what this would mean to us."

Indeed, without Manila and its facilities there was no place from which the navy could effectively operate in the Philippines. Hart left aboard the submarine *Shark*, turning over command of those Asiatic Fleet forces still in the Philippines to Adm. Francis Rockwell. The miasma of disorder that afflicted MacArthur's staff and its relationships with other organizations marked the Navy as well. Dennison, on instructions from Hart, traveled to Corregidor, the new headquarters for the American defense, to meet with Rockwell. "Hart, typically, hadn't briefed Rockwell on what his war plans were, what his thoughts were. When I put Hart aboard the *Shark*, he told me the gates to the south were closed, the Japanese fleet is there; we can't get any more ships out. This was just stupid. The destroyers didn't have any torpedoes, they were running short of fuel oil, and they had to get out, or sit there and have everybody killed. I told Rockwell I didn't agree with Hart and why. And we did get the ships out."

Near chaos developed with the designation of an open city—the defenders would not use Manila for military purposes and therefore the enemy should not bomb or attack it. Thousands of soldiers with their weapons in "retrograde maneuvers," or retreat, to Bataan could only reach there by passage through Manila over a number of days after it was named an open city.

Submarine commander S.S. Murray, after receipt of the word on Manila's status, recalled returning to the Army-Navy Club where he spent his few off-duty hours. "I went down in the bar of the club and met the Army officers coming in from the east coast of Luzon. Their troops were just arriving in the outskirts of Manila and they had until midnight that night to start moving by foot to Bataan. They were supposed to be there the next night [a distance of perhaps sixty miles]."

"They had been on a forced march ever since the Japanese had landed on the east coast and I've never seen such a bitter, frustrated crowd in my life. Most of them were weeping because they said, 'They wouldn't even let us shoot once at the Japs and we had twice as many troops as they had.'" The laments notwithstanding, although the terrain may have favored the defense, MacArthur's strategy recognized that the Southern Luzon Force could not have remained viable once the Northern Army was overwhelmed.

Paul Carpenter, a bomber pilot without a plane, ate the traditional Christmas turkey dinner on the eve of the holiday. On Christmas Day he served as train commander for the evacuation of all ground troops at Clark Field. Their destination was a stop on a highway that led into Bataan. "There wasn't anybody in charge except the engineer, the fireman, and me. We pulled into a station and we stopped. The engineer said, 'This is as far as I go. I unhook and another engine picks you up.' This happened about three times and I began to get suspicious. These guys were going to turn us loose in some little stop I didn't even see on the map. About midnight, the group exec and I went up and I said, 'No, we're not going to do this.'

"[The train crew said] 'Oh, yes, we have to leave.' At the point of a .45 automatic, we said, 'You're not going anywhere' except whatever the name of the place was. The two of us held automatics on these guys until we got to this stop that turned out to be the end of the line toward Bataan." The passengers debouched swiftly when they saw an ammunition train directly ahead, an obvious target for enemy planes. Before they could move out, a colonel arrived and ordered them to unload the freight cars. "It was Christmas Day and we were starving. There were two or three boxcar loads of C rations and when we finished unloading we broke up the C rations. That was our Christmas Day dinner. We headed out and the Japs came over and blew all the ammunition we had stacked." Trucks arrived and carried the airmen, now made "ground pounders," to defensive positions on Bataan.

Carpenter and his associates also constructed an airfield to handle B-17s. "We had bombs, ammunition, gas, anything you could think of that was necessary to refuel and turn around a B-17 unit. We had engineer troops with bulldozers who made a runway 5,000 feet long, 300 feet wide. We had hardstands so we could pull the airplanes off, service them. We were convinced that B-17s were going to come in any day, maybe thousands of them, and we wanted to be ready."

For many in Manila there was neither an opportunity nor a real choice of evacuation. Mary Rose Harrington, the Navy nurse posted to the medical facility near Cavite, had left that area. "It was too vulnerable out there. They made arrangements for us to work at several places in Manila. They set up a main operating center at the Jai Alai palace and took over several schools. Mary Chapman and I set up at one of the schools where we had a few patients. On 23 December, the Army doctors and nurses told us they had orders to move to Bataan. We were told we could do whatever we wanted. We had no orders. The saddest of days was when the Army left and Manila was declared an open city. We got bombed but they hit mostly bodegas and ships on the waterfront. The Red Cross offered to send our wounded by boat to the southern islands. Someone screwed up; the corpsmen and ambulances moved only army patients." Without the means or direction to flee, the navy nurses awaited the conquering army.

Madeline Ullom, the Army nurse, saw a number of her sorority receive orders to join the defenders on Bataan. The first contingent of twenty-four Army, one Navy, and twenty-five Filipino nurses left in a twelve-bus motor caravan to set up shop at Hospital Number One at Limay in the peninsula. "The drivers waited about ten minutes between every departure to provide a greater safety factor and to try to dispel the convoy idea. Many stops were necessary to seek roadside shelter from the planes which bombed and strafed most of the day." A second batch of twenty-five nurses embarked on Christmas night to sail for Corregidor and another group boarded a boat that evening for a trip to Mariveles on the southwestern tip of Bataan. Successive shipments ferried the remainder of the Army and Filipino medics to Corregidor and Bataan.

The authorities, however, ordered Ullom and some colleagues to stay in the city to treat wounded. "Manila was declared an open city," she remembered. "The American flag was not hoisted to the pole above Sternberg General Hospitals entrance. A desolate, helpless, and unrealistic sensation gripped me. So many of my close friends departed. Officers no longer carried arms. Japanese prisoners were released. Lights of the city shone at night, although not as extensively as before the first week in December."

But on 29 December, Ullom and others received word to prepare for evacuation. "Surgery was quiet. I packed some instruments which I knew were the only ones in the department. I went to bed early. After midnight, Josie Nesbit [one of the senior staff] awakened me. She whispered to come quietly. I slipped into the fatigues, gave a parting glance to the mementos on the dresser, to the dresses hanging in the closet, slung the gas mask and helmet with the musette bag on my shoulder to tiptoe down the stairs.

"Some tanks rolled by the quarters. We moved to the door to better see them. Hope continued to exist. Josie cautioned us to keep back from the porch in the darkness. We were not certain whose tanks were rolling along Arrocerras Street." Ullom climbed into a field ambulance. The driver skirted huge bomb craters as the vehicle, without headlights, bumped along the pitted roadway to the port area. "Ships were blazing in the Bay. Buildings were burning along the waterfront. Structures of jagged concrete were still visible. Heaps of wreckage and crumbled ruins were everywhere. The sky was more vivid toward Cavite than the spectacular and vivid sunsets we often watched from Dewey Boulevard. Loud blasts punctured the quiet. A stretching flame, an exploding substance colored and streaked the horizon."

As the interisland steamer *Don Esteban* left the pier, Japanese planes hovered in the sky before bombing and shooting-up the port area. Ullom saw that the pier on which she had stood shortly before was now a blazing mass. At dawn, the *Don Esteban* increased its speed and lessened the danger of blindly colliding with a mine. After a "big, delicious breakfast," the steamer docked at Corregidor. Ullom felt secure again. "The Rock, the Eternal Rock, were the terms for the fortification. Phrases of conversation mysteriously linked its features to an unconquerable entity."

On Christmas Eve, the *Don Esteban*'s passenger list was substantially more imposing than a collection of medical personnel. When MacArthur abandoned Rainbow Five and reverted to War Plan Orange, he moved his headquarters to the Rock and the office opened for business on Christmas Day. "Manila," said MacArthur, "because of the previous evacuation of our forces, no longer had any practical military value. The entrance to Manila Bay was completely covered by Corregidor and Bataan and, as long as we held them, its use would be denied the enemy. He might have the bottle, but I had the cork."

Actually, the evacuation of MacArthur's army was very much in progress and its success still in doubt when the general announced his new location.

It was not a single but a double retrograde operation if the bulk of both the Northern and Southern Luzon Forces were to withdraw into Bataan. Wainwright, confronted with a steady erosion of his army from casualties inflicted by the enemy and desertion by the untrained, undisciplined troops, withdrew behind the Agno River, a natural barrier for anyone seeking access to Manila from the north. Wainwright actually talked of a counterattack if his boss would order up the most effective fighting force in the entire defense, the Philippine Division with its Philippine Scouts, and the U.S. 31st Regiment.

However, not only did MacArthur not accede to the request for the Philippine Division but he now informed Wainwright that Orange was in effect and that Wainwright's soldiers must fight delaying actions that would allow the bulk of his army to escape to Bataan. Although supported by the 192d and 194th Tank Battalions, a pair of U.S. National Guard units, Wainwright's army continued to recede under pressure from Japanese infantry supported from the air.

One of the strong points for a Bataan defense lay in the limited access to the peninsula. But while the choke points favored the forces established there, it posed a threat to the moves by Wainwright's North Luzon Force and the South Luzon Force under Brig. Gen. Albert Jones. The route to Bataan for both required passage across the Pampanga River over the Calumpit bridges, one of which handled highway traffic and the other served the railroad. Military vehicles, soldiers on the march, and a thick stream of Filipinos with wagons, animal-drawn carts, a few cars somehow not commandeered by the military, and civilians on foot packed the route to the bridges. In the sky, flights of Japanese planes continued to bomb and machine-gun military targets and portions of Manila. They ignored the long column snaking toward Bataan but resolutely attacked designated targets. Unlike the Germans in Europe, who understood that disruption of road traffic often prevented an effective retreat, the Japanese hewed to the prescribed plans and, as they demonstrated through the war, lacked an inclination to improvise and exploit unexpected opportunities. Indeed, General Homma, had he elected to concentrate his army upon the elements bound for Bataan, might well have destroyed the forces of Wainwright and Jones. But he, too, stuck to the script that made the capture of Manila top priority.

With some desperate defensive efforts delaying those Japanese units that were approaching the Pampanga, Wainwright himself crossed the bridge. At 1:00 A.M. on New Year's Day 1942, he heard a rumbling that signaled the approach of tanks. The anxiety eased as the armor from the 192d and 194th Tank Battalions rattled through the darkness and across the river. The main remnants of both the NLF (Northern Luzon Force) and SLF (Southern Luzon Force) continued to make their way toward Bataan. Around 6:15 A.M., twin four-ton dynamite charges dropped both spans into the deep, un-fordable current of the Pampanga. For the moment, the Fil-American Army was intact and secure.

Much worse than the shrinkage of the turf controlled by the U.S., and loss of 40 percent of the troops because of casualties and desertion, was the loss of vital supplies. As part of MacArthur's strategy, the troops evacuated Fort Stotsenburg; up in smoke went as much as 300,000 gallons of gasoline and large amounts of high-octane fuel. Tons of food, clothing, and other military gear were discarded.

John Olson, a West Pointer and adjutant for the 57th Regiment, Philip-pine Scouts, a component of the Philippine Division, while delivering a mes-sage learned of Stotsenburg's abandonment and of the vast stores left be-hind. Olson reported the news to his superior and said, "Major Johnson directed Captain Anders to investigate. He did so and returned laden with soap, toothpaste, candy, film, cigarettes, and a number of other items from the Post Exchange. Colonel George Clarke, the regimental commander, de-nied Major Fisher permission to send men and vehicles into the post on the grounds that they 'might be hit by fragments of Japanese or American bombs.' [Engineers at Clark detonated ordnance they could not carry off.]

"Major [Royal] Reynolds, whose patrols had ventured into the post, sent all the vehicles he could get his hands on to salvage whatever they could. From this trip they got large quantities of clothing and food. Among the clothing were winter overcoats that members of the 31st Infantry had worn when the regiment was sent to Siberia in 1919. Though of interest, they were left for the Japanese in favor of more usable items. The salvage party did bring back thirty-six Smith & Wesson .45-caliber revolvers. The most valu-able acquisition was enough Class C rations to fill two buses. They were to be worth the equivalent of gold later in the campaign when food became scarce. In spite of the haul, there was much more that could have been saved. But the timidity of the regimental commander prevented any further ex-ploitation of the abandoned supplies."

The items written off at Stotsenburg can be attributed to panic but a much more basic logistical difficulty arose from the substitution of Rainbow Five for Orange late in the game. To feed the army that would deprive the invaders of a foothold in the Philippines, quartermasters deposited huge stocks of food in the central Luzon plains where they would be accessible to Wainwright's forces. According to Bluemel, a Filipino captain told him that one million pounds of rice had been left at the Cabanatuan storage area. From the commander of the depot at Tarlac, Bluemel heard that 2,000 cases of canned food and clothing could not be taken by the retreating army because it belonged to Japanese companies. The refusal, allegedly from MacArthur's headquarters, to allow confiscation of items owned by citizens

of the invading nation would seem to carry the rights of private property to
an extreme. To further complicate supply problems, commanders of many
units refused to return precious vehicles that brought materials to them, re-
taining trucks and cars for their own use or for use in an emergency. The
law of the jungle infected some units that hijacked and commandeered
transportation, wrecking any systematic efforts by the quartermaster organizations. No one stepped forward to halt this anarchy. Richard Sutherland
commented that his boss never had any interest or understanding of logistics and that flaw would be crippling. The theory for WPO's premise of resistance to conquest by an army defending in the Bataan redoubt rested on
critical logistical assumptions. The strategists expected a force of perhaps
40,000 troops with appropriate equipment and other necessities to be able
to withstand the estimated Japanese army for six months.

MacArthur's plan to prevent the Japanese from overrunning Luzon had
upset the schedule for stockpiling the munitions, food, and other vital items
on Bataan. When he reinstituted the concept of a defense built there, the
supply system like some great ocean liner forging in one direction could not
instantly reverse course, but shuddered as it sought to halt its momentum.
The confusion and absence of a disciplined system might have been overcome by a forceful attention to the problem, but a monumental miscalculation overrode whatever anyone did.

Instead of the compact, well-commanded, skillful body of 40,000 troops
envisioned, tens of thousands more men reached Bataan. Some arrived as
members of the intact but unreliable Philippine Army divisions; others from
shattered units seeped through the jungle. Along with the Filipinos came a
horde of air corps and navy men; their primary mission in the Philippines
now vanished with the disappearance of the planes and ships. They now became ground forces. Under the authority of WPO, the military expected to
evacuate civilians on the peninsula. With the Japanese rushing forward and
the Fil-American forces in retreat, no one attempted to reduce the local population. Furthermore, refugees, who feared Japanese occupation of their
home areas, swelled the numbers of noncombatants on Bataan. With as
many as 80,000 uniformed men on Bataan and an extra 10,000 civilians
added from the start, the food and medical supplies on Bataan were pitifully inadequate.

7
The East Indies

Admiral Thomas Hart had acted upon a 27 November 1941, message from chief of naval operations Adm. Harold Stark that said, "This dispatch is to be considered a war warning . . ." Hart had sent much of his Asiatic Fleet to sea before the raids smashed the ships at Pearl Harbor and then devastated the Manila base at Cavite. Among the vessels temporarily removed from harm's way was the heavy cruiser USS *Houston.* Otto Schwarz, a refugee from the Great Depression in New Jersey and an alumnus of the Civilian Conservation Corps (CCC), at age seventeen had enlisted in the Navy eleven months before the war began. Originally assigned to the *Lark,* a minesweeper, Schwarz was transferred to the *Houston* in June.

As 1941 dwindled down, Schwarz said he and his shipmates groused about the frequency of long gun drills. The procedures at the time stored a number of 150-pound projectiles for the eight-inch guns on the deck with more shells stashed on a shelf five feet above the deck. A hoist with a chain theoretically brought down the reserve ammunition. "We used to ask old-timers how we were going to get those shells down during battle and they always told us, 'Don't worry about it, because there has never been a naval battle more than twenty-minutes and you'll never use the shells on the decks.' The first time we went into battle, we used every shell on the deck, and the guys were lifting the ones off the shelf by hand. It was quite a difference between what you had been taught and what you ended up doing.

"A week or ten days before Pearl Harbor, we were over in Cavite Navy Yard undergoing repairs. We had some of our boilers dismantled and parts all over the deck. All of a sudden we received orders to weld up all of the portholes. We took all the parts off the deck and threw them up on the ship and took off. At sea we hurriedly put everything back together again. From that moment on we were at general quarters and Condition Two with the guns manned all the time. On 8 December we were in condition of readiness and general quarters sounded. We all went to our battle stations and a short message over the p.a. system said the Japanese had attacked Pearl Harbor and we were in a condition of war. We were already in a frame of mind that we wanted to get at the Japanese. There was no doubt that they were an enemy of ours, embarking on a campaign to gobble up territory. It seemed to me

that we were almost jubilant about the war starting. That soon changed after we got our noses bloodied and found out what life was really all about.
We were all rather young, ready to go."

He remarked that he and his colleagues stereotyped the Japanese as
"about four-feet tall, wore round glasses, were not too intelligent, and ate
women and little children for breakfast. [The war] couldn't possibly last
more than five or six months after we got involved."

Japanese airmen had dealt the Allied naval forces a stunning blow on 10
December by sinking the British battleships *Repulse* and *Prince of Wales,* the
two biggest warships in the Far East. Meanwhile, for almost two months the
Houston engaged in convoy duty, traveling to Borneo and Australia without
coming in contact with the enemy. The American-British-Dutch-Australian
(ABDA), Command activated in mid-January, cobbled together a paltry
naval strike force to disrupt the Japanese campaign against the Dutch East
Indies.

The Dutch and Americans anted up four destroyers each and two cruisers apiece, including the *Houston.* On 4 February, operating without aerial
cover, the ABDA force came under attack from fifty-four bombers and torpedo planes. "I was down below the waterline," said Schwarz, " and I knew
nothing about what was going on except from putting two and two together.
For instance, if the 5-inch guns went off, we knew that the bombers were at
a high level; if we heard the .50-caliber machine guns go off, we got a little
worried because they were pretty close. I was in the powder magazine of the
8-inch guns, which do absolutely nothing during an air raid. We were just
manning our battle stations. We really didn't get to see anything, only hear
noises."

When a 500-pound bomb struck the *Houston* squarely on its aft 8-inch turret, Schwarz said it shook the entire ship but his area remained undamaged.
A Dutch cruiser and the other American one, *Marblehead* incurred severe
damage, forcing the ABDA flotilla to flee the Java waters. "After we secured
general quarters," noted Schwarz, "I went aft to see what was going on. There
was a lot of feverish activity, attempting to get the bodies out of the turret.
I did have a couple of friends in that turret and when I got there, they were
screaming for someone to go inside the turret to try and get out a couple
of bodies. There was a tiny room where the shells and powder come up from
below with a little window entrance or exit. They needed somebody small
enough to go in there. I was pretty small and thin so I was chosen. The two
bodies were fused together and I had to break them apart and pull them
out. That's when I first found out that it was not going to be fun and games.
It finally hit me that we were in for something distasteful, that war was not
all the glory of finishing the Japanese in five weeks. We buried something
like forty-eight men and went about putting the ship back in order."

Walter Vogel, who was on deck, said, "We were attacked by some fifty land-based bombers. We had no air support and to our surprise our five-inch AA shells were duds. That left us sitting ducks and they attacked our group for about three hours. I had my head cut open by shrapnel. At Tjilatjap I went to the hospital for seven stitches and a plaster pack on my head. While I was there, the *Houston* departed because Japs were reported making a landing. I went down to the dock and was ordered to get the hell out the best way I could. I went aboard the USS *Gold Star* [a freighter which was among the vessels the *Houston* guarded on the way to Java]. It had no guns and could do only ten knots but we made it to Darwin, Australia."

While the British Empire and the Netherlands fielded the ground forces in Southwest Asia, the United States committed its available resources in the air as well as at sea. Bomber pilot Paul Carpenter whose B-17 had been wrecked in an accident at Clark Field, had retreated into Bataan by rail, truck, and on foot. Early in January, he and other grounded pilots were evacuated to the island fortress of Corregidor in Manila Bay. "We were at Corregidor for two or three days. In the middle of one night, they took us through the tunnel and put us on the old *Sea Wolf* submarine and away we went for Java. The submarine looked mighty good to me. It was a big old black thing, long as a football field, and it was a way to get out of the Philippines and I was delighted. There were twenty to thirty Air Force types aboard, eight or nine from the 19th [his group]. All were aircraft commanders. There was a dive-bombing outfit with five or six of its pilots, some specialists, bombsight or electronics men. The submarine also had aboard a great amount of gold that belonged to the Philippine government and quite a supply of quinine seeds [extracts from the plant were used to treat malaria].

"We came right down through the Battle of Makassar Strait [where the *Houston* took a bomb on its after turret]. The submarine commander had orders not to engage in any hostilities because of all this junk he had aboard—the people, the gold, quinine seeds. His job was not to fight but get us down to Java. That made the submarine crew very unhappy because of all this activity going on around them. We got picked up [by enemy ships] on two or three occasions and I am sure they were all Japanese tin cans [destroyers]. That really shakes you up on a submarine when those depth charges come."

Running on the surface with diesel engines while charging the batteries, the voyage of the *Sea Wolf* from Corregidor to the Javanese port of Surabaya lasted eight days. "They were beginning to get B-17s for replacement through the Africa route. They flew down to Brazil, to Belem, across to Africa, then to India, and on into the East Indies. The pilots that brought those airplanes over just had a trip around the field, a pat on the back, and away they went. They had never seen a B-17 more than a week or so before they headed out for the Southwest Pacific area. They [the command] were eager to get those of us who had some experience in the airplane to get down there and fly. So we did.

"We attacked Jap shipping," Carpenter continued, "and primarily the Jap Navy who was at that point coming down from the Philippines and engulfing all of the East Indies. The Japs knew where we were, and they attacked us once or twice a day. We would try to get a flight off in the interim and you would generally land, and here the Japs would be with their fighters strafing the place when you got there. It was a dicey time. We generally managed to get about six to nine airplanes airborne every day for the month I was there. Our bombardment wasn't very effective because we didn't have much to work with. We were more an annoyance to the Japanese than anything else. Every once in a while we would make a good strike, but I am sure it didn't bother them very much."

Along with the bombers, there was a small fighter-plane force. Tommy Hayes, a member of the 35th Fighter Group who had pinned on his wings and second lieutenant's gold bars in February 1941, had been posted for Clark Field. "On December 7th, the 35th was spread a bit. About one-third had arrived in the Philippines at the end of November. One-third were in mid-Pacific and turned around to head for Hawaii and the last third had not left the States. The plans were to move fifty-five crated P-40Es, along with a like number of pilots, crew chiefs, and armorers. We sailed in mid-December and were diverted to Brisbane, Australia.

"The planes were reassembled and flown to a base prepared for us at Surabaya, Java. When we had arrived in Australia, we were met by ten or twelve veteran fighter pilots from the Philippines. They were the leaders and we, yet to be baptized, were the wingmen. Against the Japanese, who had been fighting in China for four or five years, we had leaders who had a few weeks of war and the majority of us had not even squeezed the triggers of our machine guns.

"Aboard the ship to Australia we had a Navy intelligence officer who briefed us on the Japanese air force—a collection of fixed landing gear, biwing aircraft. The P-40 pilots on board were sure we would be home in six months. Yes, they had a few of those obsolete planes, but they also had the Mitsubishi Zero and the Betty two-engine bomber. Their navy had better fighters and bombers than their army. And their disregard for human life contributed to their success over the British, Dutch, and the U.S. initial air battles. They deployed their equipment very well. Their weakness was a lack of self-sealing fuel tanks.

"The guys from the Philippines explained, 'You don't turn with a Zero.' It's hit and run and the P-40 had speed and was fast in a dive. We overcame our fears and anxieties and gained experience. The Flying Tigers in China with P-40s did a great job, thanks to their early-warning system. In Java, and later in New Guinea, without early warning, P-40s were always below the Japanese, losing the advantage of being on top where you can pound and add or subtract for your rate of climb. Learning was costly."

The *Houston* escorted a convoy of four troop transports to the besieged garrison on the island of Timor. Enroute the cruiser valiantly protected its flock as marauders off Japanese carriers and land-based bombers from the conquered Celebes Island swooped down near Darwin, Australia. "When we were attacked Captain Rooks put on a display of seamanship and guts. He used the *Houston* as a one-man defense of the four ships. Moving the ship rapidly in and out of the convoy and firing constantly we soon became the target, which is what he wanted, I suppose. The bombers really went after us. There were a couple of times when people on other ships told us later they thought we had just disappeared from the sea. Large numbers of bombs would explode, and the ship would just disappear and then come back up. We drove off the bombers without a single direct hit. There was only one near miss on one transport. After we had defended those four ships, we aborted the mission and went back to Darwin. We let the four transports go in the harbor and then the *Houston* went between them and they lined the rails and cheered at the top of their voices . . . they were so thankful for us actually having saved them."

The Japanese had reported the *Houston* sunk on several occasions and the sailors began to refer to their ship as the *Galloping Ghost*. But while it evaded hits at Darwin and the four ships shielded by the cruiser were spared, the enemy blasted a number of other vessels, shot down Allied aircraft, and wrecked Darwin's port facilities. The string of defeats weakened an already rag-tag assemblage of battered, aging ships, and even the *Houston* lacked radar. The American high command conceded the loss of the Dutch East Indies and in a bit of save-face, sleight of hand, Admiral Hart yielded the leadership to a Dutch counterpart.

The Imperial Navy now set its sights on the main prize—Java, with its vast oil stocks and its strategic location. A mighty armada of carriers, battleships, cruisers, and a swarm of lesser but still deadly warships accompanying a large invasion force, bore down upon the Dutch-controlled island. To intercept this fleet, a motley formation of five cruisers, including the *Houston* plus a few destroyers, sallied forth. David was off to meet Goliath without even a slingshot.

In the Battle of the Java Sea, on 27 February in the late afternoon, the Japanese spotted the small Allied force and attacked. The outgunned ABDA vessels raced for safety. Enemy shells disabled the Royal Navy's HMS *Exeter;* a Dutch destroyer sank after a torpedo hit. The *Houston,* with its after turret still unrepaired, maneuvered to defend itself with the six forward guns. That night star shells illuminated the battle scene and long-range torpedoes accounted for two Dutch cruisers. The Australian Navy's *Perth* and the *Houston* escaped momentarily. A day later, they headed into the jaws of destruction blundering into the convoy unloading troops and cargo at the northwestern tip of Java. Although the Allied cruisers sank four of the fifty-six transports, heavyweight Japanese warships surrounded the pair and blasted them with torpedoes and shells.

"We had very little ammunition left after the Java Sea battle," said Schwarz. "We had taken all of the ammunition out of the disabled turret and dispersed it. We were firing star shells—ones that you normally use in practice—giving them everything including the kitchen sink. General quarters had been called so quickly that night that the only clothing I had on was a pair of khaki pants. The speakers on the telephones would say, 'There's another cruiser over there; we hit one!' It was pandemonium. The ship was moving at great speeds and making all kinds of maneuvers. The *Perth* went down first and rather quickly. We were shooting everything, including .30-caliber machine guns. It became obvious we were in trouble. We knew we were being hit because we could feel all of the jarring and the explosions.

"We got word to abandon ship and there was a problem. There is supposed to be a repair party to open the hatches that were battened down very tightly. No repair party was there. Either they'd been killed or were busy elsewhere. We had a mallet which we could use in an emergency to undog the hatch from our side. We let the crew out of the powder magazine inside into our compartment.

"I led the group. I had the mallet in my hand and I opened up the dogs. When you open up the hatch, you don't know what's on the other side. Maybe that compartment has been hit and it's on fire. Maybe it's flooded. Each time you open up another hatch, you go through this trauma of not knowing whether you're going to be alive in the next instant. We got up on the next deck and started forward. Everything was filled with smoke. You could hardly breathe. You couldn't see at all; it was pitch black. I hollered back, 'Okay, everybody put one hand over your nose and mouth and one hand on the shoulder of the guy in front of you and we'll try to get out!' I led.

"Going up on another deck," Schwarz went on, "I felt the guy's hand behind me leave my shoulder. For whatever reason, he went left toward the port side and I continued through the compartments on the starboard side. A short time later, a torpedo hit on the port side. It knocked me off my feet and unconscious. I found out later that the entire group behind me that had let their hands go off my shoulder were killed by the torpedo.

"When I came onto the deck, it was like the Fourth of July at an amusement park. We were dead in the water, just drifting or floating. The Japanese seemed to be ten feet away with searchlights on us and stuff was coming at us like crazy. Shells were exploding all over the place. [Machine-gun fire raked the deck as well.] It was a duck shoot. They had us surrounded and were just sitting out there shooting. Guys were running all over the place.

"I had no life jacket and started forward to my Abandon Ship station. Some guy passed me, running. He stopped and said, 'Don't you have a life jacket?' I said no. He said, 'Here, take this one.' He had one on and one in his hand. I took it and went up forward where the rest of the guys from my division, those that were still alive, were forming. Orders came to cancel the Abandon Ship order. By then a lot of guys had bailed out already. I saw some run past me and go right off the bow, which was darn high. I looked down at the water, watching them dive in and then go past the ship like little corks.

"I went forward to await orders," said Schwarz, "and Ensign Nelson jumped on top of number two turret and ordered us all back to our battle stations. Everybody said, 'What battle stations?' We had none. Our compartments were flooded, on fire. We had no more shells left. Shells exploded all around us. Pieces of teakwood deck were flying in the air. Very shortly, we got word to abandon ship. I went to the port side of the bow where there was a boat boom that is let out when you're at anchor and your boats tie up to this boom. It is a few feet below deck level. I lowered myself onto the boom and then jumped. I started to swim as rapidly as I could away from the ship. Shells were exploding in the water; my stomach kept bouncing back and forth from my backbone. I had one objective and that was to get away from the ship because the suction would take me down. I didn't look back. I headed out, as fast as I could. Swimming with the life jacket was very difficult because they were not the modern Mae West inflatable ones but old-fashioned kapok canvas jackets that completely enveloped you.

"I kept swimming and everything started to quiet down. The ship had sunk and the ocean was dark and silent. I could hear occasional screams from some of the guys in the water. In an attempt to save my life and reach land, I swam for hours. I didn't meet a single soul. I saw a boat approaching me and became very frightened. I could hear the Japanese were machine-gunning the water, so I decided to make them think I was already dead. I tucked my face up underneath the collar of my jacket, got an air pocket there and just bobbed up and down.

"I heard the boat come up to me. They shut the motors down to an idle. I could hear a foreign language being spoken, I could hear them jabbering away. I could 'feel' a searchlight on me. I felt myself being poked with a hook or pole and the jabbering went on. I felt the searchlight go out. The boat started up again and left me. I had been born and raised Roman Catholic. I had been an altar boy and a choir boy. I was very church-oriented as a child.

I found out that at my time of need, my orientation had been one of a God that I feared. I tried to pray that night and seek help but I didn't find any feeling of association. I prayed a lot, but didn't feel it did any good."

For a brief period as he struggled toward the shoreline of Java, Schwarz swam in the company of another sailor. But when Schwarz flagged because of leg cramps the other man paddled off. "Just before dawn, a Japanese landing boat came up. They pulled me out of the water. I was glad to be out of the water. They threw us down in the bottom of the barge but did not mistreat us at that point." Taken to the beach, Schwarz joined a group of seventeen or eighteen survivors from the ship. His new ordeal, life in a prisoner of war camp, was about to begin.

The Americans still in the battle lacked the resources to carry on an effective war from the air. When the Japanese occupied Bali, the always-tenuous supply line between Australia and the bases on Java broke down. By then Tommy Hayes had shot down a pair of enemy planes but on 20 February a Zero hit him from the rear. "The tail was damaged and the canopy dislodged from its track. On landing, coming in over a coconut plantation, turning and slowing to land, the tail dropped and the P-40 fell into the trees. It stopped quickly, the tree trunks ripping the wings off. My head hit the gunsight. I was taken to a hospital with a concussion. About a week later they started evacuation for Australia. I was on a Dutch ship, the *Aberkirk,* along with about 2,000 U.S. and British from Malaysia and Singapore. The ship had about twenty staterooms for the crew but these were given over to badly burned sailors from the *Houston.*"

Because replacement parts needed to maintain the bombers were scarce, only two or three in Paul Carpenter's entire B-17 group could operate at high altitudes. Toward the end of the March, as the enemy advance inexorably swallowed the East Indies, the air fields became untenable. "We got word to evacuate to Australia," he remembered. "At that time, I again had no airplane. I was just extra crew and came out in the back end of one of the last B-17s that left. We could see the Japs coming down the road as we took off. They fired at us, and we fired back." With the remnants of planes and crews, the refugees from Java waited for reinforcements and to regroup.

The Allied efforts in the Dutch East Indies did nothing to relieve the pressure brought by the Japanese upon the hapless American and Filipino forces in Philippines. Tom Gage among the airmen refugees fleeing into Bataan recalled a hellish bomb attack. "The strike came just at lunch time. I remember getting into one of the slit trenches with my mess kit in my hand. To the best of my knowledge I finished the meal. General opinion was they were trying to hit the highway bridge over the river at Orani, which they missed completely. However, they did get two direct hits on the gasoline tanker trucks that were parked in the village. The drivers, not from the 34th, were killed and the town was set afire.

"We continued at Orani until January 7th. During this time I went back in the direction we had come from with a small truck convoy to scavenge anything we could get in the way of supplies. We moved at a snail's pace, bumper-to-bumper with trucks and overhead, flight after flight of Japanese bombers. Luckily for us they had no bombs to spare and also equally lucky no fighters were interested in us. We had no place to hide in the rice fields."

While Americans and Filipinos alike had struggled and straggled toward Bataan, General Homma savored a triumphant entrance into Manila. The soldiers moved into public buildings, hotels, university and school buildings. Japanese officers, prepared with occupation pesos, bought up souvenirs wherever they found an open store. All British and American citizens, including Navy nurse Mary Rose Harrington, were incarcerated on the campus of Santo Tomas University.

With control of the big city established, General Homma unleashed his armies on the last line of American and Filipino troops blocking access to Bataan. The available defenders considerably outnumbered the fighting men fielded by the Japanese commander, although the American commanders continued to insist the enemy had far more troops at his disposal. For their part, Japanese intelligence undercounted the defenders, figuring MacArthur could call upon roughly 40,000 or so underfed, poorly trained, and dispirited soldiers.

Only the support of artillery and heavy fire from the two American tank battalions prevented swift progress by the enemy. But the longer-range Japanese artillery blasted holes in the defensive lines and the last of the Luzon armies retreated into Bataan. Officially, defense of the peninsula began on 7 January 1942 as Wainwright assumed command of the west sector while Gen. George M. Parker received responsibility for the east sector.

The relatively easy initial success against the armies arrayed for the defense of the island had persuaded the Japanese High Command that conquest of the remnants on Bataan would not require as much force as originally planned. To consolidate and expand the control of Southeast Asia, the Japanese army command had snatched away some of Homma's best ground and air troops for the invasion of Java. In place of these experienced and effective soldiers, the 65th Independent Brigade, with 6,500 men, landed on 2 January. The enlisted personnel, all conscripts, had only a month of training and the commander, Lt. Gen. Akira Nara, a graduate of the U.S. Army Infantry School in 1927, described his organization as "absolutely unfit for combat."

The consequences of hurling men with little more knowledge than how to march into the inferno of battle showed immediately. On 8 January, advancing toward Mabatang near Manila Bay, elements of the 65th Brigade tramped along a road in a column of fours with their horse-drawn artillery trailing. Observation posts on the slopes of nearby mountains spotted them and called in the 155mm artillery, already registered for targets on the highway. A torrent of shells burst among the Japanese soldiers, killing and maiming many. Whenever the barrage slackened, the troops dutifully reformed into their columns and renewed their trudge toward death and destruction, for what the defenders could only describe as a "turkey shoot." First blood in the battle for Bataan spilled mainly from the offensive forces.

Nevertheless, the invaders continued to attack. The 57th Regiment, Philippine Scouts, with Philip Fry, recently promoted from major to lieutenant colonel, as CO of the 3d Battalion, opposed the thrust. "On the afternoon of January 10th, our patrols reported contact with strong Japanese combat patrol. Companies were notified to be on the alert and increase their local security. About 2:00 P.M., rifle and machine-gun fire commenced in the I Company sector. We had these flare up before when stray carabao wandered into minefields and set off mines. The men, on edge, would immediately fire a few shots into the darkness. As soon as the firing started, I called Captain [Herman] Gerth, I Company CO, and was informed he was on the front line. I managed to get Captain Haas, Company K, on the phone, who said his sector was quiet. I told Haas to send a patrol to look over the I Company sector and find out what was going on. Not satisfied with the information available, I started out for the observation post.

"On my way up, the firing became more severe. One of the runners was shot through the arm. In spite of his pleading and tears, I ordered him back to the first aid station, as our first casualty. By the time we arrived at the OP the firing had become even more severe and the machine guns had joined in. In fact, the entire left sector was violently active. Gerth was on the OP phone waiting for me. He told me that his entire company was engaged and the Japs were advancing through our minefield. I could see and hear the flash of the mines going off. They were supposed to withstand 600 pounds pressure, but many were homemade and went off at the slightest provocation. I told Gerth to pour it on them and help would be forthcoming if needed.

"A great shout of 'Banzai!' came from the front and the Japs started an old Civil War charge. I got Haas on the phone and told him to sweep Company I's front with his machine guns. It was slaughter. All of our guns had been carefully sighted for mutual support and the Japs were caught by terrific fire, both frontal and flanking. Even now I can't understand why the Japs launched an attack of this kind against modern weapons. My only explanation is they had not faced trained troops before and thought that if enough noise were made the opposition would simply fade away. The attack was smashed before it got underway. The Scouts were jubilant. I made a hurried trip to the front lines and warned them to expect another more serious attack soon. Our casualties were only five wounded including my runner.

"The second attack began about one A.M. It was preceded by considerable small arms and mortar fire. Our lines were smothered and the OP came in for its full share. The entire battalion front came into action. This time the enemy brought up his tanks and hit us hard. Once again the main effort was against Company I. We were forced to put our fire back along the final protective line. A few of the enemy started filtering through and circling behind the Company I sector. As soon as Gerth sensed this he very properly asked for help. I just couldn't afford to commit my reserves so early in the game.

"Captain Coe, the artillery liaison officer, was with me and designated the cane field [to the front of the defenders] as the target and asked immediate fire. Captain Grimes, the heavy weapons company commander, was nearby and directed to concentrate all mortars in the same place. The concentrated fire of these mortars alone would have been terrific. But we had World War I ammunition and averaged about six duds out of every ten rounds fired.

"We abandoned the new light mortar guns at Fort McKinley because the ammunition for them had never arrived. We were badly handicapped without our own protective weapons and forced to rely heavily on the artillery. Captain Coe had Colonel Luback on the phone and asked me to talk to him. Luback said the regiment had taken control of all artillery support, and out of the hands of battalion commanders. This was incredible. I believed some mistake had been made. My only reaction at the time was irritation.

"I asked Luback to keep his line open while I contacted the regiment and got Major Johnson, regimental S-3. I explained the situation and asked him to authorize a barrage. Johnson was evasive so I asked him to put George Clarke [the 57th's commander] on the phone. Once again I went over the situation with Clarke. He had the same line of conversation as Johnson and we ended in a furious exchange of words but no artillery!" The supposed excuse for Clarke's behavior was his fear that any use of artillery would bring retaliatory fire upon his headquarters. Harold Johnson, who also served under Clarke, described him as "phobic" about air attacks.

Outraged and frustrated, Fry rallied his forces. "Company K as well as Company I was now heavily engaged with more and more snipers, armed with Tommy guns, filtering through the lines. They were coming mostly through the 41st Infantry [Philippine Army unit manning the left flank] and circling behind us. Both Gerth and Haas were asking for supporting fire and they were badly worried. They didn't have a thing on me. The Scouts were willing fighters but after all it was their first combat experience. They were bound to be affected by fire into their backs."

The men under Fry pulled back and reestablished their lines. But the enemy seemed relentless in purpose and heedless of losses. Fry recalled, "January 11 about 10:00 P.M. there were signs of formation for a coming mechanized attack from the Nip side. The sounds of tanks couldn't be mistaken. We took preparatory countermeasures. Our mortars and artillery went into action at once. The antitank weapons, 37mm cannons, .50-caliber machine guns, and a battery of 75mms were silent. They had strict orders not to fire a single shot unless tanks were seen approaching. Otherwise they would give their positions away.

"The attack was broken up before the tanks could be used. The Japanese opened up with heavy and light mortar fire against our front lines. Not much damage was done thanks to excellent foxholes. Soon everything we had was in action. The firepower of a battalion armed with modern weapons is something. The Garand rifle is beyond my descriptive powers. It is a mystery to me how anyone can come through it [the battalion firepower] alive. But they do. And they came with the now familiar cry of 'Banzai!' The fight was on. Once again the filtering tactics, but on a much larger scale. We had men stationed in commanding positions waiting for them. Here at least, there was plenty of individual combat. The Nips poured men into the battle. They had face and prestige at stake. This Battalion of Scouts, though badly outnumbered, were desperately eager to place the number of a new American-Filipino Regiment among the war great."

Lieutenant Alexander "Sandy" Nininger, a Georgia-born youth and West Point graduate, fresh out of the infantry school at Fort Benning, had only come to the Philippines and the 57th Regiment in November 1941. According to his superiors, Nininger volunteered to accompany one party of Scouts bent on rooting out infiltrators. His company commander gave Nininger the names of six or eight of the best marksmen in the outfit but specified they must all be volunteers. The heavily armed patrol set out. Those behind them heard intense exchanges of gunfire and explosions. The party returned intact with their ammunition expended. Nininger insisted on another expedition but this time he selected only three Scouts for the mission.

"After some time," wrote John Olson, "they came running back. Shouting to his men to remain, the lieutenant grabbed some more grenades and a bandolier of ammunition and raced back into the trees. He was never seen alive again. His body was found later leaning against a tree. Lying around him were three dead Japanese, one of whom was reported to have been an officer."

Subsequently, Nininger was posthumously awarded the nation's highest military decoration, the Medal of Honor. He was the first American to receive the congressional medal during World War II. Nininger seems to have demonstrated genuine valor although the eyewitness testimony that is a prerequisite for a Medal of Honor is murky. Encomiums, like that of his regimental commander, Clarke, in the forms of letters to the dead man's family, seem inspired more by desires for reflected glory than for drafting a factual record.

While Nininger and the embattled Scouts of the 3d Battalion sought to repulse the onrushing Japanese, a renewed appeal for artillery support was not denied. Major Johnson, instead of consulting Colonel Clarke, arranged for barrages in the canefields directly in front of the Scouts. The defenders momentarily halted the offense. Captain Gerth personally went among the front line platoons, leaving Lt. Arthur Green in his command bunker. A bullet struck the company commander in the groin at 0330. Carried to the command post, Gerth tried to carry on, reporting the situation to higher headquarters. The battalion supply officer, Capt. John Compton, hearing about Gerth, received permission to go forward and aid him.

According to Fry, "A portion of the line was penetrated. Green was telling me this over the telephone when all of a sudden he exclaimed, 'They got Johnny [Compton]! There he goes down.' I told Green to hold on and I would send help to him right then. I turned to Brown who was standing right beside me and ordered an immediate counterattack in the I Company sector. I had one more call from Green, his last one, stating his company was being forced back, casualties heavy but the remainder was fighting hard. I told him of Company L entry." While Gerth continued to pass on details to Fry, Lieutenant Green, leaving the safety of the dugout, headed for the forward positions of the I Company troops. As he consulted and advised, he incurred a fatal wound to the head.

Fry continued, "Haas reported his left flank exposed, Company I shot to pieces, and his company being outflanked. I told him about Company L's entry and for him to give all possible assistance. I believed the enemy had shot the works and was hoping for a breakthrough with Brown's Company L being timed correctly. I called regiment and informed them of the situation and that my reserve had been committed. I asked that at least one company of the regimental reserve be placed at my disposal. Company E was assigned to me and ordered to report to my battalion support line and there await orders. This action on the part of regiment was a very generous one and paid big dividends. Company L under Captain Brown hit the hole in the I Company sector hard. He established contact with Haas relieving the strain there but failed to contact the 41st Infantry. Things quieted a bit."

Although a lull fell over the front, Fry remained aware of threats to his sector's positions because of an exposed flank. "The stage was set and it was a question of who would get there fustest with the mostest." [Employing a quote attributed to the Confederacy's Nathan Bedford Forrest.] Company E, borrowed from regimental reserve, and some added men would carry out the mission. Other companies set up machine guns to hammer the foe if he tried to pull back.

"The attack was a beautiful one," wrote Fry, " an inspiring sight to see. The Scouts had been trained for years in the company-in-attack and it was a model of precision and played for keeps. The reward of perfection was retention of one's life. If this attack had been staged at Fort Benning to show visiting firemen the mechanics it would not have been improved upon. I knew the outcome at once. With such leadership as [Capt. Don] Childers [E Company commander] was showing and such trained fighters as these Scouts, it couldn't fail. The Japanese were trapped. They fought bravely and tried to withdraw in orderly fashion but they were caught by the machine guns positioned for the purpose."

John Olson, as the adjutant at regiment, described the scene at daylight: "The picture that greeted the sleepless eyes of the surviving Scouts as the sun rose, was one of utter chaos and devastation. Broken and bloody bodies were sprawled all over the foxholes and open ground throughout the I and left of K Company sectors. Forward of the front lines, mangled Japanese corpses were strung on the barbed wire like bags of dirty laundry. Abandoned weapons were strewn everywhere. The occasional bursts of fire from enemy-occupied holes, while sometimes provoking retaliatory fire from the Scout strong points, served to keep down any friendly movement. . . . Everyone, even the enemy seemed content to desist temporarily." The losses to the Scouts added up to more than 100.

Harold Johnson, as executive officer for the 57th, coped with the importunings for aid from Fry, replacements for the high number of casualties among the American officers and Scout noncoms, and strove desperately to provide additional ammunition and supply. His by-the-book superiors flatly refused on the grounds that all allocations of artillery shells would be based upon a calendar basis. The schedule restricted batteries to less than one hour of fodder per day.

Johnson went over the heads of the commanders to reach MacArthur's deputy Richard Sutherland. The chief of staff, having visited the 57th two days before the opening of the attack, agreed with Johnson and forthwith directed ordnance to replace each day's expenditure of ammunition as it was consumed rather than hewing to a calendar. Furthermore, Sutherland recognized the failings of George Clarke and started a hunt for a new regimental leader.

As dawn lit on 10 January, the same day that Fry and his outfit met the Japanese attack, a PT boat carried MacArthur and Sutherland from Corregidor to Bataan for an inspection of the terrain and defenses. In his *Reminiscences*, MarArthur said, ". . . I had to see the enemy or I could not fight him effectively. Reports, no matter how penetrating, have never been able to replace the picture shown to my eyes."

This visit, the only one made by the general to the peninsula during its three-months' siege, covered an area south of where Fry's embattled forces in II Corps repulsed the initial assaults on the eastern edge of the front lines. Driven west, MacArthur conferred with Wainwright, the I Corps commander, who offered to show his boss where his 155mm guns awaited the enemy. MacArthur supposedly replied, "I don't want to *see* them. I want to *hear* them."

According to Clifford Bluemel, the CO of the 31st Division, then part of the I Corps, Wainwright summoned all of the generals to meet with their supreme leader. "We spoke to him and shook hands," recalled Bluemel. "He said, 'Help is definitely on the way. We must hold out until it arrives. It can arrive at any time. [Maj. Gen. George] Parker [II Corps commander] is fighting the enemy on the Manila Bay side [site of Fry and the 57th Regiment battle] and he'll hold them. He'll throw them back. We've just got to hold out until help arrives.'" Bluemel did not dispute the general's optimism then nor did he criticize him for misleading his subordinates. To have talked in terms of defeat could only have led to a quick collapse of resistance.

The week before the 57th engaged in its fierce series of battles with the enemy and he toured part of Bataan, MacArthur became aware of the meager food stocks available for both civilians and troops. An inventory indicated only enough to feed 100,000 men for thirty days. On 5 January MacArthur approved a recommendation of his quartermaster that placed all troops and civilians on Bataan and Corregidor on half-rations. The diet amounted to roughly 2,000 calories daily, adequate for sedentary individuals but far below the needs of troops working or fighting for twenty hours a day. Furthermore, vital nutritional elements were missing from the reduced fare. Some units temporarily supplemented the short rations with items scrounged from depots during the retreat. The troops in the field also hunted for their meals, killing a number of carabao, the domestic cattle.

"I got a call one night to come up to Wainwright's headquarters," said Clifford Bluemel, whose 31st Division protected the unchallenged section of the west coast of Bataan. "He said, 'Your division's going to be moved over to the Manila Bay sector.' I said, 'My God! I haven't reconnoitered anything over there. All my reconnaissance has been on the China Sea side and out in Zambales.'" Poor mapping, few roads, and spotty trails through thick vegetation fomented Bluemel's anxiety. Any shift of men and equipment entailed the possibility of being lost.

"There was to be a guide to show me how I was to get to Guitol [a hamlet four or five miles behind the front lines]. I was to be in reserve. General Parker told me on the telephone, 'You follow the road. There is a wire that leads up there. All you have to do is follow the wire.' But there were dozens of wires. I was in a car and I followed this wire and that wire. I ran into an artillery battery and finally someone showed me where Guitol was. I got the troops up there, but we were bombed on the way up. That was the first time the division had been under fire."

With the bulk of his soldiers in reserve, Bluemel dispatched one regiment to support the Philippine Army's 41st Division, commanded by Gen. Vincente Lim, a Filipino alumnus of the USMA. "I went up to see how they were getting along," said Bluemel. "On the way back, I ran into a Japanese patrol behind the lines. There was a truck trail through a sugarcane field. I wanted to go up through the trail to get back to my command but was cut off by the Jap patrol.

"There was a Philippine Scout engineer detachment with one machine gun and a lieutenant. I said, 'You form up a point of an advance guard here, and we'll go up that trail.' But, by God, he wouldn't move. About this time I saw a captain with thirty Filipino Army men. He said, 'General, I think the Japs are there. I'll tell you what we'd better do. Comb that tree and all that area with a machine gun. Then I'll go into the sugarcane and you can go up the trail.' He made a remark to those Filipinos. 'Go on in there. What the hell's the matter with you! Goddamn you, you can't live forever!' They went in and drove out the Japanese patrol. I started up but those engineer Scouts wouldn't move. There was a little Filipino soldier there and after that he became my bodyguard. Nobody would go up the trail but he said, 'General, I'll go.'

"I said, 'All right, we'll go. You go ahead and I'll go with you.' Then I turned to those Philippine Scouts and said, 'I'm a brigadier general. I'm going up this trail, all of you goddamn yellow sons of bitches that are cowards stay there.' They came. From then on I found I could get them to obey orders by cursing."

Even though the enemy was apparently driven off, Bluemel soon found himself under attack. "Some of my own troops opened fire on me. I got off the trail into the sugarcane field. I lay down on my stomach and I could hear the bullets cutting through that sugarcane over my head. Finally they stopped. I went to the trail and waved my hat. There were some Filipino soldiers who belonged to my division, I said, 'What the hell do you mean by shooting up your own division commander!'"

While the body of the Fil-American defense futilely sought to contain the enemy on Bataan, the brain directed movements from the 2.74 square miles of Corregidor, the Gibraltar of the Pacific. Tadpole shaped, the island's head lies two miles south of Bataan while the tail points toward Manila Bay. The bulbous end of Corregidor thrusts 600 feet above sea level and on Topside, as it was known, stood the basics of an army post, headquarters, barracks, and officers' quarters all grouped around a parade ground. A small golf course adjoined the parade ground. The cliffs of Topside, cut by a pair of ravines, dropped precipitously to the water.

Adjacent to Topside, more quarters for officers and noncoms, a hospital, service club, and schools for children occupied a small plateau, Middleside.

East of this area the land fell away to almost sea level and was only 600 feet in width. Known as Bottomside, the low area contained docks, warehouses, a small barrio, San Jose, and a vital power plant. Life upon Corregidor depended heavily on the energy generated on Bottomside to pump fresh water from wells, to refrigerate perishable foods, to move the electric railroad that supplied military installations. The topography changed radically as one continued from Bottomside toward the tailend. Another hump, Malinta Hill, almost 400 feet high, rose above the water. Beyond this outcropping, on the extreme eastern edge, lay a small air strip and a Navy radio station.

It was from Malinta Hill that MacArthur and his staff directed the struggle to preserve the American presence in the Philippines. To protect the nerve center for a War Plan Orange strategy, engineers had burrowed deep into the side of Malinta Hill to construct a 1,400-foot long, 30-foot wide tunnel. From the main shaft, with its railroad track running through it, extended twenty-five laterals, narrower 400-foot-long branches. A separate network of tunnels with a connection to the main passageway served as an underground hospital.

Blue mercury-vapor lights pierced the gloom of Malinta Tunnel, reflecting off the six-foot high, endless line of packing crates with supplies. Signs that denoted organizations identified the province of the laterals. Within the confines of stale, hot air, insects, including bedbugs, tormented the residents. People intent on their business constantly jostled against others; solitude was impossible. The claustrophobic ambience drove some to stay outside even though exposed to enemy shells. Others developed "tunnelitis," unable to leave the seeming security of underground.

To maintain fortress Corregidor, a seemingly formidable array of heavy guns, principally coast artillery, housed in concrete bunkers, menaced anyone who approached by sea. But there were acute deficiencies. The big sticks all were of World War I vintage. They were geared for action against ships, not in support of ground troops. The antiaircraft weapons lacked the best ammunition for use against planes. And although emergency generators could operate the big guns, long-term efficiency required the services that only Bottomside could provide.

Three smaller islands bolstered Corregidor's control of Manila Bay. Tiny Caballo (Fort Hughes), only a quarter-mile square in area, lay due south. It bristled with eleven batteries of artillery including antiaircraft. Also blocking access through the south channel to the bay were Carabao (Fort Frank) and El Fraile (Fort Drum), a pair that contributed another thirty-two heavy pieces to the arsenal. Carabao's own heavy weapons, beach defenses, and 100-foot-high-cliffs, made it an uninviting target for invasion.

Life on Corregidor during the first few weeks after the evacuation of Manila was subdued, broken only by the start of air raids. Food rations were more of an inconvenience than a severe hardship as boats from the southern islands ran the tightening blockade by the Japanese Navy. The vessels that reached the Rock brought fresh fruit, vegetables, and even candy along with other supplies. The population continued to grow. The 1,000 leathernecks of the Marine 4th Regiment, stationed first at Olongapo and then Mariveles, the port on the southern tip of Bataan, on 26 December boarded vessels that ferried them out to the Rock. According to one of their officers, "There was much talk among the men about its big guns and underground system of defense. Inspired by the memory of photographs of the Maginot line, they conjured up pictures of underground barracks and supply lines direct to gun positions. We watched Jap bombers steer clear of the antiaircraft barrages. It was pointed out that Corregidor's antiaircraft was so good that the Japs had not even dared to bomb it yet!"

On 29 December air raid sirens sounded on Corregidor, as they had so often in the past without incident. Convinced this was one more false alarm, the denizens of the Rock paid little attention to the planes. But then bombs rained down upon portions of the island, with several striking at Middleside. Most of the Marine 4th Regiment dropped to the floors of their buildings as the explosions testified to the limits of Japanese fear of Corregidor's defenses.

"An army officer came in the room in which we were," said one leatherneck, "and informed us that there was no need to worry because the barracks roof was bombproof. A few minutes later, a Jap bomb had penetrated the roof on the other end of the barracks." The Marines moved outdoors to tents set up near the beach areas they would be expected to defend.

With the Marines now in residence, the number of people on Corregidor added up to 5,500 men, plus assorted civilian refugees connected with the uppermost echelons of command—the families of MacArthur, Quezon, Sayre, and some Filipinos acting as houseboys. The abundant portions of butter and eggs disappeared. On the 29 December raid, the twin-engined bombers maintained an incautious level of only 18,000 feet. The 60th Coast Artillery, throwing up three-inch shells and some .50-caliber machine-gun lead made the Japanese fliers pay for their insouciance. Several planes began smoking and the enemy formations recognizing the error in judgment, climbed to a safer height. The bombardment scored heavily against barracks, warehouses, and other unshielded surface installations. It killed twenty-two and wounded another eighty, but tallied insignificant damage to the essential defensive armament of the Rock. Further aerial punches over the next week or so shattered more buildings, gouged ugly craters in the once-lush greenery but left the fortress intact. The residents, now aware of the deadly consequences if caught in the open, learned to either dig in or take shelter in places like the Malinta Tunnel.

General George F. Moore had named Col. Paul D. Bunker, nominally in charge of the 59th Coast Artillery manned by Americans, to run the seaward defenses of the Rock. At the start of the war, Paul Bunker had already worn an army uniform for thirty-eight years. A classmate of Douglas MacArthur at the Military Academy and an athletic star, he was an opinionated man freely given to the prejudices of his era, Bunker exuded spit and polish. "He appeared to walk at attention as he made his daily inspection of various batteries under his command," said one account.

Bunker jotted down his record of life on Corregidor. A 3 January entry noted: "Awoke early and went down to relieve the watch officer. Breakfast and then [for] bath and shave as usual. . . . They sprang the usual Air alarm on us which usually occurs when that lone Jap observation plane comes over every morning, thus wasting an hour . . . Bought toothpaste and shaving cream in the heap of ruins which was once our Post Exchange. Lunch at Wheeler [a battery] on Topside. . . . As all was quiet went to my dugout to arrange its contents when Wham-o! She started. This was our second dose of Jap bombing, composed of four courses across the rock, said to be by two flights of six and eight planes, some of them the largest of the Jap bombers.

"Got into my car for a tour of inspection. Arrived at barracks at 2:35 and what a scene of devastation met the eye! Huge patches of corrugated roofing missing and scattered in painfully distorted shapes all over front and rear parades [grounds]. Captain [Harry] Julian met me and smilingly reported, 'Colonel, I have no office now.' A huge bomb had landed just across the car track in the rear of his place and blew out a crater twenty-five-feet deep and forty-feet across, cutting rails and trolley wires and shattering every window on the rear face of barracks. A smaller direct hit on [the] Mechanic shop where the Mech had practically finished making me a filing cabinet! Our regimental workshop [was] burning fiercely and, of course, no water at Topside.

"One could see, from the direction of wind, that it would also burn the other buildings, including the 'Spiff Bar.' I went up into my library and found utter chaos. Glass case containing my shell collection blown to smithereens and thousands of books littering the floor everywhere and even some outside. Going downstairs I found soldiers already looting the PX like ghouls . . . Stationed a sergeant as guard temporarily."

In his diary, the coast artillery officer disparaged the Filipino soldiers. "It is an obvious fact that the Philippine Army is worthless because the Filipino will *not* fight under Filipino officers. And there are practically no Filipino officers who are worth a damn. The graduates of the 'Philippine West Point' at Baguio are sometimes pretty fair but others are political appointees whose only idea is to line their pockets. They have no control over their men."

The one resident of Corregidor who seemed totally unconcerned about the air raids was MacArthur, who, as navy officer Robert Lee Dennison pre-

viously observed, refused to seek shelter. As the siren sounded everyone
headed for the safety of the tunnels. But MacArthur insisted on walking outside to watch the attack without even a helmet to protect him from debris
or shrapnel.

High Commissioner Francis Sayre recalled an incident where he was
among a group outside the shelters with MacArthur when a sudden bombardment exploded. Everyone, except the supreme commander dropped
to the dirt. "Anyone who saw us," remarked Sayre, "must have had a good
laugh—at the General erect and at ease while the High Commissioner lay
prone in the dust. I have often wondered whether he was as amused as I. In
any event, his expression never changed." Sayre also remembered that
MacArthur once remarked "he believed death would take him only at the
ordained time." The nickname of "Dugout Doug," bestowed at a later period when MacArthur escaped from the Philippines and capture, was singularly inappropriate to describe his behavior on the Rock or, for that matter, other instances when he came under fire.

Seemingly oblivious to danger, MacArthur also exhorted his flagging
troops. He issued a letter on 15 January: "Help is on the way from the United
States. Thousands of troops and hundreds of planes are being dispatched.
The exact time of arrival of reinforcements is unknown as they will have to
fight their way through Japanese attempts against them. It is imperative that
our troops hold until these reinforcements arrive.

"No further retreat is possible. We have more troops in Bataan than the
Japanese have thrown against us; our supplies are ample; a determined defense will defeat the enemy's attack. It is a question now of courage and determination. Men who run will merely be destroyed but men who fight will
save themselves and their country. I call upon every soldier in Bataan to fight
in his assigned position, resisting every attack. This is the only road to sal-
vation. If we fight we will win; if we retreat, we will be destroyed."

The message adds further mystery about the workings of the MacArthur
mind. This was the only occasion on which he indicated numerical superiority for his own army; his reports to Washington and his memoirs constantly
spoke of the greater strength of the foe. The statement, "thousands of troops
and hundreds of planes are being dispatched" was ambiguous if not deliberately deceptive. Any men and equipment moving to the Pacific were
bound for Australia, not the Philippines. In his *Reminiscences,* MacArthur
claimed "A broadcast from President Roosevelt was incorrectly interpreted
because of poor reception in the Philippines, as an announcement of impending reinforcements. This was published to the troops and aroused great
enthusiasm, but when later corrected, the depression was but intensified."
It is hard to believe a radio broadcast would be the means to inform the Pacific War's top commander that vital reinforcements were on the way.

Paul Bunker greeted the exhortation with reserve. Of the expected additions of men and machines, he noted, "If the Navy is responsible they'll never get here! Rumors are persistent that instead of six months' reserve of food, we have only three months!"

Army nurse Madeline Ullom says she took MacArthur's statement at face value. "Every morning, before breakfast, I walked to the top of Malinta Hill to see if the promised convoy was arriving." A month would pass before she realized help would not come over the horizon.

8
The Fall of Bataan

At the start of the third week in January, Alva Fitch with his artillery battalion feared an imminent and dangerous thrust from the enemy. Fitch's direst expectations proved well founded. When he reached headquarters, he recalled, "The CP was in a stew. The gooks were chattering like so many monkeys. A force of Japanese had gone around our right flank and cut our communications exactly at the rear echelon of the Pack Battery, five kilometers back. All forms of communication were cut. [Col. Halstead] Fowler [his commander], when he heard about it, had gone back and tried to drive them out with an automatic rifle. He had been hit twice in the back and lungs, but had escaped and returned to the Regimental aid station.

"About 4:00 P.M.," said Fitch, "a gook lieutenant, unknown to me, told me the road was open. I relayed the information to Colonel Berry. He sent an ambulance loaded with wounded to the rear. The road was not open. The Japs shot up the ambulance. Colonel Fowler and one other man who could walk, escaped. The Filipinos decided the Japs were using the ambulance as a machine gun and literally tore it apart with rifle fire. Of course the wounded were still in it.

"I found myself with 700 men who had not eaten for twenty-four hours. I got a sack of rice from the Philippine Army Infantry, and found a carabao during the night; each man got a little to eat. On the 22d, the Japs began closing in on us from all sides. We had no reserves after we had committed Laird's battalion in the rear and it was rapidly tiring. During the afternoon I called a conference of all of my battalion commanders and gave instructions for the destruction of guns and other materiel when the position should fall.

"We had received no word from General Wainwright and had no communications. Our position was extremely precarious. The troops had received only one meal since the interruption of communications and the capture of our rear echelon. Our ammunition was about gone, and we knew that a heavy battle was under way on the other side of Bataan. The principal reserve of General Wainwright's Corps had been moved to support the other battle before our communications had been cut. We could expect very little help and our force was exhausted."

118

Strategists plotted a new defensive position. But what looked good on a map proved extremely difficult to achieve. Access to the designated position depended upon a trail that deteriorated into an impassable path for vehicles. "As in many situations during the early days of the war," said John Olson "no one on the higher staffs had taken the trouble to verify all of the facets of WPO-3. So no provision had been made to ensure that supply and evacuation could be effective for the organization given this portion of the line to defend."

For engineers to hack a road through the thick growth would require five days, an unacceptable delay. Regimental supply organized mule trains to pick up supplies dropped by vehicles at the point where the trail became inaccessible for trucks. Harassed by Japanese planes, the troops still managed to transport enough to sustain the infantrymen for several days. The planners worked out an intricate choreography—trucks or buses to haul soldiers as far as possible, and night marches to avoid the threat of air attacks. Military police patrolled the roads and trails but only partially prevented traffic jams. Periodic salvos of Japanese artillery rained upon critical sites under enemy observation during daylight hours and added to the difficulties.

A runner brought a message from Wainwright, directing units to, "Hold your positions. Plenty of help on the way. Food will reach you tomorrow." The besieged troops hunkered down and employed what means they could to consolidate their position. A Japanese cavalry unit slipped into the area and triggered a firefight. Far worse, the battalion committed to an attack against the enemy in the rear, slipped away. Their escape left the men with Fitch vulnerable.

Said Fitch, "We discovered [this] defection the next morning when Japs began arriving in the vicinity of our CP in buses. By 9 A.M. on the 23d our position had become untenable. All wire communication was broken. I lost all but one of my OPs. Rifle fire was coming through my CP from the front and the inland flank. About 10 o'clock, I gave the order to destroy all guns, except the 2.95" pack guns which were to be carried, and ordered all battalions and batteries to assemble about a kilometer to the rear of my CP. When I arrived at the assembly area, I found that Lieutenant Platt had been wounded. He had received bullets through one foot, and his testicles, and couldn't possibly walk. Colonel Fowler was also there. I found myself with 700 men, of which 80 were Scouts from the Pack Battery, the remainder untrained and undisciplined P.A. artillery. I had four unwounded American officers."

Not only were Fitch and his companions in dire circumstances but the entire Bataan defense was threatened by a clever maneuver instigated by General Homma. The Japanese loaded a battalion of infantrymen aboard barges and set out for Caibobo Point, one of a series of finger-like protrusions along the western shore of Bataan behind the bulk of Wainwright's I Corps. Hastily mounted, the amphibious operation miscarried during a series of misfortunes. A lack of proper maps misled the navigators. Treacherous tides and a cranky sea sickened soldiers. But the worst to befall the ill-fated troops was their discovery by PT-34, skippered by Lt. John Kelly with squadron commander John Bulkeley also on board. "We were returning to our base on Bataan early in the morning," said Bulkeley, "from a patrol off Subic Bay. We saw these barges and charged in among them, strafing them with .50-calibers and raising general hell but without very decisive results." In the darkness, a dim light, low in the water, had appeared. When PT-34 came within twenty-five yards of what was now perceived as a boat very low in the water, Bulkeley hailed it with a megaphone to determine friend or foe. A burst of machine gun fire and a stream of tracers established the relationship. Bulkeley himself took up an automatic rifle while the four machine guns on PT-34 pumped bullets at the craft now headed for the shore.

An enemy bullet ripped into the ankles of Ens. Barron Chandler, Kelly's second in command. But the enemy barge had taken too many hits to remain afloat and soon sank. According to the stripped down narrative of Bulkeley, "We concentrated, after a general dispersion, on two barges that appeared to be crippled and sank them. The last one was boarded before sinking by myself and two live prisoners were taken with a lot of papers which were delivered to Corregidor. That first gave the news of the strength and force of the attempted landing. The Japanese barge sank with me and I was in the water hanging on to the two Nips till Kelly rescued me. It was a good thing that I had been a water polo player."

The interruption by PT-34 completed the disarray of the small flotilla. Not a single man reached Caibobo Point. Instead a third of the men came ashore at Longoskawayan Point ten miles southeast of the objective and the rest of the battalion landed about three miles from Caibobo. Guarding the beaches where the latter group came ashore were the Air Corps comrades of Tom Gage in the 34th Pursuit Squadron. The official U.S. Army history, *The Fall of the Philippines,* noted "the airmen failed to make proper provision for security, for there was no warning of the presence of the enemy. The gun crews, awakened by the sound of the Japanese coming ashore in pitch blackness and unable to fire their .50-caliber machine guns, put up no resistance. After giving the alarm, they, in the words of an officer 'crept back to their CP.'"

Tom Gage offered a somewhat different version. "For several days," remembered Gage, "we could see mast tops just over the sea's horizon, coming down from the north to even with our position and then patrolling back and forth. Rumors said it was a battleship, mine sweeper, cruisers, tug boats pulling barges. No matter, during the night of the 22d, barges did land in a ravine or gully that ran down to the seashore. Our furthest northern point was a machine gun (.50 caliber) placed inside a rock barricade. In the early morning of the 23d, Japanese soldiers climbed out on top and approached the gun position. Some men thought they were Filipino soldiers, even called a greeting to them that was answered with rifle fire. Private first class John W. Morrell from Ohio was killed. The remaining men of the gun crew withdrew. Lieutenant Jack Jennings took a patrol later in the day into this area and came under heavy fire. He was wounded in the knee and Sgt. Paul Duncan was hit in the thigh by something of a large caliber. Paul died during the night in the squadron aid station. Others from the 34th incurred wounds from tangles with the invaders."

The Japanese who did reach the shore threatened Mariveles. Defense of the port depended upon one of the many improvised units, the Naval Battalion, with men drawn from the PBY Patrol Wing, the *Canopus* crew, shore personnel from Cavite Naval Base, and Battery A and Battery C of the 4th Marines. It was a collection of former shore-based torpedomen, storekeepers, yeomen, a motley crew of naval rates, and some marines under the leadership of Comdr. Francis J. Bridget—"Fidgety Francis" to some of his men because of his relentless insistence for them to "get war conscious." An Annapolis graduate, Bridget flew PBYs and had served as a squadron commander in the Philippines. But after air raids destroyed all nine planes, Bridget volunteered to form a security force that would defend the Naval Station at Mariveles.

During the week or so after the creation of the Naval Battalion, the new foot soldiers began courses in such unfamiliar subjects as marksmanship, squad tactics, and the use of the bayonet under supervision of Marines. Aware that their ordinary Navy whites made the men easier targets, the novice foot soldiers desperately attempted to dye their uniforms khaki but instead produced rather bright, mustard-colored garb. Some time after eight on the morning of 23 January, Bridget listened to a frightened call from the lookout. "Longoskawayan, Lapiay, and Naiklec Points are crawling with Japs," supposedly shouted the observer. "We're getting the hell out of here, right now!" After those few words, in spite of requests for further information, Bridget heard only the ominous sounds of rifles. Bridget briefed and then dispatched two separate outfits to deal with the enemy until he could round up more men. He failed to advise either that a second friendly force would be active in the vicinity. The two units marched off into the wilds leading up to Mount Pucot.

One platoon blundered into a small group of enemy and a firefight ensued. The Navy ensign in charge and his senior Marine noncom both incurred wounds but the invaders took off. The untrained Navy troops kept firing long after the foe vanished into the jungle. Another platoon routed a handful of Japanese with more bursts from their rifles. The first effort of the novice infantrymen wiped their sectors clean but the main element of the amphibious force were still on the scene. Still, by nightfall, Bridget's ersatz infantry had control of Mount Pucot. A dead Japanese soldier's diary reported the presence of a "new type of suicide squad" dressed in brightly colored uniforms. He marveled at their tactics. "Whenever these apparitions reached an open space, they would attempt to draw Japanese fire by sitting down, talking loudly, and lighting cigarettes."

Bridget's makeshift army, reinforced with some soldiers from the Air Corps, a chemical unit, and the Philippine Army sought to displace those Japanese still on Mount Pucot and the Longoskawayan peninsula but most of the seaborne force had advanced into Quinauan Point after passing through thin beach positions of the 34th Pursuit Squadron. Brigadier General Clyde Selleck, required to defend the ten miles of the entire southwestern Bataan coast between Caibobo Point and Mariveles, ordered Lt. Col. Irvin Alexander and his regiment to drive the invaders into the sea. After his initial mission of surveying the turf to be manned by the 71st Infantry Division, Alexander now led the 1st Philippine Constabulary Regiment.

Inducted into the Army only in December, the constabulary ordinarily served as an indigenous police force. Their background did not include infantry training. Alexander hurriedly mobilized his 3d Battalion and set out to block the enemy. Rugged terrain, overgrown trails, and a single passable road delayed movement long enough for the Japanese to dig in. Alexander ordered an attack that faltered. He recalled, "The battalion commander explained that he had attacked frontally without making any attempt to explore either flank. After I had moved to try to start the envelopment myself, the Nips must have spotted me for they opened up with a heavy machine gun which snipped off many leaves uncomfortably close to my head. I lost no time hitting the dirt, but before my head got there, a bullet struck the ground where my head hit an instant later. Wiping the dirt out of my eyes, I realized I was badly scared, my brain seemed paralyzed.

"I explained to the battalion commander the necessity for a flanking attack and assured him I would go with it. A Filipino corporal who saw the logic, jumped up shouting and kicking at his men to get them moving. It was difficult to get the men started, but we had to get results when the Nip machine gun opened up again, killing the corporal and several men, thereby putting a stop to our attack. That corporal was a gallant man who deserved recognition, but later, when I tried to find out his name, I was unable to locate anyone who remembered the incident."

MacArthur's chief of intelligence, Col. Charles Willoughby, accompanied by a member of his staff, showed up for a first-hand look at the problem. Along with the dismayed Alexander they kept meeting soldiers straggling away from the front. The Americans sent them back to their posts. But, noted

Alexander, "Finding a number of officers standing behind trees, we tried to get them to take some tactical action; we had no success." Alexander said he made another determined effort to launch an attack. "There were no Filipino officers present, and the men were not going to be pushed, so I saw I had to lead them. I crawled ahead of the line about ten feet. By shouting and waving my arms, I managed to get the line to crawl up to me. We moved a couple of times more, while [an American officer] kept shouting a description of what he could see from the flank. He said we were very close to the Nip line that was made up of individual foxholes, except for a machine gun position that had two or three men in it. He announced that he could see a Nip sticking his head up, to which I answered, 'Shoot the son of a bitch!'

"His voice suddenly sounded very excited as he yelled, 'Look out! They are turning the machine gun in your direction!' I could not see a thing as I raised up on one knee, holding my rifle in front of me with both hands. Something struck the rifle with a metallic sound, jarring my hands pretty severely. Feeling an additional jolt on my right thumb, I turned it up to see a phosphorus core of a tracer bullet burning into my flesh. Before I became aware of any pain in my right hand, I had started jerking it violently. At last the phosphorus came off, leaving the top half of the thumb almost as dark as a piece of charcoal. Not until the pain eased up did I notice that one finger of my left hand had been shot away, and another one had been considerably mangled.

"After I recovered my wits, I ran a little to the left rear of where I was hit so that my location would not be the same when the Nips fired again, and then I was sick. For thirty-six hours, with the exception of four hours of sleep, I had been going at top speed. I had made countless decisions, some of which might have been of sufficient importance to influence the critical situation and I had one scanty meal during the action while working so hard to get results with poorly trained and poorly equipped soldiers who did not even understand my language. I was in doubt as to the results of the engagement, and I was suffering somewhat from the shock of my wound."

Willoughby bandaged Alexander's hand and led him to a first aid station. A surgeon discovered a sliver of metal in his breast bone. Driven to the Bataan hospital, Alexander admitted, "I had [a] feeling of relief . . . a mixture of thankfulness for being practically still in one piece and of pleasure at the opportunity to go to a place of comparative safety and comfort. On the other hand, I had a small guilty feeling that I was running away from the boys."

General Parker ordered the U.S. 31st Infantry and the 45th Infantry, the other Philippine Scout regiment, to counterattack. The troops moved out with less than precise coordination as the Americans jumped off well before their Filipino comrades. The GIs achieved some good gains but then the attack stalled against a stiffening and increasingly numerous enemy. Even as the strategists rearranged their front, the hazard of the Japanese presence on the Points between Mariveles and Bagac required quick action. Not only had USAFFE strategists thrown General Selleck's forces into the fray alongside Bridget but, also, after Col. Paul Bunker pleaded the case, Battery Geary, crewed by Philippine Scouts on Corregidor, blasted enemy positions with huge shells from its guns. A Coast Artillery installation had not fired against an enemy since the Civil War.

The psychological effect of the big guns may have shattered the spirit of some of the inexperienced enemy, but the interdiction capacity of Coast Artillery emplacements on the Rock was severely limited. Most fired flat trajectory missiles, almost useless against an enemy hugging the reverse slope of a ridge. To support the Fil-American soldiers attempting to root out the opponents on the Points, 14,000 yards from Corregidor, the big guns at Geary lobbed shells at their most extreme range. Early in the month, a hit from an airplane had collapsed a half-completed air raid shelter, suffocating most of Geary's top noncoms. Their replacements were still learning their jobs. While a forward observer did accompany the men on Bataan to pinpoint targets, the ragged performance of guncrews led to inaccuracy and worse, several short rounds inflicted casualties upon about a dozen sailors serving as riflemen.

On another front, an infantryman well schooled in the theories of fire and movement so basic to the foot soldier, in jungle tactics, and coordination with artillery, Lt. Col. Hal Granberry, with his executive officer Maj. Robert Scholes, expertly directed the 460 men of 2d Battalion from the 57th. The Japanese fiercely resisted; some men fought hand-to-hand, but the Scouts relentlessly swept the enemy from their positions. Driven to a precipice some threw away their weapons and hurled themselves from the cliffs into the water. They either drowned or fell victim to marksmen.

The corpses of the invaders lay exposed for several days, putrefying in the sun while Scouts busied themselves cleaning out caves along the shoreline where a few Japanese soldiers sought to hide. Not until the mopping up ended could a burial detail dig holes large enough for a mass grave to accommodate more than 100 bodies. Another 200 men were estimated to have been either blown up by the artillery, drowned, or been interred by their comrades. Casualties for the Scouts numbered eleven dead and about forty wounded.

The Japanese tried to add troops with more seaborne ventures. Sam Grashio, limited to flying reconnaissance missions from the field near Cabcaben, recalled, "Somehow our Intelligence got some remarkably accurate information: on February 1 at about 10:30 P.M., a Japanese ship would tow thirteen landing barges, crowded with 1,000 troops, into nearby Aglaloma Bay. At the appointed hour, our shore batteries abruptly shone their search-lights onto the barges, turning them into sharp, silvery silhouettes against the black waters of the South China Sea. As targets they were perfect. The other pilots and I, singly and in two-ship formations, flew back and forth over them, no higher than 200 feet, strafing every barge repeatedly, from end to end with .50-caliber machine gun bullets until we ran out of am-munition. Most of the barges sank.

"It seemed to me at the time that every last enemy soldier must have died either from gunfire or from drowning, though many years afterward I read an account that stated that about 400 Japanese troops did manage to get ashore, where all but three were killed by our troops. When it was all over, around 2:30 A.M., General George was ecstatic. He grabbed each of us in a Russian-style bearhug and recommended all of us for Silver Stars." Along with the blows struck by the four P-40s in Grashio's flight, the unfortunate Japanese reinforcements reeled from a rain of shells fired by field artillery outfits and small arms fire from Scouts on the shore. Among the participants in the ground fighting was Ed Dyess, Grashio's former squadron comman-der. He led infantrymen manufactured out of former Air Corps men, some of whom, according to Grashio, could be heard inquiring how to fire their weapons even as they moved into combat.

While denying reinforcements to the enemy, hundreds of the original invasion force continued to present a risk for the defense. Poor coordina-tion marked the first experience of the Scouts with tanks dispatched to their aid. The foot soldiers, instructed to keep 100 to 150 yards behind the ar-mor could not protect the hapless tankers from mine and grenade attacks. Individual Japanese soldiers dashed from the thick cover beside the trails, plastered a magnetic mine against a tank and then scurried into the jungle before the device exploded. On other occasions, they simply pulled a con-tact mine by string across the path of the tank. The Scouts, however, learned quickly. Instructed to stick close to the tanks, the riflemen picked off would-be mine layers before they had a chance to place the explosives. The de-termined troops contained the drive designed to conquer the western half of Bataan, albeit maintenance of the Fil-American lines required a pullback beyond a stretch of major east-west road from Pilar to Bagac.

To the east, in the II Corps, the Japanese had simultaneously applied pres-sure, particularly at a point centered around Trail 2 that plunged into the heart of the peninsula. Responsibility for the area, known as Sector C, be-longed to Clifford Bluemel who understood he would have at his disposal his entire three regiments of the 31st Division. Bluemel, organizing in Sec-tor C, assigned his three regimental commanders to areas and they sup-posedly moved into place during the night. Said Bluemel. "The next morning I got an early breakfast, picked up all my staff, and headed for the front line. I made it a rule to visit the front line before the fighting started.

"I had a hole in the line which you could walk through. I had a battalion headquarters company from the artillery, fifty or sixty men, armed as infantry." They were available because a few days before, about 2,000 recruits had reported and, when asked how many he would accept, Bluemel grabbed them all. The newcomers filled such units as the artillery battalion but since they had no field pieces, they served as riflemen, equipped with obsolete Lee-Enfields.

Bluemel assigned this skimpy band of soldiers to plug the gap. The handful of artillerymen armed with rifles could hardly have been expected to do more than delay an attack by even a company of Japanese soldiers at Trail 2. Bluemel tossed in a chunk of the reserves. "I had a G-2 [intelligence officer], a very bright young Filipino named Villa. The 32d had two battalions on the line and they had one in reserve. I told Villa, 'You see all these foxholes?' I want you to see a soldier in each foxhole before you get back to my headquarters, even if you're there until the day after tomorrow.' When he got back about 7:00 that night, he said, 'The battalion is in.' A little later the Japs attacked us. Right in that place they made their main effort."

Bluemel rightfully boasted, "If I hadn't gone out to the front line, assuming it was there, the Japs would have walked right up Trail 2 and Bataan would have fallen. If I had stayed back in my command post, it would have been a bad state of affairs." Not only was the planned advance through Trail 2 halted but Bluemel organized a counterattack that eventually pushed the Japanese back across the Pilar River.

Initially, the Japanese benefitted from the confusion and weakened state of their adversaries. The 1st Division of the Philippine Army, commanded by Gen. Fidel Segundo, had taken such a beating and dumped so much of its equipment during its earlier encounters with the invaders that men who had lost their entrenching tools dug holes and trenches with mess kits and cleared fields of fire with bayonets. The Japanese secured positions behind the Fil-American lines that became known as "the Pockets." They dug in with the skill and camouflage they would consistently demonstrate throughout the war. Against the Pockets, artillery proved almost useless. Forward observers could not pinpoint targets; the absence of maps to indicate ranges and topography hampered gunners; the prevalent high-trajectory weapons only shattered treetops; and the plethora of dud mortar shells limited effectiveness of the basic piece for close support.

Wainwright personally directed the overall defensive operations against the incursions and at the Pockets as much as possible. During an inspection trip, the general's car rounded a curve that exposed it to enemy gunners. Incoming shells pounded the area and the occupants leaped out in search of cover or foxholes. Wainwright noticed a captain from his cavalry days and for eighteen minutes of the barrage calmly sat atop a heap of sandbags chatting with his old comrade.

Navy Lieutenant Malcolm Champlin, that branch's liaison to Wainwright, who had accompanied Wainwright, said he asked the general why he took such a risk. Recalled the Navy officer, "He said, 'Champ, think it over for a minute. What have we to offer these troops? Can we give them more food? No, we haven't any more food. Can we give them supplies or equipment or tanks or medicine? No. Everything is running low. But we *can* give them morale, and that is one of my primary duties. That is why I go to the front everyday. Now do you understand why it is important for me to sit on sandbags in the line of fire while the rest of you seek shelter?'"

The defenders, guided by Wainwright with his local commanders, gradually marshalled their superior manpower, brought up tanks, and squeezed the foe. As usual, gains accrued from the ranks of the Scouts—the 45th Regiment. Platoon leader Willibald C. Bianchi earned a Medal of Honor, knocking out a pair of machine guns while absorbing three wounds, including a pair of bullets that struck him in the chest. Tough fighting at a significant cost in casualties annihilated the substantial number of enemy invested in the Pockets, and the entire Japanese campaign to conquer Bataan ground to a standstill.

While the Fil-American forces had begun to decline due to the effects of short rations, fatigue, and disease, the enemy had also succumbed to the brutal conditions where the temperature averaged ninety-five degrees and the terrain was particularly inhospitable to an attacking army. Instead of the customary sixty-two ounces of food daily, the Japanese soldiers nearly starved on only twenty-three ounces in rations. Malaria and dysentery ravaged the Nipponese and medical supplies ran desperately short. Most of all, the jumble of Fil-American forces slowly, but with deadly effect, battered the Japanese. General Homma, expected to declare victory by the end of January, now saw his 16th Division of 14,000 soldiers able to field only 700 for combat. The 65th Brigade, nominally 6,500 strong, could muster only 1,000.

A temporary respite gripped the war zone during mid-February. The breather allowed replacement of forces and resupply for the Japanese, but no such restoration attended the defenders. Colonel Glen Townsend, commanding the 11th Regiment, which played a principal role in reducing the Pockets, noted, "The 26th Cavalry had eaten its horses. Rations were reduced from sixteen ounces a day to eight and then to four. Twice a week we got small amounts of carabao, mule or horse meat. There was no flour, vegetables, or sugar. The quinine was exhausted; malaria rampant. Almost everyone had dysentery. The hospitals and aid stations were jammed with sick and wounded [there were as many as 7,000 patients in Hospitals Number One and Two]."

Along with the troops on Bataan, those on Corregidor endured half-rations, but food recovered from barges and sunken vessels around the island shores supplemented supplies. Even as the troops on Bataan sucked on boiled hide, Paul Bunker on Corregidor recorded eating a dinner topped off with a piece of pie. "Probably the last," he noted, "because of the flour shortage. We are now on a ration that allows only one ounce of flour and seven ounces of bread per day." Meager as it sounds the amount surpassed that available to the soldiers on the peninsula.

Blockade runners from the southern islands or even, in a few daring forays, from Australia, increasingly ran afoul of Japanese warships. Because of their limited cargo capacity, submarines which operated with much greater impunity, were used only to bring in munitions and remove items like gold bullion and, increasingly, personnel—code experts, pilots, naval specialists deemed essential for prosecution of the war. Some of those evacuated owed their rescue to whom they knew rather than what they knew, and that engendered some resentment. The *Seadragon* scored one of the few successes at sea, sinking a fully loaded 6,441-ton transport outside Lingayen Gulf.

The administration in Washington, D.C., had already written off the Philippines. Always a longshot, the achievement of War Plan Orange required a fleet capable of carrying massive numbers of troops and gear 5,000 miles. Shattered hulks at Pearl Harbor and the imperatives of a two-ocean war, factors never introduced into the original planning calculus, reduced WPO to the irrelevant. Glumly contemplating month after month of defeat, the policy makers desperately seized upon MacArthur both as an irreplaceable strategist and a rallying figure. He had earned this stature more for his skills as a diplomat and public relations than for any smashing victories.

A disheartened, sick Quezon had proposed to accept a Japanese offer that would grant the Philippines independence. He dictated a cable to President Roosevelt in which he complained that the U.S. had abandoned the Commonwealth, and it was "my duty as well as my right to cease fighting." MacArthur persuaded Quezon not to transmit the message. However, as Quezon continued to grumble about the ineffective American defense of his land, Washington politicos offered only encouragement, but no material aid. MacArthur, as middleman, skillfully navigated a tricky course. Surrendering before exhausting all possible resources would be a terrible blow to U.S. morale. At the same time, the supreme commander endeavored to convince the Filipino leaders that their citizens were not being sacrificed to salve American pride but to provide breathing space for mobilization of resources in the U.S. Sergio Osmeña, Quezon's vice-president, buttressed

MacArthur's argument, suggesting to his president that history would perceive him as a traitor if he capitulated. For the wheelchair-bound, tubercular Quezon's protection, and perhaps to remove him from a stage where his cries of desertion might still echo, the submarine *Swordfish* evacuated the Quezon family to the southern Philippines. (Bulkeley spirited Quezon to Mindanao and a B-17 flew him to safety in Australia.)

The orders to MacArthur stipulated resistance so long as humanly possible and he expected to die with his boots on. To his aide, Sidney Huff, he confided, "They'll never take me alive." Wife Jean, offered an opportunity to accompany the Quezons, refused. "We have drunk from the same cup, we three [their son Arthur] shall stay together." Instead of the MacArthur dependents, the *Swordfish* stored a footlocker with the general's medals, the couple's wills, some investment securities, their son's birth certificate and first baby shoes, and a few similar personal items.

The doughty spirit MacArthur presented to the world was not lost on his superiors half a world away. Correspondents filed stories of his fearlessness during air raids, detailed his almost daily visits to the cots of the wounded, painted portraits of his constant sessions with his commanders to plot moves which could thwart the enemy. Winston Churchill, with only melancholy news to issue about his own nation's engagements, addressed the House of Commons: "I should like to express . . . my admiration of the splendid courage and quality which the small American army, under General MacArthur, has resisted brilliantly for so long, at desperate odds the hordes of Japanese who have been hurled against it. . . ."

American soldiers on Bataan had begun to look at MacArthur differently, however, expressing resentment at a commander seemingly safely ensconced in an impervious fortress. The GIs, increasingly cognizant no help was on the way, referred to him as "Dugout Doug" and composed the ballad, "Battling Bastards of Bataan", that mocked their status. In marked contrast, the Filipino soldiers seemed to maintain their faith in MacArthur. More important, the stories printed in American newspapers and magazines played him up as an authentic hero to the public.

Military and political leaders at home and abroad urged that MacArthur be extricated from Corregidor as an essential weapon for continuance of the war. He represented a rallying figure, and his capture or death would give the Japanese a propaganda coup. MacArthur's superior, General Marshall, on 23 February instructed him to visit Mindanao, spend a few days lining up defenses, and from there proceed to Melbourne for command of all U.S. troops in the Pacific theater.

In his memoirs, MacArthur claimed, "My first reaction was to try and avoid the latter part of the order, even to the extent of resigning my commission and joining the Bataan force as a simple volunteer [an improbable fantasy]." The assembled officers, according to MacArthur, vociferously protested the idea. "Dick Sutherland and my entire staff would have none of it. They felt that the concentration of men, arms, and transport which they believed were being massed in Australia would enable me almost at once to return at the head of an effective rescue operation." The general agreed to mull over his decision. A day later, the wishful thinking of his subordinates, based on rumors and interpretation of vague messages about shipments of men and machines, apparently infected MacArthur. He agreed to leave but on his own timetable.

Over the next few weeks MacArthur recalled, "I began seriously to weigh the feasibility of trying to break through from Bataan into the Zambales Mountains to carry on intensified guerrilla operations against the enemy." Obviously, the general was once more intoxicated by dreams of ventures far beyond the capacity of his ragtag army. In light of the condition of the Fil-American forces, piercing the Japanese lines was preposterous. More urging from Washington persuaded MacArthur to schedule his departure before the foe foreclosed any escape.

On the eve of his departure, MacArthur summoned Wainwright to whom he would turn over command of Luzon. At that moment Wainwright's control covered at most a couple of hundred square miles because the enemy now occupied almost the entire island. Separate COs were named for other portions of the archipelago—Mindanao with 25,000 men, and the Visayan grouping that had a garrison of 20,000, all under Gen. William F. Sharp. There was also a commander for the fortified islands in Manila Bay. Strategic and tactical command for the Philippines remained vested in MacArthur, about to reside in Melbourne, 4,000 miles away.

MacArthur recalled his final meeting with Wainwright: "'Jim', I told him, 'hold on till I come back for you.'" Wainwright in his memoirs offered a much lengthier version of their remarks. In his account, MacArthur addressed him as "Jonathan" and vowed he was leaving only under repeated orders of the president. "I want you to make it known throughout all elements of your command that I am leaving over my repeated protests." He did reassure his subordinate that if he got through to Australia he would come back. Wainwright, in addition to the command of a badly depleted army in wretched physical condition, received a box of cigars and two jars of shaving cream from the departing chief.

MacArthur recalled the scene at the dock the night of 11 March. "I could see the men staring at me. I had lost twenty-five pounds living on the same diet as the soldiers, and I must have looked gaunt and ghastly standing there in my old war-stained clothes—no bemedaled commander of inspiring presence. What a change had taken place in that once-beautiful spot! My eyes roamed that warped and twisted face of scorched rock. Gone were the vivid green foliage, with its trees, shrubs, and flowers. Gone were the buildings, the sheds, every growing thing. The hail of relentless bombardment had devastated, buried, and blasted. Ugly dark scars marked smoldering paths where the fire had raged from one end of the island to another. Great gaps and forbidding crevices still belched their tongues of flame."

He said he thought of those who would stay, like his classmate Paul Bunker. "He and many others up there were old, old friends, bound by ties of deepest comradeship. Darkness had now fallen, and the waters were beginning to ripple from the faint night breeze. The enemy firing had ceased and a muttering silence had fallen. It was as though the dead were passing by the stench of destruction. The smell of filth thickened the night air. I raised my cap in farewell salute, and I could feel my face go white, feel a sudden convulsive twitch in the muscles of my face . . .

"I stepped aboard PT-41. 'You may cast off, Buck,' I said 'when you are ready.'"

Bulkeley later said he had full confidence his boats and he could deliver their human cargo to safety. Although he had no sophisticated instruments for navigation through the thousands of islands, tricky currents, and in the darkness, Bulkeley said, "I had been in the Philippines for a long enough time and gone through the islands many times. I never doubted success and I was damn glad to get out of Corregidor."

Racing through a stiff wind that sent water lashing the faces of all aboard—seasickness struck all of the landlubbers—forced to stop from time to time to clean gasoline strainers, changing course to make a time consuming swing away from land after signal lights from shore seemed to inform the enemy navy, only three of the PTs reached the first stop after almost twelve hours afloat. With PT-32 unable to continue for the moment, its passengers transferred to the 34 and 41. In tandem they set out for Cagayan on Mindanao On the morning of 13 March, the boats docked on schedule, having traveled 560 miles through Japanese-patrolled waters with only charts and a basic seaman's knowledge of navigation to arrive precisely on schedule. B-17s from Australia picked up the entire party for the final 1,500 mile leg of the trip to Batchelor Field, fifty miles from Darwin, Australia.

The general said it was at Batchelor that he issued the most famous pronunciamento of World War II, "I shall return." Manchester's biography of MacArthur reports the statement went to the press that met him at the Adelaide railroad station while he was enroute to Melbourne. In light of the details supplied by Manchester, his account appears more likely. The use of the first person singular provoked considerable argument with detractors citing it as damning evidence of MacArthur's egomania. However, according to the biographer, the suggestion to use "I" instead of "We" developed from Carlos P. Romulo, then a lieutenant colonel and former newspaper editor and publisher, charged by MacArthur with handling news for the US-AFFE. Sutherland, foreseeing the immediate future, while on Corregidor had suggested the Allies should employ the slogan, "We shall return." But Romulo argued that while Filipinos believed the U.S. had let them down they maintained their faith in MacArthur. "If *he* says *he* is coming back, he will be believed."

Whatever the origins, MacArthur gloried in its use. "I spoke casually enough, but the phrase, 'I shall return' seemed a promise of magic to the Filipinos. It lit a flame that became a symbol which focused the nation's indomitable will and at whose shrine it finally attained victory and, once again, found freedom. It was scraped in the sands of the beaches, it was daubed on the walls of the *barrios*, it was stamped on the mail, it was whispered in the cloisters of the church. It became the battle cry of a great underground swell that no Japanese bayonet could still."

The American propaganda machines seized upon the slogan. Only a few days after MacArthur left, Sam Grashio and several other pilots flew over Manila and other sites to drop leaflets in which MacArthur sought to explain why he had left. "He also called upon them to be courageous, and promised that U.S. forces would return soon to rescue them," noted Grashio. Later, submarines handed out cartons of supplies bearing the three word quotation.

The looming defeat of the MacArthur defense of the Philippines notwithstanding, the general was awarded the Medal of Honor

> For conspicuous leadership in preparing the Philippine Islands to resist conquest, for gallantry and intrepidity above and beyond the call of duty . . . He mobilized, trained and led an army which has received world acclaim for its gallant defense against tremendous superiority of enemy forces in men and arms. His utter disregard of personal danger and under heavy fire and aerial bombardment, his calm judgment in each crisis, inspired his troops, galvanized the spirit of resistance of the Filipino people and confirmed the faith of the American people in their armed forces.

For the moment, regardless of how it originated and how much the phrase "I shall return" was trumpeted or inscribed, MacArthur as a figure in the defense of the Philippines was now offstage. The problem was he did not acknowledge the fact. To the confusion of the War Department in Washington, MacArthur did not clearly spell out the legacy of his command arrangements. It was assumed that he had endowed Wainwright with power over the entire archipelago forces. Made aware that such was not the case, a flurry of messages flowed from the interested parties. MacArthur told his boss Chief of Staff Marshall he still expected to control operations in the Philippines. Marshall declared the MacArthur plan unsatisfactory, advising President Roosevelt of the difficulties in managing four separate commands in the Philippines from a base 4,000 miles away. Roosevelt promptly elevated Wainwright to lieutenant general, officially notified him he now headed the U.S. Forces in the Philippines (USFIP), and carefully explained the decision to MacArthur, who for the moment accepted the new arrangements without objection.

The reactions to MacArthur's exit by the Americans who remained varied. Irvin Alexander said, "We were electrified by the news that General MacArthur and a part of his staff had gone to Australia. Of course, there was a great deal of resentment among those left behind, and the expression 'Ran out on us' was on many tongues, but if there was a single officer who would not have given his right arm to have gone with him, at least he would have settled for his left. I can never forget my elation when [word] came to my headquarters to tell me that General MacArthur intended to send for the remainder of his staff, and alerted me to be ready to go to Corregidor at an hour's notice, . . . others were scheduled to go with the next group of staff officers. It was our great misfortune that our call never came."

MacArthur's former West Point classmate Paul Bunker, initially, expressed his faith in the general. "We have been at war almost four months now and so far as we can see, no slightest effort has been made to help us. From the first, knowing the Naval War College 'solution' [reference to both WPO and Rainbow Five] to the Philippine Problem, I have secretly felt that we are slated to play the part of another Alamo. However, if anybody can help us it is MacArthur. He is our only chance. It is disturbing, however, to read that our President has appointed a 'Board' of all nations to control the 'strategy of the War in the Pacific'—why hamper MacArthur."

Sam Grashio, still flying one of the paltry stock of airworthy planes, said, "His departure occasioned some bitter remarks about 'Dugout Doug' from men who had long envied the Corregidor garrison for what they presumed was the easier life of the latter or who blamed MacArthur for the inadequate defenses of the Philippines. There were also gripes that the General had taken along the family's Chinese maid and, according to 'latrine rumors', even a refrigerator [false as was one that said the family took out a mattress stuffed with money]. I never shared that discontent. Like most GIs at all levels I felt somewhat let down to learn that the Chief was no longer with us, but it seemed to me mere common sense to save him for the rest of the war."

To John Olson, fighting with the 57th Infantry, Philippine Scouts, however, the news was depressing. He noted that a rumor had circulated of General Homma's suicide, a reaction allegedly for the disgrace in not having overrun Bataan. "Perhaps this was to counter the dishearteningly accurate report that Gen. Douglas MacArthur had transferred to Australia. While this was explained as making it possible for him to command the reinforcements that had been promised since late December, it encouraged very few who heard it. Promises and predictions were not chasing the enemy from the Philippine Archipelago."

Clifford Bluemel spoke of MacArthur as a magic talisman. "There are always soldiers who say it's nice to fight under a lucky commander. I figured MacArthur had been a lucky commander and I said to some of the American officers, 'We've lost our luck' and I think we did. I think it hurt morale all the way down to the front-line people. I had to tell them, because if I didn't, the Japs had loud speakers . . . talking to the men, telling and begging them to desert. I told them, 'Help is going to come. He's going to bring it back.' I had to lie a little bit. I didn't believe it."

Meanwhile, USFIP commander Wainwright coped with his meager resources in men and supplies. It was clear that all efforts to break the blockade had failed, that the Luzon defenders could count on only insignificant amounts of food or medicine to reach them. Already puny food rations continued to dip in February and March. The Bataan soldier, American or Filipino, by late March lived on less than twenty ounces of food a day. Rice, in barely palatable, soggy portions, replaced wheat products like bread or potatoes. Those on Corregidor ate better than the troops fighting on Bataan. Rear-echelon troops managed to siphon off some items destined for the front lines. Commanders took to inflating their roster numbers in order to draw extra rations—a division that normally counted 6,500 men, dispatched two-thirds of its men for service elsewhere, then claimed it was feeding 11,000. Squabbling over the apportionment of food stocks racked relations with headquarters, quartermasters, and those engaged in distribution. Cigarette-hungry soldiers, down to an average of one smoke a day, created a black market that pushed the price of a pack to as much as five dollars. The low-calorie diet wasted muscle, depleted fat reserves, and men acted listless after any spurt of exertion. Serious vitamin deficiencies produced scurvy and beriberi. Malaria, dengue fever, and amoebic dysentery thrived in the weakened bodies.

The progress of the war curtailed medical care. Madeline Ullom recalled, "The supply of plasma and for blood transfusion was soon exhausted. Doctors and enlisted men donated blood. The influx of many orthopedic cases used up the supply of traction ropes. Jungle vines were substituted. Backs ached from long dawn to dusk hours of changing dressings of patients on beds about one foot from the ground. Amputees without hope of prosthesis tried to learn balance and movement in their weakened condition.

Gauze was washed, sterilized, and reused. Amputees spent long hours stretching and folding gauze. The transfer of patients from Hospital Number One to Number Two could not compete with the increase in admission rates."

As Wainwright assumed command, he still could list just under 80,000 soldiers in his 200-square-mile fief. But a large proportion could not be described as fighting troops. Doctors rated combat efficiency below 45 percent. In outfits like the Scouts, the best ones that Wainwright could field, company strength dropped considerably. And not even recruitment of the most capable from the constabulary, nor the promotion of men of proven worth to upper echelon noncoms or even the ranks of officers, could compensate for the losses. Wainwright and his staff learned that reports of General Homma as a suicide had been erroneous. Actually, Homma had added 25,000 fresh soldiers, more and heavier artillery, and, equally important, a massive influx of air elements with a mission to pulverize the Bataan defenders.

"On April 3," noted John Olson, "the sun when it rose looked down upon a peninsula torn by incessant and devastating bombardment from virtually every tube of the available Japanese artillery pieces. The artillery fires were reinforced periodically by the heavy thumps of bombs that shrieked in clusters from dive bombers that flew with almost complete impunity back and forth across the lines." According to Olson, an uninterrupted, five-hour deluge of bombs and shells literally blew a hole in the sector of the jungle defended by the Philippine Army 41st Division. An ongoing barrage prevented reserves from sealing the hole. "Except in the western portion, the defenders had been reduced to a dazed, disorganized, fleeing mob. Nothing that the American and Scout advisors tried succeeded in stopping the bewildered and terrified Philippine Army personnel. A major rupture of the line had been achieved."

Exploding missiles interrupted Easter Services at Hospital Number One. The steady flow of casualties to the battered medical units became a torrent. "By five in the evening on the next day," said Ullom, "shells were raining. Word was that the Japanese had landed at Cabcaben which was only two kilometers away." Nurses like Ullom could not handle the volume. "Beds were assigned before those who occupied them were discharged prematurely to return to combat. Front lines seemed to vanish. Most of the patients suffered from gunshot and Hospital Number Two sent buses, trucks, and ambulances to transfer patients."

Alva Fitch witnessed the same overture to the final assault. "Our own news agencies kept reassuring the troops that everything was under control. By the sixth, all of our reserves had been committed and the Japs were advancing even more rapidly. At noon of the eighth, I was told to move my battalion about fifteen miles to my rear, about ten miles from Mariveles. I started my ammunition back during the afternoon. About dusk, I was told to remain in my present position, that Mariveles would be abandoned and we would make our final stand on the west side of Bataan. There was considerable confusion and no one seemed to know what was going on."

Deploying tanks and piercing the Fil-American lines in a number of places, the Japanese surrounded some defenders and swept others to the rear in a rout. This was accelerated by their air arm that blasted the trails or roads packed with men and the few vehicles and field pieces not abandoned or shoved into ravines and ditches when passage became obstructed. With the enemy about to overrun the hospitals, the authorities forestalled the capture of the women. "Around eight on the evening of 8 April," said Ullom, "nurses at Hospital Number One and Number Two were ordered to take a small bag and be ready to depart immediately. It evoked mixed feelings from the nurses. Many were reluctant to go. They felt an obligation to nurse the seriously and critically ill patients. But they knew orders must be obeyed. The doctors came to see them leave. Goodbyes were hasty with promises to see each other again.

"About midnight, the nurses from Hospital Number One were in a small open boat. It tossed about in the water as blasts hit nearby. Guns on Corregidor were hitting the Japanese on Bataan. Shells whizzed over heads repeatedly. Men on all sides were attempting to swim to Corregidor. At 3:30 the pier was reached finally, amidst flashes of gunfire and blast of bombs."

Later, evacuees from Hospital Number Two endured an even more harrowing trip. They had gathered at the Mariveles dock while in the early morning hours, defenders demolished stores of TNT, warehouses, ammunition dumps, and storage tanks rather than allow them to fall into enemy hands. For as long as seven hours, the nurses and personnel accompanying them huddled in ditches, under trucks, in an engineers' tunnel, or in a culvert. Meanwhile the orgy of destruction continued to streak the sky with streams of colored fire and smoke. Sailors scuttled the few ships and the faithful *Canopus* backed out into fifteen fathoms of water and then slowly settled to the bottom as water flooded the torpedo warhead locker and forward magazine. Even Mother Nature battered the hapless on Bataan and Corregidor. An earthquake shivered the ground, sent men sprawling, bounced the beds in Hospital Number Two, shook the walls of Malinta Tunnel on Corregidor, swayed the trees, panicked screaming monkeys.

The II Corps, defending the eastern side of the peninsula, ran out of space to back up in as the enemy advance from the north and on the western flank shoved troops under Bluemel toward Manila Bay. Bluemel supposedly had three regiments and a battalion of his own tied in with two more regiments under Col. John Irwin. In fact, surrenders, desertions, killed, and wounded had depleted approximately 10,000 combat troops to 2,500 who, said one officer, "were all so tired that the only way to stay awake was to remain standing. As soon as a man sat or laid down he would go to sleep."

As communications broke down and the defenders broke ranks to retreat, Bluemel could personally exercise command over only a small portion of the men. He spoke for many of the embittered at the front as he exploded to a handful around him, "Those goddamned bastards back there have been sitting on their damned fat asses for months, eating three squares a day before retiring to their comfy beds for a good night's sleep. They've had their heads in the sand like a covey of ostriches. They haven't known what is going on, what has happened, and they haven't listened. And now it's all down the drain. I can't pull their dead asses out of the fire, and I don't know of anyone else who can except the Good Lord, but I don't see Him taking the trouble." While Bluemel overstated the living conditions to the rear, the orders he received indicated at best wishful desperation and at worst woeful ignorance.

On 8 April, the troops led by Bluemel yielded along the Alagan River, the final natural barrier to the enemy advance. The haggard general, who had suffered the same extreme physical demands as his soldiers, had halted at night by a stream of water, waded out to a rock, and removed his shoes and socks to bathe his sore, swollen feet. When his II Corps commander and nemesis Gen. George Parker reached him by field telephone and told Bluemel to form yet another line of defense, Bluemel scalded his superior: "You sit back there on your dead tails in your comfortable, well-lighted CP and draw a line on a map with a grease pencil and tell me to hold it. I am lying here in pitch black dark, with no map and only a vague idea of where I am. I have been fighting and falling back on foot for the last seventy-two hours. I have no staff, no transportation, no communications except the phone I hold in my hand. My force consists of remnants of the only units that have fought the enemy, not run from them. The men are barely able to stagger from fatigue and lack of food, which we have not had for more than twenty-four hours. Yet you cannot send me one of your many fat, overworked, staff officers to show me where I am to deploy the handful of men I have. Where is the food we need to revive our starving bodies? Where is the ammunition we need to fire? Where are the vehicles and medics to treat and evacuate our wounded and disabled? I'll form a line, but don't expect it to hold much past daylight. OUT!" As Bluemel and his staff tried to organize a cogent defense they too felt the earth tremble beneath them. They first thought that hunger and fatigue had induced hallucinations but then realized it was a quake.

In Australia, MacArthur said, "Rumors reached me of an impending surrender. I at once radioed General Marshall, informing him that under any circumstances or conditions I was utterly opposed to the ultimate capitulation of the Bataan command. If Bataan was to be destroyed, it should have been on the field of battle in order to exact full toll from the enemy. To this end, I had long ago prepared a comprehensive plan for cutting a way out if food or ammunition failed. This plan contemplated an ostentatious artillery preparation on the left by the I Corps as a feint, a sudden surprise attack on the right by the II Corps, taking the enemy's Subic Bay positions in reverse, then a frontal attack by the I Corps. If successful, the supplies seized at this base might well rectify the situation. If the movement was unsuccessful, and our forces defeated, many increments, after inflicting important losses upon the enemy, could escape through the Zambales Mountains and continue guerrilla warfare in conjunction with forces now operating in the north. I told him I would be very glad to rejoin the command temporarily and take charge of this movement. But Washington failed to approve. Had it done so, the dreadful 'Death March' which followed the surrender, with its estimated 25,000 casualties would never have taken place."

Nothing demonstrates better than this statement the fantasies that had swathed MacArthur's thinking. From his first decision to meet an invasion with an untrained, ill-equipped army through the final moments when he proposed that the starving, sick [80 percent with either malaria or dysentery], ammunition-poor, artillery-weak, and ragtag aggregation, an army largely only in name, carry out an attack against a well-led, fully equipped foe supported by an abundance of big guns and aerial supremacy, he seemed to believe he could control reality by means of his will.

MacArthur voiced his faith in this "sudden surprise attack" even after the war. Wainwright, who had dutifully echoed his superior, years later said of Gen. Edward P. King, "[he] was on the ground and confronted by a situation in which he had either to surrender or have his people killed piecemeal. This would most certainly have happened to him within two or three days."

Irvin Alexander attended the conference at King's command post while the strategists wrestled with Wainwright's notion of an attack by I Corps. Remembered Alexander, "Calling General Wainwright's headquarters again, [King] demanded to know what the decision was with reference to I Corps in view of the fact that General Jones had reported to General Wainwright exactly as he had to General King, that he could not launch an attack. . . . There was a considerable pause, during which I assumed that a discussion was going on at the other end of the line. Two or three minutes later, General King said, 'Thank you very much' and hung up. Turning to his staff, he reported that General Wainwright could not agree to a surrender of Bataan as General MacArthur had ordered him to hold on, but that if General King did surrender on his own authority, there would be no interference with any element of his command." Wainwright later would categorically deny he held any discussion with King about the option of surrender.

Said Alexander, "The general went on to say that if he survived to return home he fully expected to be court-martialed, and he was certain that history could not deal kindly with the commander who would be remembered for having surrendered the largest force the United States had ever lost." After further review of the situation with his staff officers late during the night of 8 April, King concluded he had no alternative but to submit to the enemy. He made the decision on his own, knowing full well it directly disobeyed the orders emanating from both Australia and Corregidor. King and the enemy commander, Maj. Gen. Kameichiro Nagano, met to cover the details for a formal surrender. The first hours of the session went badly. General Homma had expected the U.S. envoy would be a representative of Wainwright and prepared to speak for all Fil-American forces in the islands. King could speak only for the Luzon army. King bargained an immediate armistice, for assurances that all prisoners would be treated in accord with the Geneva Convention, and that the sick, wounded, and weary ride in trucks with gasoline expressly saved for this contingency. The Japanese dismissed the plea for an immediate halt to the shelling, saying that their pilots, already in the air for missions, could not be recalled before noon and raids would continue until that hour. Irate because King could not yield the defense of the entire archipelago, the victors demanded unconditional surrender of those under King's command. The discussion dragged on for ninety minutes before King, desperate to spare useless bloodshed, assented. Even then, his conquerors demanded that every individual and unit accept the uncompromising terms.

The chaos continued even with the cessation of hostilities. Alva Fitch recalled, "A messenger told me to report to General Stevens's CP as Colonel Hunter's representative. " [Luther Stevens commanded the 91st Division supported by Fitch's artillery.] "When I arrived, the staff was sitting around with long faces, drinking coffee. I was given a cup of coffee and a chair. General Stevens blew his nose a couple of times, and said: "Major, General King has gone to Japanese headquarters to surrender the Bataan forces. The terms are not yet known. Be prepared to complete the destruction of your guns and material before 6:00 A.M. [There is a discrepancy between Fitch's time table and the official record but there is no reason to doubt his memory of the experience.]

"I reported this to Colonel Hunter and assembled my battalion commanders and staff. I gave them the news and instructions as to what to do to their guns and equipment. About 4:00 A.M. I received a call from General Stevens. He said the Japs had refused to accept the surrender. And that we were to fight it out on our own. My Filipinos didn't like this much, nor for that matter did I. About half an hour later, he called again and said that the surrender had been accepted.

"The next few hours were very noisy. The sound of demolitions and of burning ammunition dumps gave the impression of a fair sized battle. . . . We had a good meal, posted guards for local security, and I went to sleep. By the time I awakened on the tenth, most of the sounds of fighting had stopped. We received orders to stack arms and display white flags. All day we heard stories of how the Japs were treating prisoners. Generally, they indicated that we could expect fair treatment. My lieutenants were in favor of taking to the hills. All had malaria, some had dysentery, and we had no medicine. I feared that it would be a year or eighteen months before the Philippines were retaken. I didn't believe we could live that long among the Filipinos without being captured or betrayed by them. Eventually they [his subordinates] all took my advice and stayed with me."

When Col. Irvin Alexander returned to the 71st Division headquarters he reported to his superior, Brig. Gen. Clinton Pierce. "I informed the division commander that most of my American officers and a number of the best Filipinos had spoken of going to the hills instead of surrendering. I suggested the possibility of the general leading a picket detail through the Nip lines. He answered, 'If the commanding general had wished that I take a patrol to the mountains, he would have told me. I have received orders from my commander to surrender myself and my command and I am a soldier who carries out orders.' I asked him if he would authorize the immediate departure of a patrol if someone else led it. He answered, 'No!'"

The upper echelon officers waited for official word of acceptance of a cease fire. Word came that the enemy had started an attack. Alexander received orders to block the Japanese, using a battalion of Scouts already on hand and another battalion that would join them subsequently. "The men had been informed before noon that the war was over, and they had thrown their arms away, substituting white flags for their guns. I tried to get them off the road into the jungle but I was not successful. The story of surrender spread like wildfire, so that the newly arrived men started to throw their arms away. I appealed to the battalion commander who did get his companies into position, but I knew there was no fight left in the men.

"General King had surrendered us, yet I had command of a defensive force that was practically useless, under order to allow no Nips to pass our position. The American officer with me tried to reassure me by saying there would be at least one man to back me up when I started shooting." To Alexander's enormous relief, he received instructions to withdraw into a bivouac at their permanent camp. "I assembled all of the Americans at supper to repeat my conversation relative to taking to the hills. I told them I was not in good enough physical condition to try to pass through the Nip lines. I [explained] I saw it my duty to stay and accept surrender but I would order out a patrol consisting of all those who felt their chances were better in the hills. Moreover, I would take full responsibility for their absence in the event they did not come back. After a brief discussion among themselves, every man decided he would stay."

By field telephone, Gen. Arnold Funk advised Bluemel to withdraw his people to an isolated position where they could escape contact with the enemy while rations would be sent to them. The general with men from his 31st Division and other units formed into a column trudging toward a safe area. Bluemel recalled, "While moving on [a] trail, [I] was leading the column with a patrol of two men and came under rifle and machine gun fire in the open at a distance of about 100 yards. The troops of the 26th Cavalry were deployed and an engagement commenced. At this time the attention of the CG 31st Div. [Bluemel] was called to the fact that headquarters Luzon Force surrendered at daylight and directed firing to cease at that time, that it was now almost noon and a fight was commencing. If the command fought its way out of this situation, it would be to surrender at Mariveles or some other place as there was no place to go or other troops that could be reached—and that many casualties would be incurred for no useful purpose. It was decided to stop the fight and surrender."

9
The Death March and Morale Missions

In the handful of hours that remained before the Japanese overran all of Bataan, Wainwright endeavored to import as many as 7,500 men to Corregidor. He hoped to reinforce his garrison with proven units like the 45th Infantry Philippine Scouts, a field artillery battalion with its weapons, and other soldiers. He agreed to take all Navy personnel, mostly Americans, with their precious stores of food, fuel, and boats to the fortress. Transportation specialists rummaged a shuttle service employing a minelayer, interisland steamer, launches, and barges towed by powered vessels. The entire operation fell apart as gridlock on trails and roads as well as interdicting fire from the enemy prevented the 45th from ever reaching the docks. Through binoculars, a horrified Wainwright and staff watched servicemen and civilians improvise their own craft, sometimes as flimsy as a few bamboo poles lashed together. Others plunged into the oily, shark-infested water and swam toward the Rock while Japanese artillery lobbed shells among them and snipers picked off the bobbing heads. About 2,000 eventually joined 8,000 already on Corregidor. Had everyone whom the command authorized reached the island, the limited food supplies would have run out within ten days.

On Bataan, the Japanese bagged as many as 78,000 men, the largest number ever surrendered by an American commander. The volume staggered the victors who had anticipated only about 40,000 troops opposing them. Not only were there nearly double the amount of captives but also the speed of victory far exceeded the Japanese timetable. In little more than a week they had achieved what they believed would require at least one month of operations. Under these circumstances the absence of a plan to handle prisoners is understandable. As a consequence, there were no preparations to provide food, water, or transportation for the tens of thousands. These inadequacies alone boded ill for forces taken on Bataan.

Adding to the potential for disaster was the attitude of the winners. Resentment toward those whose bullets, grenades, and shells killed friends and associates was expectable. But racism also played a role. The Japanese considered themselves a superior ethnic strain and the subjugated Filipinos, along with the Chinese, Polynesians, Koreans, and other Asians, as inferior.

Their knowledge of the U.S., much of it drawn from Hollywood's gangster movies or westerns, coupled with propaganda, persuaded them Americans were crude, thuggish people bent on the destruction of the Japanese way of life. Perhaps most damaging to the esteem for Americans was *Bushido*, the warrior code that taught that death was preferable to surrender. For a foe to yield while still able to fight generated contempt, particularly among the officers.

What would become known as "the Death March" developed slowly; the men caught up in it had no inkling of what lay ahead. In the chaos neither American officers nor the captors provided direction. Tom Gage, the Air Corps clerk, remembered, "When we got the news that Bataan had been surrendered—something like jungle telegraph spreads by osmosis—everyone started gathering in the headquarters-supply area. We built a fire and began throwing the .45s into the fire. Rifle bolts went into the fire, too. Campbell came over and suggested we drift toward the supply trailer and see if we couldn't get ourselves some new clothes. I put on everything new and picked out several pairs of socks. I also put on a brand new pair of brown army shoes." Some in Gage's area had been approached by Filipinos offering to sell food. After agreeing to a deal, the Americans followed the natives. Gage recalled, "They found a mountainous food dump, and we had been starving for the past two months. Everyone could get all the milk [condensed], chocolate, corn beef [canned] they wanted. There were a lot of K rations, too.

"On April 9th, we were told to move out. I don't think a single officer stayed with the enlisted men. I think we were trucked in relays to area headquarters. Our truck wouldn't run so it was towed to Mariveles by another loaded truck. We were packed in standing. On the way down we saw our first Japanese troops. They were stringing telephone wire up the road. When we got to Mariveles we were not allowed off the trucks. In the morning, they would let a few off the back but we could not wander. I filled my canteen with ditch water and dosed it liberally with either chlorine tablets someone gave me or iodine. I've never understood why I didn't get dysentery or typhoid from this water—maybe I overdosed it with chlorine.

"We were put through our first shakedown, they were looking mainly for weapons. I retained my field bag and food, tin helmet and a book—*For Whom the Bell Tolls*. We were in this place the 10th, 11th, and 12th [of April]. Most of the 34th [Pursuit Squadron] searched each other out and gathered in one general area. We were all approached on turning in our chow to Mess Sergeant Hardy and having him make as many meals as he could. I recall we had something to eat every day. On April 12th, they threw us out on the main road and we started the march out of Bataan."

P-40 pilot Sam Grashio passed up two opportunities to escape by air when he saw his squadron commander Ed Dyess refused to flee. Dyess procured an automobile and a handful of companions sought to find the rest of the scattered outfit. Said Grashio, "Cold reality enveloped us within a few minutes. We met a Japanese tank and staff car. We stopped at once, threw up our hands and waved white handkerchiefs. A Japanese soldier standing in front of the tank motioned us to drive closer. We did and again alighted with our hands up. A Filipino interpreter with the soldier complained that we were violating surrender instructions because we still wore sidearms.

"The Japanese without a word proceeded to club Dyess mercilessly. For good measure, he then stole two rings of mine, a crash bracelet, and a pen and pencil set. Then he motioned for us to get back into the car and resume driving toward our outfit. As we proceeded, our captor pulled close to our vehicle, smiled inexplicably, and threw my jewelry back into our car. But as soon as we stopped, other Japanese lined us up in groups of 100, and stole my possessions all over again, save only my flying ring, which I managed to tie inside my underwear."

According to Alva Fitch, "About noon of the 11th a Jap force occupied the area of the creek from which we were getting our water. I went to pay a call on the commander thereof. He was quite civil and told me to send my Filipinos to Bagac and that he would give me a pass to take my Americans to Mariveles. I sent the Filipinos to Bagac at once and with one car and one truck we started for the Jap CP. We were no sooner on the road than trouble began. A party of Japs took our truck and car and began taking watches, money, etc.

"I walked the 300 yards to the CP and protested. The officer was 'so sorry' but 'you should bring all of your men to my CP.' After about two hours of argument and waiting, he gave me another car and a pass to Mariveles. He cautioned us not to drive after dark. We started for Mariveles, driving fast so as to get as far as possible before something happened. We went about five kilometers before we were stopped by a Jap whose car was broken down. After about an hour of arguing in a wide mixture of tongues, he took our car and told us to wait, that he would bring it back. It was just getting dark. We knew from experience that the road was no place to wait, so we crawled off into the jungle and holed up for the night.

"The next morning" Fitch remembered, "we split our last can of beans and started walking. It was a hot day, a dusty mountain road with considerable traffic. Everytime we encountered any Japs we were searched and robbed of a few more of our possessions. About 10:00 A.M. we arrived at a motor pool where we located the car taken from us the night before. We showed our pass and opened negotiations for the recovery of 'our' transportation. After thirty minutes we got[an] answer: 'Very sorry but I have no car to give you.' We resumed our walk.

"The west side of Bataan is quite devoid of rivers. The few streams were so contaminated that we didn't dare drink from them. We were unaccustomed to the sun, so it didn't take long to become thirsty. Our loads were light. All they had left me was one pair of extra socks and my empty canteen. In the early afternoon we were able to thumb a ride in an empty truck and rode for about ten kilometers. We arrived in Mariveles about 3:00 P.M. and expected to find food and transportation to wherever we were going. We found nothing, except several hundred Americans, as bewildered, hungry, and poverty-stricken as ourselves. We were herded into what had been the public square and thoroughly searched.

"After about an hour of milling around, a Jap climbed up on a truck and made a speech. 'You take a little walk to Balanga. Maybe you get food there.' Balanga was about forty kilometers away. I didn't think we could make it but I was no longer in a position to dispute with the Imperial Japanese Armed Forces." As Fitch's report indicated, one immediate policy of the Japanese was to separate the indigenous people from the U.S. soldiers.

What also soon became clear was that the occupiers of the Philippines made no distinction between rank and file. The diary of Clifford Bluemel indicated the attitude from the first day of his incarceration: "9 April 1942 Captured in company with Col. Lee Vance [CO 26th Cavalry] Col. Edmund J. Lilly [CO 57th Scouts] . . . Questioned by G-2, [Intelligence] 21st Jap Division. Hit in head by Jap. Lt. Col. believe name is Kusiamato. No food since breakfast. Slept on ground, during night moved to tent [with others] that was closed and the odor was terrible. I laid on the ground with my head near the door so I could get air.

"10 April 1942 Shortly after daylight I was again taken to Kusiamato who again questioned me. He gave me a handful of cold rice, some tea for breakfast. We marched toward Mariveles with the division. After about an hour a truck was obtained. Stopped in abandoned army camp. Here we were permitted to scavenge and I found a pair of trousers, three pair of socks, shaving brush, shirt, and mess kit. No dinner or supper. A Jap soldier gave us some sugar and water during the night. Slept on ground, no blankets.

"11 April 1942 Shredded coconut and sugar for breakfast. The five of us were put in a truck to go to Orani. Truck also contained Philippine Scouts and Philippine Army enlisted men. Truck reached Balanga, the five officers were put on a truck returning south from where we came. We were taken off about ten kilometers south of Cabcaben, turned over to a Jap detachment, told we would remain in zone of Corregidor shell fire until Corregidor fell. We were given some American canned food. Each of us was given a cot. We were permitted to go to a nearby stream and bathe."

On 13 April, a large body started toward Cabcaben. Riding in a former U.S. Army truck under guard, Bluemel and fifteen officers and enlisted men passed columns of Japanese troops. Shells whistled in from Corregidor and both the Nipponese and their prisoners scurried to cover. The truck brought them back to Balanga where Bluemel downed a plate of rice and endured another grilling about the fortifications on Corregidor. He convinced the interrogators he knew nothing of value. They lodged him in a guardhouse with Brig. Gen. Luther Stevens, an American officer with the constabulary, and Maj. William J. Priestly from the 57th Infantry. Released from the confines of the guardhouse on 15 April, Bluemel, along with Stevens and Priestly, joined an American column of fours, and started to walk toward Orani.

The terse diary entry for 16 April noted: "Left Orani a.m., no breakfast. Stevens hit by Jap on passing truck. Jap sentry made me leave him, threatened to shoot me if I did not move."

After the war, Bluemel amplified his description of the incident. "A Jap riding in a passing truck struck Stevens on the forehead with a bamboo pole. Stevens staggered and his glasses fell off. I held him with my right hand and caught his glasses with my left. We fell out of the column and sat down. He said, 'That was hard to take.' The column passed. At the end, a Jap with a rifle on his left shoulder and a .45 caliber revolver (U.S.) in his right hand, stopped, pointed the revolver at me, grunted, and motioned for me to get up. I tried to tell him in English that a general was hit and hurt. He pulled back the hammer and again grunted and motioned for me to get up. I did. He then pointed the revolver at Stevens and did the same. I helped Stevens up. I still tried to argue with the Jap. He motioned Stevens off the road and into the dry rice paddies. He went about fifteen yards. I thought the Jap was going to shoot Stevens. The Jap then pointed the revolver at me and motioned me up the road to join the column. He left Stevens in the rice paddies and then ran past me to the column. I rejoined the column."

On the road again, Bluemel heard firing to the rear. "Saw Filipinos who had been shot a few minutes before. A grueling march, no food, little water, many who fell out shot." The group stumbled into Lubao after dark and Bluemel, who managed to buy some rice and sugar enroute, gulped it down when they halted for the night. Bluemel met a Japanese officer who spoke English. "I told him I was a general and asked for a ride, as I understood all generals were given them. While talking with him, a squad of American officers marched in, halted and reported. [They were late, having fallen behind the main body of the column.] The Jap immediately accused them of trying to escape and said they would be shot. I told him if they planned to escape they would not have marched in a squad formation. It showed they had no intention of escaping. They had become tired and dropped behind. They had marched in the required formation to join the column. the Japanese officer sent them to the other prisoners near us. He gave me a meal at his mess."

Alva Fitch, having conceded he was no longer in a position to argue with the enemy, had started the forty-kilometer hike toward Balanga. Near little Baguio the prisoners managed to fill their canteens. Then the Japanese separated the Filipinos from the Americans, who spent a hungry night without bedding and hordes of insects. "A few men had some C rations," said Fitch. "That served to make the rest of us that much hungrier. At daylight we were awakened with the rumor that we were to have some breakfast. After two hours of milling around and counting and recounting, we started down the road again. This time we went about four kilometers and were taken off the road to wait for trucks or breakfast. Neither came. About noon we were back on the road. About 2:00 P.M. we arrived in Cabcaben and were herded into the schoolyard. We were very hot and thirsty. Stillman, Semmens, and I slipped away and filled our canteens at the barrio pump. We were slightly beaten for our pains, but the water was worth it.

"At dark we arrived at Limao [about ten miles from their starting point]. Most of us had a much-needed bath in the bay. We found an artesian well and drank all the water we wanted. We held a conference and decided we had enough of marching in the sunlight. We decided to get up about 2:00 A.M. and march to Balanga where we had been told we would be fed. Without taking the Japs into our confidence, we formed for the march on schedule and started. The guards came along without protest. We arrived in Orion about 8:00 A.M. and were marched into some rice paddies and ordered to sit. There we stayed until midafternoon in the heat of a bright day of the dry season. We were not allowed to get water or move around. About 4:00 P.M. we resumed our march to Balanga, arriving just before dark. [They had traveled about twelve miles.] We were placed in some open fields, already overcrowded with American and Filipino prisoners. We learned they had not been fed and insofar as they knew there were no provisions at Balanga."

Fitch continued. "I noticed an increase in the number of corpses along the road between Orion and Balanga. I noticed also that many of them had not been dead two days; they had been killed since the surrender. My friends at Balanga explained anyone who became exhausted and fell out of the march column was immediately shot or bayoneted by the guards. There were no sanitary facilities at Balanga. This did not concern most of us much as we had been three days without food and could never get enough water to spare for urine. There were two small spigots at Balanga and it was necessary to stand in line for several hours to get your canteen filled. We found there were a few small turnips in the ground. By digging for an hour with a sharp stick, I obtained one apiece for myself and my lieutenants. It is impossible to imagine how incomparably delicious they were.

"After not having any breakfast, we were formed in columns and put in open fields for another day of 'sun cure.' Late in the afternoon, we resumed our northward march. The marked increase in the number of dead along the road kept even the weakest in column. Sometime during the night we arrived at Orani. We were marched into a barbed wire enclosure so crowded that it was very difficult to sit down. The ground was well covered with the feces of the dysentery patients that had already been there. We had reached a point where little things like that didn't bother us very much. And if we couldn't sit down, we could sleep standing up.

"The next morning I found a blanket that someone had abandoned. That made me a member of the upper class, owning valuable property. In addition, I had slipped out of our cage during the night and filled my canteen. About 9:00 A.M. we started marching north again. The troops were tired and we were going at a very sharp pace. Even the Americans began breaking down and falling out along the road. I helped Chaplain Duffy along until he quit trying. I then commended him to his maker and left him to the gentle mercies of the Japanese. While we were crossing the bridge at Colis Junction, old man Uddenburg jumped off the bridge and was shot.

"I ran into a classmate of mine, Jimmy Vaughn, a signal corps major who was in poor shape. I helped him along and every now and then he'd stop and sit down, then we'd get him on his feet and move on. Finally, I couldn't get him up and a Jap came along and told me to move on. I tried to explain to him but he jabbed me in the butt with his bayonet. Then he shot Vaughn through the chest. I've been told that Filipinos took him to one of their houses where he died. I saw two American soldiers bayoneted for crawling into the shade alongside of the road. The number of Filipino bodies was shocking, even to us, who abhorred the sight of a Filipino soldier."

Although tens of thousands partook of the death march the mass of humanity dispatched from Bataan was not one endless column. Instead, packs of 1,000 to 1,500 men formed groups overseen by parties of guards that seldom exceeded twenty-five. Without any schedule or routine, the only consistent aspect was movement as quick as possible and mercilessly urged on.

John Olson, who survived the trip, recalled, "Shuffling along through powder-thin dust that was often four to six inches deep, prisoners and guards soon had their sweat-soaked bodies covered with a thick coat of tan that gave a uniformity of appearance to both groups. Half strangled by the layers of dust that clogged their noses, the pitiful victims had trouble breathing. Some Japanese wore surgical-like face masks that strained out much of the air they breathed. The haze that hung over each group billowed up into the trees as the endless processions of Japanese trucks, tanks, and artillery pieces passed enroute to positions at the base of the peninsula.

"Sometimes, if a prisoner was indiscreet or careless enough to come close to one of the troop carriers, a few of the occupants thrust menacingly at him with their bayonets while emitting animal like screams and jeers. Those who were targets of these attacks and did not move quickly enough to dodge were slashed or even severely wounded. These unfortunates were forced to tend to themselves as they continued to stagger forward.

"The Japanese guards would tolerate no stopping at any place other than the spots where they had been instructed to halt. Anyone who attempted to fall out of the march was quickly set upon with a club, rifle butt, or a bayonet. Pushed or kicked to his feet, the sufferer would be thrust back into the ranks. In the beginning, some men screamed at their tormentors that they were sick, wounded, or too exhausted to go on, and refused to move. The reaction was swift and decisive. A fierce jab with a bayonet into the chest or a bullet in the head was administered with dispatch and the body was pushed into a ditch or the bushes. This message quickly sank into the aching heads of the others. Keep going no matter how hard it is to put one foot in front of the other! He who cannot move will soon be unable to move forever more!"

Harold Johnson remembered self-protective measures and even a slightly more benign approach. "Everyone had a different pace he followed during the march because there were plenty of opportunities to hide out. You didn't know what the result would be if you got caught. Some people were bayoneted. Other people were helped into calasas, the little cart pulled by a pony and sent on. It depended on the whim or mood of the guard. Some days we covered eight to ten kilometers; others we spent the entire day in the broiling sun. Some days I just hid out, rested, and Scouts gave me a hand. There were stops at regular intervals where the Japanese tried to take care of us. There was always a water source, maybe one spigot with hundreds lined up.

"I had one advantage, the services of the Philippine Scouts. The Scouts were moving around, relatively freely. They would search for their officers and say, 'You come see me in an hour and I'll have some rice for you. You would find them an hour later with a gallon can, half filled with porridge, rice, and they would give you a section of sugarcane so you could suck it."

"I was dead tired," said Fitch of his arrival at Lubao. "I doubt if I could have gone another hour. I had been a prisoner five days, walked more than eighty-five miles, and eaten one raw turnip. My worldly wealth consisted of a blanket, a towel, a spare pair of socks, and a canteen, all except the canteen picked up along the road." Their first morning at Lubao, Fitch and his companions were tendered a half-cup of "very dirty unsalted rice porridge. We stayed at Lubao several days, continuing to receive the same luxurious rations. There was only one small water spigot for three or four thousand men. It was only with great difficulty that you could obtain one canteen of water a day. I saw one American soldier bayoneted to death for trying to buck the water line. They took another across the road and shot him. Many Americans and Filipinos died here. We had no tools for digging so the dead were simply stacked in one corner of the yard.

"One morning, two thousand were marched to San Fernando [about ten miles north]. I went along. We spent two days in San Fernando. Here again there were no sanitary facilities and only one small water spigot. The Japs gave us three meals of 'lugao' [rice porridge] a day and pointed out we should be very grateful as our own army had fed us only twice a day. Two days later we were taken by train to Capas, about twenty-five miles north, and we marched from there to the partially completed Philippine Army camp at O'Donnell. I was damn glad to arrive, little knowing that the name O'Donnell would make the Black Hole of Calcutta seem a Sunday school picnic."

The hapless prisoner drew little surcease during the short train trips to Capas. John Olson said, "These tiny boxcars were similar to the World War I French 'Forty and Eight' [forty men or eight horses]. But into each of them were forced one hundred, not forty men. Too crowded to sit, much less lie, they watched the doors slam shut. Then began three to four hours of excruciating sweltering in this fetid sweat box. Some collapsed, the weakest died. Even the Japanese guards suffered. A few disregarded their orders and cracked or even opened one of the doors while the train was in motion. In so doing, they undoubtedly saved a number of lives. Even so, when they finally stopped at the station in Capas, everyone was wobbly and totally exhausted."

According to Olson, when he stumbled from the boxcar, hordes of Filipinos materialized in the Capas train yards. While the Japanese rushed about shouting commands and perhaps counting—it was gibberish to the prisoners—the civilians eyed the gaunt, gasping, sweat-soaked human cargo. "A Filipino boy dashed over to one of the Americans and thrust a stalk of sugar cane into his hands and scuttled back behind his comrades. Others, encouraged by his success, emulated his action with bananas, sugarcane, rice wrapped in banana leaves, sugarcane candy, and cups of water. A Japanese suddenly aware of what was going on, uttered a strident command. Instantly, the guards turned on the crowd and by jabbing, shoving, and shouting, forced them back. Sullenly, they withdrew but expressed their animosity by hurling the remains of the food over the heads of the guards to the expectant Americans."

The captives formed up for the last brutal leg of the Death March, the final six kilometer hike under a broiling sun to O'Donnell. As Olson and his contingent of Americans, with a large number of Filipino prisoners, trudged toward their destination, the locals furtively flashed the "Vee for victory" with their fingers, tossed food, and even stashed cans of water along the way.

From the extremities of the Bataan peninsula, where most of the prisoners began, the Death March to O'Donnell stretched 105 killing kilometers, or about 65 miles and lasted about two weeks. The bulk of those consigned to the camp reached it between 14 and 25 April. Exact numbers on deaths from disease, thirst, malnutrition, or at the hands of guards along the way, do not exist. But hundreds of men undoubtedly perished. Even worse, the maltreatment of the Death March coupled with the woeful diet and miserable health conditions endured during the siege of Bataan weakened the prisoners to the point where massive losses followed at O'Donnell.

At the same time as they overran the Philippines, in addition to swallowing up the colonial island empires of the West, the Japanese armies advanced in mainland Asia, knifing deeper into China, snatching much of Burma, and extending control over bits of the former French possessions such as Siam [Thailand]. Nipponese soldiers backed by a formidable air arm obliged the Allied ground forces to either surrender or retreat. The only major resistance to the Imperial forces lay in the Flying Tigers of Claire Chennault.

To maintain the esprit and retain the freedom to act as he saw fit, Chennault, himself now on active duty as a brigadier general, had delayed the induction of the AVG into the Army Air Corps. Meanwhile, the Flying Tigers received some Kittyhawks, the newer versions of the P-40, ships with added firepower, more speed, and better visibility. One thrust at Japanese airfields in northern Thailand caught a large number of enemy planes packed onto the Chiengmai base and burned or riddled an entire complement of Japanese planes.

General Joseph Stilwell, chief of staff for the forces under Chiang Kai-shek and Chennault's boss, regarded the Flying Tigers as of limited offensive value. He viewed their role as one of observation, bomber escort, and as showpieces to boost the morale of Chinese ground forces. All of these roles demanded grueling long distance flights that exposed the pilots to Japanese fighters. In mid-April, the fliers stationed at the Loiwing base flat-out refused to perform what they believed was a poorly plotted raid by Blenheim bombers against Chiengmai that would, unlike the previous successful strike, put them over the target in a vulnerable position.

Chennault met with the dissidents and flashes of temper ignited ugly talk. Although they had fought for months against superior forces with meager resources, some pilots thought he accused them of cowardice. George Paxton who had absorbed five bullet wounds during an early encounter, wrote in his diary, "The pilots are bitter. They feel Chennault is bloodthirsty and will sacrifice the AVG to the last man."

When the discussion broke off, twenty-eight of the thirty-four pilots signed a petition that described the type of mission ordered as unreasonable and too perilous in light of the quality of the American planes and the strength of the enemy. Unless such operations were canceled, they would quit. Chennault faced a revolt that could spread to his base at Kunming. The AVG commander refused to accede. He declared he would not accept their resignations and any attempt to do so would be tantamount to desertion in the face of the enemy. Tex Hill was one of the few nonsigners. He argued, "Hell, we're not a bunch of mercenaries over here. Hell, since we've arrived here our country's involved in war and this is part of our war. It's not just like a coldblooded job. Whatever has to be done, we've got to do it. We've got a man who's our leader who says this is the way it should be done. We've got to advise him of all of the facts and our thinking on the thing, but if he makes up his mind and says it's still necessary, we've got to do it."

The issue turned moot as the British bombers scheduled for the affair were delayed and a few days later, the invading Japanese ground forces forced the Flying Tigers to hastily evacuate Loiwing. Some defections followed but apparently for other reasons than the aborted raid. Most notable Greg "Pappy" Boyington. An accomplished pilot whose fondness for whiskey had made him a disruptive force, he left with a dishonorable discharge signed by Chennault. Later in the war, the Marines decorated Boyington for his exploits as a leatherneck fighter pilot.

Even as the Flying Tigers rebelled against their leader, they heard the astounding news that U.S. bombers had struck at the heart of Japan—Tokyo. Under the urging of Winston Churchill that the war against the Third Reich have priority, President Roosevelt had agreed to focus on the Western Hemisphere. Stung by the succession of defeats in the Far East, Roosevelt and his advisors cast about for some way to bring the war home to the Japanese. They sought a method that might give the enemy pause while uplifting the morale of Americans shaken by the losses in the Pacific and the impending conquest of the Philippines. While none of the Navy's carriers and their short-ranged aircraft could be risked in an operation against the Japanese home islands, staff members for Chief of Naval Operations Ernest J. King proposed that B-25 medium bombers might be launched from a carrier at a viable distance and then, after dropping their bombs, land safely in China. It would have been easier for the B-25s to find refuge in the Soviet Union but that country, still at peace with Japan and mindful of the dangers of a two-front war, was unwilling to risk offending the Japanese.

Chosen to lead the expedition was then-colonel James Doolittle who began work on the project in February 1942. Jimmy Doolittle grew up in Alaska and earned his wings during World War I. He never reached France in time for aerial combat but, as an Army pilot between the wars, indulged a lust for risk-taking with acrobatics, air races, and cross country jaunts in the primitive planes of the era. He backed up his feats with studies of engineering and then quit the service for commerce. Doolittle was horrified by the growth of the Nazi air arm and the belligerence of Adolf Hitler. He quit his job and returned to the Air Corps with an assignment from Hap Arnold to head up special projects. His knowledge of aeronautics, expertise in fuel, and his derring-do all recommended him for the mission.

Pilot Robert Emmens belonged to the 17th Bomb Group (Medium) which flew the twin-engine B-25 Mitchells from a base at Columbia, South Carolina. A drop-out from premed at the University of Oregon in 1937, Emmens had succumbed to an advertisement, COME TO THE WEST POINT OF THE AIR, RANDOLPH FIELD, AND LET THE ARMY TEACH YOU TO FLY AND PAY YOU AT THE SAME TIME. By the time of Pearl Harbor, however, he was preparing for operations overseas with some antisubmarine patrols. "Somewhere between the middle of February and the first of March word came that then–lieutenant colonel James Doolittle, was looking for a group of crews for a volunteer flight, no word as to what it was to be. The Group commander called for a meeting of all members of all of the squadrons and announced there would be a picking of some twenty crews who were asked to volunteer for a very secret mission. He asked for a show of hands. The entire group stood up. Every man in every squadron volunteered for this mission."

"I had gotten my Regular Army commission and was one of the oldest men—by this time we were getting second lieutenants wet behind the ears. Some had been promoted to first already after about three or four months being on active duty. Here I was on duty since 1938, back to second lieutenant [RA status]. My squadron commander Jack Hilger looked at me and said, 'You have to stay behind—you are the oldest guy in the squadron now— and run the squadron. I am going on this mission.' All my friends left. They were ordered to Eglin Field, Florida.

"News began coming back to the group. Word started that they were practicing these strange maximum takeoffs, that the B-25 had to get off in 400 feet. We couldn't imagine why such a crazy maneuver. The B-25 loaded normally took a 1,500-foot run. We heard they were out over the Gulf flying a long mission over water, and they were allowed to fly at only 50-foot altitudes and at very reduced throttle settings. Normally a B-25 cruised at 210 to 225 miles per hour. But these [training for the mission] couldn't cruise over about 165."

Under Doolittle's supervision, auxiliary gas tanks replaced the B-25 belly turrets. Additional fuel storage came from tanks in the bomb bays, with rubber bladders holding another 160 gallons in crawl spaces above the bomb bays. Twin .50-caliber machine guns in the top turret and a single .30 in the nose was all the firepower aboard. Wooden broom sticks, painted black to simulate gun barrels, poked out of the tails to discourage fighter approaches from the rear.

Emmens could only puzzle about the bizarre doings at Eglin until he received a telephone call from Ed "Ski" York, [born Edward Cichowski], the only West Pointer attached to Doolittle's complement. His surname, taken from that of the World War I hero Sgt. Alvin C., had been adopted after graduation because Ski supposedly believed Cichowski would handicap his career. According to Emmens, York was not expected to make the mission. "He had been assigned to be the operations chief. He would schedule the flights only."

Manning the office at Columbia, Emmens answered when York rang up to explain they had just lost an airplane after an engine misfired during one of the maximum takeoffs. "York said, 'We need another airplane right away down here.' I said, 'Ski, I will see you at about 3:30 or 4:00.' I went to my tent, packed my footlocker, stenciled it to 1443 East Main, Medford, Oregon, which was my home. I packed 20 pounds; all the crews were allowed to take was 20 pounds of clothing—toilet article kits, socks, change of underclothes. I looked around and found a guy to be copilot and an airplane in commission sitting there."

To Emmens's astonishment, the field at Eglin was deserted, not an airplane in sight. After landing he found Ski York sweeping out the operations building. "There were two or three other guys there. I said, 'Where is everybody?' He said, 'They've all left for the west coast. Do you want to go on this thing?' I said, 'Ski, more than anything.'" According to Emmens, York said they could form a substitute crew. He told Emmens, "See that fellow playing solitaire? He is left over among the navigators. That guy sleeping in the corner is an engineer." Within a few minutes York and Emmens put together the full crew of five.

"We left that night about 6:00 or 6:30," said Emmens, "and never even sent a message back to Columbia. We landed at Sacramento [after refueling in Texas] about six o'clock in the morning. [York] introduced me [to Doolittle] and said, 'We would like to be the new crew to substitute.' Doolittle looked at me and we shook hands very cordially. He asked, 'How much time do you have in a B-25?' suspecting, I think, that I was brand new with my second lieutenant's bars on. I said, 'Sir, I have about 1,000 hours.' He said, 'Do you want to go on this thing?' I said, 'yes sir, I do.' 'All right, York, [said Doolittle] you are the new crew.' It was that simple."

The fliers and sixteen B-25s loaded onto the carrier *Hornet*. Doolittle allowed them one all-night fling in San Francisco and then on 2 April, the carrier bore them off toward their still-undisclosed mission. Out beyond the Golden Gate and in the Pacific, the leader held a meeting at which time he announced the target was Tokyo. According to Emmens they had not guessed their destination and instead figured they were bound for Bataan. "Sixteen targets had been picked. As the pilot of each crew walked past a table, he was handed a target folder. No specific target was assigned to a specific crew. Then the pilot got his crew together and we spent the next two weeks studying that target folder. Our target was to be a steel factory on the north outskirts of Tokyo."

Bill Bower, whom Doolittle appointed engineering officer, recollected, "Doolittle was as close as he should be. Everything was on a first-name basis. But he had all of these things to consider. You didn't go putting your arm around him telling him your personal thoughts and he didn't tell you his. There wasn't time for horseplay; it was all business. After we passed Hawaii we picked up cruisers, destroyers, a tanker, and the carrier *Enterprise* as part of a task force under Adm. William Halsey. We [each] had two 500-pound general-purpose bombs and two canisters of incendiaries. On deck, there was a ceremony where they put on the bombs some medals given to people by the Japanese in the past.

"We were going to launch the planes 400 miles off the coast of Japan [on 18 April] in the afternoon, bomb Tokyo at night, and then arrive in China in the morning. We were discovered by a picket ship [the *Nitto Maru*] about eight o'clock in the morning on the 18th. It was promptly sunk when the *Enterprise* launched their aircraft and the cruisers shelled it. They called general quarters and announced we would launch immediately." Officially, at 8:00 A.M. as the Japanese picket boat succumbed to the American guns, Admiral Halsey sent a message, "Launch planes. To Colonel Doolittle and gallant command, good luck and God bless you."

According to Bower, "We were then eight hours at forced draft from our [planned] launching point which put us somewhere in the area of 640 statute miles from [that] site. [Other estimates make the distance 700 or even 800 miles.] "I stopped and bought a carton of Lucky Strikes and went up to the plane with my B-4 bag while they were refueling the planes, topping off the tanks. They brought these tin cans on; we each got five of them, which would amount to fifty gallons of gas. They were stowed aboard and we were told to uncover and start our engines."

Emmens reported that every morning they awakened at 5:30 A.M. for a battle station drill where the Army pilots ran to their planes while the carrier's gun crews manned their guns. As the sun rose, the all clear would come. On this day, however, he said, the instructions directed, "Army crews, man your airplanes. Prepare for takeoff. This is not a drill."

"I remember running to the room where I was staying. I picked up my small bit of belongings and beat it up on the deck. Every gun on every ship was going off. I have never seen such a display of firepower. The pom-pom guns off the *Hornet,* every gun off every cruiser and destroyer at this silhouette of a freighter, and here came the fighter planes off the [*Enterprise*]."

The efforts to destroy the enemy trawler hardly qualified as a textbook demonstration. The initial salvos from the cruiser *Nashville* splashed harmlessly in the ocean. A plane from the *Enterprise* strafed the vessel but its bomb missed by 100 feet. Halsey ordered the *Nashville* to point blank range. Not until a third salvo was the *Nitto Maru* fatally hit. The "engagement" with the hapless trawler lasted twenty-nine minutes, long enough for a radio message to Tokyo to advise of the presence of an American force. The Imperial Navy mobilized ships to search for the flotilla that within minutes was steaming hastily back toward Hawaii.

Said Emmens, "I saw Doolittle take off, then number two, number three . . . I looked at that deck and it looked a little bit like a postage stamp. On a wet deck the B-25 with its brakes locked and the power full on would tend to skid forward even with locked wheels. They had put two cork pads about three or four-feet square with the wheelbase of the airplane. Each airplane had to taxi and put its front wheels on those cork pads because the procedure for takeoff was to sit with locked brakes, the power all the way on, clear up to the top, flaps all the way down that are normally used to slow an airplane down when it lands, but in this type of takeoff, it acts as a lift for a little bit. It helps to get the rise but you must get those flaps up immediately to reduce the resistance, and the stick all the way back.

"Full power it took both of us with our arms around the wheel to hold it in the full-back position, elevation position. We had absolutely no problem at all. We had at least fifty feet of deck ahead of us when we were airborne. Then immediately you let up on the stick to get your nose down where you are going to gain speed and start bringing those flaps up and your wheels up immediately. We slowly leveled out, gained speed. There was no formation flying; it was too costly [in fuel] because you juggled the throttle to get in formation. Each airplane had its target, knew where it was going, and each airplane flew individually. There was to be no talk, no intercourse between airplanes. Back down then to fifty feet and the reduced power setting."

Bower noted, "Because of the way the carrier was constructed, you couldn't takeoff until you passed the pivot point at the center of the island. Everybody therefore had the same takeoff distance. I had seen one of the planes in front of us take off with his flaps up so it was obvious that it was no problem. We maintained radio silence in a loose formation. I was with Ross Green and Ski York. We formed in threes for five flights." In the roughly four hours from the *Hornet* to landfall, the aircraft gradually separated until they saw little of one another. "We set up our own navigation. We found a ship near landfall and my gunner shot at it. The countryside had been described to us in great detail by Lieutenant Forrest.[The Navy briefing officer.] It was amazing that he had such knowledge of it. We came ashore well north of Tokyo, somewhere around the 36th Parallel, maybe 100 miles north of Tokyo. Right on the deck, there was an opportunity to look at the countryside. I thought, my God, what peaceful, pretty countryside this is. Why on earth would they want war; it was a natural thought; all countryside looks pretty from the air.

"As we approached Tokyo Bay we went across an airfield where some of the aircraft were operating and flying around the field. We cut across the bay and climbed to 1,000 feet. There were some barrage balloons [apparently the Japanese had prepared for the possibility of an attack] which we went through. Although there was a haze we broke out as we came to the western shore and could identify our target. We bombed the target. I don't recall any aircraft but I saw some shooting. We returned to the bay and set course over the water on a southwesterly direction for China. We had been concerned that at nighttime how were we going to identify [landmarks] but it was daylight and we didn't have any difficulties. About an hour or so later we came upon a Japanese cruiser that launched an airplane, but fortunately it didn't catch us.

"We got down to the southern tip of Kyushu and set course across the East China Sea. We figured we'd make landfall after dark and wondered how we'd know when we reached the coast. At dusk we could see some shoals and shallow water so we felt we were near the coastline. The fuel supply held up; our consumption was normal. Obviously we were going to have to climb because of the weather. We were scheduled to land at an airfield 200 to 400 miles inland where there was to be fuel for us. There was to be a beacon on but only at our [scheduled] arrival time and then it would be turned off. Sometime around 11:30 P.M., fifteen hours after takeoff, the red light [indicating low fuel] came on and a few warning lights, so everybody got ready [to jump]. When Waldo Bither was trying to come up from the bombardier's compartment his parachute opened and he calmly repacked it. I said, 'Let's go' and I trimmed the airplane up and jumped after the rest. Our plan was that the last man out would turn around and walk in a northeasterly direction. First man would walk southwesterly.

"I landed on a pretty high hill. Immediately rolled up in the parachute and went to sleep, which I think was a logical reaction. It was just as well, because when dawn came I was right on the edge of a cliff." Bower hid his chute and hiked down the mountain to a road. He had retained a .45 automatic carried by his father in World War I. When he met some Chinese people he attempted to talk to them with the few phrases taught to the Doolittle raiders before their takeoff. The farmers did not understand him. On a piece of tissue paper, Bower drew pictures of an airplane, an American flag, and a train, but no one seemed to grasp the meaning. He walked farther in their company to a tiny village where, wet and tired, he was fed hot soup, peanuts, and rice. After dark, his copilot came in with men in black clothes. Two more of the crew showed up. The four Americans spent an uncomfortable night in a house infested with lice where the occupants relieved themselves in a bucket in the corner. But Bower said he was well treated.

Chinese guerrillas brought in the last of the five-man crew and the group started to walk in the direction of Chungking. "We had no idea whether they were guerrillas leading us to safety or taking us into a trap. But we had faith in these people. There wasn't much you could do. I don't know what would have happened if we had seen Japanese. We were taken care of pretty well. The word was out but anytime the Japs started toward us, we were under cover."

After an arduous trek they met a man who spoke some English and owned a 1940 Plymouth automobile. He drove them to a town where they remained for a week before continuing their journey by car, train, and bus. At one point they were forced to double back because of advancing enemy troops. Along the way the Americans met English-speaking missionaries who joined the party. At one site a province chief tossed a bash in their honor. Eventually, the group reached a point where a C-47 picked them up and flew them to the Chungking base, where they were housed in Generalissimo Chiang Kai-shek's compound until they departed for the States along with other survivors. Under orders not to disclose their identities, the Doolittle raiders reached Miami where customs officials regarded them with considerable suspicion. Eventually the saga ended with a reception in Washington D.C., and a subsequent tour to sell war bonds and uplift American spirits.

Emmens related his experiences: "The last word we got on the *Hornet* was, 'Good luck, boys. I hope you make it. If you have any trouble, we will pray for you. But don't come back to the *Hornet.*' They turned around immediately after the sixteenth airplane took off and the whole business went back to Hawaii as fast as they could. There was nothing they could have done. We couldn't possibly land [a B-25] on the deck."

Ski York and Bob Emmens realized they were in difficulty even as their ship neared the Japanese coast. Their B-25 had never been adjusted to consume fuel with greater efficiency. "The first thing we saw at that low altitude was a little black blip on the horizon, which was Mount Fuji. As the coastline was coming into view, we measured [the gasoline] as carefully as we could and found there was simply no way in God's world we could fly back out to sea, down to the bottom of Japan, and all the way into the coast of China. There was a chance, if we turned slightly right over Tokyo—Russia was quite a little bit closer. Roosevelt had asked Stalin to please accept our sixteen airplanes, which would have assured the success and termination of the mission at least resulting in landings. Stalin refused flatly. We were told this in our briefings on the *Hornet.*

"There can be situations that arise that demand you do something that may not have fitted into the original schedule. The only dry land in sight was Japanese and that didn't seem to be too healthy a solution to our being short of gas. The alternative was square miles of blue ocean in enemy waters and that didn't seem very attractive for our dilemma. There was no objection on anybody's part when York [said], 'Let's go to Russia. We can make it, we think.'

"We bombed at approximately noon. We listened all the way in to a baseball game. There was no evidence that they knew we were coming. We dropped our bombs on the steel factory. Each airplane was equipped with a camera in the tail, mounted between the two broomsticks that had been painted black. The camera was set to trip to cover the trajectory drop of the bomb and its strike. Ours was the only one that was ever retrieved because all the rest of the airplanes crashed. We dropped our bombs. We felt the explosion of them even at 1,500 feet. One of them went right down the stack of the steel mill. After dropping our bombs we immediately dropped back down to the fifty-foot altitude. We had no opposition whatsoever."

Because the American bombers traveled singly and their navigation scattered their approaches, the Japanese when they finally realized an air raid was in progress, could not mount a coherent defense. The element of surprise enabled almost every plane to dump its ordnance before gunners on the ground could train their weapons or interceptors could find the attackers. Doolittle seems to have been most at risk. He spotted fighters in the sky as he neared Tokyo but managed to lose them. Over the target antiaircraft shells burst around his plane, spattering the fuselage with shrapnel, but caused no damage. The mission chief headed for China. Several others ran a mild gamut of antiaircraft fire or saw enemy planes but none incurred damage.

Emmens remarked that they carried only an outline map of the Soviet Union. Concerned that any drift to the left might bring them down in Korea, York corrected to the right and the navigator brought them over the Sea of Japan until they crossed the coast. They decided that Vladivistok might be heavily defended and it would be risky to approach the city at dusk. "As we hit landfall, we saw a great big field and as we flew over it, a big white circle in the middle indicated it was some sort of auxiliary field. About that time the engineer [Theodore H. LaBan] poked me. Here was a Soviet fighter airplane practically flying formation with us, a big red star on it, and wiggling his wings, the international signal, 'Land, or I will shoot you down.' We gave him the wiggled wings back, 'Don't bother to shoot us down; we intend to land.'

"He followed us all the way down to the ground. There was the barest chance, faintest possibility that it could be [the Japanese]. We decided we would leave the engines running until the first people came up around the airplane. We would look at them, and if they had slant eyes—even though we registered empty—we were going to take off, fly out to sea and due north toward Russia. But the guys who came up around the airplane didn't have slant eyes. They stood there grinning. They didn't know what we were. We shut the engines off, took our .45s and pistol belts off and were greeted immediately by a bunch of soldiers with at least five Tommy guns.

"We were conducted, marched, rather, across the field into this building with Tommy guns in our backs. It was about 6:30 in the evening. They put us at a table with these [four ranking] navy officers. We tried to speak to them and they tried to speak to us. We didn't know a word of Russian and they didn't know a word of English. Finally, by gesture alone, we were taken to a bathroom, a rather primitive outside trough, that slanted down and went into a hole in the ground. Also by gesture we were finally able to get over to them that we would like something to eat. We hadn't eaten since the morning on the *Hornet,* and nothing in the airplane all day long. They brought us some black bread and some soup

"I had studied German and I had studied French. I tried both of those, nothing. York was Polish and he tried to remember some Polish words but couldn't make a breakthrough. Finally, [from] one of the men came the word 'San Francisco.' So we said, 'San Francisco.' That was our first breakthrough. We shook hands all around." A man who spoke a bit of English appeared and so did a large map. York uttered "Alaska" and the interpreter nodded yes. Then York traced his finger from Alaska, through the Kuril Islands, down through Siberia to Vladivistok and said "Goodwill flight." No airplane in existence could have flown that enormous distance nonstop but for the moment their inquisitors accepted the explanation. However, a pilot appeared and when York demonstrated the route, he smiled and pointed to Tokyo.

After a dinner featuring vodka toasts, York advised a Soviet colonel of their role in the Tokyo raid. The following morning, the crew sat down to a breakfast banquet with about two dozen Red officers including several generals. The visitors swallowed numerous rounds of vodka that accompanied toasts from both sides; the Americans hailed Stalin, the Red Navy, the Red Army, and their hosts championed Roosevelt, the U.S. Navy, the respective Air Corps. Over a five-hour period they dined on a sumptuous repast. The fliers asked to be put in touch with the U.S. consul but the request was ignored. The era of good feeling disappeared after they were transported to another area and new, sterner inquisitors questioned them. Emmens and company learned they would be interned indefinitely.

At the controls of *Bat Out of Hell,* the sixteenth and last airplane to leave the *Hornet,* was Bill Farrow. The copilot, Bob Hite, actually was senior to Farrow but he and his crew had not been chosen to fly the mission. Farrow, unhappy with his deputy, asked Hite if he'd like to replace him. "I would have gone as bombardier, rear gunner, nose gunner; I would have gone in any position to be on that raid because I really felt it was going to be a great raid and I wanted to be on it. After I accepted to go with Bill, I had people offering me $500 for my place."

Bat Out of Hell, at the back of the pack, its tail hanging over the carrier's stern, nearly slid backward into the sea when the propwash of the plane immediately ahead lifted *Bat Out of Hell's* nose. As the front end of it rose, sailors and bombardier Cpl. Jacob DeShazer struggled to restrain the bucking aircraft with ropes tied to hooks. The nose dropped just as a sailor slipped on the deck and a whirling propeller slashed his arm so severely it required amputation. According to one account, once aboard, DeShazer discovered that in its gyrations, *Bat Out of Hell* had slammed its plexiglass nose into the tail of the aircraft in front of it, gouging a jagged hole.

Farrow and Hite, lifted off the damaged bomber and set a course for Japan. "We never saw one of our aircraft on the way in," said Hite. "We didn't see anyone into our target. We could have bombed Osaka or Nagoya and we chose Nagoya because we had homed in on Asahi Point. We had an aircraft factory and old storage tanks. As we approached the area we saw many Japanese fighter aircraft . . . [but] we climbed into the clouds, which were at about 7,000 feet. We stayed in the clouds to avoid detection and flew dead-reckoning courses to the area of Nagoya. Then we found a hole and let down through it. We had four incendiary clusters, 500-pounders. The aircraft factory was afire and the oil storage tank was afire when we departed the area to go across the China Sea. [The flak] was all over."

In spite of the damage to the plane and the drag from the opening in the bombardier's compartment, *Bat Out of Hell* stayed aloft for more than fourteen hours when the indicators reported empty tanks. All five men bailed out, with Hite the fourth and Farrow the last to exit the plane. "I landed in a rice paddy," recalled Hite and hit my right ankle on a rock. I hurt it pretty bad. I got my parachute off finally and I was right up to my waist, in the mud, slime, and so forth."

He climbed onto a dike in the paddy and began an aimless hike that took him into a cemetery where he jogged in place to keep his circulation flowing. In the morning, when the chickens crowed and daylight broke, Hite started to wander toward some houses. "The first two or three houses I tried, I backed off on account of the dogs. I found a house later on in the morning that sort of accepted me. There were no dogs. It was a man and his wife, and I think they had three or four children. They had cows and donkeys in the barn. I had a pocketful of Lucky Strike cigarettes and Mounds candy bars and about $5 in silver. I was prepared to offer anything that I had for help. I tried to explain that I wanted to go to Chungking. The family accepted me pretty good. They ate my candy. I didn't know the Chinese women would smoke but this Chinese lady was smoking those Lucky Strike cigarettes like they were going out of style.

"I kept insisting that I go find Chiang Kai-shek. They had taught us that 'wa-su-mei-ko-lin' was probably the way to say that 'I am an American' in Chinese. I repeated that several times. I thought they understood. The man put on a little shawl and a big flat hat and his little wooden shoes and motioned for me to follow him and I did. He led me through rice paddies and dikes for about thirty minutes to a house. In front, about twenty yards from the house, was a soldier walking. He was a Chinese soldier without saber or rifle, or any armament. He spoke English. I gave the Chinese coolie some more silver and thanked him and he went back toward his house and left me with the soldier. The soldier asked me who I was and I said that I was an American and that I was here to help Chiang Kai-shek. He was very friendly and said, 'Let's get something to eat.' We went toward this little cluster of houses. As we approached, about fifteen Japanese soldiers came running out with bayoneted rifles and surrounded me." Hite was the last of his five-man crew to be captured. All of them had dropped in an area occupied by the invading Japanese.

Chiang Kai-shek, whom Hite insisted he hoped to aid, opposed the operation at its inception. The Generalissimo asked for a delay until he could transport more troops to the landing fields expected to receive the B-25s after they struck Japan. Unfortunately, when Chiang finally acquiesced, there was confusion because of a misunderstanding of the date line. Worse, the American forces working with the Chinese could not confirm the storage of fuel, the signal systems, or the conditions at the outlying airfields designated for the Doolittle flyers. Four separate attempts to install American experts failed because of either bad weather or Japanese interception. The chances that the flares, beacons, or homing signals might guide the aircraft, feeling their way through the dark over unfamiliar territory, fell to zero. It was an appalling case of what can happen when the desire to put on a show overwhelms the necessity for careful planning and execution of all aspects of an operation.

An entire squadron of medium bombers was wiped out at a moment when the Allies could ill afford any losses. Not a single B-25 landed successfully in China. Four crash landed with two fatalities. Crews parachuted from eleven planes with one death. The only bomber that touched down intact belonged to York and Emmens. Eight Americans, including Farrow and Hite, became POWs. The Doolittle raid killed fifty people, wounded another 250, and damaged a number of buildings and installations. In terms of hurting production of war materials, the effects were minimal, but the attack did cause the Japanese to bring home some air units for protection against future raids, that would not come for another two years. To convince the people in the occupied territories not to assist Americans in such endeavors, the Japanese embarked on a furious campaign of reprisals that brought death to many Chinese.

10
Final Defeat in the Philippines

Almost immediately after the Bataan garrison waved the white flag, Japanese artillery had moved into positions where it could rain explosives upon the fortified islands still held by the defenders. The last bastion lay only three miles from the enemy guns. Air raids increased in tempo but the mounting fury of artillery exacted the greatest toll. Paul Bunker on 13 April noted in his diary, "This was another day of artillery activity. The Japs plastered us with shells from morning to night." A few days later Bunker reported, "Six heavy bombers attacked Fort Drum and dropped bombs, but all were misses, for I distinctly felt them in our tunnel. This evening a flash came in, saying that Tokyo this morning was under a four-hour bombardment. It cheered us up to think that maybe Nippon is at last getting a touch of her own medicine."

Albert Svihra, the Army legal officer who had been among those transferred from Bataan to Corregidor, described a relatively secure existence that dissipated as the intensity of attacks built. "During March and April, although we were under intermittent artillery fire and bombardment from the air, we were able to take off a little time now and then to sit outside the east entrance of the tunnel [Malinta] under a tent fly with a number of wicker chairs to have a cigarette—no smoking being permitted inside the tunnel— and to discuss the news. At 12:30 P.M. each day our radio station, the Voice of Freedom, broadcast the news from the U.S.

"About the only other pleasures of the tunnel were reading and an occasional bridge game. We were on reduced ration as in Bataan. If anything, we were on about one-third, instead of one half. Our meals, prepared by Chinese boys, formerly employees of the Officers' Club at Fort Mills, and served cafeteria fashion, consisted first [breakfast] of either a small portion of cooked raisins or cracked wheat, a piece of toast, two small pieces of bacon, and all the coffee you wanted without sugar. For lunch a cup of soup, and either a piece of whole wheat bread or a biscuit, or a small meat pie. Supper, the only decent meal, consisted of rice or a small canned potato; stewed corn beef or corn beef hash, or occasionally, fresh carabao or baked ham; one vegetable, corn, peas, or sauerkraut; a piece of bread; a small portion of dessert, usually a fruit cobbler, custard cake, or fruit; and a cup of coffee. Toward the end, the food particularly at luncheon increased somewhat but at no time did one leave the table satisfied. However little we got, still the meals were fairly well balanced and the deficiency diseases seldom appeared on Corregidor, although not uncommon at Bataan where food was more scarce and less varied."

Despite his protestations of meager fare, Svihra's description of meals tends to corroborate the image of life in the rear echelons held by the unfortunates fighting on Bataan. The presence of orderlies and mess boys rather than potential defenders on the Rock is also indicative of skewed priorities when choosing people for residence at the fortress. Conditions rapidly worsened, as Svihra observed. "Artillery fire and air bombing were increasing in intensity. Our outdoor toilets and shower baths, about one hundred feet [away] had been demolished. The shells and bombs shook the very tunnel itself, often landing just over or near the entrance, filling the tunnel with smoke, dust, and the acrid fumes of picric acid, and making it so dark inside that despite lights, one could scarcely see ten feet, and causing apprehension that the entrance had been blocked. The power plant was off for days, and the tunnel lighted by an auxiliary diesel engine that on occasions went out of commission, throwing everything into total darkness. Meals were often delayed and sleep often became impossible.

"One evening, there was quite a gathering of enlisted men at the west entrance to the tunnel, out to have a cigarette. It was a moonless but otherwise clear night. Suddenly there was heard the whining of a shell, then a burst, followed by a shower of stones from the top of Malinta Hill, just above the entrance. There was apparently a terrific rush for the entrance, in which several men were knocked down and trampled on. There followed another big shell that this time landed between the high, steep sides of the entrance, killing or injuring some fifty men. It was a grim sight to watch litter bearers carrying in armless, legless and even headless forms through the main tunnel to the hospital lateral."

To mark Emperor Hirohito's birthday, 29 April, and to celebrate it, the Japanese unleashed the heaviest bombardment yet seen. They continued to torment the occupants of Corregidor for the next six days. The puny remnants of the U.S. Pacific Fleet soon sank to the bottom of the bay as gunfire destroyed the minesweeper *Tanager,* gunboat *Mindanao,* and tug *Pigeon.* Crews scuttled several other small vessels. The defenders sensed the imminence of the final act as Japanese planes and artillery shifted their aim from the gun emplacements and installations on Corregidor to its beaches. At around 9:30 P.M. on 5 May, searchlight units equipped with sound-detection systems reported the sound of landing barges warming their motors. About 2,000 Japanese soldiers loaded the small craft for the quick run to their assigned stretches of the coast.

Unfortunately, the preparations for the assault went largely for naught. The coxswains operating the launches could not make out the landmarks by which they planned to steer. Strong currents conspired to carry them

1,000 yards away from their planned touchdown points that would locate them close to Malinta Hill. When the first waves approached the shoreline, the 4th Marines were well dug in along with a bunch of GI and Philippine Army refugees from Bataan, coast artillery Scouts, and even some Filipino messboys. Machine guns, rifles, and a few pieces of artillery slaughtered the hapless enemy trapped in the flimsy barges.

Although the defenders staggered the invaders in this encounter, the Japanese troops established a beachhead. And once they penetrated the thin crust of resistance at the water's edge, the Nipponese pushed forward. In support, batteries on Bataan raked the island and kept Wainwright easily shifting units of his diminishing army. Japanese reinforcements numbering about 6,000 started to arrive, bringing with them light artillery and ultimately a handful of tanks. Untrained sailors and airmen equipped with rifles could not cope with the determined, well-schooled foe. Although the American led forces fought hard for hours, even counterattacked, the defensive perimeter continued to shrink. By 10:00 A.M. on 6 May, the Japanese were closing in on the Malinta Tunnel. Already between six and eight hundred defenders were dead; the thousand jammed into Malinta Tunnel would be massacred if the fighting continued.

Through the siege of the Philippines, Washington had issued a series of messages that falsely raised hopes of succor and admonitions not to yield. At the time Wainwright had succeeded MacArthur, President Roosevelt directed him "to continue the fight as long as there remains any possibility of resistance." Wainwright recognized the situation as hopeless. He radioed President Roosevelt: "With broken heart and head bowed in sadness but not in shame I report . . . that today I must arrange for the surrender of the fortified islands of Manila Bay . . ." A similar message went to MacArthur.

Madeline Ullom remembered the cease-fire: "A corpsman stopped to gravely inform us he saw the white flag at the tunnel entrance. We heard the time of a broadcast was set. We gathered around Major Richardson's radio in the dental clinic. A desolate, numb, unbelievable feeling engulfed one. We listened to the words we had pushed to the backs of our minds. Tears came to our eyes. No one spoke. We walked away as though we were in an unrealistic situation. Colonel Paul Bunker, Lt. Col. Dwight Edison, and a bugler marched to the Topside parade grounds. Taps were played while they stood at attention. The flag was lowered. A white sheet was run up. Many had tears running down their cheeks."

Giving up turned out to be considerably more complicated than running up a white flag or announcing a willingness to cease resistance. The Corregidor radio station, starting at 10:30 A.M. and twice more during the next hour and fifteen minutes, had broadcast a statement to the Japanese command that the defenders would end hostile action at noon on 6 May, lower the American flag, and hoist the white one. Upon complete cessation of Japanese shelling and air raids, Wainwright would dispatch a pair of staff officers to Bataan where they could meet the Japanese and arrange a formal surrender.

The attackers continued to bombard the beleaguered on the harbor forts and the ground forces pressed ever closer to the Malinta Tunnel. Wainwright sent off three messages just before noon. One went to Maj. Gen. William F. Sharp, head of the Corps that covered the Visayan-Mindanao troops, the southern island defenses. Wainwright advised Sharp he was relinquishing his command of those forces and Sharp now would report directly to MacArthur in Australia. By this means, Wainwright hoped to surrender only the men on the Manila Bay islands.

The brief statement to President Roosevelt summarized the hopeless military situation and defended his decision: "There is a limit of human endurance and that limit has long since been past. Without prospect of relief I feel it is my duty to my country and to my gallant troops to end this useless effusion of blood and human sacrifice."

MacArthur received a similar message, in which Wainwright noted, "We have done our full duty to you and for your country. We are sad but unashamed . . . Goodbye, General, my regards to you and our comrades in Australia. May God strengthen your arm to insure ultimate success of the cause for which we have fought side by side."

A truce party chosen by Wainwright reached a Japanese officer who demanded the general come to him. Having carefully taken his pistol from his holster and placed it on a desk, Wainwright, with four from his staff, drove in a Chevrolet sedan bearing a white flag to a rendezvous point. They were met first by a Lieutenant Uemura who demanded that Wainwright surrender all the Fil-American forces in the Philippines. The general, still hoping to salvage a resistance under Sharp in the southern part of the archipelago, was not about to discuss terms with a lieutenant. He demanded an audience with a higher authority. Colonel Motto Nakayama from General Homma's staff appeared and, when Wainwright claimed he held only authority over the harbor forts, the colonel angrily insisted in Japanese that any surrender would have to include all military units in the Philippines. After one of Nakayama's lieutenants translated the harangue, Wainwright countered, "I will deal only with General Homma and with no one of lesser rank."

Nakayama agreed to arrange a meeting with Homma on Bataan. Wainwright with one of his staff was led by Nakayama and his translator toward a dock. Enroute, a barrage of Japanese shells forced the group to halt. Wainwright yelled, "Why the hell don't you people stop shooting? I put up my white flag hours ago." Nakayama replied through his interpreter, "We have not accepted any surrender from you as yet." After some delay, an armored tank barge anchored offshore; Wainwright and the others boarded it by means of a rubber raft and set off to meet Homma. From the dock at Cabcaben the general and several of his officers were driven to a battered white house with a large porch. A second boat brought in more of Wainwright's staff. Sipping cold water, they waited for Homma. From where they sat the Americans could see explosions on Corregidor, a mix of enemy shells and demolition of supplies and weapons by their colleagues.

According to a Japanese correspondent on the scene, statements by Wainwright that he possessed only the power to surrender the forces on Corregidor and the other fortified islands in the bay produced an uproar as the Japanese commander conferred with his subordinates. Homma thumped his fist on the table. "At the time of General King's surrender on Bataan, I did not see him. Neither have I any reason to see you if you are only the commander of a unit of the American forces. I wish only to negotiate with my equal, the commander in chief of the American forces in the Philippines. I see no further necessity for my presence here."

The burly Homma, 5'10", 200 pounds, started to rise from his chair. Wainwright conferred with his chief of staff, and realized that his host would not accept further piecemeal surrenders. "I will assume command of the entire American forces in the Philippines, at the risk of serious reprimand by my government following the war, " announced Wainwright.

But Homma's gorge seemed to overflow and he flatly rejected the change of heart. "You have denied your authority and your momentary decision may be regretted by you. I advise you to return to Corregidor and think this matter over. If you see fit to surrender, then surrender to the officer of the division on Corregidor. He in turn will bring you to me in Manila. I call this meeting over. Good day." The Japanese newsman said the Americans were "bewildered" by the abrupt departure of Homma. The Wainwright people had to be appalled. Assuming their war over, the garrison had already destroyed its weapons. The enemy could slaughter them with impunity.

The Americans debated alternatives until Wainwright offered to surrender the entire American forces in the Philippines to General Homma unconditionally. The Americans volunteered to send a representative to the other islands to arrange for their capitulation On Corregidor, Al Svihra, aware of Wainwright's mission, prepared himself for the inevitable. He packed his musette bag with a first-aid kit and toilet articles, some personal papers, groups of pictures of his wife and daughters and awaited his future in a tunnel lateral.

"Around 5:00 P.M., a Jap officer, accompanied by soldiers armed with Tommy guns and flamethrowers, entered the tunnel. Instructions were to stand by in headquarters lateral, to unload all arms and stack them, and have with us such articles of equipment and clothing as we could conveniently carry. We were ordered to move out of the lateral into the main tunnel which by that time was a mass of humanity, empty tin cans, discarded arms and equipment, filth, and trash. We tried in vain to make our way in a column of twos, through the mass of people to the west entrance. Even then we could hear enemy planes outside, bombing somewhere on the west side of the island. The enemy continued to shell this island with artillery fire."

Because of the danger outside, the Japanese permitted the inhabitants to remain inside the tunnel. When an officer started to inspect the area, he was followed by armed guards. "The latter stopped here and there along the way and plucked watches, rings, fountain pens from among the unfortunate lining the path through the tunnel."

By midnight of 6 May, the Japanese had completed a document of submission and Wainwright signed it. The provisions specified by Homma required the American general to surrender all forces in the Philippines, including those in other areas, within four days. All commanders were to assemble their troops and report to the local Japanese authorities. In the morning his captors pressed upon him the task of fulfillment of the terms. Wainwright had to rescind his directive to General Sharp and reassume command of the Visayan-Mindanao area. To ensure Sharp's compliance, Wainwright sent an emissary with a letter. Adding to Wainwright's humiliation, the victors ordered him to broadcast from Manila instructions to some smaller units still operating in northern Luzon. A pair of Americans also traveled to this area to personally contact the commanders. The bulk of these Luzon remnants refused to concede, however. They hid themselves in the mountains and became part of guerrilla movements.

The largest segment of Fil-American combat soldiers still under arms belonged to Sharp. While the enemy had wrested about half of Mindanao, most of Sharp's army remained intact. Even as Sharp had absorbed Wainwright's original message giving him independence of Corregidor, MacArthur, mindful of the imminent fall of the Rock, radioed Sharp, "communicate all matters direct to me," thereby assuming command of Sharp's Visayan-Mindinao force.

Upon hearing Wainwright's Manila broadcast in which he retrieved his authority over his Corps, Sharp relayed the gist of the statement to Melbourne and requested clarification. MacArthur quickly responded, "Orders emanating from General Wainwright have no validity. If possible separate your force into small elements and initiate guerrilla operations."

MacArthur advised George Marshall in Washington of the situation and stated, "I have informed him [Sharp] that Wainwright's orders since his surrender have no validity. . . . I believe Wainwright has temporarily become unbalanced and his condition renders him susceptible to enemy use." At his headquarters in Australia, MacArthur of course had not been privy to the details of the meeting between Homma and Wainwright. He could not have known that the Japanese held the entire 10,000 survivors on Corregidor as hostages against surrender in the southern islands. If Sharp failed to accede to Wainwright, the enemy might very well execute close to 10,000 soldiers, sailors, and airmen. While neither Homma nor any of his staff ever issued a threat of this nature, Wainwright and his staff feared that at the very least the Japanese would resume firing on the hapless residents of Corregidor.

Sharp reserved his decision until he met with the officer bearing a letter from Wainwright that set down reasons for him to capitulate. Once Sharp became convinced of the very real possibility that the enemy would resume its war against the defenseless garrison on the Rock he felt obliged to follow Wainwright's lead. He ordered weapons stacked, the white flag flown. Sharp issued orders to subordinates for submission on other southern islands but poor communications delayed receipt of the word. In some instances local commanders were unwilling to accept defeat. In a number of places units as large as battalions vanished into the interior for rebirth as guerrilla organizations. However, by 9 June the Japanese were satisfied that all organized outfits had yielded and told Wainwright, "Your high command ceases and you are now a prisoner of war."

Army nurse Madeline Ullom remembered scenes shortly after Wainwright acceded to Homma's demands. "Miss Davison [the chief nurse] told ten of us to report near the hospital tunnel to have our picture taken with Colonel [Wibb] Cooper [top ranking medical officer]. The Japanese officer, who was in charge, told us he was a graduate of the University of Utah. He assured us in excellent English not to be afraid. He wanted a picture of us in a line with a Japanese armed guard at each end to show we were protected. The pictures would be forwarded to General MacArthur's headquarters.

"Retinues of high-ranking Japanese officers inspected Malinta Tunnel. The white sheet that covered the entrance to the nurse's lateral was once quickly jerked aside and the delegation of Japanese attempted to enter. The alert, stalwart Miss Davison demanded a courageous, 'Halt!' They did immediately. She informed them they could not enter without previous arrangements. Heat and humidity of the lateral was intense. Many nurses were ill with malaria, dengue, and dysentery and skin conditions. Several nurses had elevated temperatures. Only a bottom sheet could be spared for the beds. Miss Davison strode to our commanding officer to report the incident. A brief time passed before a standard with a sign in Japanese was placed at the entrance. Thereafter, arrangements for inspections were made well in advance."

Al Svihra, during the first days in captivity on Corregidor, shared a large room with more than a dozen other officers. "Since we were given the freedom of the tunnel the first day, we were able to pick up a supply of canned goods cached in various parts of the tunnel. We had plenty of wet rations [cans of meat, vegetables, beans, hash], milk, coffee, some fruit, and a few odd cans of various other foods. Jap sentries guarding the tunnel came in frequently to use the toilet and bath. Although they had evidently been instructed not to molest us, some were bold enough to stop on the way out to see how they could despoil us."

According to Svihra, the Americans played bridge, read old magazines or books, did laundry, and prepared food. At the entrance to the tunnel lay the bodies of soldiers killed or who had died from wounds during the attack. As several days passed, bodies bloated, flies swarmed, and terrible odors mixed with the foul stench of a broken latrine. The Japanese refused permission for burial parties.

On 11 May, Svihra became one of the last to move to a beachfront installation of two balloon hangars and a work shed, the former home of the 92d Coast Artillery. "There were already jammed into the area about 10,000 to 12,000 officers and men. With the exception of a few hundred in each hangar, the men had hastily prepared shelters from the sun by spreading out shelter halves, blankets, pieces of canvas cloth, anything readily available, propping them up by means of poles. Most of the men were in dirty and tattered uniforms. It was no uncommon sight to see a soldier wearing an army cotton shirt, sailor trousers, marine shoes, and a Philippine Army fiber helmet.

"Sanitary conditions were deplorable. Men were using any place in the hills, forming a perimeter of the camp as a latrine. The Filipinos were even relieving themselves in the sea, the only place we had for bathing or washing our clothes. I was told that for the first two days or so, the Nips issued no food for the prisoners. Thereafter they issued limited supplies, not to exceed two meals a day and consisting mostly of rice, dry and wet rations, corn beef hash, flour, and shortening. The only source of water at first was a shallow well located near one of the hangars. Later a pipeline which had been put out of commission was repaired and from one spigot furnished an additional supply."

The captors organized the prisoners into groups of 1,000 with a pair of American officers assigned as leaders. A further subdivision created units of 100 with a captain and lieutenant in charge. The arrangement facilitated distribution of rations but without cooking utensils or organized messes, the inmates at the site ate poorly prepared meals on an irregular basis. Dysentery, diarrhea, and skin diseases inevitably spread. Svihra scrounged some sulpha tablets to cure his condition but with medical facilities limited, no general relief could be achieved until the tools to dig latrines, garbage, and trash pits became available. The increase in the water supply and proscription on use of the sea as a toilet improved health conditions.

Unpleasant and as hazardous to the health as circumstances were for the captured on Corregidor, the situation for the Bataan prisoners was far more deadly. Their life under the victors had begun with the Death March. Those who did not perish enroute, had reached the destination of Camp O'Donnell, weakened by malnutrition, dehydration, and disease, battered by maltreatment from their guards. The horrors multiplied in the camp, a site without facilities for the more than 50,000 residents, (8,675 Americans, roughly 42,000 Filipinos) with neither food, water, or, perhaps most important, the sanitation vital for preservation of already weakened bodies. O'Donnell was a sun-baked, almost shadeless, water-poor, semidesert without mosquito control and rampant malaria.

"O'Donnell, drenched in the glaring, blazing heat of a tropical sun, was certainly no place to be with a shortage of water," said John Olson. "For some fifteen days we did not have a drop of water for washing teeth, face, hands, or mess kit. I licked my mess kit as clean as possible, wiped it with paper, and set it in the sun to sterilize." Ultimately Olson compared the place to the infamous Confederate stockade at Andersonville during the Civil War where thousands of Union soldiers died because of the conditions.

Of his arrival at O'Donnell, Tom Gage said, "I remember two things: Filipino soldiers digging graves, graves, graves, and Filipinos in the river, bathing, urinating, and drinking. They died like flies." Just about every prisoner still on his feet, lurched and tottered onto the grassless parade ground in front of what was the Japanese headquarters. Soldiers, wearing fresh, clean, white shirts, khaki shorts or breeches, and armed with large sticks, pummeled the arrivals into a formation for the first indignity, a shakedown that took away blankets, pencils, pens, watches, lighters, cigarettes, shelter halves; in short, just about every personal item the men had managed to retain during the Death March.

Camp commandant, Capt. Yoshio Tsuneyoshi, an overage caricature of a Japanese soldier, decked out in very baggy shorts, riding boots with spurs, and a white sport shirt; whose printable nicknames included, "Baggy Pants," "Whistling Britches," "Little Napoleon," and "Little Hitler," then delivered what John Olson called his "goddamn you!" tirade in his native language. Through his interpreter he iterated that his sole interest was in dead Americans and those that died. They were not prisoners of war and the Japanese did not care whether they lived or died. Only the generosity of the Japanese spared their lives. The penalty for attempted escape was death.

The rationale that denied official prisoner-of-war status was that some US-AFFE units had not surrendered and would not do so until August. In addition, the Imperial government had never signed the 1929 Geneva agreement regarding the humane treatment of prisoners, although the Japanese issued statements that so far as circumstances permitted they would act in accord with the Geneva provisions. In practice, however, the handling of prisoners throughout the war fell far short of the minimum requirements of the Geneva Convention.

Initially, the Japanese specified no distinction between officers and en- listed men. All would receive the same treatment and rank conferred no power. Tsuneyoshi refused to meet with General King, the senior American, or King's opposite number among the Filipinos. Instead he would see only their representatives through whom he passed on his ukases and listened to requests and questions. Obdurate, harsh, and prone to tantrums even in these sessions, Tsuneyoshi blocked many of the simplest means to improve conditions. The death toll climbed steeply after the first week of O'Donnell's operations.

Tsuneyoshi had warned that anyone who tried to escape would be killed, a violation of the Geneva rules and one largely observed by Japan's partners in Europe. At first glance conditions at O'Donnell seemed to invite break- out. Only a few strands of wire marked the boundaries and at night the thick grass could hide a figure from sentries posted on the handful of watchtow- ers. Beyond the enclosure lay a dense jungle, ideal for evading a search party. But the ordeal of Bataan, the Death March, and the first days at O'Donnell sapped the mental and physical strength of even the most resolute of men. Men who were barely able to totter to a latrine could hardly imagine them- selves able to endure the effort required for flight.

Olson, who kept what records he could of life at O'Donnell and who in- terviewed many survivors, says there were no genuine attempts to escape. However, the Japanese executed at least a dozen prisoners, almost entirely those discovered in possession of items believed removed from the bodies of their own casualties on Bataan.

"Most days in camp were monotonously alike," said Sam Grashio. "We were awakened about 6:00 A.M. by the bugler, if we had not been already roused by the maniacal yelling of the Japanese taking early morning bayo- net practice. Then we went to the mess hall for breakfast. This always con- sisted of about half a messkit of lugao, a soupy form of rice. Many men sim- ply ate their meager breakfast, then lay down again and slept most of the day, a habit that became increasingly prevalent as we grew weaker from the lack of food. The main activity of everyone in camp who was not dead or wishing himself dead was trying to get more food. If someone was sick and about to die, others stayed close to him, less from compassion than from hope of getting his rice ration."

According to John Olson, many, many more of the incarcerated would have died of malnutrition or starvation but for truck drivers and work crews dispatched to chores outside the camp. Filipino civilians donated or sold food to the Americans on the work details. The transactions occurred when the attention of the guards was elsewhere or even with the knowledge of more humane merciful soldiers. In turn, the prisoners carried back items to the camp, ingeniously hiding the contraband during routine shakedowns. Some of the fortunate shared their treasures gratis while others sold or bartered for profit.

For more than 1,500 Americans and an estimated 20,000 Filipinos there was no help. They died, mainly during the first two months at O'Donnell. The numbers appalled the Japanese high command, if not Captain Tsuneyoshi. Starting in June, began an American exodus to a new, somewhat less malignant installation at Cabanatuan. Also, with hostilities in Bataan and Corregidor ended, the Japanese dismantled Hospital Number One and shipped the medical personnel with their equipment to O'Donnell. In addition, the cessation of fighting brought release of the surviving Filipino soldiers into the civilian population. Although the hellhole of O'Donnell did not discharge its last inmate until January 1943, it no longer figured as an element in the fate of the erstwhile defenders.

The first weeks of imprisonment for those held on Corregidor had differed significantly from that of the men on Bataan. There was no Death March for them but the time came for them to join their colleagues in camps on Luzon. After almost two weeks, the incarcerated on Corregidor, bearing backpacks made soggy from a downpour, hiked to one of the island docks. Fishing launches ferried them out to a pair of freighters converted into troop transports. The Americans anxiously observed the ships' courses, concerned the direction might carry them to Formosa or Japan. To their relief the vessels veered toward Manila.

The landing craft at the city disgorged the men in relatively shallow water, from knee to armpit depth. "It must have been a rather amusing spectacle for the Japs to see us kerplunking into the green polluted water of the bay," remembered Svihra. "We waded some 100 yards into shore where we were promptly formed into groups of 100 willy-nilly and then marched up the Boulevard. Our shoes were soaking wet, making it extremely uncomfortable to walk with the water oozing out of them at each step. A few had taken off their shoes before debarking and carried them on their shoulders to keep them dry. When these reached shore, they attempted to change socks and put on their shoes. However, the Japs had other ideas. They compelled these people, with rifle butts as prods, to put on their shoes and without tying them to form with the nearest group.

"We marched up the Boulevard under supervision of mounted Jap guards, past the Polo Club and other familiar places. There were no cars on the Boulevard and no calesas and only an occasional Jap military lorry, some of which were evidently captured in Bataan. As we approached the residences on the Boulevard, we noticed a few people, Americans and Filipinos, gathered in groups. They were kept well back from the street by sentries and Manila police, evidently to prevent any communication with us. Occasionally, someone in these groups (when the guards' backs were turned) would wave to a friend, relative, or perhaps a wife waved to her husband, for there were many American Manilans who had enlisted or were commissioned in the Army at the outbreak of war. They all looked pretty sad and we observed many tearful eyes.

"We were halted for a few minutes to permit us to obtain water from some GI cans which were very conspicuously advertised as an act of charity by the Japanese Women's Club of Manila. We had hardly taken off our packs when we were ordered to form a column again. We continued our march. As we reached the high commissioner's residence we noticed the Rising Sun flying from it. The same was true of the Elks Club. This was practically an uninterrupted march of about seven to eight kilometers, on a hot, sultry May day. As a result many were forced to drop out. Most were made to rejoin their groups by thumpings with a rifle butt."

To Svihra's shock, their destination was Bilibid Prison, a massive pile of stone and dungeonlike buildings that ordinarily housed convicted Filipino criminals. The erstwhile legal officer was pleasantly surprised by the better sanitation in the new digs and the three meals a day, although the food was limited. Prisoners supplemented their diet through what Svihra labeled, "Jap soldier-racketeer sentries" who acted as intermediaries between the inmates and Filipino peddlers outside Bilibid. The guards let down baskets from their posts atop the walls; the vendors put in bananas, mangoes, molasses, and the like. The prisoners passed up money, most of which went into the pockets of the troops before it got to the sellers.

The Japanese, who had signaled a sense of respect for the privacy of the Army nurses captured on Corregidor, continued to deal benignly with the women. Nurse Josephine Nesbit described the move from Corregidor to the mainland. "During the trip to Manila, the Jap officer in charge of the boat, graciously offered tea and rice cookies to the officers and women. It was midafternoon by the time the boat docked and the passengers were unloaded. The officers and men were taken off first and most of them marched away. Incapacitated patients went in trucks. When the women assembled on the dock, the thirty-eight Filipinos were put in one group and the sixty-eight other women in a second group. All were counted several times before trucks arrived to take them away from the dock. The Filipinos went to Bilibid Military Prison.

"The American women were taken to Santa Tomas Internment Camp [a site of a local university known to inmates as STIC] where they were excitedly received by more than 3,000 internees. While baggage was searched and the women interviewed by the Japs, they were fed their evening meal. The most satisfying food they had in months. The fresh pineapple was the first fresh fruit they had eaten since the war began."

11
At Sea and In the Air

Historians have questioned the wisdom of Germany's declaration of war against the United States but American efforts prior to 7 December 1941 had already come close to open combat. Merchant ships ran a devastating gauntlet of German submarines from the moment they left ports in the United States until they docked in Great Britain or at Murmansk, the only port open in the Soviet Union. For a time, the British Navy, coordinating efforts with the Royal Air Force, had staved off the U-boat attacks upon convoys. But after the fall of France, subs operating from French ports relentlessly prowled the western Atlantic exacting a sharp increase in the toll on shipping.

To bolster the British resistance to what Roosevelt and his advisors perceived as an inevitable threat to their country, the United States in September 1940 swapped fifty aged destroyers that dated back to World War I for naval bases on colonial islands in western waters. While Hitler scrapped restrictions for hitting cargo ships, he cautioned against incidents that involved American warships. U-boats refrained from hunts in the waters off the American coasts.

When the United States, in January 1941, accepted the responsibility to protect freighter convoys sailing the North Atlantic a confrontation with German subs became inevitable. The Roosevelt administration convinced Congress to pass the Lend-Lease Act on 11 March 1941. With a vague promise of repayment for goods provided, the United States now geared up with war materials for Britain. The Germans could hardly ignore the role being played by the officially uncommitted United States. Meanwhile torpedoes blasted ships of various registries, bearing lend-lease goods. Admiral Harold Stark, chief of naval operations reported in early April 1941, "The situation is obviously critical in the Atlantic. In my opinion, it is hopeless except as we take strong measures to save it." However, not until June 1941 was the American Navy ready to begin this role, to which had been added responsibilities for guarding the Caribbean.

American escort vessels and U-boats sparred without either side landing a punch until October 1941, when a wolf pack ravaged a convoy 400 miles from Iceland. During the wild melee, the destroyer USS *Kearny* absorbed a hit but managed to steam into port. About three weeks later, a torpedo smashed into the destroyer *Reuben James* on picket duty 600 miles from Ireland. The magazine ignited a violent blast that tore the ship in half. As it slid below the surface, several of its depth charges detonated, killing some survivors floating in the sea. Only 45 crewmen of the 160 in the ship's company were rescued.

Only in November 1941, did Congress agree to lift restrictions on freighters sailing under the American flag and allow them to not only travel in the war zone but to arm themselves and fight when attacked. Following the official state of war against the European Axis partners, the struggle in the Atlantic fully involved the United States. The losses in ships and cargo during the first years staggered the Allies. At the height of the Battle of the Atlantic, German U-boats destroyed from 7,000 to 8,000 tons worth of vessels a month, a pace beyond the capacity of shipyards. Tens of thousands of seamen perished. Submarines stalked and attacked during daylight hours, even surfacing to finish off a vessel already crippled by a tin fish. The hard-pressed navies mustered huge 100-ship convoys but even with flocks of escorts ranging from destroyers up to battleships to shepherd them, the wolf packs savaged an average of 20 percent of each group.

Convoy PQ-17 epitomized the first year of the runs to the Soviet port of Murmansk, the most perilous voyage because the route not only carried the merchantmen into U-boat-invested waters and exposed them to heavyweight German surface warships, but also put them within range of the *Luftwaffe*. PQ-17 was organized at the Icelandic port of Reykjavik in late June 1942. The initial escort consisted of six destroyers, two flak ships, a pair of submarines, eleven corvettes [miniature destroyers], minesweepers, and armed trawlers. A task force of Allied cruisers, two battleships, a Royal Navy aircraft carrier, and another flotilla of destroyers joined the procession.

German undersea raiders and aircraft, initially frustrated by the protective screen and the weather, on 4 July, scored with an airborne torpedo that reduced the Liberty ship *Christopher Newport* to a powerless hulk. It was sent to the ocean bottom by the guns of a warship. Having tasted blood, the *Luftwaffe* dispatched waves of Heinkels and Focke-Wulfs and although a number of planes were shot down, half a dozen vessels reeled from blows and several sank.

As a U.S. Navy captain, Dan Gallery commanded the patrol-plane unit stationed at Iceland. He recalled that PQ-17 only left port after a near mutiny by the crews of the merchant ships was quelled by the promise of the additional naval escort of the capital ships and heavy cruisers. "They were supposed to protect the convoy," said Gallery. "Actually they tagged along about 150 miles astern [when the attack began]. I was in the RAF headquarters and we were looking at the chart showing where the convoy was. It was up around the North Cape of Norway and it was having a bad time. We got a flash that the *Tirpitz* [one of the few German battleships] was coming out to attack the convoy. The air commander and I just rubbed our hands together and [I] said, 'Boy, this is it. The *Washington* and the *King George V* [the American and British dreadnoughts that outgunned the *Tirpitz*] will get the *Tirpitz* today.' He said, 'Boy this looks like it's going to be the best Fourth of July since you blokes declared your independence.'

"Then about an hour later, we got this message from London: 'All warships retired at high speed to the west, convoy scattered.' Everybody just slouched out of air force headquarters and went back to their huts and either cursed or wept or both. That convoy was slaughtered. The British Admiralty had withdrawn the big ships, unwilling to risk its prize assets in a showdown with the *Tirpitz*, its cruiser companions *Scheer, Hipper,* and accompanying destroyers."

Explained Gallery, "The reason behind that order from London was that our battleships had been catching hell along about that time. We had lost our whole fleet at Pearl Harbor. The *Prince of Wales* and the *Repulse* had been sunk at Singapore. All the shipyards were full of battleships that had been damaged by either torpedoes or aircraft. So the British were simply gun-shy and they weren't about to risk any more big ships within range of either torpedoes or aircraft."

When PQ-17 broke up, the freighters, like rabbits caught in an open field and beset by flocks of raptors, frantically fled for the safety of the Soviet shores, 450 miles away. Gun crews using .30- and .50-caliber machine guns futilely sought to fend off a series of assaults from the heavens. A few small but better-armed warships using 3-inch guns attempted to protect the merchantmen while the U-boats operated with impunity. Of the original thirty-three vessels carrying supplies to Murmansk, twenty-two, including fifteen under the American or Panamanian flag, went down. As a dispiriting footnote, the *Tirpitz* and its accompanying ships, misled by the information from the *Luftwaffe,* fumbled around the area without ever finding the convoy or the navy forces.

The fate of PQ-17 led to modifications and innovations that ranged from winter clothing to bigger guns and, most important, better air support. To buttress the work of the warships, aerial patrols from the States, bases in Greenland, Iceland, and Great Britain scoured the seas in search of submarines. Later, small aircraft carriers accompanied convoys, providing constant air cover against the roving marauders. Within a year the Allied forces could shift from a defensive posture to an offensive one and the balance in the Battle of the Atlantic tipped.

During this first year at war, the U.S. Navy, critically wounded at Pearl Harbor, and now engaged in a two-hemisphere conflict, faced a formidable challenge from the Japanese forces rampaging through Asia and the South and Southwestern Pacific islands. To satisfy the legitimate and political claims of the armed forces, the Joint Chiefs of Staff broke the Pacific theater into two separate fiefs. They named Douglas MacArthur supreme commander for the Southwest Pacific with responsibility for Australia, the Philippines, the Solomon Islands, New Guinea, the Bismarck Archipelago (between the Solomons and New Guinea), and part of the Netherlands Indies. His resources included soldiers, airmen, and some naval units.

Admiral Chester W. Nimitz had assumed the post of commander in chief, U.S. Pacific Fleet (CinCPAC), on 31 December 1941, the post formerly held by Admiral Kimmel. His territory stretched over the vast reaches of the Central Pacific, from the Aleutian Islands to the north, down through Midway, the last bastion before Hawaii and Fiji, and Samoa that lay along the route to Australia. To the west lay the Japanese strongholds dotting the ocean, islands grouped under headings as the Ryukus, Marianas, Carolines, Marshalls, and Gilberts.

A 1905 graduate of the Naval Academy, Nimitz had an excellent reputation among his peers, having served on a variety of ships from submarines through battleships and in staff jobs. Unlike MacArthur, Nimitz offered no showmanship; he was soft-spoken and patient. But beneath the placid exterior lay a determination that augured well for an aggressive approach. His subordinate, Adm. Raymond Spruance, complimenting Nimitz's personality, emphasized, "The one big thing about him was that he was always ready to fight. . . . And he wanted officers who would push the fight with the Japanese. If they would not do so, they were sent elsewhere."

Shortly after the new year began, the carrier *Saratoga* was plowing through the seas several hundred miles west of Oahu. Aboard was Lt. Comdr. John "Jimmy" Thach, a graduate of the Naval Academy and leader of a fighter squadron. Thach had already distinguished himself by design of a tactic that became known as the "Thachweave." Instead of the conventional Vee formation, he designed a two-plane arrangement of leader and wingman, a tactic that provided mutual protection for the pair. From a survivor at Pearl Harbor, Thach had also learned about the capabilities of the enemy. "He confirmed that a Zero could turn inside of anything we had. He said he had pulled up and was on this fellow's tail and was just about ready to shoot him and the Zero just flipped right over his back and was on his tail and shot him down." The Grumman Wildcat lacked the Zero's speed, maneuverability, and rate of climb. Americans benefitted from greater firepower, self-sealing fuel tanks, and armor plate to shield the pilot and vital points.

As the *Saratoga* moved at a six-knot pace, a dental officer remarked on the slow speed. He said, "Gee, if there was a Japanese submarine anywhere in this part of the ocean, it would seem like it could catch us easily." Thach agreed, adding, "It would take a long time to launch an airplane if you had to get up to speed to do it." The skipper had been ordered to travel slowly in order to conserve fuel.

"That evening," said Thach, "I was sitting in the wardroom eating when it sounded like the bottom of the ship blew out, a whole big explosion—a huge, loud, ear-splitting explosion. All the dishes went up in the air. I remember seeing my executive officer, who was sitting right by me, reach up in the air and catch a roll that was coming down. Everybody went to 'general quarters' immediately. We got to the ready room and word came from damage control that we'd been hit by a very large torpedo, obviously from a submarine. It had knocked out two boilers.

"The *Saratoga* cranked on twenty-seven knots and moved out with that big hole in the side. We had a hole big enough to drive two trucks through, side by side, flood two boilers, and still move at 27 knots." The torpedo actually blew up in a deserted spot on the ship, limiting the dead to a half dozen. The carrier sailed to a shipyard at Bremerton, Washington, for refurbishing.

Thach and his squadron transferred to the *Lexington,* which, a month later, plowed toward Rabaul on New Britain Island, a huge Japanese base. On the morning of 20 February, Thach remembered, "I was on combat air patrol with [Edward] Butch O'Hare leading another two-plane section and Bert Stanley leading a third. So, we had six planes on combat air patrol [There] was real, honest-to-goodness, no-fooling radio silence. No one dared open up, because we figured if we did they might get a bearing on us. I almost jumped out of my seat when this loud voice of the *Lexington* fighter director came in giving me a vector and said there's apparently a snooper about thirty-five miles away. I started out after him and Butch O'Hare started to follow me. I turned around, looked at him and motioned him back. He didn't want to go back but inasmuch as I knew there couldn't be fighters in the area it could only be large aircraft. I figured that my wingman and I could take care of that. So I made him go back. I also calculated that if there's one snooper, there'd probably be another. It was important to get these planes and knock them out before they could report the locations of the *Lexington* task group."

The direction given Thach sent him into a heavy thunderstorm and when he queried his controller he was advised the interloper was also in the squall. "Once we were in the soup, we couldn't see very much. We came into a rift, an opening in the cloud for just a second, and right below me was this great huge Japanese insignia. I saw two engines on one wing and then just as quickly we were in the soup again. Here he was right below me, like about twenty or thirty feet. About that time the fighter director called and said, 'We have a merged plot.' [Radar showing both planes in the same space.] I called back. 'We sure do. If it had been any more merged, we would have crashed into him. I just sighted him.'"

The snooper disappeared but circling about, the American caught a vague outline of the Japanese plane. Within seconds, both aircraft broke into the clear and Thach readied for an attack. He directed his wingman to move to the other side where the pair could bracket the target and guard against any turns. "I took what I figured was the proper lead on him and waited until I got close enough, coming in from the side, and opened up with all six of those guns. It was a really good blast of tracers. I took a good lead on him and on the engines on the right wing. Bullets would carry into the cockpit, through the engines, or round the engines into the cockpit. I looked back and nothing happened. No smoke, nothing! I thought, have I got blank ammunition?" His partner maneuvered for a run when the wing of the victim burst into flame.

"This was an Emily [a four-engine bomber]. We'd never seen one. We had no intelligence that they had that kind of an airplane. I knew it was huge and I could tell it had a cannon because when the cannon was shooting, it would make smoke rings. I really felt sorry for him because here he was doing his job and obviously had gotten off a message on the location of the *Lexington* task group and I hadn't hit him soon enough because I couldn't find him in the soup.

"We didn't have to make any more attacks, just watched him. He started burning and six huge long bombs dropped in the water. A few minutes later his nose went down and in he went with a splash. Made a big cloud of smoke they could see all the way to the *Lexington*. I felt sorry for the crew because some of them, maybe all, had convinced themselves they could defend with all those guns against a fighter-type aircraft. How else could they feel? It was the same sort of feeling when we were doing gunnery training and the same sort of propaganda that our big bombers were putting out to bolster their feeling of being able to survive against attack by fighters. I never believed it. We landed aboard and everybody wanted to know what it was like, what happened when we made the attacks, what kind of attacks, were they the same we did against the sleeve, and we said yes, the same thing you've been doing all the time. O'Hare was fit to be tied. He wanted to get in quick. This was the first enemy airplane any of us had seen."

O'Hare did not have to wait long before his opportunity for combat. Thach was studying charts and intelligence reports for information about the Emily when, he said, "The flight order sounded. 'Fighter pilots, man your planes.' I knew we had something coming and I figured it was an attack, or else another snooper." In fact, a large number of Japanese aircraft sallied forth from Rabaul intent upon destroying the task force. Other units preceded Thach and he sat for a time in his airplane watching. "It wasn't long before we could see from the flight deck, in the distance, some smoke and airplanes falling. I could see these bombers in close formation headed for us. The enemy was at about 8,000 feet. Later, I learned Noel Gayer [in command of a section] had called down, telling our own antiaircraft fire to please shorten their fuses to 8,000 feet because that was the altitude of the enemy bombers and he was being bothered by bursts of antiaircraft fire above them where he wanted to maneuver for attacks. We didn't have influence fuses [ones triggered by a target]. We had time-set fuses, so many seconds. This was the situation the first part of the war. We did half our fighting in the middle of our own AA fire and the other half in the middle of the enemy's."

The carrier dispatched Thach and Butch O'Hare with their wingmen. Said Thach, "I started climbing in the direction they were going so that if I ever did get to the altitude maybe I could get some of them, all the time watching these airplanes falling out of the air. Sometimes there were three or four falling at once, just coming down with dark red flame and brown smoke coming out. We didn't have a very high rate of climb, only 1,100 feet a minute when we were fully loaded with our 1,800 rounds of ammunition and full of gas. I managed to get up there and start working after I saw three of them still in some kind of formation. They split and were starting to run away individually. I made an attack on one from the low side because I didn't have enough altitude and it burst into flame and started down.

"About this time I saw one of my planes coming in dead astern [of another bomber] and a flash right on his windshield where, apparently, a cannon had hit him and he went into a spin right on in. He made a bad mistake by coming in on the tail of a bomber that had a cannon [there]. I was pretty mad at this character who had shot down one of my pilots and I wasn't going to let him get home free. I managed to get a little bit above his level before starting the approach. I was amazed; I was definitely out of his range but he was shooting all kinds of stuff at me. You couldn't see it, looking right at it. You had to look behind to see it. I put what I thought was a real good burst into his wing root and fuselage and nothing happened. I got out and made another run, pulled out, looked at him again and all of a sudden he disintegrated, just blew up.

"I didn't have my wingman with me. We were a little disorganized because we never had a chance to join up after taking off. It wasn't really necessary because against bombers you didn't have to defend yourself with maneuvers. It was all right to just go hell-bent for election and that airplane that can get there the first gets there. Then, over the radio I got the impression there was a second wave, another nine-plane group of Bettys [two-engine bombers]. We didn't know what they were because they were entirely different from anything in our intelligence manuals.

"Butch was vectored out after these people and intercepted when they were about six minutes away. We had a practice, charge all your guns and fire a short burst to be sure you've got 'em charged and your gun switches are all on. His wingman did this and nothing happened. He apparently had a short or some open circuit and couldn't get any gun to fire. Butch realized this and waved him back but he didn't want to go. Butch shook his fist at him but he came on and maneuvered to try to draw some attention to himself while Butch went in and made the attacks.

"They [the Japanese] stayed in rigid formation. That was the best thing for them to do. First they've got to have a bomb pattern if they want to hit the ship and [need] a whole proper formation for the right pattern. Furthermore, it gives all the guns from each airplane a chance to shoot to defend themselves. [O'Hare] got in, lined them up and apparently knocked down two in one pass. Then he went to the other side to work on that line back and forth. Inside of six minutes he had six down. At first he was given credit for only five. They thought antiaircraft had shot down one. Afterward one of them came down and approached like he was going to crash into the *Lexington*. We got photographs of that airplane and one engine had completely fallen out of the wing. Butch had shot that engine out. Of the twenty aircraft we met that day, nineteen were shot down." The Americans counted one pilot killed, two aircraft lost. In their zeal to hit the task force well out to sea from Rabaul, the Japanese could not dispatch short-range fighters to cover their vulnerable bombers. While the *Lexington* celebrated its aerial victories, the asset of surprise had also been a casualty and the fleet aborted the proposed raid on Rabaul.

In early March word came of a Japanese expedition into New Guinea at Salamaua and Lae, a pair of towns at either end of a horseshoe-shaped harbor. The invaders met no opposition but intelligence reported a concentration of transports, cargo ships, and naval vessels. According to Jimmy Thach, no one knew whether air cover protected the enemy but the carriers *Yorktown* and *Lexington* received a mission to disrupt the operation. The plan called for torpedo planes to attack all the shipping in the harbors with the Wildcat fighters along for protection.

The fleet hugged the south coast of New Guinea via the Coral Sea and the Gulf of Papua with the idea that the raiders would fly over the Owen Stanley mountain range to surprise the targets. Lt. Comdr. Jimmy Brett led two torpedo squadrons that included an ancient type known as a Devastator. "They were more devastating to the crews in them than they were to the enemy. They were absolute firetraps," said Thach. "They were underpowered, and carrying a huge torpedo and all the gasoline, they could just barely get off the deck if they started right at the stern and the ship making 25 or 30 knots, they could barely stagger into the air."

The jagged ridges of the Owen Stanleys stuck up 10,000 feet. No one was certain whether Brett's ships could even ascend above these. Thach watched the torpedo planes mill about in search of more altitude or a passage. Brett started to fly parallel to the lowest ridge and he noticed a sunny area over some fields. Having trained as a glider pilot, he recognized that that portended thermal updrafts. "Sure enough," said Thach, "he circled around, rising, finally got enough and just washed himself right over the ridge.

"We went into Salamau and Lae and there were the cruisers, getting underway, pulling up anchor chains. There were a lot of transports. Brett went in with his torpedo planes and I took my fighters in. I left Butch O'Hare upstairs. He didn't like that, either, but we didn't know whether we were going to run into some Zeros and we wanted to go down, strafe just ahead of the torpedo planes to give them a chance. I figured that no matter how many planes there were where we were coming in, Butch could give them a busy time before they got down to us.

"The torpedo attack was beautifully executed. You could see the streaks of torpedoes going right to the sides of these cruisers, and nothing happened. I saw one or two go right on underneath, come out the other side, go over and bury themselves in a bank on the shore. Some obviously hit the cruisers and didn't explode. We had bad fuses and very erratic depth control. I didn't see any torpedo explosions. What a heartbreaking thing after all of that effort, all of that training, the wonderful experience Jimmy Brett used to get there." It was one more instance where defective torpedoes thwarted American efforts. Only a single enemy aircraft, a float plane with a small-caliber gun, attempted to deflect the attack. It was quickly shot down. But except for some dive-bomber hits and the strafing, the ships in the harbor escaped serious damages.

Undeterred by such ineffective jabs, and on the verge of completing its conquest of the Philippines, the Japanese moved southeast to reinforce and extend Nipponese domination. The strategy, designed to isolate Australia, called for occupation of New Guinea, the Solomon Islands, and control of the surrounding waters. Intelligence reports received by MacArthur and Nimitz indicated a Japanese strike force bound for Port Moresby, New Guinea, separated from Australia's Queensland peninsula by the Coral Sea. To deny them a foothold at Port Moresby, the Americans plotted to hit the invaders at sea with land-based Allied aircraft from Australia and a naval force that would include the air groups aboard the carriers *Lexington* and *Yorktown*.

On 3 May an Air Corps reconnaissance mission spotted an invasion of Tulagi, one of the Solomon Islands. Hidden by rain squalls, a group that included the *Yorktown* approached within twenty miles of Tulagi. The carrier launched its torpedo planes, dive bombers, and fighters. The pilots and gunners scored some hits but, as so often happened, wildly overinflated the targets struck and damage inflicted. Had the tacticians acted upon this information the results would have been disastrous for the bulk of the enemy navy had gone unscathed. Both sides then followed their own agendas for the next several days. The Japanese busily deposited ground troops at various sites while keeping an eye out for the Allied forces. A formation of four B-17s from Australia came upon an enemy carrier near Bougainville Island but none of their bombs dropped close to the ship. Throughout the war, high-altitude bombers recorded little damage to ships underway.

Dive bombers from the Japanese force aimed at the U.S. destroyer *Sims* and the oiler *Neosho*. The *Sims* struck by a trio of 500-pounders from a fourth wave of attackers exploded and sank with only sixteen survivors. The battered oiler remained adrift several days before the crew was rescued and the vessel scuttled. Faulty communications led to an all-out strike by planes from the *Yorktown* against what proved to be minor elements of the enemy but before the Japanese could exploit the mistake, ninety-three American aircraft pummeled the foe's light carrier *Shoho* and a flight leader radioed the *Lexington*, "Scratch one flattop!"

On 7 May, in the Coral Sea, Paul Stroop, a 1926 graduate of the Naval Academy, a member of the U.S. Olympic gymnastics team in 1928, and a former dive-bomber pilot, was aboard the *Lexington* as flag secretary. As the carrier recovered its aircraft, he recalled, "It was a very fine, successful day. We hadn't found the main body of the Japanese and up until that afternoon they hadn't found us. Our search planes had returned and we were running a cruising formation at dusk when we sighted some lights coming over the horizon. On the *Lexington,* we thought these were some of our own planes from the *Yorktown* returning. We were not sure that they had all their planes back. We knew that the *Lexington* planes were all aboard. These planes were in very good formation. I remember noticing the port running lights of the formation all in a beautiful echelon. One of the things that struck me as odd was that the red color of the port running light was different from the shade of running lights that we had on our own planes.

"About the time we sighted these lights, one of our screen destroyers began firing at the planes. I remember a voice message went out over the TBS [Talk Between Ships system] to the skipper of the destroyer, telling him to stop, that these were undoubtedly friendly planes coming in." The TBS instructions, said Stroop, probably came from the air officer of his ship. However, he recalled, "Chillingworth [the destroyer skipper] came right back on the TBS and said, 'I know Japanese planes when I see them.' I had subconsciously noted there was a difference [but] at the moment I didn't consider them enemy planes. Actually, these were Japanese planes that had mistaken the *Yorktown* and *Lexington* for their own ships. They came in with lights on and were ready to get into the landing formation. There was a lot of confusion, but after Chillingworth identified them as enemy planes, everybody began shooting. The Japanese broke up their formation, turned out their lights, and disappeared. I don't think we hit any that night."

American search planes glimpsed the main enemy strike force with its two big carriers, *Zuikaku* and *Shokaku*. Said Stroop, "Lieutenant Commander Bob Dixon, the commanding officer of the search squadron, stayed as long as he could in the vicinity of the Japanese carriers, giving us locations, speed, and direction of their movement. He did a classic job of shadowing these carriers, taking advantage of cloud cover when he could and reporting back to us."

From the *Yorktown*, coveys of dive bombers and torpedo planes, protected by fighters and led by Dixon, drew a bead on the *Shokaku*. According to Stroop, "The distance was a little greater than we wanted, maybe something over 200 miles, particularly the TBDs, torpedo planes that were carrying heavy torpedo loads and would not have too much range. An attack was scheduled to take place about 11:15 to 11:30 and the *Yorktown* and *Lexington* were in an area of good visibility, whereas the *Zuikaku* and the *Shokaku* still had the advantage of cloud cover. A good many of our attack planes could not ever make contact with the *Zuikaku* or the *Shokaku*. Those that did were quite effective. They damaged one carrier, the *Shokaku*, considerably, and the other a slight amount. However, the Japanese managed to control the damage and get away.

"About eleven o'clock we began getting indications on the radar of a large group of planes approaching us. We figured that the Japanese were doing the same thing we were. They had their attack planes coming down." On the bridge, Stroop recorded entries in the war diary. At 11:20 he noted, "Under attack by enemy aircraft . . . They came down in a very well-coordinated attack with torpedo planes and dive bombers. [At the moment] you're a little curious and you're a little scared. You wonder what the outcome is going to be. They were fixed-landing-gear dive bombers [known by the code name "Val"]. You were convinced that the pilot in the plane had the bridge of your ship right in his sight and this didn't look good. Fortunately they were not strafing because if they had been, I'm sure they would have made topside untenable.

"The minute he released his bomb you could see the bomb taking a different trajectory from the aircraft itself, generally falling short because their dive wasn't quite as steep as it should have been. The torpedo planes came in about the same time and launched at about 1,000 yards. They were down to flight-deck level. We got, I believe, four torpedo hits, although only two were officially recorded. I watched some of the torpedo planes passing from port to starboard [the hits were all on the port side]. It was pretty discouraging. They'd launch their torpedoes and then some of them would fly very close to the ship. They were curious and sort of thumbed their noses at us.

We were shooting at them with our new 20 millimeters and not hitting them at all.

"We had fighters overhead and they were credited with knocking down some Japanese planes. We'd also taken some of the dive bombers and put them on close-in patrols against the torpedo planes, figuring they could overtake them possibly and disrupt the attack. They were not successful and the torpedo planes pretty much got through. The *Lexington* took, I think, three bomb hits. One of the most spectacular was on the port gun gallery. A bomb exploded and immediately killed and burned gun crews in that area. The Marine gunners were burned right at their stations on the guns. That particular bomb started a fire down in the officers' country, the next deck below, and it killed a couple of stewards down in the pantry. We had another bomb in the after part of the [carrier's] island and another one pretty well aft.

"All of these bombs started fires which we figured we could control and put out. We learned a lot from this action—that ships of that kind had too much inflammable stuff aboard. The furniture in the admiral's cabin was wood and fabric and that burned. Paint all over the ship had an oil base and wherever we got a fire, the paint on the bulkhead burned. We learned that our fire-fighting equipment was not adequate, that we needed to redesign our hoses and hose nozzles."

In spite of its wounds from the three bombs and four torpedoes, the carrier achieved twenty-seven-knot speed. Through counterflooding, the ship returned to an even keel and like the *Yorktown* recovered its planes. The task force formed up, heading for Brisbane, Australia. "About 2:00 in the afternoon," recalled Stroop, "we heard a rather loud, submerged explosion. My first reaction was that a Japanese submarine had fired a torpedo with an influence fuse that had gone off under the hull. It seemed like that kind of explosion, deep down, probably beneath the ship. However, we found later it was not an enemy torpedo but leaking gasoline fuel, caused by the bomb hits that had collected in the elevator well. Some spark set off the fumes. The immediate effects were quite disastrous. Communication between the bridge and central station was lost. [The damage-control officer and much of his staff in the central station were wiped out in the blast.] Fires throughout the ship accelerated. Fire developed underneath the number-two elevator.

"Word came almost immediately that the engineering spaces were untenable and had to be abandoned. The engineer crews on the afternoon watch shut down the main engines. Here was the ship, dead in the water and, worst of all, there was no fire-fighting capability. From then on it was hopeless. We had a destroyer come along to try and get hoses over but this was absolutely hopeless. The fires began increasing in size and by 3:00 or

3:30 the decision was made to get the wounded and the air-group personnel off. They brought destroyers alongside and got these people off." Because the carrier lay dead in the water, the planes could not be launched.

"We continued to try to fight the fires but it became increasingly evident that the ship not only couldn't be saved, but that it was very dangerous to stay aboard much longer. Fire had gotten increasingly violent on the hangar deck. We were beginning to get explosions, apparently torpedo heads going off from storage. Finally, Admiral [Aubrey W.] Fitch, to ease the captain's problems and ease him into making the proper decision, said, 'Well, Fred, [Capt. Frederick Sherman] it's time to get the men off.' This was around 5:00 in the afternoon. The order was given to abandon ship. Everyone sensed this was the proper thing to do and they ought to do it in a hurry. We had lines over the side; the sea was calm; the water was warm; and it was still daylight. The men starting going down over the side of these lines and being picked up by boats from other ships. We didn't have any of our own boats in the water. We lost about 150 people in this total action, many of whom were killed in the initial attacks and then from the internal explosion. I remained on the bridge with Admiral Fitch, his orderly, his chief of staff, the communications officer, and the flag lieutenant. We were probably the last to abandon ship except for the captain."

The small party with Stroop selected the port side, forward, as the best place to go over the side. As they walked toward that area across the flight deck, Stoop said they felt the heat from fires that raged just beneath them. Stroop remembered that even in this moment, protocol continued. "The admiral's Marine orderly was still with him and he walked across the flight deck with the orderly in an absolutely correct position, one step to the left and one to the rear, carrying the admiral's coat over his arm. The admiral was the only officer who arrived on the rescue ship with a jacket, just because the orderly had taken it with him. The Marine orderly also had kept all of the dispatches that were handed to the admiral during the action. When the admiral would read a dispatch, he'd hand it to the orderly who put them in his pocket. As flag secretary, my job had been, among other things, to keep the war diary that I wrote in longhand. Just before I left the bridge, I tore all the pertinent pages out of the diary, folded them up, and stuffed them in my pocket."

When they reached the rail, the sun was setting and all of the boats, heavily laden with survivors, had headed for the other ships. Stroop, who had not semaphored a message in fifteen years, wigwagged attention from a cruiser and requested a boat to pick up the admiral. "When the boat was quite close, we started getting ready to go down the lines. The admiral's orderly tried to insist that the admiral go first. He was still very proper and finally the admiral, a little annoyed, ordered the orderly to go. The admiral wanted to be the last to leave the flight deck."

The rescuers had hardly brought Fitch, Stroop, and company to the *Minneapolis* before an enormous explosion shattered the blazing hulk of the *Lexington*, sending tongues of flame the height of the mast. "We had probably fifty aircraft parked, tied down in the launching area of the flight deck. Many of these were loaded with ammunition in their fixed guns, and with fuel in their tanks they made a spectacular fire. The ammunition cooked off and the night sky was filled with tracers coming off the deck of the *Lexington* as well as the fire engulfing the entire bridge area."

The task force steamed away and a destroyer stayed behind to sink the flattop. The tally for the Battle of the Coral Sea indicated a win for the Nipponese. They lost fewer ships than the United States. But the invaders of Port Moresby backed off, reducing the menace to Australia. Encounters like these and other operations seriously attrited their experienced air crews.

Barely a month later, the two adversaries squared off for an even more critical bout, the Battle of Midway. The Americans possessed one striking advantage, intelligence on the enemy's movements. A team of expert cryptanalysts and radio operators working together not only broke the highly complicated Japanese naval codes but refined the work sufficiently to recognize the enemy ships from which messages emanated. (This was an entirely separate activity from cracking the Japanese diplomatic code known as "Purple.")

Eager to deliver a knockout blow before the Americans could recover, Adm. Isoroku Yamamoto, architect of the 7 December assault, had plotted an invasion of Midway that would allow the Imperial Navy to sweep the ocean clean of Allied vessels and might provide an opportunity to seize even Hawaii. The strategy envisioned landings upon the Aleutians, which pointed a protective arc toward Midway. The atoll had also provided a base for operations that ranged from the Doolittle raid to penetrations of U.S. ships into the Coral Sea. Some Japanese leaders considered the proposal too ambitious and preferred consolidation of earlier gains. Yamamoto threatened to resign unless his plan was accepted and associates acquiesced.

A mighty fleet of warships and troop transports assembled and sailed toward the target, designated in coded messages as "AF." Again, the Japanese believed their destination would come as a surprise. Hypo, the U.S. code-breaking operation, divined the movement and the intelligence experts interpreted the purpose of the armada. To confirm the reading, U.S. intelligence expert, Comdr. Joseph Rochefort manufactured a sting. He arranged for a message in the clear from Midway reporting that its water-distillation system had malfunctioned and a water shortage had developed. Within forty-eight hours, the Americans recorded a Japanese transcription advising that AF had water problems.

During the last week of May, Hypo produced another vital intercept, a precise account of the order of battle for the enemy fleet now bearing down on Midway. Marine ground and air units crowded onto the island to ward off landings. Army B-17s shared airstrips with Marine fighters and dive bombers. Barbed wire ringed every possible point of entry. But the principal first line of defense lay with the seagoing Navy.

Jimmy Thach and his fighter squadron landed aboard the patched-up *Yorktown* when it was 50 to 100 miles out of Pearl Harbor on its way to join the task groups that included the carriers *Enterprise* and *Hornet*. When he took off from Hawaii, Thach knew only of an impending big fight in the Pacific. Once aboard the *Yorktown*, he listened to a complete briefing on the opposition. Thach was reassured after a visit with his engineering chief who promised all planes would be ready. Leaders of the dive-bomber and the torpedo squadrons, none more senior than a lieutenant, agreed with Thach that he could only send a portion of his fighters [the bulk would remain behind to protect the *Yorktown*] to escort the torpedo planes. He explained, "If you had enough, you would stack your fighters up to and including the dive bombers. The torpedo planes were old firetraps that were so slow and awkward and no self-sealing tanks. They needed protection more than anyone else, so that governed our decision in this case."

Thach faced high noon off Midway with considerable trepidation. "I was very concerned about whether the torpedo planes could get in or not. I knew that if the Japanese were together in one formation and had a combat air patrol of defending fighters from all the carriers we would be outnumbered. We were also quite concerned that the Zero could outperform us in every way. We had one advantage in that we thought we could shoot better and had better guns. But if you don't get a *chance* to shoot, better guns matter little." He was disturbed that only six fighters could make the mission; violating the principle of the weave which was predicated on sets of fours. Because the Americans divided their forces into two groups, Task Force 16 under Spruance, and Task Force 17 commanded by Adm. Frank Jack Fletcher, a gap of more than twenty-five miles separated the *Yorktown*, with TF 17, from the *Enterprise* and *Hornet*, with TF 16. The distance between the flattops reduced opportunities for a mutual-protection fighter shield.

On 3 June, the Japanese took the first step toward implementing their plan. The bombs fell not at Midway but at Dutch Harbor in the Aleutians. The purpose was to defang any American air power there and influence the U.S. to spread its resources even more thinly. Carrier-based bombers and fighters blasted several installations, destroyed a couple of Navy Catalina PBY patrol planes and killed about twenty-five men. A scattering of soldiers then landed on the remote tundra of Kiska and Attu. Japanese intelligence vastly overestimated the U.S. military forces manning the inhospitable terrain. Kiska's "defenders" amounted to a handful of unarmed weather specialists and Attu had no military components. Strategically, the operation amounted to a waste of effort. The occupation posed no menace to Alaska nor did it divert American attention.

On that same day, the pilot of one of the PBYs that shared the long-range over-the-ocean searches with B-17s saw flyspecks on the horizon. It was the first sighting of the foe. At that distance, the only weapons immediately available to attack were the Flying Fortresses. They sallied forth. Nine B-17Es discovered a section of the enemy fleet. Armed with 600-pound bombs, the Americans dropped their ordnance from high altitude while antiaircraft gunners retaliated with great enthusiasm. Although the Air Corps announced a number of hits, it was a draw; neither side landed a punch. A slapdash scheme equipped some PBYs with torpedoes for a night run at transports. The untried, hastily improvised operation actually scored a hit on an oiler but the remarkable feat would be dwarfed by the immense scale of battle that began 4 June.

On that morning, from the main body of Yamamoto's force, a first wave of 108 bombers and fighter roared off the carriers to smash Midway. A far lesser number of Marine fighter pilots with inferior aircraft—Wildcats and Brewster Buffalos—hung about the ready shack prepared to intercept them while antiaircraft crews manned their guns and scanned the skies. Shortly before 6:00 A.M., the puny Marine outfit scrambled its obsolete interceptors against the oncoming flights. They were no match for the attackers. Of the twenty-six men who met the enemy, fourteen died and several others were wounded. In full view of the furious defenders, the foe machine gunned to death a helpless American who had bailed out. However valiant the U.S. fliers, their achievements seemed modest. They and antiaircraft knocked down perhaps ten or twelve enemy planes and damaged more than thirty. However, the bombers inflicted only moderate damage, all of it repairable. The Japanese leader of the assault dispatched a message back to the commander of the air fleet that submission of Midway required another attack wave.

Having absorbed the opening blow, the Americans sought to counterpunch. The first effort involved flights from Midway by the latest version of a torpedo plane, the TBF Avenger, plus dive bombers and twin-engine medium-bomber B-26 Martin Marauders. None of these achieved any successes and most were shot down or badly mauled by Japanese fighters and antiaircraft. Almost as futile, B-17s struck at the fleet and missed.

Even as the vast array of Imperial Navy ships bobbed, weaved, and fended off the attacks while recovering their planes from the first Midway wave, the Japanese commanders suddenly became aware of American carriers within striking distance. They vacillated whether to prepare for another whack at the island or to take on the opposing fleet. They also had to factor in how much cover they would need for their own vessels. Protection for the Japanese flattops would lessen the escort for any assault upon Midway. And although the defenders of the atoll greatly overestimated their results against the first wave, they had significantly reduced the total resources available to the Nipponese.

Intercepts of transmissions between enemy planes and carriers indicated to the Midway eavesdroppers the course and rough location of the oncoming ships. At sea Task Force 16 had closed to within 100 miles. Admiral Spruance, not an aviation expert, after consultation with his chief of staff, an experienced airman, realized if he signaled his planes to attack at this point they had a magnificent opportunity to strike before the enemy could get his aircraft aloft. The catch was the Devastator torpedo bombers operated at a maximum combat range of 175 miles. They could not expect to make a round trip. Fully aware of the grim consequences, Spruance ordered a coordinated attack of the TBDs, dive bombers, and fighters. Just before 8:00 A.M. the catapults on the *Enterprise* and Hornet began to shoot their squadrons from the decks. A total of 116 aircraft set out for the quarry.

Glitches in communications of information from Midway-based scouting planes and an American submarine trailing the enemy force almost derailed the entire venture. Some twenty planes from the *Hornet* never located the target and could only return to the flattop. But one squadron, VT-8 from the *Hornet*, followed an unerring track right to the heart of the Japanese fleet with three carriers. At this early stage of the war many of those on the mission, like Ens. George H. Gay, while schooled in theory had little practice or experience in their craft. When he took off that morning it was the first time he had ever borne a torpedo in his plane. Many of his companions were equally unversed, although their leader, Lt. Comdr. John C. Waldron, had done his best to school them through chalk talks and lectures. In the ready room as they were about to leave, Waldron, the only Annapolis graduate in the squadron, handed his men a mimeographed plan of attack to which he appended a brief message.

"Just a word to let you know that I feel we are all ready. We have had a very short time to train and we have worked under the most severe difficulties. But we have truly done the best humanly possible. I actually believe that under these conditions we are the best in the world. My greatest hope is that we encounter a favorable tactical situation, but if we don't and the worst comes to the worst, I want each of us to do his utmost to destroy our enemies. If there is only one plane left to make a final run-in, I want that man to go in and get a hit. May God be with us all. Good luck, happy landings, and give 'em hell."

Unfortunately for VT-8, the plan to catch the Japanese with their planes down failed. Aware of their approach, a flock of fighters lurked in the clouds. Gay thought at least thirty-five Zeros jumped the doomed squadron even before the antiaircraft guns opened up. The fighters slaughtered most of the Devastators before they could unleash their torpedoes. Two of the ships hit the water before Gay saw Waldon's plane flame up. Gay remembered seeing him stand up, trying to jump, but he crashed into the sea. Making a run toward a carrier, Gay glimpsed two others from his squadron but suddenly they, too, disappeared. Through his intercom he heard his radioman, Bob Huntington, murmur, "They got me." When Gay swiveled his head for a quick look back, he saw the radioman's head lifelessly lolling against the cockpit. Something stabbed the pilot's upper left arm. A hole appeared in his jacket sleeve. With his right hand he ripped the sleeve, removed a machine-gun bullet from the wound. Injured further by shrapnel, he guided his stricken plane by holding the stick between his knees.

Some 800 yards from the enemy carrier *Soryu* he discharged his torpedo. Gay thought an explosion followed but in fact the tin fish passed harmlessly by the carrier. Pulling up, Gay flew down the length of the ship, and performed a flip turn at the fantail as the *Soryu* abruptly reversed course. Passing over the bridge, Gay said he "could see the little Jap captain up there jumping up and down, raising Hell." At this point a quintet of Zeros fell upon him, shooting out his controls and ailerons. The Devastator plowed into the ocean, a wing tore off, and the fuselage sank, but not before Gay clambered out with a rubber life raft and seat cushion.

In the water, Gay artfully tried to conceal himself from the Japanese sailors by ducking beneath his black rubber seat cushion. Several spotted him but they forgot his presence as another bunch of American torpedo planes now menaced their vessels. Again, the slow-moving TBDs succumbed to the Zeros and antiaircraft fire; only four of fourteen escaped the withering fire and returned to the *Enterprise*. The squadron failed to damage a single ship and the enemy fleet steamed on, intent upon destruction of the U.S. task forces.

The *Yorktown* dispatched its torpedo planes commanded by Lance "Lem" Massey, with six puny fighters under Jimmy Thach, about forty minutes after Task Force 16 commenced its operations. Thach recalled, "I told the people who were going on the attack that nobody was going to be a lone wolf, because lone wolves don't live very long. They had to stick together because that was the best way to survive and protect the torpedo planes. I reminded them of the tricks we heard played on some people. A Japanese fighter would pose in a position a little below where it looked like you could easily go out and shoot him, giving you this so-called advantage but his friends were waiting topside to come down and pick you off if you pulled out alone.

"It was a beautiful day. There were little puffy clouds up around 1,000 to 1,500 feet that sometimes would get a little thicker and other times they'd open up and be very scattered. I could see ships through the breaks in the little puffy clouds. We had just begun to approach about ten miles from the outer screen of this large force. Several colored antiaircraft bursts [exploded] in our direction, one red and another orange, and then no more. I wondered why they'd be shooting at us because we weren't nearly in range. We soon found out we'd been sighted from the surface screen and they were alerting the combat air patrol. A very short time after these bursts, before we got anywhere near antiaircraft range, these Zero fighters came down on us. We'd been trained to count things at a glance and I figured there were twenty.

"The first thing that happened was that [Ens. Ed] Basset's plane was burning. He was shot down right away. I was surprised they put so many Zeros on my six fighters. I had expected they would go for the torpedo planes first. But then I saw they had a second large group that were now streaming in right past us and into the poor torpedo planes. Several Zeros came in on a head-on attack on the torpedo planes and burned Lem Massey's plane right away. It just exploded in flames. Beautifully timed, another group came in on the side against the torpedo planes. I had to admire these people; they were plenty good. This was their first team and they were pros. It was the same team that hit Pearl Harbor. [Meanwhile] a number were coming down on our fighters, the air was just like a beehive. It didn't look like my weave was working, but then it began to. I got a good shot at two of them and burned them. One of them had made a pass at my wingman, pulled out and then came back. I got a head-on shot at him and just about the time I saw this guy coming, Ram Dibb, my wingman said, 'There's a Zero on my tail.' He was about forty-five degrees beginning to follow him around which gave me the head-on approach. I was really angry because this poor wingman who'd never been in combat before, very little gunnery training, the first time aboard a carrier and a Zero about to chew him to pieces. I probably should have ducked under this Zero but I lost my temper a little and decided to keep my fire going into him and he's going to pull out, which he did. He missed me by a few feet and I saw flames coming out of the bottom of his airplane. This is like playing 'chicken' with two automobiles on the highway headed for each other.

"They kept coming in and more torpedo planes were falling, but so were some Zeros, so we thought at least we're keeping a lot of them engaged. The torpedo planes had split for an 'Anvil Attack.' They'd break up and spread out on a line on each side of the target so that they could have torpedo planes coming in from various points. If the ship turns he's left a broadside shot for several torpedoes and he can only comb one [head directly for the missile and barely avoid it].

"I kept counting the number of airplanes that I knew I'd gotten in flames going down. You couldn't wait for them to splash but if it was real red flames, you knew he'd had it. I had this little knee pad and I would mark down every time I shot one that I knew was going. Then I realized this was sort of foolish. Why was I making marks on my knee pad when the knee pad wasn't coming back. I was utterly convinced that none of us were coming back because there were still so many of these Zeros and they'd already gotten one. I couldn't see Tom Cheek and Dan Sheedy anymore. There were just two others I could see of my own, Macomber, Ram Dibb, and me. Pure logic would convince anyone that with their superior performance, and the number of Zeros they were throwing into the fight, we could not possibly survive. It takes a second or two to look down to your knee pad and make this mark— a waste of time. I said, talking to myself, 'if they're going to get us all, we're going to take a lot of them with us.'

"We kept working this weave and it seemed to work better and better. I haven't the slightest idea how many Zeros I shot down. I just can't remember and I don't suppose it makes too much difference. It only shows that I was absolutely convinced that nobody could get out of there, that we weren't coming back and neither were any of the torpedo planes. Then the attacks began to slack off. Whether they were spreading out and working more on the torpedo planes that were unprotected, I don't know. I saw three or four of them that got in and made an attack. I believe at least one torpedo hit. All the records, the Japanese and [Naval historian] Sam Morison's book, said none hit. I'm not sure that people aboard a ship that is repeatedly hit about the same time by dive bombers really know whether they got hit by a torpedo or it was one of the bombs. I was aboard the *Saratoga* when she was torpedoed and the *Yorktown* when she was bombed and I couldn't tell the difference.

"I was looking at a Jap fighter when I saw this glint in the sun. It just looked like a beautiful silver waterfall, these dive bombers [American] coming down. I've never seen such superb dive-bombing. It looked to me like almost every bomb hit. Of course there were some very near misses. There weren't any wild ones. Explosions were occurring in the carriers and about that time the Zeros slacked off even more."

As the enemy fighter cover appeared to fade, Thach and his flight escorted several of the battered torpedo planes away from the combat zone. Then, upon conclusion of the dive-bomb attack, he hung around. "A single Zero appeared flying slowly below and to one side of us. I looked up toward the sun and sure enough there were his teammates poised like hawks waiting for one of us to take the bait! We didn't. I saw three carriers burning furiously before I left."

Of the forty-one Devastators that lumbered off the Americans carriers on 4 June, only four battered ones staggered back to their nests. George Gay, plucked from the sea several days later, was the only survivor from his entire VT-8 Squadron. "Those pilots were all my very close friends, especially Lem Massey," mourned Thach. "I felt pretty bad, just sort of hopeless. I felt like we hadn't done enough, that if they didn't get any hits, this whole business of torpedo planes going in at all was a mistake. But thinking about it since, you couldn't fail to send them since this was a classic, coordinated attack with torpedo planes going in low and the dive bombers coming in high, although it is usually better if the dive bombers hit first and the torpedo planes can get in better among the bombs bursting."

The SBD Dauntless dive bombers from the *Enterprise* and the *Lexington* fell upon the flattops at a most opportune time. Aboard the Japanese carriers crews were busily preparing planes for the second wave attack on Midway, while the air cover, still at low altitude because of engaging the torpedo bombers, were in no position to intercept. A 500-pounder struck the carrier *Kaga* squarely on the flight deck amidst the aircraft, loaded with fuel and ordnance. An instant inferno erupted with most of the sailors below trapped. Probably already fatally wounded, the *Kaga* rocked from three more hits of near-equal magnitude.

On the *Akagi* the first Zero bound for Midway barely lifted off the deck before the first of several 1,000-pounders whistled down from the plunging SPDs. As in the case of its sister ship, the flight deck of the *Akagi* was jammed with fully armed and fueled planes. A holocaust ignited among them and magnified several times over the destructive power of the American bombs. The explosions blew 200 men overboard as its crew scrambled for lifeboats.

A third Japanese carrier, *Soryu*, drew the attention of the *Yorktown*'s dive bombers. Lieutenant (jg) Paul Holmberg, first in line, dove into the maelstrom of antiaircraft fire to within 200 feet before he pulled up. His daring was rewarded as an explosion ripped up the deck, blasting an airplane in the midst of a takeoff into the sea. Five hits and three near misses transformed a puissant warship into a blazing wreck. Elated at their successes, the crews of the TSBDs straggled back in search of their carriers. Aside from several that were shot down, a number of the Dauntlesses ran out of fuel and ditched. Other ships picked up most of the airmen.

Only one Japanese carrier, *Hiryu* remained afloat. Aware of the destruction of its three sisters, *Hiryu* stolidly followed the orders, "Attack the enemy carriers." Because no torpedo planes were ready, only dive bombers and fighters could go. The *Yorktown* radar alerted the Americans to the oncoming enemy. A flight of twelve Grumman Wildcats tangled with the Japanese, scoring some knockdowns, but still the bombers continued their run.

More of the attackers splashed into the sea from aerial combat or antiaircraft shells but one released its explosive just before the American gunners smashed it into three pieces. The bomb struck on the flight deck, killing or wounding a number of men and curtailing antiaircraft. A pack of planes pursued the *Yorktown* until they scored two more hits. Immediate preventive measures were taken upon word of the imminent attack, and the well-trained, damage-control parties enabled the *Yorktown* to resume a respectable speed and remain operational.

Undeterred by losses incurred, the Imperial Navy directed a second strike from *Hiryu* at the American carriers. It seemed to have become as much a matter of pride as of strategy for the successive engagements had sharply trimmed the quality available. Even planes already damaged had to be used while air crews were both weary and mentally stressed. Nevertheless, aware of the presence of the *Enterprise* and the *Hornet*, the Japanese commander instructed his air commanders to seek them out as well as the already-wounded *Yorktown*.

The hunters soon focused on their nearest target, the *Yorktown*. Again, radar, a device not possessed by the Japanese, signaled the approach of unwelcome visitors. On this occasion, the assault included ten torpedo planes accompanied by a half-dozen Zeros. A force of Wildcats that outnumbered the Japanese fighters, shot down three of them and several torpedo planes. As the torpedo planes started their runs a few yards above the surface of the water, American cruisers trained their big guns on the sea ahead of the aircraft, hoping to create waterspouts that might knock them out. Still, five broke through the cordon and dropped their missiles. The *Yorktown* evaded a pair, but two smashed into her side. Water flooded portions of the ship not only shutting down power but producing such a severe list that the flight deck canted down until one side almost touched the ocean. A protective screen of destroyers formed around the crippled ship. In a desperate effort to preserve the vessel a skeleton crew remained aboard.

Meanwhile, scouts advised the two task forces the location of the *Hiryu*. Just about everything that could fly took off. Not realizing they had hit the *Yorktown* on both attacks, instead of two separate carriers, the Japanese did not expect such a heavy assault. Dive bombers from the *Enterprise* demolished *Hiryu*, starting fires that raged from bow to stern.

In terms of carrier warfare, 4 June stood as a landmark U.S. victory. However, despite the loss of airpower, the enemy fleet still outnumbered and outgunned the Americans. The land-based defenses of Midway might well have folded under an invasion. During the night of 4–5 June, the fleets jockeyed for position. The weaker Americans strove to avoid any confrontation against the foe who was not only stronger but also skillful at night operations. The Japanese sought to smoke out the Americans but Spruance and Fletcher refused to snap at any bait.

During the following few days, the loss by the Japanese of all their carriers enabled the Americans to pummel other vessels with aircraft from flattops, supplemented by the Army and Marine ground-based units on Midway. They victimized enemy destroyers and cruisers. However, a Japanese sub sneaked through the screen surrounding the barely moving *Yorktown*. One torpedo exploded the destroyer *Hammann* amidships while two others that slid beneath the *Hammann* found their mark on the *Yorktown*. The destroyer broke in half and quickly disappeared beneath the sea. Although sailors worked frantically to keep the shattered carrier afloat the damage was too great. Some eighteen hours after the last injury it sank.

The Battle of Midway ended as the Japanese retreated towards the home island. Their official toll listed four carriers and a heavy cruiser sunk, heavy damage to another cruiser and a pair of destroyers. More than 332 aircraft were destroyed and the casualties in manpower, including many veteran proficient pilots added up to 2,500. The U.S. losses were the *Yorktown* and *Hammann*, 147 planes, and 307 men. The enemy did extensive damage to Midway installations, and in the Alaskan waters lesser harm to Dutch Harbor, occupying Kiska and Attu, uncontested.

It was the first great victory for the Americans in the war. The Japanese would never again venture that far east. Beyond the deaths of comrades, the one sour note for the Navy lay in the unwarranted credit given to the Army Air Corps. In fact, although the bombers from Midway air strips tried on four separate occasions to strike the ships from various levels of altitude, and despite their claims to the contrary, the Army airmen scored only minor hits.

12
American Airpower Concepts

Within twenty-four hours after the first bombs from carrier-based Japanese airplanes exploded at Pearl Harbor, the United States had entered a world-wide war in which the flying machine, largely a bit player previously, assumed an ever larger role. But, on 7 December 1941, what would become the single, largest component of the American aerial arms, the Eighth Air Force that carried the heaviest portion of war in the skies to Germany, did not even exist on paper. For that matter, the entire U.S. Air Force hardly deserved the name, so lacking was it in combat aircraft both in terms of numbers and performance capability against what the enemy mustered as well as in qualified airmen.

The inadequacies of U.S. airpower at the start of the war were due to lacks of imagination and money. As late as 1939, a Naval War College instruction to students dismissed, "the idea that aviation alone can achieve decisive results against well-organized military or naval forces," a position refuted three years later at Midway. Because of poor intelligence and racial chauvinism, military leaders also could not believe that the Japanese might produce airplanes and pilots of quality. Few believed in the need to build better torpedo planes or bombers. At the same time, air power proponents who urged programs for research and development in the field encountered stiff budgetary restrictions.

Brigadier General Billy Mitchell, during the 1920s, was driven from the service because of his outspoken faith in the concept of strategic bombing as the key to modern war. But as time passed U.S. airmen accepted his ideas and those of others who believed airplanes could blast a foe's ability to manufacture war goods, destroy means to distribute the tools of combat, and cripple armies. That led them to put their appropriations into bombers that they believed could fly higher and faster than enemy inter-ceptors. They were further inspired by the introduction of the Norden bombsight, a device that promised great accuracy for daylight raids. Accordingly, the Army downplayed the importance of what were known as pursuit planes, interceptors, or fighters because they seemed to lack offen-sive capability against the targets predicated in strategic bombing.

Only with the advent of war in Europe did the American hierarchy begin to revise its ideas. Missions to England convinced airmen that enemy interceptors could threaten their prime weapons, the four-engine bombers. The existing U.S. fighters could not compete with the best of Germany and Japan. Aircraft bombing from high altitudes posed minimal threat to moving targets like ships, a fact heavily underscored during the first year of war against the Japanese. Conditions mandated new machines, improvements on older ones, new weaponry, and new tactics.

With the British appealing for, if not demanding American airpower to add to their efforts against the Axis powers, Lt. Gen. Henry (Hap) Arnold, as head of the Army Air Corps secured approval from the War Department to activate an air force as part of U.S. Air Force in the British Isles. He chose Maj. Gen. Carl Spaatz, a World War I combat pilot, respected tactician, strategist, and administrator to head the outfit and nominated Brig. Gen. Ira Eaker, a Spaatz pal, to run the bomber command. Even before the Spaatz and Eaker team could begin to mobilize the airplanes to carry out the task, they encountered fierce opposition from the brass in charge of all U.S. Army efforts in England. The traditional resistance of ground commanders to grant any autonomy to the air forces succumbed only through the intervention of Chief of Staff George C. Marshall of the Army. The vehicle tapped for Spaatz and Eaker was the Eighth Air Force, activated in January 1942.

While the newly formed outfit initially consisted of a medium bombardment group, two pursuit groups (the designations of fighters or interceptors were not yet in vogue), and auxiliary units, other priorities reduced the Mighty Eighth to a bare skeletal form as the Japanese advanced in the Pacific. The original bomber group committed to the Eighth joined Lt. Col. James Doolittle to train for his mission against Tokyo. Other aircraft allotted the Eighth were siphoned away to participate in the critical anti-submarine warfare off the U.S. coast and for other responsibilities.

Ira Eaker took up station in England, in February 1942, as the head of the Eighth Bomber Command. But the parent organization, as such, was not in residence until 11 May 1942, when the first contingent of thirty-nine officers and 384 enlisted men set foot in the United Kingdom. Eaker, at the time, all too aware of what little of material strength he brought with him, rose to speak to an assemblage of RAF guests at an early June ceremony at the newly opened High Wycombe headquarters. "We don't do much talking until we've done more fighting. We hope that when we leave you'll be glad we came. Thank you."

Eaker's twenty-three words could hardly offend the host country as they implicitly recognized that six months after the declaration of war, the American contribution to the air war effort in Europe had been only money and goods, while British fliers continued to pay a bloody price. But while the British approved the gracious note, furious discord marked the opinions and policies of the two Allies even before they joined forces to fight.

A tour with the U.S. military mission during the Battle of Britain, opened Carl Spaatz's eyes to some of the weaknesses of the Air Corps. He quickly realized that the effectiveness of the Briitsh radar system, crude as it was, detected aircraft long before they could be seen. He understood that the protection of invisibility through distance, darkness, or cloud cover no longer pertained. His talks with RAF pilots and commanders revealed that the weakness of the German bombers that were restricted in distance, were too lightly armed to defend themselves, flew too low, and maintained level flight, created a recipe for disaster. Because enemy fighters appeared able to reach the altitude of the B-17 and B-24, the heavyweights needed rear firepower to ward off attacks from behind and armor plate to shield personnel and vital organs of the aircraft. He also accepted that escort fighters would be desirable, but the solution of how to load enough fuel on the smaller aircraft without destroying maneuverability and speed remained a problem. In contrast to earlier attitudes, the bomber specialists would welcome the P-47s and P-51s to the arsenal.

The American's approach met opposition from their allies. The RAF had seen their own fighters smash German bombers during daylight forays. They remembered, too, the loss of fifteen two-engine Vickers Wellingtons from a total of twenty-four during an early daytime raid against Germans; and noting a similar British attack on Augsburg, in which seven out of twelve Lancaster heavyweights went down, the Royal Air Force insisted that only under the shroud of darkness could strategic bombing successfully hammer the enemy. In the spring of 1941, having weathered the Battle of Britain, and now intent on carrying the death and destruction to the enemy, the British tested about twenty Forts delivered under Lend-Lease to the RAF. After training and some modifications to incorporate the local control system, a trio of Forts headed for Wilhelmshaven on 8 July. The raid was a fiasco; the bombs, dropped from 30,000 feet, missed the target, and the machine guns froze up when German fighters attacked. Subsequent missions against shipping and other objectives produced dismal results, almost half the sorties aborted, only a couple of planes reached primary targets; eight of the twenty B-17s were lost or grounded for repairs. Not a single enemy fighter had been knocked down.

British enthusiasm for the B-17 and daylight operation vanished. The Americans noted their allies insisted on operating at well over 30,000 feet, excessive even for the high-altitude bomber, leading to overloads on the oxygen systems, a freeze-up of weapons, reduction in air speed, thus lessening the ability to defend against enemy fighters. Finally, the RAF relied on the Sperry bombsight, considered quite inferior to the Norden. But, unconvinced by the arguments of the Americans, when B-24s were delivered, the RAF shunted them away from strategic-bomb operations and into antisubmarine patrols. Spaatz and his associates remained committed to their notion of daylight bombing from high altitudes. Only the U.S. possessed the Norden sight which the strategists believed guaranteed effective delivery.

The failure to convert the British to the potential of the heavy bombers for their designed purpose dogged Ira Eaker from the moment of his arrival to command U.S. forces. Not only did the ally clamor for immediate deeds by the Americans but it insisted that the proposed approach would be a disaster. Not too subtly the Brits suggested that all American aircraft come under RAF control. No one in America, certainly not Chief of Staff George C. Marshall, or Hap Arnold as boss of the Air Corps could stomach that. Spaatz and Eaker would have to prove to the British that daylight, precision bombing could work.

The Allied commanders agreed, however, on the need for a strategic-bombing campaign. Aerial assaults on production and transportation centers, combined with a blockade, economic pressure upon neutrals, hit-and-run operations by commandos, sabotage by people in occupied lands, and the murderous war between the Soviets and Germans, could bleed the Axis powers. The strategy aimed to weaken the enemy and provide prime conditions for a frontal assault by ground troops in the West. The RAF publicly wondered if intensive bombing might obviate any need to invade the Continent.

The British policy makers, aware that night attacks sacrificed precision, introduced the notion of "area" bombing. Destruction in the vicinity of a strategic site, while perhaps not inflicting all the desired damage on the target, would destroy the surrounding neighborhood, which included workers. Psychological as well as physical injury would result; the ideas of Giulio Douhet, a 1920s advocate of total war, rendered real. The approach dictated the design of British aircraft; bombers with great range, oversize loads, and, because of the presumed protection by darkness against opposition, less armament and fewer crewmen. Because of their nocturnal rounds, the Lancasters and Stirlings sallied forth without fighter escort; indeed the British made no effort to extend the short range of the otherwise-superb Spitfire. At the end of May and the beginning of June 1942, just before the first Eighth Air Force elements arrived, the RAF scrounged aircraft from training and noncombat commands to mount Operation Millennium, the first thousand-plane saturation raid upon Cologne. More than two-thirds of the attackers consisted of two-engine planes with no margin for error if they were to return to base. The bombs killed 469, wounded more than 5,000, and destroyed 45,000 homes. Subsequently, similar assaults blasted Bremen and the Ruhr with widespread havoc but relatively little effect on the German war effort, other than to stimulate production of fighters. From a propaganda viewpoint, however, the attacks seriously wounded *Luftwaffe* chief Hermann Goering who had boasted in 1939, "My name is not Goering if any enemy aircraft is ever seen over Germany, you can call me Meyer." [An antisemitic reference.]

The U.S. airmen predicated their faith in the daylight approach on the ability of the Norden sight to pinpoint targets and on the ability of the Forts and Liberators to fly high enough and fast enough to defeat efforts to stop them. Their theorists denigrated area bombing as a wasteful dispersion of resources. The British convened the Butt Committee, charged with an investigation of the effectiveness of the RAF by the War Cabinet Secretariat. It statistically analyzed night bombing through the use of photography. The results were discouraging. The averages indicated only one of three attacking aircraft over Europe came within five miles of the target, with the best achievements registered for France but a severe drop to one in ten for areas like the German Ruhr. Some of the nighttime missions struck the wrong cities or dummy versions erected by the Germans in empty fields. To enhance accuracy British scientists developed a pair of radar-based systems: Gee, and then H2S, both of which aided navigators to locate targets. Gee was supposed to locate an airplane precisely enough to bomb within a tenth of a mile of the target. In practice it was less accurate; its range was limited, and over German territory the enemy successfully jammed it. H2S used its beams to indicate ground features, giving airmen a rough picture of the territory below with readings that distinguished water, open fields, and built-up areas. Both of these tools would be adopted by the U.S. airmen operating from the United Kingdom.

The Americans argued that precision bombing could take out key elements in the enemy war effort, rendering him weak if not helpless, more quickly than area bombing could. The Air Corps stance also reflected reluctance to the inevitable slaughter of noncombatants by area bombing. Even the Japanese at Pearl Harbor had concentrated on military targets. Earlier, however, Italian airmen bombed and strafed Ethiopian citizens in 1935, and the Germans struck at the town of Guernica in Spain while supporting the rebels under Gen. Francisco Franco. The *Luftwaffe* then hurled death and destruction upon Polish cities before finally striking at Coventry and London. The actions provoked outrage about such barbarism. As the RAF commenced its nighttime area bombing that wreaked havoc among civilians, the Allies muted the talk about victims, but initially, Americans officials could argue their approach as more humane. As World

War II stretched over the years, daylight bombing eventually spared relatively few civilians in Europe, and when B-29s began massive raids on the Japanese home islands the net effect was the same as the area bombing practiced by the British.

Serious weaknesses afflicted the initial American plan. The exaggerated and legendary belief that the Norden bombsight was accurate enough to drop a bomb in a pickle barrel not only overstated the capacity of the instrument but it included no recognition of what happened under combat conditions with exploding antiaircraft shells and enemy fighters, guns and cannons blazing, careening through bomber formations. Furthermore, the Messerschmitts and Focke-Wulfs could reach altitudes above those favored by a B-17 or B-24, and flew hundreds of miles faster than any bomber. Spaatz, having witnessed the Battle of Britain, undoubtedly realized the potential for interception but he hoped that extra armor and greater firepower would rebalance the equation in favor of the Air Corps. He also counted on the newer American fighters that might provide more extended escort service than what previously existed.

Jim Goodson, Bill Dunn, and the other U.S. volunteers, as members of the RAF, did not qualify as Americans carrying the Stars and Stripes into the air war. British officialdom and the local press forcefully criticized both the absence of U.S. forces and the American ideas. Implicit in the ongoing controversy were questions of command and control. Spaatz, Eaker, and Arnold all feared that if they converted themselves into warriors of the night, they would become subservient to the RAF's bomber chief, Sir Arthur "Bomber" Harris, thus surrendering the limited independence wrested from the U.S. Army hierarchy. Furthermore, the B-17s and B-24s would require substantial changes to adapt for a different kind of work. The engine exhausts for the Forts, for example, spurted flames, making the aircraft obvious to any night marauders or even ack-ack gunners. Crews also would need considerable retraining.

The initial reticence displayed by Eaker at that first luncheon did not mollify a growing impatience with the pace of the American combat effort. Winston Churchill constantly nagged U.S. leaders to put their planes in the air, their bombs on targets. It was not simply an attempt to relieve his forces from carrying the weight of the war. The British Empire, already shrunken by the Japanese in the Far East, was losing more ground in North Africa to the German *Afrika Korps*. There was genuine worry that Germans would shortly overwhelm the Soviet Union unless the Allies applied pressure that diverted the enemy and strengthened Red Army resolution. There was even talk of an invasion late in 1942 or early 1943, preposterous and most certainly doomed to a devastating loss in light of the British Army still recovering from its mauling at Dunkirk and the lack of trained, properly equipped U.S. troops. The fortunes of the United States were near bottom, with the Japanese having swept over the Philippines, Wake, Guam, and lands formerly held by Allies.

The first units that would fly against the European enemies under U.S. insignia were echelons from the 97th Bombardment Group, a B-17 outfit, and the 1st and 31st Fighter Groups with P-38s and P-39s, respectively. They expected to sail from New York early in June, arriving a few days after the combat aircraft, with their crews and pilots, ferried themselves across the Atlantic.

Everything bound for Europe suddenly appeared in jeopardy with the discovery of the Japanese fleet bearing down on Midway. Both the 1st Fighter Group and the 97th Bomb Group reversed course and tracked toward the West Coast, prepared to reinforce the defenders of Midway. The 31st Fighter Group, whose pilots were to have depended upon the 97th's B-17 navigators to lead them over the Atlantic, now boarded ships for England.

On the heels of the victory at Midway, the British, from Churchill on down, continued to press the Americans, including Maj. Gen. Dwight D. Eisenhower, who had assumed command of the European theater of operations, United States Army (ETOUSA), to do something. In North Africa, *Afrika Korps* commander Erwin Rommel threatened the Suez Canal, while across Egypt, the British and Australians barely hung on in front of Alexandria. On 2 July, the Nazi juggernaut smashed into Sevastopol, completing the conquest of the Crimea. German radio sneered at talk of an American airpower debut.

The Nazis seemed to have better intelligence than Washington. Hap Arnold, unfortunately, to placate the British Prime Minister, had told him on 30 May 1942, "We will be fighting with you on July 4th." At the moment he made his rash promise, Arnold believed the 97th would have trained for a month over England and be ready to commence operations. Eaker and Spaatz had precious little with which to work. When word reached Eaker, he reportedly remarked, "Someone must have confused the 4th of July with April Fools' Day."

To fulfill their boss's order, Spaatz and Eaker in desperation turned to the one unit actually on hand, the 15th Bombardment Squadron. It was not a heavy-bomber outfit. Far from it, the 15th, originally intended to employ night fighters, flew twin-engine Douglas A-20s, four-man light bombers that the British called Bostons. The aircraft used by the 15th actually belonged to the RAF and carried the British insignia. One crew from the unit, with Capt. Charles Kegelman as pilot, flying with the RAF 226 Squadron, had been, on 29 June, the first to bomb occupied Europe during a raid on a marshaling yard at Hazebrouck.

With the 15th was Bill Odell, a Chicago youth born in 1915, who entered the army under the Thomason Act, an officer program established at his college, Washington University in St. Louis. Odell and his fellow members of the 15th reached England in mid-May of 1942 and the crewmen were assigned to RAF outfits that flew Bostons. "These were front-line, operational units doing battle almost every day. Every day was packed with learning opportunities. Covered were the essentials to survival in combat; aircraft identification, communications procedures, ditching techniques, discussions of all phases of aircraft operation, and combat flying."

Another member of the 15th was Marshal Draper, a bombardier. "The spirit [of the first Americans in England] was willing but the supplies were meager. The German submarine campaign was in full swing and confusion reigned. I had an abbreviated course in the Royal Air Force navigation system and did a little practice bombing."

As 4 July approached, Odell kept his diary informed. On 2 July, while at Swanton he went off on another preparatory exercise "We're practicing for a 4th of July show somewhere over Germany [occupied Europe] We expect to make an American low-level attack on fighter airdromes during daylight. General Spaatz and Eaker arrived and Keg talked to them. They wanted us to put on a 'circus' without fighter escort. Just shows how much our brass hats know or how they value the cost of mens' lives." The July 4th event brought out Spaatz, Eaker, and Eisenhower who met the crews going on the sortie. They shook hands with everyone. "It was obvious they had been told it was not going to be a 'piece of cake.' Their faces were somber, if not grim. Then to dinner and the food did some good."

The planned U.S. Independence Day affair, endorsed by President Roosevelt as a highly appropriate date for actual entrance into the shooting war, met none of the concepts behind the Eighth Air Force. Instead of a huge armada of heavy bombers soaring far above the clouds, penetrating deep into enemy territory while relying on the precision of the Norden sight, a dozen Bostons, all of which belonged to the RAF, with six U.S. crews combined with an equal number of Britons, would raid four enemy airfields in Holland at low level. British bomber command had balked at a high-level excursion because the Spitfires ordinarily assigned to escort such raids were already committed to other operations. Civilian leaders may have relished the effort by the U.S. Air Corps, but the senior RAF people recognized the operation as more show biz than strategy.

Bombardier Draper recalled, "Our assigned target was De Kooy, a *Luftwaffe* base on the northern tip of Holland. The fight was led by an RAF pilot with Capt. Charles Kegelman and 2d Lt. F.A. Loehrle, both US pilots, flying the wings. I was the bombardier-navigator in Loehrle's plane. Just before takeoff, the RAF officer who normally flew in this plane, handed me a one-inch by two-inch piece of armor plate and a steel infantryman's hat and said, 'Be sure you put the plate under your feet and wear the hat.' I have been told that this practice was vigorously discouraged later because of the added weight in heavy bombers with a larger crew. Nevertheless it probably saved my life since I was the point man of our plane.

"The flight took off, formed up, and we headed east at a height of about fifty feet above the water toward Holland. About ten miles from the target we passed a couple of small boats that appeared to be fishing craft but were picket boats, called 'squealers' by the RAF, and whose function was to alert the shore-based antiaircraft defenses, as we soon discovered.

"A few moments later, we were approaching a seawall on the shore when heavy flak opened up. Tracers were going by and above the plane and on both sides of my head like flaming grapefruit. This kind of situation, like hanging, concentrates the mind wonderfully, and everything went into slow motion. I could not see why we weren't getting hit but we cleared the seawall and I felt the plane lift as we let the bombs go. We immediately turned left and came face to face with a flak battery. [The German word for antiaircraft was *Fliegerabwehrkanone* which U.S. fliers shortened to flak. The British usually used "ack-ack", a World War I term.] The four wing guns were firing but we were so close the fire was converging beyond the battery. I glanced at the air-speed indicator, which registered 285 mph, and suddenly realized the battery gunner was shooting directly at me. We were getting ripped right up the middle as we passed over, about two feet above the gunner's head. We were fifteen feet off the ground at this point. That was my last memory of the attack."

In his diary for 4 July, Odell scribbled, "Up at 5:15 and had a cup of coffee in the mess hall. Then to the operations room and turned in papers and got packet for combat flight (concentrated food, water purifier, compass, and French, Dutch, and German money). Had no trouble but was a bit anxious on the takeoff. After getting in the air, we settled down and flew right on the trees to the coast. When we went down on the water, felt a bit uneasy because there was a cloudless sky but no fighters appeared. Found land ahead and could spot the landmark of the lighthouse a long way off."

In the diary, Odell reports, "Swung over the edge of the coast even lower than the leader and stayed right on the grass. I opened the bomb doors, yelled to [bombardier Leslie] Birleson and then it started. I fired all the guns for all I was worth and Birly dropped the bombs. I saw the hangar but that wasn't my dish. I saw Germans running all over the place but I put most of my shots over their heads." Two gunners on RAF Bostons manned single, flexible machine guns from rear, upper, and lower positions. Affixed to the fuselage also were two pairs of .303-caliber machine guns located on the lower port and starboard sides of the ship. A pilot like Odell could fire all four in unison by depressing a single trigger on his control column.

As the raiders zoomed over the airfield, dumping bombs and spraying machine gun bullets, the defenders fired back. "Our bombs were okay," Odell noted, "but I thought we would crash any moment for I never flew so reckless in my life. The next moment we were flashing past the coast and out to sea—the water behind us boiling from the bullets dropping into it all around. I kicked and pulled and jerked from side to side. Didn't look at the air speed—was trying to miss the waves. Over the target we were doing 265 but shortly after I opened it up a bit.

"'Digger' [another pilot] claims he shot his guns into a formation of groups lined up for inspection. His bombs hit well before they should have. 'Elkie' was a bit behind but he got rid of his load. He got a broken radio antenna and a mashed-in wing edge. I picked up a hole just above the pilot's step and a badly knocked-up bomb door. We zigged and zagged until three miles out, then closed up waiting for fighters. None came. We reached the coast and were the first home.

"All came back except Loehrle, Lynn, and a Britisher (Henning). Loehrle was hit by a heavy shell and hit the ground right in the middle of the airdrome. 'He flew into a million pieces,' one of the rear gunners said. And I owed him one pound ten shillings. I feel like a thief! Lynn was following before the flight hit the target but never came away from it. His wife is to have a baby in November. He really wasn't cut out for this game. At breakfast he was salting his food, trying to hold the salt spoon steady, yet throwing salt all over his shoulders. I hope he didn't crash. Henning was shot down by an ME 109 that took off just ahead of him. He tried to get it but it turned, got behind him and set one motor on fire. He crashed into the sea. Keg got his right prop and nose section shot off by heavy stuff right over the target. His wing dropped, hit the ground and he managed to right it and come home on one motor."

While a gunner said he saw Loehrle's bomber crash onto the tarmac, Draper, the bombardier on the fallen A-20, said, "I woke up lying on my back on the bottom of the North Sea in about twenty feet of water, very confused about where I was or what I was doing there. I thought I was dead and kept waiting in the gray gloom for something to happen. Then I sat up and saw my breath bubbling up through the water and finally realized I was submerged.

"When I surfaced I was opposite a small beach under the seawall and with the tail of the A-20 protruding from the water, which was all that was visible of the plane. Various subsequent reports had us crashing in flames, or disintegrating, but I saw no smoke or signs of fire associated with the plane and no debris. However, for me to be vectored nearly sideways to the plane, which appeared pointed to the west, I must have been subjected to very powerful force.

"I swam ashore, walked a few feet from the water's edge, and sat down, overcome suddenly with an enormous fatigue. Somehow I had been taken right out of my parachute harness and flotation vest and my uniform was ripped to shreds. Also, I was bleeding from an assortment of places. A path led up from the beach to the seawall and I could see several soldiers at the top of the path but they made no effort to come down. So I sat and rested for a time. After a while, my mental tiles had clattered back into place, somewhat, and it occurred to me that I might be better off starting up the path than sitting on the beach bleeding like a stabbed hog. I got to my feet with some difficulty, trudged across the little beach and started up the rather steep path. To my astonishment, the soldiers came rushing down the path and grabbed me by the arms. They were mumbling 'minen,' 'minen' as if to excuse some perceived lack of hospitality in not coming to my aid. The beach had been mined, presumably by the Dutch before the Germans got there.

"The next thing I remember I was lying on a table in what appeared to be a first-aid room. The cast had changed from the *Wehrmacht* to three *Luftwaffe* types, one of whom was holding my eyelid up and looking at my eye with a little flashlight. He straightened up, turned off the flashlight and announced to the room at large, 'Shock.' Then he asked me, 'Have you lost many blood?' I corrected him, 'That's much blood. You mean much blood. I don't know.'

"I was still functioning in an offset mode. I did notice that my clothes had been removed and I could see my shoes lying on another table. The rubber heels had been torn off—shoe heels were a common hiding place for escape materials. I thought that must have been a big disappointment. I was already acquiring a *Kriegsgefangener* [POW in German; shortened to "kriegie" by those who were incarcerated] mind-set." In fact, Draper qualified as the very first U.S. Air Corps prisoner in Europe.

The 4 July event was celebrated in newspapers and Kegelman received a Distinguished Flying Cross. But, overall, the affair was a fiasco. The tactics had no relation to the concept of strategic bombing. The three Bostons shot down represented a 25 percent loss; an insupportable rate of casualties. The bodies of the other three men with Draper were recovered. Furthermore, most of the aircraft that made their way home needed considerable repairs from the shot and shell inflicted by flak gunners and enemy fighters. One researcher, George Pames, claims that Eisenhower was so dismayed he "never again permitted men of his command to engage in needless combat to satisfy American pride or produce media events for propaganda purposes."

13
Opening Offensives

The 15th Bomb Squadron's valiant but insignificant achievements only increased the pressure for the debut of the four-engine, heavyweight bombers upon which the entire daylight strategic-bombing program of the Eighth Air Force was predicated. Furthermore, the American commanders wanted control over the fighter escorts and while RAF efforts on their behalf would be welcome, Spaatz and Eaker always planned the Eighth would field its own.

By the second week in June, after the decisive defeat of the Japanese Navy, the 97th Bomb Group resumed its path toward England. It was too late for the fighters who had also been diverted. Their pilots were already on the high seas with their P-39s to follow. The trip by the 97th to the United Kingdom was almost akin to the earliest voyages against the uncharted Atlantic 450 years earlier, although Columbus sailed through the southern climes rather than the shorter and much less forgiving North Atlantic.

The 97th's itinerary began when the B-17s headed to Presque Isle, Maine. After a pause in Goose Bay, Labrador, the flights scheduled stopovers at a pair of outposts in Greenland, then Reykjavik, Iceland before touchdown on the United Kingdom soil at Prestwick, Scotland. Several from the group crash-landed in Greenland but heroic rescue efforts saved the crews. The first ship from the 97th cleared the Atlantic on 1 July. The remainder straggled in twenty-six days after the migration began. They had lost five aircraft but no personnel.

Among those who brought his bomber to Scotland was Walt Kelly, a twenty-three-year-old tavernkeeper's son from Norristown, Pennsylvania. "When we got to England, the facilities and conditions were A-OK but we did have problems keeping the planes flying. The RAF told us we would get our butts blown off if we persisted with daylight bombing. We were told that the *Luftwaffe* was highly skilled and that their 88s were very accurate, both of which were confirmed later. For our part we were ready for action and wanted to prove ourselves in combat. We were impatient for the big day to come. We didn't have to wait long. August 17th, 1942 turned out to be a beautiful sunlit day—one of a very few since our arrival in the United Kingdom. Our very first combat briefing was full of detail about the Messerschmitt 109 and the Focke-Wulf 190 fighters, our escort (RAF), and specifics about the marshalling yards at Rouen, France, our target.

"It was cause for celebration for finally we were gonna get it done or fail desperately in trying, as many, especially the RAF Bomber Command, predicted. We in the 342d Squadron of the 97th were confident. We just wanted to be let loose to punish Hitler and the *Luftwaffe*." On this uncharacteristically bright, clear day, the lead element of the twelve B-17s, spotted Rouen ten minutes before turning into its bomb run. "I can see the target. I can see the target," exulted Lt. Frank R. Beadle, the bombardier in *Butcher Shop*, flown by Maj. Paul W. Tibbets who just shy of three years later would pilot the *Enola Gay* over Hiroshima. Also on *Butcher Shop*, in the copilot seat, group commander Col. Frank Armstrong, hearing Beadle's cry, snapped over the intercom, "Yes, you damn fool, and the Germans can see you, too."

Temporarily chastened, Beadle switched open the bomb-bay doors and as he cut loose the ordnance, sang through the intercom, "I don't want to set the world on fire . . ." Walt Kelly in *Heidi Ho* described the experience, "It was a cakewalk. We saw little opposition and it seemed to me like a realistic practice mission, like one we had flown in recent days. We were cocky when we took off and more so when we landed. There was lots of hoopla and queries from the press. Several planes buzzed the runway before landing [a stunt forbidden but often unchallenged]."

From a ringside seat in the lead plane of the second flight, Ira Eaker observed what his tiny air force wrought. He was pleased enough to announce, "A great pall of smoke and sand was left over the railroad tracks." Armstrong chimed in, "We ruined Rouen," hardly descriptive of the actual minimal damage done. Rail traffic was disrupted only temporarily and no serious impact upon the German war effort occurred. Perhaps delighted at any addition to the efforts of his forces, Bomber Harris sent a message, "Congratulations from all ranks of Bomber Command on the highly successful completion of the first all-American raid by the big fellows on German-occupied territory in Europe. Yankee Doodle went to town and can stick yet another well-deserved feather in his cap."

The debut of the U.S. heavy bombers prompted an outpouring of self-congratulatory declarations. In Washington, Hap Arnold, wrote a memorandum for the attention of Gen. George C. Marshall, and to the attention of Navy head Adm. Ernest J. King and Adm. William Leahy, an adviser to the president. "The attack on Rouen," claimed Arnold, "again verifies the soundness of our policy of the precision bombing of strategic objectives rather than the mass (blitz) bombing of large, city-size areas." In fact, the attack of 17 August proved little as the 97th encountered limited opposition, most of which was handled by the RAF Spitfires.

The euphoria dissipated rapidly. "We weren't wiped out as the British predicted," said Kelly. "But this to them was just a token raid in which the Germans were taken by surprise. Early claims of enemy fighters shot down dwindled to one as gunners were pressed for confirmation of kills. High altitude, precision, daylight bombing would have to be proven over deeper and more difficult missions. We still had to prove we could hold our own in aerial combat over continental Europe." Eaker, too, recognized deficiencies. He felt the crews lacked discipline and seemed nonchalant about combat. He voiced disapproval of loose rather than tight formation flying. He called for added drill in oxygen use, advocated lengthening the hoses to give men more freedom to move, and for improvements in the masks, which were clumsy and tended to freeze up.

In August 1942, a force of some 7,000 largely Canadian troops with a few American Rangers and some British commandos raided the channel port of Dieppe. The defenders inflicted heavy losses upon the Allied forces notwithstanding air support that included the 97th Bomb Group and the American 31st Fighter Group, the first unit from the States to meet the *Luftwaffe*. The 31st had expected to cross the Atlantic in their P-39 Airacobras chaperoned by the B-17s of the 97th that would provide navigation data. However, the flap over Midway that detoured the B-17s forced the 31st personnel to travel to England by ship. Once in the United Kingdom, their P-39s still on U.S. docks, the pilots of the outfit climbed into the cockpits of Spitfires.

Frank Hill, a New Jersey high school graduate in 1937, was initially assigned to P-40 Warhawks, then worked with the Airacobra. "The Spitfire was really a welcomed airplane," said Hill. "After only a few flights, we were unanimous in our praise for it and thankful not to have the P-39. The Spitfire was an easy plane to fly and to maneuver. Our mechanics were quick to adapt to the engine and armament. In less than thirty days, we were ready to go."

To ease the 31st into combat, it flew what Hill calls "indoctrination—sight-seeing—missions along the coast of France." Mostly these were practice "rodeos," maneuvers designed to entice enemy aircraft to put in an appearance. On 26 July during a sweep that carried him over occupied France, Lt. Col. Albert Clark, an unlucky member of the 31st bailed out after engine failure and became the first fighter-pilot prisoner from the Eighth Air Force.

Hill and the 31st participated in the 19 August action over Dieppe. "We had been over Dieppe only a few minutes when the RAF operations center that was controlling all the fighters [The Eighth Air Force relied on some British facilities, particularly during joint efforts] reported that a dozen or so enemy aircraft were approaching Dieppe from the direction of the big German airdrome at Abbeville. A few minutes later, a flight of aircraft arrived above us, at about 12,000 feet and immediately commenced an attack on my flight." Hill on this venture led four ships.

"I wanted to keep my flight together and avoid giving away the advantage. As the Germans attacked, their formation broke up into pairs. I turned up toward them and flew at them head-on as they came down. This made it hard for the German pilots to keep their sights on us, and it forced them to attack us head-on. One pair of FWs came in real close, and that gave us an opportunity to fire our guns directly into them. On this pass, my number-four airplane, piloted by Lt. D. K. Smith, received a burst of cannon fire through its left wing. It left an eight-inch hole on top and took out about two feet on the underside of the wing.

"After about three minutes of trying to keep my flight from being hit— by constantly breaking and turning into the Germans—I found myself in position to get a good shot at one of the Focke-Wulfs, so I fired all four .303-caliber Browning machine guns and both Hispano 20mm cannon at it. The German swung out to my left and I got in another good three-second burst of cannon and machine-gun fire. I fired into his left side at a forty-five-degree angle from about 300 yards down to about 200 feet. The Focke-Wulf started pouring black smoke. He rolled over and went straight down. I followed the smoking FW down to about 3,000 feet, but at that point I had to pull out because the ack-ack coming from the ground was really intense and I didn't want to lose any of my planes to ground fire. The last I saw of the Focke-Wulf it was about 1,000 feet over the Channel. It was still smoking and still in a steep dive.

"We climbed back to 8,000 feet. It was quiet for a few minutes, and then more Focke-Wulfs came down. We headed up and kept breaking into them. As my wingman and I turned into them, making it harder for them to track us in their sights and forcing them to come at us head-on, my second element was given an opportunity to fire on them. This was our first combat and we didn't know much else to do except turn into them and fire as best we could. We were fighting defensively, but we had a chance to hit them as they came down to hit us.

"It was constant look-see-turn for about thirty-five minutes. Then we started to get low on fuel. I had run out of cannon ammunition by then. I don't think I did much damage after I hit the first Focke-Wulf. I made one last attack on another Focke-Wulf from above and behind. I don't think I hit him. If I did, I didn't damage him very much. I was getting ready to turn for home when my element leader, Lt. Robert "Buck" Ingraham called, 'Snackbar Blue-three going down.' I thought he was going down after something but then I saw him bail out at about 7,000 feet. As Buck approached the water, I saw two boats heading toward him. I thought he was going to be picked up okay. I later found out that these were German E-boats and he was a prisoner for the rest of the war.

"When we got back to Kenley [the 31st airfield] we refueled and had the airplanes ready to go in about ten minutes. We picked up another pilot to fill in for Buck Ingraham and D. K. Smith got another airplane. [All units ordinarily included extra pilots and crew as well as reserve aircraft.] I was wearing a leather jacket and when I landed after the first mission, I discovered that it was soaking wet from sweat. B flight flew four missions that day, and we had quite a time. I fired my machine guns and cannon on each mission. We learned a lot. Flying and firing on each mission was quite an indoctrination to fighting."

As Hill's account indicated, the short distance to the action permitted Spits to go to work, return, refuel, rearm, and sortie again. These conditions enabled the Spitfire to dominate the Battle of Britain. The same advantage, however, would accrue to German interceptors when the Eighth Air Force began to penetrate deep into the Continent. Because no one could confirm that the German fighter he last saw smoking in a steep dive actually crashed, Hill only received credit for a "probable." Lieutenant Samuel Junkin of the 31st was the first of the Air Corps in Europe to score a kill, although Junkin was severely wounded and shot down during the same action.

For the 97th Bomb Group, the price increased sharply on its fourth mission aimed at Rotterdam. Delayed by an abort and some mechanical failures, the Forts arrived sixteen minutes late for a rendezvous with fighters. In sight of the Dutch coast, the Spitfires reluctantly peeled away to go back to base. Almost instantly hordes of enemy fighters replaced them. Several Forts were shot up and crewmen killed or wounded. On 6 September the 97th lost its first airplane to enemy fire and the first operation for the 92d Bomb Group cost it a B-17. Enroute to hammer the Avions Potez aircraft factory at Meaulte close to the French coast, escorted by Eagle Squadron Spitfires—planes crewed by Americans who had volunteered for the RAF before Pearl Harbor and still controlled by the British—the B-17s barged into flocks of interceptors. The seemingly reticent enemy had only been analyzing the American bomber procedures and developing a tactical approach. Charles Travinek, a radio operator and waist gunner said, "Midway over the water all hell broke loose. Goering's Abbeville Kids were waiting for us with 200-plus *Luftwaffe* fighter planes, ME 109s and FW 190s. They stayed with us, constantly firing away until our planes were crippled while fighting our way through direct hits over the target.

"Three of our engines were shot out as we dropped our bomb load over Meaulte. The fourth engine was feathered. Our vertical stabilizer was shot out as was the oxygen and intercom. Our plane began making spasmodic drops of 500 feet to 1,000 feet in altitude. We hit the ceiling with each sudden drop along with the unsecured equipment. Then we rapidly dropped with the flying objects to the plane's rubber walkway." In a crash landing, the right wing tore off and the ball turret smashed through the tail on impact. "Bill Warren, the ball-turret gunner," said Travinek, "was the only crew member not seriously hurt—just a gash on his head. He dragged Bill Peltier, tail gunner, away from the plane to safety but was unable to get [William] Dunbar, [Thomas] Matson [radio operator] and [me] out because we were wrapped up in the metal of the bomb bay tanks and the radio room.

"Warren then went to the nose of the plane looking for possibly injured officers. He found none Warren realized they must have bailed out. Instead, he found Paul Drain, bombardier, trapped in the cockpit with a broken leg. He got Drain out and over by Peltier. Matson, Dunbar, and [I] managed to extricate ourselves from the twisted wreckage and crawl to safety."

According to tail gunner Peltier, "No bail-out alarm was sounded. Whether due to pilot failure, or the electrical system being damaged by shell fire is open to debate. Anyway, four of them jumped, pilot, copilot, navigator, and the engineer. Six of us were left behind, four gunners, bombardier, radio operator. The plane was in a steep glide, pretty close to the ground, when the bombardier [Drain] managed to straighten it out a little. We crash landed in a wheat field. I've never explained the miracle of how all six of us survived that crash."

A band of French Maquis, guerrilla fighters, reached the scene an hour or so after they came to earth. Recalled Travinek, "When they saw the shape we were in they explained that they couldn't take hospital cases which would have slowed them up in their work. Warren and the French officer destroyed the bombsight. Warren also gave him five submachine guns with about 5,000 rounds of ammunition and all Colt .45 automatics."

The French freedom fighters slipped away as German soldiers located the wreck and the survivors three hours later. The troops transported the wounded to hospitals for medical treatment before the entire bunch headed for the stalags. Officially, the reports on the first Fortress shot down listed nine men as MIA. But in fact there were ten. Staff Sergeant William Dunbar, an armament chief in the ground crew wanted to get an idea of a combat mission. He had approached the crew led by pilot Lt. Clarence Lipsky and asked to go along. Qualified as a .50-caliber gunner, he was welcomed aboard and stationed at one of the waist positions. Under these circumstances, his presence went unrecorded and he may have been carried as AWOL for the three years he endured as a kriegie. Dunbar was by no means the last ground crewman to volunteer for combat missions although the regulations expressly forbade such guests.

The 15th Bomb Squadron had resumed its strikes on 5 September. Odell, with his bombardier off in London, stood by as a reserve. On the following day he joined a concerted effort after a briefing on the target, Abbeville. "I led the second box [a formation of aircraft]. Met the fighters, mostly American Spitfires [from the 31st], and cruised across the channel at sea level until I thought sure we were going in low level. The visibility was remarkable. We climbed and had a very peculiar bomb run. Brown told me to open the bomb doors and no sooner were they opened than Brown said the bombs were gone. We turned, diving away and not until we were almost to the coast did any flak appear. It was way off and I saw only a few bursts at all. The trip home was uneventful except we were a bit off course."

On the following morning, Odell was summoned to appear at Wing headquarters with squadron commander Maj. John Griffith. "It seems we had missed the target—by about twenty miles! Thank goodness I couldn't be blamed. I gave my ideas about where we bombed and it turned out to be a dummy airdrome near Dieppe." Odell recalled the hearing before a board of five U.S. officers and an RAF wing commander, all of whom were senior to the squadron commander and Odell. "Griffith was grilled sharply. From the beginning, the tone of the questions made it apparent that no excuse would be accepted for his flying on a heading that would cause him to lead the twelve-plane formation to a dummy airdrome instead of Abbeville.

"When Griffith proposed the most likely fault was a miscalibrated compass, he was then blamed additionally for failing to oversee required instrument maintenance and compass checks in the squadron aircraft. I squirmed a lot, watching Griffith take the heat. The senior board member made it clear that the Eighth Air Force could not condone the failure of any aircraft to locate its assigned target. Such a gross error smacked of poor training, sloppy navigation, and inept squadron commanders unable to lead and accomplish a simple mission. That kind of conduct was not acceptable and contrary to the standards being set by what would be the mightiest air armada ever assembled [and] which boasted of unerring 'pickle barrel' bombing accuracy.

"When the ordeal seemed close to a conclusion, I was asked to describe the mission, and had to admit that about midway across the channel, Lt. Cecil Brown, my bombardier, advised me over the intercom that he thought we were off course. My cockpit compass reading did not correspond to the plotted course, but not all that much and Griffith may have deviated momentarily and would make a correction. I added that flying under fifty feet at midchannel, no land was in sight to check our position visually to verify we were off course.

"When I hesitated after being asked why I didn't advise Griffith of the situation, Maj. James Beckwith, supported by the RAF wing commander, came to my defense on that crucial question. They noted I had acted properly, having no other choice but to follow established operational procedure by maintaining radio silence. Not to do so would alert enemy defenses; the formation would come under attack and I, more than anyone present, knew the consequences."

Griffith was relieved of his command and Odell believed he got a raw deal. "He made an error but, as it turned out, making an example of him did nothing to prevent the same situation from occurring time and again. Postwar strategic bombing survey studies cite numerous instances, particularly after the Germans began emphasizing camouflage and dispersal of industrial facilities, of flawed Eighth Air Force bombing missions launched at or lured into attacking simulated targets." The review also revealed numerous samples of poor bombing accuracy.

"These errors were not made public by the Eighth Air Force during the war. Censorship was the shield, justifiable for intelligence and morale purposes. [Reading] the Strategic Bombing Surveys, I did not run across any case of disciplinary action meted out to squadron, group, or wing commanders to equal the brusque way Griffith was stripped of his command that curtailed his career opportunities from that time on." Actually, the unfortunate Griffith eventually earned the silver leaf of a lieutenant colonel in command of a B-29 squadron. He and his crew were lost during one of the firestorm raids upon Tokyo in 1945.

The role of lighter bombers as part of the Eighth Air Force began to phase out as new B-17 and B-24 units entered the war. Two Flying Fortress groups, the 92d and 301st began operations against the enemy. The 97th with Walt Kelly continued its runs. "It did not take long before an opportunity to prove we could hold our own in aerial combat over continental Europe." According to Kelly, on 6 and 7 September, "We smashed our way through heavy *Luftwaffe* opposition to bomb targets in France and Holland, knocking off seventy-seven Nazi fighters in the two sweeps." Official totals for the three bomb groups were 16 kills, 29 probables, and 22 damaged.

Jim Goodson, the survivor of the *Athenia* sinking, had not immediately switched from the RAF after Pearl Harbor. But in the summer of 1942, he remembered, "I got a call from Charles O. Douglas of Fighter Command who said, 'Before, we invited you to join the Eagle Squadrons. Now I'm ordering you to report to the 133 Eagle Squadron of the RAF tomorrow morning. I turned up at Debdum [the airdrome], walked into the officers' barracks to find every room empty. There were half-finished letters, toothbrushes, shaving mugs, but no pilots. Every single one who had gone out with the 133 on a mission had been shot down. No planes returned. This brought the war home very sharply. We had the job of reforming the 133 Eagle Squadron virtually overnight, which was accomplished by bringing in pilots from RAF squadrons.

"The ground crew was all British and they were wonderful people with great dedication. I became close friends with my mechanic and I remember when I came back from a mission, he'd say, 'How did we go?' I would say, 'We got two' or 'We got one.' [Goodson became an ace.] It was always a team effort. We both had our names on the plane; it was our plane."

The operations of the Eighth Air Force during the summer of 1942 marked the first American offensive effort against European adversaries. Army chief of staff George Marshall and his planners had proposed Bolero, a quick build-up of men and supplies in England that would lead to Sledge-hammer, a landing on continental Europe in 1942, followed by Round-up, a full-scale invasion for the spring of 1943. British leaders considered the scheme somewhere between unrealistic and preposterous. Prime Minister Winston Churchill anticipated another Dunkirk. He dissuaded Roosevelt and argued in favor of an approach through "the soft underbelly"—Italy via North Africa.

Meanwhile in the Pacific theater, the success at Midway emboldened the high command there to plot their own aggressive thrust. Driven away from the coast of Asia and out of the islands stretching to the south and south-east, the Allies clung to Australia none too firmly. The four best Australian infantry divisions were engaged thousands of miles away, three of them in North Africa and one retreating in Malaya. Still up for grabs lay 600-mile-long New Guinea, which hung over Australia. However the Nipponese Imperial forces already held a strong position with conquests of adjacent New Britain and New Ireland. Furthermore, the Japanese had established footholds on New Guinea at Lae and Salamaua, preparatory for an advance upon Port Moresby located on the other side and facing directly at Australia.

To complete their occupation, the Imperial Army placed 11,000 soldiers on the northeastern coast of the island in the vicinity of Gona and Buna, Papua New Guinea. In an astonishing military feat, a force of Japanese soldiers trekked up and into the rugged Owen Stanley Mountains, the same range that had almost thwarted the American naval flyers aiming at shipping in the Gulf of Papua. Australian units also in the Owen Stanleys at first refused to believe any army would attempt such a march along the Kokoda Trail, but once convinced they fought off the invaders in a series of jungle battles among desperately hungry and malaria-stricken soldiers.

To the east and southeast of New Guinea lay the Solomons, several hundred islands of volcanic origin, ranging in size from a few hundred square feet to substantial land masses that form a set resembling footprints. Bougainville anchored the northerly end while ninety-mile long Guadalcanal stood at the other extremity. Douglas MacArthur sketched out a scenario in which he would direct a joint operation that employed amphibious troops, carrier- and land-based bombers against occupied Rabaul, on New Britain. The port had acted as a staging platform for future expansion into the South Pacific including the conquest of New Guinea at the peril of Australia itself. Eager to capitalize on the Midway victory, Army chief of staff George Marshall, his Air Corps chief, Hap Arnold, and Roosevelt himself were intrigued. But the Navy quickly pointed out that enemy air bases ringed the area and it opposed putting its carriers at risk and under the command of MacArthur. He, as Southwest Pacific theater commander, modified his proposal, drafting a scenario in which he would begin by capturing bases in the Solomons where Japanese had begun to appear, and evicted the foe from New Guniea before taking on Rabaul.

While the strategy struck everyone as feasible, the notion of control by MacArthur infuriated the Navy, and particularly Adm. Ernest J. King. A 1901 Naval Academy graduate, King had worked on surface ships, submarines, and in his mid-forties qualified as a naval aviator in order to command a carrier. Extensively versed in technical knowledge to accompany his vast experience, King was caustic, and known for a vitriolic temper. He brooked little disagreement from subordinates and freely disputed his superiors. Like too many of his contemporaries he drank more than moderately. In line to become chief of naval operations, to his great disappointment the post went to Harold Stark. On the verge of retirement, King performed so well as the director of Atlantic operations during the period in which the U.S. acted as the arsenal for Great Britain in return for bases, King was named to the post of Commander in Chief, U.S. Fleet. In effect he became CNO while Stark dealt with the civilian policy makers.

Given King's personality and the traditional rivalry of the two services, MacArthur's grandiose drama with himself as central actor drew less than rave reviews. His proposed moves poached on territory designated for the realm of the Navy's Admiral Nimitz. Furthermore, RAdm. Richmond Kelly Turner, chief of the Navy's War Plans Division advised King, "It is a far different matter attempting to establish advanced bases in the Solomons than in the islands heretofore occupied." King and Marshall fought out the issue in Washington. The admiral wrote his own script for dealing with the enemy outposts like Tulagi in the Solomons. He included dispositions of Army outfits and told Marshall that Navy and Marine units would proceed even without support of Army forces in the Southwest Pacific. Now MacArthur was outraged. He accused the Navy of seeking to reduce the Army to a subordinate status, which he divined had long been part of a sinister plan to gain control of the entire defense establishment.

King and Marshall worked out a compromise. The Navy would be responsible for the Tulagi area and in addition take on a slice of the Solomons, the island of Guadalcanal. In return the Army would get full cooperation from the Navy for a campaign against the enemy already on New Guinea, Rabaul, New Britain, and New Ireland. The Air Corps, broken into a pair of mobile units, would be available anywhere needed in the Pacific through the control of the Joint Chiefs.

The prize wrested by the Navy from MacArthur was a dubious one. Ancient volcanoes, superabundant rain, year-round humidity, and tropical heat had made Guadalcanal into a mountainous, thick jungle whose constantly rotting vegetation in the mucky soil acted as a giant petri dish for the cultivation of bacteria and bugs. But like the Americans, the Japanese had also recognized its strategic potential despite the inhospitable climate and terrain. A small Nipponese detachment set up shop on Guadalcanal's northern coast at Lunga Point, across from Tulagi, to construct an airfield.

Watchtower was a hastily mounted navy operation focused on putting more than 11,000 Marines ashore on Guadalcanal, with additional leathernecks to seize Tulagi and two smaller Japanese-occupied outposts, Gavutu and Tanambogo. From the start glitches in coordination hampered Watchtower. Command for various phases was split among VAdm. Robert Ghormley, designated as overall boss; RAdm. Frank Jack Fletcher, Expeditionary Force chief who divided his fleet into two elements, adding more layers of command; and the leader of the 1st Marine Division, Gen. Alexander A. Vandegrift. The parties had their own notions of objectives and Ghormley viewed the project pessimistically. Indeed, most of the senior navy people thought it jeopardized the remnants of the Pacific fleet.

Nevertheless, almost 100 vessels, including carriers and a small task force ordinarily under MacArthur's Southeast Asia command, sailed from New Zealand. Fortunately, Japanese patrol planes, frustrated by thick clouds and rain, never saw the fleet. On 7 August, following offshore bombardments, Marines of the 1st Division simultaneously waded onto the beaches of Guadalcanal and the three other objectives—the two-mile-long Tulagi, and smaller atolls, Gavutu and Tanambogo that were connected by a 500-yard-long causeway.

The 1st Marine Raider Battalion waded through armpit deep water over a coral reef onto the Tulagi beach at 0800. No hostile fire greeted them as the Japanese expected an invasion in a different sector. Raider exec officer Lt. Samuel Griffith, a 1929 Naval Academy graduate who had studied under the British Royal Marine Commandos, led the initial arrivals. But overall command of the battalion rested with hard-bitten career Marine, Merritt Edson. As a captain he had helped wield the big stick when the U.S. intervened in Nicaragua in the 1920s during what some referred to as a civil war and others a struggle between the government and bands of banditos. Reporter Richard Tregaskis described Edson, "He was a wiry man with a lean, hard face, partly covered by a sparse, spiky growth of grayish beard; his light blue eyes were tired and singularly red-rimmed in appearance for he was weary now from long days of fighting . . . his eyes were as cold as steel, and it was interesting to notice that even when he was being pleasant, they never smiled." On the eve of the invasion of Tulagi, the soft-spoken red-haired Edson quoted to his troops a Japanese propaganda broadcast of the previous evening. "Where are the United States Marines hiding? The Marines are supposed to be the finest soldiers in the world, but no one has seen them yet [a regiment had been in the Philippines]." He drew a predictable response from his men.

For the first few sultry hours, the Raiders pushed into the dense bush without firing a shot. But the advance brought them within range of enemy positions embedded in a ridge and the Marines received an indoctrination in how the Japanese would fight the war. The 500-man garrison manned a series of well-constructed dugouts, caves, and tunnels, entrenched positions that required extreme measures to overcome. At this stage of the war, there were no flamethrowers—later the standard means for dealing with the concealed emplacements. On Tulagi, they improvised with pole charges shoved into the enemy positions under the cover of smoke and heavy small-arms fire. Bogged down before a hill, Edson called for help from the sea. The cruiser *San Juan* blanketed the site with 280 5-inch shells enabling the Marines to advance until darkness arrived. Again, the Japanese showed one of their favorite tactics, the night charge. The invaders clung to their positions and the following day wiped out the enemy. Only three were taken alive.

The 1st Marine Parachute Battalion approached Gavutu by boat instead of from the air. As the first wave dashed across the sandy strand they came under light but deadly enough fire to kill the battalion intelligence officer. Considerably heavier resistance met the second wave. Fierce firefights enveloped the invaders and again the defenders burrowed into the hardened fastness of caves scooped out of the coral. Reinforcements from reserve elements and a few tanks weathered withering fire until both the defenders of Gavutu and neighboring Tanambogo were subdued.

In contrast, the first hours of the Guadalcanal invasion passed without opposition. The leathernecks swiftly moved inland a few miles before they encountered the thick jungle with its overarching canopy of huge trees. A cacophony of bird calls sounded from above the men, soon panting for breath in the sweltering humidity. Through the thick vegetation they glimpsed rats the size of rabbits, wild dogs, pigs, and lizards ranging up to crocodiles slithered in and out of the streams. Woefully poor intelligence misled the Americans about the roughness of the terrain—hills turned out to be mountains—and only with machetes could the troops slash trails through Kunai grass whose razor-sharp, man-size stalks concealed the foe and cut into exposed flesh.

In Rabaul, the Japanese forces received word of the Solomon operations and reacted. Coast watchers scattered through the islands alerted the Allied headquarters in Australia of bombers and fighters headed toward the invasion area. Wildcats from the carriers *Saratoga* and *Enterprise* dueled with the aerial armada. While the Japanese Zeros destroyed half of the U.S. fighters, the Americans disrupted the bombers enough to prevent serious damage to the fleet disgorging men and supplies on the Guadalcanal beach. A second raid later in the day was no more effective. The ability of the Japanese to mount these air attacks worried those in charge of the ships.

Vandegrift received word the carriers would remain only two days, then depart, leaving his men short of food, ammunition, and weapons and naked to aerial assault. He pleaded for more time and grudgingly was granted one additional day of protection. by the flattop planes.

By the end of the second day, the Marines had advanced far enough to capture the airfield site. Correspondent Tregaskis who accompanied the 1st Marines onto Guadalcanal noted considerable booty—trucks, food, clothing, tents, and even the newly built wooden barracks that had been expected to house Japanese soldiers. "When we entered the Japanese tent camp we knew why we had been able to sail into Tulagi Bay and under the Jap guns without being fired upon. The enemy had been caught completely unawares."

Shortly after midnight, on 9 August, Tregaskis and the Marines in the Japanese tent camp heard an airplane and saw greenish white flares floating in the sky. A few minutes later furious cannonades, salvos that flashed in the sky followed by the boom of explosions, rent the night heavens. "We knew that there was a sea fight going on. Possibly it was the battle for Guadalcanal. Possibly if our people out there lost the battle, the Japs would be ashore before morning, and we would have to fight for our lives. We knew the fate of all of us hung on that sea battle. In that moment I realized how much we must depend on ships even in our land operation."

What Tregaskis had seen was the first of the engagements in the Solomons between the Imperial Navy and the Allied seapower. Gaps in a surveillance net designed to detect the approach of Japanese warships, and a weather front that hampered reconnaissance, enabled a cluster of cruisers and destroyers to slip into the passageway between the double line formed by the Solomon Islands. The section of water became known as the Slot with Savo Island marking the north end of the channel between Guadalcanal and Tulagi. Coast watchers who reported the flotilla could not track the vessels and pinpoint their target. Fletcher, apprehensive about the strength of the Japanese bomber and torpedo plane attacks, and having lost a fifth of his fighters, yanked out his carriers with their escorts. The cargo ships also fled, leaving the Marines severely short on food, ammunition, and other materials.

To forestall an attack on the Guadalcanal landing site, a sizable Allied task force remained to prowl the Slot. However, it was broken into two, in order to cover both approaches around Savo. Again, faulty communications and poor intelligence led the commanders to believe no attack was imminent. Around 1:40 A.M., as the Australian cruiser *Canberra* meandered along with an American equivalent, the *Chicago,* plus some destroyers, the flares seen by Tregaskis silhouetted *Canberra* to the enemy force. Within five minutes, twenty-four shells from the Japanese blasted the cruiser into a pyre. Even as flames mushroomed from the *Canberra,* a torpedo smashed the bow of the *Chicago.* Guns from both sides erupted furiously before the Japanese broke off to seek the other Allied components.

Within a few minutes, four of the Japanese cruisers opened up on the American counterparts *Vincennes, Quincy,* and *Astoria.* The crews and captains of these ships had noted gunfire and explosions to their south but still were late to sound general quarters. Searchlight beams from the enemy fixed upon the trio of American cruisers, and expert Japanese gunners fired accurate salvos at the ships. Torpedoes and shells punished the *Quincy.* An officer sent to the bridge for instructions recounted, "When I reached the bridge level, I found it a shambles of dead bodies with only three or four people still standing. In the pilothouse itself the only person standing was the signalman at the wheel . . . On questioning him I found out that the captain, who at that time was laying [*sic*] near the wheel, had instructed him to beach the ship and he was trying to head for Savo Island, some four miles distant on the port quarter. I stepped to the port side of the pilothouse and looked out to find the island and noted that the ship was heeling rapidly to port, sinking by the bow. At that instant the captain straightened up and fell back, apparently dead, without having uttered any sound other than a moan."

The *Vincennes,* like the *Quincy,* foundered during the battle. The *Canberra* and *Astoria* remained afloat a few hours, but the former was scuttled while the latter gave up the ghost on her own. Two destroyers and the *Chicago* survived although badly battered. An air attack sank the destroyer *Jarvis.* All 247 hands died. Aside from several hits on attackers, the Allies scored only one notable success when a submarine sent a cruiser to the bottom. More than 1,000 sailors died defending the Slot. In the months ahead, battles in the passageway bestrewed so many ship carcasses on the floor of the Slot that it became known as "Iron Bottom Sound."

Except for Pearl Harbor this was the Navy's worst hour of the war. Yet, the task force which could have ravished the Guadalcanal landing site unopposed retreated. Unaware that Fletcher had absconded with his carriers, the Japanese admiral in command feared his force vulnerable. Meanwhile, for the moment, the Marines were totally on their own, limited to half-rations for five weeks, short on ammunition, without artillery, and exposed to air attacks.

Walter Vogel, the sailor who had left the *Houston* for medical treatment of a head wound, had not returned to the ill-fated cruiser, and when he reached Australia was assigned to the destroyer *Blue.* It partook of the patrols in the Slot until late in August when, while escorting vessels, Vogel, who was on the bridge, recalled, "The sonarmen picked up the sound of high-speed propeller noises. Immediately two big torpedo wakes appeared. They were coming right at us. The skipper gave full-speed ahead and full right rudder. But we were struck on the starboard side aft. The explosion was tremendous. It shook the destroyer from bow to stern. Our screw shafts were damaged and also the steering room destroyed. We had temporary loss of power and electricity while our stern was almost blown off. We lost eight men killed, twenty-two wounded. We were flooding aft. I thought this is another ship I've lost."

Another destroyer attempted to tow the *Blue* but the lines parted. When a dispatch reported a large enemy naval force heading down the Slot, the crew received orders to scuttle the ship. After Vogel and his shipmates abandoned the *Blue*, the *Henley*, a companion vessel fired a torpedo that missed and then sank it with a barrage of 5-inch shells.

Lacking reinforcements and bereft of support from the big guns of the Navy, the 1st Marine Division on Guadalcanal reverted to a defensive stance, protecting the beaches and still-under-construction Henderson airstrip. The one saving grace was the thinness of the enemy ranks on the island. The Japanese could not mount a strong attack without more troops. Nor could Rabaul dispatch air attacks until planes and crews arrived to replace those lost earlier.

Interrogators of several captured Japanese convinced the division intelligence officer, Lt. Col. Frank Goettge that a substantial number of starving, disease-ridden troops and laborers wandering about the bush could be induced to surrender. Instead of a heavily armed combat patrol originally scheduled to sweep the area, Goettge took a smaller team with limited firepower. Led by one of the prisoners, the Marines traveled by boat and went ashore shortly before dusk. As Goettge gathered his officers to discuss their next move, an ambush slaughtered almost the entire patrol, including the leader. Before he died, a sergeant blew off the head of the Japanese guide. Only three of the twenty-four Marines escaped. One of the survivors witnessed knife- and sword-wielding Japanese savaging the members of the patrol.

The incident set a tone for dealing with the Japanese, one in which no quarter would be given. Subsequent experiences, like that of Marine Don Zobel who came upon an American corpse with at least thirty bayonet wounds provided more evidence. "His penis cut off and shoved into his mouth in the Japanese way of the ultimate insult," confirmed, to the Marines, the barbarity of the foe.

The inability of the enemy to evict the Marines enabled the 1st Engineer Battalion, improvising with abandoned Japanese equipment, to complete the rudiments of an airfield. On 20 August, a dive bomber and a fighter squadron, launched from the escort carrier *Long Island*, flew 190 miles to land at Henderson Field. General Vandegrift personally welcomed the Marine pilots to residence on Guadalcanal.

Unwilling to concede Guadalcanal, the Imperial Army, diverting some resources from the New Guinea campaign, started to ship fresh troops to the island. Misled by faulty intelligence on the American strength of nearly 8,000, a total force of 2,000 soldiers, commanded by Col. Kiyano Ichiki boarded ships bound for Guadalcanal. A detachment of some 900 slipped ashore west of the Marine beachhead. They headed toward the perimeter set up along a tidal lagoon known as Alligator Creek to the leathernecks, but which in fact contained crocodiles. A large sandbar blocked outlet to the sea. Parallel to the stream ran the Ilu River, erroneously listed by the poor American maps as the Tenaru River.

On the night of 19–20 August, some sixty Marines patrolling the bush suddenly bumped into a Japanese unit. After a thirty-minute firefight, the Americans counted more than thirty enemy dead and among the corpses found map cases, documents, and other paraphernalia that seemed out of the ordinary. At headquarters, intelligence experts deciphered enough of the material to find these troops had only been on the island a day and already seemed well versed in the defenses around Alligator Creek. The Marines hastily added some artillery, dug in deeper, and settled in behind barbed wire to await hostile visitors.

The enemy attacked the well-entrenched U.S. forces and after initially being repulsed, regrouped in a stand of coconut trees. Dick Tregaskis made his way to the front. "Out in the glassy blue water I saw globs of water jump up where the bullet struck. 'They've got a Jap out there,' said my friend. 'He's trying to swim around and get in behind us. We've killed a lot of 'em that way.'" Three more leatherneck rifle companies led by Col. L. B. Creswell arrived to surround the Japanese.

"The volleys of machine gun and rifle fire," reported Tregaskis, "from the depths of the grove across the river, grew louder. Colonel Creswell's people were rolling the Japs toward us. Suddenly I saw the dark figures of men running on the strip of beach that bordered the palm grove. The figures were far off, probably a half mile down the light ribbon of sand, but I could see from their squatness that they were Japs. There was no time for any other impression. In a few seconds the black, violently moving blobs were squashed down on the sand and we heard a fusillade of rifle fire. The Japs did not get up again.

"A rumbling of powerful motors came from behind us. We turned to find a group of four tanks moving down the trail through the coconut palms. . . . We watched those awful machines as they plunged across the spit and into the edge of the grove. It was fascinating to see them bustling amongst the trees, pivoting, turning, spitting sheets of yellow flame. It was like a comedy of toys, something unbelievable to see them knocking over palm trees which fell slowly, flushing the running figures of men from un-

derneath their treads, following and firing at the fugitive. It was unbelievable to see men falling and being killed so close, to see the explosions of
Jap grenades and mortars, black fountains and showers of dirt near the tanks
and see the flashes of explosions under their very treads. We had not realized there were so many Japs in the grove. Group after group was flushed
out and shot down by the tanks' canister shells."

To add to the carnage, fighter planes from Henderson had strafed the
coconut grove. The engagement lasted until about five in the afternoon before the Battle of Tenaru River ended with wary Marines, rifles in hand,
heads swiveling constantly, cautiously moving among the shattered land and
the bodies. Colonel Ichiki committed suicide rather than be taken captive.
Wrote Tregaskis, "Japanese dead are dangerous, for there are usually some
among them alive enough to wait until you pass, then stab or shoot you. Our
marines had by this time learned to take no chances. The dead were shot
again, with rifles and pistols, to make sure."

The next round involved naval vessels and aircraft. Hoping to inveigle
the Americans into exposing their carriers while simultaneously ousting
them from the island with a much larger landing party, the Japanese sent a
convoy of transports accompanied by major naval units, including a trio of
carriers—*Ryujo, Shokaku,* and *Zuikaku.* When coast watchers notified the
Americans of the advancing ships, swarms of dive bombers, torpedo planes,
and fighers from the *Saratoga* rose to the bait. Unfortunately they could not
locate the target because the Japanese had slyly retreated.

In a counterstrike, Betty bombers from Rabaul combined with airplanes
from the flattop *Ryujo.* The operation proved a bust; Marine fighters from
Henderson Field destroyed sixteen Zeros and Bettys at a cost of three Wildcats. Far worse for the attackers, in the exchanges between carriers, while
Enterprise quit the scene with moderate damage, *Ryujo* added her hulk to the
growing junkyard at the bottom of the sea. The Japanese Navy prudently
withdrew the *Shokaku* and *Zuikaku* rather than risk further carrier losses, leaving the transports and their destroyer escorts open to air attacks.

The Cactus Air Force—Cactus was the code name for Guadalcanal—dive-
bombed the oncoming warships and transports on 25 August and blasted
the largest vessel, the cruiser *Jintsu,* forcing it to retire to the base at Truk.
Hits on a transport, the *Kinryu Maru,* by the Marine flyers caused a destroyer
to come alongside for rescue. A flight of Army B-17s dumped its load close
enough to the ship to sink it. Rabaul recalled the Japanese expeditionary
force, affording the Marines on Guadalcanal a brief respite.

During the interlude, Seabees carved out a second strip but amenities for
the airmen remained scarce. Correspondent Robert Sherrod wrote, "Living
conditions were appalling. Pilots had to fight and fly all day on a diet of dehydrated potatoes, Spam, or cold hash—and sometimes Japanese rice. . . .

Sleeping in a mud-floored tent was constantly interrupted by Japanese planes ('Louie the Louse' or 'Washing Machine Charlie') that flew around murdering sleep and dropping occasional bombs, or by destroyers or submarines that stood offshore and lobbed shells at Henderson Field. When a man could get away for a bath in the Lunga River, the only time he could take his clothes off, he frequently found there wasn't any soap. If he didn't catch malaria from the anopheles mosquitoes that swarmed into his foxhole, he was almost certain to get dysentery that tormented his bowels."

Marine units on Tulagi and Gavatu, including Edson's Raiders and the Parachute Battalion added their weight to the embattled leathernecks on Guadalcanal. They arrived none too soon because the enemy demonstrated renewed vigor in his effort to end the American presence. Actually, the commander for the task forces in the area, Admiral Ghormley had notified General Vandegrift he deemed his resources insufficient to support the Guadalcanal operation. Ghormley believed a massive ground, sea, and air attack organized from Rabaul and Truk would overwhelm the American fleet and the Marines. Admiral Richmond Kelly Turner, Ghormley's subordinate in charge of the amphibious forces and nominally Vandegrift's immediate superior, in his typical fashion, over a bottle of whiskey, told the Marine general that he believed he could deliver reinforcements in the form of the 7th Marine Regiment. Vandegrift cringed as Turner then counseled a strategy to sprinkle the fresh troops around the island where they could repel each attempt to land. With the Japanese already in strength on Guadalcanal, the recipe spelled disaster for such small, separated units. Vandegrift sidestepped the bizarre proposal, and continued to plump for a landing at the established beachhead by the 7th Marines.

Japanese ships bombarded the Raiders by night and planes raided the area during the daylight hours. The fighting intensified; the Americans now went on the defensive. Tregaskis back at a command post, observed, ". . . this morning the din of firing grew so tremendous that there was no longer any hope of sleeping. Our batteries were banging incessantly, the rifle and machine-gun fire from the direction of the Raider lines had swelled into a cascade of sound. Louie the Louse was flying about and flares were dropping north, south, east, and west.

"We were drawing up a strong skirmish line on the ridge-top. Reinforcements were on the way up. We knew that the Raiders . . . out on the ridge had their hands full. We knew then that a major Japanese effort to break through our lines and seize the airport had begun." The original aim of Edson's mission had been to seize a supply area and eliminate the garrison there. But now the Japanese had brought in thousands of well-armed troops whose positions lay less than 2,000 yards from the vital U.S. asset, Henderson Field and General Vandegrift's command post.

"Snipers were moving in on us," said Tregaskis. "They had filtered along the flanks of the ridge and taken up positions all around our CP. Now they began to fire. It was easy to distinguish the sound of their rifles. There were light machine guns, too, of the same caliber. Ricocheting bullets skidded amongst the trees. We plastered ourselves flat on the ground."

Subsequently, he reported, "As the first light of dawn came, the general was sitting on the side of the ridge, talking to some of his aides. A Jap machine gun opened up, and they high-tailed for the top of the ridge with me right behind. We were heading for a tent, where we would at least have psychological shelter. Just as we reached the tent, a bullet clanged against a steel plate only two or three feet from us. It was amusing to see the rear ends of the dignified gentlemen disappearing under the edge of the tent. I made an equally undignified entrance."

The standoff reached a climax on 14 September as waves of Japanese soldiers rushed the Marines dug in on "Edson's Ridge." Officers flourishing swords led their warriors who shouted Banzai and sought to challenge within bayonet range. Some did engage the Marines in close combat but the leathernecks held their ground or relinquished only a few yards at a steep price in enemy lives. Tregaskis noticed that Edson, who had spent the night at the lead edge of his people, had a bullet hole in his collar and at the waist of his blouse. "Along the flank of the hill, where a path led," said Tregaskis, "we passed strewn bodies of marines and Japs, sometimes tangled as they had fallen in a death struggle. At the top of the knoll, the dead marines lay close together. Here they had been most exposed to Jap rifle and machine-gun fire, and grenades.

"At the crest of the knoll we looked down the steep south slope . . . there were about 200 Jap bodies, many of them torn and shattered by grenades or artillery bursts, some ripped, a marine told us, by the strafing planes which we had seen this morning. It was up this slope that the Japs had sent their heaviest assaults many times during the night and each time they tried they had been repulsed." Sporadic attacks occurred in the next several days but the fury of the assaults diminished and then the Japanese retreated deep into the bush.

On the water, however, American fortunes nosedived. A task force that included the carriers *Hornet* and *Wasp,* supplemented by the fire power of the powerful new battleship, *North Carolina,* steamed northwest from the island base at Espíritu Santo to bring fresh troops and supplies. On 15 September, the flight decks teemed with fully gassed and armed planes, prepared to ward off any aerial assaults. Everyone remained at the ready, scanning the skies, but from beneath the sea, a submarine fired a spread of four torpedoes at the *Wasp.* Two struck home with tremendous explosions reducing the aircraft to fiery wrecks while below deck, water mains ruptured, fuel in the pumping system fed the fires, and seawater poured into the hold. Another undersea boat loosed its tin fish and one gouged a huge hole in the hull. More explosions from its ammunition and ordnance stores created an inferno. Recognizing his vessel was dying, the skipper gave the order to abandon ship. An escorting destroyer delivered the final blows with torpedoes. Nevertheless, the convoy sailed on.

On 18 September, Tregaskis strolled down to the beach where cargo vessels, warships, and transports hove in sight. Thousands of reinforcements in clean fatigues marched inland to relieve the embattled Marines of Edson's Ridge. The fight for Guadalcanal was a long way from over but the U.S. forces were there to stay.

14
Paratroopers, Raiders, Rangers, Marauders, Alamo Scouts

Until the Industrial Revolution, fighting men came in two simple models, on horseback or on foot. Over time the mounted knight exchanged his lance or sword for a cavalryman's Mauser; the yeoman swapped his bow or pike for a rifle with bayonet. The age of science, invention, and machines created refinements in explosives, innovations in weapons, massive firepower. In addition, the new techniques of manufacturing introduced specialization, a concept naturally manifested in modern warfare.

Beyond the obvious tasks associated with artillery, armor, and electronics—gunner, loader, tank-driver, wireman, the literally hundreds of military occupational specialties—also was born the notion of the singular unit. Designed to carry out unique missions they received special instruction, weapons, and gear tailored for an individual purpose. With one exception, these were all relatively small outfits. Separated from the general run of the military, they accrued a sense of élan which members and their superiors exploited.

Of all of the World War II special units, the largest by far was the airborne. Men who served in the armies of America during World War II may recall the nearly ineffable aura that enveloped the label of "Airborne." Paratroopers received extra instruction in infantry tactics, use of explosives, and survival behind enemy lines. They had a reputation for toughness, for daring as well as for brawling with nonjumpers or "straight legs." To be sure there were some tangible trappings to envy or relish, the highly burnished boots and the silver badge marked a "trooper"—even that name distinguished him from the common "soldier." Many GIs with long military experience as well as raw draftees, perceived them as harboring a death wish. Sensible people would hesitate to hurl themselves from an altitude of several thousand feet, dependent only upon yards of silk or nylon to prevent a fatal plunge. They drifted helplessly toward the ground, unable to unlimber their weapons, while the enemy could slaughter them in their descent.

Still, the army never lacked recruits. Mel Trenary, a member of the 517th Parachute Regimental Combat Team, was one. "I volunteered for the paratroopers because I wanted to prove to myself that I had the ability to build my body into something worthwhile and at the same time I could do something that the average person wouldn't want to do. My first jump was a surprise. We put on our chutes, sat on benches until finally we walked to the plane. The harness was so tight I could hardly stand up right. As the last person on board, I sat right next to the door, looking out. This was my first time in an airplane and I was fascinated. It was hard to believe, at that time, that a heavy machine like this could go up into the air. I had of course seen planes but it was different being inside one as it went up.

"They had trained me right. It was all automatic. When the red light went on, I got up and stood at the door. I didn't look down, but I could see the horizon anyway because of the plane's movements. When the green light came on, I felt a tap on my leg and I jumped out, just like they had taught me. I had my eyes closed, but I could feel my body going upside down. When the chute opened, it flipped me right side up and I knew everything was working right. I opened my eyes and watched others come out of the plane. I was the first one out of the plane and I had felt that if I didn't go then some of the others might chicken out. Later, one of the guys told me that as he saw me get ready by the door, he thought, 'if Trenary can do it, so can I.'"

Even before Pearl Harbor, while the notion of such airborne units barely existed beyond the paper stage, U.S. paratroopers already bore the status and the stigma almost inevitably stamped on an elite outfit. James M. Gavin, an orphan, enlisted man, then graduate of West Point, who led four combat jumps in Europe and finished the war as commanding general of the 82d Airborne Division, was part of the tiny group that created the paratrooper role. "We had an idea. We wanted to tell these guys that they were the most capable guys on earth. And when they land, it doesn't matter who they meet; they can really lick them under any circumstances. And any parachute squad is worth a platoon of anybody else. We want these guys to find out that there's nothing too good for them; no bed too soft, no food too good, no conditions too good for them to live. But, by God, when combat comes, then there's not too much to ask from them. We really expected to ask anything of them and we expected them to come through.

"We tried to give a whole dimension of how to train human beings and how to get them committed and dedicated and believing in what they were doing and how to make them very combat effective, consistent with trying to find the kind of leadership that could lead these guys. You had to be as good at anything as they were, and oftentimes better and be quite willing to do anything you asked them to do."

The parachute itself wasn't that new: Leonardo da Vinci, along with his designs for manned flight, in his fifteenth century *Codex Atlanticus* noted the possibility for safe passage from the skies. "If a man have a tent of linen of which the apertures have all been stopped up . . . he will be able to throw himself down from any great height without sustaining any injury." Da Vinci sketched four triangular panels jointed at the top from which a human figure dangled.

During World War I, only the Germans, in the waning days of the fighting, equipped some of their pilots with parachutes, although both sides outfitted balloonborne observers with chutes. However, in October 1918, Col. Billy Mitchell, chief of the American Expeditionary Force airmen, approached Gen. John "Black Jack" Pershing, who commanded all U.S. forces in France with a daring plan. ". . . he should assign one of the infantry divisions permanently to the Air Service . . . we should arm the men with a great number of machine guns and train them to go over the front in our large airplanes which would carry ten or fifteen of these soldiers. We would equip each man with a parachute, so that when we desired to make a rear attack on the enemy, we could carry these men over the lines and drop them off in parachutes behind the German position." The November armistice quashed further consideration. Still, under Mitchell's prodding, a standard, practical parachute was developed for use at least by pilots.

During the 1930s, Soviet, French, and Italian forces embarked on parachute programs in varying degrees. Nazi Germany, forbidden to rearm by the Treaty of Versailles, sponsored glider clubs whose craft showed an obvious potential in warfare and secretly started to build a paratroop corps. The notion of airborne fighting men, "a sword of silk" in the rhetoric of one advocate, languished in the U.S. But in 1939, George Marshall, as Army chief of staff, enlightened by intelligence reports of the European interest in airborne and parachute soldiers, ordered a feasibility study. The hasty research study, while it supported an experimental program to develop infantry traveling by air, remarked that combat groups dropped behind enemy lines could well be on suicide missions.

William Yarborough, USMA 1936, was among the pioneers of American parachute troops. "Some of the best training material in the early days on parachute techniques was Russian," said Yarborough, "and it was translated by my father, a Russian linguist and intelligence officer who served with the 31st Infantry in Siberia during World War I. As a kid I saw a picture of Russians lying on the wing of an airplane, jump at the command 'Turn loose.' I remember thinking of all the stupid ways to make a living, or the most tenuous ways to go into combat."

Not until fighting broke out in Europe was there an American effort to create paratroop units. The entire project received a boost with the news of the German successes, using parachutists, to overwhelm the Netherlands and Belgium on the way to overrunning France in the spring of

1940. On 25 June of that year, the very day the French admitted their defeat to Adolf Hitler in the same railroad car that witnessed the German surrender in 1918, an order to the commandant at Fort Benning, Georgia, called for a platoon of recruits for parachute training.

In 1940, jumping out of an airplane, in spite of Leonardo da Vinci's theoretical assurance that given enough canopy one could throw himself down from a great height without fear of injury, seemed a highly dangerous business. The offhand suggestion by those who first investigated the use of such troops that their roles could become kamikaze-style missions added to the sense of risk. Sensitive perhaps to excessive demands upon men while the country was not yet at war, the brass decided that no one should be forced to be a paratrooper. Those first candidates for the new type of soldier, like the Commandos, Rangers, and other elites were thus asked to break the First Commandment of the soldiers, "Never volunteer!"

Those in charge of those first volunteers screened for both attitude and athletic ability. A recruiter might perform a series of tumbles and then ask the potential trooper if he could manage a similar stunt. That provided insight into physical agility but according to Gavin, the gymnastics were really designed to show off the trooper. "It impressed young kids, who thought if a guy can do that and with that sharp look, it must be a pretty good outfit." Once in training, the regimen required intensive conditioning. The original platoon exercised, marched, and ran beyond the norm. In the absence of towers* to learn how to cushion the impact with the ground, would-be troopers jumped off the backs of trucks and for advanced practice leaped from moving vehicles.

The art of tumbling to avoid injury seemed critical. Anyone who failed to roll in the prescribed manner immediately received a critique that ended with a command of "Gimme ten!" on the basis that extra pushups cured carelessness. Well before behavioral scientists publicly proclaimed the virtues of "aversive training," those running the infant paratroop program thus employed punishment as a way to instill an instinctive resort to the right techniques.

Even the tumbling evolved through painful experimentation. That same sort of trial and error marked landing techniques for actual jumps.

---

*Major William Lee, who commanded this first detachment, discovered that the makers of the grand parachute tower installed at the New York World's Fair in 1939, had a pair of towers in Hightstown, New Jersey. He arranged for his unit to spend ten days at nearby Fort Dix and train on the two high platforms. Eventually, similar but higher towers were erected at the major paratroop training sites, Fort Benning and Camp Mackall, North Carolina, with a minisize one at Toccoa.

Originally, the experts instructed recruits to strike the ground with feet spread to the width of the hips. Only after countless sprains, cartilage damage, and broken bones did anyone realize that touching down with feet close together better distributed the shock and reduced injuries.

Those first volunteers spent hours learning how to pack their silk. Not until well into World War II did the art of parachute rigging become a responsibility of specialists while the troopers themselves concentrated on their roles as airborne fighters. The gear issued to the would-be paratroopers consisted mostly of hand-me-downs. Each volunteer for that first platoon received two pairs of Air Corps mechanics' coveralls, a leather flying cap like those sported by World War I aces, and a pair of boots with a strap across the instep designed to give support to ankles stressed by that first contact with the earth. One genuine innovation made at the very start of the program was the reserve chute carried on a man's chest. Throughout World War II, American troopers were the only ones afforded a second chance if the main chute failed to deploy.

The instructions placed great stress upon the way in which a man exited the airplane door over the drop zone. Charles La Chaussee, who served with the 517th, described the method as calling for "a quarter-turn in space toward the tail of the plane, head bowed, knees slightly bent, and with both hands on the reserve parachute. Correctly executed, the good body position eased the opening shock and lessened the chances of the parachute snagging on equipment as it opened." However, as La Chaussee noted, in a mass jump, only the first man had an opportunity to follow the manual. The rest were lucky if they went out feet first, many wound up diving head down. Any delays, counted even in seconds, meant that even if the pilot throttled down properly, the stick of twelve to fifteen troopers would be strung out over a great distance, seriously reducing effectiveness.

Following the first successful jumps of the test platoon, the brass scheduled a mass demonstration to indicate the tactical potential of airborne. Several members of the platoon on their way to the barracks after watching a Western film at the Fort Benning post theater discussed the added dangers of such an untried maneuver. One man teased Pvt. Aubrey Eberhardt that he would be so scared he wouldn't remember his own name. Eberhardt, in a sudden inspiration said he would shout the name of the Indian warrior bedeviled by the U.S. cavalry in the movie. True to his word, Eberhardt, as he exited the door of the C-47 the next day, yelled, "Geronimo!"

Although celebrated in the popular media, the invocation of Geronimo was a short-lived tradition. Experts in the field soon taught men to forget about the chief and count, "One thousand, two thousand, three thousand . . ." and if the main chute had failed to open, it was time to yank the ripcord of the reserve. Furthermore, succeeding classes of paratroopers considered the cry juvenile. Russel Brami, a member of the 517th and who made a career of being a paratrooper, says, "I never heard anyone yell 'Geronimo!' We used to claim the translation of Geronimo was, 'Who pushed me?' The usual comment, if any, when a guy jumped was, 'Oh, shit.'"

The tangible morale builders for paratroopers followed soon after the graduation of these initial recruits. In January 1941, the men received authorization to wear their boots with trouser legs tucked into the tops while in dress uniforms. The patch with the white parachute against a blue background for the soft overseas cap followed. Airborne artillery used a red backdrop. The silvery badge with the wings curving up from the base of a chute to meet the canopy added an adornment. Bill Yarborough developed the design of a two-piece jumpsuit with plenty of pockets that replaced the mechanics' coveralls. Redesign of the boot improved its function and style, the leather's potential for burnishing gave new meaning to spit-and-polish.

Airborne training stressed hand-to-hand combat and demolition. Yarborough explained, "The philosophy we built into those outfits was that wherever you land, you are liable to land in the wrong place. It's a coin flip. You are to do the kind of damage to the enemy that you are trained to do and don't let it worry you that you may end up in twos or threes, or a half a dozen. That's part of the racket."

Along with chutists, soldiers ferried to the battle scene in gliders came under the rubric of airborne. Unlike troopers, glidermen were not volunteers although their exposure was arguably as dangerous. Moreover, not until well into World War II did they gain the right to wear their own winged insignia.

Even as the American and the British enthusiasm for airborne units swelled, the German version staggered from a near-fatal blow. The Nazi war machine, rushing to the rescue of its ally, Benito Mussolini's Italian army floundering in its invasion of Greece, drove the British to a last-ditch defense on Crete, the largest island of the Mediterranean Sea and a strategic block to the Aegean Sea. Among other things, Crete offered an airbase for Royal Air Force planes to bomb the Romanian oilfields, so essential to Hitler's panzers. General Kurt Student, the German airborne commander, convinced Hitler he could conquer the British forces—mainly New Zealanders—with his glider soldiers and paratroopers descending on Crete's three major airfields. The battle demonstrated the vulnerability of such units. The first error lay in sending gliders that were not preceded by paratroopers. As the first fragile sailplanes swooped to the tarmac, the heavily entrenched defenders slaughtered the occupants almost before they could tumble from their bullet-riddled craft. When the paratroopers arrived at the airdromes the British wreaked heavy casualties while many invaders still hung in their harnesses. However, a handful of the airborne gained a toehold. A withdrawal by the New Zealanders due to poor communications allowed the Germans to bring up massive reinforcements. The battle tide ebbed for the British who performed a mini-Dunkirk to rescue many of their forces.

The victory notwithstanding, Hitler lost faith in airborne assaults. Of the 13,000 jumpers and gliderborne, 5,140 had been killed or wounded. The losses to the *Luftwaffe* in planes was also enormous, 350 aircraft were destroyed including many transports that would be desperately missed when the Nazi armies headed east into the Soviet Union.

While the Germans all but abandoned the use of airborne, the British and the Americans, however, continued to have faith in the concept. From the Crete defeat they learned that a heavily defended position fell against a determined airborne operation that numbered less than half its foe. Furthermore, strategists perceived the importance of the tactical mistakes of the Crete paratroopers and glider forces that landed directly on well-entrenched opposition rather than to their relatively weaker rear.

The decision to build up U.S. airborne outfits received a final boost with the raid on Pearl Harbor. By the summer of 1942, airborne outfits had grown from the original platoon-size unit up to 3,000-man regiments. The powers at the top decided operations of full divisions were feasible and chose the 82d and 101st Infantry Divisions to be the forerunners of the new breed.

The granddaddy for World War II glamour was of course the British Commando. The phenomenon sprang from the fertile brain of Prime Minister Winston Churchill in 1940, after the fall of France and with the British troops thrown back to England. Immediately after the completion of the Dunkirk evacuation, Churchill told the House of Commons, "We shall not be content with a defensive war." He told his War Cabinet, "We should immediately set to work to organize self-contained, thoroughly equipped raiding units. Enterprises must be prepared with specially trained troops of the hunter class who can develop a reign of terror down the enemy coasts."

Because missions would require participation of air, naval, and ground forces, the British created the organization known as Combined Operations, headed by Lord Louis Mountbatten. Within a relatively short time, Commandos stung the enemy with hit-and-run raids that, while of very limited strategic value, at least buoyed morale.

In the United States, these exploits inspired some adventurous and highly aggressive souls. The Marine Raider Battalion that stormed Tulagi was one such copy, although the results were not always what was expected.

Merritt Edson's battalion resembled an assault force rather than a commando-style group. The members had all received extra training in close combat and physical conditioning. They also organized their platoons differently with extra firepower. There was a premium upon strong leadership, as exemplified by Edson whom correspondent Robert Sherrod described, "He hated the Japs, as only men who have met them in combat hate them. Whenever, during his hour-long lecture to correspondents the day before we left Base X [this account was written during the war], he used the phrase 'killing Japs' or 'knocking off Nips' his eyes seemed to light up, and he smiled faintly."

Harry Manion of the 4th Marine Raider Battalion had volunteered for the duty. "The Marine Raiders were formed with ten men to a squad, a squad leader and three fire teams. The teams could have two submachine guns and one M1 rifle, a Browning automatic rifle, and two M1s, or two BARs and one rifle. BAR men also carried a .45-caliber pistol and two magazines. "I was a BAR man and in the Raiders you always had a buddy. We did almost everything together. You must protect and help your buddy at all times. We became almost as one. Sometimes a nod of a head would suffice for many words. This could mean the difference.

"War in the Pacific seemed to have a time schedule. Fight in the daylight and dig in at night. The Raiders went around the clock. Whenever the enemy was most relaxed, we liked to hit him. On patrol we could lie within a foot or so of the enemy and breathe normally. Weapons ready if needed. Knives, rifles, etc., but never used unless absolutely necessary. This 'trick' is not easy to learn." Manion commented on a common aspect for all elite outfits. "Many senior officers were totally opposed to the concept of Raiders. We knew we were a breed apart from other Marines. They had artillery, naval gun-fire support, air support, heavy mortars, and good resupply, or at least better than ours. Their medical support was much greater. Most of our beans, bullets, and bandages were personal items."

Another well-publicized Raider leader was Evans F. Carlson. A marine officer whose career included a stint at the Roosevelt White House as an attaché, who retired from the Corps and then, as a member of the diplomatic service, spent some time with the Chinese Communist Army, he exploited his acquaintance with the president to organize the 2d Marine Raider Battalion in his own unorthodox style. Carlson stressed the Chinese Red attitude, "gung-ho," pulling together with much less attention to the usual hierarchical structure of the military. The romantic sense of the adventure, and his father's favor, apparently inspired James Roosevelt to sign on with Carlson's Raiders as executive officer. In a high-risk venture while the struggle for Guadalcanal was still in doubt, 222 men under Carlson and Roosevelt traveled by submarine to Makin Island in the Gilberts, a thousand miles northeast of Guadalcanal. Although the Japanese garrison numbered only eighty-three soldiers, a shot accidentally fired during the landing aroused the defenders. In a muddled battle, the Raiders erased the smaller force. But upon returning through a ferocious surf to their submarines, confusion led to nine Marines being left behind. When the Japanese reoccupied Makin they discovered the nine and beheaded them.

The U.S. Army equivalent of the Commandos began with the agreement of Chief of Staff Marshall and Lord Mountbatten for the training of Americans to replicate the British version. A veteran of World War I, Lucian K. Truscott, a colonel in April 1942, after having spent nineteen years at the company-grade level, joined Mountbatten's staff. General Russell P. Hartle, commander of the first American soldiers stationed in the United Kingdom—the 34th Infantry Division and the 1st Armored Division—nominated his aide, an ambitious 1929 West Point graduate, Capt. William O. Darby to run the new outfit. "He was the right man in the right place at the right time," said Warren "Bing" Evans, a member of the 1st Ranger Battalion and sergeant major for Darby. "He was a helluva combat soldier, a good leader who didn't hesitate to break the rules if he thought it would help him."

Darby quickly selected several officers as his cadre and began to interview volunteers. The first recruits underwent a rigorous physical examination and an interview to ascertain whether they seemed mentally and emotionally suited. Evans, big and agile, in 1938 had graduated from South Dakota State, which he attended on basketball and football scholarships. "We were all a bunch of egotists, volunteers, good physical specimens, and intensely patriotic," recalled Evans. "We'd all heard of the Commandos and that's what initially inspired us. Most of us were farm boys from the Midwest and the Commandos thought we were soft. They underestimated us because we broke every record that had been set during training."

The 1st Ranger Battalion consisted of fewer than 400 soldiers, less than half the size of a normal infantry battalion, divided into six companies. They learned their craft at Achnacarry, a castle in Scotland and a Commando depot. Physical conditioning through arduous marches, climbing exercises, and stream crossings built strength and endurance. Intensive work with weapons that ranged from .45-caliber pistols, rifles, BARs, sub and fixed machine guns, through light mortars enabled the Rangers to deliver maximum firepower. They studied map reading, demolition, fire and maneuver, amphibious landings, and hand-to-hand combat. Ordinary infantrymen might be lightly schooled in several kinds of ordnance and activities, but the focus of the Rangers was much more thorough.

James Altieri, an original member of the 1st Battalion, remembered,

"Every morning was spent on a long speed march or mountain climb. We were driven relentlessly until it seemed our aching bodies could take no more. The sight of men dropping out on the marches, broken and beaten, was disheartening. Each day the distance of our march would be lengthened until we were doing twelve miles in two hours, which included a five-minute break. At the breaks men would drop like sacks of beans, tired and exhausted. Each day I thought would surely be the last for me."

Along with the physically grueling regimen, the Commandos directed live fire during exercises. "When Company F made the practice landings," said Altieri, "machine-gun bullets, fired from shore positions manned by Commando marksmen, would splatter rowing paddles to splinters in the hands of men that held them as our collapsible boats neared shore for landings. As we hit the beach, charges of dynamite exploded almost in our faces as we dashed madly for cover to evade the snapping Bren-gun bullets that kicked up dirt between our strides."

Allen E. Merrill, as an eighteen-year-old growing up in Buffalo, New York, in the first surge of patriotic fervor that enveloped young men of his age, attempted to enlist in the Marine Corps on 7 December 1941. Rejected because of color blindness he applied to the Navy with the same result. "Spring came and I tried the Army. They welcomed me with open arms. Merrill's path to the Rangers included qualification as a paratrooper and flunking out of OCS, an opportunity that he said he never wanted. Neither commissioned nor a member of an airborne outfit, he sailed to England for duty with the 34th Infantry Division and engaged in amphibious training. While stationed in northern Ireland, Merrill saw a notice on the bulletin board about a new Commando-style unit being formed. Two officers would interview volunteers.

"What the hell, I decided to give it a try. What could I lose? I joined to fight a war and was just taking up space here, and Americans were fighting and dying out in the Pacific. They asked me things about my past life. Like, did I have many fights as a boy. Did I have a temper. Did I see anyone die or get killed. How did I feel about blood, my own or someone else's. They asked if I ever killed anyone. The answers were what I assumed most everyone would say. I had a few fights, won some and lost some. Then the tall lieutenant asked me if I could ever kill anyone, either with a weapon at close range or with my bare hands. I replied that if it came down to it, I could kill an enemy who was out to get me or to save another buddy's life. They asked if my being part German would affect me in fighting Germans. I said I would be able to kill them as a duty of a good soldier in wartime. I was not sickened at the sight of blood. They asked if my Catholic religion would stand in the way of my doing my duty as a combat soldier. I said, 'No, sir, it would not. That's what they had confession for.'" Merrill explained that his brief, involuntary OCS tour had kept him from remaining a paratrooper although he had attempted several times to return to the airborne ranks.

Accepted and transported to the Achnacarry site, Merrill noted, "Whoever had set up this operation had a devious one-track mind. All the important functions of living were strategically placed on separate hills. We were billeted on a good-size hill. The orderly room was located on another; the latrine on yet another, and the mess tents a fourth hill. You had to negotiate each hill during your 'off' hours when not on duty. Even being in good physical shape I found myself panting and breathless once we got to the 20/30-mile speed marches and the constant double-time in which we performed our tasks. Pushups were as common as eating and sleeping. Early morning PT wasn't ordinary PT as I'd had back at Fort Bragg. Innovations were added. We lifted tree trunks, ten men to a log, by the numbers, in rhythm and coordination. If any man goofed off, the rest knew it at once and that man was called to task then and there. We learned to work together from day one and if you couldn't, you were sent packing. There were grueling hours on obstacle courses designed for mountain goats, cliff scaling, hand-to-hand unarmed combat, day and night exercises under live ammunition and in the harshest of weather. After the first week or so, many men fell by the way. They were returned to their units and replacements joined our ranks for their shot at this program. The officers got no special favors. Our leaders went through exactly the same rigorous training we did." There were casualties; one man fell to his death from a cliff; another died when struck by a bullet during a live-fire exercise.

After six weeks as a Ranger, Merrill developed pneumonia. While he convalesced in a hospital the 1st Ranger Battalion departed Achnacarry. He wound up in an engineer battalion. His new outfit refused to aid him in his quest to rejoin the Rangers, and on more than one occasion his pleas infuriated his CO, whose ire infected the first sergeant as well, all to Merrill's detriment. All the Ranger hopeful could do was await an opportunity to rejoin the outfit.

Dwight David Eisenhower, the rapidly rising star of the Army, in his capacity as chief of the War Department's Operations Division had counseled Truscott, "I hope that you will find some other name than 'commandos' the glamor of that name will always remain—and properly so—British." A number of individuals would claim they suggested the name for the American facsimile of the Commandos and Truscott noted in his memoirs, "Many names were recommended. I selected Rangers." (The term dated back to the French and Indian Wars prior to the American Revolution and had been popularized in a best-selling novel by Kenneth Roberts, *Northwest Passage*.)

Early in the summer of 1942, the Allied High Command in London drew up Jubilee, a plan for a large-scale raid at Dieppe on the occupied French coast. The purpose was to test equipment and techniques for a full-scale invasion, evaluate the response of the enemy, and put on a show that might drain some German forces from the Russian front, or at least indicate to the Soviets good-faith intentions. To carry out Jubilee a combined force of some 5,000 Canadians, 1,000 British Commandos, and 50 Rangers [the official count, although Evans believes one more man was involved] boarded ships and boats for the cross-channel excursion.

The 262 vessels started across the channel the night of 18–19 August, nearly two weeks after Edson's Raiders struck Tulagi. Although enemy trawlers blundered upon the Allied convoy in the dark hours of the morning and opened fire, doing some damage, a number of Commando units came ashore and neutralized the Josef Goebbels Coast Artillery Battery (named for Hitler's minister of propaganda). But that was among the few triumphs. Shore gunners shot out boats from underneath Commandos and some Americans attached to Number 3 Commando had to swim for shore. They advanced a few hundred yards inland and Ranger Lt. Edward Loustalot charged an enemy emplacement. A machine gun cut him down.

Wehrmacht soldiers rallied and inexorably shrank the beachhead. Only about a dozen of the Rangers ever got to the beach. Lieutenant Joseph H. Randall working with a Canadian regiment died from enemy fire right at the water's edge. He and Loustalot were apparently the first two Americans to be killed in ground action in Europe. Within a few hours, the Dieppe raid developed into a catastrophic event for the invaders. More than two-thirds of those in the operation became casualties, with nearly 500 dead, 800 listed as missing, and 1,800 taken prisoners. There were no boats to extract the surviving Commandos with their Ranger associates. The Rangers counted two KIA and another man succumbed to his wounds in England. Taken prisoner, most of the first Rangers to enter combat began almost three years of stalag life.

The 1st Ranger Battalion briefly renewed its training with the Commandos and then in September began to work independently toward a new mission. According to Evans, the experience at Dieppe only confirmed the necessity for the kind of intensive preparation common to Rangers and Commandos. With the German *Afrika Korps* punishing the British Eighth Army in North Africa, the Rangers prepared for the first major Allied campaign against the Axis power of Germany and Italy, an invasion of North Africa under the code name Torch. For this operation they became attached to the 1st Infantry Division and responsible for providing a secure beachhead area.

Elite units also participated in the Asian war. In order to keep the Chinese forces viable, the Americans and British created a military supply life-line that extended from India through Burma to the forces of Chiang Kai-shek. While the American-trained and equipped Chinese troops were directed by American general Joseph Stillwell a force of 20,000 elite sol-diers, skilled in guerrilla warfare embarked from India to be inserted into the wilderness behind the Japanese lines where they would clear a path through Burma. More than three-quarters of them were Britons or men from the empire, and in command was Orde Charles Wingate, a noncon-formist general. In parallel with Wingate's "Chindits," the Americans fielded a much smaller, 3,000-strong brigade, known officially as the 5307 Composite Unit. Stillwell's headquarters knew them under the code name Galahad and reporter Jim Shepley of *Time-Life* pasted on the label of Mer-rill's Marauders, in honor of their leader, Frank Merrill.

The men were all volunteers but apparently not screened for any partic-ular skills or virtues. They were drawn from the professional army ranks as well as the citizen-soldiers who trained for jungle warfare after being sta-tioned in India. They benefitted from two highly qualified leaders, Col. Charles Hunter, a 1929 West Point graduate who schooled them in the most useful infantry skills, and his classmate Frank D. Merrill, a former cav-alryman with the insight to recognize the superior military ability of his deputy, Hunter.

During the China-Burma campaign, instead of hit-and-run units de-posited by boats upon coasts, then extracted within a matter of hours, the Chindit-style operations kept the fighters in place until they used up their supplies. Then, they melted back to bases where they restocked weapons, and replaced casualties before returning to the jungle.

In the South Pacific, the Army would form a temporary special group known as the Alamo Scouts. They were not established until 1943 when Gen. Walter Krueger, commander of the Sixth Army, became concerned about the lack of intelligence on enemy soldiers occupying the islands des-tined for invasion. He proposed to form a small group who would surrep-titiously insinuate themselves into enemy-controlled islands and bring back vital information on the disposition of troops, the fortifications, and con-ditions facing invaders.

Colonel Frederick W. Bradshaw, a former lawyer, and Krueger designed the program to manufacture the scouts. Bradshaw said, "We picked out a training center, a little paradise called Ferguson Island. Then we began selecting men. First we called upon the 158th Infantry—justly famous as jungle fighters—the Bushmasters of Panama. We asked for volunteers with qualifications beyond their prowess as foot soldiers. We wanted men of individual initiative and competitive spirit. They had to be men attracted by a game of great risks. They had to be crack marksmen, experts with the grenade, the knife, the Tommy gun and carbine, and also able to kill with their hands if necessary. All our men had to be steeped in woodlore and the techniques of individual camping, in signaling by numerous devices, in map reading and drawing maps."

The candidates underwent a rigorous six-week course that Bradshaw candidly admitted could not hope to instill all of the knowledge and skills required but would provide the basic qualities for their missions. As with the Rangers and Marine Raiders, survival of the rugged competition for membership generated an esprit de corps.

15
Torch

Persuaded that a small-scale invasion of continental Europe in 1942 was beyond their means, the Americans had agreed with the British to mount Torch, in which Allied forces would relieve the British Eighth Army sorely beset by the German *Afrika Korps* and Italian troops. In the Pacific, those desperately fighting to hold Guadalcanal bitterly resented the operation because it denied arms, ships, planes, and men for the war with Japan. Many American leaders believed the British had manipulated the United States into a policy designed to preserve their empire at the cost of American resources. General Joseph Stilwell, among those attempting to develop a strategy for the War Department, referring to the objectives of Torch, groused, "[Roosevelt] had been completely hypnotized by the British who have sold him a bill of goods . . . The Limeys have his ear, while we have the hind tit. Events are crowding us into ill-advised and ill-considered projects. The Limeys want us in with both feet. So the answer is, we must do something *now*, with our hastily made plans and our half-trained and half-equipped troops." Stilwell's superior, George Marshall, also doubted the wisdom of the strategy and when the British surrendered at Tobruk in Libya, giving up 33,000 soldiers, the effectiveness of an invasion seemed questionable. At a dinner in London, Churchill explained to Eisenhower, "When Stalin asked me about crossing the Channel I told him, 'Why stick your head in the alligator's head at Brest when you can go to the Mediterranean and rip his soft underbelly.'" Using this argument Churchill had wooed and won the support of Roosevelt for Torch.

Torch presented the first major test for the newly named commander of American forces in Europe, Dwight D. Eisenhower. Unlike MacArthur, Eisenhower, a 1915 West Point graduate, remained stateside during World War I and never exercised a field command. During the 1920s and 1930s he held a series of staff positions, where he distinguished himself with his diligence, good humor, and appreciation of the chain of command. Undoubtedly his most taxing job was as assistant to Chief of Staff MacArthur from 1930–34 in Washington, and as chief of staff for MacArthur after he assumed the post of field marshal responsible for building the newly created Commonwealth of the Philippines. Eisenhower neither privately nor publicly criticized the crucial decisions that revised War Plan Orange and reduced the ability to resist the Japanese.

While in Washington during the 1930s, Eisenhower came to appreciate certain qualities exhibited by MacArthur. He described him as a "rewarding man to work for, who never concerned himself with how many hours one put in so long as the task was accomplished." Indeed, many who knew Eisenhower saw much of the same in him. But the two were totally dissimilar in their relations to other human beings. Aloof, humorless, enormously impressed with himself and his positions, MacArthur never had any confidants save perhaps his mother and then his wife. Eisenhower, on the other hand, was more often one of the boys; he laughed easily, enjoyed poker or bridge with colleagues, and seemed unconcerned with the niceties of rank.

Drawn to Washington at the birth of World War II by General Marshall, another man whom MacArthur had alienated, Eisenhower's skills quickly became apparent to the Army chief of staff. In those first weeks after the war broke out, Washington, and the various military arms, was, in the words of one historian, a "tower of Babel." The public and the press expected quick action and revenge. Powerful men rushed about, holding secret meetings that fomented wildly improbable schemes. Eisenhower at the War Plans Division maintained his equilibrium and displayed a keen insight into practical possibilities while tactfully dealing with influential if wrong-headed individuals. When the moment arrived to name the top American for European operations, there was no hesitation about the choice of Eisenhower. When he arrived in London in June 1942, he believed, along with Marshall and Secretary of War Henry L. Stimson, that he was there to run Operation Sledgehammer, a limited invasion of Europe to be followed by an all-out assault—Operation Round-up. Eisenhower was shaken by Roosevelt's agreement to substitute Torch for Sledgehammer; he had to proceed in haste.

"The decision to invade North Africa," wrote Eisenhower, "necessitated a complete reversal in our thinking and drastic revision in our planning and preparation. Where we had been counting on many months of orderly build-up, we now had only weeks. Instead of a massed attack across narrow waters, the proposed expedition would require movement across open ocean areas where enemy submarines would constitute a real menace. Our target was no longer a restricted front where we knew accurately terrain, facilities, and people as they affected military operations, but the rim of a continent where no major military campaign had been conducted for centuries. We were not to have the air power we had planned to use against Europe and what we did have would be largely concentrated at a single highly vulnerable base— Gibraltar—and immediate substantial success would have to be achieved in the first engagements. A beachhead could be held in Normandy and expanded, however slowly; a beachhead on the African coast might be impossible even to maintain."

Although Eisenhower later agreed that those opposed to Sledgehammer were correct in their argument that such an operation in 1942 was not feasible, his insistence that Torch presented more problems than a cross-channel beachhead is hard to understand. On D day, 1944 in spite of the enormous build-up of Allied forces, the German losses on the Eastern Front, the huge investment of Nazi troops in Italy, and the devastation from two years of strategic bombing, the Normandy venture faced far more powerful resistance.

North Africa in 1942 was a complicated mix of warring armies, intensive espionage, and a strange diplomatic protocol that portended the political independence and neutrality of the Vichy government in France. The Axis permitted Vichy to run French Morocco, Algeria, and Tunisia through its colonial appointees, backed by the French military, so long as the puppet leaders remained neutral if not hostile to attempts by the Allies to invade. German and Italian intelligence and the gestapo supervised the Vichy-backed officials. Still, the situation enabled American consular and embassy people in North Africa to move about rather freely. They accumulated intelligence about beaches, tides, bridges, railways, troop deployment, and coastal defenses,

A critical issue lay in the reaction of the local armed forces to an invasion. After France collapsed in 1940, the British, fearful the warships might become part of the Axis booty, attacked a portion of the fleet in the North African port of Mers el-Kébir. One battleship was destroyed, two other heavyweights disabled, and as many as 1,200 French sailors were killed. In ports controlled by the Royal Navy, ships flying the Vichy flag were seized and the crews interned. The Vichy government was enraged and the French Navy grew extremely hostile to the British.

A combined operation of Free French troops, under Charles de Gaulle, and British ships had sought to seize the West African seaport of Dakar, only 1,600 air miles from Brazil. Control of the port could shorten distances for the flights from the U.S. to the European theater. The colonial authorities arrested emissaries of de Gaulle when they came ashore and the coastal batteries fired on the British, who retaliated. The enmity of Vichy toward the British and de Gaulle increased.

These unhappy events occurred almost two years before Eisenhower assumed his command in London but the antipathy toward major elements of the Allies remained. The American precursor to the Central Intelligence Agency, the Office of Strategic Services (OSS), advised the British and Free French to remain in the background to avoid offending the colonial forces. With 125,000 men stationed in North Africa and 500 aircraft available for their support, the Vichy French potentially posed a formidable obstacle to

Torch. The American diplomat Robert Murphy, chargé d'affaires at Vichy, and associates delicately felt out high-ranking representatives of the French government in North Africa in an effort to ascertain their reactions to a U.S.-led invasion. The French colonies seethed with internecine intrigue and conflict and, although Murphy developed promising leads, the Allied command wanted to nail down commitments from military leaders and top officials that either they would join the invaders or at least not resist.

Mark Wayne Clark, a boisterous, outspoken West Point graduate of the Class of April 1917, had been named second in command. According to Clark, Roosevelt urged the planners for Torch that a senior officer be dispatched to North Africa to negotiate with the various parties. Murphy, through his contacts in Algeria, contacted the representatives of the French. Clark was the obvious candidate for the meeting. To accompany him he chose Col. Julian Holmes, a former diplomat fluent in French; Brig. Gen. Lyman Lemnitzer, Capt. Jerauld Wright from the U.S. Navy; and Col. Archelaus Hamblin, responsible for the operations supply and shipping.

"The first thing we had to do was get a submarine," reminisced Clark. "We met with Prime Minister Churchill and told him what we had in mind. He had Mountbatten, all of his chief cabinet officers there. When Ike revealed to him I had been selected to go, someone brought up the question of a British representative. I said the British will be represented by the submarine and any Commandos that will help us. He turned to me and said, 'What do you want? The whole resources of the British Empire are at your disposal.' He loved it, just loved things like that. I said I need a British submarine of sufficient size that will pick us up at Gibraltar, put us ashore, and get us out. We'll need all the paraphernalia to get ashore, kayaks, and Commandos."

Headquarters for Torch staff had been established in the tunnels of Gibraltar and Clark informed Churchill that a pair of B-17s would bear them there. The journey required a protective escort but at the same time had to be handled discretely to avoid German surveillance. When the bombers touched down, cars picked up the passengers right at the ramp where they could not be seen by German agents lurking at the Spanish border only 300 yards off.

Said Clark, "I wanted some gold pieces, about $10,000 worth, in case we needed to bribe someone. [Jerauld Wright reported they each carried about $300 worth of gold Canadian coins.] We had passports in case we needed them to get out. I wanted civilian clothes cached someplace where we could get them." At Gibraltar, Clark met the British admiral of the fleet, whose attitude changed abruptly when informed Churchill enthusiastically supported the mission.

The admiral introduced Lt. Norman Jewell, commander of the submarine *Seraph*. "He was a magnificent fellow," said Clark. "Just radiated confidence. I talked with him about the mission. I asked if he knew what it was all about. He answered, 'No, sir. May I be frank? All we have been told is that we are going to take a bunch of screwy Americans who are to be landed on the coast of North Africa.' I said 'is that all you've been told?' He said, 'Yes, sir.' I said what about getting us out? He said, 'Oh, yes, that's just as important, too.' He had a keen sense of humor."

It had been arranged for them to arrive at midnight when a light from a house on a cliff overlooking the sea would signal it was safe to come ashore. But because the flight to Gibraltar had been delayed by inclement weather, they did not reach the site until dawn was breaking. Rather than risk detection, the submarine remained underwater throughout the day. That evening it surfaced but no signal showed and the group had already retired when around midnight Clark was awakened and told the welcome bulb was lit.

"We went in sort of a diamond formation," recalled Clark. "One kayak got smashed against the waves, busted up. Only four of us could go in; one had to come back [to the sub]. We guided on the light in the house and had no problem. We picked up our kayaks and ran across the beach. We learned that [the people they were supposed to meet] had gone when we didn't show up [the night before]. They were risking their lives; they would be called traitors and would only come when we were there. They had arranged to get word to these fellows after daylight and they soon showed up." On hand, too, was Robert Murphy. The host, a man named Henri Tessier, had sent off all of his Arab servants to eliminate any gossip about his guests. Clark recalled, "There was a four-star general named [Charles] Mast. There was an admiral also; all the services were represented. There were five or six Frenchmen and we sat around a table. Everything had to be interpreted. I couldn't tell them we were coming in but I said eventually my country and the British hoped to come to North Africa and if we did we wanted to get their ideas on how we should do it." Actually, as Murphy and Clark knew, the first convoys sailing directly from the United States to participate in Torch, were already at sea.

The French participants, said Clark, provided excellent intelligence. "They were prepared to give us everything. They had maps and all the information I needed, location of all the airfields, what harbors were mined, what beaches were mined, which commanders were more friendly than others." Clark lacked the knowledge or temperament to delve into the schisms among the French leaders. Murphy's responsibility was to sort out the most promising candidates for Allied support.

"I wanted to get out of there that night because the longer we stayed the more trouble we could expect," reported Clark. "About three o'clock in the afternoon I recall looking out the window—they had put me in a French officer's blouse in case anybody happened to see me from the beach. The waves were coming up and there was a storm. It looked bad. The windmill was going a hundred miles an hour. I saw there wasn't much chance of getting out [to the *Seraph*]. So we went back and talked some more. The phone rang and a lookout in town informed Tessier that something was cooking in the police station. They were suspicious of the house because some Arab had gone down to the beach and observed footprints in the sand coming in from the sea. They had reported it and the police were on their way. We hid in the wine cellar. I sent one of the Commandos down to the beach and with the walkie-talkie to radio the submarine."

As the other Americans concealed themselves, Murphy said, "I posed as a somewhat inebriated member of a raucous social gathering. Fortunately, the police were not looking for military conspirators but for smugglers."

"The police came but they didn't find us," recalled Clark. "I decided we'd get out of the house, get into the woods and then down on the beach. We tried to get out when our boats sank and we lost everything. I had stripped down to nothing except the gold in a belt. [Clark felt he could swim better pantless.] We spent most of the night there in a little perimeter defense."

The police returned, inspected the house, and even looked over the beach, but did not see Clark's group and departed. "I went to the house; I had no shoes and my feet were cut from jumping on some sharp rocks" said Clark. "I got [Tessier] to turn his lights on. We got down on the beach. [Jerauld Wright] said there was a stretch where it wasn't as rough. I said we'll try it. Jerry and I went stripped down The rest of them pushed us through the waves, big ones. Finally, we paddled out. We knew the submarine would be standing by because we had a message, a flash, one word, one letter that they'd be standing by. After about an hour, all of a sudden—there were no lights—they appeared and they grabbed us. One by one [the others] came out until the last one which smashed into the submarine and the boat sank. The fellows could swim and they had life jackets. I had a lot of stuff, maps and things strapped to me, but the kayak that went down carried weapons, infra reds, walkie-talkies, and papers with information about French officials. I was afraid it would be washed up on the beach.

"Ike met me when we got to England and he wanted to take me right away [to see Churchill] but I said God almighty let me have a little rest. They let me take a short nap and then we met with the prime minister. God, he loved it, just loved it. The king wanted to see me and he loved it . . . I told how the police had raided the house while we hid in the empty wine cellar and the king said wasn't it too bad it was empty." Clark said he had been told that the best choice to command friendly French forces was Gen. Henri Giraud.

"Giraud wouldn't ride in a British submarine so we put Jerry Wright in charge of a British sub and picked up Giraud off southern France and brought him to Gibraltar." Clark's mention of Giraud as "the man we wanted" far oversimplified the situation. In the delicate interchanges with the French, the absence of specific information about the coming invasion prevented a commitment to any individual, such as Giraud. The French general, senior in standing to de Gaulle, had avoided disgrace during his nation's defeat, escaped from a German prison camp, and had never publicly supported the Vichy government. He seemed to have the proper credentials for what the Allies had in mind. However, he proved to have as grand a sense of himself as did the nettlesome de Gaulle. With the landings only ten days off, Giraud demanded he be named commander in chief for the campaign. At the same time, General Mast, when notified of the imminent arrival of Allied forces on the Algerian shores, expressed anxiety and displeasure. Looming over all was the question of how Adm. Jean Francois Darlan, commander in chief of all French military forces and the executive in charge of the North African territory, would behave. Darlan was a bitter foe of the British, receptive to the Nazi philosophy concerning Jews and a willing collaborator with the Germans. No one knew how much authority or influence Giraud, Mast, or Darlan could exercise over subordinates in the resident French armed forces.

From the United States, soldiers in the 3d and 9th Infantry Divisions and units from the 2d Armored Division boarded ships bound for North Africa. From England, the 1st and 34th Infantry Divisions plus the 1st Armored Division loaded onto transports. Attached to the 1st Infantry Division was the 1st Battalion of Rangers. Other vessels carried British fighting men. The Allied navies gathered round to ward off submarines and to add their punch with offshore bombardment. At a British airdrome, the 504th Parachute Regiment readied itself for Torch.

For the most part, the GIs going off to battle had spent at least a year in uniform and many came from the regular army. But their combat readiness was another matter. For example, Capt. G. V. Nicholls, a British veteran of tank warfare against the Germans, spent three weeks with the 2d Armored Division in February 1942, and noted, "The outstanding impression I had . . . was the supreme overconfidence of all ranks. From General [George S.] Patton downward, they seemed confident in beating any enemy with whom they were confronted and were fully prepared to begin operations at once." Nicholls quoted junior officers and enlisted men: "I would like to see German Panzers stop us."; "Give me a Light Tank and nothing will be able to stop us."; "These 75mm guns will smash anything the Germans have." Commented Nicholls, "This attitude is encouraged by General Patton's constant allusions to that imminent departure for the theater of operations. The junior officers thought the six-months continuous maneuvers in 1941 had fitted them for active service, and were satisfied that their individual training was well up to the standards of the British and Germans. In this opinion they were entirely wrong."

The British officer blamed Americans' assumptions for superior equipment and "better education and living conditions [which were] more than a match for the Japanese and the tired and unfit Germans. Any attempt to point out the German aptitude for mechanized warfare and the British experience during the past two years was discounted by most of the junior officers."

Hamilton Howze, a 1930 graduate of the USMA, had become a staff officer for the 1st Armored Division. Much of the North African campaign would be waged in desert country but Howze noted "We did not have the privilege of desert training. We did not anticipate that there is no cover, or practically none in the desert against aircraft. The aircraft can easily spot you and knock the hell out of you. We suffered badly from German air attacks. Any vehicle running across the desert leaves a plume of dust behind which can go 300 feet high. We had bad training, unusual visibility, [were ignorant of] the ranges in which tanks could engage each other. These things came as a surprise. Going to Africa, we were thinking about Europe. The morale was very high. Everyone was excited and full of beans and anxious to go to war. The equipment we had wasn't as good as we thought it was, simply because we hadn't run up against the superior equipment of the Germans. But at the time we thought it was great stuff."

The 1st Infantry Division, a regular army outfit, was among the best-trained American organizations in the early days of World War II. Many of the soldiers were career military men. George Zenie, a Long Island, New York, native, unable to find a job, joined the outfit in 1940. "When I enlisted, my original company officers and indeed the officers of the 1st Infantry Division, were, for the most, West Point graduates. They ran their outfits by the book, but we expected that and we respected them. Our division commander, Maj. Gen. Terry Allen, and Brig. Gen. Teddy Roosevelt Jr., the assistant division commander, were revered. Our noncoms were also old army. They drilled us and worked us very hard. Later, in North Africa, Sicily, France, and Germany I thanked God they had pushed us." Zenie noted that the huge expansion of the army required the 1st Division to ship many of its better officers and noncoms to recently activated units. The replacements received by the 1st Division were "a mixed bag."

The 3d Infantry Division included Lt. William B. Rosson, a 1940 ROTC graduate of the University of Oregon, who chose to enter the service as a regular. He recalled training as "rather rudimentary. It was a peacetime oriented affair with more emphasis on spit and polish, cleanliness of barracks and what not, rather than combat readiness. We had no information on the German forces before embarkation. They kept us in complete secrecy of the destination and didn't know where we were going when we boarded the ships. We had 37mm guns [for antipersonnel and antitank purposes]. On the ship was the first time we saw and fired the bazooka. The CO wore an asbestos firefighter's uniform for the first demonstration."

Amphibious landings, practiced by the GIs in England and the United States, only marginally resembled what lay ahead on Mediterranean beaches. Leisurely picking a route through rocks would not be an option when under enemy artillery and small-arms fire. A shortage of experienced crews to operate the landing craft further troubled those in command.

Operation Torch also offered the American airborne its first opportunity for combat. Chief of Staff Marshall had picked William Yarborough to become a member of the London Planning Group as the authority on airborne operations. "I suppose," said Yarborough, "because I was extremely enthusiastic about airborne operations and maybe having been one of the early, early officers in the activity. I went to England in July 1942 with more enthusiasm than real background knowledge, intelligence, and strategy. We didn't really know what the airborne goal or objective was." At the same time he became increasingly aware of problems with the Air Corps, which was supposed to transport the troopers. "They resented being taken off the kinds of jobs that provided support to air or army units. The installation of navigational gear to keep in formation had been delayed [because of lack of interest in hauling airborne]. The troopers themselves were superbly trained. The air group was gallant, fine, young, tremendous people but certainly had not had the kinds of training that the Germans had to go into Crete or someplace else."

Imbued with pride, the neophytes and uncertainly prepared combat troops headed for North Africa. Meanwhile, it was up to Eisenhower to pick which French steed to back. At one point, dispirited by his talks with Giraud, Eisenhower unleashed Clark upon the prickly Gaul. Clark informed the French general that he could either accept the limited role proffered or sit the entire affair out. When Giraud haughtily declared he would return to France, Clark claimed he said, "Oh, no, you won't. That's a one-way submarine. You're not going back to France on it," and left it to the interpreter to tell Giraud, "From now on your ass is out in the snow."

"Finally," said Clark, "we got him to come 'round. I would take him with me as soon as the Algiers airfield was captured and I would set up the command there as Ike's deputy. Giraud would be the supreme French commander for political, military, and everything else. That evening, Ike and I went back to our room where we got undressed and in our pajamas. Ike said, 'Let's have a drink before we go to bed.' He said, 'I wish I could go in with you but I can't.' I said, 'Of course you can't. You've got to stay at your headquarters.'"

As head of the American ground forces, Eisenhower had chosen Gen. George S. Patton Jr. A veteran of the expedition that hunted Pancho Villa in Mexico and the American forces in France for World War I, Patton had a well-established reputation for emotional outbursts and fractious conflicts. He quarreled with most of his contemporaries, regarded few if any his equal at strategy, and rarely tempered his criticisms of others with praise. Nevertheless, he gained the confidence of even those offended by his conduct, perhaps because of the strength of his belief in himself. His units were regarded as the most disciplined and well trained.

Still, fearful the personnel were insufficiently schooled and the plans equally inadequate, with typical bombast, Patton boasted he would "leave the beaches either a conqueror or a corpse." To a British admiral he sneered, "Never in history had the Navy landed an Army at the planned time and place. If you land us anywhere within fifty miles of Fedala [a site near Casablanca] and within one week of D day, I'll go ahead and win." He covered his reputation, however, by sponsoring a statement that warned, "This [the invasion of Morocco] cannot be considered a militarily sound operation of war."

Considered critical to the success of the strike into Algeria was the capture of the Tafaraoui and La Senia airfields near Oran. Shortly before midnight on 7 November, thirty-nine C-47s bearing paratroopers from the 2d Battalion of the 503d Parachute Infantry Regiment rose from the British base for a long night flight to the drop zones of the airports. Lieutenant Colonel Edson D. Raff commanded the battalion and Bill Yarborough, as the chief planner for the mission, accompanied the outfit. For guidance to the target the operation relied on the Rebecca-Eureka navigation system. In practice, the Eureka component on the ground transmitted a signal to the Rebecca aboard aircraft, enabling the planes to home in on the sites. Whether the C-47s landed at the airdromes or the troopers jumped depended upon whether the local military would fight or welcome the Americans. While still in the air, intelligence sources advised headquarters the French troops would be hostile. Unfortunately, efforts to relay the vital information to the planes were never received. The airborne had no clue whether to land or leap.

"Some of the pilots only arrived at the airdrome the night before they were supposed to take off," recalled Yarborough. Without the equipment to help maintain formation and without running lights because of the need to avoid observation, the untutored aerial chauffeurs lost contact with one another. Instead of an organized group, the flight broke down into small units of from one to six aircraft. On the ground, Lt. Howard Hapgood, disguised in an Arab burnoose, waited near Tafaraoui with his Eureka. He had been given civilian status as a member of the diplomatic service and had smuggled the navigation aid into the country . But when the time for the arrival of the airplanes passed without any sight of them, Hapgood, "wisely," said Yarborough, "blew the thing up and vanished. He had been sitting there for several hours operating this device. His chances of survival would have been pretty low."

At dawn Yarborough looked out and saw only one other airplane on his flank and no others on the horizon. "I stood in back of Col. William C. Schofield, the Air Corps commander, and tried from my knowledge of the terrain models and the maps to figure out with him where we were. We saw lots of mountains but it wasn't until we saw a particular section of the coast of North Africa that we realized we were well south . . . and west of where we should be. We decided to turn toward our objective. We flew over Spanish Morocco and saw two of our airplanes down. One with what appeared to be spahis—troops on horseback rounding up the guys who had gotten out of the airplanes. We knew that was not the place."

Another group of C-47s headed toward the objective of La Senia. Any notions of a friendly reception evaporated when French antiaircraft guns started to bark. The flight set down at Sebkra d'Oran, a dry salt lake west of Oran. The crews of six more planes, including one with Raff, observed a column of tanks approaching the aircraft on the ground. Raff ordered his troopers to jump. Only after they landed did they recognize the armor as American.

At this point the three planes with Yarborough spotted the Sebkra d'Oran aggregation and they joined the people on the dry salt lake. Raff, although injured when he crashed into rocks after his jump, along with Yarborough organized an overland attack on Tafaraoui. They were twenty-five miles from the airdrome when word came by radio that other U.S. units had already seized the field. The armor commander asked if troopers could be flown in to relieve his tankers for pursuit of the enemy. Yarborough agreed to return to the planes and find some with enough fuel to make the trip. "It was unbelievable, the mud of Sebkra d'Oran," said Yarborough. "You couldn't move, you couldn't drive. It was like walking in flypaper." Nevertheless, they made their way to the C-47s, jammed seventy or eighty troopers into three with enough gas and flew toward Tafaraoui. As they approached at low altitude, three French fighters zeroed in on them. "We didn't have far to go and hit the ground. But it was enough to wash out the landing gear on the airplane I was in. We were hit broadside by the first pair of the Vichy fighters. They made two passes while we were in the air and they hit something every time. Then when we hit the ground, they flew over us one final time and peppered us as we lay there. The airplanes were a complete loss." They were still fifteen miles from the objective but after an all-night march, the men took over Tafaraoui.

In terms of the objectives of the mission, the first airborne effort was a flop. Not a single trooper had parachuted into combat. Only about a third of the airplanes remained operational. Yarborough commented, "The Rebecca-Eureka supposed [to bring us in on target] was put out of action because of the complexity of the plan. It is something that soldiers will never learn; that if a plan is simple, it's liable to work. If it's complex, its chances of working go down astronomically." Still, he noted, "We confounded the criticism of some experts. We were in North Africa with thirty-six or thirty-seven airplanes and almost a whole parachute battalion. There weren't all that many casualties. We got our parachutes together, and five or six days later made another drop."

The first of those to come ashore near the city of Algiers were men from a British infantry brigade. They encountered no resistance and the French troops, in accord with word from General Mast, did not fire. More than 4,300 GIs with 1,000 Commandos struck three other sites near Algiers. For the most part the uniformed inhabitants responded passively with General Mast personally welcoming Commandos to Fort de Sidi-Ferruch. One garrison refused to put down its weapons but submitted after intervention by British planes from a carrier.

For the U.S. 1st Division, however, mistakes by those steering the assault boats created serious difficulties. The overloaded soldiers set down in deep water waded or even floated ashore. If opposition had been on the scene the situation could have been deadly. A third group, its numbers reduced when a submarine torpedo damaged a troop ship, also reached its destination in some disarray. Fortunately, their initial landings did not meet serious resistance.

Terry de la Mesa Allen, in command of these 1st Division troops, was a dropout from West Point in his final year before he earned a degree at Catholic University in 1912. Allen's background, his intense solicitude for his troops, and his less-than-abstemious enjoyments in off hours, set him apart from his contemporaries. He cheerfully admitted to a lack of interest in the academic end of a military education. When he attended the Fort Leavenworth Command and General School in the same class as Eisenhower, Allen graduated 221st while Eisenhower came out first among the 241 students.

Reporting for the *New Yorker* during the North African campaign, A. J. Liebling said that in the eyes of superiors, Allen had come across as "slapdash and reckless" during peacetime. However, one of his staff officers, a USMA graduate himself, noted, "There are some generals that if they find the enemy in strong positions, they will go ahead and get you killed [a frequent critique of Patton]. But old Terry will find the way around and kill them all."

Ernie Pyle, the reporter for the Scripps-Howard newspaper chain, who ordinarily preferred the company of the lower echelons, said, "Major General Terry Allen was one of my favorite people. Partly because he didn't give a damn for hell or high water; partly because he was more colorful than most; and partly because he was the only general outside the Air Forces I could call by his first name. If there was one thing in the world Allen lived and breathed for, it was to fight. He had been all shot up in the last war and he seemed not the least averse to getting shot up again. This was no intellectual war with him. He hated Germans and Italians like vermin, and his pattern for victory was simple; just wade in and murder the hell out of the low-down, good-for-nothing so-and-sos. Allen's speech was picturesque. No writer could fully capture him on paper, because his talk was so wonderfully profane it couldn't be put down in black and white.

"Allen was shot through the jaw in the last war. That wound causes him to make an odd hissing noise when he is intense. He breathes by sucking the air in between his teeth, and it sounds like a leak in a tire. . . . As far as I know, Terry Allen was the only general in Tunisia who slept on the ground. All the others carried folding cots. General Allen wouldn't allow any of his staff to sleep on a cot. He said if everybody in his headquarters had a cot it would take several trucks to carry them and he could use the trucks to better purpose."

At Saint-Cloud on 9 November, French artillery wrought so many casualties on the 1st Division's 18th Regimental Combat Team, that Col. Frank Grier pulled back his three battalions to regroup while American artillery prepared to blast the town. Terry Allen, hearing of what had happened, tore out of his command post at Renan, a few miles off, sped to the regimental forward headquarters for a thorough examination of the entire situation. It was his first big decision. "No," said Allen, "We're going to bypass the town. We're not going to bombard it. I don't want to kill civilians. There are four thousand of them in there. Regardless of sentiment it would make a bad political impression. Third, if we bombard it and yet failed to take it by attack that would be disastrous. Fourth, it would [expend] too much ammunition. Fifth, it isn't necessary since we can reach our objective Oran without it." It is difficult to believe that in the same situation Patton would have hesitated to use the artillery. However, to some high-level critics, Allen's decisions smacked of pampering his men rather than strategic moves.

The first serious resistance on opening day had erupted in the Algiers harbor, where two British destroyers flying U.S. flags, bearing troops from both nations, all of whom wore American uniforms, raced toward the docks to seize the anchorage and prevent any French warships from being scuttled. Commandos assigned to knock out coastal batteries that protected the port were unsuccessful. A fusillade hammered both ships, forcing one to retreat. The other, having cleaved a boom blocking the entrance, raced to a berth where the infantrymen could debark and capture the major installations.

GIs of the 2d Armored Division assaulted Safi, a Moroccan town about 100 miles from Casablanca. Ernest Harmon, USMA Class of April 1917, in command, said, "Upon arrival at the beach we found about 200 men lying there with water lapping against the soles of their feet. There was a little sniper fire coming toward us and bullets were striking the sand here and there. I asked the captain of the troops on the ground what they were lying there for and he stated they were being fired at. I said, 'Yes, I realize you are, but how many people are firing at you?' He replied, 'About six.' I directed him to attack the house where the fire was coming from with a squad of twelve men and to get going with the remainder of the company on their objective as planned. The men were just having initial stage fright that all men have the first time they come under fire."

The opening phase of Operation Torch dismayed Patton, who stepped ashore shortly after noon at Safi. Bullets from stubborn French holdouts still smacked the surf as the general made his way onto the shore. He harshly criticized the actions of the soldiers. "The beach was a mess and the officers were doing nothing. I cursed and at last got a launch off to catch the boats [with reinforcements] and show them into the harbor. Had [General Jonathan] Anderson showed the proper push, this would have been done earlier. Just as I got the launch out, a boat turned end-for-end and drowned sixteen men. We only found three—they were a nasty blue color.

"The French bombed the beach and later strafed it. One soldier who was pushing a boat and got scared, ran onto the beach, assumed the fetal position and jibbered. I kicked him in the arse with all my might and he jumped right up and went to work. As a whole the men were poor, the officers worse. It is very sad. I saw one lieutenant let his men hesitate to jump into the water. I gave him hell. I hit another man who was too lazy to push a boat. We also kicked a lot of Arabs."

Tanks from the 2d Armored rolled ashore and with infantry drove some six miles inland. This would put the Allied ships in the harbor beyond artillery range while leaving behind scattered resistance within Safi to be mopped up later. When word reached Harmon of French reinforcements heading for the town from Marrakech, sixty miles off, he called for an air strike that destroyed the column.

Even as the first soldiers climbed onto the Algerian shores, Robert Murphy brought news of the assault to Admiral Darlan. Furious that he had not been consulted and brought into the drama earlier—although whether he would have gone along or alerted the Germans is not clear—Darlan accused the Americans of being as stupid as the British. About the same time, French

Army headquarters, now fully aware of the invasion, staved off an uprising intended to aid the Allies. The accommodating General Mast was relieved of his command. A detachment loyal to Darlan overwhelmed rebels who had grabbed Admiral Darlan and Robert Murphy. The small force of Allied troops in Algiers harbor withdrew as the French Army counterattacked. Nevertheless, the expeditionary force had effectively isolated the city.

Some 200 miles west, an invasion enveloped the smaller city of Oran. The 1st Ranger Battalion, led by Darby, assaulted the harbor fort and a pair of French coastal batteries that guarded the port of Arzew. Manned by naval personnel, presumably with a grudge against the British for their bombardment of French ships, the battery had to be regarded as hostile. Darby split his unit with Herman Dammer, his executive officer, who led the 1:00 A.M. charge of Companies A and B against the bastion at sea level. The defenders offered little fight although snipers killed one Ranger and wounded another.

Darby himself landed half an hour later with the remainder of the Rangers silently working their way up the hill in the darkness. "I was with Darby," said Bing Evans. "He went about a quarter-mile past our marker and I told him we've gone too far. He didn't want to believe me but then he talked to Roy Murray and Max Schneider [the COs of E and F Companies]. They verified what I said. We got our bearings and went to the right place."

While James Altieri and his fellow Rangers fixed bayonets preparatory to an assault on the French positions, the 81mm mortar teams set up some 500 yards behind them. Two men with wire cutters crept forward in the darkness to open a path through the barbed-wire fences. Altieri noted, "They were gone only a minute when the darkness crisscrossed with orange-and-green tracer fire. The crisscross was joined by two more angles of machine-gun fire. Dirt was splattering all around us from the impact of the bullets." The defenders had been alerted by the fire down in the harbor where other Rangers under Herman Dammer engaged in a skirmish.

Altieri remarked, "Strangely, I wasn't scared. It was just like the Commando training. Close-landing bullets by now were a familiar experience. Also the drama of the battle was so completely absorbing, that there was no time to be concerned about personal fears."

Darby took charge calling for a mortar barrage. Recalled Altieri, "In an instant the air overhead was filled with loud swishing, fluttering mortar shells speeding earthward on their mission of destruction. The entire hillside shuddered as the shells came crashing down, their flaming bursts illuminating the area in eerie shadows. For two minutes the mortar bombardment continued, then the order was passed down, 'Prepare to assault.'"

The Rangers rushed through the openings in the barbed wire and in the dugouts discovered French soldiers dazed by the explosions. Swiftly, they bagged some 150 captives including the commandant of the still-untouched

Fort du Nord. Darby demanded the colonel surrender the bastion but was momentarily nonplussed when his prisoner said the French could not yield until they displayed valor. Darby then proposed token resistance. The troops in the fort could fire their rifles in the air once before coming out. On that note resistance at Fort du Nord ended. By noon Arzew was officially secure. Terry Allen, as commander of the 1st Infantry Division, to which the Rangers were attached, commented, "Their initial mission was accomplished with great dash and vigor."

Bill Behlmer, as an antitank crewman with the 1st Division, said, "We were briefed that we'd land at a seaside resort, Arzew, and our objective was the railroad station in Oran. The English crews dropped some of the trucks and guns in deep water and it was a mess, but we made it to the beach. This was the real thing, artillery shells, machine guns, mortars, small arms. We had our first taste of the gnawing feeling in the pit of the stomach. Fear! We secured the beach, but that first night was terrible. Everybody had an itchy trigger finger and fired at anything that moved, shot up half of the grapevines in North Africa. The corporal of the guard shot one of our sentries in the stomach."

Harold J. Taylor, a pre–Pearl Harbor draftee and communications technician with headquarters of the 3d Division's 15th Regiment, heavily burdened with a rifle, combat pack, ammunition; half of a two-man, two-piece radio set, scrambled down the side of a cargo net into the landing boat in the darkness off the port of Fedala. "Beads of sweat covered my forehead while many things were racing through my mind—might I be killed!!! I also realized that I wasn't alone in this ordeal; there were many others with me and they too were experiencing similar feelings. Together we were supportive of each other. The knowledge that we would be together added comfort and a sense of security.

"As we approached French Morocco in the dark it became apparent that trouble was ahead. We were not approaching land in the designated area . . . large protruding rocks became visible in front of us. It looked like sure death as our landing craft was buffeted by the large waves that kept rolling off the rocks. The craft rolled back and forth on its sides, throwing men and equipment about. Had it turned over all aboard would surely have been killed.

"How the Navy man was able to stay at the control and move us out of the area and back to our convoy, I will never know. We picked ourselves up off the floor of the craft and retrieved our belongings. No one was seriously injured." Daybreak revealed that other landing craft also had problems. The beach, littered with debris as far as one could see, had the appearance of a major disaster. But in fact, Taylor and his unit quickly set out toward Casablanca.

Ships bearing men from the 7th Regiment of the 3d Division, also destined to go ashore at Fedala, rendezvoused at sea. William Rosson, assigned as assistant regimental S-3 [plans and operations], recalled, "A certain amount of fire from ashore and Casablanca began. It was quite exciting and a bit unnerving to see the tracers heading into the ship areas. Operations began at night for a dawn assault. There was no problem boarding the landing craft, but we spent what seemed an eternity circling about. I had the uneasy feeling we were off course going in as the naval gunfire began . . . as dawn broke. I could see explosions and some return fire from the French positions. As we approached the beach we came under scattered machine-gun fire from the Fedala strong point. The surf was fairly turbulent and quite a large number of craft had broached. I was amazed to see how many boats had ended up on the beach sideways."

Support for the amphibious assault at Fedala came in the form of airplanes catapulted off the decks of three escort flattops and the bigger carrier *Ranger*. Among the smaller carriers was the USS *Suwannee*. Torpedo bombers and fighters from the *Suwannee* accompanied by air groups from sister ships hammered submarine pens and targeted the Port Lyautey airfield. Rumors that French pilots would refuse to fight Americans proved false. Four U.S. planes were lost in dogfights that also brought down eight French aircraft. Two Wildcats off the *Suwannee* blasted a twin-engine bomber out of the sky only to learn they had knocked off a British Hudson.

David Jones, the pilot with the Doolittle Raiders who reached safety after parachuting from his B-25 over China, had returned to the States where he received command of a B-26 squadron in the 319th Bomb Group. In its early versions the twin-engine bomber known as the Marauder earned the nickname of "the widow maker." Said Jones, "We were in Baton Rouge about a month, and in that month the group lost seven airplanes, none out of my squadron. Guys flying into trees, the blind leading the blind."

The Martin Company produced a modified version, and equipped with new Marauders, the 319th headed for England via Presque Isle, Maine; Greenland; and Iceland. A series of crashes convinced the authorities the two-engine aircraft could not manage the long journey with normal gear and crew. "We had a crew of six on the B-26 with guns, armor plate, and the whole bit. [The order came] unload all your guns and you are going to take your armor plate out. Three of the crew, the pilot, copilot, and crew chief were all we had." While Jones was marooned for eighteen days in Greenland because of bad flying weather, the experts decided weight was not the problem. "Four C-47s came in to give us all the equipment we had taken out of the airplanes. We took the armor plate, the guns, and we threw them all in the bomb bay, wired them down, and waited for the weather to change. We finally made it to Iceland and were there about ten days waiting for weather and then went to England."

Because the fighters were ill equipped to navigate the long trip from Land's End on the southwestern coast to North Africa, Jones, in his B-26, led a dozen P-38s to an air base in Algiers. "Christ, there were bomb craters and it was a mess, a big mess. We landed in all directions and straddling bomb holes and God knows what all. We must have ended up with almost two or three hundred airplanes on the field. No organization, no nothing. We just lived by our airplanes. In the morning you'd see hundreds of little fires. Everybody was cooking, even the fliers beside their own airplanes. We were loading 250-pound bombs when we could because we could muscle those in."

One of the first raids struck an enemy base at Sfax. "We went across the field with nine airplanes. We were on the deck and I missed the airfield. I could see it on the left so I made a 180 and by this time everybody was waiting for us. They shot everything at us. My left wingman fell off. We got home but we had lost this airplane and I felt pretty bad. The next morning, here this crew walks in. I had P-38s escorting us. They had seen and followed this airplane when it landed in the desert. The crew stayed with it. The P-38s then went home where the A-20s squadron with Charles Kegelman [a participant in the 4 July 1942 inaugural raid of the Eighth Air Force] was and they got to talking, yakking. They fired up an A-20 and one guy went out and the guys were still at their airplane. The A-20 picked up seven people and took them home."

Flying into the Blida airport near Algiers on D plus one, Mark Clark nervously watched as German bombers attacked the installations now controlled by the Allies. No sooner did his B-17 touch down before another wave of enemy planes sent everyone scrambling. The French in the captured city ignored, if not insulted, Giraud. "We found that the Arabs would shoot Giraud on sight. He wasn't the right guy at all," said Clark. "Darlan was." As Eisenhower's deputy indicated, a cease-fire from the French forces required the cooperation of the admiral who detested the British and who had easily fitted into the collaboration with the Axis countries.

"I had to meet with Darlan who was in full command," said Clark, "while we had to hide Giraud. We kept him hidden for weeks. I had to get Darlan to issue two orders; one to bring the French fleet out of Toulon [a seaport in southeastern France] and the second to stop the fighting." The British worried that the French warships might become Nazi property and then ravage Allied shipping in the Mediterranean. "Before he [Darlan] would stop the fighting between French and Americans he wanted certain guarantees. After four hours with him I sent a message home, using for the first time YBSOB [Yellow-bellied son-of-a-bitch, the code for Darlan]. I met him some more and finally got to the point where he wouldn't cooperate at all and I got tough. I had [Maj. Gen. Charles] Doc Ryder there with his 34th Division. We took a company of infantry and surrounded the place. I told him he'd be under arrest until he came around. He did come around. He issued orders and it stopped, although for about 48 hours there was still some going on."

Darlan, technically still subject to the government of Petain in Vichy, nevertheless instructed the French vessels in Toulon to prepare to sail in the event the Germans overran unoccupied France. When the Nazi leaders learned of Darlan's surrender they immediately threatened Petain who relieved Darlan and cancelled his orders. The admiral vacillated, talked of revoking the commitment made to Clark who informed Darlan that that was not possible.

To his chief of staff Gen. Walter Bedell Smith, Eisenhower, confronted by the rivalry of Darlan and Giraud, wrote, "I've promised Giraud to make him the big shot, while I've got to use every kind of cajolery, bribe, threat, and all else to get Darlan's active cooperation. All of these Frogs have a single thought—'Me.' It isn't all this operation that's wearing me down—it's the petty intrigue and the necessity of dealing with little selfish, conceited worms that call themselves men." To a friend he confided, "I am a cross between a one-time soldier, a pseudo statesman, a jack-legged politician, and a crooked diplomat. I walk a soapy tightrope in a rainstorm with a blazing furnace on one side and a pack of ravenous tigers on the other."

While Eisenhower found it difficult to comprehend the attitudes of people whom his armies had come to liberate from the Nazi jackboot, Giraud understandably was miffed because he had been deceived by Americans like Murphy on his status. De Gaulle was equally furious because he had neither been involved nor informed about Operation Torch. When he heard the news, he huffed, "I hope the Vichy people will fling them into the seas! You don't get France by burglary." It required Churchill to stroke de Gaulle until he converted into a supporter of Torch.

All of the dissembling, the "acting" he studied under a prima donna like MacArthur, taxed Eisenhower, but the experience probably helped him later in the war when he dealt with conflicting personalities and hard-held positions. But the stakes were huge; men's lives and the success of the venture depended upon how the North African French acted. The advance word was that those defending the various areas would meet invasion forces with all the firepower available.

Fortunately, although Vichy had fired Darlan, the French of North Africa decided to take their cue from him. As a prisoner of the Allies, the admiral had little choice but to call upon those within his former jurisdiction to cease-fire and, on 11 November, the French military did lay down their arms. Unwilling to trust even the Vichy French, the Nazi armies then fully occupied the former satrapy with help from Il Duce [Benito Mussolini] who sent his legions into southern France and Corsica. Crews aboard the French ships in Toulon, unwilling to fight for either side, scuttled their vessels. With the capitulation of the French and Rommel in retreat, Churchill crowed "We have a victory—a remarkable and definite victory." The triumph was short-lived.

While *Wehrmacht* strategists considered an Allied invasion of North Africa high on the list of probabilities, *der führer*, who believed himself the best judge of military actions had not taken the notion seriously. In fact, in the weeks before the opening salvos of Torch, as the reinforced British Eighth Army under Bernard Montgomery opened an offensive against El Alamein with a 1,000-gun barrage. Spearheaded by 1,000 tanks compared to the 240 available to the Germans and 280 obsolete Italian ones, the British also mustered 1,500 planes against the 350 of the *Luftwaffe*. Hitler refused to permit an evacuation to Europe but allowed the embattled Rommel to retreat from Egypt to Libya. Without authorization from Hitler, Field Marshal [Alfred] Kesselring in Italy amassed troops and aircraft and within thirty-six hours of the invasion the first of them debarked at an airfield in Tunisia. French soldiers on the scene might have repelled them but Vichy instructed its underlings in Tunis not to resist. Subsequently, Hitler ratified Kesselring's decision with orders to drive the Allies out of Algeria.

16
Grim Glimmers

With Torch drawing so heavily on U.S. resources, the campaign in the South Pacific dragged on, short in manpower, rations, ammunition, and firepower. Admiral King, as the boss of all naval operations, and Admiral Nimitz, commander of the Pacific fleet, unhappy with the timorous approach of Adm. Robert Ghormley, replaced him with Adm. William "Bull" Halsey. A member of the USNA Class of 1904, Halsey, an indifferent student who almost flunked out in his third year, shone on the football field and in social situations. During World War I he commanded a destroyer in the war against German U-boats. Like a number of others of senior rank he learned to fly while in his forties in order to earn command of an aircraft carrier. Although he needed spectacles, Halsey nevertheless passed the eye exam, the beneficiary of some finagling with the medical records.

Unlike Nimitz, his junior by a year, Halsey, while well versed in technology and tactics, was an impulsive, hunch-driven commander with a penchant for blurting out his opinions, a characteristic one reporter called, "an affinity between his foot and his mouth." But what recommended him for the job was the same sort of aggressive approach to war. Speaking to midshipmen and officers in 1942 during a brief stop at the Naval Academy, he glossed over tactics in favor of blunt bellicosity, snarling about "yellow-bellied sons-of-bitches." His election to command was welcomed by the Marine commanders. General Vandegrift described the admiral's visit to Guadalcanal as being, "like a wonderful breath of fresh air."

The Japanese again determined to evict the enemy from Guadalcanal. Fortunately for Halsey and the defenders, the code breakers intercepted intelligence detailing the order of battle plotted by the Nipponese. Immediately, the Americans beefed up the forces in residence through the Americal Division, the only large-scale Army organization activated overseas. These GIs, graduates of former National Guard outfits, began to join the Marines on the island during the first week of November. More Air Corps bombers and crews took up station on Espíritu Santo from where they could batter enemy positions.

Convoy and task-force vessels steamed toward Guadalcanal from both directions. The two sides traded punches in the air as American fighter planes tangled with torpedo-laden Bettys bound for transports carrying more Americal infantrymen. The Grumman Wildcats and the antiaircraft fire knocked down almost all of the bombers and some of their Zero escorts. That band of attackers inflicted little damage. Pouring into the Slot, however, was a formidable flotilla of Imperial Navy warships, including a carrier, two battleships, cruisers, and destroyers. They considerably outgunned and outnumbered the opposing U.S. vessels, a force without a functioning carrier or battleship to block a bombardment of Henderson Field and its environs.

During the night of Friday 12–13 November, General Vandegrift said, "For nearly an hour, we watched naval guns belch orange death with such rapid vehemence that the island seemed to shake beneath us." The two groups of warships apparently stumbled into one another while darkness covered Ironbottom Sound, the nickname for the water bed strewn with sunken ships. The Americans operated without the most modern radar aboard the vessels at the head of their column. In the confusion, the gunners exchanged huge shells—14-inches from the Japanese battlewagon *Hiei*, 8-inchers from the biggest U.S. cruisers—torpedoes, and 20mm cannon with foes. In a number of instances, ships flying the same flag opened up on one another. Charging about in the black of night and rain squalls, they passed within point-blank range, enabling machine gunners to rake decks and superstructures. "It was like a barroom brawl after the lights had been shot out," said one survivor.

Shattering news filtered into Halsey. First, the cruiser *Portland* reported her steering room flooded, her rudder jammed by a torpedo blast. Then the cruiser *Atlanta* sounded a cry for help. The cruiser *Helena* announced itself the command ship of the task force, indicating terrible injury to the anointed flagship the cruiser *San Francisco,* and advised that "All ships are damaged." Before the action ended four American destroyers and two cruisers added their carcasses to the collection in Ironbottom Sound. Several other vessels absorbed such extreme hurt they were dubious candidates for repair. When dawn broke, small boats from Guadalcanal picked up hundreds of Japanese and Americans, many burned or wounded, floating offshore. More than 1,400 American sailors were killed, including the five Sullivan brothers who went down with the light cruiser *Juneau.* That loss caused orders to be promulgated against allowing siblings to serve in the same unit. In terms of tonnage, ships, and lives the Japanese appeared victorious but they were prevented from hitting the objective, Henderson Field.

Still intent upon a naval strike at Guadalcanal, Adm. Isoroku Yamamoto mobilized another fleet to sweep the Slot clean, annihilate positions around Henderson Field, and bring fresh troops into the fray. Halsey now relied on his partially repaired carrier *Enterprise,* a pair of battleships, *Washington* and

South Dakota, and the airmen at Espíritu Santo and Henderson for the main defense of the sea lane and the turf. Cruisers, the first elements in the Japanese armada, approached close enough to Guadalcanal to lob nearly 1,000 shells at Henderson with no significant results. For their pains, they drew the attention of aircraft from the island and the Enterprise that scored major hits and sank a cruiser. Even more important, they ravaged the group of transports. The Nipponese regrouped, and upon the arrival of a battleship plus other ships the fleet aimed another blow at Guadalcanal. While they outnumbered the Americans by four to one in destroyers, the two U.S. battleships, armed with 16-inch guns, packed the most power.

Once again, it was nighttime in the Slot, just below Savo Island, when the opponents squared off. Although the longer range weapons of the South Dakota and Washington commenced firing before the enemy could close near enough to retaliate against them, the American destroyers in the van quickly succumbed to the avalanche of torpedoes and shells. Two slid beneath the surface almost immediately after being hit and the surviving pair limped away seeking to stay afloat in spite of their wounds. One of them began to break up and subsequently was sunk by its sister ship.

Japanese cruisers and destroyers approached the South Dakota, hampered by mechanical failures that blacked out its radar functioning. Shells and torpedoes crashed into the battleship but its thick armor plate limited the damage. However, explosions in the superstructure killed, wounded, and destroyed systems required for gun control. More than twenty fires burned aboard the South Dakota. Unable to fight effectively, it withdrew, leaving the still-untouched Washington to cope with the entire Japanese force. It had already battered a destroyer and now took under fire the overmatched heavyweight cruiser Kirishima. It subsequently rolled over and sank. The aroused Japanese destroyers, like a pack of wolves after a particularly meaty specimen, unsuccessfully pursued the Washington now retiring from the scene.

The naval battle of Guadalcanal was over. Overall, the Japanese lost more at sea than the Americans. But it was in terms of ground forces that the victory truly counted. Only about 2,000 soldiers of the Imperial Army, short on food and ammunition, were deposited on the contested island. During the same period almost three times as many American fighting men joined their comrades. Halsey, unlike his predecessor, risked major assets on the gamble that he could stop the enemy and he won. Instead of another Bataan this was the first success in the island-hopping strategy. The Japanese high command wrote off Guadalcanal but to their troops on the island their duty to fight remained constant and the agonizing struggle continued.

Robert Muehrcke, a corporal with the Americal Division, remembered conditions that would persist for another six months. "After the sun set, there was no smoking, no talking, and most of all, no above-ground movement. No one left the foxhole to defecate. Only one's eyes were above the foxhole edge. Firing at a Japanese ruse gave away one's position. One prevented this at all costs. The Guadalcanal full moon was a blessing. The light was bright enough to distinguish movement. Any unusual movement seen in the bright moonlight had a grenade thrown at it.

"Facing the enemy from a foxhole night after night, across a small strip of jungle measuring fifteen to twenty yards, was a true test of the emotional makeup of any fighting man. His prior combat experience, his military training, his emotional stability, as well as his preparation for each specific encounter, all influenced his reactions. At night, odors filtered down the defense line. One became especially aware of one's own body odor as well as that of his 'buddy.' It was distinguishable from the enemy's odor, so entirely different from the living Americans. The body odors of the living were mixed with the stench of the decaying dead, both Japanese and American—an odor never to be forgotten."

The losses at sea and on Guadalcanal enabled the Allies to focus on New Guinea. MacArthur had committed the newly arrived American 32d Infantry Division to fight alongside the Australian 7th Division. Fred Johnson served as a medic with the 128th Infantry Regiment [32d Division]. The outfit reached Adelaide, Australia, in May 1942. "Around September, we flew to Port Moresby and they sent us to the Goldie River near the foot of the Kokoda Trail. We ran patrols, looking for Japanese stragglers but never encountered anyone. The climate was extremely hot and humid with a lot of rain."

As the Japanese fortunes on Guadalcanal declined, they abandoned their quest for Port Moresby and dug in on the northeast coast. MacArthur sought to eliminate them. "In November 1942 we flew to a field on the north coast," recalled Johnson, "a short runway strip usable during the dry season. We marched along the beach toward Buna. Everyone felt real confident this would be a real short victory. We were led to believe it would be lightly defended by a lot of sick, starving Japanese. But they brought in a lot of men from Rabaul and it was heavily fortified, lot of bunkers, tremendous amount of machine guns. They didn't have artillery or big mortars so we didn't get a lot of wounds that caused amputations. That would come later in the Philippines.

"We could see the airfield they held and U.S. bombers hit the place. One came flaming down, crashed, and exploded. It was a sobering sight. The rainy season set in; rain kept pouring down. We didn't have shelter halves or raincoats. We were constantly wet. As medics when we first went into New Guinea we wore the brassards [Red Cross insignia], but they were removed quickly because we lost half of our medics who were killed in line companies around Buna and you didn't know whether the brassards made a good target or what. Almost all of us also carried weapons, Tommy guns or M1s, the whole war.

"I didn't see a lot of hatred toward the Japanese, not by the wounded or anyone else. The boys just felt they had a job to do. Everyone developed a lot of respect for them as infantry fighters who were extremely adept, courageous. We didn't know of any atrocities. There weren't a lot of prisoners taken. Most of them fought to the very end. The aid station was just set up alongside the road. Any wounded brought in would just wait there in the rain. There isn't a lot you can do at a battalion aid station under the conditions where often you are, at most, 300 yards or so behind the front lines."

Embattled Americans in the Pacific—from foxhole soldier to MacArthur speaking for his fief, and almost the entire naval command beginning with Admiral King down through the likes of Nimitz, Halsey, and Vandegrift—bemoaned the focus on Europe to the detriment of their concerns. But within the Western Hemisphere Torch also drained direct operations by the Eighth Air Force in England against the European enemy. The escort service provided by the first American squadrons, the 31st Fighter Group in Spitfires, was bolstered temporarily by the 1st Fighter Group manning P-38 Lightnings. These U.S.-built, twin-engine, double-boomed aircraft were blessed with speed and great range. As the first fighter unit to cross the Atlantic under its own power, the 1st Fighter Group, like its bomber predecessors, encountered serious problems. In mid-July six P-38s, confounded by the weather and misled by directional broadcasts from German radio, had no recourse but to land on the icecap of eastern Greenland. The Lightnings' wreckage couldn't be salvaged but the fliers all survived. Over time the accident rate during passage to England via the North Atlantic route would fall drastically and by January 1943, 920 planes had attempted the crossing with a loss rate of 5.2 percent, below the anticipated 10 percent.

However, the 1st Fighter Group, which went operational at the end of August and started full-scale sweeps in mid-September, left Europe for North Africa in November. In preparation for this departure and its P-38s, the Eighth Air Force in late September incorporated the American pilots of the Eagle Squadron into the just activated 4th Fighter Group. Spitfires continued to be their aircraft. On 9 October, the Eighth Air Force mounted its most impressive show yet. "Against Lille and other objectives," said Walt Kelly, "we sent 110 of our own bombers, 27 of which were B-24s. We downed 56 enemy fighters with 26 more probables. Our escort was credited with only five. Four bombers failed to return to the U.K., three B-17s, and one B-24 with one crew picked up in the channel. We had now provided ample evidence of who was to be boss of daytime air over Western Europe. This action was against some of Goering's most experienced pilots—some German aces had more than 300 kills [three years of war including duty on the Soviet front].

Our squadron morale was very high. We considered our flying and bombing skills to be the very best and were particularly proud of our tight formation flying."

Kelly's declaration of victory may have been premature but the thrust at Lille presaged the style that would become a hallmark of the Eighth Air Force. Eaker put up 108 bombers, the first occasion in which a raid exceeded the century mark, but unfortunately a total of 29 B-17s and B-24s turned back.

For their inauguration into combat that 9 October, twenty-four brand-new B-17Fs, designated as the 306th Bomb Group, warmed up their engines at the Thurleigh Field for the trip to Lille and their first mission. In the command seat of one of the 368th Squadron's planes was a twenty-two-year-old native of Boise, Idaho, Lt. John Regan.

Regan flew one of the first of the 306th's Forts from Wendover to Maine, then to Gander, Newfoundland, before the final leg to Prestwick and the hop to the base at Thurleigh. "We had not been told about flak and German fighters because the people with us hadn't any experience in combat. The first mission of our group was against a factory in the city of Lille, not a very deep penetration but one that required us to be in formation. I had been a football player in high school and college and my feeling was like that. I was really excited. This was what I trained for. I was over here to fly combat. Boy, I was young, eager, ready to go.

"When we crossed the coast, we didn't have fighter escort. We climbed to altitude, went toward our target and we started getting attacked by fighters and the ground antiaircraft was shooting as us. I thought, 'My God! Those people are serious.' From that point on, combat was never thrilling to me. It was a job that had to be done and a job that turned out to be extremely tough. I imagine the rest of my crew felt very much like I did. Nobody was unsatisfactory and nobody did anything particularly outstanding.

"After we departed the target, I lost my number-two engine, which suffered some minor damage from flak. We had to drop back from the formation and were attacked by about 20–25 yellow-nosed ME 109s, Goering's own airplanes. Fortunately for me at the time, the Germans didn't know how to attack the B-17, still an airplane with which they were not familiar. They stood out, forming an echelon on my left side and they would peel off and try to attack us from that side. They just were not successful. When they did this, I would pull up so I would get the prop wash from the airplanes that were much farther ahead of me and these people would have to fly through it. I would then go from one side to another to keep them from attacking us as well."

Another first for Lille was the B-24s mentioned by Kelly. They came from the 93d Bomb Group. Among the new crews was Luther Cox, the twenty-four-year-old son of a Baltimore executive. Lu Cox was a navigator for the Liberator *Shoot Luke* in the 93d Bomb Group. Cox said the crews received limited preparation for combat. "The main emphasis was on formation flying. No aerial-gunner work. No instructions on strategic or tactical bombing. We had absolutely no idea how much weather flying we could get involved in when we were sent over to England." The name of the plane derived from the oft-heard cry in innumerable barracks crap games, "Shoot, Luke, you're faded." On the nose of *Shoot Luke* a painter depicted a hillbilly leaning against a tree while holding a long rifle.

Cox recalls the morning of his and *Shoot Luke*'s first mission, the raid on Lille. "After breakfast we all went into the briefing room, which was dimly lighted. The hustle and bustle of crewmen entering and finding their seats together was overpowered by the undertone of conversation that hung above the flyers. The lights on the stage in front of us came on and flooded the walls upon which hung some air-navigation charts. The fact that it was ice cold in the room didn't seem to be recognized, so intent was everybody to hear what the target would be. Throughout every mission ever flown, I am certain that the most important words offered from the briefing stage were, 'Gentlemen, the target for today is . . .' In that tense atmosphere we could clearly see our target and the course we were to take in and coming out. It was very important to be aware in great detail of your position at all times while over enemy territory for although you might not be the lead aircraft, all that had to happen was for you to have to drop out of the formation and then you would hear the voice of the pilot asking for a heading back to England and our base.

"As all the planes warmed up their engines it seemed as though the entire base had turned out to watch this great moment in the history of the 93d Bomb Group. We were lined up in snake fashion waiting for the signal from the control tower. At ten o'clock sharp, KK [Maj. Kenneth Compton, operations officer] pointed his Very pistol skyward and fired a flare, signaling number-one aircraft, the lead ship to take off. One after another they staggered down the runway that seemed so short and finally lifted off the ground, each just barely clearing the perimeter fence.

"Finally it became our turn to line up and take off. Earlier, back when we were in our parking space, Murph [pilot John Murphy] had run each engine up to its fullest rpm, checking the array of instruments before him very carefully. Our faithful ground-crew chief stood by each engine in turn with a fire extinguisher, as Murph cranked up each one, waiting for the right speed of prop rotation and compression before he would energize the starter. Starting these huge engines could be anxious moments as each engine seemed to stubbornly defy being kicked in. They seemed to come to life with a grunt, a puff of smoke, and then that roar as she caught. The aircraft shuddered each time this happened.

"Now, at the beginning of the runway and with a crew at a peak of anticipation and excitement, Murph locked all four throttles and gradually moved them forward, as those four mighty engines began to come to life and roar, both Murph and [Frank] Lown [copilot], pushed as hard as they could on the brakes trying to hold *Shoot Luke* down. Finally, with the airframe of the plane fairly jumping up and down, they released the brakes and she seemed to leap forth as she charged down the runway. Carrying twelve 500-pound demolition bombs and 2,500 gallons of fuel, the gross weight of the aircraft was more than 70,000 pounds. Murph held her on the runway as long as he could in order to get her moving faster and faster until at almost the last moment he eased back on the wheel and she staggered off into the sky. He quickly called for wheels-up and Lown flicked the switch to bring them up. This greatly reduced drag and *Shoot Luke* took to the air like a huge bird."

For Cox's flight to Lille, operations decreed a bombing altitude of 22,000 feet. As soon as he saw the coast of France, Cox alerted all gunners to watch for enemy planes. "Our lead navigator brought us in too close to Dunkerque and they threw everything at us but the kitchen sink. One of the very first planes to cross the coast of France received a direct hit in its bomb bay. Their plane seemed to disintegrate in midair. It was not until months later that I discovered that Captain Simpson and Lt. Nick Cox were the only two members of the crew to survive such a mighty explosion. One can only surmise that the force of the blast blew their aircraft apart and they fell free. The same concussion evidently opened their parachute packs. They survived practically unscathed."

Even as he witnessed his group's first loss in combat, Cox himself nearly became a casualty. As the plane approached the target, enemy fighters started to appear, and with bombardier Ed Janic, he manned a machine gun in the B-24 nose. Suddenly he fell unconscious on the floor of the nose. Janic saw what happened and immediately secured a walkabout bottle of oxygen to Cox's face. According to Murphy, "The bombardier called to say the navigator was sick and that it was suicide to go into combat with him in that condition. We had a hurried talk over the interphone and then saw there was nothing to do but turn *Luke* around and go home. It almost broke the hearts of the crew when they headed back for England [the bombs were dumped] and saw the rest of the group continuing into enemy territory. When the other ships and crews returned they told of flak like huge clouds and fighters in swarms, some of the ship had been shot to hell, but *Luke* was so far a virgin."

Ramsay Potts, a former college instructor in economics, commissioned and awarded his wings four days after Pearl Harbor, piloted one of the B-24s that continued on to Lille. "I was flying element lead, a twenty-four-plane formation," said Potts. "It seemed to me that we had no sooner formed

up and turned toward France than we were over there. This was due to a
100-knot tailwind at 23,000 feet. We were supposed to have fighter escort
but we never saw them. Very shortly after we penetrated the coast of France,
we ran into some FW 190s and they attacked from different directions. It
seemed to me most of the attacks were coming in from the rear. I had a tail
gunner who was a pretty good man but shortly after the first attack, I could-
n't contact him on the intercom radio. I thought perhaps he had been hit.
I sent the engineer back to find out. He reported the man was in a state of
shock, not from being hit, just from fright and he had frozen up. He wasn't
firing his guns; he wasn't talking to anybody on the intercom.

"Then my left wingman got hit and his airplane caught on fire. I got a report nine chutes were seen. This coming on the heels of the problem with
the tail gunner was another sort of psychological shock, because Simpson,
the man flying the plane on my left, was my closest friend in the squadron.
We overshot the Initial Point to turn into the bomb run because of the very
high wind at our altitude. As a consequence we actually made a very poor
bomb run. We were subjected to severe fighter attacks during that time. We
dropped our bombs and later learned we had not hit the target.

"We turned and now were going back against that wind. Until this time
it seemed as if we had been flying for a very short time. Now I kept looking
down at the French landscape and it seemed to me we were hardly moving
at all. Minutes after minutes rolled by and it was an interminable amount
of time throughout which we were catching sporadic fighter attacks. There
had been flak over the target, which, since this was our first time, was a little nerve wracking.

"Finally we got home and we had two airplanes make crash landings on
the field and they tore off their landing gears and one lost its wings. Then
we got news that another one had crash-landed on the beach. Altogether I
felt it was a pretty tough operation.

"I went back to my quarters after the interrogation and was trying to light
the small pot-bellied stove we had with some sort of cinders that passed as
a form of charcoal. I was so cold. I think it was not only because it was damp
and chilly, but also I suppose I was experiencing a kind of shock reaction
from this mission plus evidence of fear. I don't remember throughout the
whole rest of the war ever again feeling as fearful about going on missions
as I did right after this first one. I couldn't get warm. I put on all kinds of
sweaters and heavy jackets and even wrapped a big tartan blanket around
myself while I tried to get the fire going.

"It was a typical early mission and later there were ones that were really
tougher. But I never felt as badly afterwards as this time. My friend Simpson
and the copilot and about five other members of the crew were captured by
the Germans. Two of the members of the crew were killed and one was un-

accounted for, a tech sergeant named Cox." The latter succeeded in evading capture. He worked his way to Spain before returning to the United Kingdom more than a year after his plane was shot down.

W. J. "Red" Komarek, after a radio flash about the attack on Pearl Harbor, left his home in the Yorkville section of New York City to enlist. Komarek first sought the Navy but when he couldn't pass their eye exam walked a half block to the Army recruiting station and signed up for the Air Corps. Initially, Komarek signed up for a radio operator's course but when too many applied, he gladly dropped out in favor of gunnery school. Conditions at the gunnery instruction field were less than ideal. "The pilots were staff sergeants who thought they were going to gunnery school, not to ferry aerial gunners," recalled Komarek. "We had no helmets and no intercom with the pilots and flew in AT-6s and O-47s. You sat with your back physically separated from the pilot and your .30-caliber machine gun was stowed in front of you on a tracking swivel. The instructions amounted to the pilot telling you to fire when in position with the tow target, that is, when he waggled his wings, and to stop firing when he waggled his wings again. He said at no time should you release your seat belt. On the first flight you learned you can't substitute a handkerchief tied on your head for a helmet, you can't reach a stowed machine gun without releasing your seat belt to get the gun to the quarter position against the wind, you had to struggle like hell against the slipstream to clamp the gun down for firing at the tow target."

Komarek was assigned to the 93d Bomb Group equipped with B-24s and became a tail gunner for a Liberator named *Globe Trotter*. After four months of antisubmarine patrol over the Gulf of Mexico, Komarek, along with other airmen, sailed to England on a troopship. The B-24s practiced for their encounters with the enemy in mock combat with RAF Spitfires. "The Spits barreled in and we tracked in our sights and pretended leading and firing. Although the turret was equipped and fitted for gun cameras, they were not available to us. We had no way to evaluate our effectiveness." Nor did he relish the high-altitude flights. "I was cold and my seat seemed tiny and we appeared to go slow. I had to get used to adjusting oxygen for altitude and the heat suit. The door of the turret was a real obstacle. I never seemed to get enough heat in the suit and the electric gloves were worthless. I was getting the impression that we should know these things by osmosis. If it weren't for the bull sessions with other combat men, we would have had a helluva time."

On the 93d's maiden mission to Lille, Komarek said, "Seeing my first flak burst I called the Skipper. Imitating John Wayne, I said, 'It looks like they're shooting at us, but the bursts are low and behind.' No sooner said and big black bursts with a whoosh and pebbles hitting the window sounds seemed to be all around us. I quickly forgot John Wayne. They found us and I had better imitate a tail gunner. I didn't see any fighter escort but a fighter was diving down on us. I watched fascinated as he dove below and disappeared. I didn't fire! Why? Buck fever? Then there was another. I tracked him firing short bursts. I wasn't leading him enough. My tracers were arching away from his tail. I led the next, firing short bursts when suddenly my sight was filled with a B-24, our left wing ship. I stopped firing momentarily. Did I stop in time or did I put a couple of fifties in its nose? I strained to see if there was any damage.

"I kept squeezing the green balloon on my oxygen mask. We were told to do this to prevent your saliva from freezing the vent, since this was a constant-flow system, the green bag would burst with the vent clogged. My green balloon was growing larger. What the hell am I doing here, anyway? I should be back in high school."

The tail gunner on *Globe Trotter* gaped at the sights and coped with his own problems. "God Almighty, what is that! A 24 trailing smoke . . . going down. I see chutes, one . . . two . . . three . . . watch for fighters . . . short bursts. The balloon on my mask is now twice as large. Pull the feed line off the intake and stick the hose in your mouth. I don't feel so good. Then it had to happen, biting down on a hose with pressure building, the hose spewed out of my mouth. Where did it go? Grab it from the turret valve and trace it down to the end. Am I seeing purple dots? Put the hose back in your mouth . . . don't bite down on it. Look for fighters . . . There they are, twin booms, they're P-38s and Spits, just like the cavalry. What a sight! I had a seat on the fifty-yard line watching our fighters roaring in to attack. A fighter was going down . . . for every German there was a Spit or 38 on its tail . . . An intercom check from the pilot . . . all okay, thank God, nobody got hit. I got through the mission, oxygen trouble and all."

Almost two weeks later, the 97th Bomb Group, on its final assignment for the Eighth Air Force before transferring to the North Africa–based Twelfth, reeled from punishment meted out over the Lorient U-boat bases. The tally showed 3 aircraft shot down, with 30 airmen missing, 6 planes damaged, 5 crewmen wounded. Worse, even direct hits with five one-ton bombs made no dent in the submarine pens. A navigator who saw the explosives fall dead on target reported, "They bounced off those massive concrete U-boat shelters like Ping-Pong balls."

Walt Kelly survived the Lorient debacle but the new place of business challenged even the most optimistic. "We were to be led to North Africa to participate in Torch by Jimmy Doolittle, the newly designated commander of the Twelfth. After several days [in transit] we flew on to Africa where the ground forces were still in the midst of skirmishes with the Vichy French who were supporting the Germans.

"Amid sniper fire and bare base conditions, we struggled to load bombs and refuel the planes from five-gallon cans. Some were hopelessly bogged down in the mud at Tafaraoui and couldn't operate. The turf field was a soggy mess. We off loaded the bombs and managed to fly out to Biskra, an oasis resort on the edge of the Sahara. We went from mud to sand. Every takeoff left a sandstorm behind. Some air crews, mine included, were lucky enough to have rooms at the Palace and other hotels in town." For the others, living standards dropped far below what they experienced in England. The flak and enemy fighters remained as dangerous as ever.

The 97th was not the only outfit lost to strategic bombing by the Eighth Air Force during this period. Ramsay Potts took a squadron from the 93d to a southern RAF base to perform sweeps and searches into the Atlantic, antisubmarine patrols as part of the preparation for Torch. The British had long advocated use of the B-24s with their extended range for combating U-boats.

"We didn't know anything about any invasion of North Africa," said Potts. "We were trying to locate submarines and use our depth charges to kill them. On a very long patrol down into the Bay of Biscay, we were returning. I'd gotten up out of my seat and looked over the ocean to the left and for just a moment I mistook what I saw for a flight of birds, way off, close to the water. This flock of birds turned out to be twin-engine German ME 210s. There were five of them. I jumped back into the pilot's seat and noticed a split in the flight. I was getting reports from the rear gunner and it quickly became apparent that two of them were trying to move ahead of us and two were turning in toward us. One had moved to get into position for an attack at the tail.

"As they started climbing, so did I because we had been below a ragged cloudbed that was maybe 2,500 to 3,000 feet above us. The first airplane came in toward us and as he approached, I turned sharply toward him. He then came right across the top of our airplane. It seemed I could practically reach up and touch him. Our top gunner just split him open and he burst into flames practically atop our airplane. At the same time the waist gunner was claiming that he was firing at another plane making an attack and the tail gunner was firing on a third. The waist gunner claimed he'd shot down his man and so did the tail gunner. Nobody saw the plane coming toward the tail go down except the gunner but one other crewman saw the plane shot down by the man at the waist.

"By the time I completed the maneuvers, I had done about a 270-degree shift, a part circle climbing and getting up and approaching the cloud cover overhead. When I ducked into the clouds we didn't have any attacks from the two ME 210s that had streaked out in front to intercept us. I stayed in the cloud cover, set a course that finally brought us to Land's End where we landed in high spirits because we knew we had shot down two airplanes and were claiming three. A message had gone on ahead of us. They knew we had been under attack and that we'd had an engagement. All of our squadron was out there and the RAF permanent party when we landed. They counted 156 .30-caliber holes in the airplane. No vital part had been hit and we felt pretty good. I had not been flying precisely as our operations procedure indicated. I should have been closer to the clouds but the deck had been lifting and I'd been careless and hadn't changed my procedure.

"Instead of congratulating me, the squadron commander said, 'What the hell were you doing, flying so far below the cloud cover?' He was not happy. Instead of being gratified that we had shot down two or three German aircraft, he was angry that I had exposed the plane. The RAF interrogated the intelligence people. They were skeptical. They did not believe one bomber could have an engagement with five fighter aircraft and survive. They questioned my crew for a very long time. Finally, they seemed to get a story that satisfied them. So they gave us two probably destroyed and one possible. Later, through communications intercepts, the coastal command established that we shot down three planes and the RAF considered it quite a feat.

"That evening I was sitting in the mess when an RAF corporal came in with a message for Captain Potts. It was a teletype from Air Chief Marshal Joubert who was head of coastal command. It congratulated me and my crew for a fine performance. He commended us so naturally I took it to the squadron commander and said, 'Look at this message from Joubert. Perhaps this will cause you to change your mind a little bit about what happened today.'

"He looked at it and said, 'You know what this proves?' 'No,' I said. 'What does it prove?' He said, 'It proves Air Chief Marshal Joubert doesn't know his ass from third base.'"

The use of B-24s as part of the antisubmarine campaign actually preceded the assignment of Potts and his unit by several months. Bill Topping, a native of a small town near Roanoke, Virginia, piloted during a tour with the 19th Anti-Submarine Squadron that patrolled the waters around Gander protecting convoys and searching for submarine wolfpacks. "I never saw a German sub but we did see what happened to ships getting torpedoed while in convoys."

When the U.S. Navy assumed responsibility for that sector of the Atlantic, Topping flew to England to perform antisub work in a B-24 off the southeast coast. Attached to the RAF, Topping and the officers lived comfortably in a hotel. "We had tea servings. I had a batman who took care of my clothes and shined my shoes. Next door lived a group of Land Army girls. The missions and techniques were the same as those of the RAF. Stay in cloud cover as much as possible, use radar to indicate someone was out there. We had depth charges and in an attack were to dive down to about fifty feet, and as bombardier I was to string out five depth charges. It was hours and hours of boredom, flying the Bay of Biscay, sometimes going to Gibralter to refuel. I belonged to the whale and ale club, getting a couple of whales we dove on. The British were quite concerned about whales in the Bay of Biscay, always asking how many we saw and in what direction they were headed. But one day, it all came together.

"I spotted the subs, there were three, followed by four all on the surface going toward France probably for supplies including torpedoes. We broke radio silence and the navigator gave our position. Then we attacked. We dove on them and I tried to string out the depth charges. As we pulled out and swung away from them, we were taking a lot of hits from the subs. We had attacked the first three subs and were getting ready for another depth charge run when the tail gunner said, 'Nothing came out, no depth charges.'

"I rushed back to the bomb bays and I found out what had happened. We were helpless. We had been shot up so bad on the left side of the bomb bay that the main wiring system along the top left was shredded. There was nothing we could do and we had to stay out of range of shells from the subs, which could throw up a lot of lead.

"We waited until other planes came in, the first a British Sunderland. I said, 'Bring me some ammunition from the back.' I had a .50-caliber nose gun and I figured I can at least fire if we attack. We dove and I was shooting at the Germans on the subs who were firing at us and trying to get the Sunderland behind us. I don't know how many I hit; they looked like ten pins in a bowling alley, just being knocked off the sub. The Sunderland dropped some depth charges and the tail gunner told us he had dropped them and was still with us. Six or seven other planes came in and we proceeded to lead, telling them to follow us. They started hitting the other subs. One of the Wellingtons went into the water, losing all but one of the crew. Some Royal Navy sloops showed up. They fanned out, went through throwing their depth charges and firing off their decks. It was a long battle, lasted six hours, but it seemed like all day."

The British Air Ministry announced the engagement sank three U-boats but Topping upset his commanding officer. "Back at the base, my CO wanted to know why I didn't drop any depth charges. He was a West Pointer and we did not get along too well. I made the snotty remark, 'I just missed getting the Congressional Medal of Honor.' He asked, 'How come?' I said, 'I should have gone back into the bomb bay, grabbed one of the depth charges and dove out, giving my life.' That comment gave me a lot of trouble. I deserved it; I was always causing him a lot of headaches." Topping saw no more subs while posted to southeastern England.

Absorbing painful lessons on the job, group and squadron leaders realized their aircraft lacked protection for the crews. Enterprising engineering officers of one B-24 squadron arranged for a local contractor to pave the nose compartment floor with boiler plate, not only adding protection to the navigator and bombardier but apparently also providing better balance to the aircraft. All planes began to receive similar modifications. Sheet-steel plates added to the side of the ships shielded the pilots. In fact, engineers, maintenance workers, and factories responding to the complaints, critiques, and requests of air crews, constantly tinkered or changed in varying degrees all of the planes flown by the Eighth Air Force throughout the course of the war.

Ground crews improvised. Whit Hill, a mechanic with the 91st Bomb Group, recalled, "When we first arrived on the scene, our equipment was limited by a 'table of authorization' that was inadequate to say the least. We had no aluminum sheets to use for patches, rivet guns, or even hand-rivet sets, to rivet on patches. In Hangar #1, however, there was an RAF maintenance shop whose friendly personnel were more than ready to assist us all they could. We 'borrowed' sheets of aluminum and used their machine shop to make hand-rivet sets and other repair equipment.

"One day I was ordered to attend an airframe school at the Eighth Air Force's Burtonwood supply depot. While there, Captain Larson, our engineering officer, appeared, and together we reviewed the depot's supply bins. While he distracted the depot guide, I was busy loading up Captain Larson's staff car with much-needed but unauthorized equipment such as straight and offset electrical drills, rivet guns, rivet sets, bucking bars, etc. On return we were ready to meet the action. Meanwhile, the group sheet-metal crews had obtained surplus bomb-loading carts and modified them into portable sheet-metal workbenches that included electric and air compressors, a floodlight, workbench with vise, storage for sheet metal and parts, and room for eight toolboxes used by the sheet-metal crew, all towed by a Jeep assigned to the crew chief.

"At the end of each mission the battle and mechanical damage of each returning aircraft was assessed and time to make necessary repairs was estimated. The planes requiring the least amount of work were the first to be repaired. Then there were many shot-up aircraft, the sheet-metal crews would help each out. There were times when the sheet-metal crews did not get to bed for seventy-two hours. None of the men from the ground crew—mechanics, electricians, prop specialists, bomb loaders, sheet-metal repairmen—had any set daily working hours. Everyday was Monday; it was 'work until you drop' and the password was 'how soon?'"

Frequent thick fogs, towering mountains of clouds, capricious winds, and sudden shifts from crystal-clear skies to ground-obscuring murk frustrated all Eighth Air Force pilots and navigators. Routine practice flights or trips to other bases could be as dangerous as a mission. The conditions forced innumerable unplanned landings, led to crashes, lost planes, and killed crewmen. For bombers shot up during missions, with hydraulic and electrical systems out of whack, and desperately wounded men aboard, the weather extended the nightmare beyond the zone of combat.

The efforts of the first heavyweight bombers, the airmen, and their ground support did not impress Winston Churchill, still unconvinced of either the quality of U.S. bombers or the daylight, precision-bombing campaign. In a letter to Air Chief Marshal Sir Charles Portal on 2 November, Churchill complained, "The number of American Air Force personnel [in England] has risen to about 55,000 . . . So far the results have been pitifully small . . . Far from dropping bombs on Germany, the daylight bombers have not ventured beyond Lille." [RAF Lancasters had already paid their disrespects to Berlin and Cologne among other German targets.] The British prime minister expressed frustration with the political currents that defeated what he considered the Allies' best interests. "Considering the American professional interests and high reputation which are engaged in this scheme, and the shock it would be to the American people and to the Administration if the policy proved a glaring failure, we must expect most obstinate perseverance in this method." He gloomily concluded, "for many months ahead large numbers of American air personnel will be here playing very little part in the war."

Oddly enough, Eaker's opposite number in the RAF, Air Marshal Arthur Harris, the bomber chief, was one of the few Britons who approved of the U.S. theory and practice. He wrote to a subordinate commander, "I have never been apprehensive about the ability of the heavy bomber to look after itself in daylight vis-à-vis the fighter. There is not the least doubt in my mind that if we and all the available Americans started daylight attacks against the less-heavily defended targets in Germany by big formations of heavy bombers now, we should knock the German fighter force out of the sky in two or three months, by the simple process of shooting them down. . . . It has all along been our experience that whenever the rear gunner, even at night, sees the enemy fighter first, he either destroys it or the fighter refuses to come in and attack."

At the time Harris made these comments, December 1942, the U.S. Army Air Corps for all of its 55,000 people in the United Kingdom, could never mobilize much more than seventy-five effective bombers for a mission, in contrast to the several hundred from the RAF. Harris, a man with a reputation for deviousness that masked his own implacable ideas, never showed any real willingness to switch his forces from night to day. Furthermore, as he should have known then and certainly was shown shortly, the contest between bombers and fighters was anything but weighted in favor of the heavyweights.

If anything, the situation for American airmen in North Africa was even more tenuous. Early in December 1942, David Jones, temporarily leading the 319th Bomb Group after its official commander was shot down and killed, received orders to hammer Bizerte. A newly designated group commander, Walter Agee, arrived, and to familiarize him with operations, Jones put him in his copilot's seat. "We were bombing at about 1,200 feet because we didn't have any bombsights. I get out to the airfield and whappo, they knocked out my left engine, and the trim and engine instruments, the bloody works are gone. I am cranking all the rudder and all the wheel I can get into it and it didn't have any air speed. I couldn't advance the throttle. I headed north to the coast, afraid the thing would snap on me.

"The terrain is like it is around El Paso, just a bunch of little nobs, sand hills. I went down in a kind of clear area and between two little sand mounds, sort of took the wings and then slid forward. The poor guy in the nose was thrown forward and out and then we ran over him. Agee was knocked out in the copilot seat. When we finally came to a halt I shook him a little bit, got him awake and out the top. Everybody got out and we went back, picked up the guy who was still on the ground. We took a piece of flap, put him on it as a stretcher, and headed north for the coast.

"We hadn't walked 200 yards and looked up and here is a whole line of skirmishers, German. I had a pistol in my pocket. I pointed at the pistol. [The soldier] took it out. Sam [Agee] was hurting a bit and kept saying, 'Don't let them give me any sulfa because I am allergic.' We got that point across. I think my nose was broken, my back was hurting. They took me and one other guy to Bizerte to the fighter headquarters and Sam and the other guys to a field hospital."

Fed cheese and wine, set in a deck chair, Jones went through a cursory interrogation that in his memory mainly consisted of questions about why the U.S. had allied itself with the "Russians" and a request not to run off. He was expected to leave for a European prison lager [camp] aboard Junker-52 transports the following day. But just as he walked toward his plane with a guard, "Here the sirens go and I looked up and saw the goddamn B-26s right at the bomb-release line. Everybody started running. I was hobbling like hell. There was a little depression and I fell in this damn ditch. The airplane I was supposed to get in had received a direct hit. There was nothing left but a hole."

Loaded aboard another ship, Jones flew to Italy where he rode a train bound for Germany. "We had lots of room in our compartment, while people outside were standing in the aisles. We stopped someplace and the Red Cross girls were just like everywhere. They were running around and giving out doughnuts and coffee. We were still pretty much gentlemen; we were combatants and they treated you that way." Later on in the war prisoners endured much harsher handling from civilian and military personnel.

17
Defeat

Despite Darlan's agreement to a cease-fire for French military on 11 November, uncertainties remained about the reactions of military outposts. Anxious to secure forward footholds at airfields that could intercept enemy planes before they reached the jammed harbors at Casablanca and Oran, the 509th Parachute Regiment boarded C-47s to drop on Youks-les-Bains, close to the Algeria-Tunisia border. "We had two or three Spitfires escorting us," said William Yarborough. "It was real hostile territory. A German airfield was not far away. We could see on the ground fortifications that the French had thrown up and we felt these guys were the same caliber as those that had shot us down [near Tafaraoui] and didn't really like Americans. We felt we'd have to fight and they had all the advantages. They had the high ground overlooking the drop zone. It was a very tense moment after we hit the ground and marched up the hill toward these French fortifications, weapons in hand.

"Finally, Colonel Berges, got out of his foxhole, came down to meet Ed Raff, stuck out his hand and embraced Ed. Then the troops came out of their holes and it was that way all down the line. They took the Zouave badge—they were the Zouave regiment—and pinned it on us. We joined together in picking up the parachutes and all signs we were there. There was a new spirit in the French. It was the first time they could turn and fight the Krauts. When a German JU 88 came the next day, expecting to land, he was shot down by French antiaircraft."

Amid the self-congratulations and puffery of the first successes against the Vichy French and some Italian troops in North Africa, some foresaw a much tougher war ahead. Lieutenant Colonel John Waters, a son-in-law of Patton, cautioned his exuberant 1st Armored Division tankers, "We did very well against the scrub team. Next week [figuratively] we hit the Germans. Do not slack off in anything. When we make a showing against *them*, you may congratulate yourselves."

By 24 November, Eisenhower had established his headquarters in Algiers and the augmented forces in North Africa began a campaign to push the enemy out of Tunisia. He delegated British lieutenant general Kenneth Anderson to lead an offensive of combined troops from his own country with the American 1st Infantry Division. As Waters had warned, the foe showed considerably more strength and counterattacks stalled advances. Increasingly, the weaknesses of the U.S. troops surfaced. They were not scrupulous enough in maintaining blackouts; they did not dig adequate foxholes; camouflage was perfunctory; reconnaissance was weak; communications broke down; vehicles in convoys followed too closely, offering prime targets for German planes. But in December, weather stopped the drive on Tunisia. Rain pelted down in torrents that mired tanks and wheeled vehicles. When Eisenhower, already troubled by a stretched-out battle line and supply shortages, watched four soldiers struggle fruitlessly to extricate a single motorcycle from the muck beside a road, he called off the offensive for two months.

On 24 December, an assassin fired a fatal bullet into Darlan. The vacuum in leadership enabled the Allies to broker an arrangement between Giraud and de Gaulle. The former would soon fade into the background while the leader of the Free French gradually strode to center stage.

The 44th and 97th Bomb Groups, with Lu Cox and Walt Kelly, in Liberators and Fortresses, as well as the 15th Bomb Group of Bill O'Dell flying lighter bombers, attacked enemy shipping and airdromes. The air war increasingly pitted fighter planes against one another or deployed fighters for tactical ground support. But the downpours transformed grass airstrips into little more than swamps, curtailing operations. The Germans enjoyed hard-surfaced fields.

Among those involved early in the game was the 33d Fighter Group, commanded by Lt. Col. Philip Cochran. An Erie, Pennsylvania, product, Cochran in 1935 enlisted in the Army Air Corps. With his experience Cochran earned command of the 33d. "I left the United States about October 28th," recalled Cochran. "I was on the British carrier *Archer,* a slingshot [catapult] job. I had thirty-five P-40s and I was in charge of the advance element of the 33d Group. These boys were very inexperienced and knew nothing about what we were heading into. The catapulting of the P-40s was very successful. Out of 103 we catapulted, we lost four.

"We landed on an airdrome where there were still snipers, but the armistice had been signed and we had no fighting to do. Our boys were in a state of what, for want of a better name, is called war hysteria. Why it occurs I don't know. Everybody seemed calm enough—but we wrecked airplanes on the landing at Port Lyautey. We lost nine airplanes from our own action. Boys who had never shown any tendency to be nervous or do erratic things, suddenly, through some peculiar human reaction, did unlooked-for things—in landing the airplanes, mostly.

"We found we were terrifically in need of training. We trained very diligently for about three weeks on what we had heard from the front, mostly on formations. Then suddenly we were sent forward to the Thelepte area [just over the Tunisian border]. Our move forward was very, very confused. We ended up with two halves of two squadrons and, having brought seven people forward, I was the ranking person. We first lived in a French house and the first night we had the thirty-five pilots all sleeping in this house to get out of the cold. While lying there shaking with cold, I thought I would be the horrible example of the man who put all his pilots in one house and one bomb got every one of them. The next night we slept in the ground and I don't mean *on* the ground. At Thelepte there is a large ravine and our enlisted men went back to the primitive cave man method—they actually dug into the sides of the ravine and lived that way. Officers themselves dug— anybody who wanted to live there dug himself a hole—and, if he could get two fellows he liked and wanted to be that close to, those two helped him dig a larger hole. It was hard digging, too. Some of our little abodes went eight-feet deep. If you left the place where you lived, there was no way you could orient yourself in the dark and get back. Nobody moved after five- thirty or six o'clock in the evening. We spent all the hours of darkness in the holes and all the hours of daylight either jumping into other holes, or being on mission."

"We found right off the bat," confessed Cochran, "that the Germans knew an awful lot more than we did and all we had was our eagerness. We started out with very, very poor formations. We built formations tactically based on the defense you have in the P-40. We learned the P-40 was quick in a turn and you couldn't find a guy on the field who wasn't ready to send a testi- monial to the people of Curtiss Wright because the quick turn of the P-40 saved every one of their necks every time they turned around. I think I can count ten times when, if the P-40 wouldn't turn, I would have been gone long ago." Like Jimmy Thach, Cochran opted for a two-plane unit.

Lacking radar, the airmen relied on an early-warning system that resem- bled what Chennault employed. French gendarmes stationed in towns be- tween the lines would telephone the airdrome, advising the approach, di- rection, and the number of aircraft. Unfortunately, Cochran noted, "Any airplane was enemy to them. They were hard for them to distinguish. They had us running like mad—chasing our own planes some of the time." Still, the P-40 pilots frequently intercepted the JU 88s as they began their run from 11,000 feet down to 4,000. At first the Americans discouraged the raids by knocking down a substantial number forty or fifty miles from their target. But then the enemy started an escort service and the air war escalated.

While the Allied drive into Tunisia halted in December 1942, the Eighth Air Force resumed its buildup of men and planes. To buttress Torch, the British-American high command had dispatched the 93d, 97th, and 301st Bomb Groups along with the 1st, 31st, and 82d Fighter Groups to Doolit-

tle's command in Tunisia. With the 92d Bomb Group committed to training, the transfers depleted the thin ranks of warriors and machines available
to Eaker. As winter approached he could muster only recent arrivals from
the 44th, 303d, 305th, and 306th Bomb Groups and the only American-flown
escorts, Spitfires of the 4th Fighter Group.

Captain Billy Southworth Jr. commanded one of the 303d's B-17Fs. Southworth, whose father led the St. Louis Cardinals in 1942 to a World Series
championship, had himself shown promise as an outfielder and played for
a high minor-league team before enlisting in the Air Corps nearly a year before the Japanese attack. After a training flight in which he deftly handled
his plane with only three functioning engines, he noted in his diary, "Sergeant
Means who has been with me for about two and a half months, said, 'You are
good, aren't you, sir?' Hell yes, Means. They have confidence in me. Schueler,
my navigator, nervous type, but a solid guy, wasn't at all bothered."

In addition to comments about the poor condition of the aircraft, the
journal frequently notes the efforts of the Cardinals in the pennant race,
the failings of superior officers, and romantic entanglements of himself and
his associates. Southworth courted and broke an engagement before pursuing numerous "swell gals." He remarked on navigator Jon Scheuler taking "the fatal step" proposing by telephone, and later bombardier Milt Conver also married.

In Michigan, Southworth picked up a B-17 that would carry him to England. During a layover, he noted, "Had a party last night. We're all confined
to the post so the girls came to see us. 'Spook' Hargrove threw a bottle
through a window at the end of a BOQ. Lieutenant Mitchell put his hand
through another and cut it badly. The boys were high. Colonel Hughes
wanted to know who was baying at the moon at 2:20 A.M. Stockton was out
with [name deleted by author] who likes to spread her affections about.
Seems that all of the girls did.

"I'll never marry Helene hard as she's trying. Babs proposed persistently
to me last night, second date. She's very pretty but wouldn't have her on a
silver platter. There's Ann, wealthy in looks but lacks something. Ruth had
everything but was too fond of herself. Betty a swell gal but too set in ways
and lacks oomph. Cliffy might be a possibility, haven't known her long
enough. I'd like to get into this damn war and return so I can settle down."

On the final day of October, Southworth could scribble notes about the
last legs from Newfoundland to a field near Liverpool. "Got off on instruments and was in the soup three-quarters of the trip. It took us ten and a
half hours. Dillinger, my copilot, slept most of the way. Means, the sergeant
engineer, did likewise, while Doughty, Radio, and Schueler, Navigator, did
a bang-up job. Jon missed his ETA by one minute. Land was sighted, all men
were alert at their stations ready to fire (save Means, asleep). We were im-

pressed by the jagged shores [Ireland], green hills, hedge fences, beautiful estates, picturesque, with ancient moats of King Arthur's time surrounding them. Airports then littered the way to Prestwick."

The 303d made Molesworth its home and Southworth said early in November, "Rained every day since we've been here. These muddy days, a foot deep in places I'll never forget. Cold, wet, and black nights, cold wind stinging your face while your feet just get used to that dead cold feeling. The British are a fine people. Take the bitter with the sweet, defeat and victory without feeling—they hang on, just keep hanging on. They aren't deceiving, love their country, and are proud of it. We'll win this war but it will take a long time."

Southworth expressed unhappiness with his superiors. "Lieutenant Joe Haas got Dumbbell [award for a blunder] after Captain Blythe and Maj. Calloway snafued a situation worse than Joe. Told Col. Wallace [group commander] of a desirable landing procedure, also the desirable way to fly a formation. It wasn't appreciated nor listened to, but I'll wager that they'll adopt it as their own idea. . . . God damn!! Flew with Maj. Calloway's outfit and he snafu as usual. He led a very poor formation and was lost nearly all the time. . . . Flew No. 2 with Maj. Sheridan. Dillinger is the poorest excuse for a copilot that I've ever seen. He went to sleep three times this morning on our flight." The Southworth crew named its B-17 *Bad Check* in the obvious hope that it, too, would always bounce back. Throughout the war, however, crews often flew different aircraft, sharing them with others and switching because of malfunctions or combat damage.

The winds of war blew together an unlikely companion for Southworth in the person of Jon Schueler, the navigator for Southworth's plane, son of a businessman who struggled through the Depression. Astigmatism in one eye eliminated pilot training and Schueler graduated flight training as a navigator. Like Southworth and the other young males in uniform, Schueler, too, partied enthusiastically when not carrying out his flight duties. "All of us knew we were flirting with death from the moment we saw the planes. It was like the feeling at the beginning of a love affair, when all of the enticement is joy, yet one senses also the excitement of unknown possibilities, sadness, treachery, death. Larry [another bombardier in training] and I had seen the two planes crash on that first day and the image didn't leave our minds."

A third member of the crew was Milt Conver, a native of Columbus, Ohio. A graduate of Staunton Military Academy in Virginia, he was an excellent boxer, swimmer, and college football player. After washing out as a pilot, Conver elected to become a bombardier.

Neither as opinionated as Southworth, nor as eloquent as Schueler, Conver filled his diary with matter-of-fact accounts of his days, noting whom he

saw, problems in getting paid, festivities at the officers' club, and classes connected with his craft. In his accounts, on 22 August 1942, he noted Schueler's
marriage. "Jean and I stood up for them. Gene Rochester took my hat by
mistake." His entry for the following day reports the death of several friends,
killed in a crash. "Bodies were so messed up they were hard to identify. My
hat was found and they thought that I was on the ship." The sources of the
error lay in the cap taken by the unfortunate Gene Rochester at Schueler's
wedding. On 24 August he announced his wedding to Jean. "I suppose both
our families will be sorry and I know they'll say we're crazy." In fact, neither
set of parents greeted the news with enthusiasm.

A soldier formed from still another mold, SSgt. Bill Fleming, a Jenkins,
Kentucky, coal miner's son, one of eight children, born in 1924, operated
machine guns from the waist of the Southworth plane during its first missions. "We got along pretty well. Billy Southworth was a very good pilot but
he did not associate with his crew very much. He gave you the feeling that
socially he was above you. In October 1942, at Battle Creek, Michigan, we
received our new planes from the factory and flew them to Bangor, then to
Gander and, finally, to Prestwick. Molesworth became our base of operation
until the end of the war. None of the crew, myself included, at this time had
ever fired a .50-caliber machine gun from a B-17. Most of our training was
on .30-calibers out of small planes. We were due for some on-the-job training. At Molesworth we had a few practice missions. We were so young we
didn't realize what we were getting into. Orders came for us to go 17 November on our first mission, Saint-Nazaire."

Bombardier Conver described the facilities at Molesworth. "There is a
great deal of mud. The rooms are large enough, but the heating system—
one small coal stove—isn't good at all. Being in a combat area, the Group
is scattered all over the four parts of the field, as are the airplanes. The
weather is as expected, rain and cold. I can't see how we can operate around
here in B-17s and I wouldn't be surprised if we moved out of England in the
near future."

On the eve of the first mission an exuberant Southworth declared, "On
the morrow, pilots and crews will spring into action, all looking forward to
a day of 'Success!' We bomb Saint-Nazaire submarine base, a heavily protected area. It will be our first combat experience. We expect to find opposition without looking too hard. It's not like patrol. Last raid on Saint-
Nazaire, three Forts were lost."

According to Fleming, however, "Success!" was denied because, "Somewhere in the lead plane, the navigator got off course and we missed the entire target. We didn't come close and had to return to base with all of the
bombs on board. We weren't allowed to drop them over occupied France.
It was a big disappointment. There was no antiaircraft fire or enemy air-

planes. Germans flew around us a couple of times wondering who we were. I guess they were as curious about us as we were about them."

On the morning of 18 November, Southworth awakened at 5:30 A.M. In his diary, he wrote, "Seemed as if I were going on a hunting trip back home. Carefully selected clothes, papers, pencil, oxygen equipment, pistol, etc. Off to eat a quick breakfast, then to the briefing room where we get the dope. The target La Pallice, French seaport, sub base, workshops, factories. Secondary is Lorient. I missed my place in the taxi procession as the wind and takeoff position had changed. All seemed to be taken care of before turning 'em over. Jenkins, a damn good man, to be my waist gunner, bombs loaded, crew intact. Twenty minutes before takeoff time I am told the primer is broken. I did all in my power to start them. It worked. Then due to some poor headwork on Lt. Robey's part, I lost my spot taxiing. I was mad, damn mad.

"We took off at 10:00. I quickly got into formation and stuck tight—no help from Dillinger [the copilot]. I did all the work that day. We were over an overcast, then there was the French coast. Peaceful, pretty country but we had been warned what would come. Approaching Nantes we were hopped by German pursuit and heavy flak. One of the boys said on interphone, 'Here they come, 6 UP.' Guns started to chatter, formation tightened. Bursts of flak came close. We began our evasive action. My arms began to ache, steam and sweat rolled off me. Dillinger sat there, looking out of his window, either scared to death or bored with it all. Flak would bounce our ship now and then. I just bore down harder, just flew tight automatically.

"We began to circle as though we were lost. Jon called up and said we were over Saint-Nazaire, a big Nazi sub base—good target. An FW dived at the 306 [Bomb Group] formation, then made a feint at us. We were being attacked from the rear. Our outfit downed three ME 109s of six attacking planes. Fleming and [Waldo] Brandt [tail gunner] sighted thirty FW 190s keeping out of range. We kept on circling. Flak made large bursts above, below, to the side, just a few feet from us. We flew through their smoke. Bomb doors finally opened, we were on our run. Flak bursts were intense— Bombs away.

"We started ours after the colonel had let his go. They were excellent hits. Ten 500-pounders in each ship, twenty-one of them after Roby turned back. They sure looked good. We then headed out to sea and home. I let Dilly handle the throttles to give one arm a rest. Soon enough he was asleep and we all but passed the colonel up. I was damn mad, hit his heavy flying suit with the back of my hand. The colonel landed at Chelveston, me and Goetz behind. It was the wrong target but a good one. Won't be much good for several months to come."

Conver reported, "About 12:10 P.M., we arrived at what the lead ship thought was La Rochelle. Both myself and Jon [Schueler] knew it wasn't. The antiaircraft batteries had opened up by this time but they hadn't gotten our range yet. We flew around and around waiting for the lead ship to do something. During this time, Jon and I figured out that we were at Saint-Nazaire . . . The lead ship opened their bomb bay doors and the rest of us did likewise. We started on a bombing run but turned off due to the fact the sun was in our eyes, so they told us later. We then made a large circle and started another run. By this time the flak was getting very heavy and very close. We finally let our bombs go and I'm sure they hit the target even if we didn't get a picture of them. We returned by the way of water. My ears hurt; I was very tired and hungry."

The postmortem criticized the 303d for having struck at Saint-Nazaire instead of the briefed objective, La Pallice, 100 miles away. Furthermore, the 500-pounders could barely have scratched the concrete walls of the enemy sub base. At that the crews were fortunate the enemy was still apparently not well organized or proficient with its antiaircraft.

Along with the 303d Bomb Group, the 305th, led by Curtis LeMay, had added its weight to the still-slender resources of the Eighth, making its first strike on 23 November. While junior officers like Southworth expressed satisfaction with their results, senior officers like LeMay, braced with the data provided by photo reconnaissance and other sources of intelligence, were aware that the strategic-bombing campaign was not inflicting serious damage. Furthermore, the enemy, having studied the tactics of the U.S. raiders was raising the price of each foray.

LeMay decided that better results could only be achieved if the bombers maintained altitude and flew a straight course in the final moments before the drop. Evasive actions in the face of flak, implied in Southworth's descriptions of his first missions, defeated the work of the Norden bombsight and the concept of precision bombing. LeMay subsequently explained that he calculated, using an old artillery manual and compensating for the improvements of the German 88, that flak gunners would need to fire 372 rounds in order to guarantee a single hit on a B-17 in level flight. Whether his arithmetic was corrrect or not, LeMay believed the figures enough to like the odds. On the very first mission of the 305th LeMay announced to his dubious pilots they could take "no evasive action" over the target. He sought to allay their fears by announcing he would fly the lead aircraft. To be sure, the first ship over had a much better chance for survival than the tail-end Charlie when gunners had time to adjust for range and speed. Still, willingness to do what he asked of his subordinates gave him some credence.

American bombers, previously, also broke away from the bombing path when enemy fighters charged. LeMay directed his subordinates not to deviate from course because of the *Luftwaffe*. His luck and theory stood up in that initial raid; the Eighth Air Force intelligence photos showed that the 305th laid down twice as many bombs on target as any other group and lost no planes. It would take several months before the principles established by LeMay for his group, buttressed by the insights of other commanders, would become gospel.

Overall, however, the bombing continued to be erratic, with most of the ordnance missing the aiming point. LeMay also blamed inadequate training of navigators and bombardiers and the difficulty of concentrating upon the target while beset by the enemy fighters. He advised his superiors of the need for intensive instruction in navigation and target recognition under poor visibility or to pierce the veil of camouflage. He wrote to his mentor, Gen. Robert S. Olds, "There is a lot of difference between bombing an undefended target and running through a barrage of six-inch shellfire while a swarm of pursuits are working on you . . . On our arrival here our gunners were very poorly trained. Most of them had not received enough shooting, especially at altitude, to even familiarize themselves with their equipment . . . due to weather and missions, the only practice we have had so far is shooting at FW 190s and ME 109s."

While the on-the-job education indicated improving marksmanship, LeMay searched for a way to circle the wagons when facing an attack by fighters. He theorized that the best means for bombers to protect themselves against interceptors lay in a modified staggered formation with the aircraft tightly packed. The arrangement pointed the maximum number of machine guns at would-be marauders. The combat box, for a bomb group based upon three squadrons, placed six to nine aircraft in the lead with a similar number as a second echelon 1,000 feet higher and to one side while the third squadron flew 1,000 feet below the leaders and on the opposite flank. When in proper array, a group could bear as many as 200 .50-caliber machine guns on any interlopers while a wing composed of several group boxes could respond to attack with between 500 and 600 machine guns.

The key for both bombing accuracy and for protection through tight formation flying was discipline, maintaining position no matter what the opposition did nor how difficult climatic conditions were. Gunners also needed to control themselves; indiscriminate shooting amid the tightly packed formations could and did result in deadly friendly fire. Other aerial warfare thinkers concocted similar schemes, but LeMay put his theories into practice. He personally supervised training runs from the top turret of a B-17. His insistence upon practice while other bomb-group crews enjoyed a respite from flight duty generated resentment. But the results achieved as a result of LeMay's demands impressed even those who scorned him as "Iron Ass."

Many months later, with all planes expected to follow the leaders and further ensure accuracy, the theorists developed the notions of lead navigators and lead bombardiers, with deputies in a position to take over should the guide abort or be knocked down. Unfortunately, at the time LeMay began to implement his ideas, there were so few units and crews in England, that opportunities to practice innovations were limited. The close-in formations, as Southworth experienced, demanded skill, knowledge, and concentration. Buffeted by winds, the turbulence of prop washes, and the jolts of ack-ack, it was inevitable that the huge aircraft, laden with heavy explosives, sluggish to respond at upper altitudes would, even in the hands of the most capable pilots, collide as the margin of distance between them shortened. With just five full groups on hand, the numbers for mounting a wing-size box in the grand scheme projected by LeMay simply did not exist in the winter of 1942–43 and the early months of spring.

On 6 December, Milt Conver went on his second raid after having been unable to fly because of a head cold. He reported, "Someone saw an FW at 12 o'clock and at our same level. I scraped what ice I could from my window and got ready for him to come in. He dived a little to our right, then came directly at our ship from one o'clock. When he got in range I started to fire. I could see my tracers going into him, but he kept coming in at terrific speed until he was not more than seventy-five yards away. All this time Belk and Means were also pouring lead into him. Billy Southworth, who was sitting in the copilot's seat, said the Hun's prop started to stop. Fleming said the tail fell off, also part of the right wing, then the FW burst into flames. I must have fired more than 100 rounds without stopping and fear that I might have ruined my gun. We were all afraid we were going to be rammed. As Billy said, 'I could see his gold teeth.' Well, the fellow's a good German now. The thing that impressed me most was seeing the fire coming from his guns and the fact he only hit us twice."

The ebullience drained from Southworth as the missions continued. His diary refers to drunken brawls among the squadron officers and his frustration as the 303d's superiors refused to accept his recommendations for better tactics. Regular crewmen became unfit for duty. He noted his bombardier Milt Conver left *Bad Check* because of chronic ear infections. Respiratory problems felled navigator Jon Schueler. Flight surgeons scrubbed two of the regular gunners for what Southworth listed as "a dose," the GI slang for gonorrhea. The pilot himself sought treatment for a cold and sore throat, a threat to his own readiness.

Nevertheless Southworth was at the controls on 12 December for the run at Rouen/Sotteville, the same marshaling yards stung by the first Eighth Air Force heavy bomber attack in August. "Twenty-one planes were scheduled for takeoff, twenty took to the air. Two were knocked down before reaching target, nine turned back, and twelve dropped their bombs, mind you," groused Southworth, "only twelve. Smells like fish. Two minutes over the French coast here come the Jerries, attacking in pairs and large numbers. Six of our ships took positions on our right and an even level (piss poor). Another bunch [was] on our left and level—stinks. The Huns bore in. Here come four at me, firing across my nose from one and two o'clock. Our guns, top turret and more guns blasted a steady stream. My window, already cracked, became streaked with cracks, at which I became furious at Sgt. Means [top turret] for disobeying orders, firing forward as his zone was rear. The ball turret reported out of order.

"Flickenger received the shots meant for my ship. One engine smoking, he disappeared behind me. Another moved up into his place. Frequent attacks came from the rear. The Spitfires had left us to return home. Continual attacks were made by the yellow-nose FW 190s, often from the nose." Southworth had observed the latest wrinkle in enemy tactics. The Germans had become aware that the front end of the B-17F was highly vulnerable if one attacked from that direction and at a slightly elevated angle. Only the top turret then had a clear line of sight. The .30-caliber machine guns used by a bombardier could not focus on hostile aircraft directly ahead.

Southworth's complaint about his bomb group maintaining the same altitude was justified. He remarked, "Our Forts were so close and on the same level that [they] seemed to lose effectiveness as the gunners couldn't fire and few turrets could be brought into play. We made a turn for evasive purposes and L—— slid over, into me, missing by inches. I tried to get Dilly to watch him but he didn't and then again this numbskull slid fifty yards out of his formation and into ours. I skidded out of danger, extremely lucky to avoid a terrible crash. He hit our horizontal stabilizers, putting a damn good dent in it. I'll take a bow for being on the alert and saving our necks there."

Bad Check managed to dump its cargo in the vicinity of a railroad complex and fought off enemy fighters until Spitfires met the returning bombers. Although they had lost two aircraft with their crews, the surviving pilots buzzed the airdrome before settling in. "There was Schueler to meet us," wrote Southworth. "He's my boy." He proudly contrasted the 303d with that of the 91st assigned to the same target. Only six of its twenty-one aircraft crossed the Channel.

On 3 January, as dawn neared, an exultant Southworth scribbled in his diary, "Will be copilot with Col. Wallace [group CO]. We will lead five groups, 21 planes each. General [Haywood] Hansell, two-star boy will fly with us." Hansell served as head of Eighth Air Force planning. Southworth, blithely remarked on the briefing data . . . "Smile lady luck. Over flak area of 56 heavy guns plus mobile installations of guns. Loads of fighters and loads of fun. Submarine installations and torpedo docks will be 'leveled.' What a red-letter day."

Indeed it was a momentous occasion. Acting as copilot while Wallace sat in the left seat, Southworth maneuvered a different plane than *Bad Check* to the French coast. In an elliptical and disjointed account he reported, "It seemed to be deadly peaceful. There was no escort. The general seemed to be a good stick. We got on a four-minute bombing run. The colonel thought he heard someone say, 'Bombs away' and he turned off the run a couple of seconds early. He had a fit but cooled down. All going too perfect, then here they came. Four FW 190s from the front. [They] shot two down. Of our first nine ships over the target, four were shot down; they got seven in all. We've lost nine crews and ships in combat on eight missions.

"The general served sandwiches on the way home. The general said that we had some good Indians on our ship. 'For plain unadulterated guts,' he said, 'You boys have it.' Scheuler did a fine job. Was pleased until I found out our losses. Sheridan and Goetz gone. Sure will miss Goetz, one of my best friends. We were all at the club after dinner. Bought Schueler a drink. Then a bunch of us began to flip coins. Loud singing began. More liquor was ordered. At 10:00 we left for Diddington and the nurses. I was drunk for the first time. Don't remember a thing. Guess we tore things up, running in and out of huts while girls screamed. One walked me around while I staggered. Wow! Got home—said 'Do I live here?' Froze at night, had a cramp."

According to Fleming, the facts of war came stunningly home to him on this, his third mission, after he missed several with the *Bad Check* crew because of illness, including one sudden onset of severe pains enroute which earlier had forced Southworth to abort a mission. "By this time we had experienced some antiaircraft fire, but not enough to make you think somebody was trying to kill you. It wasn't that bad. The third mission [for Fleming] to Saint-Nazaire was the shocker for all of us. Over the target the antiaircraft fire was very heavy and it was hitting the planes, we started to realize somebody was really shooting at us. All of a sudden the plane on our wing, the squadron leader, Major Sheridan's took a direct hit and completely blew up. Pieces of it flew all over our plane, knocked holes in the wings and the stabilizer. It was a terrible shock to see. None of us could believe what had happened. But by the time we got off that target we knew Germany was no playground anymore. When we got back to our field, the ten empty beds from the lost crew made everybody realize what could happen."

Navigator Schueler described the routine of these first forays and his reactions. "We'd be awakened at 2:30 A.M. and we'd dress in the cold of the room and slog outside into the rain and muck and we'd have our breakfast and then we'd go to the briefing room. 'Attention!' We'd pop to and the colonel would stride down the aisle and mount the platform and announce the target.'Saint-Nazaire' and we'd groan and laugh at the same time. From then on it was business. We'd be told the time of takeoff, the time and place of rendezvous, the point of crossing the channel, the initial point, the target, the procedure, and route back. Then we'd go to individual briefings, navigators' briefings, gunners' briefings, pilots' briefings, bombardiers' briefings. All night long the bombs were being loaded and the ground crew was working on the planes. We could hear the engines being revved up.

"As long as the momentum of activity was going, everything would be OK. I felt the excitement, the blood coursed through my veins. I felt the intensity of it. We would start the engines revving and I'd lay out my charts and have everything ready, oxygen mask, parachute. Check all the dials. Computer, pencils, Weems plotter [a navigational tool]. Milt Conver would be making wisecracks. We could feel the plane being readied, we could feel the vibration of readiness of men moving back and forth at their dials, controls, and guns. Everything was OK. We were a team and we knew each other and loved each other. The men were truly noble. The planes were noble.

"The B-17s are scattered around the field and it is seven in the morning, the first dim light of day. The first dim, gray silver light, mists rising from the fields. And then you hear engines starting here and there, some close, a roar, and then rrrrrrmmmmmmm, ready on one, ready on two, contact, ready on three, ready on four. And the four engines of the B-17 slowly throbbing, vibrations increasing, a spitting and grumbling, a lust for the morning air, a waking from the dead, a waking from the night, a waking to life, the life of the new day, of the throb, the heart throb of the plane, four engines beating, four propellers whirling, engines revving, echoing each other.

"The olive-drab B-17s would slowly move, brakes screeching, the ground crew watching, one of them helping to guide the plane around the circle onto the tarmac path to the perimeter track. One after another, lumbering out onto the track and then all of them, single file on each side of the field, two files moving, lumbering slowly toward the takeoff point at the end of the runway. All of them, engines growling and propellers twirling. The nose of the B-17 in the air, the body sloping down to the rear tail wheel, already in an attitude of urgency, of wanting to rise into the gray morning sky. Because of the morning light, because of the vast, flat stretch of the field, the planes looked larger and more powerful than they actually were.

"Men. Each an individual who lived and suffered, who had a woman or women, who sweated, crapped, lusted, who drank and got cold in the damp billets, who tried to light the stoves, who sat around and talked into the night, talking about the raids, and latterly, about the chances for survival. It really was beautiful, beautiful in many, many ways."

In a more prosaic tone, Bill Fleming reminisced, "Some of our equipment bothered us as much as the Germans. Our planes were open [at the waist positions for the machine guns] so the temperatures at 30,000 to 32,000 feet were forty to seventy degrees below zero. We had to dress very heavily. I wore long underwear, and a uniform shirt and pants, an electric suit over that, plus a fur-lined flying suit on top of it. On my feet I wore silk stockings, wool stockings, electric shoes, and fur-lined flying boots. My hands had silk gloves, wool gloves, electric gloves, and then the fur-lined flying mitts. You could barely move a finger and you always left one free to work the trigger of the machine gun. We didn't dare unplug the electric suits which were connected to the battery system. Without heat you would freeze to death in a matter of minutes. It was funny to look at the man next to you and see his eyebrows white with frost. There were several severe cases of frostbite. You did not dare fly while you had a cold because if you did, your oxygen mask, which was the old bag type, would freeze with ice and cut off your oxygen. We lost two gunners out of our squadron that way. One a ball turret and the other a tail gunner.

"We had to clean our guns after every mission using the solvent carbon tetrachloride. That kept the guns dry because any kind of moisture on them and they would freeze up. Later, of course, in the U.S. factories carbon tetrachloride was banned as a deadly poison. I wonder how many of our guys got sick from it. I remember over Halle, Germany, when it was so cold that our guns wouldn't fire. Fortunately for us, the Germans couldn't fire theirs either."

The astute if acerbic Southworth expressed his continuing exasperation with his superiors for their refusal to consider more effective formations, "What a bunch of little tin gods. I like the colonel but there sure are a lot of deadbeats running this outfit." He shifted his attention to the other major weakness. "Went down to see how progress, if any, was being made on the new nose gun mount. We can't get that too soon. It's a sheer waste of men and airplanes to attack without nose guns. Just sit and wait to get shot down." Eighth Air Force tacticians had realized the enemy's approach and they asked for modifications to protect the planes. Subsequently, B-17Gs would come to Europe with a chin turret whose pair of .50-caliber guns significantly improved a Fort's ability to defend itself against those who attacked at twelve o'clock high.

Whatever the formation, maintaining position demanded strenuous effort at the controls. Southworth, an exceptionally skilled pilot, speaking of an excursion to Lille, said, "I fought and fought prop wash. As we neared the French coast, it was so bad that when I turned one way, with all my strength applied, the ship was going the other way toward Buck [Glenn Hagenbuch] who was also flying formation prop wash. I managed to push my nose down in time to break out of it. I was 200 to 300 yards out of formation and then had to battle my way back in there. This went on for an hour or two, a battle all the way. We'd get out of formation and nearly dive into other ships. The FW 190s didn't bother me. It was the 17's prop wash. The plane felt loggy and flew like a truck. We saw two B-17Fs ahead of us crash in midair. The tail section came off one, broke in two and damaged the wing of another so that it too spun in."

Subsequently, Bomber Command dispatched the 303d with the South-worth crew to Lorient and Brest and their severest test yet. "Little happened until we reached the target," said the pilot, "where huge puffs of heavy flak broke in close proximity. It sounded like rain blowing on a tin roof, or a limb cracking, a bolt of lightning. We had passed through a solid bank of haze at 25,000 feet and then it was clear as I have ever seen it over the target. There were about fifty to one-hundred fighters in the area. We watched groups of 190s at 30,000 feet. They would peel off, leaving beautiful vapor trails but soon to spell the end for some of my buddies.

"We dropped our bombs and turned off when the fighters attacked. Hagenbuch's engine failed and Colonel Robinson pulled off with another group, Cole and Reber with him. Both squadrons on our side left us, the three of us alone. We were sitting targets when the attacks came. Over the interphone a constant position report came through. 'Nine o'clock, lower six, upper five, two, low five, up three, eleven, low ten, twelve o'clock.' There was continuous shooting. An FW gained position eight to ten miles forward and started a long head-on attack. Upper-turret firing felt like someone pounding on my head, a loud noise with heavy vibration. My glass cracked in front of me. I bent my head slightly in case she let go. Our .30-caliber from the nose sounded like a toy or an electric sewing machine. The FW firing lit up like an electric sign. Robey, to my left was being hit in the fuselage and vertical stabilizer. Looked as if we would crash head on, so I raised my nose to allow my lower turret to fire back but instead pulled up violently, throwing everyone on the floor as the enemy grazed below me. At that moment, Dillinger pushed my controls forward trying to talk through his oxygen mask and the drone of the engines. I put the ship under control. Robey missed our tail by inches as he peeled off into a dive straight down, many thousands of feet, his tail gunner hanging on, firing both of his weapons.

"Attack positions kept coming in, and brief reports of an FW shot down and its clock position were briefly sounded off. We were headed toward Brest, heaviest flak-defended area in that section. We took slight evasive action. Our interphone went out and only the roar of the engines and the bark of the .50s could be heard. FWs were attacking furiously.

"Two miles to our left the 305th Group was moving up. We came within 200 yards of the 305th as flak pounded up in large black puffs. I covered Buck taking more violent evasive action as the 305th bombs fell. They pulled away from us like [Ernie] Lombardi and [Terry] Moore in a foot race." The former was a Cincinnati Reds catcher known for slow speed afoot and the latter an extremely fleet St. Louis Cardinals outfielder. Unable to gather with the B-17s of the 305th, Southworth and the remnants of the 303d huddled together hoping to mutually fend off further assaults.

"There were only a few attackers left. We had little ammunition. One waist gunner was out of the same as was the lower turret and the .30 in the nose. Low on gas and with an unpredictable radio, we landed at Exeter. Fleming had shot down two planes and Kirkpatrick shot down one from the ball turret. Upon our arrival at Molesworth, we learned of Reber's tough luck and the others' fate. Hate to lose the lot of them." [The 303d listed a staggering five aircraft shot down, with fifty airmen MIA. And those B-17s that reached the United Kingdom bore one dead and nineteen wounded.]

Conver noted the furious exchanges with enemy fighters. "Our gunners shot down three FWs. Fleming got two and Kirkpatrick got the other. We had three head-on attacks; one would have rammed us but Billy Southworth jumped our ship right over him. I thought sure I was a goner or else I was going to have a Jerry in my lap."

Captain John Regan of the 306th Bomb Group was awakened at 3:00 A.M. on 27 January and advised breakfast would be served an hour later, with the briefing at 5:00 for a mission against a German target. "This was somewhat routine," recalls Regan. "We had already bombed German targets in occupied Europe—routine, that is, if one could adjust to the tremendous pressures of combat and the all too often loss of close friends. Frankly, I knew of no one who could truthfully say that any combat mission was just routine.

"I wish it were possible to accurately describe the tension, the emotion that was evident in our thirty-five-man crew huts on those mornings when we were awakened for combat missions. One would have to be present to feel the electricity that filled the air. Some men shouted to relieve tension, others laughed out loud when nothing was really funny, and others were silent with their thoughts, probably fixed on coming events, or on loved ones. I even knew some who would silently slip outside in the darkness to become ill—they didn't want their buddies to see them. Everyone wanted to appear strong and tough—it is normal, we were all so young—but we had learned that war is hell and that the only romance or glamour associated with it is fiction.

"All was as usual until the 5:00 A.M. briefing. This took place in our combat-operations hut that had become very familiar to all of us. We sat together as combat crews and exchanged small talk while we waited anxious to find out what our target for the day was to be.

"A large map of England and Europe that took up most of the front of the briefing room was covered as usual with a blue cloth so that crews would only find out what the mission of the day would be after the briefing had started. At 5:00 A.M., our commanding officer and the operations briefing officer entered the hut. We came to attention and then sat down. After a few short, opening comments, our commander paused, then said, dramatically, 'Gentlemen, this is it.' and with that drew back the blue cloth covering the map, so we could see it and the telltale ribbon that would show our course to fly and the target for the day.

"Initially, there was a stunned silence and then the room erupted with shouts of exultation and wonderment, as the significance of the mission sunk in. Yes, we actually were going to hit the enemy near his heart. The excitement was intense. For a moment, even the fear of combat was forgotten, as exultation reigned. The historic meaning of this event sank in even further when we were told that our group had been selected to lead the mission. I was doubly thrilled as my squadron was to lead the total American bombing effort."

The mission that so galvanized Regan was the Eighth Air Force's first assault upon German turf in the form of the shipyards at Vegasack outside the city of Bremen. The 1st Bomb Wing, composed of the 91st, 303d, 305th, and 306th contributed fifty-five B-17s. The planners had expected the B-24s of the 2d Bomb Wing—the 44th and 93d Bomb Groups—to participate but all twenty-seven Liberators returned to base, defeated by the weather and an inability to navigate to the target. But despite the failure to unload their ordnance, the B-24s would endure a terrible pounding from enemy fighters.

Regan remembers, "The rest of the briefing was anticlimactic, as were the preparation of aircraft, the takeoff, the rendezvous with other aircraft, and the initial flight to target. As the bombers crossed the coast of Germany and headed for the primary target at Vegasack, it became apparent that the complex to be attacked was covered by low clouds, which made bombing impossible.

"What a dilemma! Over Germany for the first time, all aircraft with a full load of bombs and the ground at the target hidden by low clouds. To return to home bases without bombing would have turned this momentous event into a failed sortie. A choice of action had to be made. The air commander, Col. Frank A. Armstrong Jr., weighed the alternatives and elected to try to bomb the secondary target, the shipyards and docks at Wilhelmshaven.

"As this secondary target was approached there fortunately was a break in the low clouds that allowed the bombardiers to see the target and successfully drop their bombs. Although the size of the bombing effort that day was relatively small, it was a great morale booster for the young Eighth Air Force and all Americans. The Germans had been taken by surprise. They had not anticipated this attack and had probably felt that bombers would not dare penetrate the airspace over their homeland in daylight. There was some antiaircraft fire over the target, but it was not accurate, and a small number of fighters attacked our bombers, which attested to the success of the surprise aspect of the mission."

The critique of the mission, organized by Southworth's former passenger and sandwich purveyor General Hansell, sounded some ominous themes. "The Combat Wings on this mission did not keep close enough together to give shielding protection, one to the other. Fifty-five aircraft in a formation are not enough aircraft to be able to defend themselves. It is felt that most of our losses were the result of poor formation flying which resulted in aircraft becoming separated and an easy prey to fighters. Gunnery must be stressed . . . even when a formation brought all its guns to bear on some of the attackers during this mission, the enemy continued to come in firing. Poor visibility at the target made the bombing very difficult . . . a target as small as this one should only be assigned when the weather is very clear and visibility is good." For all of the theories of LeMay and the high command that agreed with his precepts, the air crews of the Eighth obviously required continued training and a more focused effort.

As January drew to a close, Southworth recorded a dismal inventory. "We arrived as a complete group on October 31. In three short (or long) months the group has completed some eleven raids and lost over 50 percent of the [organization]. We average about fifteen planes per raid, which means that we have lost about 120 percent of our combat equipment and are operating [by using] reserve. We still lack nose guns. Eighty to 90 percent of our losses have been from nose attacks on our squadron. Nine pilots were lost. L——— doesn't count as he has been on no missions. A white feather might be in order."

A bout of the flu mandated a hospital stay for Southworth. In his absence, Jon Schueler volunteered to fill in with another crew out to slam Saint-Nazaire once again. The experience shattered Schueler. Years later, he wrote a surrealist account of an extended nightmare. "Billy had been sick and was off flying. I had a cold, too, and was off flying but I wasn't in the hospital. We were called upon for a raid and we could only get a few ships out of the group in the air—because of lost ships, because of badly shot up ships, because of shortage of personnel. Either shot down or sick. Two minutes before Saint-Nazaire, the squadron is seven ships. At Saint-Nazaire it is two. This was the raid in which we headed into a steep descent down to the deck from 20,000 feet after dropping our bombs and pain shot through my head like I had never before imagined."

Savage as the reception at Saint-Nazaire was another calamity that struck on the voyage home—a headwind of 120 miles per hour. The hapless bombers, reduced to the pace of a tortoise, crawled toward sanctuary while predators stalked them. "I see the clouds, the clouds building up so that we couldn't see the ground, we had no sign of movement, the B-17s standing still and the Focke-Wulfs and Messerschmitts coming in to meet them, coming in to knock us out of the sky.

"For a moment, for a long moment, I was not navigating, I was watching the planes falling, the head-on crash of a fighter into a B-17, the exploding, burning, war-torn falling planes, all too often no chutes in sight, the lonely men held to their seats, to the walls, to the roof of the plane as it twisted and fell, sometimes with machine guns blazing, and a spume of smoke for a long moment. It seemed endless. It seemed as though we would never get home. I was looking out of the window at the endless blue sky and white cloud beneath us. We waited for the Focke-Wulfs and the Messerschmitts and we watched the Fortresses fall. Falling Forts. I wanted to hold them. I wanted to go down with them. I wanted to go home. I prayed. I prayed, please God, I'm bored, please don't make this go on and on and on, it's boring, it's ennui. I can't stand this boring repetition, please God, get us out of here and get this over with. I was probably frightened, too, although I was seldom scared while actually flying.

"Had I been able to feel the fear, call it that name, I might have been able to feel the rage. Had I been able to feel the rage, I could have poured out the machine-gun fire. I could have slammed bullets into the sky, into the waiting Focke-Wulf. In combat, I could not feel the fear or the rage and therefore the love, and excitement of what I was doing. I was quite cool in combat. I'd always be so goddamned busy with charts, mental averages, counting, and noting falling ships. I was a cool cookie. And I lost everything in my cool. I drowned myself in it. I lost my way."

Upon his return from Saint-Nazaire, inner demons overwhelmed Schueler. "I started to feel guilty, responsible for every death. I was afraid, not sleeping, that I'd make errors and cause the death of many. It could happen—navigation errors, pilot errors. Ending in death. Planes falling, planes shot down. So many were dying and I felt responsible. But I felt more responsible for those who might die. The flight surgeon gave me sleeping pills and talked to the group commander about taking me off combat for a while to rest up. I had lost twenty pounds or more and was skinny as a rail. They needed an operations navigation officer and I was made that.

"We sent out as many planes as we could muster on a mission and instead of being on it myself I was left on the base. At the end of the day I was on the tower, looking to the sky, watching for the returning planes, counting when they appeared. One, two, three, four . . . nine, ten, eleven, twelve . . . twelve . . . twelve . . . there are no others. We look anxiously, scanning the sky. Then the planes are flying in low over the field. Then there is a flare from one and he's moving right down the runway without permission. He's floating down, landing, another flare denoting wounded on board and the ambulance is rushing toward the plane even as it rolls to a stop. . . . The group is badly shot up. One plane is missing."

Transferred to the VIII Bomber Command in High Wycombe, Schueler became increasingly uncomfortable in the almost luxurious surroundings: a private room, "superb food," and an office in an air-conditioned hillside burrow. The meetings and briefings took on the atmosphere of theater. "It was as though I was moving onto a stage, parts to be played until no one could clearly remember the reality. The reality of fight and fear and death, but also the reality of comradeship and effort, and aliveness, and meaning, and strength. I felt dead amongst the living. I felt weak, washed out, through." Schueler contracted mumps and collapsed into a depression complicated by a second childhood ailment, chicken pox. He entered a hospital.

Conver's diary noted a depressing discussion. "Diff and Barker are now having a heated argument on whether to spend all our money or save it. Diff says spend it, 'cause it won't be long until we're knocked off and our wives will marry again and some other guy will [get the money]. 'Barker says to send it home and save it 'cause even if we are knocked off, he knows where his is going and his wife will see that his family will get what they need.' I'm inclined to agree with Barker. I'll send what money I can to Jean and I know she'll help my folks, if they need help."

Fleming commented on the status of the outfit. "In March of 1943, Lt. Schueler and Lt. Conver had left our crew. It was nothing against Schueler that he was grounded. All of our nerves were affected. We were now down to only three of the original nine crews in our squadron. No replacements. It wasn't anything to see some guy break down and cry. I felt like doing it myself many, many times." Conver underwent batteries of medical examinations until the doctors declared him unfit for high-altitude flight. He was sent back to the States. Schueler also went home and after hospitalization received a medical discharge.

Subsequently, the waist gunner himself began to fall apart. "Things were not looking good," says Fleming, "I was having blackout spells, running a high temperature. They put me in a hospital. They couldn't find out what it was. After six weeks, a young doctor discovered I had an infection of my inner ear that upset my sense of balance. They treated me and released me. By that time I had completed fourteen missions."

The brutal first months in the Solomons, the frustrations of strategic bombing, the disappointments in North Africa could all be marked up to necessary learning experiences. The Aleutians campaigns, conducted in the cruel Arctic climate, a frigid version of hell, off the southern tip of Alaska, offered nothing in the way of genuine rewards and seem to have more to do with bragging rights than any contribution to winning the war. The Japanese, perhaps with an inflated view of their power because of victories in 1942, occupied Attu and Kiska, a pair of islands of no strategic importance to either side. Unwilling to allow this incursion into the Western Hemisphere to pass, the Americans responded with a buildup of forces in the area.

Air Corps pilot Stanley Long said, "I think the Aleutian Islands were perhaps the worse place in the world to live because of the high winds, fog, and rain. You lived in a sea of mud all of the time. We lived in pyramidal tents without a floor. The floor was wet all the time and would sometimes be ice it was so cold. If you stood, your head was practically in a steam bath."

Charles Pinney flew B-25s from another base where the crews lived in Quonset huts. He added, "We had our little outhouse that was a tent but it wouldn't stay up very long because we'd have winds that would get up to ninety miles an hour. Having a three-holer out in the tundra got to be a chore. Our mess hall at Cold Bay was a quarter to half a mile from the Quonset hut. It got to be too much of a drudge to even fight the weather to go there to eat. You didn't need an awful lot of food and the food was horrible. A lot of times we'd stay in our [hut] and eat crackers and some fruit juices. [When] things got better we had Vienna sausage and Spam."

Everytime the pilots took off they were at considerable risk of being lost. "We had no navigational aids at all in the Aleutians," said Long. "We were just green pilots out of flight school. I had no instrument training except for maybe four or five hours in Link trainer during flight school. Some of the charts were made from very early Russian surveys. And the Rand-McNally maps weren't accurate at all. I know of one instance where a big mountain showed up fifty miles away from where it was indicated on the map. We lost a lot of our boys over there—flying into situations like that. I know in our squadron we had twenty-five P-38 pilots come up and out of the twenty-five only nine lived to return to the States. [The main cause] was weather. A lot of times [after] we'd get a briefing, by the time we walked down to our airplanes, got in and started the engines, and started to taxi off, the field was socked in again and we couldn't go. We cancelled more missions than we actually flew. [In several instances] where we were able to find the field, the B-17 or B-24 went up, picked us up, and took us down through the overcast." According to Pinney, perhaps four times a year was there CAVU—clear air, visibility unlimited. Along with some B-25s the P-38s struck at the major Japanese installation on Kiska. "We did a lot of the dive-bombing and skip-bombing there," said Long. [They] were trying to build a runway near the camp area and we'd let 'em go for a couple of days and then we'd come over and drop a couple of 500-pound bombs on it and they'd have to start from scratch again, just manual labor. They didn't have big equipment."

Against this backdrop, Long, in 1942, and a companion became the first P-38 pilots in the theater to shoot down the enemy when they downed a pair of flying boats.

The following spring, the 7th Infantry Division, although trained in the Nevada desert for use in North Africa, abruptly embarked on ships for an assault on the Japanese ensconced in the hilly frozen wasteland of Attu Island. At that time of the year, daylight stretches toward twenty-four hours. Ed Smith, a 1939 graduate of the USMA, led a battalion across the small sandy beaches. "We had trained for the desert and had no experience in north climates or living. The equipment was unsuitable, particularly bad for the feet. I had close to 1,000 people in the battalion when we started the assault. At the end of a week we were down to the size of a company, little more than 200 men. Men kept being taken out because of their feet, from trying to live on Attu and from being shot by the Japanese. They were always above us. Wherever the fogline was, we knew the Japanese were behind it. It was foggy most of the time. It got dark at about 2:00 A.M. and cleared by 5:00 A.M. We knew they could see us to fire but we could not see them to fire back."

Against the well-dug-in defenders, the GIs advanced very slowly. The foe took full advantage of steep ridges and sharp ravines to shield themselves against the offshore salvos of the American Navy. Unhappy with the progress of the campaign, RAdm. Thomas Kinkaid, commander of the North Pacific Fleet, fearful of an attack by a Japanese fleet, replaced the 7th Division commander. The decision typified the concerns of naval strategists versus those of Army commanders intent on overcoming the enemy with minimum expenditure of men and equipment. Placing the prerogative to judge ground-combat leadership in the hands of an admiral was as absurd as if the division chief had been handed control over the fleet. Ed Smith, more than fifty years later, criticized the relief of a man he considers "an outstanding commander."

The change had little to do with the final outcome. The fewer than 3,000 defenders could expect neither reinforcements nor evacuation. Squeezed into an ever-smaller piece of turf, about a thousand of those Japanese still on their feet erupted into one of the biggest banzai charges of World War II. Eyewitnesses swore the suicidal soldiers screamed such imprecations as "Japanese drink blood like wine!" The onslaught surprised several units and overran some American positions.

Bob MacArthur was with the division's 13th Engineer Combat Battalion. "It must have been about 4:00 A.M., and we were in our tents playing poker, having a great time when suddenly these guys come streaming back, yelling, 'The Japs are coming.' The battalion commander, Lt. Col. James Green, a West Pointer, drew his pistol and said, [to the fleeing GIs] 'This is as far as you go.' Grenades were being thrown back and forth, a lot of rifle, carbine, and pistols firing."

MacArthur improvised a firing line that drove off the first wave before organizing a withdrawal to a sounder location. His immediate superior, Capt. George Cookson, whose feet were in such wretched condition he merited evacuation, played a major role in mounting the defense. "It went on for most of the next day," recalled MacArthur. "They penetrated as far as the tents for the medics and field artillery." MacArthur then saw the remnants of the enemy kill themselves. "It was the damndest thing. I watched them up on a ridge, taking their grenades—they had a button that detonated them—bang them on their helmets and hold them to their chest while they went off. I couldn't fathom it. I heard they had been told that if they surrendered, we'd run them over with bulldozers." Only twenty-eight enemy soldiers were taken prisoner.

About three months later, the 7th Division GIs hit the beaches at Kiska. But to their astonishment no resistance greeted them. They fanned out in search of the enemy but found only deserted emplacements and booby traps. A flotilla of destroyers and cruisers, under the cover of a thick fog, had slipped into the harbor and the well-disciplined sailors and soldiers evacuated a garrison of 5,000. The Japanese presence in the Aleutians had ended with considerable cost to both sides and at a profit to neither.

18
Tunisia

On 14 January 1943, President Roosevelt and Prime Minister Churchill met with Eisenhower at Casablanca where the political leaders formulated "unconditional surrender" as the only terms under which the Allies would cease fire. The conferees still talked in terms of a cross-channel attack later in the year. However, Churchill, to Marshall's concern, appeared to have talked the American president into a strategy that would send Allied troops to Italy before France. Of more immediate consequence was a strategy that placed the British Eighth Army, pressuring Rommel from Tripoli, under the overall command of Eisenhower in the campaign for Tunisia that would begin as soon as the weather became more friendly for armored vehicles and aircraft.

Promoted with a fourth star, yet still only a lieutenant colonel in the permanent ranks, Eisenhower was dismayed to discover that his II Corps commander, Gen. Lloyd Fredendall, had established his headquarters a full sixty miles behind the front. He was further distressed to observe the Corps of Engineers there engaged in a mammoth tunneling project. "It was the only time during the war, that I ever saw a divisional or higher headquarters so concerned over its own safety that it dug itself underground shelters." With his forces spread thinly Eisenhower would have preferred the engineers to be engaged in building front-line defenses. However, he did not instruct Fredendall to shift his attention and his resources closer to the foe. Nor was he happy with the attitudes of those nearest the enemy and who exhibited "a certain complacency." Discerning an overall slackness, Eisenhower ordered tightened training and battle discipline: "Every infraction, from a mere failure to salute, a coat unbuttoned, to more serious offenses, must be dealt with; or disciplinary action taken against the officer who condones the offense."

Symptomatic of the haphazard operations in the early weeks of Torch, Phil Cochran recalled a small group of paratroopers who suddenly arrived at his base. They told him of a plan sketched out in Algiers to disrupt German supply lines by blowing up a railroad bridge at El Djem. Because Cochran had flown over the area on several occasions they queried him on the bridge structure and the ground at the drop zone. Their transport pilots inquired about landmarks and how difficult it would be to find the bridge at night. It did not occur to the planners in Algiers that the excellent German radar would track the transports and that when no bombs fell the enemy would realize what was happening.

Cochran volunteered to fly over El Djem at dusk, pick out check points and compass courses. "I found the bridge," he said, "protected by only four men with two machine guns. They lived in holes conveniently located so the paratroopers could give them the hands-on-the-shoulders and knees-in-the-back business. I found the spot where they intended to drop and there were ravines as deep as a building. It would have broken every kid's legs on landing." Cochran asked the troopers how they intended to get back. "They answered, they would simply walk west. I know my mother could know this was wrong because they hadn't planned it at all."

Cochran informed Edson Raff who requested headquarters in Algiers to cancel the operation but the rear-echelon strategists insisted on proceeding. Cochran stuck his neck out by going along as copilot on one of the C-47s. For a few moments he confessed he was lost but then he saw a lake he recognized and headed for the drop zone. El Djem contained the ruins of an ancient Roman coliseum and when Cochran spotted the crumbling remains he directed the planes north to a point on the left side of the railroad before announcing, "Let them go. Then they rang the god-awful fire bell and the kids, one after another, counting to themselves, jumped. They were wonderful guys. One right after the other. You could feel the airplane lurch after each one. As soon as the last one went out my pilot jammed the throttle forward and said in the most awful voice—like he didn't want to think about it, 'Let's get the hell out of here.'"

The next day, Cochran flew over El Djem and glumly noticed the bridge still intact. "We figured we must have dropped them into enemy hands. Out of the thirty-five, only five came back. Instead of dropping them going north, I had dropped them going south. When they got to the railroad, they turned the wrong way and walked into town, four miles away. They blew up the railroad tracks in a few places and then most were captured sleeping in a haystack the next morning. It was complete stupidness throughout the whole thing."

For roughly six weeks the Allied foot soldiers manned static positions. When weather permitted, the small band of P-40s at Thelepte, led by Cochran, harassed the enemy troops in Tunisia. "Our action started out trying to force an air war," said Cochran. "They wouldn't do it. We could go right over Gabès [site of an enemy air base] and they would watch you, say, 'go ahead.'" The *Luftwaffe* remained intent upon its objective of supporting the soldiers on the ground and attacking bombers aimed at Axis ships and installations.

"Then we started strafing. We made it our point to burn anything we saw in the way of equipment, including trains, trucks, locomotives. We had complete air superiority except around [the coastal area north of Gabès]. We were successful enough at this to have the Germans stop any movement on these highways at all in the daytime. We actually got so we could hunt the whole area and not even find a motorcycle rider. One day we caught a hundred Italian trucks who attempted to hide in an olive grove. Out of a hundred we burned, in five missions, eighty-seven of them, and lost one pilot. They didn't move any more in the daytime so we started going out at night."

Beginning in January, the enemy struck hard. A quick blow into the Ousseltia Valley was followed by a two-pronged thrust that overran the American positions through Faïd Pass and Gafsa before smashing Allied positions near Kasserine. The advance threatened to swallow up a large number of Allied soldiers, eliminate air fields like the one Cochran used at Thelepte, and capture a major supply base at Tébessa. The *Afrika Korps* under Rommel and another army led by Gen. Jürgen von Arnim initially routed the Allied soldiers. "We were told," said antitank crewman Bill Behlmer of the 1st Infantry Division, "we were to stop Rommel and his *Afrika Korps* from breaking out. We dug in our guns all night long. Other guys dug in their machine guns, mortars, etc. At dawn we decided to light up a cigarette. A few minutes later, a mortar shell hit behind us. Then another in front of us. We dove for cover, because we knew where the next would land. All hell broke loose, and we didn't stand a chance. The Germans had gotten there first and were dug in on the slope ahead of us. The out-of-action signal came and we took off, leaving everything behind."

John Waters, Patton's son-in-law, who had warned his men that they would be up against much stronger adversaries, was well aware of the inadequacies of U.S. tanks such as the M3, eighteen- to twenty-ton light model known as a "Honey." Their 37mm cannons had a range of only 1,800 yards while the 88s mounted on German tanks could blast away from twice that distance. Toward the end of November Waters and his battalion fought the much heavier Panzers and escaped only because the Germans failed to press their attack. At Kasserine Pass, however, the German armor destroyed two battalions from the 1st Armored Division and bagged Waters as a prisoner.

Sergeant Clarence W. Coley, radio operator for Col. Louis Hightower, a battalion commander of Combat Command A of the 1st Armored Division, recalled that 14 February began "just like any of those beautiful African days we had been having there in the 'cactus patch' near Sidi-Bou-Zid for the past week or so. We had been taking it easy, knowing the enemy was over there, somewhere the other side of Faïd Pass. We had all been instructed to dig holes, deep holes to sleep in because of reports of big guns moving into position to shell us. I, like the rest, slept as well as ever because everything was quiet that night."

In the morning at daybreak, the troopers performed their customary "stand-to," checking radios, engines, and guns. Coley climbed into an M4 Sherman named "Texas," and when the colonel arrived, the tanks moved out. They were patiently awaiting further instructions near the CCA's headquarters when Coley learned from the radio that the Germans had attacked Company G near a place known as the "oasis." Hightower returned from headquarters and with two companies of tanks the armor cranked up toward the oasis.

"We hadn't gone very far when we ran into blistering fire from many guns, including a lot of 88s," said Coley. "I didn't know much about what was going on but I did see many of our tanks get hit. Sometimes two or three men got out. Sometimes no one got out. Most of the tanks burned when hit [the Germans referred to Shermans as "Ronsons" because of their high flammability when struck in certain areas]. The artillery got so hot and heavy and we were losing so many tanks due to being outranged, that the colonel decided to withdraw. We started backing out, keeping our thickest armor toward the enemy. The colonel told the driver to zigzag, and when we reached a suitable place, to turn fast and get going. I remember two men got on our tanks to ride out of the battle area—but I guess we were moving too slow for them because pretty soon they jumped to the ground and took off on foot.

"We moved on back toward Sidi-Bou-Zid and learned by radio that the Germans had put up a roadblock there. We were expecting to have to fight our way through it. I loaded my .30-cal. machine gun and was ready to fire at anything that looked suspicious but the roadblock did not materialize. Back in Sidi-Bou-Zid we pulled in beside a building and the colonel left us on foot to check the situation. As we had started before breakfast that morning, Clark, Bayer, Agee and I warmed up some C rations and had us a feast. It was around noon.

"We mounted up and moved out toward the desert. I don't know in what direction but away from the enemy, which had all but wiped us out. The *Luftwaffe* paid us many visits that day. They seemed to have a twenty-minute schedule, just time enough to go back and load up again. It was getting up into the afternoon now, and was pretty hot and smoky in this whole area. As we were moving along we could see many other vehicles moving in the same general direction across the desert, half-tracks, peeps [the nomenclature for Jeeps in armored units], motorcycles, and trucks. About five tanks of Company H had moved on out ahead of us. As far as we knew, we were the only tank back there and the colonel seemed to want to bring up the rear, keeping between the enemy and our withdrawing forces.

"I suddenly got a call on my SCR-245 [radio] set. [The] message was that a bunch of German tanks were shooting up the column, knocking out trucks and half-tracks one after another. I passed the message up into the turret to Colonel Hightower who immediately tried to contact the tanks of H Company. But no luck. The colonel then said we would just have to take them on by ourselves. He immediately rotated the turret until the 75mm was pointed over the left rear fender at the German tanks . . . there were seven of them. Corporal Bayer, the gunner, started firing at them. I could hear [Hightower] complimenting Bayer on getting hits. Clark, the driver, was craning his neck trying to see the action. Agee, the loader, was busy keeping the 75 loaded. All the time we were firing at the Supermen, they were not wasting any time. We were getting it hot and heavy. I did not keep count but we received many hits on our tank. I could feel the shock and hear the loud noise as those projectiles bounced off.

"The rounds were running out in the turret racks but we had a few left in the racks underneath the turret. I took off my headphones, laid them up on the receiver, took the back of the assistant driver's seat out, very deliberately. It is when you have nothing to do that you are afraid. Sitting backwards on my seat, with my feet on the escape hatch, I began pulling the rounds from the racks underneath the turret and passing them up to Agee. I remember other times when I had needed to take rounds from those racks, it was very hard for me to get them out, because I was afraid of hurting my fingers, but this time those rounds came out easy. I didn't worry about my fingers. In fact, I wouldn't have given two cents for our chances to get out of that mess alive. I kept passing the ammo. Agee kept loading and Bayer kept firing that 75. Every once in a while I could hear the colonel tell Bayer that he had hit another.

"Our luck finally ran out. A round got stuck in the gun, wouldn't go in or come out. The colonel told Clark to move on out, and about the same time, one of the enemy guns got a penetration in our tank. The projectile came in the left side, passing through the gas tank, ricocheting around and winding up on the escape hatch just behind my seat. Thirty seconds earlier I was bent over in that space pulling ammo from the racks. I remember sitting there, watching that bit of hell standing on end, spinning like a top, with fire flying out of the upper part of it like it was a tracer. Our tank was on fire inside.

"I heard the colonel say, 'Let's get the hell out of here.' We started bailing out. I remember trying three times to raise my hatch but it wouldn't go up but about four inches. The colonel, Clark, Bayer, and Agee were all out of the tank while I'm trying to get my hatch open. I finally gave up trying and got across the transmission like a snake and up through the driver's hatch, diving headfirst out of that burning vehicle. Hitting the ground on my shoulders, I rolled over and before I got to my feet, I noticed the tracks were burning also. I took off after the rest of the crew who were not letting any grass grow under their feet. When I was between twenty-five and fifty yards away I heard an explosion. Looking back I could see fire shooting skyward from old 'Texas,' ammo or gas blowing up."

The crew hiked through the desert, "sweating out small arms fire from the German tanks." But the smoke and dust hid them. They reached a half-track with other refugees from the battlefield and made good their escape. "Texas" was credited with having knocked out four enemy tanks and distracted the enemy sufficiently for much of Combat Command A to evade capture.

The fighter planes and the ground personnel at Thelepte hastily abandoned their strip for an airdrome safely behind the fluid lines. Cochran and his associates flew off unharmed, leaving behind only some supplies. Then–Maj. Gen. Omar Bradley, as deputy commander to Fredendall, remarked, "There were pockets of gallantry, but for the most part our soldiers abandoned their weapons, including tanks and fled to the rear." General Ernest Harmon, head of the 2d Armored Division, ordered by Eisenhower to evaluate the ineffectiveness of the 1st Armored Division, recalled, "It was the first—and only—time I ever saw an American army in a rout."

Upon hearing of the calamitous events, Eisenhower issued orders for Harmon, already on the scene, to act as his deputy at the front. Harmon recalled, "The only thing I could think of was that when troops were running away, the first thing to do was to stop them, have somebody in authority tell them to stop and turn around. And the next thing was to try to win back the ground they had lost. My motto all day long was, 'We're going to hold today and counterattack tomorrow. No one goes back from here.'

"I told [this to]all detachments that I met on the road. On the way to Thala where the British were located I ran across a colonel of the 26th Infantry of the 1st Infantry Division. He had about a battalion plus around him and he was gathering up more people. I told him to stay right where he was, that we were going to hold today and counterattack sometime tomorrow. He assured me he would hold, and I could depend on it. I put his unit down on my operations' map.

"We finally arrived at Thala; the Germans were shelling the town. We had some difficulty getting in among the alleys and between the houses to the British Command Post, and for the first time I ran into the British. I was unshaven and dirty from my long trip all night long, no sleep, no breakfast and finally found my way into the command post of Brigadier Nicholson of the 6th British Armored Division. The British general as was usual was shaven, clean and spick and span. He looked me up and down and I'm sure I didn't make a very favorable impression on him. I showed him my orders and told him that I was in command of the front and asked him what his situation was.

"He replied, 'We gave them a bloody nose yesterday when they attacked and we are damned ready to give them another bloody nose this morning.' This seemed like very good news to me. Here was a man that had no idea of going away. I said, 'All right. Improve your position today; we are going to hold on all the front today and counterattack tomorrow. I have a battalion of tanks that are coming from Tèbassa and I am going to put them right behind you here on this hillside with orders not to move under any circumstances. They are to support you. They will be here almost momentarily, under Colonel Hightower.

"About this time there was a commotion and a brigadier general of the American Army, General [Stafford LeRoy] Irwin, who commanded an artillery brigade [from the 9th Infantry Division], came in. I had known Irwin at West Point, and he said, 'I have just got an order from General [Kenneth] Anderson the British commander to the north ordering me to pull out of here with my artillery brigade.' Nicholson spoke up, 'Oh, my God. You can't do that. If my men see your artillery brigade pulling out of here it will be bad on their morale.' I said, 'Indeed, it will. Irwin, you stay right here,' and I countercommanded the order. I figured if I won the battle I would be forgiven and if I lost the battle, the hell with it. Irwin smiled and said, 'That's just what I wanted to hear.' I was greatly heartened by the fact that nobody wanted to run, everybody wanted to stay and fight. All they needed was somebody to give them some positive direction."

Harmon checked in with II Corps boss Fredendall to report that the front appeared secure and he intended to counterattack in the morning and take back the Kasserine Pass. "He looked at me rather strangely," said Harmon, "but made no further remark." Harmon resumed his travels, with just his executive officer, a communications officer, his aide, and a driver. "Sometimes I think it is just as well to have a small staff. I think we have so many people on our staffs sometimes that they become cumbersome. It was sort of enjoyable to work with just a couple of people and we ran the battle just as well as if we had had a big headquarters of fifty—probably better."

The enemy opened up with what Harmon described as a rather weak artillery barrage. He sensed there would be no all-out drive at the Allied defenses. Several months later, intelligence studies of German documents found that Rommel had previously decided that if he could not reach Tèbassa within two or three days he would have to withdraw in order to meet Montgomery's Eighth Army advancing from Cairo through Libya.

Returning to Thala, Harmon met Hightower and his battalion of tanks. "Colonel Hightower complained that his people had never fired the tanks, had never even bore-sighted the guns. Harmon ordered the armor onto a hillside and climbed atop one vehicle with the colonel, and said, 'I want you to stay right here. You can bore-sight to beat hell, there is nothing in front of you but the Germans to shoot at.'

Harmon then conferred with 1st Armored Division commander Maj. Gen. Orlando Ward and other high-ranking officers to draft a script for driving the enemy out of Kasserine. "One time in Morocco, Uncle George Patton and I had a little talk on what to do in case we wanted to capture a pass, and both decided the thing to do was to get at least one, and if possible two promontories overlooking the pass. So we staged a counterattack that was to start at midnight that night, two columns with a double pincer movement. On the right the 1st Armored Infantry Regiment and the 26th Infantry Regiment would attack for the high ground to get the promontory on the right. The British had the Coldstream Guards and the Hampshire Infantry Regiment and were going to do the same thing on the left. We would pound the plain, the center, and, when our infantry got to the heights overlooking the Pass, we would move forward with the tanks and drive the Germans through the plain. It was rather simple but a very effective plan.

"The Germans had already started vacating the area during the night and by morning most of them had gotten out of the Pass and were in full retreat. We organized a pursuit as early as we could but they had mined the roads and mined the Pass. We had to lift all these mines before we could proceed so they made a getaway. We have been criticized for not [moving faster] but I took command of troops that were running in the opposite direction and within twenty-four hours we turned them around to attack."

"We went back to General Fredendall's headquarters and gave him the news that the Germans were on their way out. He was in bed at the time and feeling no pain after a few drinks he was having in celebration of the occasion as word had already gotten to him. He called the British commander, General Anderson, and said a few unsavory things." Fredendall got on poorly with many people and perhaps worst of all with his British opposite number.

Having snapped at Anderson, Fredendall then encouraged Harmon to recommend relief of Orlando Ward, an obvious scapegoat for the Kasserine debacle. Harmon declined, defending Ward and obliquely suggested that if Fredendall would allow Ward to operate his division on his own the results would be satisfactory. Amid the jubilant atmosphere at Torch headquarters, Harmon noted, "General Ike asked me if I was to go to relieve General Ward and I told him no. I thought [he] was doing very well but had been very badly handled by General Fredendall. General Ike then asked, 'What do you think of Fredendall?' I said, 'He is no damned good, you ought to get rid of him.'" According to Harmon, Eisenhower invited him to take over II Corps but Harmon believed it would be unethical since he was the one who advised, "my superior was no damned good and it would look like I sold him down the river." Instead, Harmon recommended Patton and subsequently Patton replaced Fredendall, with whom, perhaps not incidentally, he had a long and frequently testy relationship. Fredendall, curiously passive as a combat commander, went home with a medal and a promotion.

In four short days, the Axis forces had lost the power to mount a sustained offensive. However, by the time Rommel broke off the engagement, the U.S. II Corps counted 6,000 casualties, including 3,000 men captured and 200 destroyed tanks. It was such a sudden reversal of fortunes that although the Allied forces had engaged in a pell-mell retreat, the enemy could not remain long enough to exploit the booty. "A few days later," said Behlmer, "we returned and recovered our guns and equipment intact. We were losers again at Kasserine Pass, but we were getting smarter. 'Old Blood and Guts' General Patton took command of the II Corps, and we knew he was there to win even if he had us all killed doing it."

Hamilton Howze commented, "Patton quite wisely elected to make his presence felt as dramatically as he could . . . the whole Corps needed the impact of a new and vibrant personality . . . a new broom that was going to sweep hard and vigorously. He initiated some fines that probably would have had a tough time standing up in a court of law. He said that anybody who was caught standing outside a building without a helmet on would be subject to a $25 or $50 fine."

The installation of Patton as II Corps boss elevated the matter of form to its zenith. Omar Bradley, who disliked Patton for his profanity and bravado, nevertheless approved of the measures he took to build discipline. "Each time a soldier knotted his necktie, threaded his leggings, and buckled on his heavy steel helmet he was forcibly reminded that Patton had come to command the II Corps, that the pre-Kasserine days had ended, and a tough new era had begun." Patton even insisted his officers wear their insignia of rank upon their helmets although that certainly helped to make attractive targets of them for the enemy.

As part of the new attitude, Patton generally disdained actions that smacked of a defensive posture. Carlo D'Este in *Patton: A Genius for War* reported that he "shamelessly humiliated his friend Terry Allen during a visit to the 1st Division. . . . When he discovered a series of slit trenches around the perimeter of the command post, Patton demanded: 'What the hell are those for?' Terry Allen replied that they were for protection against air attack by the *Luftwaffe*. 'Which one is yours?' When Allen pointed it out to him, Patton walked over, unzipped his fly and urinated into it. 'There,' he said, 'Now try to use it.'"

According to D'Este, the bodyguards for Allen and his deputy, Gen. Theodore Roosevelt Jr., snapped the safeties off their submachine guns, ready to gun down Patton on a word from either of the two 1st Division generals. Patton quickly departed.

Patton's impetuous nature frequently carried him right to the brink of disaster. Hamilton Howze led the II Corps commander on a tour of the forward area. "He was in a command car behind us," said Howze, "and we came to a place with some U.S. Army engineers and some light tanks parked off to one side of the road. The engineers were probing with their bayonets and sweeping mine detectors back and forth across the road. They had already dug out some Teller mines, a terribly effective German antitank mine. I stopped my Jeep short of where the engineers were. I told General Patton, 'Sir, the road is mined. We can't go any farther.' He characteristically said, 'Damn the mines! Go on.' Hesitantly, I got in my Jeep, went past the engineers thinking that any moment might be my last. His command car followed me. His driver made sure that one of his set of wheels was in the track of my Jeep; the others were [on the road] where no one had been. It was a foolhardy thing to do. Then a few hundred yards, actually much less than that, behind us a light tank hit a mine and blew up. At which time General Patton changed his mind and we very gingerly came about and back down the road. I am a great admirer of Patton. He had to exhibit a certain amount of flamboyance. He had to make a determined effort to make his personal presence felt. If this involved a certain amount of theatricality, so be it."

The changing of the guard also caused Maj. Gen. John Lucas to replace Bradley as Eisenhower's "eyes and ears." Almost immediately, Lucas and Eisenhower focused on the 1st Infantry Division for alleged deficiencies. In his diary Lucas noted, "He [Eisenhower] is not satisfied with the 1st but neither am I. The division has been babied too much. They have been told so often that they are the best in the world, that, as far as real discipline is concerned they have become one of the poorest. They look dirty and they never salute an officer if they can help it. They should be worked over by II Corps."

Lucas noted that he personally, "drove out and told Terry to get after the saluting in his division." Lucas explained, "The military salute is the sign of fraternity and is important because it indicates the pride the individual takes in being a soldier and wearing the uniform of the great Republic. It has always seemed significant to me and I know this from my own experience that military courtesy—saluting, proper reporting, etc. improves as one approaches the front.

"Terry was rather on the spot because of the discourtesy of his men when the commander in chief drove through his area. It was hard to understand how a car with four stars on it could fail to be noticed . . . It was reasonable to suppose that if General Eisenhower were treated in that fashion, one of lesser rank would hardly be treated any better."

With everyone unhappy about the slow progress in North Africa, even before Eisenhower sacked Fredendall, Gen. Sir Harold Alexander, of the British Army, took over command of all land-based forces. Respected for his military expertise even by Patton, Alexander was dubious about the U.S. forces whom he regarded as ill-trained, poorly disciplined, and weakly motivated. While still coping with North Africa, Operation Husky, the invasion of Sicily, was already starting to take shape on the Allied drawing boards, but there still remained the conquest of the *Afrika Korps*.

The stage was set for a decisive advance toward the coastline via Gafsa and El Guettar, towns on the Eastern Dorsal, the final mountain range before the sea. Hell bent on confounding Alexander's low opinion of the American forces, Patton directed an ambitious and successful campaign that routed the Germans and Italians from the objectives and beyond. Patton, dissatisfied with the 1st Armored Division's performance, had sent Orlando Ward packing and, with the 2d Armored Division training for Sicily, brought in its commander, Ernest Harmon, to take charge.

Harmon's description of his meeting with Patton on this occasion is indicative of a kind of manic-depressive quality about Patton. "I was shown to Patton's rooms," said Harmon, "where he apparently had lain down to sleep in the middle of the day. It was terribly hot and there wasn't a breath of air. Upon opening the door, General Patton was just sitting on the edge of his bed, putting on his boots. His dog Jimmy, with one black patch over his eye, was in the room and the whole room smelled fetid with dog smell and hot air. Patton wasn't in a very good mood, having just woke up from sleep. I reported to him and he grunted that he was glad to see me. He told me to get on out to Maknassy, some 40 miles to the east and relieve General Ward.

"I asked him what I was to do, attack or defend, and with this he flew into a kind of rage and said, 'What have you come here for, asking me a lot of Goddamned stupid questions!' I said I didn't think it was stupid. I simply asked two very fundamental questions, whether I was to attack or defend. He said, 'Get the hell out of here and get on with what I told you to do or I will send you back to Morocco.'"

Harmon then visited with Patton's chief of staff who attributed Patton's behavior to his disgust with Ward and a reaction to being aroused from a nap. Ward apparently had backed and filled over a critical mountain pass for a period of time and Patton worried that the enemy might slip behind the Americans. Patton's deputy told Harmon his mission would be to retain the pass.

When Harmon arrived at his command, Hamilton Howze, the American operations officer, quickly apprised him of the situation. The new 1st Division CG directed his forces, including infantrymen from the 9th Division, to attack, with an objective of gaining several miles each day. "Patton called me up and said, 'What in hell are you doing out there?' I said, 'Nothing. We are just attacking here.' He said, 'I told you to stay on defense.' I said, 'You didn't tell me a damned thing. You just told me to get the hell out. We are just making limited-objective attacks to keep the Germans off balance and we are going to hold here, as [your chief of staff] said that's what you wanted.' He then replied, 'That is fine, okay, Harmon.'"

The new leader of the 1st Armored was hardly less quick-tempered than Patton. He angered many in his organization with a talk to his staff that implied the division had been less than exemplary. He instituted fines for any officer late for one of his meetings. He had very harsh words for a British unit that blocked his progress when it took time out for afternoon tea. He only barely contained himself when General Anderson, the Briton in command of the army that included the 1st Armored, made some slighting remarks.

Later, members of an advance guard discovered a cellar full of wine and nearly drank themselves into a state of stupor. "That made me very mad," said Harmon, "so I told Colonel [Lawrence] Dewey, my operations officer, to get the names of the men who were drunk and have them shot right away. Colonel Dewey was a fine officer and with me pretty much during all of the war. He often softened the blow and he knew when I was mad and he knew what to do about it. I asked him about sundown if the men had been shot and he said, 'I think we ought to let the men live until sunrise, as it is usually customary to allow them to live until sunrise to say their prayers and what not.' I said, 'All right, but have them shot at sunrise for abandoning their mission in the face of the enemy.'

"At sunrise the next day I asked if they had been shot, and by this time I had cooled off a bit and when he said, they hadn't, I said to hell with it and that ended the matter. I don't blame the men so much, but at the time it seemed a very poor moment for anyone to incapacitate himself, especially when he was covering the movement of the column."

In mid-April, Patton passed the baton for II Corps to Omar Bradley and busied himself in preparations for Husky at Seventh Army headquarters. The combined drive by the Allied forces squeezed the enemy into an ever-shrinking area. The British Eighth Army under Montgomery advanced from the south and east, while that country's First Army operated north and west. In the center, the II Corps, including Harmon, pressed forward.

Bill Kunz was an enlisted man in headquarters battery of the 39th Field Artillery, part of the 3d Infantry Division, as it closed in on the enemy. "We were in a column with some infantry which did encounter scattered resistance. This was nothing more than machine-gun fire at some little crossroads. At the time, being relatively 'new' at the game [although involved in the original landing, his assignments had restricted his exposure to hostile action], the engagement seemed significant. A little later, we met some Australian troops. We were a source of amusement to them as we were towing 37mm antitank guns—small-caliber equipment. 'Where are you Yanks going with the popguns?'"

The final offensive, begun early in May, brought the 1st Armored Division to the outskirts of Bizerte. Harmon recalled coming up on the crest of a hill overlooking the city. He watched his tanks clamber into position for the final assault. "My aide and I got into a Jeep and drove to the edge of the plain where I saw some tanks firing but none moving to the front. I got ahold of the commander. He said they were under heavy machine-gun fire. I said, 'Follow me in the Jeep,' and that sort of shamed him. We all went forward and after I had gotten the tanks started, I moved off to see what my right tank force was doing. As we pitched over the brow of a small rise I ran into a whole company of German soldiers who were hugging the side of a cut to keep from getting slaughtered by our artillery. We had one of our artillery liaison planes hovering overhead directing fire into them. Captain Moody [his aide] and I dove off the Jeep and landed right among the German soldiers. They hugged the ground and alongside of them was ourselves. I said to myself, 'I've really stepped into it. I've gotten myself, a division commander, captured. I yelled to the German captain, '*Hauptmann,* I've got to go back and have this artillery fire raised and arrange for your surrender. You come with me.' We got in the Jeep, turned around, went down the road about a mile where we ran into the forward observer for our artillery and arranged for some of our own infantry to go up and take the Germans prisoners.

"I sensed something drastic was about to happen. I rushed back to my command post, just in time. Colonel [Maurice] Rose, my chief of staff, told me we had three German officers who had just come in under a flag of truce and wanted to know what the terms of surrender were. The only thing I could think of was "unconditional surrender. We propose to move immediately upon your works," as my great Civil War hero, General Grant, said in front of Fort Donaldson. I told the Germans there weren't any terms except unconditional surrender. It was 9 o'clock. I would give them until 10 o'clock to make up their minds. If they hadn't surrendered by 11, I would move the attack forward and drive them into the sea. If anybody blew up any of the equipment or tried to escape we'd shoot 'em down. The senior German asked if I'd send one of my staff officers along with him so he could tell the German commander my terms. I said, 'All right, you go with them, Colonel Rose.' I don't think Colonel Rose cared too much for this but Colonel Rose's command car, with a flag of truce with three German officers blindfolded, rolled off toward the German lines. I telephoned General Bradley. He said, "Your terms are all right, Ernie. Have you any idea how many of them there are?' and I said, 'No, probably three or four thousand.'

"Pretty soon, Colonel Rose's voice came over the radio, 'The Germans accept your offer and wish to have you cease firing at once.' I said, 'How about those bastards on the left?' The first request had come from the Germans on my right flank. I hadn't heard from the commander on my left flank. My reference to the Germans as bastards coming in over the clear sort of nettled Rose who had accepted an offer of a drink of champagne with the Germans. Soon Rose's voice came in, saying the left-flank commander accepted. I issued orders all along the line cease firing, everybody hold his place, no forward movement. This ended the battle.

"Next thing was to collect the prisoners, and I was able to tell Bradley that a conservative estimate indicated we had at least 20,000 prisoners. I kept calling him and finally we had nearly 42,000 Germans, including nine general officers. It was a mighty big haul. We had all the roads blocked by tanks. We had the German people handle themselves. We told them to go into camps, stack their arms, bring their own rolling kitchens up, feed their men and stay in these temporary camps until we could evacuate them to the rear. They couldn't go anywhere. There was sea on three sides of the peninsula and we had tanks covering the other side. We shipped in truckloads of rations when they were needed. They were very orderly and well disciplined. I think most of them were glad the war was over. They were part of Rommel's *Afrika Korps*, Panzer troops, the elite of the German army. They were the best soldiers I've ever seen in appearance and behavior."

It was the first significant victory for an Allied campaign in the West and a prerequisite for the strategy aimed at the so-called soft underbelly.

19
Husky

At Casablanca when the Allied leaders had congratulated themselves on the start of Torch they had also agreed upon the capture of Sicily. Initially Eisenhower favored bypassing that island in favor of Sardinia and Corsica as better suited for a campaign in Italy. On the flank of Italy, operations from these islands would require the enemy to disperse his forces rather than concentrate them against an attack from Sicily. But Sicily guarded Mediterranean sea lanes and the size of the island suggested that once captured it could be more easily held against a counterattack. The port city of Messina, separated from the mainland by a narrow strait, could serve as a base for an assault upon Italy proper.

To carry out Husky, the Allies amassed a huge army. The Americans contributed the 1st, 3d, and 45th Infantry Divisions, the 2d Armored, elements from the 82d Airborne, and the Rangers. They would be joined by Canadian and British soldiers as well as the naval and air forces. General Sir Harold Alexander, respected even by Patton, assumed command of ground troops. Montgomery would lead his countrymen while Patton drew the honors for the GIs.

Studies convinced the Allies that the small island of Pantelleria between Tunisia and Sicily if under enemy control would allow Axis aircraft to hammer the Husky forces. In friendly hands it would provide a base for air operations. A rocky coastline, however, boded ill for a seaborne invasion and the rugged countryside denied opportunities for paratroopers. Perhaps because of its apparent impregnability, the enemy high command stationed a garrison of 11,000 Italian defenders, even though the growing disaffection of Mussolini's legions for the war had become obvious in North Africa. The Allies gambled that an all-out series of air raids might discourage any resolute defenses. For six days and nights in the early days of June 1943, the combined air forces rained some 5,000 tons of high explosives upon the area inhabited by most of the Italian soldiers. On 11 June, as assault troops started to climb into the landing craft, Pantelleria capitulated, the bastion falling without a single casualty for the invasion force.

Among the outfits that engaged in the aerial attacks on Pantelleria was the 99th Fighter Squadron, the first of the unique African American Air

Corps units known as the Tuskegee Airmen. The tradition of segregation in the armed forces, and restriction of blacks to largely service and labor organizations, afflicted the U.S. military throughout World War II. Pressure from African-American leaders like Walter White, A. Philip Randolph, and Mary Bethune along with the support of whites like Eleanor Roosevelt breached the military color line in a few places. With great reluctance, the Air Corps had agreed to form what was sneered at as a *Spookwaffe,* in an experiment to see whether "Negroes" possessed the intelligence and ability to fly combat.

Under the command of Benjamin O. Davis Jr., a 1936 graduate of the USMA, the first of his race in more than forty years, the 99th reported to the fighter command in North Africa. They were not regarded as qualified nor were they welcomed by most on the scene. However, Phil Cochran, now part of the Training Command, said, "I found that they were a delightful group of guys to be with; they were a lot of fun. I found out that they could fly formation beautifully. They could land an airplane with more expertise than any young pilots I ever saw. They were trained to the hilt. When I converted them to new formations, they caught on quicker than other squadrons.

"But they lacked aerial judgment. Physically they could fly the airplane exceptionally well, but if they were to be criticized—it wasn't their fault—they were lacking in such things as navigation. They didn't know how to get from here to there properly, and especially in a tough district where there isn't a lot of civilization. It's easy to fly from Buffalo to Cleveland, because you followed the damn lake. But when you get on one of those desert things, and get a little disoriented, there aren't any rail lines to follow and there aren't any highways to follow and there aren't any towns to look down on and say that is [such and such] city. So they would get lost." In fact, because of the hostility to them at air bases around the States, the Tuskegee Airmen rarely had an opportunity to hone their navigational skills in cross-country flights.

Cochran noted, "They were exceptionally eager. Man, if there was a group that ever wanted to prove themselves, they were it. And they would get embarrassed when one of their men would do something that any young, inexperienced pilot would do. They would say, 'We are not supposed to do that; we can't afford to do that.' They didn't want to make mistakes because they had been made special. I always kind of felt for them. I had a fine time of just sitting with those guys. I got to know their wives. I drank beer with them at night. I just lived right with them and I kept talking to them and talking to them, and then going up with them, taking them up one at a time, two at a time, and making them fight each other and fight the winner. They were just so anxious to learn something, and eager to go and eager to fight."

Cochran's affection for the 99th was reciprocated. "He was a great guy," said Spann Watson, one of the original twenty-six pilots of the 99th. "At Tuskegee we more or less trained ourselves. They would just send you out to practice. But Cochran helped the 99th learn how to fight." In their P-40s, the African-Americans were in the skies over Pantelleria and the area commander, Col. J. R. Hawkins, offered them "Heartiest congratulations for the splendid part you played in the Pantelleria show." Nevertheless, the naysayers never shut their mouths throughout the war nor after, no matter what the achievements of the Tuskegee Airmen.

The Pantelleria success enabled Husky to go forward on schedule. But no one believed that the experience would be replicated at Sicily. While the Italians had not shown great determination in North Africa, in Sicily they would defend their native turf. To overwhelm the stalwart defenses, which included a substantial number of first-rate German soldiers backing up the Italians in coastal positions and supported by the *Luftwaffe,* the biggest airborne effort ever launched would begin on the night of 9 July. The attack would include both paratroopers and gliders.

Bill Yarborough expected his own regimental command after the drop in North Africa, but he received only the 2d Battalion of the 504th Parachute Regiment under Ruben Tucker. Aside from his hurt feelings, Yarborough said there was another aspect to Husky that perturbed him. "The planning was done by the staff of the 82d Airborne, a part of which were not airborne officers but straight legs. My distress was even greater when the debacle occurred, because I felt I had something to say about recognition signals, maps, and even equipment."

The order of battle for Husky I scheduled the 505th Parachute Infantry Regiment, commanded by then-Col. James Gavin, reinforced with the 3d Battalion of the 504th, to jump east of Gela, on the southern coast where the 1st Infantry Division expected to come ashore. The remembrances of paratrooper Bill Dunfee indicate the appalling vagueness of the plot. Dunfee, an Ohio high school dropout, led a rifle squad for Company I, 3d Battalion in the 505th RCT [regimental combat team]. "Our CO was Capt. Willard Follmer and I jumped in Follmer's plane. Major Edward Krause, the battalion CO, had informed Follmer of I Company's mission, giving him an airphoto of the area where they were to land. He didn't tell him where but instructed him to pick a drop zone two or three miles from where the 1st Division would be landing and about the same distance from the drop zone of the rest of the battalion. I Company's mission would be to reduce several pillboxes in the area, kill or capture the Italians manning them, set up roadblocks, and then light bonfires to signal the 1st Division offshore that was clear. After studying the airphotos, Follmer picked a narrow valley just over and north of Lake Bivier. Krause approved and said the Troop Carrier Command would be notified.

"Despite Krause's order to the contrary, Follmer, remembering all too well the misdrops and mishaps that had occurred in practice jumps, took it upon himself to contact the Air Corps. In the middle of the night he left our camp in the olive grove and went to the airfield about a mile away. Locating the lieutenant colonel who was to lead the I Company flight, getting him out of bed, showing him the airphotos, Follmer was not surprised to learn that the colonel knew nothing of our mission. He was very cooperative. They agreed to put I Company at the rear of the 3d Battalion's flight and [travel] in a line of three Vees, instead of the standard nine-plane-wide Vee. This would put I Company into the narrow valley. Follmer thanked the colonel and returned to the olive grove, with no one the wiser as to his circumvention of Krause's order.

"July ninth started with an early breakfast. We were issued a basic combat load of ammunition, grenades, and rations. Two items were unique to the Sicily operation, Mae West life preservers and gas masks. The Mae Wests were left on the planes and the gas masks discarded shortly after landing. We had an early supper at 1600 hours. Trucks carried each group to their C-47s. After the equipment bundles were checked and loaded, we crawled in the shade to relax. At this time we were given the password and countersign, 'George'—'Marshall' and told our destination in a mimeographed note to each of us from Gavin. Time came to chute-up and board the planes. The first took off at 2010 hours and by 2116 the complete combat team was airborne. Since my squad was jumping [from] Captain Follmer's plane, I was put at the end of the line as the last man out. I was concerned when Follmer put one of the new men between me and the rest of the squad. We had a direct order from Krause to shoot any man that refused to jump. That presented a problem since my M1 was in a canvas container under my reserve chute."

To protect the transports, gliders, and troopers, Husky I exploited the cover of darkness. Unfortunately, nighttime operations exposed the airborne armada to jittery gunners aboard the great invasion fleet moving through the Mediterranean. Antiaircraft crews tended to regard the sound of motors in the sky as a signal to open fire. As a consequence the transports took off from North African fields but instead of a straight northeast course to the island, they flew east to pass over the small island of Linosa and then the British outpost of Malta before a turn north toward the southwest corner of Sicily, and the ultimate leg, northwest to Gela. Unfortunately, a thirty-five-mile-per-hour wind blew many aircraft off course, carrying numerous planes beyond Malta, and the pilots approached Sicily well off the mark.

"The pilots were as green as ourselves," said Dunfee, "and the navigation pretty primitive. They established a heading and flew for it X number of minutes and then turned as indicated to another heading. This did not take into account the gale over the Mediterranean. Many flights became separated and missed the check points of the small island of Linosa and the larger island of Malta [from where Eisenhower and his staff saw them in the sky]. Most of the flight that missed the checkpoints dropped our guys along the southeast coast of Sicily in the British zone." A worse fate met the British gliders destined for Siracusa. In spite of the scheme to avoid friendly fire, Allied ships shot down ninety of the flimsy craft, which crashed in the sea.

"As we approached Sicily," said Dunfee, "for reasons unknown, the others of the 3d Battalion flight turned back out to sea, subsequently returning to drop on the wrong DZ. Our pilot and Follmer, seeing the Acate River, were satisfied we were on the proper course. As we crossed the coastline, Follmer told me to pass the word back, 'Stand up, hook up, and check equipment.' This done, we sounded off the equipment check, starting with me and moving toward the door. About this time, over Lake Bivier, Captain Follmer, moving by me, said, 'About five minutes,' and took his position by the door. Being crowded when we stood up, it became necessary for me to step through the bulkhead into the radio operator's area. My attention was called to the new man who had sat down. I told him to stand up and he started giving me conversation. I made it very clear to him in four-letter words that he damned well better stand up.

"I had noticed the green light was on when Follmer yelled, 'Let's go!' We started moving toward the door. The man in front of me went past the door into the tail section of the plane. I grabbed his back pack and pulled him back to the door. He started to back off again so I grabbed the sides of the door opening and pulled us both out. I had no more felt the shock of the parachute opening when I was going through pine trees, hitting the ground going downhill. Getting down so fast, my thought as I hit the ground was that I'd had a malfunction but I was able to stand, get rid of the parachute harness, and, securing my equipment, move out.

"Being unable to find the man that went out ahead of me I thought he may not want me to find him. I started back the way we flew in to 'roll up the stick,' but I couldn't find anyone. I spent the night searching for my company. Since I had no idea how far the plane had traveled during the mixup at the door, my assumption was I had landed over the crest of a mountain beyond the valley. By daylight I traveled back over the crest and headed downhill into the valley. By noon of D day I noticed movement on the far side of the valley that I thought to be part of my group. Not sure of who they were I took a route that would eventually intersect their path. By early evening I'd made contact with four men from the 2d Battalion. They too were lost and after comparing notes we decided we didn't know where we were. Being tired, hungry, and frustrated, we sacked out for a few hours. On awakening, we could not agree on our next move. My suggestion was to move south, believing we would contact either I Company, friendly troops, a road, or the Mediterranean. My idea was dismissed and they had none better, so I took off by myself. I found a larger group of troopers, what was left of the 3d Battalion, and finally my company. Less one planeload and myself, I Company had accomplished its mission. Although Follmer had broken his leg, he directed the troopers from the back of a confiscated mule."

Husky I strewed paratroopers from Licata to Siracusa, a distance of eighty miles. The demolition team that was to prepare the Acate River bridge for demolition was dropped sixty miles east in the British zone. The 3d Battalion, less I Company, was scattered between Scoglitti and Vittoria, a few miles southeast of the Acate River. Gavin himself landed twenty miles from his drop zone. He, two of his staff, and three equally lost troopers spent the night wandering in search of the main body of the regiment. They blundered into an enemy position that cost them their first dead man, then sneaked off to hide during daylight. While Gavin, Dunfee, and similarly lost souls could contribute little or nothing to the operation, others among the 3,400 troopers in Husky I, mostly in small groups, improvised to disable the local communications network, knock out some objectives, occasionally call in effective naval support, and delay the rush of the Herman Goering Panzer *Fallschirmjäger* Division to reinforce beach defenses.

Eisenhower's "eyes," Maj. Gen. John Lucas, reached the Gela beachhead at about 7:30. He was disturbed to see enlisted men and officers crouched in slit trenches rather than moving inland. He told his diary, "If I ever command troops again I will teach them nothing about digging. The slogan, 'A soldier's best weapon is his shovel' has taken a lot of fight out of our Army.' He shared this sentiment with Patton who habitually excoriated GIs for resorting to foxholes. Neither man seemed to appreciate the difference between the general officer's behind-the-lines vantage point and that of the combat soldier exposed to artillery, mortars, and small arms.

On his second night in Sicily, Gavin located as many as 250 paratroopers under Krause along with units from the 45th Infantry Division. He struck out for Gela but enemy troops barred the way. Tanks from the Herman Goering Panzer Division clanked to the front, oblivious to bazooka rounds that bounced off their thick skins. A fierce firefight at Biazza Ridge stalled Gavin's people and they were in danger of being overwhelmed. With only a single 75mm piece from the Parachute Artillery plus a pair of 81mm mortars Gavin and cohort were severely outgunned. In his book, *On To Berlin,* he wrote, "About four o'clock a young ensign who had parachuted with me the first night came up with a radio and said he could call for naval gunfire. I was a bit nervous about it because we didn't know precisely where we were and to have the Navy shooting at us would only add to the danger . . . We tried to fix our position in terms of the railroad crossing over the road, and he called for a trial round. He then called for a concentration, and from then on the battle seemed to change." Not for the last time would the big guns of the Navy aid the invaders. The tide in this encounter turned with the arrival of half a dozen Sherman tanks.

Gavin ordered an attack, employing anyone who could carry a weapon, riflemen of the paratroops, engineers, clerks, cooks, truck drivers. The Germans withdrew but not before they killed forty-two Americans, including the forward observer from the Navy and wounded another hundred. The enemy losses were greater but more important, the beachhead had remained intact.

Jay D. Northrup, son of a Wall Street executive and an OCS graduate, volunteered for the Rangers after he reached North Africa. He joined the 4th Battalion. "For the invasion of Sicily at Gela we sailed from North Africa on British Commando invasion boats. They were great to work from since each platoon was assigned its individual LCP [Landing Craft Personnel] and was boarded from the main deck simultaneously by all platoons and when loaded dropped to the sea at one time." Other systems required men to climb down cargo nets to landing vessels or travel across the Mediterranean on the boats that would beach them. The Commando boats allowed better coordination among groups traveling separately.

Northrup explained, "When loaded, the boats were ready to head for the beach in Vee formation following a submarine with a red light. When near the beach, the sub left and the LCPs fanned out in a straight line to land on the beach simultaneously. At Nemours a fellow kidded that they were going to tie a rope with fishhooks on it to my belt so that when we hit the beach, I, going first, would have the opportunity to trip the mines on the beach. I never gave this a second thought until I hit the beach at Gela. I was a few feet on it when I went face first to the ground, thinking about the rope and fishhooks. [I had tripped] over a cable of some type that took me out of the antiaircraft searchlights that were covering the beach and soon to be taken out by the Navy. There was no hesitation of the Rangers hitting the beach and moving into the city. The heavy storm that preceded our landing [which had so disorganized the airborne] was a blessing as the waves brought considerable sand onto to the beach and packed it tight over the teller mines, saving many lives, I am sure."

While rampant surf neutralized mines in the sector of the 4th Ranger Battalion, the surge of the first wave from the 1st Ranger Battalion carried it into a very live field of antipersonnel Bouncing Bettys. The first explosion shredded platoon leader Lt. Walter Wojic. In swift succession more mines detonated, killing and mutilating. First Sergeant Randall Harris, his stomach held in only by his tightened cartridge belt, assumed command. He picked a path through the deadly ground, moving the men to positions where the Rangers seized an opportunity to wipe out pillboxes and machine-gun emplacements that were firing on compatriots still pouring ashore.

Among those in the 4th Battalion now hitting the beach was F Company platoon sergeant Jim Altieri. His boat had been delayed when it slowed down to pick up Rangers dumped from a craft hit by fire from defenders. He was surprised when his ramp dropped and he waded through two feet of cold water to the shore. "I couldn't believe it. Nobody was shooting at us; no mines were exploding. It was not supposed to be this easy. Before I knew it we were safely across the beach, climbing a wide path leading up to the cliff. A path, unguarded, unmined! Right past two pillboxes still acrid with grenade smoke, we climbed. Some outfit had beaten us to the punch." At terrible cost, D Company had preceded them and eliminated potential heavy opposition.

Darby, who apparently seldom missed an opportunity to personally combat the enemy, had met up with a Ranger unit assaulting Italian defenders barricaded inside a hotel. The painstaking rehearsals for house-to-house, room-to-room operations featuring grenades and submachine guns paid off and the Americans overcame the *fascisti*. Meanwhile, Altieri and his platoon approached their objective, the cathedral square at the center of Gela. A burst from a machine gun cut down the point man. "Every building bordering the square seemed to be crawling with persistent Italian gunners," remembered Altieri. "It was still pitch-black night and we could hardly see the Rangers alongside us, let alone the Italians. But we knew the difference between a Ranger walking or running and an Italian; we knew the distinctive contrast between our automatic fire and theirs, our grenade bursts and theirs; even the sounds of our men reloading their clips."

In the darkness, Altieri heard Italians talking and then the distinctive noise of leather footwear approaching. "On an inspiration, I held [Corporal James] Hildebrant's arm and yelled, *'Veni qua subito!'* [Come here quickly]. Within seconds four stocky Italians carrying their rifles at the port double-timed up to us. Their leader, thinking I was an Italian officer, actually clicked his heels to attention. Hildebrant and I jammed our rifles at them and quickly disarmed them."

Allen Merrill, the Ranger dropout assigned to an engineer battalion, had rejoined the Rangers as a scout for Altieri's F Company. He recalled the first moments of the operation as his boat bounced and splashed toward the shore. "A new replacement in our squad, Ben, whispered that he was scared shitless. I told him we all were but that didn't seem to help him. He told me he had a gut feeling he wasn't going to make it. I lied and said most of us had that feeling going into combat for the first time. As 1st Scout I was to be first man out. It was 0425 hours as we ground ashore and the ramp slapped the water. Muzzle fire from machine guns echoed in staccato blasts and tracers seemed to float overhead at the waves of troops behind us. In addition to my Thompson submachine gun I carried extra ammo, a pouch of grenades, both high-explosive and smoke, thirty feet of half-inch rope, a pair of wire cutters, and a nasty-looking four-foot pipe, three inches in circumference, called a bangalore torpedo, in the event we needed to blow anything up that impeded our advancement. My normal weight was 160. With this gear I weighed 220.

"I stepped off the ramp and into three feet of water. A wave covered me before I regained my footing and I spit out the water I'd swallowed and started forward, waist deep, then thigh and knee and finally onto the sandy shores of Gela Beach. Flares lit and floated above in the night sky. As we moved toward the cover of a seawall and a series of small structures, the machine gun found our range and its fire swept across the landing area. Our platoon made it to the structures along the road that slanted from the beach upward toward the town of Gela, some two hundred yards ahead." Merrill encouraged Ben, "See, you made it."

Merrill continued, "From the eerie light of bursting shells and flares I could see the face of my platoon huddled among the rubble of structures along the beach road. It was the composite face of fear, mine undoubtedly included. But there was no time to be fearful. Orders were quietly passed down. As we moved up the road keeping a low profile, the platoon leader called me and the second scout to lead the column some fifty feet ahead. I moved out; Bob [second scout] followed. The platoon moved out a few seconds later." Merrill reached the town square, but darkness hid the fountain, promenade, and marble benches carefully carved in the sand replica. Dawn broke, outlining buildings in the square, including the cathedral, across from where the Rangers huddled.

"The CO summoned Ben to act as company runner between us and those still moving up the beach road. He issued instructions for the rear company. Ben took the message and seemed to turn toward the rear. Then before anyone was aware, he ducked low and started running. But he ran in the wrong direction. In momentary confusion he ran past the wall I was behind and right across the open area. I was ready to call out but before I could he had taken perhaps three steps when a machine gun opened fire and cut him down in midstride. It was just one rapid series of shots and then all was silent again. I was looking straight ahead when he zipped past me. I saw where the shots came from across the square. There was no doubt about it; they came from the cathedral. I reported what I observed."

Quickly the Rangers devised a plan for the two squads to attack the church gunners. As daylight brightened Merrill said he plainly saw the machine gun on a tripod in the main doorway with some figures behind it. According to Merrill, he crept to within five feet. "There was still almost about ten minutes till our planned synchronized convergence on the doorway. I took one step up the three steps to the doorway. I reached out with my left foot and lifted the barrel [of their machine gun] high in the air as I tossed the grenade into the doorway. They were so surprised they never got off a single shot. When the smoke and debris settled, I stood in the doorway with my submachine gun ready. There had been thee men nestled behind the gun, all were sprawled in death. Men ran from the cathedral holding their ears. I let one quick blast go from my Thompson. More men ran toward me, yelling something in Italian I did not understand. Most of them had their hands up high over their heads. My squad ended up taking more than forty prisoners."

For nearly an hour the Rangers besieged the church where a hard core of defenders answered shot for shot. Captain Walter Nye directed Altieri, "Clean 'em out." The order shook Altieri momentarily. "Now I must spill blood on consecrated ground in a holy cathedral. Of all the situations a soldier can face, this to me was the most unpleasant. But Rangers can't waste time debating moral issues. A few more rifle pings from the tower apertures were convincing reminders that the enemy inside the holy ground was very much alive and very tenacious. I kicked the door open wide, threw in a grenade, flung myself back as the grenade exploded and, before the debris had cleared, fired eight fast rounds into a corner of the cavernous cathedral. Wincompleck, followed by McKiernan, Merrill, and Big Pruitt, rushed by me, bounded over the altar rails, shot it out with two Italians holed up in a sacristy, then fought their way up the winding tower stairs. When it was all over we had flushed out three diehard Fascists of the Livorno Division; sprawled grotesquely by the altar were two dead Italian soldiers." Altieri crossed himself, knelt, offered a silent prayer before the altar, then returned to the fighting. In the glow of morning at 6:00 A.M., the Rangers counted more than fifty prisoners and untold numbers of dead. Medics began to patch up the wounded including Randall Harris with his exposed innards. Evacuated to a hospital ship. Harris earned a Distinguished Service Cross and a battlefield commission for his leadership at Gela.

With the Gela beachhead seemingly secure, the GIs of the 1st Infantry Division waded ashore. Bill Behlmer, as an antitank crewman for the 1st Infantry Division recalled, "We moved inland after the first day and the Hermann Goering Panzer Division encircled us. Tanks everywhere. We stood our ground and thought we could outlast them. The 57mms [cannons copied from the British 6-pounder] that had replaced our 37mm cannons performed beautifully. Finally their big guns had us zeroed in and the German armored infantry was advancing. We knew we had to change our positions, but we couldn't get the trucks up the hill to move our guns. I could see we were surrounded and got going. The Germans captured our guns and spiked them. The heavy cruiser *Savannah* and our own artillery saved the day. The *Savannah* steaming back and forth off the beach knocked out the tanks."

The 3d Infantry Division zeroed in on Licata for its objective. William Rosson with the 7th Regiment noted an extremely high sea. One officer on his LCI [Landing Craft Infantry] was washed overboard. He was saved by the next boat. Sailors swam to the beach and set up lines that the troops used to struggle ashore. The opposition was light and the soldiers captured Agrigento quickly. Bill Kunz, with Headquarters Company of the 39th Field Artillery Battalion [3d Infantry Division] as part shore fire-control section, on 9 July sailed from Bizerte on an LCT [Landing Craft Tank]. "A severe storm separated us from the main convoy and we were in danger of sinking for some time. A destroyer found us and we headed for the beach at Licata very early in the morning of 10 July. Our LCT beached and was disabled by gunfire. The tank moved out to Green Beach and so did we with some Rangers and the 3d Division, 15th Infantry. We received welcome fire support from the *Nicholson, Edison, Buck, Ludlow, Roe, Swenson, Woolsey, Wickes* [destroyers] and the cruisers *Brooklyn* and *Birmingham*. The Navy ensign in charge of our disabled LCT went with us and marched the 120 miles to Palermo, on the northeast coast. He had a rough time and remarked he would never leave a Navy ship again if he lived to return to one."

Toward afternoon, a Ranger outpost noticed tanks backed by foot soldiers, some eighteen to twenty miles off, making their way toward the Ranger perimeter. Some 1st Division troops appeared to be retreating from the armor. Binoculars identified the tanks as Renaults, lightweights used by the Italians. About ten feet from Merrill, a high-level conference of brass at Darby's command post appraised the situation. Patton, immaculate, a necktie neatly tucked into his pressed gabardine shirt, his trademark ivory-handled pistols hanging at his sides, shod in knee-high brightly burnished boots, surveyed the scene with Terry Allen, Teddy Roosevelt Jr., Lucian Truscott, and others. Biographer Carlo D'Este said Patton glimpsed a naval officer with a radio and shouted, "Hey, you, with the radio!" Extending his arm in the direction of the Italians, he ordered: "If you can connect with your Goddamn Navy, tell them for God's sake to drop some shell fire on the road." Soon the cruiser *Boise* obliged and began hammering the enemy tanks. Before departing, Patton instructed a captain to "kill every one of the Goddamn bastards."

The general, however, left the area before the armor came within range of the Americans in Gela. According to both Merrill and Altieri, Darby commandeered a lone 37mm gun in the possession of some engineers and as the first tank rattled up the road fired the cannon. He knocked off a tread and then put a second round through the thin-skinned vehicle. The crew climbed out to escape but Ranger sharpshooters picked them off. Darby and his 37 victimized a second tank while Ranger bazooka shells knocked out a third. A Ranger leaped atop the disabled Renault tank, lifted the hatch, and dropped in a grenade. "In the stark silence of my soul," said Merrill, "I can still hear those men scream, momentarily and then nothing." A ricochet off the concrete roadway by one of Darby's missiles stopped a fourth tank. When a crewman emerged from the hatch with a burp gun in hand, a Ranger BAR decapitated him. Now a barrage of 4.2 chemical mortars with white phosphorus shells, "liquid fire," landed among the enemy troops and remaining armor. The soldiers fled. "In the field glasses," said Merrill, "you could see them panic and a look of terror filled their agonized faces, as they ran helter-skelter trying to avoid the spreading smokelike substance. The weapon was operated by men from the 1st Division."

Having fought off the Germans at Biazza Ridge, Gavin, expecting a renewed attack, deployed his troopers for the remainder of the night. "It must have been about 2200 hours," he said, "when all hell broke loose in the direction of the beaches. Antiaircraft fire was exploding like fireworks on the Fourth of July, tracers were whipping through the sky, and as we were observing the phenomena, the low, steady drone of airplanes could be heard. They seemed to be flying through the flak and coming in our direction. Everyone began to grasp their weapons to be ready to shoot at them. A few of us cautioned the troopers to take it easy until we understood what was going on. Suddenly at about 600 feet the silhouettes of American C-47s appeared against the sky—our own parachute transports! Some seemed to be burning; and they continued directly overhead in the direction of Gela. From the damaged planes some troopers jumped or fell. At daylight, we found some of them dead in front of our positions."

Yarborough's choice of the word "debacle" was most appropriate for Husky II. Whatever could go wrong did, and much was due to ignorance and error rather than the uncertain weather or bad luck. Yarborough remembered, "I went into the Sicilian operation on the second lift and from a personal view it was a traumatic experience. I didn't even have a map as Battalion CO. Ruben Tucker had the only one in the outfit. The briefing consisted of drawing on the ground with a stick. 'We're here. They're there. You're going to do this and they're going to do that.'"

During the daylight and early evening hours of Husky's D day, the vast array of Allied Navy ships and transports coped with repeated forays of German aircraft. There was word of German parachutists dropped as reinforcements against the British. Allied antiaircraft batteries on the ships were primed for attacks from above. Anxious not to miss the designated drop zones of Husky I, the air fleet attempted to use the invasion armada as the reference point for passage over Gela. On the night of D plus 1, a burst of gunfire from an Allied warship at the convoy of C-47s bearing the remainder of the 504th signaled open season to other vessels. The slow-moving airplanes broke formation, wheeled in desperation, tried to veer away from the deadly friendly fire. Altogether twenty-three planes were shot down, killing 318 troopers along with the air crews. Among the dead was the 82d Airborne's assistant division commander, Brig. Gen. Charles Keerans.

The surviving airplanes dispersed over the island scattering troopers in their wakes. Tucker's airplane with 2,000 flak holes, traveled the length of the coast twice before finally dumping the regimental commander and his stick reasonably close to his drop zone. Wherever they landed, the troopers ambushed enemy soldiers, blew up defenses, transport, and communications. As would occur in the future, the widespread dispersal of the men fooled enemy intelligence into the belief that the attackers numbered many more than actually landed.

A graduate of the Civilian Conservation Corps, Ed Sims, as a twenty-two-year-old second lieutenant and platoon leader for Company F of the 2d Battalion, remembered standing by the open door as his aircraft neared Sicily. "The night was calm and the light from the quarter moon reflected off the white caps of the Mediterranean Sea below. Suddenly against the dark background of the sky, a gradual buildup of fiery red tracers from below were engulfing our formation. I felt a shimmy go through our plane and then pandemonium reigned as antiaircraft guns of our own forces at sea and on the beaches were blasting our slow-flying aircraft.

"As my plane flew through the heavy flak, I could hear the hits as they penetrated. From my door position, I scanned the sky for other planes but could see only those going down in flames. My plane developed a distinct shudder and banked away from the flak with one engine starting to sputter. I had my men stand up and hook up then, before going forward to talk with the pilot. I instructed my platoon sergeant to get the men out fast if the plane started to go down.

"From the pilot I learned he had lost the formation and had a damaged starboard engine. We decided, since there was land below, that he would stay our present course and allow me a few seconds to return to the door, then turn on the green (go) light when in jump altitude. We both realized that with the heavy load he had, it would be difficult for him to fly back to North Africa. [He did make his home field with a badly damaged plane.] I rushed back to the door yelling to my men to get ready to jump. As I arrived at the door, the red (warning) light came on followed within seconds by the green light just as I hooked up. I immediately released the equipment bundles from under the plane, then jumped into the darkness with my men following.

"Landing was quick and rough. My parachute had just opened seconds before landing. The plane must have been less than 300 feet above the ground. When assembled, I learned that one man had been injured when he hit a stone fence. I sent patrols in opposite directions on a nearby road to look for signs and landmarks. One patrol located a road sign indicating that Augusta was forty kilometers. This was sufficient to locate our general position on the map as about twenty-five miles from where we planned to land in the vicinity of Gela. Also we were several miles behind the German forces opposing the landing of the 45th Division. I had fourteen men with me so we moved in a southwesterly direction toward Gela. At one point we had a short firefight with a small German force, but they soon fled. Later we spotted a company-size German force moving north but since they did not see us, we held our fire and let them pass. Our next contact was with advance elements of the 45th Division. They opened fire on us and for a few moments the situation was dangerous. We had a tough job convincing them we were U.S. paratroopers."

Lucas offered a highly negative appraisal of the air drops, four days after Gavin and his regiment struck Sicily. "Judging from this operation, I am extremely doubtful of the value of airborne troops. The losses in men and planes are heavy and not paid for by the results accomplished. The results would be of great value, of course, if the Air Corps could put these people where the plan calls for them to be. They don't seem able to do this.

"The paratroopers knocked out a Mark VI tank with a 75mm howitzer. It must have been a lucky shot. The bazooka didn't hurt it. The other Mark VIs we got were knocked out by the 75mm antitank guns. We lost six tanks to their three. The paratroopers spread over a huge area and many of them like Gavin's battalion [that of Dunfee] east of Gela did excellent work . . . But they were not landed where they were supposed to be . . . Some paratroopers were shot by an outpost last night when they did not know the proper countersign."

Lucas attributed the Husky II disaster to the tardiness of the Air Corps in providing the routes for their planes and for them being so far off course. "These planes have a knack for coming over at the worst possible time. One group came over a unit that had just been bombed and strafed by the Germans and the poor devils thought, which I can understand, that the Hun was on their backs again so they opened fire." He added the comment, "Air refused to bring any more airborne in, because of the unfortunate fact that some planes had been shot down by ground troops." [Lucas ignored the major source of friendly fire, the navy ships.]

Although the first counterattacks had been beaten back by the paratroopers and the Rangers, the infantry divisions seeking to drive deeper into Sicily coped with stiff resistance and the ambitions of British and American generals. The Husky chief, Alexander, considered the GIs inferior combat soldiers. He sought to use them as a blocking force to protect what he considered the superior army under Bernard Montgomery. The top brass bickered over who should attack along which axis, without regard for which units enjoyed the best opportunity to hammer the foe. The squabbling cost lives as American artillery that could have aided a Canadian brigade held its fire rather than trespass across the demarcation line separating the Allied armies.

John Lucas scorned the ally: "The British are rather surprisingly slow. Two reasons . . . 1. Strong opposition. 2. Montgomery is notorious for the meticulous care with which he prepares for his operations. This virtue . . . can become an obsession that finally defeats its object. He will not move until everything, every last ration and round of ammunition, is ashore and in its proper place. This was needed in the desert against Rommel. Here [Sicily] speed would seem to be the better part of wisdom. Destroy the enemy before he can be reinforced from the mainland.

"Patton has done a splendid job in this operation but neither Eisenhower nor Alexander have mentioned that fact as yet." Indeed, D'Este notes that the supreme commander had reservations about his Seventh Army commander whom he blamed for both the airborne disaster and the inadequacy of communications to Malta about the progress of Husky. To individuals like Lucas who found fault with Alexander, Eisenhower confided, "[that] he had never seen a case where the British tried to put anything over on us. He said, put myself in Alexander's place. He first came in contact with American troops when the fighting at Kasserine and Gafsa was going on. They did so poorly that the British lost confidence in us as offensive troops. Later the same division [the 1st] did well in Tunisia but in Sicily there were two new divisions, the 45th had no combat experience and the 3d with only a little . . ."

According to Lucas, Eisenhower felt Patton should stand up to Alexander. "He would not hesitate to relieve him from command if he did not do so." When Eisenhower praised Bradley [II Corps commander] and Truscott [in command of the 3d Division], Lucas disagreed. "Terry Allen's 1st Division had done most of the fighting. I pointed out that while other division COs received Distinguished Service Medals, Allen, who had been much more involved, did not."

While the generals politicked and sniped at one another, the men in the field hustled forward. Bill Dunfee's airborne regimental combat team marched up the west coast. "It was increasingly obvious," said Dunfee, "that the Germans were sacrificing the Italian Army in a delaying action. This allowed them to evacuate most of their units across the Strait of Messina into Italy. The Germans did abandon huge quantities of materiel. The Italians were something less than enthusiastic fighters, and gave up after a token effort of defense. This was of little comfort to our wounded and was *very* frustrating to those of us that had to take them prisoner."

The American foot soldiers, reinforced by the arrival of the 2d Armored Division, steadily advanced. Bill Kunz of the 3d Division was with an infantry column bound for Palermo on the northwest coast. "We were learning some hard-taught lessons. The enemy were masters with booby traps. Enemy bodies may explode if moved. Also equipment, and the same went for enemy weapons. Any likely looking resting place is dangerous. One GI picked up a soap bar and gave it to a family. Later it went off. We took a lot of casualties from mines and booby traps."

Patton's Seventh Army rolled up the western half of Sicily rapidly and within two weeks occupied Marsala on the extreme western tip and Palermo on the north. Montgomery's Eighth Army to the east moved slowly against defenders protected by emplacements on towering Mount Etna and their determination to buy time for the evacuation of men and gear through Messina. Montgomery, aware of the strength that prevented his army from breaking through to Messina, invited Patton to cross the hitherto sacrosanct boundaries and capture the prize of that port. For all of the flak about "God Almonty" and the image of an overbearing, conceited Briton, Montgomery was a general who, said Carlo D'Este, abhorred the "senseless waste of men so casually practiced by the British leadership [of World War I]." Patton, who had uncharacteristically bided his time, snatched the opportunity. He sent the 3d Division along the northern edge of the island toward Messina while the 45th and 1st battered the enemy from the center of Sicily. The going was particularly difficult for Terry Allen's GIs who received help from the 9th Division.

Patton himself raced back and forth to the various fronts and on 17 August, less than six weeks after the beginning of Operation Husky, he led a convoy into Messina, where an advance guard from the 3d Division beat an amphibious force dispatched by Montgomery. The city was in ruins from constant shelling and aerial bombardments and now the new residents ducked incoming from the Germans in Calabria, just across the strait.

More than Sicily was devastated at the end of Husky. Bill Dunfee remarked on the anger against the supposedly unenthusiastic Italian defenders who nevertheless inflicted serious casualties. Because of the killed and wounded, as well as the unpleasant experiences with booby traps, attitudes harshened and triggered at least one war crime. At Biscari a sergeant and a captain from the 45th Division murdered seventy-three Italian prisoners. The shooters faced separate court-martials. The sergeant offered a defense that combined the claim of extreme emotional stress with an impression that Patton and lesser officers had directed the troops to take prisoners only under limited circumstances. Found guilty, he received a sentence of life but higher authorities commuted the term, simply stripping him of his stripes.

The captain argued that his actions reflected instructions from superiors and cited his memory of a Patton speech. "When we land against the enemy, don't forget to hit him and hit him hard. We will bring the fight home to him. When we meet the enemy, we will kill him. We will show him no mercy. He has killed thousands of your comrades and he must die. If you company officers in leading your men against the enemy find him shooting at you, and, when you get within two hundred yards of him, he wishes to surrender, oh, no! That bastard will die. You will kill him. Stick him between the third and fourth ribs. You will tell your men they must have the killer instinct. Tell them to stick him . . . We will get the names of killers and killers are immortal. When word reaches him that he is being faced by a killer battalion, a killer outfit, he will fight less . . ."

Subsequently, a soldier swore, "We were told that General Patton said, 'Fuck them. No prisoners!'" An officer reported Patton as having said, "The more prisoners we took, the more we'd have to feed, and not to fool with prisoners." In a letter to his wife Beatrice, Patton wrote, ". . . these Boches and the Italians that are left are grand fighters, [they] have pulled the white flag trick four times. We take few prisoners." The officer in the dock insisted, "I ordered them shot because I thought it came directly under the general's instructions. Right or wrong, a three-star general's advice, who has combat experience, is good enough for me and I took him at his word." Acquitted, the captain later was killed in action.

While engaged in the final campaign to capture Messina, Patton visited the tents of the 15th Evacuation Hospital outside Nicosia. In the wards lay the latest casualties of the fighting, mostly GIs from the 1st Division. Among the patients, Patton encountered Pvt. Charles H. Kuhl with no visible wounds. When Patton inquired why Kuhl was there, the soldier answered, "I guess I can't take it." Patton instantly flew into a rage, berated Kuhl as a coward, and ordered him from the tent. When the soldier failed to move, the general slapped him in the face with his glove, grabbed him by the collar, shoved him out, and kicked him in his backside. On the scene, John Lucas noted in his diary, "We stopped at an evacuation hospital to visit the wounded and try to cheer them up. Brave, hurt, bewildered boys. All but one, that is, because he said he was nervous and couldn't take it. Anyone who knows him can realize what that would do to George. The weak sister was really nervous when he got through."

Patton's ire still raged when he wrote his diary that night, "Companies should deal with such men, and if they shirk their duty, they should be tried for cowardice and shot." Two days later, he distributed a memo decrying the presence in hospitals of soldiers "on the pretext that they are nervously incapable of combat. Such men are cowards and bring discredit on the army and disgrace to their comrades, whom they heartlessly leave to endure the dangers of battle while they, themselves, use the hospital as means of escape." He ordered commanders to prevent them from hospitalization and arrange courts-martial "for cowardice in the face of the enemy."

His rampage against GIs diagnosed with "battle fatigue," "shell shock," "combat neurosis" continued at the 93d Evacuation Hospital. There he blasted Pvt. Paul G. Bennett, a shivering artilleryman who confessed his problem was "my nerves." The general snarled, "Your nerves. Hell, you are just a goddamned coward, you yellow son of a bitch. Shut up that goddamned crying. I won't have these brave men here who have been shot seeing a yellow bastard sitting here crying." Patton went so far as to draw one of his ornately handled pistols from his holster and threaten, "I ought to shoot you myself right now, God damn you." He ordered the quivering Bennett out of the tent, slapped him in the face, and heaped curses upon the bawling soldier. The general started to walk off, then turned and smacked Bennett a second time with such force that he knocked his helmet liner off. Before he finally left, Patton addressed the hospital commander, "I won't have those cowardly bastards hanging around our hospitals. We'll probably have to shoot them sometime anyway or we'll raise a breed of morons."

Patton was anything but regretful about the incident. He drove to the II Corps command post and breezily told Omar Bradley he had just slapped around a malingerer. When the hospital authorities through the chain of command notified Bradley, he filed the papers in his safe on the grounds he would not approach Eisenhower over Patton's head. But too many individuals had witnessed these scenes for them to pass without notice, and the press picked up the story.

Subsequently, Patton would confess to an associate he had been "a damn fool" in both cases. But his admission of an error in his behavior never meant that he believed battle exhaustion acceptable, but only that he had lost his composure in striking an enlisted man. Ironically, he himself may well have been a victim of the same type of emotional distress he despised in others.

John Lucas continued to dismiss the occurrence, referring to it as, "the slapping incident which created so much furor in the papers in the States. I saw nothing serious about it at the time. There are always a number of such weaklings in any army." He added, "George has never grown up and is still about eight years old. He can't see that commanding an army is different from commanding a division. All the men in a division know the commander and understand his peculiarities."

After an investigation into the facts, Eisenhower tried to save Patton's career. "I felt that Patton should be saved for service in the great battles still facing us in Europe." He tried to lift him off the hook through a strong reprimand and directed he apologize to the patients. Patton complied, although D'Este says it was on the advice of John Lucas, rather than because of a demand by Eisenhower. However, the furor in the States forced Eisenhower to relieve him.

The ax also fell on Terry Allen. According to Omar Bradley, "Early in the Sicilian campaign I had made up my mind to relieve Terry Allen at its conclusion. This relief was not to be a reprimand for ineptness or for ineffective command . . . Under Allen the 1st Division had become increasingly temperamental, disdainful of both regulations and senior commands. It thought itself exempted from the need for discipline by virtue of its months on the line." Bradley added, "Allen had become too much of an individualist to submerge himself without friction in the group undertakings of war. The 1st Division under Allen's command had become too full of self-pity and pride. To save Allen both from himself and from his brilliant record and to save the division from the heady effects of too much success, I decided to separate them."

As early as 28 July, Lucas's diary reported, "I gave [Eisenhower] a letter from Patton recommending the relief of Allen and Roosevelt from the 1st Division. Terry's relief is to be 'without prejudice' and I hope he will be given a command at home. The boy is tired." Why the knives were honed for Terry Allen is a matter of conjecture. He was never a part of the club, having quit the Military Academy just short of graduation. His enjoyment of carousing with his staff in off-duty hours would not have endeared him to the straightlaced Bradley. As D'Este points out, the public thought of Bradley as a "plain, soft-spoken general with whom the average civilian could readily identify. If truth is the first casualty of war, so was the pretense that Omar Bradley was a general of the masses, an image that Bradley himself gladly encouraged for the remainder of his life. The real Omar Bradley was somewhat narrow-minded and utterly intolerant of failure." Physically, Bradley may have appeared almost grandfatherly and he never displayed the flamboyance of Patton but he was equally demanding for the niceties of the profession.

Although Allen was respected by Patton, who demanded he have the 1st Division for the critical attack on Gela, theirs was a testy relationship, perhaps a natural result of competition and ambition. Allen would have proudly agreed that he had enormous concern for the welfare of his people. He would have had compassion for those who broke down under stress; it is difficult to imagine that he would ever have struck a hospitalized soldier. Indeed, when Allen returned to combat in Europe to command the 104th Division he received a letter from a father worried about his son. Allen wrote back, "I can readily understand your worry regarding him and your anxiety to secure accurate information regarding his welfare. I have just sent for your son, have talked to him and find he's in fine shape and doing well. The division has been fighting hard since 23 October and so far have had marked success without excessive losses when their accomplishments are considered.

Your son and the other boys like him have been largely responsible for the combat success of the division." There are no similar letters to be found in Patton's file and very few if any among the papers of other World War II commanders.

The choice for Allen's successor, Maj. Gen. Clarence Huebner, probably delighted all of Allen's detractors. Lucas had noted with approval that the British "fired Huebner who was on duty at General Alexander's headquarters. Too virile an American." Bradley praised the new commander as "a strict disciplinarian." The GIs in the 1st Division, however, felt they had lost a fine leader and the Rangers attached to the Big Red One agreed.

20
Island Ventures

On 8 December, Marine general Alexander Archer Vandegrift, taking with him the 1st Marine Division, relinquished his command over the ground forces on Guadalcanal to Army general Alexander M. Patch. To root out the remaining Japanese, Patch would field all of the components of the American Division, some lingering Marine units, and troops from the 25th, 37th, and 43d Divisions. The quality of American air power in the Pacific improved dramatically. The twin-engine P-38 fighter replaced many of the P-40s. The Lightning flew high enough and fast enough to contend with the Zero even if it gave away some advantage in turns. The F4U Chance-Vought Corsair, a misfit for carrier warfare, gave Marine pilots at Henderson Field a weapon superior to the Wildcat. The latter was itself supplanted by the much faster F6F Hellcat. The Army bomber command, accepted the futility of high-altitude attacks against ships and innovated low-level skip-bombing by the two-engine B-25s and B-26s, much to the detriment of enemy shipping.

The capture of islands and advances in New Guinea allowed greater use of land-based planes and participation of the Air Corps along with the Marine and Navy flyers who used flattops. Robert DeHaven, a P-40 replacement pilot, wore the wings given his father for World War I. In Australia, he entered a combat replacement training unit [RTU]. "We had about three or four weeks working on combat formation and tactics before we were sent up to the line at New Guinea. When I got to the squadron and actual combat I had just shy of fifty hours in the P-40."

The indoctrination was rudimentary. "You didn't try to dogfight with a Zero. We had a lot of classes in aircraft recognition. One of the major discussions about the war in New Guinea was the problem of survival. If you went down in the water you could expect sharks. Everybody had shark repellent, which didn't work. If you went down [over land] you hoped to find friendly natives. Living in the jungle, escape planning and routes was essentially meaningless. The idea of anybody trying to walk out by himself was just ridiculous. We carried little pidgin English books, where, if we could find a friendly native and talk to him, the chances of getting out were improved. The .45 we wore in a shoulder holster was meaningless. In twenty-four hours the gun would be so rusted it would be useless. If you used it you gave yourself away. The Aussie liaison officers, former territorial wardens or representatives of mining companies before the war, emphasized that the jungle is a harsh place but also your friend. If you felt you had to fight your way out, use a knife. Keep it quiet. Strike and get back in the bush. Five feet off a trail you couldn't be seen."

To discourage Japanese soldiers in the wilds of New Guinea, the natives received bounties in mother-of-pearl shells, their medium of exchange, for each set of Japanese ears brought in. DeHaven said he saw local people hiking down roads with a string of such trophies, as many as two dozen hanging from their loin cloths as they went to collect. "But as far as intimate combat information, we got very little until we reached our squadrons. Then the older heads in the outfit [got] us into innumerable sessions about tactics, strategies, conditions, engagements, etc."

DeHaven joined the 7th Fighter Squadron, 49th Fighter Group at Dobodura. "The first thing we had to do was build our own house. All of the quarters were sixteen by sixteen pyramidal tents set up on six-foot posts so the insects and snakes couldn't get in. The posts and platform for the tent had to be built by somebody and that somebody was the fellows going to occupy them. They had a practice of putting one old head in with three new pilots." DeHaven recalled the chief amenity was a fresh egg once a month and no matter how late an individual had stayed up or how severe his hangover, when the ration of eggs arrived, every man was roused from bed.

The 49th Group consisted of two P-40 squadrons and one P-38 unit. The limited range of the P-40 required the enemy to meet the Americans halfway in most instances while the P-38s flew and fought over much greater distances. DeHaven remarked that the kill ratio for the P-38 9th Squadron was greater by almost two to one. "The 9th had as many, if not more, aces than any other squadron in the Pacific. The 49th Fighter Group became the highest-scoring fighter group in the history of the Air Force. That is strictly in aerial kills. In the Pacific we did not count aircraft destroyed on the ground, half victories, quarter victories. If there were two people that had shot at an airplane and it was a question of who was to get credit, they flipped a coin."

DeHaven remembered his elation when he was given his own P-40 and allowed to paint his name and personal insignia on it. "I was the proudest son of a bitch in the world. Here I am in combat. My own airplane, my very own crew chief. The crew chief was a very helpful force facing into combat. For instance, the kind of damage that he had seen, what he knew the airplane could absorb. We had an armament section but the armorers only worked on the airplane with the forbearance of the crew chief, as did radio or anyone else. When he said the ammunition was loaded and he'd checked out the guns, you didn't have to fire a burst. You knew they were going to work. He was God on that airplane. When he said it was ready to fly, you didn't make a walk-around check. That would have been insulting. You got in and you flew."

For most of his first half-dozen missions, DeHaven flew under a leader named Ray Melikian, the operations officer who apparently was blessed with superkeen eyesight. These first sorties carried DeHaven toward Lae, in search of shipping, but the newcomers all yearned for a crack at enemy fighters. "On occasion, Ray called in 'bandits high' when nobody else could see them. After a fast circle climb eventually the rest of us would see the gaggle, eight or ten Zeroes or Oscar fighters. We would continue circling full bore but we didn't attack and pretty soon Ray decided he just couldn't get an advantage and took us home.

"We young bucks would get excited as hell and irritable because we hadn't taken them on. He would sit us down and say, 'Gentlemen, give me just one tiny advantage—airspeed, altitude, or both—to make one run through them and you'll get your shot . . . and we're going to keep right on going, nobody turns around.' He wanted that flight intact. He didn't want people scattering on their own and getting picked off. He drilled firmly on formation integrity."

Melikian reiterated the common wisdom that advised against trying to climb away from a Zero or seek to turn into one. He warned against solo combat but in DeHaven's first opportunity to shoot at an enemy plane, he violated the precept. Along with the operations chief he dove on a pair of low-flying Val bombers. DeHaven remembered, "Ray came in astern of the Val, snapped off a shot with no apparent effect and pulled up as we overran him. There was scattered cloud cover, and we busted out on top of that, made a big fast turn and came around again. As we did I saw a P-40 go by underneath me, almost inverted and shooting at the second Val. It was also in a turn so the P-40 overshot him. Ray didn't appear to see this, so I broke formation and made a descending roll. I was directly behind the Val—overtaking him. I pulled the power back some and as I slowed down, I noticed these funny-looking little red balls zipping by over my canopy. The God-damned gunner in the back of the Val was shooting at me. First time I'd ever been shot at and at first I didn't realize what it was. I was really surprised. Not scared, just surprised—and indignant. The adrenaline was really flowing. I settled slightly below and behind him, watched him fill the sight, then cut loose. In the barrage I burned up five out of six guns, but he slowly rolled over and went straight into the water. Later, I got my ass chewed royally and rightly. I was forcefully reminded but gratefully not belabored about it. The older heads recognized that there was a degree of impetuousness about youngsters in combat—you could expect many were going to get excited and do something they had been told not to do."

That same encounter also saw a veteran of the squadron forced to bail out after the rear gunner on a Val shot out his coolant. "When Bob Lee went into the water, we saw him inflate his vest but not his seat raft. We all had both. We didn't know at the time but one of his arms was broken and he had tucked it inside his vest. He couldn't get to the lanyards on the raft with only one good arm. We put in a call back to base to try to get a PT boat to pick him up. There were one or two that were working along the coast. Then we started circling to begin our shark-strafing session. It was inevitable, those waters are loaded with sharks and, good God, some are massive. We got a couple. You would see a big splotch of red and then a great thrashing as other sharks tore into the one that was hit. It only took a moment and then they would go back to circling Bob. We tried other things. I got my seat raft out from underneath me and started down. I wound back the canopy, laid the raft on the crook of my left arm, holding the lanyard in my hand. I got the airplane just as slow as I would get it and level about twenty feet off the water. I got lined up on Bob and when I thought I was over him, I flipped that raft out, holding onto the lanyard so the raft would open up as it fell down to him. What I didn't consider was that the raft was packed in a preservative powder. I had on a pair of sunglasses. When the raft went out, the powder flew back and the world disappeared. There I was, sitting five knots above stall and maybe twenty feet off the water. I jammed the throttle forward and, as frequently happens when you jam a throttle, the engine coughs momentarily. Mine did and that got my attention." While Lee was unable to retrieve the raft, a PT boat rescued him while DeHaven cleared his glasses and made it home.

There, in addition to the scolding from his superiors, he also absorbed a lecture from the crew chief. "He explained to me how one could become defenseless with frozen guns. It meant you fired in bursts too long, causing the barrels and breeches to overheat. When the shells slammed into the chamber, they'd expand and jam. The eject mechanism would not pull open the spent cartridge shells. So concentrate on firing in short bursts.

"When you've got one in your sights and you know you're hitting him, it's the most difficult thing in the world to release that trigger. The tendency is to keep pouring it on. Soon you've got four guns firing, then three, then two . . . that really doesn't take very long. In a P-40, a five-second burst would put all six guns out of commission. You never wanted to fire more than one- or two-second bursts if you wanted to stay in business. Another lesson the crew chief gave was getting the guns out and changing all those barrels. He made me attend the entire procedure."

Like most fighter pilots, DeHaven found air-to-ground work less rewarding than aerial combat. "There's rarely anything to score in air-to-ground," he remarked. "It's not a mano-a-mano situation. For the most part, at least in the jungle, you are shooting at a blind target. You can't see anything; you are shooting at a grid mark, a set of coordinates, or a smoke bomb. Once in a while, early in the war, 1943, we had many opportunities for shipping targets. That was fun because, if good enough, you could sink a boat with P-40 gunfire. We did an awful lot of dive-bombing. The basic problem was you never knew where your opposition was. There's nothing more irritating or distracting than to suddenly see 20mm or 40mm bursts coming up on you right out of a clump of coconut trees and you can't shoot back because you can't see the guns. You might see some smoke coming out of the bush, go down and strafe it but while you're doing that another clump over there suddenly opens up. It's distracting and hardly fun.

"Air-to-air is something else. This is essentially a man-to-man proposition. Actually, I can't say man-to-man because you never consider an airplane as occupied by an individual or human. It's just a piece of machinery. There were times when air-to-air combat was a little more personal, when a man bailed out, a rare occurrence in the Pacific. It was quite common in Europe and the Mediterranean. But in the Pacific, I don't think I saw more than half a dozen enemy pilots bail out during two tours. The situation was magnified by the brevity of Pacific combat. You rarely engaged more than a minute or two. Ninety percent of your fights were hit and run."

The limited number of parachutes observed by DeHaven may have had something to do with increasing savagery. He admitted shooting one enemy in his chute. "They actually started the parachute strafing in China. They pulled it on us first, too. Moreover, since most of our combat was over enemy territory, the possibility of a Jap who bailed out getting safely home was pretty good. The rationale was, why give him a second chance to come back and get you? If we bailed out, we expected to get shot at and the possibility of coming home was nil. If you were captured by the Japanese you were essentially dead. They didn't ship prisoners from New Guinea all the way back to a prison. They couldn't afford to do it. They executed prisoners; that was well documented. Those they didn't [kill] they starved or beat to death. The farther they were from the home island, the less likely they were to keep prisoners because they were a burden. They had to feed them, care for them, and the Japs were having enough trouble feeding their own troops."

The dismal prospects if shot down bothered some airmen enough so they were sent home. "We had two," recalled DeHaven. "They had chronic engine trouble—almost every flight they would turn back before they got fifty miles from the field. Back on the ground, the crew couldn't find anything wrong with the engines."

The code breakers scored a great coup when they intercepted a radio message from Rabaul detailing a forthcoming inspection of Japanese facilities on Bougainville by the architect of the Pearl Harbor attack, and the man considered the guiding light of Imperial Navy warfare, Admiral Yamamoto. Nine Zeros accompanied the two bombers bearing the admiral and his staff. Eighteen P-38s ambushed the covey, scattering the escorts. The U.S. flight leader, Capt. Thomas G. Lamphier Jr., blasted Yamamoto's plane with his 20mm cannon. The aircraft burst into flame and crashed in the jungle. There were no survivors.

Having occupied Guadalcanal and turned away the Japanese seeking to expand their hold on New Guinea, the American forces in the Pacific pursued the strategy of island hopping. The losses at sea while trying to land soldiers on Guadalcanal set the Imperial Navy far enough back on its heels to allow bloodless conquests of the Russell Islands close to Guadalcanal. Admiral Nimitz and his staff agreed the next logical target was New Georgia, another link in the Solomon chain bordering the Slot. New Georgia, and a clump of islands closest to it—Rendova, Arundel, Kolombangara, and Vangunu—were obvious stepping-stones for the offense, not only because of the location, but also because the enemy had chosen to build an airfield at Munda Point on New Georgia. That base could threaten the American forces on New Guinea as well as block progress toward points closer to the Philippines and eventually the home islands.

Over a period of months small groups of Americans slipped ashore on New Georgia to scout out the terrain, examine the beaches, pinpoint optimum locations for artillery, and pick up intelligence on the deployment of the enemy troops. Although the turf came under the jurisdiction of Nimitz, the most available ground force was the Army's 43d Infantry Division, which went ashore on Guadalcanal too late to encounter the Japanese. Also scheduled for the initial assault on New Georgia were some Marine Raiders and elements of the 37th Infantry Division that had been dug in around Henderson Field to protect the base against infiltrators or snipers.

On 22 June 1943, leathernecks from the 4th Marine Raider Battalion carried by destroyers, stepped onto a secluded beach at Segi, where a small enclave of native constabulary under Maj. Donald Kennedy, a New Zealander, acted as coast watchers and guerrilla fighters. After getting their bearings, a company led by Tony Walker, a Yale graduate, in rubber boats and canoes set out for an objective, the harbor at Viru along the coast away from the Slot. Raider Roger Spaulding recalled, "The third night ashore, we assembled in the quiet lagoon waters for the raid on Viru. Fifty assorted boats gathered in the darkness, were boarded by the Raiders and about thirty natives. Heavy equipment like the radio and mortar shells were loaded on a magnificent native canoe that carried about twenty men, mostly native paddlers and the native sergeant.

"Under the mangrove trees at times and under the brilliant stars, we paddled until well past midnight and finally landed at a tiny shore village [some eight miles from Segi] where huts had been built above the water on stilts. We pushed our rubber boats through the mud and pig pens and moved on up to dry land. The boats were quickly pulled back on the water and tied to each other. They were towed back to Segi before sunup. We tried to eradicate any evidence of our passing by wiping the mud behind ourselves and praying there would be a heavy rain before dawn [to conceal their presence], but it did not rain. The Japanese did find our tracks and a small patrol harmed the natives even though the natives participated not at all either for or against us. Truly hapless innocents of the war.

"As miserable as was the edge of the swamp outside the village, the place was a Garden of Eden compared with what we went through the next four days. Mud was ankle- to knee-deep all the way. Every step was slippery and the muscular action required to stay afoot was exhausting. The farther back in the column a Raider was, the harder [it was]. Hundreds of feet stirred up the mud and made it deeper as we went. Then, too, the rains came and went and the trail became a long necklace of small, deep, mud puddles. Rivers were almost welcome as a time to cool off and rinse off the muck. We crossed one river, the Choi, at least three times, as we went in sort of a straight line, but the river coiled like a snake through the jungle. At each crossing the banks were a special hardship because entry and exit slopes on the banks became a mud pit waist-deep. It had to be crossed for several feet before the bank dropped off into shoulder-deep water.

"Only Raiders who were close to six-feet tall could cross with head above water. Shorter Raiders were lifted by the man in front and behind to keep their heads up. Rifles, machine guns, and BARs were hoisted above our heads to keep out the mud and water. All else went underwater, packs, bullets, and all. Things like cigarettes, matches, and coffee grounds were tied tightly in rubberized pouches to keep dry and usable." Through the pitch-black nights, the Marines, led by their native guides, tied pieces of phosphorescent twigs and pieces of luminous rotting wood to the person in front in order to follow him.

"I was on the point with Corporal Tower and Private Harbord," said then-private Milton J. "Cajun" Robert. "We crossed the river [Choi] and kept going until we came to the crest of a hill where the native threw up his head as he smelled the Japs and said, 'Japs come.' He took off immediately on the right of the trail and so did Harbord and I. Tower was killed immediately on the trail. Harbord emptied his M1 from behind a large banyan tree. I turned my BAR sideways so it would not walk up as I fired and let the first twenty rounds go. I think we were about fifteen minutes ahead of our outfit. The Nips were chattering a hell of a lot. A hell of a lot of them went to my left as I continued firing. Could even hear their hobnail shoes hitting the roots of trees. They opened up with a machine gun no more than thirty-five to forty yards away. I threw grenades, holding [them] three to four seconds because they were so close.

"[I] was about to raise up and fire again as a head started to rise on the other side of the root I was behind. Backed up a little and shot his head off!

I also popped a shot at a Jap officer with a sword, shot at his head as he came up behind his men. Horse Taylor later told me that I shot the back of his head off and that he, Horse, had placed his machine gun right by him and shot him again with his .45 because he was still alive." That firefight cost the Raiders five dead and one wounded, but with further resistance suppressed, Tony Walker's company continued toward Viru Harbour. After Cajun Robert killed the enemy machine-gun crew he saw a boat below a 150-foot cliff begin to pull away. He immediately opened fire and Taylor joined in with his machine gun. Robert learned later that seventeen Japanese soldiers, accompanied by three pregnant Tonganese women, had been aboard.

Private First Class Bill Thompson, in the antitank section, participated in the attack. His leader ordered, "Bill, go back and tell Captain Walker to knock off the mortar fire. We now have men in the enemy positions." Thompson zigzagged toward the captain's position and a sniper put a bullet clean through his pack. When he reached Walker's approximate location, Thompson said he called out the code name for the commander, "'Cold Steel! Cold Steel!' I received no response so I kept yelling. Finally, I committed the unpardonable sin—I yelled, 'Captain Walker! Captain Walker!' I heard him yell back at me, 'Right here, Major, what the hell do you want?' That was the fastest promotion and demotion I ever had."

Cajun Robert cautiously explored the scene. "Corporal Green called to me about the machine-gun position I shot out and said, 'Cajun, this one is alive and playing dead. What are we going to do with him?' I told him to stick him. Just then Father Redmond [the battalion chaplain] came up and I said ix-nay to Green. Father Redmond wanted to know what was the matter and we told him that this one was still alive. He made the sign of the cross and said, 'May God have mercy on his soul,' and kept going. Green then looked at me and I said, 'Stick him, dammit!' We then threw him over the cliff. Before leaving, we formed a seven-man squad and fired a twenty-one-gun salute to our dead." Altogether the expedition to Viru and environs left thirteen Americans dead and another fifteen wounded.

On 30 June, the first elements of the U.S. invasion force occupied Vangunu and effectively eliminated the garrison. The Japanese, apparently unaware of the American success, dispatched three barges packed with reinforcements and supplies to Vangunu from New Georgia. Marines from the 4th Raider Battalion and infantrymen from the 103d Regiment of the 43d Division ambushed the landing craft, killing all but a few of the 120 estimated passengers.

On 1 July, GIs from the 43d's 172d Regiment and elements from the 103d widened their beachhead on Rendova. Separated from New Georgia by a narrow strait, Rendova had been chosen as a staging area for the invasion to capture the Munda Point air base. Because the distance between Rendova and New Georgia was so small, the former could provide a platform for long-range shelling of the Japanese. No one, however, had counted on what the rain would do to such well-laid plans. Seabees from the Navy labored to create roads over muck that drowned huge logs and steel mats. Foxholes became bathtubs as the rains pelted down. Artillerymen struggled to dig firm emplacements and clear the towering palms for fire lanes. A surprise attack by Japanese bombers killed a number of Seabees, destroyed earthmovers, and blew up supplies. A covey of enemy warships that pumped hundreds of shells onto the water-logged tenants of Rendova inflicted much less damage.

On 2 July, just after midnight, the 1st Battalion of the 172d Regiment loaded into landing craft to cross the treacherous, reef-ridden channel to New Georgia itself. The soldiers expected to wade ashore at Zanana Beach, undefended according to intelligence. When the canoeborne native guides vanished with their signal lamps, chaos followed. Boats piled up on a reef. In the blackness of night, coxswains bawled questions and directions to one another; engines reversed and then thrust forward; boats collided. The disorder so appalled the commander that he ordered a return to Rendova, while sending a couple of hardy souls to furtively examine Zanana.

A few men never got the word to head home and together the Americans scouted the area, coming away with the knowledge that no enemy troops protected the shores of Zanana. To avoid another nighttime fiasco, on Independence Day 1943, the 1st Battalion stepped onto the beach during daylight hours and quickly advanced far enough for a perimeter some 500 yards beyond the water. By 5 July, the 43d Division could commence its drive to Munda Field. At the same time, the Japanese commander, now fully aware of the American intentions, drew in whatever troops he could to repel the Americans.

Private First Class Sam LaMagna, who as a former National Guardsman remembered wrap leggings, World War I rifles, and stove pipes to represent mortars, at Zanana wore and bore the latest equipment, but nothing had prepared him for the ordeal. "The first couple of nights gave us a taste of what jungle warfare was all about. The Japs were experts. They were Imperial Marines, the elite armed forces of Japan who had fought in China for many years. Munda Trail was thick with trees, brush undergrowth, vines. Sound was more important than sight. You could hear someone before you could see him. After many casualties, we learned to fight a Jap war. At night, stay in your hole until the surrounding area has been sprayed with machine gun and BARS. Sort of like spraying for mosquitoes. You can't see them but they're there. At first daylight, Jap snipers would shoot anyone walking around or into our foxholes. They tied themselves up in trees and it was a great morale booster to see Japs hanging after machine-gun and BAR bursts.

"At night it was an individual war with everyone fighting for his life. The screams pierced the jungle night and sent chills up my spine. Art Delorge, Syl Bottone, and Gildo Consolini stayed in different foxholes. Farmer Bederski and I shared one. At first break of dawn we'd peek over and wave, as if to say, 'Hey, I'm okay.' One morning Syl and Gildo waved back but not Art. Farmer came back and notified us Art was killed by his foxhole buddy who thought Art was a Jap and panicked. Art was bayoneted. Later Gildo was killed by a Jap at night. Every morning I'd hear who was killed or wounded. Company F [172d Reg.] had about 30 percent casualties and the men were getting jittery. Rumors went around that the Japs were yanking GIs out of their holes by the helmets and to keep helmets unbuckled. At night I could hear teeth chattering. "

LaMagna remembered a soldier he called Joe who clearly showed signs of distress. When LaMagna shared a foxhole with Joe one night, he awoke to find his companion about to toss a grenade, followed moments later by a loud tirade that pinpointed their position. LaMagna eventually quieted him by rapping him in the mouth with a .45 pistol and threatening to blow his head off. The platoon sergeant volunteered to control Joe the following night. Shots erupted from the sergeant's foxhole along with cries of "Shoot him! Shoot him, or he'll kill us all!"

"By now all the Japs knew our positions," said LaMagna, "and sent in a barrage of artillery and mortar rounds. My first thought was Joe and when shells started to explode all around me I drew my knees up against my chest and prayed. A shell landed near my hole and felt like someone hit me across the head with a baseball bat. My hole caved in and I passed out. In the early morning, two guys dug me out. I was covered with dirt, my nose stuffed with mud and blood, a cut on my right shin and knee. I was dazed, glassy-eyed. I passed out on a litter and was sent to a hospital on Guadalcanal.

"I awoke on a cot next to the platoon sergeant. I asked him what happened. 'Joe grabbed my .45, thought he saw Japs, and started shooting. A bullet went through my knee into my chest. The other sergeant had to shoot and kill Joe or they both would be dead.'" His injuries kept LaMagna under treatment for five weeks. Tagged for shipment to the States he begged to return to his company. When the medics agreed and discharged him as fit for duty he rejoined his outfit, down to less than one-third of its complement because of the fighting on New Georgia.

To fill up the ranks, replacements like Leonard Glenn Hall, who hailed from Oklahoma and Texas, became members of Company F, 172d Regiment. He and other newcomers picked up their weapons from a salvage pile a few hundred yards from the front. The best that Hall could find was a Springfield with a rope sling that replaced the standard leather one. Each replacement received only a single canteen but they threw away their gas masks. On his first day on the line, a well-concealed machine gun zipped bullets along the trail. "No one had told the replacements that the first rule of survival," said Hall "was to get off the trail." The enemy fire stitched his trousers, burning his calf with a grazing shot. Veterans offered no sympathy but scorned them for not having immediately formed a defense.

Within a few days, Hall and another novice, Trinidad Borrego, drew assignment as lead scouts. "Only the depleted condition of the company," said Hall, "could justify two green soldiers as advance men on an unknown, forbidding ridge. Both of us knew something was wrong when we reached a rusted, barbed-wire fence, but neither wanted to be considered a coward, so we kept moving forward. Ten feet into the clearing behind the fence were pillboxes. Suddenly shots rang out and I saw smoke curling from the rifle pointing out of the nearest emplacement. Quickly raising the old bolt-action '03 I placed a shot at the butt plate of the Japanese rifle without ever seeing the enemy. The rifle fell and a thrashing sound came from the enclosure."

From his vantage point Hall saw more Japanese soldiers entering the pillboxes. He continued to fire, providing cover for Borrego who leaped to his feet and raced back to the safety of the jungle. The gunfire died out and Hall saw a Japanese helmet on a stick, a lure for him to fire and show his position. He held back. Tiny pebbles struck the ground around him, and Hall, who said he was already resigned to his death, summoned the courage to glance backward. He saw Borrego beckoning him to retreat. The 6' 4" Hall sprinted to the rear, leaped the barbed-wire fence, and tumbled into a half-dug foxhole as machine-gun bullets whizzed overhead. "Repeated attempts to capture this strong point in the days ahead," said Hall, "were disastrous. This ridge became the final resting place for many American soldiers."

With the 43d Division stymied by the enemy, the American leaders committed the 37th Infantry Division to the New Georgia enterprise. Cletus J. Schwab, who would put his ability as a high school baseball pitcher to good use with hand grenades, climbed the ranks, rising to staff sergeant, second in command of a forty-two-man platoon in the 148th Infantry Regiment. He had been under fire from snipers and air raids while guarding Henderson Field at Guadalcanal. Again that did little to ready him for the resistance on New Georgia. "The first day, to gain over a hundred yards we faced twenty-five machine guns, small and large mortars, and 75mm field-pieces. During the night we dug foxholes while ships brought in more supplies. As we moved northeast we met the 5th Marine Raider Battalion of about fifteen hundred men. Their mission was the same as ours and the 145th Regiment [a 37th Division unit] was moving in from the southeast. It took twenty-eight days to secure the island. When the battle started we had only ten days' rations. For eighteen days we lived on jungle plants, Japanese rice, and fish."

The advance on the Munda Point objective stalled in the face of fierce opposition and counterattacks. The battle planners inserted parts of a third Army division, the 25th. To envelop the foe, the 4th Marine Raider Battalion returned by sea to Enogai, New Georgia. Their objective was Bairoko, a village that barred the way to the Japanese air base. The attack opened with rebel yells or, according to one participant, an Indian war whoop. John Dennis Hestand, a member of a fire team in C Company recalled, "After we'd gone about a mile or maybe two, we stopped and formed a skirmish line across the trail. Until then everything was real quiet, but after we all got into position, it sounded like every gun within miles went off and everybody was screaming and hollering. We started moving on. We'd run a little way, hit the deck, shoot some, get up, and go it again. On one of my get-up-and-run periods I felt like I'd been kicked in the stomach by a mule. I grabbed my stomach and went down. Corporal Harold Pickett saw me go down, came over and said, 'Let me see.' I took my hands away and smoke was coming from my cartridge belt just to the left of the buckles, the left half of which was gone. We finally figured a bullet or something had hit an M1 clip, blew it up, and set my belt afire. My belly-chest stung some, but there was no big-hole penetration. So we got up and continued on.

"Some time later, I was on my belly shooting some and I felt like somebody had hit me on the right leg just above the knee with a red hot poker. There were mortars bursting in the treetops and on the ground all around us and all kinds of other stuff was flying around, coming from all directions, twinging, whirring, and thunking. A lot of our guys were getting hit and needing corpsmen. Pickett was again nearby and heard me yip, came over, dumped some sulfa in the hole on the side of my leg, bleeding pretty bad, tied on a big bandage, and I took off for the aid station.

"After a while I found it and there must have been a hundred guys, bleeding, hurting, being bandaged. One I saw was Captain Walker. He was on his belly and a corpsman was picking at something in the captain's right hip pocket area. He said, 'Hi, Hestand. Where'd they hit you?' I told him in the leg and he said, 'The dirty little bastards shot me in the ass.'

"A corpsman said they were sending about fifty of the walking wounded and some of the litter cases back to Enogai for evacuation. He asked if I thought I could walk it. I was hurting but could still walk. We formed up and started back down the trail. Before we left, somebody took my M1 away and gave me a BAR with a bunch of ammo so I could sort of ride shotgun as most of the other guys were arms and chest wounds.

"We started back later in the afternoon, going real slow with the litter cases, and got maybe half a mile or so when it got dark. We settled down but didn't sleep or rest much because there were still a lot of explosions around with flares [and from] planes. During the night my leg started getting stiff and really hurting. Come daylight we started moving back to Enogai but I couldn't walk anymore. I tried to keep up but, hobbling and crawling, wasn't doing so good. Wasn't alone because there were some other troops on the trail. After what seemed like forever, and me not getting very far, two big, fuzzy-haired natives came down the trail from Enogai and made a chair with their crossed hands, got me aboard supporting my stiff leg, really hurting now, and being real gentle and easy, got me back to Enogai. There they checked my leg, put on a new bandage, and then onto a rubber boat to a PBY. Some Zeros came over and strafed. Some of the wounded guys were wounded again and some of the plane crew, too."

Cajun Robert, armed with an automatic rifle, labeled Bairoko "one hell of a fight." He remembered, "running out of ammo four times that day and got more from the dead and wounded. On the last time looking for more ammo I came across Pfc. [Jeff] Watson dead, turned him over, took his ammo and drew my Ka-Bar [knife] and cut his belt to see where he was hit. He was hit in the stomach and I tried to see if he had any life in him." Robert paused to give water to a wounded leatherneck, "then went forward again and put out a machine gun that had my outfit pinned down. I'm proud to say I put that gun out with ammunition taken from Watson. Watson was my friend and he had begged me to arrange for him to carry a BAR."

The company received orders to retreat. Roger Spaulding noted, "We had just barely enough men still standing to carry out the wounded and protect ourselves while we did so. Further attacks were impossible. On the way out those with rifles walked the flanks, protecting the column of stretchers that dripped blood all the way back to Enogai."

Among those limping in retreat was Robert, hit in the legs by a mortar burst. For all of his scavenging he was down to his last seven rounds but he shot the head off a lurking sniper with one of those few bullets. Robert climbed into a PBY with a crew of six and forty wounded leathernecks. He flinched as a Japanese fighter sprayed the PBY with its machine guns although six on his ship incurred more wounds. Marine Corsairs shot down the interloper.

Having repulsed the initial Marine assault at Bairoko, the Japanese astonishingly mounted a furious counterattack, punching away at the ridge position occupied by Cletus Schwab and others from the 37th Division. "There was a storm of rifle, machine gun, and mortar fire coming from the direction of our company outpost," recalled Schwab. "Snipers were moving in on us. They had filtered along the ridge during the dark of the night. We heard Japanese firing weapons from several new directions. They were all around us, trying to break through our barbed wire.

"We were only protected by jungle grass. The Japanese were firing from the cover of the jungle. One of my sergeants reported to me that six or seven of his men had been hit by machine guns and mortars and two were dead." Only the intercession of another company from Schwab's battalion relieved the pressure. "Six Japanese made banzai suicide charges with bayonets. They were all killed. We had stopped the attack and I estimate about 800 or 900 Japanese were killed or wounded. A patrol reported that forty or fifty of their dead were lying in the barbed-wire fence. I had forty-two men in my unit when the battle for New Georgia started. At the end I had twenty. The rest were either dead or wounded. I was wounded in the back but remained with my platoon."

The combined forces of the Americans ground up the defenders of Munda Point with the field listed as officially captured on 5 August. The Japanese had lost another valuable outpost. Neighboring Kolombangara, a refuge for some of the Japanese facing extinction on New Georgia, was effectively neutralized. When the American strategy indicated that Halsey and MacArthur intended to bypass the place, the Japanese removed some 12,000 soldiers to fight elsewhere.

The Marines also learned a lesson; the light infantry of Raider battalions that brought to bear nothing larger than a 60mm mortar could not defeat a well-dug-in enemy without heavy support from artillery, navy ships, or airplanes. The concept of the Raiders lost currency and, in a reorganization, their four battalions reconstituted the 4th Marines, a regiment lost when the Japanese overran the Philippines.

Meanwhile, the campaign against the Japanese on New Guinea continued. MacArthur plotted to seize Lae, a port on the northeast coast of the island, and another enemy center, Salamaua. His script involved an attack by the Australian 9th Division transported to within twenty miles of the city by air. The operation depended upon seizure of an airdrome at Nadzab, and the 503d Parachute Infantry Regiment on 5 September 1943 would drop on-site.

"It was a delicate operation involving the first major parachute jump in the Pacific War," said MacArthur. "I inspected them and found, as was only natural, a sense of nervousness among the ranks. I decided that it would be advisable for me to fly in with them. I did not want them to go through their first baptism of fire without such comfort as my presence might bring to them." He observed the drop from a B-17.

Hugh Reeves, a Mississippi youth, had volunteered for airborne after being told he was ticketed for military police duty in New York. Rod Rodriguez, a former Florida National Guard soldier, volunteered for paratroops because, he said, "The challenge of testing myself in an elite unit appealed to me. Also the jump pay of $50 a month seemed a princely sum when a private's monthly pay had just jumped from $21 to $31 a month."

"There were bombers above us, fighter planes above them, and A-20s all around us," said Reeves. "As we approached our destination we could hear the B-24s with their machine guns chattering away, strafing the jungles below. I was in the sixth plane in our group, and when I went out the door I could see nothing but treetops. My chute opened, made one pendulum swing, and I felt myself crashing through limbs. All I could do was fold my arms to cover my face, keep my feet together, point my toes down, and say a quick prayer that I would not hit a large limb, for, just as I reached the outer edge of that one swing, I saw my chute collapse like a busted paper bag as it hit the top of the tree before I did.

"When I came to, there was a medic standing over me, pointing a Tommy gun and saying, 'Lager.' Our answering password was 'Label' because the Japs had trouble with the ell sound. I looked up at my chute still hanging to a large vine with thousands of one-inch needles sticking out. My guardian angel had looked after me for that tree was well over a hundred-feet high and that would have been a free fall had that pine not been there to slow me down."

His good friend Rodriguez said, "The airfield was seized without opposition, being manned by service personnel who fled on our arrival. I quickly became a jump casualty when I landed in a tall tree and drove a branch sharp as a spear completely through my thigh, emerging in my groin area. Doctors later told me it had grazed the main artery flowing into my right leg, and had it been cut I would have bled to death in seconds. For two days I was kept hopped up on dosages of morphine, until the airport was opened and I could be evacuated."

The Australian infantrymen aided by troopers from the 503d hacked and shot their way toward Salamaua and Lae. The two towns yielded on 12 and 16 September. It was Halsey's turn to expand American control and his goal was Bougainville, a big island at the northern head of the Solomon chain. Its airfields could support Air Corps bombers from New Guinea bases and Navy torpedo bombers from Munda against the huge depot of Rabaul.

Adroit raids by Halsey's forces, flying from carriers and shore bases, along with the heavyweights contributed by the Air Corps, battered enemy vessels and diverted the Japanese from interfering with the landings at Empress Augusta Bay by the 3d Marine Division on 1 November. The beachhead grew and within three weeks the 37th Division had joined the leathernecks. The Americans on Bougainville consolidated their positions, leaving the way clear for MacArthur to make his move on the island of New Britain and its vital center, Rabaul.

21
Pointblank, Blitz Week, and Ploesti

The 56th Fighter Group officially debuted on 8 April 1943 with a rodeo along the French coast near Dunkirk but nothing of consequence occurred. An original pilot with the 56th Fighter Group was John McClure, an instructor with a class of students at the time of the Pearl Harbor raid. The group had originally flown P-35s, P-36s, and the P-39 but, when, in 1943, it arrived at Horsham Saint Faith airdrome in Great Britain, the pilots occupied the roomy cockpits of P-47 Thunderbolts. "We'd started our operations in early April and I was on my seventh mission, the 29th of April," recalled McClure. "It was our first major contact with the enemy. In the mess we had a little confusion and we got separated. I got hit and managed to get back out over the coast. The one set of instructions we had was for heaven's sake don't let 'em get a hold of a Jug [P-47].

"I got out over the North Sea and I was down to about 400 feet when I bailed out. A German coastal patrol picked me up. In the water like that you lose your sense of time, but from my watch, which stopped when I hit the water, and the Germans figuring from their own watches, it was about an hour and a half. They shook their head, 'No way,' because at that time of the year, twenty minutes is about average survival time. I had discovered that my life raft was full of holes and my Mae West had a puncture. I pulled the emergency kit off the raft and proceeded to float. I didn't have time to be afraid on the way down because there are so many things to do, you don't have time to think. And you suffer from shock. I couldn't move, almost paralyzed, they drug me up over the side of the boat and took me to an island along the Dutch coast."

McClure was issued a skimpy blanket and then taken by train to Amsterdam with a trio of guards. There he was imprisoned in solitary confinement. "It was absolutely black, no light, about six feet long, three or four wide with an iron bench on one side. You lose all concept of time under such circumstances but I later figured out I was there a little over two weeks. I'd get a little piece of ersatz bread—half sawdust—and a cup of ersatz coffee, twice a day. That was it.

"Periodically, they'd take me up for an interrogation by an officer who spoke very good English. He didn't mince too many words. They asked ques-

353

tions and beyond name, rank, and serial number, they wanted to know what you were flying, who was your CO, where you were located, what kind of armament does this aircraft have, and technical questions. They seemed particularly interested in organization, who was there, and how many. When you didn't go beyond name, rank, and serial number, they encouraged you with the old rubber hose. When you didn't answer, they'd say, 'We'll give you a little time to think this over.' This was repeated, every day or so.

"They came down at the end of about two weeks and took me for interrogation. The guy told me that if they didn't get some answers out of me, they'd call in the firing squad. They weren't going to fool with me any more and he'd give me a couple of hours to think it over. They pulled me back after some hours and it was almost a repeat of the same thing and then the third time there were three guards with bayonets drawn. They herded me up and out into the courtyard of the prison. About then, here comes a ten-man rifle squad and they lined up just opposite me. They led me down a flight of steps and suddenly turned, took me out the gate, placed me on a train for Frankfurt, and *Dulag Luft* [the center for interrogation of downed Allied flyers]."

Another member of the 56th Fighter Group was Robert Johnson, a twenty-three-year-old Oklahoma native. Said Johnson, "The P-47s were like big Cadillacs, a super big old Cadillac. It would fly itself." When one landed a Jug, which seemed to come into a field and squat, Johnson said, "It was just like you were approaching a cold toilet seat." Johnson struggled to learn gunnery. "One training technique was for another guy to fly 100 to 200 feet over the water and then we'd come in and shoot at his shadow. It was a matter of a quick burst and than a break because you could be in the water real quick. We did a lot of skeet shooting to teach us how to lead a target. From time to time, they took us to shoot at flying targets. I never did qualify because I could not hit the flags. I learned my combat shooting, firing at airplanes."

When the 56th Fighter Group arrived in England, he listened to an RAF pilot who advised, "If a German gets on your tail, don't sit still. Move, shake your airplane, get all over the sky. Don't sit still because then he's got you." Men who'd flown with the Eagle squadrons taught some tactics. "The P-47 was a very comfortable airplane—big cockpit, very warm, so we wore our typical woolen OD [olive drab] uniform. We put a silk scarf around our necks inside the shirt collar to keep from cutting our necks on those wool shirts while constantly turning our heads. That was the purpose of the scarf, not flamboyancy. You had to look backward 90 percent of the time when flying."

As the newest entry to the war, the Thunderbolt, said Johnson, confused the Germans. "We got a lot of them because the elliptical wing of a P-47 at first glance looked like a Spitfire if you didn't happen to notice that big, bulky nose. The Germans might fly under us or maybe we would catch them beneath and they'd simply roll over and dive because they could always out-dive a Spitfire. We'd roll over, throttle back, slide right up their ass, and shoot them down. They were not going to get away from the P-47s straight, level, or down. Our guns narrowed around 400 yards until the eight .50s came to-gether in a two-foot-square box."

Johnson remembered his first operational sortie. "It was simply a fighter sweep and it was a little bit unreal—you were anticipating something but you did not know what. We didn't really believe they were shooting to kill over there. We thought it was a big game. All we had done was shoot cam-era gunnery and then always you would come in and land with the guy you shot at. You could not believe that you were shooting to kill and you were being shot at to kill.

"That first mission, I was flying as [a wingman]. There were forty-eight of us altogether, sixteen per squadron, with three squadrons at different lev-els and we made a sweep at 35,000 feet back to England. We were way up at the top and I was way to the right of everyone else when they made a turn. I was following orders, 'Stay on your leader,' and I was looking around and did not realize they had turned a little bit sharper and really left me. So when I looked back and saw them leaving me, I pulled in the stick and hit my gun trigger. That scared the hell out of me; of course, there was no one around.

"I had heard about flak and seen two or three airplanes up above us quite a ways back. I wasn't worried about them because they were quite [far off]. I saw all these little white things popping all around me and thought, 'That must be the antiaircraft they are talking about. I wonder where my buddies are.' I looked to the right and out of the corner of my eyes saw something blinking at me. There were two 109s! I rolled that thing over and instinc-tively to the left. [I had been told] never fly a straight line. I started to split-S and then as I got halfway through it, I realized this was enemy country that I was split-S-ing into. So I straightened it up and at a good 45-degree angle—I was kicking rudders at the same time—upside down. I was really slashing that airplane all over the sky. I had the throttles bent forward; got home a good thirty minutes before anyone else."

Johnson flew a number of missions without engaging the enemy. One evening, after a day on which he saw German fighters pass apparently un-observed by flight leaders, Johnson, mindful of the requirement to main-tain position, asked one of his seniors, "Suppose I am not the leader but I see an enemy and he is a perfect spot for me to bounce [attack] and there is just not time to do anything but call him in and bounce him. If I call him in and then we [the flight] try to maneuver so that the other planes are in position to bounce him, he is gone. What do you do?

"He said, 'That's a good question.' And that was his answer. But to me it was enough—go get him. Call them in and then go get 'em. The next day, [Hub] Zemke was leading the whole group. I was on [Paul] Conger's wing, sitting up there on the top and I saw about twelve Focke-Wulfs pass under us. I knew someone had to see them. I wasn't the first. I called them in and said 'Come on, Paul.' I went right down through our guys. I pulled up behind their Vee echelon.

"I took it very slow, easy, and casual, my airplane was really coming in, overtaking them. The pipper [on the gunsight] was on the cross piece of the rudder and the elevators. I thought, nice and gentle, and then, that is not right. I remembered in our camera gunnery, you always put the pipper on the back of the pilot's head. I put it up on his head, calmly checked the needle ball. It was centered and I pulled the trigger. My whole airplane vibrated. All this smoke and fire—all this noise. I released it immediately, because I thought I am hit. Then I realized it was my own guns and I saw what was happening to the guy ahead of me. He went all to pieces. This was the leader of that German formation. If I had any experience at all, I could have gotten one or two more, but, as it was, I was rolling out through the sky, having a great time. Then suddenly I realized that it was easy and I should go back and get some more. I ended up alone over there wandering around enemy country—Belgium and that area.

"I got home thirty or forty minutes later than anyone. They weren't sure what happened to me. When I landed, flight commander Jerry Johnson right on through [Francis] Gabreskie and Zemke really reamed my butt and rightly so—I was wrong. But after they all chewed me out, they congratulated me on getting my first one."

Because of his eagerness, Johnson admitted he quickly earned the reputation of "a wild man. Everyone said, 'Don't fly with Johnson, he will kill you.'" Even when not in the cockpit, Johnson personified the stereotypical image of the swaggering fighter pilot. "We were confined to the base one time. It was cold, too cold to get up and put out the lights. I shot them out with my .45. It became a standard joke, fusillades of bullets to put out the lights. One man had a Tommy gun, another a rifle." After rain leaked through roof holes, higher echelons firmly requested less violent means to extinguish the bulbs.

Just shy of three weeks after his first victory, Johnson's career almost came to a crashing halt. "I was so badly shot up that had I been able to get out of the airplane, I would have been a prisoner, or dead, or an evadee. I couldn't get out of the airplane. My oxygen had been shot out and flash-flamed my cockpit. That singed the side of my head a little. My wrist bone was part of the damage that I did to myself trying to fight my way out of the cockpit.

"This was the one mission on which I had not worn my goggles; I had cracked them the day before, so I'd left them at home. One of the 20mms had exploded in the left-hand side of my cockpit and knocked out my hydraulic throttle or control. Hydraulic fluid was all over the floor of the airplane and flying around in the air of the open cockpit and getting into my eyes, which were starting to swell. I was flying half the time with my eyes closed and part of the time with my head sticking out of the window, getting air blown into my eyes just trying to see.

"I had dropped down to about seven or eight thousand feet and my head was beginning to clear. I was heading north, going toward England and I had to cross the Channel. I looked back to the right at about four o'clock and slightly high, and saw a beautiful, dappled, blue gray [plane] with a yellow nose coming in at me. Black crosses on it. I recognized it of course as a Focke-Wulf. I was sitting there, thinking about it as he kept coming right at me. I waited for him to move the nose of his airplane forward of my airplane but he kept his nose directly on me, which meant he was taking pictures. Then when he got about fifty yards from me, I thought, 'Now what would I do if I was in his shoes? I would stick my guns in the guy's cockpit and blow him out of the sky. That's what that bugger is going to do to me.'"

"I turned and went under him real quick and headed again to the north. I didn't know how badly my airplane was banged up and didn't know whether I could fight him or not—so I didn't try. As I went under him, he pulled up, pulled back around, came directly in on my tail, and emptied a lot of .30-caliber machine-gun shells into me. They all hit me. All I could do was sit back there, leaning against the armor plate and take it." As Johnson turned his head, a bullet nicked the end of his nose. Another passed through the side of the cockpit, split, and half of it pierced the upper part of his right thigh while the rest entered several inches below.

"I held my course. He overshot me and just out of anger, I stuck my head out of the window and hit hard right rudder, and skidded a little bit and fired at him. I got two bullets into his left wingtip. It didn't really hurt him, but he at least knew I still had a little fight. He came back around and got in formation with me. I could have reached out and touched his wingtip. He was sitting in there the way we flew when going through weather. He probably saved my life. We went over Dieppe at 4,000 feet, a P-47 and a Focke-Wulf in tight formation. So, no antiaircraft. He took me out over the water. He was looking at my airplane up and down. He'd just shake his head. Incidentally, he had black eyes. He shook his head and kind of waved at me, tipped his left hand like a little salute, and pulled off. I thought, 'Thank God, he's going home.' Then he pulled in behind me and emptied the rest of his .30-calibers. It sounded like a goat on a tin roof. This time he didn't make the mistake of overshooting me. He came back in formation with me, stayed with me until I was down to about 1,000 feet over the Channel, then waved his wings and went home.

"I was directed to an air base in southern England. I had kicked out my instruments trying to bail out. I had thrown my feet up on the dashboard and leaned back as I tried to yank the canopy open but it was jammed shut. I was brought over the air base in southern England, but I couldn't see the field when I looked down, partially because my eyes were swollen and partially because it was so well camouflaged. I told the controller I'd just go on up to another base where all my buddies were, at Manston. I called Manston and told them I expected to make a gear-up landing because I had no brakes, no hydraulics, no flaps, and I wasn't sure I could get the gear down. I was told if possible to bring the airplane in gear-down because there were a lot of crashed airplanes coming back. I dropped the gear. The doors popped open and the tires were okay. I landed and ground looped the airplane to stop it—I had no brakes—and backed it in between two British aircraft, just like I'd parked there.

"I crawled out of the airplane and kissed the ground, then got my chute out. I went to the flight surgeon. He doctored my nose. Later, as I was taking my trousers off for a shower, I discovered the two partial bullets in my right leg. I put iodine on the holes thinking that would cure everything." To his enormous satisfaction, Johnson heard over the radio a German flier describing how he had seen a P-47 with Johnson's number going into the water.

In January, Eaker could call on only six bomber groups but by the end of June he commanded thirteen of these plus three fighter groups. But the statistics hide a scarcity of operational strength. The Mighty Eighth could dispatch little more than 200 of the heavyweights. The number fell short of what the strategists on the scene deemed necessary. Eaker, eight months earlier, had written Hap Arnold that his people were "absolutely convinced that . . . 300 heavy bombers can attack any target in Germany with less than 4 percent losses." The magical figure of 300 seems to have been plucked from the air, like a .300 batting average as a magical talisman in baseball, for no evidence supported Eaker nor, as became woefully apparent later, the idea that the German defenders would be overwhelmed by 300 or more aircraft.

Furthermore, the top command clung to another deadly misperception. The battles in the early months of spring persuaded the brass that the strongest German fighter defense lay near the channel coast, a crust that once pierced opened up the heartland to a more lightly resisted attack. That theory was obliterated within a few weeks with the discovery of an intricate web of German airfields arranged in depth. Moreover, the *Luftwaffe* had also developed its own radar and early-warning apparatus, much like that which helped preserve England in 1940, and intruders found the defenders ready and waiting. To knock down bombers, the Germans, in addition to machine guns and cannons, added rockets, explosives dangling from parachutes, and even tried unsuccessfully to deploy an infantry mortar shell as part of the air-to-air ordnance.

Archie J. Old Jr., a thirty-seven-year-old Texan, brought his 96th Bomb Group to a base at Grafton Underwood that spring. Old had abandoned his career in construction and won a commission in 1929. He left the Air Corps but signed up for the reserve. Called to active duty in 1940, Old progressed up the chain of command. Following activation of the 96th in July 1942, Old became its CO within a month. He faced two major problems immediately: inexperienced pilots and a shortage of aircraft. Old instituted a rigorous regimen based on eight hours in the air, eight hours of schooling, eight hours reserved for sleep. He scheduled airmen to fly on rotating shifts that gave them experience both day and night. To avoid any downtime, recalled Old, "If the airplane didn't need any particular maintenance, we would actually change crews with the engines running to save time. We refueled with engines running. It was dangerous as hell, but never did we burn one up. We were getting the maximum amount of flying time, since we had only twelve planes and thirty-five crews who needed to fly. We were flying those damn aircraft twenty hours a day."

According to Old, common sense taught him that evasive action in the face of flak brought no real protection. It inevitably led to missing the target because the changes in airspeed and angle among the bombers in formation significantly altered the direction of ordnance. He insisted on no evasive action during bomb runs. "If you were a German fighter pilot leading a bunch of fighters out there, you would start looking for the ones split out a little bit, not in line. Every man in my outfit heard me harp all the time, 'Get that goddamn formation in there and keep it there if you are interested in a long life and doing a good job. The tighter the formation is, the better the bomb pattern. And those damn fighters looking at you, if you have a nice, tight, compact formation, they know there are a hell of a lot of guns that can start unloading on them.' The idea would be, 'Don't go for that guy. Look at the outfit yonder that is scattered all over the sky.' I didn't pass this information right on because I knew it would be unwelcome and have to be sold."

The ideas of the 96th CO meshed with the thinking of Curtis LeMay, who had ascended to the leadership of the 4th Bombardment Wing. "LeMay invited me up invariably after I led a mission," said Old. "We also had critiques on every damn mission where the lead crews would critique a half-dozen missions at a time. We would go over them in detail and discuss the mistakes. One of the things that made LeMay a great leader was that after I had just led a mission he had me up at his place for dinner. We had a drink or two and we were talking about that mission. We ate and we talked about that mission. We had an after-dinner drink; we talked about that mission. I'll guarantee you that by the time we got through, he knew as much if not more about that mission than I did. I felt like I had to keep flying missions to stay abreast. That's why I flew a lot until LeMay would ground me. He would say, 'You're flying too much. Let someone else lead a few of them for a while.'

Hell, the low group, the low squadron of the low group, that was the hotspot. Everybody was always talking about it, so I would go down there and fly it. I would fly the low airplane of the low squadron of the low group. If you wanted to see a lot of fighters, that is where you saw them, particularly the head-on attack that the Germans primarily used." Old believed that he actively participated in seventy-two missions—often riding as an unofficial observer.

Billy Southworth continued to praise some and blame others in his diary as he and those who had come to the 303d and the United Kingdom with him approached their last missions. He remarked, "Just back from Kiel, where I dropped incendiaries, 4,000 pounds of them, tired as hell and glad to be alive. Fighters greeted us at sea and a continued two-hour battle ensued. Before it was ten minutes old I saw two fighters and three B-17s shot down. The fight out was fierce, ME 110s shooting from the front, side, and rear, FW 190s bursting in from head-on. What a day, Cards lost to the Dodgers 1-0. Henderson shot one down at 200 yards."

A few lines later he confided, "An interesting question asked of me. 'Do you feel the same before each mission?' The answer is no. It used to be a big thing like the opening game of the season with the bases loaded, only more so. As we taxied down it was all business. The night before it was on one's mind, anxious to go but sleeping light as a mouse. First time over enemy territory seemed like a new world waiting for the big fight to follow. Once it came, I worked harder than ever before and keen as a razor. It's all the same now, except preceded by a sound sleep, mindful of the crew, target position in formation, and characteristics of the ship [I am] scheduled to fly. Mind on the new boys on my wing. Are they new? Green? Fly close? Stick in on evasive action? Do they understand their job and their ship? Today I heard from Dad, the Cards beat Brooklyn. Took pictures of Clark Gable and met him." Toward the end of June, Southworth wrote of a number of farewells as various members of his crew recorded their twenty-fifth mission.

Desperate as the Bomber Command was for bodies, they could not at this point extend tours without crushing morale. In the summer of 1943, as the number of missions piled up, so did the bodies. The 306th Bomb Group, for example, which had become operational on 19 October 1942 with 35 air crews consisting of 315 men, lost 27 of its crews and only 8 completed the full 25-mission tour. KIAs added up to 93 and POWs covered another 88. More than 12 men died in training accidents and 29 had to be relieved and reassigned. Other groups recorded similarly dire results.

Drained of men and aircraft by punishment meted out by the foe and the need to siphon off assets for the Twelfth Air Force operating out of North Africa, the Mighty Eighth hardly offered the prospect of a long life to its members. On 19 May, the publicity flacks could trumpet the news of the 91st

Bomb Group's *Memphis Belle* as the first bomber to complete a twenty-five mission tour without losing any of the crew. The feat, celebrated with a documentary film and later a fictional movie, emphasized the fragile lifeline. Many other crews had preceded the 91st to Europe ten months earlier and yet only this solitary bunch had completed a tour.

The 95th Bomb Group had the ill luck to be chosen for an experiment devised by Gen. Nathan Forrest. Instead of the box at staggered altitudes formulated by LeMay, Forrest drafted a blueprint that flattened the setup, placing the planes wing tip–to–wing tip. He was convinced that could concentrate firepower ahead, below, above, and to the rear. For two weeks the 95th practiced the new system and when the outfit headed for Kiel, the huge German naval base on the Danish peninsula, Forrest occupied the copilot's seat of the lead airplane.

Lieutenant Robert Cozens, deputy leader of the group for the mission, said, "I was instructed to keep the nose of my B-17 tucked up under the tail of the lead aircraft. The Forrest formation underwent the 'true test' when, as we completed the bomb run, the formation received a massive diving frontal attack from the German FW 190s and ME 109s. In our position in the formation, as well as that of our wingmen, we were unable to clear any of our guns on the attacking aircraft because of the line of sight through our lead echelon aircraft. Consequently, the lead aircraft was raked with enemy fire from one end to the other and immediately fell out of formation."

A total of sixty bombers from the 4th Bomb Wing, hewing to Forrest's arrangement, attacked Kiel. "Goddamn," said Old, "The fighters blew him [Forrest] out right ahead of me. They took his whole squadron out at one time." Indeed, the enemy shot down ten of the twenty-four effectives of the 95th Bomb Group with whom Forrest rode as an observer and rendered one more fit only for the salvage heap. Nor did the other raiders fare much better; the 94th Bomb Group lost nine and Old's outfit another three, a daunting 37 percent casualty rate.

The Casablanca conference of Churchill and Roosevelt, set in motion around-the-clock bombing against the Third Reich's war industry. The massive British assaults upon Ruhr Valley installations hampered production sufficiently and killed enough civilians to persuade the enemy to deploy increased numbers of fighter aircraft for defenses. FW 190s and ME 109s battered the Eighth Air Force. The Allied high command decided that continued operations in the face of this formidable resistance demanded a shift in emphasis.

On 10 June 1943, RAF bomber commander Air Marshall Arthur Harris and his counterpart, the Eighth Air Force's Ira Eaker, received a directive which read, "It has become essential to check the growth and to reduce the strength of the day and night fighter forces which the enemy can concen-

trate against us in this theater. . . . First priority in the operation of British
and American bombers based in the United Kingdom shall be accorded to
the attack of German fighter forces and the industry upon which they depend." The program, known as Pointblank, delineated a series of sites for
bombers to visit. Means to carry out Pointblank against enemy fighters already on the wing, however, remained unavailable because the proposed targets for bombers lay well beyond the range of Allied fighters. Furthermore,
to guard the limited number of U.S. bombers, the outriders were forbidden
to leave the herd in pursuit of marauders. Frustrated pilots watched packs
of hostile aircraft, lurking in the distance, awaiting the moment when the
P-47s or Spitfires would be forced to return to base. Once the shepherds departed, the wolves would ravage the flocks of Forts and Libs fending for
themselves against the savage onslaughts.

On 24 July, the Allies opened a subset of Pointblank, Blitz Week, combined strikes by the RAF and the Eighth Air Force, upon a wide-ranging series of targets, Norway, Kiel, Hannover, Hamburg, Kassel, and Warnemünde.
Hamburg indicated one exception to the concentration against aircraft. The
port city held shipyards that built and assembled U-boats as well as merchant
and naval vessels. As the Battle of the Atlantic, the threat to the seaborne
lifeline from the U.S. to the United Kingdom, raged, submarine pens and
production centers stayed on the target list.

The raid by the British upon the port of Hamburg at the beginning of
Blitz Week witnessed the first use of chaff, also known as window, tens of
thousands of strips of aluminum foil that confused ground and air radar into
the belief of a massive 11,000 instead of the actual 740 bombers. The local
radar-guided searchlights wandered futilely through the night skies, antiaircraft batteries fired aimlessly. One German night-fighter controller was
heard to shout, "I cannot follow any of the hostile; they are very cunning."

The British dumped 2,400 tons of explosives upon Hamburg during the
night. When the Americans came the following day, their 350 tons, a fraction of the RAF contribution, nevertheless kept the pressure on the weary
firefighters. Successive waves of British planes over the next three days with
incendiaries ignited a firestorm. "The last day that we went," said Southworth's erstwhile gunner, Bill Fleming, "You could see the smoke from a hundred miles away. When we flew over the city at 30,000 feet, the smoke was
coming up through the formation. On July 26th I was making my fourth trip
to Hamburg, flying with Lieutenant Lefevbre on the bomber known as *Flak
Wolf*. At 28,000 feet over the target the plane was hit by I do not know what,
either antiaircraft or a fighter plane. We went into a diving spin and the pilot rang the bail-out alarm but nobody could jump out because the cen-
trifugal force was holding us. The experience is impossible to describe. Once
I couldn't move, I knew there was no way we could come out of that dive

and I was going to die. The fear I felt was unbelievable. As we came down, somehow, even the pilot couldn't say later how he did it, he pulled that plane out of the dive. We started at 28,000 feet and leveled off only at 6,000.

"Once he leveled off, everybody was very quiet. I realized I had a terrific pain in my left leg, a searing pain. I thought I'd been hit by antiaircraft. I tried to paw along my clothes to see where the hole in my clothes was but couldn't find it. Then it dawned on me. I had wet myself and shorted out my electric suit and it was burning me from my crotch down to my ankle, resulting in a solid blister all the way down. When we got back I spent two weeks grounded on that account. It wasn't that funny when it happened."

The holocaust at Hamburg reached 1,000 degrees centigrade, creating a tornado of fire that yanked trees from the ground, burned up asphalt streets, sucked human beings from buildings into its vortex, cremated alive citizens who had sought refuge in bomb shelters. Those who did not succumb to fire died of smoke inhalation or asphyxiation from carbon monoxide. The official figures counted 50,000 dead but no one really knew the count because the city held vast numbers of slave laborers, displaced persons, and foreigners. An estimated 900,000 residents were homeless. When Fleming read an account in the GI newspaper *Stars and Stripes,* he said it disturbed him. "German children and old people were there. Of all my experiences that's the one that continues to bother me, even though I never spoke to my wife about it."

Hamburg cost the RAF 2.8 percent of the dispatched aircraft, 87 of 2,592 sorties. The Mighty Eighth paid a much higher price for Blitz Week, 8.5 percent of its attacking force, or 88 aircraft from 1,720 sorties. Worse, the Eighth could not even muster 200 heavies upon conclusion of Blitz Week. For that matter, the Hamburg effort also exhausted the RAF. According to Dudley Saward, a former RAF group captain and author, who visited Albert Speer, Nazi Germany's minister of armaments production, after the war, similar sacking of a half-dozen other German cities immediately on the heels of Hamburg might have actually ended the war. Whether this would have been the case is questionable but in any account the British bombers could not return in force for another two weeks and in markedly lesser numbers.

The most notable first for the Americans during Blitz Week was the use of auxiliary fuel tanks on the Thunderbolts that had previously been restricted to about 200 miles from home bases, able only to escort as far as Amsterdam. The VIII Fighter Command contracted locally and slung a cardboard tank that could be jettisoned on the P-47s. However, these added a mere sixty miles, leaving the big planes still unprotected when they ventured any significant distance beyond the coastline. The newest B-17s installed "Tokyo" wing tanks that allowed them to travel considerably farther, eventually enabling them to reach anywhere in Germany. Overall, however, Blitz

Week may have done more damage to the Eighth Air Force than to the German war effort. When the period ended, the heavyweights basically stood down for nearly two weeks.

In principle, Pointblank set a limit to the types of targets that the Allied air arms would strike; but in practice, the spectrum of targets widened as almost any kind of industrial or manufacturing site could be related to the enemy air strength. Certainly, the huge oil refining plants located at Ploesti in the heart of Romania qualified as vital to the German fighter effort. If this source of petroleum could be eliminated the Nazi war machine would be forced to rely on costly and scarcer synthetics extracted from coal. Ploesti lay beyond the longest-range RAF bombers in England, but the Allied conquest of Rommel in North Africa that led to bases at Benghazi put the Romanian oil complex within reach of B-24s equipped with extra fuel tanks.

Strategists plotted a low-level attack that might evade early detection, conserve fuel for the extended run, and enhance bombing marksmanship. Leon Johnson, the commander of the 44th Bomb Group, said, "We went to General [Uzal] Ent [the Ninth Air Force bomber chief] and asked him if we couldn't go in at high level and were turned down. We said we thought we could hit the target from high level and wouldn't take the losses we'd have at low altitude. If there is anything as large as a bomber flying at low level, [and] someone is in a position to fire at it, they are very apt to hit it. But General [Lewis] Brereton, [Ninth Air Force commander] said it would take a campaign to knock out the targets from high level and they wanted to do it in one fell swoop. They assured us that if we knocked it out adequately, the war would be over in six months. Brereton did not think up the low-level attack; that came from Washington."

In preparation, at the end of May 1943, two B-24 bomb groups in England, the 44th and 93d, halted missions for the Eighth Air Force to practice low-altitude flights and maneuvers. They were joined by the 389th, which had yet to go operational. Within a few weeks all three outfits flew to North Africa, temporarily attached to the Ninth Air Force, for a strike at Ploesti. Ramsay Potts, now a major and squadron leader for the 93d Bomb Group recalled, "We were told there was some sort of special mission coming but not what it was. While we were training, the higher echelons were holding their conferences, discussions, and arguments. Conditions were not very good. The food was terrible, C rations, maybe some canned fruit salad, and it was terribly hot. Sand storms, frequent high winds during the day forced us to work on the planes at night, after six o'clock, and before seven in the morning. The sand blowing in the engines was difficult to deal with. We had a large number of diarrhea cases; everyone lost weight.

"We flew a few missions up into Italy and one long one to the Messerschmitt plant at Wiener Neustadt. Then we settled down to practice low-level runs over some dummy installations in the desert. The planning, training, and briefing preparations were quite thorough. We were briefed on our approaches. We had dummy mockups for targets. Everything that we could do within limitations was done. The mission was recognized as being of utmost importance and everyone had a real keenness that it had to be accomplished at any cost.

"We had some RAF bomber pilots who had flown through barrage balloons in Germany and they briefed us on balloons surrounding Ploesti. Operations officers and the command were a little skeptical but we accepted the hazard of the balloons as one of the things you had to go through. We had been briefed on the balloon barrages, the flak defenses, the fighter units, and their locations. We had been briefed on the hazards of exploding oil tanks and distillation units. The low-level aspect didn't frighten anybody. Many of us looked forward to this because it was the only way to get the necessary range out of the airplane.

"It was to be a thirteen-hour mission. Even with an extra tank in the bomb bay, you couldn't have done it flying at a high altitude. Five groups were going and attacking seven targets. The 93d was split into two forces. The main one was to be led by Colonel Baker, the group commander, and the other by our former group commander, Colonel Timberlake, who'd just been promoted to brigadier general. He was going to fly in the copilot seat of my airplane. Just prior to the mission, General Brereton decided there were too many generals going and he told Timberlake not to go. That meant I had to act as commander of the force as well as be the pilot."

The top echelons were aware how precarious the business could be. Brereton emerged unscathed from his stint as MacArthur's Air Corps chief. This despite the fact that during his watch the Japanese caught half of the entire B-17 fleet in the Philippines on the ground and destroyed it eight or nine hours after word of the events at Pearl Harbor. Brereton said, "We expect our losses to be 50 percent but even though we should lose everything we've sent, but hit the target, it will be well worth it."

Lewis Ellis, a pilot for the 389th, temporarily transferred to the 98th because his own outfit had more crews and ships than its quota. He recalled practices at extremely low altitudes. "I guess we frightened every Arab off every hay wagon and blew down half the tents for fifty miles around. The British engineers erected a 'target' on a clear space in the desert . . . a large number of long, low wooden buildings with an occasional circular one and a few towers. We always dropped a few one-hundred-pound practice bombs, but on the last day we put in some live five-hundred-pounders and blew the whole thing sky-high. Every airplane had a *specific* building or a part of a building on which the bombs were to be placed. Our target was the *left* end of a boiler house; the ship behind us was assigned the *right* end. We had draftsmen to make drawings and sketches of every route, every target, every building. They constructed wooden models of every building and every oil storage tank. We had pictures, maps, and drawings galore. Every pilot, navigator, and bombardier knew exactly what he was supposed to do."

At 4:00 A.M. on 1 August, tower controllers fired flares into the dark skies and, to begin Operation Tidal Wave, *Wingo Wango,* the leader for the entire attack, rolled down the runway. Like the other planes it was laden with extra fuel and ammunition as well as the maximum bomb tonnage, but it also bore the lead navigator for the attack. Of the 175 Liberators that headed for Romania—one crashed on takeoff, killing most of the crew—ten aborted enroute. Potts, piloting *Duchess,* recalled, "We formed up and started over the Mediterranean, seven different task forces numbering about 175 planes. We were flying at low altitude, maybe a few thousand feet over the Mediterranean and quite a bit spread out. Looking out, I saw the lead airplane suddenly turn off to the right and then he fell into the water and burst into flames. It was a shock and my radio operator, who was pretty callous, stood up and said, 'Look at that fire.' I was so indignant that I turned around and knocked him back into his seat."

Unfortunately, the doomed *Wingo Wango* not only carried the mission lead navigator to his death, but also the wingman pilot disobeyed the rules. The wingman descended to scout for survivors and drop them rafts. He found none but the time and fuel spent in his search made it impossible for him to climb back into position. He headed back toward Benghazi, taking with him the deputy route navigator. Other B-24s filled the empty slots but key personnel were now gone.

Undeterred, the B-24s skimmed the water until they crossed the coast where Albania and Greece meet. "We started climbing up to get over the mountains," said Potts, "and ran into a few cumulus clouds. I stayed in close on the heels of the leader of the second group and we wound our way through these clouds, finally either climbed on top of them or skirted them, over the mountains and then started to let down to the minimum altitude over the Danube Plain. But the four task forces behind us had disappeared. We didn't know what had happened to them. They vanished while we were passing through those cumulus clouds. We in the first three groups were still together but couldn't see the ones who'd been following."

In *Teggie Ann,* Col. Keith Compton, the Ploesti expedition commander, flanked by Brig. Gen. Uzal Ent, IX Bomber Command boss, anxiously studied the landmarks that delineated the last navigation keys before the final bomb run. The topography, the streams, even the villages and towns looked similar, and the leaders became confused. Believing they had reached the final marker, Compton instructed *Teggie Ann*'s pilot to bear right. "We were all getting keener and keener," recalled Potts. "My navigator and I were coordinating with each other. On the intercom he gave me the time of nine minutes to the Initial Point. Just after he said this, the leader started to turn to the right. I was behind him, a little bit higher and about the same altitude as the number two group, which was in echelon off to the left. When both turned to the right, I did also, because I couldn't do anything else. I was boxed in. I checked again with the navigator and he said that wasn't the right place. We were still short of the Initial Point. At the same time as we completed the turn, the descent to treetop level started."

Lewis Ellis, flying *Daisy Mae*, reported, "Bombardier [Guido] Gioana pointed out a Romanian festival in full swing with girls in colorful dresses. They were unaccustomed to air raids and waved. Farmers were plowing in the small square fields. Some fields were green with wheat. In others, sunflowers were growing between rows of corn. Occasionally we passed yellow haystacks that reflected the bright sunlight. It was a beautiful country and looked peaceful."

Potts was disturbed by the direction of his group. "This was part of the bomb run up to the target. The plan was to do this in line abreast with each task force assigned its own refinery. Within the task force you had elements come across in line in a sequence. The leaders, first over each target, had delayed-action bombs in the hope they wouldn't have anything blowing up in front of the planes coming behind in their attack. As we came down to the minimum altitude, seeming to have made a mistake with the turn, I broke radio silence and talked to the leader."

Norman Appold, piloting one of the B-24s, broke radio silence to shout, "Not here! Not here!" Potts reportedly exclaimed, "Mistake! Mistake!" Other aircraft now chimed in. Remembered Potts, "He [Compton] said he was aware they had made the wrong turn and now were going to turn back to the left. It was unclear to me exactly what he was going to do at this point, making almost a 180- or perhaps 165-degree turn to go back to the IP, but he did start his turn. You could see Bucharest up ahead. We had good visibility but were going along at 210 miles per hour right on the deck, with confusion everywhere. After we turned, [we saw] that the leader was coming in on his target by skirting the Ploesti area and at a heading of 180 degrees opposite the one he was supposed to follow."

The change in course shifted the Liberators to a path directly over the heaviest flak concentrations in the area. As the ground batteries opened up, gunners on the B-24s sprayed the installations with countering fire. The second result of the error on *Teggie Ann*, more fortunate for the air armada, lengthened the distance between it and the enemy fighter fields, delaying the arrival of hostile interceptors. Because of the deviation, ground spotters issued alarms not only for Ploesti but also Bucharest, thereby confusing the defenders. According to Ellis, the delay enabled the enemy to sound the alarm. "Haystacks opened up and turned into gun nests, machine guns and flak guns were on every hill. By now we were down to two hundred feet but we knew instantly that we were still much too high. Down we went to one hundred feet, fifty feet, twenty-five feet, just clearing bushes and shrubbery. As we got closer we were surprised to see B-24s from another group bombing our target."

Leon Johnson, leading the 44th Bomb Group said, "We were quite low, about 100 feet or so. You could see about the time we got some thirty miles away, all kinds of smoke and flames down in our target areas. We didn't know what damage they had done and we didn't know how successful they had been. We started in on our course. As we got within ten to fifteen miles I could see this gun firing at us. You could see the flash of the gun; you didn't see any shells break around you because those were down low. Right ahead of us, right over our target area, was this complete flame and black smoke. It looked like a solid wall. The thought ran through my mind for a moment, 'My God, we are going to have to go into this?' There didn't seem to be much of an alternative. We all said we were going to hit our targets if we made the trip. I had briefed the crews, we don't go that far and not hit our targets. I had explained that I didn't want them to go on to the target if their planes were in bad condition and they couldn't make it. But I expected to go to the target and didn't want to look around and find myself [alone].

"As we got right over it, there was a kind of steeple, almost like a church, and it was the cracking tower, our aiming point. Went right under us. We were directly on course, still running into this wall of flames and smoke. Just as we got ahead, there was a hole big enough to get about three planes through that wall. We turned and went through and everyone else came through. It probably wasn't as large for the planes that came after us. Some got singed going through, but that was the only opening. There was not a single turnback for the whole thirty-six aircraft [of the bomb group], which is remarkable for a trip that long with all that can go wrong on an airplane. I later found that one of the planes pulled out at the last minute and didn't drop his bombs.

"I believe we got our bombs off right in the cracking plant. As we turned off the target and got through this mass of smoke and fire, we could see planes from the other group. Planes were going in all directions. It was almost as you see in a war movie. You could see planes going, some crash landing. I remember one going straight up off to my right, one from another group. Two chutes came out of the open window, then the plane went into a complete stall and went in.

"I looked over and there was a German 88 millimeter aimed right at us. We were so close and so low and I yelled at Brandon, 'Pull left fast!' We turned and went right over it. I figured it couldn't traverse as rapidly if we went over it [instead] of in front of it. Fighters came in at us from the nose and various places. It was pretty touchy as you went through but it didn't last very long, fifteen minutes was the entire operation."

Ramsey Potts said, "I was coming up and running over some refineries, and we were being shot at by a lot of small antiaircraft weapons on the ground—machine guns, 40mms, and that sort of stuff. We gradually approached our target for an attack on it. Some other planes in my outfit actually dropped their bombs on the refinery we had just passed over. I think they may have been confused, believing maybe this was the target, or else maybe they were hit because quite a few planes in my formation were shot down. They may have simply jettisoned their bombs at the earliest target of opportunity. We made our [prescribed] attack but I don't think more than three airplanes in the unit actually hit the refinery they were supposed to. We had made our drop on the primary target because I had a very good navigator and he knew at all times exactly where we were. Some others had either been hit and felt it necessary to jettison or else did not know where they were because we had come in from a totally unfamiliar direction. There had been no study or planning for a run-up from the southerly direction. I had no trouble with the barrage balloons but one plane in my group hit one, partially shearing off his wing. My airplane was hit several times."

Others fared much worse. A direct hit in the bomb bay of *Euroclydon*, ignited an auxiliary tank needed for the return trip. Flames sprouted from the tail and amidship as bodies hurtled free. One chute opened; another did not. The B-24 smashed to earth and burned. *Hells Wench*, bearing Col. Addison Baker, the 93d's CO, struck a balloon cable, then absorbed four punishing blows in the nose, wing, wing root, and ultimately set the cockpit ablaze. Fire raged in the now mortally struck B-24. To remain in the air and lead to the target, *Hells Wench* dumped its ordnance, a few minutes before the bomb-release point. The flaming aircraft bore on, passing up an opportunity for a crash landing in wheat fields to aim at an opening between a pair of refinery stacks. Another pilot saw a man tumble out of the nose-wheel hatch, his parachute burning as he drifted by so close they could see his burned legs. By Herculean effort, the pilot at the controls held the fiery wreck on its course until it fell to earth. Even though several tried to jump at the last moment, no one survived. A third doomed B-24, both wings sheared off, careened toward the ground and another suddenly exploded into a gaseous red fireball.

"While others were dropping on different installations," said Potts, "My target lay right in the middle of the Ploesti defenses. I went through those on the southern side of the refineries and then through the main defenses, passing over the northern side batteries before we finally got through. On the way home, as we were turning at low altitude in the target area, we came abreast of what appeared to be a distillation unit, a cracking plant. My left waist, a young fellow about nineteen years old, let loose with a barrage of .50-caliber machine gun at the unit, which suddenly burst into flames. That was sort of a dividend."

Ellis also steered *Daisy Mae* to its destination. "When the smoking target was almost in the windshield, Cal [Fager, his copilot] and I both hauled back on the wheel, held it a few seconds and then pushed it forward, barely clearing the chimneys as we plunged through the smoke. I felt the bombs go and saw several balloon cables snap as they struck our wings. A ship on our left waited too long to pull up and flew directly into a storage tank. Burning pieces of it disintegrated into the air and crewmen were thrown in every direction." Appalling as the carnage from antiaircraft, the nightmare entered a new phase. Enemy fighters now arrived on the scene just as the first B-24 elements from North Africa completed their runs and fled. A substantial number of the later Americans, battered by the ground batteries, were victimized by savvy German fliers.

Said Potts, "We came out of the target area, turned left to head home. I regrouped the remaining airplanes in my formation and we started back. It seemed to me I had ten or eleven planes in my formation at that point; I think we had fifteen when we began. We had lost four or five in the target area. As we climbed over the mountains coming out of the Danube Plain, we ran into those cumulus clouds again but they seemed thicker. I gave the signal to loosen up the formation to go through them. As we came out of the clouds, my right waist gunner reported that parts of an airplane were falling down through the clouds. One of the best pilots in my squadron, flying with a very good formation pilot on his wing, but who always tried to fly a bit too close—I'd warned him about it—flew in very tight, not loosened up enough. When they went into the clouds, the two planes came together. After the war I learned that three or four of the crew survived.

"When we got home," said Potts, "I believe there were seven airplanes from my formation that landed at the base and some landed elsewhere. A couple went down in Turkey and another was lost. It was a very gloomy base that night."

Daisy Mae, with Ellis in the cockpit, staggered toward its home field. Over Ploesti the plane had lost its number-three engine; the nosewheel was knocked out; the hydraulic system inoperative; the top turret no longer worked, and one of the .50s in the tail had been lost. In a ragged formation with eight surviving B-24s, several hours into the return, and just as the crew felt it had escaped, a coven of ME 109s appeared. They commenced a well-organized attack with a quintet charging head-on. "We either had to shoot them down, be shot down ourselves, or wait for them to run out of gas. At one-thousand yards we started firing and at eight-hundred yards everyone was firing. Tracers literally covered the sky and 20mm shells exploded all through our formation. Our gunners got the range and the two ME 109s on the right were hit hard; one exploded immediately, and the other blew up just after passing the formation. But we didn't exactly win that round. One B-24 was burning furiously, and the crew members were already bailing out. That left eight B-24s in formation for the second attack. The Jerries tried the same tactics, this time six abreast. Again they all fired together and the lead ME 109 completely disintegrated as it was caught in our deadly crossfire. Another was smoking and again a B-24 went down in flames. This time we only counted five chutes out."

The enemy fighters changed their tactics, buzzing from all directions. Holes appeared in the fuselage and a 20mm shell injured bombardier Gioana and engineer Sgt. James Ayers. A direct hit smashed the tail turret. Another 20mm ripped the left rudder, a chunk of the elevator surface disappeared, and two more shells into *Daisy Mae* sprayed Gioana with shrapnel. The damage included severed control cables and the ME 109s, now short on fuel, departed. Over the ocean, the crew jettisoned most of their machine guns and ammunition. Ellis hoped to avoid going down at sea since Gioana had lapsed into unconsciousness. *Daisy Mae* wobbled to a night landing fifteen hours after it had left the desert. Four of the crew merited Purple Hearts.

Of the 1,600 plus airmen who got off the ground for Operation Tidal Wave, more than 300 died, hundreds more were wounded or captured, seventy-nine were interned in Turkey. From the 178 Liberators assigned to the affair, only thirty-three could be listed as fit for duty the following day. It was altogether the worst day in the Air Corps' war so far. Perhaps conscious of the impact upon morale, the authorities conferred four Medals of Honor (two posthumously). No other mission during World War II brought more than a single such decoration upon the men involved. Two subsequent attacks on Ploesti added another pair of Medals of Honor (both recipients KIA on scene), a bleak testament to the ferocious defenses that surrounded the oil complex.

The fire, smoke, and destruction observed by the aircrews and shown on reconnaissance photographs taken after 1 August indicated a serious blow to enemy facilities. President Roosevelt apprised Congress of the casualties, but declared, "I am certain that the German or Japanese High Commands would cheerfully sacrifice tens of thousands of men to do the same amount of damage to us, if they could." But in fact, Ploesti prior to Tidal Wave functioned at only an estimated 60 percent of capacity. While some installations

had been reduced to rubble, the production pace quickly resumed a normal rate. Ploesti registered one essential fact with the Air Corps. The surest,
most awful route to disaster lay in low-level attacks by its heavyweights. Within
a few weeks, an event of almost equally terrible magnitude would befall the
Eighth Air Force.

To directly implement Pointblank, the Eighth embarked on twin strikes
at the Messerschmitt factory in Regensburg and the ball-bearing plants at
Schweinfurt, both of which lay deep inside Germany. Curtailment of enemy
fighter-plane production at an installation that supplied 200 MEs a month
was an obvious goal. Schweinfurt churned out 42 percent of the country's
ball bearings, the antifriction mechanisms vital to aircraft, tanks, weapons,
ships, subs, and other manufacturing operations. For the first time, the mission would reach the magic figure of 300 heavy bombers with 376 from 16
bomb groups assigned to the runs.

Actually, the strategists had planned a three-point attack. While the U.K.-
based heavyweights slammed Regensburg and Schweinfurt, planes from
North Africa, including those that attacked Ploesti, would return to England
via Wiener Neustadt, site of a Focke-Wulf factory. However, the bomber
groups based in England, busy pounding airfields in hopes of suppressing
fighter attacks, and plagued with habitual weather problems, postponed
their effort. Carl Spaatz, in charge of the Ninth, impatient with the delay,
and probably prodded by Hap Arnold in the States as well as his RAF colleagues, ordered the strike against Wiener Neustadt 13 August without waiting any longer for the Eighth to dispatch its aircraft.

Ramsay Potts, flying one of the 93d's B-24s to Wiener Neustadt recalled,
"It was another thirteen-hour mission, with no fighter escort like all those
flown from North Africa. When you got attacked by enemy fighter planes
it was just a question of trying to fight it out. Because of previous strikes at
the Wiener Neustadt plant, the Germans knew it was in range of our
bombers. Therefore, they increased the flak defenses as well as enemy fighters in the target area. It was very important that we compress our attack time
in order to have minimum exposure to flak. I led the third group. As we
flew up toward the area, the second group lagged behind and I closed in
as much as I could trying to get them to move up. When we finally got to
the target area and the second group still hung back, I closed the gap. Finally, we were over the target and I was now number two in sequence rather
than number three.

"If you have the maximum amount of planes going through over the target at about the same time, the ground guns can only fire at the lead ones
and by the time they reload, resight, and reaim, a number of planes have
passed over. The gunners then must pick up someone from the rear. So the

number of shots any battery can take at a formation is more limited than if you are spread out. We came off the target and there was a very severe fighter attack from the rear. It centered on the original number-two group that now occupied the third position. If I hadn't closed in, the fighters would have hit us. The other group had very heavy losses, as much as half their force. I think my group lost only two airplanes.

"We got home and the other group commander was very upset about his losses to severe antiaircraft plus aggressive fighter opposition. He and I had rather strong words about what happened. There was a board convened to analyze whether there was any fault or blame. Finally, they said I'd done the right thing closing in. But for a while that didn't relieve the tension between the other commander and me. After a while when he had thought about it, he realized it was just one of the things that happen in a war. If he had been where he should have, my groups would have caught the heaviest part of the attacks, not his."

Meanwhile, the script organized the B-17s into a single compact force that would split south of Frankfurt, with 230 ships from the 1st Air Division destined for Schweinfurt. The remainder, drawn from the 3d Air Division commanded by LeMay and all of which had the Tokyo tanks, would continue toward Regensburg, 110 miles southeast. They would then fly over Austria and Italy to bases in Algeria. The crews who attended the predawn briefing, and saw the maps with the extended ribbons into southern Germany, understood what they faced.

On 17 August, exactly one year after the very first B-17 paid a call on occupied Europe, the Eighth Air Force gave the go signal. At the scheduled takeoff times, a ground fog so thick as to make it impossible even to taxi aircraft to the runways, halted operations. The opaque clouds extending high above the United Kingdom obscured the skies rendering formation assembly too susceptible to midair collisions. Bomber Command delayed the beginning of the mission to Regensburg for ninety minutes. LeMay, who had insisted that those in his 4th Bomb Wing practice instrument takeoffs, advised Bomber Command he believed his outfit could get airborne if he used ground crews with flashlights to guide the aircraft as they taxied to the end of the runways. Any further wait meant the aircraft would be hunting for the unfamiliar Algerian fields as darkness came. LeMay himself scrambled aboard the lead aircraft of the 96th Bomb Group.

The assembly above the overcast skies went off relatively smoothly but an angry LeMay demanded of Bomber Command the whereabouts of the escorts and the 1st Bomb Wing (assigned to Schweinfurt). The P-47s, socked in by the weather and without the navigational tools installed in the bombers, never connected with his 4th Bomb Wing. The Schweinfurt groups, also bowing to the restrictions on visibility, delayed departure. Disgusted, LeMay headed for Regensburg without the others. The 1st Bomb Wing took off almost four hours late, eliminating any possibility of the two forces entering Germany as a united phalanx to divide German predators and mitigate concentration upon either element. In fact, having hammered LeMay's troops bound for Regensburg, the *Luftwaffe* refueled and rearmed to savage those targeting Schweinfurt.

The 100th Bomb Group, one of the most recent additions to the Eighth Air Force, part of LeMay's contingent, took off from its base at Thorpe Abbotts, northeast of London. Operations officer Maj. Jack Kidd, occupied a copilot's seat as the group filled the unenviable position of the last outfit in the formation. Harry H. Crosby, a navigator for the 100th, an outfit that had a reputation for slack discipline and sloppy formations, credited Kidd with having brought to the outfit a more disciplined attitude. "I remember once during a briefing the air crews were acting up and making smart-ass, ribald remarks. Jack pointed to one and said, 'Stand up.' Jack said, 'You're the kind of person who does not listen. Unless you shape up, you will be the kind of person who does not come back from a mission.' The man sat down and the briefing was quiet."

Like all staff officers, Kidd flew selected missions. "Somebody else was scheduled to lead that shuttle mission from the 100th [Regensburg] to Africa, but at the last minute I was put in as the command pilot to lead our group, which was the last and the lowest in the 3d Division." Some 240 P-47s sought to provide safe conduct for the B-17s as they entered enemy air space. Unfortunately, those assigned to protect the 3d Division never caught up with the bombers bound for Regensburg. "The enemy fighters," reported Kidd, "seemed to gang up on us. It took less fuel for them to get up ahead of the group and come on back in. The farther ahead they flew, the less fuel they would have. Their fire was murderous."

Harry Crosby, as navigator in Kidd's aircraft, noted the appearance of the first Focke-Wulfs over Holland as the fifteen-mile-long fleet of B-17s flittered across the foe's radar screens. "Gaggles of ME 109s and FW 190s came up behind us, paused, and then slid up and under us. Arcs of our .50-caliber tracers and their 20mm cannon fire scorched the sky. Beams of horror threaded our formation. The tail gunner reported, 'The whole last element in the low squadron went out.'" Crosby wrote in his logbook the names of the crew commanders who were shot down and counted thirty lost friends from the three aircraft. As the opposing aircraft flailed away at one another, both sides scored kills; the ball gunner reported over the intercom that he had counted sixty parachutes in the air at one time, men leaping from bombers and fighters.

In the copilot seat of a B-17 of the 100th sat Lt. Col. Beirne Lay, a veteran of just four missions but expected to command a bomber group. He was on hand as an observer, charged with drafting a first-hand account of events along with recommendations for improvements in procedures. Lay, gifted with reportorial skills, later would coauthor with Sy Bartlett, another Eighth Air Force staff officer, the screenplay for the film *Twelve O'Clock High*, based upon what Lay saw. (Veterans of the air war over Europe consider it the best movie on the subject.)

"At 1017 hrs," said Lay in his official report, "near Woensdrecht [Holland] I saw the first flak blossom out in our vicinity, light and inaccurate. A few minutes later . . . two FW 190s appeared at 1 o'clock level and whizzed through the formation ahead of us in a frontal attack, nicking two B-17s of the 95th Group in the wings. . . . Smoke immediately trailed from both B-17s but they held their stations. As the fighters passed us at a high rate of closure, the guns of our group went into action. The pungent smell of burnt powder filled our cockpit, and the B-17 trembled to the recoil of nose and ball-turret guns. I saw pieces fly off the wing of one of the fighters. . . . For a few seconds the interphone was busy with admonitions; 'Lead 'em more' . . . 'short bursts' . . . 'don't throw rounds away' . . . 'there'll be more along in a minute.'

"A coordinated attack followed, with the head-on fighters coming in from slightly above, the 9 and 3 o'clock attackers approaching from about level, and the rear attackers from slightly below. Every gun from every B-17 in our group and the 95th was firing, crisscrossing our patch of the sky with tracers to match the time-fuse cannon-shell puffs that squirted from the wings of the Jerry single-seaters. I would estimate that 75 percent of our fire was inaccurate, falling astern of the target—particularly the fire from hand-held guns. Nevertheless, both sides got hurt in this clash, with two B-17s from our low squadron and one from the 95th Group falling out of formation on fire with crews bailing out, and several fighters heading for the deck in flames or with their pilots lingering behind under dirty yellow parachutes. Our group leader, Maj. John Kidd, pulled us nearer the 95th Group for mutual support."

The dismayed Lay looked out his window at two entire squadrons of interceptors climbing to a parallel position, and ahead of the 100th, preparing to turn and slash through the formation. Over the interphone he heard reports of a similar situation building on the other side while down below more enemy planes rose into the air. Off to one side, out of range, an ME 110 radioed information on the disposition, route, speed, and other vital information on the Americans.

"At the sight of all these fighters, I had the distinct feeling of being trapped—that the Hun was tipped off, or at least had guessed our destination and was waiting for us." Americans frequently insisted the Germans learned of missions through spies, but more likely, early-warning radar stations tipped the *Luftwaffe* to operations. "No P-47s were visible," continued Lay. "The life expectancy of the 100th Group suddenly seemed very short, since it already appeared that the fighters were passing up the preceding groups, with the exception of the 95th, to take a cut at us.

"Swinging their yellow noses around in a wide U-turn, the twelve-ship squadron of ME 109s came in from twelve to two o'clock in pairs and in fours and the main event was on. A shining silver object sailed past over our right wing. I recognized it as a main exit door. Seconds later a dark object came hurtling through the formation, barely missing several props. It was a man, clasping his knees to his head, revolving like a diver in a triple somersault. I didn't see his chute open.

"A B-17 turned gradually out of the formation to the right, maintaining altitude. In a split second, the B-17 completely disappeared in a brilliant explosion, from which the only remains were four small balls of fire, the fuel tanks, which were quickly consumed as they fell earthward.

"Our airplane was endangered by various debris. Emergency hatches, exit doors, prematurely opened parachutes, bodies, and assorted fragments of B-17s and Hun fighters breezed past us in the slip stream . . . I watched two fighters explode not far beneath, disappearing in sheets of orange flame, B-17s dropping out in every stage of distress, from engines on fire to control surfaces shot away, friendly and enemy parachutes floating down, and on the green carpet far behind us, numerous funeral pyres of smoke from fallen fighters, marking our trail.

"I watched a B-17 turn slowly to the right with its cockpit a mass of flames. The copilot crawled out of his window, held on with one hand, reached back for his 'chute, buckled it on, let go, and was whisked back into the horizontal stabilizer. I believe the impact killed him. His 'chute didn't open. . . . Our B-17 shook steadily with the fire of its .50s and the air inside was heavy with smoke. It was cold in the cockpit, but when I looked across at Lt. Thomas Murphy, the pilot, sweat was pouring off his forehead and over his oxygen mask. He turned the controls over to me for a while. It was a blessed relief to concentrate on holding station in formation instead of watching those everlasting fighters boring in . . . Then the top-turret gunner's twin muzzles would pound away a foot above my head, giving a realistic imitation of cannon shells exploding in the cockpit, while I gave an even better imitation of a man jumping six inches out of his seat."

"After we had been under constant attack for a solid hour," continued Lay, "it appeared certain that the 100th Group was faced with annihilation. Seven of our group had been shot down, the sky was still mottled with rising fighters, and it was only 1120 hours with target-time still thirty-five minutes away. I doubt if a man in the group visualized the possibility of our getting much farther without 100 percent loss . . . I had long since mentally accepted the fact of death and that it was simply a question of the next second or the next minute. I learned firsthand a man can resign himself to the certainty of death without becoming panicky. Our group firepower was reduced 33 percent, ammunition was running low. Our tail guns had to be replenished from another gun station.

"Near the IP at 1150 hours, one hour and a half after the first of at least 200 individual fighters attacks," said Lay, "the pressure eased off, although hostiles were still in the vicinity. We turned at the IP at 1154 hrs with 14 B-17s left in the group, two of which were badly crippled. They dropped out soon after bombing the target and headed for Switzerland . . . Weather over the target, as on the entire trip, was ideal. Flak was negligible. The group got its bombs away promptly on the leader. As we turned and headed for the Alps, I got a grim satisfaction out of seeing a rectangular column of smoke rising straight up from the ME 109 shops, with only one burst over the town of Regensburg." Beirne regarded the trip to Africa as anticlimactic. Only a few fighters pecked at the planes and a single burst of flak greeted them over the Brenner Pass. "At 1815 hrs, with red lights showing on all our fuel tanks in my ship, the seven B-17s of the group still in formation circled over Bertouz [a Tunisian airfield] and landed in the dust."

Kidd recalled, " We lost on that mission seven out of our twenty-one airplanes. [Official figures say nine.] One of ours belly-landed on a lake in Switzerland and they spent the rest of the year there. The flight to Africa was about twelve hours, quite a number of planes hit the water. We landed at a little dirt field that was hard and smooth. We stayed for a week. At a postmission critique, General LeMay asked me where the rest of my airplanes were. I said, 'They were shot down, sir.' That ended the conversation."

The scorecard for the 3d Division appalled everyone. Of the 127 "effectives" after 19 aborted, 24 B-17s went down and one more could not be restored. Fifty aircraft needed repairs. Aircraft could be replaced relatively quickly and painlessly as the war plants in the States accelerated into high gear. The human cost of Regensburg was another matter. The aircraft that survived brought back 4 dead or mortally wounded, and 9 men who required hospitalization. Two hundred MIA were either dead, in prison camps, or enemy hospitals.

Regensburg was only half of the savagery visited upon the Eighth Air Force on 17 August. An even bigger armada consisting of 188 B-17s (a whopping 42 from those originally dispatched chose to call off their participation for mechanical or other reasons) struck at the ball-bearing center of Schweinfurt. The long interval between the start of this mission and LeMay's enabled the enemy fighters to rearm and greet the day's second stream of

B-17s with fury. For ninety minutes, from the Belgian coast to the target, the MEs and FWs battled the stolid procession of Forts.

More than 424 tons of ordnance exploded amid the ball-bearing factories. The return from the target eased only near Eupen on the German-Belgian border where squadrons of P-47s appeared to fly shotgun. When back on the ground, the 1st Bomb Wing counted 36 B-17s missing with 352 airmen. Three aircraft that crash landed in England went on the scrap heap and another 118 required the attentions of mechanics and sheet-metal workers. The maximum effort drained so much strength from the Eighth Air Force that for the following two weeks, the magnitude of missions dropped below 100 bombers per objective.

22
Avalanche, Shingle, and Defeats

An immediate result of the capture of Sicily was the end of Benito Mussolini's dictatorship over Italy. In his place Field Marshal Pietro Badoglio assumed the mantle of premier. Although Badoglio publicly said he intended to continue the fight alongside the Germans, whose troops pervaded the country, he secretly sought to negotiate a surrender. Cloak-and-dagger plots abounded, with representatives of the premier in clandestine meetings with Allied officials in neutral Portugal, and Gen. Maxwell Taylor slipping undercover into Rome in an attempt to set up an airborne coup that would liberate the Eternal City.

While diplomats conferred and secret agents schemed, on 3 September, from Messina, Montgomery put two divisions ashore near Reggio Calabria, the toe of the Italian boot. When Badoglio temporized about surrender, Eisenhower forced the issue. With four American divisions scheduled to strike at Salerno in the early hours of 9 September, the supreme commander informed Badoglio he would announce Italy out of the war shortly before the GIs landed. The Italian leader capitulated.

Operation Avalanche, the Salerno attack, united the Rangers and the British Commandos who came ashore north of the city to block enemy forces concentrated toward the Naples area. "Our landings went like clockwork," said Allen Merrill. "We had the total element of surprise. We started down the coast road while dawn's first light was in its earliest stages." Through his field glasses, Merrill saw the panorama of ships streaming toward the harbor, with the small craft filled with troops already assembling. "I heard shellfire and the loud ka-boom of our naval guns beginning the softening-up process. If they had the element of surprise, with this bombardment, they had lost it."

The sound of a vehicle alerted the Ranger scout. A motorcycle with a sidecar approached him. Merrill vaulted into its path. "I levelled my Thompson submachine gun at the driver's head and yelled in my best German, *'Alt, Ve gast!'* The motorcycle skidded to a stop within ten feet of me. I ran up to it and pushed my Tommy gun into the ribs of the driver and yelled, *'Hanz oiten!'* I saw the unmistakable look of fright in his face. Beside him sat a German officer, no helmet, his officer's dress cap at a jaunty angle, and a sneer upon his otherwise handsome face. I motioned for him, saying the same *Hanz oiten. He* did not raise his hands. I was close enough to reach out and touch him. I did, with the butt end of my Thompson. He got the message. His hand fingered the blood dripping from his bruised lip and both hands raised. A scabbard held a rifle on the motorcycle. I took it out and flung it as far as I could."

The prisoners were led off while Merrill and the second scout cautiously explored the road in search of the German officer's destination. They discovered steps leading down from the road to a building. The company commander decided it was an observation post, and a squad, with Merrill and Bob, the second scout, in the lead, carefully approached a concrete structure behind a closed gate. "Bob and I unlatched the gate and slowly entered the courtyard. We stepped to the double door and called out again to come out [in Italian and German] but got no reply. I raised my foot and smashed the doorknob with the heel of my boot. It never budged. In a matter of seconds, two objects came flying out of the open window and landed with a tremendous roar in the sheltered courtyard. The concussion deafened me. The shrapnel tore into our bodies. I don't remember seeing Bob nearby. I rose after being knocked down and ran for cover.

"I yelled for cover fire as I ran behind some of the mountain jutting into the courtyard. I would be safe here from our own guns that would be opening up on this place. My squad had orders to hit the place with everything they had, bazookas included. I could not hear a thing. But from the vibration, smoke, and debris falling around, I knew the squad were hitting them with all the firepower we had. I sat on a rock and kept my eyes on the space between the fence and the mountain. My Tommy gun was trained on that space.

"Slowly I tried to ascertain my injuries. I felt a burning sensation in my legs. It seemed to be where most of the damage was. I used my first-aid kit and sprinkled sulpha on all the wounds I could see. I gave myself a shot of morphine from the break-off vials we carried. I was not aware of time passing. Something very heavy had hit the concrete building. The vibration and rocks scattered high and far. But they were in another direction away from me. I wondered about Bob and what had happened to him. I stood and found I could move around. I decided as long as I could walk I would have to move away from here. The only way was up the side of the mountain. It was steep and boulder-strewn with outgrowths of small trees and shrubs. The pain wasn't too bad as I made my way. The sun was up fully. It may have been ten or eleven A.M. Slowly I trudged upward. After some time, I found a small flattened hollow of ground and lay down to catch my breath. When all the shooting stopped and the OP was taken, the CO sent a couple of guys to look for me. They found me asleep in the noonday sun, in the small hollow.

"They carried me topside and a medic bandaged my legs. I explained what had happened. The CO already knew. Bob had run the opposite way from me and back to the squad waiting on the stairway. They had taken him to a medic and then notified the CO, who brought the company to deal with the OP and its inhabitants. There were four Italian soldiers in it and a German officer. It was at his insistence that they fought it out. They had had a white flag ready for total surrender when we approached. The German is the one who threw the grenades out the window. After the barrage from the company, one of the Italians shot the German from behind in the head. Then the rest ran out with hands up. Only two of them made it to surrender. Mortars have no way of discriminating between the good guys and the bad."

Merrill, his legs bandaged from toe to hip, rode to a field hospital in the motorcycle that he had captured a few hours earlier. As he awaited evacuation, he saw Bob, lying on his stomach, posterior and back swathed in bandages. The following morning both boarded an LST to the British hospital vessel, *St. Andrew*. "The ship was taking on wounded soldiers all through that day and most of the night. There were two air raids that night; the *Luftwaffe* was out in strength. On the second raid, around midnight, our ship took several bombs amidship and started to sink. Many were killed that night. Some who had been wounded ashore thought they were out of harm's way on this well-lighted ship, plainly marked with red crosses. The bombardment of the *St. Andrew* sent it to the bottom of Salerno Bay, along with hundreds of Allied wounded and the gallant crew that worked feverishly to take as many of us littered wounded off before it sank with a gurgling, horrible sound.

"We hovered alongside another British hospital ship for hours, each waiting his turn to be hoisted up the side and bedded down in the ship's hold. Many were treated again for shrapnel wounds from the air bombing. Some of the wounded did not make it to the new ship, the *Newfoundland*. It left the battle zone the following morning, heavily shelled but sailed under its own power to North Africa where it discharged its human cargo."

Mark Clark nominated the 36th Division, a former Texas National Guard outfit, to lead the U.S. VI Corps into Salerno. The division commander, Maj. Gen. Fred L. Walker, declined a prelanding barrage from the Navy because he expected minor opposition and wanted to spare civilians in the city. His decision exposed the first waves, crawling and cutting through barbed wire, to considerable German fire. Nevertheless, the troops overcame the defenses and gained a four-mile-deep foothold. The 45th and 3d Infantry Divisions were to follow the 36th.

The Germans quickly recovered and applied increasingly strong pressure upon the narrow foothold carved by the 36th and its Ranger attachments.

At some places the beachhead shrank to only two miles into which the enemy concentrated artillery and air raids. With his forces in danger of being divided, Clark drafted emergency plans to evacuate his command.

In Sicily, the prickly William Yarborough, executive officer for the 504th Parachute Infantry Regiment, joined Mark Clark's staff to plan the use of airborne forces. Yarborough visited the Salerno beachhead. "We were bombarded by Kraut airplanes both day and night. It was a real, nerve-wracking thing and Fifth Army headquarters would be crawling around on hands and knees in the weeds, no higher than the waist, four stars, three stars, all of us together." Clark requested reinforcements by the 82d Airborne. "We'd gone through the terrible experience of Sicily, where our planes had been shot down by our own gunners, so I picked out a section of beach where we'd have this great cross marked by five-gallon containers of gasoline-soaked sand and light them.

"General [Alfred] Gruenther put out instructions urging that no anti-aircraft battery on the beachhead would fire at anything under any circumstances during the period when the airlift was coming in from Sicily. Didn't matter whether we were being attacked. There was a real dramatic business waiting for them to arrive. Everything was quiet on the beachhead. Finally hearing the hum of the motors in the distance. Because we had no mechanical means of picking them up from that distance we were wondering whether they were German bombers or our planes. Finally, the first of the C-47s came over." In at least one instance the gasoline-impregnated signals were only ignited after the troopers jumped, having recognized from the moonlight their target. Two regiments dropped on 13–14 September, while the third jumped the following evening.

Lieutenant Ed Sims, the paratrooper, after a few months as a military governor in a Sicilian town, returned to Bizerte as a platoon leader for Company H of the 3d Battalion of the 504th as it prepared for a special operation. "Early in September Company H loaded onto an LCI and left Bizerte for Rome. Our [the entire 3d Battalion] mission was to enter the Tiber River, south of Rome and then land and capture a nearby airfield so the remainder of the 82d Airborne would airdrop and seize Rome. The Italian Army in that area was to assist. As we approached the area of the Tiber, orders canceled our mission. Subsequently we received new ones to head for Salerno." Maxwell Taylor had realized he could not arrange a strong enough commitment from Italian officials for support against the Germans in the Rome area.

Sims's outfit coordinated its operations near Salerno with the Rangers in the locale. "We moved inland and went into the mountains where we seized some high ground near the Chiunzi Pass area, including a vital tunnel. My platoon occupied positions at the tunnel on the right flank of the company.

Our strength at that time was about 120 men." The rugged mountain area was not difficult to defend. There were only two roads by which Germans could move heavy equipment. "During [our] ten days in this area, the Germans made a number of attempts to get through but were repulsed. For our action, the company received the Presidential Unit Citation."

Yarborough said, "I went up to see [Ruben] Tucker and his people the morning after they had gotten in. The results of combat were all over the place. There were a lot of dead lying around. They didn't have a chance to bury them. They were fighting too hard." Yarborough plotted an airborne assault upon Avellino, a town nestled in a mountain pass twenty miles inland. It was a choke point for traffic toward Salerno. The action failed to follow the plan. The pathfinders, dropped earlier to home in the main body of the C-47s, missed their marks and there was no time for an adjustment. The devices designed to guide in the aircraft either did not work or functioned only intermittently. The scattered troopers harassed the enemy but while making their way back to the Fifth Army lines, the battalion commander, Doyle Yardley, was wounded and taken prisoner. Yardley's misfortune, however, enabled Yarborough to achieve his goal, command of a battalion.

Meanwhile, the British Navy ferried that nation's 1st Airborne to the port of Taranto on the east coast. Eisenhower has argued that the move drained away opposition to Montgomery coming from Reggio Calabria but some military historians suggest the troops and the scarce landing craft could have been more useful at Salerno. Still, although the Nazi forces in Italy considerably outnumbered the Allied troops, heavy support from the Air Corps, the fleet offshore, and the timely introduction of the 82d Airborne elements established the U.S. Fifth Army under Mark Clark as a going concern on the mainland. The Allied purchase on Italy continued to expand and by mid-December the ground forces pushed nearly 100 miles up the shin and calf of Italy. Three British divisions fought under the banner of the U.S. Fifth Army along with five American ones. Montgomery led six more divisions including units from the British Empire as well as Englishmen. The Allies captured two vital objectives: the great port of Naples on the west coast, and the airdrome at Foggia in the east near the Adriatic.

Sims and the entire 504th Parachute Infantry Regiment attacked north to help oust the enemy from Naples. He characterizes the resistance there as sporadic, with three days of house-to-house combat against small groups of enemy soldiers who had been cut off. Behind them the Germans left numerous booby traps that brought additional casualties, particularly among civilians. The advance, however, slowed until progress was measured in yards. In place of the "soft underbelly" promised by Churchill the soldiers fought a skilled, well-armed enemy in mountainous terrain optimally suited for defense and in increasingly wretched weather.

Bill Kunz, with a 3d Division artillery battalion, said, "We began many weeks in the miserable Italian rainy season. We got cold and stayed that way. The mountains seemed endless. Mule trains with ammo, rations, radio supplies moved up, the dead and wounded back down. Much of this was night activity. We would establish an OP on a hill, fire some missions, move down into a valley, up another hill, and repeat the operations. Mud was everywhere; sometimes the only things that could move were men and mules." After the GIs crossed the Volturno River, in mid-October, the Italian winter worsened.

While all other elements of the 82d Airborne left Italy for England, where they would ready themselves for the cross-channel invasion, the 504th PIR, with Ed Sims, pursued the enemy northeast of Naples into the rugged Apennine Mountains. "We were restricted to movement by foot," said Sims, "and had to carry our equipment and ammunition. The few mules we had were a big help, but progress was slow in these treacherous mountains. The numerous booby traps and destruction of trails made it more difficult. Near Colli Lazali, Company H was ordered to attack and seize Hill 1017. The attack started by fording a raging stream, then up the south slope of the hill. Resistance was moderate but the entire area had been heavily mined with antipersonnel devices. The first casualty was the company commander who had his heel blown off. The officer who then took command, within minutes fell from a cliff when he tried to avoid incoming artillery and broke his leg. At that point I assumed command of the company and continued to direct the attack. Due to enemy fire and the mines we had to proceed slowly and cautiously. While doing so, many S-mines were activated causing a number of casualties. Of the three mines I stepped on, the first one angled up under a mule in front of me and demolished his rear end. The second one, while I was carrying a wounded man, exploded in the ground when it failed to bounce up, and the third bounced up but failed to explode. By late afternoon, we were able to take the hill and set up a defense. I ordered everyone to stay in place until I could get our engineers to clear the mines."

In the increasingly frigid, rainy winter, fighting in the mountains, crouched in foxholes for extended periods, men developed trench foot, a World War I malady. Wet, near-frozen feet, with no opportunity to dry, developed circulatory problems that could cause gangrene, loss of toes, or even the foot itself. Harold Taylor observed, ". . . a caravan of stretchers winding its way down the side of the mountain to a clearing. These were men killed in action . . . their corpses were in white bags. In this clearing the tagged bodies were stacked like a cord of wood until they could be removed to a burial sight. It brought a prayer to my lips and sadness to my heart."

Ernie Pyle, who accompanied the 36th Infantry Division as it drove north into the mountains, wrote, "Dead men had been coming down the mountain all evening lashed onto the backs of mules. They came lying belly-down across the wooden packsaddles, their heads hanging down on one side, their stiffened legs sticking awkwardly from the other, bobbing up and down as the mules walked.

"The Italian mule skinners were afraid to walk beside the men so Americans had to lead the mules down that night. Even the Americans were reluctant to unlash and lift off the bodies when they got to the bottom, so an officer had to do it himself and ask others to help." Pyle's column describing the recovery of a company commander's body and the sorrow of his troops, inspired the film, *A Walk in the Sun.*

In late November, Bill Kunz and his section dug in on the side of a draw looking down on the village of Mignano. "Normally, you stay out of draws because Jerry has his mortars zeroed in on them. We thought this one a little safer and there was an aid station located across from us. It had about thirty or so wounded, plus a few medics located under shelter halves [half a pup tent] spread out over the dugout area. It seemed okay until one of *our* fighter planes dropped a bomb short of the bomb line, a direct hit on our aid station. All wounded and medics were buried. It was raining so hard and was so muddy that a rescue attempt was useless."

Unhappy with the pace of the offense, the high command had replaced the VI Corps leader with John Lucas. Bespectacled, gray-haired, habitually chomping on a corn-cob pipe, Lucas hardly sprang from the leadership mold that formed his friend Patton. The change in command failed to generate any momentum. The Allied armies faced a series of German positions known as the Winter Line that stretched across Italy. It actually consisted of three separate defense systems, the Barbara Line, the Bernhard Line, and the most daunting Gustav Line. These barred the path to Rome, a glittering attraction because of its prestigious status, its equal importance as a hub for roads and trail lines, and as the home of the Vatican.

The strategists pondered a way to drain off the formidable forces that blocked passages through the steep ranges between the Allied soldiers and Rome. Mark Clark and his staff proposed to strike the enemy head-on and simultaneously leapfrog beyond the Winter Line with an amphibious operation that would put a minimum of two infantry divisions ashore at Anzio and Nettuno. These were Tyrrhenian Sea towns sixty miles beyond the coastal positions occupied by British units, but only thirty-five miles from the outskirts of Rome. The theory held that the Anzio encroachment would force Field Marshal Albert Kesselring to withdraw elements preventing further advances from the south. That retreat would be cut off by the troops based at Anzio. And if Kesselring did not pull his defenders back to Rome, the GIs at Anzio could head for the Eternal City. Anzio drew the enthusiastic backing of Churchill. Eisenhower, in *Crusade in Europe,* indicates he was

less sanguine, warning of shortages in means of supply and reinforcement
for the beachhead.

The quickest route for the main body of the Allied armies from the south
lay through the wide plain of the Liri Valley along the axis of Highway 6.
But the Germans, entrenched in the hills and mountains on both sides,
mounted stalwart defenses at the gates. In particular they infested Monte
Cassino, crowned with a historic Roman Catholic abbey. The town of that
name, at the base of the slope, bristled with enemy troops and guns. As the
two sides organized themselves in front of Monte Cassino considerations
other than military ones governed their actions. Neither wanted to antago-
nize the Vatican by destroying a venerated piece of religious ground and its
artistic treasures. Franklin D. Roosevelt, as a political animal, was always sensitive to complaints of insensitivity to ethnic voting blocks such as Roman
Catholics or Americans of Italian descent.

On 29 December, Eisenhower informed all commanders, ". . . If we have
to choose between destroying a famous building and sacrificing our own
men, then our men's lives count infinitely more and the buildings must go.
But the choice is not always so clear-cut as that. In many cases the monu-
ments can be spared without any detriment to operational needs. Nothing
can stand against the argument of military necessity . . . But the phrase 'military necessity' is sometimes used where it would be more truthful to speak
of military convenience or even of personal convenience." That proscription notwithstanding, some Roman Catholic institutions had been hit and
church personnel killed.

The Germans also appeared to refrain from exploiting Monte Cassino's
massive stone walls as a ready-made defensive fortress. They did remove art-
work, ostensibly to protect it from damage, but some of it was consigned to
Hermann Goering's private collection. In addition, livestock had been requisitioned as food for the *Wehrmacht*. Even as both sides pledged to respect
the integrity of the abbey, their artillery whistled overhead, generally targeted
upon each other. However, errant shells struck the monastery buildings and
a steady stream of injured civilian was brought for care by the clerics.

Ernest Harmon, as CO of the 1st Armored Division, attended the conference where Fifth Army boss Mark Clark and the other senior military
honchos considered possibilities for a breakthrough. Clark proposed a plan
for crossing the Rapido, establishing a bridgehead, and then pushing the
1st Armored up the Liri Valley to Highway 6 which led directly to Rome. "Everyone in the meeting except Clark was opposed to the plan," remembered
Harmon, "because they felt you couldn't possibly cross the river with the enemy holding both ridges and looking down your throat. We felt you had to
have at least one of the ridges. We were overridden and the 36th Infantry
Division was assigned to make the crossing." Clark and his staff drew up a

plan in which the French Expeditionary Corps and the British would strike at the high ground while the GIs forded the Rapido River. That icy stream, thirty-five to forty feet wide, about four feet deep, coursed swiftly between six-foot banks. The heavily entrenched enemy had sown mines on both sides.

General Fred Walker of the 36th regarded the enterprise with trepidation. He told his diary, "I do not know a single case in military history where an attempt to cross a river that is incorporated into the main line of resistance has succeeded. So I am prepared for defeat." News that the attacks on either side of him by the French and British had flopped added to his gloom.

John Goode entered the ranks of the 36th Division as a replacement officer about a month after the start of Avalanche. As the executive officer for K Company, 141st Regiment, Goode had endured six weeks on the line before the outfit started a ten-day R & R as 1943 ended. "When we reentered combat about January 10th," said Goode, "we moved close to the Rapido. Our first forty-five-day combat tour had seen K Company reduced to sixty men for duty. I was the only surviving officer because of transfers and casualties. Our losses were more from weather, mud, and cold than battle casualties, although we had our share of them. We had never been used in an attack, such as our 2d Battalion at San Pietro. Forty-five days of K rations had taken its toll. I developed night blindness because of a vitamin deficiency, where my vision declined with darkness to a point and then to total blindness. Discouraging for a combat officer. It would come and go, and it didn't seem to make that much difference. Our second tour of combat saw a company filled with replacement officers and enlistment. We were no longer a team. Gone was the feeling that you could rely on your people.

"On the night of January 19 I was ordered to take a patrol across the Rapido and take prisoners or kill a Jerry and get his 'Pay Book' so that his unit could be identified. I did get to see a bit of the German sector just north of our position but didn't learn anything.

"The next night we were ordered to proceed north on a road just east of the Rapido to a point about one mile north of our position, just west of Mount Troccio. We were told that we were to cross the Rapido and take the town of Pignataro, some distance west of the river. No field order was issued. You might have thought we were off on a stroll in the park, from the mood of the occasion. We were ordered to send a detail of riflemen to guard the Battalion CP. We should have learned something from that. We were not shown a map of our crossing area, which would have revealed we were crossing an 'S' bend in the river. We were not advised that this peninsula was sealed off by a double apron, barbed-wire fence. German barbed-wire fences were usually rigged with mines and trip wires to antipersonnel mines.

"On our way from below San Angelo to the point above it we were very close to our artillery pieces, which laid down an artillery concentration of at least ten minutes. You could have read a newspaper from the muzzle blasts of light produced by these guns. The artillery seemed to always fire shells with super-quick fuses, rather than delayed-action fuses. One had only to turn a screw in the fuse to set on five-second delay. Super-quick fuses are best when firing on an attacking enemy. Against dugouts and the heavy emplacements of a German deliberate defense only delayed-action fuses could hurt them. In addition, each such shell would have dug a place for a man to hide, while advancing under fire.

"We picked up an 'assault bridge' at this point. It was made of three or four inflated rubber life rafts or boats from ten to twelve feet long, with a slatted catwalk connecting each boat, and tied to it by rope. A conventional infantry assault bridge was not available for this attack. Ropes were strung along the side of this bridge so that with about fifteen men on each side it could be moved to the river. With engineer people as guides, we moved across our access road, down a 'cleared' lane through the mine field running parallel to the river. I led the way, little knowing I was like a Judas Goat, leading the sheep to slaughter. Then Sgt. Herbert W. Caulery of Alice, Texas, stepped on a Schuh mine. I was knocked flat on my face and stunned by the half-pound blast of TNT. We withdrew in confusion, jumping on the catwalk of the bridge to avoid mines. The first of the inflatable rubber boats had been deflated by debris from the explosion. Aid men went to treat Cauley and perhaps others wounded by the first mine. Several more mines were detonated. One of these men lost both eyes. I don't know how many others were wounded.

"Whether these Schuh mines were missed by our engineers or replanted under cover of darkness by subsequent Jerry patrols, I don't know. This 'cleared' mine lane was marked by white tapes as wide as ones used to mark a tennis court and would have been visible to German positions across the river. I believe they were replanted. There ought to have been camouflaged tape for marking mine lanes. White on one side only, to be reversed at night to show that side.

"I remember standing on the catwalk and meeting a major from the 141st. I [believe] I told him that with the bridge destroyed, the attack was off and we ought to get some orders to get out of there before the alerted Germans began their artillery. About that time the Germans did begin to shell the area with mortars, artillery, and *Nebelwerfers* [multibarrelled rocket launchers]. The major told me the attack was very important, because we were landing forces at a place called Anzio, which of course I had never heard of.

"When the German fire began, I found a large culvert under the road and crawled in. We were still waiting orders to stay or withdraw. Some projectile went off near the drainage ditch leading to my culvert. The blast blew me flat against the bottom. Close explosions leave one vibrating like a tuning fork. We were finally told to return down the road to our old position."

Clark directed a second assault on the Rapido. The 36th's commander, Fred Walker, glumly scrawled in his diary. "I expect this attack to be a fizzle just as was the one last night."

Goode wrote, "The next night we were ordered to run the same 'play.' Back up the road, pick up the same type bridge, down the same mine lane. Noted a dead soldier just beside the mine lane this second night. Found the river bank; slid the 'bridge' into the river like one might launch a canoe, bow first. An engineer walked upstream with a rope attached to the bow to keep it from being swept downstream. Another engineer crossed the bridge and flopped a piece of catwalk up on the German shore and we crossed. It was nighttime. There was fog along the river. I learned later that smoke pots had also been used. Visiblity was ten feet at most. The single file of men stopped. I went forward to see if I could find 1st Lt. Robert L. Davey and learn what was holding up the column. I found him in front of the double apron, barbed-wire fence, where it joined the bank of the river on the downstream side of the river. I suggested we send a man out to see if there was a gap in the wire through which the Jerries might be going out on patrols. I didn't know I was on an 'S' bend and now fenced off from the rest of the west bank on a peninsula. There was nothing to do but start cutting the wire with our cutters. The Corps of Engineers had bangalore torpedoes. We didn't have a bangalore torpedo. Our own engineers could have improvised a similar device with a length of pipe or a thin plank and explosives. Placed under barbed wire, it could have exploded and snapped the wires.

"Some Jerry on outpost near the wire heard us. We heard him sound the alarm as he ran away from us toward the German positions. Shortly thereafter came the first, small explosion of a grenade or rifle grenade. I remember how the fragments glowed in the dark as it exploded. Then the orchestra began to tune up. Dark, foggy, no targets. There was a bit of machine-gun fire. At 100- or 150-rounds-per-minute cyclic rate of fire, you only have to hear it once to remember it! Twice as fast as our MGs. By now we were prone and started to crawl for what little cover could be found on the flat ground. I decided that to stay here and wait for daylight would be suicidal. I told Lieutenant Davey I was going back across the bridge and get permission to withdraw. I had not gone twenty feet when a lieutenant colonel I had never seen stopped me and asked where I thought I was going. He ordered me back where I came from. He said he was Lieutenant Colonel Gault of the 88th Division. He was part of an advance party of 88th officers sent to observe us 'battle-tested veterans.' I heard he was killed at the Rapido.

"I went back downstream along the dike that the Italians had erected to contain spring floods and started to dig in, into this dike directly on the bank of the river. The dike had been made from white, marble gravel, and as fast as I dug, the gravel would collapse into the hole. About this time a Jerry whose MG was sited along my bank of the river (with the fog and smoke he could not see us, but the sound of digging might have alerted him), fired a burst of rounds. They struck the river downstream, about five yards from me. The splash of those bullets in the river was spectacular. I now realized I had to get out, and must take the company with me. I went down the bank to the bridge, crossed, and bumped into Major Mehaffey. I explained the situation. He phoned regiment and I think spoke to Lieutenant Colonel Price. Price ordered him to send me back 'and set up a base of fire.' This was ridiculous. We had minutes to spare to get our people out before the Jerries realized the enormity of the 'barrel of fish' they had before them.

"I returned across the bridge," wrote Goode, "and tried to find other officers and noncoms and see what we could do about moving inland. It was then, for the first time, that I discovered this sprawling horde was not just K Company but also L, and E, and F, as well. I shall never forget shaking a man to find that he was dead. A not uncommon occurrence in such a situation.

"Now, more than ever I was convinced that when the sun rose and burned off the mist—I didn't know about the smoke pots at this time—that a minor concentration of artillery and mortars would wipe out what I now felt was about 450 people. It did, as it turned out. I returned across the bridge, by now partially deflated, and reported to Major Mehaffey that there was complete loss of 'control' among our people and I saw no hope to get them forward through that barbed-wire fence and the increasing volume of MG fire. As I had crawled and crouched my way around, across the river, I had seen bullets striking the damp sod and decided I would be safer if I jumped into the Rapido and made my way back to the bridge holding onto the stumps of brush along the bank. The water was very cold. By the time I had finished talking to Major Mehaffey my legs were locked by cold. I was now convinced that I had 'sold' Major Mehaffey and through him, the regiment, that the only practical thing was to get those men out. This was the bulk of what was left of the 141st, as A and B Companies had been largely lost the night before. Perhaps three companies of the 141st were uncommitted at this time. I asked permission to go back to an aid station and try to thaw out. It was granted. I walked through the famous 'cleared' land-mine lane and found an aid station. I walked back down the road to our previous position downstream of San Angelo. By that night, the enormity of what had happened fulfilled my prediction. Very few of our men came back to join us in our position."

Sergeant Bill Kirby, a twenty-two-year-old machine-gun section leader who was caught in the Rapido slaughter, recalled, "We were under constant fire. I saw boats being hit all around me, and guys falling out and swimming. When we got to the other side, it was the only scene that I'd seen in the war that lived up to what you see in the movies. I had never seen so many bodies—our own guys. I remember this kid being hit by a machine gun; the bullets hitting him pushed his body along like a tin can. Just about everybody was hit. I didn't have a single good friend who wasn't killed or wounded."

From the 143d Regiment, Carl Tschantz, a lieutenant with Company I, said, "When word of the attack was finally passed down to the rank and file, it was readily apparent that a deep sense of futility prevailed among the men. Everyone knew that the Germans had had months to prepare a deep belt of dugouts, concrete bunkers, and slit trenches protected by barbed wire, booby traps, and thousands of mines. No matter which way you approached the Cassino front, the Germans on the highest ground were going to be looking down your throat. To make matters worse, the division was in bad shape. The 36th had been clobbered at the invasion of Salerno and shattered at San Pietro. Reinforcements of green recruits were hastily sent to patch up [heavy losses]. A high percentage of officers were new and did not yet know their men. The final blow was to have to go it alone without any protection on our flanks by other outfits.

"The attack began at 8:00 P.M. January 20, in a heavy fog that cut visibility to only a few yards. Almost at once, while we were still a mile from the river, German shells began to fall all around us. At the same time, our men had to lug the bulky twenty-four-man rubber rafts down through safe lanes marked by tapes. In the darkness and fog, guides lost their way and stumbled into minefields. By the time our outfit was approaching the crossing site, about a third of our boats had been destroyed and we had suffered about 30 percent casualties. Foreseeing annihilation, our battalion commander requested permission to withdraw, which was granted by higher command.

"Our period of recuperation was not long," Tschantz continued, "because late [the next afternoon] under cover of a heavy smoke screen, laid down by artillery, we were attacking again. Only this time Company I of the 143d was the leading company to cross the river. After much of the same pounding from enemy shells as the night before, we somehow managed to reach the crossing site. We launched our boats and immediately came under fire from both artillery and small-arms fire. I saw boats being hit all around me, and men were falling out and trying to swim. I never knew whether they made it or not. I only knew it was impossible to swim in the rapids with a full field pack and equipment. After we got to the other side and regrouped, I was surprised that approximately half of my men had made it.

Our only hope for survival was to move forward, stay dispersed, and at the same time remain coordinated. This was easier said than done. Because of the smoke and the fog, visiblity was about zero. In spite of the conditions, we moved forward and overran German positions, but with heavy losses. By this time, the most I could count were about a dozen of my men, and about five or six who had strayed in from other companies. Later that night a sudden quiet developed with only an occasional burst of an artillery shell.

"Early the next morning we were joined by a couple of officers and about twenty men from various other companies. No sooner had we started to move forward again when all hell broke loose. The Germans were hitting us with everything they had and, to make matters worse, our own artillery was dropping shells in our midst. We had a couple of battery-powered radios but neither would work, so we had no way to communicate our positions to our artillery units. I know that some of our men were hit by our own artillery. The situation was now getting even more desperate. Our ammunition was running out when we heard German tanks moving to form a ring around us. We tried to break out several times but each time lost more of our men.

"I could see no way out and began to feel that maybe my number was up. I thought of only two alternatives. Either I would get killed or wounded. Somehow it never dawned on me that I might be taken as a prisoner of war. It was early afternoon on January 22 when the ranking officer and another officer crawled over to my position and advised me that, since we had no means to fight the enemy and had no chance of being liberated by our own forces, it would serve no useful purpose getting ourselves killed. He recommended we take our chances as prisoners of war. Finally an agreement was reached. Ironically, we negotiated our surrender with the Germans by using a couple of German prisoners we had captured early in the day to act as our intermediaries. In our sector, three officers and nine enlisted men became prisoners of war."

According to Goode, "The situation of the 36th Division was now so precarious that they ordered artillery and all remaining machine guns to fire into the general area of German positions to pretend that we were attacking again. A small force of Germans, as few as a company, could have pushed right through the thin, demoralized remnants of the 141st and 143d."

The German booty from the ill-fated assault included carrier pigeons. They sent one back addressed to the 36th Division, and taunted, "You poor nightwatchmen, here is your pigeon back so you won't starve. What do you plan in front of Cassino with your tin-can armour? Your captured syphilitic comrades have shown us the quality of the American soldiers. Your captains are too stupid to destroy secret orders before being captured. At the moment, your troops south of Rome are getting a kick in the nuts—you poor nosepickers."

Said Goode, "I had now gone for three nights without sleep. After the debilitation of the first forty-five-day tour of combat I found I could not get to sleep. I had a small, painful infection on the knuckle of my right hand and went to the aid station for treatment. I also asked if they had anything to help one sleep. The battalion medical officer sent me to the rest area at Caserta. There I was given barbiturates to help me get some sleep. I returned four days later to find the division had moved. I found the headquarters of the 141st and was told to report to the regimental surgeon. He asked me how I felt I would handle myself if returned to combat and how long I had spent in combat. During my rest time at Caserta, the 36th had verged on mutiny, and rightly so, in my judgment. I answered the surgeon, 'as well as I always had.' He said he was sending me back to Naples. I ended up in the 45th General Hospital and was declared a 'battle fatigue' case. Everyone but one of the officers in my room were 36th Division officers.

"During my trip back to Caserta I had begun to wonder if I had crossed the vague line between 'cowardice in the face of the enemy' and showing commendable initiative, to get those people out to fight another day. General Patton had said, 'We're not here to die for our country, but to kill some S.O.B. for his country.' I looked up Major Mehaffey in a field hospital. He was severely wounded and so narcoticized that I wonder if he knew who I was. He did show me his Purple Heart and Silver Star. I looked up First Lieutenant Davey in an evacuation hospital where he was being treated for a shell fragment wound of the lower leg. We compared notes and felt there would be no investigations. There was no one left in Battalion or Regiment who knew what had happened or gave a damn.

"The blame for the Rapido has been shoved upward to [Geoffrey] Keyes [II Corps commander], Clark, Churchill, etc. But a lot of K Company problems were right in the 141st CP. What other infantry regiment in Italy had its CP shot up by the Jerries twice?" In his critique, Goode questioned the structure of infantry divisions, the reliance upon untested replacement officers from the Naples depot instead of battlefield commissions for experienced senior noncoms, and the system that filled depleted ranks with individual replacements rather than cohesive units. The latter point was made by Stephen Ambrose in his book *Citizen Soldiers,* which detailed the American advance across Europe after the invasion of Normandy. Goode also noted that during the Italian campaign company officers became casualties before they could be promoted to the battalion or regimental level. "No number of months behind the front-line rifle companies can give an officer the 'feel' or the insights that being out on the line can give one.

"The aftermath of the battle left an awful feeling of having been betrayed by our leadership. Stupid tactics. Oversights such as those mines in the 'cleared-mine lane.' Why had the attack been launched so quickly that no adequate patrolling could be done? The double apron, barbed-wire fence.

Why didn't we in K Company know about the barbed wire? Did Regiment know? Why cleared-mine lanes were not guarded at night against Germans replanting new mines. All those men, their lives, their training gone for no impact on the Germans or the war. The feeling of how utterly unprofessional we looked. How stupid. I wavered between feeling justified for leaving the scene and not returning to face my fate with the men of Company K."

Many survivors from the stricken 36th Division blamed Mark Clark for the catastrophic results. Hamilton Howze, in a position to observe the assault and to question participants, blames others. "They made this attack in an extremely awkward way. It was very badly done. We had a tank battalion a few hundred yards back in the woods and its mission was to cross over the bridges behind the infantry once they were established and exploiting the gains they made on the far side. We had three more tank companies available and they could have been used to assist the infantry in the assault. The tanks could have been brought up right against the banks of the river. They would have had most excellent defilade because they could have just hung their guns across the banks, and tank commanders with the benefit of their field glasses could have watched the hills on the far side. These were usually about 100- to 200-feet high. Germans had put wire and mines on the bottom by their side of the river and they had infantry positions in the low hills, mostly treeless. The tanks, using overwatching fire, could have done an enormous amount of good whenever they saw one of the infantry units receive fire. Tank commanders could have whomped the German position very effectively from a range of no more 600–800 yards, an ideal position to use tanks in overwatching fire support of infantry on the far side of an obstacle.

"Another example of incompetence was the assault bridges brought down by the engineers and infantry. One was named Yale and the other Harvard and they were put down on mines, which blew them up. It is an indication of how inadequately the area was swept. In my interviews of two infantry battalion commanders after they had brought back only a handful of men from each of their companies, I was told that most of their people had gotten on the other side where they were either killed, wounded, or surrendered; large numbers surrendered. The battalion commanders obviously had the most confused ideas of what they were supposed to do and what happened to them. I asked what was the artillery-fire plan and both replied in approximately these words. 'It was falling out in front of us for a while and then it lifted.' I said do you know the details of the artillery-fire plan? They both answered, no, they didn't tell us. These things present a picture of a division attack which was so inept that the fact that it failed can't be laid to the belief that the concept was improper. We watched this division come streaming back, having accomplished essentially nothing, and lost very heavily. It was a very bad show."

While the Allied armies stumbled if not fell in their first steps of the winter offensive for Rome, Operation Shingle, the invasion at Anzio, began 22 January, the day of the final disaster at the Rapido. John Lucas commanded the VI Corps at Anzio and vacillated between dire forebodings and great optimism. At a conference shortly before Shingle's onset, Lucas met with top echelon officers including Gen. Sir Harold Alexander. Two of the staff had been to Marrakech where Prime Minister Churchill personally questioned them about the forthcoming action. "Sir Harold started the conference by stating that the operation would take place 22 January with the troops as scheduled and there would be no more discussion of these points," Lucas wrote. "He quoted Mr. Churchill as saying, 'It will astonish the world,' and added, 'it will certainly frighten Kesselring. Overlord would be unnecessary.'" Alexander spoke to Lucas about an advance that would seize heights known as Colli Lazali, twenty miles inland, and that he should be prepared to march on Rome. "I felt like a lamb being led to the slaughter but I thought I was entitled to one bleat so I registered a protest against the target date as it gave me too little time for rehearsal. This is vital to the success of anything as terribly complicated as this. I was ruled down." Lucas believed politics, the desire to capture Rome for nonmilitary reasons dictated the timetable.

"I have the minimum of ships and crafts. The ones that are sunk cannot be replaced. The force that can be gotten ashore in a hurry is weak and I haven't sufficient artillery to hold me over. On the other hand, I will have more air support than any similar operation ever had before. A week of fine weather at the proper time and I will make it."

At a subsequent meeting, Lucas reported expectations scaled down. "The primary mission is to seize and hold the beachhead." Rome as an objective was not even mentioned. At a boozy dinner with Lucian Truscott, the 3d Division commander, Lucas celebrated his fifty-fourth birthday buoyed by word that, "The general idea seems to be that the Germans are licked and fleeing in disorder and nothing remains but to mop up. I think we have a chance to make a killing. I have misgivings and am also optimistic."

Upon recovering from his wounds at Salerno, Allen Merrill located his old outfit, the 4th Ranger Battalion, which occupied a ridge. Merrill felt the men seemed "sullen," "morose," "listless" during the early winter, stalemated campaign. Withdrawn from the front lines, the Rangers embarked on another training regimen for Shingle. They practiced landings, worked on endurance. Merrill relished a three-day pass in Naples, where he and several friends, "got ripped, laid, and re-laid." Then back to the grind, which intensified early in January. "I got to know some of the replacements pretty well. I had sworn that I wouldn't do that anymore. That way you don't miss them if they are killed. How can you not miss a guy you served with. Replacements or not, they all mean something to you once you go into combat with them.

"The night before we boarded the boats for our fourth invasion, I could not sleep. I thought of everything I had been through, all the places I'd been, and all the people I'd seen killed or maimed. I thought too of all the soldiers I killed and thus rendered them fatherless. I wondered in that long dark night if I ever made it back in one piece would I ever be able to handle the guilt of it or be able to justify any part of my actions.

"I was as frightened on this my fourth landing as I had been on my first. I relaxed in my usual way, reading from my small volume of poetry. At 2:30 A.M. we went over the side into the small LSTs. Colonel Darby's husky voice could be heard plainly as the flare signaled onward to the landing zones, 'Rangers lead the way.'" As the first scout of F Company, the lead Ranger unit at Anzio, Merrill said, "I was the first man to step across the beach that morning. There was no opposition waiting for us. No shots were fired in either direction. Nothing moved but us. The only movement of the section of beach I landed on was an old, grizzled man pissing against a seawall. He bade us 'Buon giorno' and finished what he was doing. We knifed through the town of Anzio in the predawn hours without mishap. Farther down the beach, a momentary firefight erupted. Some German officers on leave from their units and enjoying the talents of a few of the local females were caught literally with their pants down and captured in position *indelicato,* so to speak." Merrill was one of almost 34,000 to cross the Anzio shore the first day.

He reported, "On the second day, Ranger companies had advanced to within six short kilometers of the Holy City and not a German soldier in sight. In another hour we could have been in the outskirts of Rome itself. Our captain radioed back for confirmation to begin the final advance to the city limits. That confirmation never came. Instead the commanding general of the beachhead chastised us for extending our lines too far ahead and instructed us to fall back to the factory town of Aprilia, dig in, and hold. Colonel Darby was livid but he was a West Pointer who took and gave orders without question. There was absolutely nothing of any military importance showing signs of resistance in those foothills of the Colli Lazali.

"The 82d Airborne were on our right flank and the No. 6 British Commandos under Lord Lovat were on our left. Together we could have been in Rome by nightfall of that D plus 1 day. Instead, where we were told to dig in and hold was eight miles inland and that became the limit of the 'doormat-size beachhead that remained static until five months later."

Merrill mentioned the 82d Airborne on the Ranger flank; the unit was the 509th Parachute Infantry Battalion, under the command of Bill Yarborough. Like the Rangers, the troopers whored and brawled, but mostly prepared in the Naples area in the weeks before Anzio. Having expected extensive casualties Yarborough said he had requested a large number of replacements. "When they arrived," he said, "we isolated them behind wire like they had measles and then sent a guy with the badge of the 3d Zouaves [awarded for valor in North Africa by the French] who talked to them about the history, the honor, and the integrity of the unit. It gave them pride and it would pay rich dividends when they went into combat."

Yarborough personally felt comfortable to be working alongside the Rangers. "I had known Darby and had high regard for him. But mixing paratroopers and Rangers was like oil and water. There was bad blood between our units. We went for the traditional esprit of the soldier based on the military service. Even in foxholes, every man shaved, every day, no matter what. Our people looked sharp. I required them to take pride in their parachute uniform, their barracks, the whole bit. Darby's guys looked like cutthroats. They looked like the sweepings of the bar rooms. They had stubble beards, they wore any kind of uniform; some of them tanker uniforms. Darby and I approached leadership from two points of view. When you have an extraordinary mission, there is a traditional one, which I prefer, and the other was his approach, which offers only blood, sweat, and tears. It would offer you nothing except the hardest bloody job and the smallest recognition. You would get guys who would go for that sort of approach."

At Salerno, members of the 3d Infantry Division drilled for Anzio. Bill Kunz recalled in mid-January, Operation Webfoot, a practice landing. "We were to come ashore in DUKWs [Ducks, or amphibious craft dispatched from LST ramps, capable of carrying men and heavy weapons]. Our artillery was to have one gun per Duck and to fire on the way ashore. There was an argument, Army v. Navy. 'The waves were too rough,' said the Navy. 'This is our operation,' the Army said. 'Launch them!' The Navy was right. The Ducks were too low in the water, were swamped, and sank. Men, guns, and equipment to the bottom. None of the guns were fired enroute. Our battalion lost twelve guns, 105mm [howitzers]."

At Anzio, the 3d Division batteries borrowed guns from the 45th Division to replace those lost during the Webfoot fiasco. Said Kunz, "Our artillerymen spent time 'zeroing in' and learning the quirks of the 105mms from the 45th. Guns have individual characteristics that you have to know to fire them with pinpoint accuracy."

William Rosson, shifted from a staff position at regiment to command of the 3d Battalion of the 7th Regiment, recalled no fire at all as they crossed the beaches and reached their objectives. The 3d Division struck off east to seize the seaside town of Nettuno, widening the turf controlled by the invaders. Rosson remembered he had been instructed that there would be "a rapid, sustained drive inland once we had established a beachhead." The advisory noted his unit might be forced to operate independently for periods of time. "Presumably, this landing would dislodge [the enemy] from the Gustav Line. . . . He would be forced to give combat where he found us. But no orders were received to move in a major offensive position toward the distant objectives. Several days passed. Then came information from regiment there was to be an attack carried out by the Rangers under Col. Bill Darby."

Harmon said British intelligence mistakenly advised there were no German divisions available in the north to reinforce the Italian-based garrisons. According to Corps Commander Lucas, on 29 January his 61,000 soldiers were opposed by a force of 71,000 still being reinforced. Harmon noted that a second flaw of the Shingle plan lay in the inability of air forces to destroy the bridges and rail lines from the north into Italy.

Against this largely undetected strength, the Rangers kicked off the Allied attack. As a lieutenant in C Company, 3d Ranger Battalion, platoon leader Clarence Meltesen said, "On 29 January [a week after the troops landed] orders were received and reconnaissance initiated for a night-penetration march and dawn attack on Cisterna di Latina. We were to move in a column of two battalions, entering the Mussolini Canal and then the Pontana Ditch to exit immediately southwest of Cisterna. We were to seize Cisterna and hold until linkup with attack elements of the 3d Infantry Division." Because of a shortage of ships and the start of the buildup in England for the cross-channel invasion, the 1st Armored Division only began to debark at Anzio on that day.

Initially, the Rangers advanced with no significant opposition and sentries who might have sounded an alarm were eliminated. The Americans slipped beyond German emplacements, close enough to hear conversation among the enemy. But lying in wait for them were massive forces, undetected by patrols or from the air, that had come from Austria through the Brenner Pass to seal off the small plot held by the Allies and systematically grind up the entire II Corps. When morning came, the 1st and 3d Ranger Battalions found themselves cut off and battling against far superior forces that included artillery and armor. The Germans blocked the 7th Infantry of the 3d Division from linking up with the Rangers. Nor could the 509th paratroopers gain ground. The 3d Rangers bought some protection with their machine guns that swept the ground by using a deep drainage ditch, but the enemy in houses and elevated roosts unleashed fusillades upon the Americans. Mud into which the heavy base plates of the 4.2 mortars sank limited the usually effective mortar support. A handful of the attackers actually broke through to the Cisterna railroad station but, according to Meltesen, most were caught in the open and pinned down by fire from several directions. Meltesen himself fell with a neck wound inflicted by a sniper. The 4th Ranger Battalion vainly tried to break through to the encircled troops.

Because of casualties, Jim Altieri, upon whose shoulders Mark Clark pinned lieutenant's bars on Christmas Day, now commanded Company F. Supported by a couple of half-tracks and tank destroyers, Altieri attempted to halt a counterattack. "Ground-grazing machine-gun fire covered every ditch and their mortars crashed all around us," said Altieri. "In one attack I lost one of my platoon lieutenants and four key noncoms as well as ten men badly wounded. We were desperate; we knew we had to crack through to save the 1st and 3d—but each attack in broad daylight over open ground brought frightening casualties."

Allen Merrill recalled, "The Rangers were surprised in their attack upon Cisterna by the Germans, recently reinforced by two divisions, the elite Green Devil Paratroops and the Herman Goering Panzers, both up to full strength. In the early morning ground fog, the first two battalions realized they had walked into the middle of a German counterattack planned for that very morning. Rangers fought valiantly in small pockets and by ones and twos until their ammunition was gone. They faced point-blank tank fire and were outnumbered four to one.

"In the village in the suburbs of Cisterna, called Femminamorta [dead woman in Italian] I was wounded [in the lower leg] and captured. I had saved one round of ammo for myself in case this happened. But a kick in the ribs deflected my weapon and two Germans carried me to a farmhouse with many other Ranger wounded and they dumped me on the floor with the others."

Platoon leader Clarence Meltesen, with C Company in the 3d Battalion, still dazed from a morphine injection after being wounded, said, "I had decided that with my right lung affected by my rifle-shot wound I should not try leading my platoon back. I prepared to surrender and after two minutes of absolute quiet, I saw a German three-man patrol headed my way. I had been informed that the large shed [nearby] contained a fair number of our wounded. I waited and tried to surrender at a distance of fifty yards. I could only raise my left arm and was given an overhead machine-pistol burst. I dodged behind the medical collecting point and pulled out my new Red Cross handkerchief, took my helmet off, and wiggled a white flag on a tattered end of a piece of cane. I made another appearance and was allowed this time to surrender. In my schoolbook German I tried to tell my captors my condition and that there were wounded in the shed. My captors were very happy capturing Rangers. One did a little jig and said he had been in Sicily when the 1st Battalion had shellacked them. They told me to go 'thataway' and they went on."

Other Rangers recalled the sight of their comrades being used as hostages, hands held high in front of armed Germans who called on the GIs to surrender. Bing Evans, as CO for F Company of the 3d Battalion, prepared to order his troops to shoot the guards when suddenly an artillery shell burst nearby. "I remember my face in the dirt" said Evans, "but nothing else for the next two months until I was in a prison camp."

Enemy barrages bracketed the command post occupied by Darby. The blasts killed a staff officer and Darby's runner. German armor relentlessly attacked and counterattacked. Darby briefly lost his composure at the realization that nothing could save the more than 750 men from his two trapped battalions. Fewer than 20 Rangers from the 1st and 3d Battalions evaded capture. Statistics of the Ranger Association list only 12 from the two battalions killed, 36 wounded, and 743 captured. The figures seem low. The 4th Ranger Battalion itself had 30 KIA and 58 WIA.

Post-mortems blamed the failings on the strategy, the poor intelligence, and the use of Rangers for such a mission. Mark Clark stated, "Neither Truscott [3d Division commander] nor I knew of the organized defensive position they would run into." Lucas absolved himself for the destruction of the Rangers. "Instead of performing their assigned mission, [they] seem to have advanced without proper security and were surrounded and captured by hostile forces outside the town." However, he admitted he approved the plan of attack.

Absent was coordinated tactical support from the air and sufficient artillery. Harmon, whose armor had only bivouacked for the first night on 29 January, later said, "I always felt that if the 1st Armored strength had been assigned to the Cisterna sector, instead of the British one, my tanks could have supported the Rangers. It would have made the sacrifice of these crack troops unnecessary. We certainly could have gone in and got them out." The Cisterna attack failed but the furious fighting prevented the enemy from eradicating the beachhead.

23
Solomon Finales, Galvanic, and Flintlock

Farther up the northwest trajectory from Guadalcanal lay more stepping-stones toward the expanded Japanese Empire. The Solomons' Bougainville was the northernmost footprint at the head of the Slot and New Britain and New Ireland stood off the coast of New Guinea. Bougainville attracted Allied strategists as an excellent site from which to batter the massive enemy concentration at Rabaul. Aware of such a prospect, the Japanese had already begun a buildup on the southern end of this replica of Guadalcanal. To retain control of Bougainville, the Imperial Army gathered 45,000 soldiers with all of the arsenal necessary for a protracted struggle.

Instead of directly confronting the foe at the southern tip, the 3d Marine Division on 1 November 1943, scrambled ashore in midisland at Cape Torokina on Empress Augusta Bay. To divert the enemy the 2d Marine Parachute Battalion attacked neighboring Choiseul Island. [They came by sea and the outfit never performed as airborne during the entire war.] At Cape Torokina, only a single infantry company, albeit with well over a dozen pillboxes, defended the beach. The prelanding naval bombardment missed its mark and the Japanese gunners shot up many of the landing craft. Marine airplanes helped quell the resistance but hard fighting occurred before Cape Torokina could be declared secure.

The enemy, determined to hold Bougainville, countered with naval and air assaults as well as bringing in a battalion of soldiers from Rabaul. In swamps so deep with ooze they could completely swallow a bulldozer, the two sides fought it out. The 3d Marine Divison expanded its grasp of territory, aided by the insertion of U.S. Army forces from the 37th Division in early December. With tanks, flamethrowers, heavy artillery, and control of the air, the Americans hammered a stubborn foe. Months of dogged fighting slowly whittled away the Japanese defenders, who, as at Guadalcanal, could not count upon reinforcements or resupply. The struggle for Bougainville would drag on for a year.

As part of the further isolation of Rabaul, the strategists focused on two more former pieces of the British Empire, New Britain and New Ireland. Ed Andrusko, bloodied with the 1st Marine Divsion on Guadalcanal, recalled Christmas Day 1943, as his company sailed toward New Britain. The public-

address system summoned the leathernecks to an assembly on the fantail
for some last-minute instruction. There an intelligence lieutenant with a
background in biology, a Navy doctor, and a coast watcher instructed them
on some of the perils that awaited them.

The lieutenant began, "Men, you will be in the first wave of the invasion
tomorrow. When your attack boats drop you near the shore be careful *not*
to stay in the water too long. The sharp coral can cut you badly, and this will
attract sand sharks, barracuda, and poisonous large eels. Watch out for giant clams; if you step into one, it will close and lock on your foot with a vice-
like grip, breaking your leg, causing excruciating pain." He continued with
warnings about large biting ants, scorpions, and small scrub typhus bearing
fleas. He spoke of a variety of poisonous snakes, spiders, and centipedes hidden in the thick jungle.

According to Andrusko, the doctor added, "Remember, if you're bitten,
we don't have antidotes, so try to recall the color of the snake or spider; it
might be a helpful warning to the next person. There are giant wasps and
thousands of other insects that can bite or sting you day or night. The
anopheles mosquito can give you one of four types of malaria. All types will
make you very sick; two will make you sick for a long time; the other types
will kill you in a few weeks. We have some medication called atabrine but it
has limited use—mainly because the men won't take it. It has a tendency to
turn your skin, eyes, and clothing a bright yellow color and rumor has it that
it will make you permanently sterile."

The Australian coast watcher added his comments about massive, dangerous, almost impassable swamps. "These swamps contain the large sea-go-
ing crocodiles. Please be sure of where you step! I can assure you that there
are also alligators that will attack a person with deadly results. Be on the lookout for sink holes and quicksand under the dark brackish swamp water.
You'll need help pulling each other out of the mud and removing the blood-
sucking leeches off your bodies. Unfortunately, it is the monsoon season and
you are five degrees south of the equator so you will be constantly hot and
wet. The continued torrential rain and the high sweat-producing humidity
will cause mold and you will soon acquire the infamous jungle rot, a skin
condition that will be ulcerated, painful, and itchy. It will never heal until
after you leave here. And large blowflies will constantly try to get at your
sores. These same swarms of biting flies will bring amoebic dysentery."

The briefing noted, "Not too many natives live [here] due to dengue
fever, scurvy, beri beri, leprosy, and many other diseases we have never heard
of. Plus the large, smoking, rumbling volcanoes and daily earthquakes
frighten them off. They feel it will erupt any day."

The Marine lieutenant then called for questions from the troops—
"[they] sat stunned by what they had just heard," recalled Andrusko. "A

young Marine raised his hand. 'If all you say is true about this place, why don't we just let the enemy have this horrible island—the enemy will be dead in no time. All we have to do is sit out here on the ships and wait, or go back to Australia.'

"A chorus of agreement and obscenities filled the air. Voices yelled, 'Who needs this God forsaken place. Let them have it. It is Christmas time. Let's give it to them as a Christmas present.'" But on the morrow, Andrusko and his comrades went over the side. To their delight they met almost no opposition when they touched down at Cape Gloucester. They headed inland to find the "Damp flats" about as advertised. On their third day, sixteen inches of rain pelted down. Bolstered by Sherman tanks the Marines steadily drove the enemy ever deeper into the jungle.

"On the seventeenth day of the battle for Cape Gloucester," said Andrusko, "our battalion had fought through the thick jungle and monsoon rain since landing. Our destination was a hill called '660.' As our company advanced, enemy shells rained down and we sustained heavy casualties. A large enemy shell exploded nearby and I was wounded, then evacuated." Through amphibious operations, the Marines enveloped the enemy on New Britain, controlling the perimeter while enemy soldiers remained at large in the interior.

High on the American agenda stood the necklaces of coral atolls known as Micronesia that lay athwart the sea-lanes from the U.S. to the major Pacific objectives. Operation Galvanic proposed to conquer within five days the atolls of Makin and Tarawa, in the Gilbert colony. Flat and sandy over coral bases, unlike the densely vegetated and mountainous terrain of Guadalcanal and New Guinea, these islets provided surface cover for neither defenders nor invaders. But the Japanese had tunneled deep in the coral to provide excellent protection against bombs, shells, and small arms. The timetable called for landings to start on 20 November.

The traditional inter-and intra-service rivalries sorely afflicted Galvanic. Naval airmen complained of exclusion from key planning sessions, even as more carriers with improved airplanes and radar-control systems bolstered the fleet. Admiral Richmond Kelly Turner and Gen. Holland M. Smith squabbled over the precise point at which authority over the operations shifted from the Navy to the Marines. In a bizarre twist, an Army Air Corps officer, aboard a Navy ship, was to direct the naval and marine aircraft supporting the leathernecks on land. Evans Carlson's ill-fated 1942 Marine Raider sortie against Makin had triggered an intensive effort to create excellent defenses with interlocking fire to sweep every inch of terrain. The intelligence on Makin estimated a relatively small garrison and the American strategists figured a massive strike from the sea and air would soften up the inhabitants sufficiently for a quick victory. Instead, when the 6,500 soldiers drawn from the Army's 27th Division reached the Makin strand, 500 resolute Japanese soldiers and 300 laborers staunchly fought from almost-impregnable bunkers. They pinned the invaders on the beaches and a battle dragged on for four days, to the dismay of the two overall commanders, the Navy's Admiral Turner and the Marines' "Howlin Mad" Smith. From this point on Smith regarded the 27th Division as unreliable.

The Americans expected a much tougher fight at Tarawa. There the enemy numbered 5,000 and they brought to bear everything from 8-inch naval rifles, prizes taken from the British at Singapore, to infestations of machine guns. The most important item in the atoll was Betio, a 291-acre fortress with an airstrip, girdled by a three-to-five-foot-high seawall, and stuffed with concrete and coral emplacements that housed numerous artillery pieces and troops. The approaches from the sea bristled with concrete tetrahedrons festooned with mines and wire. As troubling as the man-made defenses was the coral reef that entirely ringed Betio. The hard, jagged, natural obstacle could hang up landing craft, even rip open bottoms, forcing leathernecks to wade through deep water to gain the shore. The experts who had guided ships in the Gilberts, predicted five feet of water over the reef at high tide, adequate for the Higgins LCVP [landing craft, vehicles and personnel] that ordinarily drew four feet. However one aged British civil servant, who had lived on the atoll for fifteen years, warned that in November, tides frequently fell below the norm. The Pacific fleet had begun to deploy Alligators, or LVTs, new amphibious tractors that could crawl across a reef if necessary; but a limited stock was available for Tarawa. Nimitz and the staff delegated to carry out Galvanic fretted over the problem. They were urged not to postpone operations until more favorable tidal conditions. Allied momentum in the Pacific was quickening. Delay might allow the enemy to regroup and reinforce the objectives.

Questions about tactics stirred debate, particularly in the matter of air and naval bombardment. General Julian Smith, whose 2d Marine Division would ride the Alligators and LCVPs, wanted a lengthy preparation from the big guns offshore and in the air. Navy brass worried that this would alert the Japanese to the intentions of Galvanic and bring ships and planes down upon the fleet. In this concern, U.S. intelligence had failed to discover that the enemy, hard hit by previous engagements, could not react with any substantial force.

Reports from Air Corps bombers that struck Betio and met weak anti-aircraft opposition elicited hopes that most of the Japanese had been evacuated. About 4:00 A.M. the amtracs, loaded with leathernecks, chugged toward the line of departure, the rendezvous point from which the first wave would frantically jounce toward the beach. Overhead, shells from some Japanese shore batteries testified to life and fight on the island. The battleship *Maryland* answered with the full-throated roars of its 16-inch cannons. Two other dreadnoughts, four cruisers, and some twenty destroyers cascaded 3,000 tons of ordnance upon the target, pausing only to allow carrier planes to swoop in and deliver their own explosives. It was the heaviest bombardment of any invasion beach to date.

Correspondent Robert Sherrod watched the overtures to the Tarawa venture aboard the transport *Zeilin*. "At 0505, we heard a great thud in the southwest. We knew what that meant. The first battleship had fired the first shot. . . . The curtain was up in the theatre of death. We were watching when the battleship's second shell left the muzzle of its great gun, headed for Betio. There was a brilliant flash in the darkness of the half-moonlit night. Then a flaming torch arched high into the air and sailed far away, slowly, very slowly, like an easily lobbed tennis ball. The red cinder was nearly halfway to its mark before we heard the thud, a dull roar as if some mythological giant had struck a drum as big as Mount Olympus. There was no sign of an explosion on the unseen island—the second shot had apparently fallen into the water, like the first.

"Within three minutes the sky was filled again with the orange-red flash of the big gun, and Olympus boomed again. The red ball of fire that was the high-explosive shell was again dropping toward the horizon. But this time there was a tremendous burst on that land that was Betio. A wall of flame shot five hundred feet into the air, and there was another terrifying explosion as the shell found its mark. Hundreds of the awestruck Marines on the deck of the [*Zeilin*] cheered in uncontrollable joy. Our guns had found the enemy. Probably the enemy's big eight-inch guns and their powder magazine on the southwest corner of the island.

". . . This was only the beginning. Another battleship took up the firing— four mighty shells poured from its big guns onto another part of the island. Then another battleship breathed its brilliant breath of death. Now a heavy cruiser let go with its eight-inch guns and several light cruisers opened with their fast-firing six-inch guns. They were followed by destroyers, many destroyers with many five-inch guns on each, firing almost as fast as machine guns. The sky at times was brighter than noontime on the equator. The arching, glowing cinders that were high-explosive shells sailed through the air as though buckshot were being fired out of many shotguns from all sides of the island . . . the whole island of Betio seemed to erupt with bright fires that were burning everywhere. They blazed even through the thick wall of smoke that curtained the island.

"The first streaks of dawn crept through the sky. The warships continued to fire. All of a sudden they stopped. But here came the planes—not just a few planes: a dozen, a score, a hundred. The first torpedo bombers raced across the smoking conflagration and loosed their big bombs on an island that must have been dead a half hour ago. They were followed by the dive bombers, the old workhorse SBDs and the new Helldivers, the fast SB2Cs that had been more than two years a-borning. The dive bombers lined up many thousands of feet over Betio, then they pointed their noses down and dived singly, or in pairs or in threes. Near the end of their dives they hatched the bombs from beneath their bellies; they pulled out gracefully and sailed back to their carriers to get more bombs. Now came the fast, new Grumman Hellcats, the best planes ever to squat on a carrier. They made their runs just above the awful gushing pall of smoke, their machine guns spitting hundreds of fifty-caliber bullets a minute.

"Surely, we thought, no mortal men could live through such destroying power. Surely, I thought, if there were actually any Japs left on the island (which I doubted strongly), they would all be dead by now." Sherrod forgot the warning from the former Raider leader, Merritt Edson, now chief of staff for the 2d Marine Division. "We cannot count on heavy naval and air bombardment to kill all the Japs on Tarawa, or even a large proportion of them."

The gigantic blasts flung smoke, sand, coral, chunks of wood, concrete, and steel into the air. Concussive effects momentarily stunned the well-shielded defenders. Unfortunately, the Marines could not exploit the brief period when the enemy was dazed because the first waves required longer than expected to make it to shore. Smoke and haze from the preinvasion barrage prevented the naval observers from using their heavy guns to the best advantage of those in the landing craft. Likewise, the strafers from the air quit too soon. Only the first group of the assault teams reached the beach before the Japanese recovered and commenced to fight.

The timetable scheduled the first wave to hit the beaches at 0830 but miscalculations on the distances and the rate of speed through the choppy waters delayed the arrival until 0913. Aware of the tardiness, the naval commander revived the offshore bombardment for a few minutes but, nevertheless, the defenders had almost twenty minutes to recover their wits and man their weapons. Some groups of amtracs met relatively minor opposition but at Beach Red 1 devastating fire greeted the Marines. Private N. M. Baird remembered, "Bullets pinged off that tractor like hailstones off a tin roof. Two shells hit the water twenty yards off the port side and sent up regular geysers. I swept the beach [Baird had a machine gun], just to keep the bastards down as much as possible. Can't figure how I didn't get it in the head or something.

"We were 100 yards in now and the enemy fire was awful damn intense and gettin' worse. They were knockin' boats out left and right. A tractor'd get hit, stop, and burst into flames, with men jumping out like torches. The water here was only about three feet deep, just covering the coral reefs that the tractor'd bounce onto and over. Bullets ricocheted off the coral and up under the tractor. It must've been one of these bullets that got the driver. The boat lurched and I looked in the cab and saw him slumped over, dead. The lieutenant jumped in and pulled the driver out, and drove, himself, till he got hit.

"That happened about thirty yards offshore. A shell struck the boat. The concussion felt like a big fist—Joe Louis maybe—had smacked me right in the face. Seemed to make my face swell up. Knocked me down and sort of stunned me for a moment. I shook my head. Shrapnel was pinging all around. Nicked the hell out of my face and hands. One piece, about an inch long, tore into my back. A fella later pulled it out onshore. I looked around. My assistant, a private with a Mexican name, who was feeding my gun, had his pack and helmet blown right off. He was crumpled up beside me, with his head forward and in the back of it was a hole I could put my fist in. I started to shake him and he fell right on over.

"Guys were sprawled all over the place," said Baird. "I looked across at my buddy who was only five feet from me. He was on his back and his face was all bloody and he was holding his hand over his face and mumbling something. Our boat was stopped, and they were laying lead to us from a pillbox like holy hell. Everybody seemed stunned, so I yelled, 'Let's get the hell outa here!' I grabbed my carbine and an ammunition box and stepped over a couple of fellas laying there and put my hand on the side so's to roll over into the water. I didn't want to put my head up. The bullets were pouring at us like a sheet of rain. . . . Only about a dozen of the twenty-five went over the side with me, and only about four of us ever got evacuated."

The first three waves, riding Alligators, could not move off the narrow beach. Pinned down, they lay at the base of the coconut-log and coral-block seawall unable to advance or retreat. A murderous storm of bullets and shrapnel pelted across the strip and out to the reef where the carcasses of twenty disabled amtracs and a pair of LCVPs loaded with dead and wounded piled up. The tide stubbornly refused to rise sufficiently for LCVPs with tanks and artillery to navigate the coral ridge. The Marines ashore could attack pillboxes only with their small arms, a few flamethrowers, grenades, and blocks of TNT fashioned into pole charges. One Marine special outfit, an elite Scout-Sniper Platoon led by Lt. William Deane Hawkins, somehow went on the offensive. The thirty-four leathernecks, sharpshooters, and experts in close combat, shot numerous snipers from their perches in trees and blasted those concealed in foxholes.

Deane Hawkins, as Sherrod knew him, had attended the Texas College of Mines before the war, married, and divorced before he enlisted as a private around Christmas of 1941. "Hawk" to the troops, he won a battlefield commission in the Solomons and at twenty-nine was among the oldest of the junior officers. He had told Sherrod, "We're going in first. We are going to wipe every last one of the bastards off that pier and out from under that pier before they have a chance to pick off the first wave." But although the Scout-Sniper Platoon eliminated defenders far beyond their own limited number, they could not prevent the carnage inflicted upon the first waves. The Hawk continued to fight even after being wounded by shrapnel. He reportedly shrugged off medical treatments, "I came here to kill Japs: I didn't come here to be evacuated."

The LCVPs bearing 37mm cannons could not pass the reef and were forced to wait until nightfall to make their approach. Sherman tanks, disgorged at the outcrop, climbed over that natural barrier and through three or four feet of water. Eleven of them rattled onto the beach and added their firepower to that of the beleaguered invaders.

Sherrod, scheduled to accompany the fifth wave, climbed into an LCVP. He peeked over the ramp even as water splashed over the bow and to his dismay saw very few boats on the beach. A naval officer came alongside and announced they would transfer to an amtrac in order to get through the shallows. Combat soldiers boarded the first Alligator before a second craft took the remainder of the men and Sherrod close enough to hike the last several hundred yards.

"We started wading," said Sherrod. "No sooner had we hit the water than the Japanese really opened up on us. There must have been five or six of these machine guns concentrating their fire on us—there was no nearer target in the water at the time—which meant several hundred bullets per man. I don't believe there was one of the fifteen [in his group] who wouldn't have sold his chances for an additional twenty-five dollars added to his life-insurance policy. It was painfully slow, wading in such deep water. We had seven hundred yards to walk slowly into that machine-gun fire, looming into larger targets as we rose onto higher ground. I was scared, as I had never been scared before. But my head was clear . . . I recalled that psychologists say fear in battle is a good thing; it stimulates the adrenal glands and heavily loads the blood supply with oxygen."

Sherrod and a few companions crept to comparative safety beneath a pier that jutted out into the sea, then scrambled the final distance over an expanse of twenty feet of sand and brown-and-green coral, the width of the beachhead. Nearby lay the dead driver of an Alligator, a Marine whom Sherrod learned had only recently married a girl in New Zealand. From behind a beached amtrac he watched as "a Jap shell hit directly on an LCV that was bringing many Marines ashore. The explosion was terrific and parts of the boat flew in all directions. Then there were many Marines swimming in the water. Two pairs of corspmen brought two more dead men and placed them beside the dead boy who had been married to a girl from Wellington."

He saw a sniper's bullet go through the helmet of a nearby leatherneck but the only wound was a scratch where the helmet was torn off the Marine's head. "Another Marine walked briskly along the beach. Again there was a shot. The Marine spun all the way around and fell to the ground, dead. From where he lay, a few feet away, he looked up at us. Because he had been shot squarely through the temple his eyes bulged out in horrific surprise at what had happened to him, although it was impossible that he could ever have known what hit him."

Sherrod labeled this the most gruesome sight he had yet seen. Many good reporters like Ernie Pyle, out of delicacy or regard for the censors, ordinarily never detailed the agonizing nature of the wounds made by white-hot, jagged pieces of shrapnel traveling at tremendous speed when they ripped into bodies; nor the excruciating pain of burns from napalm, oil, and gasoline fires aboard ships; nor the terrible trauma to human organs from a stream of machine-gun bullets.

At Tarawa Sherrod recorded only an inkling of the horrors. "The number of dead lined up beside the stalled headquarters amtrac grew steadily. But the procession of the wounded seemed many times greater. There went a stretcher with a Marine whose leg had been nearly torn off; another had been hit in the buttocks by a 13mm bullet or a 20mm shell—a man's fist could have been thrust into the jagged hole; another was pale as death from the loss of much blood—his face seemed to be all bones and yellowish-white skin and he was in great pain."

The delicacy in describing the killing extended only partially to enemy casualties. Sherrod reported that immediately after the sniper felled the grinning Marine, the Japanese soldier was flushed from his dugout by TNT and then, as he ran, a flamethrower caught him. ". . . the Jap flared up like a piece of celluloid. He was dead instantly but the bullets in his cartridge belt exploded for a full sixty seconds after he had been charred almost to nothingness."

In a huge shell hole that served as a command post, Sherrod heard the senior officer order the Marines crouched around them, "You men, get on up front. They need you out there." The correspondent watched a few men pick up their weapons and go over the seawall, "singly and in two and threes, but many were reluctant to move."

By the end of the first day, 5,000 Marines were on the island with an estimated 1,500 killed or wounded. The Navy warships had continued to fire missions, and carrier aircraft also struck at the defenders. While the Marines held their positions, the first 75mm pack artillery began to land during the night along with medical supplies, water, and ammunition. Reinforcements straggled in. The Japanese, notoriously skilled in night attacks might have tried to eliminate the beachhead, only 300 yards wide at most places. However, the constant barrages from the battleships, cruisers, and destroyers, plus what the planes unleashed, and the small arms and explosives of the ground forces, had destroyed the communications links between the Nipponese commander and his units. Half of his force was now dead or wounded.

To Col. David Shoup, in his sand shell-hole CP, the issue remained in doubt as the sun rose. He radioed a number of "imperative" messages calling for ammunition, water, rations, medical supplies, and evacuation of the wounded. Sherrod, on the scene, reported, "Colonel Shoup is nervous. The telephone shakes in his hand. 'We are in a mighty tight spot,' he is saying. Then he lays down the phone and turns to me, 'Division has just asked me whether we've got enough troops to do the job. I told them no. They are sending the 6th Marines, who will be landing right away.'"

Word circulated about Deane Hawkins. A lieutenant recounted to Sherrod, "He is a madman. He cleaned out six machine-gun nests with two to six Japs in each nest. I'll never forget the picture of him standing on that amtrac, riding around with a million bullets a minute whistling by his ears, just shooting Japs." But in addition to the shrapnel of the previous day, he was hit twice by bullets, and loss of blood from the three wounds would eventually kill him.

The 6th Marine Regiment, building on the gains achieved by their predecessors, forged ahead. By four o'clock in the afternoon, Shoup's spirits had lifted and he announced, "We are winning." Terrible as the losses to the invaders, the defenders could not match the manpower and firepower thrown at them. "On the third day," said Sherrod, "the question was not, 'How long will it take to kill them all?' but 'How few men can we expect to lose before killing the rest of the Japs?'" Without letup, the deluge of shot, shell, and fire ravished the dwindling enemy.

Aware of impending doom, the last radio message from the garrison said, "Our weapons have been destroyed and from now on everyone is attempting a final charge . . . May Japan exist for ten thousand years!" On that third night, bands of survivors staged suicidal attacks that were repulsed with everything from artillery to bayonets. Seventy-five hours after the first leathernecks waded and crawled onto the thin strip of beach, Betio was declared "secured." Some killing continued; holdouts, hidden in bunkers or bypassed, potshotted unwary leathernecks before they were eliminated. A number blew themselves up rather than surrender. The official totals for Americans were 685 killed, 77 who died of wounds, 169 missing, and about 2,100 wounded. Conquest of the remaining bits and pieces of coral that composed the Tarawa atoll brought additional casualties, albeit on a much lesser scale than Betio.

The bittersweet taste of victory turned to ashes less than twenty-four hours after Betio became "secure." Because the conquest of Makin lasted four days instead of one, the naval task force had remained on station in the nearby waters, rather than steaming away from any Japanese submarines that might lurk in the area. In the early-morning hours of 24 November, the escort carrier *Liscome Bay,* in the company of some other vessels, prowled the area. The thin, four-ship screen around the *Liscome Bay* included the new destroyer *Franks.* Radar detected bogeys, unidentified aircraft, and the admiral in charge dispatched the *Franks* to investigate, punching a hole in the protection for the task force's three carriers.

Another radar contact registered a surface vessel but that blip vanished, indicating either the presence of a submarine that had just dived or perhaps a false image. The convoy started to execute a planned maneuver just as the *Franks* spotted a light on the water. Later investigation revealed that an enemy airplane had dropped a floating flare to advise a Japanese sub of nearby targets. At 0513 a torpedo ripped the *Liscome Bay* midships. From a distance of some two or three miles, Michael Bak, on the bridge of the *Franks,* saw a gigantic explosion of fire soar into the sky as the initial detonation of the torpedo ignited the aircraft bombs stowed in the carrier's hold. Fragments of steel, clothing, and human flesh showered the deck of the battleship *New Mexico* almost a mile away. Little more than twenty minutes later, the shattered hulk sank. "It was just like putting a candle out," said Bak. "The ball of fire was snuffed out as the ship sank. We were just dumbfounded. That's the first time we experienced the horrors of war. I think it sort of scared everybody. They just sort of felt, 'My gosh, this is for real.' We knew it was a lot of men lost because of the way the ship blew up and looked like a ball of fire. It happened so fast."

In fact, 642 officers and men went down with the carrier; only a hundred or so fewer than died wresting Betio from the determined Japanese. Among those who perished was Dorie Miller, the African-American steward who shot down a pair of enemy planes at Pearl Harbor. In the segregated Navy, he died still a food handler.

For all the bloodshed in the Gilberts, the Nimitz braintrust coveted much more highly the Marshall Islands, in particular Kwajalein and Enewetak. The ultimate plan went under the heading of Operation Flintlock. Mindful of the experiences at Tarawa, Richmond K. Turner issued a paper that prescribed considerably heavier advance bombardment from the sea and air. He also demanded increased training to ensure getting one's shells' and bombs' worth. Submarines, which had been invaluable in collecting intelligence for the invasion of the Gilberts, performed the same service in the Marshalls. Reconnaissance flights from the new U.S. air base on Betio, named for Deane Hawkins, brought detailed photographs enabling the strategists to plot the attack more precisely; a small return for the high investment of life at Tarawa. Underwater demolition teams made their debut, swimming in to check out the shoreline defense systems. Flintlock mounted an assault force of 54,000 as against half that number in Galvanic. Amtracs, without which Galvanic might have totally flopped, became a top production priority. The latest models added armor plate to protect drivers and machine guns for inshore fire support. One version carried no troops but its turret, equipped with a 37mm cannon and machine guns, acted as a kind of seagoing light tank. Following the lead of the RAF and the Atlantic air arm, the Pacific fleet laced its fighters with rockets to strafe beach emplacements.

The shipyards in the States had been busy; Task Force 58, commanded by VAdm. Marc A. Mitscher, boasted twelve carriers, eight new battleships, and a host of cruisers, destroyers, and lesser vessels. From the flight decks, 650 planes were available for Flintlock. The attack on Kwajalein actually involved not only that coral atoll, but also two smaller ones in the vicinity, Roi and Namur. The 4th Marine Division drew the Roi and Namur while the Army's 7th Division, bloodied during the Aleutian campaign, swapping its parkas for lighter-weight khaki, struck at Kwajalein.

The hapless garrison on Kwajalein could do nothing to prevent the enemy from occupying islands that flanked the main objective. On Enubuj, the 7th Division installed forty-eight pieces of artillery that quickly zeroed in on Kwajalein. Simultaneously, missiles delivered from the battleship-stuffed fleet rocked boomerang-shaped Kwajalein for two days. Unlike many other amphibious operations, Flintlock proceeded with almost paradelike precision. The Navy and Army smoothly coordinated supply and troop buildup.

Samuel Eliot Morison, commissioned by Navy buff President Roosevelt for the purpose of providing an eye-witness history of seagoing operations, frequently displayed prejudice toward the brother service. He had been acutely critical of the 27th Division at Makin and only slightly less so in recounting the Aleutian campaign of the 7th Division. Describing Kwajalein operations, he credited the 7th Division with professional skill but nevertheless held to his bias. He noted that by the afternoon, while the Japanese were admittedly putting up well-organized resistance, "the troops had advanced only 950 yards . . . The 11,000 men ashore by 1600 might have rushed the enemy lines, but that was not Army technique. In contrast to the Marines, the Army was taught not to advance until all possible fire had been brought to bear on the path ahead of the troops."

Throughout the war, the "experts" debated the philosophies behind the operations of the Marines and the Army. Leatherneck tacticians insisted that plunging head-on against the foe which, while the approach piled up dead and wounded initially, resulted in fewer men lost over time than the more gradual approach of the Army.

Bob MacArthur, as a 7th Division engineer officer, participated at Kwajalein. "The assault was a classic one on fortified positions. I went in on the third wave and there was no opposition at first [testifying to the improved preinvasion barrage]. We worked with small teams of infantry. They kept the ports [for pillboxes] covered with small-arms fire and we had these seven-second fuses on the fifty-pound satchel charges—dynamite [another improvement over the improvised means at Tarawa]. We'd blow doors open and then the flamethrowers would come in through the smoke and dust. It was all over in six days."

While this part of Flintlock required less than a week, only 265 enemy soldiers were taken prisoner; the remainder of the roughly 4,000 fought to their death. American casualties numbered nearly 2,000, with 372 KIA.

A truly intensive bombardment by battleships and aviation, almost triple in tonnage to what fell upon Betio, blasted Roi and Namur, devastating the defenders. The first Marines ashore met enemy soldiers still disoriented from the concussions. On Namur, a Marine platoon led by Lt. Saul Stein crept up to a large blockhouse. One leatherneck placed a shaped explosive against a wall blowing a sizeable hole. Suddenly, Japanese soldiers rushed out of the place. Stein ordered satchel charges thrown into the inside. The concrete building erupted, with enough force to hurl a fighter plane overhead a thousand feet higher. The Marines had detonated a warehouse of torpedo warheads. The explosion killed forty Marines, including Stein and most of his men, while flying debris wounded another sixty.

On Roi and Namur, the Japanese soldiers stubbornly fought back from their wrecked blockhouses and rubble. TNT, flamethrowers, and other assorted weapons vanquished them. The entire operation required little more than a day. During the brief but deadly twenty-six and one-half hours, three Marines won the Medal of Honor, posthumously.

The greatest prize in the Marshalls was Enewetak, a rough circle of some forty islets that surrounded a lagoon twenty-one by seventeen miles. It was capable of serving as a staging area for assaults on two major enemy strongholds, Truk and Saipan. A joint Marine-Army assemblage of 10,000 sailed to the atoll and again the outnumbered, outgunned Japanese succumbed to a coordinated assault by ships, planes, tanks, and troops with massive firepower.

During this period, the 37th Division on Bougainville carved out a fifteen-mile-long, seven-mile-wide stretch as a safe haven for supplies, a hospital, radio station, and large airfield. Once the Americans established strong perimeters with open fields of fire and barbed-wire barriers, they assumed a defensive stance. "It became a waiting game," said Cletus Schwab, a lieutenant in the 37th, "because we knew the Japanese forces would try to drive us into the ocean."

Around Empress Augusta Bay, the Americal Division similarly fortified its perimeter. Matters reached a crescendo in March. Bill McLaughlin, as a private with the Americal Division's 21st Recon Company, recalled, "They attacked and we had a grand fight as they piled up some thousands of bodies on the wire, penetrating to within a half mile of the sea. Every man in the Army was fighting them that day and they buried them with bulldozers when it finally ended."

In a two-day battle, the enemy lost as many as 4,000. Henceforth, those Japanese still on Bougainville could only mount small-scale operations while a combination of Americans, Australians, Fiji Scouts, and the New Guinea "Police Boys" gradually wore them down. For the first time in World War II, African Americans who had been trained as combat soldiers but shunted to labor and service duties, confronted the enemy. Private First Class Thomas E. Lewis left the safety of a tank to rescue three wounded GIs; he was hit by a mortar burst. He received a Purple Heart and a Silver Star. Subsequently, the black soldiers from the segregated 93d Division and the 24th Infantry Regiment, except for a few more encounters, returned to menial tasks.

The Army Air Corps, in its efforts to support the ground troops, however, still labored with substandard weapons. The P-40 had always been at a disadvantage against the Japanese fighters and while the P-38 provided a powerful tool, the debut of the P-39 Airacobra added nothing useful to the arsenal. William Turner, who flew one for the 36th Fighter Squadron, called it a decent enough strafing plane with its four .30-caliber machine guns in the wings, two .50s firing through the propeller, and a 37mm cannon that shot through the propeller hub. "You could fire the wings, the .50-calibers, or the cannon, or any combination, or all of them at once," said Turner. "It was awesome firepower but the .30s were too light.

"The Allison 1150-horsepower engine sat behind the pilot with a ten-inch drive shaft running from the engine to the gear box in the nose." Some said that made an uncomfortable cockpit. "The engine had no supercharger, making poor performance at high altitudes. The engine in the back made flying at stalling speeds tricky—controls were very sensitive. It was not suited for the Pacific but was the tool at hand and used."

Turner's tour of 250 combat missions illustrates the changeover to more effective weapons. He did his first 61 in the Airacobra; then progressed to the P-47, in which he completed another 54, before finishing with 135 in P-38s, with which he knocked down 3 enemy planes. By 1944, the Japanese ability to trade punches with Americans on an equal basis in the sky was over.

24
Burmese Days and Skip Bombing

The China-Burma-India theater was a backwater for the American war effort, particularly in terms of ground forces. Operating on the theory that the Chinese had abundant if untrained and ill-equipped manpower, the U.S. supplied advisors, weapons, and direction. From the beginning, overall Allied command dealt with a roily stew of factions—the forces of Chiang Kai-shek, internally wracked by corruption and a war-lord philosophy; the Chinese Communists with their own agenda; the American Army and its rambunctious junior partner, the Air Corps; and the British with their interests of empire. The highest-ranking American, Gen. Joseph Stilwell, nominal commander, as chief of staff to Chiang Kai-shek, thought poorly of his patron and seldom spoke favorably about anyone.

Running the British units in Burma was a highly unorthodox soldier, Gen. Orde Wingate. His prewar background of counterinsurgency against Arabs seeking to oust the English from Palestine, his open support for undercover Zionists, and a brief covert job rallying Ethiopians against Mussolini's armies, apparently qualified him as the man to direct guerrilla-style operations in Burma against the Japanese. Bearded, careless of uniform, and with a corruscating tongue toward even his superiors, Wingate had developed the "Chindits" into an effective fighting force. The U.S. Joint Chiefs of Staff met Wingate at a Quebec Conference in 1943 and he impressed them sufficiently for Hap Arnold to offer air support to the Chindits, to the chagrin of Stilwell.

The specially trained Chindit Brigade of 9,000, drawn from a variety of units including native Britons, Ghurkas from India, and Burmese, had spent many months in action. They hiked deep into the jungles of Burma where they conducted hit-and-run raids and fought off the Japanese columns seeking to block passage between India and China, the lifeline for the Chinese armies.

Flip Cochran, rotated back to the States from teaching aerial combat to newcomers in the Mediterranean theater, visited Hap Arnold, the Air Force chief, to correct an error about the newest fighter plane, the P-47, just being introduced in Europe. He said he told him, "There's a misconception. I hear from England that the P-47 will only fight at high altitude.

These kids are being told and believe they won't ever fight down near the ground . . . below 12,000 feet, because they have this wonderful super-charger. I said any airplane with eight .50-caliber machine guns in it is go-ing to be used on the ground." Cochran lectured Arnold on the need for instruction on how to properly school new fliers in the virtues and capa-bilities of the P-47.

Arnold listened politely but then proposed that Cochran take command of the air group that would work with the Chindits and Merrill's Maraud-ers. Cochran balked; he preferred to go to Europe to work with the first squadrons flying P-47s, including his good friend Hubert Zemke, already an ace. He called the other assignment, "some doggone offshoot, side-alley fight over in some jungle in Burma that doesn't mean a damn thing." When Cochran argued further and remarked, "It's my destiny and I think it's my life," an exasperated Arnold became "a little irked." According to Cochran, he growled, "I don't know what kind of an Air Force office I'm running here when guys come in and tell me they are not going to do something . . . You are going."

Arnold made it plain that Cochran had no choice and the pilot yielded, "Where and when?" The Air Corps boss answered, "That will come later. I want to get that other monkey in here." The "simian" in question was John Alison, as outspoken as Cochran. The pair received orders to lead the 1st Air Commando Task Force, designed to support Wingate's operation.

Cochran explained, "He [Wingate] would effect long-range forays into enemy territory. He used mules as transport and the jungle as protection. They would get in, disrupt the enemy, and take over whole territories. He called it 'long-range penetration.' He felt that if he had some air support, it would make him more effective. We were told by General Arnold to study General Wingate, find out all we could, his ideas, his plans, how we could support him. Originally the idea was light airplanes, because Wingate had brought that up with Churchill, Arnold, and Lord Louis Mountbatten at the Quebec meeting.

"Wingate had said, 'if you could pull out my wounded; because when we get a man wounded, we can't carry him, because he becomes a burden. We have to prop him up against a tree, give him a gun, or let him stay there and give him money and stuff, hoping that the natives would take care of him. Our attrition rate is terrible. When a man gets wounded, his chances with this kind of warfare aren't very good.'" Operations were also hampered by the requirement that the Chindits carry on their bodies, or their mules, sup-plies and equipment which, when expended, forced the troops to withdraw for refurbishing.

Alison remembered Arnold's instructions slightly differently on two oc-casions. "He gave us a free hand in choosing our equipment, and his only directive to us was, 'I want to see the United States Army Air Forces play a large part in Wingate's coming operations.'" In another official interview, Alison reported Arnold as saying, "I am giving you 200 L-5 and L-1-type aircraft [single engine planes ordinarily used for liaison and observation]. I want you to go in there and take out General Wingate's wounded." Allison added, "Then with a twinkle in his eye he said, 'I not only want you to do that . . . but I want the USAAF to spearhead General Wingate's operations.'"

After conferring with Wingate, and having personally seen the mountainous terrain, the absence of roads, and the streams from the air, the Americans identified movement on the ground as the principle difficulty. "The obvious answer was to move the troops by air," said Alison. "We asked for gliders and transports and light planes. We knew there was not enough fighter aviation in that theater, nor bomber aviation to take care of the present commitments and also to give our force the protection we wanted them to have." The fledgling 1st Air Commando Task Force eventually included a squadron of P-51s, another of B-25s, along with roughly 100 gliders with seventy-five pilots, plus a squadron of troop carriers [C-47s] capable of parachuting men and supplies or towing the gliders, and about 100 of the L-1s and L-5s.

Wingate still thought in terms of trekking to the interior but at a meeting with Mountbatten and him, Cochran boldly announced that the U.S. airmen would fly the brigade into Burma. Alison, present at the conference, remarked later that Cochran had nothing to back up his word other than his reputation. An operation of this nature had never been attempted and the assembled strategists seriously doubted him. However, the Americans worked out the details and conducted a large-scale maneuver that convinced the British leaders.

"General Wingate was an officer with vision," said Alison. "We had no sooner sold him on the idea of moving the troops by air than he immediately began to expand upon our operation and press us to do more. Instead of flying in a small percentage of his troops as first planned, General Wingate called on the Troop Carrier Command to carry almost his entire force after the troops of the Air Commando Force landed and built airdromes.

"On the night of 5 March 1944, we started out from India with our force of gliders. These gliders were loaded with bulldozers, tractors, jeeps, mules, soldiers of General Wingate's forces to guard the area in which we were to land, and members of the Air Commando Force to direct the building of airdromes."

Cochran recalled one unusual problem. "How were these animals [the mules] going to ride? They [the Chindits] depended a great deal on them. [The mule] was their mobility in the jungle. Going along in the jungle, you'd be within a hundred yards of the enemy and the enemy wouldn't quite know exactly where you were. The soldiers were trained to strap all their military utensils, everything so they didn't clank. If the mule brayed or hee-hawed, he would give you away. The poor fellows had to be 'debrayed.' [Severance of their vocal chords. Merrill's second in command, Charles Hunter, flat-out refused to silence the animals used for the American operation Galahad, insisting the only pleasure the sexless mules enjoyed was braying.] We had these mute mules to put in gliders and aircraft and we didn't know how they were going to take to that sort of thing. We knew something of the nature of the mule and we were a little apprehensive. We had all manner of wild schemes of how we would do this. We searched the outfit to find any farm boy that had any experience or knew anything about mules. We found a couple of our guys who had mules on a farm. We had attacked the problem as though it were something you would have to sit down from square one and design something, as though it were one of these terrible, insurmountable things. This kid just cut that all out and said, 'Why don't we just try walking them in and see what they do.' Lo and behold, the mule took to it just like they take to everything else. It didn't concern them one bit. We asked the mule to go in the glider. He walked in and he stood there. We did take some precautions. We had a mule tender to go along and he had a ready revolver to clunk the guy between the eyes if he started tearing the glider apart. It wasn't necessary at all. The mules took off and enjoyed the ride, landed and did nothing. As the guys in the glider said, 'They even banked on the turns.'"

Alison noted, "We were to land in areas far in the enemy's rear which had been previously selected and carefully photographed and mapped. Elaborate plans had been made so that nothing would go wrong. The gliders took off just at dusk so as to cross enemy lines after dark. We had selected two sites; half our gliders to go into each and build an airport for transport planes at each site. Just prior to takeoff, photoreconnaissance showed that the Japanese had gotten wind of our plan and completely blocked with logs and trees one of the jungle clearings. Plans were immediately changed, and all gliders were [routed to] the other area [code named Broadway] and if the enemy really had gotten hold of our plans to land in such force we would be able to overwhelm him." Cochran said the enemy action at one place suggested the possibility of an ambush at the second.

In sharing the command of the American air unit, Cochran grounded himself and assumed the administrative duties while Alison, as the hands-on operations chief, flew missions. He described the first insertion of Chindits into Burma by air, probably the most difficult glider tow ever tried. "There was a three-quarter moon shining, and although this was good light for night flying, the haze was bad over the mountains and over Burma, which made it difficult to see the planes from the gliders that they were towing. The DC-3 [C-47] had to climb 8,500 feet to cross the mountains through turbulent air on a flight into enemy territory that lasted three hours and fifteen minutes." Back at Wingate's headquarters ground observers flashed word of red flares, the distress signal for downed gliders. Three tow ships returned to base with the disconsolate news that the ropes to their birds had snapped, meaning a total of six gliders lost even before passing over the border into Burma. Alerted to the broken lines, the home base messaged the convoy of transports and gliders to fly "high tow," a maneuver that stationed the gliders above the towship and less likely to break off.

Alison said, "The gliders were overloaded with men and machinery; parachutes were not worn. Every pilot left our home base knowing that once he was committed to this flight the airplane that was towing him did not have enough gasoline to turn around and tug his glider all the way back home. Every pilot knew that no matter what the outcome of this venture, he was going to be deposited 200 miles [officially the distance was 165] behind the enemy lines and if everything did not go right, 200 miles is an awfully long way to walk through jungle country. The glider flight was led by Capt. William H. Taylor, who trained our pilots for many months for this operation. His was the first glider to hit the ground; two gliders were towed behind each airplane. I flew behind the second airplane to reach the landing ground.

"From the photographs we had estimated two logical places on the field where the Japanese might have machine guns. The first two gliders were down and their crews out immediately and on the dead run for these two points. Fortunately, the enemy machine guns were not there, and as my glider came over the field I saw the green flare which meant that the first two gliders were not being fired upon and my landing could be accomplished without that harassing thought. The pilot on the end of the other rope from the airplane cut, and I followed right behind him. He came into the field and had to purposely crash his glider to keep from running into the first one [there]. My landing was uneventful. I have the solution for successful glider landing at night; I use the close-your-eyes-and-pray method."

The pathfinder gliders, first to touch down, set out flare pots to facilitate succeeding waves of gliders. However, the field proved far less accessible than expected. For many years, the local people had logged teak and during the wet season, slid the huge logs across the ground down to a river. Over time the technique gouged deep ruts that elephant grass covered, making the trenches invisible in aerial photographs or reconnaissance. "They formed perfect glider traps," said Alison, "and there was no way to avoid them. The gliders arrived overhead in large numbers and when a glider starts down there is no way to stop it. As each one hit the trenches the landing gears would come off and the gliders would go in a heap. We tried to arrange the lights to spread the gliders all over the field to avoid collisions, but this was impossible—they were coming in too fast to change directions and glider after glider piled into one another in the landing area.

"It was dark, and standing on the field you would try to shout to the gliders as they whizzed by at 80 to 90 miles an hour to give the pilot some directions after he hit the ground. You would try to get the injured out of the wrecked gliders, but there just wasn't any way to stop it. You had to be on the alert at all times for gliders rushing down the field and be mighty quick to get out of the way. You don't hear a glider coming toward you—it doesn't make any noise; then all of a sudden it's on the ground and you hear the rumble of its wheels and you look out into the darkness and try to tell where it is going to go. There is not much use starting to run until you know that. It was a dramatic evening but we lived through it, got our equipment down, and got our men down without too many casualties." Actually, 31 men were killed at Broadway, including Capt. Patrick Casey, the engineering officer expected to clear debris and construct the airstrip. Another 30 individuals suffered serious injuries. Only 31 of the original 68 gliders launched actually reached Broadway and virtually every one was beyond salvage. A handful went down in enemy territory. But there were more than 500 men, 3 mules, and 30 tons of equipment on hand.

Realization of the hazards at Broadway forced those already there to send a radio message using the prearranged code to halt all flights, "Soya Link, Soya Link, Soya Link!" [The British hated an ersatz sausage manufactured from soy beans.] "The entire second wave of gliders was stopped by radio and returned to base," said Alison. "In the first wave we had enough equipment to build an airfield and it wasn't necessary to jeopardize other mens' lives as our patrols reported no Japanese nearby. The next morning, the field was a mass of wreckage. Looking at it, it was impossible to believe we could put an airfield there. I talked to our engineer [Casey's deputy], Lt. Robert Brackett, and said, 'Can you make an airfield in this place?' He replied, 'Yes, sir, I think I can.' and I said, 'Well, how long will it take?' He replied, 'If I have it done by this afternoon, will that be too late?' He wasn't just kidding— that night the first DC-3 landed at Broadway at 7:20, and altogether sixty-five sorties arrived that night bringing in fighting troops, mules, machine guns, and equipment. From then on it was just another operation—taking transports off from India at night and landing them 200 miles behind enemy lines at night. Before long we had quite a sizable army."

Indeed, less than one week after the first glider bounced to a halt at Broadway, more than 9,000 Chindits had flown in and then moved out to hit the Japanese. Eight days after the Air Commandos first arrived, the Japanese struck at Broadway with fighters. Fortunately, a flight of Spitfires happened to be on hand and they shot down half of the attackers and drove off the others. The success at Broadway inspired the creation of two similar installations behind the enemy lines, Piccadilly and Chowringhee, employing the same technique of gliderborne men and equipment.

The Japanese quickly recognized the threat of these air bases. Not only had they magnified the capabilities of the Chindits to disrupt supply lines and mount guerrilla attacks upon the Imperial Army, but also they enabled aircraft to fly offensive missions deep in Japanese-controlled territory. Said Cochran, "They had to come in and try to get them out. There was hand-to-hand fighting to protect these bases. Both sides knew how to jungle fight. Many a time we would land airplanes in there and the Japs would be right on the end of the strips. There would be a gun or two, a party of Japanese the British hadn't been able to get out of there. You'd be taking an airplane off and someone would say to you, 'Hey, Colonel, when you go out, don't turn left, because if you do, they'll get you.' It was that close, that kind of warfare. It surprised our guys but you got so used to it that it became a way of life. At night you didn't sleep too well, because you knew there were crawly things running around and that there were Japs who could crawl right into your place, throw grenades, and start shooting up the place.

"One night we had a DC-3 run a little too long on the strip and in trying to turn around, he got stuck. He and his crew got out and started to walk back to get help. They hadn't walked very far until their whole airplane blew up. The enemy was that close they sneaked in and planted explosives."

Alison also introduced the helicopter to combat. Having heard that the first few of these machines had come off the production line, Alison plotted to add them to the 1st Air Commando Task Force. While engaged in England, and then in the Soviet Union on the Lend-Lease program, he had met Harry Hopkins, the confidant and aidè to the president. Hearing of Alison's assignment to the China-Burma-India theater, Hopkins invited him for a chat. Alison seized the opportunity to ask for the helicopters, even as the Air Force brass tried to figure how best to deploy them. When Hap Arnold demanded of a bemused Cochran how these suddenly became part of his command, Cochran said he responded, "General, you just have to know the right people!"

Cochran said, "We didn't use them as tricks. We used them in the jungle for serious business. They were terribly underpowered. But they were effective for what we used them for. If you got a pilot in them, that was about their capable load. Then you would add another person. A couple of times we were able to get two wounded out at a time by using a stretcher on a sling attached on the side. We pulled out and documented the saving of eighteen lives that we couldn't have gotten out in any other manner."

Perhaps nowhere during World War II was there more internal strife than in the China-Burma-India theater. At Quebec, in an effort to establish a firm chain of command, Mountbatten had been named Supreme Allied Com-

mander Southeast Asia. The highest-ranking American on the scene, Lt.
Gen. Joseph Stilwell had a pathological dislike for those he continually called
"Limeys." He was equally disdainful of most other racial and ethnic groups;
his diary is sprinkled with references to "frogs," "niggers," "coons," "wops,"
"gooks," and "chinks." He considered the British effete, snobbish, and reluctant warriors. Mountbatten professed his dismay when Stilwell said to
him, "Gee, Admiral. I like working with you! You are the only Limey I have
met who wants to fight." When Lord Louis praised Gen. Sir Harold Alexander as a model soldier, "[Stilwell] staggered me by saying, 'General Alexander was a coward and retreated all the way and never stood and fought.' I
pointed out that Stilwell had retreated all the way and that nobody so far
had called him a coward." Mountbatten was referring to the 1942 defeat of
Stilwell in Burma, a campaign in which the Japanese forces chased the Americans and their Chinese soldiers out of the country, shutting off the supply
route from India. The only way to get vital materials to the armies of Chiang Kai-shek was through the perilous airlift over the Himalayas, the fabled
"hump."

Stilwell sniped at and criticized not only the British but also Chiang. He
showed little interest in Chennault's Fourteenth Air Force or the potential
of the outfit led by Cochran and Alison. For the most part, Cochran and Alison got along famously with Mountbatten and Wingate. However, on one
occasion, Cochran lost his temper with the leader of the Chindits. Unknown
to the American, Wingate arranged for some RAF Spitfires to set down at
one of the airfields during daylight hours. "The worst thing to do would be
to land fighters on that field in the daytime and have the Japs see them.
You're just waving a red flag at a bull. He did it and don't you know the Japs
came in and got them and just about wiped them out. They got one guy who
was just taking off. They got one on the ground. They had to come in and
beat that place up and those airplanes were just like drawing flies. This in-
censed me probably more than anything ever had in my life. I felt Wingate
had betrayed me. I said, 'you do that anymore and we're off you. You did a
thing you shouldn't have and you doublecrossed us. You undercut us.' He
looked me straight in the eye and said, 'I did, didn't I.'

"That just about cut me off. Naturally I was fuming and I imagine my language wasn't that good. I learned later that the office was not soundproof.
The walls had ears, and I was told later that his whole staff and all the soldiers, everybody in the place, heard my tirade. I was accused of very bad man-
ners by those who didn't know the seriousness of it. I can see I did sound
like an arrogant Yank. We had a little bit of a different relationship after that,
but still a solid one, because we had it out.

"Wingate was man enough to [take criticism. He] brought in an aide and
he used his peculiar archaic words to the man who had a poised pad and

pencil, 'Take a screed to the Prime Minister of Great Britain . . .' Then he started out . . . to the Prime Minister, to Lord Louis Mountbatten, to General [J. W.] Slim [the British Army head in the CBI theater] to General Marshall, to General Arnold, and went all down the list. He read off a very concise signal of admission that he had done it, that he had been wrong and he apologized. Whether that ever got to the Prime Minister, Lord Louis, or General Arnold, I don't know, but it sure was a good show. It satisfied me, and I stormed out a little bit placated. I got those Spitfires the hell off that landing strip. We had been planning to put our P-51s there but we were going to fly them in late in the evening so the Japs wouldn't see them. During the night [we would] load them with bombs and do close support in the early morning, fly on back to the bases, stay out in the daytime so they would not be seen."

Ideally, the 3,000 in Merrill's Marauders would have been mated with Wingate's brigades, but Stilwell refused to allow the GIs to serve under the Briton. When that news reached Wingate he reacted in fine American style, ". . . tell General Stilwell he can take his Americans and stick 'em up his ass." The bitter relationships spilled over into crucial matters affecting the lives of those engaged in the fighting. Stilwell, rather than seek transport by air, marched Merrill's people deep into Burma in a flanking maneuver aimed at cutting off the Japanese long enough for slower-moving Chinese infantry and tanks to trap them. Aided by some native Kachin tribesmen, recruited by American officers of the Office of Strategic Services, and who provided excellent intelligence on the enemy, Galahad fought a sizable battle near the village of Walawabum repulsing an attempt by superior forces to break through.

Unfortunately, the main body of Chinese soldiers under Stilwell, only ten miles off, failed to exploit the momentary success of the Marauders. Hindered by poor communications, he exercised the same excessive caution he so often denounced in others, delaying marching orders until the enemy escaped the trap. A pattern developed in which the men of Galahad thrust themselves behind the now-withdrawing enemy but, on each occasion, there was no follow-up of the opportunities to crush the Japanese. Using the few 81mm mortars they packed, along with small arms and bayonets, the Americans inflicted severe losses, far above their own. Still, the campaign under wretched climactic conditions, the usual hostile microbes, and enemy fire, exacted a heavy toll upon the Americans.

"Those fellows took an awful beating," said Cochran. "The jungle got them and the Japs got them. In one of their early contacts with the enemy, they had a lot of guys hurt. They said, '[there's] Cochran's outfit. He has got some L-1s and L-5s. We'll just send him down here and he can start working for us. I said, 'No, I can't do that.'

"They said, what the hell, you're American Air Force guys and here our American guys are in there suffering and you're withholding a capability. I said, as I know my instructions, I am sent here as a project to support Wingate's penetration into Burma. That is my job. If I start using my airplanes and start losing them down there . . . by the time Wingate gets in position and I am needed there, I won't have the aircraft. I went back to the rule that I was a one-purpose outfit and was to hold my capability until the time it was to be used. Certainly those kids needed it. Hell, I wanted to do it as badly as anybody, but I also didn't want to break the orders given to me . . . Stratemeyer [Maj. Gen. George, head of the Eastern Air Command] said Cochran is right and he doesn't have to do that." In fact, the Galahad battle at Walawabum happened during the period when the Broadway field was being created.

With the big airfields in business, Wingate's people created small simple airstrips close to where the Chindits were warring. According to Cochran, "You would fly airplanes [the L-1s and L-5s] in and out of the strips. They would collect the wounded at the immediate site, come into the big bases of Chowringhee or Broadway, off-load, and go back with a replacement and some ammunition, and bring out another wounded. Then when the DC-3s came in at night with supplies or personnel or equipment, the wounded would go into the DC-3s and be taken to hospitals in the rear. Wingate's first request was more than adequately supplied. The wounded not only didn't lie in the jungle anymore to die, they were the best cared-for guys in the business. They would get out the same day and they'd be in hospitals.

"This was the very necessary and very proud work of those liaison guys. They were the beloved of the British soldier. I remember when I would go in, you had a load to take in and a load to take out. I remember bringing one kid whose leg was all shot up. I got him out and I've never seen such appreciation from that boy. There were many instances where the kids on stretchers, pretty well shot up, would kiss the hands of the pilot. We not only amazed them, but they were mighty proud to be associated with us, and a great camaraderie was set up between the forces. We admired each other."

The Americans had very little time to savor the successful combined operations with Wingate. His B-25 crashed, killing all aboard only three weeks after the establishment of Broadway. Within a few months Stilwell added the remnants of the Chindits to his command.

At the time of the campaign in Burma, the Air Corps was also assuming a more prominent role in the island campaigns of the South Pacific. Robert Smith, the offspring of Norwegian immigrants, a graduate of Bowdoin College, Maine, graduated as a pilot a few days after Pearl Harbor. Early in 1942 he sailed to Sydney, Australia, as a member of the 43d Bomb Group. "They had no aircraft for us. Most of the other pilots were in the ferry command."

Smith expected to fly B-17s but upon transfer to the 22d Bomb Group climbed into the cockpit of a B-26, the Martin Marauder, a plane with a somewhat dubious reputation. Crashes at the Florida training site led to the motto, "One a day in Tampa Bay." A two-engine, medium-range aircraft, the B-26 was characterized by a relatively smaller wing area. It became known as "the flying prostitute"—no visible means of support [lift].

Smith defended the B-26. "Limited support was given to our area of the war. Everything had to go to Europe. We had good mechanics and our B-26s were well maintained. We had excellent pilots. Unfortunately, the attrition rate was quite high, mostly due to combat losses. We flew B-26s for about nine months but then stood down because we had lost roughly over half our force. We were retrained and picked up B-25s. I had flown the short-wing model, the A. New B-26 B and C models were going to North Africa and Europe. I have a lot of respect for the B-26 because it was a very, very fine airplane but it was a tricky airplane to fly. I have flown the B-26 on one engine very successfully but on takeoff, if you lost an engine you had a problem."

Smith's early combat days illustrate the primitive state of tactical support in New Guinea. "The idea of a forward air controller [FAC], which we developed to a high degree during the Vietnam War, did not occur. We were never FACd. We had preplanned targets. Usually, it would be a section of the jungle marked out in grease pencil. We would bomb the target area from an initial point [IP]. We would usually come in off the coast and would have our IP and our course well identified. If we were supporting the military, they would fire mortar shells to identify by smoke flares the precise target."

Smith's group flew out of Australia and Port Moresby for its runs. "We would strike targets from one to three days, but we were bombed quite often by the Japanese. I recall one raid where there were something like eighty Betty bombers overhead. Unfortunately we had the P-40s and the P-39s and of course the Zeros knocked them off like flies because they couldn't get up high enough. We were escorted a few times but not very often because the B-26 was a little bit too fast for the fighters and, as a result, they had to burn too much fuel. We went more or less on our own.

"In the Bismarck Sea battle against Japanese, we bombed on several occasions Japanese destroyers, which were very difficult to hit because they were doing figure eights usually. [My squadron] had originally been a recon. We bombed airfields because you could see them and then see the results. There were some excellent missions flown. I think they got fifty-two aircraft at Wewak [a Japanese base] one day." Promoted to a staff position with the Fifth Air Force Bomber Command, Smith put in time as a pilot for both B-17s and B-24s.

Richard Ellis, like Smith, a 1930s college graduate [Dickinson], was drafted and immediately applied for flight training. Ellis flew B-25 submarine patrol out of Massachusetts after earning his wings, but then shipped out to the South Pacific and participated in the New Guinea campaign. "We were flying against the supply lines of the Japanese. There was a target, Wairopi Bridge, a rope bridge that swung over a gorge. Here we were trying to bomb something that was maybe three-feet wide from 18,000 or 20,000 feet. We dumped I don't know how many tons on that thing day after day."

He was amazed by the feat of the Australian 9th Division crossing the Owen Stanley Range, over which he flew on numerous occasions. "I had never seen any place quite like that, high mountains and deep, deep rain forests. I know it was so bad because I can remember some of them [the Aussies] coming back. When they left they were guys that were normal and healthy, but when they came back they were walking dead."

Ellis, like Smith, recalled the frustration because the American fighter planes could not compete with the enemy. "One day there was a big raid. There were P-39 fighters stationed on our strip. We could see the P-39s taking off and we headed for the slit trenches. They banged the hell out of us. We lost all of our aircraft except one or two of them. The P-39s were up against the Zeros and the P-39 was not an aircraft that could be used very well against the Zero. It wasn't an airplane that gave a lot of confidence against the Zero. I remember some of these fighter pilots coming back, and the tapes would still be on their guns. [They never could maneuver into position to fire.]

"We used to think of those enemy fighters as having first-class pilots, usually navy pilots. They were flying out of two bases on the north side, Lae and Salamaua. Once in a while we would get mixed up with them. One day, by ourselves we had just gotten over the other side of the mountains and were headed out to sea to do a little ocean surveillance and we got jumped by four Zeros. I saw the fanciest flying and the poorest gunnery I saw during the whole war.

"The first time we saw them, there was a flight of B-26s, about nine airplanes, headed up to Lae to bomb their base. These four fighters had a go at the B-26s and decided they were too tough and too many. They saw us sitting out there and said, 'Here's our meat for today.' Captain Klein [Ellis was copilot] put the aircraft into a fairly sharp descent altitude and those Zeros were all over us, coming in and rolling all the way through. I could see them out of the side and they would come up underneath us with their bellies up. We had a top and lower turret, a gunner in the top and the bottom turrets. How we didn't get the hell shot out of us, I don't know. I could see this guy come up underneath us and he was right on us. Our lower gunner just stitched him right down the belly. We nailed him. The other three sort of moved off, made a few feints at us like they were coming in again but never did. When we got down, we had been hit in only one place, one hole."

Dismayed by the poor results against enemy ships, the Air Corps, under the direction of Gen. George Kenney, revised its tactics and equipment. Ellis remembered, "One squadron of B-25s had been converted to the low-level B-25, where we had eight machine guns in the nose, two on each side, for a total of twelve .50-caliber machine guns. We flew those right down on the deck, ten or fifteen feet above the water. We would fly into the target, firing our guns and then would drop our bombs, which would have a four-to-five-second-delay fuse. You would drop the bomb and then before it went off you would have four seconds to get away. We used the technique for the first time at the Bismarck Sea battle."

Along with the increased gun power, the B-25s added racks to carry as many as six 100-pound bombs and smaller fragmentation explosives, all with delayed fuses, for what became known as "skip bombing." According to Ellis, "You would go in usually broadside to the ship. When you got within machine-gun range, you would strafe, which would help contain the flak from the ship. When you got close enough—this was all a matter of judgment; there wasn't any bombsight—you would drop the bomb, pull up over the ship and hope the bomb hit the water and skipped into the side of the boat. If you got close enough, you couldn't miss the boat. But you had to get really close. When you pulled up over the ship, there was a wrenching, you just heaved back on the controls. When you went over the ship, you immediately got down on the water again. You didn't have a lower gunner. You had a top gunner and he would strafe to the rear as you departed. It was very successful and great against merchant ships because they usually weren't very heavily armed. From then on we did everything at low level, including attacking airfields, regardless of the type target."

Piloting his own B-25 on 2 November 1943, Ellis went on a highly successful skip-bombing operation against Rabaul. An elaborately planned affair, the mission dispatched several squadrons to dump smoke and fragmentation bombs that would provide concealment for Ellis's group. "We were the first that went down into the harbor," said Ellis. "As we came between these two volcanoes, there was the harbor in front of us. I was credited with sinking two ships. We got jumped pretty heavy by Zeros as we were coming out of the harbor. Our top gunner got another confirmed kill on that mission." For his performance Ellis earned a Silver Star.

The new low-level approach surprised the Japanese at their big Wewak complex. Ellis recalled, "They were just about to launch a big mission of their own because, as we came over the hill, we could see the airplanes lined up wingtip-to-wingtip along the runway. It was a dream target. We had 23-pound fragmentation bombs with a little parachute on them. We had somewhere between thirty and forty of those on a B-25 and you would just string them out as you flew over. It took long enough for the bomb to float down, even though you were at low level, for you to get away." The growing achievements of the Air Corps under Kenney's command won the respect of MacArthur, who had previously regarded aircraft as a minor component in his arsenal.

25
Big Week, Berlin, and Assaults and Batterings in Italy

The New Year brought profound changes to the Eighth Air Force in En-gland as Lt. Gen. Jimmy Doolittle replaced Ira Eaker on 6 January. For months Hap Arnold had grumbled about the progress and achievements of the biggest of his commands and the one charged with bearing the heaviest burdens of strategic bombing in Europe. Arnold brushed aside excuses, largely legiti-mate, for the many aircraft grounded because of mechanical defects. He chafed at constant demands for more of everything from Eighth Air Force headquarters. Instead of lessening enemy opposition through Pointblank, the *Luftwaffe* seemed stronger. For all of the devastation supposedly visited upon the manufacturing sources, the Germans actually rolled out more planes per month than they lost during 1943. Although during the final weeks of that year the bomber fleets of more than 500 B-17s and B-24s—far in ex-cess of the original magic figure of 300—struck several times, the appalling tolls for the final six months of 1943 demanded a scapegoat.

Doolittle's first vital policy decision reversed Eaker's dictum that fighters could never leave the bombers. Even when the enemy appeared vulnerable because of numbers and position, standing orders dictated that the Little Friends maintain their place as escorts. Doolittle announced that the P-38, P-47, and P-51 groups could engage the *Luftwaffe* on sight. When he visited the office of Maj. Gen. William Kepner, boss of the Eighth's fighter com-mand, and saw on the wall the motto, "Our mission is to bring the bombers back" he ordered it removed. "From now on," Doolittle declared, "that no longer holds. Your mission is to destroy the German Air Force."

While the fighter groups heartily endorsed the new directions, the bomber people naturally reacted negatively to what they perceived as a pol-icy that would leave them naked to enemy onslaughts. Their fears were not allayed by initial explanations that offensive action by fighters was condi-tional upon having enough aircraft to remain with the bombers in the event interceptors showed. But as the flow of planes and pilots from the U.S. swelled, the Mighty Eighth would enjoy increasing luxury to go after the foe whenever he appeared.

Doolittle demonstrated his command at the end of January in the form of an 806-bomber assault upon Frankfurt, the most massive strike by the

Eighth yet. More than 630 fighters roamed the skies in support. Encouraged to seek and destroy, the Americans punished the *Luftwaffe* severely and gun cameras from both bombers and fighters confirmed more than 120 enemy planes destroyed and an additional 90 or so probables or damaged.

Frankfurt seemed merely the flexing of muscle when in the third week of February, the four-engine bombers dominated what was called "Big Week." Meteorologists had forecast several days of clear weather over Germany. The Eighth and Ninth Air Forces, working with British Bomber Command and the Fifteenth Air Force in Italy, drubbed the Continent in a six-day cycle of round-the-clock destruction that emphasized aircraft factories. On opening day, 880 heavyweights with an almost equal number of fighters visited the targets. Thick cloud cover, in spite of the predictions of the weather specialists, obscured some objectives. Poor visibility may have also limited the defensive effort but thick swarms of U.S. fighters covered the Big Friends. The enemy knocked down twenty-one aircraft, a ratio of 2.2 percent, compared to the horrendous 29 percent downed on Black Thursday. Unlike earlier days, when a maximum effort left the bomber command supine for days, the combined air forces mustered intensive operations in the following days, including massive tonnage dropped on two notorious sites, Regensburg and Schweinfurt.

Doolittle displayed no hesitation because of bad weather. Ralph Golubock, a replacement pilot with the 44th Bomb Group, after his briefing for one of the missions, looked at the forbidding skies, thick black clouds, low ceilings, and heavy rain, mandating a tricky instrument takeoff and the always dangerous jockeying into formation. He and his colleagues believed the brass would scrub the affair, even as they taxied out to their assigned positions.

"The first two planes took the runway and awaited a takeoff flare that we were sure would never come. But it did! Right on time. The lead bomber raced down the runway and took off and was almost immediately enveloped in clouds and disappeared from sight. We all followed in turn, the planes spaced apart by thirty seconds. When my turn came I advanced the throttles and immediately went on instruments. The copilot tried to watch the runway to prevent accidentally drifting off and onto the grass. The engineer stood between the pilot and copilot to carefully monitor the engine instruments. He also called out our airspeeds so I could concentrate on taking a whole lot of airplane off the ground safely.

"Upon leaving the ground we were immediately immersed in rain and clouds. The tail gunner was back in his position with an Aldis lamp that he blinked on and off so that following planes would see the light and keep their distance. The climb was long and grinding, and to our horror, we saw a huge flash of light in the sky. We all knew that two planes had collided and exploded." His Liberator broke through the clouds at 17,000 feet to a deep blue sky and a sun bright as a ball of fire. "I drank in the beauty surrounding me and wondered why I was carrying a load of death to be dropped on people I didn't even know. My meditations were shortlived. There were hundreds of airplanes around us and this was not the time for daydreaming. We had to find our proper spot in formation. The procedure was to fly a racetrack course around a radio signal called a buncher. The lead plane was constantly firing flares so we could identify him. Each group had their own buncher. Out of all of this confusion, we began to form up. First as elements, then as squadrons and groups, finally as wings and divisions.

"The outside air-temperature gauge on the instrument panel was against a peg at -50° Fahrenheit. The biting cold was almost unbearable. We did not have heated flying suits or heaters that worked. We only had sheepskins that just could not keep the cold out. It was a numbing and strength-sapping cold that made concentration on flying and staying in proper formation difficult." Over the primary target, the bomb guidance–equipment system aboard the lead plane malfunctioned. Golubock's flight sought out a secondary site and dropped its ordnance. For all of the massive numbers and airmen involved, Golubock counted that Big Week expedition a "screwed-up mess. Three aircraft and crews lost. We bombed a secondary target and probably achieved nothing. All to fly a mission that should have been scrubbed in the first place."

Nevertheless, Big Week demonstrated that strategic bombing now meant sustained campaigns. The mounting production of bombers on U.S. assembly lines and the thousands of airmen completing their training was vital to Big Week's success. But the numbers were only part of the story. Technological advances that allowed the Little Friends to come along on even the most distant excursions made a substantial difference.

The P-51 Mustang, endowed with a Rolls-Royce Merlin engine that had a supercharger, was transformed from a mediocre, low-level, ground-support ship into a superb, high-altitude fighter with enough speed and maneuverability to outfly anything the Germans offered until the advent of the first jet fighter. External wing tanks extended the original scant 200-mile combat radius. In mid-December, P-51s chaperoned bombers to Kiel and back, a distance of nearly 1,000 miles. Engineers then crammed an extra fuel-supply tank in behind the pilot's armor plate enabling P-51s to go the distance of the bombers throughout the Continent.

Tommy Hayes, after his tour in the South Pacific, where he knocked down a pair of enemy planes but suffered through a period of flying the P-39, had earned a month of R&R back in the States. He was reassigned to the 357th Fighter Group, again committed to P-39s. "The P-39 was an aircraft you flew with a cerebral sense. It did not warn you how close the P-39 was to the edge.

Zap! and you're in trouble. We had too many crashes in a short time, evenly spread among the squadron. Maybe we commanders and flight leaders were pressing too hard. It was usually the newer pilots who bought the farm."

To Hayes's amazement, after his group sailed on the *Queen Elizabeth* for England instead of the P-39, they were ticketed for Mustangs. The outfit, on its fourth mission, scored its first kills during the first day of Big Week. Colonel Henry Russell Spicer, a new group commander, known as "Hank," "Russ," or "Pappy," quickly endeared himself. "He was a natural leader, a Pied Piper," said Hayes, "having the qualities absent in his predecessor. Appearance, posture, caring, respect, voice, eyes. His arrival was an example. We were called to a personnel meeting. Spicer took the stage, introduced himself, related that he was familiar with our past, said we were a great group and, weather permitting, our mission tomorrow would show just how great the 357th is. He had physical presence and personality. After seven months, we had a commander again."

Beginning with Big Week, the air war visited the Third Reich with an intensity previously unseen. Whereas the sacking of cities and factories had earlier been spaced by intervals of days, even weeks, the Forts and Liberators showed almost daily and with them came hordes of fighters prepared not only to protect their Big Friends, but also to seek, pursue, and destroy any enemy planes that ventured aloft. For the first time in the war, the German aircraft industry could not match or surpass their losses of fighters. That deficiency was temporary as manufacturing installations pushed up their pace of production. But the *Luftwaffe* could not churn out capable pilots fast enough to offset the loss of experienced and skilled hands in the cockpits. Bob Johnson, the veteran fighter pilot from the 56th, said, "As time went on, we were knocking the best boys the Germans had out of the air. We were knocking off some of the best German pilots, primarily because we didn't know any better. We didn't know we were supposed to be afraid of these guys and that they were so much better than we were. We went after them and we got them."

At the same time, a number of American fighter pilots using P-38s and P-47s quickly saw the virtues of the latest entry, the P-51. "We all wanted the P-51," said Jim Goodson. "It was the most remarkable plane of the war. It had as much range as a B-17, was about the size of a Hurricane and only slightly larger than a Spit." His boss, Col. Don Blakeslee, commander of the 4th Fighter Group, which had started out with Spitfires and then Thunderbolts, pleaded with Kepner for Mustangs. Kepner balked, noting that the Eighth in the midst of its huge offensive could not afford to stand down a fighter group while the pilots accustomed themselves to the new ships. Blakeslee supposedly pledged, "Give me those Mustangs and I give you my word—I'll have them in combat in twenty-four hours. I promise—twenty-four hours." His guarantee persuaded Kepner.

When the first P-51s arrived at the Debden airdrome, Blakeslee informed his subordinates of his promise to Kepner. "You can learn to fly them on the way to the target." In fact, the 4th's pilots squeezed in about forty minutes of flight time to familiarize themselves with their new equipment before heading out on a mission at the end of Big Week. Within a matter of weeks, group after group converted from P-38s, which continued to develop problems in the frigid climes of upper altitudes over Europe, and from the dependable but less agile P-47. Only the 56th Fighter Group in the Eighth Air Force, led by Hub Zemke, retained the Jugs. All fourteen other groups in the Eighth eventually manned Mustangs, although the Ninth Air Force, with heavier tactical responsibilities, continued to operate a number of P-47 outfits.

Little more than a week after Blakeslee's outfit adopted the P-51, the 352d Fighter Group, with Punchy Powell, switched. "I flew the P-47," says Powell, "for about half my eighty-three missions—all with the Thunderbolt were shorter than those in P-51s. I loved both airplanes for different reasons. The 47 was a flying tank, most durable, more firepower, and absolutely the greatest for strafing attacks and excellent at the higher altitudes for air-to-air combat. However, it lost a lot in aerial combat at lower altitudes. Its number-one weakness was its limited range. It was a big sweat returning from almost any penetration of the Continent because of lack of fuel, particularly if you got into a fight or misjudged your time over the Continent. The Mustang doubled our range and eliminated this problem, except on a few extralong missions to which we were assigned. It had range and firepower, particularly the D models with six guns instead of the four in the Bs and Cs." Actually, the ability of the P-51 to travel greater distances stimulated the devotees of the P-47 to enlarge its combat radius, and while never quite the marathon performer of the Mustang, Thunderbolts eventually journeyed ever deeper into enemy territory.

The 357th, which went into combat flying P-51s on 11 February, was jolted by the loss of their commander less than three weeks later. Even as the *Luftwaffe* tottered under the weight of firepower poured out by the near tidal wave of bombers and fighters, and the Third Reich earth shook from the thunderous rain of explosives, the Germans continued to draw blood. Henry Spicer, who in the eyes of Tommy Hayes transformed the 357th Fighter Group into an effective instrument, had led fourteen missions and been credited with three enemy aircraft destroyed when a burst of flak struck his P-51 on 3 March. He bailed out over the English Channel, hauled himself from the frigid waters and into his inflatable dinghy. But search-and-rescue units failed to find him before he drifted onto the beach near Cherbourg. There he lay on the sand, with frostbite of hands and feet until German soldiers discovered him. After medical treatment and interrogation, the Germans lodged him in Stalag Luft 1, an encampment of downed aviators.

The pressure for fewer drop-outs because of mechanical difficulties was reflected in an experience of Golubock. "During one assembly over England, we developed a problem with one of our props malfunctioning. We left the formation and radioed the base that we were returning and explained our problem. We were ordered to land and to taxi over to one of the maintenance hangars. It was still very early in the morning and I was looking forward to returning to my room and hitting the sack. The engineering officer told us to stay in the airplane. They wheeled out a new prop and within fifteen minutes they removed the unserviceable one and replaced it with a new prop. We were told to take off and try to catch the group at Beachy Head. That's what we did. My record for no abortions remained intact. I would much rather have been in the sack."

On 4 March, the VIII Bomber Command dispatched 238 B-17s for a run at Berlin, the first strike by the Air Corps at the German capital. As the navigator for *Spirit of New Mexico*, 95th Bomb Group, housed at Horham, Lt. Vincent Fox, remembered, "If Berlin could be attacked in daylight, then all of Germany would become accessible to the full weight of American bombs. For us, the bomber crews who were assigned the mission, Berlin was a giant mental hazard, the toughest of all missions, for which we had little genuine enthusiasm. However, the briefing officer, Maj. Jiggs Donohue, the silver-tongued lawyer from Washington, D.C., had the ability to make it sound like a gallant adventure into the wild blue yonder to be cherished.

"But the procedure wasn't new to us. We were on our twenty-fourth mission. We'd been briefed for Berlin on five previous occasions, but each time the adverse European winter weather had forced us to abandon the mission short of 'Big B.' The previous day we'd climbed to 30,000 feet over the Danish peninsula only to be confronted by a solid bank of swirling, turbulent clouds. The meteorology officer glibly promised better weather for today's mission but our faith in his predictions had suffered numerous setbacks before. At our takeoff time of 0730 hours, scattered snow squalls limited visibility down to a scant 300 yards as we peered apprehensively into the eerie predawn light while we spiraled up to group-assembly altitude. During the tension-filled climb, the English countryside was visible only momentarily through multilayered clouds."

The 95th formed up successfully but other groups were defeated early on by the towering overcast in their assembly areas. Shortly after Fox and associates crossed into Germany, Eighth Air Force supposedly sent out a recall signal. However, the mission commander of the 95th, Col. H. Griffin Mumford, leading a wing, resolutely slogged toward Berlin. Puzzled by the failure to turn back, one pilot broke radio silence to advise Mumford there had been a recall. Still the 95th's B-17s continued on the pathway that carried them over the Rhine River. Unhappy crewmen watched other groups turn back and radio to the 95th, "You'll be sorry."

Grif Mumford, however, advised by his superiors that combat wing leaders could use their own discretion, continued toward the target. Subsequently, it appeared that the recall attributed to the Eighth Air Force headquarters came from an enemy transmitter. The colonel, relying on the word from Curtis LeMay's 3d Bomb Division, decided he and his aircraft were already in too deep to simply reverse course and escape enemy fighters lurking along the pathway. Instead, he reasoned that the poor visibility might hide them until they struck Berlin. Then if they flew a different course back to England they might escape unhurt. He was obviously aware of the morale and propaganda value of a hit upon Big B.

Navigator Fox said, "We soon had the chilling realization that we were alone in our undertaking. Our ball-turret gunner could identify squadrons with the 95th 'Square B' tail markings and elements with the 'Square D' of the 100th Group [part of the wing led by Mumford] still maintaining the integrity of the formation. It seemed incredible that our token force was still bearing east toward the German capital. We got a brief glimpse of the ground near the city of Brunswick and were greeted by a barrage of enemy flak bursts."

Indeed, the ground fire began to exact a toll. Lieutenant "Doc" Thayer, a copilot said, "I could see the vivid red flashes of flame from the gun barrels and then, for the first time ever, I saw the 88mm flak shells themselves, distinct against the white snowing background, coming all the way up as if in slow motion, then rapidly accelerating the closer they got. Fortunately the flak barrage burst above us. Then another flak shell came up through the bomb-bay doors, knocked the fuse off one of our bombs, and kept on going, completely through the top of the fuselage.

"Our bomb ended up on the catwalk between the two bomb bays, making a noise like a volcano-type sparkler and spewing out what looked like small shiny pieces of aluminum. How we got the bomb-bay doors open and that smoldering bomb out of our aircraft in less than ten seconds, I will never really understand. Apparently, there was another B-17 almost directly below us that the falling bomb missed by a matter of inches." A further hit from antiaircraft punched a hole in the wing of Thayer's B-17 and damaged the engines.

Grif Mumford, in a stream of consciousness after the fact, noted, "4 March 1944, 28,000 feet over Berlin. The first of many. God, it's cold at that outside air-temperature gauge—minus sixty-five degrees, and it isn't designed to indicate anything lower. [On at least one B-17, the bomb doors froze.] Forget the temperature. Look at that flak. The bastards must have all 2,500 guns operational today. This has to be the longest bomb run yet. Krumph . . . boy that was close and listen to the spent shrapnel hitting the airplane. Look at the gaping hole in the left wing of number-three low element . . . an 88 must have gone right through without detonating.

"Wow, look at our Little Friends. Love those long-range drop tanks! That old 'escort you across the Channel' crap just wouldn't get the job done. Not to worry in the target area today about the ME 109s and FW 190s. [Others on the scene counted a dozen P-51s that apparently drove off the enemy fighters.] I wonder if they realize the significance of this mission, that it could be the turning point of the war. Stinking weather, fighter attacks and flak over Berlin so heavy it could be walked upon is enough to make one anxious to get out of this wieners-and-krautland and back to Jolly Old . . . We made it. Wonder what old 'Iron Ass' LeMay will think of the show his boys put on today."

At the end of the month, LeMay issued a commendation to the 95th that paid tribute for completion of 100 heavy-bombardment missions and specifically stated, "On 4 March 1944, this intrepid group led the first daylight bombardment of Berlin by American heavy bombers, a feat for which it has already won world renown." While perhaps scoring a propaganda victory for the folks in the States, the raid barely laid a glove on the city. Only thirty aircraft from the 95th and 100th reached the objective as the remainder of the 502 planes assigned, thwarted by the weather or mechanical breakdowns, toted their ordnance back to base. Actually, British heavyweights had been hammering Berlin for months but from this day on the Americans also called upon Berlin regularly and with far more weight. What's more, to the dismay of the *Luftwaffe*, they came accompanied by fighters. Hitler allegedly scoffed that they must have benefitted from favorable wind currents but Goering later admitted that when he saw American fighters in the skies over Berlin he realized the air war was lost.

"As of March 6," says Tommy Hayes, "we [his fighter group] were not experienced veterans. We were still learning. Up to that date we had thirty victories with seven our high for a mission. The weather enroute to Berlin on that day was bad. The bombers flew a dogleg north of us while we flew a straight line to our rendezvous point west of Berlin. Colonel [Donald] Graham, [elevated to group commander upon the downing of Spicer] had to abort over the North Sea and passed the baton to me. We were flying time and distance [a navigational technique] because of a solid overcast below. A cloud obscured our left as we passed the rendezvous time. Were we early or the bombers late? Or was I south of the rendezvous point? Geez, I screwed up. A little later, someone called out, 'Bombers, nine o'clock.' There they were, B-17s coming out of the poor visibility. *But* we were to escort B-24s, the 2d Bomb Division. It entered my mind to look for our 24s but then someone called out, 'Bogeys at two o'clock.' When they appeared, it was fight now.

"I called, 'Let's fight. Drop tanks.' The 109s, 110s, 410s, and FW 190s were estimated at 120–150. They were going head-on for the bombers. We turned left onto their rear. Some turned into us. Some continued for the bombers.

Then a top cover of thirty or so 109s entered the fight. My high squadron, up-sun, engaged the top cover. The score was twenty kills and no losses. It was important for us because it was our first big fight against a large force. And we kicked ass. We were still learning. It was good timing, good for morale. But it wasn't the best work. We didn't escort our assigned bombers. We lucked out, getting a distinguished unit citation."

"I was on three of the first Berlin raids," remembered Bob Johnson of the 56th Fighter Group. "I was the lead airplane on March 6. I had only eight airplanes to protect 180 bombers; the 62d Squadron had dropped off to take up battle over the Zuider Zee. Gabreski had moved off the top and south to try to find some enemy. [A freelance hunt not permitted under the pre-Doolittle regime.] I was circling overhead. As I got to the front of the bomber line and made my orbit to turn left, I saw a gaggle, not any particular formation, just a group of airplanes, coming in from the north. At first I thought they were P-47s, a new group had just gotten over there and was flying all over the sky. As I came up, I said, 'Christ, they're Focke-Wulf 190s.'

"We were in line abreast, all eight of us, and we just opened fire and went right through some sixty or so 190s and 109s. As we turned to get on their tails, we saw another sixty or so above and another sixty or so to their left. Probably 175-180 German aircraft. Eight of us. We followed the first gaggle through our bombers, head on. We had no idea how many we hit. We were firing, airplanes were falling out of the sky all over, from bomber gunfire, from their gunfire to our bombers, from them ramming into our bombers. Burning bombers and fighters and parachutes filled the sky. There was no space; they weren't ramming purposely. You never saw such a sight in your life. Bombers falling, parachutes falling, fighters falling.

"I didn't have to think about the situation. It was there. I thought only of survival, and hitting the enemy. If there are crosses, shoot at them. So much damage was being done in the air there, at that moment; it took place in seconds. We lost sixty-nine bombers, and I was right in the middle of it. How many of the bombers were shooting at me and my buddies, I don't know. But they were shooting at airplanes. That's all they cared about. And I don't blame them.

"A heck of a lot of those [bomber crewmen] were out in parachutes and in burning airplanes that were falling with flames two thousand feet deep. The bombers scattered all over the sky trying to get home. We went after the 109s and 190s who were still attacking. We did not have radio contact with the bombers but we got a lot of waves from waist windows as we crossed the North Sea and a lot of free drinks in London from some of the bomber crews. I lost one guy of the eight. I think our boy ended up a POW. We got sixteen or seventeen Germans."

Two days later, Johnson immersed himself in what started out as a replica of his first trip to Berlin. But this time, as he headed into the enemy fighters with his eight planes in a line-abreast formation, he said, "All the time I was calling over various buttons [frequencies], slowly and distinctly calling our exact location on all the different channels, even the bomber channels, so they could call other fighters and get them there. When we hit them, our eight little guys scattered their fighters all over the sky. Other batches of our fighters came down to help and there was a bunch of confused Germans. Just that few minutes that it took me to get out and hit them, then brought in P-38s and P-47s all over the sky. That was one hell of a battle. We stopped the Germans at least two miles away from the bombers."

Although the loss ratio of heavyweights fell from about 10 percent during the previous attack on Berlin to less than 7 percent, that still meant close to 400 Americans were MIA, KIA, or WIA. The Eighth insisted it had destroyed or damaged as many as 400 enemy fighters in these two encounters. During the 4 March foray against Big B, assembly problems thwarted a number of groups including the 388th. Larry Goldstein's crew already had finished twenty-four raids and had hoped for a milk run. Berlin hardly seemed like a soft touch, but now that they were on the verge of ending their time in combat, the men were willing to take dangerous chances. "Our crew elected to fall out of formation, pick out a target in Germany, drop our bombs, climb back into the formation, and all would be okay.

"We did drop out, we did bomb a railroad yard, and when we attempted to climb back to the group, we were attacked by a FW 190 who hit us several times with 20mm shells. We were able to escape by diving into the clouds. My pilot asked me for an emergency radio fix from the British rescue net. Despite German jamming, I was able to get a position report, pass it on to the navigator. He plotted a course for England and when we broke out of the clouds, we were over the English Channel. When we landed we had no brakes and went off the end of the runway, ending up in a plowed field. When we left the plane, we saw the extensive damage and realized how lucky we had been to escape disaster, especially when I saw a hole in the radio room just above where my head had been. This was twenty-five and we all kissed the ground when we realized that our flying combat was over."

Even as the P-51 forged ahead as the weapon of choice the 364th Fighter Group continued to operate P-38s. Among those in Lightning cockpits was Montana-born Max J. Woolley, who said, "I chose the P-38. I liked the two engines, probably for safety, the speed of the aircraft, and I red-lined [pushed to or past the manufacturer's limit] a number of times, and the firepower. With four fifties and a 20mm cannon up front, the Jerries knew that you could hurt them."

Placed in the 384th Fighter Squadron, one of the three operational units that composed the 364th Fighter Group, Woolley said, "I had about four or five hours of training in England before I went 'active.' A pilot learns combat by being in combat," he noted. "None of my flight instructors had been in combat so they had no firsthand experience to pass on. No one can tell you about the feeling, the tenseness, and your grinding guts. You have to have been there and felt it firsthand. Although I had quite a bit of target shooting in State-side training, nothing takes the place of shooting at an ME 109 or FW 190 while it's moving better than 400 miles per hour for a split second across your gunsight.

"My first encounter with the enemy was on my first mission [15 March]. From the Allied viewpoint, historians have classified this particular battle as one of the five greatest air battles of the European war over Germany. It wasn't great because I happened to be over Europe that day, but because of the great effort that Hermann Goering put forth with his air force to break the back of the Allied fighters. Our group was near Hannover, Germany, around 23,000 feet and heading east. A gaggle of German fighters were below us around 18,000 to 19,000 feet, set there as a decoy. Several thousand feet above us was a much larger group. Undoubtedly, this was the main strike force intent on reclaiming the skies for the Fatherland.

"The signal was given to drop belly tanks, close flight to our tactical position, increase rpms and manifold pressure as we headed down to intercept the Jerries below. This being my first mission, I was assigned the flight's most protected position—number two on my flight leader's wing. The enemy above us came down for the attack as we knew they would. Within seconds there was one massive hornet's nest stirred up in the German skies. I immediately knew that I was in a battle for my life. Planes were going everywhere, red flashes streaked the sky, puffs of black smoke started to curl upward as Orville Myers, my flight leader, called, 'Red Two. Tighten your turn. Jerry on your tail.' At that moment, streaks shot past my canopy. In my mirror I saw a 109 that appeared inches behind me tighten his turn to put me in the 'has-been column.' I had everything forward exceeding the red line, hit the flap handle again, and stood her on a point, desperately trying to save my skin. A 109 slid in front of me, intent on taking Myers. He crossed my gunsight. I hit the trigger button as four fifties and a 20mm cannon belched their hate for a fair-haired Superman. Part of his tail swished past my wing, only a superfical nick but enough for him to wing over and head below.

"P-47s in the area heard the chatter and came rushing to the fray. Friend and foe now were desperately trying to annihilate one another. 'Red Two. Tighten your turn.' Again I hit the flap handle, kicked left rudder, fought the control wheel to shake him with all needles vibrating beyond their safety zone. Soon it was over. What seemed like an hour lasted only minutes. They saw, they came, but they didn't conquer. The sky was now void of the Reich defenders. Only white-streaked contrails left by the angry hornets seeking their adversaries fluttered in the brilliant blue. Down below, a few broken machines jabbed back and forth amid the rising acrid smoke, soon to take their place in the graveyard of broken dreams. Both friend and foe paid dearly for this exercise in self-determination. The fight was a great lesson. Classroom instruction can never take the place of flak and live ammunition trying to separate a man from his inner soul."

Woolley attempted to shield himself against the impact of losses. "I tried not to become emotionally attached to any one person, as a pilot never knew when his name would be called by his maker. It was tough seeing your friends taking the worst of things, but so much harder if you were extremely close to them. Most of the pilots from our original group in California were outstanding fliers. Some had personalities I didn't care for but I never questioned any of their technical flying ability."

Joseph Bennett, in a P-47 for the 56th Fighter Group, through an accident, splashed down in the Channel. On 15 April he was briefed for a mission that might last six hours. "I had always flown with my seat belt tight and on one long mission, the bottle for inflating the rubber dinghy that was packed with our parachute cut off blood circulation, causing numbness from the knees down. To prevent this, I loosened my safety belt, giving me room to change my position and be more comfortable. We took off with a man flying his first mission on my right wing; the other two of the flight were on my left wing. We went into a cloud soon after takeoff and flew on instruments. At 21,000 feet, my supercharger cut in and I pulled the throttle back to maintain a constant airspeed. The wingman's wing made light contact with my canopy and it popped off.

"I jammed the stick forward unconsciously and in seconds I was vertical. The loose seat belt allowed me to slip up until my head was sticking out of the plane. My little and second fingers were still on the stick at the last knuckle but when they slipped off, I was sucked out through the harness or else the belt broke. When I left the plane I was falling so fast I could not breathe so I pulled on the rip cord and it slipped out of my hand. I grabbed it again and pulled so hard that when my arm extended past my body, the wind jerked it straight upward. The chute opened with quite a jerk and I was sitting on air.

"It suddenly came to my attention that I could not see. I put my hand to my face and couldn't see it. It was quite unlike anything I had ever known. Something warned me to prepare for landing. I uncoupled one leg strap and twisted the connector on the other when I hit the water. When my head came out of the water, my eyesight had returned and the parachute was folding up on the water beside me. I unbuckled the chute waist connector and reached for the dinghy but it wasn't in the pack. Part of the plane was floating about fifty yards away so I started swimming toward it. My left shoulder was hurting, the water was cold, and the swimming pretty slow.

"After about thirty feet I found the dinghy, less than a foot under the surface. I got it in position and pulled the pin for inflation, then tried to roll it under my body but it slipped out of my cold hands as it was inflating, which would make it more difficult to mount. Grabbing the dinghy I gave another roll with all the strength I had and got a part of it under my back but didn't make it to the center. Finally, I could feel it inflating where my hand was gripping and I began to rise out of the water. I slid to the center and began to put the hood on and fasten the windbreaker. I was so cold I began to shake and my teeth were clattering so hard I though they might break. I was having trouble breathing and started to blow my nose only to discover that more than half of it was almost severed. My upper body began to warm up, but my butt and feet ached and were cold.

"Opening the windbreaker, I discovered about four inches of water in the bottom of the dinghy. I took off one of my GI shoes and bailed until it was almost dry, then fastened the windbreaker. I had been there about an hour when I heard a plane go by. The clouds had lifted to another 300 feet. On the third or fourth circle he spotted me and stayed around for about an hour. It was McKennon, from another squadron in our group. That perked me up. However, I knew chances of being picked up by air-sea rescue were slim. A slight breeze had started and if I could live through the night, I'd possibly drift to Belgium.

"I fell asleep to be awakened by a sea gull standing on my head with my nose in his beak, shaking his head from side to side quite violently. I don't know how long before I fell asleep again, but the noise from a rescue-boat engine woke me. It was about seventy-five yards away, headed toward me. A native of Norway was in command of the vessel in the service of British Air Sea Rescue. I never did know how they got me aboard but they wrapped me in blankets, gave me two cups of hot buttered rum and I drifted off into a sound sleep. I awakened hours later as I was carried up a gangplank on a litter. I learned later that the boy on my right wing had called in a distress May Day." Bennett, unlike the unfortunate Henry Spicer, would fly again.

Some three weeks after Spicer went down, another squadron commander in the 357th was KIA and the musical chairs of replacement elevated Tommy Hayes, who says he now perceived the effects of the incessant pummeling of the enemy. "The all-out air war in February and March paid dividends by April. Hitting their oil was serious enough so that pilot training was reduced drastically. At the same time they were losing their most experienced people. During the period of March 2 to May 29 I shot down several who were still green. I also had engagement with the 109 and 190 where it was a toss up. Some flew the 109 like it was a P-51. Then there was an FW 190 that outran my flight of four, all of us with the throttle against the wall gave up after five minutes. This pilot outflew me from 22,000 feet to the deck as he slipped, and skidded, power off, power on. Sometimes our pilots on the tail of a 109 or 190 saw them release the canopy and bail out, some without ever firing a burst. A victory is a victory. Some 190 pilots couldn't really handle their fighter. The 190 had a high wing loading, but when on the deck, if they pulled it too tight, they stalled and went in. Again, a victory without firing the guns."

In Italy, Shingle, rather than draining away German strength from the Winter Line, had instead become almost a liability for the Allied forces. Maintenance of a small tract required a regular infusion of replacements, reinforcements, and scarce equipment. Additional GIs and armor that might have been deployed for the Liri Valley effort went to Anzio. To abandon that beachhead would have been a propaganda as well as a strategic defeat.

The victors at Cisterna had paraded the captured Rangers through the streets of Rome by way of proclaiming to the local people that the Reich ruled. (German medics treated seriously wounded Americans before they were shipped to POW camps in Germany.) The 1 February POW show, according to some participants, was not quite what the producers expected. Captain Chuck Shunstrom, who had been leader of an antitank platoon for the Rangers, said, "The Italians were supposed to boo us and cheer the master race as we marched five abreast through the streets. Instead, the Italian women cried and the men flashed us surreptitious Vee-for-Victory signs. They would stroke their hair or brush off a sleeve with fingers shaped to a Vee. When a dumb German guard wanted to know what the Vee sign meant, none of us knew a thing about it. We marched along singing 'God Bless America.'"

Some of the local citizens, provided with garbage or rotten vegetables, however, threw them at the Americans and one prisoner recalled being spat upon. But for the most part, the Rangers under heavy guard felt the Italian people radiated good will toward them. The march through Rome began a long journey on foot, by truck, and by rail to the POW camps. (A number managed to break away while in Italy and hide long enough to be freed by the Allied advance.)

Allen Merrill missed the humiliation in Rome. Dumped by German soldiers on the floor of a farmhouse with other wounded, Merrill bandaged his leg wound and stopped the bleeding. "The first night I was alert enough to realize that only one fat Kraut soldier sat, back against the door, guarding us as if the men couldn't go anyplace anyhow. They fed us once with some kind of crackers and a broth that was mostly water. I had two D-ration bars [a high-calorie chocolate] for emergency. The next morning I raised to the window and saw the lay of the land, some trees, shrubs, and a woods about a hundred yards back of the house. Overnight, two men died in that room. We pounded on the door and told the German about it. He just said, '*Ja wohl*' [Yes, sir] and went back to his chair against the front door.

"I made up my mind I was going to try to escape after dark. I told Frank [a seriously wounded soldier] and some of the others. A sergeant said I'd better not try it. They could shoot you on sight. I said it didn't matter. I was still going to try. These Germans had no record of how many of us were there, so what the hell I had to give it a shot. I went through one of the dead guy's pockets and found another D bar. He wouldn't be needing nourishment anymore. Frank asked if I would help him and we could escape together. He was hit in both legs and there was no way I could manage the two of us. He felt bad and so did I. But what the hell, it was every man for himself in a situation like this."

Merrill did not know which direction to take but believed that with his compass and by moving only at nightfall he could avoid a sojourn in an enemy hospital and a prolonged stay in a POW camp. In his pockets he packed his D bars, several cheese tins from K rations, and a tiny can opener. He practiced crawling around the farmhouse room and found the pain tolerable. He downed the last of the sulpha drugs to ward off infection, said goodbyes, and shook a few hands.

After dark, Merrill felt his way through back rooms in search of a rear entrance. "I was aware of a steady draft from one wall. Sure enough, there was an opening to the outside of what appeared to be a kitchen. It was a potato bin where canvas covered the opening from the weather. If I could squeeze through I could crawl to the woods and be on my way. After three tries and repiling the potatoes I made it through by removing my jacket and pushing it ahead of me. Once I was free of the house I crawled in the direction of the woods. It was so dark I couldn't see my hand in front of my face. [I heard] heavy vehicles moving, tanks, probably, or large trucks. Occasionally there were voices, the low guttural sounds of German spoken nearby."

Merrill paused to rest. "Two sharp sounds made me hold my breath. They were unmistakable, from a bolt-action rifle reloading. I held my breath for as long as I could, then let it out in short, irregular exhales. Then gulped air and held that as long as possible. Not ten feet to the right of me a figure sat on a small shed roof. By the outline of his helmet I could see he was a Kraut. I felt the urgent need to urinate. I held that, too. I could smell the faint odor of cigarette smoke. The Kraut was stealing a puff or two while on guard duty. Then I heard him crush the butt out with the toe of his boot and his outline disappeared. I could hear his footsteps fade away."

Merrill resumed his slow passage toward the forest. At 2:00 A.M., when he checked the luminous dial of his watch, he saw the roof of the farmhouse some distance off. Doggedly he crawled on, his pace reduced as the underbrush became thicker. By four o'clock, shortly before the first streaks of dawn began to illuminate the area, he was deep enough into the trees to seek a hiding place. He fell asleep in some thick brush cover. When he awoke in midmorning he discovered himself covered with ants. "I must have crawled over an anthill. As slowly as possible I brushed them off my exposed skin. I felt crawly all over. But any sudden moves might make me a sitting duck. I was bleeding in several places. I gazed slowly around; the bushes had thorns the size of straight pins. There were no human sounds anywhere in the vicinity. My numb left leg ached but it wasn't unbearable. I shivered; my clothes were damp and my hands and fingers were coated with caked mud, and sore. I retrieved a D bar from my jacket and munched on it as I slowly made a 360-degree turn. Somewhere behind me vehicles moved in the distance but I couldn't tell if they were theirs or ours. Nothing else was moving anywhere I could see."

In a grove of olive trees amid oozing mud Merrill settled down for another day of concealment. "I slept soundly until my bowels again exploded in another siege of the running shits. My stomach churned in discomfort and I shivered under a gray, cold, sunless day. I would have loved to just stand up straight and stretch my limbs but I dared not. In the late afternoon I gnawed on my D bar and had two sips of tepid, stale water. My bowels rustled and ached and only liquid came out in dribbles.

"After about an hour of crawling I thought I would try hobbling. This meant double work on the right, unwounded leg. That was both good and bad. Good because I hopped faster than I crawled, but bad because the ground was uneven. After two falls the left one started to bleed again. I could feel the warm, oozing blood. I had to stop and reapply my belt tourniquet until the bleeding stopped. I lost precious time in my advance up the gully beside the road. Before dawn I crawled to a small stream crossing the road. There was a culvert and I decided to stay there. For the first time in three days I slept the daylight hours away in a flat position."

As Merrill continued his travels, a hard rain pelted down, soaking him and reducing his passage through cold, slippery mud. The pain in his left leg reached a point where he sought refuge in a farmhouse that was unoccupied. Although aware his building might become a target, Merrill decided he would have to take his chances and rest there. When he awoke, there was light outside. To protect his wounded leg against the hard floor of the house, he tried to wrap a small blanket about it. "I saw into the wound for the first time in three days. There was a white moving mass in that wound. It was maggots. I gagged once and threw up. I would have screamed and don't know why I didn't. In training they don't tell you about things like this. I used a long-handled wood spoon to scrape them out of that wound. I retched each time I pushed them off my leg. The knee had started to bleed again. I found a towel and pulled it tight around the area. When I pulled the towel away, many maggots fell away also. I had nothing inside to vomit but bile. There was some blood in it. My lungs and stomach ached with a fury I could not control. I lay on the floor of that farmhouse kitchen and cried until I must have fallen asleep."

When he awoke again, Merrill rediscovered his resolve and started out again. As on earlier nights he passed or bumped into fallen soldiers from the battle for Cisterna. "Several times I felt for the patch on their shoulder. It was there, with the Fifth Army patch just below it. The Rangers had left a trail of dead wherever they went. This time, however, they were the trail. The cold, near-freezing temperatures of late January had almost preserved these bodies. But now rain and warmer weather had started the rotting process and the smell was something you never forget. The consoling factor was that it had to be the road we came on."

Toward dawn he hid himself in a shed beside another farmhouse. That night, in spite of almost unbearable pain and in a steady rain, he started to pull himself along. "Several times I thought about crawling out of the gully onto the road and giving up. Something kept me going. Whatever it was, it is not part of Army training. It comes from a higher source, perhaps from the Creator Himself. As I crawled and thought about these things I was not aware it was growing light. I was oblivious. When I opened my eyes it was bright daylight. Two pairs of eyes were looking down at me, as though I was an illusion. Then a voice, distinctly American, yelled to others in the vicinity. 'Hey, guys, lookit what crept into our area.' Then another one said, 'Jesus H. Christ, it's a Ranger and he's hurt bad.' More GIs came running. One carried a litter and before I knew it an ambulance was pulling up. The last thing I recall before dreamland was the medic saying, 'Son, your Colonel Darby is over at our battalion headquarters right now and he'll sure be glad to see you.'

"Then I slept. An hour or so later I was aware some guy was shaking my hand and hugging my shoulder. Either I was dreaming or it was Col. Bill Darby. I was amazed to learn it was him. Hatless, jacketless, with those sawed-off leggins." Shipped to Naples for hospital care, Merrill received a Silver Star recommended by Darby.

Despite the negative results of the Ranger-led assault, Gen. John Lucas advised his diary a day or so later, "I was sent on a desperate mission, one where the odds were greatly against success and I went without saying anything because I was given an order and my opinion was not asked. The condition in which I find myself is much better than I ever anticipated or had any right to expect."

That roseate view could hardly be justified by the situation as February began. At Anzio, as elsewhere, the rain-soaked dirt mired American armor. Ernest Harmon recalled, "When tank commanders attempted to skirt gullies, they found themselves bogged down in the mud. January rains made the place a gooey mess. Four tanks became stuck in the mud and I ordered an armored wrecker to pull 'em out. The wrecker was ambushed by the Germans. I sent four more tanks to rescue the wrecker; then I sent more tanks after them. I finally learned the Anzio lesson the hard way, not to spend good money after bad. I lost twenty-four tanks while I was trying to succor and rescue four." Harmon said he visited one of the British units, the Sherwood Foresters, who had captured a bluff overlooking the enemy positions. "They'd gone up there with 116 men and there were 16 left, the highest-ranking man was a corporal. I had never seen so many dead men in one place."

The Allied forces settled in for a prolonged defensive siege. Men awaiting evacuation for treatment of their wounds crammed the tents packed around the beach while aerial predators and long-range guns worked the area over. It became known as "Hell's Half Acre." Said Harmon, "Some men hid their minor wounds so they would not have to be sent to that plague spot. At Anzio there were no goldbricks, no wooden Indians. Truck drivers, stevedores, ammunition passers, ordnance men, quartermasters, medics, engineers were shoved forward into the front line to fight as infantrymen. Ski troops fought in swamps; cooks dropped their skillets and picked up their guns. Officers were in the same boat. I never saw anything like it in the two world wars of my experience. There was an Anzio community of selflessness, a willingness of troops to help one another that I never saw again. We were there to stand or die."

The remnants of the Rangers had been integrated into a new organization, the Special Services, under Gen. Robert Frederick, leading to reassignment of Ranger-head Darby as commander of the 179th Regiment of the 45th Division. The losses at Anzio also gave Michael Davison, the West Pointer on the division staff, an opportunity to enhance his career under the former Ranger boss. Darby named him exec for the 1st Battalion, telling him to report the following morning. "That night," said Davison, "the CP of the 1st Battalion got the hell shelled out of it and the commanding officer was seriously wounded and evacuated. When I arrived at the regimental CP the next morning, Darby was going out and he stopped his Jeep long enough to say, 'Johnson got wounded last night and you are now the battalion commander.'

"At Anzio we slept during the daytime and did all our fighting at night because the Germans were looking right down our throats. You couldn't move in the daytime because of their observation. We were all dug in; everything was underground. We would sleep until about four in the afternoon and then as soon as it got dark we would send hot cereal, oatmeal, or Cream of Wheat and coffee and bread up to the front-line companies. You couldn't [bring that up] during the daytime. After that we would send out our patrols for the night. Usually they would come in, three or four in the morning. You would feed them a hot meal and everybody would go to sleep."

Ed Sims, acting CO of Company H, 504th Parachute Infantry Regiment, hung in despite reversals of fortune. His battalion moved to the British sector along with the U.S. 1st Armored Division where mud, terrain, and heavy enemy fire bogged down the attack. Subsequently, he was much discomfited to find that the Britons supposed to anchor his flanks had pulled back several hundred yards leaving the Americans overexposed. While reorganizing his lines, a shrapnel fragment struck his lower right leg.

In their new positions on 5 February, the company rocked from German fire. "Numerous rounds landed in my command-post area causing everyone to seek shelter. I jumped into a large open slit trench next to a building, and two men came in behind me just as an explosion took place directly above the hole. The fragments came into the hole, killing the two men and I was hit in the right shoulder. The trench caved in on us and after [they dug us out] I was taken to the hospital near Anzio. That evening the hospital was shelled by German artillery, so I located my clothes and equipment, got dressed, and hitched a ride in an ambulance back to the front line and my company. Medical installations were bombed and shelled frequently. On one occasion, a German fighter bomber dropped a load of antipersonnel bombs on the 95th Evacuation Hospital, killing twenty-eight patients and hospital workers, including three nurses."

According to Lucas, his II Corps was losing a fearful 768 men per day while replacements averaged only 462. The GIs of the 3d and 45th Divisions, who had previously engaged only in offensive operations, assumed the unfamiliar stance of defensive warfare. By 12 February, three weeks after the start of Shingle, Harmon said there were 120,000 crack German soldiers squeezing the ten-mile deep pocket around Anzio. On 16 February, said Harmon, the Germans at dawn opened up a massive attack against the beachhead. "These were the finest combat units in the Reich Army. Captured prisoners told us they went around and even the sick were routed out of their beds and thrown into the line, those who could fight. We had about 50,000 Americans and more than 400 pieces of artillery and it was artillery fire that saved the beachhead. I had one of the toughest decisions a commander can make. My chief of artillery reported that a battalion of the 45th Division for reasons unknown was in front of what we called the 'no-fire line.' If we laid down a barrage we'd kill our own troops. There are times when the responsibilities of a military commander involve the true meaning of the word 'awful' and this was one of them. The artillery attack might mean the death of many fine, brave American soldiers. To abandon it might mean abandoning an effort to save the beachhead. To me the choice was between the losses of some hundreds of men against the possible loss of many thousands. I ordered them to fire." Subsequently, he learned the soldiers were never where communications had placed them.

According to Harmon, the hard fighting around Anzio ended by 8 March. "Both sides lay down, you might say, panting and with their tongues out." For the next two months the opposing forces were content with raids, skirmishes, artillery, and air attacks.

Hamilton Howze analyzed Shingle as largely mistakes in both strategy and logistics. He noted the Germans were able to concentrate large forces against Anzio more rapidly than was thought possible and that the Allied troops halted before the defensive strength was sufficient to block them. "We stopped simply because the troops available couldn't man any [greater] perimeter and maintain proper tactical strength. The Lord granted the operation total initial success. Yet the planning was such that there were not enough forces to exploit the beachhead and push sufficiently far inland to cut the lines of communications to the south. I won't say the Anzio beach forces did not contribute a lot to the breaking of what was called the Gustav Line in the Cassino peninsula. Primarily the Anzio beachhead occupied a lot of German forces."

The unhappy results of Shingle, as is usual in military campaigns, mandated a change of command. Mark Clark had initially urged his VI Corps commander, Lucas, to be aggressive. "He must take chances," Clark informed his diary three days after the arrival at Anzio. He believed Lucas possessed sufficient forces to "advance on the the Alban Hills." The fuzzy instruction at the time of the invasion did not specify whether the VI Corps should seize the heights or merely reach them. The Fifth Army commander later remarked that he had never believed Anzio was a potential springboard to Rome. "They said you could have driven in your jeep to Rome. You might have but it would be the end of the war for you. There was no possibility of capturing the Alban Hills. I didn't have many reinforcements, the fighting was so hard down on the southern front. The assault at Anzio occupied many German soldiers. Nobody met us with any force at the landing and you could advance as far as you wanted to until you met opposition. The resistance amounted to eight divisions that were ordered by Hitler."

William Rosson, as a battalion commander of the 3d Division, felt that a more aggressive effort during the first few days could have secured an additional five to ten miles of defensible turf. "We failed to produce the impact on the German situation that I think the operation was intended to produce and could have done."

Below the besieged VI Corps, the gunnery between the Allied and German forces around Monte Cassino intensified. Shells struck the monastery with increasing frequency and except for a handful of monks and people too badly hurt to be moved, all residents had left. American soldiers tentatively advanced up the ridge, capturing some Germans, coming under fire from others closer to the monastery. But the GIs, too weak to extend their real estate all the way up to Monte Cassino, retreated. The monastery now occupied a no-man's-land and became exposed to the kind of treatment normally accorded such territory from both sides. As casualties accumulated, conviction that the Germans were using the monastery as an observation post, a sight for homing in artillery on them, grew stronger. To relieve the exhausted and depleted American forces, the Allies had inserted New Zealand and Indian divisions. Again a frontal assault produced only casualties. The commander of the Indian outfit, with the concurrence of the New Zealander in charge of both units, Gen. Bernard Freyberg, requested intense bombing of the monastery.

Under the chain of command for the polyglot forces in Italy, although Alexander was Clark's superior, the final decision lay with Clark, who was mindful of Eisenhower's strictures on "military necessities." Clark remarked that his allies called for bombing and shelling of Monte Cassino because "they just looked at it so long." Clark claimed he protested that all his intelligence sources agreed there were no Germans in the abbey. Field Marshal Kesselring wrote that all of his people were strictly forbidden to enter the monastery. After the war Clark spoke to the abbot, who reiterated there were never any soldiers in the monastery except for an army doctor who treated the civilian wounded seeking refuge there. Furthermore, the American general claimed he perceived that the ruins would make even better defensive positions for the enemy. Nevertheless, after Alexander approved Freyburg's request, Clark acquiesced. The bombardment of Monte Cassino began on 15 February with an air raid that dumped 442 tons of explosives and incendiaries.

In a colossal mistake in timing, the aerial effort was not coordinated with the ground forces. Instead of immediately charging up the last few hundred yards of mountain slope to occupy the monastery, the assorted New Zealanders, Ghurkas from India, and Britons, already discomfited by some bombs that fell within their precincts, crouched in their positions to await their H hour several days later. The massive air raid killed and injured many civilians taking refuge around the monastery, destroyed roofs, started fires that blazed up, and transformed walls into jumbles of rock, perfect nests for would-be defenders. After repulsing attempts by the New Zealand Corps to gain a firm purchase on its way to occupying the high ground, the enemy seized the advantage of the delay to fully invest themselves within the shattered complex. The siege of Monte Cassino would last nearly three months.

26
Galahad's Joust, New Ventures, Minor Gains, and Overlord

To preserve the corridor through Burma to China, the Chindits and Merrill's Marauders plotted maneuvers that would enable a large Chinese army to crush the main body of Japanese troops. The American objective was an airdrome at Myitkyina. The men of Galahad had now endured two arduous campaigns in the debilitating jungle struggles. Casualties from enemy action, disease, and an inadequate number of replacements had reduced the brigade to less than half, with Merrill himself on a curtailed regimen after a heart attack.

As disorganized as the Japanese appeared, they still outnumbered the forces available for Galahad as well as the Chindits. Stilwell, always anxious to disparage the British, crowed in his diary after the Americans grabbed the Myitkyina airfield, "Will this burn up the Limeys." The British hierarchy, up through Churchill, questioned how the small American brigade had pulled off such a prodigious feat. Unfortunately, Stilwell and his staff gravely underestimated the enemy troops available to defend the town of Myitkyina. There was a series of bloody encounters in the vicinity. Stilwell demanded that the Chindits in their sector, in terrible shape from disease, fatigue, and wounds, fight on, and he constantly harangued Chiang Kai-shek to commit more of his soldiers. Under these circumstances he could ill afford to spare the remnants of Galahad. To maintain Galahad, Stilwell transferred engineers, untutored in jungle warfare, to fill the ranks, and ordered Marauders from their hospital sickbeds to the front. Dysentery afflicted some men so severely they cut away the seats of their pants to enable them to function in combat. Those engaged in the actual fighting lived on short rations and husbanded their ammunition and other vital needs. The capture and full occupation of Myitkyina and its environs dragged on for another three months.

As in Italy and the CBI, there were no easy victories in much of the Pacific. The jungles of tropical islands soaked up troops like a blotter. MacArthur hatched a scheme to bypass a number of enemy bases with a 580-mile leap to Hollandia, on the north coast of Dutch New Guinea. The giant step avoided confrontation with a string of Japanese installations, but it also stretched the air cover to the edge. Nimitz and his people fretted about exposure of their carriers but the Air Corps eliminated the danger of torpedo bombers by intensive air raids upon enemy bases on Dutch New Guinea. The Army's 41st Division, blooded in the Buna campaign, and the 24th Division, a newcomer to battle, boarded ships destined for Hollandia, Dutch New Guinea. Also on the menu was Aitape, a locale in Papua New Guinea, about 125 miles east of Hollandia.

Han Rants, a wireman for the 34th Regiment of the 24th, said, "My greatest concern was that I would freeze or lose control when faced with extreme fear. Publicly, no one would discuss having fear. Some who boasted the most courage and told what they would do, turned into jelly as we started to climb over the side of the ship into landing barges. Others lost control of bowels and bladders as we hit the beach. Without really knowing Christ in a true sense, I considered myself a Christian and I prayed in my way that I would not show fear or be a coward when facing death. Some of the sailors told how in earlier campaigns the officers had to hold a gun on some of the marines to get them to go over the side into the landing barges. I believe this helped our green outfit because we had to tell them to watch our smoke and generally smothered any sign of fear that might otherwise have been shown."

The 34th's Hollandia venture began, however, without any sign of resistance. The 24th Division advanced about five miles before nightfall and then, while the riflemen dug foxholes, wiremen like Rants set up field telephone lines between battalions. "The first night of combat for a green outfit is a nightmare for everyone within rifle range," said Rants. "Knowing that the enemy preferred to sneak in at night, we were all overly alert to any movement or noise. Although our training taught us to hold fire unless absolutely certain, thus not giving away our position, we threw hand grenades and fired rifles all night long. Dogs, monkeys, water buffalo, birds, snakes, land crabs, and everything imaginable except the enemy were fired upon that night."

Bruce Pierce, a South Carolinian and graduate of his home state's National Guard, had graduated from the Fort Benning OCS academy and become a platoon leader with the 19th Infantry, 24th Division. "There was no problem with the sense of responsibility for men under me and decisions that would mean life or death to them. Being an enlisted man for more than two years and an officer for two and a half helped me know how the enlisted men thought and established a rapport with them. They knew I was subject to the same results of my decisions that they were and knew I would not act foolishly.

"I was not in the invasion at Tanahmerah Bay [Hollandia] as I was in the hospital on Goodenough Island. I rejoined the regiment a week or so later. There was no heavy fighting as there was not much opposition. Most of our time was spent on patrols around Lake Sentani and mountain trails leading toward Finchhaven. The Japs' 18th Army had been cut off and a lot of them tried to come up the trail thinking they still held Hollandia. Most of the ones we found were dead of starvation or killed by the natives because the Japs were raping their women."

Among those introduced to combat in Dutch New Guinea was a former refugee from Germany, Eric Diller. Denied an opportunity to enlist because his parents' attempts to obtain U.S. citizenship were delayed by investigation of German, Italian, and Japanese aliens, Diller nevertheless was drafted in June 1943. "When processed at the Camp Upton, New York, induction center, an 'Enemy Alien' stamp in bold letters was printed on the cover of my papers, causing some unfriendly glances." Assigned as an ammunition bearer for a .30-caliber machine-gun section in the heavy-weapons unit, Company H of the 34th Infantry, Diller said, "Most GIs with the outfit had spent nineteen months protecting Waikiki Beach against an invasion which never came. Then they trained for seven months in Australia, preparing for jungle combat, all without seeing a single day of combat. They must have been waiting for me." The waiting ended as the battalion embarked for the Hollandia campaign.

Pennsylvania draftee, Cpl. Joe Hofrichter went ashore with the 1st Battalion of the 339th Engineers near Hollandia. He recalled the scene during the invasion of the New Guinea beach overlooked by a site dubbed Pancake Hill. "An hour of shelling from our ships was followed by aerial bombardment. Going over the rail of the troop transport, we descended into LCVs, (Landing Craft, Vehicles). About halfway down the rope ladder, a man froze. He had things tied up, at a standstill. The poor man was so frightened, he couldn't even speak. Two men were sent down to pry his locked fingers from the rope in spite of his pleas to stop. When his fingers were freed, he fell backward. He landed on the eighty-pound jungle pack we carried. While this cushioned his fall, his helmeted head hit the steel deck with such force, the back of his helmet caved in. He lay unconscious. Resistance was relatively light. But [if there had been] a few artillery pieces, some mortars, and well-placed Japanese machine guns and we would still be trying to land and secure Pancake Hill."

Kansan Phil Hostetter, immediately after medical school in 1942, qualified for a commission as a first lieutenant in the Army Medical Corps. He spent a year interning in Wichita before he reported to the Medical Field Service School at Carlisle Barracks, Pennsylvania. "Medical schools," says Hostetter, "had taught us very little about the actual practice of medicine in civilian surroundings and nothing in the military. Our teachers at Carlisle, talented and hard working as they were, had no knowledge of combat conditions." Assigned to the 407th Medical Collecting Company upon completion of the Carlisle course, Hostetter's duties mainly involved physical exams for men scheduled to go overseas. Just before the 407th itself embarked for the Pacific, the medics went through the standard infiltration course, climbing obstacles, crawling under barbed wire, and live machine-gun fire at night. They also practiced climbing cargo nets.

In February 1944, the outfit docked at Milne Bay, New Guinea. They lived fairly comfortably in a tent city; gawked at the indigenous Micronesians; dined on Spam, dehydrated potatoes, and eggs; listened to the Armed Forces Radio; and awaited the opportunity to treat casualties. While staging for the Hollandia invasion, personnel like Hostetter learned to use the .30-caliber carbine, an indication of the status of medics in the eyes of the enemy.

Behind the infantrymen of the 24th Division and the engineers attached to it, amphibious vehicles, "Ducks," brought Hostetter to the beach. "We stood around wondering what to do next. The first casualty we saw was a man crushed to death by a boulder. He was bathing at the water's edge when the boulder rolled down the cliff from high above where a soldier was building a road with a bulldozer. We sent a litter squad to get the body. 'Lay him on the grass,' I said. 'The Quartermaster Department will take care of the body.' We were not responsible for the dead, only the disabled. Inland, a little farther, an enemy soldier lay on the ground. He was mortally wounded, unconscious and gasping for breath. I knew he would soon die. We felt no sense of exhilaration over the small victory. It was not small to him."

Hostetter continued to see few U.S. casualties. Detached to an evacuation hospital he began treating patients in two large tents. "All had a psychiatric condition. It was up to me to determine what their condition was, treat them if feasible and evacuate them to other hospitals if necessary. Those who had broken down under exceptional stress and exhaustion we called 'battle fatigue' cases. In a state of chronic anxiety, exhausted, they could not relax. They were so jumpy you could practically see daylight between them and their cots when a truck backfired. They had little appetite and when they did eat they were apt to have stomach cramps and perhaps vomit. Their sleep was fitful, marred by vivid nightmares of battle experiences and friends being mutilated. Some told of 'fugues' when they would become conscious after running for miles and not knowing where they were.

"Battle fatigue cases constantly asked when they could return to duty. They would hear reports of their units on the radio and feel required to return as quickly as possible. They felt obligated to help their buddies and guilty because they had failed when needed most. To help my patients rest I prescribed huge doses of the sedatives, Nembutal and phenobarbital. The other doctors thought my doses excessive but I had seen these amounts used in mental hospitals for the severely disturbed and knew they were suitable. Before long, the other doctors agreed with me.

"We would assess their fitness for combat by estimating the severity of the stress that put them in the hospital. If it had been great, as often it was, they recovered in about two weeks and returned to their outfits. The Army had a wise policy of keeping the men as close as possible to the combat zone. They still had high motivation to return to duty. The farther away they got, the less they cared about recovery and the poorer they did."

The Japanese expected invasions closer to the major U.S. bases and most of the garrisons at Aitape and Hollandia consisted of service troops rather than combat soldiers. When the fleets showed up offshore and commenced their prelanding bombardments the third week of April, the surprised defenders mostly fled the scene. Their departure left the Hollandia area secure but the Japanese in the jungles surrounding Aitape organized for an attack upon the Americans.

Early in 1944, halfway around the world in Italy, a standoff characterized both the Allies' Anzio beachhead and the situation at the German Winter Line throughout the first months of spring. With the enemy burrowed in the rubble there was nothing to restrain air attacks upon Monte Cassino. On 2 March, Dick Gangel, a replacement pilot in a P-38, *Chattanooga Choo Choo*, for the 82d Fighter Group stationed at Foggia, flew his first combat mission patrolling the sky over Anzio. Gangel flew another one covering B-24 bombers hitting the marshaling yards at Florence and then he and his group shepherded B-17s in a heavy raid upon Cassino. His diary noted this was supposed to be the "largest on record for any small target. It spearheaded a ground attack by American infantry and tanks."

As a fighter pilot, Gangel at Foggia shared a four-man tent with wooden floors and jerry-built gasoline heaters. "Everytime a plane crashed at the field, the first thing would be to make sure the pilot or crew were okay and then try to get the copper tubing from the wreck either to improve the heater or to make whiskey." Unlike those airmen in either North Africa or the Pacific, flyers like Gangel rarely saw what was happening on earth. Operating at great altitudes and frequently with thick clouds below, there was little opportunity to gauge the effect of the air war. "You didn't want to spend your time looking down anyway," said Gangel, "because you were always watching for German fighters. They could hear us coming and get to their top altitude and pop down on us." During his first five missions, however, Gangel never saw an enemy plane and in several succeeding ones the Germans declined to engage.

Eli Setencich, a Sacramento native and son of Yugoslavian immigrants, chose to fly rather than "being an infantryman slogging around." Graduated as a fighter pilot, he reached Italy as a replacement where he put in a few weeks in a night-fighter outfit. "I couldn't wait to get out of that because I didn't want to fly at nighttime. I had a hard enough time *driving* at night. I got into A-36s [a P-51 without a supercharger, designed as a dive bomber]. The dive brakes enabled you to go straight down. We were strafing and diving, going after trains, trucks, and resupply—anything we saw on the ground. Also repple-depples [replacement depots], railroad terminals, ships in harbors, like Genoa. Mostly it was railroads, tanks. We usually had a target when we took off but they would also say targets of opportunity. We go out in a flight of four and see what we could find. We'd look for trains, marshaling yards near the bigger cities. If we were supporting troops, we did a lot of close-order support; they'd say there were tanks in the woods holding our troops from going farther north. We'd circle around, see if we could find the tanks, go down and drop bombs on them if we could find them. Or if it was a bridge, it would be farther inland, that might be used for supplying their troops. Four of us would dive down and try to hit the bridge, knock it out. Generally, we had a pair of 500-pound bombs. It was all low, dirty work. We had .50-caliber machine guns with tracers every five rounds that helped our aim. You could see trains blowing up with all the steam coming out. Sometimes you hit an ammo train and that would really blow up." Unlike the Navy and Marines in the Pacific, the Air Corps in Europe did not use trained ground observers to direct and control their tactical operations.

Setencich recalled, "I crash-landed twice. My airplane was shot up near Pisa by ground fire. I didn't 'jink.' I remember my first flight. Jackson Saunders was leading it. We flew over Cassino and I could see these black puffs in the air, and no one told me what the hell they were. It was flak, bouncing around the sky. All I could hear was Jackson yelling at me over the earphones. 'Jink, for chrissakes, jink!' I didn't know what the hell he meant but I could see him jumping all over the sky. You were supposed to get your airplane going every which way so they couldn't track you with those 88s." From his testimony, it would appear that the precombat instruction he received did not include some vital advisories.

The efforts at air-to-ground support were not enough to protect the embattled forces at Anzio. Bill Kunz, as a member of the communications section with the 39th Artillery Battalion, had come off the line and was in reserve, about midway from the Anzio harbor and the front. "Gene Baron and I had dug in a fairly comfortable foxhole, almost a dugout, complete with sandbagged top, but what happened next illustrates what can happen if you relax and get a bit careless. I took one of our radios outside our 'home' to check transmission, etc. There were about half a dozen infantry in the area—enough to bring us to the Krauts' attention. They say you never hear the one that gets you! It was true in my case. While standing, I felt a hard blow in front of my right hip, like being hit with a baseball bat! Knocked flat on the ground, I heard the shell hit a dozen feet away. Instinctively I listened for the sound of the gun and heard it—at a distance, not close. The round had landed on our far side, between us and some infantry, killing two and injuring three more. I was the only one hit on our side of the shrapnel spread—usually in a V-shaped cone from the ground up. Since we were in reserve, there were medics nearby and in a few minutes one got to me. He bandaged the torn hip, gave me a shot of morphine and said I had a 'million-dollar wound,' serious enough for a possible trip home but not totally disabling. Had I been standing or turned a fraction to my right, I would have received the dreaded 'lower-gut shot.' Four of us were loaded in an ambulance and we began a rough ride to the 95th Evacuation Hospital. The ambulance was peppered with shrapnel; enroute I saw the arm of the man in the stretcher above me fall limp. He may have taken another hit."

Kunz arrived at the medical center in midafternoon and by midnight he was on an operating table while the surgeons temporarily repaired the damage. "The next morning, an orderly went between the two rows of cots in our tent, tossing Purple Heart medals (in boxes) on the foot of each cot. About two days later we were taken out, stacked up on the pier awaiting transfer to a hospital ship. It was a British ship, clean, and we received excellent attention."

Allied political and military leaders grew increasingly impatient with the status in Italy. More than three months after the first soldiers stepped onto the Anzio beaches, 70,000 men were still tied down and the highway from Rome to the Winter Line remained securely in enemy hands. Freyberg's attempts to break through at Cassino had stalled despite the enormous effort mounted by the Air Corps. The countdown to Overlord, the invasion of France from England, had begun and the overall strategy included capture of Rome and release of the VI Corps for Anvil, landings in southern France coordinated with the cross-channel assault.

Under General Alexander, the British-dominated Eighth Army had regrouped and now prepared to take on the defenders in the Liri Valley. Alexander drafted Diadem, in which the VI Corps, instead of banging its head against the stalwart positions that blocked access to Rome, advanced east toward Valmontone to meet the Eighth Army. Diadem kicked off on 11 May with a massive artillery barrage along the fronts of the Allied Fifth and Eighth Armies. Again the Rapido River crossing cost many lives. The victims belonged to Indian, British, and Canadian units. However, the attacks persevered until the Eighth Army established a bridgehead enabling it to muster sufficient forces to drive the Germans backward. Meanwhile, on the right flank at Monte Cassino, the Polish II Corps, an army of exiles, at great cost in lives, captured the ruins.

Mark Clark's Fifth Army, spearheaded by a French Expeditionary Corps on the left flank of the Eighth Army, penetrated the German defenses and pushed deep enough to require the enemy to withdraw in an effort to straighten its front. The American 85th and 88th Divisions drove up the coast against considerable opposition. The Fifth Army in very difficult circumstances broke down the formidable Gustav Line but the British Eighth Army lost momentum. After more than four years of war, the British could not keep up with the rate of attrition. Clark directed Truscott's VI Corps to advance toward Valmontone through Cisterna. Unfortunately, that nemesis of the Ranger battalions was if anything an even harder nut to crack, because the *Wehrmacht,* in falling back from the Allies to the south, settled in that area. The first blows at Cisterna by elements of the 3d Infantry Division, 1st Armored Division, and 1st Special Service Force [created from the remnants of the Rangers and Canadian troops organized into three 750-man regiments] were repulsed. The stymie continued.

From the onset of the American entry into World War II, the two prime leaders, Roosevelt and Churchill, had agreed that the first priority for peace required a tramp through Germany itself. The boasts of both British and American airmen that their day and night bombing might crush the enemy, or at least knock him to his knees, did not pan out. While the British prime minister spoke of the "soft underbelly," the brutal campaign in Italy had not provided easy access to Germany. Nor did the struggle that had begun in North Africa, proceeded to Sicily, and then onto the mainland, and which occupied a considerable amount of the Third Reich's resources, qualify in Joseph Stalin's mind as a second front that would alleviate the awesome pressure on his country. It was clear that a cross-channel attack, which the Americans always believed in, must go forward.

Churchill, whose attitude toward an invasion of France seesawed between wild enthusiasm and brooding despair, initially had thought a 1943 operation feasible. The American generals, with the enthusiasm of ignorance, had even talked in terms of 1942. But, as the dimensions of the problems and the resources available revealed themselves, a more realistic timetable evolved. Eisenhower, in fact, was not even named as supreme commander for what was dubbed Overlord until December 1943. And by the spring of 1944, the blueprints for the operation had gone back to the drawing boards and conference rooms innumerable times.

Where to actually strike turned on a number of factors. The beaches needed to be large enough to accommodate masses of men and materials. The distance from British airfields had to be within the radius of land-based aircraft—all operational aircraft carriers were committed to dealing with the Japanese in the Pacific. Ideally, the location would be the one with the fewest numbers of enemy soldiers in the weakest defensive positions. Into the decision-making mix poured a welter of information—intelligence from aerial surveillance, tidbits supplied by Resistance fighters and spies, intercepts of telephone and radio communications on the Continent, and even what could be gleaned from postcards, snapshots, and prewar vacationers' memories of the prospective beaches.

Theoretically, the most inviting target was Pas de Calais, the portion of France directly across the English Channel from Dover. It was the shortest distance from Germany itself and highly suitable for the swift deployment of armor. But the Germans would be expected to know all this. Allied observers detected extremely strong defenses in that sector. The extreme west coast of France, at Brittany, while shortening the sailing distance for supplies from the United States, lay beyond the range of some fighter planes based in Britain. The Cotentin Peninsula could fall under an umbrella of air cover and boasted the prize harbor of Cherbourg. However, it would be relatively easy to pinch off that neck of land, trapping the troops. The ultimate compromise choice was Normandy, whose beaches lay between the Pas de Calais and the Cotentin Peninsula. The major drawback lay in the absence of a port suitable for reinforcements and supplies.

To hide the target from the defenders, Eisenhower named Patton to command a paper organization listed as the 1st U.S. Army Group whose location in England indicated a Pas de Calais approach. To lend credence to the Patton figment, tent camps without soldiers were erected; trucks drove through the deserted area to make it seem populated; dummy tanks and landing craft added to the deception. German intelligence, which often astounded the Allies with knowledge of such intimate details as when troops turned in their winter blankets, bought the package, and nineteen enemy divisions battened down to defend Pas de Calais. Almost alone in his hierarchy, Adolf Hitler intuited Normandy as the bullseye, but military logic, for once, overcame his imagination. German knowledge was severely handicapped by the defensive posture forced upon the *Luftwaffe*. Aerial reconnaissance could not pierce the curtain drawn by Allied fighters around England.

Had the Anzio operation and the drive of the American Fifth and the British Eighth Armies achieved their scheduled advances, Overlord would also have been accompanied by Anvil, a thrust into southern France. But the latter invasion, which would become known as Dragoon, was postponed because the units designated for it remained tied down in Italy. Originally, the strategy for Overlord plotted a twenty-mile front but that was expanded to fifty miles. The British assumed responsibility for the three easternmost beaches, designated in code as Gold, Juno, and Sword at the extreme left of the Allied line. The Americans would come ashore west of the British at two beaches, code-named Omaha and Utah. Committed to Omaha were GIs like Bill Behlmer and George Zenie from the veteran 1st Division, the unblooded onetime Virginia National Guard 29th Division, and Rangers from the 2d and 5th Battalions. The pair of Ranger units, formed in the United States under Col. James Earl Rudder, a Texas A&M football star, college coach, and teacher, then further schooled in England, recruited officers and enlisted men while in the United Kingdom. Utah Beach would receive the 4th Division, a regular-army organization, but, like the 29th, without combat experience.

To forestall efforts to reinforce the beaches once the attack began, both the British and the Americans plotted roles for paratroopers and glidermen who would precede the seaborne soldiers, seize highways, choke points, and destroy communications. Sir Trafford Leigh-Mallory, the Briton in command of the Allied Expeditionary Air Force, argued vehemently against the scheme, prophesying a minimum of 50 percent casualties and perhaps as high as 90 percent for the airborne. The trooper generals persuaded Eisenhower they were vital to success. The American contingent included the 82d Airborne, with combat-experienced people like Bill Dunfee and Jim Gavin, as well as the virgin 101st Airborne and the 508th Parachute Regiment Combat Team. Glidermen would also be heavily committed.

The enemy, although expecting the Allies in the vicinity of Pas de Calais, attempted to make the entire coast impregnable. Field Marshal Erwin Rommel, named by Adolf Hitler as commander of the Army Group for Special Employment, held primary responsibility for the coastal defenses. But Field Marshal Gerd von Rundstedt, as commander in chief in the West, controlled dispositions of the troops. To complicate planning, command, and control further, Gen. Geyr von Schweppenburg oversaw panzer forces with their tanks and mobile armored infantry.

Rommel and von Rundstedt differed on a basic principle of the defense. The former believed it imperative to prevent the Allies from gaining a foothold on the Continent. His strategy, based on mines, beach obstacles, and gun emplacements proposed a defense four or five miles in depth. Von Rundstedt considered the coastline far too long to fend off invaders before they established a beachhead. Instead, he posited an approach that would deploy massive, mobile forces that could be rushed to any area under attack. But the panzer boss von Schweppenburg, acutely aware of the damage done to his armor by offshore naval guns at Gela in Sicily (where the cruiser *Savannah* saved the hides of Bill Behlmer and his associates), insisted on keeping his forces beyond warship range. Because Allied bombers and fighter planes ruled the air, anything that traveled by daylight, particularly over roads, was at risk. Swift reaction by German reserves was questionable. Hitler also decreed that some armored units could move only on his direct orders.

The differences between Rommel and von Rundstedt were never resolved. Both commanders received some of what they wanted but less than they believed essential to carrying out their strategies. The most important asset acquired by Rommel was the shift of some reserves, particularly elements of the veteran 352d Division closer to the Normandy beaches. Their presence escaped the notice of Allied intelligence, which referred to many of the defenders as raw youngsters, overage, or wounded vets from the eastern front, and unenthusiastic conscripts from occupied territories.

Deprived of all he felt necessary, Rommel still invested his considerable energy and tactical brilliance to deterrence of seaborne assault. He arranged a series of deadly barriers in front of the beaches. Metal stakes driven into the Channel floor could rip the hull of a landing craft bouncing through the water. He installed iron bars welded into the shapes of giant jackstraws to block access to land. Huge metal gates—"Belgian doors"—anchored offshore, guarded the approaches. Engineers festooned all of these obstacles with mines.

Behind the shoreline, in spite of a shortage of materials, the defenders labored to casemate large-caliber guns overlooking the beaches. Inland, Rommel directed the implantation of *Rommelspargel*, ("Rommel's asparagus") poles garnished with explosives and embedded in open fields to deny gliders a place to set down.

The extent and type of defenses were largely known by the Overlord planners. Navy reconnaissance patrols put small teams ashore where they examined the obstacles and pinpointed some of the emplacements. Navy people argued for an invasion at low tide when the landing craft would ground before encountering the obstacles and traps lurking in the water. However, the Army strategists pointed out that would increase the stretch of open land necessary to cross while under heavy fire. A compromise set H hour for one to three hours after extreme low water. To facilitate the nighttime airborne operations, full moonlight was desirable. The astronomers could specify those days precisely but much less certain was weather prediction. High winds could endanger those on the water as well as men in gliders and parachutes. Thick cloud cover could blot out drop zones and bombing targets. Based on the readiness of the forces and the conditions required, the high command named the period of 5–7 June as the primary target dates. The next favorable tidal time would be 18–20 June and no one cared to give Rommel any extra time to strengthen his defenses.

Furious debate marked the discussions on the magnitude of naval power. Appalled by the preliminary order of battle, Adm. John L. Hall Jr., who had responsibility for the transport and support of Omaha Beach, met with Adm. Charles M. Cooke, the chief planning officer for Ernest J. King. Hall remembered, "I banged my fist on the table and said, 'It's a crime to send me on the biggest amphibious attack in history with such inadequate gunfire support.' Roosevelt and Churchill had agreed that the English would furnish the naval gunfire support for the Normandy landings. I didn't give a damn what they'd agreed on in conference. I wanted to give my troops the proper support."

Cooke scolded Hall for his impertinence but Hall refused to back off. He recalled his reply, "All I am asking you to do is detach a couple of squadrons of destroyers from transoceanic convoy, give them to me, [and] give me a chance to train them in gunfire support for the American Army on the Omaha beaches." Hall obtained his destroyers as well as other warships including the battleships *Nevada, Texas,* and *Arkansas.* Hall's account was somewhat contested by Harvey Bennett, a Yale graduate whose specialty was shore fire control and served on the staff of RAdm. Alan G. Kirk, the senior U.S. planner for the Normandy landings. Bennett said that, on his advice, Admiral Kirk specified a quantity of ships with certain capabilities and received *almost* as many vessels as requested. Bennett agreed that Hall was correct in noting that compared with operations in the Pacific, the allocation of firepower for Overlord "was pretty puny."

To boost the firepower ahead of the GIs, the U.S. Navy converted British-made LCTs to rocket launching platforms. The Royal Navy, which employed these in Sicily, reported, "Prisoners taken during the Sicilian operation were awed by the effectiveness of the projectiles and told Allied military leaders that they had been able to stand up under ordinary shellfire but were not able to bear the fire, explosions, and destruction of the rockets. Nine such LCT (R)s were to blast away at Omaha Beach and five would hammer Utah.

Lieutenant (jg) Larry Carr, a reservist called up by the Navy in July 1941 was appointed commander of the rocketeers, and in December 1943 began to train crews on the missiles. Said Carr, "Each rocket weighed sixty pounds, was five inches in diameter and thirty-six inches in length. They were mounted in racks at a fixed, forty-five degree angle with a fixed range of 3,500 yards [slightly less than two miles]. Every ship mounted 1,440 rockets, fired in banks of forty. All were to fire in about two minutes. There were no specific targets; the mission was to blanket the beach areas, destroying barbed-wire defenses, pillboxes, etc." The sound, fury, and sight of the rockets would supposedly pile terror upon physical destruction.

To compensate for the absence of port facilities, engineers designed artificial replacements known as Mulberries. Hollow, floating concrete caissons, six stories tall, towed across the Channel, then submerged, would form piers extending out into the water. To provide a breakwater, the Allied navies scuttled obsolete ships labeled Gooseberries. To ensure a steady flow of fuel, the innovators prepared PLUTO—Pipeline Under the Ocean.

At Slapton Sands, on the southwest coast of England, a major area for amphibious training, the armored units learned of a secret weapon, the DD (duplex drive) tank, which was covered with canvas and an inflated rubber wrapper that enabled it to float. Aside from those devised to be fully amphibious, a second type of tank was waterproofed to the extent that the vehicle could be launched in shallow enough water for it to track across the sea bottom until able to climb up onto the beach.

The threats atop the cliffs that overhung Omaha Beach generated another ingenious scheme. In particular, two sites attracted the attention of the strategists. Near the hinge between Omaha and Utah stood a 100-foot high precipice, Pointe du Hoc (erroneously named Pointe du Hoe on maps). A reported emplacement there of a six-gun battery of 155mm cannons menaced the approaches from the sea. Another height, Pointe et Raz de la Percée also provided defenders with a natural stronghold.

Jack Kuhn, a sergeant with the 2d Ranger Battalion, remembered being summoned from a game of darts in a pub for a special assignment. He and Pfc. Peter Korpalo rode in a Jeep driven by their company commander, Duke Slater, to London. Enroute, Slater explained that amphibious trucks, officially known as DUKWs ("ducks" to GIs) were to be fitted with 100-foot extension ladders. The intention was to mount a machine gun on a small platform atop the ladder. When the DUKW crawled up onto land, the ladder would rise and extend, lifting a Ranger and the weapon. From that height he could provide covering fire for those Rangers ascending the cliffs.

"I was taken to a large factory," said Kuhn, "where I met with firefighters, military personnel from the British forces, and two British soldiers who would drive the DUKWs. I learned the fundamentals of the ladders and the British Lewis machine gun. The British were very high on the concept and we worked together with great enthusiasm, through trial and error, to make the systems function. In the first experiments I walked up to get acquainted. I had climbed cliffs from one hundred to three hundred feet, and this was a scary proposition. I would much prefer to hold a rope. Then I stood on the platform while the ladder was extending, giving me a hundred-foot free ride. We had a communications system so that I could speak to those on the DUKW and they could answer.

"On a cloudy, cold day with a pretty heavy sea running we gave the vehicle a trial run. The two British soldiers and I went out on the water, turned about and came ashore. That answered my first questions, whether the duck would float. Then the Lewis gun was mounted, and with me on the platform, they raised the ladder, extending it its full hundred feet. I fired the machine gun and everything worked to perfection. Feeling the experiments successful, Korpalo and I returned to the battalion with our DUKW. I believe altogether we had four of them on D day."

"On May 20," said Bob Edlin, a lieutenant who had won Rudder's approval as a Ranger recruit by his commonsense declaration that if surrounded and out of ammunition he would surrender, "the 2d and 5th

Ranger Battalions moved into the marshaling area at Weymouth on the English Channel. The weather was beautiful, sunshine; we knew the time was getting close for the invasion. The first four days were pretty much carefree. We could go into any nearby town, do just about anything, drink, gamble, or whatever. We had the usual arguments with the paratroopers of the 101st Airborne. On May 25, the party was over. We were locked in the marshaling area for a briefing. The area was surrounded by barbed wire. Armed guards, MPs and British, were stationed outside the fence. We were ordered not to communicate with them. We couldn't have any conversation with anybody who wasn't more or less imprisoned in the compound. In fact, we felt more like prisoners than we did invading troops.

"We were briefed by Colonel Rudder on the complete invasion, including the roles of the British, Canadian, Americans, paratroopers, 29th Infantry Division, the 4th and 1st Infantry Divisions, and what the Ranger Battalions were to do. We were told the date, time, and location of the invasion. I can remember someone saying, 'Hitler would give ten million dollars to know what I know.'"

Captain John Raaen Jr., a West Pointer who graduated in 1943 as an engineer officer, grew up in the same Fort Smith, Arkansas, neighborhood as William O. Darby, his senior by about ten years. "I heard of Bill Darby most of my life. When the article in *Life* magazine came out about Darby and his Rangers, I wanted to be one, too." While on maneuvers with armored engineers he learned of the new Ranger battalions being organized, so he volunteered.

Assigned to the 5th Ranger Battalion, Raaen took an almost instant dislike to Maj. Max Schneider, the CO of the 5th and one of the few Rangers in England who had combat experience in North Africa and Sicily before coming to England to work with Rudder. Raaen said, "He wanted to command the 5th but he was stuck with a love of the 2d Rangers. He was often insulting to us and always extolling the quality of the 2d's officers and men while deriding us. I commanded Headquarters Company and had much to do with Schneider." According to Raaen, "Prior to boarding the *Prince Baudouin* [his D-day vessel] we had many training sessions on sand tables and maps that had no names on them. Not until we boarded the *Baudouin* were the names uncovered so we could see the exact location of the invasion."

Behind the barbed wire of the marshaling area Sgt. Bob Slaughter of the 29th Division realized, "This was serious business. Brand-new equipment was issued and new weapons had to be zeroed in on the firing range. Unlimited amounts of ammo were given for target practice. Bayonets and combat knives were honed to razor sharpness. Food not seen since leaving the United States was fed to us, and it was all-you-can-eat. Steak and pork chops with all the trimmings, topped off with lemon meringue pie, were items on a typical menu. One of the wags said, 'They're fattening us up for the kill.' The officers became a bit friendlier and it seemed that the men were kinder to each other. First-run movies were shown; *Mrs. Miniver* with Greer Garson and Walter Pidgeon was one of my favorites. Touch football, softball, boxing, reading, and letter writing were popular pastimes. Bible verses were must reading for most of us and prayers were said many times a day.

"New Yorker Francis 'Skeets' Galligan put on a Broadway skit, *Yankee Doodle Dandy,* portraying himself as George M. Cohan. Skeets, agile and a fair tap dancer, concluded the routine by jumping high in the air and clicking his feet together. Semi-nude, hoochie-coochie dancers grinding hips to a beat on a tight canvas cot brought smiles and cheers from a captive audience."

Captain Norval Carter, a thirty-three-year-old battalion surgeon with the 115th Regiment of the 29th Division, a psychiatrist by training, who volunteered for the Army Medical Service, wrote home to his wife Fernie, "We shall hit our objective in the morning. Today is Sunday and we are practicing loading our rubber life craft. Letters from various generals have been read to us showing their faith in us and telling us our mission is to go in very fast and hold what we get *at all costs.* Religious services were held for the last time today. There was probably 100 percent attendance. Most of us have a strong spiritual feeling about this affair. We realize we are up against a well-trained, well-equipped, and a well-disciplined enemy who will resist and counterattack with great zeal. But we realize we are fighting for a way of living that is fundamentally right in the eyes of God and man, and the ideals of the enemy are wrong . . . Fernie, my sweetheart, I feel that I shall see you again. You and the boys. But if I don't I want you all to remember that my love for you cannot be said or put on paper. It can only be felt. You have meant everything to me that is good and happy . . . May God help us in our mission."

A 1940 graduate of Presbyterian College in South Carolina, George Mabry, as a reserve officer, went on active duty with the 4th Infantry Division stationed at Fort Benning, Georgia. He subsequently earned a regular-army commission. Mabry had moved up from a lowly platoon leader to the post of S-3 of the 2d Battalion of the 8th Regiment. His responsibilities included preparation of the boat-loading tables to ensure that the proper number of troops, equipment, vehicles, and supplies were allocated for the available landing craft.

"Eventually all personnel were briefed on where we would land and the specific tasks for each battalion and company. Security at Torquay became even stricter. We had only one man in the battalion administer a self-inflicted wound to avoid combat. He shot himself in the foot. During one meeting between officers of the 101st Airborne Division and the 4th Division, Colonel

[Robert] Sink chided Colonel [James] Van Fleet, 'Be sure, Van, that members of the 8th Regiment hurry and make contact with my troops at the causeways that cross the inundated area behind the beaches because we have other objectives to capture.' Colonel Van Fleet's reply was 'Bob, you just be sure your troops get there, because mine certainly will be there.'"

27
Overlord Overtures

At the end of May and during the first week of June, at a great sacrifice of life, the Allied armies finally ruptured the Gustav Line and bore down on the Italian capital. The forces trapped in the Anzio environs broke out. The various legions picked up their pace, spurred not a little by the competition to be the first in the Eternal City. Clark, in particular, wanted his Fifth Army to beat out any British unit. The Allied high command also believed an announcement that Rome had fallen combined with the D-day invasion would radically dampen German morale.

Howze remembered, "We went up a valley, the 1st Armored Division units working with the 3d Infantry. At one point infantry of the Hermann Goering Division came into the sights of the tankers and they killed a lot of Germans. We just sat in our tanks and killed Germans trying to get beyond where we were to establish a defensive position." The swift ebb and flow of battle bedeviled efforts to avoid the peril of friendly fire. American armor complained that the Air Corps bombed and strafed their units seven times in a single day. When told the ground forces were not properly reporting their positions, Howze retorted that there were Army liaison spotter planes over the tanks and the messages simply were not reaching the proper authorities.

"We made twenty-five miles a day," he recalled. "Get in a firefight every so often, kill a few and lose a few then go on. I'd lose patience. I'd tell my tanks, damn it, there is nothing out there, just get on the road. They'd run two miles and then a mortar would blow up and they'd get cautious and fan out. It was a hard go, the terrain was so broken it made bad tank country." To trundle over the misshapen ground, the tankers improvised, using bundled oil drums and poplar trees to fill deep troughs in their path.

Michael Davison, of the 1st Battalion of the 45th Division's 179th Regiment, recalled, "We had very tough fighting on the breakout. One day on the road that led to the capture of Rome I had nineteen battalions of artillery firing on my battalion's front—every single battalion of the division, battalions from the Corps artillery and from neighboring divisions. The casualty rate was high in the first couple of days. We fought like hell for three or four days getting out of Anzio. It began to ease the third day and on the fourth we had been passed through by another regiment."

Bill Kunz, still in a Naples hospital ward at the time of Diadem, said, "We knew when the 'breakout' from the beachhead occurred, as the wounded were stacked up in the hallways and any other spaces they could find. I learned later my division sustained 995 casualties the day of the breakout and 665 the following day. My injury maybe was really the million-dollar wound."

On the heels of the armor spearheading the advance on Rome came the Special Services Force. This unit was composed of survivors of the three Ranger Battalions and Canadians, and led by USMA graduate Brig. Gen. Robert Frederick, who had the authority to enter Rome. On the morning of 4 June, Frederick halted at the city's outskirts because of mobile antitank guns that repulsed the tanks. When II Corps commander Gen. Geoffrey Keyes demanded why Frederick did not advance, the head of the SSF explained the problem. Keyes, a protégé of Patton, blandly asserted that Clark expected to be in Rome by 4:00 P.M. "Because he has to have a photograph taken." Although the SSF and a recon platoon from the 88th Division, followed by a motley of Allied troops, surged into Rome starting at dusk, Clark could not publicly celebrate the victory until the next day. The ceremonial occupation degenerated into a farce when the Fifth Army's senior party lost itself in the maze of the city's streets until an English-speaking priest pointed them in the right direction to Capitoline Hill. Furthermore, it was a triumph not over a defeated army but one that retreated to new defensive positions north of Rome.

During the first days of June, with Overlord scheduled to begin on the fifth, the airborne contingents bedded down at the airfields. The huge fleet, numbering 5,000 vessels, milled about in the Channel waters. The weather refused to cooperate, with rough seas matched by a turbulent night sky. Eisenhower accepted a twenty-four-hour delay while meteorologists formulated a prediction for the following night. Troops who had been aboard the lurching ships for several days coped with seasickness. The airborne forces settled in for another twenty-four hours of waiting.

Ed Jeziorski of the 507th Parachute Infantry Regiment said, "Normandy would be my first combat. As foolish as it sounds today, I, among many, felt relief that we would be committed, and excited over the prospect of tangling with Jerry to show what we could do. I felt let down when we were told the invasion was held off for a day. While in the hangars, before moving out to the planes, we gathered around a small radio as the 'Berlin Bitch' came on. Her words still live with me. 'Good evening, 82d Airborne Division. Tomorrow morning, blood from your guts will grease the bogey wheels on our tanks.' Then she played tear-jerking songs."

Dave Thomas, a battalion surgeon in the 508th Parachute Infantry Regiment, was among the thousands behind the barbed-wire fences. "I was always an odds player and won a lot of money playing poker. This night I wasn't doing that well at the table so I thought I might as well go hit a lick with Jesus. I sat down in the last cot; the place was sold out. Chaplain James Elder was really getting the troops in. As I sat down, he said, 'Now the Lord isn't particularly interested in those who only turn to Him in time of want.' I thought, what the hell am I doing here? I got up and went back to the poker game, but still didn't do all that well. Some time later, back in England, after Normandy, I told Chaplain Elder about the incident. He was mortified."

Bill Dunfee, recalled, "I was disappointed and let down when the mission was postponed twenty-four hours, I was emotionally ready to go. I did my sweating before a mission. Once airborne I was apprehensive but became very calm and accepted whatever was to come."

Turk Seelye, like Dunfee already a veteran of combat with the 505th, recalled the same uneasiness. "We had spent a couple of days and nights living in barracks close to the landing strip. We spent the time getting our equipment ready, sharpening knives and bayonets, and in general having feelings of apprehension of what was to happen next. On the third or fourth of June we had been billeted in the airport hangar itself. Our beds were blankets spread on the concrete floor. We were issued the grenades, ammunition, and other supplies that we would carry. Briefings consisted of studying maps and using sand tables, as well as showing each unit the scope of its particular mission. That's when we had learned that the invasion would take place in Normandy. Other activities at the airport included shooting craps and playing poker, using the French invasion currency, watching a movie in the evening, and attending religious services."

Matthew Ridgway, the 82d Airborne leader, said, "About forty-eight hours before D day, they told us what they had just discovered. The 91st German Division had been moved into our drop zone. [Clay Blair's book, *Ridgway's Paratroopers* reported the intelligence on the 91st actually came to the attention of the strategists on 25 May.] Bradley asked what will you do. It was too late to change things or planes. My chief worry was enemy air interference. I was confident there would be no planes or night fighters but we might come over unlocated and unneutralized concentrated flak. We would be down so low we would be just sitting ducks."

In the G-3 section [Divisional Plans and Operations] of the 82d Airborne, Tom Graham, of the 505th Parachute Regiment, noted constant revisions. "It was a day and night project because of changes made where we were supposed to jump. Aerial photos would come in to the war room and things had to be changed. No one knew exactly where we were going to drop until shortly before takeoff."

Both the British and American airborne operations were designed to forestall any German deployment of reserves against the soldiers storming onto the beaches. The beneficiaries of the paratroopers from the U.S. 82d and

101st Airborne Divisions, as well as glidermen, would be the GIs from the 4th Infantry Division on Utah Beach. No airborne forces would be deployed behind Omaha Beach. Gavin, among others, believed the flat ground behind Omaha would expose the paratroopers to the crush of an expected advance by German armor. The area picked out for the elements of the 82d straddled the Merderet River five to ten miles behind Utah Beach forming a rough triangle whose perimeter measured about ten miles. The major objectives included the town of Ste.-Mère-Eglise, which sat astride a crossroads and a rail line that connected Cherbourg in the northwest with Paris.

The 101st Airborne Division under Gen. Maxwell Taylor would form a racetrack-shaped position parallel to Utah only two or three miles behind the beach. The 101st's troopers and their glider component, drawn from the 327th Glider Regiment, were expected to hold a coastal road that ran toward Carentan, a known stronghold of enemy reserves. The flight plan for all U.S. airborne components carried them on a southwest course toward the Channel Islands of Guernsey and Jersey. There, a submarine-borne beacon light would signal the transports to veer east over the Cotentin Peninsula for the final run to the appointed areas.

For recognition purposes, the troopers in the 101st Airborne carried tiny noisemakers, spring-steel crickets of the type usually included in boxes of Cracker Jack caramel popcorn. One click was the challenge and two snaps was the appropriate response during Overlord. General Maxwell Taylor, the former Screaming Eagles commander, explained, "It rose out of my experiences earlier in the Mediterranean and from our Eagle [practice] exercise in England. There was so much dispersion in Sicily," said Taylor, "that I realized we needed some method of identification behind enemy lines. Eagle convinced me more than ever. We needed a little noisemaker a man could carry in his hand. The cricket seemed just right."

While the 7,500 men of the 101st clicked together in Normandy, the troopers of the 82d Airborne, according to Gavin, relied solely on the passwords of "Flash" and "Thunder." "There was a lot of gadgetry around," Gavin responded, "and a lot of it didn't make much sense. In Normandy, the 82nd used only an oral password. It's always more important to carry more ammunition . . . to stay alive . . . to fight . . . to get there. I even cut the fringes off the many maps I carried so there'd be more room for ammunition. I myself carried 156 rounds of ammo, four grenades, a knife, a rifle, and a pistol, in case I had to fight my way through enemy territory, which once I did."

Of the top U.S. airborne commanders, only Gavin was a fully qualified paratrooper who had earned his wings at jump school. When the 82d and 101st leaped in Normandy, the most senior commanders, Ridgway and Taylor, had only jumped once or twice. Taylor's deputy, Gen. Don Pratt, could only join the division on D day as a glider passenger. Another novice jumper was the commander of the 101st's airborne artillery unit, Gen. Anthony McAuliffe.

As Lt. Homer Jones and his platoon prepared to board their plane after hearing a message of good luck from Eisenhower, Jones said he felt impelled to address the troopers. "I had tremendous respect and feeling for them. In the paratroops the normal walls between officers and enlisted men broke down. You did everything the men did, and I often finished marches carrying a mortar or machine gun. There were lots of country boys, poor kids, ones with different backgrounds, and they'd all become close. I looked at them and realized there were a lot I wasn't going to see again. This would be a final goodbye. I said, 'I'd like to add a few words.' I began, 'We've been together a long time . . .' and then it got to me. 'Oh shit!' is what I said.

"Trooper Japhet Alphonso said, 'That's okay, lieutenant. We know what you mean.'"

For both divisions, pathfinders, equipped with the Rebeccas-Eureka system and signal lights, would jump first to guide in the more than 13,000 men. Their aircraft roared down the runways and lifted off while the skies were still light, before the midnight prefacing 6 June. Because of double daylight saving time, darkness arrived very late. The first pathfinders touched down as early as ten minutes into 6 June.

The flak thrown up by the defenders drove most pathfinder-bearing planes off course. As a consequence less than one-third of the 120 troopers assigned to guide in their fellows achieved their targets. Even those who reached the proper place operated on the edge of disaster. German soldiers, alert to the presence of strangers, made the use of illuminating devices suicidal. Radios were damaged or malfunctioned. From the beginning, plans for a strategically effective airdrop went awry. The enemy, gradually aware of extensive activity overhead, filled the skies with exploding shells and bullets. Pilots ferrying the airborne units then sought to evade the fire. Simple navigation errors compounded the growing disarray.

Ridgway, somewhat overstating the case, claimed, "These kids that were flying the troop carriers, C-47s, they hadn't much flying training. They had done the minimum number of hours in the air. The glider pilots still less and so what happened was to be expected. I had fifty-four planes in my serial and they were using only these little violet lights, no navigation lights at all."

Tom Poston piloted a C-47 packed with paratroopers. "D day, it was black, pitch black. I think it was one A.M. when we crossed the coast of Normandy. The moon was bright through the clouds, it was *gorgeous*. We came in, drifting down through those clouds, plane after plane after plane after plane, down through this pitch-black dark and then there's a flaming 'Tee' there that those brave guys that go ahead of the drops set out there and that's the target for the paratroopers. But, oh, my God, they were dropping paratroopers from hell to breakfast because the formations were so spread out. Pilots don't like to fight prop wash too much [the air eddies created from the propellers of nearby aircraft].

"The ideal thing is to come in at 400–500 feet, drop the paratroopers. They just go bustling out, the chute opens, slows them, and they hit the ground. That's ideal because nobody can pick them off. But the guys [pilots] behind them don't want to go in at 400–500 feet because they're fighting the stick like crazy, trying to fly in formation, flying in the prop wash. So they stack and the next group comes in twenty feet higher than the first group. By the time the last groups are dropping, those guys are coming in at 1,000, 1,500 feet in the air, hanging there.

"I don't know what the Germans could see from the ground but we couldn't see anything. It was pitch black when we went in. But when we left it was a *sea of flame*. Everybody woke up down there and went, 'What the hey!' Boom! Boom! Boom! Antiaircraft and machine-gun fire, tracers all over the sky, every which way. The tracers look like they're coming right at you. You'd see a flare coming right at your nose and then it trailed off to the side."

Wallace Swanson, an Oklahoma State football star in Company A, 1st Battalion, of the 502d Parachute Regiment, described the ensemble he wore. "The parachute jumpsuit had these baggy pants with large front and rear pockets, two each, plus two more big, front-side pockets. One could easily carry twenty-five to fifty pounds of necessary ammunition, K rations, and personal items. The jacket had four pockets, two on the upper chest, and two lower that went to hip level. These were also wide enough for more stuff. I carried an officer's Colt .45 and a .30-caliber carbine. My favorite was the .45. I was quite accurate with it up to fifty feet. While I used the carbine numerous times, my second choice for combat was the semiautomatic M1 rifle. I had an escape kit with some hacksaw blades, a compass, a map of France, and a knife. Most of the men in my jump stick had a similar kit. An inspection before we left prevented anyone from throwing away items necessary for survival and got rid of any beer or liquor in canteens.

"There was little conversation during the flight. The leaders checked to see that the individuals for whom they were responsible were ready and alert to what they were to do. Most of the talk was along the lines of 'Are you ready?' and 'This time it's for real.' Maybe among a buddy-buddy group of two or three there was a laugh over a remark from one of the comedians on the plane. I dozed off for a while during the flight and saw many others relaxing in similar fashion. My feeling was, get some rest while you can because we might be on the go for many hours through the next day or two. With all that combat equipment on, one snuggled into the most comfortable position possible, sitting up, leaning against others or the fuselage supports. A few stretched out nearly flat in the middle of the aisle and hoped no one would step on them.

"Although I was a platoon leader and second in command of the company, I did not have any info on the flight rendezvous area after takeoff nor the path to our destination. In general I understood we would rendezvous over England, head south in a safe, tight pattern until we would gradually turn east to cross the Cotentin Peninsula well above Ste.-Mère-Eglise, north of Carentan, south of Foucarville to our drop zone. The ground of the Cherbourg or Cotentin Peninsula was in darkness, in contrast to the Channel waters, which reflected the moonlight. I knew we would jump soon. As we crossed the lower portion of the peninsula, we came under antiaircraft flak fire. Visibility was good with moonlight and scattered clouds. I could see ground fire coming up at our planes. I could hear bullets or pieces of flak hitting the fuselage of the plane but so far as I know, none pierced it or came into the troop area. Two or three bursts of flak came pretty close; we saw the bright explosion lights from the doorway. Occasionally the blast of a cannon or an artillery battery from below reached our ears, but we could hear very little from the ground because of the roar of wind blowing past the door.

"The pilot took two severe and one slight maneuver to escape the antiaircraft fire. When the green light went on, I heard the crew chief yell, 'Green light! Jump!' Our plane was probably at the right airspeed, 95 to 100 mph, when I jumped. But because of the evasive actions we were probably down to 500 to 800 feet. Once outside and dropping, I could see very little because almost everything was dark. The sparse light from the moon and stars scattered, showing only vague outlines. What I could clearly see were tracer bullets coming up from gun positions and flak bursts that exposed things with a blast of light.

"When I jumped I wondered where I would land since I couldn't affect whether it would be a low area, a rise, hill, bank, or whatever. To manipulate a chute, one needs a reason or a purpose, such as an obstacle. In any case, I had practically no time to try and guide my chute. It was jump; plop open, then me swinging in the air. I had only pushed back my helmet from over my eyes because of the jerk of the chute opening and then checked to see that I had not lost any of my equipment when I hit the ground, probably five seconds after I left the plane.

"Actually, I landed in three or four inches of water covering a grassy area. My chute collapsed; I collected it and hid it. The moonlight enabled me to see the outline of certain terrain features such as higher hills, trees, and bushes. Because the more elevated ground lay on one side, I figured out it was to the west and near the first target for our mission, the big offshore guns that the Germans would use to protect the beaches. When daylight came a few hours later, I saw that we were only a few hundred yards from that objective. Further study of my map indicated it was less than a mile to our second important mission, capture and holding the right flank of Utah Beach at Foucarville.

"I took about fifteen or twenty steps and suddenly felt I had stepped into a bottomless pit. I went down in water over my head. Hanging onto my equipment I managed to crawl up the bank of what was a drainage ditch by clinging to the tall weeds, grass, and brush." Shortly after touching down and soaking himself, Swanson began collecting his troopers. With a number of men from his own platoon and the company plus some stragglers from other outfits, he directed a line of march toward the gun emplacements.

Platoon leader Bernard McKearney with E Company of the 502d looked out. "It was a clear night over the Channel. The invasion fleet below appeared as toy boats. Everything seemed so unreal. I had to keep reminding myself that this was it, the day for which we had waited and sweated so long. The men were very quiet. Some dozed, others were on their knees watching history being made below. Then landfall. Fog swirled in. Then the ack ack started coming up. It didn't look a bit deadly. Strangely enough I thought of July Fourth. One burst clipped us in the wing. The plane lurched and nearly threw me out of the door. Then the warning red light. Stand up and hook up! No dramatics, no shouting. The men's faces were grim and tight. I tried to relax them by kidding a little. Then the green light. I shouted, 'Let's go, girls!' and I piled out.

"The air was criss-crossed with tracers. I couldn't see a soul below. I was over an orchard. I slipped frantically to miss the woods under me. Oh, God, don't let them catch me in a tree. I hit with a thud. I could hear shouting in German and English. With all of my equipment, I would have been helpless in my chute. I tried to keep cool. I gathered up my chute and ran sixty yards before plunging into some thick undergrowth. I placed three hand grenades in front of me and took off my equipment. After some hesitation I started out. Someone challenged me with his cricket. I fumbled for mine. I had lost it! I started swearing at him in good old Jerseyese. I knew an American GI would recognize it. He did and burst out laughing. It was our company exec, Lt. Ray Hunter, a Carolina boy.

"Finally, we collected a force of about sixty men. All this time we had no idea where we were. We had become hopelessly separated from the rest of the battalion. The men were wonderful. After about an hour we were fired upon by a German machine gun. Someone yelled, 'Stay down, Lieutenant Mac,' and then I heard an American Tommy gun chatter. One of our boys, Staff Sergeant Brosseau from Boston said, 'Come on, I just erased them.' It was the same all through the campaign. The men fought like veterans from the very beginning.

"As it was just getting light, I was looking for some place to hole up. There was sporadic firing going on all around us. I was getting worried. These men trusted my judgment completely. Finally, we came to a little village. As it was surrounded by a stone wall, I decided to move in. As we approached, we were challenged in English. Inside the place we found a medic captain from our own battalion and three aid men. These were the unsung heroes of the paratroopers. Since we had three or four men shot up and in bad shape, I was mighty happy to see the medics. We set up a perimeter defense around the village and remained tight until dawn. With typical Irish luck, I had stopped just short of a battery of eight German fieldpieces."

"On the night of June 5," says Lou Merlano, elevated to corporal when his Company A of the 502d had entered the marshaling area, "we marched out to our planes and there was an eerie silence about us. There seemed to be a smell of death in the air. We were all fully aware of what the twenty-to-thirty-mile-per-hour winds would do to our jump pattern. When word finally came down the jump was canceled, we were all happy about the situation. When we got the go signal for June 6, I had my M1, musette bag full of rations, ammo and grenades, an infraray gun about three feet long to use for Morse Code communications, and a map case. I expected to jump last, but Sergeant Perko, in charge of the radio and whom I was to help, saw how heavily I was loaded and moved me to second place in the stick. The rest of the guys in the plane were riflemen.

"The formation of the flight was tremendously impressive. I could look out the window and see the beauty of it. Few of us dozed off. There were conversations about how much we hoped the talk about French gals was true. There was a good feeling about the whole operation. During all our briefings in the marshaling area, I clearly remember how this would be like a sneak attack in the pitch of night. However, after we started across the peninsula from west to east, it became like night and day all at one time. For a while we could see planes alongside us. When the antiaircraft shells and stuff began to come up, the pattern scattered.

"Now I saw no other planes. I know of no shells hitting our ship. The first plane, the one with our CO, Capt. Richard Davidson, supposedly was hit and went down in the Channel after only half the men got out. Captain Davidson, the rest of his stick, and the C-47 crew were lost. In my plane, only eight of us landed on the ground. I presume the rest, including Sergeant Perko, who had given me his position in the jump, had dropped in the Channel and drowned. There were no instructions from the pilot, crew chief, or jumpmaster about what was happening. All I remember is 'Go! Go! Go!' I must have jumped at about 300 feet because after one-and-a-half oscillations and I hit the ground with a thud. I was in Normandy, in a field marked 'Minen.' At the time I did not know it was a dummy minefield and I moved very cautiously. I crept through the field toward a little farmhouse I spotted.

"When I got out of the field, I ran toward the house where I met a man and a woman. They apparently were farmers who seemed jubilant to see an American. They quickly poured me a glass of Calvados. They were anxious to help and I pulled out my map, asking for directions to St. Martin-de-Varreville where our objective, the German artillery, lay. Not speaking French, I couldn't understand what they said but they pointed in a direction of an awful lot of firing. I figured I must be about three to five miles from St. Martin-de-Varreville. I heard quite a number of planes in the area, so I left the house and headed where I thought [there] was some action. I jumped over a fence and lo and behold, I was in an area infested with German soldiers running about the courtyard. From a loft a machine gun fired at planes, probably now flying east back to England. There was much firing, much commotion everywhere. I would have to say that at this point I was terrified, realizing that I had nowhere to go except into the German hands. I sat quietly and devoured my little code book."

Bill Dunfee, with Company I, 3d Battalion of the 505th, remembered, "There was a bright moon, but it was very foggy. As our flight crossed the coastline, all hell broke loose. We were receiving antiaircraft fire in abundance. Machine gun, 20mm cannon, and AA artillery was bouncing us around. The pilot took evasive action adding to our problem of a stand-up position. It was not a pleasant ride and it seemed to take forever to our DZ. I felt machine-gun bullets penetrate the aircraft wing. Someone shouted, 'Let's get the hell out of here,' but no one moved. At about 0200 hours, the green light finally came on. It did not take long to empty that airplane.

"Jim Beavers and I were in the middle of the stick and the equipment bundles were to be released when we jumped. When my chute opened, I figured I had it made. We were still drawing AA fire but I was out of that flying coffin. Looking around I spotted Jim Beavers next to me and our equipment bundle off to one side. When I looked down, I saw C-47s flying *below* us. That scared the hell out of me and I started cussing. Those rotten bastards were trying to kill us. They had jumped us at over 2,000 feet and now dove down on the deck. I didn't want to be turned into hamburger by our own Air Force. That had happened during regimental maneuvers in the U.S. when a plane lost flying speed and dropped down, running into three of our guys and killing them.

"While descending, I regained my composure because it appeared we were going to make it down in one piece. I had told Jim I would meet him at the equipment bundle. He landed on one side of a hedgerow and the bundle, and I on the other side. By the time Jim joined me I had the bundle unrolled and the bazooka and ammo out. We loaded up and headed for Ste.-Mère-Eglise. It was easy to locate. That's where most of the firing was coming from."

Turk Seelye, a rifleman and first scout for Company E of the 505th, toted the full load: His M1, ammunition, grenades, gas mask, a pick mattock entrenching tool, and some intimate personal items—twenty-four sheets of toilet paper, a French phrase book, tablets to purify water, a billfold with invasion currency, toothbrush and tooth powder, a bar of soap, a spare pair of undershorts, two pairs of socks, a handkerchief, and a safety razor with, optimistically, five extra blades. "The name on our plane was *Miss Carriage,* and no sooner had I sat down on the aluminum bucket–seat benches than I had to urinate. There were no latrines on these flying boxcars. So I had to get up, be helped down the boarding ladder, and then relieve myself under the wing. It is not an easy task when bundled up in parachute straps and equipment. The 'nervous pee' syndrome was shared by almost all. There was a steady file of troopers going up and down the boarding ladder. As we neared the Normandy coast, the jumpmaster, seeing the red warning light, issued the order to stand up and hook up. At this point, each trooper attached his own parachute static line to the steel cable that ran the length of the plane. When one jumped out the door of the aircraft, the static line pulled the parachute from the backpack, causing it to be exposed to the propeller blast and open properly. The next order was, 'Sound off for equipment check.' Then each trooper checked with his hands the static line and other equipment of the man standing directly in front of him. When my turn came, I shouted, 'Number six, okay!'

"The cruising speed of the aircraft was about 150 mph. I could see very little standing in the aisle, trying to look out the small windows. I did see some tracers whiz by, and also what appeared to be a burning plane on the ground. As we neared the drop zone, the pilot flashed the green light and the whole stick of sixteen troopers exited in less than thirty seconds. The pilot, no doubt anxious to return to safety and comfort in England, failed to reduce the speed of the aircraft to the normal jump speed of ninety miles an hour.

"After I left the door, the plane nosed downward and I watched the tail pass a few feet over my head. Then, as the prop blast forced air into my chute, I got the strongest opening shock ever. The chute opened with such a violent jolt that a Beretta pistol I took from an Italian naval officer in Sicily was torn loose, along with my new safety razor. Since I reached the ground in no more than half a minute, I estimate the altitude of the plane was no more than 325 feet, very low.

"I was shaken up a bit, nervous and scared when I hit the ground. I immediately rolled up my parachute, stuck it in under some bushes along with the reserve chute and then put together the three pieces of my M1—trigger assembly, barrel, and stock. I put a clip of ammunition into the chamber and fixed my bayonet. I heard automatic weapons and saw some tracer and antiaircraft bullets headed skyward. The first human sound was a cry for help from a squad member. Two others from my group also heard the voice and found our friend, Maryland J. Golden of Tallahassee, Florida, lying on the ground, unable to move. His left leg was broken. He received a shot of morphine and we carried him to the protection of a hedgerow to await medics.

"We walked in the darkness seeking other Americans. Somehow I became separated from the other two squad members and I was alone in a French farmyard. I used my cricket for identification and happened to run across three Yanks from another airborne unit. We moved about still looking for other Americans and trying to avoid contact with the enemy. We saw none of either. But in the distance we heard the sounds of war. At dawn we came across several troopers who seemed to know what was going on. We joined with them and walked the several miles to Ste.-Mère-Eglise, site of the C Company [505th Regiment] command post. The company occupied an open area about the size of a football field. We spent the day setting up a perimeter defense."

James Gavin had elected to jump with the 508th Parachute Regiment. "I was asked to act as his G-3," said Tom Graham.* "William Walton, a *Time* correspondent had put on an army uniform and was on the plane. Captain Hugo Olson, the general's aide, was also part of our stick. We had all been shocked to hear that four men from Headquarters Company of the 1st Battalion had been killed even before takeoff when a grenade one was carrying exploded.

"As we crossed over the Channel and into France, the general kept contacting the pilot and copilot, and he went up and down the aisle assuring everyone as he passed that everything was all right. He told us we had run into some fog, but that the flight was going according to plan. When we neared the DZ, I looked out the window and saw the river, but things did not look quite right in terms of where we were supposed to be. The green light went on and all went out the door with Gavin, as the leader in the plane, first. It was a moonlit night and you could see quite a distance once the chute opened. You could see others dropping close by.

"All at once, firing from a château on one side of the river streaked toward the bundles, which had lights on them, and then at paratroopers. It was an odd scene when the quiet of the night was broken by the guns. As I came close to the ground I thought I was looking at a big pasture. It turned

---

*In his book, *On To Berlin*, Gavin notes, "Lt. Thomas Graham and Capt. Willard Harrison [also aboard] were picked for their combat experience and reputation for toughness and courage in combat."

out to be water with grass growing up through it that broke the shine of water. I had never made a water landing and I didn't know how deep this would be and what it would be like. As my feet came down and struck this grassy water, I pitched forward as my parachute pulled me to my knees in water that was above my waist. I stood up but when I had gone under the water I lost my helmet. I fumbled around for the helmet and found it quickly. My rifle was wet, my map case wet, and my pockets full of water. I was anxious to get to a shore that I could see some distance away. Meanwhile, the firing grew heavier with tracers tracking other chutists and gliders now coming down. When I reached the dry ground, there were some other troopers there along with General Gavin."

According to Gavin's recollection, when he gave the signal to exit the C-47, they were more than half a minute beyond their scheduled time to leap. The stick with him, as well as many others, came down several miles east of their drop area. Not only were the American paratroopers misled by the ineffectiveness of the pathfinder operation and the intense antiaircraft fire that drove the C-47 pilots off course, but they were betrayed by faulty interpretation of reconnaissance photos. During the spring thaws and rains, the two principal rivers, the Merderet and Douve, had poured over their banks. The aerial photos indicated the length and breadth of the flooding, but not the depth. The tall grass that grew up through the water fooled observers into believing the swampy area was at most a few inches deep. "Ground here probably soft" was the optimistic conclusion of the report. In fact the water was over a man's head.

A considerable number of troopers, burdened with chutes, laden with weapons and extra ammunition, and toting heavy radios bags, with equipment stowed in bags strapped to their legs, fell into the deep ooze and drowned. Many of the equipment bundles with precious bazookas, machine guns, and mortars also disappeared into the marshy depths.

The party that included Gavin and Graham moved away from the river while the gunners in the château targeted the marshes. Graham remembered, "The general had seen a glider halfway under water. He said there was a 57mm gun in the glider and asked if I would take three or four troopers to see if we could retrieve the weapon. I didn't have to ask for volunteers. They were all willing. We waded out to the glider in the water. We could not raise the front end. It was wedged into mud and grass. The occupants apparently had gotten out through the side of the glider.

"Unable to lift the nose, we reported back to General Gavin. He told us he'd take a group down the road toward the château and take them under fire if we would try again to remove the 57mm. We started for the glider and the fire from the château became so intense I didn't think we could even get there. We made it without being hit but we still could not budge the nose.

"Gavin directed us to leave the area, and rightfully so, because the Germans had begun closing in on us with heavy fire. We crossed through open water and the river itself; you could not tell when you actually left the flooded field and were in the stream. I looked back while we were partway across and the bullets from the Germans were kicking up water and sometimes you heard them go overhead but you never knew how close."

Gavin surmised that he had dropped several miles northeast of Drop Zone N, the target plotted for the Red Devils. He was on the far side of the wide expanse of water sluiced from the Merderet by the Germans to impede invaders. Furthermore, the troopers he collected were not from the 508th but mostly belonged to the 507th. Gavin led his small force toward the la Fière Causeway across the Merderet, because, "It was a terribly important causeway. It was really the only feasible way to get across the Merderet all the way from Montebourg down south." Movement in this direction by enemy forces would place them directly behind Utah Beach.

But before Gavin could take command at la Fière, the situation lay in the hands of lesser figures much closer to the objective. Among the handful of troopers in the vicinity was the 507th's Raider Nelson. Nelson was of the relatively small number of paratroopers to land near the designated drop zone. "Our objective was to use the Merderet River, which ran parallel to the beach, as a defense line preventing German reinforcements from reaching the beachheads. Each of us carried an eleven-pound antitank mine below the reserve chute. This was to be buried about fifty feet from the river. We would then dig in along the river. But because of our wide dispersal upon landing in the dark, this plan was not implemented. I was separated from my company and in the darkness found other lost troopers. There was no enemy in our area but plenty of small-arms fire around us. We set up a defensive perimeter and by early light had gained several more troopers, but still none from my company. An officer took charge and we started to march single file, spread out, along a road. The second man in front of me was hit by sniper fire and from then on, enemy resistance built up."

Trooper Ed Jeziorski of the 507th recalled: "My light machine gun was in a pararack under my plane's belly. I carried eight clips of ammo in my cartridge belt plus two bandoliers draped over my shoulders, one Gammon grenade [a British device using plastic explosives], two fragmentation grenades, a phosphorous grenade, an antitank mine in my musette bag, a bayonet, a jump knife strapped to my right boot, two antitank rifle grenades and my trusty M1 rifle with 'Jean' carved into the stock. When I jumped over the Rhine later, I carried Jean IV.

"It seemed like eternity before we were able to get above treetop level. There was little or no talking. I had a certain amount of tenseness but I know it was not fear. Instead I was apprehensive as to what lay ahead. I did say a prayer, asking God to let me do the job for which I had been trained, and not to let my buddies down. We had been briefed, no lights or smoking but I had a momentary lapse and lit a cigarette. [Lieutenant] Parks yelled instantly, 'Put that goddamn cigarette out!' Someone else then said, 'Do we really have to go?' That brought some real and some fake laughs and the tension eased. As we came over Normandy, the whole sky lit up with sheets of multicolored antiaircraft tracers. Parks had us stand and hook up. We were bouncing and heaving from side to side as our ship tried to dodge the tracers. I lost my balance, went down and somebody had to help me up. Our plane was taking violent evasive action and hadn't slowed a bit when the green light flashed. Parks shouted, 'Let's go!'

"We shuffled out as fast as we could behind him. Just as I cleared the door and before my chute popped open, a great ball of red fire and black smoke erupted directly underneath me. Without thought as to how ridiculous it was, I shouted a warning, 'The bastards are waiting for us!' I pulled my knees up to make myself as small a target as possible; the bullets were crackling that close. I pulled on my risers to try and slip away from the fire. I landed near the hamlet of Hebert, nowhere near the intended drop zone. As soon as I hit the ground, a machine gun began covering me, very closely. Everytime I moved, the gunner opened up on me. I must have been pretty visible because of a burning plane nearby. I pulled my jump knife and cut the leg and chest straps. I rolled over and as a clip was already in my M1, I eased off the safety, then squeezed off a couple of shots at the Jerry gunner. I don't think I hit him but his firing ceased.

"Working my way toward a large hedgerow, I heard a good bit of thrashing about. As the sound came closer, I came close to pulling the trigger. But I called out softly, 'flash.' Quickly, the response was 'thunder.' It was my assistant gunner, Grover Boyce. All of a sudden, the world was a lot more friendly. Our stick had jumped right on top of a German concentration. Some were immediately surrounded and had no choice but to surrender while still in their harnesses. Lieutenant Parks was captured but escaped to rejoin the regiment. My squad leader, Greg Howarth, became a POW, as did Jack Kessler and Marshall Griffin. But Boyce and I teamed up with Dante Tonneguzzo, who later was awarded a DSC, and our aid man, Andy Manger.

"We moved on, trying to hook up with other troopers. Germans fired at us and we scrapped back. We took a prisoner and the firefight eased off. As Doc Manger was interrogating the Jerry, the whole left side of his face disappeared. Apparently, one of the Jerries still hidden in a building was not about to let our prisoner give us any helpful information. We stretched the Kraut out on the ground and Doc gave him a heavy dose of morphine. He was turning gray and his eyes were glazing over when we left him.

"We found a parapack, opened it up, and it had a light machine gun with two boxes of ammo. It was just like old home week. Boyce said, 'Here come the Krauts.' About two hundred yards away advanced a small line of Jerries with a machine gun in the center. They spotted us about the same time we saw them. Their gunner went into action fast and Boyce and I scrambled to get a belt loaded. Most of their bursts went over our heads. I know my fire was a helluva lot more accurate, but damn that gun of his could throw a bunch of lead in a hurry. They broke off the scrap and we didn't go chasing them."

C.B. McCoid commanded B Company in the 507th's 1st Battalion and was scheduled to lead his unit in the vicinity of Amfreville, a village west of the Merderet. "Our C-47, with six jumpers and six bundles in pararacks mounted on its underside was heavily laden. It struggled to get into the air. It seemed about to go down at one heart-stopping moment. A couple of men cursed with relief as the plane steadied and resumed climbing. I spent much of the flight in the pilots' cabin of the C-47 leading B Company's part of the formation. As the coast was neared, the pilot ordered the crew chief to open the jump door. I shook the men awake. Attaching my static line to the anchor-line cable, I stepped to the open door to watch the coastline north slip beneath us.

"All was as it should be. We were droning along at about 125 to 130 knots and holding an altitude of some 800 feet. The formation was intact. Then the red light came on. The order to 'Stand up and hook up' was issued. The heavily burdened men struggled to their feet with difficulty, most receiving and giving pulls and pushes to get in place in line. Meanwhile we flew steadily toward Drop Zone T. The ground was dimly visible below, with tree lines and open fields identifiable without much trouble. I felt we would surely be able to drop on target.

"Suddenly, we passed over a bank of white fog or smoke, extending north along the midaxis of the peninsula, which totally obscured the ground. We may have taken as much as half a minute to cross this surprise—it seemed much longer. But once we did, the action began. Machine-gun fire was coming from everywhere. The tracer rounds arced slowly toward us and then flashed by with a sharp, ripping sound that turned into uncountable cracking noises as they came close. This was our first experience with the German MG 42 and its amazingly high rate of fire.

"Now the area was being lit up by fires I associated with crashed aircraft. Just how many I cannot say. At the time I would have said ten although there may have been as few as five. Sticks of open parachutes started to appear in the illumination, including some that seemed headed into the flaming wreckage. A low bang then exploded beneath our ship, as if a 37mm or at least a 20mm antiaircraft round had struck. I felt a sharp pain at the right knee and a sudden loss of my ability to stand. As I fell to the floor, so did the entire stick. We had been battle damaged and were crashing, or so it seemed. The plane leveled out at 200 to 250 feet. Its speed was so high it was shaking and we may have reached 150 knots. The sprawled troopers untangled themselves and regained their feet, under the urging of the NCOs and by the help of medic, John Vinski.

"I tried to use the rear bulkhead intercom to reach the pilot and order him to get into drop posture. The system didn't work. The crew chief was useless, or dead. He lay curled up against the bulkhead and didn't respond to prods and shouts. Knowing that the Bay of the Seine was coming up fast, and getting the stick out safely would be a near thing, I stepped to the door, salvoed the six parabundles, and shouted, 'Let's go!' I got out, followed quickly by O'Neil Boe, the company runner and the others.

"We seemed to exit the C-47 at treetop level. Our chutes opened so violently that any gear that was not fastened exceptionally firmly on our persons simply tore away and disappeared into the darkness. In my own case, almost every item not encompassed by the T5 Parachute assembly belly band, and the reserve parachute was gone. Anything in my jump pants pockets burst through the reinforced bottom seams. I lost K rations, canteen, spare magazines of carbine ammunition, three grenades, a folding-handle entrenching tool, and my musette bag along with its contents of a Hawkins mine [a British antitank weapon], toilet articles, spare socks, and underwear.

"Fortunately, we carried our individual firearms under the reserve chute, so I had my carbine with its inserted ten-round magazine on landing. The other items I still possessed were maps, escape kit, switchblade jump knife, first-aid packet, and the Gammon grenade. I also still had on the Mae West life vest that I gladly tossed away after I was down. I landed on a stony road about one-third mile south of the small village of St. Martin-de-Varreville. This, after oscillating wildly under my canopy and crashing to the earth on my knees. Stunned initially, I soon was able to check my injuries. I found I had a crushed right kneecap where a wound already existed from the anti-aircraft round that hit our plane. I still had my chute on. It was tough to remove in the darkness. I thought it impossible for me to stand, so I wallowed around in a web of harness, canopy, and suspension lines on the road. Finally the reserve and belly band were off, the snaps unfastened, and I was free. More important, my automatic carbine was in hand, although with only one magazine. As I took inventory of the few items still with me, a series of low-flying aircraft passed over at very high speeds. Although these seemed to be ours, they were headed on many azimuths and probably lost.

"I wished them well but I had a problem of my own. The sky above was fairly light so anything higher than one's self tended to be visible in dim outline. The road was a sunken one, placing me in the darkness. A shadowy figure approached from the south. As he came up, I could make out his bayoneted rifle, as well as the shape of his coal scuttle helmet. By this time he was on the dike, or berm, on the east side of the road. Without any thought beyond, 'characteristically shaped helmet,' I thrust up on my good knee and shot him dead.

"There was nothing heroic about the act. We had an intensive series of classes on enemy equipment and the *Stahlhelm* [steel helmet] was easy to remember. My reaction was an example of useful training. Now, perhaps because the dead man was not alone, I had to get going and damn quick. Since there was no way of knowing where I was, any direction seemed as likely as another. By crawling over the dike, I got into a large field with a bunch of curious cows. By now I had found it possible to hobble along by keeping my right leg stiff and swinging it from the hip.

"I made slow progress for about fifty yards before I reached a dense hedgerow, through which it was impossible to pass. Now, with the first light breaking in the east and in considerable pain, I abandoned caution. I returned to the road leading north. Shortly, two Germans appeared immediately in front of me. Neither bore weapons or wore headgear and they seemed disoriented. Because I had only nine rounds left in my carbine, I decided to bluff them and capture them, if possible. About the only useful German phrase I remembered just then was *'Hände Hoch,'* had a magical effect. They turned in alarm, with hands raised. I don't know whether they or I were closer to wetting trousers. Certainly they didn't have the look of elite troops. It later turned out they were Russians who had been impressed into German service.

"When we moved forward we came to the outskirts of what I subsequently learned was St. Martin-de-Varreville. Now I was really scared. Some desultory fire was coming from several directions; I had no way of knowing the situation. I forced the Krauts to lie down in a ditch, which they were glad to do. I then hobbled forward to the edge of the village and met a group of privates from the 502d Parachute Infantry. They informed me that the rest of the built-up area was clear and they were checking out the last few houses. I was happy to turn my prisoners over to them. Then I slowly made my way through a typical Norman farm village with its stone structures and piles of manure. In one building was a battalion-level command post. I reported in."

Private Jim Kurz, as a member of B Company's 1st Platoon, 508th Parachute Infantry, said, "When the red light came on, we all stood and hooked up. Corporal Theis was the last man and I was right ahead of him. He turned around and I checked his chute and anchor line. Then I yelled, 'Fourteen o.k.!' He checked my chute and yelled, 'Thirteen o.k.!' I did the same for Wolfe's chute; he was twelve. As the plane broke out of the clouds, the call, 'One o.k.!' came. The green light went on. Lieutenant [Homer] Jones yelled we were over water. After a few seconds' delay, he shouted, 'Let's go!' All of the troopers left the plane. We had jumped at a very low altitude, maybe 300 to 350 feet. When my chute opened, I hit the trees and hung there. I got my knife out, cut my harness, and dropped to the ground. It was pitch black and I landed in a bunch of stickers. I had only been two feet off the ground.

"I started along the line of flight; planes were still flying overhead and you could see tracers going up to them. I heard a sound in front of me and ran into Private Wolfe. He had broken his leg. I told him I would return with a medic. When I reached the edge of the field against a hedgerow, I found Lieutenant Jones and part of the stick. The medic who jumped with us was there. We went back to Wolfe who told us he had heard others nearby. We discovered Theis and one other man. All three had broken a leg. We put them in a hedgerow ditch and left them. The only reason I wasn't hurt was I had landed in the tree and been saved the shock of hitting the ground."

Sergeant Bud Warnecke, mortar squad leader, said, "I looked around the hangar at the troopers of Company B who nineteen months ago were mostly recruits. Now they were ready to jump into combat as a family. I knew we were the best trained we could be and capable of beating the Germans in battle. Our morale was high. We had a meal fit for a king and then went blackface, using soot from the stoves in the kitchens. I waddled out to our plane. I had a Mae West in case we had to jump into the Channel. The reserve chute added extra weight and bulk but it would be useless because of the altitude we jumped at. My squad loaded into the plane with the company commander, Capt. Royal Taylor, who would be jumpmaster.

"A few minutes before takeoff, the battalion commander's runner came to the plane with a bicycle and cargo chute attached. He informed us that Colonel [Herbert F.] Batcheller wanted us to drop the cycle into Normandy so he would have transportation. We had our plate full of bundles but Captain Taylor said okay. As our plane joined the formation before crossing the Channel, I thought about what guys from the 505th had told us about what it would be like jumping into combat. I thought about where and how we were to assemble. I reminded myself of the sign and countersign, 'flash' and 'thunder,' and the cricket issued. [Although Gavin would insist no one in the 82d Airborne used the devices, Warneke's memory contradicted him.] I reminded Captain Taylor to release the pararack bundles under the C-47 when the green light came on. There wasn't much talking among the troops but a lot of smoking. All the men prone to air sickness had taken preventive pills.

"We reached the English Channel and Captain Taylor had the troops stand up and hook up. In case we were shot down we would have a chance to get out. In the middle of the Channel we looked out the door on a beautiful moonlit night at a sight no one will ever see again. Ships, so many ships, it looked as if you could walk from England to France without getting your feet wet. About this time, Captain Taylor or I asked what the hell are we going to do with the damn bicycle. Simultaneously, we kicked it into the Channel without hooking up its chute. Flying between the Jersey and Guernsey islands we could see the German antiaircraft gun flashes. The flight was in good formation until we reached the coast of Normandy where we ran into a thick fog. The formation broke all to hell. It seemed as if they speeded up. We were now under heavy German fire; it seemed as if we were engulfed in red and green tracers. Now, I was scared.

"The red light came on, Captain Taylor was standing in the door and said something like, 'I don't know where the hell we are.' The green light came on, he jumped and I bailed out right behind him. It took only a second to realize somebody was mad at us. It seemed unbelievable that I would live through this night. We had jumped at 400 feet or less because it could not have been more than thirty seconds before I'd gone through an apple tree. My canopy had draped around and caught the top. My feet barely touched the ground for the easiest landing I ever had. Using my jump knife, I cut myself out of my harness.

"Using the sign, countersign, and cricket, the first trooper I found was Captain Taylor. He was lying in a ditch beside a hedgerow and injured from the jump. I saw one of our bundles about fifty yards away and wanted to recover it. Taylor told me to forget it because it was covered by German machine-gun fire. Taylor instructed me to roll up the stick, then find Lieutenant Jones and tell him he was now acting company commander. It tells you something about Jones when you realize he was not the senior lieutenant under Taylor.

"I oriented myself by the aircraft still flying overhead, which gave the direction our troops should land. It was about 0230 when I started moving in and around the hedgerows. [We had not been briefed on finding hedgerows as thick or high as these.] In about an hour I found most of my stick and by luck stumbled upon Lieutenant Jones and our exec officer with about half of B Company. We realized we had jumped several kilometers from our drop zone and our objective.

"We waited and searched for others until Lieutenant Jones said it was time to go. He organized us into two platoons. He designated me as one platoon leader. Lieutenant Jones had us ground our heavy musette bags so we could travel faster—I never saw it again—on our way to our objective, the causeway at the Merderet River. On the way, I saw troopers in trees, shot while still in their harnesses. It was dog-eat-dog, and anger for the Germans turned into hate. There were American and German dead everywhere you looked."

"The three planes with my platoon," said Lt. Homer Jones of B Company, of the 508th, "had managed to stay together. In fact, when we came through a break in the clouds over Normandy, they almost ran into one another. After I got out of my chute on the ground it was surprisingly quiet. We used the recognition signals of 'flash' and 'thunder.' Later, though, one of my guys told me he heard someone running toward him and called out 'Flash' and the other trooper answered, 'Flash, my ass. They're right behind me.'" After his superior, Royal Taylor, assigned command to him, Jones headed his roughly seventy men in the direction of the Merderet Causeway.

Paratrooper Bill Dean said, "It was past 3:00 A.M. when we got to the la Fière Causeway, leading to one of the two bridges over the Merderet. Here, the rigors of the preceding day and night made us first sit down and not long after, lay down in a ditch and go to sleep. After a two-hour fitful doze, we were joined by Lt. Homer Jones, who was leading another small group of B Company men. Lieutenant Jones had met our regimental commander, Colonel Lindquist, who ordered him to attack and take the la Fière Manoir, a group of strongly defended buildings that guarded the approach to the road and bridge over the river."

Battalion surgeon Dave Thomas, still smarting from indifferent success at the poker table, enjoyed a brief moment of optimism in the sky. "In the nice bright moonlight, as far as I could see behind me were echelon upon echelon of C-47s, each filled with a bunch of troopers. I thought, boy, this is going to be a piece of cake. We are really organized. We turned to the coast and hit a cloudbank. When we came out of it, the airplane I was in was the only one I could see in the sky. When the flight hit those clouds they just split up like a bunch of ducks being shot at.

"Trying to find out where we were, I kept looking down and finally I saw a stream. I was jumping number two, behind the battalion commander, Colonel [Henry] Harrison, and I said, 'That has to be the Merderet. Let's get the hell out of here.' We jumped and I landed in a field. As I got out of my chute, I saw something white. I crept up to it, a cow chewing its cud. The first guy I ran into was Bill Ekman who'd been the exec in the 508th but when Gavin was promoted to a brigadier they made Ekman CO of the 505th [the regiment of Bill Dunfee]. Ekman wanted me to come with him and one of his battalions that was moving on Ste.-Mère-Eglise. I said no, I would follow the railroad line, which was west of where I came down near Beuzeville-la-Bastille. I picked up about nine or ten troopers and then bumped into a group with Colonel Harrison and a red-headed major from the 507 with thirty or forty men. Soon, we were fighting on the edge of the Merderet, which was flooded, and on our other three sides were hedgerows. These guys had been kicking a little ass before I got there because they had a lot of German prisoners. But there was no place for us to go and the enemy was all around.

"We took positions manning the ditches and hedgerows and threw the captured Krauts some entrenching tools. We told them to get out in the orchard and dig in. They had the dirt flying soon. I had one patient, a trooper in a ditch with his leg almost blown off, except for his patella tendon. I had very little to work with, a small kit, a few instruments, a bit of morphine but no way to anesthetize him. I said, 'Son, it's like the days in the Wild West. You're going to have to bite the bullet and I am going to have to separate the leg.' I cut the patella tendon and put a dressing on it. He never whimpered. We put the wounded in a little farmhouse. There wasn't much we could do for them. We didn't have a one of our equipment bundles, only what we carried."

Like their subordinates Generals Maxwell Taylor and Matthew Ridgway plunged into a miasma of confusion far from their objectives. Taylor said, "I dropped halfway between Ste.-Marie-du-Mont and Vierville, just west of the highway connecting the two villages. I landed alone in a field surrounded by the usual high hedges and trees with a few cows as witnesses. The rest of my stick went into an adjacent field and it took me about twenty minutes to find anyone. The area into which I wandered was covered with field fortifications, newly constructed but fortunately I encountered no Germans. Gradually, I picked up a few men of the 501st and later contacted General McAuliffe, who had a group of artillery personnel with him.

"Still under the cover of darkness, we worked our way eastward for about a quarter of a mile and finally halted in an enclosed field where we began to gather stragglers. It was here that I first ran into Colonel [Julian] Ewell [CO of the 3d Battalion, 501st Parachute Regiment]. We outposted the field and sent out patrols in all directions. They, however, learned very little in the darkness and were driven back by enemy fire that seemed to be on all sides. Colonel [Gerald] Higgins [Taylor's chief of staff] soon turned up with Lieutenant Colonel Pappas the division engineer." The concentration of big brass and the paltry number of enlisted men caused Taylor to remark, "Never in the history of military operations have so few been commanded by so many."

Matthew Ridgway landed in a pasture bordered by the ubiquitous hedgerows. "I felt a great exhilaration at being here alone in the dark on this greatest of adventures." After challenging a shape in the dark that proved to be a cow, Ridgway spotted another figure. "We had these little crickets and I had one in my hand but I didn't use it. I used the challenge of 'flash.'" The respondent was company commander Willard Follmer, by some lottery-size long shot, the same man Ridgway first encountered in Sicily. Ridgway was no lucky talisman for Follmer, however, for the captain had fractured his right ankle in Sicily and now in Normandy he broke his right hip.

Ridgway was in no better position than Taylor or Gavin to exercise true command and control. Instead of conducting precise well-planned maneuvers, the troopers initially performed like gangs of desperadoes, buccaneering through the countryside. The dispersion of the airdrop sowed great confusion among the enemy as the invaders seemed all over the place and difficult to pin down. During the darkness the parachutists ravaged communications by blowing telephone wires, to add to the disorder among the Germans. The defenders themselves had also lost much of their command and control, particularly because Erwin Rommel was back in Germany on a joint venture to visit his family and plead with the Führer for more resources.

For those coming to Normandy by glider, conditions were at least as chaotic. At 12:19 A.M., pilots of the tow planes at Aldermaston Air Base throttled up and the gliderborne troops began their trip toward Normandy. "Lieutenant Colonel Mike Murphy was in the lead glider to my immediate left," remembered Vic Warriner, "and to my right in the four-ship echelon was Capt. Jack Willoughby, CO of the 434th Group. The takeoff was uneventful except for the fact it seemed to take much longer than normal for Murphy's glider to become airborne." Warriner, at the time, knew nothing of the installation of heavy metal plates in Murphy's glider. These were to protect his passenger, General Pratt, and seriously compromised its flight dynamics.

"Our takeoff," continued Warriner, "was smooth and we quickly pulled into formation on the leader's wing. My copilot was Robert (Bob) V. Kaufman. He was more than qualified to pilot a glider himself but agreed to sacrifice that spot so that we would be assured of having a competent replacement if something happened to me. My glider was important because we carried part of a top medical team from the 101st Airborne who would immediately set up a field hospital upon landing. Captains Charles O. Van Gorder and Albert J. Crandall, and several medical technicians were in my glider. In addition we carried a two-wheeled trailer loaded with medical supplies that was to be towed by the jeep carried in General Pratt's ship.

"The flight proceeded as envisioned but the night was so dark, we never knew when we left England and headed southwest, out to sea. The weather wasn't really that bad but occasionally rain would splatter against the plexiglass windshield. Bob and I alternated flying for it was rather a long haul for one pilot, considering the stress. [Contrary to some published accounts, none of the gliders invading Normandy lacked a qualified copilot.] We knew when we made the rendezvous with the submarine stationed in the Channel for we made a ninety-degree left turn to head east-southeast toward the coast of France. And sometime later we made another slight turn to the left that lined us up directly with the Normandy area. From this point on, the trip became much more exciting. As we approached land we could see several fires burning that we thought had been ignited by the pathfinder crews for the paratroops. Wrong! They were bonfires built on top of flak towers by the Germans to help them stay warm on a chilly night. We encountered heavy machine-gun fire but it was mostly inaccurate and caused very little deviation in our planned route. At one time I thought we had been hit, for the controls suddenly were very stiff and unresponsive. I glanced at Bob and he was flying the glider, too. He grinned sheepishly and let go of the wheel.

"When we were at about 500 feet, the light in the dome of the tow plane signaled for us to release. I could see the one from the plane towing Mike Murphy flash at the same time. Even though it was still dark, there was enough light for me to see Murphy release and immediately turn left in a steep climb, using the velocity of the tow to gain enough altitude. He disappeared into the black sky. His actions puzzled me for during all our training and briefing it was stressed that we were to maintain level flight when released until the glider slowed enough to reach its normal gliding speed.

"With Bob calling out the speed and altitude, we descended into darkness. Finally, we could see the vague outline of a row of trees and I put the glider into a slip to kill off excess altitude. We actually brushed the tops of the trees as we went in. We touched down almost immediately and I put the glider up on its skis and applied full brakes. It seemed that instead of slowing down, we were gaining speed. As we hurtled through a herd of terrorized dairy cattle, I could see through the darkness the end of the field coming fast. Luckily, we slowed up enough so the crash was only minimal. We hit a large poplar tree on my side of the cockpit and only hard enough for me to end up with my chin against the trunk of the tree.

"Even before the plexiglass stopped falling, Captain Van Gorder asked if everyone was okay. We were, and all I got was skinned knees from the bark of the poplar. We had been on the ground for an interval of perhaps only fifteen seconds when we heard a tremendous crash close to our left side as a glider smashed into another huge poplar at deadly speed. The impact actually shook the ground. At the very same moment, we spotted the blackout lights of vehicles traveling along a little dirt road just beyond the nose of our glider. We knew they were Germans for the briefing had stressed that no Allied vehicles would move before dawn. The convoy of three vehicles halted by the glider that had crashed next to us. A couple of soldiers emerged and entered what remained of the glider. We could see their flashlight beams as they poked around the wreckage. Soon they left in their vehicles and disappeared down the road.

"Van Gorder said he was going to the smashed glider to see if he could help anyone, although he doubted anyone could have lived through such a crash. He had no more than stated his intentions when we heard another glider thump down in the field and rumble toward us. As it got close we noticed it was up on its skids and gradually slowing down. I then realized that the field we picked sloped downhill severely and was covered in lush, wet pasture grass. The incoming ship hit the tail of our glider, but with little speed, did minimum damage and injured no one. Meanwhile, Captain Van Gorder ran toward the stricken glider.

"The rest of us started to pull away the latest arrival from our tail so we could move it away from the tree and perhaps raise the nose to get the medical supplies out. Our efforts were to no avail. Van Gorder returned and told us it was Mike Murphy's glider. Two of the people aboard, General Pratt and copilot Butler were dead. Murphy was seriously injured and Van Gorder doubted he would survive. Only General Pratt's aide came through relatively uninjured." Pratt died, apparently of a broken neck, either from the impact of the glider against the tree or as a result of his jeep shifting forward to crush him.

"I learned later," said Warriner, "about the sheet iron on the cargo compartment floor. It completely upset the balance of the glider and constituted a gross overload. And that's why he used so much runway to get airborne. Years afterward, Murphy told Van Gorder, 'It was like trying to fly a freight train.' He hit the landing field like a meteor. Combine that with the downhill slope of a wet, grassy field and they had no chance of avoiding a crash. It's a wonder anyone survived. Murphy never complained publicly about a disaster for which he was not to blame. Ironically, the measures Pratt's staff took to guarantee his safety actually killed him."

In the dark pasture Warriner and the other able-bodied crews pitched in to unload their cargo. "After that we were on our own and took off trying to establish contact with the rest of our glider pilots. We had all been issued the clickers. The whole Normandy peninsula that night sounded as if it had been hit by the greatest cricket infestation in history. And it wasn't unusual to hear someone shout in the eerie darkness, 'Don't shoot! I lost my Goddamn clicker!'"

At the moment of D day, still the youngest man to earn his glider pilot wings, Pete Buckley flew Glider 49 in the same Glider Serial [52 CG 4As altogether] as Warriner. "Thirty minutes before takeoff the engines of the tow ships started up. The muffled noise and throbbing from their motors spread around the field like a distant, approaching thunderstorm, and contributed to our uneasiness. We all climbed aboard trying not to show our true feelings. My own were that in roughly three and a half hours I might be dead. It was a very sobering moment and I wondered why I had been so foolish as to volunteer for this job. When I first went into the glider program, nobody had ever explained to me how gliders were going to be used.

"My copilot was F/O Bill Bruner. Our passengers were Pfc. Paul Nagelbush, Pfc. Stanley Milewiski, and Pfc. Russel Kamp antitank crewmen from the 101st Airborne. The cargo included their 57mm antitank gun, ammunition, entrenching tools, a camouflage net, rations, and some supplies. Our tow ship gunned its engines and started down the runway through a light rain shower and into the black of night. As the wheels of the glider left the ground, someone in the back yelled, 'Look out, Hitler, here we come!' This helped break the ice for a moment, after which no one said a word as I trimmed the glider for the long flight ahead.

"For the next three and one-half hours, we would be alone with our thoughts and fears. It wasn't too bad for me because I was busy flying the glider. But the airborne men in back and Bill Bruner, with nothing to do, must have been going through hell with their thoughts. We settled into position behind the C-47, keeping the faint blue formation lights on the top of the plane centered up in line between the glow from the tow plane's engines' flame dampeners. The longer you stare at them, the more your eyes start playing tricks. I turned the controls over to Bruner occasionally so I could look away and refocus my eyes again. An added problem was the extreme turbulence from the prop wash of the forty-eight planes ahead of us.

"Shortly after we crossed the coast of France, small-arms fire and heavier flak started coming up at the planes in the front of the formation, These intensified as we came closer to our landing zone. It looked like fluid streams of tracers zigzagging and hosing across the sky, mixed in with heavier explosions of flak. You wondered how anything could fly through that and come out in one piece. After the lead ships had passed over the Kraut positions and woke them all up, we at the tail end of the line began to be hit by a heavier volume of small arms fire, which, when it went through our glider, sounded like corn popping, or typewriter keys banging on loose paper.

"I tried to pull my head down into my chest to make myself as small as possible. I tucked my elbows in close to my body, pulled my knees together to protect vital parts of my manhood and even was tempted to take my feet off the rudder pedals so they wouldn't stick out so far. I really started to sweat it out. A few minutes after crossing the coast, and before we reached the glider-release point near Hiesville, the group plunged into some low-lying clouds and fog banks. All the planes started to spread out to avoid collisions. This caused many of us to land wide, short, or beyond our objective when we got to the cutoff point. In a very short time, too soon for me, the moment I dreaded arrived. The green light came on in the astrodome of the tow plane, indicating we were over the LZ and it was time to release. At this moment, I had a very strong urge not to cut loose. I'm sure I wasn't the only one who felt this way on that night. It was dark; everything but the kitchen sink was coming up at us from the Germans below, and that tow rope, as long as it was hooked up, was my umbilical cord. The steady pull signified safety, and a nice ride back to England out of this mess, if I hung on. I quickly put this thought out of my mind and waited about ten seconds before I released the tow rope.

"As soon as the rope disconnected from our glider, I made a 360-degree turn to the left, feeling my way down through the darkness. I held the glider as close to stall speed as I could. It is almost impossible to describe my feelings. I knew the ground was down there but I couldn't see it. I didn't know if I was going to hit trees, ditches, barns, houses, or what. And all the time, the flak and traces are still coming up. The only thing for sure was that Krauts were shooting at me and they were going to be right there, waiting for me when I climbed out of the glider. They say fear has no bounds and at this point in my life, I was in full agreement.

"Finally, out of the corner of my eye, I noticed a faint light patch that looked like an open field, outlined by trees. By this time we were so low that we had no choice in the matter. There would be no chance for a go-around. With a prayer on my lips, and a very tight pucker string, I straightened out my glide path and headed in, while Bruner held on full spoilers. We flared out for a landing, just above stalling speed and touched down smooth as glass. How lucky can you get.

"Just as we thought we had it made, there was a tremendous, bone-jarring crash. We hit one of those damn ditches that the Germans had dug across the fields. This ditch was ten to twelve feet across, five to six feet deep, with water at the bottom. The main purpose was to prevent gliders from landing in one piece and it sure worked with us. We plunged down into the ditch and when the nose slammed into the other side, the glider's back broke as it slid up over the opposite bank. The floor split open and we skidded to a halt in the field on the other side. For a split second we sat in stunned silence and then I breathed a sigh of relief because none of us seemed injured. We bailed out fast because there was rifle and machine-gun fire going off in the fields around us. Fortunately, none seemed aimed at our area at the moment. It took us almost thirty minutes to dig the nose of the glider out of the dirt so we could open it up and roll out the .57mm antitank gun. Midway through this task, the Germans set off a flare right over our heads. Low and behold, we saw Glider Number 50, piloted by F/Os Calvani and Ryan on the other side of the ditch without a scratch on it. They were carrying the jeep to tow our antitank gun.

"You're supposed to trust the tow pilot but I did hesitate and it was a good thing, because I still landed about half a mile short of the LZ. If I had let go at the first signal from the tow plane, I would have come down in the swampy area that the Germans had flooded, where many paratroopers and glidermen drowned in the dark."

Transport pilot Tom Poston noted, "We dropped paratroopers, went home, refueled, got the gliders hooked on, went back, and dropped them. It was extremely ill advised. The hedgerows there are very tall and the fields are not all that big. So the poor bastards in the gliders get released and here they are looking at a little patch, surrounded by these high hedgerows. It was a disaster. We had guys come back—Creasy, I think his name was, a glider pilot. He hung upside down in a glider that flipped over, with everybody in it dead as a doornail and the Krauts were checking. He was hanging upside down pretending to be dead. After the Germans left, he crawled under the glider [until] the Americans took that piece of earth."

28
Daylight at Omaha Beach

For all of the sound and fury of the night, the enemy still seemed uncertain whether this was to be a full-scale invasion and where it would take place. The landings were scheduled for "nautical dawn," an astronomical designation based on the position of the sun when it is two and one-half degrees below the horizon. With double daylight saving in effect, the first faint streaks of light appeared at 3:00 A.M. But those ashore could not have seen the vast fleet more than nine miles away nor could those on board pick out the coastline. Admiral Alan Kirk, the U.S. fleet commander, said his ships opened up at 6:00 A.M., but those vessels hitting the British beaches commenced firing as much as half an hour earlier. By the time the first shells from the naval guns crashed down among the German installations, the landing craft packed with the first waves for the forty miles of beaches had rendezvoused at sea and started for the shore.

At about the same hour, the huge armada of U.S. and British warplanes began opening bomb bay doors to unload their explosive cargoes. But a thick overcast hung over the ground, obscuring targets. Fearful of another deadly deluge of friendly fire from the planes working at high altitudes, the U.S. Eighth Air Force obtained permission from Eisenhower to ensure they did not hit the GIs. Aiming at Omaha Beach, 329 B-24 heavy bombers dumped 13,000 bombs, all of which missed both the beach and the enemy defenses behind it. Tons of high explosives fell as much as three miles inland. At Utah Beach, medium bombers relying on visual sightings achieved only slightly better results. Prior to D day, however, Pointe du Hoc, where the intelligence experts believed the German artillery threatened both the fleet and the beaches, had been visited several times by bombers. Because concentrated efforts might tip the Nazis to the area chosen for Overlord, these attacks were infrequent and more in hopes of delaying full operation of the battery rather than destroying it. The Ranger assignment to climb and conquer Pointe du Hoc's defenders was accepted with confidence by Rudder, but a high-level officer in Overlord planning declared, "Three old women with brooms could knock the Rangers off the cliff."

Those committed to the attack reacted with resolution and anxiety. Medic Frank South with the 2d Ranger Battalion had entered a marshaling yard near Dorchester. "There was an intelligence tent set up with a detailed sand model of the Pointe du Hoc cliff and the objectives down to gun emplacements, bunkers, tunnel works, and minefields. Stereoscopic slides gave us pictures in 3-D. Each of the noncoms was instructed to copy the layout of Pointe du Hoc on cigarette papers that could be destroyed easily or swallowed if necessary. At sea," said South, "I did not go through any religious preparation, but I did repeatedly go over the plans and where every item of equipment or supply was in the huge pack I had. I compulsively and repeatedly inspected and cleaned the .45 Colt automatic I buried in the pack, and I sharpened my knife. All the while I chatted with the Combined Operations medic with whom I stayed in the ship's surgery during the night.

"Most of the men and noncoms remained quite sober, reviewing their mission and checking their arms on board the ship. Some did a bit of gambling. Morale was high and most of us felt confident in our abilities and those of our comrades. There was one exception. Our recently appointed battalion commander had been drinking a bit too much. He either originated or supported the opinion that the assault group of the 2d Rangers was being sent on a suicide mission and that there was no chance we would survive. Communicating this sort of notion would have been devastating. Word of the problem was sent to Rudder on a nearby ship. He immediately transferred to our *Ben Machree* and assumed direct command of the Pointe du Hoc operation."

Ranger Sergeant Jack Kuhn, who had experimented with the machine gun mounted atop a firefighter's ladder, was aboard HMS *Amsterdam* "I could not envision myself going into combat. It seemed so detached from me, as if it were happening to someone else. The one thing I feared was not being able to face the test. I didn't want to coward out. Then everyone else said the same thing, and I was okay. I never had the apprehension that I would be killed or wounded. As tension mounted, Tom Ruggiero, who had studied acting, and I decided that a skit was needed. We had put on short, crazy ones as gags during training, and with Bill Hoffman and Bob Fruhling we put on a show and it helped. Sometime after, when I got into my bunk, I lay there and listened to my men talking. They all expressed anxiety at not being able to face the unexpected, and were fearful of running."

"I was never seasick," said Len Lomell. "But after a couple of days on the ship, I was getting a bit stir crazy. I am a Protestant but wasn't particularly religious. I never saw anybody praying. We had so much to think about in performing our job; there didn't seem to be time for prayer. I had a good relationship with Father Joe Lacy, the Catholic chaplain assigned to the Rangers. I made everyone in D Company [2d Ranger Battalion] attend services, usually. Late on the eve of D day, I was in a hot poker game in the mess hall when someone announced a midnight mass by Lacy. Here I was with a good hand and I figured I'm entitled to a few more minutes, so I said I'm staying. Three of the eight guys at the table got up and went. The next morning, all of them died."

Battalion surgeon Walter Block told his diary: "This is the last entry to be written before D day. If something happens to me, see that my wife Mrs. Alice Block gets this book. Kiddo—I love you."

Now as dawn crept over the coast and the 2d Ranger Battalion bounced in the choppy Channel seas, a more sustained fury broke over Pointe du Hoc. Naval salvos and aerial ordnance pelted the target. The barrage was to begin twenty minutes before H hour, at 06:30, and end with the arrival on Beach Charley of the 2d Ranger Battalion. Naval guns would remain available for support through communications from a shore-fire control party accompanying the Rangers.

The 2d and 5th Ranger Battalions acted under the overall command of Rudder with Lt. Col. Max Schneider serving as his deputy. From his 2d Battalion, Rudder deployed boats bearing men from E and F Companies for landings on the eastern or left side of the precipice while D Company struck from the other direction. The plan for the Rangers envisioned that if Rudder and his group scaled Pointe du Hoc successfully, they would advise the 5th Ranger Battalion and Companies A and B of the 2d Battalion still in their landing craft, by means of colored rockets or a radio message. Max Schneider's outfit would then follow Rudder's people up the cliff and pass through inland. If that assault on Pointe du Hoc failed, Schneider would head his men toward Dog Green Beach with the aim of breaking through the Vierville-sur-Mer coast exit at that point.

"We put on a show of confidence boarding our assault crafts, ready to be lowered into the water," says D Company's Jack Kuhn who had turned over his fire-department ladder job to another Ranger. "We tried to impress the British sailors with our seeming disregard for what was coming. They kept calling out, 'Give them what for, Yanks.' Our departure from the *Amsterdam* went smoothly. But the moment we hit the water it was apparent this was to be a most hazardous trip. The seas were high and rough. The swells were big and the winds shipped the water into massive rollers, tossing our crafts severely. These were the smallest boats I had ever seen used. When you stood up, the upper part of your body was exposed to the enemy and the elements. There was very little room in the heavily loaded craft. Men who had never suffered seasickness did that day."

The boats were roughly twelve feet wide, thirty feet long, with seating along the sides. In the middle sat the boat team leader, a second in command, and a radio man. D Company traveled on three craft; one commanded by Duke Slater, a second under Lt. George Kerchner, and the third led by 1st Sgt. Len Lomell. Said Kuhn, "Almost as soon as we left the mother ship, the men became apprehensive about the boats sinking. First Sergeant Len Lomell and I, at the rear of the boat, discussed this possibility. Well aware that we were already shipping water, we instructed the men to start bailing, using their helmets. Nobody had much, if any, sleep the night before. The guys were sick, cold, and turned apathetic. Lomell and I verbally forced them to keep bailing water. Captain Slater's boat was very low in the water, in danger of foundering. It was losing speed and dropping back from the formation.

"As soon as I mentioned it to Len, we saw the boat start to go down. We didn't want our men to see it so we pretended to spot the Pointe and told them to keep watch. I don't know if anyone else was aware that the Duke was now out of the invasion. I wondered whether we should try to rescue him but the time lost would have made us late. Len and I agreed the mission came first. It was his decision to make and personally I felt I was deserting our commander. We spotted our fighter planes overhead and saw the navy ships blasting the shoreline and inland. We saw the rockets projected. We had never seen these before. I realized now that we were taking part in the greatest battle in history and felt proud to be in it. As we got closer, it became my job to arm all six rockets that would carry our ropes up the cliff. When I armed them I saw that everything was underwater or very damp from being exposed. I doubted they would fire at all.

"Still trying to see Pointe du Hoc, I noticed the boat was taking on less water and realized we must be much closer to the shore. The swells subsided slightly. When I armed the rockets, I had leaned my Thompson submachine gun against the bulkhead. Now I couldn't find it. I yelled to Sheldon Bare, a young man from my hometown, who was bailing water if he could find it. Bare groped around in the knee-deep water of the boat, found my weapon, and handed it to me. I fired into the air and it worked fine. Later in the day, Sheldon Bare would suffer a bullet wound in the neck, then returned to the company only to be hit again. About this time, we spotted a cliff jutting out into the Channel and it looked just like the pictures of Pointe Du Hoc. But the lead boat turned right and started a course parallel to the cliff and the shoreline. We surmised we had come toward the wrong site—Pointe el Raz de la Percée [a good three miles east]."

Rudder, in the lead landing craft, discovered the error and directed the flotilla toward Pointe du Hoc. But the assault was behind schedule. Instead of the Rangers being the first to strike the Normandy coast, that dubious honor fell to Sid Salomon leading Company C of the 2d Ranger Battalion and the 116th Infantry of the 29th Division, targeted for Dog Green Beach and the promontory mistaken by the helmsman for Pointe du Hoc. "When we boarded the *Prince Charles*," said Salomon, "Colonel Rudder shook hands with company commander Ralph Goranson, the other platoon leader, Lt. Bill Moody, and myself. Rudder said, 'You've got the most dangerous mission.' There had been detailed planning. We looked at postcards, travel material on what was a resort area. We had sand tables. But we never met with anyone from the 29th [Division] to go over the mission.

"In all our training, we had never gotten on a landing craft with all of the weapons, ammo, food, and other supplies required for the actual invasion. Suddenly, we found ourselves so jammed in that I couldn't sit down. I stood behind the steel doors in the bow. Our two landing craft looked forlorn and lonesome as they splashed forward toward the shoreline. I was looking ahead when suddenly I heard pings on the side of the boat. It was machine-gun fire from the shore. There were splashes around the craft, whitewater cascades, then concentric circles as shells landed in our vicinity. I saw a barge with rockets. They made a tremendous amount of noise, a huge whoosh and then the shells burst like fireworks. But every one fell short, splashing down right at the water's edge. I saw no flashes erupting on the cliffs."

Salomon continued. "The British sub-leftenant nodded to his helmsman who opened the throttle a notch. The intensity of the pings against the outside of the steel hull increased. Everyone kept his head down. When the words, 'Get ready' were passed, everyone inched forward a little. All were tense. The sub-leftenant had his hands on the ropes that would release the catch for the steel ramp. 'Now!' he called out, and the ramp flopped down into the water. I immediately jumped off the landing craft, the men following one to the right, the next left. I knew [the] first [person] off was the safest since the guys aiming didn't know when the ramp would go down and it takes a second or two before they squeeze off a shot. My section sergeant, Oliver Reed, right behind me, was hit in the stomach. I was in water up to my chest and I pulled Reed out from under the ramp to keep him from being crushed.

"I told Reed, 'You've got to go on your own from here.' I was running across the sand, with the mortar section behind me, when a mortar shell exploded. It wiped out those around me, killing or wounding them. Some pieces of shrapnel hit me in the back and knocked me flat. I thought I was finished. My platoon sergeant ran up to me. I was about to turn over my maps to him when bullets kicked up sand in my face. I jumped up and ran to the base of the cliff, which gave some cover against the machine guns.

"In the shelter there, I took off my shirt and jacket. An aidman sprinkled on sulfa powder and said, 'That's all I can do now, Lieutenant.' So we started up Pointe el Raz de la Percée. The Germans threw grenades down while the Rangers returned small-arms fire. First, two men inched up, using ropes, hand and footholds. Then another pair followed them, while the men at the bottom continued firing at the top, taking off some of the pressure and direct attacks on the climbers."

Turning his gaze to the beach for a moment, Salomon beheld bodies strewn about, blood in the sand. He saw some wounded crawling toward shelter with looks of despair upon their faces. Others who tried to get back on their feet went down again from enemy bullets. At the water's edge, bodies rolled back and forth in the ebb and flow of the Channel.

The second boat, with Goranson, Moody, and the remainder of C Company, took a direct hit in the bow as it reached the beach. A number of Rangers were killed or wounded from the blast but the two officers at the rear of the craft remained sound. Observing the carnage and the enormous casualties among C Company, Salomon thought the invasion had failed. The still able-bodied Rangers, including Salomon, Moody, and Goranson, mounted to the top, joining the remnants of C Company. Salomon counted nine men from the thirty-nine packed aboard the landing craft only minutes earlier. Nevertheless, the Rangers doggedly advanced. Moody led an assault that cleaned out a battered stone building housing some enemy gunners. In a shell hole, Salomon and Moody met to determine their next moves. "We were shoulder to shoulder," says Salomon, "I was pointing toward a series of trenches when suddenly he rolled to one side, a bullet struck him directly between his eyes. I told Ralph [Goranson] I was going ahead. Stooping down and with two men, I walked through a series of trenches. We worked our way to a dugout. A white-phosphorus grenade was tossed in and when the Germans came out, the Rangers turned their Tommy gun and rifles on them. Farther down the line we silenced a mortar crew. Then we withdrew back to the rest of the platoon. C Company now held Pointe et Raz de la Percée."

The choreography for conquest of Omaha Beach called upon the 1st and 29th Infantry Divisions, including amphibious tanks, and with the aid of the Rangers companies to head for the shore at H hour, 6:30 A.M. The naval and aerial barrage on the defenders would blast off forty minutes before. The parade toward the 7,000-yard long, crescent-shaped strand was to be led by amphibious tanks, followed by more armor to be put shore from landing craft, and then the first 1,450 infantrymen. Those first soldiers were expected to provide adequate protection for demolition task forces assigned to clear and mark lanes for the main body of troops to be ferried onto the beach.

Bob Slaughter of the 29th Division, with his fellow GIs from the 116th Regiment, heard the steady drone of bombers in the darkness overhead. "We saw bomb explosions causing fires that illuminated clouds in the dark sky. We were twelve miles off shore as we climbed into our seat assignments on the LCAs [Landing Craft Assault] and were lowered into the heavy sea by davits. The Navy hadn't begun its firing because it was still dark. We couldn't see the armada because of the dark but we knew it was there.

"Prior to loading, friends said their so-longs and good lucks. I remember finding Sgt. Jack Ingram, an old friend from Roanoke. He had suffered a back injury and I asked him how he felt. 'I'm okay. Good luck, I'll see you on the beach.' Another Roanoker, a neighbor and classmate, George D. Johnson, who'd joined the army with me, asked, 'Are your men ready?' I couldn't imagine why he asked me but I answered yes. Sergeant Robert Bixler of Shamokin, Pennsylvania, joked, 'I'm going to land with a comb in one hand,' running his hand through his blond hair, 'and a pass to Paris in the other.' The feeling among most of the men was that the landing would be a 'walk-in affair' but later we could expect a stiff counterattack. That didn't worry us too much because by then the tanks, heavy artillery, and air support should bolster our defense until the beachhead grew strong enough for a breakout."

"All of us had a letter signed by the supreme commander, General Eisenhower, saying that we were about to embark upon a great crusade, etc. A few of my cohorts autographed it and I carried it in my wallet throughout the war. The message was also read over loudspeakers. "We loaded into our assigned stations on the landing craft and were lowered by davits. The Channel was extremely rough and it wasn't long before we had to help the craft's pumps by bailing with our helmets. The cold spray blew in and soon we were soaking wet. I used a gas cape [a plastic sack for protection against skin irritants] as shelter. Lack of oxygen under the sack brought seasickness.

"As the sky lightened, the armada became visible. The smoking and burning French shoreline also became more defined. At 0600, the huge guns of the Allied navies opened up with what must have been one of the greatest artillery barrages ever. The diesels on board our craft failed to muffle the tornadic blasting. I could see the *Texas* firing broadside into the coastline. Boom-ba-ba-boom-ba-ba-boom! Boom-ba-ba-boom-ba-ba-boom! Within minutes giant swells from the recoil of those guns nearly swamped us and added to the seasickness and misery. But one could actually see 2,000-pound missiles tumbling on targets. Twin-fuselaged P-38 fighter bombers were also overhead protecting us from the *Luftwaffe* and giving us a false sense of security. This should be a piece of cake.

"A few thousand yards from shore we rescued three or four survivors from a craft that had been swamped and sunk. Other men were left in the water bobbing in their Mae Wests, because we did not have room for them. About 200–300 yards from shore we encountered artillery fire. Near misses sent water skyward and then it rained back on us. The British coxswain said he had to lower the ramp and for us to quickly disembark. Back in Weymouth these sailors bragged they had been on several invasions and we were in capable hands. I heard Sgt. Willard Norfleet say, 'These men have heavy equipment, you *will* take them all the way in.'

"The coxswain pleaded, 'But we'll all be killed!' Norfleet unholstered his .45 Colt, put it to the sailor's head and ordered, '*All the way in!*' The craft kept going, plowing through the choppy water, until the bow scraped the sandy bottom. I thought, if this boat doesn't hurry and get us in, I'll die from seasickness. I had given my puke bag to a buddy who already had filled his. Minus the paper bag, I used my steel helmet.

"About 150 yards from shore, I raised my head despite the warning, 'Keep your head down.' I saw the boat on our right taking a terrific licking from small arms. Tracer bullets were bouncing and skipping off the ramp and sides as the enemy zeroed in on the boat that had beached a few minutes before us. Had we not delayed a few minutes to pick up the survivors of the sunken craft, we might have taken that concentration of fire. Great plumes of water from enemy artillery and mortars sprouted close by. We knew then this was not going to be a walk-in. No one thought the enemy would give us this kind of opposition at the water's edge. We expected A and B Companies to have the beach secured by the time we landed. In reality no one had set foot in our sector. The coxswain had missed the Vierville church steeple, our point to guide on, and the tides also helped pull us 200 hundred yards east. The location didn't make much difference. We could hear the 'p-r-r-r-r, p-r-r-r-r' of enemy machine guns to our right, toward the west. It was obvious someone down there was catching that hell, getting chewed up where we had been supposed to come in."

The "someone catching hell" on Dog Green was Company A; which like much of the 116th, a Virginia National Guard unit, contained men who had grown up with one another. The GIs from battalion headquarters that followed A Company ashore were shocked to see their beach empty of living men. Slaughter remembered, "The ramp went down while shells exploded on land and in the water. Unseen snipers were shooting down from the cliffs, but the most havoc came from automatic weapons. I was at the left side of the craft, about fifth from the front. Norfleet led the right side. The ramp was in the surf and the front of the steel boat bucked violently up and down. Only two at a time could exit.

"When my turn came, I sat on the edge of the bucking ramp, trying to time my leap on the down cycle. I sat there way too long, causing a bottleneck and endangering myself and the men to follow. But the ramp was bouncing six or seven feet and I was afraid it would slam me in the head. One man was crushed and killed instantly. When I did get out, I was in the water. It was very difficult to shed the sixty pounds of equipment, and if one were a weak swimmer he could drown before he inflated his Mae West. Many were hit in the water and drowned, good swimmers or not. There were dead men floating in the water and live men acting dead, letting the tide take them in. Initially, I tried to take cover behind one of the heavy timbers and then noticed an innocent-looking Teller mine tied to the top. I crouched down to chin-deep in the water as shells fell at the water's edge. Small-arms fire kicked up sand. I noticed a GI running, trying to get across the beach. He was weighted down with equipment and having difficulty moving. An enemy gunner shot him. He screamed for a medic. An aidman moved quickly to help him and he was also shot. I'll never forget seeing that medic lying next to that wounded soldier, both of them screaming. They died in minutes.

"Boys were turned into men. Some would be very brave men; others would soon be dead men, but any who survived would be frightened men. Some wet their pants, others cried unashamedly. Many just had to find within themselves the strength to get the job done. Discipline and training took over. For me, it was time to get the hell away from the killing zone and across the beach. Getting across the beach became an obsession. I told Pfc. Walfred Williams, my number-one gunner to follow. He still had his fifty-one-pound machine gun tripod. He once told me that he was so strong from daily cradling an old iron cookstove in his arms and walking around with it. I felt secure with Williams on the gun. A Chicago boy of nineteen, he was dependable and loyal. He loved the Army and didn't believe a German weapon could kill him. I didn't think so either. We were both wrong. Enemy shrapnel killed him six weeks after D day. Part of me would die with him.

"Our rifles were encased in a plastic bag to shield them from salt water. Before disembarking, because I wanted to be ready, I had removed the covering and fixed the bayonet. I gathered my courage and started running as fast as my long legs would carry me. I ran as low as I could to lessen the target, and since I am six-feet five, I still presented a good one. It was a long way to go, 100 yards or more. We were loaded with gear, our shoes full of water, our woolen, impregnated clothes soaked. I stumbled in a tidal pool of a few inches of water, began to stumble, accidently fired my rifle, barely missing my foot. But I made it to the seawall.

"I was joined by Pvt. Sal Augeri, and Pvt. Ernest McCanless and Williams. Augeri lost the machine-gun receiver in the water. We still had one box of MG ammo and the tripod. I had gotten sand in my rifle so I don't believe we had a weapon that would fire. I felt like a naked morsel on a giant sandy platter. I took off my assault jacket and spread my raincoat, so I could clean my rifle. It was then I saw bullet holes in my jacket and raincoat. Until then, I didn't realize I had been a target. I lit my first cigarette. I had to rest and compose myself because I became weak in the knees."

Already dead were many of Slaughter's childhood playmates and brothers in arms in the 116th. In the preinvasion hours, his D Company commander Capt. Walter Schilling had confided to a fellow officer, "I don't believe I will make it." He was right. A German 88 slammed into his landing craft killing him instantly. In fact, the COs from three of the four 1st Battalion companies perished without ever setting foot on dry land along with sixteen of the other junior officers. Dead, too, were Sgt. Russell Ingram, who shrugged off a back injury in order to participate; Cpl. Jack Simms, who stuffed himself with bananas in order to achieve the minimum weight; the Hoback brothers from the hamlet of Bedford, Virginia; and T.Sgt. Ray Stevens, another Bedfordite whose twin brother, Roy, had waved off a handshake as they walked up the gangplank on the eve of the invasion. "I'll see you at Vierville-sur-Mer," said Roy, but he would never lay eyes on his twin again. Because the regiment originated in southwestern Virginia, the first wave enrolled a number of young men from Bedford, and 23 out of a total population of fewer than 4,000 died on that first day at Omaha Beach.

Bob Sales, who donned the 29th's National Guard uniform at fifteen, had, upon his return from Ranger training with Bob Slaughter, received the post as radio operator and bodyguard for B Company's leader, Capt. Ettore Zappacosta. "About 100 yards from shore, the English coxswain said he couldn't get us in closer. As the ramp lowered, enemy machine guns opened up firing directly into our boat. Captain Zappacosta, a great leader, was first off and the first hit. Staff Sergeant Dick Wright was second and he also was hit as he left the boat, falling into the water. A medic was third and I didn't see what happened to him. I was fourth, caught my heel in the ramp and fell sideway, out of the path of that MG 42 and this undoubtedly saved my life. All of the men who followed were either killed by the Germans or drowned. So far as I know, no one from my craft was ever found alive."

Sales dumped his heavy radio in the water. A log bearing an unexploded Teller mine drifted by and Sales clung to it as the tide carried him to the shoreline. On the beach he saw the badly wounded Sergeant Wright succumb to a sniper bullet in his head, and then the battalion surgeon cut down by a machine gun. "I crawled on my belly, using the dead and wounded as a shield." But when he saw some other B Company men sheltering themselves by the seawall he started to administer help to the wounded. "I kept crawling back to the water's edge, dragging out still-living men. You can't imagine how helpless it was to be lying on that beach and those snipers shooting everything that moved."

Felix Branham, with Company K of the 116th, climbed into a landing craft at 0420. Like Slaughter, he and his mates quickly found the Channel rough, with rain and spray soaking them, the swells turning many men ill. "Each time a boat hit the water, it joined a circle that became larger and larger. We circled around until finally we headed for Normandy. One guy in my boat raised up and looked over the side. We weren't within machine-gun or rifle range and there was only an occasional artillery shell that would splash down. We were getting near enough and the sky lightening enough to see the contour of the bluffs and skyline. They looked just like Slapton Sands. He was disgusted and said, "Goddamn, another dry run. I thought this was the real thing.'

"About fifty yards from the beach, we hit a sandbar parallel to the shore. Back at the marshaling area, we had been told there was a sandbar there and were not to let anyone stop there and lower the ramp to let us off. We were to make them close it up. The two fellows from the Navy moved to let down the ramp but Lieutenant Lucas, our boat-team commander, hollered, 'No, no,!' He ordered the coxswain to go over the sandbar sideways, as we had been instructed. Unfortunately, some of the guys in my company, in another boat team, didn't remember their homework and left the landing craft when it reached the sandbar. With all of the heavy equipment they had, with the waves coming, and the tide rising a foot every ten minutes, they drowned. Other boats stopped at the sandbar and were demolished; seasick men who'd stayed on board were blasted to smithereens.

"I got out in water at the top of my boots. People were yelling, screaming, dying, running on the beach; equipment was flying everywhere; men were bleeding to death, crawling, lying everywhere, firing coming from all directions. We dropped down behind anything that was the size of a golf ball. Colonel [Charles] Canham [CO of the regiment] was screaming at us to get across the beach, and Lieutenant Cooper and Sergeant Crawford also were urging us off the beach. I turned to say, 'Let's move up, Gino,' to Gino Ferrari, but before I could finish the sentence, something spattered all over the side of my face. He'd been hit in the face and his brains splattered all over my face and my stuff. I moved forward and the tide came on so fast it covered him and I no longer could see him. Canham previously had a BAR shot out of his hand. The bullet went through his right wrist and he wore a makeshift sling. His bodyguard, Private First Class Nami, followed closely behind the colonel, keeping his .45 loaded. Canham would fire a clip and hand the gun back to Nami, who would inject another into the weapon. Back in training we used to call Colonel Canham everything not fit to print. When he took command of the 116th, he made life miserable for us. We thought he would be another rear-echelon commander. After seeing him in action, I sure had to eat a mess of crow."

Antitank squad leader Bill Lewis was twelve miles offshore on an LST when he and his crew with their weapon loaded aboard a DUKW for the trip to the beach. "We had never trained on a DUKW," says Lewis. "The DUKW was like a truck and we had a big load on. The guy driving it was busy trying to keep it heading in. If we got into a trough, we were going to turn over. He let the waves coming from behind push it along.

"When we got to the metal obstacles there was a man hanging on one. He hollered for help. We couldn't control the DUKW very good and when we got close to him, Lieutenant Van de Voort yelled, 'We're out here to kill people not save lives. Jump, if you want on this damn thing.' He leaped and came on board. Then we sheared a pin and lost power. We were adrift in the Teller-mine area and going right into them, sideway. They were sticking out two or three inches above the water. We hit one mine more than once, kept bumping it, but the salt water had deteriorated it. It didn't explode.

"It was about thirty minutes after the first wave and they started to machine gun the DUKW. We jumped out and there went the DUKW with the AT gun and everything else. When I jumped out, I could stand on my toes except when a wave crashed over me. The natural assumption was the closer you went toward the shore, the more solid it would get. That wasn't true because sand had built up around some obstacles and I stepped off into a hole. I kept paddling. I wasn't about to go back the other way but just kept coming in. The water around me was dancing to that damn machine-gun fire."

Lewis and another man managed to run to the seawall where, cold and scared, they lay until a third man piled in on top of them. "He said, 'Is that you shaking, Sarge?' I said, 'Yeah, damn right!' He answered, 'My God, I thought it was me!' I could see him and he was shaking, all right. Both of us were. We huddled there, just trying to stay alive. There was nothing we could do except keep our butts down. There was no place to go and the automatic fire became heavier. Everyone coming up could see that seawall, so they got on top of you, piling up and trying to get below the damn thing."

The Rangers intent on capturing Pointe du Hoc recognized the costs of their delay. "Now we realized we would land late," said Kuhn. "The enemy would have time to regroup after the bombing attacks. The landing would be contested heavier than expected. To save time, instead of our boat rounding Pointe du Hoc to land on the right side of the cliff, we went in to the left of the Pointe. It was time to fire our rockets and I prayed for success. I pushed the switches and all of them fired. I couldn't watch where my ropes landed as I was busy under the cover of the boat sides, firing the rockets. Later, I learned that three of the six made the cliffs."

Len Lomell, in the same boat with Kuhn, recalled that as the flotilla maneuvered for its run toward the shore, "It was cloudy, foggy, dawn breaking. When we got within a mile, I could see a little dark line across the horizon. Then our rockets lit up the whole sky, the biggest display of fireworks you would ever see. Boom! Boom! Boom! Thousands of explosives and as you got closer the louder the booms. I said to the men, 'Guys, look on this as a big game, hit them fast and hard and keep moving faster. Never stop, because that's when they're going to pinwheel you."

"The ramp was dropped presumably where you could stand. But there was a bomb crater eight to ten feet deep I stepped into and I got soaked." As he emerged, Lomell swiveled about to take stock of his boat team. "I felt a burning sensation in my left side. I spun around and didn't know who it came from. I didn't see anyone shoot me. But behind me was a Ranger, Harry Fate, with whom I had a nasty confrontation a few days earlier. It was my idea to break him from the rank of sergeant because I didn't think he was hacking it the way he should.

"At the time Harry said, 'You know, Top, what they do with first sergeants in combat.' I made light of it at the time, but here I was the first guy shot. Fate was about fifty feet away and I yelled at him, "You son of a bitch.' But he protested, 'Honestly, Len, I didn't do it.' We couldn't waste time to sort this out—later Fate and I became very good friends—we went hell-for-leather up the cliff. The Germans held up some of the guys behind us but, using two sections of ladder on the sharpest incline, we got to a portion of the cliff that was bombed out. We started to use a rope. The first guy up, Lieutenant [Gilbert] Baugh from E Company [2d Ranger Battalion] took a bullet that went through his hand. He was hurt badly and said to me, 'I can't get up. Keep going, Lomell, keep going!'

Lou Lisko, assigned to Headquarters Company and responsible for communications, breakfasted on a single pancake and a cup of coffee before embarking. "Seventy yards from the cliff, a Ranger who was sitting across from me was hit by a bullet in the upper left chest. He lost a considerable amount of blood and started groaning and moaning from the pain. Bullets from machine guns and rifles were flying from the top of the Hoc and nobody dared help him. Another Ranger sitting by my side got sick. Though we all had paper bags under our field jackets near the throat in case of vomiting, this man did not have time to reach it. He threw up all over my left leg, my carbine, and radio equipment. That made me sick, too. I vomited into my paper bag and threw it overboard.

"When our LCA 722 came close to the beach, the Rangers began disembarking. I watched and saw some of them jumping neck-deep and unable to walk. The two Rangers ahead of me jumped and disappeared, so I decided to go to the left. I fell chest-deep with all my equipment, radio, ammunition, carbine. At the same time bullets were hitting the seawater around us. I struggled toward the base of the cliffs, not far away but so difficult to reach."

Lisko managed to get to the base of the cliffs and set up the radio. "After being so scared about this terrible ordeal, we were so emotional that we lost all our saliva. My tongue was stuck to the roof of my mouth. My friend, Steven, gave me a stick of chewing gun and we chewed until we had some saliva and were able to talk. We could see Rangers climbing the cliffs, pulling themselves up on ropes and aluminum ladders. The Germans were throwing hand grenades, the potato mashers, because they were shaped like that kind of cooking tool. It had a wooden handle and a canlike container with explosives. We looked back at the sea. Our LCA 722 was stuck on the sand

and couldn't return to the transport. Then we saw two British sailors come out of it and start running toward an LCA moving out. Steven and I yelled as loud as we could that there was an injured Ranger in 722. They heard us and although they had almost reached the outgoing LCA went back to ours to bring the Ranger out. While a machine gun fired at them, they carried him, one by the knees and the other by the arms. Later we learned the Ranger was wounded twice more but the sailors escaped any injury.

"Although our radio was set up, we couldn't contact anybody. I went to inform our communications officer, Lt. Ike [James] Eikner. As I started to move to find him, a machine gun and a rifleman on the left flank fired at me. First I thought I saw pebbles; then I realized they were bullets. I ran fast and jumped into a crevasse. Eikner was there where he couldn't be seen and he had twelve German prisoners. One of the prisoners stood up, as if he wanted to escape. The lieutenant and I grabbed our carbines and said, 'Halt!' When we stood, we exposed ourselves and drew fire again. Eikner shouted, 'Down!' but I was already down. One bullet struck the cliff between our heads. That's the way it would be for two and a half days with German soldiers everywhere. You never knew when you would be fired on by a German who was in a position a Ranger had not reached."

All along the narrow ground beneath the towering precipice, Rangers struggled to make their way up. In some cases, climbers ascended thirty or forty feet on a rocket-launched rope only to fall to the beach as their grapnel gave way, a rope slipped, or was cut. Attackers dropped back as the enemy hammered at the vulnerable Americans occupied with scaling the wall of earth, clay, and stone.

The Rangers from LCA 668 tried to exploit the success of the three rockets fired by Jack Kuhn that carried two smooth ropes and one with toggles to the heights. To expedite the ascent, he ordered that sections of extension ladders be put in play. They reached high enough for agile Rangers to scramble the remainder of the way by free-climbing over the debris caused by the bombardment. "We were shot at as we climbed," says Kuhn "but it was possible to get some cover by climbing behind chunks of cliff dislodged by the shelling." The innovation of a machine gun elevated on a fire ladder was one more casualty of circumstances. Only one DUKW bearing the gear got far enough onto the beach to deploy the weapon. For the most part, individual Rangers, using rifles, submachine guns, and BARs doggedly exchanged fire with enemies who showed themselves while shooting or flinging grenades.

Lieutenant George Kerchner of D Company recalled departing the *Amsterdam* at 4:30 A.M. He noted in his diary, "Heavy seas, began bailing immediately. Motor launch led us to wrong point. Sailed along under machine-gun fire, bailing all the time." Some years later, Kerchner amplified his terse first recollections. "We passed not far from the large warships. About five o'clock, the battleship *Texas* started to fire. It was a terrifying sound, the fourteen-inch guns shot far over our heads but still close enough for us to hear and feel some of the muzzle blast. When we were a little better than half way in, the rocket craft fired their barrages, salvos of ten or fifteen at a time. It, too, was terrifying, one continuous sheet of flame going up from the rocket-firing craft. How could anybody live on the beaches with all this fire landing there from the warship and the rocket-firing boats. Our air force bombers were overhead; we couldn't see them because there was a low overcast in a dull gray sky with clouds down to one or two thousand feet. But we could hear the bombs dropping on the shore and see them exploding as we came closer to the shore.

"We had been told these landing craft were unsinkable. They had large air tanks along both sides, supposed to support the craft even if holed by a shell. At first we did not worry about shipping water. The heavy seas hit the ramp in the front. and washed right over the top, and shortly we had six to twelve inches of water in the bottom of the boat. I saw the one boat from D Company [Duke Slater's] carrying a group of men with whom I was very friendly sink because of shipping water. That convinced me our landing craft were not unsinkable. We began bailing with our helmets and managed to keep us afloat, even though we were taking on a lot of water as the boat speeded up."

Acceleration was vital because of the navigation mistake. To Kerchner, the change in course seemed, "a catastrophe. We were due to land at 6:30 on the dot. In the forty minutes before that time, the heavy bombers would drop their sticks on the Pointe and the *Texas* would deliver several hundred rounds. Then medium bombers would plaster the area and only three minutes before 6:30, fighters would strafe the Pointe. The attacks were designed to keep the defenders pinned down, so they wouldn't see us approach the Pointe. They would be kept from the edge of the cliff. Otherwise while we were climbing they could cut our ropes before we even managed to get halfway up the cliff.

"Although we were about half a mile offshore and sailing parallel for half an hour under fire by German antiaircraft guns, 20mm and 40mm, none of the men in my boat were wounded. I believe several other craft were struck, one sunk. As we neared Pointe du Hoc I looked at my watch and saw it was 7:00 A.M. and we were far behind schedule. All of the preparatory fire on the Pointe had been lifted. The Germans who were in their underground shelters were now coming out and starting to look about to see what was happening. As we turned to make our approach, I looked up and saw Germans standing atop the cliff. I thought, this whole thing is a big mistake. None of us will ever get up that cliff because we are so vulnerable. The Germans could just stay back from the edge and cut the ropes.

"When we were about twenty to twenty-five yards offshore, I gave the order to fire our rockets. All of them fired and five actually cleared the cliff. Some other landing craft had a great deal of trouble, firing too soon or, because the seas had wet the ropes and made them too heavy, they couldn't clear the cliff. The ramp was lowered immediately after the rockets fired. It was our hope and desire to run right up on the beach for a dry landing, not because we were afraid of getting wet but because if we were soaked it would have added weight to carry while climbing. The British navy man had promised to put us down dry but suddenly we ran aground with the ramp dropped. The officer said, 'Everybody out.' Looking ahead, I could see fifteen or twenty feet of water, a muddy, dirty gray stretch. The entire area was marked by craters, shell holes from the guns on the *Texas* and the bombers.

"We had run up on the edge of one of these shell craters as I discovered almost immediately. I figured the water was only a foot or two deep because the landing craft drew only about two feet and we could run through it. So I yelled, 'Come on, let's go!' I rushed ahead, first one off, and fell into eight feet of water. It had to be at least that deep because I couldn't touch bottom. When I came to the surface, I started to doggie paddle, keeping my head above water while I tried to reach the beach. The men behind me realized what had happened when I went under and they went off both sides of the crater, getting nothing more than their feet wet. Instead of being the first ashore, I was one of the last. I looked around for someone to help me cuss out the British Navy for dumping me in eight feet of water but there was nobody to sympathize with me. They were all busily engaged.

"I tried my SCR 536 hand radio. It wouldn't work and I threw it down on the beach. Then I realized we were being fired upon by a machine gun off to the left at the top of the cliff, several hundred yards away. Sergeant [Francis] Pacyga, [William] Cruz, and [Lester] Harris were all hit. I don't know how they missed me since I was right next to those who were wounded. I felt rather helpless with my .45 pistol. I picked up the rifle dropped by Harris. My first impulse was to go after the machine gun but I realized this was stupid. Our mission was to get to the top of the cliff and destroy the guns up there. The men all knew what they had to do. They had their ropes, the order in which to climb, and they were all starting up. The only command I gave was for the platoon messenger to stay with the wounded after we got them close to the cliff so they were protected.

"I thought I had better inform Colonel Rudder that the boat with our company commander and a number of men had sunk. I located him about twenty-five or fifty yards down the beach as he was beginning to climb one of the rope ladders. He had his hands and his mind full and did not seem particularly interested in my information that I was assuming command of the company. He told me to get out of there and climb my rope. Getting up the cliff was very easy after all the training we had in England. The shells

from the warships and the bomb damage at the edge of the cliff caused dirt
and large chunks of clay and shale to fall. You could almost walk up the first
twenty-five feet. Using a smooth rope, I had no trouble getting all the way
up."

In spite of the loss of boats to the sea, the small arms and grenades of the
defenders, and the rigors of the climb, a number of Rangers, like Kerchner,
completed the frantic race to get up the cliff in less than fifteen minutes.
Within half an hour of setting foot on Beach Charley, the bulk of Rudder's
task force moved out in search of their objective: the casemated big guns.
(According to Lomell, of the 225 Rangers assigned to assault Pointe du Hoc,
about 175 actually reached the top.) To their surprise and chagrin, the battered emplacements on Pointe du Hoc were empty of artillery.

"Upon topping the cliff," said Kuhn, "I was shocked to find nothing that
resembled the mock-ups and overlays we had studied prior to D day. The
terrain was in complete disarray. Since there were no guns, D Company's
second objective was to travel to the highway directly ahead and hold it
against the German troops. I was at this time alone, trying to contact my men.
As I neared the exit road from Pointe du Hoc, I spotted John Conaboy. We
were running from a shell hole to the exit road when a sniper hit Conaboy.
We reached a communications ditch and I checked Conaboy. He insisted
he was okay and I should go on. I could tell his wound wasn't serious, and
not seeing any blood, I asked him where he was hit. He laughed, and said
in his canteen. Actually he'd been hit in the hip.

"About ten yards farther, I spotted a column of D Company Rangers
where I made contact with Len Lomell. We split into groups to make our
way to the road. Heading for the main highway, Len and I walked up the
road, scanning it and the hedgerows to our sides. Just as we came abreast
of the battered remains of a small French farm building, Lomell grabbed
me and threw both of us through the doorway. 'Didn't you see that Jerry
kneeling in the road aiming at us?' I had not and went to check him out.
I took a quick peek and the German was still kneeling. He was combatwise
and figured one of us would probably do this. He fired once and the slug
hit the door frame above my head. Len went through a window or a door
to cut the Jerry off. I looked again a few seconds later and he was running
away. I stepped out to cut him down but the Tommy gun wouldn't fire.
When I checked it, I found my clip had been hit right where it inserts into
the gun.

"I yelled to Len I was going back to the communication trench where
they'd left a pile of our weapons. I retrieved another Tommy gun and then
found Lomell setting up the men in the hedgerows along the road. Larry
Johnson and I settled down in a very shallow rain ditch that was pretty well
hidden by hedge and high grass. We had excellent vision over the three sites

we were to guard. Lomell took a position across from us covering the same area. We felt the Germans would probably use an opening in a stone wall across the way.

"We heard movement from behind the stone fence. A German soldier appeared, stood at the opening, looking up and down the highway. Seeing it apparently clear, he came through the wall and ran across the road right up to me. I saw a German burp gun slung across his chest. I jumped up and fired point-blank, hitting him in the chest. My slugs must have cut the strap on his weapon for it fell to the ground about three feet in front of me. The German ran a few steps then dropped.

"Larry Johnson said, 'Hey, Jack, get me his gun.' I leaned out and picked up the weapon. As I did, I noticed movement and saw another German soldier standing in the opening of the stone fence aiming at me. I had no way to protect myself and felt I was about to be shot. Len saw it all and got the German just as he shot at me. His bullet struck the road near me. For the second time on D day, Lomell had saved my life. I learned the hard way to observe and proceed with caution."

"Because we couldn't stop until we reached the road, we had moved fast," recalled Lomell, "with the wounded men helping one another. Once we set up our roadblocks, there were maybe thirteen of us, Jack and I made up a two-man patrol in one direction, while another two Rangers went the opposite way. I saw some wheel tracks in a dirt lane. We followed them and about 200 yards from the highway, I found the five guns, all in place, pointed toward Utah Beach, but with not a soul around them, not a single guard. It was about 8:30 in the morning and maybe they hadn't realized that there was anyone landing on Utah Beach. But another 100 yards off were a bunch of Germans forming up, putting on jackets, starting their vehicles. I think they were the gun crews getting organized.

"'Jack,' I instructed Kuhn, 'Keep your eyes on them and if one starts toward here, get him between the eyes.' While he watched the Germans, I took his thermite grenade and the one I carried. I put them in the barrels of two of the guns. They just made a light popping noise that couldn't be heard by the enemy but destroyed the barrels. Then I ran back to the rest of the guys, got their thermite grenades and did the remaining guns. For good measure, I busted out the sights.

"Just as we returned to our hedgerow, there was a tremendous roar, like the whole world had blown up. There was a shower of dirt, metal, ramrods. I figured that a round from the *Texas* or some other warship had hit the ammunition dump for the artillery. When we first came over the top of the Pointe, we were a lot of disappointed guys when there were no guns there. But now, just by a piece of luck, we had found them and were able to destroy the pieces."

Medic Frank South said, "The medics had a problem. It would be impractical for us to carry all the equipment and supplies we would need in our aid kits or simple packs and we did not know when we would be able to retrieve the rest of our materials from a supply boat. We decided each of us would carry an enlarged kit. Because I was the biggest and presumably strongest, youngest, and perhaps the most naive, Block asked me to work with him putting together a *very* large pack of medical gear and supplies to be carried on a mountain packboard. On its horns I coiled about fifty feet of three-eighths-inch line in case I had to ditch it in the surf and pull it to shore. The pack contained plasma, sulfa-based antibiotics—there was no penicillin yet—drugs, additional instruments, bandages, suture material, and whatever else I could think of. God knows how much it weighed, perhaps sixty-five or seventy pounds. I was a walking aid station and I don't recall any other medic making or carrying such a pack. In addition, I carried my regular aid kit, side arm, knife, canteen, an Argus C-3 camera that I lost in the surf, and a D-ration bar.

"As a medic on the LCA, I was to be the last one off. There was not much conversation around me, a little black humor maybe—'Now if the lieutenant and I get hit, you know who to take care of first, Doc.' Then someone lamented that the army had never issued bulletproof jockstraps. 'After all, I got married just before we left. Could you requisition one for me, Doc?' Approaching the beach, our LCA was able to fire its grapnel-bearing rockets in good order, and most men got off in about two or three feet of water while under almost continuous MG fire from the cliff. Expectably, as the boat load lightened, the LCA rose and shifted its position. When my turn came, I jumped off the ramp into an underwater bomb or shell crater that was over my head. Before either the pack or I became waterlogged, I scrambled out and crawled into a drier crater ashore when I was able to shuck my burden.

"Immediately, there was the first call of, 'Medic!' My regular aid kit was still attached to my pistol belt. Opening it, as I dodged the fire from the cliff, I reached the fallen Ranger who had a chest wound. I was able to drag him to an indentation in the cliff face and begin to help him. The call 'Medic!' was now repeated time after time. For a while it seemed as if I were the only one retrieving and working on the wounded, which of course was not so. Block and another medic had worked their way up to the cliff base and were beginning to treat men as fast as they could. However, it was not possible to actually set up a proper aid station on the beach. The highest priority went to scaling and securing the cliff. Also the wounded were too scattered. I worked along the entire beach area, covering all three companies. Block devoted most of his attention to the most critically wounded.

"Although the LCA I was on got its grapnel rockets off effectively, the one with the 1st Platoon [F Company] was in the wrong position to launch the rockets. They were designed so they could be removed and fired by hand, a risky procedure. Sergeant John Cripps took off the LCA four rockets, and while exposed to machine gun fire from above, mounted them on the beach. He hot-wired and fired one, receiving a blast in the face. With terrific determination, he fired the rest, just as successfully.

"Nearly blinded, almost fainting, Cripps stumbled over to Block and me. His face, neck, and hands were covered with powder burns and imbedded with black unburned explosives. He said to me, 'Jesus, South, didn't you ever stand too close to a big firecracker?' All we could do was blot his face and neck with water from our canteens and pat on, as gently as possible, some burn ointment I found in the bottom of my aid kit. He immediately left to rejoin his platoon and the attack. For all that courage, willpower, and determination that Cripps displayed while under direct fire, he never was cited or decorated. Very early on, while I was finishing working on someone near our left flank, Sgt. Bill (L-Rod) Petty, his BAR slung across his shoulders, was struggling with a straight rope. It was slippery with wet clay and he was having a terrible time getting a purchase on it and ascending the cliff. During a pause, while he was trying to dry his hands and catch his breath, Block appeared and said in a loud, commanding voice, 'Soldier, get hold of that rope and up the cliff!'

"Petty, face flushed both by anger and his efforts, replied something like, 'What the hell, if you think you can do any better, you can fucking well try!' Short-tempered, Captain Block was stymied by the equally short-tempered Sergeant Petty, one of our most effective noncoms. Somehow Block did control his temper and realize his charge was unjust. He looked at Petty, turned, stared at me for an instant, and then stalked down to the beach where he was needed."

From Pointe du Hoc, Rudder dispatched Rangers to capture other troublesome bastions belonging to the enemy. One was the command post, presumably for the big guns that Lomell and Kuhn found elsewhere; the other was an antiaircraft battery emplacement doing considerable damage to the invaders. In both instances the defenders were too numerous and strongly entrenched to be overrun by the limited number of men Rudder could muster. The German command post, which included a series of underground tunnels, troubled the invaders for many hours, as enemy soldiers disappeared in its warrens only to surface in some protected place and fire. The gun battery, however, yielded to the U.S. Navy. The destroyer *Satterlee,* earlier had help drive off Germans atop the Pointe. Now, with the guidance of a shore fire-control officer it blasted the antiaircraft guns.

When Rudder and his headquarters party achieved the heights of the Pointe, they set up their command post in the revetments of that antiaircraft post. Unfortunately, a round from enemy artillery smashed into their position, wounding Rudder in the arm—down on the beach a bullet had passed through the fleshy part of his leg. The same explosion killed the naval observer. Lou Lisko assumed the responsibility for contacting the warships to enlist their aid. "I had a signal lamp," says Lisko. "I was able to get in touch with the *Satterlee* but the Navy guys were much too fast with their lights for me. Finally, they told me the wave length to use. We began to communicate by radio. When the *Satterlee* used up all its ammunition, the destroyer *Harding* took over. Their fire support saved our necks, breaking up counterattacks."

What the Rangers and all of the soldiers assaulting the beaches lacked was any tactical aid from the air. American fighters either flew air cover for the bombers or else devoted themselves to keeping the inland highways clean of any would-be reinforcements. There were no means of air-to-ground or air-to-ship communications. The absence of coordination sharply contrasted with naval operations in the Pacific, where U.S. Navy warships worked closely with their air arm.

The bloody reception that greeted the Rangers climbing Pointe du Hoc was mimicked by that encountered when A and B Companies of the 2d Battalion attempted to fulfill their mission. Bob Edlin remembered, "The navy had opened up. It seemed as if the whole world exploded. There was gunfire from battleships, destroyers, and cruisers. The bombers were still hitting the beaches. There didn't seem to be any way that anyone could live on the beaches with the amount of firepower laid down by the American forces. As we went in, we could see small craft from the 116th Infantry that had gone in ahead, sunk. A few bodies were bobbing in the water, even out three or four miles.

"I took stock of the men in my boat. They were vomiting on each other's feet and on their clothing. It was just a terrible sight. They were so sick from the action of the waves. There was a deep silence. All the gunfire had lifted for a very short time. The navy was giving way to let the troops get on the beaches. The only thing I could hear was the motor of the boat. It was dawn. The sun was just coming up over the French coast. I saw a bird, a seagull, I guess, fly across the front of the boat, just as if life were going on as normal.

"Then there came something like a peppering of hail, heavy hail on the front of the ramp. I realized it was enemy machine-gun fire. All hell broke loose from the other side, German artillery, rockets, and mortars. It was just unbelievable that anybody could have lived under that barrage. It came in through our boat and the other boats. We crouched in the bottom of the boat in the vomit, urine, and seawater and whatever else was there.

"The assault boat hit a sandbar. We were at least seventy-five yards from shore. I told the coxswain, the operator of the boat, 'Try to get it in farther.'

That British seaman had all the guts in the world, but he couldn't get the assault craft off the sandbar. So, I told him to drop the ramp or we were going to die right there. We had been trained for years not to go off the front of the ramp because the boat might get rocked by a wave and run over you. So we went off the sides. I looked to my right and saw a B Company boat next to us with Lt. Bob Fitzsimmons, a good friend, take a direct hit from a mortar or mine on the ramp. I thought, there goes half of B Company. It was cold, miserably cold, even though it was June. The water temperature was probably forty-five or fifty degrees. It was up to my shoulders and I saw men sinking all about me. I tried to grab a couple but my job was to get in and to the guns. There were bodies from the 116th floating everywhere. They were face down in the water, packs still on their backs. They had inflated their life jackets. Fortunately, most of the Rangers did not inflate theirs or they also might have turned over and drowned. I began to run with my rifle in front of me. I went directly across the beach to try to get to the seawall. In front of me was part of the 116th Infantry, pinned down and lying behind beach obstacles. They hadn't made it to the seawall. I kept screaming, 'You have to get up and go! You gotta get up and go! But they didn't. They were worn out, defeated.

"I continued across the beach. There were mines and obstacles all up and down the beach. The Air Force had missed it entirely. There were no shell holes in which to take cover. The mines had not been detonated. Absolutely nothing that had been planned for that part of the beach had worked. I knew that Vierville-sur-Mer was going to be a hellhole, and it was. When I was about twenty yards from the seawall, I was hit by what I assume was a sniper bullet. It shattered and broke my right leg. I thought, well, I've got a Purple Heart. I fell, and as I did, it was like a searing, hot poker rammed into my leg. My rifle fell, ten feet or so in front of me. I crawled forward to get to it, picked it up, and as I rose on my left leg, another burst of, I think, machine-gun fire tore the muscles out of that leg, knocking me down again.

"I lay there for seconds, looked ahead, and saw several Rangers lying there. One was Butch Bladorn from Wisconsin. I screamed at Butch, 'Get up and run!' Butch, a big, powerful man, just looked back and said, 'I can't.' I got up and hobbled toward him. I was going to kick him in the ass and get him off the beach. He was lying on his stomach, his face in the sand. Then I saw the blood coming out of his back. I realized he had been hit in the stomach and the bullet had come out his spine and he was completely immobilized. Even then I was sorry for screaming at him but I didn't have time to stop and help him. I thought, well, that's the end of Butch. Fortunately, it wasn't. He became a farmer in Wisconsin.

"As I moved forward, I hobbled. Your legs after you have been hit with gunfire, slowly, stiffen. The pain was indescribable. I fell to my hands and knees and tried to crawl forward. I managed a few yards, then blacked out for several minutes. When I came to, I saw Sgt. Bill Klaus. He was up to the seawall and when he saw my predicament, he crawled back to me under heavy rifle and mortar fire and dragged me to the cover of the wall. Klaus had also been wounded in one leg and a medic gave him a shot of morphine. The medic did the same for me. My mental state was such that I told him to shoot it directly into my left leg as that was the one hurting the most. He reminded me that if I took it in the ass or the arm it would get to the leg. I told him to give me a second shot because I was hit in the other leg. He didn't.

"There were some Rangers gathered at the seawall—Sgt. William Courtney, Pvt. William Dreher, Garfield Ray, Gabby Hart, Sgt. Charles Berg. I yelled at them. 'You have to get off of here! You have to get up and get the guns!' They were gone immediately. Sergeant Bill White, my platoon sergeant, whom we called Whitey, an ex-jockey, took charge. He was small, very active, and very courageous. He led what few men were left of the first platoon and started up the cliffs. I crawled and staggered forward as far as I could to some cover in the bushes behind a villa. There was a round, stone well with a bucket and a handle that turned the rope. It was so inviting. I was alone and I wanted that water so bad. But years of training told me it was booby-trapped.

"I looked up at the top of the cliffs and thought, I can't make it on this leg. Where was everyone? Had they all quit? Then I heard Dreher yelling, 'Come on up. These trenches are empty." Then Kraut burp guns cut loose. I thought, 'Oh, God, I can't get there!' I heard an American Tommy gun and Courtney shout, 'Damn it, Dreher! They're empty, *now.*' There was more German small-arms fire and German grenades popping. I could hear Whitey yelling, 'Cover me!' I heard Garfield Ray's BAR talking American. Then there was silence.

"Now I thought, where are the 5th Rangers? I turned and I couldn't walk or even hobble anymore. I crawled back to the beach. I saw the 5th Rangers coming through the smoke of a burning LST that had been hit by artillery fire. Colonel [Max] Schneider had seen the slaughter on the beaches and used his experience with the Rangers in Africa, Sicily, Italy, and Anzio. He used the smoke as a screen and moved in behind it, saving the 5th Ranger Battalion many casualties. My years of training told me there would be a counterattack. I gathered the wounded by the seawall and told them to arm themselves as best as possible. I said if the Germans come we are either going to be captured or die on the beach but we might as well take the Germans with us. I know it sounds ridiculous, but ten or fifteen Rangers lay there, facing up to the cliffs, praying that Sergeant White, Courtney, Dreher, and the 5th Ranger Battalion would get to the guns. Our fight was over unless the Germans counterattacked.

"I looked back to the sea. There was nothing. There were no reinforcements. I thought the invasion had been abandoned. We would be dead or prisoners soon. Everyone had withdrawn and left us. Well, we had tried. Some guy crawled over and told me he was a colonel from the 29th Infantry Division. He said for us to relax, we were going to be okay. D, E, and F Companies [2d Ranger Battalion] were on the Pointe. The guns had been destroyed. The 2d's A and B Companies and the 5th Rangers were inland. The 29th and 1st Divisions were getting off the beaches.

"This colonel looked at me and said, 'You've done your job.' I answered, 'How? By using up two rounds of German ammo on my legs?' Despite the awful pain, I hoped to catch up with the platoon the next day. Someone gave me another shot of morphine."

29
Getting Off Omaha

Sharing the horror of Omaha Beach with the GIs of the 29th Division were the men from the 1st Infantry Division. Bill Behlmer and his antitank platoon headed for Easy Red Beach with their half-track, *Hitler's Hearse,* up front. "We were to be first off and I was to lead my platoon on Omaha Beach. My driver Stan Stypulkowski, who had come all the way through North Africa and Sicily, sat and talked with me all night. We knew this was it for us. On the way in, another LCT, not far from us, just disappeared. An LCI on the other side with red crosses on the side took a couple of hits. Medics were hanging onto the ramp and in the water. As far as the eye could see was wall-to-wall boats headed for Easy Red near the small town of Colleville-sur-Mer.

"We neared the beach and the ramp dropped. Small arms, machine guns, mortars, artillery raked across the ramp. The Navy CO said we were pulling out to try again. We came back in, and the ramp dropped, I told Stan to gun the half-track. We hit the ground, turned right, and headed down the beach, a big turkey at a turkey shoot. Every gun covering that beach zeroed in on us. We didn't stand a chance. I stood up and turned to the back, told the guys to get out. Stan and I jumped from the hood to the ground. On the way down, it felt as if someone jabbed me in the legs with a red-hot poker. Stan, his arms across his chest, oozed blood. I must have gone into shock, because I drifted in and out. Shells were falling everywhere. But for me the war seemed to have gone away."

Fred Erben, a Brooklyn youth who joined the 1st Division as a seventeen-year-old, was a member of C Company and destined for Easy Red. "As luck would have it," said Erben, "we were in the first wave and hit the beaches at low tide. We were fortunate because we could see the underwater obstacles and skirt around them. However, we hit a sandbar and had to unload. Beyond the sandbar there were obstacles we did not see. Our craft made it out of there in a hurry but some boats that got over the bar, struck the mines and blew up. It was horrible seeing men blown all over the place. Some were swimming ashore. The ones not so lucky floated ashore.

"We had to wade in with all of our equipment: a pair of twenty-pound TNT bangalore torpedoes and ammo. Our flotation devices helped. My squad made it intact, but the beach was rocky and there was no chance to dig in.

Many men were hit all around us from the intense crossfire from two pill-boxes on either side of us. That's when Omaha Easy Red became known as Bloody Red. We got the word to advance and get the hell off the beach. We had barbed wire and land mines in front. One of my scouts, Private Tripoletti, set his ammunition down on a mine and was killed. This was where the bangalores—we called them stovepipes—came in. They were assembled under fire, one by one, with three-foot lengths pressed into one another until they passed through the barbed wire. The pipes were loaded with high explosives and an ignition cap placed in the last one. A man would lie directly behind the tube, pull the cap, setting off an explosion that caused the tubes to burst sideways, cutting the wires. It also blew up any buried mines. We kept passing them forward and the tubes made a large enough hole for us to pass through.

"This was about twenty minutes after we landed. We inched our way up the hill toward one pillbox. Myself and another man put a charge attached to a wooden pole into the aperture of the pillbox. It sounds crazy but it worked. We moved into a wooded area and went on a recon mission, moving forward to a hedgerow. Peering over it, we saw a group of men on our left flank. Thinking they were another patrol, we waved to them. They waved back; then we motioned for them to come over. They must have realized we were Americans because they dropped down behind their hedge and opened fire. No one was hit at the moment.

"Then they started to drop in mortars on us. We opened up with rifle grenades fired from an adapter on our M1s. I told my squad to withdraw when a mortar shell struck near us. A piece of shrapnel hit me and knocked me out. I came to and heard German voices nearby. They must have thought I was dead and they left. Now I heard Americans but I didn't move. Someone said, 'That's Erben. Is he dead?' Gene Greco came over and bandaged my head. After he patched me up, I headed back toward the beach. It was devastation, littered with bodies, with wounded being tended to. Sunken boats lay on their sides. More troops were coming ashore. Finally one of the medics directed me to a ship, where I saw more bodies being put in body bags."

Fred Erben and his squad were among the very few Americans to blast an opening for themselves and actually get off the beach and move inland. Most of the men, whether from the 116th, like Slaughter and Branham, the 1st Division or the Rangers detailed for Omaha, huddled below the seawall seeking shelter from the prolonged savage rain of death and destruction.

George Zenie, another 1st Division vet from North Africa and Sicily, was aboard an LCT with three half-tracks, three 57mm antitank guns, and the crews to man them. They also were to come in at Easy Red. "Finally, our LCT landed, dropped the ramp, and we disembarked. It was around noon and we had been scheduled to land between ten and ten-thirty. We followed the two other half-tracks onto Easy Red. Artillery and mortar fire were falling around us. A piece of shrapnel flew through the driver's slit and cut the side of his face. He screamed and stopped the half-track. I put my first-aid gauze against his face, told him to hold it there, moved him over, and drove the half-track down the beach as planned.

"When the whole line halted, I got the driver out and told one of the men to drive, to follow the other vehicles. I helped the driver to an aid station, taking the wounded aboard an LCI. The scene around me depicted the real horror of war. Dead bodies floated in the water and were scattered about the beach. Wounded lay everywhere. All types of equipment were broken and abandoned. A gasoline truck ahead of us was in flames. The entire beach was under constant fire from small arms, mortars, and artillery. The guns of destroyers, cruisers, and battleships were still battering at heavily fortified beach emplacements and pill boxes that blocked the important exits from the beach. A bulldozer trying to clear our exit was a target for enemy fire. Two drivers had been wounded; a third soldier tried to restart the machine. Our line was still contained.

"When I returned to the half-track, another of my men had been wounded, in the buttocks by shrapnel. 'Pappy' Henderson, a sergeant in our platoon, and a very close friend of mine, came along. He was called 'Pappy' because he was a little older than most of us—earlier 30s—and sought after for all kinds of advice. He and I put the wounded man in a blanket and carried him close to the bluff where a first-aid unit was set up in a gully. We left the wounded man there. I told the rest of the men to get into the gully where they were better protected. Pappy and I carried another soldier with chest and arm wounds to the aid station in the gully. Pappy said he was going to see if we could move forward. When he left, I maneuvered the half-track close to the gully. I never saw Pappy Henderson again. To this day he is listed as MIA."

Rifleman John Bistrica, a replacement who joined the 16th Regiment of the 1st Division in England, was forced to disembark in water over his head. He inflated his life preserver to keep himself afloat. Pinned down with others, he remembered, "Our regimental CO, Col. George Taylor, came on the beach and he started to get the officers and noncoms organized, getting us going. He said, 'There are two kinds of people on this beach. Those that are dead and those that are about to die. Let's get out of here!'" [The quote has also been imputed to Gen. Norman Cota, assistant division chief of the 29th Division, or to Col. Charles Canham, CO of the 116th.]

The 1st Division's Lawrence Zeickler, combat savvy after North Africa and Sicily, never succumbed to the optimism voiced by Bob Slaughter and his fellows, who thought it would be a "walk-in." Zeickler, with E Company, also destined for Easy Red, remarked, "We knew the German soldier was a fighter. And especially when we heard Rommel was in charge of the beach, we knew it wasn't going to be a picnic. There is always a sense of fear when you go into combat, particularly before you hit the beaches. Anyone who said he wasn't scared isn't kidding anyone who knows. You should be scared when someone is shooting at you, hoping to hit you.

"The one nice thing about this invasion was we didn't have to climb down the side of the ship. We in the first wave were lowered over the side in our LST without using a cargo net. When we looked over the sides of the landing craft as we started in toward the beach, we could see tanks, some of them still afloat, with the [flotation] rafts holding them up. It was weird to see a tank in the water and floating. Others had gone down; the crews were sitting in their little dinghies after the tanks swamped.

"When we reached the beach, things were not busted up as we expected. The tide was out, and we could see obstacles. The air support had missed the beach, falling inland, and the rockets fell short. We hit a sandbar close to shore and the sailor tried to get us loose to take us all the way in, but small-arms fire and mortars were coming in heavy. Our boat commander, the battalion exec officer, hollered for them to lower the front of the boat so we could get out. The longer we sat there, the more chance we had of being hit by either a mortar or artillery shell.

"I got out of the landing craft but I must have hit a hole at the end of the sandbar because I sank down into the water. We had on the new combat jackets where you only had to pull three or four tabs and you could shed your equipment. But my fingers were so cold I couldn't do it. My helmet flew on the back of my head and was pulling on my neck. As I started down in the water, I thought, 'What the hell, North Africa, Sicily—it seems as though there's nothing to look forward to but being killed.' I thought I'd give up as I went deeper and deeper.

"Suddenly, it came to my mind someone saying that drowning is a helluva way to die. I started to tread water and I finally got my equipment loose and could shed it. I was a fairly good swimmer and made it to shore. My objective was to go to the left with my squad across the beach. I saw men taking cover behind the underwater obstacles. But the tide was coming in now and to stay there was sure death. We started kicking butts to get 'em out of the water, up on shore. Those who were wounded, we drug up behind. Right off the beach was a pile of rocks that looked like a stone fence. We could get down behind it and try to figure out where the hell to go from there.

"When I set my helmet back on my head and put my hand beneath it, there was dried blood. A bullet or piece of shrapnel strafed the top of my head; another half inch I wouldn't be here. Right to the front was a German gun bunker that was supposed to be blown to smithereens but the Air

Force wasn't able to do it. All this time, the Navy is coming in, bringing more men, and stuff piling up on the beach. I found Private Ratti and we headed up the beach trying to find the others from our group. We found some medics and they told us the rest of the company had gone up a nearby wadi. The man who had broken the barrier to an exit from the beach was a sergeant from our company, Philip Streczyk. Almost everyone followed him through."

Bill Lewis of the 29th Division credits someone like Streczyk with preparing the way for his departure from the killing ground. "This 1st Division boy who had been in combat, said, I see what they're doing—from the big bunker by the exit. He said, 'Get some fire on that baby.' A shore control man got on his radio but the shells wouldn't even touch it. He [the 1st Division GI] said, everybody get up and start firing on the embrasures and get them back away from that hole. He knew what he was doing. We started firing on the embrasure. He took some men and went up there. I didn't go. They took some bangalore torpedoes and put them under that baby. That was the thing that was murdering us, an 88 or 75mm gun. That stopped the gun, blew it over. He was a 1st Division sergeant who blew it up. He had a big red one on his shoulder."

There were four such exits on Omaha Beach through which the assault companies had been expected to drive inland. The Allied high command had anticipated that even if the big ships and sky fleets failed to demolish the barriers and fortifications defending these openings, the duplex-drive Sherman tanks would overwhelm the enemy. But the rough water ripped away the fragile canvas flotation devices. Seaborne armor sank almost instantly upon launching while still thousands of yards offshore. Of the thirty-two the U.S. expected to launch, twenty-seven quickly disappeared below the waves, many of the crews unable to escape entombment. Just two with the wraparound flotation mechanism actually gained the shore under their own power. Three others made it to land only because an accident aboard the LCT prevented them from trundling down the ramp into the water. On the British beaches, the command realized the sea was too much for any flotation devices and did not attempt to use the amphibious tanks.

Armor came to Omaha Beach later in the form of dual-drive tanks that scuttled across the sea bottom, rather than plowing through the waves on canvas "bloomers." Eddie Ireland, a Calumet City, Illinois, high school grad who chose armor because he didn't care to walk to war, drove the second type of DD tank. "We started out sitting on top of the vehicles. But when we came close to the shore, we were told to get inside the tank. They let us off in water that was about turret-high. I had a camera and I wanted to take pictures of the beach. So I cracked the hatch open and just then we hit a shell hole. Water poured in and I got soaked.

"The tide was in and we rode through the water for quite a bit. The engineers had made a path for us [through the obstacles]. When we did come ashore, the infantry guys had to move the bodies lying at the edge so we wouldn't run over them. The troops were still hugging the shoreline and there wasn't much land between the hill and the water. There was a lot of mortar fire coming down, not so much small arms. We didn't have much trouble there on the beach. But once we got over the hill, we started to catch artillery fire."

The 5th Ranger Battalion's Charles Parker, CO of Company A, Lt. Frank Dawson of D Company, and John Raaen testified to the wisdom of Max Schneider. Lost in the waterborne assault of the Rangers upon Pointe du Hoc were colored rockets to inform Schneider of the success or failure of the mission. A radio carried by Rudder's party would not transmit. Ranger John Raaen, the CO of Headquarters Company, explained that with no information about events at Pointe du Hoc, Schneider had to make a decision. "As we approached the beach, Schneider had a clear view of what was happening on the beach. The survivors of the 1st Battalion of the 116th Infantry were clinging to their very lives in the wreckage of their landing craft and behind the seawall of Omaha Dog Green Beach. As A and B Companies of the 2d Rangers touched down slightly left of the [29th Division GIs] they were hit by enormous fire directed at their LCA ramps. Those Rangers who were to survive went over the side, using the LCAs, DD [dual drive] tanks, other wreckage, and obstacles as a shield against enemy fire.

"We were delayed maybe thirty minutes, and it was about 8:00 A.M.," said Parker, "This is where Max Schneider's leadership and experience paid off. He saw what had happened to the 116th, which was cut to pieces, disorganized; the support elements like tanks, transport, artillery, and supply smashed together in a jumble. The enemy fire from casemated guns, pillboxes, and fortifications was just butchering them. Schneider swung the entire group farther east, from Dog Green to Dog White. We had fewer casualties and the command group was intact. We were the only cohesive force in that vital invasion area. The coxswain of our boat put us off in waist-deep water. He then held his boat in and used his machine gun, trying to suppress enemy fire to give us a better opportunity to cross the beach. I don't think it helped much because the Germans were all shooting from massively prepared positions. Still, it was an incredibly brave thing for him to do.

"We had to get across what seemed an endless expanse of sand and then an area of shingle, small rocks with bad footing. Behind us boats were being blown up and burning, artillery and mortal shells were exploding, machine-gun bullets ricocheting around. The water looked dimpled from the shrapnel and bullets. In addition to Schneider picking Dog White, we got another break. The grass and low bushes that grew on the flat portion of the land behind the beach and up the sides of the bluffs themselves was on fire. Smoke covered the whole area and the Germans couldn't put much observed fire on us. The fire also revealed the mines when the grass burned off. Later I heard the engineers removed about 150 of them from the areas.

"There was concertina wire behind the seawall and we had to blow that with bangalore torpedoes. The assistant division commander of the 29th, General Cota, came strolling up the beach to where Schneider was. He asked who was in command and then supposedly made his famous line, 'Rangers, lead the way.' Schneider gave the word to us, 'Tallyho,' our planned signal to move out and assemble at the rally point south and west of Vierville."

Ranger lieutenant Frank "Buck" Dawson, a 5th Battalion, D Company platoon leader, occupied a ringside seat during the drive for Dog White beach. "I saw several large ships moving toward the beach. One fired a volley of rockets and I noticed a destroyer had cut across our front between us and the beach and was firing at gun positions as it moved along. Finally, the signal came for us to move out. The LCAs formed a skirmish line parallel to the beach. I could not make out the shore due to the haze and smoke. I began to notice the obstacles. Just ahead were four posts set at an angle with mines attached to the tops. We were just about in them and in the boat no one was talking. I imagine each had his own thoughts of what would happen when the ramp fell.

"We were very lucky. The landing craft was heading straight toward a pole obstacle with a large mine attached to the top and leaning seaward. The skipper on the LCA steered sharply left and the breaking waves just lifted our craft over. We came to a halt in knee-deep water. I could see my immediate destination, a seawall about fifty to seventy-five yards across a flat beach. I was completely pooped from the dash, wet boots, and equipment, with an ammo bag of .45-caliber magazines for my Thompson, gas mask, light pack, and entrenching tool. I was running but still noticed machine-gun rounds hitting near. The ones who stopped to take shelter behind obstacles and stayed at the water's edge were unlucky.

"I saw disabled tanks, one was burning. The noise of gunfire was everywhere, incoming and outgoing. Mortar rounds were falling between the seawall and the water's edge. At the seawall there were other men besides Rangers. You had to push in to get to the wall. I wanted to see what was on the other side. No effort was being made in my sector to get off the beach. I was busy getting my platoon head count and then sending my runner off to contact the company commander, telling him where we were, and finding out any order he might have for me.

"I would not have known General Cota from anyone else. [If Cota indeed said, "Rangers lead the way," the man who did as directed never heard him.] The confusion was enormous. When the word 'Go' was given, my two bangalore-torpedo men, [Elwood] Dorman and [Ellis] Reed set off the charge. Before the dust cleared, I stepped into the cupped hands of my company first sergeant and platoon sergeant and was lifted over the wall through the area just blown. I began my run for the high ground. The ground was very flat, grassy, and in full view of the enemy.

"Knowing I was being fired on, I twice hit the ground, rolled over, sprang up, and continued. I chose to go to my right about fifty yards and then picked a route to climb. The bluff was steep but not a cliff. I knew there were mines in the area but I took a chance. I was alone while climbing the bluff, having outdistanced my platoon following in single file. I hadn't looked back because I was too busy looking forward, right, and left. I knew they were coming behind me; I just had that feeling. Beyond the top lay a battery of rockets that were firing. As I neared the crest smoke started to drift toward me but not enough to block my sight. So far, I had not seen any Germans and I continued to climb, using my hands on the ground to help me. Suddenly, I reached the top, traversed to the right where there were trenches and German soldiers. One, in particular, a huge man came straight at me. He was my first kill. Having a Thompson sub, I kept it hot. Several prisoners came out of a trench and I had them spread-eagle on the ground. By then, members of my platoon took over. One young German emerged with a hand blown off. We were not instructed regarding prisoners. We were attacking in a narrow column so we passed the prisoners back, hoping they got to the rear.

"As I continued along the ridge I saw below active machine-gun positions still firing on the beach. These Germans had not seen my platoon. My BAR man was near and I pointed out the positions to him. But he exposed himself too much and a German crew killed him. I retrieved the BAR and killed that crew. Others in the area were making a hasty retreat toward Vierville." Later, Dawson received a Distinguished Service Cross for his efforts and the two bangalore-torpedo men, Dorman and Ellis, were awarded Silver Stars.

Ranger captain John Raaen contended that in the amphibious aspect of the operation, "Schneider was outstanding. He waited as long as he dared before he diverted to Omaha. He watched the destruction of A and B Companies of the 2d Rangers and then brilliantly diverted to Omaha Dog White. That last move I credit for saving the Omaha beach operation. Without the 5th on the beach, the Germans would have stopped the 29th Division cold (they already had) and swept them back out to sea. Perhaps the 1st Division could have saved the left flank of Omaha, but I doubt they could have done it without the 29th Division's success, which came from the 5th Rangers being in the right place at the right time and in sufficient strength."

Company A, led by Charles (Ace) Parker, meanwhile, advanced upon the bluffs mentioned by Dawson as the eastern anchor of the Ranger line.

Parker, with his runner William Fox and a lieutenant from E Company, halted to investigate a field with trees on the far side from them. "We didn't know it," said Parker "but there were snipers in those trees. One of them got us in his sights and we all went down. Fox squatted while the lieutenant and I went prone. A bullet hit Fox in the shoulder, leaving a small blue hole, and then angled down. Another one struck the lieutenant in the right side of his head, blowing out a piece of his skull, leaving his brains partly exposed.

"I kept trying to wriggle out from under my pack while lying flat. It was a huge pack; with enough in it for me to have survived for a month. I finally got my pistol and unbuckled the pack, although, meanwhile, that sniper put several bullets in it. I rolled over into a ditch and we roped the legs of the two wounded and pulled them into the ditch also. We stayed in that ditch for about three and a half hours before we could get to the rallying point, a château. Every man behind Fox had to crawl over him in that ditch. He waved to everyone and smiled. We gave him a canteen of water and went on our way, on our bellies. There wasn't anything we could do for them. Later, they picked up the lieutenant, who somehow survived, hospitalized him, and he eventually regained his ability to speak and function. We didn't know on the other hand that the bullet that hit Fox had ranged down and cut his spine. He died in that ditch."

At the château, Parker counted his troops and discovered he had only twenty-three of his normal complement of close to seventy. Parker reasoned that the remainder of the 5th Battalion must be ahead, on their way to Pointe du Hoc. He led his troops through a series of hedgerows and secondary roads, hoping to catch up with the main body. "We kept switching directions, getting in small-fire fights, killing a few Germans each time, picking up some prisoners. I accepted the surrenders but I really didn't want 'em. We got to a small village, then the Germans started crawling along hedgerows on both sides of us. We could hear them and they were getting behind us. I turned all of the prisoners loose. We retreated at double time until we got well beyond where the Germans were. Eventually, we made contact with the outposted people of the 2d Rangers on Pointe du Hoc." Parker and his slim band now united with the meager forces that included Len Lomell, Jack Kuhn, and George Kerchner.

In his wallet, the chief executive for Overlord, Gen. Dwight D. Eisenhower, carried a brief, hand-written statement. "Our landings in the Cherbourg-Havre area have failed to gain a satisfactory foothold and I have withdrawn the troops. My decision to attack at this time and place was based upon the best information available. The troops, the air, and the Navy did all that bravery and devotion to duty could do. If any blame or fault attaches to the attempt it is mine alone." If his 1948 memoir *Crusade in Europe* is to be believed, he never felt he would need to release this message. There, Eisenhower wrote, "As the morning wore on, it became apparent that the landing was going fairly well." The statement, however, squares neither with the facts nor the reactions of those of his own high command.

Aboard the flagship of the American naval forces, the U.S.S. *Augusta,* Gen. Omar Bradley, as commander of the U.S. First Army, anxiously awaited word on the invasion's progress. In his autobiography he wrote, "As the morning lengthened, my worries deepened over the alarming and fragmentary reports we picked up on the navy net. From these messages we could piece together only an incoherent account of sinkings, swampings, heavy enemy fire, and chaos on the beaches."

Bradley's timetable expected the two assault regiments, the 116th from the 29th Division, and the 16th from the 1st Division augmented by the Rangers and the waterborne tanks, to have passed a mile inland by 8:30 A.M. But at 10:00, the first report from Gen. Leonard Gerow, commander of the V Corps, charged with the conquest of Omaha Beach, brought gloom and fear. Gerow advised, "Obstacles mined, progress slow . . . DD tanks for Fox Green swamped."

Admiral Kirk and Bradley dispatched aides RAdm. Charles (Savvy) Cooke and Brig. Gen. Thomas Handy for a firsthand look. The latter remembered an appalled Cooke exclaiming, "My God, this is carnage!" Handy was equally dismayed. "It was terrible along that damned beach because they were not only under mortar fire but they were under small-arms fire. The amphibious tanks were all sinking and the beach obstacles blocked access."

The V Corps commander, Gen. Leonard Gerow, asked Handy, "How about it?"

"G, it isn't very good," was the reply. When Gerow pressed for advice on what to do, Handy said he responded, "The only thing you can do and you've got to do, regardless of the losses, you've got to push your doughboys [Handy dated from World War I] in far enough to get that damned beach out from under small-arms fire and if possible, mortar fire, because it's just terrible."

The anxious brass at sea, concerned with Omaha Beach, heard only a series of discouraging words about troops pinned down at the seawall; a beach swept by deadly enemy fire; assault and supply craft milling about offshore because of the failure to open more than six pathways through the honeycomb of mined obstacles. Navy UDTs and Army Engineers trying to blast lanes for the invaders suffered casualties estimated between 50 and 75 percent. Not only did they have to contend with what the foe threw at them but they were frustrated by GIs who clung to the mined obstacles. Detonation by the demolition experts would kill the hapless soldiers. The sole good news from the area was the report that Pointe du Hoc had fallen. Handy remarked, "At Omaha, we just hung on by our eyelashes. For several hours, I don't believe they ever realized how close that things were."

As noon approached, V Corps reported the situation "still critical" at all four of the avenues to a breakthrough on Omaha. Bradley admitted, "I reluctantly contemplated the diversion of Omaha follow-up forces to Utah and the British beaches. Scanty reports from both those sectors indicated the landings there had gone according to plan."

Navy lieutenant Harvey Bennett, serving as assistant gunnery officer for Admiral Kirk aboard the *Augusta* insisted he saw no evidence of any wavering by Bradley. "I sat very close to him and at no time do I recall his intent to pull troops off the beaches." According to Bennett, the responsibility for bombardment of the beaches, rather than the dugouts, pillboxes, and emplacements guarding the approaches, lay with the U.S. Army Air Corps. "AAC decided on D day that visibility was not suitable. As far as I know, no other command was notified of this omission." Because of this apparent failure to communicate, the shoreline at Omaha Beach remained a pristinely smooth surface without shell holes that might have preserved the lives of those in the first waves.

Bennett also emphasized the serious flaw that marked combined assaults by Allied forces in Europe. "It would have taken more than a joint command to provide the same sort of air support the Navy had in the Pacific. The Army Air Corps and the RAF were basically concerned about their own war against German industry. In no operation in which I have been concerned has there ever been any liaison with the Army Air Corps." In place of a tactical partnership between aircraft and ground forces, the navy dispatched sailors equipped with radios to serve as shore fire-control parties. These teams acting as forward observers for the ships, accompanied the earliest invaders, including the Rangers' attempt to scale Pointe du Hoc. As soon as minesweepers cleared the seas nearest land, destroyers moved in so close as to risk grounding in order to hammer targets named by the shore fire-control parties. In some instances where the navy personnel were killed or wounded, GIs such as Ranger Lou Lisko assumed the role of liaison with the seaborne gunners.

One of the first sailors to navigate the treacherous Channel waters to Omaha Beach was Dell Martin, coxswain aboard the last of thirteen LCMs [Landing Craft, Mechanized] bearing the spearhead forces around 6:00 A.M. "We circled around waiting to form into a line. I passed alongside a large French ship as she fired some very big guns. As the coxswain, I was in an enclosure by myself. When those shells went over my head, it felt as if someone had socked me in the jaw. My ears started ringing and have ever since. I get a 10 percent pension as a result and the VA also gives me hearing aids.

"It was low tide and the men on our ship got off in knee-deep water after we hit a sandbar. All the obstacles were high and dry. Each boat carried fifty men, half army and half navy. Their job was to blow 100-yard gaps at 50-yard intervals to open lanes for succeeding boats. The army men were responsible for the landward obstacles and the navy the ones in the sea. We ran into very heavy opposition. I understand losses went as high as 85 percent.

"We left the beach and went to a hospital ship to put off a man we had picked up on our way in. He was from one of the amphibious tanks that sank. From there we returned to a rendezvous area, circling about until called to shuttle the 1st Division and Rangers into the beach."

Gil Miller was a member of the crew on one of five boats that made up LCM (fifty-footers) Amphibious Force 88. Traveling under its own power about six miles an hour and pausing once for fuel, Miller was at sea fifteen hours once they departed from England. "Our job would be salvage and we were to go in at Omaha Beach one hour after H hour with the mission of keeping the lanes to the beach open. Six waves were to precede us and they would do any fighting that was necessary. We had a twenty-ton bulldozer that, once dropped off, would push aside anything that blocked the movement of troops or vehicles.

"The obstructions to the beach, crossed steel beams imbedded deep in the sand and with mines on top were eerie-looking and sinister. I didn't have time to take notice of what was happening on the beach. Once we unloaded the bulldozer, we backed off with a load of wounded. Our starboard engine shut down; the shaft became caught in camouflage netting and the shaft bent in an S shape. It wasn't a big problem, one big engine could do the work of two. I happened to look up for a moment and lost my helmet. I then went down into the well of the LCM and talked to the wounded, passing out cigarettes. An officer called me over and offered me his helmet, saying, 'Here, you need this more than I.' He was badly wounded, his right hindquarter was gone. I went down between the engines and got out of our kit a clean undershirt. We patched him up the best we could. I put on his helmet and it had the bars of a lieutenant or captain on the front. Everytime I passed any of our crew they saluted. With my knife I scraped off the markings. After we passed on the wounded, an LSD repair ship pulled us up out of the water and in half an hour we had a new screw and shaft."

As the engineering officer, Richard Wilstatter, a lieutenant jg on LST 133, was below deck as his ship proceeded toward its position two or three miles off Omaha Beach to await instructions. The invasion plans slated LST 133 for a kind of triple duty. On board were men from the 1st Division with an attached unit of five DUKWs, each packed with seven tons of munitions as well as trucks, jeeps, ammunition, and weapons carriers. In addition, the vessel's personnel included a hospital unit with a pair of navy physicians and roughly twenty pharmacist mates to assist them. An army doctor and his two assistants rounded out the team designated to treat wounded taken off the beach. In its third role, an LST had towed a Rhino ferry [a barge constructed from pontoons] bearing a navy Construction Battalion (CB), more commonly known as Seabees, and its personal tug to the outer anchorage for the fleet off Omaha Beach.

"When we reached our position off Omaha and anchored while awaiting further instructions, it was realized that the situation on the beach was far from 'proceeding according to plan.' A great many ships had been set afire and sunk in the region of the beach. The beach itself was badly infested with obstacles and mines and was still under heavy 88mm and machine-gun fire. Most of the LCTs and LCIs that had hit the beach that morning were casualties there and blocked the further approach of other landing craft. As we learned later from a colonel of the army amphibious troops, the first soldiers had sustained heavy losses and hardly any reinforcements had been able to land.

"Some time during the day, we received orders to beach at utmost speed—your cargo urgently needed. We could see that the beach and nearby water were still very much under 88 fire. However, we weighed anchor and proceeded in toward Dog Red. We were stationed at general quarters and in the engine room we received the following, 'All engines ahead flank!'

"On our ship, the 'captain's talker' (an enlisted man with a set of sound-powered phones, who stands alongside the captain where he can instantly communicate with any section of the ship) was a yeoman, married, who when ashore indulged himself extraordinarily and was not an admirable person. On the way to the beach he was very loudly praying to God to protect us/save him and us. Everyone on the phone system was deluged with this outpouring of begging. Then there was a loud voice from some unknown quarter, 'Oh, Allen, shut the hell up!'

"About the time we figured we should be hitting the beach, came the orders, 'All engines stop!' Then immediately, 'All engines back emergency!' Later, I learned we had been approached by a control boat that gave us contrary orders and commanded we retire from the beach at once. We were so close in that it would have been impossible for us to turn, normally, without going on the beach sidewise. We returned to our anchorage area close off the beach.

"Very shortly thereafter, small boats and DUKWs came to us, carrying wounded from the beach. Since we were an auxiliary hospital ship, we received all casualties brought to us. Because all the troops and cargo still remained aboard, our crew vacated their aft quarters for use as bunks for wounded. A makeshift operating room with operating lights was installed on a raised platform on the aft end of the tank deck. A second site for surgeons was a starboard table in the wardroom.

"Somewhere around eighty patients, all on stretchers in the small craft and DUKWs, were lifted through a sling arrangement that raised a litter by electric power. Once aboard, stretcher-bearers took the litter through a hatch from the galley passageway, passed it through the window over the galley steam tables, and then down the ladder into the crew's quarter. Patients so badly injured that they probably could not survive this treatment went immediately into the wardroom for attention. Too much credit cannot be given to a Captain Ely, the army surgeon who worked endlessly and with great skill on these badly shattered men.

"Shortly before dark, the DUKW officer on our LST decided his loads of ammunition must be badly needed and he would try to get through. The captain gave permission for the attempt. The bow doors opened and the ramp lowered. The lieutenant and his five ducks rolled out and headed for the beach. They made it."

Aboard LCI 491, Bill Hughes, a ship's electrician learning his duties on the job, watched about 100 good-humored soldiers settle in on his vessel for the ride to Omaha Beach. "On June 5th we fed them all their last hot meal. We were told to destroy all letters, mail, any papers we carried with us. By 0200 of the 6th we were off the coast of France. The word from the beach all morning was bad. Until noon, the rumor was they were all going to come off the beach and that's why we didn't go in. We were held back and did not land our troops until 1400 hours. It was high tide and none of the obstacles were visible. On the way back, we saw all of them sticking out of the water with bodies, missing their shoes, floating among them. A British LCT broke in half; we pulled out the survivors."

By the time Dick Conley, an officer replacement with the 18th Infantry Regiment of the 1st Division, in the second wave of infantry, arrived, Easy Red was less lethal. "We climbed down rope cargo nets from the sides of the Liberty ships [cargo and troop vessels specially designed for World War II] around 0700. The waves were so high, the LCVPs going up and down, many feet, you had to time the moment you let go of the net to drop into the boat. If you hit it while it was going down, that was okay. But it you dropped while it was coming up, that was not good. Altogether, we had about thirty soldiers.

"We spent four and a half hours in the LCVP [Landing Craft, Vehicles and Personnel]. We were supposed to keep our heads down but everybody had to stand up to take a look at what we were facing, what was waiting. When we looked at the beach, all we could see was a haze of smoke. As we closed in on it, the place was so crowded with debris, wrecked craft, and vehicles that we had a great deal of difficulty finding a place to get in. But we had a good crew that dropped us in fairly shallow water.

"It was about 11:30 and about an hour and a quarter later than scheduled. As the leader I charged off first. It was knee-deep and when I hit it, my feet didn't keep up with the rest of me. I went down flat. But I didn't get any wetter than I already was. As soon as we got ashore, we stripped off the plastic covering from our rifles and carbines and I assembled my platoon. We dropped our life belts and I directed that pole charges, satchel charges, and bangalore torpedoes be discarded because I could see the beach had been breached, we wouldn't need them. I saw my first dead American soldiers as soon as I got ashore. Most were in the water at the shoreline."

Dick Biehl was an infantry replacement with B Company of the 26th Infantry Regiment. He arrived in North Africa too late for an encounter with the *Afrika Korps* but entered combat in Sicily. The 26th was to advance to Omaha Easy Red upon orders from the commanding general of the V Corps, behind the assault waves from its two brother regiments in the 1st Division. Biehl did not feel particularly reassured. "I cannot recall if I was more sick than scared. I was very seasick and frightened. Mentally, I knew I had to accept where I was and what was expected of me. On the way in I could see smoke, some fire, hear shells exploding. Lots of friendly aircraft passed overhead with the black-and-white stripes on the wings and fuselage as we were told they would be. Those planes were somewhat of a comfort.

"About 100 yards from the edge of the water we ran aground. The young officer commanding the vessel wanted us off the ship as soon as possible, so he could back off the sandbar and proceed away from the artillery fire that was hitting the water around the craft. I don't think he was chicken. From his vantage point he could tell wounded were being brought out to his ship to be taken back to England or hospital ships, and he needed to lighten his load and so ordered us off. I am six feet, one-half inches, and as the first one off the ladder on the port side I stepped into water neck- deep. I do not understand how the fellows shorter than I made it. Some things I saw remain quite vivid. I recall two medics, dragging out to the ship we had just vacated, a wounded GI with a hole in his forehead I could have laid my fist in. I saw burning landing craft, a jeep bobbing on the water like a cork . . . a lone sailor who I suppose survived a damaged or sunken landing craft, appearing very confused . . . one of our guys wandering into a mine area but being retrieved okay by two engineers with mine detectors . . . a dead engineer still in a kneeling position with his shovel in his hands, trying to dig into some cover.

"We had a few wounded on the beach but training paid off as reactions became automatic in given situations. Assigned missions were scrubbed. The resistance was greater than anticipated because the German 352d Infantry Division had arrived just prior to the landings. Those guys were scattered but pockets of resistance were numerous."

Leo Deschamps, a 1st Engineer Combat Battalion replacement, via Algiers and then England, was assigned to a thirty-man assault team. Even though it was H plus 5 hours when his group arrived, the enemy resistance continued. "As the landing craft neared the beach, a shell hit the lowering mechanism and the gate fell down. The Navy [coxswain] told us this was it; he couldn't get any closer. We stepped off 300 yards offshore. As I entered the water, DeLuca stepped into a shell hole. I grabbed him by his Mae West and squeezed the belt to activate the air unit. He bounced back up and treaded water until his feet touched ground. Dave Perlie went to the left up a ravine; his body was found three days later. The others went right. The beach itself was a madhouse; bodies lay where they fell and shouts for medics were in the air. Some corpses were half in and half out of the water and as the waves rolled in the bodies would sway back and forth like dolls.

"There was a depression in the beach, a tank trap, and we had to go through the water a second time to get to the beach proper. A sergeant directed us and we assembled at the battalion command post. We were sitting eating our rations by 1:00 or 1:30 P.M. I am not ashamed to say I prayed all the way in and I prayed also till the next day whenever I had free time."

Some time after the fire on Omaha slackened, Bill Behlmer regained consciousness. "I heard voices. Sailors were on the beach. One of them rolled me over and said I was still alive. He took me out to the troopship, the *Samuel Chase,* which was now a hospital ship. It was around noon, I later learned. That probably saved my life. The war was over for me. The next morning I was in a hospital in England where they amputated my right leg above the knee due to gangrene. No one was at fault or could have done more for me." His driver Stypulkowski also recovered from his wounds.

30

Utah Beach

To the west of Omaha Beach lay the shelf of yellow sand roughly nine miles in length with the code name Utah Beach. At low tide it was 300–400 yards wide with a low concrete wall inland. Beyond the beach lay the heavily inundated areas into which the troopers from the 82d and 101st dropped. Ordinarily eleven causeways led toward the heart of France but the flooding left only three dry. Once inland, the 4th Infantry Division, with tank and artillery support, would advance over these causeways, secured by the paratroopers against any attempt by German reserves to push the infantrymen back into the sea.

Captain George Mabry, and a naval officer designated for the task, coordinated the loading of boat teams from his ship onto landing craft. "We ran into trouble when the men began climbing down the nets to the boats below. The Channel was extremely rough and cold. Soldiers climbing down this slippery, cold net, attempting to enter into the small LCVPs bouncing up and down in the pitch-black dark was quite a chore. On two occasions, just before men were to turn loose and jump into the LCVP, a foot would get hung up in the rope and hang the man upside down. The boat would come up and smack the soldier on the shoulder or the head, even while those already in the boat tried to push the man up. You'd see the landing craft high up on a wave, almost halfway to the rail of the ship and then suddenly so far down in a trough you could dimly see it."

The assistant division commander, Terry Allen's former deputy, Brig. Gen. Theodore Roosevelt Jr., had chosen to accompany Mabry's battalion. When the moment for his boat team was about to come, Mabry hastened to notify Roosevelt. "He thanked me," said Mabry, "and then hollered to his aide, 'Stevie, where is my life belt?' Stevie said, 'General, I don't know. I've already given you three.' General Roosevelt said, 'Damnit, I don't care how many you've given me, I don't have one now.'" Mabry and the aide searched and found one for the general. When Mabry asked whether Roosevelt had all his armament, he patted his shoulder holster and responded, "I've got my pistol, one clip of ammunition, and my walking cane. That's all I expect to need."

The assistant division commander expected to accompany part of E Company, scheduled for the first wave. Mabry recalled, "Even though Roosevelt's boat was to be rail loaded, it still required a jump of four or five feet down to the deck of the LCVP. When a soldier reached up from the boat and said, 'Here, General, let me help you.' Roosevelt took his walking stick and lightly tapped the young man on the arm. He said in a friendly growl, 'Get the hell out of my way. I can jump in there by myself. I can take it as well as any of you.' Although tension ran at fever pitch, the remarks brought smiles and a few chuckles."

Compared to Omaha Beach, Utah was less heavily defended. Two casemated positions overlooked the shoreline but only one actually held big guns. The Germans had not completed installation of barriers in the water and there were fewer mines. Underwater demolition teams blew up much of what posed a threat to landing craft. Furthermore, the naval bombardment, in contrast to what happened off Omaha, pounded the shoreline, punishing the existing German positions and also providing convenient shellholes in which foot soldiers could take refuge.

Although Bradley spoke of the assault on Utah going "according to plan," in fact, Utah, assigned to the 4th Infantry Division, did not follow the blueprints, and that deviation had much to do with the success enjoyed there. Nor was it a "walk-in." The commander of the 22d Regiment's 3d Battalion, Lt. Col. Arthur S. Teague, described the initial wave. "We came ashore on LCMs operated by Navy enlisted men. On our LCM [a sailor] remarked this was the third landing in which he had participated and that he didn't mind the initial landing as much as the one afterward because he would have to keep bringing in supplies. Just as we were coming in to shore, I saw a shell fired from up the beach and I knew some of us were going to be hit. I saw spurts of water coming up. I saw one small landing craft hit, and thinking the same might happen to us, I told the Navy man to ram the beach as hard as possible. He held it wide open for about 200 yards and we hit the beach and stepped off on dry soil. A couple of boats behind us—about seventy-five yards back in the water—were hit and then I saw a number of casualties. Many were killed and quite a few wounded.

"I started up by the seawall on the sand dunes and stopped for a moment. I heard someone call me. It was General Roosevelt. He told me we had landed way to the left of where we were supposed to have landed and he wanted us to get this part of the beach cleared as soon as possible. He wanted action from my men immediately after landing and asked me to get them down the beach as soon as I could. This was about 0930."

Roosevelt had quickly realized the helmsmen's errors delivered the initial wave some 2,000 yards south of the prescribed location. Instead of seeking to correct the mistake and shift his forces laterally, Roosevelt, observing the relative ease of the landing, deemed a hookup with the airborne troopers paramount. He ordered the troops to advance inland. Following Roosevelt's directive, a skirmish line organized by Teague rousted some German soldiers. When they surrendered they claimed ignorance of the minefields beyond the beach. Forced by Teague to accompany the Americans over the seawall, the prisoners quickly revealed safe pathways.

George Mabry, with his battalion commander, Col. Carlton McNeely, occupied a "free boat," one that could come in at any stage of the invasion. McNeely decided to arrive behind the third wave, when some idea of the progress of the assault could be determined. "As light began to improve," said Mabry, "the first casualty I saw was a Navy boat that apparently had hit a mine. One sailor was lying on the keel of the boat, holding onto a man who was obviously either critically wounded or dead. That boat had been stationed to mark the lanes for approaching the beach. Soon after, I saw a large transport hit a mine; the front just rose up into the air and bucked like a horse, rocking from side to side. You could see personnel jumping off the ship.

"About this time, the bombers began to bomb the beaches. Wave after wave came parallel to the beach dropping their bombs. Smoke and dust obliterated the area. We couldn't see the shore or any distinguishing features that we had memorized. As bombers went away, naval gunfire opened up. They began to pulverize the beaches and behind them. Rocket ships began to discharge toward the beach. As we got closer to the beach, a German ME 109 fighter came out of the clouds and seemed to me to be diving directly at our landing craft. Right behind that ME 109 came a British Spitfire that fired three bursts of its machine guns. That German ME 109 just disintegrated in the air and the propeller fell right in front of our landing craft.

"The coxswain, a Navy man piloting our craft, kept falling farther and farther behind. Colonel McNeely hollered for him to speed it up and then we slowed down. About this time we passed some of the floating tanks from the 70th Tank Battalion, which had worked closely with the 8th Infantry Regiment in England. They'd been discharged 800 or 900 yards from the beach. Unfortunately, they didn't work too well in the rough Channel. They'd have been fine on a millpond. They were kind of wallowing in the sea and every once in a while you'd see them start to sink. They had a rubber raft and you'd see the crew take it out and jump on it and get away. As we passed the company commander's tank, the crew bailed out, all except the company commander. I assumed he drowned. Later I found out his foot got caught, he went down with the tank, doubled himself up, freed his foot and then swam to the surface and was evacuated.

"When for the third time Colonel McNeely told this coxswain to speed it up and we slowed down again, McNeely pulled his pistol and pressed the barrel against the sailor's head. 'Look, you son of a bitch, I told you to speed up. I'm not going to tell you again. Move it, now!' The young fellow understood. He really moved out. We went through the third wave, traveling fast. I was trying to pick up landmarks; the bombing apparently knocked them down but we figured there was something wrong. The terrain, the beach, didn't look right. We were coming too far to the left, we could see the mouth of the Merderet River and we were supposed to be a thousand yards farther to the right.

"As we approached the beaches the pillboxes became more clear, the tetrahedrons stood out like bristles on a hog's back. We landed right behind the second wave, elements of E and F Companies [of the 2d Battalion, 8th Regiment]. Just as the bottom of the landing craft touched the ground, this coxswain dropped the ramp. He wasn't going any further. Men began to jump off the left and right corners of the ramp. Right ahead of me was this short fellow, 'Smoky' David. He jumped and just disappeared. Seeing this, I jumped in front of the ramp. When I hit the bottom and came up, water was up to my neck. I looked behind and suddenly Smoky David's bald head appeared behind the landing craft. Somehow he had gone under the boat, missed the prop. He got rid of his equipment and began swimming toward the beach. We moved through this water to the beach. We'd been trained that once you hit the beach, you run across that thing; never lie down on it and don't crowd up against the seawall. You've got to push on inland. That was drilled into us.

"Walking through that water, dragging along, we met with something we hadn't reckoned with—right adjacent to our left was Pointe du Hoc, next to the Merderet River. Germans had artillery batteries honeycombed in that Pointe. The Rangers [who were to neutralize the guns] had difficulty and German artillery and mortar fire was raking the beaches. Companies E, F, and G were issued black rockets to signal the navy gunfire to lift from the beach and shift it inland. I saw a black rocket from E Company go off. Later I saw one from F Company go off. As we were coming ashore, German artillery was just raking the beach. When I and the other fellows heard a shell coming, we'd duck down in water and let it splatter over us. Then try to run again. But when we got to waist-deep or less, you couldn't duck down far and the water was so cold that our muscles had become cramped. You'd run six or seven paces and there was no way you could go farther. You'd hit the beach, lie there a second or two, then get up and run again.

"Just before I got out of the water, Corporal Speck, one of my baseball players when I coached the team at Fort Benning, was lying there. He had been hit in both legs. I reached down to help him but he stopped me. He said, 'Captain, your place is inland. Leave me alone and get moving.' It was a tough thing to do, to leave him there. But he kept insisting my place was inland. I moved forward. Ahead of me was a man carrying like a cloverleaf of 81mm mortar ammunition. This he was to drop at the seawall so that H Company with the mortars would then run down the seawall and gather up the ammunition for their use. As we were struggling to cross the beach, I was standing up trying to run and this man was doing the same. A mortar round came in and hit this soldier right on top of his head. That caused the 81mm mortar rounds to detonate also and this man's body completely disappeared. I felt something hit me on my thigh and it was this man's thumb. It was the only discernible part of a human being you could see. To my left I saw a human stomach lying on the beach. No one dead or alive was near it. It was a stark, grotesque sight." According to Mabry, those on the beach believed the shells falling in their midst belonged to the offshore fleet, but the most damaging artillery came from the defenders.

Mabry knew for certain they had come ashore some 800 to 1,000 yards to the left of their original proposed site because of the location of the Merderet, the absence of the expected number of tetrahedrons, and the abundance of barbed wire in the water. The navigational error happened due to miscalculation of the effects of the weather and speed of the tide. Mabry remembered briefly spotting Roosevelt, waving his cane, urging troops to keep moving.

Although separated from other troops, Mabry now sought to implement the plan devised with McNeely. The strategy called for troops to proceed directly inland over sand dunes, perhaps half a mile, to an inundated area. There, three causeways crossed the flooded low ground. Seizure of these was vital because if the enemy could destroy them and then counterattack while the Americans were trapped between beach and inundated area they would be in serious trouble. He and McNeely divided up supervision of their attacking companies.

"Having finally gotten to the seawall," said Mabry, "I followed a squad of about six men from G Company being led by a red-haired sergeant. As they went over the seawall, they began moving toward a fence. The sergeant started through the barbed wire. A tremendous explosion occurred. Obviously he had stepped on a mine. All six men fell to the ground, some killed, some wounded, some screaming. I ran beyond them because my mission was to follow G Company and ensure that Causeway I was secured. Naval gunfire was now falling inland and German artillery was coming in the area where we were located.

"I was by myself and didn't see anyone else. I began to run over a sand dune and started to receive small-arms fire from some Germans dug in on the sand-dune line. Periodically I would hit the ground and try to survey the situation and pick up the smoke from the German rifles to locate the enemy. After about two short rushes from one sand dune to another, I looked around my feet and noted I was in a minefield. The wind had blown away the sand and uncovered some of them. Having seen the squad killed and wounded by the mine, I thought, if I turn around and try to go back to the beach I'll probably step on a mine. My mission is inland so I'm going to take my chances and continue to move toward the enemy firing at me. I got up, made another dash, landed successfully and safely. The next time I jumped up and ran, the small-arms fire was cracking around me pretty close. I made a long leap to a shell hole I had spied and while in midair, my right foot apparently caught the trip wire attached to a mine. The mine exploded, and the force of it slammed me against the shell hole I was headed for. It numbed my right leg and I thought I had lost a foot. Looking around carefully, I found I had not been touched. My leg was intact. I regained my composure and decided to continue the advance.

"By this time the German rifle fire had subsided a little bit. I assume they thought I had been killed by the mine explosion. I jumped up and ran directly toward the position the Germans were firing from. Apparently I startled them. When I reached the top of the dune line I saw several individual foxholes. The first one was empty but hand grenades and rifle ammunition was all around the edge. I jumped into it and quickly realized this was a rather precarious position because they must have seen me jump into this foxhole. I scrambled out and saw, about eight yards from me, a German in a foxhole who had a hand grenade, a potato masher, in a position to toss it into the foxhole I had been in. I turned on the German and shot him. Germans started getting up on all sides of me; the total count was nine. They raised their hands quickly. I corralled them in a group, I noticed two non-comissioned officers and the others were of lesser rank. I looked over my shoulder toward the Channel. The sight bewildered me. It appeared the entire Channel was choked with ships of all sizes and descriptions. I thought these Germans had a lot of guts to be shooting small-arms fire at even one individual, when they had spread out before them a panorama of the largest invasion force that a human being had ever seen.

"I really did not know what to do with these prisoners. I saw a soldier about a hundred yards away with a bloody cloth wrapped around one hand. He turned out to be Corporal West of G Company I asked where the company was and he told me they were halted by a minefield behind me. I had assumed they were in front of me. I instructed West to escort the prisoners back to the beach and warned him to make a semicircle to avoid the minefield I had negotiated."

Mabry now searched for G Company. After about 300 yards, he met a pair of enlisted GIs, including a BAR man named Ballard, whom he knew to be an excellent marksman. They came upon a huge German pillbox. "Machine-gun fire opened up on us and we dove into a deep ditch nearby. We crawled down the ditch to within one hundred and fifty yards of the bunker. I told Ballard to spray the slits of the bunker with his BAR to determine whether these Germans inside really meant business. He gave a few well-placed bursts and ducked down in the ditch. Two embrasures of the pillbox began delivering machine-gun fire over our heads. This was a formidable emplacement and they meant business. I asked the other soldier if he knew the route back to the beach and could bring back one of the DD tanks and other soldiers."

The first U.S. DD tanks had finally crawled ashore. According to Mabry, about half an hour later, his emissary led in two DD tanks and they began to blast the pillbox. After shells pierced an opening, a white flag poked out of an embrasure. Mabry and Ballard counted thirty-six Germans. The tanks continued to knock off enemy fortifications. Barriers to prevent an exit from Utah fell under the onslaught of the tankers. A flamethrower drove twenty-five defenders from their pillbox, as well as two American paratroopers being held prisoners. Unlike Omaha the Germans were unable to pin down elements of the 4th Division in a beach killing zone.

Harper Coleman, a member of heavy weapons H Company in the 8th Infantry Regiment, stepped from the transport directly into an LCVP. "Being with the first waves had some advantage. We were not required to go over the sides of the ship. In the water, the small craft began to form groups. We circled under one of the battleships. It was firing the big guns. You could actually see the projectiles going through the air.

"As we moved toward the shore in lines, we passed rocket-launcher ships and they were releasing salvos on the beach, still some distance ahead. It was almost hidden from view by smoke and shell bursts. I saw the craft ahead of ours going up with some sort of direct hit, which left us first. Before we reached the shore, something came through the side of our craft and tore a hole, in one side and out the other. It also ripped a good size piece from my backpack. I saw a Navy ship lying on its side with many people on the side. We did not stop to render assistance.

"The history books say we landed some distance to the left from where we were supposed to be and this made it one of the easier landings. It did not seem good at the time. We went into the water more than waist-deep. If you're being fired on by small arms and artillery, light or heavy, it does not seem to make much difference at the time. Our first casualty was just behind me with a serious wound to the stomach. A second man was in front of me when he stepped on a land mine. After this we found out that the mines were all marked with a wooden stick. It seems they did not have time to remove the markers or else didn't expect a landing could take place. Those wooden sticks saved many from getting into the mines.

"When we came ashore, we had a greeter. Brig. Gen. Theodore Roosevelt was standing there waving his cane and giving out instructions, as only he could. If we were afraid of the enemy, we were more afraid of him and could not have stopped on the beach had we wanted. Our squad of six was down to four very early, one person on the beach and one when we came to a higher ridge, just beyond the sandy area. We made a left turn as we came over the top of the beach on what seemed to be a path. Moving as fast as we could, we came to a road that led to the beach and this took us through the swamps, which had been flooded by the Germans. We came up on the small town of Pouppeville. This is where we began to see the results of our work, our first dead enemies. Shortly beyond the town, we began to meet some of the airdrop people."

While Coleman, as a member of the same battalion as George Mabry, advanced inland, Mabry, having dispatched BAR man Ballard to escort the prisoners to the beach, grabbed another GI to accompany him toward Causeway I. They reached a point where Mabry noticed a hedgerow that he believed put them close to the objective. However, a field surrounded by a barbed-wire fence, which frequently indicated a minefield, lay dead ahead. "I recalled a piece of intelligence given while in England that stated that if a length of straight wire extended skyward from the corner posts, the minefield was a dummy. On the other hand, if the wire curled like a corkscrew, it was a live field. I saw a straight line extend from the corner post closest to us. I explained to the soldier about the wire and said I would test the veracity of our intelligence. If I hit a mine, the soldier was to head back and contact G Company.

"I crawled through the wire fence and into the field. Talk about walking on eggshells, I was really tiptoeing. I detected no bumps in the grounds and saw no disturbances of the earth, either fresh or old; the minefield was indeed a fake. I motioned for the soldier to follow. We quickly reached the hedgerow and keeping low began to creep down it. I peered over the top and there, only 150 yards away, I saw our Causeway I. At this time we began to hear rifle fire coming from across the flooded area opposite the causeway bridge.

"When we reached a point only forty-five yards from the causeway, we were forced to stop. To get closer we would have to go over the hedgerow to a parallel ditch on the other side. Although there were only two of us, the causeway had to be held at all costs. I decided to make a dash for it and told the soldier to cover me. If I did not get pinned down, I would wave him across. I made it to the ditch, which was filled with nearly two feet of water. I had received no fire, so the soldier promptly followed me. I noticed then that the rifle fire had begun to pick up on the far side of the bridge. We had moved up to a position just thirty yards from the causeway when two German soldiers began running down the road from the direction of village of Pouppeville. I told my companion not to shoot until they got very close to the bridge. When they reached within ten yards of the far side of the bridge, we opened up. Both men fell. Immediately, a squad of seven or eight Germans appeared and moved off the road to their right. They approached the bridge in skirmish formation. They were clearly trying to outflank us and we began shooting at them.

"The gunfire on the far side of the bridge intensified. I felt some of the shots were directed at the same Germans we had engaged. Some of the firing, however, seemed to be aimed at us and had the sound of an M1 rifle instead of a German one. I believed American paratroopers must be closing in from the other side of the bridge. I pulled out my square of orange cloth that identified us as allies and hoisted it on a stick over my head. A few more rifle bullets cracked around but then an orange flag waved back and forth from beyond the bridge. It had to be the paratroopers. All the rifle fire concentrated on that squad attempting to outflank us.

"Several minutes passed and the German rifle fire tapered off and then ended. I decided to run across the bridge to contact the airborne forces. If I didn't get any trouble, I'd wave my companion forward. The soldier covered me as I dashed across. As I ran, I spotted a huge aerial bomb wired for detonation lashed onto the bridge. The Germans we had shot had probably been on their way to blow the bridge. When I reached the far side I saw the two Germans sprawled on the road. They were dead. Several yards away I noticed other German soldiers all around. Some were lying on the side of the road, some in the bushes, and others in a slight ditch a few yards away. One of them appeared to be shaking so I gave him a hard kick in the thigh with my boot. He quickly jumped up and surrendered. Suddenly all the Germans around me began standing up. I gathered them into a group. I had a total of eight prisoners.

"Before I could even consider what to do with them I heard a noise in front of me. An airborne soldier jumped over a hedgerow with his rifle at the ready. I hollered to him, 'Don't shoot, I got some prisoners.' I marched them up to him and he was a member of the 101st Airborne Division. We shook hands and he told me that Maj. Gen. Maxwell Taylor, commanding general of the 101st, was just across the hedgerow and would surely be glad to see me. Seconds later, General Taylor, preceded by two men, crawled over the hedgerow. I saluted and we shook hands. I glanced down at my watch. It was 11:05 A.M. As far as I know, this was the first official contact between airborne troops and seaborne troops. Minutes later, Brig. Gen. James Gavin, the assistant division commander of the 82d Airborne Division came over the hedgerow along with Lt. Col. Julian Ewell, a battalion CO, and ten airborne soldiers."

Bob Meyer, the BAR man with G Company, 2d Battalion of the 22d Infantry Regiment, stepped from his boat onto the sand of Utah Beach. "Wet feet were the least of our worries. The beach was being shelled by artillery and it was a very serious reminder that someone would like to kiss us to prevent the success of the invasion. As we were moving forward, a shell exploded near us and Kinser hit the ground. But if the shell has exploded and you're still going, there is little point of hitting the ground, although it is one's first instinct. I grabbed his shoulder strap and helped him to his feet so we could continue running.

"In one of our early engagements we ran out of ammunition for our BAR. Fortunately, a machine-gun crew gave us some to keep going. The BAR has a crew of three. One is the gunner who carries it, ten magazines with twenty rounds each and some bandoliers of ammunition. The assistant gunner, who has an M1 rifle and bullets for it, plus bandoliers for the BAR, takes over the weapon if the gunner is hit. The third man is the designated ammunition carrier, and he also has an M1 with its ammo, plus bandoliers for the BAR. We started out with something like 200 rounds each in addition to what I had in my ten magazines. But after we ran out of ammunition once, we increased our load to all we could carry. I would take about 600 rounds, plus the magazines to add up to 800 rounds. That meant about forty pounds to carry, plus the BAR, which was around twenty-one pounds. Then there were things like hand grenades, an entrenching tool, canteens and other stuff. I was so heavy that when I stepped down from a little curbing or the like, I often just fell in a heap and had to pick myself up.

"Shortly after we landed," Meyer continued, "we came upon the weapon the GIs named the Screaming Meemie [*Nebelwerfer*], because of the soul-wrenching sound it made when launched. It was a kind of rocket that could be fired right out of the crate and originally they fired them from six barrels. We saw individual ones, about the size of a five-gallon can. When fired from their six-barrel mortar, everything in the circular strike zone could be killed by the concussion alone. If you happened to be where one landed, there would be nothing left to indicate you'd ever been there. We had a scout hit and all we found of him were his shoes.

"We had a person in our company named S——, who was more animal-like than anyone I had ever seen before. When he stood, his arms and hands stretched down past his knees. I never heard him speak. If he had to respond, a sort of grunt was all you would get. It took several trips for him to qualify with an M1, and I wondered if he really did qualify or whether they tired of taking him out to the range. He would sit in the mess hall and with those long arms just reach for what he wanted. Once he reached across Sergeant Garner's plate and Garner stabbed him in the back of his hand with a fork. He didn't even say 'Ouch.' Just became a little more careful where he put his hand.

"There'd been several tries to get him out of the army on a Section-8 [the regulation that allowed discharge for mental problems], but our captain was convinced he was faking. During our early confrontation with the Germans, S—— was still with us. Bullets were flying everywhere and we were all keeping as low as possible. Suddenly, he stood up and said the only thing I ever heard from him. It was something like, 'To hell with this,' and walked to the rear. We watched him disappear over the little hill behind us as he walked back to the beach. Bullets were everywhere but S—— didn't get hit. God must have been watching over him. We were sure that back on the beach he was seen for what he was, a Section-8, and sent home.

"I think it was at the end of this firefight, when we routed the Germans, that a German SS officer hid in ambush and opened fire with a machine gun, practically cutting in half our captain, Robert Russell, a VMI graduate. Then he dropped his weapon and threw up his hands. This might have gotten him captured, except that, as he put up his hands, he was laughing. It was his last laugh. Our executive officer, Joe Jackson, who weighed 240 pounds with no fat, stuck him with a bayonet and pitched him like a bundle of grain. We weren't too fond of our captain but he was one of us. We were certainly motivated by his death, which we thought cruel and unnecessary. We went through the rest of that German group like a hot knife through butter."

Marion Adair, the surgeon of the 8th Infantry Regiment's 2d Battalion, clambered into an LCVP at 2:30 A.M. In his diary he wrote: "We churn around about 22,000 yards offshore and for a while I think we are lost. Eventually our wave forms and we start toward the beach about dawn. It is terribly rough. We are all drenched, and all but another and myself get terribly seasick.

"We pass Îles St. Marcourf [an offshore spit of land seized just before the invaders struck the mainland], past battleships and cruisers firing, past rocket LSTs that loose a defeaning barrage. There is so much smoke and dust that we can hardly see. Finally, soaked to the skin, we brace and our boat touches land. We jump off into three feet of muddy water and wade to the beach, which is extremely wide at this time (the tide is just past ebb and coming in).

"We hear shells whining in and think at first it's our own Navy. But it isn't. The time is 7:00 A.M., thirty minutes after H hour. I see my first casualty, gunshot wound of the mouth. We keep working to the seawall, diving into shell holes every time a shell whines. I get very muddy and my pack weighs a ton. We see the engineers blowing up the beach obstacles and logs are sailing through the air. Finally, I make contact with Vic [battalion surgeon Sam Victor] and Chaplain Ellenberg, and we set up a temporary aid station on the beach. Our next patient that comes was blown up by a mine and dies. After about two hours, the engineers have blown a path through the seawall and cleared a path through the minefield.

"We clear off the beach and work inland. We set up an aid station just off a little road, eat our rations, and begin to treat some casualties, including a

Jerry. We move south and I'm glad because the Jerries are shelling the beach quite vigorously. I see my first dead German and we have a few casualties, including Stark, who lost his foot due to stepping on a mine. We cross the flooded area into Pouppeville where we run into some wounded from the 101st Airborne and some Jerry wounded. After this we keep walking to Ste. Marie-du-Mont, pass through that town, and follow the highway toward the Carentan-Cherbourg Highway."

The progress made by Adair indicates the success of the Utah landings. Malcolm Williams, a North Carolinian who had tea with King George V, as a member of the 12th Infantry Regiment, was with the later arrivals at Utah. In contrast to Coleman Harper, Williams and his fellow GIs experienced considerable risk just transferring from their LC to the assault boat. "We had to go down a rope ladder with both boats rocking like hell. Everyone was seasick and scared shitless, but we knew what our job was and we were ready to do it. The craft hit bottom and that moment the ramp went down."

Roosevelt was still acting as a kind of host to the newcomers. "He said to us, 'How do you boys like the beach?' After we got off the beach, the trouble started. The heavy equipment on the only open causeway was drawing enemy fire. So we decided to cross the flooded area. We'd been told it was about three to five feet deep and if we stepped in over our heads to swim for about six feet and we would be back where we could walk. We did that until we reached the other side. We could hear machine-gun fire in the distance but it was on the causeway.

"Our first wounded was a major but it wasn't serious. Sergeant Noe, who I always paired off with when digging a hole, had a bullet hit the stock of his rifle, clipping off a piece of wood that struck him in the face. Boy, that got the attention of all of us. The worst thing I saw on D day were some men from the 82d or 101st, tied by their feet, hung up a tree and then cut all the way down their bodies with a knife. I also saw where wounded had been tied to a bed and then the house burned down around them."

Sam Frackman, who manufactured jewelry before being swept up in the draft, said of his voyage to the Normandy shore, "We were crouched low and did not see anything except some planes and we heard the sounds of the big guns from our ships. We were let off in deep water with heavy loads of mortar and machine-gun ammunition we were supposed to deposit on the beach. We had life preservers, but why, I don't know. If you fell over, the preserver didn't help. There were many bodies floating by and a lot of shots being fired.

"On the beach, lines had been marked for the mines. One of my best friends was killed when he ignored the markers. When I had gone about 100 yards inland, I heard crying coming from a crater. I went over to investigate and one of the men from my company lay there with blood spurting from his hip or thigh area. I had no first aid experience and we had orders to move up. I couldn't get a tourniquet around his leg so I called for a medic and went looking for my platoon. Later, I found out he had died and was the first casualty from B Company [22d Regiment].

"Most men just did their job. Some prayed for a 'million dollar wound' and others were too scared to move. As far as our training was concerned, you can shove it. It amounted to a zero. We had on-the-job training and we learned quickly. We learned when to hit the dirt, when to run, where to cross, when to lie still. Crossing a road with the first sergeant leading the way, he was hit slightly by a machine gun. We then waited and ran. On my turn, I ran and then came the machine-gun fire. When I got across, not hit, I looked for a cigarette but they had been shot out of my pocket. My gas mask case had also been hit."

Nathan Fellman, who transferred to B Company of the 12th Regiment in the 4th Division after a sergeant in another unit directed his anti-Semitism at him, was an ammunition sergeant responsible for three jeeps with trailers. For his ride to Utah, Fellman separated from his usual companions and rode in the boat bearing C Company. "There were LCIs to the right and left and we got off in water that was up to my waist. I am six feet tall and while wading quite a distance to the beach, two of us taller men put our rifles across to pull in a very short GI until we got to shallower water. We did not suffer any casualties on the landing. I quickly separated from C Company and began studying my map. I wanted to get to my own unit. I looked up and saw some sand fly in the air. A lieutenant started to give me hell for not taking cover from those 88s. I informed him that I didn't know the sound of 88s. But I decided to get off that sand beach.

"I found myself joining up with some 101st Airborne men. That brought my first combat experience. A sniper fired on us. The paratroopers quickly took cover but before I realized what was happening, three or four more shots came at me. The paratroop sergeant asked me where I thought they were coming from. I pointed out a tree. We all turned our weapons on that tree and fired many rounds. Then the sergeant sent one of his troopers up the tree. He cut down two German soldiers. They were very much dead.

"Shortly thereafter, the sergeant was taking us up a trail when he gave the signal to disperse and take cover. We did while he and his second in command pointed to a barn. The pair of them quickly ran to the barn and threw a hand grenade inside. Before it could explode, five German soldiers rushed out with their hands up and yelling *Kamerad*. The young sergeant lined up the prisoners while we covered them. He asked his assistant what he thought they should do with the Germans. Without hesitation, the paratrooper answered, 'Kill them!' A GI with a small machine gun mowed them down in Chicago-gangster style. We promptly resumed our march.

"On our first rest, I sat down next to the sergeant and asked him how he knew there were any Germans in that barn. He grinned at me and said he could smell them. [Many veterans claim they could detect the odor of the enemy from their diet or the aromas of their uniforms when damp.] I voiced an opinion about shooting prisoners, that if they knew they would get shot, none would ever surrender. He said his landing instructions were to kill all enemy and he merely followed his orders. There were no provisions for taking captives. And none of his commanders had changed these instructions. I shook my head but he told me not to worry. In his mind he did the right thing. But even though I had no love for the Germans I would rather not have had this experience. I never talked about this incident either with my officers or the men in my company."

While the 4th Division was the only infantry organization of its size to cross Utah on this first day, the 359th Regiment of the 90th Division, temporarily attached to the 4th, also was committed on 6 June. As platoon leader for the 359th Regiment, Company A in the 1st Battalion, J. Q. Lynd, a native of Oklahoma, remembered the wet chilly morning when he and his forty companions climbed into their LCVP. "Our grouping contained three craft; we were the middle boat. Almost immediately as our group started the run toward the beach, the LCVP to our right 'blew.' A brilliant flash, thunderous crack of explosion, we ducked, our craft lurched, seemed to lift in a quick bucking motion, then dropped, slapping the ocean surface with a terrific impact. We couldn't fall to the deck, we were wedged together like sardines in a can. We looked to the right—nothing! No LCVP, no debris, no smoke, no nothing! Looked to the left, white shocked faces were looking at us in disbelief! Everybody immediately looked to the front—Utah Beach was approaching. We tensed for debarkation as rapidly as possible, as soon as the ramp dropped.

"Utah Beach was a confused array of metal hedgehog obstacles, crumpled barbed wire, columns of thick black smoke, the pungent odor of burning rubber, bodies of dead and wounded soldiers, scattered equipment and supplies in the sand and signs marked 'ACHTUNG! MINEN.' When we reached the water's edge, we quickly ran zigzag through the smoking debris toward the high sand dunes, dodging a burning jeep, an abandoned tank, and the jagged shell holes in the sand. German artillery was shelling the beach area and some of our soldiers were hit. Our orders were to keep moving, attack, *do not stop*, move to the high ground as rapidly as possible. The units that followed would care for the wounded. Our soldiers obeyed as they had been trained."

The Utah Beach venture was the most successful one achieved by the Americans. Roosevelt had transformed the lemon of a navigation error into something approximating a refreshment for the hard-pressed U.S. strategists. General Handy credited the GIs. "The performance of the 4th Division was remarkable. It was a new division that had never been blooded. We all thought Utah was going to be more of a problem than Omaha—the damned terrain swampy with causeways; one gun at each could stop tanks from coming through."

For the Air Force, D day was almost a milk run, with the major threats coming from midair collisions in the crowded skies and overanxious gunners aboard the armada in the Channel. John Hibbard, a waist gunner and assistant radio operator on a B-17 in the 385th Bomb Group, remembered returning from a mission along the French coast on 5 June, with an alert for the next day. "There was something unusual about the alert. All of us felt it. At briefing time the next morning, 6 June 1944, we found out! Colonel Vandevanter [the 385th CO] addressed us. Everyone was tense with excitement, trying to catch every word. 'Gentlemen, you are about to embark upon a very important mission, the success of which will greatly affect the outcome of this war. Today is the day we've all been waiting for—D day.'

"A cheer went up. This was it! Everyone was bursting with excitement and pride because we were all to be there to help assault the enemy beaches. We made two successful operations that day. One was to bomb gun installations at Caen and one to bomb road junctions and railroad bridges. It was a great day. The *Luftwaffe* didn't dare show itself. We were all out, both the Eighth and Ninth Air Forces as well as the British RAF."

Allied fighter pilots scoured the skies for predators almost entirely in vain. Punchy Powell, in a P-51 that day said, "The 352d Fighter Group flew several missions on D day, but these were probably some of the easiest we flew. Our job, like most of the fighter groups, was to provide a wall of aircraft from the deck to 30,000 feet in a semicircle about fifty miles south of the beaches to make sure no enemy aircraft reached the shoreline. In this we were successful."

According to Jim Goodson, who interviewed one of two German pilots who managed to break through the cordon, the enemy explained, "We were right down among the weeds and when I got back the tips of my propeller were bent where they struck the ground. Only my wingman and I got through. We got over the beachhead and saw several thousand troops on the beach, several thousand ships at sea, and looked up above at several thousand aircraft. My wingman asked what do we shoot at. And I said, just spray and we'll go home." [George Mabry, however, insisted he saw an ME 109 destroyed by an RAF Spitfire.]

Martin Low, the P-40 pilot caught on the ground at Pearl Harbor in 1941, and whose car was shot up as he sped to the airfield, had the unique experience of having been on the scene for that disastrous start of the war and involved in the biggest single event of the war, D day. Having completed his tour in the South Pacifc, he received a month's leave in the States and then trained P-38 pilots. Low had come to England and the Eighth Air Force. "On June 5, I had a date in town and I took a jeep to drive from the base. The sergeant at the gate had a machine gun and he said, 'Sorry, sir'—I was now a lieutenant colonel—'the base is closed.' I started to argue and he unlimbered the gun. So I went back and saw men from the ground crew painting black-and-white stripes on the planes. [To help the Navy recognize friendly aircraft.] We always expected the Navy to shoot at us and they always did.

"At the briefing we were told it would be an early morning mission. Because the P-38 was easier to identify, we were to be at the bottom of the stack. We had never before taken off in the dark but we had no problem. From the air it looked as if you could walk from Southampton to Omaha Beach. We could not see anything on the beaches, other than explosions and flashes of guns. It was enormously exciting to see the power, the size of what we'd all been waiting for. From June 6 until about ten days later, we flew three missions a day, bombed and strafed anything that moved within fifty to a hundred miles of the coast, mostly trains. We did not do much close, tactical support for the troops. The Ninth Air Force handled most of that."

Bill Dunn, who had started the war as a foot soldier with Canadian troops, gone to the RAF, and finally the Ninth Air Force's 406th Fighter Group, flew a P-47 on D day. "It was black and rainy over England, bloody awful. About 4:00 A.M. we got up, got ready to take off, and thought sure as hell they wouldn't send us off in that rain. But sure as hell they did. Off we went into the black, climbed up through 20,000 feet of soup, three squadrons of twenty-five airplanes each, all hoping we wouldn't run into one another. We all made it, broke out halfway across the pond where it was clear as a bell. Over France the sky was absolutely full of airplanes, all ours. I did about four missions on D day, and three the following day, strafing or striking with bombs, napalm, rockets, areas that requested it."

Martin Garren, a copilot for the 94th Bomb Group and among the youngest aviators to sit in the cockpit of a B-17, recalled their target lay in the Utah Beach area. The schedule mandated bombs-away about fifteen minutes before the first waves were to strike the shore. "That meant taking off around three A.M. and assembling in the dark, which was very hazardous. There was a lot of apprehension because we had never practiced that kind of thing, although we all had experience flying at night. We got off all right and began to form up. The tail gunner had an Aldis lamp, a very bright lamp that he kept flashing to indicate this is the tail of a B-17 here and don't bump into it. We also flew with wing lights, which would have been of great help to German fighters or antiaircraft.

"Soon after we took off, the sun was in the sky, although none on the ground. We could see each other and we turned off our lights. Things were normal. We assembled into our thirty-six-ship formation, then the combat box of our wing, and headed for Utah Beach to bomb the concrete fortifications the Germans had built. I kept looking out and all I could see was our wing, close to 108 planes, and I thought, now they've really screwed up. Then, a minute before we were to bomb, I looked to the right and to the left and out of the high-altitude haze I suddenly saw what looked like the entire Eighth Air Force, maybe 1,500 planes, almost in a line abreast like the kickoff of a football game. We went on and dropped our bombs. We had expected the *Luftwaffe* to put up everything they had because once we got our men ashore—we had two million in England waiting to invade—it would be all over. We did not see a single enemy plane or burst of flak.

"To make sure that nobody mistook who we were when we returned to England, we had a specific course to fly over France and then make a big, wide U-turn. We came over Ste.-Mère-Eglise, where a few hours earlier our paratroopers had dropped. As we were passing over Ste.-Mère-Eglise, I was thinking of what might be happening to the paratroopers—anyone who came swinging down in a parachute was likely to be shot at. Suddenly, we developed a fire in our control panel. Si, our navigator, and Tim, our bombardier, started tearing away insulation. Barehanded, they pulled some wires loose and stopped the fire. We all thought, 'My God, what a place to have to bail out.' We returned to base without further incident. Actually, we were scheduled for a tactical mission later on D day. But they had time lines and you couldn't attack a certain area after a specific hour because our guys might now be there. So after we took off we were called back and landed with our bombs."

According to historian Roger Freeman, "an estimated 11,000 aircraft were in the air over southern England." Only a single U.S. bomber went down because of enemy fire. Two others collided and another crashed on takeoff. Fighter losses amounted to twenty-five planes. Most important, the enemy was unable to move reinforcements and armor to bolster Normandy defenses.

31
Hanging On

Behind the shoreline, the parachutists and glider troopers played a critical role in securing the Normandy turf for the American forces. Of those who entered enemy territory during the dark, early hours of the morning, one of the first GIs to encounter the 4th Division soldiers was paratrooper Lou Merlano, whose C-47 so vigorously changed course to evade flak that Merlano and some of his stick dropped into the Channel.

In his nocturnal wanderings, Merlano had blundered into a German compound. He hid himself until he could chew up the pages for his radio code book and, now, in the last hour of darkness, gathered his wits sufficiently to creep through the shrubbery until he was beyond the immediate vicinity of the enemy. "Around the crack of dawn, I ran into Eddie Stiles and Danny Steinbach. The three of us cautiously searched for others. We finally teamed up with Bob Barnes and Sgt. George Barner with a bunch of people. We now had a complement of a dozen or so troopers. We were still considering our next objectives, such as a crossroads, when we encountered a flight of bombers intent on softening up the beaches for the landing forces. We were caught right smack in the middle. A number of us jumped in a creek for no purpose except we were scared to death.

"After the bombers left, we headed out to the road near us. It was just behind the beach and we could see quite a bit of ocean. Something was going on south of us and we started to destroy whatever lines of communication were still standing. We used hand grenades to blow telephone poles and any wiring around. We split the group in an effort to find the rest of our company and to secure crossroads to the causeway. Stiles, Steinbach, and I took one of them. We brought out carts and anything else we could find that would serve as an obstacle, then took positions in a farmhouse right at one corner.

"In no time at all, the Jerries found us. From inland we received heavy fire, mortars and machine guns. In hopes of confusing the Germans, not letting them know how many people were at this crossroads, two of us went upstairs, while one stayed down below. We would run from window to window, firing our M1s. More and more shells hit the house, practically obliterating it. We took positions in the courtyard, using the craters made by the bombers. Every so often, one of us would sneak out to the causeway just to keep them off guard.

"We felt an ambush was coming and decided I should cross the road, go through the hedgerow to the Channel side, while they held the ends of the yard. There was an eerie quiet and we felt something was abrew. Danny Steinbach first noticed someone coming up the road from the south. Crouched down, we couldn't determine whether friend or foe. Much to our surprise, he was from the 4th Division, proceeding in a crouched position with his rifle at port arms, just as a first scout should. When I surprised him, I screamed and hollered, 'What took you so long.' I said we had expected them at six in the morning and here it was eleven or twelve.

"We were jubilant and I said I wanted to speak with his CO to let him know what was up ahead. I explained to a major that because he had a battalion he should be able to move on and take over completely. The officer asked us to act as point men for him but we felt we should get back to our own outfit. The three of us decided to ride some vehicles that had just come in and I jumped on a tank. I thought we were all together but I soon found myself alone with the tankers while looking for A Company. The first gathering of paratroopers I came across was F Company of the 501. I jumped off the tank and joined them. It didn't take long to get into firefights and sniper chases around the hedgerows. During this period, I saw many of our troopers who had been caught in the trees, butchered. At no time in the marshaling area, where all aspects of combat were covered, was it ever said we should take no prisoners. However, on the scene with so many troopers so brutally killed, without question we had no intention to take prisoners. That happened in numerous skirmishes over the next two days in the hedgerows."

Bernard McKearney, as a platoon leader for E Company in the same 502d Parachute Regiment was similarly struck by the savagery visited upon invaders. After the drop, he gathered some sixty men and staked out a small village with a stone wall as his group's redoubt. Dawn displayed an enemy artillery position.For several hours, the two forces exchanged small-arms fire. "About ten that morning, a considerable force of paratroopers passed through us and the Jerries retired. We were assigned the mission of destroying the fieldpieces. I took a demolition squad to carry out the detail. What a scene of carnage! This was my first intimate association with violent death. A man at one hundred yards seemed so impersonal. About ten paratroopers had landed amid the gun emplacements. We had expected sudden death or capture. But not this! Mutilation! Horrible, terrible, vicious mutilation of dead soldiers. Most of the men were slashed about the face and body. One man was wrapped in a chute, a thermite grenade applied to his unholy shroud.

"The men said nothing. Words are so useless at a time like this. We removed the bodies from the trees and covered them with their chutes. Your mind functions oddly under stress. I tried to think of a suitable prayer. All I could think of was my Mass prayers in Latin. So, very slowly, I said, '*Requiescat in pace.*' A solemn Italian boy standing by responded, '*Deo gratias*' That broke the tension. We moved on to complete our mission and returned to the village.

"All during the day snipers harassed us. One was especially dangerous, wounding three men during the morning. We could pick out his approximate location by the sound of his rifle and the thud of the bullet as it hit. Finally, Sgt. Richard Willburn, a lanky Texan, decided to go after him. He spotted the Jerry up in a tree, wrapped in one of our camouflaged chutes. Willburn's first shot tumbled the sniper from his perch. But before Willburn could reach him, he disappeared. A little French boy, no more than seven years old, took Willburn by the arm and pulled him into a barn. Inside, the sniper cowered and trembled. This Nazi superman presented a very sorry picture."

For Wallace Swanson with A Company, 1st Battalion of the 502d Parachute Regiment under Lt. Col. Pat Cassidy, 6 June presented a hectic series of encounters. Following his landing, Swanson had engaged in small-arms fire exchanges, mostly from a distance, with enemy forces. In some instances the foe were Germans pulling back from the Utah Beach area. "I had started with about sixty-five men with me and was moving north toward Foucarville, a tiny village of maybe eight to ten houses surrounded by farms. I was collecting men and combat gear on the way but as we continued toward the objective some troopers withdrew to go to their own units. My number dropped to about twenty men. Foucarville was our main assignment after the coastal batteries. I suppose the French underground had given the Allied command a pretty good description of what was at and around Foucarville. It was heavily guarded."

Unknown to Swanson, Baker Company GIs of the 502d had already battled the Germans at Foucarville, withdrawing because of the enemy's vastly superior numbers and fortified positions on a knoll overlooking the village. Before backing off, Lt. Harold Hoggard, who took charge of the Americans there after his CO was felled, captured several prisoners. Upon interrogation they revealed the deployment of the Germans. "I could never countenance killing unarmed men," says Swanson, "and prisoners can be a valuable source of information as Hoggard found. He obtained information that enabled us to maneuver our platoons and company-size forces. Later, when a group of Germans surrendered to troopers from C Company, and someone said, 'Let's shoot these bastards now,' their CO, Capt. Fred Hancock, squelched them with, 'Don't you think we've had enough shooting for one day?' That shows how a good dedicated officer can put a stop to the consequences of bitter feelings."

"When I got to Foucarville, most of the Germans had retreated to their fortified spots in the nearby hills. But a wasp's nest of snipers occupied well-protected positions in the village church steeple. Any troopers who tried to cross open areas to get at the snipers were cut down by withering fire from the hillside venues—concrete pillboxes, dugouts, and machine-gun platforms erected up in the trees with deadly sight lines into Foucarville. Hoggard's actions, placing riflemen and setting up machine gun positions, provided us with strong security. What followed at Foucarville was Company A's first organized confrontation with the enemy. Until then, the Germans we encountered were scattered or in flight. Here we needed to be organized into effective fighting forces as squads or platoons. The Germans were always famous for counterattacks and our men had to be readily for that kind of action. Some of our people attached their bayonets, prepared for close contact.

"We had been told that jumping behind enemy lines we would be in situations where an individual or small force would find enemy on all sides of him, and up against rifle and machine-gun fire. We had trained to meet this kind of engagement. Furthermore, we had some very fine soldiers among us. Sergeant Cecil Thelan, our company communications noncom, who had a strong knowledge of explosives and demolition, was in charge of a roadblock to the north. In midafternoon, Germans tried to outflank Thelan's block but, with two machine guns and a dozen riflemen, Thelan's group drove them off. But the enemy now turned a small cannon, sited by dugouts on the slope, toward Thelan's group. On his own, Pvt. John Lyell moved to take offensive action. He crawled up the slope through the brush until he spotted the gun. Holding a grenade in his hand, Lyell yelled for the Germans to surrender and three of them emerged from the dugouts. Behind them came a fourth soldier and Lyell saw him starting to pitch a potato masher. Lyell tossed his grenade, which killed the Germans, but the one thrown at him badly wounded him in the shoulder. He went down.

"For a while we couldn't get to him. Finally, two troopers, Privates Richard Feeney and James Goodyear, covered by fire from Sgt. Thomas Wright, tried to drag Lyell away. Feeney eventually managed to pull the wounded man back while Goodyear and Wright pinned down the enemy. But it took too long to get effective cover fire and by the time we reached Lyell he had lost a lot of blood. He died of his wounds several hours later. He had stopped one spot of enemy fire on us but they were able to replace men and weapons and we couldn't silence that machine gun."

The snipers in the church tower winged a bunch of men at one roadblock. Swanson's people tried to suppress the threat with their own assortment of weapons, while the Germans holed up in the steeple sought to slip away by a side door. Unfortunately for them, a misdropped trooper from the 82d Airborne lay quietly opposite the exit. He dropped them all with several bursts from his Tommy gun.

A German artillery column, racing to reinforce Foucarville, headed for one of Swanson's roadblocks. A well-placed charge blasted the lead vehicle into a pile of flaming wreckage. Two machine guns sprayed the artillerymen in the trucks behind and a pair of bazookas destroyed the remainder of the convoy. But the German soldiers who survived attempted to shoot their way through the small group of paratroopers. They did not succeed.

Rather than remaining in a defensive stance, Swanson and his group began to pound the remnants of the enemy still hunkered down on the fortified hill looking down on Foucarville. "Private Charles, an American Indian," said Swanson, "was an outstanding 60mm mortar man and he hammered the works. I also had several machine guns working the area over. Just before ten o'clock at night, the enemy stopped firing. A white flag was raised. Eighty-seven Germans came out with their hands up, along with the French widow of a soldier killed that day."

Behind the surrender, the startled Swanson and his companions watched an eruption of gunfire in a surprise appearance by a batch of U.S. paratroopers shooting at Germans who elected to flee. Seventeen Americans, misdropped during the earlier hours had been seized and held by the enemy. Sergeant Charles Ran, an A Company operations noncom, participated in a series of conversations with the captors as the Germans steadily lost confidence in their capacity to resist. Ran informed them that his fellow invaders planned to unleash a huge artillery barrage on the hill at 10:30. As the alleged zero hour approached and the Americans continued to talk up the tale, the garrison became increasingly apprehensive until finally most decided to yield.

But not all of the enemy were prepared to give up. The GIs learned that a considerable number hoped to run off to fight another day. When the main group left their positions, dropping their weapons behind them, the paratrooper prisoners snatched them up and opened fire upon the fugitive Germans. Others also turned their sights on the retreating foe and about fifty Germans died while on the run. Foucarville, strategically important to the western end of Utah Beach, now belonged to the 101st Airborne and, soon, advancing infantrymen from the 4th Division.

Bazooka man, Sgt. Bill Dunfee, of the 82d Airborne, with his buddy Jim Beavers, retrieved their equipment bundle, loaded up, and headed for Ste.-Mère-Eglise. "Jim and I joined a group on the outskirts of the town. Our battalion CO, Lt. Col. 'Cannonball' Krause, ordered all bazooka teams forward. We went to the designated area and were told to stand by. There was a fair amount of rifle and machine-gun fire, but the firing I heard did not indicate major resistance. Ste.-Mère-Eglise did not appear to have a large force in town or else they hauled ass when we started dropping. I was in reserve and didn't observe or engage in the firefights. I believe our men pushed through the town, outposted it, then returned to mop up any enemy bypassed. Considering we dropped around 2:00 A.M. and by 4:30 secured the place, it was quick.

"I was shocked by the sight of the men hanging in the trees. It became apparent they had suffered more than jump injuries. They were cut down immediately. I'm sure each of us said a silent prayer, 'There but for the grace of God am I.' My hatred of the enemy ratcheted up several notches to the point of shoot first and discuss it later. I accepted the enemy as another man fighting for his country but never lost sight that we were there for one purpose, to kill each other.

"Prior to my first day in combat I had accepted the possibility of my early demise. A close friend of mine was killed on D day and that changed my feeling that I possibly would die to a sense that it was probable. My acceptance of my fate was because of what had happened to this friend. I had seen him become emotionally unstable. He had changed from an anything-for-a-laugh extrovert into a subdued and withdrawn shell. He seemed to have a premonition of his death. This was the same man who had exhibited great strength and courage in Sicily and Italy. I assumed that each of us has a breaking point and I prayed I could die like a man and be spared the horror of coming unglued. Personal vanity took over, making death acceptable but certainly not desired.

"I have no idea of any context in which 'Take no prisoners' was issued but it sounds like bullshit to me. We were instructed in the Geneva convention rules of our rights as a POW, and how we were to treat enemy POWs. No responsible officer or noncom would issue such an order. You would most certainly be court-martialed and spend the rest of the war in Leavenworth. General Maxwell Taylor, who was the 101st Airborne commander, in Normandy was formerly the 82d's artillery commander and then assistant division commander. I don't believe he would tolerate the suggestion of such an order. Most of our field-grade officers and all senior officers were West Pointers. They were career military men and to be a party to such a thing would have ended their careers. At Ste.-Mère-Eglise, we established a perimeter defense, dug in to await the counterattack that came all too swiftly. The enemy really socked it to us with 88s and Screaming Meemies. The 88s must have use timed fuses because we were getting air bursts. The *Nebelwerfers* were so erratic you couldn't tell where the rockets would land.

"We learned in a hurry to cut laterally into the side of your foxhole for a safe place to hide the family jewels. My bazooka became a casualty when shrapnel penetrated the tube, blowing away the firing mechanism. My musette bag was hit, and a Gammon grenade destroyed, but without setting off the Composition C it contained. I acquired a BAR; my .45 seemed inadequate.

"We also found that the safest place to relieve one's bladder was in the bottom of your foxhole. If Mother Nature required further relief you were in serious trouble. We were being shelled almost constantly. During a brief letup, I yelled to Louis DiGiralamo who was dug in nearby, 'Are you okay, Dee Gee?' His response was, 'If blood smells like shit, I'm bleeding to death.'

"We suffered a number of casualties during these bombardments. The most gruesome came when a rocket landed among three men in a mortar squad. They were all killed but the explosion must have detonated a Gammon grenade in the leg pocket of one man. The secondary explosion blew him to bits. His head, chest, and right arm were all that remained intact. One of our men remarked, 'That's what you call going to hell in a hurry.' He wasn't being callous or unfeeling; his statement seemed appropriate at the time.

"By midafternoon of D day, I Company was ordered to move south toward Fauville. We didn't actually know where we were going nor why. But not too far along the way, fire on the point killed four men, our CO Capt. Harold Swingler, Sergeant Sandefur, Privates Irvin and Vanich. Edwin Jones, the lone survivor in the group, crawled back to us under our covering fire, and reported the news of those KIA. I was really close with both Sam Vanich and George Irvin. Sam and I shared a pup tent in Oujda, French North Africa. He was mischievous, always good for a laugh. George was the strong, silent type, the kind you wanted with you when the going got tough. Their deaths were a deep personal loss. I couldn't help but think of my mortality. Swingler was an excellent leader and could have remained safe in a hospital for his knee operation.

"I don't think Swingler anticipated running into enemy between Ste. Mère-Eglise and Fauville because our 1st Battalion supposedly held the bridge at la Fière. However, there must have been a corridor between our forces that enabled a German battalion to move in between. The entire situation was in flux those first few days in Normandy. On the platoon level we were pretty much in the dark. At times you get the feeling that nobody knows what the hell is going on."

Battalion surgeon Dave Thomas, with a band of troopers hemmed in by the flooded Merderet and ducked down beneath the hedgerows or in ditches, tried to reach friendly forces. "Using anything we could, blankets, barn doors, tree limbs tied together, we carried the wounded into our aid station. We had German prisoners carrying some wounded who couldn't walk. A machine gunner brought in his buddy who'd been shot. There was a German prisoner who wasn't badly hurt making a lot of racket. The trooper kept telling him to shut up but he wouldn't. The GI said, 'To hell with it!' He stuck his bayonet in the German's guts, threw him over his shoulder, and carried him outside the aid station, dumped him in a ditch, and went back to his machine gun. However, we weren't going anywhere. We were surrounded."

The bridge across the overflowing Merderet at la Fière was critical for the Allies to hold St. Mere Eglise, a crossroads town through which German armor would need to travel. Once he had determined his location, Jim Gavin mobilized a patchwork assortment of troopers to seize both ends of the la Fière span. In the peculiar nature of the dispersed airborne drop, the opposing forces in effect surrounded each other. Gavin had maneuvered into a position that placed him on the Channel side of the river. Behind him, however, enemy still defended against the incoming 4th Division. Across the Merderet, elements of the 507th and 508th Airborne Regiments would attack their end of the bridge, while to their rear marched a regiment of German reserves intent on throwing all of the Americans back into the sea.

The 508th's Sgt. Bud Warnecke, whose B Company CO, Capt. Royal Taylor, hurt his leg upon the landing, was named a platoon leader by Lt. Homer Jones when Jones assumed the leadership of the eighty men collected. "Our objective," says Warnecke, "was on the west side of the Merderet. But we had landed north of Ste.-Mère-Eglise and the river. We passed through Ste.-Mère-Eglise some time after daybreak when the American flag was flying over the first town on the Continent to be liberated. Chills went down my spine. Shortly after noon, we ran into a strong German roadblock at la Fière Manoir, controlling the causeway and bridge, our objective across the Merderet. We got into our first real firefight. The Germans were holed up in a house and several barns. We had more firepower and after what seemed like an hour, the Germans who were not killed, waved a white flag, came out, and surrendered. We would have liked to have shot them, but didn't. We treated them as prisoners of war.

"We started through the marshes near the causeway until the water got too deep and then used the bridge before getting concealment and cover from edge of the causeway to the other side of the marshes. There Lieutenant Jones had the company, now of about sixty men, strung out along a hedgerow with instructions to dig in. We heard tanks coming down the road. All we had were light weapons, really no defense against armor. The order to withdraw came.

"The only route to retreat was by way of the marshes back toward the Merderet. It was an unorganized rout; control over my platoon was impossible. I kept contact with as many men as I could while the Germans fired at random into the reeds. I finally reached the Merderet with about half of my platoon. I didn't think there was a chance to swim the river, even if we were good swimmers. It wasn't very wide nor was there much current. But the banks were very steep. I ordered my men into the river and to move along the bank, using their hands with only their heads out of the water. I was scared, fearful of us drowning, but hoping to find a safe way out.

"The next thing I heard was machine-gun fire coming from a long way off, from a small French Renault tank on the causeway. Like in the movies, the bullets were dancing off the water near our heads. Out of nowhere, a 57mm antitank gun blew the tank away. I soon had my men around a bend in the river and out. I took a head count and there were at least two men missing. One of them was Tooley, the squad comedian, who entertained us once by smoking five cigarettes at one time. He had been concerned about going into combat and had asked me to promise him I would take care of him. The promise has haunted me for years. The other fellow who was gone was Forrest 'Lefty' Brewer, a professional baseball player, property of the Washington Senators and at the time he entered the service, playing for the Charlotte Hornets."

Bill Dean, radio man for Homer Jones, was among those engaged in the firefight at Le Manoir and the la Fière causeway. "Le Manoir was a typical Norman house-and-barn combination of stone and concrete, and rather large. The Germans considered it important enough to defend it with a full platoon with many automatic weapons. Our equipment bundles with machine guns and mortars were scattered and lost. We had to make do with what was available. Our heaviest artillery consisted of two hand grenades we each carried hanging from our rifle-belt suspenders. There was one hell of a firefight. Point scout John McGuire, who was beside my right elbow, was shot through the head and killed. I just stared down at him, not wanting to believe what I saw. My shock was short-lived when several more volleys whizzed by my head.

"It was about 2:00 P.M. when Lt. Jones led an inspired attack on the place. By 2:30 P.M., the remaining fifteen or so German troops surrendered. After hastily eating a K ration in the presence of eight or ten dead Germans we crossed the bridge that we had just captured. When we got to the west side of the river, we turned south toward Hill 30 and came under heavy fire from tanks, mortars, and machine guns from our right rear. They had us in a pocket. We couldn't go back across the bridge. Straight ahead or to the right put us in their gun sights. To our left was the flooded river.

"At this point, Lieutenant Jones yelled for us to pull back. When the tank machine guns opened fire, Lefty Brewer and I broke for the water. Brewer had been one of the original cadre when I came to Camp Blanding in October 1942. We all admired and respected him because he had already been through Fort Benning and wore the wings. The Lefty tag remained from

his stint with a Double-A baseball team. For some reason, Lefty had memorized every verse of Rudyard Kipling's "Gunga Din," and at night in the barracks he would recite them with such enthusiasm that I was prompted to visit
the library at Camp Mackall to learn the poem. Now, an instant after we
plunged into the water, Lefty Brewer lay face down in the water, dead! I swam
the river back to the east shore, like a porpoise going down and up, down
and up, because they were firing on me the whole way over and even beyond since I had to climb a ten-foot-high bank to leave the river.

"I lost my rifle, ammunition, and all my gear during the frightful swim.
After my breathing returned to normal, I headed north along the river until I came upon a makeshift aid station where twenty or more troopers were
being attended to by several medics. The weapons and gear of the wounded
had been stacked in a corner of the room, so I went to the pile and
reequipped myself. I traveled north again to the la Fière Bridge and re-
crossed during the night."

The man who led the attack on the la Fière Manoir, Homer Jones, offered
an account that differs slightly from those of others involved in the firefight
at Le Manoir and the subsequent withdrawal dictated by the confrontation
of superior numbers and heavier weapons. "Lieutenant Lee Frigo was with
the support group on a hill close by the Le Manoir. I had already worked
my way into the basement and the Germans and I had been exchanging fire
through what was the ceiling over my head and the floor underneath their
feet. Someone, I believe it was Lee, shouted to me that everyone should cease
fire in order to let the civilians in the building get out. He spoke fluent
French and he arranged the cease-fire. Once the French had left, the firing
from the hill and within the house started again, including the exchanges
through the floor.

"Lee dashed into the basement, a most welcome sight. There were no
other troopers there. The two of us continued to fire up and watch the bullet holes appear above us. We decided they had organized a line and were
advancing in an orderly fashion. Since the Germans had bolt-action rifles,
there was a pause between volleys. Lee and I figured that during one of those
pauses, we could skip to the half of the cellar already covered by the German fire. I may be giving them too much credit for a methodical procedure
but in any event they never hit us.

"There was another small room in the cellar; a light machine gun fired
on us, cutting my trousers and bruising my leg. I tossed a grenade in and it
killed three Germans. Inside there were some barrels spouting what I presume was Calvados from the holes made by the grenades and bullets fired.
Frigo and I started up a narrow flight of stairs and just as he was about to
toss another grenade through an inside window without glass, we heard
shouts that the Germans had surrendered. We escorted seventeen prison-

ers, leaving eight dead or badly wounded in the house. A couple of the prisoners had been hit in the testicles by our fire coming up from beneath them."

After two groups led by Jones and Lt. Hoyt Goodale pushed across the bridge and causeway Jones quickly realized they lacked the strength to maintain their toehold. "I discovered that Goodale and his people had left. Our right flank was totally exposed. I didn't say 'Every man for himself,'" recalled Jones. "I simply told everyone to get out and get back. Frigo, Bill Dean, and I were the last ones to leave. I swam across, hearing the crackle of small arms in the bulrushes." Jones earned a Silver Star while others received Bronze Stars. La Fière Bridge and Causeway witnessed a murderous series of punches and counterattacks for four more bloody days.

For glider pilots Vic Warriner and Pete Buckley, the remainder of the hours of darkness and the day meant a tense waiting game. Although schooled in combat, they were expected to rejoin air-transport operations. Vic Warriner recalled, "By daylight, we had made contact with and were joined by about a dozen glider pilots. We kept busy unloading gliders and doing messenger work for the airborne. We all realized that the next flight of gliders coming in that evening was going to have great difficulty landing the huge Horsas in the small fields that had destroyed our small CG 4As. We borrowed some plastic explosives from the airborne and blew down the larger trees dividing the pastures so the Horsas could have a longer glide area. That was partially successful but many still crashed that afternoon with severe losses for pilots and passengers.

"I spent my first full night in Normandy in a foxhole in a little French cemetery. It had a stone wall around it and was easy digging. A German 88 blew the front gate off during the night but outside of that it was peaceful. The airborne command had taken over a château for headquarters. We glider pilots gathered there to act as a perimeter guard for as long as was needed. A field nearby served as the area for casualties who were brought in for identification and burial. It seemed like acres of dead, row on row, covered with blankets, or tarps where available. It took away the excitement and enthusiasm I had been feeling and made me realize that this was a pretty rough game we were playing. From the field hospital we heard that [Mike] Murphy was going to survive but his would be a long and painful recovery. I was told by our surgeon, Capt. Charles Van Gorder, 'It looked like Murphy had undergone an explosion inside his body.'"

Pete Buckley, whose glider brought in an antitank cannon, left the gun crew shortly after daylight. "I started on foot to find the 101st Division CP at Hiesville. On my way I stopped a jeep driven by a paratrooper headed in what we hoped was the right direction to the CP. I hopped on the hood and we went up a narrow path between the hedgerows. About five minutes later, some Krauts opened up on us with machine pistol and rifle fire. I fell off and the jeep almost ran over me. I got up and began walking on my own. While still going up this narrow lane I glanced to my left and saw a rectangular opening with a rifle barrel sticking out, pointing at me. I froze in mid-step, waiting for the bullet I thought had my name on it. Nothing happened. The gun didn't move. I crawled over the hedge and looked in. It was a complete German bunker, big enough for five or six soldiers. Its sole occupant was a dead German, his rifle poking through the slot. Thank God for the paratroopers who had taken care of him earlier.

"The next German I ran across lay at a crossroads in a pool of blood. He had just been hit by a mortar or shell fragment and was still alive. But his gut was ripped open, his intestines spilling out onto the road. I felt horrible while I stood there watching him die, knowing I could do nothing for him. I had not yet developed the hate for the enemy that would come to me as the day progressed and I saw and heard what they had done to some of our airborne. This German dying on the ground in front of me, was a young kid and sure didn't look like a Nazi superman.

"At 8:30 that evening, some of us were asked to go back into the fields to meet and cover the landing of the second serial of gliders. a large force of Horsa gliders were expected by 9:00 P.M. They came right on time and the Germans in the fields around us, who had been playing possum, opened up on the gliders with everything they had. Their heavy AA guns outside the perimeters were firing airbursts over and into the fields while the gliders landed. The fields around Heisville were much too small for these big British gliders and those that weren't shot down, crashed head-on into the hedgerows. Some were fortunate, making it down in one piece. Others came under heavy small-arms fire after they landed. Many glidermen and pilots were killed or captured while climbing out of their Horsas. For an hour or so, it was a god-awful mess."

Glider pilot Tip Randolph had not been a party to the Chicago mission in the early, dark hours of the morning. Instead, he was assigned to Elmira, the evening operation employing Horsas to tote supplies and added weaponry. "I had a jeep, a 75mm pack howitzer, twenty-two rounds of ammunition for it, and five men from the 82d Airborne. Our squadron carried a battery of these guns, six in all, with their jeeps, crews, and ammunition. We were all excited. We were going off to win the war. Before we left Col. Adrien Williams, the CO of the 9th Troop Carrier Command—we called him 'Big Willie'—made a little speech. I have no idea why, but he told us, 'Be good Presbyterians' and finished with 'we'll see you in a few days.'

"The trip was uneventful until we came to Normandy. Over the Channel—it was dusk and with double daylight saving time, visibility was unimpaired—it looked like if you landed in the water, you could take a step either way and put your foot on a boat. They were all headed the same way, toward France. I saw the battleships firing, a lot of stuff was being poured in. There had been some dark and light clouds but just after we turned over the beaches the sky turned black. I could see ahead of me the first echelon of Elmira and about five minutes in, started to see tow ships catch fire. We also saw fires on the ground, tracers flying up.

"It was seven or eight miles inland to our LZ, and when we got the green light it was off we go into the blackness. I thought, there's no way I'm going to make it into the field. I couldn't see anything. All you could do is a 270-degree landing, count five, and then turn the 270 degrees which should line you up. The most important thing now was the altitude. The Horsa had flaps that looked like billboards and could almost put the thing down on its nose, like letting you down in an elevator. We kept watching the altimeter. Flying in the dark there's no sense of where you are until you come level with the horizon. Tracers crossed in front of us, some coming up—that indicated ground fire. We were eighty feet in the air when we finally saw the horizon. We made the decision to drop her on her nose when we were at sixty feet and we felt ourselves brushing the tops of trees in the hedgerows. As we came down farther, we could see streams of light from tracers, people were firing across the field. We set down in the field and went past one glider but didn't hit it. We rolled farther and now could see we were near the end of a field, with less than 800 feet, while we were traveling eighty miles per hour. Bullets hit the Horsa; the sounds were like thuds; in a CG 4A the noise was like a snare drum.

"We came to a stop and got out as quick as we could. One man, the radio operator, sitting in the jeep, had been hit in the arm. When everyone was out and on the ground, I got behind a glider wheel as there was a lot of firing going on. We didn't know who was doing what but figured if they were on our side, they'd stop. We were sprawled there for ten minutes to half an hour when all the shooting stopped. We started to hear the sound of those crickets. Someone put a patch on the wounded man. He was okay, having been hit in the fat part of the shoulder.

"We figured we were near Ste.-Mère-Eglise. What we didn't know was that a division of the Germans that wasn't supposed to be in that area was between us and our objective. Those 75s might just as well have stayed in England. All they could do is move half a mile, and then stay put. They would set their pieces up, ready to fire, then have to knock the gun down, move to another quadrant, but never got a firing order. Meanwhile, a bunch of paratroopers came along and captured the Germans who had been firing at the gliders. Things were so mixed up that Germans were captured just moving down the road not realizing where the GIs were."

From the beach, Max Schneider directed his 5th Battalion Rangers to advance across a blacktop road and sweep southwest toward the Château Vaumicel. Intense machine-gun fire from hedgerows halted the Rangers who sought to outflank the resistance. However, according to John Raaen, Schneider spread out the GIs in the wrong direction. "Clearly, Schneider was completely baffled by the hedgerows. These were like nothing any of us had ever seen before. A hedgerow was a long thick mound of earth, six to ten feet high. On top of the mound was usually a hedge of some sort, old, gnarled, heavy, with huge roots holding the mounds together. Tanks could not drive through these monsters. The Germans dug holes in the back side of these natural barriers and hollowed out small machine-gun nests and fighting positions. Because of the natural camouflage and overhead cover, it was impossible to see these positions as they fired at you."

After four fruitless hours attempting to move on Château Vaumicel to the south, the Rangers followed the coastal road that took them west toward Vierville-sur-Mer where they contacted the advance elements of the 29th Division. Although the defenders closest to the beach had been eliminated, German soldiers infiltrated through gaps in the lines to renew their attacks. Buck Dawson, as a platoon leader for D Company, was on the Vierville Road when a machine gun opened up. "We failed to eliminate this gun, because they moved it back through the hedgerows when we attacked. We withdrew and then sought to skirt the enemy and strike out for Pointe du Hoc. But as night fell, we were not too far from Vierville. We dug in, reinforced by elements of the 116th Infantry and other remnants to form a perimeter for the beachhead. I had lost only one killed and several wounded, but an eighteen-man Ranger platoon can't afford to lose a single soldier. That night at Vierville, I heard a rumor of the possibility of a pullout, but it was only a rumor."

Perhaps the most isolated outfit among the invaders were the Rangers clinging to their small piece of turf atop Pointe du Hoc. When Lt. George Kerchner finally scaled the heights he was dumbfounded by the sight. "It didn't look anything like I thought it would. We had a number of aerial photos, maps, and sketches of what was supposed to be there. But the tremendous bombardment from our ships and planes had torn up the terrain until I could not recognize things. It was one large shell crater after another. When I headed toward the portion of the Pointe where the guns were supposed to be, the Germans began shelling us from inland. This was my first time under artillery fire and it was a terrifying experience. I kept going in the direction of the emplacements because I felt this was safest. Most of the shells were falling near the cliff edge. I figured inland a way I could be away from shell bursts.

"I began picking up men. Some were from my own company and others from different ones. You would jump into these craters twenty-five feet wide and there might be one or two Rangers there. As soon as a shell had landed, you would get out of the hole, run and jump in the next one. The faster you moved, the safer you felt. I couldn't see any Jerries but saw Branley, Long, and Hefflebower trying to locate mortar targets. About 200 yards inland, I saw a Jerry in a 40mm gun emplacement, the first live one I'd seen. I told Huff to fire at him, but he missed five times. The rest of the men set out for the road. I stayed behind to get the Jerry but I couldn't get a shot at him and left when he turned the AA gun on me.

"I crawled through a communications trench to a house. As I went through it, a shell hit it and a sniper fired at me. I found some E Company men pinned down and asked them where D Company was. They said some of my men were up ahead. I set out up the road as two Jerries came in with hands up. A sergeant reported that the guns were not in the casemates. That eliminated our initial mission. I decided to set off for our second objective, a roadblock along the coastal road running from Grandcamp-les-Bains to Vierville-sur-Mer behind Omaha Beach.

"The men took off in small groups," Kerchner continued, "I followed and as I crossed Pointe du Hoc I dropped into a communications ditch, two feet wide and eight feet deep. My first impression was, I'm safe from artillery fire. But the trench zigzagged every twenty-five yards. You couldn't see any farther ahead and as you went around a corner you never knew whether you would come face to face with a German. I never felt so lonesome before or after. I became all the more anxious and started to think in terms of my being captured. I hurried to reach the coastal road and the other men. You felt better when there were others around.

"Pointe du Hoc was a self-contained fort. On the land side it was surrounded by minefields, barbed wire, and machine-gun emplacements, all to protect it from a land attack. I don't think the Germans really believed anyone would come from the sea and scale the cliffs. Now we began running into the German defenders along the perimeter of the fortified area. As I came on, I saw one of my Rangers, Bill Vaughn, a machine gunner, and a real fine boy. As soon as I saw him, I realized he was dying. He had practically been stitched across by a machine gun. He wasn't in any pain. He knew he was dying. All I could do was tell him, 'Bill, we'll send a medic up to take care of you.' There was no point in my staying with him since I could do nothing for him.

The 'cavalry,' in the form of the 116th, never arrived during the day nor that evening, as Bob Slaughter and the others in the Blue and the Gray [29th] Division barely survived their day at the beach. On the Pointe, Ranger lieutenant George Kerchner, who with the remnants of his own platoon, had joined Lomell, Kuhn, and a handful of Rangers in the fortifications of Pointe du Hoc, endured a desperate cat-and-mouse affair with vastly superior numbers of enemy. "About six o'clock," said Kerchner, "we realized we were not going to be relieved by the 116th. The hours had passed so fast that what some call the 'longest day' was to me the shortest. For a while, we weren't even sure that the Americans had not pulled everyone out, gone back to England, and left us there alone. We only knew of a group of Rangers at the CP with Colonel Rudder, where they were also treating the wounded. [We also were aware] that a naval shore fire-control party and a couple from the 29th Division Recon were on hand. Meanwhile, we were about three-quarters of a mile inland and there were a tremendous amount of Germans around, several hundred at least. They had the advantage of knowing the terrain, having underground rooms and passageways. They seemed able to pop above ground, shoot, then duck back down, and come up somewhere else.

"A little later, however, a platoon from the 5th Ranger Battalion, with Lt. [Charles] Parker in command, broke through and joined us around this time. We were so happy to see them, the first men from Omaha Beach. Now we realized the invasion was here to stay and that other men would come forward. Parker and his troops helped contribute to our perimeter." As anticipated, the Germans counterattacked. Said Kerchner, "It was the most frightening moment of my entire life. From all quiet and silent to this tremendous outbreak of firing, exploding grenades, furious yelling. And it seemed there were hundreds and hundreds of Germans running toward us. From their firing, we began to see their outlines; it was not real dark. We started firing and although they did not break our lines, we suffered casualties."

Charles "Ace" Parker from Company A of the 5th Battalion explained his passage to unite with the embattled Rangers on Pointe de Hoc. "We kept switching directions in the hedgerows, and as we did we would meet up with small numbers of Germans, killing some, accepting others' surrender, although we did not want prisoners. About three-quarters of the way to the Pointe, we reached a small village. Germans began crawling along each side of the road on the other side of the hedgerows. We could hear them and then they began to got behind us. We turned all of the prisoners loose and retreated. We cut off into a field toward the beach and about nine at night made contact with the outposted people of the 2d Battalion. There were three officers there, and since they knew the positions, our men were integrated into the line. When the German counterattacks came and finally broke right into our ranks, some of the 2d Battalion people began pulling out without giving us notice. It was extremely difficult to get our men out, because they were scattered along the line but we managed."

On the beach, Bob Edlin of the 2d Ranger Battalion, after being knocked down by two bullets and receiving a second morphine shot, had fallen asleep. "When I awoke, it was late afternoon. The sun was shining and there was a lot of incoming artillery fire. The tide was going out, taking bodies and debris. It kept reaching back to pick up another body, but they didn't want to go. They had earned this part of the beach with their lives.

"Other troops were coming ashore, I couldn't walk but as a light tank came by, a wounded sergeant and I got on. They were going up to the Vierville exit. If we went that far, maybe we could find out something about the rest of the battalion. Then the tank stopped. A motionless tank in front of a Kraut pillbox is not a healthy place to be. We bailed off the tank and crawled a few yards. It got popped. Now we were in a hell of a fix. A burning tank a few yards away and we couldn't get to the seawall. Artillery, mortar, and rockets are still pounding away inland.

"I looked at the exit again. The large pillbox was still there, a big stone dinosaur. Because of the heavy artillery fire, people were taking cover under the seawall. They wouldn't come and help us. Finally two black soldiers, part of an engineer battalion came out under heavy fire and dragged us to cover. They would have made good Rangers. Things began to loosen up as it got toward four or five in the evening. There was still artillery, mortar, and rocket fire on the beach, but it was obvious that we had established a beachhead. As it got toward dark, a boat came in to evacuate the wounded. I was immobilized by this time. A full colonel said they would only take the walking wounded out to the ship. Two or three of the Rangers put me on a stretcher, and they informed the colonel I was the one man on a stretcher who was going to leave. He agreed.

"It was almost dark when we reached the small landing craft. We went out on the landing craft coming up beside a ship. Sergeant Ted James of B Company, 2d Battalion, had lost some or all of the fingers from one of his hands. It was impossible for him to climb the ladder. I was lying in the bottom of the boat and just about everyone had gone up except James and me. A German fighter came in, strafing the living hell out of the boat. I saw Sergeant James go up the ladder with no problem. His hand got better in a hurry. Now I was the only one left. The strafing and bombing around the ship became so heavy I thought they would leave me.

"I looked up. It seemed a long distance. There was a redheaded, heavyset American sailor. He said, 'I'll get that son of a bitch.' He dropped a big net, climbed down the ladder, and put me, stretcher and all, into the net, almost single-handedly forcing the Navy to take me. I'll never know who he was but he was a good man.

"All night long the Germans continued to strafe and bomb, it seemed unfair. They took me down into the hospital section of the ship. I was given more morphine, and as I lay there on the operating table, I heard a conversation between an Army and a Navy doctor. One said, 'We're going to have to take his leg off.' The other answered, 'It's not going to get any worse. Why don't we just leave it alone? We don't have time to fool with him anyway. Let's get to the seriously wounded people first. Let's get this man back to England and they can decide what should be done.' Thank God they were busy, because that leg still works.

Sid Salomon, the C Company platoon leader atop Pointe et Raz de la Percée, found the heights lonely after ousting the German defenders. "There was nobody around. We had so many killed. We were supposed to go after Isigny that night, but we had only nine men left from the thirty-one in our boat. The other platoon had ten men. We didn't have a sufficient force for an effective firefight. It wasn't until sometime in the afternoon that I felt that the tide of the invasion seemed to change. Until then it had seemed a failure, but I could look down on the beach and see wave after wave of manpower come in, with tanks firing from the beach. We spent the remainder of the day on the Pointe."

Frank South, the Ranger medic under Captain Block, stayed on the beach for an hour or so after Pointe du Hoc fell. "Block ordered most of the medics to the top, but I was to tend any new casualties on the beach and protect those that couldn't be moved until we had a place for them—which turned out to be the bunker above." Fire on the beach diminished to an occasional outburst as patrols sought out isolated defenders. After helping to move the wounded up to the aid station established by Block, South climbed to the Pointe. The medics there used flashlights until gas lanterns were received. As ammunition ran low, Rudder assigned Block to ration the supply and the surgeon delegated the job to South. "By then many of our men had resorted to German arms because we were so short of ammunition. One supply LCA had foundered and another pulled out too soon. I was still working in the aid-station bunker at midnight. I do not remember where or if I slept. I doubt that I was thinking any profundity at the moment but instead tended to my job. I did have a sense of wonderment that all this was actually taking place and that we had made it to the top and appeared to be holding on at the time."

While the situation of the Rangers atop Pointe du Hoc was still precarious, things were improving for Overlord. Utah Beach was secure. The airborne forces that remained behind enemy lines continued to repulse efforts to wipe them out. There was no reason, as Bradley had feared, to pull the troops out of the Omaha sector even though they still struggled to widen their grasp. And to the east, the landings by United Kingdom forces were going reasonably well.

A rescue launch plucked from the water a sailor who jumped overboard from the shattered battleship *West Virginia*. (National Archives)

During the infamous Death March after the fall of Bataan, captives improvised litters for those unable to complete the hike to a prison camp. (National Archives)

The U.S. carrier *Yorktown* listed badly after being hit during the Battle of Midway. (National Archives)

Battle-weary and malaria plagued, leathernecks from the 1st Marine Division relaxed behind the lines on Guadalcanal while fresh forces relieved them. (National Archives)

P-40s flew off the deck of a carrier to support the ground forces in North Africa. (National Archives)

Working with a Sherman tank, infantrymen expanded the beachhead on Bougainville in the South Pacific. (National Archives)

Shattered palms and flame-thrower smoke marked a marine assault upon a sand-banked blockhouse on Tarawa. (National Archives)

Torpedo bombers from U.S. carriers ranged the skies over a Japanese armada in the South Pacific. (National Archives)

Near Italy's Rapido River, an antitank squad defended against an enemy counterattack. (National Archives)

Crewmen aboard the U.S. Coast Guard cutter *Spencer* watch a depth charge explode during a successful attack upon a German submarine, the U-175 which menaced a North Atlantic convoy. (National Archives.)

During the bomb run of B-17s from the 94th Bomb Group over Berlin in May 1944, *Miss Donna Mae* drifted beneath another Fort as it released its 500-pounders. The camera in the aircraft dropping the ordnance captured the images. (Bottom) The doomed *Miss Donna Mae,* still level has lost the elevator and the plane soon plunged to earth. There were no survivors. (Wilbur Richardson)

Half-drowned soldiers in the English Channel on D day were hauled on an inflatable raft to Omaha Beach. (National Archives)

In September 1944, U.S. infantrymen first broke through the formidable German defensive wall known as the Siegfried Line. (National Archives)

The aircraft carrier *Princeton* suffered a mortal blow from a suicide raider during the Battle of Leyte Gulf. (National Archives)

Boyd's Boids, a B-17, managed to stagger back to England before it crash landed and broke apart. (Dick Bowman)

Troops fought house-to-house to capture Cologne. (National Archives)

On Iwo Jima, marines crawled over the black volcanic ash deposited by Mt. Suribachi whose summit overlooked them and provided a deadly observation post for the enemy. (National Archives)

The capture of the Remagen Bridge over the Rhine hastened the Allied advance into Germany. (National Archives)

Soldiers in an amphibious truck broached the last formidable natural defenses of Germany in March 1945 as they crossed the Rhine River. (National Archives)

Marine Corsair fighter planes operated from landing strips in the Philippines to provide ground support for army troops. (National Archives)

Flames threatened to explode a Navy Hellcat fighter aboard the carrier *Enterprise* after an errant anti-aircraft shell aimed at a *kamikaze* sprayed the deck with hot shrapnel. (National Archives)

Struck by a kamikaze off Okinawa, the aircraft carrier *Bunker Hill* spewed fire and smoke as more than 350 men died another 250 were injured. (National Archives)

32
The Normandy Campaign Begins

The "beginning," as Churchill labeled Overlord, could be called a success if establishing a foothold were the sole criteria. By the morning of 7 June, the Allied forces, with the fleet still lobbing huge ordnance at inland targets and the air arms dominant—only 100 German planes operated against the invaders—controlled enough ground to beat off any effort to throw them into the sea. Well over 100,000 Allied troops occupied positions in Normandy (the seaborne gridlock and the aerial-drop confusion prevented precise statistics), with the deepest penetration some eight miles in the British sector and the narrowest as thin as 1,000 yards for the American area beyond Omaha Beach. Inland pockets of airborne GIs and Tommies continued to beat back counterattacks, solidifying and enlarging lodgments on the Cherbourg peninsula.

Casualties among the Allies for that first twenty-four hours included as many as 2,500 on bloody Omaha, fewer than 200 at the less fiercely defended Utah Beach, and 2,499 among the U.S. airborne. Several hundred sailors who went down with their landing craft or were hit by fire as they approached the beaches added to the losses. Because estimates of the dead, wounded, and captured had been pegged as high as 80 percent for the airborne, and from 25 percent upward for others, the numbers were acceptable to the commanders, if not to kin and friends.

For the soldiers now on the continent, 6 June indeed was only a beginning. The Utah Beach losses for D day amounted to only 197 casualties, and these included about 60 men missing from the sinking of a landing craft bearing a portion of an attached field-artillery battalion. (In contrast, the German E-boats that interrupted one of the Slapton Sands preinvasion exercises inflicted losses of some 700 men.) However, in the days that followed, the 4th Division encountered fierce opposition and the KIA, WIA, and MIA numbers rocketed. By the end of the month, the total for the 4th Division mounted to 5,452. Other VII Corps units, including the 82d and 101st Airborne and three infantry divisions brought in by sea, sustained brutal losses.

During the first day or so after climbing Pointe du Hoc or scrambling through the Omaha Beach firestorm, most of the Rangers struggled under similar conditions to those of the airborne forces. Isolated, and operating

as small units against severe counterattacks, they clung to their meager portions of French soil. On 7 June, from the command post in a bombed out
German position on Pointe du Hoc, Lou Lisko watched the U.S. destroyers
Harding and *Satterlee* throwing their weight at the nearby enemy emplacements. German guns responded. Offshore observers decided the Rangers
no longer occupied the Pointe. "In the afternoon, several American fighter
planes flew in a circle over Pointe du Hoc," says Lisko. "We became very concerned they might think we were Germans and start bombing and killing
all of us. I took off my field jacket and waved it. One plane approached so
close that the motor was hard on my eardrums. One Ranger had an American flag and started to stretch it out, using stones to keep the wind from
blowing it away. A machine gun from the left flank opened up at this Ranger.
He fell down but wasn't hit and crawled up again to put more stones on the
flag. That enabled the flight leader to see the Rangers were still alive. He
flew in a circle several times. We waved at him and he waved back. He and
the other six planes left without throwing any bombs or firing any shots. Several hours later, three or four planes returned and pulverized a dangerous
target, the machine-gun nest on our left flank. They dropped six or eight
bombs on it. The defense of Pointe du Hoc was thus fought by a team that
included Rangers, the U.S. and British navies, and the U.S. Air Corps.

"By June 8, we were waiting to be relieved by the Rangers from Omaha
Beach who had run into a lot of German resistance. We had run out of ammunition and two Rangers were using a German machine gun. About
noon, Schneider and his 5th Ranger Battalion heard the distinctive sound
of a German machine gun. They assumed we had been wiped out. In the
confusion, they started to fire in our direction with mortars. Tanks attached
to the 116th Regiment joined in. After two and a half days of fighting the
Germans, now we were being attacked by our own troops.

"Colonel Rudder was yelling as loud as he could to the Rangers to stop
firing the German machine gun but he was not close enough for them to
hear. My buddy and I were trying to contact the friendly troops over the radio and tell them they were shooting at their own troops. Finally, we succeeded. Colonel Schneider ran out into the open and told his men to cease
firing."

Lieutenant Charles Parker from the 5th Ranger Battalion, who received
a DSC for D day, was heavily engaged on 7 June with counterattacks. "There
was a very nasty fight three or four days later. We had to cross a flooded
swamp area where they had the targets painted on their emplacement walls.
They could fire two or three mortar rounds from trenches and pits under
manhole covers without exposing themselves. They had four years to prepare for us. In the Rangers we practiced an elementary principle. Once you
jump off, there's no place to stop until you arrive at the target. If you halt

halfway there, then you become pinned down. So we were right among them very soon, working our way down in the trenches using fire and grenades. They started to surrender and a lot of them had been gathered out of their holes but there were several SS men among them. They began killing those who surrendered and that brought chaos. The entire thing had to be done again. One SS officer held a grenade to his head and blew off most of his face rather than surrender. I lost my first sergeant and a dozen other men there."

Subsequently, the Rangers entered a bivouac where they sought to fill their ranks. "I interviewed hundreds of volunteers," said Parker, "and we rejected most of them. Regular-army organizations always hate special units. They didn't know what to do with us. They would use us for smash-and-grab operations. We were to take positions but we never had enough men or firepower to hold them for any length of time." Parker recalled at least four subsequent encounters with the enemy that struck him as equal to the perils of the invasion. "But I went through the entire war and never missed a day at the office."

John Raaen remembered that on D plus 1 orders directed his 5th Battalion Ranger unit to relieve the 2d Battalion at Pointe du Hoc. When he stepped out to the road beside the farmyard where he'd spent an uncomfortable night in a manure-laden haystack, he was pleasantly surprised at daybreak to find that several tanks from the 743d Tank Battalion had arrived. "Suddenly there was a lot of firing directly to our south. A German counterattack of at least company size. I could see through the hedgerow that our troops were being beaten back by a superior force. I could also see that the tanks were doing nothing about it.

"I climbed up on one of the tanks and banged on the turret with my rifle. The hatch opened and the tank commander asked what was up. I pointed out the firefight about 300 yards away and asked that he bring the building the Germans were using for cover under fire. He spoke on the radio, unlimbered his .50-caliber machine gun, and all the tanks began firing. I got his attention again and asked why he wasn't using his 75mm guns. 'Target doesn't call for it. Might hurt friendlies,' was his answer. The 50s must have been enough, for the attack soon died down."

Few American infantrymen, including the Rangers, had practiced coordinated operations with armor. It was another vital skill that GIs learned on the job, at cost. Not until late in the war did someone think to install systems by which a foot soldier could get the attention of a tank commander by other means than banging upon the turret.

Instructed to contact 29th Division headquarters on the situation of the Rangers, Raaen made his way to the beach command post. Having reported the disposition of the organization, Raaen requested machine-gun and mortar ammunition to replenish the expended supply. Given a barely functioning jeep, Raaen and Jack Sharp, an enlisted man, loaded up and drove along a road that showed evidence of fighting. Occasionally, rounds from unseen adversaries struck the jeep—Raaen counted four hits on his helmet, either by bullets or debris. After distributing their cargo, partly by lying under the jeep and passing back ammunition while enemy fire whizzed overhead, Raaen and Sharp motored toward advance elements. They halted near a huge crater across a road when suddenly a heavy artillery barrage erupted several hundred yards to the front.

"It was clearly enemy fire and it was devastating. Rangers began streaming back across the crater to get away from the fire, officers among them. At first, they were orderly in their withdrawal but soon it became a panic. I stood on the edge of the crater shouting at the men to slow down, swearing at them to stop and reorganize. I knew many of them and calling them by name stopped the rout. My standing there above them as they came out of the crater had a very salutary effect as well." Even the most doughty of troops occasionally broke.

Pressure from the swelling U.S. infantry contingent supported by tanks, artillery, and naval guns offshore cracked the defense at Grandcamp, one of the major objectives for the Rangers. Elsewhere, the invaders encountered similarly stubborn resistance. "We got off the beach well enough," said Charles Mastro from the intelligence section of the 2d Battalion in the 22d Infantry Regiment, "but then we hit a wall." The entire offensive that included the 4th Division shuddered to a halt as an entrenched enemy, backed by the dreaded 88s and Tiger tanks, fiercely defended its turf. Unhappy with the progress, the top brass sacked commanders. Colonel Hervey Tribolet, whom Mastro described as a leader who talked to the lowest privates like a father, was relieved of command over the 22d, although most of his officers and enlisted men retained confidence in him. "We had one battalion commander," noted Mastro, "who was not a leader. Omar Bradley, watching our progress from a hilltop, relieved him on the spot."

George Mabry recalled that his battalion met sporadic resistance while approaching Ste.-Marie-du-Mont. "Eventually we got into the little village. Once in a while we heard a rifle with a muffled sound from it. This was coming from a church in the middle of the town square. It had a very tall steeple. I dodged around, got myself to the square. There was a kind of half-track German vehicle with two dead Germans. The vehicle having turned the corner and the driver having been shot, it was angled across the street. I contacted a member of the 101st Airborne who told me they had some casualties. I asked about the muffled fire from the steeple. He said, "Oh, sir, that's the first sergeant up in the church. He shot these two Germans." In a few minutes he appeared and I commended him. I told him to round up the casualties so that medical personnel would take care of them. Sitting on the base of a pump in the town square was a U.S. airborne soldier wounded in the hand and face, apparently from a hand grenade and small arms. Both hands were wrapped in bandages and his entire face was covered with blood-soaked bandages. He was able to mumble through the gauze covering everything but his nose. It was shocking to see a man sitting there completely wrapped in bandages covering every part of the skin that was ordinarily visible. Yet he was conscious and made no complaint.

"Having passed through Ste.-Marie-du-Mont. it wasn't long before we met stiff resistance from Germans dug in along the hedgerows, and the dairy farms that had a stone wall as well as the hedgerow. I don't recall ever having any briefing from our intelligence that mentioned the hedgerows or the formidable obstacles the trees and underbrush on these hedgerows would have on airborne and restrictions upon any vehicle, tracked or on wheels. We soon learned the tactic the Germans would use. We'd run up against a prepared position. The riflemen would lean against the hedgerow and shoot while machine guns would be put atop the hedgerow for enfilade or flanking fire into German positions. The Germans would hold their machine guns in reserve and once we got ours in position, they would run down the field and take a position and give us enfilade fire. We'd be shooting at what [had been] a German machine-gun position, but to our surprise, to our flank would come machine-gun fire. It didn't take long to figure out what they were doing and we began to do the same thing. Fire with MG, then take it down and put a BAR man in the position and run down and move our own MG.

"Daylight at that time of the year prevailed until almost 11:00 P.M. Eventually we stopped to give everyone an opportunity to dig in around 10:00 P.M. We dug in, set out mines, and antitank weapons. But no attack occurred. Apparently, Hitler did not think this was the main invasion force and he held his armor in reserve. In addition, our air force was quite active and caught some German convoys on the road, including some tanks.

"The next morning," Mabry remembered, "we jumped off at first light. We were getting along fairly well until we ran into a complex of dairy farms, each separated by a road and a big stone wall around its house, barn, silos. The Germans had been using these buildings and stone walls for defensive purposes. We began getting a terrific amount of small-arms fire. I was near F Company on the left. We were shooting mortars at these houses and artillery had been brought in. I crawled up by a hedgerow where some of F Company was. Very close to me was Mickey Donahue, [a highly skilled boxer on a team coached by Mabry while at Fort Benning]. I was peeping over the hedgerow and saw a German run down the field and I shot at him and so did some others. He went down. A tremendous explosion happened close to Mickey Donahue. I had seen a German's arm. I figured the German had thrown a potato masher hand grenade. What I saw was his hand coming down after having hurled the grenade. He stuck his head up and I took a crack at him and I never heard from him again. I crawled down to Mickey and he had been hit. He was bleeding and looked as though he was going to die pretty soon. I dragged him up the little road, turned him over on his back, put his helmet under his head, took out his canteen and put [it] by his right hand. A couple of other enlisted men were there and called for medics. Elements of the company began to move. We crushed the enemy immediately ahead of us and I had to abandon Mickey. I thought Mickey Donahue would die, but some years later I found that he was at the Valley Forge [Pennsylvania] hospital, paralyzed from the waist down.

"Three Germans came running around a stone wall and I hollered 'halt,' they threw up their hands, I made them lie down. If they stood up I knew someone seeing their uniforms would let 'em have a blast. I ran on, telling them to stay there. When I ran inside a courtyard inside a stone wall I noticed a Frenchman making all kinds of signs with hands, indicating someone inside, wounded. I went in with some enlisted men. There was a middle-aged woman and a small boy. The woman had been hit in the abdomen by a shell fragment. She was bleeding profusely. The little boy was sitting in a chair, staring. She was making no noise, other than breathing heavily. I calmed down the man who was quite excited, telling him we'd get a medical person to tend to his wife. I checked later; they assured me this lady was taken care of.

"When we got within 1,000 yards or so of Ste.-Mère-Eglise we met a very stiff defense. The 3d Battalion [of the 8th Regiment] was supposed to be on our left flank as we began to receive quite a bit of fire from that direction. I suggested to Colonel McNeely we try to contact the 3d Battalion. We couldn't reach them by radio so I took two enlisted men with me to see if I could find them. We started up a dirt road and saw many German vehicles on the paved road leading to Ste.-Mère-Eglise. There must have been twenty to twenty-five trucks, strafed and riddled with .50-caliber MG bullets. [This was a convoy shot up by the Air Force.] As we approached, we saw a paratrooper hanging from a telephone line, his feet about a foot off the ground. His throat had been cut. It angered us. The enlisted men made threatening comments. I told them we will never do this, that's what we're fighting against. As we went on we saw a couple more hanging and killed the same way.

"We spied a group of houses on the other side of the road and heard rifle fire from that direction. I figured the 3d Battalion were attacking this group of houses. We got into the big ditch, crawled along it until we noticed some Germans were in the house directly in front of us. Some were looking out of a second-story window, some peeping around the corner on the ground floor. I told [some] enlisted men we'd take 'em under fire and help the 3d Battalion. We sneaked closer behind a hedgerow. I told 'em I'd take the man on the ground floor; the men to take the others. We shot simultaneously. A couple of them fell to the ground. At that time a German on the top floor stuck his head out of the top-floor window. I shot at him; he disappeared. Another soldier stuck his rifle out of the window trying to determine where fire was coming from. I shot at him; he fell back.

"About this time a few rounds of artillery started to land near these houses. I didn't like this artillery, coming from the beach [friendly] area. I told the enlisted men we'd better turn around and get back into our area. We were too far over and too far in front of the 3d Battalion. Just as we started back up the ditch, the U.S. artillery really started coming in. It was massive, flying through the air like a flock of ducks. Rounds hit all around us. We began running back up the ditch. A round hit in a mud puddle, covering us with mud from head to foot. I said, 'On my count to three, let's take off!' We jumped up and ran as hard as we could across an open field toward the 2d Battalion, then flopped down. Meanwhile the artillery was coming in, Brrrmm! Brrrmm! Brrrmm! We ran again. Nobody shot at us because they were taking cover from the artillery. We ran as hard as we could and fell down again with the artillery shells starting to fall behind us. We hit the ground one more time. On the third rush we were able to get out of the artillery concentration, but we were covered from head to toe with mud and dirt. I was visibly shaking when I explained to Colonel McNeely how we'd been caught in that artillery barrage. Since then I studiously avoided getting into somebody's else's area without notifying them.

"I told McNeely about seeing how paratroopers had been killed while hanging from wires and trees. He said he'd seen the same. I recommended that we pass the word to company commanders to inform all officers down to the last enlisted man we did not condone such barbaric behavior. Members of the 2d Battalion would not take out their frustration and anger against German prisoners. Individuals caught doing this would be subjected to a general court-martial. Colonel McNeely agreed and word was passed to every man to preclude any reprisals. Something like this can get out of hand and it was inhumane treatment, a violation of the Geneva convention."

Eventually united with the 3d Battalion, the GIs of the 4th Division advanced to positions on the left of Ste.-Mère-Eglise. Mabry searched for the airborne commander and troopers directed him to Lt. Col. Benjamin Vandervoort, 2d Battalion, 505th Parachute Infantry. "Lieutenant Colonel Vandervoort was sitting in a wheelbarrow, obviously wounded in his leg, and an enlisted man was pushing him around. He remained in command even though injured. I asked him how secure his position was. He said fairly tenuous with the Germans massing for counterattack. I showed him where our people were. He asked us to move forward and protect his flank. He informed me where he anticipated the counterattack would come. We said we might make a limited, flanking attack, to thwart the Germans who would be surprised to find another battalion in place. He thought it a great idea.

"As luck would have it, the enemy did counterattack head-on. Realizing this, our 2d Battalion conducted a flanking attack and sweep toward the front of the airborne unit. We moved parallel, along a sunken road, worn down by travel, with hedgerows on both sides. The vision of anyone moving up and down this road was obscured. When the German counterattack came across a wide-open field we caught them and began shooting them down in the field. They came running across and reached the sunken road. German bodies were piled up in the road—a sight hard to believe. After they pulled back and we started to dig holes to button up for the night, the troops had to stack German bodies two or three deep in order to have room for a foxhole. On the following morning three Germans gave themselves up, punching GIs to take them prisoners. These live ones mixed in with the dead, feigned being dead before giving themselves up.

"As we attacked inland from the beach we would often run into groups of parachutists. Some were from the 82d and others the 101st. Some would be holed up in a corner of a hedgerow and I'd ask if any enemy were around. No, they hadn't seen any. I asked who's over on right or left; they didn't know. They were waiting, not knowing what to do. I classified those individuals as the nonfighters. Go further and you'd run into another group, walking around, sneaking about, men from a combination of the two airborne divisions. You seen any enemy about? Oh, yes, we had a firefight, killed some. They were out looking for enemy. These were the fighters and the fighters had gotten together. The nonfighters were holed up, eating K rations, waiting. This was not peculiar to airborne; it was typical for infantry, armor, Marine Corps. There is a definite category of individual who will shoot and close with the enemy. There's another group that will shoot but not close with enemy. And there's a third that will neither shoot nor close."

The bodies piled up rapidly. Much of the diary of Marion Adair, the 4th Division battalion surgeon, is a book of the dead.

"June 7: I set up an aid station in a field where two gliders have crashed and there are casualties. Meanwhile, two more gliders of the 82d crash within fifty yards of where I am, ten men are killed, and as many are wounded. After taking care of this mess, I push on up the road where there are a number of casualties including the Colonel's runner, Tom Sullivan, who has been killed. . . . The woods are full of snipers and a man next to me in the ditch gets shot.

"June 8: Jerry shells our area during midmorning and sets fire to our ammunition trucks and several vehicles. Fortunately, only several men are hurt.

I explore a nearby road and there are more than two dozen dead Germans. I also run across Lt. Vill, killed by rifle fire.

"June 9: . . . the battalion attacks about 6 p.m and E Company suffers heavy casualties, including the death of Lt. Wilder. We work far into the night, on our hands and knees under blankets, with flashlights. It's gruelling, tiresome and the boys are really in bad shape . . . This has been one of our worst days yet.

"June 11–20: We hold a defensive position west of Montebourg. We receive our first replacement. Lt. Wilson gets killed and Lt. Couch is wounded. Capt. Haley is hit. We [shifted] place in the line with the 1st Bn and then the 3rd. Capt. Watkins is wounded. . . . I write my first letters home and receive my first mail. We get better rations, a chance to drink cider, and clean up.

"We make a night attack [June 19] commencing at 3 a.m. It's rough going at first but we drive the Jerries out of a dug-in place . . . Twice we go through an artillery barrage. Lt. Col. Steiner is killed, but our casualties are not too excessive.

"June 22: I am awakened at dawn because a German patrol sneaked in the C.P. and shot and killed Lt. Marquard. Our boys kill five of the Krauts and wound the officer. They reoccupy the crossroad behind us, and cut us off. We are having casualties and I send some back in an ambulance, which is machine-gunned. I also send a jeep back, which is stopped and then permitted to go ahead after a Kraut casualty is removed. I accumulate about twenty casualties during the day which I cannot evacuate. We are shelled thrice and one actually hits the top of the aid station. Shell fragments destroy several units of plasma.

"June 23: Our battalion attacks this afternoon, and E Company sustains about 35 wounded and 15 dead."

"June 25: Chaplain Ellenberg holds a service this morning and I enjoy it. The Lord has been kind."

A day later, Adair drove to the medical clearing station for "a wash and a rest . . . the boys there slip me a shot of real whiskey. Tonight it's mighty fine to sleep under plenty of blankets on a cot above the ground." Returning to the front, Adair passed through the site of one of the earlier battles, a meadow laced with drainage ditches. "There are at least 40 or 50 dead soldiers partially buried in the muck and slime and a few dead Jerries in the rise near the swamp. This was the most depressing thing I saw in all of France."

Already at sea when the first Americans jumped into darkness over France, the 2d Infantry Division, at midnight 6–7 June, prepared to climb down the cargo nets from transports into the landing craft bobbing below. Their destination was Omaha Beach. George Duckworth, a platoon leader with Company F of the 23d Regiment remembered, "As we were standing by, the Navy crew of our transport distributed steak sandwiches as a gesture of goodwill and good luck. They realized that we could use a morale booster and it was appreciated.

"Company F descended the nets without any real trouble and settled down for the run to the beach. It seemed like an eternity before we grounded just a few yards offshore where the Navy coxswain lowered the ramp and we piled out into knee-deep water and waded ashore as quickly as we could. The distance from the water's edge to the high ground on the far side of the beach was about 200 yards and I think we covered it in record time.

"The higher ground was steeper and more rugged than anticipated, but we finally found a place where we could traverse back and forth until we reached level ground. At the top we encountered considerable confusion among some of the first assault troops, who had just cleared the beach and were behind schedule. Our designated assembly areas had not been cleared of enemy troops. We had to wait for daylight to clear the area so our units could reorganize and proceed with our attack inland.

"We moved forward very cautiously until we came across a narrow black-top road that ran parallel to the beach and gave us some bearing as to our location. At first light we moved forward through some assault units from the 29th Division that were beginning to withdraw. Evacuation of the dead and wounded was taking place as we prepared for our attack."

Duckworth and his outfit pushed ahead while snipers harassed them. Serious opposition surfaced at a roadblock but still the GIs from the 2d Division progressed until 10 June when ordered to take the high ground in the vicinity of Hill 192. "The area we had to cross was mostly open with little in the way of cover or concealment," said Duckworth. "Company F moved forward with Company E on our left. Everything went according to plan as the troops moved out to the forward slope of the valley, then without warning, all hell broke loose. F Company's position was completely blanketed by enemy artillery, mortar, and automatic-weapons fire. There was no cover or concealment and men were falling like ten pins. Our casualties were so heavy that our advance was halted. We had no artillery or mortar support to suppress the enemy fire. The deadly rain of fire continued until it was obvious that our attack was ended."

After a short discussion with his wounded company commander, Duckworth was ordered to try to outflank the enemy with his platoon. For a brief period the maneuver enabled the troops to advance under cover but when they broke into a clearing, they were spotted and subjected to intense volleys of small-arms fire. Only the fact that they had come so close to the entrenched defenders prevented an onslaught of artillery and mortars. However, Duckworth and his people remained pinned down in firefights until dark when they retreated. Astonishingly, no artillery backup for the battered battalion was available even though Duckworth advised headquarters he could guide forward observers to appropriate positions.

"Very early the next morning, the battalion received orders to mount a full-scale, all-out, bayonet charge in an effort to break through the enemy and capture Hill 192. Considering our heavy casualties on the previous day, this order was a real shocker. Especially to me because I was aware of the open terrain, the distance to the enemy's positions, and the lack of artillery and mortar support. However, the word was that the order came from 2d Division headquarters."

The operation was a murderous fiasco for the soldiers who charged with bayonets fixed. Duckworth said, "We were deluged by concentrated artillery and mortar fire together with some direct shelling from enemy armored vehicles on the high ground across the valley. This concentration of high explosives was devastating, men were falling everywhere, some killed instantly by jagged artillery and mortar fragments, while many others were wounded and screaming in pain. Before midday it was obvious that our attack had failed and we had to withdraw what was left of the company."

With all the other officers in the company either dead or wounded command passed to Duckworth. "It was not so much of a shock to find myself the only surviving officer, as was the realization of the awesome responsibilities I faced in getting the company reorganized, our wounded evacuated, the dead recovered. This while maintaining the morale and combat capability of a unit that had sustained a 50 percent loss of enlisted personnel and most of the officers in its first days of combat." Although still functioning, Duckworth himself seemed considerably worse for the wear. "I was bone-tired, dirty, and sweaty. The entire left side of my combat jacket was ripped and torn away, my canteen had been shot off my left hip, my trench knife, carried strapped to my right leg, had the handle shot off at the hilt, my carbine had a four-inch piece of razor-sharp shell fragment embedded halfway through the stock, my helmet had two deep creases on the right side with a large dent on the left and I had cuts and scratches all over my body, probably from crawling around the company area during the battle."

A few days later, with the American lines almost twenty miles inland, the 2d Infantry Division assumed a defensive stance, exchanging artillery, mortar, and tank fire with a stationary foe. Duckworth's company had dropped to fewer than 100 men when efforts to restore the outfit occurred. "First Sergeant Henry Gratzek notified me that we had fifty replacements coming in. That was good news at first, but less so when I found that they were from a deactivated antiaircraft defense unit, were only armed with .45-caliber pistols, and with no infantry training. I pulled some of my officers and NCOs out of the front line to take them back to a rear area, arm them with M1 rifles, teach them to shoot, and give them some basic infantry tactical training. They were all good soldiers and learned quickly, but time was critical and there was no room for mistakes at the front. As a company commander, it hurt me to have untrained men get killed or wounded before I even got to know them by name."

Throughout the war, the system to funnel replacements for casualties provided mostly unsatisfactory results. Rather than replace entire units with well-trained equivalents, the personnel command chose to insert individuals into line companies. [A stateside-bound cadre that would never need to depend upon recruits for their personal survival taught replacements the rudiments of combat life.] There was little incentive or urgency felt by this cadre who converted newcomers fresh from civilian life into fighting men. They often lacked the most basic instruction in tactics and weaponry. By contrast, the first divisions involved in Overlord had all schooled their foot soldiers in fire and maneuver exercises, how to make the best use of bazookas, antitank grenades, and working with the modest hedgerows of England. Most organizations tried to provide some additional training for replacements before they came under fire, and frequently paired them off with experienced GIs. That generally did not compensate for their ignorance of their tools and understanding of how to operate as a cohesive unit. The memoirs of headquarters staffs and generals in the field show little or no concern for this weakness, but the comments of junior officers, NCOs, and GIs at the front frequently refer to the inadequacies of fresh fodder.

Still harnessed to the 4th Division, the 359th Infantry, normally part of the 90th, coped with the frustrating hedgerowed fields of the Cotentin Peninsula. J. Q. Lynd, a platoon leader of Company A said of the terrain that, "deep ditches at the base of each hedgerow provided runoff [for the marshy land with high rainfall] . . . The narrow trail-like roads were usually completely overgrown with arching treetops. These formed a cavelike canopy, termed 'sunken roads.' They effectively hid the well-concealed enemy weapon emplacements from artillery forward observers and aircraft spotters. These boxed-in, solid, earthen-dike hedgerowed fields completely limited tank and armored vehicle maneuver and support fire for attacking infantry. The deep swampy bogs further prohibited heavy tank travel."

The Château de Fontenay, a 200-year-old great house surrounded by massive stone walls, protected a pivotal road junction from the invaders. On 10 June the 2d Battalion of the 22d Infantry, part of a task force directed by the 4th Division, initiated another frontal attack on the château. The violent response of the Germans killed or wounded a great many junior officers, noncoms, and enlisted men. Company L alone lost 159 men in a series of attacks.

Ordered to advance on the château as part of a relief force, Lynd said they had made good progress until, "Two flights, each with six B-26 twin-engine bombers, suddenly appeared out of the clouds from the east over Utah Beach. They made a precise banking turn heading right toward us with opened bomb bays. Our lead scout, Pfc. Ebar Manriquez, hollered, 'Bummers! Big Bums!' We scrambled into the deep drainage ditches, jumped into the mud, and then really got a pounding with their intensive bombardment. Then the German artillery at Ozeville renewed firing on us in anticipation of a close follow-up of attacking U.S. troops immediately behind the bombing. One of the big trees toppled across the moat. The large, heavy wooden door in the adjoining stone wall was blown ajar. We clambered out of the ditches, across the downed tree, and through the loose door. Two rapid-fire machine guns were burping at us from the big stone barn. We held up behind the piles of bomb debris but close enough to heave some hand grenades through the near window. Privates First Class Bill Hazuka and Louis Rossi charged through the dark barn door opening and crash-plunged headlong over a low, circular, stone apple-crushing millstone. The German soldiers fled through the rear door and escaped into the stone-wall maze of the extensive garden tract. Shortly after that, Rossi's foot and lower leg were crushed from an antipersonnel mine near the barn. Private James Lemon and Pfc. Claude Gilbreath were hit with sniper fire. Sergeant Glen Ahrendt, Pfc. Howard Meek, Pfc. Gunder Stavlo were killed. Lieutenant John Sisson's platoon was just about wiped out. Lieutenant Herb Lawson's platoon was hit pretty hard and lost most of S.Sgt. Bill Russell's squad. We attempted to find and give aid to as many of the 22d Regiment wounded as we could stumble across in the darkness.

"About midnight the burning château was an awesome flaming pyre. Two German aircraft flew in from the north and circled twice around the now-vivid, blazing buildings. We couldn't see the planes up in the dark sky but their engine noise was distinctly different from any U.S. airplanes. During each circle, the planes dropped clutches of small antipersonnel, butterfly fragmentation bombs only to the south of the burning château buildings. The German intelligence staff had surmised quite correctly that U.S. headquarters, reserve units, supply, and vehicle concentrations would be around the road junctures south of the château.

"The ingenious butterfly bombs opened precisely at release with the parachute-like shell caps winding upward on the stem as they fell. These shell caps detonated the bombs upon contact with the stem terminal tips. When dropped from a specific altitude the entire bomb clutch would begin exploding as air bursts that detonated fragments about 50 to 100 feet above the ground. These were certainly effective antipersonnel explosives . . . The casualties numbered almost 200 in wounded and killed among the rear-echelon troops."

Bob Slaughter, who had survived the terror of Omaha Beach, joined the remnants of his 116th Regiment. "Insigny was the division objective and we suspected we were between the 1st and 2d Battalion sectors. We hooked up with others who were separated and organized a leaderless, rabble force that served merely as psychological support. Any friendly rifle or machine gun was welcome. I felt extremely vulnerable and lonely during the early hours after the invasion." Disheartened and uncertain though they were, the patchwork bands of foot soldiers formed from elements of the 1st and 29th Divisions and the Rangers doggedly inched toward the designated objectives. Those innocent of combat received instant educations if they survived.

"Snipers, machine guns, and 88s interrupted movement on the road into Vierville. The column took cover and waited for an officer or noncom with the initiative to collar a few riflemen and clear the obstacle. While lying in the warm sunshine, the rabble smoked K-ration cigarettes or rested. A young rifleman accidently pulled the pin on one of the many hand grenades hanging on his belt. The explosion and shrapnel blew most of his buttocks away. He screamed in agony until an aidman gave him a shot of morphine. Word spread that heat from the sun had ignited the grenade. Many began discarding their precious grenades.

"As we entered the tiny resort village, Vierville-sur-Mer, less than a mile from the beach, sniper and burp-gun fire came from the bombed-out Norman châteaus. We were trained to make every shot count and German targets were hard to find. Smokeless powder was a tremendous advantage. Gunsmoke billowing from our weapons like cumulus clouds helped Jerry spot our positions. We fired in the direction from which rounds came but camouflage and smokeless powder made it difficult to locate the enemy. Following an exchange of fire, three or four enemy soldiers appeared waving white flags, hands over heads, yelling, *'Kamerad!'* With them appeared a young French female civilian whom we suspected of collaboration. Thinking she was one of the deadly snipers, we didn't treat her or the other prisoners gently. I doubt they made it back to the beach alive.

"After the Omaha Beach massacre, I vowed never to take a German prisoner. During the fight for the beachhead, hatred intensified." Slaughter was steadfast in this resolve until a few weeks later when he encountered a young German paratrooper. "His right trouser leg was bloody and torn, the limb almost severed by shrapnel. Remembering my vow taken back at the beach, my first reaction was to put him out of his misery. I believe he sensed what I was thinking. He said, tearfully, *'Bitte'* [please]. He was an impressive-looking soldier and I just couldn't do it. Instead, I made sure he was unarmed and then I cut away his trouser leg and applied a pressure tourniquet. I gave him a shot of morphine, a drink from my canteen, and then lit an American Lucky Strike cigarette for him. As I departed, he smiled weakly, and said in guttural English, *'Danke* very much, may *Gott* bless you. *Gute* luck.' That changed my mind. I still hated the German soldier but I couldn't kill one at close range if his hands were over his head."

Fellow Virginian, Felix Branham, as a squad leader with Company K of the 116th, also hiked through Vierville toward the German strongpoint at Grandcamp on D plus 2. "As we began the attack, we found some 2d and 5th Rangers digging in. They told us they had been stopped cold by a heavy concentration of German fire and two of their support tanks knocked out. There was a company of German infantry in an elaborate communications trench from which they directed heavy machine-gun fire. Several attempts by our company and some Rangers failed to neutralize this fire. Sergeant Frank D. Peregory stood up and began firing his rifle from his hip as he moved in the direction from whence the enemy fire came. Upon reaching the trench, he leaped in while firing his weapon, with fixed bayonet. He paused only to reload and throw hand grenades. Frank soon emerged from the trench with three German prisoners. [Peregory had killed eight of the enemy in the course of his charge.] After handing them over to someone else he leaped back into the trench. After what seemed an eternity, he again emerged from the trench, this time with thirty-two German prisoners.

"I had known Frank for twelve years. He married while we were still in the States, and once told me, 'Felix, I should have married this damned BAR, because I have had more nights with it than I have had with my wife. For his action at Grandcamp, Frank won a Medal of Honor. But six days later, near Couvains, while he attempted to capture a German machine-gun nest single-handedly, he lost his life."

In the vicinity of that village, Branham said the hard ground prevented him from digging in. "Three of us were on watch, two guys would sleep while the other stood guard. We figured if we heard incoming mail, we'd just duck down against the hedgerow. I had just seen a medic not far away and I asked him about a friend of mine from his company. He told me the guy had been killed that morning. I started to feel bad and then everything went black for about ten minutes. You never hear the shell that hits you. A German 88 had landed. My face was streaming blood; my left leg had been torn and something was protruding from my thigh, a piece of shrapnel. I looked over and the other fellow was lying on the ground, his face quiet, his leg lying up over his shoulder. The third man, sprawled on the ground, covered with blood; I could see his lungs or heart on the ground.

"The medic came up and started to patch me up. He used a morphine Syrette above my leg wound, wiped my face clear. There were small pieces of shrapnel in my ear and jaw. I told him, go help the other guys, some are worse off than I am. But he stayed with me until he stopped the bleeding, using a tourniquet above the leg wound. I was carried back to the platoon CP, then a jeep picked me and a couple of others back for a ride to the beach. As they got ready to fly me to England, Major Howie, who became the 3d Battalion CO, said to me while I was on a stretcher, "'You're going home, son.' I answered, 'I'm going back to France.' 'No,' he insisted. 'The war is over for you.' I said, 'You're nuts, sir.' He looked at me and winked."

Frank Wawrynovic, having bolted across the exposed beach "like a deer when hunters are shooting at it," lasted less than two weeks. "When any special scouting mission was necessary, with my Ranger training, I volunteered, or was 'volunteered.' After many close calls, I was beginning to feel like the legendary buck deer back home who, time after time, season after season, escapes the hunters' bullets. But I knew the deer was not eternal, nor was I.

"The morning of D plus 12, arrived and I was still alive. It was the beginning of an unordinary day. We had dug our foxholes near the safety of hedgerows at the outer edge of a large meadow. Other troops were moving forward past us. It was to be a day of rest for us. I was dirty, smelly, and very tired. I looked very ragged since my trousers had been torn to shreds. A week before, when the Germans opened up, I had dived for the ground and I had no choice but to leave part of my trousers and some skin on barbed wire that I didn't know was there. After much crawling on the ground in the days that followed, there wasn't much left to my pants.

"Things were looking better this day. Our cooks finally caught up with us and from one, I got a new pair of trousers. We got our first cooked meal since before we left England and enough water to shave and wash ourselves. As we relaxed and cleaned our weapons, I felt very lonely. Most of my friends were gone by now, either killed or wounded. I realized it was only a matter of time before I, too, would be either killed or wounded."

The following day, the members of Wawrynovic's C Company of the 115th cautiously advanced toward an unseen enemy whom they knew, sooner or later, would challenge them. "There were only two alternatives, one to be killed, the other to be wounded," says Wawrynovic. As he approached one of the ubiquitous hedgerows, a loud noise startled Wawrynovic. He dove for the shield of the earthen and shrub breastworks. A machine gun spattered the ground less than a foot away from his trembling body. A significant force of enemy troops exchanged heavy fire with the C Company GIs. In a highly vulnerable position, Wawrynovic realized his only chance of survival lay in the darkness, still many hours away.

"From one of the patches of weeds and grass in the apple orchard nearby came a loud cry, so loud even the Germans had to hear it. 'Help! I'm bleeding to death.' In the movies I would have rushed to him. But this was the real thing. I knew the slightest movement would bring a volley of German bullets. After he called out again, in a low tone only he could hear I cautioned him to wait until dark for our only chance.

"Everything was quiet for a while. Then he or someone with him panicked and got up and ran toward me. As he reached the open alley between the last row of apple trees and my hedgerow, the Germans opened fire. His limp and probably dead body fell. My cover was broken and I had to act fast. Even as his body toppled, I rose to get over the hedgerow to my right. Fast as I was, the German bullets were faster. I felt their shock and pain. Fortunately, my momentum carried me over the shoulder-high hedgerow and into a ditch beside the road. I lay motionless, face down, thinking that when the Germans saw me, they might think me dead.

"I realized I couldn't wait for darkness now, because I might get weak from loss of blood and pass out. I remembered the advice of an old-time deer hunter back home. 'If you hit a deer and he doesn't go down, don't get too anxious and start tracking him, for he will just keep moving ahead of you. Give him some time and he will lie down and get so stiff and sore that you'll be able to walk right up on him.' Not wanting to get 'stiff and sore,' I understood the danger I was in. I had to get back to my company. I had lost my helmet and rifle. My feet were useless to me. My left shoe was full of blood and blood was running out the top of it, seeping through the bullet holes on each side of my ankle. I thought my lower right leg was broken; there was a deep wound across it. I didn't think I was hurt internally by a wound on the front of my stomach. I padded it as best I could with my first-aid kit, my handkerchief, and the lower part of my shirt, pulling up my trousers and belt. I didn't realize it, but the wall of my stomach had been cut all the way through.

"I removed my pack and cartridge belt as excess weight and started a slow, long, painful crawl back through the dusty ditch. By grasping the clumps of grass with my hands or digging my fingers into the ground, I slid along, inches at a time, my progress almost imperceptible. After many hours of crawling, daylight began to fade. I was getting very weak from exhaustion and loss of blood. I reached a wounded soldier lying in the ditch. He begged me to stay but I felt I had to move on in case the Germans should counter-attack.

"When I reached a place where friendly forces were just yards away, and with no shooting for several hours, I began to feel secure and got careless. I thought I had better let my presence be known, so I called for a medic. Very shortly two arrived, the Red Cross bands on their upper arms still very visible in the fading daylight. They stopped by me and the other wounded soldier and both went back saying they'd send up litter-bearers. In a few minutes they returned, accompanied by Captain [Norval] Carter, our battalion medical officer, also identified by his Red Cross armbands. He said it was too dangerous to bring in litter bearers. They checked my wounds and went to the other soldier. I had my head turned, watching them, when from the woods across the road came a long burst from an automatic weapon and all three medics fell to the ground. The Germans had killed all three who were protected under the international law of war. These men answered my call for help and died on account of me. To them I owe a debt I can never repay.

"I was so weak, I knew I couldn't last much longer. But with possible help so close, I could not give up. I pulled myself up to where I was just across the hedgerow from GI voices. I saw a hole through the bottom of the hedgerow, quietly called out, and they pulled me through. It was dark now and I continued to move back, inches at a time. Finally, some unfamiliar American faces came up. As they gathered around me, I felt they were going to help me and I lost consciousness. When I awakened next, I was riding in an ambulance and it was morning."

In a tent field hospital, medical personnel dressed Wawrynovic's wounds and then dispatched him by plane to England. He would spend the next nineteen months in military hospitals and endure a series of operations until his discharge with a permanent disability.

A few days before he attempted to treat Wawrynovic, Norval Carter had written his wife Fernie, "I ache for home and you and the boys—the present circumstances make the ache even more acute. Life is now very precious and dear and home is what life means to me.

"The morale of the men in my battalion is high even though the losses of officers & men have been heavy. We are very tired physically and mentally. Sleep is a rare elixir. Hot meals are non-existent. A bed is a memory. I haven't had my shoes off my feet but once in 10 days. We have been under heavy fire but are giving more than we receive—in other words, we are winning."

On 16 June he wrote his parents, "We have had a few terrible experiences in this battalion and quite a few of us are shaken up. I have never been so nervous and frightened in my life, yet we are able to push on. Some of my aidmen have been killed or wounded & my section sergeant & I were blown off a road by a near-hit from a mortar. Since then I have had bullets all around me but my luck is good. My men have shown admirable courage & heroism in removing wounded under fire."

His final letter to his wife reported, "Today we are resting in an orchard & things are fairly quiet but snipers are 100 yards south of us & I have treated 6 gunshot wounds this morning. . . . Excuse this writing 'cause I am in a foxhole with the litter on a water-can. I have collected a few souvenirs so far from the German dead. They are really well equipped. Their dead outnumber ours. But it is a very sad and distressing thing to see (& smell) so many mangled men. It seems to be so useless for nations to do such things to each other." The following day a bullet snuffed out the battalion surgeon's life.

Side by side with the hard-hit members of the 29th, were foot soldiers of the 1st Division. Lawrence Zeickler described his first week in France as "just defensive, trying to teach replacements how to handle their weapons, the mortars and machine guns. Other companies moved up while we got ourselves organized and up to strength again."

John Bistrica, with C Company of the Big Red One's 16th Regiment, had awakened on D plus 1 to find, only yards away, enemy soldiers who surrendered quickly. "As we marched on, the French came out with wine, cognac, brandy, milk. We emptied our canteens and put in whatever they gave us. We were hugged and kissed as we went through the small villages. Mostly, we fought snipers; they did not bring up tanks. The mortars and machine guns from the German 352d Division, whom we were not informed about, were bad. The hedgerows became bigger and thicker and we encountered more and more resistance. Finally, we stopped at Caumont and held. We dug holes in the sides of the hedgerows that were large enough for four men. We patrolled and swapped with the other platoon.

Tom McCann, as a member of an I&R platoon with the 18th Infantry Regiment, also halted at Caumont. "The division had penetrated farther inland than any other one and we stayed in the Caumont area for a week or more while surrounded on three sides by the enemy. In this static position we ran patrols both day and night into the enemy lines. You would be on one side of the hedgerow and the Germans on the other, going in an opposite direction. We had observation posts in houses, churches, on the edges of clearings, any place where we could see what the enemy was doing. A static position like the one in Caumont was hard on the soldiers. It's much better to be on the move. We lost one fellow to a nervous breakdown.

"Because the weather played havoc with shipping in the Channel and destroyed the artificial port, we were short of supplies. We supplemented our C rations by fishing, catching eels, and frying them. I wrote home for some fish hooks and a friend wrote back and asked what I wanted them for when I was supposed to be fighting a war. The hooks came after we had left the area."

Bob Meyer, with the 22d Infantry, swung to the north as the post–D day offensive strove to roll up enemy forces toward the tip of the peninsula. Of particular importance now was the port of Cherbourg. The mid-June gale had destroyed the artificial harbor that had been towed to Omaha Beach and severely handicapped shipments of supplies and replacement troops.

"The Germans sent a bicycle battalion to hinder our advance. However, their G-2 [intelligence section] apparently had no idea where we were. In their ignorance they were moving along in a column with no caution and they ran right into an ambush. Four tanks lay in wait. As the bicycle troops pedaled into this area, two tanks in the roadway, and one on each side in a ditch beside the hedgerows, moved against them, firing all forward machine guns as well as their 75mm cannons. It was a complete slaughter. They were gunned down and then ground up beneath the tank treads. We had all seen dead before but none of us had seen what tanks were capable of. We felt sick as we walked through that carnage. It was hard not to feel sorry for them, even if they were German SS troops."

As the "Double Deuce" trudged forward, Meyer's closest friend fell victim to a malfunction of his own weapon that put a bullet through his ankle. "After he left it was more difficult for me. We'd done everything together and now he wasn't there. My motivation was very dependant upon esprit de corps. As our numbers dwindled, that feeling faded and each casualty was a personal loss. I had mixed emotions. He was gone but I also felt a sense of relief. I knew where he was and his wound was not life threatening. Had he been killed, I would have probably gone completely mad before I did."

Subsequently, a German machine gun had ripped away his pants leg before he turned his BAR on the nest. Then he survived a thrust by seven German Tiger tanks, constant shelling by the enemy, and friendly fire. Combat fatigue infected Meyer. "The 8th Regiment moved up and we were relieved. When we started the attack, we had 185 men in our company and when we were relieved, we took 27 men off the line. When we got to the rear, it was dark and some guides led us to foxholes that were already dug. Two of us were taken to an elongated one that would accommodate both of us.

"Everything seemed great but just as we were thinking all was serene, we were almost blasted out of our hole. We were located right under the muzzle of one of our artillery pieces. They fired missions all night, and by morning, I was a crying, babbling idiot. But before they sent me to a hospital, they wanted to know if I could give some instructions to the boy who was to replace me. I tried to tell him about the care and operation of the weapon, but about all I did was show him how to take it apart. Later, I thought about that poor boy. Not only did he have to witness my breakdown, but there was so much more I should have told him about the field tactics of fire and movement, which is what keeps a BAR team alive.

"At the hospital, the first thing I had to do was take off my clothes. I had changed socks and gotten a new pair of pants when the leg of my old ones had been shot off but otherwise they were the same ones I had worn since June 6. The smell was terrible. After a shower they weighed me. I was down to 105 pounds; I had been 165 when we made the invasion. The treatment then for combat fatigue was a drug-induced, deep sleep for seventy-two hours. They were supposed to administer twelve grains in the morning and twelve in the evening to keep the patient in a deep sleep. But someone misread the instructions and they also gave us another twelve grains at noon. When the seventy-two hours ended, we didn't wake up the way we were supposed to. The idea of total rest was supposed to restore your outlook as well as your body. While it went a long way toward the recovery of the fatigued body, the psychological problems remained. I had still lost all my friends; I had still experienced all that blood and gore; I had still been blasted by artillery, theirs and ours.

"I was only slightly improved but according to theory well enough to be sent back to my outfit. I vaguely remember being brought to the company kitchen to wait until I could go up front. The kitchen was well behind the lines and they gave me a hole that was more like a den. It had a cover and I recall huddling in there for what may have been several days. A plane came over real low one day and I don't remember whether it fired or not but I slipped into total oblivion. I have no idea of how long I was away from the kitchen group but I was wandering around in the roadway when a jeep driven by a guy from my company came by. He took me back to a hospital that was an 'exhaustion center.' They ran me through the sleep therapy again but they were beginning to suspect there was much more to it than originally suspected. I and many others were sent out to provisional companies where it was thought work would restore our sense of well-being better than drugs. We did have resort to sodium amatol, and they sort of left it to the individual to decide when things were catching up to him and he needed the drug. I took it only a couple of times, just to sleep through the night." The labor theory of therapy failed to cure what ailed Meyer. He passed through a series of hospitals before shipment back to the States. The Army discharged Meyer in March 1945 with a 50 percent disability pension.

Taken prisoner late in the afternoon of D day, Jim Irvin, the CO of B Company in the 505th, remained at the German held hospital in Valognes for four days. Meanwhile, other captured GIs were marched farther behind the enemy lines. "Some were killed while on the roads by American aircraft," says Irvin. "I was moved by night. There were twenty-eight officers on a bus taking us to Germany. Some were from other divisions and regiments. Three from the 505th, Bob Keeler, B. Hendrickson, and I escaped. We were the only ones who did; the others spent the rest of their time in Europe as prisoners of war. The three of us were fortunate in that a French family, M. and Mme. Frenais, supplied us with clothing and papers. Together, we started across to Brittany. The French would stop and watch as we went through small towns but the Germans paid no attention to us. On July 1, we separated and on July 4th I met a young boy, Henri Brandilly, who took me to his grandparents' home. I stayed as a family member on their farm until the Brittany peninsula was cut off. On August 15 I returned to England and B Company. My exec officer had taken the company through Normandy, where approximately 70 percent were KIA, wounded, or captured before returning to the base camp in Great Britain."

Bernard McKearney and others from his unit advanced into the countryside. "A more colorful caravan never traveled the rocky roads of Normandy. The men looked more like Gypsies than twentieth-century soldiers. With faces still blackened, heads wrapped pirate-fashion with pieces of camouflaged chutes, and roses behind their ears, they must have seemed very strange to the French. We had horses and carts from the artillery outfit we had captured. Loading up wagons with rations, and mounting our nags, we started out. About twenty men had horses; the rest rode in wagons. I myself had a huge bay. Being a subway kid, I had trouble handling him, but it was much easier than walking.

"The night passed uneventfully but then occurred something that could only happen on a battlefield. Across the road from us was a field hospital and I could see wounded lying on the ground. Major John Hanlon, our battalion exec, who knew both of us, told me my brother Jim was there among the wounded. I was granted permission to go and see him. But before I could leave, word came for the battalion to move. We were to go through Carentan and take positions west of town. Rumor had it that a liaison plane had flown down the main street without a shot being fired. The men were laughing and shouting. This was to be a setup."

To the east of the troopers and glidermen of the 82d, the members of the 101st Airborne indeed drove on the important hub of Carentan. With the beachhead established and reinforcements flooding ashore, the initial defensive posture against a German counterattack shifted over to an offensive. Capture of the Carentan causeway, a long stretch of elevated road that bridged rivers, canals, and a soggy marsh in four places leading into Carentan, would unlock a gate through Normandy and into the heart of France.

The 502d Regiment, "the Deuce," numbering Bernard McKearney, John Hanlon, and Wallace Swanson in its ranks, drew the dubious honor of winning the causeway. The rumor that buoyed the hearts of McKearney and his fellow troopers was pitifully false. Instead of limited resistance they confronted elements of the crack German 6th Parachute Regiment plus pieces of an infantry outfit. The defenders occupied tactically strong positions under the command of a highly skilled German paratroop commander, Col. Friedrich von der Heydte.

McKearney's fantasy cracked and then shattered. "In a long column, with our battalion at the rear, we hit the road. We were strafed and bombed by German aircraft. Our ack-ack downed three of them, one falling end-over-end like a flaming leaf. However, one bomb landed smack on the road, costing I Company a lot of men. We moved slowly during the night. Shots could be heard up front. No one worried especially. Hadn't a plane flown down the main street? Didn't you hear the guy say there was no one in town?

We're going to just hold them from the flank. Some other outfit's going from the rear.

"The stories passed up and down the column. Carentan is already ours. We were actually moving toward the beach. Then the word came, 'Dig in.' You could hear it increasing in volume as it passed back. 'Dig in, dig in,' and as it went on by us, it became softer and softer. Then the clink of entrenching tools, not a word while everyone was busy digging. Then another command, 'Moving out.' Muffled curses. 'Why don't they make up their minds?' 'If this is war, I'm turning them war bonds in.' Then the shuffling of feet and we trudged on.

"We had advanced about a half mile when, Whoosh! an 88 was shelling the road. Everyone bit the dirt. To others, dirt's dirt, but to the footslogger, dirt is home, sweet home. The firing up front increased. You could hear the growl of our machine guns, then the snap of Jerry's machine pistol. The rate of fire is so fast it sounds as if someone is ripping heavy canvas. You could pick out two of our guns and three of the Jerries'. They would answer one another back. Then you could almost hear ours talking the Jerries' down. The firing ceased. Back came the word, 'On your feet, moving out.'

"The column had no sooner started up when mortar shells began dropping around us. The firing up front had become a storm of sound. God help the 3d Battalion, I thought. Now the wounded straggled back. At first, just a trickle, but then in groups. Wounded men somehow cling together. By now we were moving from slit trench to slit trench. These had been dug every few yards by the troopers up ahead. We passed through St. Côme-du-Monte; a cluster of rubble that had once been a village. This was a regimental aid station. I heard someone call my name. It was a lad who had fought on the regimental boxing team that I had managed. I asked him how he was feeling. He said, 'Okay, doesn't seem to hurt much.' After he was evacuated the doctor shook his head and said he hadn't a chance. His middle was all shot up. Ordinary boys do extraordinary things in the most ordinary manner. The wounded don't cry. They seem a little dazed. Many have a surprised, hurt look in their eyes, but they don't cry.

"Just as we cleared the town we came to the first of the four bridges guarding the causeway to Carentan. The Germans had blown the first one. Mortars, 88s, and machine guns were zeroed in on all four crossings. The 3d Battalion had repaired the blown bridge to some extent. The bridges had to be crossed, and the only way was to jump up and run like hell to the other side. One at a time we went over. I timed the man ahead of me. It took him seven seconds. Why I did this, I don't know, but you do funny things in combat.

"Then my turn came. I sprang up and started tearing across when from the other side came a wounded trooper. He had been shot through the neck.

In a dazed condition, he just stood up and started to walk back. He was still walking when we passed one another on the bridge. I yelled at him: 'For God's sake, get off this bridge!' He just looked at me with a crooked smile and walked on. The People upstairs must have been looking out for that boy that day." The Fates also gazed benignly upon McKearney who not only made it across all four bridges without a scratch but also endured the entire war without ever qualifying for a Purple Heart.

Actually, the battle for the causeway and Carentan continued from 8 June through 12 June before the combined efforts of the 101st Airborne's three regiments and heavy support from artillery units finally routed the defenders. John Hanlon, with the 2d Battalion of the 502d described the engagement as "the most devastating battle I saw. The turning point came when Col. Robert Cole, CO of the 3d Battalion, led a bayonet charge. Because of the noise and confusion, not everyone got the word. And when Cole blew his whistle and started to run while firing, as the signal to begin the assault, only a handful of troopers followed him at first. Cole was awarded a Medal of Honor for what he did at Carentan."

33
Superforts and the Marianas

Those engaged in the Pacific, while applauding the successes in Italy and Normandy, undoubtedly felt that they were denied resources vital to continuing the march toward Japan. And they were correct in this assumption; neither Churchill nor Roosevelt and their closest advisors saw any reason to shift priorities. MacArthur had continued to leap toward the Philippines in the Southwest Pacific. Navy brass, particularly Ernest J. King, thought in terms of the Central Pacific, the turf ceded to them when the Pacific was split between MacArthur and Nimitz.

The B-17s and B-24s protected by the P-51s flew the longest distances required for strategic bombing in Europe. Development of the B-29, the supersize edition of the B-17 Flying Fortress, able to travel 1,500 miles, dump a massive load of explosives, and then return an equal distance to a home base, offered a weapon geared to the war against Japan. Richard Carmichael, who had been in a B-17 approaching Pearl Harbor at the time of the Japanese attack and later led the 19th Bomb Group during raids upon the Japanese, had returned to the States to fly a B-29. "We all liked it. It was an easy, honest airplane to fly. It didn't spin out, or do anything you didn't expect. It was just like the old B-17. Both airplanes would get you home under really bad conditions." However, in its first inception, the B-29 engines had a tendency to overheat and catch fire. Carmichael noted, "The engine problem got progressively worse after we got to India because of the heat, humidity, and the dust. When we got to China we had different conditions and we had to fly over the Hump [the Himalaya Mountains]. To get over the Hump was touchy; only one out of five airplanes had radar."

Nevertheless, in the spring of 1944, the first Superforts took up stations in India to fly missions against the Japanese homeland, with a stop in China to refuel. The conditions were daunting. Every gallon needed to refuel the B-29s in China was flown over the Hump. The enormous amount of gasoline burned by the huge planes required a full load of fifty-five gallon drums loaded on six C-46s or C-47s ferried over the Hump from India. All of the bombs dumped upon Japan also traveled by air over the same perilous route.

Carmichael was on his fifth B-29 mission and over Japan when, he fell below the assigned altitude of 25,000 feet. "We were hit on the run-in from the

Initial Point to the target, which wounded my central fire-control officer, Chester Tims. It may have started a little fire or something in the back end. There was a little confusion in the cockpit, trying to find out or help do something about what had happened. Instead of turning left, as I should have, out from Yawatahama over the sea, because it looked like there was more flak and more fighters that way, I elected to turn right, and I kicked my butt all the way through prison camp for making that decision. I was picked up immediately by a Betty, a Japanese twin-engine bomber, above me about 2,000 feet. Nobody saw this plane up above us. We didn't expect to be attacked by bombs. Finally Ed Perry, the navigator, hit me on the leg and pointed up there. When I looked, the bombs were falling from the Betty. All I could do was try to make a steep turn. I always said I missed them all but one. That got us in midship and started a fire in the bomb bay.

"Ed Perry grabbed a fire extinguisher, squeezed himself around the four-gun upper turret that extended vertically all the way down through the fuselage only to find the device empty." Nor could Carmichael get rid of his bomb bay fuel tanks. "I pulled every lever supposed to release those tanks and they wouldn't go. It may have had to do with the temperatures, dust, and all the crap accumulated in India and China. Something could have gone wrong with the electrical and manual release systems. But we couldn't put the fire out and couldn't get rid of the tanks."

Carmichael flew out to sea toward Iki Island while his radio operator tried to contact a submarine stationed offshore for emergency rescues. "We were getting lower and lower and faster and faster and hotter and hotter and burning more and more. We started bailing the crew out a little before we got to the island, because the first three people out of the rear end hit in the water. We lost Chester Tims because he was wounded and he hit in the water; we figured he must have drowned. The copilot hit by gunfire in the water. He was lost, not because he drowned, but because Japanese fighters came around and shot him. They attacked everybody they could in a parachute. The radio operator also was lost. Just as I jumped out, the airplane broke apart and hit the island in two pieces. I landed in a field. The first person I saw was a little Japanese soldier coming toward me. I had a pistol and he had a rifle. Behind him I saw a whole bunch of angry farmers coming with long sticks. I knew I wasn't going to put up any resistance. I let that little soldier, who couldn't have been over sixteen or seventeen—but he had a rifle—come up and gave him my pistol." Several farmers managed to rap Carmichael with staves but the soldier drove them off and along with the seven other survivors of his B-29, Carmichael became a POW.

The difficulties of the arduous haul from India via China to Japan convinced the Air Corps that the conquest of the Marianas Islands, particularly the four largest of the fifteen volcanic atolls—Saipan, Tinian, Rota, and

Guam the former U.S. possession, would bring Japan to within 1,200 miles, a more effective range. Saipan already hosted a new airfield and the Japanese had constructed three more on Tinian. Overall, Adm. Raymond Spruance bossed the operations in the Marianas. Crusty Adm. Richmond Kelly Turner commanded the forces designated for Saipan. The 2d and 4th Marine Divisions composed the basic ground forces for that mission, with the Army's 27th Infantry Division in reserve. The equally irascible Gen. Holland M. Smith of the Marines directed the show once it moved ashore at Saipan

The brutal battles of Guadalcanal, Tarawa, and other sites led the Marines to reorganize their forces. In place of the usual twelve-man squad still employed by the army, the Marines added a leader to a trio of four-man fire teams. Each of these toted a BAR plus three rifles. Extra mortars replaced the less fearsome pack howitzers, adding greater closequarters firepower. From a modest two-dozen flamethrowers, the leatherneck divisions now operated 243 portable ones, and additional 24 longer-range ones on light tanks. Fire as a weapon dated back to British experiments in 1915. During the Italian campaign in World War II, both the British and Canadian forces employed portable, mechanical flame throwers. American experts in ordnance and armor disparaged placement of a fire cannon on a vehicle. After viewing a demonstration of the British Crocodile tank, which mounted a flamethrower in the place of the bow machine gun, Patton had sneered at the result as a "piddle." In Europe, the leading proponents of armor thought in terms of tank-versus-tank warfare rather than assaults upon deeply imbedded bunkers.

While Crocodiles accompanied British troops to Normandy on D day, June 6, 1944, U.S. soldiers in the invasion of France relied on the individually manned system, a canister of napalm on the back of a soldier who carried a spray hose and ignited the fluid. GIs disliked the weapon, both for its cumbersome weight and ability to attract enemy fire. As early as Guadalcanal, Marines, however, enthusiastically adopted the flamethrower, even though the first versions often failed to produce the requisite conflagration. Negative comment arose from those who labeled the weapon as excessively cruel, while advocates ingenuously promoted the flamethrower as humane since, they argued, it killed instantly. The horrendous loss of Americans at Tarawa and Iwo squelched complaints and Marines continued to employ the devices.

For months, Adm. Marc Mitscher's Task Force 58, composed of fifteen fast carriers and seven new battleships, along with land-based Air Corps bombers, had hammered the Marianas and surrounding areas where Japanese air power might attack invaders. Only a week after D day in Normandy, American battleships stood offshore from Saipan and commenced an impressive bombardment in terms of tonnage. But fear of minefields and shore batteries kept the dreadnoughts at least six miles from the shoreline. Sixteen-inch shells blasted the island but the gunners received poor advice on targets. The explosions rocked the prominent structures but the low-lying, deadly pillboxes escaped the notice of the spotters and the fury of the guns.

Although the roughly 32,000 Japanese soldiers on Saipan doubled the count by U.S. intelligence, aggressive air and submarine raids destroyed ships bearing materials and heavy weapons essential to erect the most devastating defenses. At the same time, because of the problems encountered earlier, the Marines relied much more heavily upon amtracs, some of which carried artillery pieces. As these swam through the sea they added their 75mm cannons to the chorus from the warships and planes. These water-bugs eliminated the highly vulnerable problem of wading ashore and deposited 8,000 troops on the beach within the first twenty minutes. But not even the steel skins of the amphibians could stop the fierce volleys of shells and small arms from the defenders, who inflicted heavy casualties. By midday, the 6th Marine Regiment, having penetrated only 400 yards, counted 35 percent of its men dead or wounded. When night fell, 20,000 Americans occupied a beachhead no more than 1,000 yards deep. Fortunately, those who were dug in so close to the water were backed by tanks, artillery, and the naval gunfire that erased light-skinned Japanese tanks leading night counterattacks.

While the Nipponese military had fought fiercely wherever they came under attack, the Marianas were a special case even for them. By a stroke of luck, Japanese intelligence knew of the B-29. During a test flight over the Solomon Islands in 1943, a Superfort was shot down. Interrogation of the pilot revealed enough information for the Japanese to realize the capabilities of the airplane. A message from the emperor informed those on the island, "Although the frontline officers and troops are fighting splendidly, if Saipan is lost, air raids on Tokyo will take place often; therefore you will hold Saipan." Thus, fully cognizant of the strategic importance of the Marianas, the Japanese dispatched a fleet of battleships and cruisers to knock out the American armada. Alerted to the threat bearing down on his responsibilities, Spruance asked his deputies if it would be possible to withdraw the transports and cargo ships from harm's way. Turner, remembering how the departure of vessels from Guadalcanal left those on the island desperately short of ammunition and supplies, answered no. Spruance decided to intercept the enemy with Mitscher's Task Force and its fifteen carriers. Valuable intelligence on the approach of the flotilla came from American submarines like the the *Seahorse*, skippered by Lt. Comdr. Slade Cutter, and the *Flying Fish* under Lt. Comdr. Robert Risser while they prowled the Surigao Strait and San Bernardino Strait near the Philippines.

For their part, the Japanese mustered nine flattops with 222 fighters and 200 dive or torpedo bombers. Opposing this were the nearly 500 Hellcats and more than 400 dive and torpedo bombers available to the Americans. Adm. Ozawa Jisaburu's aircraft, because they dispensed with such items as self-sealing fuel tanks and armor to shield the pilots, possessed greater range. Furthermore, the Japanese believed their aerial operations would be enhanced with land-based planes from Guam and Rota. A shortage of experienced and well-trained pilots, however, seriously handicapped the Imperial Navy. The high command in Tokyo had not envisioned a protracted war and the schooling of flight crews lagged far behind American efforts.

Both sides prowled the skies seeking to locate the foe, and Ozawa's searchers picked up the American task force position first. That information paid no dividends. The U.S. system that combined radar with fighter-direction teams, aided by the unintended help from a Japanese scout hovering over the area, dispatched Hellcats in a well-coordinated strike that knocked down as many as two dozen enemy planes with only a single American loss. The surviving marauders met a murderous hail of antiaircraft fire when they came within range of the battleships. Another twelve planes were splashed with only minor damage to one heavyweight.

A second wave of more than 125 planes incurred very heavy losses from American fighters and scored no hits. Similar defeats met two more attacks and, of the 373 aircraft launched by the Japanese, fewer than 100 returned safely to their carriers. With a ratio of almost ten to one favoring the Americans, the encounters became known as "the Great Marianas Turkey Shoot."

Adding to the deadly score, two U.S. subs, the *Albacore* and the *Cavalla* torpedoed a pair of carriers, including the largest one in the Imperial Navy.

For all of this success, Mitscher's task force still had not made direct contact with the enemy fleet. But late in the afternoon of 20 June, reconnaissance from the *Enterprise* located Ozawa's flotilla. 280 miles away. That was the extreme range for the carrier-based attackers. On their return, the Americans would be required to land at night, a speciality at which they had little or no training. But delay of another day would probably prevent any strike at Ozawa, and Mitscher ordered his planes in the air. The operation destroyed two tankers and a carrier, damaged two more carriers, and a battleship. Down almost to the fumes in the tanks, the flyers returned to their flattops illuminated on Mitscher's orders, even though that could have made them easy meat had any enemy submarines been nearby. While twenty planes went down because of enemy action, another 80 crashed or ditched trying to reach their homes. Intensive search-and-rescue efforts reduced the total of missing air crews to forty-nine.

On Saipan itself, however, the Japanese continued to fight far more effectively. American casualties hovered above 10 percent, an intolerable rate to sustain for any period of time. The inability to gain headway and the maneuvers of the Japanese warships convinced the command to delay the scheduled 18 June landing on neighboring Guam. On 17 June at 3:30 A.M. a counterattack spearheaded by forty-four tanks smashed into the leathernecks of the 2d Marine Division. The Americans, with no armor to speak of, unable in the darkness to summon help from the sea or air, fought as foot soldiers, using bazookas, grenades, and other weapons. In spite of the superior strength of the enemy, the Americans vanquished them, knocking out almost three-quarters of the tanks and killing more than 300 soldiers in a four-hour battle.

In his memoirs, Holland Smith wrote, "Although they resisted from caves and hideouts in the ridges, and tried to harass us at night from bypassed pockets, we dug them out and smoked them out in hand-to-hand combat. With flamethrowers and hand grenades, the Marines ferreted the Japanese out of their holes and killed them. Patrols covered the terrain yard by yard, combing thick vegetation and rocky fastnesses for snipers. It was war such as nobody had fought before; [an obvious overstatement considering Guadalcanal, New Guinea, and Tarawa] a subterranean campaign in which men climbed, crawled, clubbed, shot, burned, and bayonetted each other to death."

Doggedly the Marines thrust toward the major objective, Aslito Airfield. Howlin' Mad Smith threw in his reserves; the 27th Infantry Division with its 165th Regiment first to face the defenders. The insertion of these reinforcements set the stage for further friction between the two branches of the armed forces. Marine doubts about the 27th initially arose during the invasion of Makin Island. In the capture of that island, the division operated under Rear Admiral Turner, called by naval historian Morison a "man of steel", whose command included the amphibious corps led by Marine general Smith. The 27th's CG was Maj. Gen. Ralph Smith. The joint operation of Marines and the 27th at Enewetak again generated negative comments from Morison. He chastised the soldiers. "Too long they were held up by groups of defenders not one-tenth their strength. The men were all right but their training and leadership alike was poor." Under the circumstances, the assignment of the 27th to join the Marines under Howling Mad Smith in the assault upon Saipan seems a dubious choice.

Charles Hallden, with a career in banking and finance, had spent ten years in the New York National Guard and had gone on active duty with the now federalized 27th Division. At Saipan, Hallden held the post of CO of Company L, 106th Regiment. "The first mistake was aboard ship as we sailed toward the Marianas," says Hallden, "for the invasion of Guam. We had maps, photos, landing area, objectives, and general information about roads, buildings, harbor installations, natives, on Guam. All of these were intensely studied. After about a week at sea, plans suddenly changed. We would now participate in the Saipan operation as reserve for the 2d and 4th Marine Divisions there. When we sailed on June 1, there were nineteen alternate plans for possible employment of the 27th. On June 9, they added three more."

With the Japanese artillery, mortar, small arms, and nightime counter-attacks pinning down the two Marine divisions well short of their objectives.the 27th no longer could be kept in floating reserve. One day after the Marines set foot on Saipan, the Army troops arrived. "All previous twenty-two plans," says Hallden, "were now discarded."

The defenders retreated slowly, and after a week of bitter fighting a line of Americans stretched across the island. The two Marine organizations took the flanks while the Army occupied the area between them. This area would become known to the 27th as "Death Valley" with adjoining terrain dubbed "Hell's Pocket" and "Purple Heart Ridge." That set the stage for the great Saipan dispute. "To me," wrote Charles Hallden, "it was a mistake to have a divisional boundary or dividing line along the top, on the eastern edge of Mount Tapotchau. In my opinion, the 27th should have had control of the top of the mountain so it could flush out an enemy in the caves overlooking Death Valley. The Marines made no attempt to clean out these caves and the Army was afraid to fire into the mountain or caves which technically were in the 2d Marine Division zone.

"A third mistake was that the Army could never make contact with the 2d Marine Division on its left even after the regiment sent out an entire company to contact them." As the CO of Company L, Hallden, with only 133 soldiers, relieved two Marine units that included 185 leathernecks. Hallden was disconcerted to find the positions occupied by his predecessors did not square with the locations on maps. He later concluded, "Marine officers never report problems or losses of ground when pulling back, and several I met didn't understand the lines on their maps or were poor map readers. Seldom did they report critical information to higher authority."

In the period of three days, 22–24 June Hallden and the rest of the 3d Battalion of the 106th Regiment suffered about 100 casualties as the enemy hit them with small arms, mortars, artillery and tanks. "During the entire day of action, June 24," noted Hallden, "Maj. Gen. Ralph C. Smith [division CO] was at the front-line keeping in touch with every phase of the critical situation. With his front line riflemen and small-unit commanders, he studied and tried to solve the terrain puzzle in the area. It became evident that to push forward in a frontal attack, without cleaning the Japs off the cliff side that infiladed the valley, would mean a heavy cost in lives."

Efforts to break through wrought fearsome costs. Hallden reported, "The L company attempt to seize Hill King [designated objective] had not stopped. It had simply melted away. The commanding officer [himself] soon found himself all alone with none of his assault platoon left." When he finally dodged from cover to cover and safety, he discovered the first and third platoons each numbered only twelve able bodied men, nominally the number for a rifle squad.

Perhaps the worst of the Saipan experience was the fate of a five-man patrol from Hallden's outfit. "I was requested to send them out through the front lines, with the mission to capture a prisoner for interrogation. They failed to return. Several days after the fierce attack in the vicinity of Death Valley, our men came across the five-man patrol, legs bound with wire, hands behind their backs tied to bend them over, with a bullet hole in the backs of their heads. This was a shock and the troops soon turned angry. They said, 'We'll never take another live prisoner.' I myself was very angry and disturbed by what happened. Prior to this incident we had turned over to battalion intelligence prisoners who surrendered. Word of our take-no-prisoners stance filtered through battalion and the upper echelons of command. An officer from division visited us, stating we were to adhere to the voluntary surrender code. But to put it bluntly, the experience demonized the enemy."

The Marine counterargument to the criticisms of Hallden complained that a late start by the two Army regiments and subsequent inability to advance as part of a straight American line left the Marines on either side vulnerable to flank attacks. Holland Smith chastised the 27th for not moving swiftly enough and its leader Ralph Smith agreed that his outfit had to accelerate its pace. But when the GIs could not achieve the desired results, Holland Smith, commander of the ground forces on Saipan, became choleric over the inability of the 27th Division's pace through Death Valley to keep up with the Marine progress on either side.

Although Holland Smith later professed he considered Gen. Ralph Smith "a likable and professionally knowledgeable man," he advised his superiors, Admirals Raymond Spruance and Richmond Kelly Turner. "Ralph Smith has shown that he lacks aggressive spirit, and his division is slowing down our advance. He should be relieved." The Navy brass concurred and the 27th received a new commander. Dismissal of an Army general by a Marine could be expected to breed rancor among the ordinary GIs as well as the highest circles of the Army.

Nobuo Kishiue, a Nisei member of the 27th Division, explained the dismissal of Ralph Smith, "The Marine General Smith, known as 'Mad Dog Smith' wanted glory. He wanted to finish the campaign in a few days in order to turn the fleet loose. It was said—I did not hear it directly, but from other sources—that he ordered the Marines to advance into enemy fire as they were 'expendable.' Army general Smith wanted more naval and artillery bombardment to soften up the front lines. Saipan was cut off from reinforcements and twenty-four hours did not make a difference in the outcome. The Army general thought about his troops and because of this, every one of them would have, as they say, 'gone to hell and back with him.' Which is why the Marines had more casualties in all conflicts. I don't care who he is, if a person tells me to cross a field when it is zeroed in, I would tell him to lead the way and I'd follow." The "Marines are expendable" quote may not be factual but Kishiue's sentiments mirror those of many.

Much of the unfavorable comment on the 27th Division stemmed from basic differences in the approaches taken by the Marines and the Army. Morison critiqued, "The Marines consider that an objective should be overrun as quickly as possible; they follow up their assault troops with mop-up squads which take care of any individuals or strong points that have been bypassed or overlooked. Marines dig in at night and attempt never to fire unnecessarily, because night shooting seldom hits anyone but a friend and serves mainly to give one's position away. They allow the enemy to infiltrate—keeping good watch to prevent his accomplishing anything—and when daylight comes, liquidate the infiltrators. Such tactics require good fire discipline of seasoned troops who have plenty of élan but keep their nerves under control. The Army, in World War II, preferred to take an objective slowly and methodically, using mechanized equipment and artillery barrages to the fullest extent, and advancing only after everything visible in front had been pounded down. Army tactics required enemy infiltrators to be shot on sight."

This is, of course, a view from an expert whose main sources and affinities lay with the Navy and Marines and who had the luxury of a military life well removed from foxholes on the front lines. Throughout the way the debate raged over whether one should operate on a "damn the torpedoes, full-speed ahead"—the doctrine accepted by Marine officers Martin "Stormy" Sexton, a graduate of the 3d Marine Raider Battalion on Bougainville, who warned about being "too careful," said, "An offensive can only be successful it it is conducted in an aggressive, unrelenting mode. In many situations such an attack results in saving lives." There were Army leaders, particularly in the armored forces, like Gen. George Patton, who enthusiastically endorsed speedy advance as a means of minimizing overall casualties, while accepting initially higher ones. Other strategists insisted haste wasted men and pointed to the low losses absorbed by men under Douglas MacArthur's more deliberate campaigns. The body count issue becomes further confused by the nature of the missions assigned to Marines and Army troops—small coral atolls like Iwo Jima and Tarawa presented problems different from the Philippines or Okinawa.

The shift in command of the 27th Division notwithstanding, the battle for Saipan dragged on. Three weeks after the opening rounds, some three thousand of the enemy struck at the 105th Regiment of the 27th in what is believed to be the biggest banzai charge on record. (The word means ten thousand years, a proclamation by the warrior of willingness to enter eternal life in the service of the emperor.) The soldiers, bearing only small arms, bayonets, and grenades, attacked with such ferocity they burst through the American lines. Behind the shattered lines of the GIs, leatherneck artillerymen, used small arms and blasted at very short range with their 105 mm howitzers. Men from the 27th Divisions's 106th Regiment pitched in along with some Marines. A counterattack by the 106th recaptured the lost ground, but its brother regiment counted almost 1,000 casualties and the Marines lost another 130.

Aboard the destroyer *Downes*, Walter Vogel, who, after abandoning the doomed *Blue* in the seas around the Solomons, had been wounded again while on another ship, had been an eyewitness to the great Marianas Turkey Shoot. In this action the *Downes* fired its five-inchers steadily, while intermittently plucking fifteen downed U.S. pilots from the water. Now at Saipan, the *Downes* hugged the shores of Saipan to assist the leathernecks and GIs. "The Japs were committing suicide, jumping off the point," said Vogel. "I'd say 400 or more bodies were in the water. We had a spotter plane assigned to us. He spotted five Jap tanks heading for the airfield the Marines took and he called the grid to us. We fired our five-inch armor piercing shells when he'd tell us up or down so many yards. When we hit one he'd say, 'splash one tank,' and we got all five. Late one evening he was flying along the shoreline and he called us about a pocket of Japs in a cave. He was just circling overhead. When we spotted the cave, we fired phosphorus shells into it. About twenty-five came out burning and naturally the 20mms finished them off."

On Saipan, the 45,000 Marines listed more than 2,300 dead and missing, and an additional 10,500 wounded. The 27th's 16,400-man force recorded killed and missing of more than 1,000 with another 2,500 wounded. In percentages the Marines took more of a beating than the Army.

Morison's remarks about infiltrators seem less supportable. With one incendiary bullet, a single infiltrator on Saipan blew up an ammunition dump resulting in numerous Marine dead and wounded. The notion that any combat troops could allow enemy infiltrators to freely roam among them until daylight is less credible and that became particularly true on Okinawa. A case can be made for the strategies and tactics of either branch of the services. But when plans and operations called for cooperation and a unified effort by Marines and Army the differences could lead to devastating consequences.

Lying about 100 miles south of Saipan, Guam proved another hard case. Larger and more rugged in terrain than Saipan or Tinian, Guam offered defenders room to maneuver and to spread themselves in ways that avoided concentrated targets for bombers or naval shells. The garrison also profited from the three-day delay forced upon the Americans because of the stubborn resistance on Saipan and the necessity of meeting Ozawa's naval threat.

While UDT [Underwater Demolition team] teams swam in to destroy obstacles barring entry to the beaches, a massive preinvasion bombardment by sea and air preceded the actual landings. Primed to assault Guam were some 30,000 Marines from the 3d Marine Division and the newly activated 1st Provisional Marine Brigade composed of the 4th and 22d Marine Regiments. "Partly because of our failure at Bairoko," said Tony Walker, "higher authority decided early in 1944 to reorganize the four Raider battalions as the 4th Marines, a regular infantry regiment. There had been no active 4th Marine Regiment since it was lost at Corregidor." Walker served as operations officer for the 3d Battalion of the recreated 4th Regiment on Guam. The Army's 77th Division was in reserve.

To the sound of "The Marine Hymn," on 21 July, the first leathernecks loaded into amtracs with rocket-armed gunboats and 37mm cannon firing, landing craft sped toward the beaches. They met withering artillery and mortar fire wherever they came ashore, and by nightfall the purchase on Guam extended at best little more than a mile. The standard night counterattack of the Japanese, which employed tanks, grenades, and swords, penetrated the thin Marine lines in several places At 3:00 A.M. they hit a sector of the 4th Marine Regiment commanded by Lt. Stormy Sexton. Although the foe threw mines at the leathernecks, while firing rifles and sticking bayonets into foxholes, Sexton's outnumbered band held off an estimated 750 attackers.

Sergeant Harry Manion, a Marine Raider alumnus, served with a reconnaissance unit attached to the 4th Regiment. "Colonel Alan Shapley had us in his cabin and gave us our first day orders. Push inland as fast and as far as possible. Stay in contact. Get some prisoners. The recon platoon, full of steak and eggs, climbed down into an LCVPT and made for the beach and Mount Alifan. Transferred to an LVY [amphibious tractor] for the final run over the coral to the beach. We took a hit from a small gun on our right flank. Into the water and made the beach. Moved past the infantry. Up a draw, moving a few shell-shocked Japanese out of the way. Moved into a graveyard on a hill. Got fired on by some of our flyboys."

Manion and colleagues were sent forward to tie in between the 22d Marine Regiment and the 4th. "Picked up some ammo and grenades and moved back to the designated draw. By this time it was very dark. At regiment, we had picked up a young 2d lieutenant who was to take over as platoon leader. Recon formed a Vee facing the enemy. Three of us were at the apex. Two Johnson light machine guns [were] handled by Privates-first-class

Roy Ownes and James Ware. I had a Thompson submachine gun. We were getting settled when we heard some conversation to our right. The men were from a naval gunfire team. The USS Salt Lake City was about to send up some rounds. Overhead came a star shell. In the light we could see an entire Japanese army about a grenade throw ahead of us. I went back and found the lieutenant. He thought we shouldn't get excited. Pulled his poncho over his head. He was either crying or praying, maybe both. The cruiser started firing some heavy explosives. The Japanese were yelling and running toward us. Recon moved up to the near flank of the 4th Regiment. The Japanese came through. We could see them very clearly and threw grenades and fired ammo until our barrels were too hot to touch. Next morning there were many bodies in the draw. No doubt the cruiser's shells did a yeoman's job. Gunnery Sergeant Cutting took the lieutenant back with a few men to get ammo and water. It's amazing how much water a person can drink in a fire-fight. We never saw that lieutenant again."

Merrill McLane already had four years as a Marine when he graduated from Dartmouth with a reserve commission in 1942 and was a platoon leader in F Company of the 4th Marines. "A few days after our landing, a tragic event occurred in the platoon. At night, when in combat, we remain in our fox-holes which we dig before dark. Two men sleep in a hole, taking turns staying awake. No one leaves the hole until daybreak. If someone has to go to the bathroom, he has to do it in his helmet and then scatter it with his arm outside the hole. Anyone observed crawling, walking, standing, or running is considered to be a Japanese, and is to be shot at without warning. This is because the Japanese favor nights for their fighting, and they are very skill-ful at using darkness, much more than we are.

"That night we were all in our foxholes by dark and I had made my rounds of each one, chatting with all of the platoon. In the foxhole with me was Sergeant McCain. Everyone was expecting a counterattack to try to push us back into the sea, or at least to the beach. Nothing developed early in the evening, and I had dozed off while McCain remained awake.

"Sometime around midnight, I was awakened by a rifle shot near our fox-hole. No other sound followed. McCain, a veteran of the New Georgia cam-paign, whispered to me that he was worried and would like to crawl to where the shot had come from. My concern was that he would be fired at by other members of the platoon. We discussed it and I gave permission. Before he crawled away, I passed the word around in a low voice what McCain was do-ing. He wasn't long in returning. He told me that ——— had got out of his foxhole and been shot and killed by ———. What a shock!

"There was nothing further to do except to stay alert for an attack and wait until morning. When it was light, the body was removed. I talked with the platoon member who had done the shooting. He was experienced and well liked by the other marines. I had two problems. Should the man who had fired be punished? Second, what kind of a letter should I write to the parents of the lost marine? I solved this at once. It would be the same as parents of other platoon members killed on Guam;that he'd been lost in combat and no mention of the incident that caused his death.

"I needed guidance about the other problem. I talked to the company commander who informed the battalion commander, who called back with word that the situation should be handled at company level. The company commander talked it over with me, finally saying the decision was mine. There was no time to give a lot of thought to the matter. The company would soon be moving out. I shuffled about headquarters for a few minutes and reached my decision. No official action would be taken nor would what happened appear in written reports. The man who had done the shooting would remain in the platoon in his old position.

"After McCain and I informed him of this and reassured him that what he had done could have been duplicated by any one of us, I added there would be no further discussion of the subject. McCain passed the word around the platoon. It was one of the most difficult decisions I ever had to make and I'm pleased to say it was correct. Although the marine we lost that night was not forgotten, the platoon operated smoothly during the remainder of the campaign."

On 22 July, when the Marines began to advance through the positions of the Japanese. Gen. Roy S. Geiger, in charge of the ground forces, had already committed his reserves from the 77th Infantry Division, a well-schooled organization with a background of desert, mountain, and amphibious training at various locales in the U.S. The 305th Regiment went ashore behind the 1st Provisional Marine Brigade near Agat. Dick Forse, who'd attended radio school, was attached to Cannon Company and part of a crew on an M8, an armored, self propelled 75mm that the men called a tank even though its protection was limited to high steel sides.

"I felt apprehension going into combat but was super alert. My insides jumped at fire in our direction or any sustained fire. Sometimes I started to sweat. I had a small feeling of security surrounded by the steel side of an M8. I hoped the Japanese didn't have anything larger than machine guns. That first afternoon, the platoon sergeant and I were digging our slit trench. It was halfway completed when two artillery shells, incoming, exploded about seventy-five yards away. Both of us dove to the ground. The platoon sergeant was closer to the slit trench so he jumped in there. I was headed there also but there wasn't room for both of us so I just hit the ground where I was. My cartridge belt twisted and my canteen was in the front. I landed so hard the canteen knocked the breath out of me. As I tried to recover, the platoon sergeant was yelling, 'Oh, God, oh, God!' We remained prone and when there were no more shells we got up to finish the trench.

"A few minutes later, two more shells exploded. I thought they were close and we both hit the ground in the same places. This time I was the one yelling, 'Oh, God, oh, God!. The sergeant looked at me with eyes big as cups. He thought I'd been hit. When it quieted down and the trench was completed we went back to the company. We'd been digging sort of an outpost and when we returned, we found the lieutenant had changed his mind. The slit trench wasn't even used. We were usually up soon after daybreak. I was seldom the first out because if there were snipers, I wanted them to use up their ammo at someone else.

"After breakfast rations we'd start the M8 and work usually in support of the 1st Battalion of the 305th. Most days were spent attacking, which meant going forward, sometimes in a skirmish line, sometimes in columns, depending upon the terrain. When they hit resistance, we were committed, depending on whether we were close by if they needed the tanks. Usually we fired machine guns unless the resistance was tough. Then, if we had a good field of fire, we'd use the 75. After that spot was cleared, we'd continue on the attack.

"In the late afternoon, we would eat when we could. When we stopped for the day, we'd all dig in as part of the battalion defensive perimeter. Our driver slept under the tank with one other man from Cannon Company. The other three of the crew either slept in the tank or pulled guard, one hour on, two off. If the situation was considered dangerous at night, the driver stayed in the tank with guards on either side of the turret. There was seldom any combat at night.

"We acted like a tank infantry team. One infantry spotter on each side of the M8 as it moved forward. The squad followed and surrounded us at times. They used us as an outpost, ahead of the line at night. We had a machine gun or a BAR section with us, plus three of four riflemen dug in nearby. Our artillery fire was very good and fierce, although sometime the impact was too close for comfort. Air support looked and sounded very good. Generally, it consisted of bombing and strafing Japanese positions several times by eight or more planes. Mostly it was naval aircraft used to break up Jap resistance. We seldom had naval gunfire after the first day of combat. On Guam we were never under attack by Japanese planes."

A former sportswriter, Ed Fitzgerald wore the six stripes of a first sergeant in Service Company, 307th Infantry Regiment. On 21 July, 1944, a nervous Fitzgerald, whose responsibilities were administrative rather than combative, joined the other GIs in "endless, queasy hours circling offshore before we were sent in. When they finally told us to move up topside, we watched the shelling and the bombing in awe. They told us there were four battleships and three heavy cruisers out there where we couldn't see them, relentlessly firing broadsides of shells ranging from five to sixteen inches. We could see a long line of slender, graceful, quick-turning destroyers patrolling a steady beat to protect the big ships, and turning spitefully every once in a while to fire their own guns at the island. Agat Bay and Agat Village stood in plain view. Clouds of black smoke and leaping sheets of red flame showed the ferocity of the attack. 'There won't be anything left alive on that island by the time you guys get there,' said a sailor standing near me. That's what he thought. It was our first lesson in the exaggerated confidence the Navy had in the effectiveness of offshore shelling. What we found out was that when it started the Japanese went into their elaborate caves, and when it stopped, they came out and started shooting. They fired their rifles and lobbed their mortars down on us from high ground and even opened up with artillery pieces that they had made room for in the same caves they hid in.

"But before we learned this hard lesson, we had to go over what is considered the greatest barrier reef in the Pacific. Our landing craft couldn't go over it, so we had to walk over it. We lost a lot of men before we ever got close enough for the Japanese to shoot at us. Everybody was carrying a lot of weight. It was a helluva long distance from the boats to the beach. Some men were too seasick to keep themselves upright, some stepped into holes in the reef and disappeared from sight. The first worry we had, in the boats and after we got out of them, was that our own planes would aim short and hit us. They were coming in right over our heads. But when we saw the first guys go down in the water without a sound and we reached for them and they weren't there, we realized our biggest worry was just making it to the beach without drowning."

Following orders, Fitzgerald and his associates settled in about five hundred feet beyond the beach line. They dug in for the night. "I learned another lesson that first night," said Fitzgerald. "Some people could stay in their holes, but some of us had to move around the company area and deliver messages and the orders that the colonel gave the captain to give the lieutenants and me. That's what Charlie Bauer's two silver bars and the bars our lieutenants wore, and my six stripes were for. I 'volunteered' a lot of people to do things during the war. I made up my mind that was what I was there for.

"Guam was our high school. Everything before that was kindergarten or grammar school, or if you want to give weight to things like the obstacle course and the infiltration course and amphibious training, junior high school. On Guam we learned the big thing wasn't getting mail or something hot to eat, but staying alive. Charlie and I stood on a hill above Agat on the second day ashore, talking to a warrant officer, Warren Pepple, when the first Japanese planes hit us. They were the first we'd ever seen and suddenly they were right over our heads. Machine gun bullets came first and then shells, digging deep, angry holes in the dirt around us. We threw ourselves down. Pepple got hit in his behind by a shell burst.

"'Don't worry,' I told him. 'You're only bleeding on the side of your ass.' Charlie called for an aidman while I gave Pepple a drink of water and rubbed some of it on his sweaty face.

'He needs help,' Charlie said to the medic. 'No, he doesn't,' the medic said after a minute of working on him. 'He's dead.'"

"Our regiment [the 306th]," recalled Buckner Creel, a twenty-year-old platoon leader, "landed on the second day on Guam. Our first night on Mount Alifan was a disaster. Much panic and indiscriminate firing of individual weapons. No enemy could be seen, just shadows and strange noises in the jungle. In our own company headquarters, Pvt. John Loughead was killed by his own foxhole mate when Loughead stuck his head up and was silhouetted above the foxhole. This was quite a personal loss to me. Loughead had been a trifler and always in trouble. But during training in Hawaii he had developed into a good soldier. Although there was the officer-enlisted man relationship, we had developed a closeness and he was slated to become my radio operator.

"I believe training took over and allowed me to cope with my normal fear as I reacted automatically to situations. In addition, I had added responsibilities. I was not only exec for the company, but also had taken command of the 1st Platoon. One cannot show trepidation and lead troops in combat. The soldiers will willingly follow an assured, confident leader, so any fear had to be 'cooped' up. In our first action, my carbine had jammed. I got rid of it and started to carry an M1. The additional firepower gave me more confidence when actively leading the platoon on our many combat patrols. And my leading gave the troops more confidence in my ability to lead, react, and get the tasks done most expeditiously. In my first two contacts with the Japanese on Guam, I found that I did react immediately and with the proper action. First, while on patrol, we located a group of enemy soldiers in a defilade position. I responded with a hand grenade. It had the desired effect, killing five of them with no losses to us.

"On the second occasion, I rounded a bend in a jungle trail. I came face to face, at a distance of perhaps ten to fifteen paces, with an enemy soldier. We both dropped to our knees and fired. Apparently, I was the more accurate since I am still here and he isn't. Both times instinctive reactions took over and governed the situation."

Three days after the first marines went ashore at Guam, Henry Lopez, a sergeant in C Company of the 307th Regiment, well beyond his thirtieth birthday, waded through three-to-five-feet deep water onto the black sand beach. "Huge craters, partly filled with water; debris; uprooted, riddled,and shredded coconut trees; destroyed landing craft, and abandoned equipment strewn about testified to the intensity of the invasion. The indescribable stench of death contaminated the air, stinging and offending the nostrils."

Company C hiked a mile and a half to spend its first night on the island. "Out of sheer curiosity men left their holes to see what a dead Jap looked like. In a large shell crater three corpses lay sprawled upwards, their bloated, blackened bodies blown up like gruesome balloons. Hundreds of small, slimy white maggots squirmed on top of one another and ate their way in and out of this stinking, rotten mess. This disgusting sight, as well as the stench, made many men sick and caused them to throw up their recently eaten rations." The outfit pressed on, engaging in desultory small skirmishes with the enemy. "I am not ashamed to say that when I first came under fire I was scared to death. The only way I could cope with the fear was to think of the platoon, keep busy, and not let anyone know my feelings."

Lopez and his company were pushing north after the Americans had breached the beach defenses. "We moved in a skirmish line with visual contact on one side with a marine unit and on our other side was another company from the battalion. Entering very dense woods with heavy undergrowth, the skirmish line became a single-file column. We lost all contact with those on our left and right sides. We found ourselves past our objective. There was some firing from our left flank and rear. Suddenly, we heard a voice demanding, 'Who the hell is firing at us!' I replied, 'Not us.' The voice then asked, 'Who the hell are you?' 'Americans, who the hell are you?

"Without answering my question, he said, 'If you are Americans, throw up your helmet or come toward me.' I threw up my helmet so he could see it. Whereupon, we were greeted with a heavy volume of fire. I didn't have to think twice. We also opened fire and at the same time took off in the opposite direction. We didn't locate the rest of the platoon or the company that day but did come under mortar fire. We ended up with K Company of the [1st Marine Division] just before dusk and dug in with them. There was Jap equipment in the area where we had been and I believe that the man was a Jap who spoke perfect English and pretended to be a marine.

"We had been told that the Japs would not surrender, which very few did, and to kill them before they killed you, that they would rather die than surrender, so long as they could take you along with them. During our jungle training course in Hawaii, a large sign read, 'If they don't stink, stick them.' The civilians we encountered on Guam were treated with kindness and respect along with medical care and food."

When the 706th Tank Battalion trundled ashore on Guam, William Siegel, as a staff officer for the unit, acted as liaison from the division advance command post. "It was there that I attended all of General [Andrew]

Bruce's [77th Division CG] briefings with his staff and the regimental COs. Also, I was able to observe the few Japanese prisoners that arrived. When captured, they were very polite, docile, and humble as a rule. We in our unit never considered the Japanese as demons, but rather as sly and treacherous. Furthermore, our instructions were that if we captured any of the enemy, we, as officers, would be held responsible for their well-being as provided by the Geneva convention."

The third major objective in the Marianas, Tinian, fell more quickly than the others. In eight days, the 4th and 2nd Marine Divisions wiped out more than a thousand Japanese, many of whom preferred suicide to surrender. The expanding Pacific operations involved intensive ground support from naval and marine aviation. Tom Hartman, a Princeton freshman, had taken advantage of the Navy's policy in the spring of 1942 to enlist as an aviation cadet with only one year of college. Trained as a carrier pilot, he recalled, "The Navy had to decide whether they needed fighters or torpedo-bomber or dive-bomber pilots. My straw came up dive bomber. They then asked us to choose between the Marine Corps or the Navy. The Marines sent the most gung ho officer in the Corps. We were on our feet cheering when he finished. I rushed over to sign up."

In the cockpit of a Douglas Dauntless dive bomber, he joined the oldest squadron in the Corps, Ace of Spades, technically VMSB231, which had already fought with distinction at Midway and Guadalcanal, under Maj. Elmer Glidden. "Elmer was a very precise man, a taciturn New England Yankee who was a graduate engineer from RPI [Rensselaer Polytechnic Institute]. He was all business, never much emotion. He was an iron man who flew more dive-bombing missions than any other, anywhere. He was a warrior and a most decent man."

Hartman began his tour stationed at Midway, escorting submarines. As the Japanese Empire shrank, the base for the squadron shifted to the Marshall Islands. Flying out of Majuro, he went on his first combat operation against bypassed atolls in the Marshalls. "The first mission was one of apprehension for the unknown, but we had trained so often it was a relief to go on a mission. I was apprehensive, but like all young guys I thought I was indestructible. We knew how to dive our planes at the target, release the bombs at a certain altitude, pull out against many Gs of force, how to close the dive flaps immediately in order to insure a maximum rate of speed at our low level; how to join up in close formation on the way back in case any fighters appeared. The SBDs were so well armored and so underpowered they were slow. We had to fly in tight formations so that all of the rear seat machine guns could fire almost as one against enemy planes.

"We bombed antiaircraft gun placements, barracks, and other buildings. The return fire was intense and a number of planes were hit but there were no casualties. I was well trained and in a unit with experienced leadership; fear was never my particular concern. Our equipment was superb. My radioman-gunner was a cool customer and very good at everything. He trusted me as he had to; there were no real controls in the back seat. The strategy and tactics were absolutely appropriate for the task. We dove from 10,000 feet at an angle of seventy degrees. We opened our dive flaps at the top—they helped us control the planes and limited the speed (350 knots) in a steep dive. We released the bombs as we passed through 1,500 feet. We were an accurate squadron. We had practiced hitting circles 150 feet in diameter."

Hartman and his squadron participated in the suppression of efforts to reinforce or support objectives upon which the Pacific command had designs. "In the spring of 1944 we were told to pack up and be prepared to go to the invasion of Saipan once a third of the island was secure. We were to fly close support for the Marine troops. We had not been trained in close air support but our accuracy was legend. Then, late one night, Elmer called us together. Orders were changed because the Army wanted to use P47s for that purpose." Morale dropped sharply with the breakup of the squadron and particularly for Hartman when his new skipper, a raging alcoholic, directed the pilots to fly one above the other rather than in a formation in which the flyers could see the plane ahead of them. Hartman refused to follow the tactic and the men ignored their commander's order. The drunkard was relieved soon after.

In the wake of the Marianas campaign, the war seemed to pass Hartman's squadron. "We were bored. The worst thing that happened to us was that a finely tuned bombing squadron such as ours never had a chance to help in the real war effort. Bypassed islands were no threat. We lost pilots and gunners for not so much of a reason except we were doing our duty."

34
Breakout

On the tip of the Cotentin Peninsula sits the great harbor city of Cherbourg. As the most western port of France with the shortest sailing distance from the United States it figured as a prime objective. The 9th and 79th Infantry Divisions, which entered France shortly after D day, along with the 4th, focused their attentions upon Cherbourg. Two stalwart *Wehrmacht* divisions plus other units ringed the city. Inside, a port and labor garrison acted as a reserve. Hitler ordered them to fight to the death, and also directed Rommel to "strike into the rear of the First American Army advancing on Cherbourg." The Germans fought doggedly but rocked from artillery, armor and savage raids by Ninth Air Force dive-bombers and strafing fighters. Allied battleships, cruisers, and destroyers, offshore unloosed tons of destructive explosives.

The most obstinate and formidable obstacle was Fort du Roule, a bastion carved out of a rocky cliff above the city. From there coastal guns faced the harbor approach, while abundant mortars, machine guns, and an antitank ditch defied a landward assault. From the 79th Division's 314th Infantry, Cpl. John Kelly crawled up a slope to set off a pole charge against a pillbox that pinned down his platoon. When the explosive failed to detonate, Kelly repeated his maneuver, destroying a pair of machine guns. A third sortie with grenades convinced the Germans to yield. Lieutenant Carlos Ogden of Company K took charge after his superior was hit. Alone, he climbed a hill to knock out an 88 and blasted other defenses, while absorbing two separate wounds. Kelly and Ogden were each awarded the Medal of Honor but the former died of injuries in later action.

The defenders turned about their gigantic coastal defense guns to fire inland against attacking GIs, including George Mabry and the 4th Division. Mabry, highly gratified by a skillful capture of a pair of two well-camouflaged pillboxes housing these massive weapons, showed his battalion commander, Colonel McNeely how the GIs of E Company, "had crawled up so close, charged by short rushes; it was almost a perfect military formation, these bodies—all killed while the wounded had been evacuated—to attack these positions.

"After we had gone back to the CP, while I was checking something, I missed Colonel McNeely. Someone said he had walked off in that direction, behind a little hill. I went behind the hill and found him sitting behind a tree, with his head in his hands and crying. I sat down beside him and he began to say, 'George, it tears me up to see so many of our fine young men being killed like that. I agreed with him and, then said, 'Colonel McNeely, only by the grace of God there lie you and I. It's tough to steel one's feelings in a situation like this but you must establish some attitude that would preclude death of your comrades and close friends from affecting you so much. The only way I can do it, when we look at these men, whom we served with so long and whose names we know, my attitude is, you German SOBs you killed my buddies, I'm going to get ten more of you for that. Also, remember, you and I could be lying there dead in the next five minutes but we cannot afford to let the death of our friends affect us so much because it will affect our ability to fight.' After talking a while he regained his composure."

Although the overall commandant at Cherbourg surrendered 26 June, some soldiers, obedient to the Führer, fought on in isolated groups, and not until the end of the month did the skirmishes within Cherbourg end. During the siege, the Germans executed a masterful destruction of facilities, blowing up piers, sinking ships, and setting out mines to deny use of the harbor. Three weeks elapsed before repairs enabled the first vessels to unload at Cherbourg.

During the first months, Dick Gangel flew missions out of Foggia. He noted a number of missions in which enemy fighters met them during bomber-escort duty to Northern Italy, Ploesti, and Bucharest. On 5 May he remarked, "Got jumped by twenty-five ME 109s. They had an advantage of 5,000 feet on us. They got Klos and he bailed out. Tuffy Leeman came in on one engine. Lucky that another flight shot one off my tail." A day later, over Romania, he wrote, "Were jumped by six ME 109s. Coleman got one. Chased two to the deck and two flights shot one down. Several of us tossed for the victory but Cardimona won. Blakely also won a toss." Only in the Eighth and Ninth Air Forces, did pilots share victories if doubt arose about who scored the kill.

The tide of battle in Europe changed the nature of the air war there. Between the onslaughts of the United Kingdom-based bombers and fighters, and the territorial advances on the continent in both France and Italy, the depleted *Luftwaffe* could no longer dispatch swarms of interceptors to meet the enemy and was forced to operate ever deeper within the Third Reich. Gangel's log increasingly reported "uneventful" missions. On one occasion he described the enemy as "not eager to mix it up." He also raided more ground targets, hitting locomotives, shooting up parked aircraft. "Flying an intruder mission in Northern Italy, I saw a German staff car with a big Maltese Cross on it. I was determined to get it and blew it away. I was so low that I hit a tree and knocked a hole in the wing, but I got home. When we were dive-bombing I could put a bomb in a bushel basket. When I saw all the photographs of the dead soldiers on the beaches at Normandy I couldn't understand why they hadn't knocked out the bunkers from the air."

On 26 June Gangel laconically entered, "Shot down ME 109 after a five-minute chase on the deck." He knocked down two more before his final shuttle mission to Poltava in the Soviet Union. Enroute, while strafing German airdromes, he destroyed one plane on the ground. Others on the mission accounted for forty more. But Soviet citizens hardly showed appreciation. "We visited Kharkov and the people were very antagonistic. We went for a walk and a man and his family insulted us. A guard with us walked over and hit them."

On the long trip back to Foggia, half a dozen fighters attacked his flight 100 miles before they reached the Danube. "Sognier and I fought five of them, each getting one e/a. We had a running fight home with two, due to the need for conserving gas." He completed his tour of sixty missions without a scratch, although he counted a number of bullet holes in his ships. Credited with four victories, he earned an Air Medal with ten oak-leaf clusters and a Distinguished Flying Cross. "I never had any feeling that there was a human being in the other plane."

As fewer enemy aircraft met the Americans in the sky, fighter pilots sought them on the ground, missions conceded more dangerous than dogfights. Jim Goodson, now a 4th Fighter Group squadron CO, engaged in this type of warfare. As May ended, his crew chief had painted fifteen swastikas beside the cockpit of Goodson's P-51 for confirmed kills on the ground. But on 20 June, while spraying an enemy airfield, Goodson was forced to belly in his Mustang.

"After I got shot down," said Goodson, "I was taken prisoner by the Gestapo [Nazi secret police]. "I persuaded them to get in touch with the Luftwaffe which sent a party to take me in handcuffs to the interrogation center near Frankfurt. Going there, we had to change trains in Berlin. I asked the officer in charge of me where we were going. He said the Friedrich-strasse Bahnhof. I asked the date and then remembered that 1,000 planes were scheduled to hit Berlin with the main aiming point that railroad station about noon. What time did we get there? About noon!

"We took refuge in bomb shelters. Because I had taken part in planning the raid, I knew who would be leading the different boxes of bombers and my own fighters would be escorting. It's a very different view of the war, when you're up there at 30,000 feet and you see only little flashes and puffs of smoke. You don't think of people. Sitting in an air-raid shelter with Germans all around you, and the crashing, deafening noise above you is something else. About halfway through, the all-clear sounded and everyone was about to leave the shelter. I said, 'No, no! It's not finished yet. The second wave is going to come in. They looked at me peculiarly but the officer with me said, 'He knows.' Sure enough, another wave of bombers came over. I saw devastation a hundred times worse than the London blitz which I went through. There were hundreds of bodies of people who had not been able to get into the shelters. It brought home a war that pilots very seldom see. Digging women and babies out of the rubble we had caused was profoundly affecting."

Goodson was caught in Berlin by a raid with an added wrinkle to it. While the main bomber stream headed for the German capital, two wings of the 3d Bomb Division, accompanied by their P-51 shadows, hammered the oil refinery complex at Ruhland, then continued east with the intention of landing in the Soviet Union at Poltava and Mirgorod. The bulk of the two wings reached the Soviet Union. On the ground in Red territory, Harry Crosby, a navigator with the 100th bomb group, slept on a hard bench covered with hay, the guest accommodations for the visiting firemen. "That afternoon," he remembers, "a problem developed. German reconnaissance planes droned over the field looking at us. The Russians had no antiaircraft. Russian pilots in American Airacobras went up, and the Germans, apparently Stukas [dive-bombers], went away. Colonel Jeff [Tom Jeffrey, the 100th's CO] was uncomfortable. 'We're naked in front of those guys.'"

He was not the only one disturbed by the sight. On the ground at Mirgorod, Col. Joseph Moller, the 95th Bomb Group leader for the expedition, also became alarmed by the appearance of a German photo-reconnaissance plane. The Americans had been instructed that while at the Soviet airfields, they would be under the local commander. Moller and the 13th bomb Wing commander requested permission from the ranking officer for their P-51 shepherds to knock the intruder out of the sky. Moller saw a few meager flak bursts that hardly disturbed the spy plane.

"After a lengthy discussion with another Russian, he refused. I asked him why. He replied that if we did shoot down the German plane, it would always be said that we had to defend ourselves on Russian bases. I then asked how he proposed to defend us and our parked aircraft against a probable air attack. He had no answer, except merely to shrug and turn away." Moller and the wing commander persuaded their hosts to allow them to fly to a different location.

Using a road map supplied by the base commander, the Americans took off from Mirgorod by the light of the moon and fled to other airfields. For several days, Moller and his people then waited for bombs and fuel required for the return trip. Crosby and the other airmen circulated among the Soviet soldiers, male and female, admired the prominent bosoms of the latter, heard tales of the vicious battles endured and the murderous behavior of the German occupation troops. They swapped souvenirs, partied briefly and saw nothing of the enemy.

At Poltava Archie Old brought in about seventy-five bombers from his 45th Bomb Wing. "We hadn't much more than gotten on the ground before we were met by a General Permanov, the Russian commander at Poltava and a General [Robert] Walsh, I believe his name was, from our embassy at Moscow. [Walsh's assignment had been to arrange resupply and refueling.] I noticed this aircraft that looked like it was up 10,000 to 12,000 feet, not more than that and I was pretty sure it was an ME210. I mentioned to the American general and General Permanov, through his lady interpreter, that the plane could signal trouble. But there wasn't a helluva lot we could do about it. We had empty tanks, and there was no way, if we started to work then, that we could fill those things up and go to some other base. We had been told this was the only base readily available. I questioned that it couldn't be done but I had no authority to challenge any Russian decisions there. It was their country and their bases. But they said [the Germans] wouldn't come in and bomb or anything like that. But it looked like an awfully juicy target to me, sitting down there with these silver airplanes. It was a moot question. We could never have gotten the aircraft refueled until, probably, hours after the first Germans arrived.

"We were having a pretty big dinner in honor of myself and some of my key staff people from the 96th, the 388th, and the 452nd bomb groups, at General Permanov's mess. The dinner was progressing with probably too-frequent toasts to toss off some vodka. They would make a toast, 'Long live Stalin.' and you were supposed to chugalug, toss it off. Then someone else would [say] 'Long live Roosevelt.' We got a report that there were some aircraft coming in from the west. They were bringing reports into General Permanov. Finally, it was pretty obvious that these were German bombers coming in to bomb at Poltava and Mirgorod. Dinner immediately ceased and [people] went down into a bomb shelter. The first German aircraft over the field was a pathfinder, dropping flares. Those silver airplanes stood out like a sore toe. Then the Germans proceeded to bomb; they did a superb job. Of course those silver airplanes, sitting out on the ground with those silver wings, silver bodies, was like shooting fish in a barrel. It was rather insulting. They were using some of the oldest damn equipment that they had available. They wouldn't have dared, I don't think to go over England with anything like that.

"I could have done something about it but I had been thoroughly briefed that we would cooperate fully with the Russians. I had somewhere around seventy-five P-51s sitting over there at either Mirgorod or Piryatin [another field] and they had been refueled. It was my understanding, we could have put them up and shot down every one of those German bombers before they did as much damage as they did. However, when I discussed this with General Permanov, he said he would have to get in touch with Moscow. I can only presume he did try but we were unable to get permission to put our fighters up. I was not about to put the airplanes up to shoot down aircraft over Russian territory when they had told me I would have to get permission from Moscow to do that. I didn't go into the bomb shelter but walked to the edge of the field. There was no danger as long as you stayed off the field. I stood there watching. My people, the crews were in an area adjacent to the airfields. We had two or three casualties." While very few Americans were injured, when the last of the unmolested enemy planes departed, only seven or eight of the seventy-five aircraft of the 45th Bomb Wing were flyable. At Mirgorod, the Luftwaffe flares illuminated only an empty airdrome as the 13th Bomb Wing had flown the coop.

The introduction of the first jet fighter, the ME262 shocked and even frightened many Allied airmen. Some historians insist that the German jet might have turned the tide of the war if it had appeared in sufficient numbers. Development of the first jet fighters was detoured by Hitler's request for modifications to create a swift bomber that could exact revenge upon the Allies. They produced a worthless version and delayed manufacture of the ultimate jet, the deadly dangerous ME262. However, even without the ME262, the German air force could deploy the latest versions of the ME109 and FW190 in sufficient quantities [the Luftwaffe counted as many planes in its inventory as from the previous years] to have battled the Allies, but the severe attrition that began with Big Week had robbed the defense of proficient pilots and created a scarcity of oil and its products. No matter how many jets rolled off the assembly lines in 1944 there were nowhere near enough adequate individuals to fill the cockpits nor fuel for the rocket engines. By the end of the first month following D day in Normandy, the Allied Armies had developed their real estate along a front some seventy miles wide and twenty to thirty miles deep. The invaders counted about one million soldiers in France by 2 July, but after seven weeks of fighting, they had bitten off basically the territory expected on only D plus 5. Stout German opposition, aided by weather that favored the defense—it was Normandy's wettest July in 40 years—along an axis that stretched from Caen through Caumont and St.-Lô, thwarted advances. The most frustrating natural barrier was the hedgerow whose berms and thick vegetation defied the batterings of tanks and bulldozers. American engineers, mechanics, and farmboys experimented with contraptions attached to armor. According to Stephen Ambrose in his book *Citizen Soldiers,* the two most successful devices were a bumper for Shermans devised by tanker Lt. Charles Green and a cutting mechanism created by former cab driver Sgt. Curtis Culin.

Bud Warnecke, a platoon sergeant with B Company of the 508th Parachute Infantry Regiment, and among those forced to withdraw through the marshes and Merderet River, soon joined an isolated group with whom he fought for four days. "All our initial objectives were taken and held by make shift companies and battalions. We were placed in reserve and there I learned our first sergeant, hung up in the trees when he jumped, had been shot and the battalion commander killed during the drop. I also heard of one man from our company evacuated for combat fatigue or, as we called it, 'shit in his neck.' Our seaborne tail caught up with us bringing rations. The black bread and Normandy butter the Krauts carried had been real good. We unshaven, motley-looking troopers cleaned up."

On 4 July, Warnecke's battalion prepared for an attack near the strategic heights commanded by the town of La Haye-du-Puits, as part of the break-out from the now secure Cotentin Peninsula. Warnecke recalls, "Sergeant Call and I were standing behind a hedgerow being briefed by Lieutenant Homer Jones. A German machine gun cut down on us. I went down as if hit by a sledgehammer and, as I fell, a slug ripped through my canteen. I got up dazed and saw Lieutenant Jones had been hit through the neck. Blood was squirting out both sides and he was in horrible pain. We called for a medic. Jones was saying, 'Let me die! Let me die!' and Sgt. Roland Fecteau who was nearby, immediately stuck two fingers in the lieutenant's neck and plugged the holes. When the medic came he shot him up with morphine. The spinal cord hadn't been severed and the wound was directly behind it. As Lieutenant Jones was loaded on a stretcher, he was smoking a cigarette and said, 'I'll see you boys in Wollington Park.' [The 508th's home base in England.]

"My wound turned out to be much more superficial. It busted the skin, looked as if maybe two or three bullets just grazed me. The medic threw some powder on it, put a big patch over it and said, 'Well, you got a Purple Heart.' The shoulder turned black and blue but it wasn't enough to get me evacuated. By the time the fighting stopped for us on July 9, we in B Company, which started with 148 troopers, were down to thirty-three."

As a platoon leader for the 90th Division, Lt. J.Q. Lynd grappled with the enemy entrenchments that blocked advances. "Natural vegetative cover, concealment, and camouflage were used with well-prepared observation and weapon 'dig-ins' to attain the greatest destruction of attacking troops. The basic Wehrmacht defensive tactics were to block tank and armor advances, halt the infantry with grazing small-arms and MG fire, then to bombard the standstill outfits with destructive artillery and mortar fire. Thus it was absolutely necessary for the attacking [troops] to determine the specific locations and capabilities of the many, varied strong-point, observation-weapon sites before launching their attack . . . in order to exactly adjust preattack artillery and mortar fire to destroy [these] strong-point locations before the infantry attacks. The only means to determine the enemy location and capabilities was by probing with night patrols. This hazardous task was achieved with officer-led night combat patrols that penetrated the enemy lines and found the Main-Line-of-Resistance weapons' layout and strong-point entrenchments."

Patrols of this nature were high-risk ventures. Early in the Normandy campaign, Lynd led one of three such ventures dispatched by his battalion. As landmarks disappeared in the mist hanging over a swampy wooded area, they followed the path of an elderly cow bent on reaching its pasture. "A combat patrol that doesn't know where you are at, which direction you're going, and how to get back, is lost. The only thing that can be worse is getting caught in an enemy shoot-up mouse trap and the dense pea-soup fog saved us from that." Their guide "Granny Bossy" started grazing in the pasture "fair warning that very shortly we were going to be on our own." Fortunately, the ground fog had begun to lift. "We could now make out the distinctive tree and hedgerow features that we *must know* to get back, without our now beloved Granny Bossy."

"We picked up our azimuth reading again and began a very cautious trek roving among those hedgerows. Granny Bossy had put us in enemy territory for sure. It was still pretty foggy and we tried to be a noiseless part of the landscape. Abruptly we smelled the unmistakable, sharp, pungent smoke odor of a German cigar or pipe. Then there was the stink of fresh human feces. Behind the hedgerow to our front, a diesel engine started up, revved up, idled some moments. We could hear a chain clinking, then it accelerated again. Most likely that had been stuck in the mud, probably one of their 88mm pieces."

Lynd and his companions cautiously retraced their steps through the pasture and then along the path taken by Granny Bossy. They reported to headquarters their meager information. The bodies of all of the eleven men in the two other patrols were discovered a few days later. One of them had been led by a newcomer, "An instance of higher HQ thoughtless, costly blunders," remarked Lynd. "Newly assigned replacement officers were extremely limited in capabilities for effective patrol action, even with daylight missions. Reconnaissance patrols absolutely require individual soldiers operating as a dedicated team with total confidence in their buddies. One goof can completely wipe them out." The perils of patrols often induced men to fakery, moving only far enough to conceal them from superiors and then returning with bogus information.

Lynd mentioned that the Germans behaved slightly better than Americans when dealing with the bodies of the foe. Speaking of the corpses of the missing patrols, he noted, "The men had been stripped of equipment and personal effects, but the enemy did leave their ID dog tags intact . . . U.S. GIs in the follow-up support units were not equally respectful for an identification of the German dead. They would strip the enemy corpse of everything that could be sent home (free postage) as token souvenirs, including the German disk ID tags. As a result almost three fourths of the German soldiers killed in France are interred as unknown."

During the first week of July, Lynd's division absorbed devastating damage. His battalion under Capt. Leroy "Fireball" Pond managed to penetrate enemy lines around an objective listed as Hill 122 and bring in artillery that sustained the outfit even though it was cut off from the other regiments by the opponents. During this battle a machine gun shattered bones in Lynd's left arm and chest, necessitating evacuation to a hospital in England. Severe as the casualties were in this engagement, brothers in arms from the 357th Regiment sustained their highest single-action losses when a German counterattack almost annihilated two companies.

Along the Allied front, the 2d Infantry Division set about to occupy Hill 192, a 140-foot-high elevation on the right flank of St.-Lô. George Duckworth, as CO of F Company, 23d Infantry, flew over Hill 192 in an artillery spotter plane to survey the enemy front-line positions. "I could see the enemy in foxholes, machine-gun emplacements, trenches, and their armored vehicles. I could also plainly see enemy troops looking up at us and firing small arms at the plane." Duckworth also saw a heavily wooded approach, lined with the ubiquitous hedgerows and crossed by stream beds. Intelligence described dugouts that ran as much as twelve-feet underground and constructed so the Germans could sit out artillery and mortar barrages, and when the fire lifted, to pop up like jacks-in-boxes to confront any advances.

On the other hand, the Americans enhanced their artillery capability. The VT, or proxmity fuse, placed in the nose of a shell, relied on a miniature transmitter and receiver that detonated the shell at a predetermined distance from its target rather than upon impact or at a set time after being fired. The device used a radio beam that, upon striking a solid object, reflected back to the receiver, which then tripped the fuse switch. Proximity fuses made artillery shells lethal to anyone above ground and stripped away the protection ordinarily afforded by trenches or foxholes. The technique of Time-on-Target (TOT) added devastating effects. In a TOT barrage all of the artillery pieces fired with synchronization. This delivered simultaneously explosions of all shells whether in the air or at point of contact. TOT, with both proximity fuses and the usual impact-type ordnance, would precede a coordinated tank and infantry assault by Duckworth's battalion.

According to Duckworth, the officers and key enlisted men when briefed reacted with enthusiasm. "It was almost as if the air was charged with electricity. The constant shelling we had endured, the daily casualties, and our intensive training were at an end. We were exhilarated at the thought of engaging the enemy with the prospect of inflicting heavy casualties as a measure of revenge for the pounding we had taken. After several delays because of bad weather, at 0500 on 11 July, the 2d Division artillery, supported by four other attached battalions, opened fire on Hill 192. The noise was deafening as we watched the fiery explosions. Dust, smoke, brush, rocks, and debris of all kinds erupted over the entire surface of the hill and the surrounding area. This tremendous concentration of firepower continued for approximately an hour and it did not seem possible that there could be anyone left alive in the targeted area. When the firing ceased, the tanks made their initial run and then returned for us.

"As we charged into the enemy front line positions, we found many still in foxholes, dugouts, and hedgerow positions. Even though they were somewhat dazed and deafened by the artillery bombardment, they were able to bring a heavy volume of small-arms fire down on us. As well-trained, veteran troops they held their ground and fought almost fanatically as we closed in and overran them with our tanks and infantry. It was a fierce, no-quarter-asked and no-quarter-given battle, often man-to-man with rifle butts, bayonets, and trench knives. There were no enemy offers of surrender and I do not recall that we took any prisoners in the initial penetration of their defenses. Some may have surrendered or been taken prisoner after we moved forward.

"Our artillery and tanks gave us a definite advantage and Company F's men fought with ferocity and grim determination as we followed the tanks and broke through line after line of defense, often cutting them down from the rear before they could recover. The tanks, with their plowshare attachments, were awesome and a complete surprise to the enemy. When a tank hit a hedgerow at full speed, the plowshares threw dirt, rocks, brush, and other debris into the air. The tanks then roared on into the next field or open area and, once through, opened fire with the cannons and machine guns on the next hedgerow to the front.

"As the battle progressed, enemy troops were plowed out of their hedgerow positions and fortified bunkers, while others were covered up in their foxholes. One five-man machine-gun squad was plowed completely out of the corner of a hedgerow as the tank burst through and ran over them. One of my BAR men braced his gun on top of a downed tree stump and mowed down a line of enemy troops before they knew we had penetrated behind them.

"The assault on Hill 192 was a textbook attack, with the full power of artillery, tanks, and infantry working together as a team. It came down to face-to-face, hand-to-hand combat with cold steel and it was kill-or-be killed in our area. By 1200 hours we had completely destroyed the enemy front-line positions and by nightfall consolidated our own. Casualties had been heavy but Company F was still an effective fighting force and morale was high. Later, an intelligence report stated we had virtually wiped out the entire 9th Parachute Regiment."

Despite overcoming the hedgerows, the twelve divisions of the U.S. First Army bogged down in front of St.-Lô. General Omar Bradley scripted a plan named Cobra. The strategy envisioned an opening gambit of intensive bombing across a patch of ground three and a half miles wide and one and a half deep, starting with a road that ran from Périers to St. Lô. In his memoirs, Bradley wrote, "Indeed, it was this thought of saturation bombing that attracted me to the Périers road. Easily recognizable from the air, the road described a long straight line that would separate our position from that of the German. *The bombers, I reasoned, could fly parallel to it without danger of mistaking our front line.* "[Italics Bradley.]

Until drafted for a role in Overlord,—the invasion and conquest of Normandy, the Eighth Air Force had pursued its own objectives, the strategic goals designed to knock the enemy out of the war by demolishing the inventory, production, and distribution of the tools of combat. The preparations for D day and the missions flown on 6 June had been the first tentative attempts of United Kingdom-based air units and the American ground forces to focus on the same objective, the German forces in the field. Even here, the airmen in the big bombers were mostly not engaged in direct support of ground forces but in a more general collaboration. The responsibility to play a tactical role in a specific campaign like Cobra was something new. Unlike the Navy, the Air Corps had neither trained nor practiced for this sort of function.

Early on the morning of 24 July, Cobra started in earnest. The most forward of the Nazi troops noticed that the Americans, for no obvious reason, had withdrawn from the field to positions behind the line of the Périers highway. Shortly thereafter, the German infantry heard aircraft, invisible through a thick ground haze, overhead. The poor visibility—the operation had already been postponed three days because of overcast—prevented almost two-thirds of the 903 planes from reaching the target. Some held their ordnance because they could not see the target and the others obeyed a recall. Those bombs that were dropped exploded mostly in a no-man's-land although, by error, some hit U.S. troops, killing twenty-five and wounding more than sixty.

On 25 July, with the skies clear, the Eighth Air Force, preceded by fighter groups from the Ninth Air Force, carrying high explosives, fragmentation bombs, and napalm, struck with the full fury of more than 1,500 heavy-weights. After they departed, Ninth Air Force medium bombers and fighters rained down tons more of devastation. For the German soldiers it was an awesome demonstration of what bombers could achieve in a tactical situation. Commander of the crack Panzer Lehr Division, Lieutenant General Fritz Bayerlein, reportedly said, ". . . back and forth the carpets were laid, artillery positions were wiped out, tanks overturned and buried, infantry positions flattened, and all roads and tracks destroyed. By midday the entire area resembled a moon landscape, with the bomb craters touching rim to rim . . . All signal communications had been cut and no command was possible. The shock effect on the troops was indescribable. Several of my men went mad and rushed round in the open until they were cut down by splinters. Simultaneously with the storm from the air, innumerable guns of the American artillery poured drumfire into our field positions . . . " Bayerlein remarked that 70 percent of his soldiers were "either dead, wounded, crazed, or dazed." But again, a number of bombs exploded in U.S. positions, most notably among troops from the 4th, 9th, and 30th Infantry Divisions.

Heath Carriker, a North Carolina farmer and former draftee into an armored unit, had switched to flying. His first combat mission was Cobra. "According to my best memory, the Army [ground troops] would outline an area four miles by one mile astride the German front lines, by firing different colored smoke shells one-mile apart showing the beginning of the bomb drop. An all-out effort by the Eighth Air Force heavy bombers and medium bombers from the Ninth Air Force would bomb in squadron formations beginning at the smoke line and ending one mile deep. Two hundred fifty-pound antipersonnel bombs were used so that great craters would not result in hindrance to Army equipment [e.g., armor] and, second to kill and demoralize enemy troops. It was reported to us that the bomber stream was to be about eighty miles long.

"The next morning at the group meeting for briefing for another mission, the map showed the American armor and troops many miles past the starting point. The breakthrough was successful. This was a very satisfying and proud moment for me and the beginning of a feeling of power and eagerness for more of the same. Later, we were told that our bombs had killed American soldiers, including General [Lesley] McNair; very sad and a dampener of our spirits." Successful as it had appeared, the first close-in support by the big bombers to the ground troops was, as Carriker recalls, a disaster for some U.S. units, specifically the 9th and 30th Divisions. Several hundred men were killed or wounded. Among the dead was McNair, chief of the U.S. Army ground forces and the most senior man with the forces astride St.-Lô.

The painful friendly fire results at St.-Lô are traceable to blunders, ignorance, and perhaps bad luck. The blueprints drafted by Omar Bradley specifically directed that the attack pathway follow a horizontal route centered on the Périers road. Disturbed when he learned of the slaughter of Americans on 24 July, Bradley had demanded an explanation. To his outrage, he was informed that instead of following the generally east-west line of the battlefield, the raiders flew north to south, perpendicular to the front. The American First Army commander had contacted Air Chief Marshal Sir

Trafford Leigh-Mallory, head of the Allied Expeditionary Air Force, for further explication. In Bradley's account, Leigh-Mallory said, "I've checked this thing with the Eighth [air force] and they tell me the course they flew today was not accidental. They are planning to make it a perpendicular approach over the heads of your troops."

"But why, I [Bradley] asked, when they specifically promised us they would fly parallel to the Périers road? That road was one of the reasons we picked this spot for the breakout." Leigh-Mallory had responded that it would require two and one-half hours to funnel 1,500 heavy bombers down a narrow path like the road, to say nothing of the time demanded if one included the hundreds of fighters and medium bombers. And if Bradley insisted on his approach, the mission for 25 July would need to be scrubbed in order for the Eighth to brief the crews that perpendicular was now out and horizontal in. Bradley says he was "shocked and angered" by the answers, for they seemed a breach of good faith in the agreed-on plan. Against his better judgment, he consented to the north-south vector rather than postpone Cobra further.

With the bomber stream operating along a perpendicular axis, the 1,500 planes indeed could dump within a far shorter period of time than if they had to come in almost single file to the designated zone. Bradley reasoned that the road provided a clear marker to guide the bombardiers from dropping on the friendlies but, somehow, no one had ever pointed out to him that such a path would weaken the effect because it would lessen the concentration over a period of time. On the other hand, given the vagaries of the European weather, dependence upon a landmark seen from 12,000 to 18,000 feet up—altitudes described by some airmen as their distance above the target—would also seem rather chancy. Nor does anyone seem to have considered what the wind might do to the guideline color smoke shells, particularly over a period of time, as squadron after squadron from the eighty-mile-long bomber stream queued up for its shot.

Herb Shanker, the engineer/top-turret gunner with the 303d Bomb Group, agreed that the perpendicular approach to the front enhanced the opportunity for error. He noted, "We carried cluster bombs that opened and released twenty pound bombs after leaving the plane. The propwash scattered those twenty-pounders all over the place. We had three hit our wings."

Despite the Third Army breakout, the top generals remained dubious about closely coordinated ventures with the Air Corps. According to Bradley, Eisenhower said he would no longer involve heavy bombers in tactical situations. "I don't believe they can be used in support of ground forces. That's a job for artillery. I gave them a green light this time. But I promise you it's the last." And it would be until the ground forces needed them again.

The ferocity of Cobra's saturation bombing literally blew open the gateway for the American advance and the ground troops poured through the shattered German lines for what would become known as the St.-Lô break-out. Harper Coleman, in the 4th Division, recalled that a three- or four-day respite brought shower tents, new, clean uniforms, and kitchens with hot meals. Trucks then bore Coleman and his colleagues to the area near St.-Lô. "The Germans fought for every inch of ground. Everything was destroyed, all buildings, bridges, and equipment of all kinds. The roads and fields looked like a junkyard, dead animals in all of the fields. Some civilians had not been able to escape. Occasionally we would find dead ones in buildings.

"During this period, we lost quite a few people. How anyone made it I still do not know. I saw one of the battalion commanders killed by a sniper as he stood near our position. A member of our squad was killed by a sniper and a bullet came across my shoulder, cutting the top of my hand. We came across a column of German troops caught in an artillery barrage and still on the road when our tanks went through. They did not have time or take time to move any out of the way. It was not a pretty sight but I don't think we gave it much thought. Sometime in this period, I saw a wounded German begging for water. One of our lieutenants seemed to have lost all control. He said, 'Water, hell!' and shot him in the head."

Robert Johnson, son of a former North Carolina tenant farmer, had enlisted in the Air Corps shortly after Pearl Harbor and become a crew chief for B-17s in the 401st Bomb Group. He spent seven months servicing the bombers. In April 1944, with D day two months off, Johnson said, "Word came around on the bulletin board asking for ground crewmen to sign up for active combat duty. Me still being only a twenty-year-old kid, I thought it a great idea." Assigned to the 4th Armored Division, Johnson informed an officer that his experience with the vehicles used to tow B-17s indicated he could drive a tank. He trained for a month, learning how to handle a Sherman. "In July, after the invasion of France, we were going toward St.-Lô. A German colonel with a company was holding a huge concrete pill-box. He had defeated everything that had tried to take his fort until us 4th Armored tanks rolled against him. He was soon taken."

The almost continuous infusion of fresh forces such as the 4th Armored Division imperiled the entire Wehrmacht forces along the western front. For two days, a thin crust of the German defense had held up an advance of the 4th, 9th, and 30th Infantry Divisions west of St.-Lô. But the overmatched defenders could not sustain their resistance particularly after the 2d, 3d, and, 4th Armored Divisions battered enemy strongpoints.

Captain Tommy R. Gilliam was an Indiana University ROTC graduate, with Company B, 2d Infantry Regiment, 5th Division. He participated in the St.-Lô breakout where, after fierce fighting against a veteran German outfit, they captured their objective and then made a forced march to position themselves for support of the British at the Vire River. "It was around mid-

night and we were moving along a country road with about five yards between each man, men on both sides of the road. Company B was the advance
guard and I was marching with my first platoon which was providing the
point. The road, more a rutted trail, was thick with dust and the small
amount of noise from the occasional clank of equipment was muffled as we
entered a dark and foreboding woods, described on our map as *Le Forét Mil-
itaire*. The forest was dark and heavy and we were marching with trepidation,
not knowing what to expect around the next turn of the trail.

"My first sergeant, Tom Miller, a Regular Army veteran with close to
twenty-five years of service, was on the opposite side of the road, and I could
tell that even his normally unemotional visage was concerned with our security. At almost the center of this forest, we were startled by the sound of
people clapping, quietly and gently but continuously, as we marched along
the road. For several hundred yards we could make out the shadowy figures
of French men, women, and children, apparently from a village in the
woods, on both sides of the road. They were here at midnight to welcome
us and thank us. No words were spoken. The applause was not loud enough
that it would have attracted attention from more than a few feet away, but
it was continuous as the company passed through the area.

"It was an eerie feeling, but also a deeply emotional one. It was our first
welcome from the French people [the division had been in France for nearly
three weeks], almost as if the ghost of Lafayette was saying '*merci*' through
the hands of these French peasants. Although there were to be many more
welcomes, most with cheering, flowers, wine, and kisses as we spearheaded
the Third Army across France, none was as heartwarming or as poignant as
the one we received from the villagers of the little town somewhere between
Vidouville and the Vire River."

On 4 August, Patton's Third Army included Leonard Loiacono, of the
5th Division's 50th Field Artillery Battalion. During the next twenty-seven
days, Loiacono traveled 700 miles in a race through France. "The infantry
rode with us in our trucks," said Loiacono, explaining how foot soldiers managed to keep pace with armored divisions that spearheaded much of Patton's sweep. Other GIs climbed on tanks, tank destroyers, jeeps, ambulances,
and anything tracked or wheeled that could carry them forward. Loiacono
recalled a similar welcome to Gilliam's. "Going through towns, the civilians
would cheer and give us anything from flowers to bottles of wine. Some
places we went through, men would be shaving the heads of girls who were
friendly with Germans, or the girls would be walking out of town, nude, bald-
headed, carrying only a handbag."

As the VII Corps sought to wipe out the remaining, but still potent, German forces from the Cherbourg Peninsula, along the line running from St.-
Lô through Périers to the Channel, battalion surgeon Marion Adair, chose

a house for an aid station. He dispatched his sergeant to bring up the rest of the medical section. His diary reported: "About 10 P.M., I sit on a wall next to the road, reading my map and watching the vehicles go by. Suddenly, something slams behind me about ten feet away and blows me onto my feet. Then my right leg gives way, and it is bleeding. I have to lay in the ditch. I expect more shells but none come. When the smoke and dust clear a bit, I get my breath. I see a couple of men and shout for an aidman. They are too befuddled to help. But it doesn't matter because Vic [Samuel Victor] and the boys come running up.

"By this time, I'm hurting like hell, until I get the morphine syrette. The boys bandage up my thigh (right), left buttock, and back and make out the E. M. T tag. I'm put on a litter and start back on a jeep to the collecting station. We're slow going back because we are meeting 3d Armored Division vehicles bumper to bumper. Fresh replacements with clean uniforms are going forward. One asks the other if I am a German and I rise up and say, "Hell, no! I'm an American.

"I get to Company A station and Captain Smith and Captain Scuka see me. I get sulfadiazine and am then loaded into an ambulance and taken to clearing station. There Captain Miller anesthetizes all my wounds and pulls the clothing out of them. He also gives me tetanus toxoid, a clean dressing, and an initial dose of penicillin. 27 July: . . . After an interminable ride I get to the 44th Evac. Hosp. about 2 A.M. At dawn they X-ray me and I lay around all morning, quite uncomfortable on a litter. In early afternoon, they take me to the O.R. and give me pentathol. I go to sleep easily and when I wake up, I feel good—almost inebriated.

"The surgeon who operated tells me no fragments were removed, only debridement done. I have five wounds on my back. He dissected into one as far as my right subclavian artery, then gave up the search for the fragment. I have a wound on my left buttock and the one in my right thigh is fairly large . . . none of the fragments were removed as it would have involved extensive exploration into the remaining muscle. All the wounds are packed with petrolatum gauze. I am most uncomfortable . . . Later they bundle me into an ambulance and off I go. I stay all night at an airstrip and it's a tough night." Adair underwent months of work repairing the damage before his return to the U.S. for more treatment. In December 1945, he received his honorable discharge.

The rush through the Germans at St.-Lô by Patton's armor, coupled with the advances achieved by First Army, now commanded by Lt. Gen. Courtney Hodges, pinched the already retreating *Wehrmacht* between the Americans, the British Second Army, and the Canadian First, driving from the east pincers. Hitler, who had held in abeyance his strongest armored reserves in the mistaken belief that the main invasion was yet to come at Pas de Calais, had compounded his blunder with one as memorable by ordering an attack upon the Americans between Avranches and Mortain. Unfortunately for the Panzers, 7 August, in contrast to much of the summer weather, dawned with full sunshine and few clouds. The main American outfit, the 30th Infantry Division, could clearly see the massed attackers and summoned a concentration of artillery. Simultaneously, the P-47s streaked through the sky to unleash a torrent of rockets and bombs. The air cover expected from the *Luftwaffe* hardly left the tarmac before Allied predators fell upon them, rendering their contribution nil. German forces renewed their assault, but the GIs of the 30th Division repulsed any efforts to advance. The defeat broadened the avenue for Patton. The only route for escape or reinforcement lay in the Falaise Gap, a corridor less than thirteen miles wide.

Although Eisenhower, only a few weeks before, had dismissed the use of the heavy bombers for ground support, the strategists called upon the big planes to stop German traffic in both directions, trapping the tens of thousands being enveloped in the Falaise Pocket, and blocking off any attempt to relieve the pressure on the beleaguered troops. While not at the same close-in level as at St.-Lô, the mission again had a tactical purpose rather than a long-range strategic one.

Irwin Stovroff, having bombed major targets, D day, Munich, Hannover, and Peenemünde had completed thirty-four missions on 13 August when his 44th Bomb Group was posted for his last combat flight, a road junction near Rouen, a choke point for enemy movement in either direction. "It was supposed to be a milk run—easy in, easy out," says Stovroff. "Hell, we'd never be out of sight of the English Channel. I'd already packed my footlocker that morning at the base. I was supposed to go to Northern Ireland to be an instructor when I came back."

Stovroff belonged to the crew of the *Passion Pit*, a B-24 given that name in honor of a basement bar of the Santa Rita Hotel in Tucson where the men training together under pilot Lt. John Milliken relaxed when on pass. Bombardier Stovroff described the trip to the Rouen target as "a long, straight bomb run, no evasive action. We never dreamed there would be antiaircraft like that that day. But the time they hit us, we were at about 18,000 feet. Our number one and two engines were on fire. I toggled the bombs through the bomb-bay doors so they wouldn't explode. We all saw the flames and it wasn't long before we got the word to bail out. The bomb bay doors were still open so everyone could get out there."

"I put my chest chute on. We didn't wear chutes when flying because we had so damn much clothing, heavy equipment that you couldn't move around if you had a back chute on. We did wear a harness to which we hooked our chest chutes. We had practiced on the ground how to put it on. But I'd never jumped before. There was no hesitation on my part or the others."

In a Liberator in the squadron behind, John McLane Jr. saw the heavy and accurate flak burst within the formation that included *Passion Pit*. "I was looking directly at it when one of their planes [*Passion Pit*] started to burn. The plane fell out of formation. As I looked directly at it, there was a monstrous explosion and the plane disintegrated before my eyes. The motors were torn from the wings and went tumbling through the sky with their props windmilling as they fell. The wing, fuselage and tail were torn to shreds. As the pieces of aluminum drifted and twisted while they fell, with each turn, the sun reflected off their surfaces back to my eyes as if they were mirrors. The most spectacular sight was the tanks that had been torn from the wings. The gasoline did not explode but rather burned in huge orange flames streaming out behind the tanks as they fell in wavy fans to the earth below."

McClane assumed all the occupants perished in the fiery detonation of *Passion Pit,* but everyone including Stovroff had already exited, when *Passion Pit* blew apart. "I landed right in the front lines," said Stovroff. "I hit a fence coming down, got up and got out of my parachute. Germans were coming in all directions. I threw away my dogtags, which had an H [for Hebrew, as his religion], and I threw away my .45 pistol. I put up my hands and surrendered.

With the *Luftwaffe* no longer able to protect the German ground forces, the American dive-bombers, primarily in the form of P-47s and, to a lesser extent, P-51s, wreaked havoc with the Nazi legions in their bunkers, and savaged anyone on the road in retreat or trying to reinforce the defenders. The Germans referred to their tormentors as "Jabos," a short version of *Jäger Bomber*—hunter-bombers. They learned to work closely with ground observers. Stephen Ambrose quoted Capt. Belton Cooper when a pair of Panther tanks menaced his unit. "Within less than 45 seconds, two P-47s appeared right over the treetops traveling like hell at 300 feet. It seemed like the bombs were going to land square in the middle of our area." As Cooper and his men dove into foxholes, the P-47s followed up on their bombs with their .50-caliber machine guns. They apparently exploded a German ammunition dump. "The blast was awesome; flames and debris shot some 500 feet into the air. There were bogie wheels, tank tracks, helmets, backpacks, and rifles flying in all directions. The hedgerow between us and the German tanks protected us from the major direct effects of the blast, however, the tops of trees were sheared off and a tremendous amount of debris came down on us.' "

Walter Konantz had owned his own airplane since his high school senior year and entered the Air Corps with 250 hours of flying time. As a replacement shipped to the 55th Fighter Group, Konantz discovered, "They had changed from P-38s to P-51s only a few days before my arrival. At the 55th we had another ten hours of tactics, formation, and strafing practice before our first combat mission." The log of Konantz's early sorties suggests the still-prominent role for fighters in aid of the campaign through France during August. On the eighth of the month, his first time on the aerial battlefield he served as one of the chaperones for B-17s hammering the Romilly-sur-Seine airfield south of Paris. He described the affair as "uneventful." On 12 August he participated in a pair of ground strafing and dive-bombing ventures. In the first he noted at the time: "Southern France. Destroyed one locomotive and damaged several boxcars—lost two pilots due to flak. Time logged: 3:15." He wrote of the second mission in the Verdun-Nancy area. "Destroyed 15 ammunition railcars and a city water tower. Aircraft badly damaged by flying debris from exploding ammo cars but made it back to base. Dented the leading edges of the wings and tail as well as knocking off the propeller spinner. Lt. Gilmore shot down by flak. Time logged: 3:15." On 13 August he reported, "Dive-bombing and strafing south of Paris—Hit a railroad station with my two 500 pound bombs and strafed a German staff car. Time logged: 3:00."

Patton, dubious about the value of air support while in North Africa, now relied heavily upon the Jabos. He expressed confidence that they could ward off any attacks upon his flanks. The Third Army commander gloried in his role, speeding about in a jeep, constantly popping up to figuratively boot his forces in the rear end, exhorting, demanding them to move forward ever faster, Thor hurling multiple thunderbolts at the enemy. Success emboldened him to entertain grandiose strategic visions. If he could head due east to Paris, then dash northwest, the Third Army would seal off a huge chunk of territory, trapping more prisoners than bagged in North Africa. Eisenhower and Bradley—now Twelfth Army Group head and Patton's boss—focussed on Brittany rather than what they considered a highly risky venture. Their more limited objectives would include the port of Brest, as well as shutting down Lorient and St.-Nazaire, the two biggest hives for U-boats. In spite of his reassurances, they worried over Patton's exposed flanks. Intelligence intercepts gleaned from ULTRA, the code-breaking system, hinted at a counteroffensive. They foresaw an acute gasoline shortage for his armor. Indeed, to keep the vehicles rolling, the Third Army stole fuel from stores reserved for other organizations, impersonated officers from the First Army, bribed quartermaster people with truckloads of souvenirs, and salvaged captured materials. The "midnight requisitions" reduced shortages, but the supply pipeline could not keep up with demand. The Red Ball Express itself consumed huge amounts of fuel. A thriving black market seduced greedy American soldiers who siphoned off vital oil, gas, and food rations as well as amenities like cigarettes and coffee.

Unable to scold, cajole, or steal the necessary resources, Patton grudgingly accepted the mandate of his superiors, grousing, "Brad and [Courtney] Hodges [First Army chief] are such nothings. Their one virtue is that they get along by doing nothing." Patton's army dutifully advanced as far as Le Mans, then veered west to pinch off the entire Brittany peninsula.

Even this did not fully exploit the potential for victory. To close the escape roads, Canadian troops advanced on Falaise but were slowed by strong enemy resistance. With Field Marshal Montgomery's acquiescence, Bradley agreed to use Patton's XV Corps to pinch off the Falaise Gap. The Americans began to work their way toward the objective when again Bradley erred on the side of caution. He halted the advance for fear the two Allied forces would collide. Some 35,000 enemy soldiers, albeit bereft of heavy weapons and armor, escaped. Still, 50,000 German soldiers went behind the POW wire and perhaps 10,000 more died during the campaign.

The decision to restrict Patton's sweep was partially due to a genuine fear that he would overreach. To those who expressed worry over his vulnerable flanks, he snapped, "Forget this goddamn business of worrying about our flanks . . . Some goddamn fool once said that flanks must be secured and since then sons of bitches all over the world have been going crazy guarding their flanks . . . Flanks are something for the enemy to worry about, not us." He denounced any effort to hold one's position instead of "advancing constantly." But in the eyes of some military experts it reflected a difference in philosophy. The traditional view was based upon the conquest of territory. Patton, however, never wavered in his belief that the way to win was by killing; his speeches are replete with references to eliminating the opposition—whether by their deaths or by capturing them. Like the Marines in the Pacific, he advocated blunt force, head-on confrontation, arguing that in the long run it would kill more enemy and cost fewer American lives. It was not a simple issue; the top political and military leaders undoubtedly recalled that the failure to occupy Germany in World War I allowed the Nazis to argue that the Fatherland had not been defeated. Unconditional surrender in Europe was unlikely unless Allied soldiers tramped the *strasses*. In the Pacific Theater, areas were bypassed because there was no value to planting the flag, but the prevailing sentiment held that only invasion of the homeland would squash the Japanese empire.

Absent a call on the heavyweights for ground support the B-17s and B-24s again concentrated upon strategic objectives. A major, and dreaded, target was the heavily defended synthetic oil complex at Merseburg. Well over 300 miles east of the coastline. Bill Ruffin, from a broken family in a tiny Kentucky coal mining town, saw Merseburg, from the air on four occasions and of all his destinations came to fear it most. "My first mission, July 28, was to Merseburg, as they say, 'the flak was heavy enough to get out and walk on.' I did not realize the danger. I didn't know that these little black clouds that suddenly appeared around our plane were there to destroy me until we returned to base and counted the holes in our plane. I soon learned that if I could see the red center of those little black clouds, I could count on some damage. On very rare occasions, I could hear and feel the explosion of those shells and knew we had suffered some major damage. On one such occasion, three feet of nose section was blown away, wounding our navigator and bombardier. They were dragged up into the pilot compartment where after being attended to, the navigator sat on the hatch to stop the air coming through. The German 88 was a remarkably accurate weapon, particularly at 25,000 feet where the B-24s were normally assigned, while we in B-17s drew 29,000 to 31,000 feet."

Ruffin, like so many of those who entered the European war in its final year, speaks more of flak than he does of the enemy fighters. Although the latter appeared sporadically and in lesser numbers than earlier, the casualties among bomber crews continued to be substantial as the enemy invested heavily in antiaircraft batteries, both fixed and mobile. The percentage of losses had fallen well below the double digits of Black Thursday to 2 or 3 percent and occasionally less than 1 percent. But with thousand-plane raids now commonplace, hundreds of young men died, disappeared, or were maimed each week. The Air Corps hoped to balance its payments in blood with a shutdown of the enemy war power. Indirectly, the savage exchanges aided the Soviets because even before D day the mammoth aerial attacks on the industrial areas forced the Germans to deploy guns, ammunition, and troops away from the eastern front.

35
Dragoon

At the time Overlord went on the drawing boards, a companion piece, Anvil, was plotted for southern France, deploying troops drawn mainly from the Mediterranean theater. When the Italian campaign bogged down at the Rapido, before Cassino, on the Anzio beachhead, the Allied forces could not provide the resources to mount an invasion of the two proposed sites, Brittany or the Riviera coastline. Anvil required more fine tuning to harmonize with the efforts in Normandy. In fact, Winston Churchill had always opposed Anvil. The British leader prophesied catastrophic casualties, although intelligence reports indicated sparse German troops in the area. The Americans correctly perceived that Churchill's real objective in Italy was to drive up into the Balkans and block the entry of the Soviet Union into the region.

Eisenhower, the American Chiefs of Staff, and Roosevelt insisted upon Anvil. The only concession was to rename it Dragoon to allay the British prime minister's worry of a breach in security. The final scenario rejected Churchill's plea for an assault in the Bay of Biscay, closer to the main Allied forces already in Normandy, and fixed upon the Riviera from Marseille to Nice. As in the cross-channel attack, airborne elements under the code of Albatross would drop during the night of 14–15 August to wall off the beaches from reinforcements.

Dragoon initially committed elements of three U.S. infantry divisions, Free French armored units, and both British and American airborne. Among the regiments listed for Albatross was the 517th Parachute Regimental Combat Team. Introduced as ground troops north of Rome late in June, the 517th had been lightly blooded and gained a reputation for itself as carousers with minimum regard for some of the niceties of soldierly behavior.

In addition to the infantry-trained troopers, the 517th included a field artillery battalion equipped with pack howitzers, and a combat engineer company, all told about 3,000 men. A few troopers arranged for the 1944 equivalent of a Mohawk haircut. Almost everyone applied liberal amounts of green and black greasepaint, from tubes bearing the logo of the Lily Daché cosmetics company, to their faces for camouflage and prevention of reflections that might alert the enemy to their presence.

Assembled at the Orbetello airfield the 3d Battalion heard an address from CO Mel Zais. "I told them, and I really meant it, that I would much, much rather be in our position than that of anybody on the ground, because we knew where we were going, where we were coming in, how many of us there were. We knew what we were going to do, and we had the advantage of having the initiative. Meanwhile, those on the ground would have descending upon them at night, out of the heavens, innumerable people. Those on the ground had only three alternatives. They could lie still and be captured. They could run and probably be shot. Or they could shoot at us and if they got one or two, they would be lucky but they would never live after that because all of our attention would be directed toward them. I told this to all of my men. Of course they were up, high, just cheering." Some, like engineer Allan Goodman, however, regarded Zais's declamation as just a "Knute Rockne style pep talk." Neither Bill Boyle nor Dick Seitz, who commanded the 1st and 2d Battalions chose to make any speeches to their people.

Something of a special meal was served; boneless chicken from a can and three cans of beer were issued to each trooper. There was debate about whether to drink it on the spot or carry it along. Most, like Phil Di Stanislao opted for the bird-in-hand approach. The troopers of the 1st Battalion watched a movie, *Stage Door Canteen*, a highly improbable romance between a soldier on leave and a celebrity appearing at a Stateside canteen. Before the last reel, however, the loudspeakers called upon them to report to their planes. The pathfinders, like Dick Robb and Jack Burns, toted the Eureka system.

Said Robb, "In practice and total darkness, we had jumpers landing on us, breaking the Eureka's antennae. On one drill I landed twenty feet from the Eureka operator and I was the twelfth man out." The pathfinders also bore special lights mounted on a tripod that created a five foot-by-three foot target area in the drop zone, as well as luminous panels to aid a daylight glider landing. This also showed wind direction. The teams took two of everything in the belief that redundancy compensated for any mechanical or electronic malfunction.

While waiting to take off, an extra beer ration was served. "About ten o'-clock," said Robb, "Lieutenant Fuller stood up, and with a slight weave and a bit of a slur said, 'Lesh go over thish one more time.' Someone said, 'Oh shit, Lieutenant, we've been doing this for a month. If we don't know it now, we never will.' He said, 'Right, so let's have another beer.' We gathered at the planes around 11:30 for a midnight takeoff. I put a can of beer in each side pocket of my jacket. Jim Kitchin was ahead of me. He was laughing and fumbling with his gear and couldn't get his foot up to the first step onto the ladder. The crew chief boosted him up into the plane. The Air Corps types thought it a riot we were all so smashed we couldn't get into the planes without help. We were having a ball, too. However, I can assure anyone that a flight time of 3 hours and 30 minutes, and an altitude temperature drop of fifteen or twenty degrees, did a lot to sober up all concerned. The adrenaline and fear of what was in store added much to the process. Vaso constriction from the latter, plus the beer, gearing up, and flight time left almost no chance to pee. There were thirty-six fellows almost in tears begging to get out of the three planes to perform the mission. Later, I suggested to Lieutenant Fuller that beer might be one of the surest means to eliminate jump refusals."

To confuse potential hostile reception parties, six aircraft hauled six hundred rubber parachute dummies and dumped them to the north and west of Toulon, well away from the actual drop zones. Battle noise simulators, devices that exploded upon hitting the ground with a sound resembling rifle fire, accompanied the dummies to further convince the enemy. Planes also scattered tons of metal strips that would deceive enemy radar. The official Allied report claims that German radio transmissions indicated the tricks fooled the enemy, but events conspired to confuse all sides.

Altogether, the 405 C-47s under Troop Carrier Command lifted off ten Italian airfields with 5,630 paratroopers bound for Southern France among these, the largest single outfit was the 517th Combat Team. Not only were its three major combat components aboard but also some men not ordinarily considered as ground forces. From the Service Company, eighteen parachute riggers volunteered to accompany the combat team. They were assigned to assist the 460th Parachute Field Artillery in setting up howitzers. In the tradition of airborne, the two chaplains, Protestant minister Charles Brown and Roman Catholic padre Alfred J. Guenette, went along.

As the flights of aircraft bearing troopers from the three Rome airfields droned toward their targets, the Pathfinders prepared to descend. The strategists had arranged for boats spaced thirty miles apart in the Mediterranean to provide checkpoints for the air crews. These enabled the planes to make their landfall accurately. Unhappily, as their planes flew over the coastline, a heavy fog obscured the ground. Navigational problems due to poor visibility, shifting winds, and perhaps some pilot error, handicapped the Pathfinder operation. The entire affair was jeopardized. Even after the results of the overall operation were recorded, Troop Carrier Command boasted this was the most successful drop of the war with 85 percent accuracy. In fact, only four out of ten of the flights of planes unloaded their sticks anywhere near their DZs.

Robb recalled, "The Pathfinder pilot-commander, a who led the Normandy Pathfinders, advised us that he could not locate our DZ exactly. The beer we consumed had nothing to do with the fact that we landed about six miles from the DZ. And when we were immediately discovered by a company of Germans, we got into a running firefight that gave us no chance to guide in the other planes." His companion Jack Burns was wounded as he touched down but managed to free his weapon and wipe out his attackers. Without the Pathfinders and the Eureka-Rebecca system to guide them, the pilots relied on their airspeed and the navigational checks they managed to make before the fog blotted out the ground

The contingent that included Engineer Ernie Kosan had been separated from the 517th Parachute Regiment Combat Team. The 1st Platoon of the 596th Parachute Engineer Company was detached from the 517th to work with the 509th Parachute Battalion, a veteran combat outfit that had participated in the invasion of Italy nearly a year earlier. "I was proud to be attached to an outfit with the reputation of the 509th," said Ernie Kosan. "The objective was to secure the bridges into Le Muy for the advancing seaborne troops. It seemed like a simple, classic operation. But we were naive.

"While we waited on the tarmac to take off, we received a welcome bonus, grapefruit juice with a good, stiff shot of medicinal alcohol. Also we were given four condoms and four prophylaxis kits. These had to be shown to the officers as we boarded the planes. Failure to display them would eliminate you from the jump which would then be treated as a case of desertion. On the way to the drop zone we sat quietly on the plane, lost in our own thoughts. We were also completely bushed after the physical exertions and emotional stress prior to boarding the plane. We were discouraged from leaving our positions to look out the door because of the sheer bulk of our equipment. Anyway, the overcast and fog made it impossible to see anything.

"Then came the final command. 'Stand in the door!' The engines throttled back and the nose was dropped and the plane began to shudder. The red light continued glowing, for an eternity it seemed. Suddenly the green light came on. The jumpmaster screamed, 'GO!' The jump seemed like any other, except in this case it was a relief from tension. My chute opened and it was quiet—eerily quiet. There were no shouts, no laughter, no banter. I knew there were others out there but I couldn't see them. We were descending in a dense, cold fog. I assumed the 'prepare to land position' and waited. Suddenly, I heard below noises that chilled me to the marrow of my bones—these were crashing sounds. I thought, God, no, a water landing. I began saying my prayers because very few troopers can survive a water landing. The equipment is like a pair of concrete boots. Add to that the drag of the parachute and you're a goner.

"Then I hit a clump of shrubbery and the ground. It is impossible to describe the feeling of relief upon being safe on terra firma. All was quiet. I freed myself of the riser lines and took off the chute harness. The gas mask went into the bushes. Abruptly, I froze. I heard a crashing sound from the bushes. I couldn't remember the password or countersign. I crouched with my carbine and waited. Incredibly, a British paratrooper came striding through the brush. He saw me and without any preliminaries asked in a normal voice, 'I say, have you seen anything of my chaps?' All I could answer was, 'No.' 'Cheerio,' he said, and disappeared into the woods."

While Dick Robb and his Pathfinder comrades were engaged in a firefight far from the place pinpointed to bring in parachutists, troopers of the 3d Battalion started their journey to the earth. Without the expected help from Robb's team, the pilots could only guess where they should give the green light. In contrast, however, to the Normandy air drop, the ground-to-air fire was not heavy and the airspeed of the aircraft, if not the altitude [because of ignorance of the terrain], was appropriate. Mel Zais, who'd fallen asleep once his airplane took off, immediately sensed a problem. "I jumped as soon as the green light went on. I swung twice in my chute before I hit and I knew then we were in the wrong place because we should have been at 1,100 feet and over a vineyard. It had been nowhere near 1,100 feet and this was no vineyard that I landed in."

Zais was, in fact, twenty-five miles east of his appointed drop zone. "I started to unstrap my chute after taking my pistol out and laying it beside me in case there was any shooting. I could hear thuds from here and there as the bundles from the planes dropped. About twenty yards away I saw a yellow chute. That was one that carried a radio and I knew I must get it because I was in the wrong place. A soldier came out of the gloom, pressing his little cricket for identification. I said, 'Hey, trooper.' A voice answered, 'What do you want?' Then he added, 'I'm looking for a blue chute.' [The color signified a machine gun.] I told him the yellow chute had a radio. He said, 'You can't shoot no radio.'"

At dawn, Zais, using his maps, located himself and determined that his troopers were spread over the landscape in three segments roughly four miles apart. He started collecting troopers and marched toward a road junction through which the enemy could bring reinforcements. "My exec, Bob McMahon had landed against a wall, ripping open his knee so badly I could see white cartilage. He insisted on walking so I carried his musette bag."

Lieutenant Howard Hensleigh, who had joined the 517th and G Company as a platoon leader in November 1944, was part of Zais's lost legions. Having tossed two bundles with bazookas from his plane, he also lost his dinner for the first time in a plane. But he avoided serious injury even as he caromed off a tree onto a couple of rocks. "I got the chest snap, leg straps, and bellyband unbuckled, just as they taught us in jump school, pulled the M1 out of the bag, and assembled it, inserting a clip ,and putting her on safety."

Hensleigh started to round up men from his scattered stick. Aided by Sergeants John Podalac and Charles Boyer, Hensleigh accumulated seventy to eighty enlisted men. One of them discovered a house. "After placing five or six men behind cover. I banged the big brass knocker on the door. When I heard a female voice in French from the balcony just above, I said, 'American parachutists' in my bad French. The house seemed to shake. Soon half a dozen men and women greeted us with kisses on both cheeks and strong handshakes. We went in, had a glass of wine. I asked where Le Muy, the town we should have landed near, was. They showed signs of distress and, through a conglomeration of sign language, English, and French, told me we were thirty-three kilometers away." The column continued to swell, although the most senior officer was 1st Lt. Ludlow Gibbons of Company H. The battalion Headquarters Company commander, Capt. Joseph McGeever, appeared with several troopers. McGeever had met up with eighty Brits and, between the GIs and the Tommies, a German truck convoy bearing infantrymen had been wiped out. The union of the two American groups brought the total to 400 troopers heading for their assembly area near Le Muy.

The 2d Battalion, led by Dick Seitz, came down closest to their drop zone. "I saw fog over the water as we approached the French coast," recalls Seitz's exec, Tom Cross. "Then I saw some islands, then more fog. When the green light came on for 'go' I really wasn't certain we were over land, so I prepared for a water landing, or tried to, but I really couldn't. I had too much equipment on. I never saw the ground but, unfortunately, I grazed a tree and then landed unevenly in a ditch. I thought I sprained my right leg but I broke it above the ankle. The trench knife strapped to my right boot may have helped snap the leg but now it acted like a splint. It hurt like hell when I started to walk, but the name of the game was to get going. All of us were aware of how the Germans had killed troopers whose chutes caught in trees or were wounded during the Normandy invasion. That was a highly motivating factor toward meeting the rest of the men.

"As I hobbled along, I saw T5 Victor Cawthon, of Headquarters Company's communications platoon and hailed him. He said he had to find his radio and scooted off in search of the communications bundle. I gathered everyone that I could find and we headed for where I thought the assembly area would be. It was still foggy and difficult to establish our position. A Frenchman on a bicycle wheeled up and I asked him for directions to La Motte in my fractured French. With the greasepaint smeared on our faces, all I did was scare him. Suddenly, a German machine gun started up. We couldn't determine the direction of fire or its location but it was too damn close for comfort.

"I had a sizable force with me, about the size of a company, when I met Dick Seitz. He took over and we marched on our initial objective. I tried to start out at the head of the column but couldn't keep up until they halted because of enemy machine-gun fire. That allowed me an opportunity to hobble up to the front. When we finally reached our objective, I sat down beside a tree. Then I could not get up when it was time to move out. Someone helped me to a nearby château that became an aid station of sorts. A French family took care of us temporarily."

Company A's 2d Platoon under Lt. James A. Reith had been assigned a movie-style piece of heroics. Remembered Reith, "We were to slip into the *Wehrmacht* stronghold of Draguignan before the enemy realized that Southern France was under parachute attack. We were to capture Gen. Ferdinand Neuling, commander of the LXII Corps. And if we couldn't kidnap him alive, we were to kill Neuling and then get out of Draguignan anyway we could.

"My platoon and I had studied the details of the capture plot for a long time. Neuling's residence was Villa Gladys, a stately old mansion that nestled among a stand of towering pines on the outskirts of the town. From our study of the aged architectural plans, stolen for us by the French underground, and a sandtable reproduction of the house, we knew the site well. We were also well briefed on Neuling's daily routine and personal habits."

From his plane, Reith splashed down into a watery ditch. In the nearby darkness he heard voices speaking German. He struggled desperately to get out of his harness. He was on his back, unbuckling his reserve chute, when he heard footsteps approaching through the underbrush. "Just as I freed myself, I looked up and saw a Kraut aiming a burp gun at me. I pulled my .45 pistol and rolled over just as a burst of machine-gun fire struck where I had been. I squeezed off several rounds and the German toppled over, dead from chest wounds. Knowing the firing would alert his comrades, I hurried away toward the main highway. A glowing red light on an equipment bundle attracted my attention. I headed toward it and saw the dim outline of a paratrooper standing near the bundle, gazing up at the C 47s in the sky. I edged closer to the figure, who remained focused on the planes. Moments later, I grew suspicious of my new-found comrade because the man gave off a fishy odor. I had encountered Germans in Italy who had the same odor, apparently from their diet of smoked salmon.

"I stooped to gain a better look at the man's silhouette. My heart skipped a beat when I discerned the coal bucket shaped helmet. He was no American paratrooper but a German. Almost at the same time, he became aware of my presence and his hand flashed toward his P38 pistol. I beat him to the draw, sticking the muzzle of my .45 in his stomach and firing. He let out a gurgling grunt before collapsing in a heap. As dawn came I saw from my watch it was 5:35. I had been in France only an hour but it seemed an eternity. But how could I hope to carry out my mission of capturing the general? I was alone and had no idea of my location, and the *Wehrmacht* between me and Draguignan were certainly on full alert now that thousands of paratroopers had fallen from the sky. A short time later, I ran into Joe Blackwell, my mortar sergeant, who told me we were at least twenty miles from Draguignan."

As daylight pierced the morning fog, Waco gliders, carrying infantrymen, antitank weapons, and 4.2-inch chemical-mortar units, were now coming in to their landing fields. To forestall such airborne incursions, the enemy had planted a full crop of *Rommelspargel*. Some but not all of the antiglider obstacles had already been hacked down by paratroopers. The gliders plowed into them but by serendipity many poles had been poorly installed. They snapped off wings but acted almost like brakes. Nevertheless, a total of 108 men from the more than 2,250 passengers were injured and a number were killed by crashes.

The combat team's own artillery quickly added its resources to those of the line companies. John Kinzer, the exec of the 460th Parachute Artillery, rode in the same plane as Rupert Graves but when he jumped he touched down on the other side of a ridge from Graves. "I prepared for a tree landing," says Kinzer "after hearing the bundles hitting trees. I ended up with my toes against a large rock on the mountainside. When I opened the Griswold container, one of my submachine-gun magazines fell out and I heard it bounce from rock to rock down the hillside. Therefore, I proceeded with caution until hooking up with other troopers below. Since I was not an infantryman, I led our first small group walking in front, until the trigger-happy guy behind me fired a shot between my legs. From that point, trigger-happy led and I guided him from behind.

"Upon arrival at our assembly areas I assisted Col. [Raymond] Cato [the unit's CO] in organizing our battalion command and control. The most impressive thing about our operation was the delivery of our major artillery power in one serial of aircraft, rather than breaking it up into batteries in support of battalion combat teams. That gave us coordinated fire support in position on D day. Three of our four gun batteries were in action within twenty-four hours of the landing." It was a prodigious achievement considering that a quarter of the artillerymen and their pieces dropped several miles from their designated area. Everything from weapons through the ammunition piled into small, hand-pulled carts moved only by straining legs, backs, and arms. Phil Di Stanislao, one of the troopers of A Company, of the 517th came to earth well out of sight and sound of his buddies. "I had decided that when the red light lit, if we had passed over the coast, I would discard my Mae West. When I went out of the plane and looked down I said 'Oh, Christ!' I wanted to climb back up the suspension lines of the canopy and retrieve the Mae West. But my landing was dry, heavy, and hard. I didn't see anyone nearby. When I went to get my rifle out of its container, the trigger housing slipped out of my hands. I searched on my hands and knees until I found it. My compass was smashed. I didn't know where north or south was. I tried to locate my position from the pattern of planes overhead but they were going every which way.

"Scattered as we were presented some tactical advantages. We were all over the area, in groups as small as two or three, sometimes even as individuals. As my friend Joe Blackwell, who was a sergeant with a mortar crew, insisted, we all thought we were capable of being officers. We all felt we had the leadership ability. We knew what to do, as a result of both training and ego. And we believed in each other. I came across two or three British troopers and since I was the ranking noncom they followed me. We ran into a group of Germans entrenched behind a huge bramble patch. We killed them. The Brits went their way and I continued by myself. Even though my compass had been smashed, I had lots of maps. In the dark I couldn't find out anything. But with daylight I came across what I could see was a small irrigation canal, and I plotted a route toward my primary target, where we would rendezvous or capture, whichever came first. In my travels I met up with a team from the 460th, pushing and pulling their howitzer. I stayed with them a bit, helping them move toward their target.

"I headed for where I was supposed to be and ran into Joe Chobot. We were not the best of friends. In Toccoa, [Georgia] one night, while I was charge of quarters, I went to his barracks and told him to turn the light out. He told me to shove it and we had at it outside. I believe I bruised him pretty badly and he was never warm toward me. But situations like this make strange bedfellows. Together, Joe and I started up the path of a wooded, not very steep hill. He ran ahead and suddenly dashed back. 'Goddamn, there are Germans up there.'

"The two of us hit the ground, preparing to fire. Then they rolled concussion grenades down the path, little black eggs. One rolled almost against my head. I did a complete flip-flop and it exploded near my boot. My foot went temporarily numb but it wasn't a fragmentation grenade or I'd have had it. I asked Joe how many there were but he said he couldn't tell. I said, 'Let's stand up, fire into the area, and then haul ass.' They rolled a few more grenades at us, all concussion. I could never figure out why they didn't use fragmentation ones and didn't fire. We stood up, emptied our rifles and then scrammed." Di Stanislao gave up on reaching the primary objective and decided to head for the secondary target.

Jim Reith had reluctantly abandoned any hopes of kidnapping the enemy commander. Instead, he rounded up a large band of troopers until he brought fifty to sixty soldiers to an assembly area. There the party united with a band of troopers including Erle Ehly from the 1st Battalion Headquarters Company and C Company's top gun, Capt. Charles La Chaussee. The group set its sights on a position that would block Highway N7, a vital artery that led to the beaches. Along the way, Reith led a patrol into the woods after sniper fire harrassed the advance. He came upon an entire stick of British paratroopers whose chutes failed to open. Reith counted bodies horribly mangled from the impact of their falls. Apparently, some breakage in the static-line cable caused the terrible accident. The American safeguard of a reserve parachute would probably have saved all, of them but only U.S. troopers wore a spare.

Captain Walter Plassman, the 3d Battalion surgeon, with a Sergeant Harvey and six other medics, traveled with I Company. John Chism, a newly recruited assistant battalion surgeon, Daniel Dickinson, who quit a safe spot in a military hospital to become a paratrooper, and a half-dozen medics accompanied G Company. Plassman noted, "I carried two aid kits strapped to my legs, two canteens of water, one unit of plasma, and my musette bag with medicine strapped below my reserve chute. I could hardly get in the plane. Four bundles with plasma, litters, and other stuff were loaded on the pararacks beneath the wings but we never found them. We landed far from our objective and those who could walk left to join the main forces. About six men and myself were unable to do more than hobble. One man had a fractured leg. My left knee had banged against a rock wall next to a road. With the help of two civilians, we managed to reach Montoroux, which was about one kilometer off.

"I set up a casualty station in a building that had been a TB sanitarium. There were only three cots there but people brought in mattresses. While I was there, I met a French dentist who happened to be visiting his in-laws. He was great. He managed to scrounge food and water for us. Another very helpful person was the local priest. Things were quiet except for a few artillery rounds that fell quite close. That night, around 1:00 A.M. about twenty-five German soldiers came into the town. They had one old truck and they were part of an engineer company. Their captain spoke some English. He said we should stay put and later they would try to evacuate us to their hospital. The Germans remained all day. They had one wounded man with them, a gut shot. I examined him but explained I could do nothing except give him morphine. He died in a few hours. That night, around 2:00 A.M. they pulled out, taking their dead man."

After medic Charles Keen and rifleman Melvin Biddle touched down they had no idea of their location and as they wandered about "trying to find where in hell we were, or someone who knew," they came across other troopers. "Near daylight, we met Captain [William] Young, [the battalion's S-3]. About thirty of us started out to see just what we could tear up. First we passed under a long string of heavy, cross-country electric cables running from the coast to the interior. Young must have been out of his mind because he sent a man up the high metal towers to cut the one-inch cables with a pick mattock. The poor fellow hit once and then raised himself up and really gave it a whack. When he hit the second cable a flame or spark jumped from the overhead cable about a foot, sounding like a cannon.

"The man's body went rigid. He fell stiff as a board to the ground, bouncing off a small building and knocking off some of the tile roof. His feet were still on the metal support of the tower when he stopped falling. The next thing I heard was 'Keen, see if you can help him!'

"I knew nothing about electricity so I used a tree limb to free him. But even then I knew it was all over for him. His helmet was still on and when I removed it, it was hot and burned black. All the hair on his head was burned off. His skin was black. There was no heart or pulse beat. Our leader decided we should attack the cables with a rifle grenade. That failed and we also lost some of our crowd who apparently did not like the direction of our leader."

The remainder of the group pressed on until they bumped into a young Frenchman. "I was chosen to ask him where was the railroad. '*Où est la gare?*' is what I think I said. He answered with a long series of French words and hand gestures. I confessed I had no idea of what he was saying. Trooper John Garcia, a 110 percent American Indian, who learned a lot of the language at the reservation school, informed me the Frenchman wanted to know what state in America I was from. So much for my college French course."

Making do as best they could, Keen and company piled into the back of a flame-spouting, smoky, charcoal burning truck. The driver headed for the village of Les Arcs. "At the edge of town we disembarked because no one knew whether the Americans, the FFI or the Germans controlled the town. In a very military manner we crossed through the streets until stopped by a man who spoke perfect English. He had come there after World War I from Boston.

"He explained to Captain Young that the land beyond the railroad bridge was in German hands. In the middle of the bridge sat a burning 75mm howitzer that had belonged to our own 460th. Later we learned that a crew from the 460th had assembled the gun after their landing and were pulling it through the town when the Germans hit them. Our commander decided we would all climb aboard the fire-belching, charcoal-burning, slow-moving truck and storm across the bridge to carry the war to the enemy. While the fireman was stoking the burners of the lorry, I spotted an old man in the uniform of the French foreign legion. He had ribbons down to his belly and he was waving his arms, yelling 'Suicide!' 'Suicide!' My French may have been poor but suicide happens to mean the same in French and English. I took one look at Captain Young, then looked at the old, decorated legionnaire. Without another moment's hesitation, I climbed over the side of the truck and down to the street. All of the other troopers followed.

"God, observing our predicament, saw fit to have Colonel Boyle appear, from God only knows where, and assume command." Keen, like De Stanislao, Chism, and others, marvels still at the omnipresence of Bill Boyle. They insist he invariably surfaced at moments of crisis and, in fact, wherever he happened to be of a moment, firefights broke out. That Boyle stepped on stage at Les Arcs at that moment was almost a miracle, considering the start of his role in Dragoon. When the group of aircraft ferrying his troops was perhaps twenty to twenty-five minutes from the drop zone, Boyle glanced out of the open door of his C-47. The formation of some fifty planes seemed in order. He turned his attention to his stick and the equipment bundles that included the vital radio gear necessary for communications. Boyle himself was weighted down with his individual needs, plus a can of machine-gun ammunition. He required every man not a member of a crew-served weapon to bear either a mortar round or the machine gun ammunition. Officers were included not only because of the value of the extra rounds, but because Boyle also reasoned that if the men saw that officers bore the added weight it would maintain morale.

"When we jumped," Boyle said, "I discovered that my plane was the only one in the sky I could see. The fog bank below me looked like the sea and I started to prepare for a water landing." On the ground, Boyle realized his troops were scattered very widely. In fact, he could find only half a dozen troopers. Fortunately, a pair of French civilians provided directions to Les Arcs, his target. There he discovered the small group that included Charlie Keen. Unfortunately, when Boyle sought to advance toward his objective, control of a rail line near Le Muy, his force of perhaps forty troopers met a strong German attack comprising as many as 400 soldiers. Boyle and his crew fell back to a defensive stance on the edge of Les Arcs.

Ed Johnson became one of the eighteen troopers from C Company dug in at Les Arcs with Bill Boyle's outnumbered band. "We held the town for a day and a half," reported Johnson, "although there were ten of them to every one of us. At the height of one of their attacks, Pvt. Jim Dorman spotted three Jerries coming up the railroad tracks on the left flank about fifty yards away. Depressing his rifle, he let go a muzzle-aimed antitank grenade. It caught the middle man squarely in the back and killed all three Krauts. Patrols led by Sergeant Landsom, Corporals Perkins, and Lathers and Privates First Class. North and Shaddoz gained vital information about the disposition of the enemy and the whereabouts of friendly troops." And in spite of casualties, Boyle's forces actually increased as 1st Battalion jumpers sifted into the Les Arcs redoubts.

The enemy took heavy casualties from a machine gun operated by Privates. Richard Jamme and Albert Ernst. Boyle deployed Johnson as part of a machine-gun team to guard one avenue leading to the embattled troopers' position. The strategy worked for a while but then German snipers infiltrated some of the taller buildings in town, making the spot untenable. Indeed, the only way to avoid death or capture lay in a retreat. Boyle skillfully extricated his troops. A major reason for the American escape lay in the courageous act of Al Ernst. Both he and Jamme were killed during the Dragoon fighting.

Russ Brami of 517th Regiment, E Company, fortified with dexadrine (other troopers do not recall receiving any amphetamines or other drugs), said, "Using my cricket, the first man I saw was Rupert Graves [regimental commander]. He had banged up his nose. He made me carry a bazooka, the 2.3-inch, which was a lousy weapon. As soon as we could, we started using the captured German *Panzerfausts*. I joined up with some others from E Company and we headed for La Motte. We were on our way when the kid in front got one right between the horns. We started pushing out patrols. With some others I was outposted on a hill where the gliders from the 551st were to come in. We pulled out some of the poles put into the earth to prevent gliders. There were mines on wires between some. We shot at them but we had no real tools for removing the poles."

The immediate concerns for Dick Seitz upon the assembly of his troopers were to take over in front of the command post established at Château Ste.-Roseline and to help break out Boyle's small garrison before the enemy enveloped it. On D plus 1, Lt. Carl Starkey, led a pair of the 517th's D Company platoons into Les Arcs from the north. One of the units then pushed through to contact some of the embattled Boyle troopers. The still outnumbered Americans hung on, fending off the enemy with their own small arms and aided by 4.2 mortars as well as marauding Air Corps P-51 Mustangs that dumped 500 pounders on the foe.

The 596th Airborne Engineer Company not only did not jump as a unit into Southern France but the 1st Platoon was parceled out to the 509th Combat Team, an entirely separate organization. One batch fell at Le Muy, a town designated for future assault and which lay four miles from the planned DZ. The jump brought serious injuries to two men, one of whom was Pvt. Henry Wikins, Ernie Kozan's fellow refugee from Germany. Heavy mortar fire on the Americans forced them to pull back. Because of the severity of Wikins's injury, a broken leg, he could not be removed. A day later he was found dead, apparently executed by the Germans. The murderers cut off his penis and stuffed it in his mouth, perhaps because they knew he was Jewish since he wore a Star of David on a chain around his neck.

"This had a profound effect on our attitude toward the enemy for the rest of the war," said Charles Pugh. As both a radioman and a demolition specialist, Pugh had made his jump with a forty-pound radio strapped to him, several blocks of TNT, and the usual field pack, weapon, and extra ammunition. With his two chutes, Pugh figures he bore between 130 and 140 pounds. "My group, missed its drop zone more than anyone else. About sixty of us landed some thirty miles off. We marched, mostly at night and after three or four firefights with Germans trying to retreat, we contacted the main unit on D plus 2. We ate K rations but we had all the wine we could drink, which came from the French people as we marched through their villages. We also picked up some potatoes, tomatoes, and onions, even an occasional chicken while traveling on foot."

Weary 3d Battalion troopers, having marched more than twenty miles along mountain roads, plunked down their exhausted, sweating bodies on the slopes by Ste.-Roseline. Sprawling under anything that would shield them from the sun, the men expected to have a night to recover their strength. However, Rupert Graves believed any delay in the operations around Les Arcs might jeopardize the entire mission. He ordered the 3d Battalion to attack.

Bereft of sleep for as much as thirty-six hours, H and I Companies led the assault. Cato's 75mm howitzers, bolstered by the 4.2 mortars flown- in by glider, poured 1,000 rounds upon the enemy in a period of twenty minutes. To some of the 460th it seemed like a contest to see who could fire the most. Everybody assisted in the loading, including captains and lieutenants. While the guns were still in recoil after firing, another shell was being loaded for almost immediate refiring. German prisoners later asked whether the victors had belt-fed howitzers.

The troopers jumped off a few minutes after 8:00 P.M. It seemed unlikely that anyone could have withstood that avalanche of fire, smoke, white hot phosphorus, and shrapnel. But Zais's forces met stiff fire. The attack bogged down as the Americans hugged the ground. Zais, said, "I knew I had to get them to move up into position, to cross the line of departure. I was just breaking out into the open and I kept walking. When I walked out there and said, 'Come on, let's go. Everybody get up, the firing for whatever reason stopped.' "

There were two companies up ahead that had halted in their tracks. "First Sergeant Gaunce had been shot in the throat and when Lieutenant Freeman went to help him he was hit in the belly. Then a third man went down. I thought, 'Boy, this is bad. I wasn't sure what to do. Everytime someone tried to get up on the railroad embankment ahead they were shot. I called for mortar fire from the chemical battery that had come in on gliders because the 460th with its pack 75s couldn't get the right angle.

"My S-3 had been injured and the acting S-3 was a kid named Ludlow Gibbons, a great youngster but getting very nervous. 'Colonel, I'll do anything you want to do, but this is suicide.' I said, 'What would you suggest?' He answered, 'We can't go over the embankment. Gaunce has been killed. Freeman has been killed.' He sounded almost hysterical.

"I said, 'We'll do what we've got to do. They're not going to shoot if all of us appear at once.' The mortars put down a barrage and then we attacked. The enemy came out running, hands up. There were about eighteen of them and they all surrendered." The citation that accompanied his Silver Star award stated that Zais, "completely disregarded the enemy fire and moved out into the open in direct observation of the enemy, shouting to his men to continue forward. Inspired and encouraged by the actions of their battalion commander, the men rose to their feet and continued the attack with vigor." The Germans surrendered and among the trophies, were a handful of GIs from the 45th Division who had been captured.

Ed Johnson from C Company and part of the original band with Bill Boyle which had almost been destroyed at Les Arcs was among the victory party that occupied the town. "I confess my view of the enemy changed when we took about fifty German military students prisoners. They were just kids, like us. Their small equipment bags spewed out pictures of their loved ones, just as ours would have. We turned them over to the French FFI where I am sure the sentiment was different."

All along the front the Germans died, surrendered or retreated. British troopers captured Draguigan and Reith's intended victim, General Neuling. From out of the hills came several hundred members of the 517th, these were men who'd been listed as missing and were feared dead or prisoners, but who, in fact, had fought small skirmishes with the enemy on their own, or on some occasions tied in with scatterings of the FFI. Actually, few members of the 517th found the French helpful for much more than intelligence. "If you saw them around waving their weapons," remarks Di Stanislao, "You could be pretty sure the enemy was long gone."

Contact with armored units of the 45th Division in the vicinity of Le Muy marked the success of Dragoon. The soldiers who had waded ashore on the Riviera had linked up with the airborne forces holding the interior. John Forrest was with the group controlling Highway N7 when they observed armored scout cars working their way along the road. "At first we thought it was another German attack but then we recognized them as from the 45th Division. When the lead one pulled up, a red haired soldier stuck his head out and asked, 'Does anybody here know "You Are My Sunshine?" I can sing the harmony.'"

With hostilities temporarily reduced to the occasional sniper, Howard Hensleigh requisitioned a handful of troopers to scout Montoroux. "I found Doc Plassman with a white uniform, just as if he were a part of the small hospital. All the boys were there and that was a relief since we heard all kinds of rumors how the Jerries had treated them. I made arrangements to have them evacuated by ambulance."

Now that the shooting temporarily died down and the opening phases of Dragoon were coming to a close, the 517th Parachute Infantry units counted the toll absorbed. It added up to 19 dead, 126 wounded, and 137 injured, which is a high 14 percent of the complement. Furthermore, the casualties occured in less than a week of action and do not include the losses suffered by both the 460th Parachute Field Artillery and the 596th Parachute Engineers.

The foot soldiers of the 3d, 36th, and 45th Divisions, all veterans of Italy, who invaded from the sea as part of the U.S. Seventh Army, under Lt. Gen. Alexander M. Patch, met much less opposition. Alongside of them eventually moved six Free Fench outfits of similar size. These units eventually were organized into the French First Army. Both armies became the charges of the Sixth Army Group headed by Gen. Jacob L. Devers. They moved inland smoothly and soon headed northeast while the 517th drew the task of driving east through the champagne country into the torturous terrain that led toward Italy.

Communications Sergeant Harold Taylor of the 3d Division said, "Prior to our landing on the St. Tropez peninsula our heavy navy guns shelled the coastal area. At the same time our aircraft kept the German forces off-guard, strafing them and bombing their defenses. My regiment, along with other regiments of the 3d division, met moderate gun and mortar fire as we came ashore. We made our way up the Rhone Valley. The division, accompanied by French and American divisions, expanded the beachhead over several days into several hundred miles."

"The entire VI Corps," said William Rosson, who left his post as a battalion commander in the 7th Regiment of the 3d to become assistant G-3 of the corps, "followed the Route Napoléon, parallel to the Rhone, covering 300 miles in seventeen days against light resistance by the German garrisons. Near Montélimar, a German column was destroyed by air strikes. They had a lot of horse-drawn equipment. Dead bloated horses were all over the place. Destroyed vehicles and bodies were scattered about. It was a ghastly mess."

The battalion commanded by Michael Davison of the 45th Division was designated regimental reserve for the invasion. "We simply made a walk-in landing," said Davison. "It was not an assault because we were in reserve and the regiment met no resistance on the beach. We had a couple of fairly tough scrapes just in from the beach but they loaded my battalion up in trucks one night and we drove all night to Grenoble up the Route Napoléon. We made bivouac about three in the morning, right alongside of a main road into town. I will never forget the next morning, watching those French girls pedaling by on bicycles to work. The soldiers were really excited. Those French girls were wearing long skirts, but when they rode their bicycles they let those skirts fly right up around their hips. God, those soldiers, they were growling."

His battalion deployed to hold the city of Grenoble while the battle for Montélimar went on. "A German reserve division up the valley was moving toward Grenoble. G-2 claimed its total strength was like 3,500, but I only had 800 guys and I got together with a Commandant Le Barbier of the French Forces of the Interior who had about a thousand men. We decided on a plan in which my battalion would place a roadblock and stop the head of the division. Le Barbier, the commander of the FFI, would take his guys, who were totally familiar with the terrain, up in the mountains and they would circle around to get on the flank of this German column. We would ambush it because the best way to protect the city was to ambush the whole bunch before they had a chance to deploy and assault us. We did it and we captured more than 1,000 prisoners."

36
Silent Service, Peleliu, Mars

Although the Japanese attack at Pearl Harbor shattered most of the Pacific fleet, no bombs blasted the U.S. submarine fleet. Admiral Stark ordered the submarines, along with other naval units, to execute unrestricted warfare upon enemy shipping. The early, swift Japanese conquests wiped out precious fuel depots and torpedo stores, but the main problem lay in the quality of the American sub fleet, its armament, and the thinking of the day. A substantial number of the undersea vessels on duty in 1941 were obsolete. Defective torpedo mechanisms plagued the undersea warriors for two years. Although a modernized building program had begun late in the 1930s some pigboats dated from another era. S-class boats lacked air conditioning and sailors sweated out a stifling atmosphere during patrols in tropical zones. The elderly subs fired a World War I-vintage Mark X torpedo that swam at a maximum thirty-six knots, slow enough for enemy ships to evade them. The newer model submarines used the faster, longer range Mark XIV which, to save money, and perhaps for security purposes, had never been test-fired with its detonator set to explode a warhead. During the first two years the torpedoes frequently failed to explode, even as exasperated submariners heard them clunk against an enemy hull or saw them run deeper than directed. Not until 1943 did the Navy correct the problems of depth mechanisms and detonators.

Pre–Pearl Harbor tactics called for submarines to hug the bottom, out of earshot of the the sound-detecting sonar, and out of sight of air patrols able to spot objects 125-feet deep in the clear Pacific waters. The concern for safety canceled out effective attacks, which were based upon the submarine's less exact sonar rather than its eye, the periscope. Too little periscope experience and a lack of night surface practice, plus an absence of tactical intelligence and aerial reconnaissance seriously handicapped U.S. submarines during the early war years.

Naval Academy graduate Slade Cutter, after observing the destruction at Pearl Harbor, was the navigation officer aboard the *Pompano* as it carried the war to Japan. On the first cruise toward Wake Island, a PBY spotted the sub. There were no recognition signals and, Cutter explained, "You were on your own and you expected to be attacked by any aircraft." The PBY relayed information about the unidentified submarine and planes from the *Enterprise* actually bombed and slightly damaged the *Pompano*. It continued its patrol until it saw a big transport, a former luxury liner *Kamakuru Maru*. "We reported sinking it, because we heard the hits, and saw the splash of water. Lew Parks [his skipper] assumed it was going to be sunk. When we came up there was no *Kamakura Maru* around. She had just bailed out, hadn't been hurt at all. Two duds bounced against her and caused the splashes which Parks took to be hits."

Unlike a number of the American submarine commanders early in the war, Parks was anything but timid. He insisted on driving the *Pompano* dangerously close to breakwaters for enemy-controlled harbors. But as navigator, Cutter said he was handicapped by turn-of-the-century charts that could be in error plus or minus five miles. At one point, a pair of Japanese destroyers started to prowl the waters, possibly suspecting the presence of the *Pompano*. "Parks maneuvered all day long, trying to get in position to hit them, but they never settled down to get a good firing position. Finally, in desperation, he decided to shoot. He took a sixty-degree gyro angle, which was much too much for those torpedoes at that time. I was on the TDC [Torpedo Data Computer] and got from Parks, 'Range 1,200 yards, speed 25 . . . 'I put on the solution light, 'Fire!' We fired both torpedoes and both of them prematured. About this time Parks said, 'Slade, did you ever have so much fun before with your clothes on?' Over the loudspeaker system.

"I wasn't worrying about having fun with clothes on or off at that stage of the game. Looking at this thing on the torpedo data computer, this target at 1,200 yards would be over [us] in a minute or so. He came and that's the first depth charge we ever heard. We had never had one fired in practice. I didn't know what they sounded like. A barrage came over and I knew what it was like to face death right then because we heard the water rushing through the superstructure. We learned later that is normal but we thought we had been holed. I figured that's the end and you don't feel anything. We realized very shortly that we hadn't been holed. Lew Parks maneuvered the submarine around, all ahead full, starboard back full and port ahead full, to evade those guys up above dropping their depth charges. Then he shifted to hand steering to reduce our ship's noise and had two men turning the steering wheel by hand. That was our baptism of depth charges. Parks thoroughly enjoyed it. He was having a hell of a time. After that, every time we went out on patrol, one of the prepatrol training exercises was to have a destroyer drop one or two depth charges 100 yards away so everybody could hear what they sounded like."

On the *Pompano*'s second voyage, it ventured into the China Sea. "We were on the surface one night," said Cutter, "and we picked up a contact. We shut off our engines and put our stern toward it. We didn't want to be picked up but the contact saw us and turned toward us. Parks sent for me to man the .50-caliber machine gun that we had aft and I got the thing ready.

"'Put it on them,' he said. We made another course change and the guy turned toward us again. Parks said, 'Let him have it.' That's what he would say instead of 'commence fire.' I pulled the trigger. They had tracers on and were going right into it; I guess he was about 300 yards. It was a fishing boat, good size, probably twenty men aboard. After the first burst of probably fifty rounds, a guy held up a lantern to show the rising sun on their flag. He thought we were the Japs. The captain said, 'Let them have it,' so I opened up again and we just kept firing. Finally the thing caught fire. I guess the tracers set off the fuel and it burned. We got out of there. It was a fisherman. I think about it lots of times. That's one of the terrible things of war. He was harmless."

Parks left the *Pompano* and Lt. Comdr. Willis Thomas succeeded him. On 9 August 1942,the sub sneaked near the entrance to Tokyo Bay. An intercept of Japanese naval transmissions indicated ships would be coming through their area. "It was after sunset and I looked through the periscope and thought it looked dark," remembered Cutter. "You can't tell because you don't get much light transmission through a periscope, not as much as through binoculars. We got on the surface and, my God, we thought we were naked. It was daylight. Since we were on the surface and nobody was around, we thought we would wait it out because it was going to be dark in a little while.

"All of a sudden, on the starboard quarter, searchlights illuminated us and six shells came out from two 8-inch turrets. A cruiser fired at us. They went over. We didn't stay to see the next salvo. We got under, and the destroyers came and they worked us over. The battery was down because we had been bucking the current all day, all we could do was dive, go down there and hope to God they weren't lucky. We couldn't take much evasive action. We didn't have enough battery for it. We couldn't run our pumps for fear the Japs would hear them because they made a hell of a lot of noise. Water was coming in aft through the inboard exhaust valve, leaking from the engine room, and flooding the engine room bilges. The main generators were attached to the engines so water got up into the generators. The *Pompano* was 252 feet test-depth. We got down to 407 feet and there were all these crackling sounds. The cork started to buckle loose on the bulkheads.

"All of a sudden they left us, lost contact, I guess, and they were gone. I was navigator and had no idea at all where we were. The captain blew all main ballast in order to come to the surface. I was the first one out; I don't know what I was looking for [as navigator] but I was the first out of the hatch. I looked up and Jesus, here was what I thought was a searchlight right on us. I said, 'Oh, shit!' which is a good expression under the circumstances. I thought it was a cruiser with that searchlight high above us. It was the Miko-moto Light [a Japanese lighthouse]" The submarine slowly limped away; only two of its four engines started and with the fuel pumps grounded out by the water leaks the *Pompano* could not afford to dive. The crew impro-vised, taking a working motor from one device to drive the fuel pumps, slowly building a battery charge, and repairing damage with the mechani-cal ingenuity that came from years of submarine duty.

Promoted to executive officer on the *Seahorse* now under Lt. Comman-der Donald McGregor, Cutter left Pearl Harbor for a patrol around the Palau Islands. A frustrated Cutter recalled, "One night off Toagel Mlungui Pass in Palau, we picked up a convoy coming out. They had a big, three-stack transport, about 15,000 tons. It was heavily escorted and they were heading toward the Philippines. They went past us. We could have attacked but we didn't. That was all right with me. The captain said, 'We'll get more of them on the surface at night. If we attack now, they will hold us down and we'll lose them.' So we surfaced and got way ahead of them. The captain went into the wardroom and there he stayed. He let me maneuver and stay ahead.

"I kept going down to tell him, 'Captain, we are in position to dive.' He delayed it. There was a quarter moon. Finally, I said, 'Captain, it's getting toward daylight, we'd better dive now. The moon is going down.' He hadn't even dark adapted, didn't have on red goggles, which you were sup-posed to wear at night. He was just sitting there in a lighted room. [Ulti-mately] I said, 'The moon is set, Captain. It's two hours before sunrise. We've got to go now.'

"He said, 'All right, dive.' We dove and he came to the conning tower, not dark adapted, put up the periscope, and said, 'I can't see anything. Take her down.' We went to 300 feet and the convoy went right over us and we didn't do a thing about it. It was terrible. We let them get away. I was sick. We surfaced and again he went below." For several more hours, the *Seahorse* tracked the enemy ships, maintaining visual contact through the periscope. Having been on duty for twenty-four hours without sleep, Cutter yielded his post to another deck officer who awakened him with the news that they had lost contact. The skipper had changed course, sending a message to Pacific submarine command reporting the breakoff from the quarry being pur-sued. A curt response ordered the *Seahorse* to resume its stalking at the Toagel Mlungui Pass.

According to Cutter, "We ran into an unescorted tanker coming out of Palau. He was 150 to 200 miles off the coast, no escorts, no planes. We picked it up at about 10,000 yards. The officer at the periscope sent for me instead of the captain. I took a look and said, 'Right full rudder, all ahead two-thirds. I took another look and we were about 2,500 yards off the track, range 10,000 yards. We were in a beautiful spot. All we had to do was keep coming around, get ourselves on a 90-degree track, go dead slow speed, and wait for him to come on. We were going to fire at about 800 yards, like shooting fish in a barrel. This guy wasn't zigging, a big ship. I sent for the captain and told him the situation. After we had steadied course for a 90-degree track shot, he said, 'Right full rudder, all ahead two-thirds.' I said 'Captain, what are you doing?'

"'I'm coming around for a stern tube shot. I want to give the after room some practice.' We hadn't given the forward room any practice yet. I couldn't believe it. By God, we opened out and fired four stern torpedoes at a range of 4,500 yards instead of 800. They were steam torpedoes. The guy saw the wakes and he maneuvered to avoid. I couldn't believe my ears again. [McGregor] said, 'Make ready the bow tubes, set all torpedoes on low power.' That gave about a 9,000-yard run at twenty-seven knots as opposed to forty-seven knots at 6,500 yards. By God, he came around again and here is this tanker going with a 180-degree angle on the bow—in other words we were looking up his rear end and we fired six torpedoes. They were smoking along and this guy was making about 15 knots and the torpedoes could never catch him. There went six more torpedoes down the tube. I couldn't believe it. We had wasted ten precious torpedoes."

The disastrously nonproductive excursion of the *Seahorse* required explanation to the sub command. While the *Seahorse* sailed back to Midway after fifty-five days at sea with zero results, McGregor drafted a patrol account to exonerate his performance, politely relieved Cutter of his duties, and filed an unsatisfactory fitness report on him. Cutter for his part wrote a letter putting his superior on report for his behavior. The submarine command identified McGregor as the real culprit for the *Seahorse*'s failures. McGregor was only one of a number of overage sub commanders unsuitable for their posts. Another skipper adamantly refused to rise to periscope depth to attack enemy destroyers that were oblivious to the sub's presence. A third, during an engagement, locked himself in his stateroom and told his second in command to take charge.

When the *Seahorse* tied up at Midway, a radio dispatch sacked McGregor, elevating Cutter to the top position. With Cutter in command the *Seahorse* put to sea. Unknown to him, on the trip back to Midway, McGregor had disparaged him to the crew who, as a result, had zero confidence in him. "He [McGregor] said words like, 'He isn't in his right mind.' That I was nuts. I never found that out until much later. Those kids were loyal. They didn't say anything about the captain." The chief of the boat, the top enlisted man in a submarine, who is sort of an assistant executive officer, informed Cutter that if they had been anywhere else but Midway, half of the crew would have gone AWOL. But since there was no place to go, they remained with the sub."

The *Seahorse*, led by a skipper desperate to prove himself to his people, entered enemy waters. "The first thing we ran into were some fishing boats, trawlers. They had about fifteen to twenty men aboard, pretty good-size ships. We were told to knock them off because they were supposed to serve dual purposes, fishing and outpost. This was after the Jimmy Doolittle 1942 raid; supposedly they had all these boats out there with radios. I didn't like the idea of attacking what I thought was an unarmed ship." Whatever Cutter's preferences, as the commander, he felt obliged to obey an imperative that declared, "You shall attack all enemy ships encountered with either gunfire or torpedoes." Dutifully, the *Seahorse* knocked off three such vessels.

"There were no survivors," remembered Cutter. "I said, 'Goddamn it! I'm not going to do this anymore.' We moved into the area where we were firing torpedoes and it was sort of forgotten." With his boat now lurking off the Japanese-controlled Tsushima Strait, Cutter said, "We got desperate—we had to sink some ships. I was chicken about going in there until I just had to. I figured if we picked up a convoy and followed it in, it wouldn't go through mineable waters. We decided to go at night on the surface so we would not have to dive where the mines might be at about 150 feet. We'd follow them in, and after we made the attack, come out the way we went in. We sank a tanker that disintegrated in a tremendous explosion. They were carrying gasoline."

The submarine also blasted a second tanker and then as they sailed back toward the open sea a destroyer noticed them. "He started signaling us, sending a recognition signal. All we had left were the torpedoes aft, so I made a 180-degree turn and fired as soon as we steadied up. I had to fire at long range, a torpedo run of 4,200 yards. We bailed out of there at full speed and I called for a cameraman to come up and take a picture. If this thing went, I wanted to see it. I was starting to swear because so much time had gone by. It seemed forever. At 47 knots, for 4,000 yards it took about two or three minutes. Finally, the kids below heard it, which you always did through the water—an explosion hit. I heard the cheering from below so I knew we hit him and then fingers of flame ran the whole length of that ship. Red flames came out. All of a sudden it went up just like a huge mushroom, sort of a dark beige, lighted from beneath, I guess. That thing hung there in the air and in the end turned into a brilliant blue white. You could read a newspaper. We saw pieces of this ship falling into the ocean. We were then more than two miles away."

When the *Seahorse* came back to Pearl Harbor, Cutter raised the subject of the fishing boats with Adm. Charles Lockwood, commander of all submarines in the Pacific. "I said, 'Admiral, I sank three of these things with gunfire. Jeez, it was just murder. We went aboard one before we sank it and there were fifteen-and sixteen-year-old kids aboard. What would you do?'

"He said, 'Slade, let your conscience be your guide,' a hell of an answer. I said, 'I'm not going to attack any more.'" While at Pearl Harbor, Cutter was asked by Comdr. Richard Voge, Pacific submarine operations officer, where he would like to go on his next voyage. Mindful of the missed opportunities with the convoy at Toagel Mlungui, Cutter answered, "The *Seahorse* has unfinished business down in Palau. I want to go back there." He noted, "[Voge] held the area open for six days to let us get in. It was another hot area [where they] wanted a submarine there all the time. We never got there. We picked up a convoy before we got there and messed around with it, got a couple of ships."

Still bent on revenge at Palau, Cutter, as the result of intelligence intercepts on Japanese naval traffic, sought out another convoy and the encounter evolved into a prolonged epic. "I was in the conning tower 82 hours and 33 minutes except for when I went down to the toilet, never changed clothes. I was in pajamas when I was called to the conning tower and I was in pajamas when it was all over 82 hours later. It was a terrible strain. I lived on benzedrine. You get along on benzedrine. We couldn't get in good position until the last day and we sank two of them on the final attack. Our torpedoes were gone and we headed for home. We sank only three ships—should have done better than that but it was pretty heavily escorted. I was exhausted. The crew was wiped out, too. We dove, leveled off, and everybody was secured except the bare watch just to keep the submarine going." Cutter, however, could not fall asleep, even though he downed a pint of whiskey and swallowed sleeping pills. He gradually wound down while the *Seahorse*, empty of torpedoes, combed the ocean near Wake Island to act as a lifeguard for downed bombers.

He took the *Seahorse* out for one more patrol. It was while on this voyage that Cutter observed a portion of the Japanese fleet bearing down on the Marianas. After five tours, Cutter was rotated back to the States. Upon completion of leave he waited out the construction and commission of a new submarine *Requin*. Submarines skippered by Cutter accounted for nineteen confirmed vessels sunk, making him tied with Dudley "Mush" Morton of the *Wahoo*, who disappeared with his sub and second only to Richard O'Kane's twenty-four on the *Tang*. O'Kane became a POW after an errant torpedo ran in a circle blasting the sub while on station in the Formosa Strait.

The gathering momentum of the march toward the Japanese homeland at sea, in the air, and on land induced one of more egregious errors of the campaign, the invasion of Peleliu, a six-mile long, two-mile wide island in the Palau group. Nimitz disregarded Halsey's advice and insisted his command using the 1st Marine Division would invade Peleliu, site of an enemy airfield. Not only was Peleliu of dubious strategic importance but the intelligence gathered on its terrain and garrison proved appallingly wrong. Thick scrub hid the tortuous surface from aerial observation and photos. Major General William Rupertus of the 1st Marine Division confidently predicted conquest within four days. He apparently had no inkling of the resolve of the 15,000 defenders hunkered down in the usual honeycomb of caves dug into the soft coral of the atoll.

In December 1942, E. B. Sledge, an Alabamian who chose to drop out of the Marine Corps V-12, officer-training program attended boot camp before assignment as a replacement to Company K, 3d Battalion, 5th Marines, 1st Marine Division. On the island of Pavuvu he studied the trade of a 60mm mortar man while gaining insights into the attitudes of his fellows. "A passionate hatred for the Japanese burned through all Marines I knew. The fate of the Goettge patrol was the sort of thing that spawned such hatred." (The Guadalcanal patrol led into ambush by a Japanese prisoner.) Sledge also said the enemy tactic of feigning death or injury and then attacking a medic, along with memories of the raid on Pearl Harbor, inflamed Marines.

According to Sledge, "We had been told that the 1st Marine Division would be reinforced to about 28,000 men for the assault on Peleliu. As every man in the ranks knew, however, a lot of these people included in the term *reinforced* were neither trained nor equipped as combat troops. They were specialists attached to the division . . . They would not be doing the fighting." In addition to the leathernecks, the Army's 81st Division would be involved.

From his place in the amtrac bouncing on the water, a nauseated Sledge saw an inferno envelop the beach as the fleet offshore bombarded the strand. Around him great gouts of water spouted from missiles fired by Japanese guns. Then the American shells moved deeper into the island as the landing craft's moment arrived. Sledge wrote in *With the Old Breed*, "My heart pounded. Our amtrac came out of the water and moved a few yards up the gently sloping sand. 'Hit the beach!' yelled an NCO moments before the machine lurched to a stop. The men piled over the sides as fast as they could. I followed Snafu (a fellow leatherneck), climbed up, and planted both feet firmly on the left side so as to leap as far away from it as possible. At that instant a burst of machine-gun fire with white-hot tracers snapped through the air at eye level, almost grazing my face. I pulled my head back like a turtle, lost my balance, and fell awkwardly forward down onto the sand in a tangle of ammo bag, pack, helmet, carbine, gas mask, cartridge belt, and flopping canteens. 'Get off the beach! Get off the beach!' raced through my mind.'"

After falling in the sand, Sledge regained his feet, then scuttled across the strand while enemy guns scoured the beach. The entrenched defenders had recovered from the shock of the preinvasion barrages. When the young Marine glanced back, he saw a DUKW disintegrate into pieces of metal from a direct hit. No men left the shattered amphibian. "I caught a fleeting glimpse of a group of Marines leaving a smoking amtrac on the reef.

Some fell as bullets and fragments splashed among them. Their buddies tried to help them as they struggled in the knee-deep water.

"I shuddered and choked. A wild desperate feeling of anger, frustration, and pity gripped me. It was an emotion that always would torture my mind when I saw men trapped and was unable to do anything but watch as they were hit. My own plight forgotten momentarily, I felt sickened to the depths of my soul. I asked God, 'Why, why, why?' I turned my face away and wished that I was imagining it all. I had tasted the bitterest essence of war, the sight of helpless comrades being slaughtered, and it filled me with disgust."

Crouching low, Sledge ran across the sand; one foot barely missed a pressure plate set to trigger a huge mine. He joined men from his company as they were pinned down by a torrent of mortars and machine-gun fire. Haplessly, the Marines burrowed into craters where they sweated, prayed, and cursed the enemy. "Under my first barrage since the fast-moving events of hitting the beach, I learned a new sensation; utter and absolute helplessness." When the shelling waned he saw walking wounded making their way back to the beach. A friend with a bloody dressing on his arm paused to brag, "'I got the million-dollar wound. It's all over for me.' We waved as he hurried on out of the war."

He soon saw his first dead enemy, stared in horror at the glistening viscera of a ripped-open stomach. Almost in a trance he watched veterans come along and strip the corpses of souvenirs, spectacles, a flag, a pistol, and other items. He later became inured to the sight of Marines routinely, methodically looting bodies, extracting gold teeth—in one instance, from a badly wounded but still living soldier. A few yards from his introduction to that behavior Sledge noticed a medic beside a dead leatherneck. "The corpsman held the dead Marine's chin tenderly between the thumb and fingers of his left hand and made the sign of the cross with his right hand. Tears streamed down his dusty, tanned, grief-contorted face while he sobbed quietly."

The attacking forces slowly overwhelmed the defenders closest to the shoreline. Japanese soldiers tried to flee and riflemen cut them down as they bolted from a mangrove swamp or from behind rocks. As a mortar man, armed with a carbine which was ineffective at the distance from the foe, Sledge did not fire. "We headed into the thick scrub . . . I completely lost my bearings and had no idea where we were going." The dense vegetation concealed trails, hid snipers, and denied contact among units. In contrast with previous engagements, the Japanese on Peleliu abandoned the usual concentration of forces at water's edge to build a formidable defense in depth.

Ed Andrusko, recovered from his New Britain wound, said, "Our company was in the first wave landing on Peleliu. During the amphibious landing, enemy shells burst near our tractor. We received incoming shells starting at the reef, across the harbor, and on the beach. We were pinned down on the beach for some time. When we finally advanced inland, I stepped on a land mine. While others were killed, I was wounded in the legs and back and evacuated to a hospital ship." His was not quite a million-dollar wound; he would recover and return. But he escaped the carnage that followed in the days immediately after the initial landings.

A former drill instructor, Jim Moll, early in 1944, as a buck sergeant, joined A/1/7, Able Company, 1st Battalion, 7th Marine Regiment. Moll recalled, "My first taste of combat was Peleliu. We went in on a Higgins boat, which meant we had to climb over the sides—later models of landing craft had ramps that were lowered. Nobody was talking because there was so much noise, you couldn't hear. As you passed between all the big battlewagons, cruisers, etc, they were all blasting away with all their big guns. As you looked toward the island, all you could see was explosions, smoke, fire, and overhead planes, were diving to drop bombs, fire rockets. You wondered how the hell anybody could be alive on the island when you hit the beach.

"You looked at the men on the landing craft and everyone was solemn. Some were staring in awe at all the fireworks. Some had their eyes closed. Some were talking to themselves; you could see their lips moving, probably praying. I said a few prayers myself. As we got closer to the beach, we could see the enemy's shells dropping and some of our landing craft being hit. I could hear machine gun bullets hitting the armor plate in front of me. As we got closer, my heart was beating like a jackhammer. I was sweating profusely and I was waiting for the boat to hit the beach, as I was to be the first one out on the right side. There was so much anxiety, anticipation, hope, and other things whirling around in my brain, I don't think there was room for fear. One of my thoughts that consoled me was that this is what I had asked for and if I died, I wanted to go like a good Marine. I knew every guy in that boat felt the same way.

"Fortunately, most of the men in my craft made the beach. Other boats carrying men from our platoon weren't so lucky. When we hit the beach, my legging caught on something as I was climbing over the side. I fell head-first into the water. I quickly got up and waded onto the beach. About fifteen feet off to my right a Jap machine gunner located in a shallow pilbox was firing on some Marines wading through the water. I crawled over to the pillbox and aimed my Tommy gun into it. The damn thing wouldn't fire because sand got into the mechanism when I fell into the water. I pushed a hand grenade in the hole and eliminated him.

"About two minutes later, I was hit in the upper arm by shrapnel, about one-inch square. It went through my sleeve and lodged an inch from where it punctured the skin. It didn't even hit the bone as it traveled almost parallel to it. The shrapnel was red hot and burned like the devil, so maybe it cauterized itself. I was able to dig the piece out with my Ka-Bar knife, so I never turned into sickbay with it. My only regret is that I never will receive a Purple Heart for being wounded.

Another A/1/7 replacement, Philadelphian Earl "Rags" Rice, said, "The night before we left for Peleliu we had a big drinking party, home-brewed stuff. Everybody got drunk. A fellow named Boland, a big, good-looking sergeant, talked to me about what I was going to do after the war. I said I thought I'd travel and just see the rest of the world. He couldn't believe that I wasn't going to get more education. He'd already been to college and was a very smart guy.

"When we went in to the beach at Peleliu, it was terrible. I had never seen dead bodies like this, lying on the beach, floating in the water, mangled. Cat Allen was in a hole with another marine who saw a Jap soldier but froze and couldn't fire. He told Cat there was one out there. Cat stuck up his head to look and took a bullet right through his skull. They called me as a stretcher bearer to get him. I carried him back and dropped him off at a collection place. There wasn't anything to do for him."

After depositing Allen's body, Rice returned to the outfit's position and, as night fell, was directed to occupy a vacant foxhole. Only after he settled in did Rice realize that he was alone. There would be no one who would stand watch if he slept. "It was a most terrifying night. I was dead tired from the day and I couldn't stay awake. I started to doze off and then I could hear them out there crawling toward me on my right and left. I tried to peek out but I couldn't see a thing; all I knew is that they were coming toward me. Around 5:00 A.M.. It finally became light enough to see and when I looked out what I had heard were land crabs, crawling all over the place.

"It became very hot, and not having slept, and with all that heat while I carried men on stretchers, around midday I just went down. That hurt my pride. They took me to the hospital ship, stayed overnight. [I decided] my days as a stretcher-bearer were over. I was going back to my outfit as a rifleman, come what may. I missed two days, the only two days I missed combat while I was in the war. When I got back, a guy told me I had missed the biggest day there, when a lot of guys got killed. Boland, who talked to me about getting educated, had been sick and they told him to get behind some trees until he felt better But he wouldn't do it. He came forward and was killed. MacDonald, a weight lifter, who wrote letters to his wife regularly and who'd been so good to me, had his whole chest blown out. My squad leader, Joe Gallant, stood on top of a tank blasting away with his submachine gun when he was killed. They were both brave men who will live in my memory until I die."

Shaken but unhurt, by late afternoon, E. B. Sledge had reached the edge of the Peleliu airfield. Japanese tanks stirred up fear of a counterattack just as some American Shermans arrived to take them under fire. Sledge and

Snafu set up their 60mm mortar. He and his fellows prepared for the usual Banzai suicide counterattack. Instead, the enemy countered with a well-coordinated tank-infantry thrust eventually driven off by leathernecks on the left flank of Sledge's outfit. Although the Japanese had been repulsed, their actions indicated they would not necessarily rely on futile gestures but instead could defend with careful calculation.

Orders directed Sledge's 3d Battalion to charge across the fire-swept airfield while; on an elevation known as Bloody Nose Ridge, Japanese gunners poured devastation from their well-emplaced weapons. Sledge said he mumbled the first verse of the twenty-first Psalm as he scurried across the open area. Bullets snapped past him, explosions hurled bits of coral that stung his face and hands, shell fragments spattered about on the rock like hail. "Through the haze I saw Marines stumble and pitch forward as they got hit. I then looked neither right nor left but just straight to my front. The farther we went, the worse it got. The noise and concussion pressed in on my ears like a vise. I gritted my teeth and braced myself in anticipation of the shock of being struck at any moment. It seemed impossible that any of us could make it across. We passed several craters that offered shelter but I remembered the order to keep moving. Because of the superb discipline and excellent esprit of the Marines, it had never occurred to us that the attack might fail."

Four days after a mine wounded him just beyond the beach, Ed Andrusko returned to duty with his company, some of whom huddled in a steep ravine, while above them Japanese troops occupied entrenched positions. Andrusko said, "It was high noon, 110 degrees, no shade, and a merciless tropical sun. The hostile defenders were now firing down on us from all sides. The cross-fire was deadly and we were trapped.

"As the message runner, I returned to the command post and reported our new losses and serious situation to the top sergeant. He radioed for reinforcements, for medical corpsmen, water, and as many stretcher-bearers as he could get. The word came back negative. No reinforcements. No stretcher-bearers. All reserve units were committed in an all-out battle throughout the island with heavy casualties. There was no help available."

Desperate for aid, the sergeant ordered Andrusko and one other marine, nicknamed "Ski," to accompany him on a dash to the beach area to recruit anyone available. Under covering fire they sprinted to the rear and vainly sought succor from other unit commands. "Exhausted from the heat, we rested near the beach in the shade of a damaged supply truck. A young black sergeant who had overheard our plight, walked up and said, 'I heard you all were looking for some troop replacements.'

"Our top sergeant looked a little stunned and speechless at the black, uniformed sergeant. The Top cleared his throat and asked, 'Who are you? What unit or company are you with? Are you Army, Navy, Seabees, or what?'

"'I am a U.S. Marine platoon sergeant. My men and I are all U.S. Marines.' I remembered seeing and talking to the black troops on the beach when I first returned to battle weeks before. He continued, 'My men have all finished their work on the beach. We are cleared with the division headquarters to volunteer where needed. We are Marines from an ammunition depot and have had some infantry training.' Our top sergeant appeared very puzzled. How could he bring in an all-black unit to rescue members of a line company that was part of the famous, all-white 1st Marine Division? It was heavily complemented with Southern officers and men, home-based at New River, North Carolina, and 'the pride of the South.' He tried to discourage the volunteers, stating they were not trained nor qualified for the terror of battle. But by now the black marines had armed themselves heavily and lined up behind their platoon sergeant, who insisted we lead the way to the front lines. Our top sergeant said, 'Well, don't say I didn't warn you people.' When we reached our mauled company area, it looked like Custer's last stand. The top sergeant came upon our new replacement officer in command of the company and said, 'Sir, I have a platoon of black—I mean a platoon of Marine volunteers who came to help.'

"The young, new commanding officer said, 'Thank God. Thank you, men. Sergeant, take over. Get our wounded and dead out.' We gave covering fire and watched in awe as our new, gallant volunteers did their job. Some of these new men held a casualty stretcher gently in one hand as true angels of mercy. Then, when necessary, they would fire an automatic weapon with the other hand, while breaking through the surrounding enemy. The grateful wounded thanked the volunteers as each was brought to the rear aid station and safety. One badly wounded Southerner said, "I felt like I was saved by Black Angels sent by God. Thank you. Thank you all!'

"The platoon of black Marines made many courageous trips to our area for the wounded. With each return from the rear they brought back badly needed ammunition, food, and water. It was nightfall when the evacuation of all the wounded was completed. The volunteers moved into our empty foxholes and helped fight off a small, nighttime enemy counterattack.

"The next morning, our company commander ordered us to take the hill. After several bloody hours of fighting, Item Company survivors and our black volunteers did just that. We were relieved from the gruesome mountain by a U.S. Army infantry company. As the soldiers passed, they asked sarcastically, 'Who are the black guys in your outfit?' Our top sergeant bellowed, 'Why some of our company's best damn Marines, that's who!'"

On several other occasions, African American leathernecks participated in combat but the Corps never assigned them to such duty. The Marine Corps, dominated by a Southern-bred hierarchy, stoutly resisted even admitting blacks to its ranks until 1943. Forced to accept them, the Marines consigned them to service, supply, and labor units, with the exception of a provisional combat group toward the end of the war and which never went into the field.

The treatment of dark-skinned Americans by the Navy was hardly better. At the start of World War II they were restricted to food handling and valet service. Later, they also performed as laborers and on supply duty. To appease critics a handful graduated from officer training programs and a destroyer escort, the USS *Mason*, and a subchaser were the only seagoing vessels with deck ratings and officers drawn from men of color.

The Army enrolled the most blacks but it, too, limited the opportunities to engage in the fighting. The Tuskegee Airmen struggled mightily to overcome discrimination and flew with the Fifteenth Air Force in Italy. The segregated 92d and 93d Infantry Divisions, with a fair number of African Americans as junior officers under white superiors, were trained for combat. But when the latter reached the Pacific theater, after its first few engagements, it was broken up for use in base maintenance, stevedore work, and similar menial duties. The 92d, under an openly racist commander, shipped to Italy to replace one of the outfits taken away from Mark Clark's Fifth Army for Dragoon. Although individual soldiers and small units performed creditably, the 92d achieved mixed success in combat and white enlisted personnel and officers lynched its reputation. The Army also fielded a few smaller combat units such as tank destroyer, tank battalions, field artillery battalions, under white commanders. Some of these won recognition for valor while others were tagged as ineffective or worse.

General Rupertus, so cocksure of a swift victory on Peleliu, brought in the 81st Division's 321st Infantry Regiment to relieve the badly chewed up 1st Marine Regiment after the first week cost the leathernecks just under 4,000 casualties. The 5th Marine Regiment, with Sledge, carried on, and he learned just how nearly impregnable enemy pillboxes were. With several mates, Sledge advanced on an enemy bunker. The Nipponese inside tossed out their own grenades and any lobbed through openings by the Americans. Not even explosives dropped down a ventilator pipe neutralized the inhabitants because their engineers cleverly installed concrete baffles that shielded the occupants. The Marines sent a runner to the beach for a flamethrower and an amtrac with a 75mm cannon. Some of the Japanese began to flee their stronghold while the Marines cut them down with rifle and machine-gun fire from the amtrac. "They tumbled onto the coral in a forlorn tangle of bare legs, falling rifles, and rolling helmets. We felt no pity for them but exulted over their fate. We had been shot at and shelled too much and had lost too many friends to have compassion for the enemy when we had him cornered."

After the 75mm piece whammed three armor-piercing shells into the target, occupants emerged. "Even before the dust settled," wrote Sledge, "I saw a Japanese soldier appear at the blasted opening. He was grim determination personified as he drew back his arm to throw a grenade at us. My carbine was already up. When he appeared, I lined my sights on his chest and began squeezing off shots. As the first bullet hit him, his face contorted in agony. His knees buckled. The grenade slipped from his grasp. All the men near me, including the amtrac machine gunner, had seen him and began firing. The soldier collapsed in the fusillade, and the grenade went off at his feet.

"Even in the midst of these fast-moving events, I looked down at my carbine with sober reflection. I had just killed a man at close range. That I had seen clearly the pain on his face when my bullets hit him came as a jolt. It suddenly made the war a very personal affair. The expression on that man's face filled me with shame and then disgust for the war and all the misery it was causing." Sledge quickly rejected what he called "maudlin meditations of a fool" for feeling ashamed because he had killed someone about to kill him with a grenade.

"Near the end of the battle for Peleliu, I had my 'bells rung' pretty good. Late on one afternoon, Baker Company attacked up a hill but got pinned down with very intense fire. They sent our company (Able) up so Baker could withdraw. By the time Baker left and we started back, it was getting dark. The Japs were laying down some of their big mortar shells. As I was coming down the slope, one of these came down near me. All I can remember is that I was airborne. When I came to it was pitch dark. Fortunately, I wound up in our own lines. My whole brain seemed numb and everything ached, from my toenails to the hair on top of my head. I wasn't able to shake off some of the effects of that concussion until we got back to Pavuvu. To add to the misery, the few of us left from our platoon all had bad cases of dysentery."

On 13 October, nearly a month after the first Marines hit the Peleliu beaches, Ed Andrusko said, "Our company was battling in caves, valleys, and the limestone hills of a moon-looking mountain range. After the capture of a large treeless mountaintop, there was an ominous quiet, a lull that comes in battle. It was time for a well-needed rest in 115 degrees heat. I unslung my rifle, removed combat equipment, and a sweaty shirt, laid my helmet down next to me, and nestled down near some large boulders to read my mail. This would be a real happy moment, a cherished personal one. Suddenly there was a loud sharp crack from a nearby sniper's rifle. The calm had been broken as a bullet pierced the air. The bright streak of a tracer bullet burned across my right forearm, hit my holy religious cross on a rosary I was wearing around my neck, tore across my left forearm, continued, and ricocheted off a large boulder only to come at me again—this time across my back. This same bullet incredibly hit me for the third time. It expended itself by landing in my helmet which was lying on the ground next to me.

Three days later, I was evacuated aboard the hospital ship USS *Solace* for home."

E. B. Sledge and his fellows were delighted to greet GIs from the 321st Infantry Regiment as their relief. Two weeks later, Sledge boarded a transport that carried him back to Pavuvu. But it would be another six weeks before elimination of the last vestiges of enemy resistance on Peleliu. Between the Marines and the Army, American casualties amounted to almost 1,800 dead and more than 8,500 wounded. The Japanese lost approximately 11,000. Peleliu was a useless acquisition; its airfield of no consequence. In contrast, elsewhere in the Palaus, Ulithi, occupied with no resistance to the 81st Division six days after the assault upon Peleliu, supplied an excellent base for staging operations against the Philippines and Okinawa.

In the European and Mediterranean theaters many GIs whose ethnic backgrounds provided fluency or at least a smattering of the local tongues helped gain intelligence. In Pacific operations, fear that anyone with a Japanese background was untrustworthy deprived American forces of the talents of Nisei—Americans born of Japanese ancestry—a prime source for interrogations of prisoners and translation of captured documents. To compensate for the shortage of Japanese language experts, the Army ran a crash program to train its own linguists.

Gerald Widoff, as a nineteen-year-old graduate of the City University of New York in 1942, had studied elementary Japanese and, with additional instruction at an Army language school, received a commission. As head of a small team of enlisted Nisei he reported to CBI headquarters in New Delhi. "CBI was primarily a British operation [Stilwell was in China] and the Americans were decidedly in the minority. Someone decided that more token American presence was needed in the Allied effort and I was selected —I know not why—to work in the war room every morning. Very early each day I would meet with a British lieutenant and we would go over all the dispatches that had come in overnight, and climbing on ladders would move pins on a huge map of the theater. About 9:00 A.M. some British generals and some Colonel Blimp-types would show up, along with a few American colonels. Shortly after, two large doors would swing open and in would stride Lord Louis Mountbatten, the supreme allied commander, resplendent in a white admiral's uniform glittering with honors and decorations. Never in my years growing up in the Bronx would I have imagined that laundry could ever come out so blindingly white! Mountbatten was movie-star handsome, had enormous presence, and most impressive of all, actually seemed highly able. He spoke for ten or fifteen minutes, reviewing the situation, without referring to any notes and without any hesitations, in perfectly formed sentences."

Although no one ever officially told Widoff that his duties included checking the honesty of the work done by his subordinates, Widoff understood this to be a basic demand upon him. "I always assumed that most of the Nisei, but not all, knew more Japanese than I did. Many however were not particularly fluent in English. Once I got to know the members of my team I never doubted their integrity. I checked every translation before passing it up the line and almost all of my input was an effort to put it into intelligible English, which required going back to the original document. Any alteration of meaning or insertion of extraneous material would have been easily spotted. There never was any. It was foolish of the Army not to have granted commissions to the capable ones although that was rectified toward the end of the war. Most of the work we did consisted of translating captured documents."

Widoff replaced a Caucasian officer, KIA, assigned to vet the work of the intelligence Nisei with Merrill's Marauders. "The most difficult part of the early weeks of the Burma campaign for me was merely to fend off total exhaustion and keep up with the unit. There were no roads. The Burma Road was being built behind us as we advanced. The one time I saw it, it was an impenetrable cloud of red dust. There was no transport. We had mules but they were only used as pack animals. We would walk up a trail to a mountaintop and then go down a trail on the other side. Everyone from the general on down walked. For the first few weeks I thought I would not make it, that I would reach a point where I could no longer place one foot in front of the other. I would fall by the side of the trail and either die or somehow become a Kachin tribesman. I frequently started the day at the head of the column and ended it with a group of stragglers at the tail. Some of the guys who were having difficulty would tie their hands to the harness of one of the mules and the poor beast, in addition to carrying a heavy load of artillery shells, would also be dragging a GI. I thought that was too humiliating to even contemplate and struggled on. By the end of the week, I was only halfway back in the column and by the end of the second week I was enjoying the hike each day. Sometimes we walked through fields of elephant grass taller than I. [He was more than six feet tall.] The blades of grass had razor-sharp edges and we used our machetes all day but still wound up with lots of little cuts and nicks. Sometimes we slept in little clearings surrounded by rather sweet-smelling mounds, which we later learned were elephant turds.

"There was a fever, common in Burma, which was known to everyone by its Japanese name, tsutsugamushi fever, and it took quite a heavy toll. Malaria was quite common and many guys in my outfit had severe cases, in spite of the fact we all took atabrine tablets. These were supposed to prevent it but just seemed to turn us all yellow. Amebic dysentery was quite widespread and there was a fear of cholera and smallpox, for which we seemed to receive an excessive number of vaccinations, but which must have worked because I never heard of a case of either."

In the company of 4,000 Chinese soldiers and several hundred Kachin Rangers, the Americans, with Widoff as a member of the headquarters staff, crossed a 6,000-foot mountain to outflank the enemy. The expedition caught the garrison dozing and the principal goal at Myitkyina yielded with modest resistance. "Prisoners were hard to come by," said Widoff. "When I first joined the Marauders I went around to many patrols and gave a little talk on the importance of prisoners, the lives that could be saved by what could be learned, etc. Frequently, someone in the back would say, 'Hey, Lieutenant! Ya wanna prisoner? Go get him yourself!'" The campaign in Burma went through another reorganization and Widoff became a member of the Mars Task Force, a piece of an elaborate plan to trap the main body of Japanese troops. "The war in Burma was a very small-time affair compared to Europe, North Africa, or the South Pacific," said Widoff." There were no large masses of troops and no great sustained battles. My impression is that most of the action occurred when small groups on patrol stumbled into one another, unawares. There was no heavy artillery and no heavy barrages. We (HQ) sometimes heard small-arms fire nearby but it never seemed directed at us, although most of the time we were never quite sure where we were in relation to everyone else.

"During the entire six months of the campaign we were supplied exclusively by air drops. Cargo planes would fly low over us and boxes of supplies would be pushed out of the plane with small parachutes attached and would more or less float down to a prearranged field. Sometimes they would float a bit too much and wind up supplying the Japanese. Sometimes they drifted into areas where it was too dangerous to retrieve them. Most of the time we got them and there was always plenty for our basic needs. We lined our foxholes with the parachutes."

37
Paris, Brest, and Market Garden

The breakout by the Third Army and the advances along the entire Allied front swept northeast in a fashion that obliged the Germans to retreat to lines that left Paris vulnerable. Wary of the high costs of a block-by-block, house-to-house ordeal that would destroy a jewel of civilization, Eisenhower intended to bypass Paris and enter it at a propitious moment. Once the war swept beyond Paris, the enemy trapped there might be induced to surrender without a fight.

Hitler had hurriedly dispatched a new commander to Paris, Gen. Dietrich von Choltitz, and typically called upon von Choltitz, to defend to the ultimate. "Paris must not fall into the hands of the enemy except as a field of ruins." For the task, the *Wehrmacht* mustered about 25,000 soldiers, most of whom deployed outside the city. No armor and scant artillery supported these troops. Emboldened by the proximity of the Allies, citizens of Paris walked off their private and public jobs. Roaming bands of FFI seized police stations, newspapers, and even city hall. Von Choltitz prepared to deal forcibly with the weakly armed insurrectionists. After a truce collapsed, resistance factions fanned out for a full-scale fight with the occupiers.

Alarmed that Paris, packed with unarmed civilians might now become enveloped in a conflagration of shot and shell, Charles de Gaulle threatened to send his own Free French units into the city. Indeed, the French 2d Armored Division, acting on its own, moved a reconnaissance group of 150 to the outskirts of the capital. Although some American outfits had been closer to Paris, Eisenhower with his customary diplomatic discernment, authorized the French armor to enter the city. With the aid of the local resistance, after a day of hard fighting, the soldiers, on 25 August, drove out the main body of enemy forces, capturing von Choltitz. For his part, the defeated German general had refrained from the scorched-city policy ordered by *der Führer*.

Motorized units from the 4th Division were the first Americans inside Paris while de Gaulle staged a parade to celebrate liberation and his Free French operations. Three days later, on 29 August, the population enjoyed an opportunity to cheer Eisenhower and a march down the Champs-Élysée by the 28th Infantry Division, which had not fired a single shot on behalf of the liberation. Originally destined to make the D day invasion, the 28th had been spared that dreadful experience and on 22 July arrived, dry-footed, in Normandy. Although baptized by enemy fire, the 28th was still a relatively unblooded outfit. Ralph Johnson, in a service company with the 110th Regiment, said," "It was a nine-hour parade with bands playing and all colors flying and the men had the time of their lives—wine, women, song (and bicycles by the hundreds) was the unofficial order of the day. Late that afternoon our point ran into the rear guard of the German Army evacuating the city and a firefight broke out causing many casualties. My feelings as we marched along in the parade were that surely the war must be nearly over, as how can we have a parade like this . . . I could not have been more wrong. So many of my friends and comrades were to be killed before that happy moment would arrive. Hitler just would not give up."

Although Dragoon struck along the Mediterranean coast, the Brittany ports remained attractive, particularly Brest. The assignment to oust the Germans fell to a portion of Patton's Third Army, the VIII Corps under Gen. Troy Middleton. One of Middleton's assets was the 83d Infantry Division. After bouncing about storm tossed seas in the Channel for six stomach-churning days, the "Thunderbolts" finally debarked 21–24 June at Omaha. Within less than a week the organization relieved the hard-hit 101st Airborne around Carentan. Subsequently, it was assigned the objective of St.-Malo, a small Brittany seacoast town.

Tony Vaccaro, served in the intelligence section for the division's 331st Regiment. Born in Pennsylvania, Vaccaro had lived in Italy from 1925 to 1939, until the advent of war forced Americans to return to the States. Schooled as a rifleman, his knowledge of French, German, and Italian qualified him for intelligence work. Before leaving for Europe he attended a course in techniques to capture prisoners and interrogate them. The instructions emphasized not to fire a weapon but if necessary use a knife. "We would go out at night, in a group of four, try to capture one of the enemy, talk to the farmers or members of the underground. It was from a Frenchman who had been in hiding that I first learned that the Nazis were killing the Jews. Until then it was all rumors, but this man said he had seen what they were doing. I already had a great hatred for the fascists but this increased my dislike for the Germans. One night, we went out to try and find a route for our regiment to cross the Rance River, where all the bridges had been blown. Another regiment needed our help because they were trapped. We were in a jeep when suddenly we saw a truck full of German soldiers drive by. We quickly headed down a road away from where the truck was going. Suddenly the roadway ended and our jeep was bumping along railroad tracks on an embankment. We stopped and then we heard noises. I had learned to tell the differences between Americans and Germans. American shoes didn't make sounds but the Germans had nails in their boots and you could hear them on pavement or stones.

"We got out of the jeep and we could see in the moonlight, the clear outline of a German soldier's helmet coming toward us. We jumped him; somebody grabbed his hands, another man put a hand over his mouth and I took the bandanna I carried and tied it over his mouth. One of our guys George Goodman was Jewish. He had heard how the Germans were killing Jews and he really hated them. He took out his pistol and said, 'I'm going to kill him.' I said, 'No, no, we have to take him back. If you fire that pistol they'll know it is a .45 and they'll be after us.' But Goodman was acting crazy, making a lot of noise. The sergeant who was in charge did nothing. I took my bayonet, and put the point against his neck. I said if you shoot him, I will kill you.' Back at headquarters I tried to question the prisoner. He didn't respond to French, Italian, or Spanish. Finally, I mumbled the few Polish words I knew. His face brightened and I yelled for someone who spoke Polish. He gave us everything we needed to know."

In his knapsack, Vaccaro packed an Argus C-3 camera, a modest 35mm impersonation of a Leica. "I shot ten rolls in Normandy that I tried to send home but the censor destroyed them. Other rolls were ruined by the contaminated water. Because I went out mainly on night missions I had time to shoot pictures during the daylight hours." To procure film and chemicals for processing, Vaccaro would ask French civilians if the Boche were still in a village or town. When they answered in the negative he would hurry ahead of his comrades, who thought him daft for entering an area that might contain the enemy. "I would find the local drugstore or chemist and buy the materials. Many of the Germans we captured carried cameras and film and the guys would give me the film. I had no scales to weigh chemicals but I remembered the size of the mounds my high school teacher, Mr. Lewis, used. To process the pictures I borrowed some steel helmets."

His odd linguistic background saved the life of an ancient Frenchman accused as a saboteur who cut the division telephone lines. "The division interpreter, who was born in France, could not communicate with the man who was illiterate in French. They called me in and I tried but nothing seemed to work until I made a sign that I remembered from the period when I lived in a small village that had once been occupied by the Normans. He responded and I started to talk to him in the dialect of that town. That was the only language he knew. He had come across wires lying in the mud alongside a stream. Having lost a cow to mines, he cut the wires and used it to tie up his cattle to prevent them from wandering. I showed our officers what he had done and they let him go. In a one-in-a-million shot, I, who happened to have lived in that one village, gone to America, and come back as a soldier, had been on hand when he could have been executed."

Robert Edlin, the Ranger struck in both legs on the beach and evacuated to England during the evening of D day, although not fully recovered, talked his way back to his outfit.

Shortly after he rejoined his company, he and his associates opened fire on an enemy antitank crew. "Afterward, I rolled over the man I had shot. I see his face at night, even after almost fifty years. I wondered then and now what happened to the beautiful little boy and girl in the picture that the proud father carried to show his friends."

Rudder nominated Edlin to take a reconnaissance patrol, locate minefields, and bag a prisoner or two for intelligence about those manning, a fortress at Lochristi. "Along about dawn, September 10, we came down to within 200 yards of one of the largest pillboxes I had ever seen. The fort itself stood above us like a ten-story building. The big guns had been largely silenced and we were in so close that not even the 88s or mortars could fire on us. Only machine guns and rifles could get at us. We paused at a high stone wall. I told my platoon sergeant, William Klaus, to hold the rest of the platoon there and cover us. Sergeant Bill Courtney, Sgt. Bill Dreher, and my runner, Warren Burmaster, and I came within fifteen or twenty yards of the pillbox. There was an open doorway and we could hear Germans talking inside. I motioned to Burmaster to cover our rear. An excellent man, he would report back to the company if something happened to us. We entered the pillbox with no opposition. They were surprised to see American soldiers. They were unaware any of us were within several miles. We captured the emplacement with forty men, some machine guns, and the radio equipment before they could use it. There was no firefight at all.

"There I was, a twenty-two-year-old lieutenant, sitting with prisoners in the shadow of the strongest emplacement on the peninsula. I called in Burmaster and told him to have the radio man notify Colonel Rudder and Captain Arman that we had captured the pillbox and were within 200 yards of the fort itself. I knew if I asked Colonel Rudder if we should go ahead and try to enter the fort, he would likely say no. It would just be too much of a risk. I also thought, if I wait for permission and don't get it, there will be an all-out assault and a lot of men will be killed. There were only four of us and we had a chance to prevent it.

"I decided to go into the fort. Courtney had been speaking to a lieutenant we captured and who spoke fluent English. He said he could take me directly in to the fort commander. The German lieutenant guided us through a minefield and to the fort entrance. We came through a tunnel like in a football stadium and when we opened the door, the German was in front with me directly behind him, a Tommy gun in his back. We walked into a hospital room, a large ward. There was an operating room and a lot of white-clad doctors, nurses, and patients everywhere. When we showed up in American uniforms with guns in our hands it was just turmoil.

"Courtney, who spoke pretty good high school German, yelled, '*Hände Hoch!*' All hands went in the air. The German lieutenant asked if he could speak to them in German and I agreed as long as he spoke slowly enough for Courtney to translate. He told the Germans to remain calm, to sit down. He would lead us to the battery commander to try to negotiate a surrender and avoid more casualties. Everybody quietly went about their business and we passed through the hospital section, the German in front, my gun in his back, and Courtney behind me. As we passed several German soldiers on guard at the cross corridors, the lieutenant would speak to them and they would immediately lower their weapons. Courtney explained to me he was telling them I was being taken to their commander and not to cause problems or trouble.

"We came to a doorway and the German started to open it. I stopped him when he told Courtney it was the commander's office, I instructed him to step aside. I turned the knob and stepped into the office with Courtney right behind me, both of us with Tommy guns. A middle-aged colonel sat behind a large ornate desk with carpet on the floor. He was apparently surprised that anyone would enter without knocking. I immediately said, '*Hände Hoch!*' He raised his hands and we closed the door behind us. I told Courtney to talk to him in German but he answered that wouldn't be necessary. He spoke English well. I said the fort was completely surrounded by American soldiers. The air force attacks and artillery had lifted to give him a chance to surrender. He should immediately use the P.A. system and announce that the whole fort should give up.

"He reached for his telephone and I said for him to leave it alone. He told me he just wanted to check how many Americans were there. About the only alternative I had was to shoot him and that wouldn't gain anything. So we let him call. He asked if we would care to have a drink. I couldn't have taken a drink or anything else. My stomach was so upset, my heart up in my throat. I don't know who was the scaredest, me or Courtney. We were in a position which we couldn't back out of. If he surrendered, we'd have done a great job. If he didn't, then we obviously would become prisoners. The two of us with Tommy guns could hardly defeat the whole garrison.

"The phone rang after a couple of minutes and he spoke in German. Courtney looked over at me and shook his head. The officer hung up and said, he'd found out there were only four Americans, two, at the pillbox and us two and we were his prisoners. For half a minute Courtney and I were prisoners but we were very dangerous ones. I had made up mind we would shoot him, barricade the office with desks, and wait until either the Germans got us out or until our guys attacked the next day and when they came in, we'd still be alive.

"Something struck my mind. I don't know where the idea came from or why I did it. But I told Courtney to give me a hand grenade. I took the grenade, pulled the pin, walked around the desk and shoved it into the colonel's stomach. I told him either surrender or he was going to die right there. He said I was bluffing. I said, 'I'll show you how much I am bluffing. I'll count to three, turn loose the lever.' It would flip off and the grenade would splatter his stomach and backbone all over the wall. He just sat there. I counted, 'One, two,' and he said, 'All right, all right. I believe you.' I told him to get on the phone, use the P.A. system to announce to his men he had surrendered the fort, given up and the combat was over. We would immediately get word to our battalion commander and stop any action coming in.

"Over the P.A. system he spoke in German. Courtney understood him and it was plain and clear that he had ordered his people to lower their arms and not take any hostile action against the American forces. He said he would prefer to surrender to a higher ranking officer than a lieutenant. I didn't give a rat's ass who he surrendered to. I said I'd take him to my battalion commander and he could handle it." By radio, Edlin informed Rudder what had happened and the Ranger CO assured him there would be no artillery or air action.

"We went back to the pillbox and took out the prisoners we had obtained there while Rudder entered the fort to deal with the colonel. When I looked back, the sight was unbelievable. There were 850 men coming out. I had figured may be 150 or even 250, but 850 lined up in military formation, stacked their arms, and there was sort of an old-time formal surrender ceremony. While we were inside, Courtney had talked the German into calling the Brest commander, General Ramke, and advising him he had surrendered the fort and, on Courtney's suggestion, telling him he, too, might as well give up. That didn't work. After the ceremony, and we started to march off the prisoners, Colonel Rudder congratulated the four of us and told us we had done a wonderful job. Then he called me aside and proceeded to tear me a new butthole. He was nearly crying about the tremendous risk we had taken. I asked him what he would have done and Rudder answered he hoped he would have done the same as I did."

There was talk of a Medal of Honor for Edlin, who insisted that, while he appreciated the tale of four Rangers capturing 850 men and four artillery pieces, the men of the 29th Infantry Division, the other Rangers, the artillery, the engineers, and air corps were what achieved the results. The recommendation for the nation's highest military honor was knocked back to a Distinguished Service Cross, with Edlin's three associates receiving Silver Stars.

While the defenders in Brittany were effectively cut off from any reinforcements or resupply they nevertheless fought "fanatically," according to Eisenhower. To maintain a solid front, the commander of the enemy garrison spread through the ranks a contingent of SS soldiers. "At any sign of weakening," said Eisenhower, "an SS trooper would execute the offender on the spot." The draconian discipline may have been due to an infusion of Italian, Russian, and Polish men, like Vaccaro's captive, whose enthusiasm for the fighting probably was less than wholehearted. Manning the fortifications and barricades were as many as 50,000 soldiers from portions of three divisions, a motley collection of naval and marine units, all backed by considerable field artillery, as well as big coastal guns swiveled about to fire inland.

George Duckworth's company, in the 2d Infantry Division, which occupied a strategic hill, could testify to the tenacity of the foe after repulsing a bloody, two-day counterattack. Given a few days to recuperate, his unit assaulted through the hedgerows toward the city. "The strength of the company at this time was about 170 enlisted men and 7 officers [about 20 percent below the normal complement]. Approximately 30 percent were veterans who had landed at Omaha Beach on D plus 1. The others were replacements but had seen considerable combat in Normandy and Northern France. I was the only officer who had landed with the company on D plus 1. Besides being individually well equipped, the men had extra allowances of special weapons consisting of two Thompson submachine guns and two Browning automatic rifles for each squad. This additional firepower was necessary in hedgerow fighting." Throughout the war, experienced soldiers toted extra automatic weapons, bazookas, and other items not specified in the table of organization and equipment.

Duckworth and his people worked their way through barbed-wire entanglements mangled by artillery blasts. They entered the town of St.-Marc fairly easily only to meet concentrated enemy fire from a large château. In a coordinated attack, F Company of the 23d Infantry Regiment overran the site, killing a number of defenders and capturing two dozen prisoners. The full battalion followed and 200 of the enemy, mostly Italians, Poles, and Russians surrendered. Although the fighting had been intense, when the 2d Division GIs settled down for the night, a hot meal was served.

Further progress entailed house-to-house combat. Duckworth recalled, "It was sudden death to step into the streets and the bodies of several civilians lay in the streets where they had been shot down by the Germans. The only way the streets could be crossed was by throwing a smoke grenade and dashing quickly from one covered position to another." To knock out a pillbox surrounded by trenches, tank destroyers and heavy machine guns hammered the emplacement hard enough for assault platoons to rush forward and clear the pillbox and the trenches.

Throughout the campaign for Brest the big guns on both sides relentlessly banged away. The fury of the American artillery gradually reduced everything to a shambles and the foot soldiers scrambled through the ruins of shattered, burning buildings until the fires at one point became so hot that the attackers were forced to wait until they burned themselves out. When the GIs resumed their efforts, Duckworth noted, "The buildings were still hot and smouldering in many places but some areas were passable and the walls that were still standing provided protection for the men as they advanced. The hot ruins burned the soles of the men's shoes but no casualties from burns were reported." After five days of this operation, another company relieved Duckworth's unit. Four more days would pass before the battle of Brest ended.

Despite the impressive capture of Paris and the rollback of the enemy forces, the Allied armies racing east, crossing the Seine, Meuse, and Moselle Rivers, were literally running out of gas. The Red Ball Express, an operation in which 60 percent of the drivers were African Americans, labored mightily to maintain a river of trucks containing fuel, food, and ammunition but the advance began to grind to a halt short of the German border. Ahead lay some formidable obstacles, the defense in depth of the Siegfried line, a thickly infested chain of interlocking fortifications chock-full of weapons and troop bunkers fronted by "dragon's teeth," the man-made concrete tank barriers. However, the Siegfried line had been neglected and seemed more menacing than real. Natural barriers included the mountainous terrain of the Vosges, the steep hills and deep ravines of the Ardennes, the thickets of the Hurtgen Forest, and the approaching winter that would render roads and fields inhospitable to enemy armor.

Bernard Montgomery had always presented a prickly problem for the American generals. He was as strongly convinced of his own theories of warfare and his superiority in putting these into practice as Patton or any other of the hubris-infected top ranks. Unlike Patton, the British general ordinarily refused to commit to battle until he believed his forces achieved a total readiness in manpower, armor, and logistics. To Americans he seemed agonizingly slow to act and they complained frequently of the Briton's pace. He had lost some of the reputation gained in North Africa by the inability of the British forces to march inland following their gaining of the Normandy shore. Having captured Antwerp, a major port whose Scheldt Estuary to the North Sea stretched sixty miles, the British squandered a great opportunity to occupy the lightly held turf around the Scheldt. When enemy forces recovered, they quickly brought in sufficient forces to control passage through the estuary, making Antwerp all but useless.

In September, as the Allied drive stalled, Montgomery proposed to jump start the advance. He sketched a plan for combined Allied airborne forces to drop along a narrow corridor some fifty miles behind the enemy in the Netherlands. The parachutists and glidermen placed in the rear of the Germans could seal off the region through the capture of vital water crossings, and the British Second Army would outflank the Siegfried line and punch into the Ruhr industrial centers. Montgomery astounded Eisenhower, Bradley, and the others with this bold, imaginative adventure that displayed none of the caution associated with him. Aside from an opportunity for Montgomery to reclaim his prestige with a stunning victory, the scheme offered attractive strategic and political rewards. A surprise thrust of this nature had the potential for a great military victory. If successful, the maneuver would enable the Allies to free up Antwerp. Eisenhower had also been urged by Washington to use his airborne forces, now unemployed at bases in England. Furthermore, the contested area contained sites for V-2 rockets launched at London, and there was pressure to put an end to this terror.

Code named Market for the airborne element and Garden for the ground portion, the operation went from proposal on 10 September, to reality on 17 September, only one week later. During the frantic preparations, disquieting intelligence from the Dutch underground reported the presence of two panzer divisions being outfitted with new tanks. Montgomery waved off fears of heavier resistance. The 82d and 101st Airborne Divisions along with their British counterparts geared up to drop on three principal places, Eindhoven, closest to the foot soldiers, Nijmegen some miles north, and Arnhem, across the Rhine, the farthest intrusion. Americans were assigned to the first two areas A lack of aircraft reduced the size of the airlift, with only half of the totals scheduled for the first day. Because of fears of severe losses in planes and gliders in the initial efforts, the Air Corps granted the transport carrier request for only one flight per day. Unlike previous airborne operations, Market would occur during daylight.

The troopers of the 101st Airborne looking out the doors of their C-47s could see the massed columns of tanks, half-tracks, armored cars, and personnel carriers of the British XXX Corps, poised on the Belgian-Holland border, awaiting the moment to rumble toward the objective of Eindhoven. Heartening as the vast deployment of Allied might may have been, any euphoria quickly dissipated as they approached their drop zone north of Eindhoven. Enemy gunners opened up on the aerial armada. The usual saturation of bombs, rockets, and strafing had preceded the 101st troop carriers. While many antiaircraft weapons were destroyed, great quantities of them, some well camouflaged in haystacks, devastated the C-47s. In *A Bridge Too Far*, Cornelius Ryan recorded the words of Pfc. John Cipolla, awakened by "'the sharp crack of antiaircraft guns, and shrapnel ripping through our plane." The GI draped with ammunition belts, bearing a rifle, knapsack, raincoat, blanket, grenades, rations, plus his two parachutes, also toted a land mine. He could barely move and as he watched, "A C-47 on our left flank burst into flames, then another, and I thought 'My God, we are next! How will I ever get out of this plane!' After Cipolla jumped he glanced back at his plane. It was afire and heading toward the ground.

All about the drop zone, the transports, their pilots desperately attempting to keep them on course, shuddered and lurched from hits. Engines burned, fuel tanks flamed up. On one ship only three troopers, severely burned, and the two-man crew, escaped. Out-of-control planes chewed through those dangling from the silk and the propellers chopped into the hapless troopers. Although a staggering 16 of the 424 C-47s crashed and many more were damaged, almost the entire complement of 6,700 troopers landed close to the appointed locations. When glider forces arrived later, clusters of ground fire also battered them hard but they added their forces and vehicles to the 101st's forces.

As the last of the serials bearing airborne passed overhead, Gen. Brian Horrocks, the XXX Corps commander, signaled his Garden to grow. A tremendous bombardment preceded the tanks cracking into the enemy lines. Behind strong fortifications, the Germans waited out the barrages and then zeroed in on the lead tanks. The entire advance halted as disabled armor blocked the road to Eindhoven. The 101st leader, Gen. Maxwell Taylor, expecting the XXX Corps to supply the heavy firepower, brought no artillery in his gliders and soon engaged in fighting without the aid of British tanks or big guns. Fierce firefights inflicted heavy casualties upon both sides. Lieutenant Colonel Robert Cole, recipient of a Medal of Honor for valor at the Carentan causeways, was among those killed. The inability of the ground troops to reach Eindhoven enabled the Germans to hold out against the paratroopers long enough to blow a pair of critical bridges at Son and Best, guaranteeing further delays in establishing the alley north through Nijmegen and Arnhem. The advance was well behind schedule before the first elements from the XXX Corps linked up with the Screaming Eagles in Eindhoven.

Bill Dunfee, now an 82d Airborne veteran of three drops, Sicily, Italy, and Normandy, said, "I looked forward to this as perhaps the last airborne operation. I had mixed emotions about a daylight jump. It would certainly expedite assembly when we hit the ground. However, we would make pretty good targets in the air. Then again, the Air Force might get us on the right DZ. My feeling was two out of three were positive for the daytime drop. The Army used reverse psychology on this one. They allowed us to go to town the night of the fourteenth, telling us we would move to the airports the next day for a combat jump. From that we assumed it would be another 'dry run' but it wasn't. When we got to the airports in England on September 15, we were briefed and confined to the area around the hangars. It was the most thorough briefing I had been exposed to. On the sand tables they showed the town of Groesbeek, the German border, the forest and fire towers, all of which I noticed while descending in Holland.

"After taking off from England, and formed up over the English Channel, we could look out the door—C-47 doors were removed for combat operations—and as far back as we could see there were C-47s. At the very end of the formation, gliders carried personnel and equipment for a field hospital. There were P-51s flying cover for us and about halfway to our destination, we passed a group of B-24s returning from a bombing raid, we hoped in Holland. It is impossible to convey how impressed I was with this display of power. As we crossed over the Netherlands, we picked up a little AA fire. However, the farther we went inland, and the closer to our drop zone, the more intense it became. At 1305 hours, we jumped near Groesbeek. I noticed quite a bit of antiaircraft fire on our DZ from the direction of Nijmegen. After hitting the ground, we assembled rapidly. Due to the intensity of the AA fire, everyone was very anxious to clear the DZ.

"While moving on Groesbeek, I watched a C-47 heading back. It had been hit and was burning from the tail forward. As the fuselage burned up to the wing, only one parachute came out of the plane. At that point the wing and cockpit started fluttering down. I quit watching. My thought was, 'You poor bastards.' Two if not three men perished. We secured and outposted Groesbeek. We occupied the area without incident, other than receiving 88 and artillery fire from the direction of Nijmegen and the Reichswald. The Dutch people welcomed us with open arms. I knew from past experience that the honeymoon would not last long. Usually, within a few hours of our landing, the enemy would bring everything he could muster against us.

"A Dutch man told me there was a German soldier hiding in his barn. Taking a Thompson submachine gun, I entered the barn very cautiously. Inside there was a loft with a stairway leading up to a tack room. I figure, if he were still in there, that's where he would be. I went to the bottom of the stairway and sprayed the doors and sidewalls of the room with the Thompson. Then I called out in my best German, *'Deutsch Soldaten, Komen sie here, Hände Ho!'* There was no response only the noise of harness and wooden shoes falling around me. I yelled again and punctuated it with another burst from the Thompson. Shouting at him again, I could see movement through the door I had shot away. My concern was he would roll a potato masher—grenade—down the stairs. He exposed an arm waving a handkerchief. I told him to come on down and took him outside. Turned him over to Jim Beavers to take to regiment for interrogation. I told Jim, 'If he as much as blinks, blow his fucking head off.' The German understood English. When Jim returned, he told me the poor bastard had shit himself."

After being wounded at the Anzio beachhead, Ed Sims missed the Normandy jump but had returned to duty in time to make his second combat leap during Market Garden. "Over the Scheldt Estuary, German antiaircraft opened fire on our formation. Our fighter planes were on them immediately and able to neutralize most of them. One plane in my formation was hit and the men forced to make an emergency jump from the crippled aircraft. All but two who jumped were taken prisoner. The pilot and copilot went down with the plane.

"The remainder of Company H [504th Parachute Infantry] jumped at about 1305 hours on the designated area near Grave. Initially we supported other units in securing the Grave Bridge over the Maas [Meues] River and bridges over the Maas Waal Canal. Intelligence reports placed some 4,000 SS troops and a German tank park in the Grave/Nijmegen area but resistance near Grave was light. All of our initial objectives were secured by 1800 hours that first day. Upon landing, I had reinjured my back but did not go for treatment because I felt nothing could be done. I carried on in less than top physical condition. We set up a company command post near a small cluster of homes. There I met a Dutch family and their fifteen children. The mother made room for me to stay with them and in the evening she prepared a delicious stew, using beef she had previously preserved. They wanted to celebrate our arrival and their liberation from the Nazis."

With the enemy seeking to close down the route from Eindhoven back to the border, Maxwell Taylor directed the 101st in a mammoth attack that deployed the 502d Regiment and the 327th Glider Infantry, backed by British armor. They swept the defenders from the area, killing some 300, capturing another 1,000 along with artillery pieces and smaller arms. Even as that victory was being concluded, the Germans struck in another area. Taylor, mobilized his headquarters troops—ordinarily dedicated to staff and administration—who knocked out several tanks to preserve a route over the newly installed bridge at Son.

"On 19 September," said Sims, "we moved to an area west of Nijmegen and received a briefing on a new mission that included crossing the Waal River in assault boats and seizing the north ends of the railroad and road bridges spanning the river at Nijmegan. The south end of each bridge had not yet been taken as the Germans were fiercely defending them. We heard that the British parachute units (Red Devils) who had the mission to seize the bridge over the Neder Rijn [Rhine] River at Arnhem were unable to accomplish this. Elements of the German 9th and 10th Panzer Divsions were mauling them. Because of this tense situation, before the Germans destroyed both of the bridges over the Waal, it was imperative that at least one be taken. This would allow British armor coming up from the south to cross and rescue what was left of the Red Devils.

"For our crossing the British provided twenty-six assault boats. My company was on the right nearest to the railroad bridge. Company I [506th Parachute Infantry] was to our left. The remainder of the 3d Battalion would cross in subsequent waves. Our first objective was the north end of the railroad bridge. The plan included support from artillery and a smoke screen, neither of which helped. We did get good supporting overhead fire from our own 2d Battalion and a few British tanks that had arrived early from positions along the south bank of the river.

"The time for crossing had to be moved to 1500 hours on 20 September, because the boats arrived late. We were all amazed at these flimsy assault craft that had folding canvas sides and wooden bottoms. Each had a capacity for sixteen and each had eight paddles." According to Cornelius Ryan in *A Bridge Too Far,* in some cases there were not enough paddles and the troopers improvised by using rifle butts to stroke through the water. Said Sims, "It took us a few minutes to adjust and secure the canvas sides and then move to the river's edge for launching. Within minutes we were receiving incoming enemy fire from the north side of the river and the railroad bridge. As we progressed, it became more intense. Many boats received direct hits and sank. A number of boats had trouble navigating, but the men with me, including two engineers who had to return the boat, were calm and rowed in unison. (Only eleven of the twenty-six made it back to the south bank.) It seemed like eternity before my boat landed on the north bank but it was only ten minutes. My group landed some distance west of the railroad bridge and disembarked rapidly into a skirmish line. Another boat that landed nearby had many casualties. I ordered those who hadn't been wounded to join my group. I led this combined bunch, eighteen men, in a frontal assault on the dike that was several hundred yards farther north. I carried an M1 rifle and directed an assault forward by bounds with rapid fire from all, including myself. Enemy fire was heavy but the men did not falter. Because of these few soldiers, the dike was seized within a short time and those German defenders, still alive, were routed or taken prisoner. I later learned there were numerous enemy dead on this part of the dike."

Safely across, Sims said, "I was joined by other members of Company H. Lt. [James] Megellas took his platoon [half of whom had been lost when their boat sank] and moved out to seize a nearby old fort. I took my eighteen men and headed for the north end of the bridge. Lt. [Richard] La Riviere, with a few soldiers, moved east to flush out a sniper who had shot and killed one of his people. Resistance at the north end of the bridge was light and it quickly fell into our hands. I directed a few men to look for explosives and to cut all wires. We set up a defense around our end of the bridge. Lieutenant La Riviere and the few with him, joined us, not a moment too soon, because German troops, en masse, were coming across the bridge toward us." They apparently were fleeing an attack by the British at Nijmegen. "We let them come within range, then opened fire and continued to do so until all enemy movement stopped. After we ceased firing, we allowed those still alive to either withdraw or surrender. We held the advantage because the Germans on the bridge had nowhere to deploy. They suffered a large number of casualties. I was told that the bodies of 267 were removed from the bridge and the number that jumped or fell from the bridge into the river will never be known. We had little concern about destroying the large enemy force opposing us. My men and I were tense and angry because of the strenuous fighting and the loss of our own men during the crossing. Often, in my mind, I relive this particular action and always conclude that this terrible slaughter of humans is not something to be proud of or to brag about. It continues to bother me that I had to make the hasty decision that led to the death of so many young men, our own and those opposing us."

The bloodshed inflamed anger to a murderous level. Ryan's book quoted Cpl. Jack Bommer who, when he climbed over the crest of the embankment, saw, "dead bodies everywhere, and Germans—some no more than fifteen years old, others in their sixties—who a few minutes before had been slaughtering us in the boats were now begging for mercy, trying to surrender." Bommer said that some of these "were shot out of hand at point-blank range."

Bud Warneke, of the 508th Parachute Infantry Regiment, having weathered the D day drop and the succeeding weeks in Normandy, accepted a battlefield commission as the unit added replacements and refurbished its equipment in England. On 17 September, about two weeks after he pinned on his gold bars, Warneke acted as jumpmaster for half his platoon destined for Market Garden. "It was a nice Sunday afternoon, no problem seeing all the landmarks. The whole company jumped right on our objective. My platoon was in battalion reserve when the British linked up with us. My platoon received an order to join a British tank platoon with the mission of going into Nijmegen. We were to capture a German headquarters and post office where intelligence thought switchboxes to blow the main bridge over the Maas Waal River were located. We took the buildings without any resistance. The Germans had vacated before we got there. A search found no switchbox and we returned to our unit that night. This had been the first time I worked with British troops. They were good soldiers, but compared to us I thought they had a nonchalant attitude about the war. They would stop whatever they were doing, brew some tea with crumpets but then again I did not work with them much."

A column of British tanks waddled across one of the bridges secured by Ed Sims and associates with the 504th Regiment. However, the armor paused on the road to Arnhem for a day before advancing forward. Seething over the ferocious losses his outfit absorbed, Col. Ruben Tucker, the CO of the 504th confronted an officer from the British armored division. Tucker was overheard to snarl, "Your boys [the British paratroopers] are hurting up there at Arnhem. You'd better go. It's only eleven miles." The Briton demurred on the grounds he could not proceed until his infantry arrived to accompany his tanks. Tucker voiced the frequent criticism of the ally. "They were fighting the war by the book. They had 'harbored' for the night.

Sims commented, "By then the Red Devils at Arnheim had many more dead and wounded. As usual they stopped for tea. I will never understand why the British did not take advantage of the turmoil we created and immediately push north. Company H had fifteen men killed in action and thirty-eight wounded. In my opinion, this specific operation was poorly planned [many paratroopers had never trained in river crossings with boats of this nature] and lacked adequate support. It was accomplished only because of the courage and determination of the junior officers and the fine men they led. For my part I was awarded a Silver Star."

American leaders also came in for criticism from their troops. Bill Dunfee reported, "If the Army operated on the democratic principle of consensus, the orders we received would have been dismissed for being so stupid that no rational person should comply. But being good soldiers, there was no question that we would obey. I was ordered to lead a daylight patrol into a town we could see from our vantage point in Groesbeek. It was on the German border, approximately two miles from our outposts. We were to check it out for enemy presence and report back. I took Roy McDaniels, Bill Curley and five others with me. It was about 2:00 P.M. when we started out. I decided to go straight down the road and into the town. There seemed no point in attempting to sneak there. The sun was high in the sky; there was no natural cover, and the area was flat as a pool table. There was just no place to hide. My reasoning was, if we boldly walk down the road, a column spread out on each side, the enemy might fire prematurely and we could get the hell out of there.

"We made it to within a quarter mile of the town, McDaniels leading one column and me the other. I observed three Germans with a light machine gun walk out on the road at the edge of town. I called McDaniels's attention to them. He replied, 'Hell, that's nothing. Look to the field on your left (his side).' There was a company-strength group of Germans spread out as skirmishers moving toward Groesbeek. I told my patrol to do an about-face and head back to our lines. I told them, begged them, to 'walk as fast as you can but PLEASE don't run.' I prayed to myself, 'Please, Dear Lord, don't let anyone panic and start running.' I didn't want to draw fire any sooner than we had to. I was hoping the Germans would think we were the point of their attacking force, and ignore us, or at least not shoot us. I kept looking over my shoulder, checking on the MG squad that was about a city block distance behind us. Should they stop and set up that damned MG, I intended to tell my guys to hit the side of the road (no ditch). We were able to move back toward Groesbeek about a quarter of a mile before the riflemen on McDaniels's side of the road wised up and popped a few rounds at us. It was not necessary to tell our guys to haul-ass out of there. We ran, zigzagged, fell down, got up, and ran again. We all made it back in one piece. I dove through a hedgerow into our position. I lay there, exhausted and scared. When we were within our defensive perimeter, the company opened up and stopped the German attack. At that point, a spontaneous phenomenon occurred, something that happens rarely in a combat situation. Without orders from anyone, we charged out of our foxholes and drove the enemy back through the town they had occupied. We then withdrew to our original positions."

Glider pilot Vic Warriner went along as observer in a C-47 paratrooper drop on the first day of Market Garden. He had been assigned to bring in Anthony McAuliffe, the deputy commander of the 101st Airborne, the following day and he seized an opportunity to study landmarks. The target was the area just north of Eindhoven. Because of a shortage of qualified glider pilots, there would be no copilots. Instead, Warriner and the other aviators gave a ten-minute course to a trooper so that if the pilot were incapacitated the GI could land the ship. Because of what had happened to the unfortunate General Pratt on the Normandy trip, there was a sense of urgency about delivering McAuliffe safely and at the targeted spot. His glider was to be landed as close as possible to a schoolhouse selected as a command post. On the return from that first trip, the troopers had just exited the transport when ground fire intensified. Warriner said, "Several planes went down in flames around us. Tears came to my eyes as I saw one plane with smoke pouring from it, dive toward the ground and land on its belly in the soft dirt. The hatch over the pilot's compartment opened and I saw a man start to climb out when the whole plane went up in a ball of fire. I recognized the ID letters on the nose and tail. It was the plane and flown by the pilot that had so steadfastly towed me to France. The troop compartment of a C-47 was so big and empty after everyone has jumped. The straps and buckles on the static line flap and slap with the wind and bang on the sides of the plane. You wonder how many of the young men who just left are going to live to jump again. It's a sad and lonely place.

"My sleep that night was especially restless. I learned from Troop Carrier Command that our losses had been so heavy during the day's drop that we would go in from the opposite direction. I had made that hair-raising trip for nothing. I wasn't looking forward to going through that fire again in a glider. But you can't pass. The next morning we met at my glider with General McAuliffe, his staff. An exception was made for a copilot. In the skytrain when we assembled it was an awesome sight. There were gliders and planes as far back as you could see. It was the largest airborne operation to date. From time to time Allied fighters would buzz over our column, then pull on above us to act as guardians for our slow-moving armada. It gave us comfort. However, as we approached the coast of Holland, the fighters couldn't help. The Germans opened up with flak guns, and only the fact that they didn't have our altitude figured correctly enabled us to fly under those puffs of smoke, nasty blocks of death that burst just over our formation.

"What I saw was discouraging. The Germans had blown the dikes and water covered nearly everything, including the towns that dotted the area. We were low enough to see people. The ones who were waving were Dutch citizens. The others, who fired pistols at us, I presume were not. My VIP passenger had never uttered a word to me once we boarded but was in deep discussion with his staff. When the copilot was flying, I would turn in my seat to glance at him, he always gave me a wink or a thumbs up. He seemed completely unconcerned. I don't think he realized how serious the situation was. When we first encountered the flak and the ride became bumpy, I looked back and he was sound asleep. As we started the run to the LZ we were encountering heavy ground fire. Some ricocheted off the metal tubing of the glider and some would pass on through the fabric with a loud pop as they entered and left. Now the general was wide awake. He wanted to know if there wasn't someway we could shoot back at those 'bastards.'

"He even suggested knocking off the entry door so he could lie on the floor and fire at them. The general was a great advocate of the Thompson submachine gun. It was rumored that two nights before the Normandy invasion, after a prolonged night at the officers' club, he had returned to his BOQ, sat on his bunk, and created a plate-size hole in the roof with his beloved Tommy gun. It was also rumored that Gen. Maxwell Taylor had personally taken his Tommy gun away from him and made him go into Normandy without it. Through conversations with his troopers I learned they personally idolized him and would follow 'Old Crock' anywhere.

"We were now close to our LZ, getting down in speed and altitude, but to our dismay, smoke started pouring from our tow plane's right engine. We could see licks of flame around the cowling. I was certain that Colonel Whittaker [the tow ship's pilot] was aware of this trouble and would take appropriate measures. I knew we would have to release if he couldn't get us to the LZ and start looking around for a spot to land. I knew the colonel well enough that he would get us to the LZ if he had to get out and push. I was right between two of the toughest men I had ever known. The general suggested I call Whittaker and tell him about the engine fire. I hesitated because Whittaker had his hands full trying to douse the fire and keeping us in line to the LZ. Also the ships behind us were following his lead. The general insisted so I finally called Whittaker. I got the exact reply I expected, 'Goddamn it, Warriner! You fly your glider and I'll fly this goddamn airplane!' Click! I turned to the general and said, 'He knows.'

"We were going slower and slower with one engine and the ground fire was becoming even more intense. We could see the Germans as they fired on us and the flashes made you tend to try to get your whole body perched on the flak jacket that we all sat on instead of wearing. Then suddenly, silence, as we had crossed over the German lines and the LZ was dead ahead.

Whittaker got on us there and I glanced at some smoke on the ground to get the wind direction and prepared to land. We had been briefed on the soft sandy soil in the LZ that could stop a glider too quickly and flip the glider on its back. We landed softly and after a short run stopped Everyone started jumping out.

"I prepared myself for a bit of critical comment from the general, for I hadn't the least idea of where that schoolhouse that he had circled on a map was. To my amazement, the general slapped me on the back and remarked that was the best bit of flying he had ever seen. I looked in the direction he was pointing and there was that schoolhouse about 100 yards away. I didn't disabuse the general of the notion that I had the least idea of what in the hell I was doing. He insisted I accompany him to meet General Taylor. I tried to explain that I had a bunch of glider pilots landing that I needed to contact and gather into one group. He answered they weren't going anywhere for a while. His jeep had arrived. We rode over to the schoolhouse and McAuliffe informed Taylor that Whittaker and I had done a great job. I saluted and shook hands with Taylor who muttered something like 'well done' and went back to more important matters. McAuliffe thanked me again, told his jeep driver to return me to the LZ. I saluted and went back to deal with the common man. Later I got a letter from McAuliffe thanking me and commenting on the great job by the glider pilots. He asked me for a statement on Whittaker's skill with a one-engine airplane. I complied and Whittaker was awarded a richly deserved Legion of Merit.

Glider pilot Pete Buckley reported to the flight line on D plus 2 to fly three soldiers from a field artillery unit with a jeep and equipment. "Little did we know that this day would turn out to be 'Bloody Tuesday.' Before the morning was over, seventeen of the gliders were forced to ditch in dense fog over the Channel. Five others crashed over land because of bad weather. Dozens of others were cut loose or broke away over Belgium, and seventeen of the C-47s were shot down by enemy flak over Holland. Of the 385 gliders that left England carrying the 101st Airborne Division, only 209 made it to the LZ.

"Shortly after we crossed the English coast, the entire formation flew straight into a heavy fog bank. If there's one thing that really upsets a glider pilot, and I'm sure the tow pilots, it's flying into a dense fog in tight formation with 700 planes and gliders. You have no way of knowing who's going where, when, or how and the possibility of a midair collision or accidental release is enough to make your hair stand on end. I could see only about three feet of the tow rope and had to fly blind for what seemed an eternity. Fortunately, I had the glider in perfect trim, so it practically flew by itself. Even so, I had no way of knowing what the tow plane would do. If he made a sudden change in any direction, we'd be in big trouble. Luckily, he did not. When we emerged on the other side of the fog bank there was not another plane or glider in sight in any direction. It was the biggest vanishing act I have ever seen.

"Our course brought us in the landing zone between the town of Best on our left and Eindhoven on our right, less than one minute away from our objective on the outskirts of Son. At Best, a battle was still raging between the Germans and our paratroopers for control of a key bridge near the town. Eindhoven was not fully secured and some fighting was still going on in the streets between the 506th Parachute Infantry and the Krauts. As we flew past Best at roughly 600 feet, a mobile flak wagon which I could see out of the corner of my eye on the left, opened up on our tow plane. I watched, fascinated, as shells went up through the left wing and into the left side of the fuselage and exited out the top right side where the radio compartment is. Small bits of aluminum from the plane and spent pieces of flak flew back and peppered the front of our glider. Just when I thought the enemy fire would move back along the rope and knock hell out of our glider, it stopped. Throughout the whole time we were under fire, our two ships never wavered, changed course, or took evasive action. I found out later that on the way back out, after we had cut loose, the plane was hit quite badly but managed to get back to England with no casualties.

"In a matter of seconds the landing zone appeared directly in front of us, strewn with hundreds of parachutes and gliders. Some of the latter were in one piece, others had crashed badly and their cargo lay scattered around the wreckage. The remains of two C-47s that had been shot down moments before were still burning in the craters they made when they crashed in the center of the LZ. I cut loose and made an approach well into the center of the area just in case the Germans were in the dense wood around the edge. I found out after we landed that indeed they were there but some of the 506th paratroopers held their attention while we landed.

"We came to an abrupt stop in the soft dirt of a potato field, which partially buried the nose of the glider. The first thing I did when I got out was bend down and run my fingers through the dirt. It was so nice to be down in one piece. After about fifteen minutes of digging, we managed to get the front section of the glider opened up and unloaded the jeep and equipment. Lieutenant Linz and the other two took off in the general direction of Best where the firing seemed to be the heaviest. I went alone on foot across the landing zone to find the road to Eindhoven. On the way I stopped at the 326th Medical Tent set up on the edge of the LZ. Inside, a surgical team of airborne medics, flown in by glider, were performing operations on the wounded and victims of glider crashes. Some of the medics were the same who had flown into Normandy on D day.

"I stuck my head in to see if any glider pilots were being treated there. Some had been and some of the crews of the C-47s, who had been terribly burned on the face, head, and hands before they bailed out, were still there. Within sight of the tent you could see what was left of their planes still burning on the LZ, and in the wreckage were crewmen unable to get out in time. While the medics and surgeons worked on casualties, the Germans outside the perimeter were shelling the LZ at random. These courageous medics never batted an eye; they kept right on working."

Warriner remembered, "Our next few days were spent as perimeter guards for the command post and feeding and guarding German prisoners who had been accumulating at a rapid rate. Using the glider pilots in this manner freed many airborne troopers to join their units on the front lines. Our area began to get smaller and smaller due to German counterattacks and the lack of reinforcements because bad weather in England grounded planned resupply missions. On D plus 2, some got through despite deplorable conditions over the Channel. On that day, it seemed we on the ground were more in danger of being killed by falling C-47s than German bullets. At least a dozen of them were shot down that day. Each went through the same fatal routine. As they were hit, the nose rose to almost a vertical attitude then over it would tumble and roar straight down into the ground with a tremendous fireball. Several times we were close enough to feel the concussion and heat. We watched intently to see chutes appear as the plane reached the high point before starting down. But very seldom did we see even an attempt at jumping. Soon after this we were very short of ammunition and food. We were reduced to digging up potatoes and other roots to make soup. The free milk we were offered began to look better and better. Before the mission we had been warned against fresh milk because of the possibility of getting tuberculosis. After a while we figured, what the hell, they'll probably come up with a cure for TB."

"We were being probed on a continual basis by patrols and artillery harassment," said Bill Dunfee, on the outskirts of Nijmegan. "My platoon had taken over the point of a small orchard that included a hedgerow perimeter facing the West Wall. There was a farmhouse with a rather large garage in the rear that held the platoon CP. We were receiving rather severe artillery fire. Suddenly mortars came in. I knew they had to be close by but the sun hadn't completely burned off the fog of the night so visibility was poor. Artillery I could live with, but the mortars having a much shorter range, indicate nearby enemy infantry.

"I saw a haystack to our right front. I thought I detected movement from its backside. I suspected muzzle blast from a mortar. [Did] not want to open fire and give our position away without being sure. I ran to the CP to get binoculars. Because of the intensity of the artillery and mortar fire, I anticipated an infantry attack. I picked up Lieutenant Carter's binoculars and headed back. Between the garage and house, Sergeant Sutherland was down. He didn't appear seriously wounded. Lupoli was with him and asked me to help carry Sutherland to the CP. I told Lupoli to put him in a wheelbarrow from behind the house or get someone from the CP to help.

"I ran around the house and back toward my squad. They were dug in about 100 yards to the front of the house. When I was within twenty feet of my foxhole, I heard the swishing sound of an incoming mortar round. I thought I could make it to my foxhole, but didn't. The concussion knocked me down. A piece of shrapnel sent my helmet flying. I crawled like hell to my foxhole and went in headfirst. I yelled to my machine gunner to open up on the haystack and set it afire. Then I started to check my vital parts— spectacles, testicles, wallet, cigars. I knew if I were hit, it wasn't serious. I called out to DiGiralamo to give me a hand. He asked if I were hit. I said I thought so. He yelled for a medic. To me, combat medics had a very special brand of courage. Their duty required them to expose themselves to enemy fire at the cry, 'Medic!' The one that showed up was very young and this was his first combat exposure. I asked him how it looked. He said, 'You've got three big holes in your back and you're bleeding like hell.' He insisted on giving me a shot of morphine. I didn't want any medication that would slow me down, in case I needed to get out of there. I finally lost patience and ran him off. DiGiralamo came over and administered first aid. I stayed in my foxhole until things cooled down a bit, then walked back to the battalion aid station. They were storing the wounded in a small building. It was hot in there and didn't smell good. I sat outside until an ambulance came for us. I still had my rifle and grenades. They wouldn't let me in the ambulance with them. We were taken to Brussels, where I spent one night in a hospital. They did preliminary and emergency surgery. The following day, we who were ambulatory, were flown to a general hospital near Bristol, England."

Ed Sims remarked, "The command was aware of our dire need of supplies so they enlisted the aid of a group flying B-24s to make a drop. Why B-24s I don't know, except perhaps they figured they were fast enough to get in and out without the casualties of the slower C-47s. Late in the afternoon we heard them coming. Everyone stood out there waving, thinking how good even K rations would taste. They dove to a very low altitude at full throttle. But they waited too long in dumping the bundles. We watched everything sail over our heads and behind the German lines. Fortunately, Dempsey's armor [Lt. Gen. Miles Dempsey commanded the British Second Army] broke through and we got our stomachs full. "

From day one, the Market Garden campaign teetered on the edge of disaster. All of the airborne endured a terrible pasting. While the 20,000 who arrived that first day, for the most part secured their objectives, the Germans rallied swiftly and effectively and Allied forces soon retreated. The British and Polish contingents lost nearly 80 percent of their 10,000-strong who dropped near Arnhem. The figures for the nine days of the operation show more than 7,500 casualties among the 82d and 101st Airbornes, with air crew losses of 424. There was no road to the Ruhr, no coup that opened up a pathway across the Rhine and straight to Berlin. Instead, the Allied forces pulled back to consolidate small gains across the Belgian-Holland borders.

38
Winter Comes to Europe

Closure of the Brittany campaign and the collapse of Market Garden opened up the gasoline taps for the American armies halted because of fuel shortages. The armor rumbled forward but the delay had allowed the Third Reich to reorganize its legions. The defenders drew further advantage from the ability to concentrate their war machine within a shrunken territory. But they no longer had the luxury of fighting on someone else's property since the Allies began to crowd the borders of Germany itself. Eisenhower, ordered the offensive to grind on throughout autumn, as the weather worsened.

At the start of October, on the northern shoulder of the U.S. lines— British and Canadian forces occupied the left flank—the First Army struck at Aachen, a sacred city in the Nazi pantheon because it housed the tomb of the revered Charlemagne and the garrison stuck by its guns and emplacements. The bombs, shells, and bullets resonated symbolism beyond the historic. For the first time, ground battles ripped into German turf. Tanks, self-propelled artillery, and flamethrowers blasted and burned pathways through the Westwall to make gaps for infantrymen who fought from the jumble of wrecked buildings against the stubborn defenders. After little more than two weeks, the GIs occupied block upon block of rubble, all that remained of Aachen.

Bitter fighting erupted in the sodden Vosges Mountains of Southern France where the American Sixth Army Group advanced after Dragoon. Patton's Third Army struck across the Marne and then the Meuse into the province of Lorraine. The struggle to feed the armor and keep it rolling continued. Specially modified B-24s, transformed into flying tank cars, flew gasoline from England to airstrips abandoned by the Germans, but the juggernaut needed more. Robert Johnson, the erstwhile B-17 crew chief now driving a tank for the 4th Armored, said. "We were just north of Metz, approaching the Moselle River. Supplies were slow coming. General Patton had sent a message to General Ike about the problem. He had told Ike that soldiers could eat their belts but the tanks had to have gas."

According to Johnson, the enemy forces were even worse off when it came to the necessities for tank warfare. "The day after the shooting, we engaged in a battle with tanks of the German 2d Panzers. They were dead out of supplies and could not move. We walked through them like plowing new ground." But outside of Metz, the Third Army, to the dismay of its leader, instead of charging east settled into a grim siege. Patton now admitted frustration with "too little gas and too many Germans, not enough ammo and more than enough rain." Casualties without significant results piled up. Carlo D'Este noted, "Patton had fallen victim to the very tactics he scorned in infantry generals. He had failed to concentrates his forces for a decisive attack that might have taken Metz, then refused to accept that he had anything to do with that setback . . . Lorraine became Patton's bloodiest and least successful campaign."

During the stalemate outside of Metz, the Third Army added the 95th Infantry Division to its complement. Carl Ulsaker, was the son of a career army officer and a 1942 graduate of the USMA. As a commander of a heavy weapons company in the 378th Regiment, Ulsaker remembered that prior to the outfit's first mission officers and a representative number of noncoms assembled to hear a speech by Patton. "Because it was a chilly, overcast fall day, 'Old Blood and Guts' wore an overcoat that concealed his normally resplendent uniform and his ivory-handled pistols. He was taller than the other two generals and wore a helmet with three silver stars prominently displayed. Erect in bearing and wearing his famous scowl he made an impressive enough figure for us in the absence of his normal accouterments.

"When Patton began to talk I was surprised at his high-pitched, squeaky voice. From such a big aggressive person one expected to hear the words roll off his tongue in deep, resonant tones. Once the general swung into action, however, what he had to say captured our undivided attention and the timbre of his voice became inconsequential. After an opening statement of welcome, he launched into a litany of how he wished us to fight and behave in the Third Army. Much of what he told us seemed very practical and, to our surprise, often ran contrary to what we had been taught was army doctrine. He spiced his talk with considerable profanity and colorful figures of speech. I understand he did this on purpose because such was the general practice of soldiers and the general wanted to communicate clearly with them."

Recalling as best he could that oration forty-three years later, Ulsaker quoted, "You men were all taught to assault the enemy using fire and maneuver; that is, some of you take cover and fire, while others advance in short rushes. Well, in practice, that doesn't work. First of all, when you get close enough to the enemy to get shot at, you'll find that half your men won't get up and rush when they're supposed to. They feel too secure hugging the ground. Second, you won't see the German son of a bitch until you're right on top of him. Therefore, I want you to use marching fire to attack from the last point of cover. Close with the Hun, get as many rifles, BARs, and machine guns as possible in a line of skirmishers and put a hail of fire in front of you. Shoot at every bush, tree, house—anywhere an enemy might be. Hell, we may be short on artillery rounds but we've got plenty of small-arms ammunition. The old Bunker Hill crap of 'don't shoot till you see the whites of their eyes' doesn't work here. Besides, the Germans don't have any whites to their eyes; the bastards have God damned little yellow pig eyes!

"On maneuvers in the States you were all taught to dig in whenever you halted for any appreciable time. I believe the slogan was 'dig or die.' My motto is 'dig *and* die.' Troops who spend all their time digging are too exhausted to fight when they finally close with the enemy. I want my troops to save their energy for our principal purpose, to kill as many of the bastards as we can. Anyhow, where we're going, the Germans have already been; and they've dug enough foxholes for all of us. I don't want you to walk if there's any way you can ride. Overload the vehicles. If you squeeze hard, you can get a dozen men on a jeep and trailer. The ordnance people would have you think that the truck would break down if you put more than a quarter ton on it. Don't you believe it; those sons of bitches have been putting overload safety factors in the vehicle specs ever since we relied on escort wagons for supply. Why wear yourself out walking when you can ride? If the damn thing breaks down, we can get another. It's a damn sight easier to replace a truck than a combat-trained soldier.

"When you were children I'll bet your mother would make you go inside when it rained. You know the expression, 'He doesn't have sense enough to come in out of the rain.' I don't want that said of anyone in the Third Army. It so happens that in Europe everywhere you look the people have built houses. I want you to take advantage of this shelter to the maximum. Now, in France we are allies and liberators, so just say politely, 'Move over.' But soon we'll be in Germany; there you tell the Nazi bastards, 'Get out!'

"If you believe what you read in the papers, you'd think that generals win wars. Hell, generals don't win wars; you are the people who do that. You junior leaders—sergeants, lieutenants, captains—do things that win wars. An army in combat is nothing more than a whole bunch of small unit actions where the issue is decided by how those small unit leaders behave. Jesus Christ, any old fart can be a general. Look at [Walton H.], Walker [XX Corps commander] here.

"With that Patton slapped the shorter General Walker across his rather expansive stomach and let out a loud guffaw. Walker looked slightly pained but endured his leader's jibe in stoic silence. I noticed that our general, [Harry L.] Twiddle, whom we knew to abhor the use of profanity, also looked somewhat pained. But Patton was in the saddle; he talked the language of the troops. Furthermore, he talked common sense. I made a mental note of the fact that much of the guidance he gave us wiped out a lot of the Mickey

Mouse stuff that we had been forced to digest on maneuvers in the U.S. Here was a leader of men worth following into battle."

The 95th made its debut with some success, according to Ulsaker, obliterating a series of forts that denied access to Metz. Nevertheless, the foe retained a terrifying capacity to retaliate. When his battalion set up an observation site upon a hilltop, the Germans reacted swiftly. "Shells began to rain down on the command group and on my mortar platoon and the battalion reserves in the Bois de Woippy. Volley after volley fell in our area, about twenty to thirty shells per volley. They appeared to come from the German equivalent of our 105mm howitzer. One could hear a sound like a giant ripping a sheet of paper in the distance; it would grow louder and louder, finally rising to a piercing shriek, then dissolving into a series of loud explosions as the shells burst all around us. We, of course would flatten out on the ground to minimize our chances of getting hit, taking advantage of small depressions and the smoking craters left by previous shellbursts.

"Not one of us was hit (the command group of about fifteen people) although in the reserve companies one man was killed and a few more wounded. The effect on one's nerves was intense. I literally tingled from head to foot from nervous tension and when a volley would explode all around me, I mentally willed myself to roll up in a little ball inside my steel helmet. If the firing had not slacked off when it did, I don't know how much more we could have endured. What saved us from being hit by flying fragments was that the shells would dig into the ground softened by several days of wet weather and burst after burying themselves a short ways in dirt."

Not everyone regained his equilibrium. A subordinate reported to Ulsaker that one of his mortar-section leaders had been evacuated by medics for combat fatigue. "He was a young fireball who I thought would hold up better in combat than most of my men. In West Virginia he had scaled rocks like a spider, seemingly unafraid where the rest of us had hung on to our pitons and ropes for dear life. In the most rugged training he had always been exemplary and an enthusiastic inspiration for those who tended to lag behind. It showed me that you can't predict how a man will react in combat."

Ulsaker's 3d Battalion focused on a bridge over the Meuse River in the village of Longeville. The line companies achieved good gains. From the observation post, the command could see the general flow of the fight but buildings obscured the bridge objective. A radio message reported I Company GIs in hot pursuit of enemy soldiers retreating along a riverfront boulevard that led to the bridge. Lieutenant Crawford, the company commander then advised that the Germans now were in full flight across the span and asked for permission to chase them. The battalion commander, okayed the advance, cautioning Crawford to have his point men immediately find the enemy soldier manning the exploder habitually installed on bridges.

"A few minutes passed," said Ulsaker, "and Crawford reported his first platoon on the bridge with the lead scouts having gained the far side. Suddenly, we heard a tremendous explosion; it was apparent the bridge had been blown up. Kelly [the battalion commander] called Crawford for a report. All that stunned officer could say was that the American soldiers were still on the bridge when it blew and that he had spent the next couple of minutes dodging large chunks of concrete that rained down everywhere in the general vicinity. Kelly turned pale, sank down on a bench in the room where we had all gathered, and said, 'My God, I sent those men to their death.'

"The radio operator announced that Crawford was calling for orders, but Kelly sat in a kind of daze, shocked by the traumatic turn of events. Lundberg and I looked at each other, then I commented to Kelly, 'I know it's rough, Colonel, but we still have a war to fight, so let's get on with it.' He did not respond, apparently in such a state of shock he didn't hear me."

With the battalion leader temporarily out of action, as the senior officer, Ulsaker radioed Crawford to consolidate his position and ascertain a way to retrieve the handful of GIs on the far side of the Meuse. Kelly gradually emerged from his funk. The entire command moved into Longeville where they learned that five soldiers actually had crossed the bridge while eight still on it vanished in the massive explosion. One man somehow survived after being hurled into the river. Platoon leader Bill Harrigan located a rowboat and under covering machine gun and mortar smoke stroked his way across. He picked up three soldiers; two others had been killed by enemy fire. Subsequently, Ulsaker wrote up all fourteen of those who had either been on the bridge or gotten to the other side for a Silver Star. He was told to resubmit for Bronze Stars. Disappointed, Ulsaker complied. However, four months later when he read in *Stars and Stripes* that engineers who unsuccessfully sought to defuse explosives on a Rhine bridge received the higher award, he clipped the item and with a copy of his original recommendations sent it to the awards board with the comment, "My men crossed in the face of enemy fire and ten of them died in the effort,!" Their Bronze Stars were upgraded to the Silver.

Ulsaker coming up behind attacking rifle companies noticed prisoners of war being led to the rear. "As I approached, I saw to my horror one of our noncoms plucking Germans at random from the POW column and sticking them in the belly with his bayonet. Several of the wounded Krauts lay groaning in the ditch. I accosted the man and instructed him in no uncertain terms to stop this mayhem, warning him that as soon as I saw his company commander, I would see that he was placed in arrest and charges preferred for court-martial."

Ulsaker met with the GI's superior and first consulted with him on the tactics for the next move. He then reported the atrocity to the company commander who agreed the misconduct warranted prosecution. "As I returned the way I had come, I passed the L Company weapons platoon, now moving forward. Not seeing the noncom who had been stabbing prisoners I inquired about him. The platoon leader informed me that a few minutes earlier they had been shelled and that the noncom in question had been seriously wounded and probably would lose a leg. Apparently, a higher court had seen fit to pass sentence.!'"

On 22 November, Metz finally passed into American hands. Ulsaker accompanied a squad of riflemen to the front entry of the railroad station, a massive door that was closed and barred. "One of the soldiers banged on the door with his rifle butt and commanded in German to open up. Someone inside peered through a small window in the center of this door and asked by what authority we demanded entrance. Another soldier pointed the business end of a bazooka at the window and said, 'By this authority.' The door opened immediately and a number of German soldiers filed out with hands in the air. By this time the streets were filling with hundreds of surrending enemy and it was apparent that the battle of Metz was over. Civilians began streaming out of the houses where they had taken refuge from the occasional shots and shells fired earlier. They greeted us with great joy, shaking hands and hugging the American troops."

Like the other organizations committed since D day, the 90th Division refilled its platoons with men processed through replacement centers. Private first class Noel Robison stepped onto Omaha Beach on an October morning after a tractor pushed sand right onto the gangplank of his LCI. Robison loaded onto a truck that carried him to a last repple depple before he reached the combat zone across the Moselle. "We twenty infantry riflemen replacements of L Company [358th Regiment, 90th Division] stood around a horse-drawn farm wagon in the barn. Captain Charles B. Bryan, in ODs, with a new-style field jacket on, stepped to the head of the wagon and said in a clear firm voice, 'You may think all American GIs are brave and disciplined but that is not so. Some Americans are yellow cowards and run when faced with enemy fire. I don't want any of you to run. We're all here to finish this job and you have to do your share.'"

Bryan inquired if anyone had medical experience and when a pair raised their hands he assigned them as medics. He asked about Signal School backgrounds. "Private first class Harry Cooley, a streetwise Brooklynite, and I had gone three days for Signal School training. Cooley put up his hand. I had always heard never volunteer in the Army. I decided to make an exception and follow Cooley's decision. It probably saved my life. It certainly made my combat days more pleasant." Posted to the headquarters platoon as a runner to the rifle units, Robison noted, "I carried messages, mail, and supplies. We generally were billeted in houses rather than enduring cold nights in foxholes as did the rifle platoons."

Beyond Metz, the defense remained stalwart and the Third Army struggled to plow through deepening mud and fanatic holdouts. In the mind of the Allied high command, the war would be won once the troops crossed the Rhine River, opening up broad flat terrain with a few serious natural obstacles. They believed it highly desirable to attain that objective before the Germans refitted their shattered phalanxes of armor and replaced the fallen infantry. But ahead of the Rhine lay a lesser stream, the Roer. To forestall the possibility the Germans might blow up a pair of dams on the Roer, creating an impassable lake, the First Army kicked off an attack through a wooded zone known as the Hurtgen Forest, a fifty-square mile area packed with tall fir and hardwood trees. Heavily overgrown hills and deep ravines created a natural redoubt. Roads were practically nonexistent except for small trails. The Germans had established solidly protected gun and troop emplacements. In the open ground they sowed deadly Schuh mines.

The Air Corps delivered an enormous volume of ordnance with as many as 3,000 Allied planes dumping 10,000 tons of bombs. But because no clearly defined front line could be established, as happened on D day, the explosive tonnage left the enemy positions closest to the assaulting troops untouched. In a follow-up, American artillery blasted the Hurtgen until, said George Mabry, "The forest was literally being chewed to pieces by the exploding shells. Trees were shot off and fell across each other making large areas absolutely impenetrable. However, the Germans were so well dug in that they suffered only slight casualties."

The first units to cross the line of departure from Mabry's 2d Battalion of the 8th Infantry hemorrhaged from a wicked amount of artillery tree bursts and mortars. The advance brought the GIs into a minefield garlanded with barbed wire that rose higher than a man's head. The German small arms fire enveloped those trapped among the mines. Mabry reported, "Men trying to dig in were blown to pieces where they lay. If a man rose from the ground he was almost certain to be hit by the machine-gun fire even if he escaped the artillery and mortars."

By the end of the first day, he reported the area of contention "literally covered with the dead and wounded of the battalion as only limited evacuation had been possible due to the heavy enemy fire. The outfit had lost all rifle company commanders and a large proportion of platoon leaders and noncoms. However, permission to withdraw was denied and regiment ordered the attack renewed the following day. The night became miserably cold and wet but blanket rolls for the men were out of the question. Everything had to be hand carried up the steep slope of the ravine and too many things took priority over the rolls. The night was pitch black and the casualties could only be found by their cries of pain. A roundtrip for a litter team required one and a half to two hours. Many of the wounded died from exposure before they could be evacuated."The killed and wounded added up to about 135. The two other battalions of the regiment remained in reserve, while Mabry's badly mauled unit attacked again.

Although supported by tanks, the outfit, hewing to the plot of the previous day, advanced only as far as a barbed-wire fence. Bangalore torpedoes, inserted at substantial loss of life to those bearing them, declined to explode because of mud and water damage to fuses. Lieutenant Bernard Ray sacrificed his life to blow one gap, earning a posthumous Medal of Honor. But individual heroics meant little against the wall of resistance. The failure to achieve the objectives brought relief of the battalion leader and Mabry assumed the top spot.

To his dismay he learned that after a single day to reorganize and refit, the disheartened GIs, supplemented by 200 untested replacements would attack in conjunction with brother battalions. Even with another fifty newcomers, the battalion's strength fell to less than 50 percent of its authorized complement. When one company encountered a deadly minefield, Mabry at great risk personally reconnoitered the area and located a pathway. His unit pushed forward and warded off counterattacks for three more agonizing days. Mabry's own efforts earned him a Medal of Honor. After the war he wrote a paper for the Advanced Infantry Officers Course in which his objective tone does not hide devastating criticism of the planning and intelligence of the Hurtgen operation. "To attack a position a second time from the same direction with the same scheme of maneuver after the first attack has failed, unless unavoidable, is unsound." He noted the upper echelons ignored the need for rest and rehabilitation of hard-hit soldiers and the lack of training for replacements. He insisted, "Higher commanders must recognize when a unit has reached the point when it is no longer capable of making a successful attack." He concluded, that while the enemy paid dearly for his defense, "The Battle of the Hurtgen Forest, as bloody and bitter a fight as any of the war, brought no glorious victory. No major breakthrough was made nor large area overrun by our troops."

The same terrible consequences befell the 28th, 1st, 8th and 9th Divisions. Bereft of their usual advantages of aerial support and armor, the GIs fought the Germans on an equal footing, using basically standard infantry weapons. At the same time, while American artillery now used the proximity fuses, the Germans improvised by relying on the tree branches to detonate their shells, with deadly consequences even for those who burrowed into the earth.

John Marshall, a tanker in the 707th Tank Battalion, attached to the 110th Infantry, remembered pulling into the Hurtgen early in November. "We had just dug a trench wide enough for two men to sleep in, side by side. We would then drive our tank so that the tracks would straddle it—giving protection to whoever may be in it. All of us then would get a chance to stretch our legs as we rotated sleeping under the tank. However, we decided to leave the tank where it was and spent the night in the tank. Two soldiers asked us if they could have the trench, which we gladly said they could. About 2300 hours the Germans saturated the area with heavy shelling. One shell landed directly in the trench, killing the two men. None of us slept that night.

"It wasn't quite daylight yet and we traveled several hundred feet when Mike Kosowitz leaned out of the turret to ask two infantrymen from the 110th a question. With my hatch closed I watched the men's expressions through my periscope. They were less than two feet away. They were dirty, tired, scared—I did not realize that they had been there for over a week before we arrived, clean and fed. At this moment there was a tremendous explosion as a heavy mortar hit our tank between the two front hatches. I was crushed with a strange numbness from the concussion. Although I had blood in my mouth, my nose was bleeding, and I was temporarily deaf, I was not wounded. I was alive. I looked over at our driver, John Alyea and he was staring straight ahead as if in a trance but I concluded that he was not 'hurt' either. I removed the shattered periscope and replaced it with a spare and peered out. All that remained of the two soldiers was a leg with the shoe still on, a head bared to the skull, and a shredded overcoat. I tried to believe this was a bad dream until I heard someone faintly calling me as though he were miles away in a cave. It was Mac, Leonard McKnight, our gunner, telling me, 'Mike got it and needs help.' I crawled back in the turret. As I tried to make him comfortable I could see that his chest was torn from his body. His last words to me were, 'Don't kid me, how bad am I?' I answered, "You won't be able to write for a while but you will be okay.' He died before I finished the sentence.

"The shelling continued, exploding so close that mud came into the tank like rain, but no direct hits. We turned the tank around and went back to the aid station and turned Mike over to the medics. They processed him and placed him with the others. The bodies were stacked four high and sixty-feet long—there may have been many more but I saw two such 'stacks.'"

The tank, now operating with a four-man crew, rolled toward a church in the village of Vossenack. "We received a direct hit in the rear of the tank," reported Marshall. "It went forward for fifteen or twenty feet down a swale and into a tremendous burst of exploding mortars. The now trackless side of the tank dropped into some of these craters, rendering it immobile. We discovered the turret could not traverse; the 75mm gun was useless but we were alive and for the moment 'safe,' because the tank now was lower than the grassy mound on our left.

"The Germans, knowing we were there, kept shooting at us many times with heavy guns. The shells would slam into the mound, tear through the earth like a giant mole, and then glance upward with a sickening 'whirring' sound raining dirt, rocks, and grass into our tank. It seemed like forever, but the shelling directed at us finally stopped. The tank was a mess with blood mixed with mud and debris. Because the gun was not working, we decided to abandon the tank. I was for jumping out while it was still daylight but John and Mac thought it would be unwise; we should wait until dark. John then suggested we set up a machine gun outside the tank and take turns on guard. We decided against that move. John often wished he had an M1 of his own. The field to our right was littered with dead Americans lying near M1 rifles. Just to hear myself talk I said to John, 'There's your chance to pick up an M1 rifle for yourself.' John thought a moment and then opened his hatch, unseen by the Krauts because it was much lower than the turret. Nothing happened until he ventured a short distance from the tank to pick up the rifle and was now in view of the Krauts. Again all hell broke loose, prompting John to throw the rifle down and run like mad back to the tank.

"Darkness comes early at this time of the year but there was still daylight left when we decided our evacuation procedure. One man at a time would exit the tank and run, diving from shell hole to shell hole for forty or fifty yards, then run again when the second man exited. We were to repeat this procedure so that we would all be heading toward the command post forty or fifty yards apart." The quartet reached safety and accepted an offer from the cooks to use their tents. As Marshall tried to relax on a cot, he realized, "We had lost all our possessions. We had lost our tank with thousands of rounds of ammunition. I nudged John[Alyea] 'Do you realize we never fired a shot?' Exhausted, sleep came quickly. So ended our first day in the Hurtgen Forest."

Antitank crewman John Chernitsky said, "I had never seen such destruction to forest land. The German artillery kept firing at the tops of trees and artillery bursts hit the trees—the shrapnel fell just like rain and the artillery was constant—day and night. The casualties in the 110th were heavy. The movement of medics and ambulances was noticeable in the Huertgen Forest. When they had a chance they picked up the dead. The German losses were heavy also, but we never could figure out what happened to the Germans who were wounded or dead. We would hear screaming and cries for help but the next morning, we couldn't see any wounded or dead."

The horrendous bloodshed in the thickets of the Hurtgen—6,000 casualties— all but destroyed the 28th Division. Survivors took to calling the red keystone shoulder patch "the bloody bucket." GIs from the 8th Division took over some of the 28th's responsibilities and the 4th Division moved up to bolster the left flank on the edge of the forest. The 500-man 2d Ranger Battalion relieved elements of the badly mauled division. Sid Salomon, the Ranger captain who participated in the capture of Pointe et Raz de la Percée overlooking Omaha Beach, noted, "Cold weather and a driving rain did not help the morale of the inexperienced American troops. Trench foot and casualties helped to add to the confusion that was rampant. After one month of fighting, the Americans had barely advanced twelve miles into Germany. The Rangers of Baker Company were amazed to see the GI equipment, clothing, and even weapons that had been discarded by the division troops who had previously held this area."

After Brest, Bob Edlin and A Company of the Rangers relished a month-long sojourn at a rest camp before trucking to the Hurtgen area. "You could always tell when it was getting time to go into combat. Good things started happening. We were visited by General Eisenhower. The whole battalion gathered around and he just flat-out asked if anybody could tell him why we didn't have the new boot packs. One of the men yelled out, 'Hell, everybody back at headquarters has got them,' which was true. Back in army headquarters and corps headquarters and division headquarters, everyone was wearing boot packs, parkas, and warm clothes. Up in the front lines [that gear] never leaked down. We were still wearing summer clothing and the temperature was now down in the low thirties, high twenties. General Eisenhower said that will be taken care of and God rest his soul it was. A few days later we received boot packs and even wristwatches. He must have raided the whole damn headquarters to get enough for one Ranger battalion."

Edlin's A Company exchanged places with units from the 28th Division's 112th Infantry. He encountered a friend from OCS who said, "Bob, this is the meanest son of a bitch that you've ever seen in your life up there. I wish you wouldn't go. I wish you'd just flat tell them you're not going any farther." He told me that there were men up there that you wouldn't believe would ever lose their nerve but have gone completely blank. They absolutely can't hold out any longer. I thought—you know how you are as a Ranger—we'll calm things down. How in the hell I thought 500 men could do what four infantry divisions couldn't, I don't know. When I left Jack he was actually crying and told me not to do any more than I had to."

Amid drifting snow, the platoon climbed a trail up a steep hill to the village of Germeter. As the Rangers appeared, men from the 112th Infantry emptied from the houses. Advised they would only be there a few days, warmed by a charcoal fire, and with a roof overhead, Edlin decided that maybe it was not such a bad situation. "Suddenly, the artillery starts coming. It's the purest hell I've ever been through. It was just round after round of crashing and smashing, beating on your head till you think there is no way you can stand it. I was lying on my back on the floor and the only way I can keep my sanity was by joking with the men on the floor around me. Most of them didn't take it as a joke and got pretty upset that I was calling directions for artillery fire on the house, hollering 'up 100,' 'right 100,' 'up.' In several hours, they literally shot the house down around us."

Colonel Rudder requested a patrol into the town of Schmidt to find out if it were infested with Germans. Edlin led the same band that had accompanied him in the capture of the fort guarding Brest. The Ranger leader suspected that the same sort of trap that had destroyed the Ranger battalions at Cisterna might lie in wait. Edlin and his crew crept into Schmidt and he became highly suspicious at the absence of any visible German presence. When he informed Rudder of what he did not see, Rudder was convinced the open town was a snare. Back in the basement of the house, Edlin with only about twenty left to his platoon endured "another hellacious shelling," including one round that penetrated the cellar. "I heard Sergeant Fronzek moan. When I got to him it was the most terrible-looking wound I had ever seen. Shrapnel had torn across his chest. I think his lungs were exposed. He had a pack of cigarettes in his pocket. I could see the tobacco shreds being sucked into his body as he struggled to breathe. I yelled at Sgt. Bill Klaus to get a jeep in here and get him out. In minutes we had a medic. They carried him to the jeep and he was gone. We heard from Dr. Block he would make it and he did."

Headquarters now summoned Edlin, who assumed his paltry few were about to be relieved. "I went down that son of a bitch fire trail, past Purple Heart Corner, artillery fire on our [his runner accompanied him] asses all the way. The trail was frozen. New snow lay ass-deep to a tall Indian. We were slipping and sliding; hell, they could have heard us in Berlin. It was early evening but darker than the inside of a black cat. At headquarters someone told me Rudder wanted to see me. I knew we're not being relieved. I don't need to see the colonel for that.

"Rudder was billeted in a small building, like a hunting shelter about the size of a small bathroom. There was a little kerosene stove, a table a couple of chairs, a double bunk bed. Colonel Rudder was huddled by the stove. Big Jim, as we called him. He was only thirty-five-years-old but he looked like a tired, worn out old man. I had never seen him that way." The Rangers CO dispensed with military formality and invited Edlin to sit. "He handed me a cup of hot coffee, looked at me for a minute, and said, 'Arman [Company A commander] is here to make arrangements to relieve B Company. But we've got a problem. I heard from Sid Salomon. A short time ago, B Company was pinned down in a minefield. They were under heavy artillery and machine-gun fire with a lot of casualties. I need a volunteer to take a patrol in, find a way to get to them, arrange to relieve them, and try and bring out some of the wounded. The patrol needs to go in now. A will relieve B tomorrow night. I'm not going to ask you to go, but that's the situation.'

"The picture runs through my mind like a kaleidoscope. I can't stand to take anymore of this. I'm tired and scared. This will be pure hell and I can't stand any more of my platoon getting slaughtered. But then I can see B Company suffering up there. We've been through a lot together. Shit, I've got to go. I looked at Arman and back to Jim. There's no rank here, just Rangers. 'God, Jim, I hate to ask my guys to go, they're pretty beat up, and I don't know if they'll make it or not.' The colonel just nodded and said, 'Yeah, I know.' 'Okay, we'll be on the way. It'll take me an hour to get back to the platoon. We should be in B's position in a couple of hours.' Rudder said, 'There will be a medical jeep at your CP when you get back. Good luck.' The son of a gun knew I would go."

After another but uneventful trek up the snowy trail, navigating the always dangerous Purple Heart Corner, Edlin asked for volunteers. He chose Courtney and Dreher. They would travel without helmets, packs, or even weapons. Accompanied by a driver and medic from battalion headquarters, they passed slowly along a hardtop road, aware that at any moment shells might fall upon them. At the point where the remainder of the trip would be on foot, Edlin told the driver, whom he did not know, to stay with the jeep. He said, 'Lieutenant, they ain't nobody gonna steal it. Let me go with you. I can help carry the wounded out. The medic handed the driver a litter, took another on his shoulder and said they were ready. I said, 'Let's spread out in single file. Keep as much interval as you can without getting lost. We don't want one round to get us all.'"

The would-be rescuers slid through ice and snow, aware of a potential mine at every step. "It was so dark it was almost impossible to move. The trees are down as if a mad woodcutter had been through with a giant buzzsaw. 'Shit, I forgot the marking tape.' Courtney sensed the problem and said I've got it and we're marking the path. I prayed Lord just give me the strength and guts to make a few more yards then we can rest a minute. A shell landed thirty-yards off; damn, that was close. A few more yards I could hear German machine-gun fire; a German flare lights up the scene. The snow is almost blizzard conditions. The flare shows trees uprooted, dead American and German soldiers, twisted bushes. No satanic artist could dream up such a sight."

Edlin faltered, feeling he could not continue. Dreher's hand clutched his shoulder and the sergeant said, "I'll get it [lead] for a while." Courtney, ten yards behind called out, "What's the matter, Lieutenant, you volunteered for the Rangers, didn't you?"

Bullets rustled through the underbrush from unseen gunmen and then a quiet voice challenged the patrol. Nobody knew the password, but when questioned on the first name of Lieutenant Fitzsimmons, Courtney answers 'Bob," and they are welcomed.

"I'm led to Captain Salomon's CP." recalled Edlin. "It's under a small bridge by a woodcutter's trail. I talk with Sid a few minutes and he tells me to go to Fitzsimmons who's got the worst wounded. I inform Sid we've marked the path and A Company will be in at 8:00 P.M. tomorrow night, November 23. He thanked us for coming and said the B Company medic would meet us at Fitszimmon's position. Artillery was still coming in and there was occasional machine-gun fire.

"We found Fitzsimmons and decided we would carry out two wounded at a time. The jeep driver and Courtney started back with the first litter. The two medics loaded another litter. I took the front end and told the battalion medic to stay with B Company. He was at the other end of the litter. As he stepped back to let Dreher replace him, he stepped on a mine. It went off. I learned later this heroic man lost a foot. Fitzsimmons was hit in the face. I saw the Ranger on the litter bounce into the air. The blast of shrapnel knocked me into a tree. I must have been unconscious. For a moment I'm completely blind and deaf. My left hand hurts. I reach over and can't feel my hand. It must be gone at the wrist. I'm going to die right here in this damn German woods. Strong arms picked me up, Dreher throws me over his shoulder. I can't see or hear. They were carrying me through the woods to the jeep.

"I woke up, lying on a stretcher. I'm not blind; there is a dim light. I heard Doc Block's voice, 'Wash his eyes with boric acid [to remove dirt and mud].' I have some hearing in one ear. I hear Doc say, 'Take him back to a hospital.' 'Wait a minute, Doc. How bad is it?' 'You ain't hurt, you goldbrick, a little shrapnel in your hand and face. They'll fix you up back at a field hospital. It's mostly shock and mud.' I asked someone else about the others and all they tell me is that everyone will be okay." Loaded into an ambulance, he lay next to the medic whose foot had been destroyed. "I don't know what route we took, but German artillery chased us a good ways. It ought to be against the rules to shoot at you when you're leaving."

At a field hospital Edlin quickly recovered his aplomb and his temper. He demanded an audience with the head doctor, pleading for quick repairs, explaining. "Major, there's about fifty men from B Company still in that woods. About the same number of A Company are going in to relieve them. I know the path into that death trap. If you'll clean up my eyes and hearing I'll take them up there." The surgeon argued that Edlin risked severe infection but eventually agreed to debride and stitch the wound. The doctor and several oversized aid men showed up to perform the work. Edlin learned that if he received an anesthetic it would require an overnight stay. Having abjured unconsciousness, he watched the surgeon remove the crusty, bloody bandage. "Shit, that hurt. Then I found out what the big aidmen were for. One held my legs, one grabbed my right arm, the nurse had my left arm. He took a pan of hot soapy water and a scrub brush and went to work, cleaning my hand. I'm raising hell, it hurt so bad. The hell with B Company and the rest of the Rangers, ain't nothing ever hurt so much. After this short period of torture, he took a knife and some tweezers. I remember he said, 'This is really going to hurt.' Right, Doc, it did. They counted forty-eight pieces of shrapnel, plus whatever is still in there. They put a bandage and sling on my arm, patched up my face and the surgeon said, 'You're on your own.' I knew he would catch hell about the paperwork but he just answered, 'Get a couple of Krauts for us.' I gave him some real German marks, one of the Krauts had loaned me. He was quite a man and one hell of a doctor.

"I knew if I went back to battalion headquarters, Block would kick my ass so I took off up that damn Germeter trail again. It hadn't changed, slick, slippery, slimy. It's one dark, cold, snowy night. My ass is dragging when I get past Purple Heart Corner. I go into our beat-up old house and it's empty. The charcoal fires are out and the platoon is gone. I realize they have gone to relieve B Company without me. It's twenty-four hours since I left. My hand and face hurt and I still can't hear. I've had about all of this bullshit I need."

Edlin staggered back to battalion headquarters where he learned Rudder had left for a meeting with higher-ups. Someone took pity on the exhausted platoon leader and told him to take the colonel's bunk for the night. Another samaritan brought some hot food from the mess, even cutting bite-size pieces, and offered to feed him. Surgeon Block checked his hand and face, then chewed him out for not remaining in the rear. When Edlin asked for a painkiller that would enable him to rejoin his men, Block ordered him to remain in the bunk, where he drifted off to sleep.

"When I woke it was still dark but it was twenty-four hours later. Colonel Rudder was dozing in a chair while I was using his bunk. They just don't make colonels like that."

The enemy meanwhile occupied dominant positions on high ground around the towns of Schmidt and Bergstein, from which it poured abundant artillery and mortars upon anyone who sought to advance through the minefields and withering small-arms fire. The locale provided the defenders with a commanding view of any movement of U.S. troops. The general in charge of the task force specifically asked Gen. Leonard Gerow, corps commander, for Rangers to assist the 8th Division's assault on Bergstein and Castle Hill or, officially, Hill 400.

Len Lomell, now commissioned, and George Kerchner, with D Company, started for Bergstein on 6 December. Morale dropped as word passed that their revered commander, Colonel Rudder was departing to lead the shattered 28th Division's 109th Regiment. In the early morning hours of 7 December Rangers sifted through Bergstein and rousted those Germans who resisted. At 0730, amidst a fearsome artillery duel, the Rangers jumped off for Hill 400.

According to Sid Salomon, "The CO at the appropriate time gave the word 'Go!' With a whooping and hollering as loud as possible, firing a clip of ammo at random from their weapons in the direction of the hill, the Rangers ran as fast as they could across the approximately 100 yards of open, cleared field into the machine-gun and small-arms fire of the German defenders. Crossing the field, and before reaching the base of the hill, the company commander and his runner became casualties, but still the remaining D Company Rangers continued their forward charge up the hill.

"The enemy defenders immediately became alert. A red flare shot in the air from an enemy outpost, apparently a signal to their higher headquarters. Shortly thereafter a heavy mortar and artillery barrage came down on the assaulting Rangers. Heavy small-arms and machine-gun fire was directed on the rushing Rangers. Casualties on both sides now began to mount, but still the charge continued. Some Germans were giving ground. Others of the enemy forces were seemingly safe in well-prepared holes or behind log emplacements. Rifle and automatic fire filled the air. A creeping German artillery barrage behind the assaulting Rangers produced more Ranger casualties. The enemy continued to offer stiff resistance. Ultimately the fast, unceasing, and determined forward momentum of the assaulting D Company Rangers stunned the German defenders, some of whom quickly moved away from the steadily advancing assaulting troops."

Within an hour, the enemy had fled but it was an onerous victory. Well aware of the importance of the highland, the foe now rained down a murderous assortment of explosives upon the new kings of the hill. The rocky, tree rooted ground defied the best efforts of entrenching tools. The only shelter lay beneath toppled trees or in shell holes. The battered able-bodied Rangers of D Company drew some comfort from the support of F Company that had secured the left flank. Lomell, now the sole officer of D Company still on his feet, reached a concealed troop shelter at the top of the hill. He threw in a grenade while another Ranger sprayed the interior with automatic fire. According to Lomell, "Survival was a matter of luck. We were under constant bombardment. Guys were lying all over the hill. We couldn't even give first aid. We were told we would be relieved and just to hold on. How long can you tell a guy bleeding to death to hold on? My God, he knew I was lying to him.

"I had tears in my eyes. We stopped another counterattack but if the Germans had known how many men, or really how few we had up there, they would have kept coming." Bleeding from wounds of his hand and arm, Lomell, offered a proposal to his noncoms. "'If we retreat, they'll take care of our wounded. We can come back and take the hill later.' They adamantly refused to consider the idea." An explosion near him caused a concussion. "I was bleeding from the anus and the mouth as a result." Under cover of darkness, he was evacuated.

Originally informed they would need to control Castle Hill for no more than twenty-four hours before infantrymen of the 8th Division would take over, the beleaguered Rangers endured more than forty hours on the heights. Of the sixty-five Rangers who started the charge, only fifteen could come down under their own power. On the morning after Lomell came off Hill 400, German artillery slammed into the Ranger positions just as battalion surgeon Walter Block left his dugout to supervise evacuation of the seriously wounded. A shell fragment killed him instantly.

As one his last acts, Block spared his medical technician Frank South the worst of the battering around Hill 400. "The day before the battalion was sent into action at Bergstein, I passed out due to dehydration and a severe gastrointestinal problem. Not knowing we were about to be committed, Block insisted that I get to a hospital. I was unaware we were in action until wounded Rangers began to arrive. I immediately went AWOL from the hospital and hitchhiked back to the battalion, only to find the Battle of Hill 400 was over, the battalion decimated, and Block dead. He was the first and last medical officer we had that deserved the name of a Ranger. I still feel both guilty and somehow cheated that I was not part of that battle."

Sid Salomon, CO of Baker Company, 2d Ranger Battalion, who saw his GIs chewed up during the first exploratory thrusts into the Hurtgen forest considered his people cruelly used. "After the invasion, there was no need for a 2d Ranger Battalion. We were used as an infantry company, attached to maybe ten different divisions. The people in command did not know what the Rangers were. They would put the Rangers first and keep their own casualties down. A Combat Command of the 5th Armored Division [ordinarily about 3,000 men with tanks and other armored vehicles] failed to take Bergstein. Three companies of Rangers [little more than 200 foot soldiers] captured it, going past burned-out tanks with GIs hanging over the sides." Salomon himself collected his second Purple Heart on Thanksgiving Day 1944, as an explosion lacerated his eyebrows and chin.

39
"I Have Returned."

Following the gains in the Marianas and New Guinea, the strategists debated the next major step. Prior to the most recent successes, the blueprints called for an orderly progression up the island stepping-stones, starting with the Palau group and then climbing up the Philippine Archipelago via the southernmost outpost, Mindanao. Buoyed by their successes, Admirals King and Nimitz argued for a giant leap that bypassed Luzon, the main Philippine island in favor of Formosa, less than 1,000 miles from the enemy homeland. Adding to King's taste for Formosa was that it lay within the Navy's sphere of control. The proposal outraged MacArthur because it condemned the Filipinos to remain under the harsh boots of the Japanese. From a military standpoint, the grandiose notion to mount a successful invasion of Formosa in mid-to-late 1944 required manpower and supplies far beyond those available.

MacArthur drew support from an unexpected quarter. Admiral "Bull" Halsey reported that his ships and planes had seen little evidence of any strong enemy forces on the islands below Luzon. Although Halsey badly underestimated the strength of the Japanese, MacArthur persuaded Nimitz to accept an invasion of the Philippine Archipelago. Actually, through the campaigns that involved the Solomons, Marshalls, Marianas, and New Guinea, MacArthur and Nimitz, while occasionally squabbling over allocation of resources, had cooperated well.

Without committing themselves to taking back Luzon, the Navy honchos agreed that for a start it would be necessary to capture the southern and central Philippine areas. Mindanao, vulnerable since the conquest of Wakde, Biak, and Noemfoor seemed ripe for the opening thrust and then Leyte, strategically sited in the middle of the islands. A tentative schedule set 1 November as the date for landings on Mindanao. During the first two weeks of September, carriers from Halsey's fleet launched a series of preparatory strikes on Mindanao and the central islands. Halsey now reported to Nimitz that his pilots had destroyed the Japanese fuel supplies, sunk almost all vessels visible, and encountered few aircraft. Moreover, a downed flier rescued by Filipinos brought back the startling intelligence from the natives that there were no Japanese soldiers on Leyte. Halsey recommended that instead of Mindanao, the combined forces attack Leyte. Although MacArthur's staff correctly pointed out that the Filipino report of no enemy troops on Leyte was dead wrong, the Joint Chiefs, MacArthur, and Nimitz concurred on an invasion of Leyte rather than Mindanao and scheduled amphibious operations to open 20 October.

To reduce the capacity of the Nipponese to interfere with operations around Leyte, a component of the U.S. Navy's Fast Carrier Force, Task Force 38, steamed into the China Sea and hammered the Formosa airfields and installations. Planes on the island engaged the carrier-based Americans in a furious, three-day affair. The attackers wrecked more than 500 aircraft, sank about forty cargo vessels, and blasted ammunition dumps, hangars, barracks, maintenance shops, and manufacturing sites. The naval air arm also rampaged across Luzon, targeting fields and fortifications around Manila. Simultaneously with these raids, the U.S. Army's Far Eastern Air Forces, taking off from Morotai, Biak, New Guinea, and other locales, pummeled enemy airdromes in the Philippines and laid waste to installations in the occupied Netherlands East Indies

During the Formosa engagement, the defenders crippled the cruisers *Houston* and *Canberra,* bounced a bomb off the carrier *Franklin,* and a flaming enemy bomber skidded across that ship's flight deck. Antiaircraft and dogfights cost the Americans seventy-six planes. While casualties among personnel aboard the three vessels saddened shipmates—the disabled cruisers reduced Task Force 38's power minimally—the *Franklin* remained fully serviceable. The losses of air crews and their machines hurt most but the overall impact upon the state of the fleet was negligible.

However, the Japanese Navy enthusiastically accepted the extravagantly false claims of success from their fliers and issued a communique triumphantly listing 11 carriers, 2 battleships, 3 cruisers, one destroyer or light cruiser sunk, another 8 carriers, 2 battleships and as many as 15 other ships severely damaged or set afire. The emperor issued a special decree to commemorate the great victory, while civilians and military plunged into in a mass celebration of the fictitious triumph. A roseate view victimized the Imperial High Command. It eagerly sought this moment when it could swing the combined, full weight of the Army, Navy, and Air Forces against the now staggering Americans. A jesting Admiral Halsey radioed Admiral Nimitz on 19 October that he was "now retiring toward the enemy following the salvage of all the Third Fleet ships recently reported sunk by radio Tokyo" but the Japanese persisted in the belief America was about to fall.

U.S. intelligence on Leyte estimated a garrison of 20,000 one month before the scheduled invasion. But with more than 400,000 Japanese stationed throughout the archipelago, no one doubted that sizable reinforcements could be rushed to areas under siege. The battle order started with the 1st

Cavalry, 7th, 96th, and 24th Infantry Divisions, plus the 77th and 32d as reserves. With the auxiliaries and service personnel, a total of more than 200,000 men headed for Leyte. Because the nearest strips for fighter cover lay 500 miles off, much of the air support lay with the Navy carriers. Also hurling its weight through the sky, the Army Air Corps would hit the Japanese with its bombers and be ready to blast ships carrying reinforcements for the island defenders.

The opening salvos from the U.S. fleet crashed down upon Leyte two days before A-day. (With D day now so firmly associated with the Normandy invasion, the planners had abandoned the tradition that dated to World War I and started to use other initials and codes to mark operations.) Planes from carriers concentrated upon neutralizing enemy airfields while the 6th Ranger Battalion eliminated installations on four tiny islands in Leyte Gulf. In the armada of 700 ships, MacArthur himself sailed on the cruiser *Nashville.*

At 0600 on A-day, battleships along an eighteen-mile line from San Jose down to Dulag on the northeast coast of Leyte, shelled the beaches. From two miles offshore, MacArthur witnessed the start of the action. "I could clearly see sandstrips with the pounding surf beating down upon the shore and in the morning sunlight, the jungle-clad hills rising behind the town. Landings are explosive once the shooting begins, and now thousands of guns were throwing their shells with a roar that was incessant and deafening. Rocket vapor trails crisscrossed the sky, and black, ugly pillars of smoke began to rise. High overhead, swarms of airplanes darted into the maelstrom. And across what would ordinarily have been a glinting, untroubled blue sea, the black dots of the landing craft churned toward the beaches."

As his F Company from the 34th Regiment, 24th Division, approached Leyte, Paul Austin, the company commander, remembered, "We were awakened about 4:00 A.M., had the usual prelanding breakfast, steak, and eggs. This was the only time we ever got that kind of food. The 24th Division landed on Red Beach with the 34th on the right and the 19th Regiment to the left. The 1st Cavalry Division landed three or four miles north of us in the vicinity of Tacloban and near the Leyte commercial airfield. Their objective was that airfield and Tacloban, the capital city.

"My company landed about 10:05, in the second wave. As we came off the boats, we ran across some shallow water and hit the sand. The first wave was still lying there. I asked what company is this and was informed K Company. I said, 'You're supposed to be about fifty yards in. What's the hold up?' "They told me there were snipers and a machine gun that pinned them down. Shells were falling all over the place. I looked out to sea and saw a landing boat take a direct hit, probably an artillery shell. That boat literally disappeared, nothing left except a few pieces of scrap and steel helmets. The entire boatload, maybe twenty-five soldiers lost along with the coxswain. Other boats were on fire, two LSTs and LCIs.

"Rifle fire was coming in pretty heavy. Our Captain Wye from regimental headquarters was killed a minute after he set foot on the beach. Another company commander from the 1st Battalion was killed very near Col. [Aubrey] "Red" Newman. [Regimental CO] I looked back and couldn't see anybody moving forward. Snipers, machine guns, mortars, artillery, had everyone pinned down on the beach sand. The beach was covered with palm limbs, fronds; the bombardment had stripped the coconut trees by the thousands. It was pretty hard to walk because of the heavy layers of limbs while the trunks of the coconut trees stuck up in the air like telephone poles. Very few had any branches."

As a telephone lineman with the 2d Battalion's Headquarters Company, Han Rants recalled a seven-day voyage to the shores of Leyte. "It was a time of great anxiety among the troops. There was much meditating, cardplaying, talking through the night. We liked going by ship because we felt the Navy food was really something compared to what we got in base camp or wherever we happened to be. While down in the hold our thinking all the time was that a torpedo hit would come right into the hold. That doesn't give you any real peace of mind.

"During the card playing, few of the fellows really had any money and they would play on the basis of IOUs As that gambling went on, there was a fellow from Gardena, California, Pfc. Harold Moon, who won lots of money. He was a real rascal as far as a garrison soldier was concerned. He would have been in the stockade all the time because he wasn't a real spit-and-polish soldier. Within the first day of our trip from Hollandia, Moon showed up with a set of Navy fatigues, their blue work clothes. On occasion, he would slip on that outfit and could go through off-limits areas to get ice water or whatever he needed. He even showed up with a first lieutenant's bar for his Army fatigue hat. Moon was quite a poker player and he won big. I think he had around $1,200 in cash on him as we hit the beach at Leyte.

"The tension builds in any beachhead convoy and the nearer the island, the more tension. The day and night before a landing are wide-awake times with more knife sharpening and gun cleaning. Some of the Tommy gunners file or cut plus [+] or x marks on the cartridge heads. If properly done, this causes the slug to split four ways when it hits the body so that a large hole and much damage results. Many GIs stand at the rail all night, some weeping, some meditating, some cursing, but all weighing their chances of getting through another campaign. It gets to be pretty emotional. Some buddies sit quietly after having lived together day and night, never more than an arm's-length away. You know the other guy's family; you know his sweetheart, you know everything about everyone. I remember so vividly the last few nights with fellows saying, 'If I don't make it, will you do this for me?'

"When the people are loaded in the landing craft (LCVP) they go away from the ships and circle until everyone is loaded. As we got into our circling position, our planes had gone in to do some bombing of the beach, and our battleships who were out deep behind us were throwing shells over our heads. The beach seemed to be one big explosion. We got to feeling confident that there couldn't be anything alive in there with all of this. The LCIs were going in closer and firing with heavy machine guns. They also had some multiple-launch rockets fired at close range. The destroyers in shallower waters would blast away with five-inch guns.

"Just before 10:00 A.M. we were circling in those boats, with people getting really sick in them. They pop around the ocean like corks and the smoke from the motors is somewhat like following a city bus, just breathing in the fumes, a horrible smell that you breathe continuously. After riding around a length of time, many of the troops would just as soon die if they could reach the beach. Right at 10:00 A.M. the shelling stopped and all of these boats spread out and started in. It was deathly quiet as there was no firing while were going in because they didn't want to take a chance on shells falling short, hitting us. As we got within 200 yards, enemy shells started coming out. Mortars sometimes hit a barge but usually missed. They turned artillery and antiaircraft guns on us. Everybody was scared. The Navy men driving these barges were on raised platforms like sitting ducks. They stood up high with a very small shield and wanted to dump us and get out. They smacked the beach and yelled at us to get out. Sometimes, some started back before the last guy got out of the barge. They had to go back and get another load and come in later.

"We were supposed to be the fourth or fifth wave but we got there second or third. As our barge hit the beach and the door flopped open, we jumped out, scared as can be. There is no pain or hurt as bad as being scared to death, and scared to death we were. There was no combat group in front of us, no troops to gain some ground and make a place for us to set up a headquarters. As wiremen we had no rifles, only our switchboard and rolls of wire for telephone communications. Our weapons were .45s, meant to defend ourselves close range. We tried to hang at the beach but as we came off that landing barge, within ten feet of us was a fellow who had been cut in half by an artillery shell. There was no bottom half of him and he was stretched out, guts pouring from the bottom half, which was half in the water, and half out. Everybody just stopped, looked at some of the dead people hit in the first wave and then looked at each other. We knew we couldn't run back into the water because there was no place there. People seemed stunned. The Navy had to stop shelling but the landing barges had .50-caliber machine guns firing over our heads.

"About this time, " Rants continued," Colonel Newman, a big redheaded man and a real tough guy with a lot of guts, jumped up on the beach twenty or thirty feet from me and said, 'Get the hell off the beach! Get up and get moving! Follow me!' It was just enough to get everybody awake. GIs started moving, crawling, jumping, running combat-style. You run a little, roll over and try to take cover before moving again. We thought we would get some sort of position before they saw us but they apparently knew we were coming because they had managed to build some pillboxes. They had coconut logs covered with dirt and machine guns shooting from narrow slits in these mounds of dirt and logs. The only way you can get people out of these places is to be close enough with a flamethrower or get in closer under the machine-gun fire and toss a grenade in.

"A hero came forth but we knew he had come to this battle to die. He was a big Hawaiian captain, one of the most popular officers. Before we left Hollandia he had received word his wife just had a baby although he'd been away for twelve months. This really shook him and we knew he was going to fight with everything he had, even if he got killed in the process. Word passed that he was really ripping and had knocked out three pillboxes. With real luck, he was jumping, running, dodging, and crawling under machine-gun fire to get hand grenades in the fortresses. At about the fifth one they got him, laced him with fire and he was hit ten times through the chest. He was the one who really broke the spell enough for our people to start moving in."

Austin's memory of the morning action was slightly different. "For all of that heavy bombardment, the enemy fire was very heavy. I heard someone yell, I'm pretty sure an officer from K Company, yelled, 'Let's go!' [Newman was about 150 yards away from Austin] and K Company jumped up and ran into the jungle off the beach. I let them move about fifty yards ahead and then shouted for F Company to move. Our two platoons on the beach started forward. My instructions were to follow the 3d Battalion, K Company, as it turned out, to a certain point and then we would pass through them to take up the attack. F Company would lead under the theory that by the time we covered 300 yards, the 3d Battalion would have suffered so many casualties, the second wave would have to take over the advance. Luckily it didn't turn out that bad, although K Company have taken some casualties. I had my men get on their bellies and crawl, trying to make harder targets for the snipers. I kept them on their bellies for at least seventy-five yards.

"A light tank came roaring down the beach and he turned into our area and drove the tank right up to the 3d Battalion line to our front. Colonel Postelwaite, the battalion CO walked up behind the tank, took the telephone in his hand and talked to the gunner and driver. He started directing fire from that tank. They put a 75mm shell into everything that even looked like it might contain a Jap or a machine gun. He'd fire at two or three targets, then move the tank forward twenty or thirty yards and repeat the process. I knew he destroyed two log pillboxes with shells right into the apertures of them. Colonel Postelwaite moved his front line right up to the edge of a big rice paddie full of water. I saw him talking to the tank and then the gun swung around, to line up on a building across the rice paddie. It put a shell into a small building a few yards away from a house and blew it to pieces. I could see chickens and chicken feathers flying."

Joe Hofrichter, formerly with an engineer unit, had been transferred to the 24th Division after a misunderstanding about returning from a leave. As an outsider and buck private, Hofrichter had worked the worst details during his first weeks with the 24th until a sergeant took him to a supply tent. "He emerged holding a flamethrower, which he threw at me. 'This is a flamethrower,' I protested. 'Right, and it's all yours,' the sergeant replied. I said, 'Sergeant, I just got into the infantry. I don't know the first thing about a flamethrower.' Starting with almost a whisper and progressively getting louder and louder he repeated, 'I know you don't know anything about a flamethrower, but by the time we hit the beach in the Philippines, you're going to be the best damn flamethrower operator in the entire Army.'"

Hofrichter underwent a two-day crash course in the operation and care of his new weapon. He was assigned to an LST that carried M8s, self-propelled artillery pieces resembling tanks. Hofrichter and four riflemen were assigned to support an M8 bent on destruction of enemy bunkers. "If fire from the M8 failed to silence a bunker," says Hofrichter, "I was to move forward under protective fire. I was to find an opening in the bunker and, at close range, hit the opening with several bursts from the flamethrower. After the briefing I felt as though I had been hit in the stomach with a sledgehammer. I kept thinking how inexperienced I was and why I had been chosen to wield such an awesome weapon. It made no sense but that was not unusual in the Army. You didn't need a Ph.D. from MIT to operate a flamethrower. Privates, especially replacements, were considered expendable, referred to as 'cannon fodder.'"

On 19 October, after a final rundown on the specific missions, Hofrichter noticed that all the joking had ceased. Few slept and, as a newcomer, Hofrichter was excluded from small groups who spoke quietly to one another. The novice flamethrower operator says he spent the night thinking of his "beautiful young wife, parents, kid brothers and sisters, and a role model from high school, a football coach." At the Mass conducted by a chaplain, Hofrichter prayed not so much that he be spared but that God grant him the strength and courage to face what lay ahead. He could not stomach the steak and eggs and munched on a piece of roll with his coffee.

Scheduled for the third wave, Hofrichter and his group donned their gear at 9:30 A.M. "A fellow by the name of Johnny Lomko, helped me get into the harness of my flamethrower. As he did, he said, 'There, you lucky bastard. No Jap will dare get close to you.' Indeed I was the lucky bastard . . . Johnny would die shortly after we landed. At 10:30 or thereabouts, the twelve LSTs headed for shore at full speed and soon attracted Japanese artillery fire. Before reaching shore, four had been hit and one was burning. The one I was on came to a grinding halt long before reaching the beach. We had hit a sand bar. Engines were reversed and the commander of the ship swung the rear of it back and forth for what seemed an eternity. We became a sitting target. Japanese artillery shells kept falling to the left and to the right, closer and closer. Suddenly they also started dropping to the front and back of the ship as they tried to zero in on us. I had never experienced such a feeling of despair and hopelessness.

"We all took cover under vehicles on deck. Some men fought for places of safety. Others prayed, out loud. I did so inwardly, as I lay with the upper part of my body under a truck, my feet beneath a jeep. The rest of me was exposed. Fortunately, a destroyer saw we were in serious trouble. They shot a line to our LST and in no time we were freed and headed out into the bay. Our second run was successful and we poured onto the beach."

Like the others, Hofrichter was astonished to find the troops from the earlier waves still burrowing into the sand of the beach. The words, orders, and leadership of Newman galvanized the men around Hofrichter. "A fellow dug into the sand not far from me, looked at me, got up, moved forward, and said, 'Give 'em hell, Buddy!'" A tank trap temporarily blocked passage for the M8 with Hofrichter, but a bulldozer filled the pit. "The bunkers were well concealed, hard to see. But the concentration of firepower coming from them gave us an idea of where they were located. The first three were silenced by fire from the fire of the 75mm cannon of the M8. The fourth, despite countless 75mm shells, was not completely silenced.

"Once we moved off the beach, things were happening so fast the adrenaline kicked in and helped ease my initial fears. Now it went into high gear. I was so focused on what I was supposed to do I didn't have time to think as I moved under protective fire toward the bunker. I reached the dirt-and-log emplacement miraculously without drawing fire. Two machine guns were still firing. I could not find an opening to use the flamethrower although the shells from the M8 had caused part of the bunker to cave in. As I leaned forward against the logs of the bunker, about four feet in front of me, I suddenly began to see dirt between the logs start crumbling. A few seconds later I saw the shaft of a sabre push through, creating the opening I needed.

"As soon as the sabre was drawn back inside, I placed the nozzle in the hole and shot three bursts into the bunker. The screams I heard were of intense agony. The machine guns were silenced and the stench of burning flesh drifted through the openings where the guns were. I vomited on the spot. Four more times on A-day I used the flamethrower and I vomited each time. After the third time there was nothing left to bring up. The last two bunkers left me with the dry heaves." By midafternoon, the team with Hofrichter had accounted for sixteen bunkers.

"At Red Beach," said his supreme commander, Douglas MacArthur, "our troops secured a landing and began moving inland. I decided to go in with the third assault wave." Actually, the moment chosen to carry out the promise to return, occurred about four hours after the third wave reached the shore and establishment of a beachhead. The general's account of the trip on his barge noted, "The coxswain dropped the ramp about fifty yards from shore, and we waded in."

In his biography of MacArthur, William Manchester reported the wet landing was unexpected after the vessel with the supreme commander ran aground. "MacArthur had counted on tying up to a pier and stepping majestically ashore, immaculate and dry. Most of the docks had been destroyed in the naval bombardment, however, and while a few were still intact . . . the beachmaster had no time to show them where they were. Like all beachmasters, he was as autonomous as the captain of a ship. When he growled, 'Let 'em walk,' they had no choice."

In the famous photograph of the event, as MacArthur strides through the shallow water, he wears a grim scowl on his face. Manchester attributed the look to a "wrathful glare" at the offending beachmaster, rather than a sign of determination. Red Beach at the moment was shakily secured. Japanese snipers occasionally harassed the invaders. Close by, automatic and small-arms weapons ripped through nearby groves as GIs pressed forward. American planes from carriers passed overhead on the way to bomb targets and naval vessels hammered at distant targets. Those responsible for MacArthur's safety sweated out his tour as he inspected the 24th Division command post, kicked a couple of enemy corpses, drafted a brief message to President Roosevelt, and then spoke over a microphone hooked to a mobile communications truck.

He declared, "People of the Philippines: I have returned. By the grace of Almighty God, our forces stand again on Philippine soil—soil consecrated in the blood of our two peoples. . . . The hour of your redemption is here . . . I now call upon your supreme effort that the enemy may know, from the temper of an aroused people within, that he has a force there to contend with no less violent than is the force committed from without . . . Rally to me. Let the indomitable spirit of Bataan and Corregidor lead on . . . ."

Han Rants held a ringside seat for the appearance of the general and had his own interpretation of the event. "It had been quiet on the beach perhaps an hour or so when some ceremony or commotion seemed to be coming from out on the water. About three landing barges were coming in, and from the flags we could see it had to be MacArthur. We really didn't have a lot of love for MacArthur because as a general he wanted to win wars fast. He wanted to push as many people as fast as he could to get it done, so he had spoken out against rotation of troops so old ones would get a leave home. He wanted to keep the veterans until the war was won.

"We had only about 1,200 yards of beach but here came the landing barge with the tide right for a good, flat, dry landing. I have an idea it was kind of staged, too, as it stopped a little short, the gate flopped down, and MacArthur, with fifty aides of his, officers of various levels, waded about knee-deep through the water.[A different appraisal than Manchester.] Cameras were grinding to film the triumphant return. Later, after the war was over, we saw the very same picture with the caption in *Collier's* magazine reading 'MacArthur leads the troops ashore.' It was quite some time later than H hour and it just hadn't been safe any sooner.

"I happened to be hanging in a coconut tree close enough to hear the speech loud and clear. He mentioned that three years ago he told the people of the Philippines that he would return and now, 'I have returned.' While seeming to be a kind of grandstand thing for a show, it really took some kind of courage for a man of that level to be there. Much as we disliked the guy [because] of his wanting to use veteran troops to win wars, we knew there was no one who knew the Philippine Islands better, and we knew that had we landed somewhere else, we probably would have had a lot more people killed than we did."

At his Collecting Company station on Red Beach, battle surgeon Phil Hostetter learned from wandering GIs of the imminent arrival of MacArthur. Hostetter elected to remain at his post for orders. A second report confirmed the general's appearance and that he wet his trousers to the knees. Casualties grabbed Hostetter's attention and he administered plasma to an infantryman with a compound fracture of his arm from a bayonet fight. "After a while, someone asked," recalled Hostetter, 'Do you know who was just here? General MacArthur and some admiral! They watched you for quite a while.' No one told me we had visitors so the general watched me but I was too busy to see him. We thought the presence of our highest officers on the beach at that time was foolhardy. We did not understand the significance our Filipino allies saw in his coming. The general said he would return and he did. The next day some guerrilla soldiers came to the beach. One said, 'I am delighted to see you here but where is General MacArthur?'

"'He was here yesterday, we all saw him,' I replied, lying a little.

"'Oh, I cannot believe it,' he answered with joy. 'This means you are here to stay. It is no commando raid.' The General understood well the Oriental regard for personal leadership."

As darkness enveloped them, the 2d Battalion of the 24th, wary of the

Japanese propensity for night assaults, prepared for the possibility. "Colonel Newman," said Paul Austin, "ordered G Company to set up a roadblock a quarter of a mile down the road toward Pawing [a Leyte village]. Approximately thirty men dug in astride the highway. I felt in my bones we'd be attacked that night. They had boasted they would throw us back into the ocean if we landed there.

"About 1:00 A.M. rifle and machine gun fire erupted down at the roadblock position. That woke everyone up. Almost immediately a Japanese mortar shell hit the roof of a building right near our foxhole. I became pretty frightened and worried about our situation as the gunfire got hotter and hotter down the road. Presently my two machine guns, set up to support each other with cross fire, opened up."

Han Rants, in the communications section, remembered, "Telephone lines were kept open so those men out on points to spot trouble could kind of whisper, 'We've got people coming in.' On this particular night, Private Moon, the guy who won all the money on the ship, was holding one of the point positions with a couple of buddies. He called in and said, 'This is the big one, they're really coming and they seem to be all around.' They used a rice paddie and not only had machine guns but mortars mounted on rafts in the water. They could move the raft quickly, and they'd fire a burst then move real quickly so when we returned fire, it wasn't there.

"They came near Moon's point and he would kill three or four of them who tried to take it. The enemy determined they would try to take that point before anything else. It was kind of fortunate they did because it bought us a whole lot of time until daylight came. The Japanese started to maneuver to get the three guys in that hole and finally killed two of them. Moon was there alone but well supplied with a Tommy gun and clip after clip of ammunition plus grenades.

"We could hear exchanges; some of the Japanese spoke English and would yell at him. He knew he should be quiet so they couldn't really zero in on him but he really meant business and called them all the names in the world. He kept yelling 'Come and get me! If you want me, come and get me!' Moon called back coordinates of enemy positions, and mortars hit these targets.

Joe Hofrichter, having completed his assignment in support of the M8, located his unit, Company F under Paul Austin. Hofrichter shared a foxhole with Troy Stoneburner, who awakened him from a sound sleep as gunfire shattered the silence in the G Company sector. "It went on for hours," said Hofrichter. "Suddenly the firing stopped. We could hear clearly an American GI cussing and taunting the Japanese to come and get him. There would be a short burst of fire, then more cussing at the Japanese. At one point Troy said it looked like the fellow doing the cussing was out of his foxhole, firing bursts from an automatic gun. 'No way,' I said. Soon Troy poked me and told me to look toward the beach between two clumps of trees. I located the spot and silhouetted against the open background, a man was standing, firing a gun in rapid bursts. We were both convinced this was the nut doing all the cussing and shouting. About 4:00 A.M. a major shootout took place in G Company's area and then it grew silent. Early the next morning, we learned that they had repulsed a night attack and that a kid named Pvt. Harold Moon had killed countless Japanese within a few feet of his foxhole before he was overrun and killed. [Remnants of Moon's platoon broke the enemy line with a fixed-bayonet charge.]

"As we moved up the road at daybreak, I saw a lot of dead Japanese and one dead American soldier. Before they covered his body with a poncho, I saw his face. It was the kid who winked at me on the beach and said, 'Give 'em hell, Buddy,' and it was Pvt. Harold Moon!"

"Moon had fought by himself at the roadblock for an hour or hour and a half," remarked Austin. "He took all the ammunition his buddies had left lying around and, with his Thompson machine gun and a box of grenades, he had fought those Japs until they finally gathered in a large group, knocked him down and killed him. That morning there were fifty-five Jap bodies all lying in front of his foxhole. Across the entire front of our battalion, we estimated some 600 to 700 Jap bodies. Part of them were from an air strike called in from a carrier. We marked the ends of our lines with red panels and the pilots coming over the area after daylight could see the area. Their bombs fell right in the midst of the Japanese soldiers. I saw one bomb go off and two or three bodies flying in the air, mixed with debris, mud, and water."

"One of the first details, after the first night on Leyte," said Han Rants, "was to go out and get Moon. One of the lieutenants headed that detail and the guys all knew Moon had 1,200 bucks on him. The lieutenant took charge of the money and as far as we know, he sent it back to the family. Moon had been shot many times, and they had cut him up with a sabere or knives, even after they killed him out of extreme anger at the number he had killed. Even in their hurry to try and take us, they took time to take out some frustration on him." Harold Moon, for his extraordinary performance, was awarded a posthumous Medal of Honor.

On A-day, after the customary pounding of the shore defenses from the air and sea, the 1st Cavalry Division using amphibian tanks raced toward White Beach, a 2,000-yard-long strand of coral sand that began almost a mile north of Red Beach. Rifleman Sal DeGaetano, newly acquired from antiaircraft duty by B Troop, 12th Cavalry Regiment, rode the first wave ashore.

"As we neared Leyte," says DeGaetano, "the Navy was all around us. As the first wave formed, I looked at some of my buddies to see if they were as nervous as I was. I was fascinated by the big smoke rings the big guns made as they pounded the beach, and then walked the bombardment inland while we prepared to land. I was amazed at the little resistance we encountered that first day. But in spite of that, in my foxhole that night, my buddy Ray York and I were shaking like leaves with apprehension until we fired at some noise and then settled down."

Compared to what the 24th Division endured, passage to White Beach and immediately beyond proved relatively easy. The pounding administered by aircraft and ships drove the defenders to abandon most of their fortifications. The most difficult task that first day seemed to be crossing a deep swamp. By nightfall, the division had achieved its objectives.

The 24th and 1st Cavalry Divisions, grouped as the X Corps, formed the right flank for the assault, with the 1st Cavalry responsible for the northern most zone. Some fourteen miles south of the edge of the 24th's Red Beach, the 600-ship convoy bearing the the XXIV Corps, composed of the 96th and 7th Divisions, zeroed in on a series of beaches designated as Orange, Blue, Violet, and Yellow. Unlike the other divisions, the 96th came to Leyte unblooded. Its GIs were also a mix of extremes in education and background. Bob Jackson, a platoon leader in the 382d Regiment, recalled "Many of the noncoms were not draftees or even early volunteers, but men who, in the severe Depression of the late thirtys found a home in the Army. While not highly sophisticated, they had learned 'the Army.' We draftee officers [he graduated from OCS] were a different lot. Most of us were recent college graduates."

The need for replacements for outfits already overseas drained the 96th of some of its people. To fill the ranks of the 96th, large numbers of men from the recently closed down Army Specialized Training Program [ASTP], an operation that sent GIs to college, entered the 96th's ranks. "It was a sad situation," said Jackson, "they had no military training to speak of. A barracks was set aside and we were charged with making soldiers of these men. They were very bright—they must have had very high IQs because they'd been accepted at prestigious universities, but they knew nothing about soldiering. We were given about six weeks to bring them up to speed. Discipline was the greatest problem. They were not used to the restraints on their individuality that the Army required. Most turned out to be superior soldiers in combat."

Dick Thom, a lawyer in civilian life and older than most at his level, was a regimental staff officer. He, too, fretted over the infusion of these raw newcomers. "They turned out to be smart kids, quick to learn, good riflemen, good shooters, solid killers, and thoroughly reliable."

The preliminaries off Orange 1 and 2, Blue 1 and 2, featured a barrage led by the battleship *Tennessee*. Within thirty-nine minutes, the ships methodically painted the area with 2,720 rounds of high explosives. Carrier planes swept over the sector, unloading more bombs and strafing targets of opportunity. As the amphibious tanks and landing craft rendezvoused for the final swing to the beaches, LCIs added a barrage of rockets and mortars to the cacophony of shells.

Bob Seiler, a former ASTP enrollee, said, "It was like a hundred fourth of Julys, all at once. The rockets were the most impressive. They looked awesome. How anything could live through that was hard to believe." George Brooks, from the same program as Seiler, recalled tense early moments. "There was very little conversation while we were loading into the amtracs and then heading for shore. On the way in, one of the guys sitting opposite me in the amtrac was very nervous, as we all were, and fiddling with the safety on his rifle. He had the rifle butt down on the deck with the barrel up alongside his cheek. All of a sudden we heard a loud bang and when we looked at this guy, his eyes were bulging way out with a startled expression on his face. There was a black powder mark up the side of his face and a hole through his helmet. Nobody laughed.

"The amtracs were supposed to carry us on shore for a hundred yards or more, but when we got to the beach there were coconut logs driven into the sand at the water's edge like pilings. There were three or four logs cabled together and spaced so closely an amtrac could not get between. So we stepped out into the water from the rear of the amtrac and raced across the beach as fast as possible. It was 10:00 A.M. when we hit the beach and 98 degrees Fahrenheit. I found one of our guys passed out from heat exhaustion. His canteen was empty. I called a medic over and went inland. That very first day our battalion commander flipped his lid and had to be taken back. We continued inland through a swamp, waist-high or more. Of course one thinks of snakes in this environment but I didn't see any. Late in the afternoon, we got orders to dig in."

"The immediate reaction when coming under fire for the first time is self-preservation," noted ASTP alumnus Norman Fiedler. "The ingrained training received through basic training caused one to immediately react as a combat man—hit the ground, seek protection behind rocks, trees, etc., and move forward. Some men lagged behind but no one stayed behind, the noncoms incessantly urging, 'move forward, move ahead.'" Fiedler's outfit apparently bumped into a more determined band of defenders. "Our company was pinned down just beyond the beach, in what appeared to be rice fields. We dug foxholes by nightfall but because of the water table, they filled up with water. Because we could not leave the foxholes, we remained in water up to our necks all night. In the morning, our entire bodies, hands etc., were wrinkled from being soaked."

"Of course no one slept that first night," said Brooks. "Off our left flank we heard a lot of shooting and noise. We heard that Japs had made a banzai charge in the 7th Division area. One of our guys, whom I knew very well, got out of his foxhole and crawled toward the company CP. Someone shot him in the head. We had been told over and over not to get out of our fox-holes at night. They thought he may have heard something on the radio and was trying to crawl over to tell the company commander."

A-day called for the 32d, 184th, and 17th Regiments of the 7th Division to penetrate the one-mile of coastline denoted as Violet 1 and 2 and Yellow 1 and 2. A swamp separated the Yellows. The strategists earmarked Dulag, a barrio beside Highway 1, and its airfield, as the principal objectives. The 32d at Violet 1 and 2 encountered fierce opposition from well-emplaced de-fenders, who temporarily held up an advance spearheaded by tanks. In-tensive fire silenced the foe. Elsewhere the GIs pressed ahead with a mini-mum of interference. By nightfall, the invaders held Dulag, occupied the turf at the edge of the air strip, and straddled Highway 1.

Douglas MacArthur now paid a second visit to Leyte, splashing through shallow water to observe the 1st Cavalry at work. His annoyance over the first day's wet steps to the beach had vanished once the dramatic photographs of the event appeared. Neither broadsides issued by the Japanese authori-ties nor the sonorities of MacArthur meant a spent cartridge to the GIs now struggling inland. The 7th Cavalry Regiment [descendant of the ill-fated outfit commanded by George Armstrong Custer] battled its way into the is-land capital of Tacloban. The Japanese, embedded in the 1,500-foot hills that overlooked the town, hiding in buildings and sniping from foxholes, fought tenaciously. Tanks, artillery, mortars, and dismounted cavalrymen routed them. The citizens of Tacloban showered the GIs with gifts of eggs and fruit and vigorously waved the Stars and Stripes.

All along its front, the 1st Cavalry expanded the American-controlled ter-ritory. Squadrons from the 8th Regiment drove northward near the shore-line to combine efforts with men from the 7th Cavalry ferried up the coast. Together they secured approaches from across the San Juanico Strait, which lies between Leyte and neighboring Samar, where a large garrison of enemy soldiers might seek to reinforce their comrades on Leyte. Some of the 24th Division infantrymen to the south struggled against large numbers of determined defenders and unfriendly terrain.

After his first night on Leyte, Paul Austin, had left the safety of his fox-hole for a quick look down the road to where Harold Moon took his stand when an enemy machine gun sent him scrambling back to safety. "I got be-hind a tree trunk and he just kept pouring bullets into it. I waited until he gave up and then dashed for the foxhole. When I got in there I looked at Cuffney [a replacement lieutenant sharing the space with Austin] and re-alized there was something wrong with him. 'I'm hit,' he said, 'in my hip here.' He pulled his trousers down and below his hip joint I could see the point of a bullet sticking out of his skin. It seemed to have come all the way through his thigh and ended up on the other side.

"'We'll get a medic, Cuff, and get you out of here as soon as we can,' I told him. He lay there, not saying anything and he wasn't bleeding. He'd evidently been struck by a ricochet as plenty of them had come off the trees and ground. Medics came and took him away. I laughed as he was leaving and said, 'It's been good knowing you, Cuff.' And he was gone, having been with F Company only a month, and after his first night on Leyte. Other fellows went all the way through the war without ever being hit."

Han Rants, who had inspected Moon's remains, observed the results of GIs' experiences with the enemy. "From our very first contact with Japanese soldiers in New Guinea we saw and felt them violate every rule of war and of humane treatment of civilians and soldiers. The great majority of enemy soldiers we faced were worse than uncivilized savages or wild beasts seeking to kill. A savage or an animal has some sense of self-preservation or desire to stay alive. To the Japanese soldiers we faced, honor and life-ever-after came only from being killed in battle for their Godlike emperor. They said they would be forever disgraced and disowned if they returned home without victory. A wounded Japanese soldier would fake death, sneak a chance to use a grenade or shoot someone before killing himself. We learned quickly after each battle to make sure all bodies left were really dead. The best way was to put one more bullet through the head if not sure, or to kick them in the testicles."

"Their barbaric torture of civilians and my buddies triggered an anger and hatred in me that resulted in my doing things that are unacceptable in the civilized world. Each of us had to cope with their butchery in our own way but for me vengeance was the answer. It took many years for me to share some of the deeds that I regret so deeply and some will go to my grave with me except for dear war buddies who respected my fighting ability. Absolutely no one can make judgment on a combat soldier's behavior until he/she has lived like a hunted animal in a hole for a year or more.

"Some of us were gold-tooth collectors, and it was helpful to be in the wire section with a good pair of pliers to collect the gold. From the minute when you knew you were going to be killed yourself to the time that it had gone the other way, the GIs were out picking up what they could find." Rants recalled, "We were all so close to being wiped out. Not much longer than ten seconds later the cleanup that happens in war, which is barbaric but releases anger, began. The live enemy were gone and our guys jumped up, ran out, and started picking up sabres, guns, watches, rings, whatever souvenirs were available."

"I thought the Japs were good soldiers. I never had the good luck to run up against one who was not," says platoon leader Bruce Price, of the 19th Infantry Regiment. "We were told that if we took prisoners, we would have to feed them out of our rations, which were not too plentiful in combat. I did not consider them to be inferior humans. They could kill me as well as

I could kill them. Headquarters also said, 'If we want prisoners, we will send out units to get them."

"The mosquitoes and other animals were awful," remembered Bob Jackson, the heavy weapons platoon leader of the 382d Infantry, 96th Division. "This swampy country was home to leeches and we had all been frightened by the medicos about the liver fluke for which this animal was the host. Our feet were a mess because we dared not take off our boots; we might not get them on again. Most of us had developed fungus—about which the medicos had warned us—but we were unable to take the correct precautions of changing socks. I took off my boots about the fourth day and was shocked at the huge ringworm-type lesions all over my feet and up my legs. The carefully husbanded foot powder was about as useful as an invocation to the gods."

Bob Seiler spoke of extreme shortage amid a hostile environment. "Supplies of food and water were nonexistent the few first days because nothing could move through the swamp we were passing through. Water was always in short supply. We got it about once a day but it was always close to 100 degrees every day and water didn't last long enough. One day we passed through some very high cogon grass and I passed out because there was no air to breathe. When I came to, my old buddy Horowitz was using his water to revive me. And water was scarce. I used my Halazone tablets [for water purification] every day. We would shoot holes in coconuts and drink the juice. Chewing on a piece of sugarcane helped. It seemed as if it rained every night and one night we had a typhoon. That time you had to bail our your foxhole to keep from drowning. You took for granted you were going to be wet all night. Some nights it felt rather cold and your teeth would chatter.

"At first we went without food for days. The first thing we got came from a small observation plane dropping something like dog biscuits and salt tablets. We had to take atabrine tablets [antimalarial drug] every day and we were all yellow and had dysentery. Looking back, I think the Japs were more afraid of me than I of them. Either that, or their plans were just to slow us down. Very few times did they stand up and fight. Once or twice we had banzai attacks but they lasted only a short time. We were asked to try to get some prisoners but we all felt the only good Japs were dead Japs. I was always fearful that the wounded or dead were boobytrapped and would rather put another round in them to be sure. Because I was cautious about booby traps, I never picked up any souvenirs."

40
The Battle of Leyte Gulf and the Kamikazes

Atop Hill 331 on Leyte, Paul Austin said, "We could turn around and see the entire Leyte Gulf, the San Pedro Beach, all of the shoreline practically from the Tacloban airfield way down to Hill 522 [held by the 19th Regiment] near Palo. We could see all the ships in the armada that brought us there, all the supply ships, sitting out there, hundreds of them. On the morning of the third day, we were standing up eating breakfast. I heard a noise overhead and looked up. There were nine Japanese Betty bombers coming directly over us and headed straight for the bay and all of our ships. They were at a pretty low altitude and we could see the rising sun on their wings. Just as I thought they're going to bomb our fleet and there is no way they can be stopped, I heard what sounded like a giant string of firecrackers going off. It came from way up in the air, above the bombers. All of a sudden, each one of those Bettys began to smoke, began to burn. As they glided on toward the beach, one by one they turned belly up, plunged into the ground within the beachhead. Some hit the highways, one went into a long glide after which he guided that plane right into the side of a Liberty ship and exploded."

What Austin and his comrades observed was the overture to the full-scale involvement of the Japanese air and sea forces in Gen. Tomoyuki Yamashita's proclaimed *Sho Ichi Go*, the victory operation. The focus of the action around Leyte shifted from the efforts by GIs to widen their patch of the island to Leyte Gulf to primarily a titanic battle between the opposing navies with land-based Japanese aircraft and the limited U.S. Army air resources in the area. On 24 October, from bases on Luzon, the defenders aired massive raids directed at the American Leyte lodgement on land and at sea. As an estimated 150 to 200 mostly twin-engined bombers approached, antiaircraft gunners peppered the skies, while U.S. combat air patrols from the carriers and land-based Army fighters pounced on the slower-moving, poorly protected foe.

Among the huge armada of American ships participating in the Leyte venture was the USS *Suwannee,* one of four escort aircraft carriers (CVE) converted out of fleet oilers. With a combat history dating back to the landings in North Africa in 1942, and a dozen island campaigns, the *Suwannee* was home for Air Group 60 with both torpedo/bombers and Grumman Hellcat fighters. Tex Garner, who flew one of the latter said, "*Suwannee* was much smaller than the *Hornet* [his previous base] and we were mostly catapult shots off it, maybe 99 percent were cat shots because of the extreme loads we carried and the very low wind condition over the deck. But it was an excellent ship. We started supporting the troops; first for me was Tarawa, then Enewetak, Kwajalein, Guam. We would come in and work an island over for about a week before a landing, become familiar with the terrain, know how to lay our ordnance in to do the most good, destroy as much of the gun emplacements as we could. and then keep the air clean of planes.

"The Japanese pilots, as far as I am concerned, when we first saw them were very good. They were seasoned, had been in China. As the war went along, those men were thinned out and the quality of Japanese pilots deteriorated fast. By the same token, ours were getting stronger all the time. Every carrier and air group had some fantastic people in it. But our being together for thirteen months was an opportunity for camaraderie most carrier pilots never get."

Garner, who knocked down his first enemy, a twin-engine "Lilly" a month before the *Suwannee* came to Leyte, was a member of a predawn patrol with three others, on 24 October. He recalled, "We had been on station about four hours and ready to return to the *Suwannee.* A radio reported, 'Tally Ho. Eight bombers at ten o'clock heading toward Leyte.' I swept the sky and spotted a formation of Lilly bombers [fast, twin-engine aircraft]. I Tally Ho'd them. We dropped our empty belly tanks and climbed to intercept them.

"Lip Singleton and I set up one line of the formation while Edgar Barber and Ralph Kalal set up on the other wing of the Vee. We all rolled in at the same time. It was perfectly coordinated and four Lillies were knocked down on the first pass. Each pilot had a bull's-eye. After that run we whipped the Hellcats around for another target and for an instant all four fighters had the same bomber and fired at him—so long Lily. All four scrambled for another bomber. Lip burned one, Kal exploded one, and the last bomber pushed over, hellbent for our landing ships. I called on my Hellcat to give her all, closing very slowly. I was trying to get to him before he got to the fleet because there was no way he would miss 'em. I began to realize some of our AA were trying for him, too. I either had to break off or go for him into our ships' AA.

"I bore in firing all six .50-caliber guns. He began to smoke. I noticed the bomb-bay doors open. There was no way he should have done that because that slowed him down enough for me to catch him. I closed to within four feet. I thought I'd ram him. I came across from his left engine, left wing spar, cockpit, right spar, right engine. On the sweep back as I crossed the cockpit area, I saw like an accordion door open and the pilot appeared. The six guns cut him in half. The plane exploded with the bombs still on board.

"I knew I was in a tight spot with all those ships still firing and if I pulled up I was a dead man. I pushed over, leveled off at about eighteen inches off the water and went zigging through the ships like a scared rabbit, hunkered down behind the armor plating and praying. I was amazed when I reached the other side, wringing wet but still alive, with 18 holes and nothing serious."

For the Japanese air arm, the first day of the Battle of Leyte Gulf was catastrophic. Sixty-six planes were definitely shot down with eighteen probable kills. Three U.S. aircraft crash-landed—two on the Tacloban strip and one in the water. The ability of the Imperial High Command to threaten the U.S. fleet from the air was seriously impaired. Notwithstanding this weakness, elements of the Japanese Navy hastened toward the area, threatening to sever the lifelines of those ashore on Leyte and provide easy access for tens of thousands of reinforcements from elsewhere in the islands. Short on seaborne aircraft, the Imperial Navy mustered massive firepower with seven battleships, including two that were bigger, faster, and mounted larger guns than anything in the U.S. Navy arsenal, and thirteen heavy cruisers as well as destroyers.

The grand strategy devised by the Imperial Navy split its resources into three fleets. Vice Adm. Jisaburo Ozawa, head of the Northern Force, commanded a convoy dominated by a pair of old carriers half-converted for flight operations, several legitimate carriers for whom few planes or pilots were available, a batch of cruisers, and destroyers. The Ozawa group, approaching from the north, would be a decoy to lure the strongest of the U.S. elements, Adm. William Halsey's Third Fleet, most notable for its mighty carriers and concentration of air operations.

Meanwhile, VAdm. Takeo Kurita, in charge of the First Striking Force, led the principal armada toward Leyte Gulf. All of the battleships and most of the heavy cruisers sailed under Kurita's banner and followed a circuitous route to avoid submarines. A smaller aggregation under VAdm. Kiyohide Shima, comprised of three cruisers and nine destroyers, departed from Formosa to add its weight to the offensive planned for Leyte Gulf.

The Japanese also brought a new tactic. By autumn 1944, the Japanese admirals charged with waging the naval air war against the onrushing Allies, accepted what Tex Garner had noticed; they were no longer a match for their adversaries in either pilots or machines. Desperate to reverse the tide or inflict severe losses VAdm. Takajiro Onishi of the First Air Fleet called for volunteers to act as suicide pilots. By crashing their bomb-laden planes into ships they could do far more certain damage than through conventional raids. The first kamikaze corps had entered a training phase 19 October, a few days prior to the start of the great victory operation.

The American admirals did not expect an onslaught in the vicinity of Leyte. Once again. the division of command created possibly serious consequences. The Leyte campaign involved the Seventh and Third Fleets, two separate organizations. Vice Admiral Thomas Kinkaid bossed the Seventh Fleet, the organization responsible for landing and supporting the invasion force, and reported to MacArthur. Flotillas of troop and supply ships, dozens of destroyers, a handful of battleships, escort carriers like Garner's *Suwannee,* and support vessels comprised the Seventh Fleet.

The air-oriented Third Fleet of Bull Halsey, consisted of the Fast Carrier Force deploying most of the Navy's big carriers, under VAdm. Marc Mitscher, plus cruisers, destroyer screens, and support ships. Halsey came under the command of Admiral Nimitz and felt little obligation toward the Seventh Fleet. "Its mission was defensive," said Halsey. "It had bombarded the beaches, convoyed the transports to the landing area, and stood by to guard them while they unloaded and it was to protect them during their retirement.

"My mission was offensive. When I received orders to cover the Leyte landings my mission did not change. It was still offensive. The tasks assigned my force were to gain air supremacy over the Philippines, to protect the landings, and to maintain unremitting pressure against Japan, and to apply maximum attrition by all means in all areas. Finally, should opportunity for destruction of a major portion of the enemy fleet offer, such destruction would become the primary task of my forces." Indeed, severe criticism had lashed Adm. Raymond Spruance for hanging about the Marianas to protect invading marines rather than aggressively pursuing enemy naval forces. Submarines attached to both fleets prowled the sea lanes searching for any enemy naval reaction to the invasion. Following a series of voyages aboard other subs, David McClintock assumed the con of *Darter* for her final two patrols. On 10 October 1944, the USS *Dace* under Comdr. Bladen Clagget, formed a two-ship wolfpack with *Darter.* Alerted to the invasion on 20 October, the pair roamed the Balabac Strait, the shortest route from Singapore to Leyte. Radar signals indicated possible enemy ships but these had vanished from the screens.

A few minutes into 23 October, after a rendezvous with *Dace*, McClintock received word from his conning tower, "Radar contact—30,000 yards—contact doubtful—probably rain." McClintock said, "*The Jap Fleet* was what flashed through my mind. Almost immediately the radar operator stated the contact was ships. *Dace* was given the range and bearing by megaphone. The answer came back, 'Let's go get them.' By twenty minutes after midnight both *Darter* and *Dace* were chasing the contact at full power. The ships were in Palawan Passage, headed north.

"It was now apparent that we had not a convoy, but a large task force, which we assumed was headed for Leyte to interfere with our landing. Three contact reports were sent—the final one estimating that the force included at least eleven heavy ships. I decided we should not attack before dawn, considering it vital to see and identify the force. The left-flank column, nearest us, consisted of five heavy ships. The last gave by far the largest radar pip. Probably a battleship. There may have been more ships in this column, but at the long range at which we were tracking, and the probably close formation, this is all that showed up on the radar screen. I picked this column for *Darter*'s target, hoping for a crack at what we thought was a battleship. *Dace*, trailing us very closely, was assigned to the starboard column. We planned a periscope attack at dawn.

"At about 0430 all hands were called for coffee before the expected attack. At about ten minutes before five we manned battle stations, and ten minutes after five we reversed course, headed down the throat of the column. It was getting faintly light in the east. There wasn't a cloud in the sky. In twenty minutes we wanted to shoot. The first periscope look showed a huge gray shape. It was the whole column seen bows on. A look to the southeast where the light was better showed battleships, cruisers, and destroyers. The gray ships kept getting larger. We would pass on almost parallel courses. At 5:25 the first ships in the column could be identified as heavy cruisers, with huge bow waves. There were sighs of disappointment that the targets weren't all battleships. A beautiful sight, anyway. I hoped the lead ship would be the flagship. It was! At 5:27 the range to the leading cruiser was under 3,000 yards. All tubes were ready.

"Then the column zigged west to give a perfect torpedo range of just under 1,000 yards. Their profiles could be seen clearly, *Atago* [class] cruisers. I had the 'scope up for what seemed like several minutes, watching. The leading cruiser looked huge now. She had a bone in her teeth. The forward slant of her bridge seemed to accentuate her speed. [It was] the *Atago* [with Admiral Kurita aboard] my favorite target on the attack teacher. Estimating the angles on the bow off her flat bridge face was easy; I had done that many times before on models."

The range dropped further and McClintock called out instructions with a final, "FIRE ONE!" He unloosed five more forward fish as a searchlight on the cruiser flickered signals. "Did she see our torpedoes?" wondered McClintock. "She was going by now. No, she wasn't zigging! 'Shift targets to second cruiser' . . . 'bearing mark' . . . 'Give me a range . . . give me a range,' yelled the torpedo officer." Finally accommodated with the requisite data, the stern torpedoes left the *Darter*. As they did, the sub rocked from heavy explosions.

"Depth charges!" exclaimed the exec officer. "Depth charges, hell . . . torpedoes!" McClintock responded. Another officer, jumping up and down with each explosion shouted, "Christ, we're hitting 'em, we're hitting 'em!"

Recalled McClintock, "After the tenth torpedo was on its way, I swung the periscope back to the first target, which had been hit with five of the bow torpedoes. She was belching flame from the base of the forward turret to the stern; the dense black smoke of burning oil covered her from forward turret to stern. She was still plowing ahead, but she was also going down by the bow. Number-one turret was cutting the water. She was finished."

McClintock knew for certain he had sunk one vessel and probably another. The crew of *Darter* had little time to exult as the enemy destroyers attacked with depth charges. But the sub escaped damage. *Atago* went down within eighteen minutes carrying 360 of the crew to their deaths. A Japanese destroyer plucked survivors, including Admiral Kurita, from the water. While *Darter* fled to avoid depth charges from destroyers, its companion *Dace* stalked the flotilla and slammed four torpedoes into another cruiser. Unfortunately, *Darter* ran aground on a reef. When efforts to free the vessel failed, *Dace* removed the crew. Most important, Halsey now had firm intelligence on the approach of the enemy armada.

On the morning of 24 October, planes combing the area west of Luzon and Leyte, spied the Japanese on a presumed course for the Leyte vicinity. The third Fleet commander directed three of his fast carrier groups into positions for attack. Limited as their resources were, the Japanese threw the first punches, even as Halsey's subordinates maneuvered their carriers. From Luzon, bombers and torpedo planes went after Task Group 3, which included the big carriers *Essex* and *Lexington,* and *Princeton* and *Langley,* lighter flattops. Hellcats from the quartet met the enemy and splashed most of them; one pilot, Comdr. David McCampbell of the *Essex,* alone knocked down nine, an all-time record for carrierborne fighters. However, a lone bomber, hidden by cloud cover, suddenly emerged in perfect position to plant a 550-pounder on the *Princeton* flight deck. The bomb crashed through the thin skin of the deck before exploding deep in the ship's innards. The blast ignited gasoline stores, then set off a series of torpedoes on planes sitting in the hangar deck. Damage-control crews on the *Princeton,* and from other ships that lent assistance, fought valiantly to squelch the inferno. A further series of detonations from munitions not only doomed the *Princeton* but wrought heavy casualties aboard the *Birmingham,* a cruiser trying to serve as a tugboat. A useless hulk, the *Princeton* stubbornly refused to founder. American torpedoes finally scuttled the ship.

Lieutenant Bill Anderson Jr., a torpedo/bomber pilot assigned to the USS *Cabot,* a light carrier with Air Group 29, a composite unit that included nine torpedo/bombers and twenty-one fighters, was one of five from the torpedo squadron who took off on 24 October. Also on the mission was exec John Williams and two good friends of Anderson's, Howard Skidmore and John Ballantine. "Somehow we became separated from McPherson and Williams and we never saw them when we reached the Japanese fleet or on the way back. Williams was shot down and rescued. The three of us came over the Japanese fleet at about 15,000 feet. We circled looking for a target and we started down. I automatically adjusted speed and altitude. The ideal was at about 270 knots and an altitude between 150 and 300 feet. The only way you could get that kind of speed in a TBM was through a steep dive at full power and when you leveled off you might be at about 315 mph. You would rapidly slow down, but if you could pick up your aiming point and drop the torpedo from 300 feet up, chances were for a good torpedo entrance. It was a fairly restricted envelope in which to work. You also had to have wings level, not nose up or down, when you released, or else the torpedo might not have the proper attitude when it hit the water."

At Leyte Gulf Anderson picked out a battleship and started his attack. "There were bursts of antiaircraft fire all around but not close enough to rattle anything in the aircraft. We lost sight of our other planes. The Japanese fleet started evasive maneuvers and it was necessary for me to pass over the battleship and pick up a cruiser target on the other side. They were shooting at us with their major-caliber weapons. A 16-inch shell is not a proper weapon against aircraft; the chances of being hit are like as those of being struck by a lightning bolt. They did throw up geysers of water and you'd turn so as not to be hit with falling water. The water would be full of color; the Japanese did this in order to tell how close they came.

"We got in pretty close, straight and low, opened the bomb-bay doors and pickled off the torpedo. Any torpedo pilot who says he saw where it went after he dropped it is probably dreaming, because after you fire it you're so busy making a hard turn to get out of there you can't stop to look over your shoulder. My gunner, Richard Hanlon, said he saw it drop and head for the cruiser before he lost sight of it. Radioman Joe Haggerty said it hit the cruiser. I was credited with having hit the cruiser and got a Navy Cross, but I'd be hard pressed to swear to the fact." Anderson and the others from Air Group 29 were part of wave after wave of Hellcats, Helldivers, and Avengers from Task Group 38.2, who sortied across Leyte against a fleet bereft of air cover. Shot and shell from every gun on the Japanese ships including the main batteries of the battleships ripped the air but splashed just eighteen of the several hundred swarming over the targets.

Still puissant with a galaxy of battleships, cruisers, and destroyers, Admiral Kurita temporarily halted his voyage toward Leyte in hopes that sorties of land-based aircraft might drive off the American carriers or else protect him from their deadly stings. Unfortunately, there were no planes available to support Kurita. He resumed his course, urged by his superior that he had "divine guidance." He steamed toward the San Bernardino Strait, which would swing his massive firepower around the northern tip of Samar and then into the Leyte Gulf, to confront the less heavily gunned U.S. Seventh Fleet. The hours wasted while Kurita's fleet dallied eliminated any hope the Center and Southern Forces could rendezvous at the appointed hour in Leyte Gulf, to form a kind of nutcracker enveloping the U.S. Seventh Fleet. Admiral Shoji Nishimura, in command of the Southern Forces, wavered momentarily but shook off the minor destruction and plowed ahead.

Meanwhile, Admiral Ozawa, to the north, artfully coaxed Halsey to chase him. He issued radio messages, hoping American intelligence would intercept them. He wandered around the Pacific Ocean off Luzon, his ships seductively languishing, visible to any prying spy plane. He even mounted a seventy-six-plane strike on a group of Third Fleet ships. Desperate to lure the Americans, Ozawa directed his pair of half-battleship, half-carrier, *Ise* and *Hyuga* to run south. American planes scouring the area finally spotted the pair around 4:00 P.M. on the 24 October. Other searchers located the main carriers an hour later; the fish had gone for the hook.

Halsey was an eager candidate for the bait. He knew the enemy retained a significant number of aircraft carriers and he salivated for an opportunity to attack them. While Halsey always insisted the Seventh Fleet possessed ample weapons to handle an enemy fleet like Kurita's, he seemingly took steps to ensure that if the Third Fleet left the area, adequate reinforcements for the Seventh Fleet would be on hand if needed. He had created Task Force 34, replete with battleships and cruisers. But it was a paper organization and not specifically charged with responsibility for guarding the San Bernardino Strait. Critical intelligence errors added to Halsey's misperception. The aviators returning from their missions against Kurita's Center Force, like the Japanese at Formosa, exaggerated their success. Halsey claimed he was told, "At least four and probably five battleships torpedoed and bombed, one probably sunk; a minimum of three heavy cruisers torpedoed and others bombed; one light cruiser sunk, one destroyer probably sunk and four damaged . . . reports indicated beyond doubt that the Center Force had been badly mauled with all of its battleships and most of its heavy cruisers tremendously reduced in fighting power and life." The first information from returning pilots indicated Kurita's fleet moving west, away from Leyte Gulf.

Halsey's information on Ozawa's armada was erroneous. The pilots who flew over the *Ise* and *Hyuga* mistakenly identified them as full-scale battleships when, in fact, refitted as carriers, the ships lost four of their twelve big guns. Instead of a fleet with a quartet of dangerous battleships, Ozawa packed much less weight. The faulty evidence, however, persuaded Halsey to sprint after the retreating Ozawa. Task Force 34 remained a figment so far as the Gulf of Leyte was concerned for all of its vessels sped north, where the Third Fleet planned to blaze away with all its big guns in conjunction with the carrier-launched bombers and torpedo planes. Even after intelligence advised that, contrary to early reports, the Central Force of the Japanese instead of retreating now seemed embarked on a course toward Leyte, the Third Fleet command refused to release Task Force 34 to guard the San Bernardino Strait, the avenue open to the Japanese.

Admiral Nishimura's Southern Force, in two sections, picked its way through the archipelago via Mindoro and then toward the Surigao Strait between southern Leyte and Mindinao. The Seventh Fleet strategists, alerted to the movement, but unaware of the gaping hole of the San Bernardino Strait in their Leyte Gulf line, plotted a devastating reception. Kinkaid, having correctly interpreted the approach of Nishimura's fleet, ordered VAdm. Jesse Oldendorf to deploy the U.S. ships in preparation for a night engagement. At his disposal Oldendorf counted six battleships, four heavy cruisers, four light ones, and almost thirty destroyers. They far outnumbered and outgunned the opponents. The grand assortment of ships of the line formed a stately procession, steaming back and forth across the Surigao Strait mouth, a scant twelve miles in width. At the southern end of the strait, where the enemy would enter, Oldendorf stationed a flotilla of forty-five PT boats that would detect the arrival of the enemy and then harass them with torpedo runs.

As a gunnery officer, James L. Holloway III was aboard the USS *Bennion,* a destroyer attached to the left flank of the American screen. "At sunset, we had set Condition 1, and we could overhear on the TBS [Talk Between Ships, a voice radio] the tactical commands and reports among our own ships as we waited tensely for the enemy during this dark and squally evening. By midnight we began to think that the Japanese would disappoint us and a general relaxing was perceptible. Suddenly, at about 0200, over the TBS [official accounts place the contact with the enemy fleet several hours earlier] we heard one of the PT boats reconnoitering in the southern strait call out excitedly, 'I've got a big one in sight!,' then a pause, and 'My God, there are two more big ones, and maybe another.' Suddenly the TBS became alive as the 'Martinis'—that was the call sign for the PT boats—got ready for their torpedo attacks."

In the hit-and-run melees that lit up the strait with gunfire, searchlights (from the Japanese ships), and exploding shells, the PTs unloosed thirty-four fish. Only one struck home, wounding the cruiser *Abukuma.* Nishimura kept coming while the gun crews under Oldendorf readied their weapons. Gunnery officer Holloway, fearful for a moment the foe would depart after the Martinis struck, was reassured as the Japanese force showed up on the ship's radar, advancing at twenty-five-knot speed. The American destroyers responded, charging toward the enemy ships as they emerged from the strait, pouring out black smoke as they cut through the water at thirty knots. "From my battle station [in the fire-control director] I had a view of the whole scene: from the panorama of the two fleets to a close-up of the Japanese ships through the high-powered lenses of the MK37 [fire] director. As our destroyers started the run to the south, we were immediately taken under fire. It was an eerie experience to be rushing through the dark toward the enemy at a relative speed of fifty knots, not firing our guns, or hearing the enemy fall of shot around us. The awesome evidence of the Japanese gunfire was the towering columns of water from the splashes of their 14- and 16-inch shells, some close enough to wet our weather decks. Star shells hung overhead and the gun flashes from the Japanese battle line illuminated the horizon ahead.

"Oldendorf's battleships and cruisers opened up with their main batteries. Directly over our heads stretched a procession of tracers from our battle line converging on the head of the Japanese column. I recall being surprised at the apparent slowness of the projectiles. They almost hung in the sky, taking fifteen to twenty seconds in their trajectory before reaching their targets. It was a spectacular display. Through the director optics, I could clearly see the bursting explosions of our battleships' and cruisers' shells as they hit the Japanese ships that were enveloped in flames.

"Our column was headed directly for the lead battleship, the *Yamashiro*, so the division had to turn in a sequential movement for a clear shot, each destroyer launching successively as it executed the turn. As *Bennion* was the second ship in the last element, at a fifty-knot relative speed, our firing point closed rapidly with the Japanese battle line. We started launching our five torpedoes at a range of about 7,000 yards. At this distance, the silhouette of the *Yamashiro* completely filled the viewing glass of the rangefinder optics. [I thought,] that looks exactly like a Japanese battleship with its pagoda foremast and then realizing that it *was* a Japanese battleship."

As the tin cans closed the distance, Oldendorf inquired the range from his flagship [the heavy cruiser *Louisville*] and upon the answer of 17,000 yards, the admiral ordered his biggest ships to open fire. "It seemed as if every ship on the flank forces and the battle line opened at once, and there was a semicircle of fire that landed squarely on one point, the leading battleship. Explosions and fires were immediately noticed. The semicircle of fire evidently so confused the Japanese that they did not seem to know what target to shoot at. I remembered seeing one or two salvos start in the direction of my flagship, but in the excitement of the occasion I forgot to look to see where they landed."

Aboard the *Bennion*, Holloway observed the turmoil. "As we retired to the north in formation at thirty knots, still making max black smoke, explosions erupted close off our port beam. It was one of our destroyers, the *A. W. Grant*, being hit by large-caliber shells. The scene of the action was becoming confused and Oldendorf ordered his battle line to cease fire for concern of hitting our retiring destroyers in the melee." In fact, Oldendorf noted that after some of his destroyers launched their torpedoes and came under heavy fire, they quickly fled directly up the Surigao Strait. Some of the U.S. fleet mistook these friendlies for the foe. "The *Grant* was hit by some of our own six-inch shells from the light cruisers, as well as shells from the Japanese ships."

With his smaller ships racing out of harm's way, Oldendorf brought his five cruisers to bear upon some battered burning Japanese ships. Salvos dispatched a pair of destroyers. At about 4:30 A.M., as dawn approached, Old-endorf directed the units that included the *Bennion* to race south and en-gage any surviving Japanese ships. "In the pale, predawn twilight," said Hol-loway, "the scene in Surigao Strait was appalling. I counted eight distinct fires, and the oily surface of the gulf was littered with debris and groups of Japanese sailors who were clinging to bits of wreckage and calling out to us as we raced past.

"*Bennion* did not pause to pick up survivors, as we had sighted the Japanese destroyer *Asaguma*, badly damaged, on fire, and limping south. *Asaguma* was still afloat, and if she still had torpedoes aboard, she consti-tuted a definite threat to our ships. With orders to destroy the Japanese ship, we changed course to close the *Asaguma* and opened fire with five-inch salvos at about 10,000 yards. We shifted to rapid, continuous fire at 6,000 and she blew apart and slipped beneath the waves as we passed close aboard. On the *Bennion*," remembered Holloway, "the crew was dogtired, but spirits were elated. As we listened to the reports come in from the TBS and witnessed the hundreds of survivors clinging to the smoking wreckage of the Japanese fleet, we all sensed that a great victory had been won." The final tally for the battle of Surigao Strait showed 2 Japanese battleships and 3 destroyers sunk with only a cruiser and a destroyer, both badly damaged, able to escape. The losses to the Americans added up to 39 killed, 119 wounded, mostly on the *A. W. Grant*, struck by its sister ships.

The celebration on the *Bennion* and the other vessels in Oldendorf's com-mand halted abruptly. According to Holloway, "Suddenly—and the trans-formation of spirits was dramatic—elation turned to real alarm, when over the TBS we heard that the Taffy groups [the smaller flattops left behind to protect other entrances of Leyte Gulf] were under attack at close range by Japanese battleships and cruisers. We couldn't believe it. We thought all of the capital ships of the Japanese reaction force had been destroyed in the night battle in Surigao Strait."

When Admiral Kincaid sent Oldendorf to block the Surigao Strait in an anticipated night action, he kept sixteen escort carriers—"baby flattops" or "jeep" carriers—steaming back and forth across Leyte Gulf to the north off Samar. These slower, smaller ships, accompanied by a screen of nine de-stroyers and twelve destroyer escorts, were organized as Task Group 77.4 and divided into Taffy 1, 2, and 3. On the morning of 25 October, the Taffies be-gan to catapult their planes for antisubmarine searches and combat air pa-trols. A few minutes before 7:00 A.M., lookouts aboard the ships noticed an-tiaircraft shells in the distance and radios picked up Japanese voices over the interfighter net. But no enemy ships were believed within 100 to 150 miles.

Suddenly, one of the antisubmarine patrol pilots reported sighting four Japanese battleships, eight cruisers, and a flock of destroyers. A skeptical RAdm. Thomas L. Sprague, chief for Taffy 1, demanded a check on the identification, believing the airman had spotted part of Task Force 38 from Halsey's Third Fleet. The answer came promptly from a source close to home. Not only did the lookouts on Sprague's ships see the unique, pagoda shaped superstructure of Japanese battleships poking over the horizon, but brightly colored splashes signaled hostile shells.

Without Task Force 34 on the scene, no one had watched the San Bernardino Strait, and Admiral Kurita, with the Center Force intact, passed into the waters off Samar without detection. Kurita packed a tremendous potential wallop in his battlewagons but he had no carriers to provide air cover. The Taffies could muster several hundred planes but their surface weapons in the destroyer screen amounted to popguns compared to the huge rifles pointed at them from Kurita's battleships and cruisers. The line-ups presented a near classic encounter between an armada of seagoing Japanese behemoths and the lighter, aircraft-dominated U.S. forces.

The unexpected appearance of the Japanese so close at hand exposed Task Force 77.4 to disaster. The Center Force had an opportunity to blast the carriers and their screens before they could assume any defensive posture. Apparently, the Japanese believed they might face battleships and full-size carriers. Admiral Kurita, still fearful of another series of air attacks, and an eyewitness to the ineffectiveness of his AA gunnery, erred tactically, ordering a general attack instead of directing his ships into position for more effective, coordinated firing.

About twenty miles separated Taffy 3 from Taffy 2 to the southeast, with Taffy 1 as much as 100 miles off. The Center Force began the action of Samar blasting away at Taffy 3, commanded by RAdm. Clifton "Ziggy" Sprague— no kin to the CO of Taffy 1. Caught in the sights of enemy cruisers and battleships, Ziggy Sprague circled his wagons; the six carriers operating around a diameter of 2,500 yards while the destroyer screen steamed in parallel, 6,000 yards from the center. All ships ran at flank speed, made smoke to hide themselves, while the carriers emptied their flight decks. Nature smiled faintly upon the Americans, adding a rain squall to help obliterate them as targets, and poorly functioning Japanese radar further hampered the enemy gunnery.

Temporarily shrouded, Sprague signaled his three destroyers to counterattack the big enemy ships, boys sent to perform men's jobs. The *Johnston* ran a gauntlet through the heavier vessels of the foe and scored a few hits from her main battery on the cruiser *Kumano*, and then let fly all ten of her torpedoes at the *Kumano*. At least one, perhaps more, exploded on target and eliminated the cruiser from further combat. Japanese gunners pinpointed the destroyer. A fusillade of shells ripped into the *Johnston*. Huge holes opened up in the deck; one explosion knocked off pieces of the radar on the mast, the falling debris killed three officers. Many died below deck as projectiles pierced the thin hull and then blew up. Still, the destroyer persevered.

Others from the Taffy 3 screen, destroyers *Hoel*, and *Heermann*, plus the "Little Wolves"—destroyer escorts—charged at their oversize foe. They dashed through the roiling, explosion-riven water, threw their much smaller-size shells at their antagonists and launched torpedoes, with little if any success. The Japanese registered hits upon the little boys. Abandon ship had sounded for the *Hoel* and a DE, the *Roberts*, when the *Johnston* engaged in its finale, an exchange with the light cruiser *Yahagi* and a destroyer. The *Johnston* scored a number of hits before a firing squad of enemy ships surrounded it and hammered away until it went dead in the water, then rolled over on the way to the bottom.

Taffy 3's screen inflicted little material damage upon its much larger adversaries but the torpedoes and five-inch guns required the Center Force to take evasive action and deal with the interlopers. While the disarray would buy time for the planes of Taffy 2 to enter the fray, four heavy cruisers with murderous intent stalked Taffy 3's six carriers. As his ships desperately attempted to steam away from the ever closer shell splashes, Ziggy Sprague advised them to use their puny, single-deck gun, "Open fire with the peashooters when range is clear." The longer-range weapons of the attackers began to find their marks. Some of the armorpiercing shells tore through the thin skins of the converted oilers and passed out the opposite sides of the ships. But multiple hits killed, wounded, and damaged. Crews immersed in as much as five feet of seawater, plugged holes, repaired engines, sealed ruptured pipes, while helmsmen hand wrestled with controls designed for mechanical operation.

The first casualty among the flattops was the *Gambier Bay*. The Japanese cruisers narrowed the gap to the American vessel and at 10,000 yards put a shell into her that ignited fires. *Gambier Bay*, slowed by her wounds, staggered as the enemy gunners peppered her. The carrier capsized and sank. A sister ship, the *White Plains*, insists its "pea-shooter' vanquished the heavy cruiser *Chokai*. The 5-inch 38 gun on the fantail claimed six hits upon the *Chokai* that knocked out both the forward turret and her engines. Whatever the *White Plains* achieved, torpedo bombers executed the *Chokai* with fatal blows amidships. It blew up and sank within five minutes.

In support of Taffy 3, Taffy 2 mounted three strikes that included both fighters and torpedo bombers. They started their raids about ninety minutes after Kurita's Center Force hove into view. The planes from the two Taffies, using torpedoes, bombs, and incessant strafing, rattled the commander of the enemy fleet. Fighter planes, including some that had expended their ammunition, dove on the enemy vessels repeatedly, forcing them to use up their shells and bedeviled the crews. Taffy 1, which included the *Suwannee*, also scrambled planes to meet Admiral Nishimura's group. Tex Garner said, "They were shooting at us before we even got to them. They shot at us in every color there was. The whole sky was just full of different color bursts. [As they did in surface gunnery, the Japanese employed color as a means of zeroing in on targets.] I said to myself, 'There's no way you're going to get through that kind of barrage.' But we did. We went in and hurt 'em as much as we could. I took my four planes in and I got my four out. We had holes in us, but we were still flying. We dropped our bombs and strafed. It was amazing how we got in and out, how they could miss. All our air groups from *Suwannee, Sangamon, Chenango,* and *Santee,* were jumping on them as they came through the straits. The sky was full of planes, Technicolor puffs, and tracer shells." The furious action and the extended flight time from the carriers to the combat area drove some of the American pilots to land on the Tacloban airstrip, secured only five days before.

Well out of range of the Japanese ships, Taffy 1 staved off land-based Japanese raids. The task group recoiled from the first successful kamikaze attacks. In the days preceding the Leyte Gulf sea battles, rumors of pilots committed to crashing into American ships circulated among American sailors. One alleged source was a deciphered Japanese message to a pilot that read: "It is absolutely out of the question for you to return alive. Your mission involves certain death . . ."

About twenty minutes or so before 8:00 A.M., on 25 October, spotters among the Taffy 1 ships saw four enemy planes breaking out of the clouds about 10,000 feet up. Gunner's Mate 3d class John B. Mitchell, son of a World War I wounded vet, and a shipyard worker before he enlisted in 1943, captained a gun mount on the *Santee*. The 40mms were not loaded, because, according to Mitchell, "On several invasion landings, men got kind of jumpy and there were occasions when guns were fired by accident, error, or stupidity. I was wearing the combat headphone set and it was reported that we had some bogeys in the area. Almost immediately the gunnery officer,

Lieutenant Commander Mills, yelled that a bogey was diving on us, dead astern. I ordered my 'pointer and trainer' to bear on the target. Both used gunsights. One man had responsibility for the horizontal and the other for the vertical position of the gun. It took a great deal of practice for the two of them to act in unison. We did have a Mark 14 sight and there were fire-control men who could automatically fire our guns, but you always needed a pointer and trainer in case the electrical system failed.

"I ordered the crew to load and cock both guns. Before we were able to bear on the target, the bogey was in a dive and strafing the stern deck. I watched it come in all the way. I could not believe that the plane was not coming out of its dive. I was screaming, 'Pull out, you bastard! Pull out!' It came in so fast and with such surprise we didn't get off a single round. The plane used our aft elevator as a target and crashed just a few feet forward and to port of the elevator."

Some seven minutes after the *Santee* won the dubious honor of first ship to be a kamikaze victim it took a blow from a more conventional enemy, as Japanese submarine I-56 executed a successful torpedo run. "It hit directly below my gun mount," remembers Mitchell. "The first sensation I had was that of the deck suddenly being pulled out from under my feet. I don't know how high in the air I went but I was told later that I was tossed above the gun mount.

"When I came down I thought I had been pitched overboard and im-mediately started to swim. I was attached to the mount by my combat phone and for some reason my helmet was still on my head. And there I was, flail-ing my arms, thinking I had gone into the drink, and all I was doing was swimming back to the spot in my gun tub where I normally would be. The gun tub was filled with wet debris and several dead bodies."

On the ships in the area, the spotters had seen three of the original four planes dive toward the carriers. Gunners had thrown up a wall of metal but, as Mitchell saw, one aircraft penetrated the curtain of fire and, blazing away with machine guns until the final moment, crashed onto the forward deck of the *Santee*. A Zero making for the *Sangamon* exploded in midair when a five-incher from *Suwannee* struck home. A third kamikaze dropped into the water after concentrated AA fire shattered its controls or else killed the pi-lot. Suddenly, from 4,000 feet up, the last of the quartet of kamikazes dropped almost straight down. It seemed as if every weapon in Taffy 1 were shooting at the Zero [some say it was a Judy, a navy dive-bomber], which trailed a thin stream of smoke, as though afire. The concentration upon him notwithstanding, the pilot held his course and drilled into the *Suwannee* flight deck, to explode into pieces, the Zero's nose penetrating three decks below, just shy of reaching the aviation fuel stores. The suicide plane carved into the flight deck an impression of its front silhouette, a round hole for the engine and slits from the wings.

Petty Officer 2d class Erich Kitzmann, a native of Detroit, bossed crews that prepared planes for operations on the *Suwannee*. When the "Flight Quarters" signal was blown at 0300 on 25 October, because of blackout conditions, Kitzmann and hands worked in the dark getting the TBF Avengers topside. Hours later, Kitzmann and half of his plane handlers were at breakfast, eating beans, the standard Wednesday fare, when general quarters sounded. He tossed aside his mess tray, carelessly slung his life jacket over one shoulder, and strapped his helmet under his chin.

He checked his hangar deck for fire hazards, saw that auxiliary fuel tanks were removed from aircraft and jettisoned. Then he headed forward to a hatch where he could look out. "I could see the *Santee* burning and listing to port. A Japanese Zero was coming in from the starboard at mast level and strafing us. I drew back behind a stanchion to get out of the line of fire when I heard this crash, which was the kamikaze hitting the flight deck. I never heard the bomb go off."

Kitzmann found himself in the sea. "I saw my helmet turning over and over under the clear blue water of the Mindanao Trench as I surfaced. I discovered that my dungarees were no longer on my body except my belt and shorts, no shoes or socks. Yet my life jacket was still on my shoulder. Trying to gain my composure, I looked around and saw smoke billowing from the stern of the *Suwannee*. It was a big blur as I was bleeding from my eyes and began struggling to put my other arm into my life jacket. My face felt like someone had hit me with a baseball bat. I regained my senses; it became apparent I was not alone. Mournful cries of help and despair were all around. A body came up near me without a head and it did not shock me at the time. It did make me aware of my situation. As my ankle began to pain, I was afraid to look down to see if my foot was still with me. I realized I was going to make it; panic and fear left me.

"The next thing I remember is the bow of the USS *Bull* [a destroyer escort] plowing through the water and her Skeeter (as they call the commander of destroyers) calling on her speaker horns, 'Rendezvous in the rafts we are going to drop and we'll pick you up later.' I don't know how many men in the water understood the message but I did. I began to swim for the rafts and when I reached one I discovered it had flipped upside down into the water. It was no small thing as I dove under it to reach the paddles and began paddling around to find shipmates.

"I don't recall how long it took but I picked up Frank Yeomans and H. O. Olson, Aviation Machinist Mates, 3d Class. Olson was holding up Yeomans as I pulled them onto the raft. Yeomans was hit hard by the blast and did not become coherent until later that night aboard the *Bull*. I picked up two black men who were burned badly. Their skin was hanging from their bodies. One had lost half of one leg and the other had a hole in his neck. I put my belt around the man who had his leg half gone to stop the bleeding. I administered morphine to both men.

"To get the morphine I had to dive under the raft to bring up the five-inch shell can that contained medical supplies. I could not open the can and asked Yeomans for a knife. I'll never know how I was able to open that container with a Navy jack knife. About that time the man with a hole in his throat asked for water. The water keg I brought up from the bottom of the raft had no cup so I opened the spigot and let the water run into his mouth. It came right out his throat.

"Later in the afternoon, it seemed like years, the *Bull* returned and sent out her whale boat to pick up our survivors. As I climbed the cargo net of the *Bull*, the little pains began to ache. But I was alive and that was all that mattered at the time. In the wardroom of the *Bull*, a pharmacist mate told me I was bleeding from my shoulder, ankle, and groin. I told him to take care of the man lying on the table whose ankle was blown away. The pharmacist mate offered me a glass that contained some liquid medicine. After I drank it I walked out on the afterdeck to identify the bodies of some shipmates. Sneed, from Redding, California, was lying there without a mark on his body. Anglin was still alive with a hole through his stomach, begging me to put a .45 to his head and end his pain. At this point, the world seemed to spin and I dropped to the deck, out cold."

While other vessels plucked men like Kitzmann from the sea and tended to their injuries, Phil Phillips, one of the three flight surgeons on the *Suwannee*, narrowly missed injury or death himself. "I had no particular instruction about handling the sick before we went to sea. There was no specific educational process to prepare except to familiarize ourselves with the ship and the potentials for dealing with sick people. The medical department on the *Suwannee* was adequate in a rustic sort of way. It had an eight-bed sick bay and a little room for holding sick call. We had about ten first-rate hospital corpsmen; most had training ashore but some didn't and they were eager learners." The medical team included three doctors and a dentist.

Phillips remembered standing in the parachute loft when the kamikaze struck. "The stretcher-bearer assigned to my battle station was wounded. The explosion was so horribly loud and the sheet of metal on the inside surface of the parachute loft where I stood, was riddled with shell fragments. There were so many dead and wounded on the hangar deck that I scrambled out of the parachute loft headed for the hangar deck to do what I could. Going by the main sick bay, I could see that our little ward had quickly overflowed with patients. Stretchers lay in the passageway and on the deck of the operating room. Others were being carried into the pharmacy and the clerical office. Quickly the wardroom became an emergency aid station.

"The hangar deck was still filled with smoke. Through the eerie light streaming in from the hole in the flight deck it was easy to see that here lay our worst casualties. Mangled bodies and portions of bodies lay about the deck, where they had been blown from the explosion. Steel decks were slippery with blood. Men followed with stretchers, and one by one we gathered the wounded from their ghastly surroundings, applied temporary dressings, and sent them to the wardroom.

"In the wardroom were six to eight long tables on which we could put patients who needed immediate care. It was a helluva bad day and we lost fifty-five dead that morning and more than that were wounded. Most of the men were doing their best under the difficult circumstances. Through the night gun crews stayed at their guns while scores of volunteers assisted the doctors and hospital corpsmen in caring for the wounded. But one senior person hid himself in an ensign's room and with a bottle, trying to intoxicate himself."

On the following day, shortly before noon, the flattop's guns began to fire amid the sound of general quarters. A few TBMs, having finished their morning's work, were being taken aboard and one was in the process of taxiing to the forward elevator. The suicide plane crashed the *Suwannee* atop a taxiing TBM, annihilating the plane, and killing all three crew members. The blast wrecked the elevator and gasoline leaked from the aircraft on the deck to spread fires. The second explosion probably resulted from rupture of the compressed air tank of the ship's catapult.

Many of the ship's crew engaged in handling planes and ordnance died outright. Others received terrible burns, some fatal. Rounds from .50-caliber machine guns, cooked off in burning airplanes. The bridge had been severely damaged, sailors stationed there killed. The detonations blew some men into the water. Others jumped into the sea to avoid the flames. The skipper, bleeding from shrapnel wounds, continued to direct damage control. The inferno created molten metal out of bulkheads and fittings.

Bill Dacus had begun his navy career as a deckhand but once assigned to quartermaster duties demonstrated such aptitude that he climbed to the exalted title of chief quartermaster. Dacus recalled that after the initial explosion, "A group of us were laying on the passageway deck in front of the chief's quarters, when someone wanted to get up and run into the hangar deck. Other sailors laying there told him to stay down. He kept getting up, wanting to run to the hangar deck where the explosion occurred. I finally said in a very authoritative voice, 'Get down and stay down!' He did and it was then we heard a second explosion, from the catapult.

"It was a good thing the man hadn't moved because that explosion killed everyone in the hangar deck. The blast went through all passageways fore and aft. They actually had to scrape a sailor off a passageway bulkhead. Shortly after, Chief Shipfitter William Brooks, came up the passageway with a hose on his shoulders. He told me to grab a hose on the bulkhead nearby. I did and followed him up the passageway to the hangar deck. As we went, we both looked out a porthole. We saw our sister ships quite a distance from us and a lot of sailors in the water with 40mm-shell containers [for flotation] spotting the ocean. I asked him if we should jump out. Brooks, who was a very chubby guy, said very emphatically, 'I don't know about you but I'll never make it.' I just followed him up the stairs with the hose."

As Dacus struggled to connect the hose to a valve, another explosion rocked the ship, knocking Brooks unconscious for a few seconds. When he regained his wits, Brooks crawled under the planes on the hangar deck and opened valves from a sprinkler system. The heavy spray prevented the fire from spreading to the gassed planes. Dacus managed to keep his poise and, following Brooks's lead, started pushing the high octane gas on the hangar deck into the elevator well, as if cleaning the sidewalk.

The conflagration heated the metal in some areas until too hot to touch, forcing some sailors to abandon ship. But with everyone, including the flight personnel, tending the fire lines the *Suwannee* remained afloat, albeit she was down four to six feet at the bow. Unable to function, with at least half of the 1,000 of the complement killed or wounded, the *Suwannee* received orders to transfer her most seriously injured to hospital ships, bury her dead, and steam for the Palaus to repair the damage. Bill Dacus recalled dealing with dead shipmates. "They brought up Robert Wilding, a good friend of mine, on a stretcher. I tried to tell him something of encouragement. One of the stretcher-bearers told me he was dead. A sailor came up to us and said we should come with him to the forward, starboard 40mm gun turret. There he pointed to three bodies in the fetus position, hugging one another and burned so badly that we could not recognize them."

Word of the Japanese thrust went to Halsey with the Third Fleet and to Nimitz as the Pacific commander. The former, upon receipt of the message, replied he was already involved with the enemy but did order a carrier group under Adm. John McCain to come to the aid of the Taffies. Unfortunately, the carriers commanded by McCain were well over 300 miles from the scene. It would be noon before their planes could hope to get over the targets.

Greatly concerned, Nimitz radioed Halsey a coded question: "Where is Task Force 34?" The yeoman assigned to transmit the query thought he detected a note of emphasis in the admiral's voice. He added a repeat of the first two words, "Where is." And when actually sent, padding was inserted on both ends of the question to mislead eavesdropping Japanese. As a consequence, the complete transmission read: TURKEY TROTS TO WATER RR FROM CINCPAC ACTION COM THIRD FLEET INFO COMINCH CTF SEVENTY-SEVEN X WHERE IS RPT WHERE IS TASK FORCE THIRTY FOUR RR THE WORLD WONDERS.

The communications people on Halsey's flagship, *New Jersey* recognized the TURKEY TROTS TO WATER as intended to fool the enemy and deleted that from what was handed to Halsey. Unfortunately, the staff believed the final three words purposely included and an irate Halsey read, WHERE IS, REPEAT, WHERE IS, TASK FORCE 34, THE WORLD WONDERS. He interpreted the final phrase as a rocket from Nimitz. Months would pass before he accepted an explanation for what he regarded as a deliberate insult.

The postmortem investigation became an argument about language. The dispatch from Halsey on 24 October that described a "Battle Plan" named the specific ships that "will be formed as Task Force 34." The seabag lawyers now debated whether a "Battle Plan" can be extrapolated to mean a battle or operation order. Critics of Halsey insisted "will be formed" meant this would now happen rather than indicating that the creation of Task Force 34 was a conditional future.

MacArthur refused to criticize any individual. Instead he reiterated his disapproval of divided commands. "The near disaster can be placed squarely at the door of Washington. In the naval action, two key American commanders were independent of each other, one under me, and the other under Admiral Nimitz, 5,000 miles away, both operating in the same waters and in the same battle." He ignored his own attempt to create a divided command when he left Corregidor.

The issue, however, became moot, due to timidity by the aggressors. Convinced of imminent defeat by superior forces, Kurita withdrew, although, had he persisted, his outfit could have thoroughly whipped the Taffies. To the north, Halsey, in spite of the distractions concerning the plight of the Seventh Fleet, destroyed what he believed were the main elements of the Japanese Navy still afloat. Admiral Ozawa now reaped the bitter rewards of his scheme. With a paltry dozen or so planes for a combat air patrol from his carriers, the Japanese admiral's seventeen ships depended upon anti-aircraft to defend themselves. The torpedo-bombers and fighter-bombers from the *Essex, Lexington, San Jacinto, Intrepid, Langley, Belleau Wood,* and *Franklin* overwhelmed the enemy. When the sixth and final air strike of the day, a total of 527 sorties, landed on the flight decks, the U.S. airmen had wiped out four carriers and a destroyer. American cruisers and submarines disposed of two more destroyers and a cruiser.

The Japanese could no longer fight from flattops. However, large numbers of navy and army planes stationed at bases in the Philippines, where intelligence located between eighty and a hundred airstrips, and other islands, menaced American ground and seagoing forces. On 30 October 1944, William "Pappy" Turner and a flight of P-38s from the Air Corps' 36th Fighter Squadron traveled from Morotai some 750 miles over water to strafe the harbor and airfield at Sandakan on Borneo. "We arrived over the target without incident and evidently without warning—who would expect a fighter strike when the enemy was so far away? I saw no Jap fighters in the air, but it didn't take those Japs down below very long to contest our intentions. Ack-ack was everywhere. We made our strafing runs from all different approaches and at airspeeds of 400 miles per hour. The .50caliber ground fire was intense.

"On a high-speed run a target is picked and that's it. You don't have time to change targets, but probably you will see another one that you wish you had chosen. So, most of us gained altitude again and made another high-speed pass. How the smoke rose from those Jap gun pits as they burned their barrels up, trying to hit those 400-mile-per-hour planes. On both my runs I picked out a plane on the runway. A fighter on the first and a bomber the second.

"As I finished and streaked off out over the harbor, I saw a camouflaged ship, a good-size one, covered with camouflage netting. As long as I was here, why not? This ship was anchored between the main shore and a small island with a rocky, perpendicular cliff on its east side. I figured I would go out to sea, out of sight behind the island, gain some altitude to convert into a high-speed run around that cliff, and hit them broadside. My strategy was good, I gained the altitude, my wingman, Lieutenant Maynard, who'd been with us only three weeks was still beside me, and two or three others had joined up. In one big string we snaked down and around the cliff.

"We were close to the top of the cliff as we cut by. How those gun emplacements sent up the smoke as we went by! You could see the men on those guns, we were that close, but they got no hits. Now I had passed the cliff, brought my plane out of its steep banked turn, and leveled off for my firing run. I squeezed off a a few rounds to make them nervous as I closed in, saving the rest for a turning run where I could stitch them the full length of the ship.

"They had other plans. They were ready for us and as I closed in I was hit by their unfire. It threw my plane out of control and somewhat spoiled my run. I leveled her up and fired my guns, just missing the mast with the crow's nest. Here a gunner was firing as I came in, passed over. I could see men in white uniforms running about; this ship was no freighter. As I went away from them, the water below was being churned up with their fire and it was rapidly going out ahead of me as they were getting a better lead on me. I pulled back on the wheel, gaining altitude sharply and with much effort made a turn to the right. Seconds later I was out of range.

"They had concentrated on me and those behind me all got their runs in without being hit. The third or fourth man's fire apparently hit some high explosives on the deck. There was an explosion that cleared the decks and left the ship helpless in the water. No one could stick around to find out its fate. We had overstayed our anticipated time; now it was time for a three-hour-plus ride for home. I limped along, slowly gaining altitude. How bad I was hit, I couldn't tell. My instruments checked out okay—engines were running, gas gauges were stable. But my controls were messed up—the plane wanted to turn to the left. It took about all the strength in my right leg to keep it leveled up and on course. Soon I had both feet on that right rudder pedal. I knew they would tire before long. Then I saw a nice long new pencil that the crew chief had missed when he had strapped me in or had shook loose from somewhere. Very carefully I experimented until I got that pencil at right angles to that right rudder and wedged in so the force was straight on it. I slowly removed my two feet and, glory be, it held." Turner fluttered toward Morotai while Maynard remained on his wing. Just short of seven hours after he took off he landed safely.

Although MacArthur and Nimitz had parceled out responsibilities in the South Pacific, jurisdictional squabbles and tactical differences ignited ugly confrontations. While army troops grappled with Japanese defenders on Leyte, according to Jimmy Thach who directed air operations for the navy units supporting the landings, MacArthur drew across an eastwest line that ran just north of Legazpi on the southern leg of Luzon that stretches toward Leyte. Thach described the gist of MacArthur's order to his seagoing partners, "The carriers will take care of the enemy air north of the line and the Army Air Corps everything south of the line. So don't attack anything south of the line and the Air Corps won't attack anything north of the line."

When a kamikaze blasted one of the carriers knocking out the flight deck, the ship's planes were instructed to land at an Air Corps base. Enroute, the navy fliers noticed an enemy field near Legazpi within the territory reserved for the army. The pilots reported to the Air Corps operations officers the malignant presence. According to Thach, they responded that they did not believe the Japanese base was a threat. The navy men protested that the attack on their carrier probably originated at this field. The Air Corps relented and, in Thach's words, said, "All right, we'll take off tomorrow morning and we'll give you some bombs and you can go with us. You lead us up there and show us these airplanes."

Said Thach, "[The Army] flew pretty high but the Navy airplanes always liked to fly lower. They [the Air Corps] said 'We don't see any.' Of course you couldn't see them from that altitude. The torpedo planes were going in, winding around the trees, picking out an airplane and dropping a little bomb on it. One of the strike leaders of the Army planes said, 'We'd better get up higher. There's a lot of antiaircraft going off down there.' They couldn't even see our torpedo planes either."

The carrier pilots persuaded their counterparts to make their bomb runs and between the two forces they wreaked considerable devastation. When the navy aircrews returned to carriers that made room for them, they reported what happened. "We sent a blistering message," said Thach. "We argued against this line in the first place. Halsey immediately saw the problem and he argued with MacArthur against the line, too. He finally told MacArthur that when his carriers were called in to do a job they had the right to protect themselves and to hit any airfield that was within range because the kamikazes were undoubtedly coming from airfields that had not been properly attacked, such as the one at Legazpi. He just told [MacArthur] and we didn't hear any more about the line."

The Legaspi boundary was another instance in which MacArthur had practiced what he had preached against.

41
The Ardennes

As Omar Bradley wrote in his autobiography, of the four paths to France open to the Nazi armies in 1940, that of the Ardennes a harsh, craggy, ravine-gouged, heavily timbered region inhospitable to armored warfare seemed least appetizing as a route of attack. But just as they had in World War I, the Germans had surprised the French and the Belgians with their blitzkrieg through that sparsely populated area, avoiding the Maginot Line and the best defensive positions. With winter on hand in 1944, Bradley claimed awareness of history, but insisted he believed that with 70,000 GIs plus the armor stationed on the shoulders of the Ardennes, the risk of penetration there was acceptable. Furthermore, he had the impression that if anything untoward occurred, reinforcements could rapidly plug any holes.

On 16 December, the enemy, under a plan devised by Hitler, who considered himself both a student of history and a military strategist, struck for a third time in the Ardennes. On that day, newly promoted to the rank of five-star general of the armies, Dwight Eisenhower attended the wedding of his valet, Mickey McKeogh and Women's Army Corps sergeant. Pearlie Hargrave, in the Louis XIV Chapel at Versailles, near Paris. General Elwood (Pete) Quesada, the chief of the tactical air forces in Europe, Bradley, and Gen. Courtney Hodges, head of the U.S. First Army, which faced the Germans on the Siegfried line, visited with a Belgian manufacturer to arrange for custom-made shotguns. For the past few days, Bradley, in a chauffeured staff car, had escorted actress Marlene Dietrich who was performing morale-building shows for American troops. He had been somewhat bemused by her complaints about the food and accommodations. She also dallied with various senior officers, most notably the 82d Airborne's James M. Gavin. Hodges had devoted some of the previous day welcoming a contingent of major league baseball stars, Frank Frisch, Bucky Walters, Dutch Leonard, and Mel Ott, building morale with visits to the troops. Maxwell Taylor of the 101st had flown to England for a conference.

The top brass acted according to the evaluations of their intelligence experts. These groped through thickets of information—intercepts of enemy communications via the code-breaking medium of ULTRA, photos and observations produced by the Air Corps, gobbets of gossip and facts coaxed from prisoners, tales from civilians who crossed the lines, and accounts of troops up on the line. The fodder fed to the decision makers also reflected a certain amount of competition and ego among the analysts. While the American Office of Strategic Services (OSS), precursor to the Central Intelligence Agency, was available to supply data, there was a distinct antipathy of some military men toward civilian input to the military hopper. And to this point, the armed forces had little reason to call on the OSS. During the drive across France, Belgium, and Holland, local civilians gladly informed on the hated occupation troops. But now, on the border of Germany, that resource dried up.

A desire to get the job over with, by the start of the New Year if possible, a sentiment heartily endorsed by the civilians and those in uniform, seemed to affect evaluations of conditions for both the civilian leaders of the Allied governments and their brass-hat subordinates. There had been, according to Gen. Edwin Sibert, the Twelfth Army Group's G-2, and a rival intelligencier to his inferior Col. Benjamin "Monk" Dickson, G-2 for the First Army complaints concerning the dullness of the reports from Sibert's realm. Officers allegedly failed to study them because the files read so dully. To remedy the situation, Sibert ordered Col. Ralph Ingersoll, a former newspaperman, in effect, to jazz up the memos. In retrospect, Sibert remarked the result was to deliver overoptimistic accounts, the kind of stuff the warriors enjoyed reading. Some of the happy talk undoubtedly also owed its origins to the air corps' penchant for overestimation of its results. Its top management insisted no one could possibly continue to work and produce with all the high-explosive tonnage dumped on the enemy. But as post World War II statistical analyses and debriefing of such Nazi officials revealed, the Germans with their slave laborers kept right on manufacturing the tools of war in spite of all the bombing.

At the Twelfth Army Group, the summary issued on 12 December followed the victory-is-imminent line. "It is now certain that attrition is steadily sapping the strength of German forces on the Western Front and that the crust of defenses is thinner, more brittle, and more vulnerable than it appears on our G-2 map or to the troops in the line." The allegedly rosy view of the "troops in the line" was made before GIs of the 2d and 99th Divisions confronted strenuous resistance to advances toward the Roer.

Over the next few days, qualms ruffled some military intelligence specialists. ULTRA, the code-breaking system, flagged down messages that roused suspicions about the German intentions. On 9 December the U.S. 83d Division had seized a prisoner who said there were strong rumors of an all-out attack within the next few days. A couple of deserters as well as two men captured by the 4th and 106th Infantry Divisions claimed they were told of an imminent big push. The G-2 office sounded a vague alarm but at most divined a strengthening of the enemy defenses in the plains before the Rhine rather than indicating an assault. On 15 December, an officer from the 28th Division scrawled a smudged pencil report detailing his interrogation of a Luxembourg woman, Elise Dele-Dunkel. She spoke of many horsedrawn vehicles, pontoons, small boats, and other rivercrossing equipment coming from the direction of Bitburg and moving west through Geichlingen. In Bitburg she overheard some military personnel saying that it had taken three weeks to get them from Italy. She described the presence of men whose uniforms belonged to the Waffen SS, the most fanatical Nazi soldiers, and she saw many artillery pieces. The intelligence officer interpreted her information as indications of an offensive operation. However, a day went by before this report passed on to higher authorities.

While some of the Americans on the front lines, like Lt. Alan Jones of the 106th Division, which had just come to the combat zone, were watchful, the complaisant attitude that pervaded the uppermost echelons seemed to filter down. There was no general order insisting upon a high state of alert. General Haaso von Manteuffel, commander of the Fifth Panzer Army, personally observed the front and from what he could see the "Amis" (Americans) stayed on guard one hour after dark, then returned to their huts to sleep, reappearing one hour before dawn. Dick Byers, as part of a field artillery observation team with the 106th Division, confirmed Manteuffel. "Before the Bulge, we were a nine-to-five army in the Ardennes."

Originally, said Manteuffel, Hitler scheduled the onslaught to begin at 11:00 A.M. However, the general persuaded his leader that with darkness coming by 4:00 P.M. the Germans would have too little daylight to achieve maximum success. Accordingly, the first salvos were to boom at 5:30 A.M. Furthermore, on the grounds of preventing the Americans from becoming fully alert, instead of a lengthy artillery preparation, Manteuffel planned for less than an hour of the big guns before sending his infantry forward. His armor, relying on searchlights bouncing illumination off the clouds, would pass through the infantry at night and ready to break out the following day.

While Manteuffel controlled the tactics of the Fifth Panzer Army, Sepp Dietrich, in charge of the Sixth Panzer Army insisted upon a full-scale softening up through artillery. In both instances, the two German generals thought in terms of foot soldiers creating wedges for the armor, unlike Patton and Rommel who used their tanks to crash through. Before the targeted hour for the attack, paratroopers were scheduled to drop. However, the requisite number of trucks needed to carry the troops to the airdromes failed to show because no one had authorized fuel for the vehicles. The entire operation was scrubbed, to be reinstated twenty-four hours later.

The Nazi armies also put into play a carefully crafted plot to hoodwink the Americans, In the train of the advance group for Dietrich's legions marched the 150 Brigade, a unit led by Otto Skorzeny, a Hitler favorite who plotted the rescue of Mussolini when Italy had surrendered. Operation Greif, Skorzeny's assignment, traveled in tanks disguised to look like Shermans, genuine U.S. jeeps, and trucks. Their assignment was to race forward and seize Meuse bridges after Peiper carved a wedge through to the river. While the bulk of Skorzeny's 150 Brigade awaited their opportunity behind a task force under Col. Jochen Peiper, a vetern panzer officer, forty-four advance men from Greif garbed in American uniforms infiltrated the Allied lines. Demolition teams sought to blow up bridges, and munitions and gas dumps. Several small squads were to reconnoiter as far west as the Meuse River to gather intelligence. These men reversed road signs, switched mine markers, and performed similar acts to mislead Americans. Others disrupted communications, cut telephone wires, blew up transmitter stations and issued false commands.

Private First Class Nolan Williams on patrol for Company K of the 99th Division's 394th Regiment, discovered the massing of enemy forces on the night of 15 December. "Shortly after dark, we made our way around enemy outposts and bumped into an enemy patrol. There were some small arms shots but I don't remember that we returned fire. We did skirt around the patrol and move deeper into enemy territory. Soon, we were hearing mass movements of tanks, tracks, and men. The sergeant tried to contact our headquarters with his hand radio but could not get a response. He believed the troop movement important enough to cut short our mission and return to report. We flopped down on the first floor of the Bucholz farmhouse. Very early in the morning [16 December] a shell or grenade exploded in the courtyard, throwing glass on us. Someone said, 'Let's go down in the basement to get out of this shelling.' I put on my belt, hung my rifle over my chest, tucked a box of K rations inside my shirt and carefully picked up my new overshoes—I had only been issued them the day before.

"In the dark, I went down the hall and started down the steps. I heard someone speaking German, very rapidly. I assumed it was one of our interpreters. But then there were several voices, all German. In the dark, I placed my hand on the head of the person just in front of me on the steps, pulled his head over to me and whispered, 'There are Jerries in this basement.' All of our helmets had netting on them and suddenly I realized that the one I was holding had no net! At that moment, a German officer in the basement pointed a flashlight on us and said in perfect English, 'Hands up, boys. The war is over.' I'll never forget the saucer-sized eyes of the young German into whose ears I had just whispered. He must have been as frightened as I.

"But I responded, 'Like hell it is!' And I shoved the young soldier down the steps on top of the officer. Up the stairs, down the hall, out toward the courtyard I practically flew, meanwhile clutching my new overshoes in my right hand. In the doorway, silhouetted by the white snow, stood a German with a burp gun in ready position. I hit him with my overshoes, ran over him from toe to head like a freight train, and on to the barn. But I dropped the overshoes. To show how important they seemed to me, I seriously considered going back to the yard to retrieve them."

"I went into the barn and began to get control of myself. I unwound myself from the rifle straps and had the butt ready to defend myself. Someone else began to enter the barn and just as I was about to smack him with the butt, I recognized the sergeant. We decided we would try to get some help. We made a dash for the road and I noticed a German halftrack parked by the house. Now I saw the road was bumper to bumper with tanks, troop carriers, and infantrymen. We hid a long time in a ditch, then dashed between the tanks. Eventually, we were reunited with nine of the others from our original thirteen-man patrol. We became part of the general withdrawal."

About the time Nolan Williams stumbled into the enemy, the big guns of the Sixth Panzer Army opened up all along their front. A murderous downpour of everything from 14-inch railway pieces to mortars crashed down upon the men of the 99th Division. In their log-and-dirt-covered burrows, casualties were few but the cascade of high explosives tore up the network of wire lines necessary for communications. The Fifth Panzer Army, in spite of Manteuffel's fear of waking up the Americans, blasted away and the Seventh Army contributed long range shelling.

Sergeant Ben Nawrocki with a brother regiment to Williams's noted, "At 4:00 A.M. on December 16, it seemed all hell broke loose with artillery shells landing all over. The ground shook. We had a wool sock in a bottle of gasoline for a light but the artillery kept blowing it out. We could not stick our heads up. Trees and branches fell all over, and shrapnel whined around. The tree bursts were very dangerous. We found it better to squat, rather than spread-eagle; squatting made a smaller target.

"When the artillery started to let up around 6:00 A.M. and we stuck our heads out of our holes, an eerie sight greeted us. There were lights of all descriptions, lighting the sky and ground. The lights pointed up into the sky and into our positions. They beamed from tanks, trucks, pillboxes, everywhere. This was to help the Germans see the terrain and us. The snow was hip-deep with a heavy fog. If the lights were intended to throw fear into our troops it didn't succeed with us. The enemy were between us, and the lights made them a good target. Some wore American uniforms, throwing grenades, a few were seen on skis. Some wore white snowsuits. We kept cutting them down. In many places the Germans piled up on top of one another like cord wood."

An entire regiment of the 277th Volksgrenadier Division had hurled itself at Company B. "On the left flank of the 3d platoon, a rifleman with a

BAR was firing at the oncoming Germans, who piled up three or four feet high in front of his foxhole. I don't know his name but he was bucktoothed and when he looked down at his feet, I heard him yell, 'Goddamn, I'm barefoot.' He had been so busy for six hours he never had time to put on his shoes." The embattled GIs in Nawrocki's sector, aided by artillery fire from the big guns to the rear, inflicted heavy casualties, The resistance stalled the enemy infantrymen, jamming up the armor behind.

Along the Luxembourg border, on the right flank and to the south, the impact and the immediate problems varied. George Ruhlen, then a lieutenant colonel commanding the 3d Field Artillery of the 9th Armored Division, recalled, "At 0615 on the sixteenth of December, shells of 105mm, 150mm and 170mm came whistling into Haller [a town on the Sauer River below its junction with the Our]. The fire increased and as all ran for cover, the rumble of enemy guns could be heard echoing up and down the Sauer Valley. It was soon apparent that this was not a local raid nor a retaliation for harassing fire delivered the previous night. Bells in the Haller church struck three high notes, then three low notes, and then incessantly for half an hour until the bell ringer was evicted. An estimated 800 to 900 rounds fell in and near the town between 0615 and 0715. Columns of smoke and dust from tremendous explosions were seen in the vicinity of Beaufort. Nebelwerfer rockets fell near gun positions with their characteristically terrifying shriek.

"An observer reported sixty Germans crossing the river on a small pontoon bridge near Dillingen, but they were not carrying weapons and it was believed they were coming over to surrender. A minute later came the report that these Germans were carrying machine guns and frantic calls for normal barrages came from all observers almost instantaneously. All wire lines were shot out except the liaison line to the 60th Infantry Command Post. A heavy ground mist made observation very difficult, let alone making close air support impossible. In the forward areas, vague figures appeared in the fog, unidentifiable even a hundred yards away."

In the area occupied by the 106th Division, the huge shells launched from railway guns thundered into St. Vith, division headquarters. Up front the amazed troops watched the searchlight beams carom off the low hanging clouds to illuminate roads and open fields. More ominously, they spotted white clad figures in the distance advancing toward them, the clatter of tracked vehicles reached their ears.

From a snow-encrusted emplacement for a light machine gun, the 423d Regiment's Pvt. Frank Raila, watched the searchlights bounce off the cloud cover. "It was a pretty sight." Sightseeing ended with the dawn. "We saw a Tiger tank in the trees to our front. Our machine gun fired tracers to point out the tank to the tank destroyer unit nearby. Two or three of them went out to get it. Then 88 shells started coming, landing in the woods behind us where we put on our backpacks. Small-arms fire was directed at us and we fired back, with machine guns, mortars. The tank destroyers came back. One had been hit. Its .50 caliber machine gun was at a twisted tangle. A dead crewman was strapped in front. He was the first dead American I saw.

"I could barely make out figures, far ahead of us, 500 to 1,000 yards, with dark, flapping greatcoats. As soon as people began to shoot, they disappeared. The place we were in apparently had become untenable. I had gone back to get ammo twice for the machine gun and the sergeant said we were going on the march. We all hit the road, passing U.S. trucks burning, with ammo exploding, an occasional shell shooting into the air, pyrotechnics! It got very confusing. We were not much of a company anymore. There were different platoons and companies. We were told to walk down a field in front of us to the right of a road. Everything was quiet. I think the Germans let the point keep walking. Then when we reached an area of a few acres, all hell broke loose. It was very surprising. There had been no sound of incoming; mortars may make a sound but I didn't hear anything until the explosions started to rock the ground. Dirt flew up everywhere, pelting you in the chest and back. We all dropped down, paralyzed. People were hollering and screaming until the sergeant said, 'Get out of here!' We crawled back until the explosions didn't follow and then we ran like crazy. We straggled back to the 'front lines,' a miserably thin line of GIs, including my own machine-gun platoon."

Initially, there was little to even hint at a cataclysm for Phil Hannon and the others from Company A of the 81st Combat Engineer Battalion. "We were roused by 'calling cards' mailed by 88s on Saturday morning. We were 'green' and so, shrugging our shoulders, said, 'What the hell, this happens every so often. And off to chow we went. Chow was good as chow always is to guys who are in good shape, and the gang was full of laughs about the close calls that had dropped in on us. The heavy firing in the east didn't register, so the talk was about Christmas and the mail that was starting to come in. We didn't think it strange that all the German civilians were up and in their basements long before the shelling started.

"The third platoon had a couple of jobs to finish up front, so we loaded up and moved out. The same old horseplay went on. The KPs got the every day razzing as we rode by the kitchen. We dropped off the second and third squads and mine went up farther to finish the corduroy road we had begun the day before. The front was quiet. The shells were going over and beyond, and we felt safer than in our little village. We felt safer until we noticed the worried looks on the faces of the officers. A major walked by with a .45 in his fist, so we woke up. No work on the road this day and we headed for home. We never got there."

John Collins, a member of A Company of the 81st Engineers, was less blasé about the first salvos. "We were literally knocked out of our beds by artillery shells landing in and around our company area. We dressed quickly and went downstairs to find the German family crouched in a rear room, fully dressed. It looked as though they knew it was coming. We crouched with them until we could collect our wits and the shelling slacked off. But not much. We now knew what it feels like to be under fire and we were scared. Really scared. Maybe a better word would be frustrated. If someone is shooting at you, you can retaliate but this shelling was for the birds.

"At about 0600 we left for the mess hall to find most of the company in line for chow. When a shell would come in, everyone hit the ground. Immediately afterward they were back in line." As Phil Hannon noted, the three platoons left the area after breakfast to perform routine chores. John Collins was temporarily left behind, assigned to bring up the outfit's equipment. He had almost finished the task when the shelling increased. The company commander decided to recall the three platoons and dispatched Collins with a Lieutenant Coughlin to retrieve the men. They reached the first and second platoons without trouble and passed the word.

"We headed to the 422d Regiment to round up my 3d platoon. As we neared a guard shack about 800 yards behind the lines, Lieutenant Coughlin, very nonchalantly said, 'Sergeant, turn around real easy and let's get the hell out of here." I swung the jeep around and slowly retraced our way back. It was then that I saw the white-clad enemy in a field about 800 yards to our left. At this point we were only about seventy-five yards from the guard shack and I really poured the juice to the jeep. We heard some rifle fire but with my sliding on the snow and the lieutenant yelling 'Faster!' we made it without any hits if they were shooting at us. The lieutenant told me that the guard at the shack had on white boots and his rifle did not look like ours."

Collins's company commander ordered everyone to pull back to the village of Heuem. Lieutenant Coughlin organized a defense from buildings behind the retreat. Accompanied by foot soldiers, a quartet of German Tiger tanks trundled up the road, blew away the houses scattering Coughlin and his men. The remnants of the 81st Engineers assembled briefly at Heuem, but the pressure from the enemy continued. Collins and the others retreated toward St.-Vith, where Gen. Alan Jones [father of Lt. Alan Jones Jr.], as CG of the 106th, sought to restore control. From a hillside, the general's namesake son, watched with dismay as the enemy battered the town of Bleialf inhabited by a brother regiment, the 424th. The junior Jones himself was not in imminent danger. "There was very little shelling on our positions the first day, and not much on the second, either."

On the night of 15 December, the observation section for C Battery of the 371st Field Artillery, which included Dick Byers, slept in a house located at the center of Murringen. According to Byers, his bedroom shared the back wall and roof in common with the barn. "Just before dawn, on the morning of the sixteenth, we were awakened by a muffled explosion and a slight tremor of the house. None of us thought enough of the occurrence to get out of a warm sleeping bag to investigate. But so far as our group was concerned this was the start of the Battle of the Bulge.

"One of the guys finally went downstairs and out to the latrine. By the early light he saw that a delayed-fuse artillery shell had gone through the roof of the barn, just two feet from the wall of our bedroom. The round had buried itself in the haymow before exploding. Throughout the morning, shells struck at seeming random around the village. One exploded among a group of artillerymen lined up for breakfast and killed several. By mid-morning, we realized there was a pattern to the explosions. They fell close to houses occupied by American troops. Later, we heard that a captured German artillery observer had a map marked with all of the occupied houses. The information must have been given to him by someone planted in the area by the Germans.

"In the afternoon I drove an officer to a command post for a conference. I stayed with the jeep and was caught in the first and worst barrage I've ever been in. I was caught flat-footed in a pine forest without any adequate cover. The shells were hitting treetops and spraying the ground all around us with steel fragments. I believe I actually pressed a slit trench into the snow and frozen ground with my body, trying in my terror to become as small and flat as possible. The noise was so incredibly loud it could not be heard. It rang in my ears and vibrated my body. Imagine putting your head up inside an enormous bell while giants pounded it with sledgehammers. Most young soldiers felt invulnerable even when their comrades were dropping all around them. When they lost that sense of invulnerability and suddenly realized the truth of their situation, terror replaced it, shortness of breath, and a pounding heart. I had a terrible feeling of my back being so vulnerable."

The quietest sector for the 106th defenses until 16 December had been that held by elements of the 424th Regiment just inside the German border above Luxembourg. Shortly before dawn on the sixteenth, a noncom burst into the cabin where Harry F. Martin Jr. bunked and yelled, "The Germans are coming! The Germans are coming! We'll be killed!" Martin and Bill Williams, snatched up their rifles and steel helmets. The ran to their position, a two-man foxhole on the extreme left flank. The remainder of the platoon took their stations in log bunkers. Said Martin, "Seconds later I could see hundreds of shadowy heads bobbing up and down, coming over the crest of the hill just before dawn. They acted as though they were drunk or on drugs, screaming, shrieking. I was absolutely terrified. They had already outflanked our company and now they were coming to finish us off.

With nothing on our left and out of sight of our platoon on the right, it felt almost as if we were against the entire German Army. I was horror-stricken. There was no thought of running away or surrendering. I had an absolute conviction to fight to the death, while being certain we would be killed. Bill tugged on my leg. I was vaguely aware he asked me to let him know when the Germans were close enough. Neither of us had ever fired a rifle grenade before and we did not have the slightest idea of the effective range. There were so many of them storming down the hill coming right for us. There was no way of stopping all of them. I had a feeling of utter hopelessness; I was panic-stricken. I felt my entire life force had left my body. I was already dead and fighting like a zombie. Sheer panic caused me to fire without thinking or aiming. I was unaware of my body, just terror, firing as fast as my finger could pull the trigger.

"They kept coming as though immune to death. Apparently I was not hitting a thing. I was so transfixed with fear and terror my eyes did not focus on the individual enemy. I was firing blindly, without thinking or looking through the sights. In my terror-stricken seizure I continued to fire in the general direction of the swarming sea of terror, the huge mass of bodies charging toward me. It was as though the entire hillside was alive, moving with huge tentacles to devour me. Bill tugged on my leg again and yelled, 'Are they close enough?' I can remember telling him no, but my brain didn't register distance. I could not even think about what he was saying. He must have tugged my leg half a dozen times during the battle and I kept telling him no. In the middle of this terrifying battle I heard a very confident, calm voice inside my head say, 'Squeeze the trigger.' I calmed down instantly, took careful aim at one of the charging Germans through my gunsight and squeezed the trigger. He flung his arms up over his head and fell down dead, shot through the head. I felt a sensation surge through my whole body. I was no longer a zombie. My life force had come surging back. I was alive and for the first time I felt that I had a chance to come out of this battle.

"At this very moment I was a veteran combat soldier. I continued to shoot the attacking Germans until they finally stopped coming. The battle was over. After such intense fighting it was very strange how suddenly the battle ended. How quiet everything had become. A feeling of disbelief it was over. At the time it seemed as if it would never end. Later I thought about the voice I heard telling me to squeeze the trigger. I failed to qualify with the rifle in basic training. I had to go back and do everything by the numbers without live ammunition, again. For the next five weeks after supper and on Sundays; the practice continued. Over and over they drummed the procedure into my head, always ending with 'Squeeze the trigger, do not jerk the trigger, slowly squeeze the trigger, sque-e-e-ze the trigger.' After awhile, at night I dreamt about squeezing the trigger. We had made fun of doing things by the numbers but it had saved my life."

In support of the 106th Division's 422d Regiment and the men of A Company from the 81st Combat Engineers—Phil Hannon and John Collins—was the 589th Field Artillery. The executive officer of Battery A was Eric Fisher Wood Jr. Within the first few hours of 16 December Lt. Eric Wood became the acting battery commander as the advancing Germans captured Battery A's nominal leader, the boyishly exuberant Capt. Aloysius J. Mencke in a forward observation post. The 2d Division artillerymen had earlier dug sufficient foxholes for all of the gun crews. But Eric Wood was unhappy to discover that there was no cover over the foxholes. He ordered his cannoneers to roof over every position. By 14 December, the troops were protected from overhead bursts by pine logs. In addition, he arranged to build some flexibility into the emplacement for his number-four gun. By this alteration, he gave the battery not only the capacity to fire in support of ground troops but also means to defend against an enemy advance along the only paved road.

The spearhead for the Sixth Panzer Army under Sepp Dietrich belonged to SS Lt. Col. Jochen Peiper, a veteran of the eastern front where his harsh reprisals against villages suspected of aiding the Red Army brought him the nickname of "Blowtorch Peiper." Kampfgruppe Peiper (Task Force Peiper) and its 4,000 men, expected to advance in a fifteen-mile long column that would reach the Meuse River. Tactically, the extended line of soldiers, tanks, half tracks, artillery, trucks, and other vehicles, weakened the task force's striking power. But the narrow, sinuous roads of the Ardennes prohibited broader movement. To compensate, Peiper sought to equip his armor component with the lighter Panther tanks rather than the heavy, underpowered, and sluggish big Tigers. The task force toted enough ammunition for four or five days, fuel for an even shorter period because two entire trainloads of gasoline never reached the assembly point. Additional supplies of fuel would have to be captured, taken from Allied dumps.

While Kampfgruppe Peiper with its impatient commander idled its engines awaiting the clearance of mines and repair of an overpass, twenty-year-old 1st Lt. Lyle Bouck and the handful of others in the Intelligence and Reconnaissance platoon of the 3d Battalion, 394th Infantry Regiment, 99th Division, remained in place on the outskirts of Lanzerath, directly in the path of the spearhead. "We had made contact with the task force from the 14th Cav," said Bouck "and knew they had some machine guns and antitank guns on our right flank and in Lanzerath in front of us. But they were in a different corps so the communication between us was limited.

"Some time before dawn, the artillery fire began. I don't know how long it lasted but it seemed like a long time. At first it went over our heads. Then they started to hit in front of Lanzerath. There was a short lull before quite a bit began to drop on our positions. I had the impression we had been bracketed. It was intermittent for more than an hour, a lot of tree bursts. Initially, we were in a shocked, stunned state. I kept wondering when we'd start taking casualties but the log coverings over the foxholes shielded us. I called regiment when it began and they'd been half-asleep when it started. But the word was artillery fire was hitting the entire regiment. The only instructions I got were to be doubly alert.

"After about two hours, the firing lifted. I went to every foxhole to make contact. To my surprise, nobody had been hurt. But we were all scared. I told everyone that somebody would attack us soon. Maybe an hour later, we suddenly heard motors, American vehicles moving. The tank destroyers pulled out, traveling toward Bucholz Station. I took Slape, my platoon sergeant, Tsak [Bill Tsakanikas], and a fellow named John Creger and we ran down the hill and into the house. Inside the place we found a civilian, using a telephone. Tsak was ready to shoot him but I said let him go. We couldn't handle prisoners and I was not going to shoot an unarmed man. From the second floor we could see where the road dipped, then crested about 600 yards away. Through my field glasses I saw German soldiers wearing the helmets of paratroopers. We had taken along a field wire and I told Slape and Creger to stay there and keep me posted. I tried to get artillery fire from regiment but they said they couldn't give us any. Just about then, a jeep pulled up. It carried Lt. Warren Springer and three enlisted men from a field artillery observation unit."

Indeed, Springer, Sgt. Peter Gacki, Cpl. Billy Queen, and T4 Willard Wibben belonged to C Battery of the 371st Field Artillery, the outfit in which Dick Byers served. Byers remembered, "We had all been worried about them. They had reported on the night of December 15 that Losheim [behind the German lines] was lit up like a Christmas tree." Springer volunteered to join his tiny band with the I&R Platoon. Bouck accepted and urged Springer to see if he could raise some artillery fire upon the oncoming enemy host. The field artillery observer, using a radio in his jeep, contacted the 371st gunners. Springer watched the results: "Some rounds came in on Lanzerath. I sent corrections, and there were more rounds. Then something hit the jeep, either mortar or artillery fire, and halted all communications."

Bouck was advised of an emergency. "Slape called to tell me that Germans were in the house. I promised help. I ran to the front of the platoon and picked three men. Aubrey McGehee was a strong, rugged man who'd played football. McGehee knew the layout of the house, and he'd knock the crap out of anybody. Jordan "Pop" Robinson was thirty-seven and he'd shoot anything he saw. I could count on Jim Sivola from Florida to back up McGehee. Slape and Creger decided not to wait. They made a break for it, ducking through a door to an adjoining barn where they hid themselves under some cows. Meanwhile, my three guys arrived at the house and quickly got into a firefight with the Germans. Slape and Creger bolted from the barn, circled into the woods, and then came back across the road, which ran north-south. A machine gun opened up and shot off the heel of Slape's left shoe. He fell hard on the road, breaking a rib and his chest bone. But he and Creger made it back to our place. McGehee, Robinson, and Sivola were cut off by the machine gun and isolated on the east side of the road.

"While all of this was going on, here comes a German column up the road, walking toward us, single file on both sides of the road, their weapons slung. They were singing as they marched. I ordered don't fire until I give the word or I start shooting. There was an advance party of maybe thirty and then the main body of troops with the command group. That's whom I wanted to hit. I was also wondering whether they would turn left and cut us off but they kept on straight ahead.

"Just as I was running all this through my head and about to open fire, a little girl of about thirteen, ran up to three officers in a jeep at the front. She pointed up the road, in our direction. I still think she was showing them which way the tank destroyers went. I don't believe she knew we were even there. But the paratroopers suddenly dispersed. As they did, Tsak opened fire and so did the rest of us. McGehee, Robinson, and Sivola saw no way to get back to us. They took off from the east side of the road and tried to reach the 1st Battalion. When they came to a deep railroad cut, they went down and then up the other side. German soldiers in camouflage caught them. Sivola was badly wounded in the shoulder, a bullet tore off most of the calf in Robinson's right leg, and seeing the situation was hopeless, McGehee and the other two surrendered.

"For us, the shooting stopped as the Germans retreated. We could see people crawling around to reorganize. Then after maybe an hour and a half they came screaming and yelling, in a direct frontal attack up the snow covered hill. They were firing at us but they had no targets. And there was a typical farm fence that bisected the hill. The paratroopers had to climb over this fence. For us it was like target practice. We had a couple of BARs and a .30-caliber machine gun manned by Risto Milosevich. Tsak and Slape took turns on the .50 caliber machine gun of the jeep, until it was hit in the breech and blew up. The other guys had M1s, while I had a carbine. I could see blood all over the snow, I heard screaming, hollering.

"Then they stopped coming. Someone waved a red flag and in poor English yelled 'Medics! Medics!' It was approaching noon. For forty-five minutes, except for the sounds of wounded men in pain, the field and woods were quiet. They tended their injured, dragged them backward. We had our own casualties. A rifle grenade had smashed into Lou Kahlil's face. It didn't detonate but it broke his jaw in four places, and hammered five teeth into the rest of his mouth. Someone stuffed sulfa powder in the wound, then rubbed snow on his face. Lou got back on his feet."

When the third attack came, Kahlil again was firing at the enemy. Risto Milosevich operated a machine gun by himself. "It was like shooting clay ducks at the amusement park. But while I was concentrating hard on a German, I didn't notice another one about fifteen yards from my hole. He had a potato masher in his hand, cocked and ready to swing it forward. He was looking right at me. I had the machine gun in my hand and fired point blank. He scared me so badly that I think I kept firing so long I cut him in half. But by myself I couldn't keep the gun from jamming.

"Slape came into the hole with me. He took over the machine gun while I fed the belt. He kept firing and firing and I was harping at him to shoot in bursts of three." The weapon became so hot that it cooked off [fired] rounds even when Slape released the trigger. He could only shut it down by raising the cover. The barrel finally bowed from the heat and became inoperable. We had to use my M1 since Slape hadn't brought his to the foxhole. It worked out well though I kept shouting at Slape to save one bullet until I loaded the next clip. I saw a German medic about thirty yards from our hole. He was working on a soldier whom I thought was dead. That made me very suspicious. The medic kept looking at us and his lips moved constantly. After the medic had appeared, mortar fire was landing right on us. I was sure he was directing it. And then as I watched him, he turned. I noticed a pistol in his belt. I asked Slape for the rifle so I could shoot him. He refused, saying there were too many other Germans in front of us. When I explained about the medic, Slape shot him." During a lull, the platoon sergeant discovered two bullet holes in his jacket. Springer and his companions also poured small-arms fire on the enemy. An enemy slug struck Cpl. Billy Queen in the stomach. There was nothing his companions could do for him.

Enemy fire had destroyed the platoon radio. Bouck detailed Cpl. Sam Jenkins and Pfc. Robert Preston to carry word of the I&R Platoon's plight back to headquarters and either return with reinforcements or permission for the unit to withdraw. The two sneaked back through the woods. But the area behind the platoon was now a hive of enemy soldiers. For thirty-six hours, Jenkins and Preston hid out, trying to reach friendly forces. They were captured on 18 December

Bouck decided to pull out. "It was late in the day, but still light, somewhere between 3:30 and 4:30 in the afternoon. I sent word that when I blew a whistle three times, everyone would leave the foxholes with their weapons. We'd rendezvous at a point on the road. We would move by night through the woods. I told Slape and Tsak to remove the distributor caps from the jeeps. Tsak was with me in a foxhole as we prepared to take off. I heard the sound of boots and Germans hollering as they fired. I had one full magazine left in my carbine. I saw two figures running toward us. I had filed the sear [metal piece in firing mechanism] off my carbine so when I squeezed the trigger it operated like a machine gun. I emptied the clip at those two. I was satisfied that I had fired my last round.

"I saw the muzzle of a gun poke into our hole. I pushed Tsakanikas to get him out of the way and then someone yelled, 'How many of you? How many of you?' I didn't speak much German but I answered 'Zwei! Zwei!' With that came a burst of gunfire. The next thing I knew I am lifting Bill Tsakanikas, who was making a horrible gurgling noise, out of the foxhole. There was an arm helping me and whoever it was, he pulled Tsak out. Someone shone a flashlight on his face. 'Mein Gott! Mein Gott!!' I heard. When I saw what a bloody mess Tsak was I couldn't recognize him. Half his face had been shot away. His right eyeball hung in the gap where his cheek had been. There was still some small arms fire going on. An officer who spoke very good English demanded, 'When are your men going to stop shooting?' I answered, 'Those must be your guys. We don't have any ammo left.' The firing ceased. I felt very hot. I had been hit in my boot."

Springer also surrendered. "I heard a mixture of German and English. We were told to throw our guns out and come out or they would throw hand grenades in. I expected that they would shoot us but I thought I would rather go that way than to be inside the enclosed space of the dugout when a grenade went off. So out we came and I was surprised when they didn't fire."

A soldier motioned for Bouck to pick up Tsak. "I don't know how I did it. There was a German helping me support him down the hill. We climbed over that fence past all of the bodies of the German dead. Another soldier was right behind us and he suddenly came around in front. He kept asking if we had been at St.-Lô. I answered 'Nein! Nein!" He started screaming about his comrades at St. Lô. Shit, I didn't know what else to say. Then he stuck a gun in my back and pulled the trigger. I don't know whether it was a misfire or the gun was empty. But someone said, 'Raus! Raus!' He disappeared and we went into Lanzerath.

"They put us in a room with a bench. They sat me there with Task who leaned on my left shoulder. He'd been bandaged and only one eye and his nose were visible. Blood seeped through my field jacket and I realized I had been grazed. I could walk okay, without pain or discomfort. The rest of the platoon showed up. Sergeant George Redmond carried in Lou Kahlil. You could only see a nose and eye on him also because of the bandaging. They brought in [Joe] McConnell. His field jacket had been cut away and he had a bad wound in the shoulder. There were German wounded all over the floor."

In the darkness, Peiper, following the road, never saw the hundreds of bodies still lying in the fields. Estimates of the German dead, almost entirely attributable to the small arms of Bouck and his platoon, range from 300 to 500. Although he claimed that except for occasional artillery rounds, he initially encountered no Americans, Peiper realized mines planted by both the Americans and left by his countrymen when they retreated threatened his column. With his timetable already badly disrupted he decided simply to roll over the mines as if they were no more than speed bumps. From Lanzerath he set his sights on Honsfeld as his first objective.

At the Café Scholzen, several hours after Kampfgruppe Peiper clanked away, and as dawn broke, his captors informed Bouck he would be taken outside. "I asked if I could speak with Tsak and Kahlil. Tsak was conscious. I told him they were taking him to a hospital and I'd see him after the war. I said 'I'm putting your Bible,' which he always carried, 'and that picture of your sweetheart in your pocket. I'll say a prayer for you.' He couldn't answer me but I'm sure he heard because he squeezed my hand. And as I stood there, they hauled Kahlil and Tsak to a flatbed truck and drove off with them." Herded by guards, Bouck, his leg still oozing blood from where he was hit at the top of his boot, started a series of long hikes that marked the lives of so many American POWs. German doctors operated upon Tsak and pulled him through.

Jochen Peiper's advance guard pushed toward Honsfeld. The route followed the road through Bucholz Station, a tiny cluster of houses. Earlier, Dick Byers from the 371st Field Artillery, which had already lost one forward observation quartet with Bouck's I&R Platoon, was dispatched to replace the captured team. The new party amounted to three men, a lieutenant, Sgt. Curtis Fletcher, and Byers. "We pulled our jeep off the road into a barn attached to a farmhouse. It was across the road from Bucholz Station. Some GIs from the 1st and 2d platoons of K Company, 394th, were dug in on the side of the woods away from the road. From their holes they could see Bucholz Station and the road from Lanzerath. A few K Company men and the aid station were in the farmhouse basement. From midnight to one o'clock, I stood guard with an infantryman on the porch of the house. We took turns ducking into the house to warm up with a cigarette. It was a quiet, cold night. We could clearly hear the SS Panzer troops shouting back and forth, the racing of tank engines, the squeal of bogie wheels as *Kampfgruppe Peiper* worked its way from Losheim, over to Lanzerath, and then on towards us. I commented that their noise sounded like a bunch of quartermaster troops on maneuvers in Louisiana."

When Peiper's column, guided by men on foot, clattered up the road hard by the farmhouse, Byers was asleep. A departing GI rifleman paused long enough to shake Byers and whisper urgently, "'Get up! There's tanks outside!' I mumbled something, rolled over and went back to sleep. Sergeant Fletcher, also asleep, never stirred. But as our lieutenant started to leave, a wounded GI called out and attracted his attention. He shone his flashlight and saw Fletcher and me, still lying there, sound asleep. He *really* woke us up! We grabbed our coats and helmets, buckled on our pistol belts and headed outside. There we pulled on our galoshes and ran for the barn, thinking we'd use the radio stashed there to call in artillery fire.

"As we opened the back door of the barn, we saw three German paratroopers silhouetted against the white snow, but they couldn't see us with the black courtyard behind us. Since they appeared armed with Schmeissers [burp guns] and had the backing of an entire panzer battle group, we decided not to argue over possession of the radio. We took off through the side gate into a patch of pine woods parallel to the road. I recall a feeling of exhilaration. We could hear them, thus we knew where they were and where to go to avoid them. And we knew where they were to kill them, if we had to. I thought, it's funny but the closer you get to the Krauts, the less scared you get. That is, when you see them, you can kill them. But when you don't know where they are and what they are up to, you fear the unknown. Fletcher had not taken time to buckle his galoshes before going out of the gate and they were clinking. He knelt down to fasten them while we went on. He was captured from behind before he finished.

"We wandered through the woods between the road and infantry foxholes and dugouts. A couple of times we approached a hole and the lieutenant said in a tense, still voice, 'Don't shoot, men. This is Lieutenant———of C Battery, 371st. Don't shoot!' Then he would remember to use the password, 'Shining.' Only then would we see the two gun barrels aimed between our eyes and hear the countersign, 'Knight.'

"Eventually, I realized this wasn't getting us anywhere. We couldn't function as artillery observers without our radio and with .45caliber pistols we weren't going to be much help against paratroopers and tanks. In fact, my pistol hand felt paralyzed from gripping the weapon so tightly that I must have permanently embossed my fingerprints on the butt. I suggested to the lieutenant that I knew the way back to our gun positions via trails. He accepted the idea and we headed north. There was still a steady stream of tanks, half-tracks, and paratroopers on the road, which was lined with big, low-limbed pines. We ducked under one into a roadside ditch and waited for a break in the convoy. Enemy soldiers trudged by, just above our heads. When an opening finally came, we dashed across the road, dove into a ditch on the other side, then made our way toward Hunningen. Now my deer-hunting expedition paid off because I knew the route from that earlier trek through the woods and fields.

"Behind us, we suddenly heard gunfire. Apparently, some GI in K Co. had opened fire. The flak panzers with their 20mm cannons and quad machine guns mowed down the woods, knocking out most of what was left of the company. Then we looked over our left shoulders and saw a tank firing. We heard small arms from Honsfeld. When we reached the edge of Hünningen we were challenged by the 1st Battalion, 23d Infantry Regiment of the 2d Division. We told the men digging in what we had seen and they answered that they were oldtimers sent down to save our inexperienced asses. It was dawn by the time we reached our gun positions. The 'march order' had been given and we were just in time to jump on the back of a truck and leave for our next position near the twin villages of Krinkelt and Rocherath. I managed to grab some cold pancakes from the mess truck and ate them on the way."

Kampfgruppe Peiper now attacked Honsfeld. Occupied by a service unit of the 99th Division detailed to provide the amenities of a near-frontline rest camp—hot showers, hot food, entertainment—Honsfeld's U.S. garrison was ill prepared to host a confrontation with the brute power of *Kampfgruppe Peiper.* The captain in charge hastily formed a provisional rifle company out of his own men and some stragglers. A handful of antitank platoons arrived to confront the enemy and a small troop of men from the 14th Cavalry Group also had retreated to Honsfeld. Sentries were posted but the majority of the men bedded down to await a possible attack later.

In the darkness, perhaps an hour after leaving Lanzerath, the Germans rolled right past the Americans guarding the approaches to Honsfeld. Those on picket apparently failed to recognize the panzers that slyly joined the stream of U.S. vehicles traveling through the village by night. A belated discovery of the enemy on the outskirts generated brief and ineffective resistance. Peiper was pleasantly surprised by the ease with which he captured the village.

Peiper barely paused in Honsfeld before rolling onward. But as the echelons behind him followed, the murderous acts associated with SS forces erupted. An officer lined up eight prisoners rousted from their beds, barefoot and in their underwear and sprayed them with a burp gun. A group of Germans disregarded a white flag displayed by five GIs and killed four, leaving one man alive. A tank then crushed the life out of his body. There were a series of similar incidents and at the very least those prisoners not used for target practice endured blows from rifle butts. The Germans slaughtered civilians as well.

The worst offense occurred at a small Belgian village, Malmédy. There Battery B of the 285th Field Artillery Observation Battalion blundered into Peiper's spearhead. The Panzers quickly overwhelmed the lightly armed specialists and more than 100 Americans were captured and lined up in a field. Peiper rumbled off, leaving the prisoners in the hands of those trailing behind. Suddenly an orgy of murder erupted, first with pistols and then from machine guns on tanks or set up along a road that ran by the killing field. When it ended, eighty-six soldiers had been slaughtered along with several civilians who sought to offer succor. A few escaped the massacre and reported what had happened. Word spread about the barbarity of the enemy, sharply lessening the willingness to give quarter.

Initially, protected by the fog of battle and American ignorance of the scheme, some teams from Greif passed themselves off as GIs quite successfully. They befuddled traffic and performed minor acts of sabotage. The advantage of American unawareness ended by midmorning, the very first day of the German attack. In the vicinity of where Harry Martin learned to "squeeze the trigger," Lt. William Shakespeare, who made sports page headlines a few years before while lugging a football for Notre Dame, captured a German captain from the 116th Panzer Division. Bagged along with the officer was a map case containing the plan of attack and papers outlining Operation Greif. The documents spelled out the recognition signals and the roads upon which the teams expected to operate. Within a few hours, the material circulated among the top echelons of U.S. intelligence. A number of the fake GIs were caught and executed.

42
Chaos

On the left flank of Sepp Dietrich's Sixth Panzer Army, Hasso van Manteuffel's Fifth Panzer Army, which struck the 106th and 28th Divisions, applied increasing pressure. The initial impact of the shelling and advance of German infantry had halted the work crew with Phil Hannon from the 106th's engineer battalion. At regimental headquarters in Schönberg, Hannon and his mates learned they were cut off from the village they occupied. "The men in regimental headquarters had been taking a pasting from the German artillery. Some of their nervousness got to us. A buzz bomb clattered over, rather low. The boys bolted from the truck. We deployed by instinct on the outskirts of the town. No one had to yell 'Go here' or 'Do this,' We did the right thing automatically. A rock pile here, a depression, a ditch, a manure pile—we made use of them. My platoon of engineers was called on to unload ammunition for a platoon of tank destroyers that pulled in. The Heinies spotted us and threw 88s at us. Thank God, a number of them were duds! After the first five or six shells landed we could judge where they were hitting. We were getting battlewise fast. The Heinies missed the boat when they didn't smack us that morning. Infantry companies fell back and set up a line on the outskirts of the village. Tank destroyers positioned themselves to cover the field and roads. We settled down to stick as long as possible. They asked for a bazooka man and since I had trained with a bazooka, I stepped out. Four of us went out on the road between the Heinies and regimental headquarters and dug in. We had one bazooka, seven rounds for it, and our rifles. By the time we finished digging in, it was pitch black, getting windier and colder by the minute. About midnight two of us decided we had enough of freezing. We were wearing field jackets, no overcoats. We left the other two as the bazooka team and returned to the village. While blankets were hunted up for us, we had a chance to clean our rifles. They were coated inside and out with mud. I doubt if they would have fired. The captain told us the mess hall was serving chow all the time. We got some stew and coffee and headed back.

"When daylight came we took a look around. We had been told the infantry was all around us when we went out the night before. Three hundred yards *behind* us we located them. We pulled back to the top of a little knoll where we could command the road and fields very well. The Heinies spotted a company of infantry that had moved into position on a hill behind us. Zing! I yanked in my head and did some worrying. Zap! Damn those 88s! The infantry on the hill behind was catching hell, but the shells sounded as if they were skinning my helmet on the way over."

Hannon gave up the bazooka slot to some infantrymen and rejoined his engineer colleagues. But the enemy artillery continued to bedevil the Americans in Schönberg. It became apparent that the small contingent in the village was trapped. "About two o'clock Monday afternoon, we got orders to abandon the town and try to break out. Two infantry battalions were supposed to be fighting to open the way and we all left the place expecting to get out. A protective barrage of smoke and time fire laid down by our artillery accompanied our pullout."

No longer a green replacement after his exposure to combat with the 28th Division's Company B of the 110th Infantry in the Hurtgen Forest, Ed Uzemack, along with his comrades, became uneasy toward 15 December after night patrols heard the ominous sounds of squeaking tank treads across no-man's-land. "The reports were dutifully transmitted to division headquarters where they were dismissed as unlikely because the terrain supposedly did not suit tanks.

"On the morning of the sixteenth we experienced an intense and longer bombardment. The quiet that followed was soon disrupted by shouts of alarm from GI lookout posts. German infantry in large numbers were moving up the hill toward our village of Clervaux, Luxembourg. The fighting that ensued was weird. It was like shooting ducks at a carnival. With a heavy blanket of snow on the hillside, the Germans wore no camouflage and the dark uniforms made inviting targets. Besides our M1 rifles, we had a couple of .50-caliber machine guns and perhaps a mortar or two. After encountering heavy fire from our vantage point, the enemy troops broke and ran for cover. The action was repeated several times during the day, in what were almost suicide missions. We retained control of our positions and retired to our quarters, in my case an inn at the intersection of three highways that served as platoon headquarters. There were about eight of us billeted at the inn, the platoon commander, a couple of noncoms, and us dogfaces.

"The next day we got our wakeup call, a barrage, a bit late but effective. As the almost one-sided infantry battle continued, the walkie-talkie crackled with requests for more rifle ammunition, casualty reports, and calls for a runner [Uzemack]. Running zigzag along the road between GI fire and that from the enemy, loaded with bandoliers of .30-caliber ammo, I turned onto an ice-covered walk where one of our squads was housed. A German machine gun opened fire to my right as I slipped and fell on my back, sliding toward an open door. A couple of GIs grabbed my legs and dragged me inside. After they found I was not wounded, they took the ammunition and questioned me on the status in other sectors. I knew as little as they did. I needed a cigarette badly after I realized how close I had come to cashing in my chips. Cigarettes were scarce and the guys suggested I get them from a guy in the next room 'who no longer needed them.' Enemy fire had killed the GI that morning. He had a nearly full pack of smokes in one of his pockets which, they felt, I was entitled to as a kind of reward for bringing the bandoliers.

"While with this squad I heard the cries of a wounded German soldier, lying a few yards away. The GIs said he'd been calling to his buddies for help for more than an hour. When the enemy retreated, though, they left the wounded man, whose cries would fade and then return, louder than ever. Finally one GI blurted, 'Why don't we put the bastard out of his misery!' He and a couple of other men slowly moved out toward the sound. We heard of several bursts fire and then no more cries from the wounded man.

"In the wake of some Sherman tanks, I returned to the platoon CP. It seemed we had successfully repulsed the enemy once more. At the inn, the platoon commander shared a bottle of scotch with those of us there to celebrate what we figured was a victory. We mixed the scotch with some canned grapefruit juice; why, I'll never know. I was in the kitchen preparing some hot chocolate when a GI sergeant burst through the main entrance to warn us of enemy tanks headed our way and only half a mile away. He left hurriedly, saying he had to warn others. We heard his jeep pull out and prepared to protect ourselves. Division HQ advised us to hold our positions.

"Our hastily formed strategy was to hide in the cellar, wait for the tanks to pass our post believing the darkened, shell-battered inn was deserted. We hoped then to join some other units and surprise the Germans from the rear. Obviously, it was both a brave and naive plan, because our heaviest weapon was a .50caliber machine gun, not very effective against tanks. It wasn't long before we heard the tanks rumbling and squeaking outside our building. They moved around the perimeter of the inn, but to our dismay, several shut down their engines and parked. Moments later, the sound of heavy boots came tromping on the floor overhead, guttural voices and loud laughter followed as they found some of our personal stuff we hadn't been able to carry with us into the cellar. It dawned on us that the GI Paul Revere was probably a Jerry scout, disguised in a GI uniform and driving an American jeep. He was checking out where Americans were and at the same time encouraging them to take off.

"Around midnight, the noise upstairs quieted down to snores and barely audible talk. Sitting amid abandoned crockery, we hardly dared to move or even breathe. A muffled radio inquiry to division HQ brought the response, 'Hold your positions.' They claimed help would come but there would be no further radio contact. At dawn, the outside door of the cellar was kicked open by a heavily armed German. A sleeping GI awakened by the intruder yelled, 'Hey, guys. They found us!' We were herded out by a handful of Germans with burp guns. As we marched to the front of the inn, we saw at least two huge tanks facing the building with their awesome 88s pointed toward the cellar. They had played cat and mouse with us all night long."

John Chernitsky, from the antitank company of the 28th Division, had hardly arrived at Wiltz in Luxembourg to serve on the faculty instructing fledgling noncoms, when orders directed teachers and pupils to rejoin their respective units. Enemy fire, however, blocked some roads. Chernitsky and others returned to Wiltz. "I stayed in Wiltz with the organized riflemen who were made up of members of the band, clerks, cooks, bakers, and any men caught between Wiltz and Clervaux. After an artillery barrage, I was hit in the back with shrapnel. I covered the wound with sulfa powder from the packet on my cartridge belt and wrapped my undershirt around my back." Chernitsky and the improvised rifle troops dug in to resist the enemy advance.

When the attack began on 16 December most of the top brass regarded it as at most a retaliation for the attack by the 99th Division and elements of the 2d Infantry Division toward the Roer dams or perhaps a gambit to relieve the pressure generated by Patton's advance into the Saar Basin. After Eisenhower attended the wedding of his valet he presided over a reception at his house, dined with associates, and played several rubbers of bridge before retiring. However, he seemed to have been the first to have grasped the possible seriousness of the challenge. He began mobilizing troops to meet the growing Ardennes challenge.

In his diary of 16 December, Maj. Gen. Everett Hughes from the SHAEF staff wrote, "Brad [Omar Bradley] says Germans have started a big counterattack toward Hodges. Very calm about it. Seemed routine from his lack of emphasis." His demeanor may have seemed unruffled but by midafternoon of that day, Bradley telephoned Patton and told him to send the 10th Armored Division, then in reserve near the Luxembourg-France border, into the Ardennes. The Third Army commander protested the loss of one of his outfits: "There's no major threat up there. Hell, it's probably nothing more than a spoiling attack to throw us off balance down here and make us stop this offensive." Bradley, however, was adamant. Furthermore, he arranged to shift the 7th Armored Division, which was also in reserve, to give Hodges more punch.

By 17 December, however, any doubts about the seriousness of the enemy attack vanished. The enemy forces quickly carved out a forty-mile deep, sixty-mile wide bulge in the American lines. On the third day of the German breakthrough, the 106th Division's 422d and 423d Infantry Regiments appeared to be encircled and the vital town of St.-Vith menaced. The latter regiment received orders to attack toward its rear. The strategy called for the enemy to be trapped between the infantrymen and the 7th Armored Division, summoned from reserve, in the rear. Colonel Charles Cavender who led the 423d supposedly mumbled, "My poor men—they'll be cut to pieces."

The maneuver required the foot soldiers to shift their positions in the dark. Lt. Alan Jones, Jr. said, "As night fell, we trekked through the Alf Valley. It was very muddy, very dark, the woods heavy, just terribly tough going. The transportation bogged down. There was enormous confusion." The Germans complicated the movement with artillery salvos. The leader of Jones's battalion was killed by shrapnel. Jones recalled, "The other two battalions went on the attack but ours seemed to lose direction. No one seemed to know what to do; finally the exec moved them out. I gathered some loose ends, put them into a company formation for tactical purposes. We had tankers, artillery, crewmen, infantry.

"By the time we were organized and caught up to the 1st Battalion, the word was to surrender. 'Tear your weapons apart and throw the pieces about.' I couldn't believe it. My battalion just had not been in that much fighting." Jones remarked his outfit was low on information and while requests for supplies dropped by air began on 17 December, the layers of approvals required before the first props would spin delayed any efforts. Inexplicably, the Air Corps handled all such missions from airfields in Britain which added flight time and interposed the volatile cross Channel weather. When C-47s finally took off and arrived in Belgium, the local airdrome said it was "too busy" to accommodate them. No fighter protection could be given and the transports with their cargo had no map coordinates for a drop. Col. George Deschenaux, commander of the 423d Regiment, convinced like Cavender, that his people would be slaughtered if they continued to fight, also surrendered. By 19 December, the exultant Germans counted more than 7,000 American soldiers from the 106th Division as prisoners.

The 7th Armored Division which rushed to support the 106th Division, also reeled under the onslaught and some units broke down into a disorganized retreat. Alan Jones, Sr., the 106th commander, decided St. Vith could not be defended and he abandoned it. Now fully aware of the seriousness of the German thrusts, Eisenhower and his staff immediately rushed whatever forces available to plug gaps. The 101st Airborne Division under its assistant commander, Gen. Anthony McAuliffe occupied the major road hub to the south, the town of Bastogne. They barely beat a strong German force to Bastogne which surrounded the place and began a dramatic siege. The 82d Airborne moved to block the foe at the Salm River, north of Bastogne and west of St. Vith. A third airborne unit, the 517th Regiment, which had been resting from its labors in the south of France joined the effort to shut down the enemy advance. The only good news lay on the northern shoulder of the Bulge where the American 1st, 2d, 8th, 9th and 99th Divisions, while in some cases absorbing considerable punishment, kept the enemy from widening his advance.

Frank South, the medic with the 2nd Ranger Battalion recalled, "The woefully understrength battalion was attached to the 8th Division and placed in defensive positions in and around Simmerath on the Sigfried Line. Headquarters and the Aid Station were located in a former German hospital that was under intermittent artillery fire. Of course the hospital's belfry was used as an OP from time to time. It was assumed that we were expected to hold our position should the push come to involve us. Most of our activity consisted of reconnoitering and combat patrolling to discomfit the enemy and take prisoners for intelligence purposes We had some men killed and a few wounded but the level was relatively low."

When the center of the American front collapsed, Eisenhower, on 19 December convened a council of top commanders and sought to set an upbeat tone to the session with an opening remark, "The present situation is to be regarded as an opportunity for us and not of disaster." Patton seemed to think similarly, saying, "Hell, let's have the guts to let the sons of bitches go all the way to Paris. Then we'll really cut 'em and chew 'em up." Some revisionist historians have suggested the Ardennes collapse was a shrewd piece of strategy that exposed the German armies to destruction. That viewpoint does not square either with the panicky reaction to the penetration nor the awful casualties inflicted upon Americans caught in the maelstrom.

The best option for relief of Bastogne and a counterattack lay with Patton's Third Army. The supreme commander asked the man-of-the-hour, "When will you be able to attack?"

"The morning of December 21st," answered Patton, obviously relishing an opportunity for a heroic achievement.

"Don't be fatuous, George," reproved Eisenhower, concerned for Patton's cockiness. "If you try to go that early, you won't have all three divisions ready and you'll go piecemeal. You will start on the 22nd." Eisenhower even allowed that if necessary the Third Army might begin a day later. Patton had promised Eisenhower he could begin to lift the siege of Bastogne within two days. His genius for putting the armor and troops on the road achieved its zenith.

Carl Ulsaker recalled a moment when his 90th Division outfit was moving forward and a procession of vehicles came down the road. "Someone said, 'Look, there goes Lucky 6.' Lucky 6 was the radio code for General Patton. Sure enough his jeep was passing by with Old Blood and Guts sitting in the right front seat behind a machine gun mounted on the dash. Suddenly, the Jeep braked to a halt and backed up to a point opposite where we stood. 'My God, I thought. 'We failed to salute and he's going to bawl us out.' We popped to attention and saluted tardily.

"Patton dismounted and approached us on foot, head thrust forward and face set in his famous scowl. Gesturing with his right hand, in his high pitched voice he said, 'Men, Von Runstedt's nuts are in the meat grinder and I have the handle in my hand."

To the north, a motley of German troops, some in standard field gray, some wearing white snow camouflage garments, and still others dressed in pieces of American uniforms with boots stripped from prisoners or yanked from deadmens' feet, battered the GIs ensconced along Elsenborn Ridge on the northern shoulder of the German salient. The Germans brought to bear whatever armor and artillery they could muster. Victory here would open up a northern road route to the Meuse. The Americans enjoyed the advantage of favorable terrain to entrench the troops and an ever increasing superiority of artillery. Ben Nawrocki with the handful of men left from B Company, labored over his foxhole along the crest of the ridge. "We had only our rifles and the ammo we could carry. The ground was frozen hard, like rock. There weren't any entrenching tools. We used mess kits, mess knives, bayonets and helmets to dig in. It was frantic, hard work but with shells flying all the time, we had to have shelter.

"We could see them shelling and attacking to our right rear in the Malmedy, St. Vith area. They were coming at us through the deep draws leading to Elsenborn Ridge. We kept beating them off. We had a good open field of fire and a lot of artillery to help us. A day or two after the 99th dug in on Elsenborn Ridge, two hundred Germans with tanks came toward our lines. The 394th Regiment was in front. The Germans carried their arms in sling position on their shoulders and waved white handkerchief flags as if to signal surrender. They were told to drop their arms. They refused and kept coming. Obviously they wanted to get closer and overrun us.

"Our officers readied all our fire power along with artillery. After they didn't respond to repeated demands to drop arms and surrender, all of the fire power on the front opened up. They tried to and did run over some of the fox holes with their tanks. But our fire power and artillery really chewed them up. There were pieces of bodies and tanks flying all over. When the fire lifted, nothing moved. They all died. The tanks and equipment destroyed."

The only surviving platoon sergeant from his company, Nawrocki became first sergeant. "I made my first morning report on a piece of toilet paper on Dec. 21. It accounted for one officer and 13 men of Co. B, 393rd Infantry. We had 210 men on the morning of December 16th. Later, we started to get back some of Co. B. who had mixed in with other troops and fought.

But there still weren't many left. We received replacements almost daily. One batch of about 50 arrived, flown to Europe from the States. Some had very little training. I told them to dig in and they just stood there in the open when a few rounds of 88s struck nearby, wounding six. The rest started to dig in, as we used sticks of dynamite to break through the frozen crust."

The U.S. big guns continued to exact a huge toll. On December 21, they dumped a cloudburst of 10,000 rounds. The German dead piled up in awesome numbers; an early count by a graves registration unit added up 782 corpses in the Elsenborn area. Furthermore, as the enemy backed off from its assault that day, it left behind the broken remains of 47 tanks and tank destroyers. The stalwart efforts of the 1st Division squelched a pivotal series of assaults around the village of Butgenbach. At Dom Butgenbach, two miles south of the town of Butgenbach, members of the division's 26th Infantry Antitank Company, wielding their underpowered, undersized, 57 mm cannons blew away a number of tanks.

To the immediate south of the stalled elements of Sepp Dietrich's Sixth SS Panzer Army, the situation threatened disaster for the Americans. The enemy rapidly exploited their breakthrough of the line manned by elements of the 106th and 28th Divisions. They swept on a west-northwest course that would both widen and deepen the salient. A rag-tag jumble of GIs from the 589th FA, the 203d Antiaircraft Battalion and some soldiers from the 7th Armored attempted to set up a roadblock at a crossroads known as Baraque de Fraiture. They were no match for onrushing German armor. As the German tide flowed around St. Vith and Bastogne, the desperate U.S. commanders tossed in more blue chips. General James Gavin, typically made his own personal reconnaissance. He was concerned that the loss of the crossroads could allow the enemy armor that his 82nd Airborne held at bay at Trois Ponts might be able to bypass the paratroopers and the soldiers pulling back from St. Vith. As a result of his survey, Gavin dispatched the 2nd Battalion of the 82nd Airborne's 325th Glider Regiment to strengthen the defenses at Baraque de Fraiture. Company F, led by Captain Junior Woodruff drew the major assignment for the defense. Since Woodruff commanded the only complete tactical unit on the scene, he assumed direction for the overall strategy. To the GIs from the 325th, the battlefield now became known as Woody's Crossroads. Woodruff's GIs took instant courses in weapons shared with nine other fragmented outfits. They learned to operate AA guns, 75 mms on the tanks and 76mms of tank destroyers.

"Captain Woody was a fine officer in both garrison and combat," remembered Joe Colmer, an ex-navy man who found himself drafted into the army and a member of Company F. "He was a natural leader and the kind of guy you wanted to follow. His people had such faith in him that while we were in Holland, there was a fellow close to me who had his arm blown off. I gave him his shot of morphine but he asked me to tell Woody to come talk to him. Most guys in his shape would have been hollering for a medic instead. When we moved into the crossroads, around noon of December 22, there were only a few troops around, a couple of Sherman tanks and some half tracks. The soldiers were mostly from the 106th and they struck me as really tired and beaten. My platoon dug foxholes in an arc around the farm houses from the northwest to southeast, about 50 yards out front. It was fairly quiet that night. The next morning, however, the Germans began dropping occasional mortar rounds, a few artillery shells, and stepped up their patrols."

Along with Woodruff's crew, Companies E and G also assumed responsibility for holding the crossroads, occupying a ridge three quarters of a mile to the northeast. Leonard Weinstein was among G Company as it hiked down an almost impassable trail choked with rocks, thick roots and mud. "Our positions were basically two lines of foxholes. There were no hot meals and we rotated, taking turns to go back to a nearby small building where you could warm up before a small fire. I was in the second line of foxholes on slightly higher ground. One night the enemy slipped in close enough to the first line to kill two of our men with either a bayonet or knife. The victims were the oldest and youngest guys in the company who occupied a single hole. "

Combat Command A of the 7th Armored Division, the outfit that included the 40th Tank Battalion with gunner Jerry Nelson, committed a platoon from the 643rd Tank Destroyer Battalion (Towed). The unit of four three-inch guns pulled by half tracks and 40 crewmen faced its combat debut. When some 3rd Armored Divsion Sherman tanks, headed in the opposite direction, passed the tank destroyers, ammunition handler Edgar Kreft heard one of the men on the Shermans holler there was "nobody between you and the Germans." The platoon reached its assigned spot and dug in. At dawn, the enemy blanketed the hapless antitank crews with mortars and artillery, killing and wounded a number of men. German grenadiers overran the Americans who lost 18 killed, wounded and missing. Kreft became a POW.

Actually, the Germans were poised to overwhelm the small garrison for two days. Only an acute shortage of fuel for their halftracks and other armor delayed the launch. But supplies arrived on the night of December 22, within hours after Colemar and Weinstein put in their appearances.

When the Germans struck the following day, the attack battered the thin ranks of GIs. The 589th artillerymen got the word to get out any way they could. Two assaults by foot soldiers were beaten off but the 2nd SS Panzer tanks, in a fierce encounter devastated the American armor.

"I think it was about five in the afternoon," says Colmer, "when they started the all out drive. We were completely overrun in 30 minutes. They had our tanks on fire. I was in a barn with three or four others and we were firing out of windows when the place started to burn. We stepped out when the place started to cave in. Someone mentioned the idea of trying to surrender but from what we could see they were shooting at everyone. I told the guys they could either try to give up or make a run for it. I headed across the road and was hit in the leg. I dove under a blown down pine tree. Hiding next to me was a man from the 106th. His name was Cook. We lay there for about 20 minutes as the Germans walked all around us. By this time it was getting dark. It had been hazy every day and that decreased visibility also. The shooting died down and the Germans began taking their tanks across an open field towards a wooded area about 1,000 yards off. Foot soldiers followed the tanks in small groups of two or three and the tanks were spread out with spaces of maybe 50 yards or so between each. After the last group passed, Cook and I took off our helmets, turned up our overcoat collars and followed the Germans across the field. Some of the Germans were wearing GI overcoats so they paid no attention to us. We passed one of our tanks, still burning with its ammo exploding.

"I was limping badly but could still walk. Once we entered the woods, we angled off to our right in the direction of some artillery flashes we took to be friendly. After about two hours, we came upon one of our engineering outfits. They were occupying a barn and some houses. They bandaged my leg, gave us food. We stayed the night with them, then caught a jeep that took us right to the 82nd command post in Spa. I was sent to a hospital and then to England. I never learned what became of Cook." Only 44 men, from the original 116 in Company F at the cross roads escaped. The rest were KIA or added to the bag of prisoners.

The GIs assembled at the crossroads, enjoined not to retreat, were committed to a hopeless mission. But their sacrifice, like that of Lyle Bouck with his I & R platoon in front of Lanzerath and a rag tag band led by Captain Tom Riggs atop the Prummerberg in front of St. Vith, bought the time, hours or days that saved tens of thousands of their fellow Americans. Baraque de Fraiture, like many similar engagements in the Ardennes, was a kind of Bunker Hill; the enemy conquered the turf but at an exorbitant cost.

The fall of Baraque de Fraiture opened Highway N 15 to the advance of the Germans. In the path of Nazi forces lay some tankers from the Seventh Armored Division, and a portion of the 3rd Armored Division led by Col. Sam Hogan. Arnold Albero, a rifleman with the unit said, "We moved out on December 19 in three columns. I think it must have been the coldest winter in my life. The roads were icy, muddy, the weather foggy in spots and always numbing cold. We lost vehicles that became stuck in the mud and all we could do was just push them to the side. We kept bitching that the column didn't seem to know where it was going. We sure in hell didn't know. On the way we picked up stragglers from other outfits which had been overrun. We also heard rumors that Germans in American uniforms were trying to disrupt our operations. It was a wild and crazy night. When dawn came we were relieved to have daylight but still confused about where we were and what was happening.

"We were now told to head towards Houffalize [a crossroads town on the Ourthe River between Bastogne and Leige] and secure the roads leading to it. But we were beaten back by a good, strong defense and retreated as our gas and ammo ran low. We moved into the town of Beffe, further west. The enemy [the 116th Panzers] engaged us with tanks, infantry supported by artillery and mortars. Forced further to the west, Task Force Hogan settled in a Marcouray, an Ourthe River village on high ground. We could look out and see the Germans moving around us. Gradually, they enveloped us while we fought back attacks and beat off their patrols."

Task Force Hogan, with Arnold Albero, was completely surrounded once the Germans forded the Ourthe behind the Americans. A state of siege commenced, Bastogne in miniature. Instead of thwarting the enemy advance after the conquest of Baraque de Fraiture, Arnold Albero and his 3d Armored GIs faced their own destruction. Food, ammunition, and medical supplies dwindled. Task Force Hogan tightened its cartridge belts and waited for air resupply and a promise that division would try to relieve the beleaguered garrison. Two attempts to parachute supplies failed because of an inability to pinpoint the drop area.

There were, of course, far many more Americans encircled in the vital hub, Bastogne. The Germans strengthened their band of infantrymen, armor, and artillery around the Belgian village and on 22 December, two German officers from the 26th Volksgrenadier Division drove up with a white flag flying. Stopped at an outpost, they announced themselves as *parlementaires*—negotiators bearing a surrender demand.

While the Wehrmacht major and captain awaited a response, their formal paper inscribed with a call for capitulation was brought to Gen. Anthony McAuliffe at the CP. In the absence of Gen. Maxwell Taylor, McAuliffe commanded the Screaming Eagles. The document from the emissaries stated: "Unconditional surrender is the only method of avoiding complete annihilation of the surrounded American units. Two hours' grace is granted hereby. Should this offer be refused, an artillery corps and six groups of heavy antiaircraft guns stand ready to annihilate the American forces." The message also appealed to the American commander to avoid further suffering for the 3,500 civilians as well as his one troops."

McAuliffe's chief of staff, Col. Ned Moore, broke the news. "We have a surrender ultimatum from the Germans."

McAuliffe asked, "You mean they want us to surrender?" When Moore confirmed that was indeed the message, McAuliffe, with a number of pressing problems, matter-of-factly reacted, "Oh, nuts!" Subsequently, when McAuliffe initiated a discussion about an appropriate response no one suggested they acquiesce. Still, McAuliffe asked, "What should I say?"

Colonel Harry Kinnard, of the headquarters staff, claimed, "I piped up and said, 'Well, General, I think what you said when we first told you about the message would be hard to beat.'"

Seemingly puzzled, McAuliffe inquired, "What do you mean?"

"You said nuts." According to Kinnard the others smiled and agreed.

McAuliffe took a plain piece of paper and scrawled: "To the German Commander: Nuts!" and appended his signature, A.C. McAULIFFE, AMERICAN COMMANDER.

The message confounded the emissaries. They asked whether "Nuts" meant an affirmative or negative reply. Col. Bud Harper, regimental commander, their escort from the outpost, informed them, "It's decidedly negative. It means go to hell."

When the men of Bastogne heard of their leader's response they were almost universally enthusiastic. As paratroopers, trained to drop behind enemy lines and fight their way out, the situation in Bastogne was not extraordinary. In addition to the full complement of the 101st, as Kinnard noted, the holders of Bastogne had recruited additional people passing through, whether in disorderly retreat or on the basis of orders. The terrain provided adequate defensive protection and there was an unusually heavy concentration of artillery available.

Word that Patton's Third Army hoped to break through in time to celebrate Christmas further boosted morale in Bastogne. The major problems for the Bastogne forces were shortages of supplies and the inability to evacuate a growing number of casualties from air raids, artillery fire, and assaults. Poor flying weather interfered with air drops and protection against Luftwaffe marauders. The skies began to clear, however. And on 23 December, Pathfinder Sergeant Jack Agnew, parachuted into Bastogne to join his fellow Screaming Eagles. With several companions, Agnew had been sent back to England to participate in experimental techniques and equipment. "When we were first alerted to the problems in the Ardennes, it was nothing new to us. Starting in the Normandy campaign, the 101st was surrounded every time it jumped. We happened to be training with a Pathfinder troop carrier group attached to the Air Corps. The living conditions were great, the food great, and we had passes to London.

"But on December 22, we drew chutes and all the armament we could get from the Air Corps people. We left on a jump mission to land in the Bastogne encirclement and guide in vital supplies. Just as we were ready to stand up, the mission was recalled. I was quite concerned about our friends in the 506th since we heard they had gone into Bastogne with no more than two or three clips of ammo, little clothing and food. We left England again on the following day and completed our combat jump into Bastogne. We started to set up our pathfinder headquarters and were blown out of the first two locations. We finally established ourselves and prepared to guide the first resupply planes in."

Although the hoped-for dash to the Meuse was far behind schedule the German breakthrough continued to expand, inflicting massive casualties, swallowing up chunks of territory, and forcing the insertion of more defenders. GIs trapped by the enemy attack retreated through an avenue of escape temporarily secured by the 30th Infantry and 82d Airborne Divisions.

Among the units engaged in the fluid defense, designed to slow the Germans while preserving their own hides, was the 14th Tank Battalion from the 9th Armored Division. It had been at St.-Vith, then Ligneuville and staved off significant gains for a day and a half before the elements of the 7th Armored replaced the 14th. Dee Paris, a tank platoon leader from the 14th coped with a maelstrom of confusion. "We'd be told what unit was on our flanks but couldn't establish any contact with the alleged units there. At one point my tanks were at least 200 yards apart. You could have driven an army between them. We were told there were Germans in American uniforms. When members of the 106th, fleeing from the front, reached us, we invited them to eat with us. A Belgian civilian pointed out a man in our chow line and said he was a German in American uniform. They took him away but I don't know what happened to him. I didn't see any German prisoners killed. But there is a moment when they start to surrender and you keep firing. There are at least two reasons. You don't trust them and you are so hyped on killing someone before they kill you that you just keep firing. There is a fine line between killing prisoners and killing men who would become prisoners if they weren't shot down."

By 22 December, the enemy seemed on the verge of swallowing up Dee Paris and his platoon. "One night I heard a noise on a nearby road. I contacted Paul Fisher and we jointly investigated. We found a horse-drawn wagon with straw in the back, driven by a man dressed as a farmer. I was suspicious; why would anyone be there at midnight? When I pulled the straw aside, I found a large army thermos container used to take hot food to the troops. That was my first knowledge that there were German soldiers in our rear. We shot the driver."

They prepared for a sprint to a more secure area. Paris had parked his tank in a barnyard, alongside a manure pile, disguising its silhouette with poles, while the others from the platoon sat on the road, 100 to 150 yards apart. "During the night, we had to take care of the occupant of the house who had insisted on repeatedly going to the barn with a lantern. When daylight came, I gave the order to pull out. I then discovered that we had sunk into the ground; the tank was frozen in the earth. We couldn't move. I radioed one of my tanks to swing into the barnyard and knock us loose. I alerted the crew to hang on. It took two good hits to get us free.

"Out on the road I started to lead the platoon. Suddenly a round passed a yard behind my tank. I wondered how long it would take the antitank gunner to reload. I waited a few seconds, and then shouted on the intercom, 'Stop!' My driver, Ray Waelchi, immediately halted and the next round passed a yard in front of the tank. I waited briefly and shouted, 'Kick it in the ass—give her hell!' Another round missed us. I still don't know how an antitank gunner only about 200 yards away could miss hitting a tank broadside."

On the ground, Arnold Albero continued to live in a hole with some wreckage from a wall around him. "We made deeper and bigger pits for the tanks and artillery. But unlike the Hurtgen Forest, there was nothing to cover the foxholes. My fear occasionally made me nauseous. I drank a lot of water, ate the snow. The thing was there was no place to run and hide. The noncoms had a lot to do with keeping us going. But nobody pulled rank. There was no saluting. Everyone knew what had to be done. We knew that the Germans had sent a surrender ultimatum to Colonel Hogan and he rejected it. We didn't expect to surrender. We'd picked up rumors that the Germans were shooting their prisoners at random. The unspoken word was to go down fighting and take as many of the bastards as you can with you."

Rebuffed by Hogan, the opposition charged the defenders huddled in Marcouray. Said Albero, "The first time they came at us up a slope. I was working a .50 caliber machine gun mounted in a jeep. I had an open view and I saw them fall. Luckily, we fended them off. The most terrifying moment was an attack with armored vehicles that broke through a roadblock where our tank's gun was frozen and couldn't shoot. Once they passed that point, they started shooting like crazy while driving through the town. However, one of our other tanks knocked them out, scattering German soldiers all over the place. We captured the ones who weren't wounded.

"After that incident, they pounded us mainly with artillery fire, guns of all calibers. We couldn't understand why they did not continue to go all out against us. We would have been overrun; our ammunition was running low; we were out of gasoline. It may be that they were being hit from other areas than ours. Also they may not have wanted to slow their advance, so they just rolled around us and waited for us to give up. The stalemate dragged on. Finally through radio contact the word came no help was on the way. We were on our own; we'd have to fight our way out, leave on foot. When they told us to destroy our vehicles and the weapons we couldn't take, rather than let the enemy use them, that's when I learned what it is to be really scared."

The XVIII Corps commanded by Maj. Gen. Matthew B. Ridgway, had recognized that the loss of Baraque de Fraiture imperiled the vital crossroads town Manhay and then Liége itself. To plug the gap on Highway N 15 from the crossroads to the village, Ridgway arranged for a group of units from the 7th Armored's Combat Command A to assume responsibility for Manhay and its environs. The task force's most potent weapon was its 40th Tank Battalion. A bit more than a mile southeast of Manhay, the Shermans from C Company deployed along the critical road. Their view down the highway from which the enemy would come, was blocked after a short distance by a curve that disappeared into the trees. In one of the C Company tanks, gunner Jerry Nelson, still grieving over the death of his tank commander, Truman Van Tine, felt the loss even more keenly as he developed an active dislike for the replacement. "Burris was friendly enough but that's all. For example, in a Sherman, two guys can lay on their sides in the loader's area and try to sleep. Against the wall there is a small gas engine that runs at night to charge the batteries. Somehow the gas leaked out on Burris who was sleeping there. Actually, it was probably because he moved a lever. But whatever, he woke me and made me take the wet spot while he took my dry one. I could live with that but he showed himself to be an asshole later.

"At dusk, Sergeant Freeman's tank and ours under Burris were set up with us slightly behind Freeman and on the opposite side of the road, looking straight down it. Around 10:00 P.M. we heard them coming, mostly track noise. On the radio, we listened to Freeman, who would see them first, say to his gunner, 'I'll tell you when to shoot. Just a little more—okay Shoot! Shoot! Shoot!'

But there was no shot. We never found out why. Burris asked me, 'Can you see them?' I answered no. He said, 'I'll jump out and fire the .50 caliber on top of the turret. Watch the tracers. You're already pointing right anyway.'

"The .50 was only half loaded, as most of the guns were before they were really needed. Burris yelled, 'It's frozen.' He couldn't pull back the bolt. He told me to start firing and we did. Right into the blackness at point-blank. We were hitting something with our cannon. We got off six or seven rounds, traversing a little each time so we didn't always shoot in the same hole. I looked around for Burris for direction but he was gone. So were the two guys down below, the drivers. I yelled to the loader to bail out.

"As I hit the road, a tank appeared from the brush to the side. I thought it was a German who somehow got through the woods but then a flare went up and I knew he was one of us. I tried to run fast and grab on from behind. But I couldn't. Then a single round, probably from the lead German tank let loose at the one I'd tried to jump on. I'll never know how close it was to me, but it seemed to me that I could feel something go by me and I can't describe the kind of noise it made. If that had hit me I would be, as Paul Harvey says, twenty years old, forever.'

Bleak as prospects may have appeared to the cold, hungry, embattled GIs, the situation for the enemy was rapidly deteriorating. In the all-out sprint toward the Meuse, the crack 2d *Panzer* Division, bypassing Bastogne, had by 22 December, advanced to within five miles of Dinant, where binoculars could pick out the objects of the *Füehrer's* desires, the Meuse bridges. A pair of British armored brigades guarded these strategic spans. In a skillful piece of work, the 3d Royal Tank Regiment destroyed lead enemy elements blocking passage of the armor behind. Long-range artillery then hammered the gridlocked tanks.

The 4th Armored Division, leading the rescue by Patton's Third Army, struck at the outposts of the 2d Panzer Division. Robert Johnson recalled that while approaching Luxenbourg his unit halted for the night. "Each of us stood patrol duty around the site. Near midnight, I wandered too near the German line and was grabbed. They took me to a house with a cellar where an officer tried to make me give him information. He hanged [sic] me by my ankles from a beam. He'd kick me and yell his questions. I never gave in to his torture. At dawn, as the 4th Armored moved forward, the Germans left, just took off, leaving me hanging. My own crew found me, stood looking at me, and laughing. They finally cut me down and I returned to duty." According to Johnson, the enemy tanks, short on ammunition and fuel, offered increasingly feeble resistance. "We walked through them like plowing new ground."

On the southern shoulder of the Bulge, the German seventh Army had never accomplished its mission, to protect the left flank of von Manteuffel's Fifth Army. They stumbled upon the rock of the 4th Infantry Division whose isolated units refused to yield key sites. As a consequence, the German Seventh Army failed to push far enough to deter Patton's Third Army charging out of the south. And by 22 December, in fact, two Third Army contributions, the 26th and 80th Divisions had begun to pummel the German infantrymen.

To the northwest, most of the 1st Battalion of the 517th Parachute Regiment under Bill Boyle, sandwiched between a pair of regiments belonging to the 75th Infantry Division, moved against the enemy surrounding Task Force Hogan and Arnold Albero at Marcouray. The line taken by Boyle's paratroopers stretched between Hotton and Soy. The battalion counterattacked toward Hotton to relieve GIs pinned there and ensure the safety of rear echelon units at Soy. B Company acted as the spearhead.

According to Pfc. Mel Biddle, on the morning of 23 December, "My platoon leader said, 'Biddle, out front.'" That simple order made Mel Biddle lead scout through dense woods and underbrush as well as open ground.

Snow lay eight inches deep as Biddle inched forward in the frigid air, crawling, then getting to his feet when he could detect no enemy. As he traveled over a field with less cover, several Germans, concealed in the brush, fired at him. Biddle flopped to the snow, wriggled toward the enemy position. From only twenty yards away, Biddle used his M1 to kill the trio who had shot at him.

Biddle doggedly pushed forward another 200 yards. He ambushed a hostile machine-gun position, dispatching the two-man crew with his rifle. Still farther on, the Anderson, Indiana, twenty-one-year-old crept up until he could lob hand grenades into another automatic-weapon nest. Biddle signaled his mates that it was somewhat safer to advance. As they backed him up, the enemy focused on him with rifles and a machine gun. Again Biddle, rapidly reloading, dropped one infantryman, scooted to another position as bullets ripped into the spot he'd just left, killed a second adversary thirty yards away. A desperate grenadier swung his machine pistol in a 360 degree arc, spraying the brush with bullets. Biddle, face down, waited until the fusillade swung by, then slew his eleventh enemy. He tossed his final grenade at the machine gunners and followed up with a successful, one-man charge, leaving the gunner and assistant dead; only an ammo bearer escaped.

"There was plenty of light during the day. I had great vision. I saw the faces of all of the German soldiers. I saw each of them, before they saw me and from a very short range. That was especially true in several instances when I was only about six feet away in the underbrush." The scout heard the sounds of armor and volunteered, with three others, to investigate. Bursts from an enemy patrol convinced the group it would be folly to continue. But Biddle chose to infiltrate the enemy positions under the cover of darkness.

For several hours he crept about, determining the enemy weapon emplacements, the deployment of the troops, and location of a pair of tanks. During the course of his nocturnal prowl, Nazi sentries and patrols challenged the paratrooper but their shots missed. In one instance, a searcher stepped on his hand. Biddle stifled the urge to cry out. After the enemy moved on, he slunk away. "I was out there for a very long time but I never thought about eating. I thought how cold I was, especially my fingers. I wasn't sure I could pull the trigger of my rifle. I thought I would try sticking a finger through and pull it with my left hand."

In the early hours of the morning on 24 December, the companies of the 517th, acting on the intelligence gathered by Biddle, struck again, with Biddle repeating his role as the point. American armor, aware of the precise location of the pair of German tanks, knocked both out. When a machine gun threatened to wither the attack, Biddle maneuvered himself to within fifty yards, killed the crew and two soldiers in support. Christmas Eve descended with Hotton's garrison preserved, Biddle was credited with having killed seventeen Germans after firing only twenty-nine rounds from his M1. The performance eventually won him a Medal of Honor. "I had reached a point where I would rather die than be thought of as a coward. I was terrified most of the time but there were two or three moments when I had no fear. That's when you can really operate."

Having lost their tank, Jerry Nelson and the rest of his crew sat out an engagement on Christmas Eve, a total debacle for C Company. The opposition now hurled themselves upon the smaller and outnumbered American armor along the Manhay road. Part of the German force included the Mark V, a forty-five-ton monster with a huge gun and extremely thick armor plate. Command and control, the watchwords of military tacticians, evaporated for the Americans that night in front of Manhay. Aware of the weight being hurled at the defenses, the strategists reluctantly agreed to pull back the outposts. But in the darkness, orders failed to reach some units. Others confused German armor with American or thought only infantrymen with rockets threatened them, rather than highly effective tankers. A bulldozer had neatly dug deep holes for the Shermans manned by Nelson's comrades. Theoretically, the emplacements in the snow lowered the silhouette. But according to one of the tank commanders, Sgt. Donald Hondorp, the Shermans "were standing out like black targets on a sheet of white because the rich black dirt excavated was in stark contrast." Furthermore, the pits curtailed swift maneuvering for the tanks. The enemy armor surprised C Company; some crews evacuated their tanks without getting off a round. Others left, then returned to gamely resist. A German tank commander borrowed from the American lexicon: "It was a turkey shoot." In the end, the nine Shermans from C Company lay wrecked and burning while the Germans overran Manhay. It would prove worse than a Pyrrhic victory, however. Cooler heads dissuaded General Ridgway from an almost suicidal counterattack. The winners, occupying Manhay, discovered themselves pinned by incessant artillery. Only those huddled beneath thick armor would survive.

Kampfgruppe Peiper, remained trapped in the town of Stavelot where a combination of engineers, stragglers, and Jabos barred it from crossing crucial bridges. Low on fuel, the Nazi unit no longer doubted its reversal of fortunes, becoming the prey. Unable to ford or bridge the Salm River and Lienne Creek with his panzers, Peiper, in a farmhouse at La Gleize, watched in despair as the American artillery shattered his redoubts, blasted his armor, and killed or wounded his troops. Several U.S. counterattacks, notably at Cheneaux, wreaked heavy casualties on both sides. Sometime after midnight, in the early hours of 24 December, *Kampfgruppe Peiper's* flak tank section leader Sgt. Karl Wortmann was awakened by a messenger insistently crying "Merry Christmas. Merry Christmas." Befuddled at first by the greeting,

Wortmann learned it was a code word directing him to blow up his vehicles and follow the escape column.

Bill Dunfee, as part of the 505th Parachute Regiment, from the moment of arrival east of the Salm River near Trois Ponts on 21 December, was, in his words, "having a very hard time with the remainder of the 1st SS Panzer Division"—Peiper's men. The American paratroopers initially ventured east of the Salm but the sheer force of numbers drove them back to a few yards of river line. To break out Peiper, the 2d SS Panzer Division advanced toward the Salm from the south. The Americans had planned to blow a key bridge near Petite-Langlir but the enemy seized the span before it could be destroyed, making it available for the oncoming panzers. A daring raid by engineers under the leadership of Maj. J. C. H. Lee Jr. penetrated enemy lines, hooked up explosives and detonated the bridge while German vehicles crossed it. Says Dunfee, "We were told that a German motorcycle, sidecar, officer, and driver went airborne along with the bridge. We 'Doggies' loved it; we were more than a little jealous of anyone who rode into battle.

"About this time my platoon leader, Lieutenant Carter, ordered me to provide riflemen to accompany a patrol led by an armored officer. We would be riding a four-wheeled armored scout car mounting a .50-caliber machine gun, pulling a two-wheeled trailer loaded with land mines. The mission was to mine an approach to a bridge. I decided Oscar Newborn and I would volunteer, since we both had BARs—never my authorized weapon, but in combat you picked the weapon you liked best. My feeling was there was no point endangering others; between us we had the firepower of four riflemen.

"We took off about midnight with the lieutenant, driver, and gunner in the scout car, Oscar and I on the trailer. We moved rather slowly, watching for German land mines. Oscar cussed me all the way, first for volunteering him, and then endangering him further by riding on top of a load of mines. I tried logic with him, explaining we were dead if the scout car hit a mine anyway, whether the trailer blew up or not. He was neither reassured nor amused.

"We made it to the bridge; it was lying in the river. Someone had already blown it. Since that bridge did not show destroyed on the lieutenant's map, he insisted we go to the next bridge, a mile farther. We were rounding a curve when we heard the crunching cadence of marching men. We knew they couldn't be friendlies. Oscar and I hopped off the trailer and headed toward the river and the oncoming troops. From there we could cover the turnabout of the scout car. That required unhooking the trailer because the road was so narrow.

"Crossing the road, I pulled back the bolt on the BAR. Not wanting to goof off a shot, I slid my finger forward in the trigger guard, hit the magazine release and dumped a loaded magazine in the middle of the road. The sound was deafening. We stopped and listened but there was no interruption in the cadence of the marchers. When the car finally turned around, we mounted up and took off. Back at the defensive perimeter, we could relax and laugh. Oscar especially enjoyed describing me crawling around the middle of the road trying to locate the magazine I dropped. In the dark I could only feel for it and besides I had a full belt of loaded magazines. It wasn't my finest hour."

The momentum of the Fifth Panzer Army swept up Harry Martin, the former Sad Sack of the 424th Infantry Regiment who, during the initial attack, had recalled the dictum, 'Squeeze the trigger'. Beyond St.-Vith, Martin, along with pieces of the disintegrated 424th, the 28th Division, and the combat commands of the 7th and 9th Armored became GI flotsam flowing through a narrow corridor of escape. The route was northwest, across the Salm River where the 82d Airborne including Bill Dunfee held the way open. "On the morning of 23 December we met CCB of the 9th Armored in the snowbound hills west of Beho. We were still not aware of what was going on. Suddenly, Captain Bartel gave the frantic order to withdraw. 'Jump on anything that's moving out! Every minute counts! Every man for himself! I climbed on a light tank.

"The tank I was on was going full speed for quite some time. Just when I felt confident that we had outrun the Germans and they were left far behind, the hatch on the tank opened and the tank commander said, 'We've just received word on the radio that there is small-arms fire ahead. Come on and get inside where you will be safer.' I was very happy to get inside the tank where it was much warmer. I sat back and relaxed. I was out of the cold and I was protected by armor all around me. I thought, 'What a difference between the infantry and the armored divisions. They carry warm clothing, blankets, and food with them.' A few minutes later, machine gun bullets bounced off the tank. I might not be alive if it were not for the tank commander."

After a time, the armor drew beyond enemy fire and halted. The tankers invited the infantrymen to share their food. Martin, who had not eaten for several days, gladly accepted. He began to make plans to stay under their protection for as long as possible. But before he could even settle down for a bite, an officer rounded up the foot soldiers and led them into a wooded area. "One of the men grabbed a chicken and cut its head off with his bayonet. While the chicken was being plucked, we started a small fire. Just as the chicken was put over the fire, word came that the Germans were closing in once again. We quickly stamped out the fire. We ran down the road, passing the chicken around with each man ripping off a piece. We were so hungry that, like wild animals, we ate the chicken raw."

The small group trekked northwest, veering from the direct path a number of times as they detected the advancing enemy. After the lieutenant roused them from their fourth barn in a single night, the exhausted Martin, burdened with two bandoliers of ammunition, a canteen, mess kit, first aid kit, bayonet, hand grenades, rifle, and steel helmet, shivering with his outer wear of ordinary army shoes and a field jacket, felt he could not go on. At the last barn, when the others walked off, he slipped back and bedded down in the loft. At midmorning, Martin awoke, cautiously stuck his head outdoors and saw no one. But when he sallied forth and rounded the corner of the barn, to his horror, a huge German tank's cannon pointed straight at him. Somehow, no one noticed the lone American and he fled through the woods. He traveled in the direction of gunfire, figuring he would outflank the German lines and circle to safety.

Walking for hours, Martin lightened his load, tossing away first his grenades and then his pair of bandoliers of .30-caliber bullets. "As I crossed a snow-covered road, I saw a C ration biscuit wrapped in cellophane. It looked as though it had been run over by a dozen tanks, but I picked it up anyway. I sat down next to a small frozen brook where water flowed over the ice. I found a small package of powdered lemonade in my pocket. I filled my canteen with ice water, mixed in the lemonade powder. I opened the crushed biscuit, taking just a nibble with small sips of my drink. I savored each little nibble and sip. I was having a banquet. All of my senses were centered on this very special meal. I was no longer cold or tired; the war was completely out of my mind. I got more pleasure out of that little biscuit than any meal I have ever had. When I finished, I said aloud, 'Well, let's go and find the war and the 106th Division."

Miraculously, Martin apparently passed through the broken lines of the warring armies. He reached a town with American soldiers and trucks. He asked an MP, "Which way did the 106th Division go?" The soldier flatly answered he had never heard of the outfit. Martin did not pause to eat, rest, or warm himself. He trudged on, intent on meeting up with his unit. Toward nightfall, he prepared to give up his hunt and return to the town.

As he staggered back, he suddenly heard someone call his name. To his delight, the voice belonged to a sergeant from his own 3d platoon in L company. The noncom led Martin to a reunion with six others from the company. "It felt good to be back with friends and just in time for Christmas Eve. I had a lot to be thankful for, to have made it back from that dreadful ordeal, back with members of my platoon, in a warm building and finally safe from the enemy. We were with a heavy-artillery outfit. The commander invited us to stay for Christmas Eve and for Christmas Day with a promise of a special turkey dinner."

On the Elsenborn Ridge, the 99th and 2d Infantry Divisions denied the German drive to widen the salient. Mortar man, Rex Whitehead, from the 99th, had been at Honsfeld only a few hours before Peiper's column captured the town and several of his buddies. He had gone through a bad patch until meeting up with elements of the 2d Division. He awoke to a pleasant sight on 24 December. "We got up and saw there wasn't a cloud in the sky, and soon we could see vapor trails coming from behind our lines. Soon we could hear and see the formations of bombers going over and you wouldn't believe anything could make a bunch of guys so happy as that sight did. Judge was waving his arms and shouting something about who said we didn't have an air corps. Formations came over for about five hours and it was a beautiful sight, the vapor trails streaming behind each motor and then the escorts weaving back and forth above them, making the sky look like a giant jigsaw puzzle. Some were shot down, for as they approached the front, the Kraut AA would open up and there were some fighters to meet them. More than anything else, we were happy to have them up there, because we didn't draw any fire since the 88s were dual, and were firing at the planes. As soon as they were gone, we started to get it though."

Dick Byers, with the 371st Field Artillery of the Checkerboards [99th] lived in a farmhouse. "The Germans had captured thousands of pounds of our mail and all the normal supply lines were disrupted. By Christmas Eve, we were feeling really lowdown and depressed without any mail for a week. A bunch of us, Cleon Janos, Bill Johnson, Gerald Krueger, Smith Eads, Henry Dewey, Paul Blackburn, and Joe Peruzzi were on the second floor gathered around a canteen full of gasoline with a rope wick that gave out twice as much soot as light. We were trying to get high on one bottle of terribly oily cognac. Downstairs, there were about five or six young children. Some of them were the farmer's, others were orphans the farm had taken in to shelter. A battery of 240mm of heavy artillery howitzers was out in the field beyond the farmhouse.

"The children were singing Christmas carols in their clear soprano voices and the sound effects went something like, 'Silent night'—BLAMM! 'Holy night'—BLAMMM! Somebody would get up and put the cardboard back in the window after the house stopped shaking from each blast. We were all just about ready to give it up as a bad job and go to bed when someone downstairs yelled, 'Mail Call!'

"There was our Christmas mail. I received two boxes from my wife [to be]. In each box was a can of candy corn and in each can was a two-ounce medicine bottle filled with good whiskey. I shared the fruitcake and the cookies with the boys, gave most of the candy to the kids. I gave just a taste of the whiskey to each man and managed to go to bed on Christmas Eve with the customary glow on."

43
End of Seige

Patton radioed McAuliffe at Bastogne that he expected to reach him on Christmas Day. The would-be rescuers of Bastogne, the 4th Armored vanguard, stalled only four miles away due to heavy resistance. Patton chafed at the delay. His diary entry for the previous day noted: "This has been a very bad Christmas Eve. All along our line we have received violent counterattacks, one of which forced . . . the 4th Armored back some miles with the loss of ten tanks. This was probably my fault because I had been insisting on day and night attacks. This is all right on the first or second day of the battle and when we had the enemy surprised but after that the men get too tired."

Major Hal McCown, from the 119th Infantry, a prisoner of the Germans for several days, had escaped while a group of captured Americans were being led east. Thrashing through the woods at night, near the Salm River he was challenged by GIs from I Company of the 82d Airborne. Bill Dunfee remembered, "It was a cold, moonlit night with good visibility. It was too light to suit us. Ray (Mike) Maikowski was out with the point. Mike noticed movement alongside the road and eased the safety off his M1. The man hiding there made his presence known, claiming to be an American.

"Mike told him, 'Put your hands behind your head and get your ass out here where I can see you.' It was an American, Maj. Hal McCown of the 30th Infantry Division. After he got over his fright—he was sure Maikowski was about to shoot him, and knowing Mike his fright was justified—he told us he had been a prisoner of the 500 to 800 Germans that charged through our lines earlier.

"By daylight, we had reached our new positions. It was bitterly cold and windy. We were told to dig in and establish a line we could defend until the end of the war if necessary. Charles Lupoli and I selected a spot just below the high ground to our rear. It jutted out far enough to give us a clear field of fire to our right and left and across a valley. "During the day of December 25, we dug a cave and covered it with tree limbs and the dirt we removed. We had three firing openings and felt we would be safe from anything but a direct hit from an 88. That evening the roof began to sag. We were outside cutting down a tree to reinforce it when a mortar round landed between us. Lupoli caught shrapnel in his foot and I was knocked down, but uninjured. I carried Lupoli back to the company CP and he was evacuated. While at the CP they brought the mail forward. I got a box of Christmas cookies. I tried to get Lupoli to take some of the cookies with him but he refused. We shared everything and were inseparable. I would miss him. His godmother owned a bar and sent him boxes of Ritz crackers with a pint of whiskey securely imbedded among the crackers. It took a long time for our guys to figure out how we got so happy on Ritz crackers." Dunfee settled in his new home for the following few days. There was no special meal for him on 25 December. "We went back, a day or two later, a squad at a time, for our warm Christmas dinners. It was really appreciated. After all those K rations, our bellies felt like our throats had been cut."

Christmas in Bastogne was business as usual. Jack Agnew, atop a pile of bricks, and his team started to guide in planes bearing vital supplies. German 88s attempted to disrupt the operation. A direct hit near Agnew killed eight men in a dugout. "The cold weather was the worst," said Agnew. "We only had field jackets we borrowed from an air corps pathfinder group. We were always hungry and thirsty but existed on very little food and drink. Our Christmas dinner consisted of hot C rations, an improvement over Ks, with cow beets and onions. It was so cold that I remember finding a pig a tank had run over and that was frozen stiff. I stuck it up against a tree and it looked like a bread-cutting board. Many of the dead on both sides lay frozen stiff where they had fallen. Burial details had problems putting them on stretchers. In places where the snow piled deep they were obliged to carry the litters shoulder-high. But in spite of the shells from the Germans, we managed to guide in enough supplies to fight off the enemy. It was a great Christmas present delivered by air."

At Bastogne, the greatest price was paid by members of the 101st. Schuyler Jackson earned himself a Purple Heart. "I got hit when a shell landed nearby, ripped a strip off my field glasses. I had a concussion, and my left arm was slashed. They put a little bandage on it and half an hour later I was fine. But when I saw all of the wounded it was tough. Goddamn, I give those doctors credit. They would work for forty-eight hours straight taking care of Americans and Germans."

On Christmas Eve, the Luftwaffe, taking advantage of the blackness of night, dumped two tons of high explosives, inflicting severe casualties. It got darker before the dawn, as Manteuffel, thinking the Americans might relax their vigilance on Christmas, sprang a massive frontal assault. Beginning a few hours after midnight with a huge artillery downpour, the enemy came on with soldiers hidden by white camouflage capes and white-painted tanks, difficult to spot in moonlight or even by day.

Wallace Swanson, CO for Company A of the 502d Parachute Infantry Regiment, had suffered a minor wound at Bastogne, after rifle fire apparently ricocheted off a tank and nicked his right thigh. Sulpha powder and iodine prevented any complications and he returned to duty without loss of time. "We were at Champs [in the northwestern perimeter of the donut-shaped defense around Bastogne] and about 2:30 A.M. there was an all-out barrage, artillery, cannon, mortar, and other firepower. It was raining, snowing, hailing down on our Company A positions. This was the strongest, most extensive, continuous barrage I was ever in. Their goal was to devastate our main line of resistance and all connection from the front to the back and around our strong points."

While Company B backed up Swanson's outfit, the enemy struck directly at the Rolle Château, site of the regimental HQ. Officers rallied cooks, clerks, radiomen, and even chaplains for a defense. The regimental surgeon collected his walking wounded from the stable that served as a temporary hospital, issued them rifles, and led them to defensive posts. Fortunately for the besieged, tank destroyers, along with bazooka-wielding troopers, broke up the armored assault.

Swanson had reported to battalion HQ that the enemy was on top of him, and was still talking when all communications lines to him were obliterated. Hand-to-hand fighting in the buildings and houses of Champs lasted several hours. Said Swanson, "The men held their positions on Christmas Day, securing protection and the enemy who infiltrated the forward positions were taken prisoners. Hot meals were provided by the battalion and regimental kitchen cooks by late afternoon and evening."

Schuyler Jackson was also at Champs. "They hadn't come at our area during the first days there. The temperature, though, was around zero. There were a couple of replacements who actually froze to death while on duty. I would always have two guys go out there to keep the men awake and prevent them from freezing. When one of our planes was shot down, I took a fleece-lined jacket from the body of one of the crew. It sounds terrible but he had no more use for it. There was a bridge in front of us. We had planted explosives but the detonator froze when they hit us Christmas Day. Their infantry rode on the tanks and we were picking them off. I got myself a bazooka and hit one in the motor. The crew came out fighting. They did not surrender. We had to shoot them.

"We had originally put mines in the road but because we expected the relief column we pulled them off to the side of the road. When the German tanks came, some of the commanders must have thought the road mined. They drove off on the side and exploded our mines. We had enough ammo at our spot and stopped them cold. The last tank was turning back and going up a rise. I fired the bazooka and it was a one-in-a-million shot, dropped right down the turret. Except it didn't explode. The loader had forgotten to pull the pin on the rocket. He got some fancy cussing from me. But the tank didn't get away. Somebody else destroyed it."

Tom Poston remembered impatiently waiting an opportunity to aid the Americans in Bastogne. "It was socked in. You couldn't fly, couldn't take off because of the weather, couldn't drop anything because of the weather. You couldn't see. Every day we'd go down to the radio room, getting ready to go, because we knew the guys were desperate. Finally, around Christmas, they said, 'Okay, it looks like it's going to open up. We flew in weather all the way, got to the drop zone and pop! it was clear. We went down and dropped the parabundles. The sounds of a plane's engines are pretty loud, and there were a bunch of us, so it was pretty noisy. But the guys came out of the woods where they had been hiding and fighting and you could hear them cheer. That's how loud they were yelling. It was gratifying as hell. It suddenly seemed it was worth doing, accomplishing something."

The Christmas Day offensive was the closest call for the defenders at Bastogne. There would be one more halfhearted push on 26 December but the enemy was now very short of men and the tools of war. During the three days beginning with Agnew and company's descent into Bastogne, a total of 962 aircraft dropped 850 tons of supplies. On the day after the holiday, 11 gliders landed with doctors and fuel. The airmen paid in blood, 102 crewmen killed with 19 C-47s shot down and 51 other planes badly damaged. On the other hand, with the improvement of visibility, American fighter bombers struck increasingly hard at the enemy, whose vehicles often left tell-tale tracks in the snow leading to seemingly concealed positions. Toward the rear of the Germans, the aerial attacks blasted any endeavor to reinforce or refurbish the German forces.

On Christmas morning, with the enemy attack halted, McAuliffe himself toured the local cemetery where he saw German prisoners, laboriously chopping holes in the frozen dirt for temporary interment of the stiffened bodies of dead paratroopers. He commented to the guards they should make certain the POWs were properly fed. Earlier, he had distributed a message to his men.

McAuliffe's communique recounted the details of the German demand for surrender and his pithy response. His Christmas message then said: "What's merry about all this, you ask? We're fighting—it's cold—we aren't home. All true, but what has the proud Eagle Division accomplished with its worthy comrades of the 10th Armored Division, the 705th Tank Destroyer Battalion, and all the rest? Just this: We have stopped cold everything that has been thrown at us from the north, east, south, and west. We have identifications from four German panzer divisions, two German infantry divisions, and one German parachute division. These units, spearheading the last desperate German lunge, were heading straight west for key points when the Eagle Division was hurriedly ordered to stem the advance. How effectively this was done will be written history, not alone in our division's glorious history but world history. The Germans actually did surround us, the radios blared our doom. Allied troops are counterattacking in force. We continue to hold Bastogne. By holding Bastogne, we assure the success of the Allied armies. We know that our division commander, General Taylor will say: Well done! We are giving our country and our loved ones at home a worthy Christmas present and being privileged to take part in this gallant feat of arms are making for ourselves a merry Christmas."

McAuliffe had caroled a less cheery tune to the VIII Corps commander, Gen. Troy Middleton on the eve. "The finest Christmas present the 101st could get would be a relief tomorrow."

Another nut that the enemy offensive had failed to crack was on Elsenborn Ridge, manned by the 99th and 2d Divisions. Sergeant Ben Nawrocki found Christmas Day painful. "it was a day of sadness. The mail delivery came in. We were asked to send a detail of men to open individual packages of those lost in each company. We were to take out all the perishable foods and eat them ourselves. The valuables were sent back to the families in the States. Most of Company B was dead, captured, or wounded. We had a lot of food, which came in handy, nutrition for half-frozen soldiers.

"We were receiving picked-over C rations, cans of hash and beans. Men were angry at people in the rear who gave us the leftovers. The crates were obviously opened and then repacked. The food we took from the Christmas packages boosted morale and health. The sweets gave us warmth. We took the hard candy, melted it, and added prune bars begged from the armored troops along with crackers to make a jelly. The Army promised us a good, full Christmas dinner and made good with all the trimmings. It was served cold, but darn good, turkey and all. I could not understand how they did it with the biggest battle ever going on."

On 25 December, Glen Strange reported to 3d Armored Division headquarters with information on the disposition of his unit. He was ushered into the presence of General [Maurice] Rose. "I had not shaved since the sixteenth of December and had worn the same clothes since then, having lost all my others along with my toilet articles. I began, 'Capt. Glen L. Strange, with the 27th Armored Infantry Battalion, 9th Armored Division, part of Combat Command B, to make a report, sir.'

"He asked, 'Captain, are you an officer in the United States Army?'

"I answered him, 'Hell, yes, and we've been through hell, sir.'

"His reply was, 'Well, you don't look like it. Give me your report,' and he turned to his aide and said, 'See to it this captain gets a bath, in my bathroom, uses my toilet articles, gets shaved and, Major, find him some clothes to wear, even if you have to give him some of mine.' After I gave him the report, I did take a bath in his bathroom with hot water, used his razor. By the time I was cleaned up, the major had rounded up new underwear, clean

ODs, and an almost new combat jacket and pants. The jacket was the general's, as it was too big and had the stars cut off the shoulder straps—you could see where they had been. This was the best Christmas present I could have received. I reported back to the battalion and was envied by many for being cleaned up and having new clothes. "

Like the 27th Air Infantry Battalion, Dee Paris's 14th Tank Battalion was also in transit. There were no Christmas dinners, only C rations. Not far from St.-Vith, D Company of the 14th paused in an open field. Tank driver Harold Lemmenes remembered, "We were washing our feet in warm water when Lieutenant Paris came by and looked at our feet and ordered us to go to the medics."

Paris explained, "I made it a point to order a number of men to remove their boots and socks, particularly when I saw a man limping. I was no expert on trench foot—just figured that anyone having his boots and socks on for several days [Lemmenes said he hadn't taken his off for four days] should air his feet." Lemmenes and others with sore feet lay at one end of a tent with their bare feet exposed to the cold air. Most of the bunks were filled with wounded men, groaning in pain. "That night," said Lemmenes, "happened to be Christmas. The next day we had our Christmas dinner. Jack Soukup our radio man and gunner and I convinced them to let us return to our company and we did."

As Christmas Day drew to an end, Task Force Hogan, the 400-man unit from the 3d Armored, at Marcouray, broke into small groups for an attempt to sneak through the enemy encirclement. "We put dirt in the gas tanks, dismantled weapons, and buried pieces," recalled Arnold Albero. "We were told that friendly troops were to the north. I looked up into the black, dark sky trying to find the North Star. Suddenly, I wished I had paid more attention in basic training when they tried to teach compass reading at night. At dusk we started to leave, in small groups at ten-minute intervals. As each left his position, they were wished well by those to follow.

"The march through the woods and hills was rough and I mean rough. We crawled across open fields with some snow on the ground, waded cold streams. When we stopped to rest, I could not only feel but also hear my heart pounding. Then when I looked back to see if the GI behind me was still there, I was relieved to see he was relatively closer than he should have been. He actually should have been at least thirty to fifty yards behind me. When you couldn't see anyone behind, you left a trail, a cartridge belt, musette bag, anything. I prayed that the guy in front of me knew where he was going because I did not. The success of our infiltration rested on our lead man, whom I did not know. He was a lieutenant and I don't know which one but to this day I pray for that man.

"At times we were so close to the Germans, you could hear them singing Christmas carols. To my knowledge, we were challenged only once during our march. After about fourteen hours, we reached friendly infantry." In fact, the entire group of about 400, including a flier shot down while trying to airlift supplies, passed into the positions set up by Bill Boyle of the 517th Parachute Regiment. The paratroop commander was told some of the task force did not contact any frontline soldiers, probably because "in that fluid situation it was impossible to establish solid lines."

The deep penetration of the Germans required a constant readjustment of the American defenses, yielding turf won at considerable bloodshed. Vance Kidwell, a supply sergeant with the 78th Armored Field Artillery of the 2d Armored Division had been behind the action in North Africa and reached Normandy several weeks after the division's arrival in France on D plus 1. "On October 1944," said Kidwell, "we reached Palenburg [inside Germany] and a week later the town of Ubach." Within the breakthrough, the division pulled back. "On Christmas Day we were in Liroux a small town built along one side of a ridge, which was the main street. The night before I had slept on the kitchen floor of a house and nearly froze. It was cold and there was lots of snow on the ground. The fellows kept their engines going to keep them from freezing up and guards stood by the exhausts to keep warm. All night long, we could hear vehicles moving into a grove of trees a quarter mile away on lower ground. We assumed they were ours, but when daylight came an officer walking on the ridge was sniped at and we knew they were Germans. Our tanks lined up on the ridge and I got a bird's-eye view of our tanks picking theirs off one at a time as they tried getting away. Some of the Germans tried running across the open field toward us with their hands in the air. Some of our fellows started taking potshots at them and one German fell to the ground like he'd been hit. But as soon as the firing stopped, he got up and ran toward us to give up."

South of the Bulge, after a two-week battle at Ensdorf that established a bridgehead across the Saar Canal the 95th Division, because of the Ardennes problem, received word to abandon its foothold and retreat to the village of Hayes, liberated weeks before. Carl Ulsaker had mixed emotions. "It was a relief to escape the hell of life in Endsdorf. On the other hand, it was disappointing to have to give up ground won with so much difficulty and the sacrifice of so many good men. Survival at Ensdorf provided me early in life with the nadir of my existence, enabling me to cope calmly with all subsequent crises; for nothing I have since faced has proved to be worse than that experience."

As the trucks hauled his outfit away, Ulsaker saw a fireworks show, created by demolition of ammunition stored in the town. "White phosphorus shells hurled high into the air burst into great white blossoms, brilliant against the dark sky. Rockets shot off in all directions leaving blazing trails of orange flames. The buildings in which ammunition had been piled began to burn, fiercely, cooking off thousands of small-arms rounds making a noise like a giant corn popper. Adding to the spectacle, machine gunners of the 2d Battalion fired long bursts at extreme range into the streets of the town we had so recently vacated, the red tracers resembling fiery streams from demon hoses. Division artillery added a few volleys. The roaring flames, the sporadic flashes of exploding shells, the din, and the smoke in the Stygian blackness of that last night of the fall of 1944 gave our abandoned bridgehead an appearance that could rival portrayals of Hell by such masters as Dante and Milton."

When he reached Hayes around 2:00 A.M., his advance party informed him that the men would sleep in barns. "Recalling General Patton's policy that our allies were to share their homes, I said, flatly, 'Like hell we'll sleep in barns; get me the town mayor.' After some slight delay his honor trotted up, pulling on a coat over his nightdress and looking somewhat apprehensive. I contrived my most devilish leer, looked him straight in the eye, and said, 'I don't want my men sleeping in places designed for animals. Make arrangements for the people here to share their homes with us.'

"'But, Mon Capitaine,' he sputtered, ' There is no room.'

"'Make room,' I said, staring at him with hard eyes, visible in the light of a kerosene lamp held by my quartering NCO who also interpreted, although I knew enough schoolboy French to get the drift of the mayor's conversation." When the latter protested that everyone was asleep, Ulsaker responded, "We can easily wake them up," gesturing toward his platoon leaders who stood about with grenades clipped to their belts and guns hanging menacingly from their shoulders. "Listen, goddamnit, in case you don't remember, we're the unit that liberated your village from the Boche a month ago. You sure as hell were glad to see us then. Maybe you'd like us to invite the Germans back." Within an hour the company occupied warm beds hastily vacated by the host town.

For Phil Hannon of the 81st Combat Engineers, the Christmas season began his life as a POW. "The Germans walked us into the square of a small village. They were too busy to bother with us. They were learning to drive our trucks and eat our chow. The gearshift on our trucks puzzled some of them, so we had a few laughs. One Kraut got a jeep going in reverse and couldn't shift it into forward. Another seemed to think second gear was the way a truck should run. It was funny but it hurt. We should have burned our vehicles.We were herded into a courtyard with a few apple trees. I was lucky and got one of the frozen apples. They told us: 'You will spend the night, here. This is where your latrine will be'; designating a corner. 'If anyone tries to escape, all will be shot.'

"For a time we sang. Christmas was just a few days off so Christmas carols filled our minds with thoughts of home. We sang until the Germans complained that we kept them awake and if we didn't cease, we'd be shot. We lay next to and atop one another to keep warm. It drizzled all night and we were soaked by morning. None of us slept much, even though we were all dead tired. At 6:00 A.M. we were lined up four abreast in groups of 100 and told we'd get a break at the end of eighteen kilometers. About noon, after steady walking, we stopped in a village full of a Panzer Grenadier outfit. We were supposed to get food and water. Instead, they stripped us of the overshoes we had. About six spuds were thrown from a window for more than 1,000 men. The men fought for them and the Germans laughed.

"All of us were thirsty. I gathered a couple of canteens and two helmets and let some guards know I wanted '*Wasser.*' Luckily, he was Polish. He took half a dozen others and me up the street to a house where he was billeted. While we filled our containers, he brought a bucket of boiled potatoes and motioned for us to stuff our pockets for our comrades. I had on my overcoat and loaded both pockets to the rim. When we rejoined the others, I had enough to hand two to each man in my platoon which had stayed together."

The march continued, becoming increasingly more difficult as hunger, thirst, and weariness gnawed at the hapless prisoners. They slaked their parched throats from dirty puddles, gobbled raw potatoes thrown to them by French laborers, felt briefly cheered when they passed through the German city of Prüm and observed the damage inflicted by the Air Corps. Day passed into night; the men stumbled along. They sought to raise flagging spirits with song but that died out. "Most of us needed all our breath to 'pick 'em up, and lay 'em down.'" The march finally ended at a railhead around 2:00 A.M., nearly twenty hours after it began.

Water became an obsession. From a nearby stream, the PWs filled their canteens, then dumped in Halazone tablets for purification. But instead of waiting for the chemical to kill bacteria, the GIs gulped down the mixture instantly. At 11:00 A.M. the guards issued food, two bags of hardtack per man and a can of cheese to be split among seven persons. Hannon squirreled away some of his ration for future use. During the trek east, Hannon found members of his platoon and soon they were hustled toward the railyards. "Somehow we made it known we were thirsty and an old man and his wife started giving us water. Those old souls worked themselves like horses hauling water for us until the guards stopped them. Those people were helping us as best they could because they were built that way. We were their enemies but they were helping us. They weren't doing it because they knew Germany was going to be beaten. They did it because they were people, not puppets. Germany as a nation was rotten but its people are human beings with hearts and minds open to good things."

The boxcars for Hannon and the others arrived, apparently fresh from carrying horses. The straw with the droppings remained as the men boarded. Jammed together, the prisoners' body heat thawed Hannon's feet. He removed his boots and twenty-four hours would pass before he could bear to touch his tender feet. The trip descended into the depths of a nightmare. Dysentery afflicted many. Hannon, with a position beside one of the small windows, would hear a yell for "the helmet, for Christ's sake, quick!" Within a few moments, a helmet passed hand to hand would arrive at his spot and he would empty it out the window. To urinate, the men used a discarded cheese can. There was pushing and shoving, cursing, cries of pain as someone trod on another's foot. A few soldiers became delirious. Pleas for *wasser* or *essen* passed unheeded by the guards.

On 23 December, the train halted in a railyard alongside another load of POWs, wearing the patches of the 28th Infantry Division. That night an engine chugging by, suddenly stopped. The engineer and fireman jumped out and ran. Hannon heard the drone of a flight of planes. "We sat there and sweated. I watched from the window and saw my Christmas tree. The lead plane dropped a flare. it burst about 200 feet in the air, took the shape of a pine tree. The burning lights were red, purple, orange, and yellow, looking quite like Christmas tree lights. Then things started to happen.

"Whomp! The first one hit and jarred us around. The engine on the track next to us kept blowing off steam like a giant hippopotamus. We prayed. Each time a bomb hit, I dropped to the floor. Guys were yelling. 'Crawl out the window.' 'If this damn train ever gets hit and starts burning . . .' I couldn't get out of the window and wasn't about to try. I couldn't see myself half in and half out when one of those babies hit nearby. Down at the other end of the car, they had better results with their helmet man. It was Corporal Stone, I think, who climbed out. A guard lying in a ditch, scared to death, spotted him and pleaded, 'Good soldier, don't run.' He ignored the guard, burrowed under our car, and unwired the door. We scrambled out as men from other cars did the same. We started looking for water and found a frozen ditch. We managed to get our fill. The bombing had stopped; the guards were worked up, shooting occasionally. We loaded back in the cars. Later, we learned eight men had been killed and thirty-six wounded during the air raid.

"On the day before Christmas, we were allowed to get water and they fed us, one-twelfth of a loaf of black bread and a daub of jam. It was more than we could handle in our weakened condition. A few of the boys were too sick to even bite it. Two of our chaplains came by and told us the bombers had wrecked the track ahead. Until it was fixed we couldn't move. They wished us a Merry Christmas and moved on to the next car. When night came, we were still in the yards and worried about being bombed again. 'They won't bomb on Christmas Eve.' 'Hell they won't! They're out to win this war. Christmas won't be celebrated this year. So we waited. From somewhere along the line of cars came a Christmas carol. Back and forth the carols went, first from our train, then from the other— *"Little Town of Bethlehem," "Silent Night," "Deck the Halls,"* and the rest of the favorites. That lasted for an hour or so. Then the Catholic boys said their Rosary while the rest of us were silent with our own prayers. The air raid siren sounded once but we weren't bothered by the bombers again."

On Christmas Day, during the morning, the journey resumed. They reached Frankfurt where another old man sought to alleviate the perpetual thirst with buckets of water. But after a dozen trips with a bucket, it proved too much for him. Hannon's car received two helmets of water before the good Samaritan quit. The train rolled on and the prisoners reached the end of the line on Christmas Day. They unloaded, and the GIs caught a glimpse of newspaper headlines that read 35,000 AMERICANS CAPTURED. Civilians gawked at them without expression. "We drew ourselves up and tried our best to look like U.S. soldiers and did right well, considering the condition of our clothes and bodies."

They disembarked in the village of Bad Orb, then walked the final three kilometers to Stalag IX B. "The column came to a halt and the gates opened. We walked in, prisoners, Christmas Day and the gates of freedom had closed behind us. As we walked in, faces peered out of barbed-wire windows. They smiled and yelled, 'Russkies! Russkies!' Russian troops, allies were greeting us. We smiled and feebly waved as we marched by."

Private first class. Ed Uzemack, the reporter from Chicago who had become a veteran after surviving the bloody Hurtgen Forest campaign as a replacement in the 28th Division, lost his freedom on 17 December. "We could see that their tanks were in excellent condition and that the enemy soldiers were pretty sharp. Our immediate captors behaved a bit like gentlemen. The black-uniformed panzer men were young, clean-shaven and very smart in appearance. They were efficient and cocky in their attitude. They had captured us and naturally attributed this feat to their 'Aryan superiority.'

"The small group of men captured with me was permitted to secure blankets and overcoats before setting out on the march. Very few other prisoners had a similar break. We were forced to march several kilometers to a hillside air-raid shelter. We went through our first real shakedown as POWs. The German guards stripped us of every grain of tobacco and every ounce of food we carried. Many of the guards took from the GIs watches, pens, billfolds, personal letters, and other items of souvenir value. A good many men lost pictures of their loved ones."

Along with 400 others, Uzemack was forced inside the air-raid shelter, designed to accommodate only half that number. As he entered, an English-speaking guard warned, "Take a good deep breath, Yankee. It will be the last fresh air you'll get for some time." For almost two days Uzemack lived in the "pitch-black, damp, foul cave in the side of a hill. We lay in this dungeon with no food and little water. The air grew foul with the cave smell and the men became extremely irritable and hungry." On returning to sunlight after almost forty-eight hours, Uzemack noticed a change in the quality of the traffic. "The Nazi column was still rolling down the road. Their equipment looked like something out of a junkyard. Vehicles that had to be towed, horse-drawn vehicles and other decrepit pieces rolled past us all day." He also marked the passage toward the front of a number of well-marked ambulances, carrying heavily armed troops. Uzemack's group, as with the other POWs, frantically hunted for food and water. Uzemack to his own horror scratched in the mud to retrieve the remains of an apple tossed away by one of the Germans. To their surprise, almost a feast of half a loaf of sour bread plus marmalade and a small piece of cheese greeted them at a stop on 20 December. Unfortunately, the guards failed to instruct the GIs that this was to last several days. Furthermore, the excess, such as it was, proved more than many roiling stomachs could handle. Quartered in a church and unable to leave the premises, Uzemack noted, "In the morning, the vestibule was almost ankledeep in vomit and other excreta. A great many of the men had become ill."

The following three days they marched, finally stopping after 100 kilometers at Gerolstein. The convoy was commanded by "a monacled son of a bitch, with natty breeches, swagger stick, and boots." He forced a twenty-man party to clean up an improvised latrine with their bare hands. He also relieved the men of all of their money, a collection that stuffed several thousand dollars in various currencies into his personal pockets. Locked in boxcars at Gerolstein, the Americans heard the ominous hum of approaching U.S. aircraft. "One plane swept lower over the train, zoomed up—and then came back. This time he meant business; we heard machine-gun fire. Men pounded on the walls of the cars, screaming to be let out. A few medics in the car behind managed to get out. They waved their red cross helmets at the planes overhead and opened a few cars. Men streamed out in droves."

"Despite their fright, pain, and weakness, most headed for a vegetable patch some distance away, fell on their knees in the furrows and began grubbing out the carrots and turnips, jamming them in their hungry mouths." When the raid ended, the Germans rounded up the prisoners, firing warning shots over their heads and hitting one GI in the back. Subsequently, he died from the wound due to a lack of medical care and the hardship of the trip. Christmas Eve brought no surcease. The men abandoned efforts at caroling; the will to carry on appeared evaporating." Late on Christmas Day, shortly before midnight at Bad Orb, the authorities relented and dumped eight loaves of bread and seven meat tins amongst the nearly sixty Americans with Uzemack. "Despite the darkness, we managed to divide the food. Like many others, I decided this was the best Christmas dinner of my life."

While the 4th Armored Division spearheaded the rescue drive toward Bastogne, other elements like the 87th Infantry Division, introduced to battle early in December, followed in the wake of the tanks and half-tracks. Private first class. Alan Shapiro of the 346th Infantry recalled a nine-hour truck ride to Rheims the day before Christmas. "We had a complete night's sleep, a wonderful Christmas present. Midway through the morning, many went to Christmas services given by the chaplains. We received a chicken dinner, with fresh vegetables for lunch. For the first time in many weeks I felt as if I had really eaten."

Shapiro spent the remaining hours before dusk, standing around warming fires, wondering what was to come next. After night fell, the men of the 346th once again readied themselves for a journey. "We piled onto the trucks, which were covered and packed them to the limit. The whole platoon was in one truck and there was plenty of bitching. I had my legs doubled up under my chin, and I couldn't move without annoying somebody. I was luckier than most since my back was against the side of the truck. The fellows in the middle rested against the knees of the person behind them.

"It was impossible to sleep. There was nothing to see so we just sat there. The ride seemed interminable. Guys hollered for the trucks to stop and allow us to relieve ourselves. But during the entire twelve-hour ride, we didn't stop once to allow us to stretch or anything else. Some men were afflicted with a bit more than kidney trouble and a lot of us suffered from bad cases of the GIs [diarrhea]. We pissed in the gas cans and shit in a pile of straw. Peeing was a delicate situation since the nozzles on the gas cans were the size of a quarter and you had to be careful not to squirt all over everyone. It didn't seem funny to us and the truck hardly smelled like a rose garden. But there wasn't anything we could do. When we finally stopped and left the trucks, we didn't know where we were or even what country we were in. There were woods all around us. We marched off into them a few hundred yards away and dug in."

On the day after Christmas, Lt. Col. Creighton Abrams of the 4th Armored Division's 37th Tank Battalion poked his head up from a Sherman atop a hill three miles from Bastogne. He radioed back "Concentration Number Nine, Play it soft and sweet." It was the code name for a Time-on-Target avalanche upon the avenue leading into the town. After 420 rounds of artillery crashed into whoever might be defending, an advance column of six tanks, followed by half-tracks packed with infantrymen from the 53d Armored Infantry started the final charge. They ran a gauntlet of small arms and heavier pieces while blasting anyone in their way.

Abrams told correspondent Will Lang, "I like to be way out on the goddamn point, where there's nothing but me and the Germans and we can fight without reporting to headquarters." The American officer was frank in his assessment of his weakness against enemy armor. "The Germans can get any tanks we have beginning at a range of 3,000 yards and we have to wait until a Panther is within 1,000 yards before we're sure of crippling it and until 200 yards to get a Tiger Royal."

He remained firmly committed to the mission. "If those people in there need help we gotta get in there. When we move, we move with everything firing. In half a day we completely wrecked Assenois. Near Bigonville woods, we killed thirty enemy in foxholes and took fifteen POWs. We lost four half-tracks between Assenois and Bastogne. The men who were not killed or wounded continued on foot." Within half an hour after the final push began the relief force bagged 400 prisoners, killed hundreds of others, and Creighton Abrams shook hands with Tony McAuliffe. The siege of Bastogne was over.

44
Causualties and POWs

The relief of Bastogne, breaks in the weather that enabled the Air Corps to blast the enemy, and huge infusions of fresh troops—the 11th Armored Division, the 17th Airborne Division and a host of other organizations—doomed the German offensive in the Ardennes. Patton had boasted his hand held the handle of the meatgrinder but the crank turned excruciatingly slowly, amid substantial costs in American bodies. In fact, rather than sealing off the tens of thousands of German soldiers within the salient, the high command chose to batter the enemy in a bloody, toe-to-toe, head-on campaign. The decision ensured a casualty strewn ordeal.

In the 87th Division, where the initiation into combat a few weeks earlier left many rifle companies with half their normal complement, Alan Shapiro tried to cope with reality. "The war still appeared peculiar to us. None of us had the slightest knowledge as to how the overall picture of the war appeared. With all our constant confusion, I couldn't see how we were winning and the Germans were retreating. I wasn't killing anybody. I didn't see any Germans and their only manifestation was in their shells and machine guns." In his only opportunity to use his rifle, Shapiro was disconcerted to learn that he and his associates were exchanging fire with another company from the division. As he trudged through the snow, the condition of his feet worsened until by New Year's Day he could barely walk. He was evacuated to England along with thousands of others afflicted with either frostbite or trenchfoot.

Similarly, Noel Robison, a runner for L Company of the 358th Regiment in the 90th Division, staggered through the snow and ice. "All of us wore 'long john' [winter] underwear, olive drab wool uniforms, cotton fatigues over the ods, and our wool great field coat. Our clothing was so thick it was nearly impossible to respond to 'piss call' when the required stops were made by trucks." Rooting about in the snow they uncovered buried helmets and weapons belts marked with the red keystone, mute evidence of the overrun 28th Division. In foxholes built by conscripted labor for the Germans, they huddled together for warmth, slept fully dressed in uniforms, overcoats, shoes, and with an occasional blanket.

"Early one morning when I tried to put my boots on, I couldn't. My feet had swollen. I forced my feet into my boots and didn't lace them up." Lagging behind the company, he staggered into a battalion aid station. "I sat in a corner and took off my boots. I looked at my feet. My toes were purple. The upper parts of my feet were red and looked like hamburger, raw from the chafing during the hike to the aid station." The war was over for Robison also.

Lieutenant Colonel Bill Boyle of the 517th Parachute Regiment had persuaded his regimental commander to delay an assignment to capture high ground near the Salm River until dark. The attack went off successfully but during the night, when Boyle tried to contact another unit, an enemy machine gun smashed three bullets into him. He said that as he lay bleeding in the snow, "I prayed, God, don't let me die. This was a moment when I experienced fear. I knew my brachial artery [in his arm] was severed and that I could not stop the bleeding." Fortunately, his intelligence specialist, S. Sgt. Robert Steele got to him, administered first aid, and then goaded him into hobbling with Steele's assistance to the aid station. Although the battalion surgeon doubted his chances, Boyle clung to life and eventually was transported to a hospital.

While Boyle slowly recovered, his fellow troopers in the 517th joined the 78th Infantry Division for a renewed effort around the town of Schmidt through the bloody Hurtgen Forest. The strategists assigned the paratroopers to carry out a diversionary attack, but instead of instructing the GIs to feint and distract the foe with minimum casualties to themselves, they were ordered to forcibly confront the enemy. Error piled on error. The 517th's 2d Battalion commander, Dick Seitz, noted, "High-echelon strategists can work from a map and aerial photos, but it is an axiom of military operations that battalions or companies should never advance without first-hand knowledge of the terrain. We never had an opportunity to make a foot recon. The plan called for a night attack, which makes the need for good recon to recognize terrain features, even more imperative. The plan said we were to advance with two battalions abreast. The book calls for adequate planning, rehearsals, and to proceed on a narrow front. We were unable to properly rehearse the operation. We violated all of the principles."

In the ensuing operations, units ran into a buzz saw of enemy opposition. Lacking real knowledge of the ground, maneuvering blindly through minefields in the dark, the affair was a disaster from the viewpoint of the 517th. Although the brother infantry outfits succeeded in breaking through, the paratrooper regiment, one more victim of the Hurtgen Forest, was so chewed up that it lost its independence and was relegated to the newly arrived 13th Airborne Division in reserve, seventy miles from Paris.

Vance Kidwell, with a 2d Armored Division artillery outfit recalled that after a break over New Year's the unit returned to combat. "We spent the first night back in a pine grove and the weather was zero and below, lots of snow. The pine trees were a hazard, for when the German shells would hit the tops of the trees they would explode sending shrapnel downward from which we had little protection. If we had time to dig foxholes, we would take doors from houses, cover the foxhole with them, except for a small opening to crawl in, and then we would cover the doors up with dirt. If there were no doors, we would use logs of some kind."

Bill Dunfee enjoyed a brief respite from combat before his 82d Airborne unit rejoined the battle to evict the Germans from their gains. Proceeding along a road, a treeburst that no one heard coming showered his squad with shrapnel. Dunfee's close pal DiGiralamo died instantly. The blast slashed another man's foot and leg. "I was knocked down and the butt of my BAR slammed my middle finger, putting a permanent kink in it." But except for the loss of his toothbrush and toothpaste from his breast pocket, he went unharmed. As the troopers advanced Dunfee saw Germans shoot their own people when they sought to surrender.

The route taken by the 82d Airborne covered the terrain where the 28th Infantry Division in the late autumn had absorbed terrible punishment before retreating. Said Dunfee, "The area became known to us as 'Death Valley,' There were trucks, tanks, jeeps, trailers, tank destroyers, bumper-to-bumper and all shot to hell. Tanks had thrown their tracks; trucks, jeeps, and trailers turned over, some burned. I had been exposed to the carnage of war in four airborne operations—Sicily, Italy, Normandy, and Holland—but I never saw anything that could compare. Freshly killed troops in various stages of dismemberment are gruesome enough for the average stomach. But these men had been through a freeze and thaw. They had lain there since November and their flesh had rotted and was peeling from the skeletons. Some were on litters. I hoped they were killed outright and not abandoned to freeze to death. There was complete silence in our column, each man handling this horror in his own way. For me, it was the most shocking single experience of the war. If anyone needed an incentive to fight, this gave him ample reason."

While aircraft production by the factories of the Third Reich continued in spite of the raids by the Eighth, Ninth, and Fifteenth Air Forces, the heavy attrition of German pilots due to the bomber and fighter guns sharply reduced capable flyers to man available cockpits. And the strategic bombing program created a severe shortage in fuel for planes. The absence of protective air cover enabled the Allied planes to freely attack the retreat from the Ardennes.

Cary Salter, a Mississippi country doctor's son, was a member of a group of replacement pilots who arrived in December 1944 at Le Bourget, the Paris airport made famous by Lindbergh's landing there in 1927. While many of the enemy had to fill its flight ranks with young men with minimal experience at the controls, Salter had accrued many hours flying time while an instructor for students in P-40s, P-47s and P-51s. Assigned to the 354th Fighter Group, a few miles from Toul, and in transition to P-47s from P-51s, he noted, "I was there a month and a half before I got to fly a mission. My first missions, we were cleaning them out after the Battle of the Bulge. I flew as an escort for A-26 bombers attacking bridges and railyards or else we went on search-and-destroy missions, hitting anything we saw on the ground, such as troops or trucks. We were not bothered by enemy fighters; whatever they had they generally used to go after the high-altitude Eighth Air Force bombers."

As the Americans advanced, Belgian civilians in a forest near Meyerode led them to the body of an American officer. From the papers on the remains he was identified as Eric Fisher Wood, the artillery lieutenant with the 106th Division. Seven German corpses lay nearby. There was considerable evidence that Wood had organized a guerrilla campaign against the enemy but no eyewitnesses to his feats ever surfaced. A claim by his father, himself a general, to gain a Medal of Honor for Wood was denied because of the necessity of firsthand corroboration. Instead, a Distinguished Service Cross went to his widow. Of the 600,000 GIs embroiled in the Ardennes, Eric Wood was one of 19,000 who died with another 40,000 wounded. Casualty figures among the half-million Germans vary from 100,000 to 120,000. Most humiliating for the Americans was the matter of 19,000 prisoners, the largest number taken captive since Bataan.

The experiences of American captives varied but at best it was uncomfortable and at worst a deadly ordeal. David Jones, the bomber pilot who escaped the enemy after the strike at Tokyo in 1942 only to be shot down in North Africa some six months later, entered Stalag III a week before Christmas. Ensconced in the East Camp, Jones recalled, "There were about forty-five Yanks. I was the first one out of North Africa so they were all from the United Kingdom. They moved British and Americans still mixed up to the North Camp in the spring of '43. It was brand new. Everything was fresh and smelled of pine and fresh air. Jeez, it was beautiful.

"It didn't last long but that's when we started working on the big plan. I was a digger, a tunneler. [There were] three Americans who were face men, who worked underground. And we had Poles and Englishmen, and all kinds of nationalities on this digging team. We had an elaborate security system, a warning system, and we had an elaborate method of dispersing sand. We had very elaborate traps. We had a square German stove that sat on a brick foundation and we lifted the whole thing and made one piece out of it and sank the tap under that. We could move the stove every time. Another trap was in the washroom where there was a slope to the center and a water trap. Someone had cut one side of it out and made it where you could lift one side, make a slab, lift that out, and we went down from there. The tunnel went down to about thirty feet, full of sand, just like Florida."

The tunnelers lay on their elbows because the confined spaces prevented them from working while on hands and knees. They carried small cans of margarine for oil and early on Jones noticed it flamed out very quickly. He kept returning it by string to those above who would relight the device. After it went out several more times he realized there was not enough oxygen to support the candle. Subsequently, as they burrowed deeper and farther, the prisoners rigged an air line using cans with the tops and bottoms cut out and then stacked to make a crude pipe. "At the bottom of the hole we had a chamber and we'd have a guy work a pump to push air into the tunnel with a big bellows. Eventually we'd tap into a light and we had electricity and electric lights."

To shore up the subterranean passageway, the captives removed boards from beds and cut them to size. Even so, there were frequent cave-ins and the trapped person depended upon the man behind to pull him out. "I was thirty feet under when a cave-in occurred. You kind of wonder, 'What in the heck am I doing here. Of course it was imperative that you repair the hole before you get out because the effort of hundreds of people depended on you. You just *have* to fix whatever it was. And you had to get out of the hole to be counted.

"The dispersal system was very complicated. We'd move tons of sand a day in two-pound lots. We put a trolley in, two wooden rails, a little cart about two feet long and fifteen inches wide, and that's what we hauled the sand in from the face back to where it went vertical. We put the sand around bunk gardens. You'd always have diversions. You'd start fights, or have games, football, volley ball, soccer, and scuffle things around. You'd have these little bags you would wear inside your pants leg and you'd pull a little pin and the sand would trickle out."

The guards knew that the prisoners were engaged in some kind of plot. The "ferret"—a guard equipped with a long steel pole—poked the floor and heard a hollow sound. "They found the big one," said Jones, "and about that time they moved the Americans." While the Yanks occupied another compound, their former comrades, the British, continued to seek freedom through digging. In what became known as "the Great Escape" seventy-eight individuals broke out of the camp through the tunnel. According to Jones, two Norwegians and a Dane escaped completely. "They shot fifty. Some of them they turned back to camp but the Gestapo shot fifty. They had two or three in the car and they stopped to let them relieve themselves and they'd shoot them in the back of the head. The British ran a very thorough investigation after the war."

From the Doolittle raid of Tokyo, Robert Hite, a copilot, was one of the crewmen who bailed out over an occupied section of China and quickly fell into the hands of the Japanese. He and his companions underwent weeks of daily interrogations, sprinkled with physical abuse, including water torture. Lodged in a Shanghai prison, sleeping on a platform of boards with little food, the flyers were afflicted with painful boils and one crewman Dean Hallmark developed dysentery.

"About 19 or 20 August, the Japanese came into our cell and they took Dean and put him on a stretcher. Bill Farrow and I carried either end and took him to a truck. At Kiangwan Military Prison on the outskirts of Shanghai, we had a farce court-martial. We were all brought in and the Japanese acting as the tribunal, about four of them, had on English wigs, which I think was a mockery. There was a guard with a rifle standing in all the doorways and windows of the area. We had brought Dean Hallmark on the stretcher. They asked each of us to give our name and rank. We gave it. Dean could not; I think he was too weak to talk. Then they announced in Japanese, our so-called sentence. We didn't really know what it was. The interpreter said, 'They asked me not to tell you.' They dismissed us and put us into solitary cells. They took Dean back to the Bridge House and apparently got him over his dysentery, somewhat.

"Our interpreter, was a Portuguese named Cesar Luis don Remedios. About a month later we were taken out of our cells, but this time there were only five of us, three were missing. They told us that the results of our court-martial had been determined and we had been given the death penalty. That was hanging over us. Remedios said, 'But you have been reprieved to life imprisonment with "special treatment," that if the Americans win the war, you are to be shot and if the Japanese win the war, you are to be kept as slave labor.'

"That was a pretty tremendous blow. We were more or less sort of stunned. We were put back in solitary confinement and stayed there until the following April. We didn't know exactly what had happened when we realized that three of our compatriots were not with us. We felt that maybe they were holding three of the people over our heads to keep us from attempting to escape. We didn't know until the end of the war that they had been executed."

Moved to a prison in Nanking, Hite used some money he still had at the time of his capture, to prevail upon the guards to buy some bread, which helped him over an illness. However, in November 1943, dysentery attacked the man in the next cell, Bob Meder, who rapidly lost weight and grew weaker and weaker. One day a guard shoved Meder, who summoned up enough bravado to throw a punch at him. He missed and fell to the ground. "That particular afternoon we tried to find out if there was anything we could do, and he said, 'Just pray.'" From his adjoining compartment, Hite heard Meder give a guard his address and ask that if he died would the man write his parents and send them his clothes. "Later, around dinnertime, when they stuck the food in Bob Meder's cell, the guard started yelling. Two or three others came running down the hall, opened the door, and went in. They kept yacking and yacking and then brought a doctor. Bob Meder had died that afternoon, sitting right in the cell."

The other Americans were given a brief viewing of their dead comrade before a cremation of the remains. We thought, 'Any of us can die at any time. We could all die and they could do away with us and nobody would ever know the difference.' It was an eerie feeling and I asked to write a letter to the prison governor. I [said] their so-called treatment of prisoners was against all Geneva conference rules [Japan was not a signatory], that our rations were outrageous or inadequate. It was a complaint letter. I asked, 'If you can't do anything else, will you please give us the Holy Bible to read?'

"I read the Bible and passed it on to Jake [Jacob deShazer]. Jake had proclaimed to be an atheist. His father was a preacher. He said he didn't believe in all that stuff. He didn't see any fruits of the so-called Christianity. It was the first time I ever—the first time any of us—had really read the Bible from cover to cover. It was sort of like a man being in the desert and finding a cool pool. After reading the Bible all of our attitudes changed. Instead of hating this enemy that we had had such hate for, we began to feel sorry for them and to see them through the eyes of Jesus or God—or through the Word, at least. It was almost a miracle to realize what happened to us. It seemed we were not afraid, to the extent we had been, at least. We no longer had the hatred. I think I lived on hate for the first year and a half. I think we were able to kind of keep ourselves living on the hate, instead of lying down and giving up."

One day while outside exercising they saw the silhouette of a B-29. "The Japanese had not seen it or heard it. Bombs dropped on the Yangtze River area and they ran us back in. These 29s were flying from way down deep in China. On Thanksgiving Day 1944 we had a P-51 raid on the airfield near the prison. When we saw the B-29 and the P-51 that really did strengthen our hope and lifted us up quite a bit."

Richard Carmichael, seized in June 1944 after his B-29 crash-landed on Iki Island, endured physical abuse from his interrogators. "They would hit me in the face with fists, books, and bookends. They would make you kneel and put these bamboo poles across your calves. Somebody would get on either end and start working on those calf muscles. They would put pencils between your fingers and start working on them."

The Japanese organized a court-martial charging Carmichael and three others with indiscriminate bombing that killed civilians. "There were three judges. We had to prove ourselves *innocent*. We were guilty until proven innocent. They had these big maps of Yawata and all the spots of the bomb burst that didn't hit the target. We didn't have any bombs on the target. We had them all killing civilians. [We were not] as in Germany deliberately bombing the cities. It was a military target, a recognized one. It was just our overage, shorts, rights and lefts. They were real serious about this. We were using high explosives. What got us off the hook was the fire raid. When LeMay brought those B-29s down to 5,000 to 9,000 feet that mass attack with firebombs, made use of the high explosive, military target type of thing, look pretty good by comparison. So they decided not to shoot us."

The Doolittle raid flyers interned in the Soviet Union spent an uncomfortable two years, even though they had landed in the country of an ally. Living conditions were spartan and their freedom severely restricted. Visited by American brass, internee Robert Emmens reported, "In a nutshell they said, 'We are doing what we can for you guys. There is a big war going on. You guys ought to be happy that you are here and not out in combat somewhere. We will do what we can.'" For the moment that amounted to carrying out letters to families and a pledge to send toothpaste, soap, and similar items. Later a U.S. general and the ambassador appeared, an occasion for a feast but the American authorities could not assure their release.

By January 1944, Emmens and his colleagues in desperation wrote a letter to Joseph Stalin volunteering to help with training Red airmen in B-25s and failing this asked to be moved to a warmer climate. No immediate response came but subsequently a piano appeared in their quarters to provide recreation and they were treated to the opera and theatricals. Their hosts moved the crew west, through Samarkand to Ashkhabad, capital of the Turkmenistan Republic and on the edge of Persia—modern Iran. Given work in a factory, but with no prospect of freedom, Emmens and Ed York schemed to escape into Iran. They enlisted a Soviet acquaintance who with some $300 chipped in by the five Americans, bribed a truck driver to smuggle them past the border guards into the town of Mashad. Once inside Iranian territory, they dashed through the gates of a British consulate. "We were transported then to Washington," said Emmens, "and we were told that under no circumstances were we allowed to say that we were part of the Doolittle raid group that was interned in Russia, that Russia was very upset at our leaving. They did not want the Japanese to know that we were out."

Initially, Emmens believed they achieved their freedom through their own efforts. But subsequently he wondered whether their escape had been a sham, a devious arrangement by the Soviets to be rid of a troublesome matter. As an added insult, the American embassy billed the quintet about $600 for parkas, tobacco, postage stamps, and medicine but no one offered to refund the $300 the escapees spent obtaining their freedom.

Those who found refuge in neutral Sweden fared considerably better. With their families assured of their safety, crews like that of Ralph Golumbock, who had been forced to land in Sweden and been interned, settled into a comfortable life as tourists restricted only by the borders of the country. Golubock even spent the Jewish High Holidays with a local Jewish family. During one excursion to Stockholm the Air Corps men noticed another group of young men surrounded by Swedes as they were. Someone who spoke English informed Golubock and his colleagues that the others were all German Luftwaffe pilots.

While none of the German stalags matched the brutality or the subhuman living conditions of O'Donnell, in the Philippines, the GIs taken prisoner endured similar shortages of food, in the Philippines, the ravages of bad nutrition, and the diseases spawned by inadequate sanitation. John Collins, who participated in a last stand before St. Vith during the Battle of the Bulge, recalled, "Seven men to a loaf of bread, a little oleo, one cup of soup called 'scilly'—good for shaving or washing your face—and their coffee—hot water. Also we receive [d] a few potatoes at noon, if available. About three times a week, a can of bully beef or maybe horsemeat for six men." Cigarettes served as the chief currency of the Kriegsgefangeners—kriegies—40 or 50 bought a can of Nescafé, 70 or 80 bought bread. A good watch might earn between 250 and 600 smokes."

In Collins's camp they slept in huts on tiers of boards. "The barracks were infested with lice and fleas. The big fat ones stay in all tight places of clothing. You cannot get rid of them so you try to educate them by ignoring them." The filth of the latrine across the street spilled on floors although prisoners from the Red Army were supposed to clean the repository. According to Collins, Red Cross parcels went only to men who volunteered for work parties. The Americans and British refused but the French agreed to perform labor in return for the packages. Through the exchange of cigarettes, the contents of the Red Cross parcels reached some GIs.

Phil Hannon from the 106th Division observed discipline enforced by the POWs. "Any man caught stealing from another prisoner was automatically put in the 'outcast barracks.' First he was thrown into the open latrine pit, and men from the quarters where he stole stood around the pit and urinated on him. Theft from the Germans was accepted practice, so long as it didn't endanger anyone else. Others who ended up in the outcast barracks were those who fought constantly or had such disgusting habits that their associates voted them out. The outcast barracks GIs pulled the 'honey dipping detail', emptying out the latrine and hauling the mess away. The punishment deterred a lot of thieves."

Hannon and his fellows developed unquenchable cravings for food. "I remember dreaming of a roast beef dinner with mashed potatoes and gravy. I could actually smell the gravy but I couldn't eat it and I woke myself up crying. Each of us would make up elaborate meals we would have when we

got home and we tried to outdo each other. When we first became prisoners, we felt cheated, being out of the war. For a while we were hard on ourselves, as if we had been captured because we hadn't done our job properly.
The attitude changed after a few days of walking and starving. We became
much more individually oriented, thinking of ourselves, instead of what we
failed to do for the army. Some of the men were loners. They didn't team
up or seem to need cozying up. They were self-reliant, able to make it on
their own. There were those rejected by everyone else because of the ways
they acted or for their personal habits. They couldn't cozy up and had a difficult time. There were those, a very few, who literally gave up in the POW
camp. They'd roll over and in a couple of days they were dead. That was their
escape, but their behavior was totally beyond my comprehension. I was just
amazed when a person would shrivel up and die; they were not being treated
any worse than anyone else."

Ed Uzemack relished a windfall of Red Cross-supplied chocolate bars,
cigarettes, meat, fish, crackers, butter, raisins, sugar, coffee, powdered milk,
vitamin pills, and soap. "It was explained that the boxes came as a loan from
Serbian prisoners—God bless them—who had a surplus. We got one box
for each four men." Uzemack said he became giddy after puffing on his first
cigarette in forty-five days. During the first month at Stalag XI B, only three
of the 4,000 prisoners succumbed, thanks in large measure to the work of
a medical officer, said Uzemack. The figure would climb steeply in ensuing
months.

Along with starvation, disease, and the deadly force from their captors,
U.S. airplanes also brought destruction. Said Uzemack, "Yank planes chasing the Heinies accidently strafed the camp. Val Casados, my last buddy here,
was killed. He was standing beside our bunk talking to me when bullets
sprayed all around us. How those .50-caliber slugs missed me, I'll never know.
One hit the bedpost a few inches from my head. Two other men were killed
and twelve more wounded."

Jim Mills of the 106th Division joined a labor gang assigned to work clearing rubble in Dresden. The prisoners lived in an abandoned abattoir, later
famous as *Slaughterhouse-Five*. When the massive raids by RAF and the U.S.
Air Corps transformed much of Dresden into a crematorium the Germans
put Mills and other POWs to work removing bodies from a basement. "There
was a body lying on the floor where a hall led to the next building, and it
had been hit right at the waistline with one of the incendiary bombs. The
body was almost burnt in half.

"The guard pointed at the corpse as one I should remove. He indicated
I take a belt off another body and put it around the one I was to remove.
It's surprising how much could be communicated by hand motions. I put a
belt around the neck of this man and started to drag it toward the ramp.

But it broke in half. That was too much for me. I sort of lost it for a bit. I began to scream, yell, and dance around. I tried to get out of there but they wouldn't let me."

Given a draft of liquor for his ragged nerves, Mills returned to his gruesome task. "The guards forced me to pick up the top half of the body, put it on a stretcher at the base of the ramp. They made another man pick up the bottom half. He didn't like it any better than I did and told me so. We carried the remains out and put them on the street alongside several others. We then got back at the end of the line. As we neared the head of it we would slip out of the line and go to the rear, trying to avoid going back into the basement. Finally the guards caught us and put us at the front. In the cellar again, I thought I would be smart. I picked a fellow who had on a gas mask. I thought all I would need do is drag him by the mask to the stretcher. But when I grabbed the mask and pulled, it popped off his head. His eyes looked as if they were almost out of their sockets. His mouth was wide open and the whole face and mouth was covered with blood. I lost my cool again and the guards had me drink some more liquor. I remember taking out the body to the pile but the rest of the day is no longer part of my memory. From there on this was our daily job. We cleaned up the rubble and removed any bodies found."

Casual and calculated killing menaced anyone in a prison camp. The Germans housed the Ranger officers captured in the disaster at Cisterna in Stalag XIII B, at Hammelburg. Clarence Meltesen recalled, "The shooting of Lt. John Weeks was cold-blooded murder by a German gate guard. On the sixteenth the guard in question had been noticed at his post and muttering to the men as they passed on their way. Later an explanation was offered that the guard had recently lost his wife in an air-raid attack. When Weeks went by, and after turning the corner, the guard steadied his rifle on the wire and shot him in the back of the head." The camp commandant apologized to the senior American officer and a brief funeral interred the lieutenant in a cemetery with a growing number of residents from XIII B. Bing Evans, a Ranger captured at Cisterna, said he witnessed so many incidents of abuse and murder that he developed a lifelong affliction of periodic black rages.

The sustained, massive bombing that did not spare civilians added to the jeopardy of those airmen shot down. German police and civilians clubbed, shot, or stabbed to death four members of a crew, including the pilot Capt. Herb Newman, after enemy fighters knocked their plane out of the sky. While evadee pilot Howard Snyder, who had trained as an infantryman before volunteering for the Air Corps, joined the Belgian Maquis, other members of his crews also hid out with local people. On the morning of 22 April 1944, eight American airmen, including George Eike, Snyder's copilot, his navigator Robert Benninger, and gunner John Pindroch ate breakfast in a hut owned by a Belgian farmer. Plans had been set for the evadees to seek safety. They were given money, some received civilian clothing. Suddenly, a party of as many as 1,500 soldiers, gestapo and Belgian collaborators descended on the area and seized the Americans along with those who harbored them.

The captives were taken to a nearby schoolhouse for interrogation. All of them still had their dog tags, which identified them as military personnel, but, except for Eike and Benninger, were out of uniform. Around 2:30 in the afternoon the Americans were loaded into a truck and under guard driven to a nearby woods. Lined up in single file, with a pair of soldiers behind each one, they were marched into the forest. Some 500 feet from the road, each airman was moved in a separate direction, still accompanied by his two Germans carrying pistols. Upon a prearranged signal, the soldiers shot the captives in the back three or four times and left them for dead. Sometime later, the bodies were buried in a common grave. A pair of Belgians who had been acting as hosts to the evadees disappeared into concentration camps.

The behavior of those held by the Germans varied considerably. Fighter pilot Henry Spicer, the senior officer in his camp until the arrival of Hub Zemke, became a sharp thorn to his captors. Interviewing newcomers Spicer heard tales of mistreatment by civilians and soldiers. He may also have had an opportunity to witness the brutality meted out to Soviet captives. In any event, Spicer soon became the instigator of resistance to the camp routine as the captives harassed guards, mucked up their roll call counts, and challenged any behavior proscribed by the Geneva convention. When Zemke came to the camp and became the prisoner leader, he supported Spicer's campaign. On a frigid November morning with the entire population rousted from the barracks to stand shivering in the open air the guards exacted their own revenge as they stretched out the count from the normal fifteen minutes to two interminable hours.

At this point, according to Lt. Philip Robertson, "Colonel Spicer dismissed us, over the loud protestations of the German guards. He then called us over to his barracks, and we gathered around him, as he stood on the steps about three feet above us and began to talk loud enough for the guards to hear."

Captain Mozart Kaufman, in the audience, and who later reconstructed with others Spicer's speech, said the outspoken fighter pilot first recounted an incident in the stalag. "Yesterday an officer was put in the 'cooler' for two weeks. He had two counts against him. The first was failure to obey an order of a German officer. That is beside the point. The second was failure to salute a German officer of lower rank.

"The Articles of the Geneva convention say to salute all officers of equal or higher rank. The Germans in this camp have put out an order that we must salute all German officers, whether of lower or higher rank. My order to you is salute all German officers of equal or higher rank." Spicer then shifted to other matters. "I have noticed that many of you are becoming too buddy-buddy with the Germans. [Irwin Stovroff saw officers, including ones of higher rank, cozy up to their captors in return for small favors, such as an egg.] Remember we are still at war with the Germans. They are still our enemies and are doing everything they can to win this war. Don't let them fool you around this camp, because they are dirty, lying sneaks and can't be trusted."

The prisoners cheered loudly and a German major, outraged at the tirade, ordered Spicer into the "cooler," a small cell about six by eight feet. The camp authorities held a court-martial, charging him with inciting a riot. The initial sentence was six months in the cooler and then death by firing squad. When the men happened to be led past Spicer's cell they yelled encouragement and Spicer would reply with words like, "Keep fighting! Don't give in to the bastards." After he had endured a number of months in solitary, his jailers relented, canceling the orders for execution and returning him to the general population.

Conditions in the prison camps had begun to deteriorate further as the Soviet armies to the east and the Americans and British to the west squeezed the area controlled by the Germans and food supplies shrank. Bombardier Irwin Stovroff, shot down in August while aboard *Passion Pit* had taken the precaution to toss away his dogtags, which identified him as Jewish. But on 19 January 1945, with the entire compound population drawn up for the usual roll call and count, the commandant ordered all Jewish prisoners to take one step forward. Before anyone could respond, Spicer, backed by Zemke, shouted for all of the Americans to step out. None of those present hesitated and all obeyed. The solidarity by his comrades in incarceration heartened Stovroff but to his dismay, he and the others of his faith were soon segregated. Luftwaffe intelligence apparently already knew the background of most of their captives.

P-47 pilot Paul Ellington recalled, "The commandant, von Mueller, went to Hub Zemke and asked him for a roster of the Jews. Zemke told him, 'We're all Jews.' I guess von Mueller thought he'd make his job easier. But they knew who the Jews were and put them in some buildings separated from us by a fence. At night, we cut up the fence so people could move back and forth and they never repaired it. Some of the Jews had been treated badly. There was a fellow named Goldstein, from the 56th Fighter Group, and he had been cut badly on his shin when shot down. He was picked up by the gestapo and they kept kicking him with their steel pointed boots in that shin. When he got to the camp, his shin was a terrible mess, all scarred. Somehow, they didn't have his name when they separated out the Jews. He went to Zemke and said, 'I feel I ought to go with my people.' Zemke said, 'You've had enough trouble already. Keep your mouth shut.'"

For the next four months, Stovroff and those with him feared the worst. Spicer, who once again had annoyed the authorities, drew no extra punishment for his attempt to shield the Jewish prisoners. Apparently, the camp officials accepted him as a hard case. Although Stovroff had been fearful of his future once the officials separated the Jewish prisoners, he experienced no ill treatment. Stovroff recalls a brief visit to camp by Max Schmeling the former world heavyweight boxing champion who said, "I wish you all luck and hope to see you in the States." He handed out photographs. "We put them in the urinals," says Stovroff.

Perhaps the most dangerous status of the prisoners was to be in transit. Jim McCubbin said, "A German army sergeant told a group of us, consisting of about one hundred that we were to be transported by train to a prisoner of war camp in Nürnberg. He [said] he had taken this trip with other prisoners twenty-six times and had been strafed by our fighters twenty-five times. The train was an ordinary passenger one with three boxcars attached to the end with a flak car between. Half of the car was roped off for the guards, and some thirty prisoners shared the other half. There was only room for a few to sit. The remainder had to stand. There were two openings high up on the side walls through which one could gain a limited view. We had only been traveling several hours when the 'lookouts' shouted that two Mustangs were strafing the locomotive. The two lookouts dived for the floor, allowing several others and myself to then gain access to the view. I was just in time to see the fighters starting a run down the length of the train. As I turned to join the heap on the floor, the only opening was on the top. I shall never forget the sound of those .50-caliber bullets crashing through the wood and bodies. It reminded me of the game played in bars where you shake five dice in a wooden cup for drinks. There were two passes, but I didn't hear the second. That time I was thankful for the German flak car. If it hadn't been for them, I know the planes would have made several more passes." McCubbin adds, "I should know. I had done this frequently.

"In all, there were about sixteen prisoners killed, about the same number of civilians, and many wounded. Later, after the bodies were laid out and the wounded identified, a German medical officer and several orderlies began to attend to those in need. I was impressed to witness how the wounded were attended without regard for nationality." Marched to another rail line to resume the journey, McCubbin endured a dive-bomb attack from P-47s. Watching the bombs leave the wings, he says, "I remembered that you were supposed to lie down but to keep your stomach off the ground. The bombs landed so far away I hardly noticed them. But that gave me a feeling of life in the infantry. I was much more scared than I had ever been in the air."

As the Soviet armies advanced toward the German border, the Nazis started to drive prisoners housed in the east toward the Americans and British, perhaps to use as bargaining chips. It became a death march as weakened kriegies collapsed from unhealed wounds, disease, or hunger and either froze to death or else guards murdered them. In some instances, the prisoners carried a sick man to the door of a house and after knocking left him there, hoping for mercy from the inhabitants.

In his role as medical officer, Lu Cox tended the sick and injured but his supplies were so limited he could mostly offer only Band-Aids for blisters. The torturous hike in the worst snowstorm Cox had ever seen covered 100 miles, and all along the way they saw a vast caravan of German refugees, old men and women, small children and babies, in farm wagons pulled by oxen or on foot, also fleeing the oncoming Soviets. At the end of a nearly six-day journey, the surviving prisoners crowded into boxcars that carried them to their new home, a huge camp that eventually held more than 100,000 Allied prisoners. In his compound Cox says, "A thousand men were flat on their backs suffering from advanced stages of diarrhea, flu, pneumonia, dysentery, malnutrition, exposure, frostbite, frozen feet, and irritated and reopened wounds. There were no doctors, next to no medical supplies, not even a place fit to lie down. After appealing time after time for medical help from the Germans, the worst patients were taken out of the camp and given showers and deloused and moved into another compound. The most serious were removed to the hospital." Cox and the others in better condition now coped with the omnipresent frigid temperatures, sanitation problems, and a diet he describes as "unfit for pigs to eat, for it contained bits of wire, wood, worms, bugs, and sometimes a dead mouse."

While some felt escape was hopeless, others persisted in their attempts. Bill Topping said, "I tried five times to escape, digging tunnels. Hell, the Germans knew we were digging them. They'd let us alone and by the time we were ready to pop out, they'd swoop in and catch us. It gave us something to do and kept us busy. I played so much bridge in the camp that I became sick of it. I played solitaire, listened to stories that got bigger and longer as you stayed there."

Marshall Draper, the bombardier shot down fourth July 1942, endured one of the longest stays of an American behind the wire. He reported, "Most of the activities of the camp revolved around escaping. The accounts I have read or seen about tunneling or other escape efforts at Stalag Luft III seem to indicate that these were primarily activities of men from the RAF. As a matter of fact, the Americans were heavily involved and supplied a good deal of labor and technical expertise for such enterprises. I was number 101 on the priority list to go through a tunnel if and when it was completed. I contracted diphtheria in the summer of 1943 and was quarantined in the sick bay for a couple of weeks, during which time one of the tunnels was discovered. A few days later, the Americans were separated from the RAF and moved to a different compound, away from the two other partially built tunnels.

He confirms the account of David Jones. "Of these two, one was discovered by the Germans, but the other, closed down for the winter, was successfully completed the following spring and resulted in the exit from the North Compound of seventy-six RAF men. Three of these, two Norweigians and a Dutchman, made it home. Fifty of the recaptured men were shot by the gestapo, fifteen returned to the camp, and eight were sent to the Oranienberg concentration camp. In point of fact, only a few men made good their escape. The remainder could only wait for the arrival of the advancing troops."

45
The Battle For Manila

The flying columns that penetrated the Manila outskirts struck from the northeast. At first the overall plan envisioned a move by the 11th Airborne parachutists and glidermen that would block any attempt to relieve the Manila garrison from the south. Subsequently, Gen. Robert Eichelberger, in charge of the U.S. Eighth Army, received permission from MacArthur to change the mission and attack Manila from the south, penetrating what was known as the Genko line. With two glider-infantry teams ashore from a seaborne operation that placed them a scant forty-five miles from Manila, the script posited an airborne drop on Tagaytay Ridge, heights that overlooked the strongest fortifications of the defenders. Building upon the former U.S. installations of Nichols Field and Fort McKinley over a three-year period, the Japanese had constructed reinforced concrete pillboxes dominating the avenues into the city. In the passage of time nature contributed vegetation to augment skillful camouflage.

The glider-infantrymen progressed swiftly toward Manila until they bumped up against an enemy dug in along the slopes of the mountains between them and the city. Medic Al Ullman scribbled in his diary for 2 February, "Tired of marching, slept on the ground last night. Expect trouble soon. At noon it happened. Jap artillery opened up, everyone dived for ditches but some were not so lucky. At least 10 killed and no wounded. Assisted major in performing an amputation in a ditch with a trench knife, artillery landing around us. A miserable day. That night was on guard, boy, was I scared."

After some debate about the risks of an airborne drop on Tagaytay, Gen. Joseph Swing's paratroopers crowded aboard C-47s on Leyte on the morning of 3 February, the same day the first Americans burst into Manila from the northeast. With only forty-eight transports available, the troop carriers flew a dangerous three-shift operation, one in which the last two serials could anticipate deadly antiaircraft fire from an alerted enemy.

William "Buzz" Miley, as leader of the 2d platoon in Company G, said, "We were in the first echelon. I will always remember the beautiful sight of Lake Taal as we approached from the south, made a wide circle around the lake, and dropped on an east-to-west pass. Even though later reports stated we jumped early, I don't believe my stick did since we landed just north of the Manila Extension Hotel, about 200-330 yards from the highway. We landed without incident, assembled, and started moving south to the highway. We smelled a terrific stench and discovered a dead Filipino next to a small fire. His feet had been burned off. We naturally assumed that the Japanese had done it but none were sighted until that afternoon."

Although Miley describes an uneventful drop, as happened so often, the deliveries significantly missed the marks. As the first seventeen aircraft dropped men right over the target, the lead ship of the second section dumped its equipment bundles. Figuring this was their cue, jumpmasters standing in the doors of the trailing planes, signaled go. The parachutes of 540 troopers blossomed and the jumpers touched down four to five miles away from the drop zone on Tagaytay Ridge. After the planes returned to Leyte and loaded up again they repeated the mistake, as the jumpmasters, peering down, cued on the discarded chutes of the earlier jumpers. Purely by luck, and unknown to the descending paratroopers, the Japanese had not posted any troops on Tagaytay Ridge. The Americans who landed there escaped serious consequences from the error. A day later, the final batch of troopers dropped in the proper place.

The men of the 11th forging toward Tagaytay Ridge on the ground joined their comrades who came by air. Troopers and glidermen attacked the foremost enemy emplacements. Hard fighting followed as the outfit forced a crossing over the Parañaque River. Al Ullman's diary reports, "Today we had 19 wounded men to be evacuated. By now a man's guts are no new sight to me. Today the first of my buddies died from his wounds. I kept saying my prayers."

As the airborne GIs slogged toward Manila, the 1st Cavalry began the job of evicting the defenders. "We beat the 37th [Division] into Manila," recalls Sal DeGaetano, "but only after crawling across bombed-out bridges and past dead civilians. We came into a courtyard and spotted some Japs across Malate Circle at a gas station and house. We crossed to the opposite side of the street to the station where the Japs had disappeared. I heard voices from a basement window, level with the ground. I recognized the language and tossed a grenade, at the same time as one came out. I had dropped to the ground and when I heard my grenade go off, I raised up and got bits of shrapnel in my wrist, head, and shoulder. Luckily, I had raised my hand or I might have been hit in the left eye." Medics evacuated DeGaetano to a hospital in Quezon City.

From southwest of Manila, the 38th Division with the 34th Regiment of the 24th Division attached, expected to cut across the top of the Bataan peninsula and meet the troops driving down from Lingayen Gulf on the highway between Clark Field and the city. Paul Austin, promoted from company commander to executive officer of the 34th's 2d Battalion, endured a miserable march of nineteen miles in the heat before his outfit reached the now-deserted town of Olongapo. From there the GIs traveled east along a road known as Zig Zag Trail. It was a mountainous area and all the terrain sloped down toward the south to the edges of the road, which zigged and zagged around each ridge.

"We were in reserve when the 38th made contact with the Japanese," said Austin. "They had had two and a half years to prepare their defenses along Zig Zag Pass and done their work very well. Back on the highway, three or four miles behind the 38th, we saw those two-and-a-half-ton trucks haul men out of there, bodies piled in the back like cordwood. They had the road under observation and as our troops moved into a certain area, all they had to do was go to their reference table, put the gun to a certain setting, fire half a dozen rounds, and literally blow men to pieces. It was that accurate.

"We moved up closer on February 3d. We hiked in under a 90mm mortar barrage. It came walking down the road and as the shells got closer and closer, I grabbed the base of a tree trunk and flung my body over the edge of a deep dropoff. I hung my body over that gully, while clinging to that tree. I was scared. There is nothing more terrifying than those mortar shells. You cannot hear them coming. You have no warning. Before you hear anything at all, it has already exploded, thrown, or torn your body. I managed to get back up and we moved on.

"The 38th was pulled back for reorganization and rest. They had suffered tremendous casualties. We continued up the road. We had a couple of tanks with us, artillery firing coming over constantly. We drove 'em back probably a quarter of a mile. The next day we made maybe half a mile. On February 6, we ran into several mortar barrages that literally destroyed the 2d Battalion. F Company walked into a forty-round barrage and they came out with just twelve men. A sergeant came to me crying, tears running down his face. He was devastated. All his friends were gone. It was a family thing and it tears at a man's guts when the family he's been living with, trying to survive with, the men he loved and respected and that loved him, and they're all gone."

Joe Hofrichter, the onetime engineer reassigned to F Company had developed a blister from ill-fitting shoes and the extended marches to Zig Zag. "We had two Sherman tanks that led our convoy of a few vehicles, and a truck with ammunition and other supplies followed. I asked the driver if it would be okay to ride on the back of the truck until we got up through the pass. He said 'Hop on,' and I did. Slowly the tanks and truck crawled forward. About three-fourths of the way to the summit, we came to a wide curve and relatively straight piece of exposed road. Suddenly, to the right and above us, all hell seemed to come alive. I saw the first tank get hit and begin to burn. Almost immediately, the tank in front of my truck was struck a glancing blow that spun it to the right. An antitank gun trained on the rear of that tank missed its target and hit the left front of our truck, blowing it and everyone in it over the side into a ravine in the dense jungle.

"As I flew into the air, I saw a shoe flying by. What's my shoe doing there, I wondered! In a split second it was over. I have no recollection of where or how I landed. After seeing the shoe, my mind went blank. When I opened my eyes, it was dark and I was lying on a cot. I had no idea where I was, how I got there, what time it was, nor for that matter, what day it was. I next became conscious that I was in great pain. My legs were numb and my back hurt so badly, I could hardly breathe. To my left I saw what looked like a huge person, lying completely still. To my right was a man on a cot, leaning on his elbow and looking at me. In a thick Southern accent, he whispered, 'How ya all doin? I heard ya moanin.'

"'I hurt,' I replied. 'Where in the heck am I?'

"'Youse in a hospital in Olongapo.'

"About that time someone walked between our beds and turned on a flashlight. I thought I had died and gone to heaven. A foot away was the face of a beautiful woman. She said, 'Hi, I see you are awake. I'm Lieutenant Powell.' She told me I was brought in late that afternoon. They had dug some shrapnel from my back, which was severely damaged. She gave me a shot of morphine and I drifted off to sleep. When I awakened I saw I was in a room with thirty wounded men. The fellow next to me with the Southern accent was a black man from South Carolina. He was a cook and was burned on the legs when a field stove blew up. After watching them administer my first injections of morphine with three needles, he would often say, 'Man, how in hell can ya take those long-ass needles.' He couldn't understand that I looked forward to them to manage the pain. The big fellow to my right had a severe wound in his stomach. He was in bad shape and had gone into shock. Brought in with me, he died three days later."

Wireman Han Rants with the 2d Battalion Headquarters Company had placed telephone lines for communications. Around 4:00 P.M. he heard the sound of heavy blasts in the E Company sector. Notified that communications were out, Rants led a wire section to repair the telephone system. "Each of the shells that had come in had been a direct hit, as if someone had been looking at the men and dropped the shells right on them. The shock was seeing a body lodged up a small tree. There were bodies blown in all directions. They had thirty-four killed and many wounded. We established a new line, got the wounded and the bodies of the dead back to Headquarters Company for the move back to regiment.

"We were just settled, the time probably about 5:00 P.M., still daylight. We heard five more thunderous explosions like those that had hit E Company. These were in the direction of F and G Companies. We just assumed they had been hit horribly with the same big mortars. It was such a sickening sound. Again we took off to be sure the line was in place. We took some able-bodied soldiers, plus medics because we knew there would be casualties again. The sight was almost the same as seeing E Company. There were many guys blown apart, badly wounded with lots of need for medics, and many, many dead. We repeated the same operation we had with E Company but just could not get all the dead because it was getting late at night."

On the following morning, the huge mortars zeroed in on the Headquarters Company position. "I was perched on a field telephone, sitting just off the ground, eating some breakfast after the days of heavy, heavy work and fighting. Even in the fear, hunger came through. As I sat there, these shells exploded and I was blown some six feet into a hole." The carnage was fearsome, wiping out close associates, exposing Rants to sights of dismembered dead comrades. One man could only be identified by a ring and watch still around the remnant of an arm.

Austin spent an anguished night in a foxhole with Major Snavely, his CO, and in the morning, greeted a handful of men on the road. "There was an artillery observation team sitting there, two or three medical jeeps with aidmen eating their breakfast, C rations. I squatted down talking with the sergeant of the observation team when I got a funny feeling. Something was going on in my gut, maybe diarrhea. It got very intense, a feeling I had to move and which I couldn't resist. I walked back up to my foxhole, put on my steel helmet, wondering why I was doing it. At that instant, three 90mm mortar shells hit in the area. One struck dead center of the forward observation team. Another landed in the road and destroyed the jeeps with the medics. The third exploded in the foxhole with the battalion sergeant major and killed him. That was it. They fired just these three rounds. I went back down the road. All of the men I had been talking to were blown to pieces. Body parts lay all around the rations; the medics had shrapnel wounds that tore their bodies up. One man was blown in two and I saw a boot with a leg still in it.

"About that time, Major Snavely and the battalion surgeon, Dr. Cameron, showed up and told me to take every man I could find down into a gully. Just as we got everybody under cover, the regimental CO, Col. [William] Jenna, rode up in a jeep. He stopped and immediately wanted to know what we were doing, standing there when we were supposed to be moving up the road in an attack. He said to me, 'Captain, get those men out of that ditch and up on the road and start moving.' I said, 'Yes, sir.' I was in a battlefield situation in the face of the enemy and my colonel had given me an order and the only thing I could do was obey.

"Dr. Cameron asked if he could speak with Colonel Jenna and when given permission told him the situation of the 2d Battalion. He said he knew where all the units were, and their approximate strength, and in effect told the colonel, 'You don't have a 2d Battalion anymore.' Colonel Jenna said, 'I didn't know this. I'll have trucks up here in an hour and you're going back to a rest area.' We went back to our holes and sure enough trucks came and carried us back twenty miles to a bivouac area on a stream with shade trees. I spent several miserable days there as I thought about our friends and what had happened to them."

"On the first night just out of Zig Zag Pass," says Rants, "I made a decision that has made my entire life a series of blessings in God's service. I had believed I was a Christian because I believed in God and lived the kind of life I thought he would want me to live. An occasional trip to church perhaps three or four times a year was a way of confirming my support. I was very grateful to God for the physical gifts I had, but I really thought that I was the one who performed the deeds and God simply said, 'Well done.' This night I realized that I was not in control at all and that I had been accepting credit and compliments for achievements which he was responsible for. The fact that I had been blown through the air and received only a small wound was one more in a series of miracles, a blessing, if you will, which I finally realized God was providing. He gave me direction in the kinds of things I did, had me in the right place at the right time. As I prayed and talked with God, I asked forgiveness for feeling that I had done so much and I surrendered all credit to his glory. I told him that whatever amount of days or nights I had left in my life would all be dedicated to his service."

The official figures reported 325 battle casualties for the 34th Infantry and 25 psychoneurosis cases in less than a week, nearly half as many as were lost during 78 days of combat on Leyte. Austin insisted the total was closer to 1,200 at Zig Zag, but he may have included the losses to the 38th Division in his count. The results at Zig Zag brought the dismissal of the 38th Division commander as well as assorted regimental and staff officers for a "lack of aggressiveness." Austin, from his perspective, responds, "From General MacArthur on down, every one of our leaders knew that place was fortified, but they sent us in there, men with rifles and grenades, and they chewed us to pieces. We had no air support, did not bomb the area before we went in, didn't napalm it, nothing to soften it up for the infantry. Later they fired the entire load of 105 ammo from a Liberty ship into the Japanese on Zig Zag Pass. They marked it off in sections and gave a section to each gun, literally blowing the area to bits. Finally, when the boys with rifles got up there, they could pretty much walk through with no problem." In addition, planes from the the airfield on Luzon repeatedly bombed the area.

While the GIs waged a deadly contest for the route from the west coast, the 37th Division, on the right flank, beaten into Manila by the 1st Cavalry with its more mechanized troops, nibbled at the edges of the city on 4 February and after a respite at a brewery, where they slaked their thirst, the GIs moved out. They walked cautiously down Rizal Avenue toward Bonifacio Monument, with nary an incident other than outbursts from cheering throngs. By nightfall, the beery battalion settled in a few miles from Bilibid Prison with its imprisoned Americans from 1942. On the following day, an advance element of the 148th approached Bilibid, bearing in mind an intelligence report that said the Japanese planned to blow up an ammunition dump in the prison when the GIs came on the scene.

As members of F Company approached Bilibid, an enemy machine gun sprayed the boulevard and snipers let fly. The soldiers, lounging on the curbs along with the Manilans showering them with greetings and offerings, scattered. A ten-man patrol led by Sgt. Rayford Anderson cautiously attained a vantage point from which they saw a pair of Japanese sentries lolling about the main entrance of Bilibid. Anderson gave the word and a fusillade of bullets cut down both guards. The commotion aroused hostile but ineffectual bursts from a nearby machine gunner.

Rather than confront that automatic weapon, Anderson chose to reconnoiter the rear of the building. A member of the patrol shot off the lock from a side entrance and broke into a storage area. Prowling the building they came upon boarded-up windows. When Anderson pried the slats off he peered out into the prison courtyard and saw about fifty people huddled together. The Americans realized these were Caucasians and probably prisoners. They called out to them, urged them to open a locked iron gate. To the inmates, the unfamiliar silhouettes of the American helmets and their rifles, gear that postdated their knowledge, generated the suspicion that the armed men were Japanese assigned to murder them. The crowd refused to budge. Not even a few verses of "God Bless America" sufficed to convince them. Sergeant Smith tossed in some Philip Morris cigarettes and the smokes persuaded the prisoners. In short order, the entire battalion, occupied Bilibid and the surrounding streets, liberating 1,200 people, including several hundred military men, most of whom were in the hospital on the verge of death from their injuries, disease, and malnutrition.

The 754th Tank Battalion with gunner Tom Howard in Company A had checked in with the 37th Infantry Division and expected to face ferocious opposition as they entered the city streets. Instead it was more like a spontaneous Mardi Gras parade than a war. "The Filipinos came from their homes, their shops, appearing from everywhere to greet us, waving and yelling. Some Filipinos invited us into their homes and set up the drinks. One elderly Filipino man brought out an old bottle of Three Feathers whiskey that he had hidden during the Japanese occupation. He said he had saved it for just this occasion. We gladly helped him drink it. Someone played the piano and others cleared the floor for dancing. To hell with the war. Forgot about eating lunch. 'Snake' [the company commander] came looking for us and even he is dancing."

The 754th tanks rambled deeper into the city, trying to draw a reaction from Japanese soldiers and their locations but fierce blazes consuming Manila kept both sides from contact. Howard's tank, Boozer 3-4, stopped at Bilibid Prison, now liberated, and then Santo Tomas before it entered the downtown section. With the rear of the tank backed into the entrance of the Commonwealth Life Insurance Building the crew overlooked the strategic Jones Bridge over the Pasig River and received orders to hold the span whatever the cost. Howard remarked, "We had to button up inside the tank because of sniper fire."

Across the Pasig, along its banks and behind fortified emplacements, perhaps 15,000 soldiers and sailors prepared to battle the Americans. To confound their attackers, the defenders detonated preset charges that ignited everything flammable. The fires on the Japanese side leaped the Pasig, raking Manila with a huge, uncontrolled blaze. GIs from the 37th coped with intense heat, ever-prevalent snipers, and pillboxes that dominated approaches to the river.

Tom Howard's 2d platoon led foot soldiers of the 145th Infantry Regiment toward their objective. Howard noted, "The tank commander reported an antitank gun and directed his gunner's fire upon it. The weapon was completely destroyed. Platoon credit for the engagement was 12 dead and was instrumental in killing 113 of the enemy." Subsequently, while protecting the Quezon Bridge, Howard halted a charge by the enemy with rounds of 75mm canister. "The state of siege had settled down into a condition where bodies of civilians and Japanese were still strewn over the streets, in gutters, on lawns, and in the middle of the pavement. Attempts to remove them were met with sniper fire, so instead of removal, when dusk came, the bodies were covered with quicklime to hasten their deterioration and to stifle the smell. Upon entering any of the buildings on sniper patrols, the halls, corridors, and rooms had scattered Japanese bodies that it was impossible to get rid of. To keep from being tricked by a sniper pretending to be dead, we pulled all the bodies to the walls and sat them up leaning against the wall. We proceeded to shoot each one in the forehead regardless of whether they were already dead. In this way, we could immediately tell upon entering a room or a hall if any bluff was being pulled. Anything that lay in the middle of the floor was shot again, then placed against the wall. It was a grotesque, gruesome picture to see these row-by-row bodies along the walls. These were the day-by-day necessities to survive one day more."

From the buildings overlooking the Pasig River environs, the tankers provided an observation post for U.S. artillery, carefully avoiding the eyes of enemy troops who would then shell the structure. "We had to watch while the

Japanese soldiers dragged out nuns in their habits and tied them to the flag-pole and proceeded to whip them. We had to endure the sight of a group of Japanese soldiers drag Filipino women out into the open and rape them. It was hard to hold fire and observe the events. There was no way to describe the emotion of hate of the Japanese and the anguish of not being able to help the women, but orders were orders."

From the southwest, platoon leader Eli Bernheim of the 11th Airborne contrasted the catch-as-catch can confrontations in Leyte, where front lines hardly existed, to the fight for Nichols Field. "We had the classic coordinated attack on Nichols Field, airborne artillery, 75mm pack howitzers, against Japanese 5-inch naval guns in concrete pillboxes and many 20mms. It was very, very difficult. My battalion took friendly fire from marine dive-bombers. A 500-pound bomb hit a platoon CP." The struggle for the airbase lasted four bloody days.

The Shimbu Group, an army under Gen. Shizuo Yokoyama, within whose purview Manila came, entertained the notion of a counterattack against what its intelligence faultily described as a limited U.S. presence in the city. At the very least, Yokoyama believed he could open an escape route for Admiral Iwabuchi's men. General Tomoyuki Yamashita, however, angry that Iwabuchi had been permitted to attempt a defense, needlessly sacri-ficing people, scotched any ambitions of an offensive. He ordered that his subordinate only attempt to extricate the naval soldiers in the city. Yokoyama achieved dismal results. The 1st Cavalry, aided by devastating artillery, slaughtered the Japanese seeking to open a route out of Manila.

At the same time, the paratroopers of the 503d Regimental Combat Team prepared for another daring adventure, the capture of Corregidor. The combined airborne-amphibious operation assigned a battalion from the 24th Division's 34th Regiment to assault the tiny island's beaches. Intelli-gence figured the Japanese garrison numbered only 850 and with 2,000 GIs dropping from the sky and another 1,000 coming from the sea, the prospects of overwhelming the enemy, particularly through the surprise el-ement of chutists, seemed excellent.

What read well on paper again missed reality and ignored critical factors. Instead of 850 defenders, Corregidor bristled with about 5,000. The high-est portion of the island, Topside, 500 feet above sea level, afforded the res-idents the most devastating opportunities to beat off waterborne invaders and anyone landing on the lower ground. For that reason the Sixth Army planners chose the small areas of the old parade field and golf course on Topside as the drop zones. The restricted size of these targets, the tricky winds and steep cliffs alongside, and the tangle of shell holes and wreckage from the 1942 Japanese attack along with the coarse vegetation, hazarded troopers falling to earth. A shortage of troop carrier planes and the tiny area for the chutists dictated a series of flights, which meant those who arrived first would have to hold off defenders intent on repelling further airborne deliveries.

In the Americans' favor, lay the conviction of the defenders that no one would be so foolhardy as to attempt an assault by air. Furthermore, the Japanese underwent a furious bombardment by Air Corps planes and from the Navy. Meanwhile, on Mindoro, paratroopers, at dawn of 16 February loaded onto their C-47s. Rod Rodriguez, as a member of G Company of the 503d recalled the drop. "The 3d Battalion was scheduled to jump at 8:40 A.M. That was H minus 2, two hours before the main assault by sea, and we were to secure the golf course and parade ground for the subsequent jump of the 2d Battalion. Our mission then was to provide fire support for the infantry assaulting Black Beach, destroy the Japanese positions dug into the cliffs of Topside, and methodically move down the island eliminating the Japanese garrison.

"On the flight over I was a bit tense. I was concerned that the men seated on the other side of the plane and facing me might note my apprehension. I nonchalantly rose and walked to the plane's door, which was removed, to look around. What I saw raised my spirit. There was an impressive array of U.S. power all around us. Above the C-47s were protective flights of P-38s and flying below us were flights of P-47s. In the sea below, the LCIs carrying the 34th Infantry to the beach were already underway. They were being escorted by cruisers and destroyers. It was an inspiring sight.

"We jumped at about 400 feet. I believe this was one of the lowest level combat jumps made by U.S. parachute troops in World War II. The purpose was to minimize descent time, during which we would be a floating target. Because it takes about 175 feet for the parachute to open, it meant the average trooper had about 225 feet of float time, not very long. The flip side is that any delay in opening may be fatal, and because one has very little time to stabilize the parachute once it opens, jump injuries can also mount. I was just a little over the treetops that lined the golf course when my parachute blossomed. I came crashing down on the edge of the course. The other guys from the platoon landed around me. I quickly slipped out of the harness, ran to the assembly area, and we established a perimeter around the golf course.

"The enemy was caught by surprise and our battalion encountered only sporadic opposition on the jump. It would be different for the 2d Battalion when it jumped two hours later. From our perimeter I could see a number of troopers hit in midair by rifle fire and ack-ack weapons. Others were hit as they landed and for the most part were men who missed the drop zone and came down in the cliffs outside the perimeter.

"A fortunate break occurred when the Japanese commander [Naval] Capt. Akira Itagaki, was killed by our troops minutes after the landing. With an armed escort he had left his command post on Topside to inspect positions in the cliffs below and observe the amphibious operations. Suddenly, paratroopers who had missed the drop zone landed in his midst. Several of them were killed but Itagaki and virtually all of his armed escort were destroyed in the ensuing firefight." Rodriguez and the others on Topside settled in for the night, setting up machine guns to help cover the amphibians, fortifying their airhead, setting up fire lanes and patrols, tending to the wounded and injured—while combat losses had been low, about 25 percent of the first jumpers had been hurt crashing into ruins of buildings, trees and the ground itself.

"About 4:00 A.M. the man on guard in our three-man foxhole nudged us awake and pointed to the road. There were, perhaps thirty yards from our position, troops moving toward Bottomside. We were pretty sure that they were Japanese, because our troops did not generally move at night. They were not moving directly at us, so to avoid giving away our position, we held our fire. At that moment a flare was fired and illuminated the night sky. It was indeed a Japanese platoon marching toward the beach. Carrying satchels of TNT they raced toward the beach and were met by withering gunfire. Several saw the folly of attempting to penetrate the beach and turned in our direction. We held our fire until they were almost on us and then riddled them. Four died in front of our position and about thirty were killed in this rather senseless suicidal attack."

To the delight of commanders, the first four waves of landing craft beached their men without opposition. The barrage by naval vessels, the bombs dropped from the air, and the parachutists stunned the defenders, who stayed under cover until the fifth wave made for the shore. By then, the GIs of the 34th Infantry held their initial objectives.

"For several days," says Rodriguez, "we were mainly busy eliminating enemy positions along the cliffs of Topside. They consisted of bunkers, underground tunnels, and caves. Usually a small team would move forward to the target after softening up by artillery or other heavy weapons. The machine guns, BARs, or mortars would lay down fire, while the squad approached the mouth of the fortification. Once you were close enough, the flamethrower or phosphorus grenade did the rest of the job. In other cases, we had air observers attached to our unit who would radio in map coordinates. Once the target had been identified, pilots would dive and drop a napalm bomb with pinpoint precision into the mouth of the bunker or tunnel. The sight of those soldiers running out of their bunkers, engulfed in flames, is a vivid memory."

The climax of the battle for Corregidor occurred about ten days after the troopers descended upon the Rock. An arsenal, cached under Monkey Point, detonated in an enormous blast, caused either by an act of suicide or a U.S.-fired tank shell. "Most of the 1st Battalion," says Rodriguez, "was on top of the hill and the explosion caused many deaths and injuries. We must have been 1,500 yards behind the 1st and yet we had huge rocks and boulders raining down on us. Fortunately, we had enough time to reach cover." The explosion tore apart the bodies of men from both sides, buried some under rock slides and threw a medium tank fifty yards in the air. At least 200 Japanese died instantly while the Rock force lost about 50 killed, 150 wounded.

When MacArthur set foot on Corregidor, nine days short of three years since he boarded Bulkeley's PT boat, more than 4,500 Japanese were counted as dead, with perhaps another 500 either sealed in demolished caves or drowned while attempting to swim for their lives. Only twenty prisoners were taken. The American casualty count added up to more than 1,000.

During the battle for Corregidor, another foray tried to save the remaining captives on Luzon, the 2,147 people, including Navy nurse Mary Rose Harrington, held at Los Baños near Laguna de Bay. For this expedition, the Sixth Army marshaled elements from the 188th Glider Infantry, paratroopers of the 511th Parachute Regiment, guerrillas, the vehicles of the 672d Amphibious Tractor Battalion and supporting tank and tank destroyer outfits.

Amtrac gunner Art Coleman recalled, "After a couple of weeks at the racetrack, we got word to make contact with the 11th Airborne. We were told we were going to liberate those held at Los Baños and could expect one-third casualties. Two-thirds of the prisoners might be lost. Going through the city, we saw bodies everywhere, mostly natives but also combatants from both sides. The sports stadium was overflowing with dead.

"At 2:00 A.M. 23 February, loaded with two companies of troopers plus artillerymen, jeeps and guns, we set off across Laguna de Bay toward Los Baños on the southeast shore. We were told paratroopers would jump at dawn. At first light we had eyes glued straight up as we neared the lakeshore. Suddenly, at treetop height, nine C-47s rounded a hill and 120 paratroopers poured out and in split seconds were on the ground. We could not believe it, dropping from planes so low. Some troopers later said they couldn't either. We crawled ashore and unloaded our troopers who went into the jungle and set up a defense of the area. We proceeded to the camp."

Eleventh Airborne commander, Maj. Gen. Joseph Swing, described the action. "The camp has a morning roll call at 7:00 A.M. Timed everything to hit at that hour. There wasn't a hitch—the recon platoon murdered every sentry as the roll call gong was ringing, barged into camp, and kept the main barracks under fire until the parachute company came in and exterminated them. [Some on the scene say the garrison was on the ballfield in loincloths partaking of morning calisthenics.] The amtracs hit the beach at 7:00, grabbed a small beachhead and kept right on inland two miles to the camp while a 75mm battery kept the Baños garrison quiet. Another battalion attacked south from Calamba and drew all reserves in that direction. We loaded the people in the amtracs and shuttled back to my lines. At 5:00 P.M., 2,134 evacuees removed—had withdrawn from the beachhead to the bridgehead at Calamba. Three evacuees slightly wounded; my own casualties, two KIA, three WIA and not a d—— Jap got away".

Navy nurse Mary Rose Harrington, one of those incarcerated at Los Baños, said, "We had word in advance that they would try to liberate the camp. We weren't given any details but we had people who regularly went through the wire and contacted the guerrillas. Of course they always made roll call in the morning. Peter Miles had been in and out a number of times and he was gone a couple of days. I was outside hanging up bandages when I felt these vibrations on the ground from the amtracs coming toward us. Then when I looked up I saw the planes and something came out of one. I thought it was a bundle of supplies—the man had his body doubled up— and thought it's going to land outside the camp. But once the paratroopers started to land, the guerrillas and the men on the ground attacked the pillboxes. It was all over very quickly."

On the whole, those at Los Baños were not as physically debilitated as the internees at Santa Tomas. "There was less competition for food out where we were," explains Harrington. "We probably ate a little better. Still, toward the end, they sent about 100 old men to us. Some of them undoubtedly needed help or had to be carried to the vehicles."

With between thirty or forty people on the amtrac, Coleman's crew headed for Laguna de Bay. "A Filipino boy pointed to a sheet-metal-covered building, mouthing, Japs in there. Every available machine gun opened up, turning the place into a junk heap. No one approached to see the results. We entered the water, instructed to stay away from the shore on the return. The 1st platoon, wanting more action, went close in with all those people on board and promptly the enemy opened up. They turned away and the bullets struck the tailgates, which could withstand the fire better. No one was injured. On reaching the safe shore, the freed people boarded trucks and ambulances. We immediately returned to Los Baños and brought out the paratroopers. As we entered the water, mortar and artillery fire descended on us but not one round found its target. The commander of the task force, Maj. Henry Burgess, later told me he could hear the Jap officers giving commands as we withdrew. The operation took less than one day."

Within Manila, however, the trapped defenders refused to quit. A considerable number holed up inside Intramuros, an old walled Spanish city that backed up on the bay. Great stone blocks piled as high as twenty-five feet and as much as forty feet thick at the bottom surrounded the mostly stone structures. Units from the 1st Cavalry and 37th Divisions with supporting outfits assaulted Intramuros and large government buildings in the environs.

The 754th Tank Battalion brought its armor and 75mm guns to bear upon the targets, blasting away at the downtown edifices. On 15 February, Tom Howard's 2d platoon had rumbled out of the Bilibid Prison yard, site of the Company A command post. As Howard's tank crossed a pontoon bridge over the Pasig River, a lone enemy plane flew over Bilibid and dropped a bomb. "It landed about five feet from the command tank, killing company commander Coy "Snake" Rogers and three of his crew; driver Earl Bartling, gunner Fred Kassman, and bow gunner Russell Cattamelata. Nine men were wounded. Since the CP had been carefully selected to hide the tanks, a spy, an enemy observer, a collaborator must have reported our whereabouts and pinpointed our exact location.

"Garbled communication had been received all morning concerning the events at the CP. It was unbelievable. We couldn't comprehend what happened. Here we were at the front, on the firing line, and those in relative safety were gone. It was definite that 'Snake' was among the dead, as his arm had been found and the tattoo PANAMA easily discernable. We felt like our head had been cut off or that we had lost a parent. We were like orphans waiting for word on what would happen next or who would assume control."

In the middle two weeks of February, Howard's A Company listed twenty battle casualties, including six dead. Other medical problems, malaria, amebic dysentery, hepatitis, and routine cuts and bruises while operating the tanks depleted ranks further. "We had started with seventeen tanks at the time of the landing but now we had eleven that would run, but only enough men to man eight, using the cooks, mechanics, and administrators. We would recruit infantrymen to fill positions of machine gunner or loader for the 75mm cannon. Although we could never get a volunteer to come back a second time, we were able to get men on direct orders from the infantry officers."

In a moment of tranquility, Howard and his mates pondered the question, "Why them, not us?" They mourned their losses, reminisced about the past—"Proud, arrogant, stately, yet one of us, 'Snake' Rogers; Fred Kassman, our prized basketball player when we were on Bougainville; Theriot, with his blond hair, handsome features and a body he was always developing by exercise and weights. We who were left were a motley looking crew, unwashed, unshaven, clothes in tatters. I existed as the rest did by stripping dead Japs of their jackets and pants and stockings. We were tired, absolutely weary. I remember I sat and cried for no apparent reason, uncontrollably, unashamed, and not cold, but spent, exhausted. I had forgotten when I had last eaten a hot meal, instead of picking on a cold can of C ration, had a full night's sleep, had taken a crap—must have been constipated since the attack of dysentery."

On 21 February, their tanks serviced, restocked with ammunition, food, water, and first-aid kits, Company A in support of the infantry zeroed in on the Manila Hotel. MacArthur was close enough to the site to watch as the Japanese inside supposedly set fire to his prewar penthouse suite. "We were told to zero in on the hotel and then hold fire until the word was given. Each of the five tanks selected a partition between two windows and sat tight. Lieutenant William Dougherty, on the ground outside his tank, was to give the command to fire. We had never rehearsed a command not to fire. When 'Junior' gave us the sign, we opened fire and the building came tumbling down. We continued to rotate our turrets so that the 75 mm cannon would pour shells into the interior with the shells exploding inside and the shrapnel tear the Japanese to pieces. Unknown to us, the order given was supposed to mean not to fire since MacArthur wanted to save the hotel as best as possible."

Impatient with any delay in the liberation of the city, MacArthur virtually trod on the heels of the combat soldier. Platoon sergeant Cletus J. Schwab of the 37th Division participated in the block-by-block fighting. "We were pushing the Japanese toward Manila Bay this day and about to be attacked on our right flank when one of my sergeants hollered to me that General MacArthur and his escort were coming up the street we were fighting in. I hurried back to stop them. I reported to the general my name, rank, and reason for stopping him. He wanted to know how long the Japanese could hold out. About that time all hell broke loose. It was about half an hour before the general and his staff could retreat to safety." About a week later, Schwab received a battlefield promotion to second lieutenant and a transfer to another company.

To better support the foot soldiers and reduce turn-around time, the maintenance and ordnance details moved closer to the tanks at the front. Armor with flamethrowers trundled forward spouting napalm that adhered to the stone and concrete sides of buildings, even flowing around corners. But the 75s could not seriously dent the walls of Intramuros. The heaviest-caliber artillery, 155mm and 240mm guns methodically blasted breaches in the walls of Intramuros and stalwart government buildings. Still, infantrymen, aided by tanks, underwent the ordeal of a room-by-room struggle against an enemy resigned to death with his boots on. Iwabuchi's men held thousands of Filipinos as hostages inside. Many died from the shelling or were murdered by the defenders. The attack halted temporarily when the GIs who ran through the shattered walls discovered 3,000 civilians who took sanctuary in the churches within Intramuros. The refugees, mainly women and children— most males had been executed— were escorted out before the Americans resumed firing. About 1,000 Japanese died in the warrens of Intramuros.

The last stages of the Battle of Manila centered around a complex of government buildings constructed along the lines of those of the U.S. in Washington, D.C. Massive piles of thick concrete, they slowly collapsed from an onslaught of heavy artillery bombardment. Late on 3 March, a month after the siege began, the corps commander, General Griswold, advised Sixth Army chief General Kreuger that organized resistance in the Manila area had ceased. In and around the city, the Americans had killed about 16,000 enemy while casualties for the GIs totaled 1,000 KIA and 5,500 wounded. One estimate claimed 100,000 Filipino civilians lost their lives. Manila itself was wrecked, without power, water, or sewage systems. Few buildings escaped damage if not total destruction. With much of the housing demolished, those residents who survived occupied condemned hulks of structures or simply camped outdoors. Men and children begged the troops for food, as women peddled their bodies for something to eat. Giant holes and heaps of debris rendered many streets nearly impassable. Little more than chunks of concrete remained of landmarks like the 400-year-old Intramuros.

MacArthur had achieved his strategic aim, isolation of the three Japanese armies on Luzon. However, although they could no longer support one another or exchange men and equipment, they fought on determined to exact as high a blood penalty as possible.

46
Firestorms

Once the Marianas were conquered and the airfields made suitable, Air Force chief Hap Arnold transferred the B-29s from their fields in India to bases at Saipan, Tinian, and Guam. David Burchinal, who had been a test pilot checking out all types of multiple-engine planes after they rolled out of a depot, and on the staff of the 73d Bomb Group on Tinian, volunteered to accompany a mission from Saipan to the target area. "It was against a place called Nakajima Aircraft, an engine factory in Nagoya. That was a long haul [roughly 1,500 miles each way]. We didn't know too much about the B-29s. We were in a new business; everybody was. Thank heavens they built those runways about a hundred feet above the water, because with the loads on those airplanes at the temperatures we were operating, you had to have a little bit of headwind. You got the plane off the ground and dove it over the runway toward the water and you could pick up enough flying speed then to clear yourself up and get on the way. We found we were literally burning fuel to haul fuel. We were loading the airplanes so heavily with fuel it would cost us fuel consumption. A lighter airplane was more efficient, had more range, and much better takeoff performance. It took us time to learn.

"On that first mission, we were bombing as high as they could get the airplane, practically in a stall, up to 31,000 feet, scared to death of the fighters. At that altitude we suddenly ran into these terrific jet winds that no one had run into before. They were well over 100 knots, sometimes you'd get up to 200. That first bomb run against the airplane-engine factory, we never saw it. We were going so fast downwind that there was no way the bombardier could get on the bombsight, look through it, using radar or anything else, and synchronize anything. It was beyond the capability of the system. The bombs would fly into the fields. It was the most ineffective mission I believe I have ever been on."

Too many times, crews and their craft were unable to deal with the hazards of long-distance flights, hampered by vagaries of weather and the continuing problems of maintenance. While operations out of the Marianas had shortened distances and eliminated the difficulty of bringing in materials over the Hump, the Japanese base on the island of Iwo Jima, midway between Saipan and Tokyo, not only provided the enemy with an early-warning site but also its fighters threatened the American bases and the bombers.

Burchinal recalled, "The bases in the Marianas would get attacks from the Japanese from Iwo Jima. They would fly the Bettys down, mostly at night. They did rip up the 73d Bomb Group pretty badly one day, early in the morning. They laid a streak of bombs right down the runway where the airplanes were parked wing tip to wing tip. [Apparently the lesson of Clark Field in 1941 had escaped the notice of the base commander.] They had a pretty good fire going on the ground. They would come over our way [Tinian] and we'd go for the slit trenches. The antiaircraft would open up. They never hit anything." To avoid interception, formations out of the Marianas navigated a fuel-burning, navigationally challenged dogleg course to their targets.

Arnold installed Curtis LeMay to improve results. At first he was no more successful than his predecessors. As in Europe, LeMay focused attention on tight box formations and extended practice to enhance accuracy. "We weren't bombing very well in that formation," said Burchinal "but we weren't getting shot down or rammed either. Then he brought us right down in altitude. He said, 'You're not going to get anything at 32,000, 30,000 feet, so come on down to 24,000, 23,000, 22,000. We started to hit targets. We weren't taking any losses to speak of. We were increasing the bomb load and the winds dropped off. We had a pretty decent attack going."

But the big change came with the conquest of Iwo Jima, some 650 miles from Tokyo. Navy strategists had long coveted Iwo as a potential base for an attack into the Ryukyu Islands—Okinawa—and the imperial homeland. LeMay and his associates envisioned Iwo as a welcome emergency field for distressed bombers and in American hands allowed superforts to fly a direct route to Japan. Capture also would end Iwo's role as an early-warning outpost.

At most only four and a half miles long and two and a half miles wide, volcano-spawned Iwo sprouted from the Pacific like a noxious wart from whose pores wafted the sulphuric aroma of rotten eggs. Its one distinguishing natural landmark was a modest 550-foot hill, Mount Suribachi, a burned-out hulk. The Japanese had scraped away Iwo's covering of volcanic ash to complete two airfields with another under construction.. The mix of the ash with cement produced a concrete divinely suited to the construction of bunkers and pillboxes. In their inimitable way, the defenders burrowed beneath the surface for extensive underground fortifications with multiple entrances and exits all connected by a weave of tunnels. The caves, shielded by thirty-five feet of overhead cover, could withstand the biggest bombs or shells. Engineers erected air shafts for ventilation and the sharp corners to the underground maze protected against flamethrowers. The garrison commander, whose own redoubt lay seventy-five feet beneath the ground led 21,000 men, well equipped with artillery, mortar, antiaircraft guns, and other deadly hardware. Neither he nor his men had any doubts of their destiny. They expected to fight to the death. For several months American aircraft regularly and ships occasionally visited Iwo blasting at the fortress. All reported significant retaliatory reactions.

While naval historian Samuel Eliot Morison wrote of the Iwo invasion, "The operation looked like a pushover," the Marines most closely involved with the affair regarded it with trepidation. The V Amphibious Corps under Maj. Gen. Harry Schmidt requested a ten-day softening-up barrage by ships before the first Marine stepped into a landing craft. But other activities, the engagement in the Philippines, and a carrier-based strike at Japan siphoned off ships. The Marines would have to make do with just three days of preparatory shelling.

The bombardment, from the sea and the air, inflicted slight damage during the first two days, but on the third, 18 February, it appreciably battered the positions guarding the landing beaches. On the following day, the battleships and cruisers approached to within a thousand yards of the shore to pour point-blank cannonades at blockhouses and pillboxes until 8:05 A.M. They paused long enough for some 120 carrier-based dive-bombers and fighters to shoot up defensive sites. A squadron of B-29s from the Marianas dumped tons of explosives, stirring up old lava and sand. Finally, gunboats cut loose with rockets and even mortars.

Observers could not believe anyone near the beaches could have survived. A wave of amtracs churned to the shore while spouting 75mm pack-howitzer shells and machine-gun bullets. The black beach seemed inert, lifeless. For a few moments, the Marines hoped for the unthinkable but the first big splashes among the landing craft signaled the presence of a malevolent enemy. A direct hit sank an amtrac, drowning some unable to divest themselves of packs and weaponry. Bullets rattled against the armor plate. Still, with relatively few casualties, seven battalions landed abreast on 3,500 yards of Iwo Jima adjacent to the right side of Suribachi.

Richard Wheeler, a corporal in the 28th Marines, undergoing his baptism of fire, stepped onto the wet sand on the extreme left flank, closest to Suribachi and where the tip narrows to only 700 yards in width. Suribachi provided the Japanese with observation of almost the entire island, and was an immediate objective for Wheeler's battalion. As they moved toward it, Wheeler remembered, "We [realized] we could hardly make a move that escaped Japanese notice. We troops in the Suribachi area would be particularly conscious of this. We would seldom be more than half a mile from the volcano and much of the time we would be plainly exposed to the view of observers, gun crews, and riflemen in the caves on its slopes and at its summit. Even when we were in holes we wouldn't feel undetectable, however low we pressed ourselves. This sensation of being watched over gunsights by hundreds of hostile eyes would be very nearly as unnerving as being actually under fire.

"The loose sand was hard to negotiate. We wanted to run, in obedience to our training and our instincts, but loaded with gear as we were, we could only plod. Our route was crowded with Marines. Some were lying prone or were digging in, while others were climbing the terrace and moving inland. Troop congestion was mounting dangerously. We were all aware of the importance of dispersion in combat . . . We passed a number of tallow-faced casualties who were being treated by corpsmen and saw a blinded man being led to the water's edge for evacuation."

Glancing back to the sea, Wheeler glimpsed terrifying scenes. A landing craft approached the beach with a large American flag flapping by a gunwale. "A bold gesture," said Wheeler, "since they must have known the flag would invite a concentration of enemy fire. The Marines were carrying their display of defiance to the limit, for they were shouting lustily as their vessel cut through the surf and thrust its prow against the shore. Then as the ramp dropped to the sand and the men bolted out they took a direct artillery hit and their spirited shouts were instantly replaced by cries of anguish and confusion. Another appalling sight presented itself. About a hundred yards to our left-front, a Marine was blown high into the air. Like a great rag doll, he went up end over end and seemed to rise a least fifty feet before plummeting back to the earth."

His unit halted before a mound of sand, innocent-looking except for a dark rectangular opening that indicated a concrete gun emplacement. The sand provided both camouflage and protection for the inhabitants. "We all knew how a rifle platoon was supposed to handle a problem like this. While one man semicircled his way to the pillbox with a demolitions charge, the rest were to deliver concentrated fire at the aperture and make it impossible for the gun crew to operate. When the demolitions man was close enough to make a dash for the aperture and push his charge inside, the others were to cease firing—but only long enough for the man to make his play. The moment he turned away, the firing was to resume so the charge couldn't be expelled.

"As we lay in our places of skimpy concealment and considered the obstacle before us, the prescribed method of dealing with pillboxes seemed suddenly unfeasible. Few of us felt like poking our heads up high enough to fire our rifles and the idea of a man's rising and venturing across that barren sand seemed absurd. But if Wells [the platoon lieutenant] gave the order the measure would be tried." To their relief, a pair of Sherman tanks clattered to the rescue. Coming around their flank the armor aimed its 75mm cannons at point-blank range, turning the pillbox into a tomb. But the tanks themselves were vulnerable to well-sited antitank guns and lacked opportunities to take cover.

During the first hour the enemy had remained almost quiescent. To make the Americans pay dearly for every yard, the commander of the detachment had established a defense in depth, rather than the earlier mode that tried to halt invaders at the water's edge. On the beach, men and machines piled up in a small area as a mounting crescendo of mortars, artillery, and automatic weapons cascaded over the area. A 5th Marine Division history reported, "Wounded men were arriving on the beach by the dozen where they were not much better off than they had been at the front . . . The first two boats bringing in badly needed litters were blown out of the water. Casualties were being hit again as they lay helpless under blankets awaiting evacuation."

Most of the corpsmen who expected to move inland to treat the wounded never left the beach area as casualties streamed back. Crawling about to sew chest wounds, bandage lacerated limbs, and inject morphine to ease pain, the medics themselves absorbed cruel punishment. In one battalion, their first day casualties ran higher than for most assault groups. Indeed, for many of the reserve outfits that followed the first waves several hours later, the onslaught was much fiercer. Captain LaVerne Wagner who brought in K company of the 23d Regiment, said, "One of the first sights I saw was a Marine blown in half. The beach was crowded with Marines as far as I could see. Enemy artillery fire was very hot and it seemed to me that almost half the men on the beach had been wounded and were waiting to be evacuated.

"We had indoctrinated all our men with the necessity of getting off the beach fast, and had even picked out prearranged assembly areas. But before we had a chance to move forward our men began to drop. The machine gun that had fired on us in the water was still in action and as we jumped from shellhole to shellhole it followed us, firing from our flank. Ahead of us were literally dozens of pillboxes and many blockhouses. You couldn't move twenty-five yards in any direction without running into some kind of position. Most of them had been knocked out and had dead Japanese in them. One blockhouse greeted us with a burst of machine-gun fire. We got one of the tanks to come up and work it over, but the walls were three and four feet thick and the tank didn't do much damage. Finally, the company on our left threw some grenades into the rear entrance. Suddenly, what seemed like about eighteen grenades came flying back at us. We kept throwing our own grenades into the entrance and finally killed the Japs—three of them. We found seventy-five grenades lined up in a row, ready to be thrown. We realized that the Japs were going at this systematically."

While fellow Marines slowly ascended the lower elevations of Suribachi, the 23d Marine Regiment concentrated upon the biggest airfield, Motoyama Number 1. By midafternoon, the leathernecks approached the twenty-foot-high slope that bordered it. Hard fighting killed many defenders and when the remainder suddenly disappeared, the Marines, accompanied by tanks, climbed the sandy embankment only to come under intense fire. The Japanese had crawled through huge drain pipes and resumed the battle from positions across the landing strip.

LaVerne Wagner and his company joined the effort to wrest control of the place. "Our first big surprise was to find that no one had started across the airfield. One reason we discovered, was that a Jap antiaircraft gunner had depressed his gun level with the field and was shooting at anyone who stuck his head up. We sent a squad of men to work around behind him and one of our men shot him in the head. The bullet went in his forehead and came out his temple and despite the fact that his brains were actually oozing out through the hole, he lived. In fact, he would walk and talk. We took him prisoner—the first Jap captured on the beach. It had taken us two hours to get from the beach to the field and join the battalion ahead of us. And this was a beach that had been fought over all morning and was supposedly cleared. Already, we had lost thirty of our men. Theoretically, we hadn't even been committed to the battle. We were still in reserve."

By the end of the first day, 40,000 Marines from the 4th and 5th Divisions were digging in, with the former still on the edge of Motoyama No. 1 and the latter having cut across the lower tip of the island to isolate Suribachi. They weathered night-long volleys from artillery and mortars and choked off a battalion-size counterattack. Sporadic rifle fire rattled the darkness as star shells from the fleet, illuminating infiltrators, lit up the night.

On the second day, the Marines resumed the effort to capture the old volcano. Flights of Marine and Navy planes roared in at low altitude to smash targets with rockets, bombs, and machine guns. Napalm erupted in balls of flame and from the sea the big ships hurled shells and rockets. Tanks and half-tracks lurched forward to blast away at the lower reaches of enemy defenses. The infantry painstakingly inched toward Suribachi and poised for an attempted ascent.

Richard Wheeler participated in the assault that began after the customary barrages from ships and planes. "For a few moments the hulking fortress remained still. Then it began to react. First came the crack of rifles and the chatter of machine guns. This quickly grew to a heavy rattle, and bullets began to snap and whine about us. Then the mortars started coming in, some being visible as they made their high arc, and shortly the area was being blanketed by roaring funnels of steel and sand. The noise and fury increased until our hearing was numbed and our thinking impaired. It was as though the volcano's ancient bowels had suddenly come to life and we were advancing into a full-scale eruption.

"We were now part of a real hell-bent-for-leather attack, the kind the Marines are famous for. But there was nothing inspiring about it. None of our ex-Raiders shouted 'Gung ho!'; none of our ex-paratroopers shouted

'Geronimo!' and none of our Southerners let go the rebel yell. We felt only reluctance and enervating anxiety. There seemed nothing ahead but death. If we managed somehow to make it across the open area, we'd only become close-range targets for those concealed guns. I was seized by a sensation of utter hopelessness.

"It is in situations like this that Marine Corps training proves its value. There probably wasn't a man among us who didn't wish to God he was moving in the opposite direction. But we had been ordered to attack, so we would attack. And our obedience involved more than just a resignation to discipline. Our training had imbued us with a fierce pride in our outfit, and this pride helped now to keep us from faltering. Few of us would have admitted that we were bound by the old-fashioned principle of 'death before dishonor' but it was probably this, above all else, that kept us pressing forward."

His closest comrades started to fall all around him and the cry of "corpsman" rose above the din of explosions. Wheeler and four others jumped into a crater left by an aerial bomb. Suddenly, a shell exploded on the rim of the big hole. "My rifle was torn from my hands and I reeled under a hard, ear-ringing blow to the left side of my face. I thought for an instant that I had taken only concussion but when my hand leaped reflexively to the affected area, the tip of my thumb went through a hole at my jaw line. A fragment had broken my jaw, smashed through the roots of two molars and lodged in the muscles beneath my tongue.

"My wound started to bleed profusely, both externally and inside my mouth. While [Howard] Snyder [his squad leader] stuck up his head and shouted an urgent call for a corpsman, I took off my helmet, pack, and cartridge belt and sat down against the crater's slope. Spitting out a stream of blood and the crown of a tooth, I wondered worriedly how my injury's two-way flow could be stanched. I was afraid my jugular vein had been hit." Corpsman Clifford Langley applied compresses inside and outside Wheeler's mouth to halt the stream of blood.

Except for one other slightly wounded man and Langley, the others who had taken refuge with Wheeler, departed to continue their climb. A few minutes later, another savage explosion rocked the crater. Shrapnel ripped away Wheeler's trouser leg, his canvas leggings, and a chunk of flesh from his left calf. Langley immediately sprinkled sulfa powder on the new wound and bandaged it. The corpsman himself was wounded slightly and the other Marine killed.

The still functioning members of Wheeler's platoon doggedly advanced toward the crater of Suribachi. Donald Ruhl, known as the unit's malcontent, threw himself on a grenade and won a posthumous Medal of Honor. Native American Louie Adrian, a close friend of Wheeler's fell, mortally wounded, while triggering his BAR. A mortar shell burst among a quintet of Marines, seriously wounding platoon leader Lt. John K. Wells. Tossing grenades almost like confetti, closing in on bunkers with flamethrowers, aided by tanks, the Marines forged forward.

The last few of the 2,000-strong force that defended Suribachi hunkered down at the edge of the crater. On D plus 4, Lieutenant Colonel Chandler Johnson, the battalion commander, dispatched a forty-man patrol composed of survivors of Wheeler's platoon augmented by men from other outfits to capture the final outpost. Johnson handed the patrol leader Lt. Harold Schrier a folded American flag. "Johnson's orders were simple," said Wheeler. "The patrol was to climb to the summit, secure the crater, and raise the flag." On reaching the crater rim, the leathernecks encountered a few holdouts but grenades and rifles disposed of them. The Marines scrounged a piece of pipe that became a flagpole from which the Stars and Stripes soon whipped about in the wind atop the volcano. Some three hours later, battalion commander Johnson decided to replace the small flag with a much larger one. Associated Press photographer Joe Rosenthal accompanied the group that bore the new banner to the top and snapped the famous picture.

There were other eyewitnesses. Offshore, Walter Vogel, promoted to the rank of chief petty officer and transferred from the *Downes*, was on the bridge of the destroyer *Hyman* where he trained his long glass on the island whenever permitted by his duties. "The commander came to me and said, 'Put your glass on Mount Surabachi.' Everyone that had binoculars was watching. All of a sudden about seven or eight Marines put the American flag that was on a pole up in the rocks. Everyone yelled. It was a great thrill to see this and then we knew it would be a short time before we left."

About 900 Marines from the 28th Regiment became casualties during the attack on the old volcano and in the 3d platoon to which Wheeler belonged, 91 percent of the leathernecks were killed or wounded. But the fight for Iwo was far from over. The northern end of the island still featured shore-to-shore caves, tunnels, bunkers, pillboxes, and obdurate defenders Fresh forces from the 9th Marine Regiment, supported by tanks, slammed up against a ridge that overlooked Motoyama Number 2, half of which still remained in enemy possession..

Three tanks, *Angel, Agony,* and *Ateball* cranked ahead only to be rocked by a fusillade of antitank shells. *Angel* and *Agony* started to burn, while *Ateball* lost the ability to move forward. Corporal William R. Adamson squeezed out of the hatch of *Agony* and dropped to the ground. As other tankers followed, looking for protection in shell holes, a bullet hit Adamson in the leg. He rendered first aid to himself with a tourniquet and then noticed the muzzle flash of the gun that had knocked out his vehicle. Adamson crawled to *Ateball* whose crew could still operate its weapons. With his arm, he indicated the position of the enemy piece. *Ateball* responded and blew it away. Adamson then detected four machine-gun nests in the rocks ahead. Again he signaled to the disabled tank and its 75mm smashed all four guns. A Japanese soldier tried to sneak up on the tank with a satchel charge but the intrepid Adamson spotted him and directed machine gun fire that cut him down. Some thirty infantrymen ran forward to destroy the nettlesome tank and Adamson, but *Ateball* repulsed them with artillery and machine-gun fire. Other tanks came forward and under their cover, the *Ateball* crew and Adamson retreated to safety.

The killing continued day after day. Gains could be measured only in yards and along with map designations such as "Hill 383" and "Turkey Nob" the sectors earned grim names, "the Meat Grinder," "Bloody Gorge" and "Death Valley." Wheeler's platoon sergeant Ernest Thomas who helped raise the first flag atop Suribachi took a fatal bullet through the head. Sergeant Henry O. Hansen who appeared in the Rosenthal photograph of the second flag was killed. A shell burst cut down the intrepid battalion commander Chandler Johnson Ambushes and stalwart defenses occasionally forced the Marines to retreat, sometimes unable to take all of their wounded. These unfortunates lay there, feigning death. Any sign of life meant skewering by an enemy bayonet.

Carrier-based aircraft attempted to aid the ground forces. Pittsburgh native Harry Jones, who flew a torpedo-bomber from the *Hornet,* said, "It was a little like watching a football game from the air. The Marines put down these orange panels so we would know where to drop bombs ahead of our people. We tried to hit the caves but we couldn't see the openings from the air."

For the most part the Japanese, offered numerous opportunities to surrender, replied with bullets, grenades, and mortars. Near the third airfield, still under construction, the Marines advanced beyond a rocky ridge. From their rear, a machine gun secreted amid the ruins of blockhouses and boulders suddenly opened fire. Pinned down, those leathernecks awaited tanks and demolition teams. They repeated the tedious but deadly job of destroying anyone in the myriad openings, Methodically, the tanks fired into each hole followed by grenades and packages of explosives. Through tunnels the inhabitants moved quickly to new positions from which to shoot. The ultimate weapon of attack, the flamethrower, threw long jets of searing napalm, which, unlike bullets and shells, bounced off the curved walls and traveled around the 90-degree angles. A correspondent reported, "The Marines heard the Japs howling. A few rushed out of the caves on fire. The Marines shot them or knocked them down and beat out the flames and took them prisoners. When the Marines began to hear muffled explosions inside the caves, they guessed that some of the Japs were blowing themselves up with hand grenades. The scene became wild and terrible. More Japs rushed screaming from the caves. They tumbled over the rocks, their clothes and bodies burning fiercely. Soon the flamethrowers paused. A Marine lifted himself cautiously into view. There were no shots from the caves. A Jap with his clothes in rags hunched himself out of one hole with arms upraised. The Marines stood up behind the rocks and waved to him to come out. The Jap indicated there were more who would like to surrender. The Marines motioned him to tell them to come out.

"Almost forty scared and beaten men emerged from different holes. Some of them had round pudding faces. They grinned nervously and said they were Koreans. They had been forced by the Japs to stay in the caves. They said that everyone else in the caves had either been burned to death or had committed suicide. The Marines sent them to the rear. Then they groped cautiously among the rocks from hole to hole, examining each entranceway. Dead bodies, some hit by bullets and grenade fragments, some burned into frightful black lumps lay in the holes. The smell was overwhelming and the men turned away in disgust." Few Japanese soldiers surrendered. At one point eleven soldiers simply stood up and faced the Americans who shot them down.

On D plus 25, the American command declared Iwo Jima officially secured. More than 20,000 of the enemy fought to their death. The Marines counted 6,821 dead and nearly 20,000 wounded. This was the only campaign of the island war in which the U.S. absorbed more casualties than the enemy. Twenty-seven Marines and navy corspmen earned Medals of Honor in providing the Air Force with the emergency landing site for which it lusted.

Anxious to prove the worth of B-29s flying out of these islands, the strategic bomb experts sought to justify their presence. Prior to the shift of Superforts to the Marianas, one mass raid on Hankow, China, wiped out much of the dock area although debriefers concluded that less than 40 percent of the bombs struck in the target area. But because incendiaries that employed napalm dominated the ordnance, fires wrought enormous damage. The bomber command decided to try the method against Japan itself.

"Toward the end of February," said Burchinal, "we were ordered to load up pretty heavily with incendiaries. It was high altitude, 26,000 feet against Tokyo. I was to fly deputy lead for the wing. Our wing led all the wings in this first 200-plane attack on Japan. The idea was to take off from all the different bases and head north of Iwo Jima. We were to assemble over the water, putting phosphorous flares out for marking the assembly point. The airplanes would come in, look at the different colors, and assemble into their formation and then a line of formation.

"I was a lieutenant colonel and had been designated the leader for the whole command. We had one brigadier general, a couple of other wing commanders, a group of colonel types along with their own outfits. They didn't like all this forming up over the water because it was going to take a while, thirty to forty minutes to bring that gang together. They said, 'We're going to head for Japan.' I got on the radio and said, 'You'll see me in LeMay's office and I'll be preferring charges. Your job is to stay and form this formation.'" And they did.

"We burned up a pretty good chunk of Tokyo that day from high altitude. We didn't have much of a bomb load on the mission but it proved a point. LeMay wanted to find out if that damn place would burn, and if it was really a prospect for incendiary attacks. That pretty well proved it. A couple of nights later, a real gutsy commander volunteered to see what the Japanese defenses would look like at night, low level. He took a B-29 by himself over Tokyo at 5,000 feet at night and didn't get a scratch. He came back and said, I think we can do it. LeMay said okay and that's when he started the low-level night incendiary attacks, first on the four major cities, Tokyo, Kobe, Nagoya, Osaka.

"The third mission was Kobe and I went on it, [on a jump seat next to pilot Bill Pitts] flying deputy lead again for the group. We came up over the bay into Kobe. At 5,000 feet we had a cloud layer so we dropped under it, which put us down around 4,200 feet. I have never seen such fireworks in my life. They were throwing everything at us in the way of antiaircraft and searchlights. My God, the night was really lit up. Right ahead of us was the lead crew—good friends of ours. We got just about a minute or so from bomb release and up he went, a direct hit from AA. That was the end of him. Then the tail gunner called that another one right behind us had been hit by AA and down he'd gone. That was two out of the first three."

Burchinal watched as his pilot, "cool as a cucumber, flew right over that town, put those bombs, all those incendiaries, right where it counted and all the other guys right after him. I was a little edgy and after we got the bombs away, he just kept driving straight. You could still see the stuff coming up and I said, 'It would be a good idea to get out of here, wouldn't it?' He said, 'The best way is to keep right on going, it's the fastest we can get out of it. All of a sudden we were back in the night, climbed up, and headed home.

"After that we began to clean up Tokyo. The first night we'd gotten a whole chunk of it but there was lots left, because it was a hell of a big city. Lots of defense industries. We got a little more scientific. At the time we were still bombing at medium altitudes, daytime, at 25,000-26,000 feet. LeMay called a critique after one of those missions because our results had not been very good. I was fairly critical of some of the tactics we were using and the ways we were bombing. I didn't like the formation he was making us use. He listened and just grunted. I said what was in the minds of a lot of the crews and the ops staffs."

The problem lay in the amount of time it took to generate fires to aim upon and bring the bomber stream into position to exploit the existing conflagration. "We would spend maybe an hour and a half over the target. By the time they got a fire going, those damn flames would be up to 15,000—18,000 feet. The area was small the updrafts tremendous. You'd bounce as high as you could see flames—it would take an airplane up like a leaf. There was one particularly bad night, attacking the Yokohama area and Kawasaki area. The naval AA was particularly good. We had planned a breakaway down Tokyo Bay, which was still in range of the naval guns. The timing had gotten screwed up and the tail end was straggling. I watched twenty-three B-29s shot down at the end of the formation. I tried to divert them to take another route but it was too late.

"We knew we were going to have to concentrate the string more. We had had one-midair collision, and at least one airplane came home with a piece of another's tail in the intake. The other airplane didn't come home. We worked to bring in parallel strings. We compressed the time of attack. They could handle singles pretty well with some of the sharp AA but they couldn't deal with the mass stuff because they all had their heads down.

"When we got on Iwo Jima, we got our first long-range fighters, P-47s. We then had escort over Japan. They would also run independent fighter sweeps. The kids couldn't navigate themselves in those fighters all the way from Iwo up to the empire and back. We arranged for them to join the bomber formations. We'd escort them up and they would break off and go in. They would make a sweep ahead of us, escort us or whatever their mission. We also developed our air-sea rescue because our crews were a long way from home if they had to ditch off Japan or even on the way back. We had submarines the Navy couldn't use because there were no targets left for them and surface craft also. My friend Bill Pitts came off the target badly shot up one day and just managed to get off the coast. We had definite rendezvous points for these subs and he called his position in with such code words as 'Nellie's Belly.' He headed for one, bailed out his crew, then bailed himself. He said he was in the water maybe a minute and twenty seconds before a submarine had come and picked up his whole crew. Of course he was out of the war for about two and a half weeks—it took that long to get back to Tinian from the empire on that submarine."

On board a B-29 named *City of Los Angeles,* radio operator Sgt. Henry Erwin had completed seventeen missions when his 52d Bomb Squadron began to congregate for an attack on Koriyama, Japan. *City of Los Angeles* usually led the unit, serving as a pathfinder on night raids, when it would light up the target for the bomber stream and as the lead during daylight raids. As radioman, it was Erwin's task during the assembly maneuvers about fifty miles from the enemy coastline to drop two or three phosphorus bombs down a three-and-a-half-foot chute that provided guidance for the bomb-approach formation.

According to Erwin, "There was about an eight- or ten-second delay from the time you pulled the pin [on the phosphorus bomb] until you threw it down the tube. On this particular mission, I recall throwing some prior, but on the last one, we either hit an air pocket or there was a malfunction in the bomb. I knew it was coming back and I tried to put my foot on it and kick it out, but it came on into the plane and exploded at my feet." After ignition, the phosphorus reaches a temperature of from 1,500 to 2,000 degrees.

"Instantly, it put my eyes out, burned my ear off, burned my hair off, and my uniform was on fire. I thought to myself, 'I can't see.' I was always taught, 'Don't panic.' If you panic you are not going to be able to do anything. The first inclination, even after all this teaching, is self-preservation; how do I get out of here? I am in this radio operator's shack, back in the corner, obstructed behind the navigator. This thing is at my feet and I'm on fire and I'm burning." The smoke quickly filled the airplane and the command pilot, Capt. George Simeral dove down toward the sea.

"I said, 'Lord, I need your help *NOW!*' And instantly, I knew that there was somebody else in that plane. I reached down. I grabbed it with my right hand. I began to crawl. I remember opening the navigator's table [to get past it], crawled by the flight engineer on the right, went up between the pilot and the copilot. I told Captain Simeral to open the window and I flipped it out. One reason—we were at 300 feet over the water—the phosphorus gives out a lot of smoke and the pilot couldn't see his instruments. He couldn't understand what was happening. They were at sort of a loss. It happened so quick. But just as soon as he opened the window and I pitched it out, then the breeze sucked all of the smoke out.

"They saw me, and Captain Simeral said, 'My Lord, what's wrong?' They instantly began first aid. The first thing they had to do was take a fire extinguisher and put out the fire. I was completely aflame. Then they began wanting to give me morphine. In addition to the radio operator I was the first-aid man on the plane. They gave me one Syrette. I never was unconscious. I was still alert; I couldn't see them, I could respond to their talking. 'Red, are you all right?' 'I'm fine.'

"Colonel Strouse [Lt. Col. Eugene O.] who was our squadron commander, did something normally no commander would ever do. He told the bombardier. 'Open those bomb-bay doors and drop those bombs right here now. We are going to head for Iwo Jima.' We turned and headed for Iwo Jima. They wanted to give me some more morphine. I said, 'Don't give me any more of that stuff; you are going to kill me with morphine.'" One of the side gunners administered plasma to the stricken sergeant.

When *City of Los Angeles* touched down, Erwin began a thirty-one-month period in hospitals as doctors treated his injuries. For nearly a month, the grains of phosphorus embedded in his eyes and skin smoldered whenever exposed to oxygen. He regained sight in one eye while undergoing extensive skin grafts and reconstruction of his right hand. For his valor he was awarded a Medal of Honor. By the time the war ended, more than 2,000 B-29s had used Iwo as an emergency field, perhaps a partial payment on the investment of so many lives and bodies to capture the island.

The campaign of fire ravaged much of Japan. The 300 B-29s that hit Tokyo on 9 March ignited a holocaust that killed 83,000 people and destroyed 267,000 buildings within a sixteen-square-mile sector. The conflagration generated temperatures that boiled canal waters while towering clouds of soot and smoke blotted out the sky. The devastation surpassed the firestorms of Hamburg and Dresden. The B-29s added minelaying to their operations, sowing them extensively in Japan's Inland Sea where they sank a considerable number of ships. Leaflets dropped from the sky rained down on the residents of cities, warning them they were next on the list for the fire raids. Many people headed for the countryside, weakening the war production effort. However, although the war had now been brought to the home islands, the Allies detected no signs of weakening resolve in the military.

47
Over the Rhine

The maps indicating the fronts of the Allies and the Germans in the west showed little change between those that charted the situation in mid-December and the first week of February. But the collapse of the attack through the Ardennes and the severe losses inflicted upon men and armor, some of which had been diverted from the eastern front, brought the Third Reich to the brink of extinction. While the Soviet armies rampaged through the depleted ranks of the Wehrmacht, the Americans and British, fortified by fresh infusions of men and materials, opened up the final drive against a much weaker enemy than had faced them three months earlier.

The last natural barrier before the Rhine was the Roer River. The 2d Ranger Battalion prepared to join an assault culminating in a crossing of the Roer. Medic Frank South said, "The day before while making sure that our aid station equipment and such were set to go, we heard the familiar cry of 'Medic!' Grabbing my aid kit, I ran out of the ruined building we were in and started across the field from whence the cry had come. Just as I heard the also familiar 'crump' of a mortar round, I felt a tug at my knee and I was on the ground. I had been hit again and while I could move my leg it wouldn't support me dependably. Within a few minutes Bill Clark was at my side, compressed bandage ready and applied, and supported me back to the aid station. After glancing at the wound, dusting it with sulfathiazole and immobilizing the leg, our new medical officer, Capt. Max Fox, had me loaded into an ambulance. The hospital was in Liége where a bit more surgery was done and I was confined to bed while the battalion was crossing the Roer and taking casualties.

"Two other recovering patients, a B-17 waist gunner and a 2d Division infantryman and I got passes to go into town. We had a fine time wandering about, two of us with an arm in a sling and one hobbling about on crutches, inspecting girls and comparing the merits of bars. All went well until while making our way down a fairly steep street, there was a loud explosion almost at our elbows. Our reaction times well polished, both the 2d Division man and I hit the ground. Looking up, we saw the gunner staring at us in puzzlement and a ring of concerned Belgians surrounding us. It had been a semitruck and trailer that had backfired. Sheepishly we continued on. I hoped the Belgians thought that my crutches merely had slipped."

The period following the Ardennes campaign revealed war at its nastiest to Dee Paris with the 14th Tank Battalion. The 9th Armored Division, of which his unit was an element, had regrouped following the Bulge and become an integral part of the first Army's drive toward the Rhine. But faulty intelligence continued to dog his tracks. "Originally, since horses do not have radios, the cavalry used motorcyclists to carry messages. When they did away with this method, our cyclist was devastated. I made him a gunner in my platoon sergeant's tank. We received some incorrect information and were caught in direct antitank fire. I was in the lead tank on a road approaching a village when an antitank round passed just above my head. The weapon fired two or three more times, each time the round just about a yard over me. I figured he had the gun dug in and couldn't lower his gun tube enough to hit me. The shell passing overhead made a fluttering sound—like when you expel air through your mouth, fluttering your lips.

"The shells missed me. But the platoon sergeant, looking out his turret, was decapitated by a round. When the motorcyclist-made-gunner turned to him for orders, he saw the headless body and just about lost his mind. We got the tank back to safety, but now the gunner was a mental case. He couldn't face that experience again so he was assigned as a driver, which placed him in the lower left part of the chassis. Subsequently, his tank came under fire and was struck by a round. I neutralized the German gun and went forward to survey the damage. The shell from a German 75mm antitank piece had hit the pavement in front of the tank and pierced the thin bottom of the tank. It split the body of the driver. I was devastated. I leaned against the tank and cried.

"The battalion commander and an officer from higher headquarters arrived. This officer peered into the hatch and I lost my temper, shouting, 'If you want to see blood, why don't you come up here and fight!' My commander restrained me until I calmed down. But no matter what you've been through before, you can still feel a loss to the point where you ignore discipline and verbally attack a senior officer. I understand that as a result of my behavior, he disapproved a valor award recommendation.

"Then there was an officer who had been wounded and evacuated during the Bulge. He returned just as we left on the mission that ended in the death of my platoon sergeant. He, too, was killed. At the time he was carried as missing in action. His wife, who'd lost a baby just before we went overseas, wrote, saying, 'God couldn't be so mean as to take my child and my husband at the same time. He can't be dead.' Against all regulations, I wrote back telling her not to prolong her grief with hope. Her husband, my friend, was dead. It was another terrible moment."

Major Glen Strange of the 27th Armored Infantry Battalion of the 9th Armored Division became part of Combat Command B, an eighteen-mile-long column, as it wound its way through Belgium, into Germany, and across the Roer River on the last day of February. According to Strange, progress slowed perceptibly. "Some of the companies had lost too much leadership. I had been told many times not to volunteer in the army but something made me feel these wonderful men whom I had helped train and been through so much needed me. I told Major Deevers, 'Give me a task force and we will move.'"

Deevers arranged for Strange to lead two companies of the 27th AIB, one from the 14th Tank Battalion, artillery support, and a platoon from the 89th Recon Battalion. The task force achieved its first objective, Lommersum on the Erft Canal, a few hours after its creation. "On the morning of March 4, a sergeant who piloted an L-5 [observation plane] landed in a turnip patch just behind my lines. I had flown with him before and he took me up. It was a hazy day but we could see the Rhine River and the Ludendorff Bridge at Remagen. I reported this to Gen. William Hoge, Combat Command B commander, and his comment was, 'It won't be there when we reach it.'"

From Lommersum, Strange's task force assaulted Bodenheim. "I took A Company from the 27th Armored Infantry Battalion and a platoon of the 14th tanks and captured it with some losses in about one hour. The history books say General Hoge led this attack. He did show up and was right with me to the end of it. But I gave all the orders and directed the attack. He never countermanded anything I said and it was nice to have him there, although he had no business being on the scene and his aide was killed during the fight."

On the following day, Strange was part of a party assaulting the village of Esch. "About 2:00 P.M. I was on foot and with the leading element. I was shot by a .30-caliber machine gun located in a church on the outskirts of Esch. My military career was over. I was evacuated and reached a field hospital in Liége on the morning of March 6." The bullet severely damaged Strange's spine and he began an eleven-month ordeal of hospitalization with a prognosis that he'd never walk again.

Glen Strange, his task force, and Combat Company B of the 9th Armored were engaged in a race to cross the Rhine, the last substantial natural barrier in the west. In the vanguard of Combat Company B was Dee Paris with the 14th Tank Battalion. On 6 March, "Colonel [Len] Engeman [Paris's CO] called me, 'Squirrel'—that was my radio code name, he was 'Gopher'—'Go up there and look at that bridge.' I tried to tell him we didn't have enough gas but he ignored me. I did not want to go in the worst way. I hated night operations, you can't see and the tanks roll off into ditches and crash into trees. At five minutes to nine, just as I told the guys to crank up the engines, I received a call to cancel the mission. The Ludendorff Bridge at Remagen, on the west side of the Rhine, was still standing but there was a big hole in front of it. Meanwhile, there were German guns on a hill that was actually behind us. We'd be sitting ducks for them if we tried to reach the bridge. I was told to take some tanks and take out those guns. I couldn't get close enough with the tanks so we dismounted and swept the hill like infantry. That silenced the guns. We moved into Remagen."

For years the alumni of various organizations have argued over who deserves credit for the events surrounding the Ludendorff Bridge. Engeman, the 14th Tank Battalion CO, offered the most authoritative account. "We made reasonable progress across the Cologne Plain toward the Rhine River, crossing the Erft Canal and the Neffel River and overcoming the German resistance. We lost ten medium tanks, and two light tanks. In the late evening of 6 March, in Stadt Meckenheim about fifteen miles from the Rhine River, I met with General Hoge. I received orders to advance at daylight 7 March to seize the cities of Remagen and Kripp and to be prepared to cross the Ahr River to join up with General Patton's Third Army advancing from the south." For the job, Engeman led a task force of tanks, armored infantry, a mortar platoon, and an engineer unit.

"When we received our orders, mention was made that the Ludendorff Bridge over the Rhine River at Remagen was still standing. We thought nothing of it as it was normal for the Germans to wait until we were almost on a bridge before they blew it up in our face. We moved out of Stadt Meckenheim at 0820 on the morning of the seventh. The city had been badly bombed by us so it took a little time to clear paths through the town. We had one tank in each company equipped with a tankdozer that would clear almost anything in a roadway. Then we had tank recovery vehicles that could tow and maneuver heavy units around. We finally left the city and Task Force Engeman proceeded on our route to Remagen. We had light opposition. Mostly roadblocks and small-arms fire. No German air nor much artillery. I was riding in my jeep as usual back of the lead tank platoon commanded by Lt. John Grimball. At about 1300 Grimball reported that the bridge was still standing. I was surprised but realized that they would probably blow it before we could get to it. I moved up with Grimball and saw the bridge. I requested artillery fire to burst over the bridge and called together Major Deevers and the other commanders involved. I decided to move the infantry dismounted down the highway into the city. We were on a high point overlooking the city and the river so we had great observation.

"I started the dismounted infantry down the hill on the left side of the roadway. A little later, about 1415, I ordered Grimball and the rest of the units to proceed down the road and told Grimball to get to the bridge as soon as possible and cover the bridge roadway with fire to prevent the Germans [from] getting on the bridge [to] destroy it. There were two trains across the river and I told him to take out the engines while he was going down the hill. About the time I was ready to head down the hill, General Hoge roared up in his jeep. I informed him of what I was doing. His only comment was to the effect that it would be nice to have a bridge. I left him and headed for the bridge. On the way, I told Grimball on my radio to get to the bridge as soon as possible. His reply was, 'Suh, I am already there.' When I arrived at the bridge I found that Grimball had lined up his vehicles on the road and was firing on the bridge roadway. I had my driver park our jeep by a house near the entry to the bridge. About this time a tremendous explosion went off on the side of the bridge near where I was standing by my jeep while using the radio. The debris from the explosion rose several hundred feet into the air. I fully expected the bridge to dump into the river and was totally surprised when the debris settled and the bridge was still standing. I immediately called Major Deevers and ordered him to get his infantry across the bridge and build up a defensive position on the other side. There was a small village and a high hill on the east approach to the bridge. We discussed getting heavier weapons up on the high ground.

"Deevers took off and I called for Lt. [Hugh B.] Mott who commanded the engineer platoon attached to me. When Mott reported in I directed him to get on the bridge with his platoon and thoroughly check to see that all demolitions were destroyed on the bridge. Then to report back to me when we could move tanks across. The infantry continued to move over the bridge as they had taken care of the German defenders in the bridge towers and most of the German defense was broken. We still got a lot of small arms and medium artillery fire. Lieutenant Mott reported that they had destroyed any remaining demolitions on the bridge and the roadway needed repair before we could get tanks across. If he could find timbers he would have it ready by midnight."

Deevers had told Lt. Karl Timmerman, newly appointed CO of Company A, to get men across the bridge. They had been about to start when the explosion mentioned by Engeman occurred. According to author Ken Hechler in *The Bridge at Remagen,* when the debris and dust settled, Timmerman waved his arm overhead signaling the troops, "Follow me." Three squads led by Sgt. Joe DeLisio, Sgt. Joe Petrensik, and Sgt. Alex Drabik sprinted over the planking in the face of fire from the other side. An American tank threw a few rounds at a tower on the opposite bank suppressing the enemy action.

DeLisio reached the towers, charged up a circular staircase in one, and leveled his weapon on three German machine gunners. They quickly obeyed his cry of *"Hände hoch!"* When DeLisio tossed their weapon out the aperture, the GIs still on the bridge dashed across. The Americans overwhelmed German engineers intent on blowing up the bridge and set up a perimeter defense on the east side of the Rhine. They organized road blocks and set out mines.

On the west bank, Engeman said, "About 1600 I realized that I had no direct orders to take the bridge and felt I needed verification that our actions were approved by higher command so I had a coded message sent back to CCB to the effect that we had sent the infantry across the bridge, which was still intact. I asked for their plans. At about 1855 [almost three hours later] I received a reply from CCB. They stated in effect that they were backing me with everything they have. I was to build up my defenses on the east side and they would protect my rear and a battalion was on the way to help me."

Engeman set up his command post in a large, empty wine cellar below street level and installed radios from vehicles to provide communications. A company of tank destroyers, a recon troop, and a battalion from an infantry regiment reached the scene. Meanwhile the engineers led by Mott labored in the black of night to repair the bridge roadway. About 1:00 A.M., said Engeman, "General Hoge stormed into the wine cellar. He was upset he had lost his radio communications on the way down the hill when his half-track tipped over. He asked me to let him use our communications, which was fine with me. We spent the rest of the night poring over maps and planning our moves to expand the bridgehead. About 0200, a platoon of Company A [a tank unit] was ordered across the bridge following a report from Mott that the bridge would hold the tanks. He had strung white engineer tape on both sides of the roadways so that the drivers could see the edges. It was pitch black. The platoon made it across and took positions on the far side of the bridge. I then ordered a company of tank destroyers to proceed across. Unfortunately, the tank destroyer had steel tread as opposed to our rubber tread, and the first one slipped off the roadway on the bridge and down onto the main support girders. We got the maintenance platoon to get a tank retriever with a hoist and they managed to get the TD out in a couple of hours.

"I later learned that when news of the bridge capture had been reported to General Eisenhower he was ecstatic and approved General Bradley's plan to put four divisions across the bridge. These units were moving piecemeal beginning the morning of 8 March. At 0635, [that day] General Hoge and I crossed the bridge and we set up headquarters downriver. I moved into a big house right on the east bank of the river. Shortly afterward General Louis A. Craig, 9th Infantry Division commander, assumed command of the bridgehead units. They began to assign my tanks to support the infantry units pushing out of the bridgehead so that I eventually had little command left. General Craig came into my headquarters and asked if he could move his command staff into a wine cellar directly in back of the house I occupied. It was the first time a general asked for something instead of ordering it."

A key figure in the exploitation of the Ludendorff Bridge was then-Lt. Hugh B. Mott of the 9th Armored's engineers. A 1939 ROTC honor graduate of high school in Nashville, Mott had married a childhood sweetheart. This prevented him from accepting a later nomination to West Point. Mott remembered, "People in town had informed us the bridge was to be blown up at four o'clock. We knew if anything was to be done, it had to be done quick. Colonel Engeman called me down to the foot of the bridge and we had the full bridge in sight and decided we'd go ahead and try to take the thing. It looked awful long and awful dangerous to me. I said, 'Lemme go and get a couple of my men and my tools.' I got two of my good sergeants, Sergeant Reynolds and Sergeant Dolan brought them back down there. There had been no Americans across the Rhine, yet. I told Colonel Engeman to give me all the fire cover he could. They had two main charges at the center of the bridge and a number of twenty pound packages of TNT in a number of places underneath where there was a scaffolding that covered everything up. Having no knowledge of the system layout we just cut all of the wires we could and hoped to get the one that controlled the whole electrical setup for all of the charges. As we started on the bridge, the infantry scouts came along with us. We attempted to cut every wire while the infantry boys were going across the bridge. We were getting pretty good fire from the other side. We really didn't know what to expect. Sergeant Dolan worked out a little bit ahead of me and Sergeant Reynolds, and he found what he thought was the main conduit for the electrical charges and blew it in two with his rifle. We never did know whether that was the right one, but the rest of the charges didn't go off.

"Our next problem was to get armor across but with that big hole in the middle of the bridge we couldn't. We worked on up into the night, pitch black night with no flashlights, with sniper fire, enemy fire hot and heavy. About midnight, we finally told them it was ready. Their armor lined up bumper-to-bumper. When the tank destroyer slid into a hole we got some cross ties, put them behind it, and they were able to pull the thing out."

As armor and men flowed across the Ludendorff Bridge—Dee Paris guided his platoon of tanks over on the morning of 8 March—the Germans attempted to destroy the span. Engeman remembered, "For the next several days the Germans blasted the bridge with artillery and tried but failed to hit it with bombs from their planes. We had moved so many antiaircraft [weapons] into the area that the Germans' aircraft had no chance. I really felt pity for the pilots who were repeatedly knocked down or dropped their bombs long before they neared the bridge."

To facilitate passage over the Rhine, GIs constructed a pair of pontoon bridges, one above and one below the Ludendorff. "The German artillery," said Engeman, "hit them repeatedly but the engineers managed to get them across. On 17 March, at 1505, my adjutant burst into headquarters and informed me that the bridge had collapsed into the river. I rushed to the site and found it had fallen and medics and others were rescuing the engineers who had toppled into the river with the bridge. In all twenty-eight men were killed and sixty-one injured. They were primarily men from an engineer construction battalion, repairing the bridge at the time. It had been closed to traffic while repairs were going on and we were using the two pontoon bridges." Although official records credited the 9th Armored Division commander Maj. Gen. John Leonard and Combat Command B's leader Brig. Gen. William Hoge, both West Pointers, with the decision to send the troops across the bridge, neither officer ever issued such an order. Erroneous accounts even place Hoge at the scene when the first GIs dashed onto the structure but it was well after dark before he arrived. Instead, it was Engeman, an ROTC product of the University of Minnesota, on his own, at considerable risk since he had been given a mission of linking up with the Third Army south of him, who directed the crossing. Major General George Ruhlen, who bossed the division artillery said, "Colonel Engeman and Engeman alone made the decision to attempt to capture the bridge. He and he alone gave the order to the 27th Armored Infantry Battalion to do it."

More than two weeks after the 27th Armored Infantry Battalion jounced across the Ludendorff Bridge at Remagen, Patton boasted that his Third Army had achieved the first successful assault crossing of the Rhine. He celebrated with several histrionic gestures, peeing into the river from a pontoon span thrown up by his engineers, grabbing handfuls of dirt on the eastern bank in emulation of William the Conqueror and topping off his performance with a telephone call to Omar Bradley, "For God's sake, tell the world we're across. I want the world to know Third Army made it before Monty starts across!"

Assault boats began to ferry thousands of GIs from the Ninth Army across the Rhine a day later. A barrage of 2,000 artillery pieces along with massive air raids preceded the crossing and the defenders offered relatively weak resistance to the 79th and 30th Divisions. Bill Kunz, as a member of the 3d Infantry Division's artillery, recalled, "Early on the assault morning, we fired a barrage of 10,000 rounds onto the Rhine east bank in less than 45 minutes. In one of my more stupid moves, I managed to get our jeep hung up crossways on the pontoon bridge. Luckily it was only temporarily stuck. Once across, our advance started to gain some momentum, and the amount of prisoners increased."

On 24 March, Operation Varsity carried 21,680 parachute and glider troops, mostly from the 17th Airborne Division, over the river for a daylight drop north of the main pontoon and assault-boat operations. Paratroopers rode in C-46s, whose doors on either side of the ship permitted a faster exit than the single entrance C-47s. But the less protected fuel systems of the C-46 resulted in deadly fires.

Pete Buckley flew a glider towed by a C-47. "It would be the first landing in enemy territory not secured in advance by our own paratroopers. My copilot, flight officer Bill Ryan and I introduced ourselves to the men from the 194th Glider Infantry whom we would be carrying. Bill and I up to this point felt secure in the knowledge that they were experienced combat soldiers, having been blooded while fighting in the Ardennes. One of the young troopers came up to me and mentioned the fact that most of them in my glider were replacements who had been transferred from another airborne unit and had not been in combat. They sure hoped that Bill and I knew what we were doing. With a sinking feeling in the pit of my stomach, I put on a very straight face and told him that Bill and I had landed in Normandy and Holland and assured him this was going to be a piece of cake. Little did I know that it was going to be the toughest mission to date for the tow plane crews and the glider pilots. It would also be the first time that the glider pilots after landing, would be organized into fighting units under the direct command of their own and senior airborne officers.

"The takeoff for the whole group went smoothly and quickly. In a very short time we had formed up and started to blend in with hundreds of other C-47s and their gliders that had taken off from fields all over France. The end result was a massive formation of aircraft that stretched as far as you could see from horizon to horizon, all headed for Germany. The only drawback was the extreme turbulence in the air caused by the prop wash of hundreds of planes ahead of us. You couldn't relax on the controls for one minute.

"About an hour into the flight, a glider on a tow ahead of me, shed a wing and then broke up completely in midair spilling its cargo of men and a jeep out where they seemed to float down in slow motion, mixed in with pieces of the glider. When all these glider pieces and the jeep hit the ground a big cloud of dust settled over the wreckage as we flew directly over it. This gave me the cold sweats for a few minutes and Bill took over the controls so that I would have a minute or two to compose myself. I didn't know whether the glidermen sitting behind us had seen this terrible accident but I hoped not.

"As the Rhine River came into view, Bill and I noticed to our mutual horror that all of the LZs and DZs on the other side were almost totally obscured by smoke and haze. Murphy's Law, which always seemed to haunt these airborne missions, was coming into play. The cause was the smoke screens the British were pumping out all along the banks to mask the crossing earlier that morning of their Commandos, who were assaulting the town of Wesel on the western edges of the landing zones. The RAF had also bombed Wesel and the smoke and dust from this combining with the smoke screens on the river had blown over the drop and landing zones.

"The moment that we crossed the Rhine, heavy flak and small-arms fire started coming up at us, the worst I had seen to date. The closer we got to the landing zones, the heavier it got. Tow planes and gliders were getting hit and going down in flames. A C-47 in front of us, with one engine out and with flames streaming back over its wing, held to a steady course, determined to get its two gliders to the LZs. In many cases they succeeded but by then their chances of bailing out were nil. All through this hell in the air, formation discipline was fantastic. The tow planes tucked in closer and bored straight on toward the landing zones with no attempt at evasive action.

"In a very short time the green cutoff light came on in the astrodome of our tow plane. I reached up and smacked the tow-rope release and started a 360-degree turn down into the smoke and flak. The closer we got to the ground, the more details became visible, details you really didn't want to see. We were looking right down the throats of the Germans who were manning their slit trenches and flak guns and were firing at us with everything they had. Gliders were coming down from all directions, at all speeds, into fields criss-crossed with tracers, artillery bursts, and mortar explosions. Some were touching down smoothly while those that came in too fast usually ended up in a twisted ball of wreckage from which no one emerged. Almost everyone became engaged in some form of hand-to-hand combat the instant they left the glider. Some poor souls never left their glider.

"Four gliders that landed in front of a well-entrenched 88 field gun were blown to bits with no survivors. Three others in this same field caught fire when the gas tanks in the jeeps they were carrying were hit by incendiary bullets and exploded. The pilots and glidermen were still sitting in their seats, burned to unrecognizable black crisps. If any place could be described as Hell on earth, this little corner of the world at this particular time had to be the place.

"By now I was so low that I had to decide fast what field we were going to land or crash on. The biggest field that we had just flown over was completely filled with wrecked, burning, and intact gliders with no opening in between except close to the 88, which was still firing. I spotted a small field dead ahead, surrounded by tall trees and with only one glider in the corner. By now we were getting hit by some small arms fire, and were so low that it had to be this field. I pulled the nose of the glider up to kill off the air speed. Bill held on full spoilers [devices that manipulate air flow over a wing] and in a nose-high sideslip just above stall speed, just before touchdown, I kicked it straight and we settled into a smooth, three-point landing. I rammed the nose down into the soft dirt and we stopped so quickly that I thought for a moment we were going to flip over. Bill and I yelled, 'Everybody out!' and when we turned around we were alone in the glider. I think the glidermen must have been jumping out while we were still rolling. I can understand this because I could hardly wait to get out myself but I couldn't because I was still at the controls. The important thing was we were down on terra firma, all in one piece, huddled in a wet ditch on the edge of the field.

"I wasn't sure where we were but for sure the enemy were in fields all around us and heavy fire was going on at all points of the compass. The sergeant in charge of the glidermen pulled out a map and I pulled out an aerial photo of the area to ascertain where we were with no luck. We all climbed out of the ditch and started off single file down a narrow dirt farm road in the direction of the heaviest firing. As we proceeded, we could hear the cry 'Medic, Medic' coming from both sides of us. There was very little we could do to help because we were under continuous sniper fire from all sides. We could see medics under continuous enemy fire bending over treating the wounded and trying to assist troopers still trapped in smashed gliders.

"As we passed a small farmhouse, surrounded by a stone wall, a sniper let loose from the upper window. We ducked behind the wall. While plotting out our strategy to cope with this problem, we heard a strange noise coming up the path. Like a Hollywood sketch, with a thunder of hoofs, six airborne troopers rode up on liberated farm horses, circled the farmhouse shooting into the windows. Finally, one trooper stopped and lobbed a rifle grenade through the second-story window and the sniper fire stopped. These crazy characters then galloped off down the road, into the sunset, as they say in cowboy movies. It seems funny but at the time it was a deadly serious game. Airborne men always seemed to find horses no matter how hot things got."

Buckley said he separated from the group to try to find other pilots. He paused briefly to reassure a wounded lieutenant that a medic would soon attend to him, then headed into the big field where so many gliders had been wiped out. "In the middle of the field I came across a glider pilot lying on his face about twenty feet in front of his glider. He was dead, with a bullet hole in the back of his head. I gently rolled him over and saw that when the bullet came out it took most of his forehead with it, making it impossible to recognize him. I checked his dog tags and much to my horror discovered that he was a friend and we had flown together during training.

"While sitting there on the ground beside the dead pilot, feeling quite depressed and downright scared, I heard a low rumbling noise in the distance. It came closer and closer until the ground began to tremble under me. Then with a horrendous roar, 240 Eighth Air Force B-24s came over right on the deck dropping supplies by parachute. It was the same outfit that resupplied us during the Holland mission. It was beautiful, awesome, and thrilling. I jumped up and waved and cheered them on. The tragic part began when the Germans in and around the perimeter opened up and shot down fifteen of them. At that low altitude it was almost impossible to bail out and most of the crews had to ride the planes down.

"Later in the day, I finally linked up with a group of glider pilots and we were assigned a section of the perimeter to hold until daylight. We settled down in some abandoned German dugouts in an apple orchard behind a farmhouse. Most of us crawled in and promptly fell asleep. Around midnight, all hell broke loose at a crossroads. Just over the hill from our position, glider pilots of other groups had been assigned this section around a key road junction to block any attempt to infiltrate into our lines. That is exactly what happened. Two platoons of German infantry with two tanks and a 20mm flak wagon were advancing straight up the road on a collision course with the glider pilots who were backed up by a .50-caliber machine gun manned by glidermen of the 194th. The battle raged off and on for most of the night before tapering off. During the fight, one glider pilot managed to knock out a tank with a borrowed bazooka.

"When the sun came up, the glider pilots at the crossroads took stock of their night's work. They found at least twelve German dead in front of their positions and more than forty wounded. Two tanks had been put out of commission; one 20mm antitank gun was destroyed and approximately eighty-four enemy infantry in and around their positions were ready to surrender. Not a bad score for a bunch of so-called undisciplined glider pilots. Their own casualties were three dead glidermen who had manned the machine gun and two wounded glider pilots. By late afternoon of the second day, things had stabilized to the point where glider pilots were authorized to withdraw back over the Rhine. They brought back with them 2,000 prisoners, some of whom they had captured themselves. A funny thing about these prisoners. A short time before, when they had their weapons, they fought like hell trying to kill you. Now with no weapons they were as docile as cows and seemed to sense that they had lost the war. It was much different in Normandy and Holland. Most of the POWs captured at that time remained surly and arrogant, convinced that they were still going to win the war."

Within three hours of the first drop, American paratroopers linked up with British forces. Three entire German divisions plus other units were destroyed between the Allied airborne contingents and the armor and infantry crossing the Rhine in great numbers. U.S. forces, however, incurred losses of ten percent and the British suffered triple that number. But it was now only a question of how far the soldiers in the west could travel before meeting the Red Army.

On 25 March, the 4th Armored Division, with Capt. Abe Baum of the 10th Armored Infantry Battalion, had advanced to the Main River, capturing bridgeheads at Hanau and Aschaffenburg. Now Patton proposed to send men of the 4th Armored on a daring rescue mission, the liberation of Stalag XIII A at Hammelburg, forty miles away, and where Lieutenants Lyle Bouck and Alan Jones Jr. were confined with other officers. Patton explained on 30 March, "I felt I could not sleep during the night if I got within sixty miles and made no attempt to get that place." He claimed the inhabitants were in dire peril since the Nazis were murdering POWs.

Patton handed the mission to Gen. Manton Eddy, commander of the XII Corps and Gen. William Hoge, promoted to head the 4th Armored. Both of them objected strenuously to the concept of a foray by a force containing 3,000 men, 150 tanks plus artillery and other support. Omar Bradley was not in favor of the raid either. In the end, Patton yielded on the numbers, but his persistence brought a deadly compromise, that instead of the equivalent of a full combat command, the strike force be little more than one-tenth that size, about two companies' worth of troops.

Although Patton professed his motivation was the welfare of all of the officers confined at Hammelburg, there are strong signals he was concerned about one individual in particular, his son-in-law, John Waters. There was intelligence that indicated Waters had been moved from a prison camp in Poland and most likely was at Hammelburg. The idea of a sudden dramatic strike to liberate American prisoners obviously appealed to Patton. MacArthur, had scored huge headlines with the operation that freed 5,000 U.S. prisoners in the Philippines. While lobbying for support with Hoge, Patton boasted, "This is going to make MacArthur's raid on Cabanatuan peanuts." Al Stiller, a Patton aide, repeated the general's comparison with the MacArthur feat, changing the "peanuts" to "look like a Boy Scout hike."

Nomination of those who would go on what he perceived as a near suicide mission devolved to Col. Creighton Abrams, newly elevated to lead the 4th Armored Combat Company B. Actually, his first choice would have been Abrams' former regular partner on missions, Harold Cohen, and members of the 10th Armored Infantry Battalion. But Cohen was still recovering from a painful case of hemorrhoids.

With Cohen not available because of his painful rear end—he was excused only after personal inspection by Patton—Baum became the choice. After Baum heard the bare essentials of the mission at a meeting, Patton drew him aside, and in a conspiratorial whisper, said, "Listen, Abe—it is Abe, isn't it? You pull this off and I'll see to it that you get the Medal of Honor."

When he learned what was expected of him, Baum says he never considered refusing the orders—perhaps a consequence of being an aggressive twenty-four-year-old. He remarked to Abrams and Cohen, "You won't get rid of me this easy. I'll be back." In retrospect he said, "When a mission is created, nobody says this or that might happen to you. There usually isn't the intelligence available to say what could occur."

Al Stiller actually supplied the details of the operation. He spoke of 300 officers being held at Hammelburg, an error that would give the affair even less chance. He reassured Baum there would be air cover where possible, and that because Patton's Third Army was headed for another sector, the Seventh Army would be prepared to render assistance once Task Force Baum broke away from Hammelburg to return to the U.S. lines. Stiller casually mentioned Patton's son-in-law as one of the inmates to Baum.

The column jumped off on 26 March. It included 10 Shermans, 6 light tanks, 27 half-tracks, 3 105mm assault guns, a medic weasel for evacuation of wounded; these and jeeps, all loaded with extra fuel and ammunition. These vehicles bore 293 soldiers, most of whom had slept but one out of the previous four days of movement and battle. The mission began on a foreboding note as Task Force Baum had to run a gauntlet through the town of Schweinheim, after a TOT artillery cannonade opened the proceedings around 8:30 P.M.

With their path brightly outlined by burning buildings, and snaking between the parked tanks down the narrow street, Baum's column bolted through Schweinheim, nicknamed "Bazooka City" for the prevalence of antitank rockets. Once beyond the fires and in the blackness of night, the column used follow-the-leader navigation, relying on the glow of exhausts and specks of illumination from blackout lights. The swifter light tanks assumed the head of the mile-long column that now hurried through the darkness at fifteen miles per hour. Overhead, a liaison plane dallied long enough to relay radio messages from Baum.

At the Berlin headquarters of the Wehrmacht, news of the fight at Schweinheim trickled in, but the defenders could not accurately report the size of the American contingent. The Germans concluded Patton had engineered another daring thrust with a considerable force, rather than the small self-contained group under Baum. The foe quickly mobilized to stop this threat.

The task force smashed through a roadblock and demolished a German truck convoy in which the main casualties turned out to be German flak girls assigned to antiaircraft duties. At Gemünden the GIs blasted several trains, but when the foe dropped the only bridge over the Saale River into the water, the armored column had to locate another less direct route. At the same time, several tanks had been disabled and about twenty men killed or wounded. Overhead, however, spotter planes appeared to track the path of the task force.

After several more skirmishes, the tanks and half-tracks reached the Hammelburg camp. German soldiers tried to defend the place from foxholes, but they were outgunned. The commandant agreed to yield. With all of the confusion and shooting, however, it was necessary to send out a truce team from the camp. John Waters volunteered and, with several other Americans plus a German officer, set out, carrying a white flag manufactured from a bed sheet. When the party passed through the gate, a German soldier suddenly appeared, leveled his rifle, and squeezed off a shot. The bullet hit Waters below the right hip, smashed off bone, and then chipped his coccyx as it exited from his left buttock. The German officer with Waters and the others engaged in a furious discussion with the soldier, who seemed inclined to shoot everyone. But at least he grasped that his commandant had agreed to the surrender. The badly wounded Waters was carried in a blanket to the POW hospital operated by Serbian prisoners. The task force battered down the barbed wire, then parked in a field just beyond the camp.

Lieutenant Alan Jones Jr. from the 106th Division says, "The attack on the camp was totally unexpected by me. I was sitting there when suddenly I heard the firing. We moved quickly to another barracks, which was made of stone and would protect us better. But we were all at the windows watching, cheering our guys on. I saw Lieutenant Colonel Waters go out with the others and I saw him being shot. Then, as darkness came, the tanks moved into the camp."

Baum was dismayed to learn that instead of the 300 officers Stiller claimed were held at Hammelburg, the number was about 1,500. He could not possibly accommodate that many in his half-tracks or on his tanks. As a kriegie, Lyle Bouck thought in terms of the Allied advance rather than a raid as the engine of his liberation. "Early in the morning, I heard small-arms fire. We thought it meant that the front lines were approaching. Somewhere before dark, we saw tanks and the next thing I heard stories that a task force had come to get us. There was much confusion. A lot of people were standing around, Yugoslavs and Americans, amid the tanks and half-tracks. We found the task force couldn't take all of us." Actually, Baum had asked the senior American prisoner, Col. Paul Goode, to pick the limited number of lucky ones who could ride with the task force, fewer than 300 because of Baum's losses. When Goode failed to make a selection, rumors circulated. "There was a story that only field-grade officers would go," remembered Bouck. "Some of the guys said to one another, 'I'm promoting you to major,' and the other would reciprocate."

Baum never sought to limit the rescue to field-grade officers. But he was forced to make the discouraging announcement to the crowd of kriegies. He explained that there were far more men than had been expected. He could take some but the rest would have to decide whether to take their chances walking westward toward the advancing Seventh Army or remain in the camp until the front lines swept past them. Those who accompanied his column would risk attacks directed at the task force. The frustrated Baum, aware of his losses in what was clearly a long shot with no real pay-off, says he fought back his tears as he spoke to the prisoners.

While Baum dealt with the main body of prisoners, Al Stiller sought out the one man for whom the entire operation was designed. He found Waters recovering from emergency surgery by Serbian physicians. He obviously was in no condition to be moved and he still faced the danger of infection or paralysis. Stiller visited with Patton's son-in-law, then made his way to the task force. Baum hurriedly ordered engines cranked up for the start back, knowing the Germans would come after his task force and its cargo. Hundreds of prisoners, evaluating the odds or considering themselves too weak to attempt to travel the forty to sixty miles to the American lines, shuffled back into the camp. Many others walked off on their own, hoping to remain free. And a generous number clambered aboard the tanks and half-tracks.

Alan Jones and a buddy, Lt. Bud Bolling, whose father also commanded a division (84th Infantry), boarded a tank but the crowd was too much for the Sherman's commander. He couldn't traverse his gun and he ordered a bunch off, including Jones and Bolling. "Bolling and I started to walk. My feet were still bothering me and I couldn't go very fast. In the morning they found me and brought me back to camp. But Bolling got away."

Lyle Bouck and a friend, Matthew Reid, stuck together, hauling themselves aboard the second tank in the column. The convoy started off, trying to take a different path to avoid discovery and roadblocks. "One of the guys gave each of us a grease gun. We were making pretty good progress when the tank in front of us exploded and started to burn. I see that I'm in the middle of a sea of tracer bullets. I'm hit in the left knee. It felt very hot and I couldn't tell where I could move. Reid and I ducked into some small saplings. From there we could see where the stuff was coming from, crew served weapons. I hollered, 'Let's charge 'em" and we did, firing the grease guns. We could see them dropping.

"I yelled to the tankers to call the commander and tell him we knocked out the road block and he could move around it. We climbed on the last tank and then pulled up in an area where they put out a perimeter defense. We had some wounded and they were all put in a kind of outbuilding made of stone. They put a white flag on the rocks."

The task force commander, aware his men had had no sleep for forty-eight hours, decided to wait until dawn to make a last desperate dash to evade his pursuers. He ordered gasoline siphoned from some half-tracks to fill the vehicles that would make the final run. Reid and Bouck got into a half-track. But during the night, the Germans had moved a substantial force into position. Bouck remembered, "All of a sudden we were hit. We took off for the woods. But they had goddamn dogs all around us and they began rounding us up. Some of the tankers took off their coveralls and the Germans got angry because they couldn't tell who was from the task force and who had been a prisoner. They went around looking at faces, trying to see who was well fed."

A salvo crashed into the building with the wounded. The walls collapsed on the hapless victims; none survived. As if in a shooting gallery, the Germans methodically destroyed every vehicle in a firestorm of shells. Baum with Stiller and another man fled to the forest. But the dogs picked up their trail. The enemy closed in. Baum was prepared to shoot his way out, if possible. "I tried to pull up my mackinaw to reach my .45 and I saw this German. While I watched him, he pulled out his P38 [pistol] and shot me inside the thigh of my right leg. 'You son of a bitch, you nearly shot off my balls,' I said. He laughed. He understood English; he was from Bridgeport and serving in the Volksturm, the home guard." Baum managed to discard his dog tags, which identified him as Jewish. He was now a prisoner, a seriously wounded one at that.

Other captives persuaded the Germans that Baum was just another inmate caught in the crossfire. They half-carried him back into camp and placed him in the care of the Serbian medics. When the 14th Armored Division overran Hammelburg little more than a week later it liberated both Baum and Waters. While they recuperated in a hospital at Gotha, Patton visited them both, presenting each with a Distinguished Service Cross. Waters earned his in North Africa and Baum's was the payoff for the task force operation. An intelligence officer had already warned Baum that the mission must remain top secret. He also realized that Patton could not afford to recommend a Medal of Honor, for that would require a public airing of the circumstances.

The great Hammelburg raid failed to free John Waters, and only a few prisoners and would-be rescuers slipped through the German lines to safety. Every piece of equipment was lost; nine men were officially identified as dead and an additional sixteen were never accounted for. Most of Task Force Baum endured several weeks in the stalags.

Some military historians point out that whatever the motivation behind it, the mission wreaked havoc upon a substantial number of German troops and caused a diversion of forces that the Americans exploited. Patton never conceded the purpose of the expedition was the liberation of his son-in-law. Abe Baum who became friendly with Waters asked him at the time if he had ever discussed the matter with Patton. "He said he had asked his father-in-law, who answered, 'If I did know I wouldn't tell you, because that would jeopardize our intelligence.'" Baum had no doubts that Patton was aware of Waters's location.

48
Operation Iceberg

The first day of April saw Allied armies in Europe on the western front sweeping across the Rhineland toward Berlin and a rendezvous at the Elbe River with the Soviet forces careening through Czechoslovakia and Austria before bludgeoning their way into Germany. The advancing troops bagged thousands of prisoners, and overran the Third Reich's war factories as the bombers of the RAF and U.S. began to run out of targets.

In the Pacific, GIs continued to liberate chunks of the Philippines while a mighty armada bore down on the Ryukyus intent upon a base only 350 miles from the Japanese home islands. The advance across the Pacific toward Japan, had almost wiped out every acquisition of the Empire, though the ultimate aim, as in Europe, was not simply to roll back the enemy but to defeat them on their home turf. Ground troops were required to achieve victory in Europe in spite of the terrible pasting delivered to the Third Reich from the air, and it was believed that only when GI boots tromped on the streets of Tokyo would the warlords accept unconditional surrender.

Beyond the Philippines lay two candidates for the last stage before an invasion of Kyushu, the southernmost Nipponese island, the large Chinese island of Formosa, (Taiwan in today's lexicon), and the biggest of the Ryukyu Islands, Okinawa. U.S. Army strategists estimated conquest of Formosa would require nine combat divisions plus the requisite service troops. With the war in Europe still blazing, there simply would not be enough men available.

Okinawa, closer to Japan than Formosa, and in an early intelligence report defended by fewer than 50,000, seemed more manageable. For the purposes of establishing supply and airbases to support an invasion of Kyushu it was eminently qualified. Okinawa beckoned with first-rate, protected anchorages for a fleet striking at Japan. The vast stockpiles of supplies required for the million men deemed necessary to shatter the last strongholds of resistance could be safely warehoused on Okinawa. It would provide an unsinkable aircraft carrier, close enough to the targets for fighter planes to shepherd the bombers. Formosa could be bypassed. Attempts to interdict the Allied operations from that island could be blocked by naval and air forces.

Known sometimes as "Loochoo" or "Lew Chew" in Chinese and Japanese dialects, the roughly 140 Ryukyu Islands consist of the remains from mountains and some now-dormant volcanoes that thrust up from the East China Sea. The biggest of the bunch, Okinawa, "the Great Loochoo," includes a quarter of the land mass and lies in the middle of the chain. Its closest companions were a clump of small islands known as the Kerama Retto and one of sufficient size to maintain a large airfield, Ie Shima. Fully vested citizens of Imperial Japan, Okinawans were regarded by those who came to govern, manage, and defend the place as rustics and perhaps inferiors. However, the soldiers stationed on Okinawa never generated the hostility manifested by the peoples of the occupied territories like the Philippines, Solomon Islands, or other lands conquered after Pearl Harbor. The native inhabitants may have resented the attitudes of those from the original Japanese country, but they considered the Allies their enemies and they were willing to fight for their homeland and Japan. To the 80,000 troops from various parts of Japan hunkering down to defend Okinawa were added 20,000 Okinawan conscripts. Their officers from the Japanese army had no complaints about their performance under fire.

The American figures on Japanese strength on Okinawa and the surrounding islands considerably underestimated the number of troops. Interrogators collected scraps of information from documents and an occasional prisoner taken elsewhere, but their knowledge of the Ryukus was scant. A submarine dispatched from Pearl Harbor to photograph the beaches disappeared. The only real source of intelligence lay in aerial reconnaissance and early in the game the enemy had gone underground. To the prying eyes of the pilots and to the lenses of the cameras, Okinawa began to look as if it were devoid of humans. Photographs indicated defenses around Naha, twenty miles behind the western Hagushi coast beaches, and along a ridge known as the Shuri line that centered on an ancient walled city dominated by a castle.

On Okinawa, subterranean defenses, as at Tarawa and Iwo Jima, burrowed into nearly impregnable coral for their emplacements, rendering themselves all but invulnerable to the usual insults of artillery and heavy naval guns. The defenders developed coordinated tactics with snipers to pick off assault teams with flamethrowers and explosives. Antiincendiary devices like wet mats or blankets smothered fires. Ventilation systems became well disguised and less susceptible to attacks. For close to two years, the Okinawa commanders drove their men to dig, ever deeper.

This industry and ingenuity created a honeycomb of underground bunkers, some as much as five stories below ground, and many of these connected through a web of tunnels, as much as sixty miles of subterranean corridors. A single cave could house as many as 1,000 men, and trucks, and even tanks, could be parked inside. Intersecting automatic weapons fire forged deadly mutual protection for entrances. Openings from inside the caves allowed positions to shift during artillery and air bombardments. Egress was artfully concealed. Spider holes—small, well-hidden pits—sited near entrances provided sentries clear and surprise fire lanes upon interlopers.

The U.S. forces focused on three other principal objectives in the Ryukyus, the Kerama Retto, Keise Shima, and Ie Shima. The first of these consisted of eight mounds of steep, rocky slopes that poked 400 to 600 feet out of the water. The largest added up to only a few square miles and provided sustenance for a handful of inhabitants. There were no roads on the Kerama Retto, merely trails for pack animals or humans. The Kerama Retto offered one irresistible asset. Lying only ten to fifteen miles from Okinawa, within the waters of the otherwise unprepossessing clumps of real estate was nestled a spacious, well-protected deep anchorage.

It apparently never occurred to the Japanese that the enemy would find the natural harbor within the Kerama Retto so attractive, for little effort had been made to install strong points capable of fending off attacks. Instead, they based only about 100 troops there, supplementing them with some 600 Korean laborers. But one additional and potentially dangerous element consisted of several squadrons of plywood motorboats armed with depth charges.

The sea raider squadron crews were trained to dump their 264-pound explosives as close to the vital areas of a ship as possible. Once the devices rolled off the racks at the back of a speedboat, the pilot had five seconds before they went off. The thin-hulled, slow-moving, and poorly built craft probably would not survive the blast, but it was not considered suicidal in the same terms as a kamikaze. Altogether there were 350 of these Q-boats squirreled around the Kerama Retto.

The island of Ie Shima, about ten square smiles in size, stood less than four miles from the tip of an Okinawa peninsula about twenty miles north of where the initial attack on the Great Loochoo would occur. Flatter than most of its sister islands, Ie Shima boasted a large plateau over much of its interior. Aware of its topographical advantages in an area where few existed, the Japanese had started to construct no fewer than three airfields on Ie Shima. Only at the southern end was the level terrain radically broken. Iegusugu Mountain, a 600-foot, sheer outcrop of rock, dubbed "the Pinnacle" by GIs, jutted above the rest of the oval-shaped plateau and its airstrips like the control tower of an aircraft carrier stationed in the East China Sea. South of the Pinnacle, in the town of Ie, many of the 5,000 civilians who remained when the war reached the Ryukyus, occupied 300 houses. Ie Shima as one more objective in the overall scheme for the conquest of the Ryukyus, also drew the attention of aerial reconnaissance.

The American strategists, using four army and two marine divisions plus naval and air forces, planned to commit 172,000 combatants supported by another 115,000 troops to invade Okinawa. That required a seagoing component of more than 1,200 vessels, including transports and warships. These would of necessity be supported by ships for screening and attack purposes. The total amphibious forces added up to more than 1,200 vessels. The number does not include ships from the Royal Navy, VAdm. Marc Mitscher's Fast Carrier [Aircraft] Force, and some other units from other groups. At least 1,500 Allied craft would participate in Operation Iceberg.

To keep the enemy back on its heels, in mid-March, the Allied navies punched away at Japanese ships and installations on Kyushu. The foe counterattacked mainly with kamikazes and conventional bombing raids. Over a number of days, the attacks scored hits on a number of aircraft carriers— *Enterprise, Intrepid, Yorktown, Wasp,* and most devastatingly on *Franklin.* A series of explosions and fires rocked the huge ship and the final count showed 724 of the crew killed or missing and another 265 wounded. Another 1,700 owed their lives to rescue efforts by nearby cruisers and destroyers that plucked them from the water after all but key personnel received the abandon-ship order. After the fires aboard "Big Ben" were extinguished, it managed to stay afloat under its own power on a 12,000-mile trip to New York for repairs.

A critical decision in the design of U.S. carriers had specified wooden flight decks rather than steel ones. The use of the lighter-weight material enabled U.S. carriers to carry a greater number of planes compared to the complement aboard British ships, which had steel decks. But Japanese bombs penetrated the thin, flammable wood and crashed through to explode amid hangar decks, munitions magazines, and power plants. (The *Wasp* had a missile smash through before going off between the second and third decks, but the crew quickly extinguished the blaze.)

The trade-off, additional firepower and speed in place of safety—the weightier decks introduced a top-heavy quality and slowed the British carriers—was partly compensated for by intensive instruction in fire fighting. Experts who had served with the New York City and Boston fire departments convinced the Bureau of Ships to issue new fog nozzles that produced a fine spray and snuffed out flames more quickly than a heavy stream of water. Big ships installed fire mains that worked independently of a vessel's power plant, which often shut down after a big hit.

The invasion of Okinawa was scheduled for Easter Sunday, 1 April, and coded "Love Day" since "D day" had come exclusively to signify the Normandy landings. As Love Day approached, the extensive casualties for the Navy continued because of the need to sweep the waters off the Ryukyus clear of mines. During the sanitation of 2,500 square miles of ocean the fire-support destroyer *Halligan* struck a mine that detonated her two forward magazines. Smoke and debris rose two hundred feet in the air and the ship was abandoned with a loss of 153 dead and 39 wounded.

On Palm Sunday, one week before Love Day, U.S. warships began a bombardment of Kerama Retto. Under the cover of this fire, teams of frogmen swam in toward the beaches to map the reefs and mark spots where coral threatened landing craft. When they completed their tasks, on 26 March amtracs raced ashore. Four battalion landing teams from the 77th Division clambered out of their amtracs in the early morning on the beaches of four islands in the Kerama Retto group. Thanks to the preparations and practices carried out in the Philippines, the troops landed at the right places and almost all on schedule. The covering fire had been so effective that not a single man or amtrac was lost.

Official accounts declare that the ragtag defenders, a small complement of soldiers bolstered by the Q-boat pilots and Korean laborers, offered only sporadic resistance with minimal effect. However, in several instances where the U.S. forces headed into the hills, the Japanese and some of their Korean conscripts fought hard. On the island of Zamami hand-to-hand combat brought out Japanese wielding rifles, pistols, and sabers. "The GIs did not think it was so easy," remarked, liaison pilot John Kriegsman. "The only way to snuff out the Japs was to walk over the rock mountains. The boat crews did not give up easily. Navy destroyers poured 5-inch shells into the caves to neutralize them." When the Kerama Retto operation ended, the Americans listed 530 of the enemy killed, 121 prisoners, and almost 1,200 civilians rounded up. The 77th Division mourned 78 dead and 177 wounded. Close to 250 suicide boats were seized and eventually rendered harmless, although one officer who attempted to joyride in one lost his life to a booby trap. As many as 300 Japanese soldiers and Korean laborers hid out in the back country hills of the rugged islands and they would not actually surrender until after V-E Day.

The 1st and 6th Marine Divisions, which composed the III Amphibious Corps commanded by Maj. Gen. Roy S. Geiger, were to be responsible for the the northern stretches of the Hagushi beaches on Okinawa itself. "I was aboard a troop transport and it was the evening before we stormed onto Okinawa," wrote Ernie Pyle. "We were carrying marines. Some of them were going into combat for the first time; others were veterans from as far back as Guadalcanal. They were a rough, unshaven, competent bunch of Americans. I was landing with them and I felt I was in good hands . . . We were nervous. Anybody with any sense is nervous on the night before D day. . . . We would take Okinawa—nobody had any doubt about that. But we knew we would have to pay for it. Some on the ship would not be alive in twenty-four hours."

Pyle awoke before a predawn breakfast of ham and eggs. "Our assault transport carried many landing craft on deck. A derrick swung them over the side, we piled into them as they hung even with the rail, and then the winch lowered them into the water. I went on the first boat to leave our ship. It was just breaking dawn when we left and still more than two hours before H-Hour. Our long ocean trip was over. Our time had run out. This was it . . .

"An hour and a half before H-Hour at Okinawa, our vast fleet began its final, mighty bombardment of the shore with its big guns. They had been at it for a week, but this was a concentration whose fury had never been approached before . . . Great sheets of flame flashed out from a battery of guns, gray-brownish smoke puffed up in a huge cloud, then the crash of sound and concussion carried across the water and hit you. Multiply that by hundreds and you had bedlam. Now and then the smoke from a battlewagon would come out in a smoke ring, an enormous one, twenty or thirty feet across, and float upward with perfect symmetry.

"Then came our carrier planes, diving on the beaches and torpedo planes, carrying heavy bombs and incendiaries that spread deep-red flame. Smoke and dust rose up from the shore, thousands of feet high, until finally the land was completely veiled. Bombs and strafing machine guns and roaring engines mingled with the crash of naval bombardment . . .

"H-Hour was set for 8:30. By 8:00 A.M. directions were being radioed and a voice boomed out to sea to form up waves one and two, to hurry up, to get things moving. Our first wave consisted solely of heavy guns on amphibious tanks which were to get ashore and blast out the pillboxes on the beaches. One minute behind them came the second wave—the first of our foot troops. After that waves came at about ten-minute intervals. Wave six was on its way before wave one ever hit the beach. Wave fifteen was moving up before wave six got to the beach."

"Word came by radio that waves one and two were ashore without much opposition and there were no mines on the beaches. So far, so good. We looked at the shore through binoculars. We could see tanks moving across the fields and the men of the second wave walking inland, standing upright. There were a few splashes in the water at the beach but we couldn't make out any real fire coming from the shore.

"It was all very indefinite and yet it was indicative. The weight began to lift. I wasn't really conscious of it, but I found myself talking more easily with the sailors and somehow the feeling gradually took hold of me that we were to be spared." With the seventh wave, Pyle chugged toward the now less ominous shore, transferring to an amtrac to cross the reef. "I had dreaded the sight of the beach littered with many mangled bodies, and my first look up and down the beach was a reluctant one. Then like a man in the movies who looks away and then suddenly looks back unbelieving, I realized there were no bodies anywhere—and no wounded. What a wonderful feeling.

"Our entire regiment came ashore with only two casualties: one was a marine who hurt his foot getting out of an amphibious truck; the other was, of all things, a case of heat prostration! And to add to the picnic atmosphere, they had fixed me up with a big sack of turkey wings, bread, oranges, and apples. So instead of grabbing a hasty bit of K rations for our first meal ashore, we sat and lunched on turkey wings and oranges."

Marine platoon leader Bob Craig, as part of the 1st Division reserve, headed for the shore with his men in midafternoon. "Our LCVP [Landing Craft Vehicles and Personnel] stuck on a coral reef about 200 yards out. Waded ashore, and moved inland about 200 yards and started to dig in. Lost one squad leader, Corporal Boris. Dropped a rifle on his foot and hurt it. He should be back.

"About dusk (6:30 P.M.) we moved up the hill toward Yontan Airfield. Were halfway up when a Jap plane came over. All the ships opened up with their AA. While we dodged falling shrapnel, the Jap landed on the airfield and got out of his plane. When he tried to run, some boys in an amtrac got him. We moved across a corner of the airfield, past a motorless Jap plane. Made first contact with the enemy. A sniper. I dived into a shell hole as two shots zipped through the grass near me. Too dark to do anything, so moved another 100 yards and dug in for the night, just east of the village of Sobe. Awake most of the night—partly in fear and partly because the fleas in the grass really bothered me. The only activity of the night, aside from the regular naval bombardment, was the appearance of another Jap plane on the Pacific side of the island. We saw a little 20mm AA but with no results."

Company A of the 7th Marine Regiment, with Don Farquhar in command of the machine gun platoon, drew the assignment of reserve. "We were in the third wave." said Farquhar, "I wasn't scared; the feeling is just like playing football in college, nervous as can be until you get in the game then the jitters are gone. It was a great relief to find the beaches not defended and a real surprise. We had been trained in kill or be killed, and I had taken some special training in bayonet fighting, so I was rather looking forward to being able to use my special training."

Jim Moll remembered, "They told us Okinawa would not be easy because we were getting closer to Japan proper. There were some larger cities we would have to take, more occasions when we would be up against larger concentrations of enemy troops than what we had met in the past, and also more concentrations of civilians. It was a blessing to land on the beach without a single casualty. I don't think anybody, including the highest brass, expected this but whoever planned the operation deserves the highest medal."

Sergeant Harry Manion, with the recon company of the 6th Marine Division, who developed his expertise at scouting and patrolling while mopping up on Guadalcanal and then applied his skills on Guam, recalled: "Recon Company went ashore and moved directly inland. Came across some caves, with civilians and perhaps some military. Called out in Japanese for the people to come out. Reply was one shot. In goes WP [white phosphorous grenade]. Out come some civilians. No soldiers. We left them for the civil affairs people. Still plenty of daylight. Moved off the left flank of the division. Dug holes, put out security, and flaked out. Later, after dark, we heard firing coming from Yontan Airfield area. We learned that a Japanese pilot landed his fighter on the field. Always some who don't get the word."

Earl Rice, who had almost been transferred out of the 1st Marine Division for misbehavior, feared another debacle like Peleliu. "There were so many boats out there," said Rice, "it was like land rather than water. Before we got on the Higgins boat they gave us only a piece of fruit and some water. Those Higgins boats went up and down, up and down, so the idea was to keep us from getting sick. I puked over the side and then I felt fine after that. The guy says, 'Fix bayonets.' You don't know who the hell is on that beach, what you're heading into. I remembered what I saw at Peleliu. You fix that bayonet and see everybody doing the same. Then you hit the ground, the boat touches the shore, you can hear it. You know you're going to be getting off. Then you see everybody, myself included, blessing their selves, everyone's full of religion."

"The religious had attended services at 3:00 A.M.," said Bob Jackson with the 96th Infantry Division. "It was a gorgeous Easter/April Fool's Day. We embarked into the landing craft and spent the usual two hours boating around in circles, under an azure sky—I can't help the cliché. There was no shore activity except that of our shore parties so we rode in basking in the cool but sunny weather that reminded me of San Francisco on such a day. The landing, with those expert seamen, was dryfooted, unlike most of our previous experiences with Army boat commanders. We came ashore, got into columns of companies, and moved inland as if it were a school exercise."

In the southwest, the 2d Marine Division loaded men from troop transports into landing craft and seven waves consisting of 168 LCVPs set course for the Minatoga beaches on the southeastern side of the island. At 08:30, as the first GIs and leathernecks stepped onto the Hagushi beaches, the vessels bearing the 2d Marines reversed course and returned to the mother ships. The feint drew one salvo of four rounds. But the official communiqué from Japanese headquarters triumphantly announced that "an enemy landing attempt on the eastern coast of Okinawa on Sunday morning was completely foiled, with heavy losses to the enemy."

By the time darkness fell on Love Day and all of the invaders had burrowed into the ground for the night, the beachhead stretched along more
than twelve miles of the Okinawa coastline. In some places the troops had
pushed inland for three miles. The 17th Regimental Combat Team of the
7th Division had occupied a now deserted Kadena airfield shortly before
noon. Patrols from the 17th gazed upon the east coast waterfront of Okinawa in midafternoon. With the two Marine divisions making swift
progress into the lightly defended north, the island had been virtually
chopped in half in less than twelve hours.

Marines from the 6th Division took over Yontan, the bigger and better
developed of the airstrips without any opposition. The booty included shattered Japanese planes and supplies, destroyed by the preinvasion bombardments. The swiftness of the advance surprised not only the Americans
but obviously the enemy, which explains the fate of the unfortunate pilot
who sought to land at Yontan after it had fallen. Statisticians figured at
least 60,000 men reached shore on Love Day. The bulk of these were foot
soldiers backed up by divisional artillery and tanks plus a generous number of service troops. The only serious opposition came from the air. A suicide plane crashed into the battleship *West Virginia,* another splashed down
close enough to damage some transports and two kamikazes off Minatoga
struck an LST killing 24, injuring 21 and a transport with a loss of 16 dead
and 39 wounded. While these losses, from a strategic viewpoint, were negligible, they signaled the coming challenge to the Navy.

Americans also had seen individual Japanese pilots try to crash into
them, or strike ships, certainly more frequently than such tactics were
employed by U.S. servicemen, but until late 1944, it was not recognized
that this was now a deliberate strategic weapon. The series of defeats suffered on land, at sea, and in the air after the loss of Guadalcanal, convinced some Japanese military theorists that the last hope lay in assaults
that would destroy the principal weapon bringing the war to Japan, the aircraft carrier. American land-based bombers could never have hoped to
reach the homeland had not the floating airfields that destroyed the
Japanese Navy provided tactical support. The fleet air arms enabled soldiers and Marines to conquer islands that now served as bases for the big
planes. And with the Imperial Navy vanquished, carrier task forces would
bring their short-range bombers to the Japanese doorstep.

The immediate inspiration for the suicide airplane came from R Adm.
Masbomi Arima, who commanded aircraft squadrons that were being
defeated in the Philippine skies. On 15 October, five days before the invasion of Leyte, Admiral Arima aimed his own plane at the carrier *Franklin* A
U.S. combat air patrol, hovering in the vicinity, spotted Arima and shot
him down, just short of his target (Some historians erroneously continue
to claim Arima actually crashed into the carrier.)

The grand if unsuccessful gesture by Arima, confirmed a program already in progress under Admiral Takajiro Ohnishi. He had been encouraging navy pilots to take such an initiative as a last resort. Now it would become the basic goal of a corps of fliers. Their acceptance and participation in the program that obligated their deaths during the final nine months of the war indicates the deeply ingrained belief in Imperial Japan with its emperor.

Onishi dubbed his group *Kamikaze Tokubetsu Kogetitai* which roughly translates as the Divine Wind Special Attack Corps. The word kamikaze bore special meaning. Japanese history told of a sixteenth century Mongol emperor who organized a huge amphibious force to conquer the country but a "divine wind" in the form of a typhoon blew away the Chinese-based fleet.

Anything that could fly, from trainers to bombers and fighter planes, eventually even pre-World War II ones with fabric-covered wings and gliders, were adapted for use by the special attack forces. In addition, engineers designed a 4,700-pound, rocket-propelled flying bomb, the *ohka* or cherry blossom (known to Americans as the *baka* meaning screwball). The *baka* launched from a Betty-model bomber, carried a pilot to guide the missile on a one-way trip.

The tactic of suicidal missions expanded to include the kind of suicide motor boats found in Kerama Retto. An even more primitive approach, the *Fukuryu*—Crouching Dragon—called for men with scuba equipment to blast ship bottoms by using mines attached to poles. To Americans all these fell under the label of kamikaze but strictly speaking the Japanese applied the term only to the naval air operations.

Neither conventional aerial raids nor kamikazes seriously interfered with the Love Day operations. But the fleet absorbed some hard punches that night. A pair of transport vessels were struck by kamikazes. One blow fell at twilight, 7:10 P.M. and the other at the seemingly safer hour near midnight. Both ships remained afloat and able to unload their cargo before steaming off for repairs. But another 21 sailors died and 68 were injured.

On 2 April, the ships in the Kerama Retto anchorage and off the Hagushi beaches reeled from lashes inflicted by the divine winds. Mindful of exposure to the enemy, a group of transports carrying soldiers from the 77th Division after reembarking them from the Kerama Retto operations, headed toward a position that would remove them from harm's way. A flock of kamikazes, at least ten planes, bore down on the fifteen-ship convoy. The destroyer *Dickerson* took a direct hit on the bridge. The fifty-three dead included the skipper and the unsalvagable ship, was towed to sea and scuttled. Two other warships escaped with lesser damage from attacks on them.

That night, the bulk of the 77th Division's 305th Infantry Regiment was aboard the *Henrico*, the flagship of Transdiv 50. Dick Forse, the crewman for an M-8—self-propelled, armored 75mm gun—remembered, "There was no general quarters signal, although there was some firing from other ships. I had noticed that the radar dish on the mast was not going around. I had been sitting on a hatch cover on the main deck, forward. I got up and went on a line for ice cream. We heard the sound of planes coming in. We couldn't see them because the ship's forecastle blocked our view to the front. But I got a glimpse of the tail of a plane as it went by. I dismissed it as the tail of a Hellcat from the U.S. Navy.

"An instant after glimpsing the tail, I heard a 'kerchunk.' I don't remember it as being very loud. The Jap plane, a Frances, [two-engine navy bomber] hit the *Henrico*'s superstructure [bridge area], near the spot where I had previously been sitting. One engine broke off and rolled, flaming, down a corridor into the wardroom where many officers were writing or just batting the breeze. One of the bombs on the plane also exploded.

"I ran to the side and saw a big hole in the superstructure with showers of sparks and clouds of heavy gray smoke pouring out. The *Henrico*'s steam whistle went off and continued one long shriek for about fifteen minutes before it finally ran out of steam. Another guy and I ran inside the forecastle to get out of the way, but we found ourselves in the way of four navy men who were getting into asbestos suits. There were several fires in the superstructure and the ship was dead in the water. There was no power whatsoever and fire hoses couldn't be used. They lowered small water pumps into the sea, but most of them stopped working when they hit the water.

"The steam whistle that continued to scream scared us. I must have checked my life preserver fifteen times an hour, hoping it would work if we had to abandon ship. I went below deck to stay out of the way. Battery power lines were being set up everywhere because there was no electricity. There also was no drinking water and no water in the heads. I realized that the ship was listing to starboard which really concerned me. Soon after, all able bodies were called topside and told to stand along the rail on the port side because of the ship's list. A destroyer passed by us up close, trying to hose down fires on our ship. But the sea was too choppy. First the hose would point toward the sky and then down into the ocean. Later they tried to shoot a line to us so we could be towed. They tried four or five times but the line missed. Everytime they fired the line I jumped a foot.

"The rest of the convoy continued on after the attack. Soon we were alone, out in the ocean. I looked out on the horizon and could see two ships burning. Then the moon came up. It was the biggest moon I have ever seen, a full moon that could silhouette the *Henrico* for the Jap subs.

My morale was not very high at this point. But no subs attacked us and we were later towed by another APA [attack transport] into the Kerama Retto anchorage. It was loaded with ships crippled by kamikazes. Four or five of us slept in the paint locker that night. None of us had any desire to sleep in our quarters, which were two decks below. For breakfast we got an apple and an orange and two cans of beer. That's the only time I know of when the Navy issued alcoholic drinks to enlisted men in a combat zone.

"The *Henrico* tied up next to another APA, the *Sarasota.* We were to transfer to it. We heard that someone was inside the pitch-black *Henrico* and would not come out. One of the last men taken off it was this soldier. He looked like a teenager, and with great difficulty, some sailors had made their way through equipment below deck, brought him up two sets of stairs to the main deck. He was very distressed, shaking, tears streaming down his face, snuffling, shuffling along rather than walking as he was helped by sailors on each arm across to the *Sarasota.*

Shortly after the plane blasted into the *Henrico,* one of the gun crews on the *Suffolk,* a nearby APA, spotted a man in the water. Joe Taranto, a member of the gun crew, remembers, "We thought he was a Jap pilot. We were ready to shoot him when he yelled, 'I'm an American GI from the 77th Division. I think that was the greatest day of my life; we were there to save that GI from dying."

But aboard the *Henrico* many others were not so fortunate. Transdiv 50's commander and the captain of the ship were killed along with twenty-one others from the Navy. Among the Army officers in the wardroom were most of the 305th's top command. The dead included the 305th's commander, Col. Vincent Tanzola and his executive officer as well as eleven more soldiers.

The *Henrico* was not the only 77th Division transport mauled. Larry Gerevas, a replacement assigned to Company K of the 307th Regiment, sailed from Leyte on the *Telefare.* "Aboard our ship, many of the army troops were assigned various duties. Some assisted the Navy gunners with the 40mm antiaircraft guns and others such as myself stood guard at various stations on the main deck. The purpose was to prevent any Japs from climbing onto the ship.

"During the air attack on April 2, I was on guard near the bow of the ship. At this location were two landing barges secured to a metal support rack about two feet above the deck. Suddenly, a terrific explosion occurred directly above me. Thinking it was a bomb, I dived under a rack holding the barges. Smoking chunks of metal rained down on the area where I had been standing a moment before. Debris was everywhere. Later I learned that a Jap bomber had dived into our ship, sheared off some of the ship's masts, fell on a 40mm gun mount, and then slid into the sea. Three Army men that manned that gun were killed."

Ed Fitzgerald, the first sergeant of Service Company, was aboard the *Monrovia*. "When the kamikazes started to come in, the captain made me chase guys off the deck. We didn't like it below decks. It wasn't comfortable, and we wondered about submarines and if something came busting in there. I was already inside on a ladder going back down when I saw the airplane coming and I knew it would hit. I wasn't that curious that I wanted to stay up there and get a look at the pilot in his white scarf. One sergeant, though, Harry O'Gawa, couldn't resist staying up there. He lost a leg from the explosion." The ship, however, suffered no serious damage.

49
Tennozan

Based upon the site of a great battle in the sixteenth century, the Japanese used the name Tennozan to mark any critical campaign in subsequent history. They considered the fight for Okinawa worthy of the designation and code-named their massive onslaught against the enemy amphibious forces Operation Ten-Go. From 3–5 April the Japanese raids on the U.S. armada amounted to no more than mosquito bites, but on 6 April, Ten-Go got off the mark as they swarmed over the targets. Endowed with the name of *kikusi*—floating chrysanthemums—ten massed kamikaze blows employing 355 planes concentrated on the Americans hovering in the seas by the islands. About the same number of conventional bombers also struck.

Minesweepers supported by a pair of destroyers, the *Rodman* and the *Emmons,* engaged in the clearance of a channel between Iheya Retto and the main island. In command of the *Emmons* was Lt. Comdr. Eugene Foss. A Harvard graduate (1934), Foss was a "plank owner," a member of the original *Emmons* crew. Said Foss, "On April 6, with a sister ship, *Rodman* number 456—our number was 457—we were providing shore-gun protection along the northwestern coast for some wooden-hulled minesweepers. When they have their gear out, minesweepers cannot maneuver. Shore gun-fire did not materialize. But this day, the Japs mounted their first major kamikaze attack. To everybody I knew, this was a totally different philosophy. It was something none of us had any education in. We knew of Marines who would storm anything, but nothing of this definitely suicidal action. But we all realized that these were very dangerous weapons and had heard about them before the Okinawa show. We'd even seen one dive on a light cruiser, coming right out from a combat air patrol.

"There wasn't anything you could do except fire at them. There were no special tactics. We did have the new proximity fuses on our ammo. These had just been issued to the fleet and we were not sure how well they worked. On this fairly mild day, with the weather overcast, around 3:00 P.M. we spotted twenty or thirty of them coming at an altitude of about 3,000 feet. We watched a dozen or so circling overhead, as if they were getting their nerve up. We did have a combat air patrol over us also.

"They started to peel off and head for us, one by one. It didn't work. We had all our guns going and our bursts would show the Corsairs where the enemy was. The *Emmons* gunners got as many as six of them and the Marine fighters dropped at least another half dozen." The *Rodman*, however, was in serious trouble. One plane smashed into the forecastle and a close-in explosion by a splashed plane or bomb ruptured a section of the hull. Sheets of flame darted to the height of the bridge and, temporarily, 456 lost power.

The *Emmons* moved to assist its stricken partner, but soon realized it now faced its own peril. The *Rodman* was in no condition to offer supporting fire nor were the minesweepers, still frantically trying to retrieve their gear. Foss recalls, "They launched simultaneous attacks, four or five at the same time. As many as five kamikazes slashed through the battery of five-inchers and the spray of 40mm and 20mm cannon fire, to smack into the thin aluminum steel of the *Emmons*. One landed in the wardroom passage and blew up with its gasoline. Another hit the fantail. We had to shut down the engines because we couldn't steer. We were drifting, like a target. But we still had our antiaircraft guns and five-inchers while they came at us from all sides." A third blow also struck aft as a Val [Japanese fighter bomber] swept away what was still working on the fantail.

"An ensign, assistant gunnery officer Ross Elliot, ordered several people to crouch down on the deck when a plane was coming in for a strafing attack. He draped himself over the men and saved them, but lost his own life." Elliot would receive a posthumous Navy Cross.

On the bridge, Foss tried to shift the steering control. But another kamikaze blasted into the superstructure. The impact shattered the bridge and blew Foss overboard. He found himself, badly burned about the face and hands, temporarily blinded, in the water. The final thrust rammed the starboard bow area. Dead in the water, fires out of control, the crew suffering the horrible wounds of molten metal, burns from searing steam and gasoline-fed fires, the *Emmons* suffered the final indignity of an erroneous 'abandon ship' command. Actually, no one gave the order but word spread that the situation was hopeless. A number of sailors jumped into the water, joining others like Foss hurled there by explosions or who because of the fire in their area had no choice but to take their chances in the sea. The sweepers, *Recruit* and *Ransom*, started to rescue those in the water. Two more planes drew beads on the wreckage of the *Emmons* but suddenly shifted their attentions to the pair offering succor. Gunners on the *Recruit* and *Ransom* splashed both.

Remnants of the *Emmons* crew, led by the gunnery officer, Lt. J. J. Griffin—the skipper was gone, the exec dead, and the next in the chain of command badly wounded—struggled to contain the fires and keep the destroyer from sinking. It was a losing effort; she continued to settle ever deeper. Griffin consulted with the few officers still on the *Emmons*. The damage-control news relayed to Griffin left no choice. One main engine was inoperable; there were no means by which to steer. The fire forward could not be controlled. Except for a pair of 20-mm guns the ship was bereft of firepower. They were still sinking and faced an imminent explosion of what remained in the magazines and fuel tanks. Griffin, around 6:00 P.M., some three hours after the first kamikazes appeared, ordered abandon ship. The last man climbed onto a small mine-disposal vessel, the PGM-11 at 8:00 P.M. Subsequently, Admiral Turner directed a destroyer to sink the burning hulk. Sixty-four died and another 71 were injured from a ship's complement of 237. Foss spent many months undergoing skin grafts and other treatments to repair his body.

Meanwhile, in the area of Kerama Retto, combat air patrols scrambled to knock down the enemy aircraft. The relentless kamikazes wreaked havoc in the harbor. To stop the suicide bombers before they reached Kerama Retto, a picket line ringed the Ryukyu chain. In midafternoon of 6 April, the destroyer *Bush* at Picket Station #1 and the *Colhoun* at #2 succumbed to a series of floating chrysanthemums, sinking with more than 100 dead. Combat air patrols had run into so many of the enemy, they could not prevent the attacks.

Destruction of the destroyers *Bush* and *Colhoun* signaled the opening round of kamikaze fury directed at those on picket duty. Jumped by interceptors summoned at the behest of the pickets, the minimally fueled Japanese planes discovered they could not evade the enemy aircraft and then fly onto the strategic targets off the Hagushi beaches and at Kerama Retto. Their meager amount of gasoline would only allow them to focus on those closest at hand, the seaborne sentinels. Furthermore, those in command realized they must destroy or weaken the advance-warning and protection network if the suicide missions were to reach the bigger targets.

With Japanese air and ground forces desperately engaged in the Okinawa campaign, the Imperial Navy threw its last remaining surface power into the Ten-Go game. Out of the naval base at Kure on the Inland Sea steamed the *Yamato*, at 68,000 tons displacement, the largest battleship afloat, and with 18.1-inch guns, more than a match for the mightiest that flew either U.S. or British standards. Their biggest ships fired 14- and 16-inch shells.

The *Yamato* sallied forth on 6 April in the company of the light cruiser *Yahagi* and eight destroyers, designated Task Force II, a puny force considering the massive number of ships available from the American fleet. Worse, the *Yamato* sailed without air cover. The notion that she could navigate the 600 miles to the Okinawa anchorages without discovery, followed by an all-out onslaught from carrier-based planes, could not even be sustained as a fantasy.

In the confused, conflicted, and frustrated direction of Japanese military affairs, some hoped that at least the small task force, as part of Operation Ten-Go, could distract the American carriers sufficiently to allow the kamikazes of 6 and 7 April to reach their targets. If *Yamato* somehow managed to reach the Okinawa area, it could train its huge turrets on anything in range and, as a last resort, beach itself where it could provide a kind of artillery support for the Japanese ground forces. The operational plans directed that when all ammunition had been expended in this last effort, the ship's crew should try to contact the ground forces and become infantrymen.

Some historians like Morison bluntly describe the *Yamato's* voyage as designed for a one-way trip with only enough fuel to carry it to the Hagushi roadstead. But George Feifer in *Tennozan* points out that officers on the Combined Fleet staff scrounged enough oil to fill the battleship's bunkers three-quarters full, more than enough for a round-trip. While few held out any hope for survival, enough navy people hoped to give *Yamato* at least a long shot at coming home.

Task Force II had barely cleared the Inland Sea at 5:45 P.M. on 6 April when the U.S. submarine *Threadfin* detected the flotilla. The sub notified VAdm. Marc Mitscher's Task Force 58 some 400 miles off, which included many carriers. Immediately, search planes began to prowl the skies peering at the sea below for the quarry. At dawn on 7 April, a pilot from the *Essex* sighted the *Yamato* and her companions. Task Force II now endured continuous surveillance from aircraft based on as many as a dozen carriers and which kept safely out of range of antiaircraft fire. The shadow team included flying boats based at Kerama Retto. Mitscher closed the distance to 250 miles and then launched a series of gigantic strikes—the first one sent up 280 dive and torpedo bombers.

Harry Jones, an Avenger pilot, with Torpedo Squadron 17 [VT-17], Carrier Air Group, flying off the *Hornet,* said, "Scuttlebutt on the ship had it that the battleship admirals who outranked the air admirals wanted to shoot it out with the Japanese. But the *Yamato's* 18-inch guns were bigger than anything we had and the air admirals won out. We would intercept them. We took off from the *Hornet,* seven torpedo bombers with fighters and dive-bombers along with us. The torpedo planes, which had search radar, did the navigation and it was a poor day for flying, rainy, misty, a lot of scud [clouds], not much ceiling. The flight leader from another carrier developed engine trouble and turned the lead over to our air group, bossed by Comdr. E. G. Conrad, a Naval Academy graduate.

"The lead pilot said they ought to be in range, but we couldn't see anything on radar. Conrad said stay on course. One plane radioed that he saw a blip off to starboard about fifty miles out and we turned right. Then we saw them. Holy mackerel! The *Yamato* looked like the Empire State Building plowing through the water, It was really big. We orbited around out of their gun range. They opened up with main batteries, 18—inch guns. What was very surprising to us was there were no Japanese aircraft around even though we were near their home islands.

"The air boss gave us the order of attack. He said, 'Shasta,' meaning those from the *Hornet* 'go in first.' We didn't have too much ceiling. I was at 12,000 feet at most, and usually liked to start at 18,000 feet for a steep approach and then right over the water, drop the torpedo, and then get the hell out of there. Meanwhile, the bombers are supposed to be going down, so we all hit the ship simultaneously. I kept diving toward different puffs of smoke, where shells had already exploded. The first two fighter planes were to strafe destroyers to suppress and draw off the fire. I saw one of our replacement pilots take a direct hit and go down. I went down, dropped my torpedo, and went right across the bow of *Yamato*. The ship was turning, but in our attack we always dropped in a fan shape so no matter which way a ship is turning it's going to get hit. Our group was credited with two torpedo hits among the planes, but the gun camera that showed my angle on the bow didn't credit me with a hit."

The hunters swarmed over the targets while Task Force II responded with fusillades dominated by the *Yamato's* half dozen 6-inch batteries, 24 5-inch guns, and 150 machine guns. But only nine minutes after the *Yamato* spotted the first wave of attackers, a pair of bombs from Helldivers struck near the mainmast and a few moments later the first torpedo exploded against the thick armor plate of the port bow. Already, the *Yahagi*, victim of a bomb and a torpedo, lay dead in the water, while one of the destroyer screen had slid beneath the sea, bow first, taking most of her crew down with her.

A brief respite ensued as the first attackers retired, but a second strike bore in less than an hour later. The hail of bullets and shell fragments toppled sailors on the supership. Its powerful engines and sleek design enabled it to temporarily dodge torpedoes. To the thick curtain of smaller guns it added its 18.1-inchers, training them low to the water where they exploded great spouts that might destroy aircraft skimming the sea as they prepared to launch their torpedoes.

For the next hour and fifteen minutes, the carrier aircraft, killer bees pouring out of many hives, stung the *Yamato*. Five more torpedoes struck home and the ship began to list. Its commander ordered flooding of several compartments to correct the ship's attitude. The combination of that water, the sea pouring in through the holes created by the torpedoes, and steam escaping from ruptured boilers snuffed out the lives of several hundred sailors. The tactic failed to correct the list and only one screw continued to work. *Yamato* lost speed and any real maneuverability for defense.

Third and fourth strikes pounded away at the crippled behemoth unable to respond to commands or to defend herself. At two in the afternoon the torment of the *Yamato* reached its peak. The assassins, with names like

Dauntless, Hellcat, Avenger, and Corsair, drilled her almost at will. It was hopeless. From amid the wreckage on the *Yamato* bridge, the admiral in command, Seiichi Ito, ordered the mission aborted. The ships still able to operate were to pick up men from the sea and from disabled vessels and try to make port. Then Admiral Ito shook hands with some officers on the bridge and locked himself in his quarters. He would go down with the *Yamato*.

With ten torpedo hits and five bomb blasts as well as countless near-miss explosions, the munitions aboard the *Yamato* administered the *coup de grâce*. Deep, subdeck blasts erupted a 6,000-foot-high tongue of fire, and the smoke rose more than four miles as the mightiest battleship in the world expired after two hours of battering. One or two U.S. aircraft, hovering over the battleship, may have been victims of the debris from detonation of *Yamato*'s ordnance. The body counts for the destruction of Task Force II range from 3,700 to 4,250 lost to the Imperial Navy. As many as 3,000 aboard the *Yamato* died. Along with the battleship, the Americans sank the light cruiser *Yahagi* and four destroyers. With the few survivors plucked from the sea, the four surviving destroyers limped away. Mitscher reported his losses at ten planes and twelve airmen.

While the splintered vestiges of the Imperial Navy fled under the onslaught of the carrier-based attack, the 96th Infantry Division rammed up against the first in the series of bulwarks of the Shuri line, the in-depth Okinawa defense. Bob Jackson, with B Company of the 382d, recalled those first days as resembling a tour of an exotic land. "We were in reserve, behind the 381st and 383d making the main attack. We crossed interesting, rather hilly country. The tombs that were to be a big part of the difficult fight ahead were deserted. On breaks we'd inspect them as best we could. We were still in fear of the highly advertised snakes [habu]. My only memory of action in these first days was watching as our company half-ton truck hit a mine and rolled over. There was small damage, but I lost a Japanese bowl I'd found beside the road.

"When the forward regiments ran into resistance, our battalion, led by A Company, was committed and began receiving fire. A small hill had been invested by A Company, from which it was trying to move forward against strong resistance. We in B Company were behind them and could see the mountains where the Japanese had fine artillery emplacements. A Company was mauled pretty badly and had barrage after barrage of artillery thrown at them. This was our first experience with concentrated artillery fire and we were scared!" In previous campaigns, the Japanese had demonstrated a serious ignorance of the most effective use of artillery, limiting themselves to a single shell at a time. On Okinawa, where they possessed ample pieces and ammunition, they showed Jackson they had learned how to use their heavier guns.

"About this time, the Japanese unleashed a previously unknown weapon, a 320mm mortar. It blew a big hole in the ground and frightened us; it sounded like a freight train coming in. But it did little damage to the troops. On this hill I experienced my first abject and shameful fear. We had now relieved A Company and were preparing to move three platoons into position when we came under a severe artillery and mortar barrage. It was awesome. I understand one becomes inured, but that afternoon I tried to dig my way to the center of the earth. When the barrage lifted, I got up, shook the dirt off my fatigues, and went back to work with my platoon. I have never forgotten, however, how I screamed in fear and how hard I shoved myself into the dirt of that Okinawa hillside.

"We had penetrated the outer reaches of the Japanese main line of resistance (MLR) before the largest city, Naha. My company commander assigned my platoon to the left flank of the battalion. I was to occupy a small knoll facing away from the rest of the outfit. Darkness was coming on as I took my messenger to the knoll while the platoon sergeant brought up the squads. The men were about fifty yards behind me as I gave instructions to a squad leader on where to place his BAR and have the men dig in. Suddenly, a Nambu machine gun ripped off a burst of fire. That has the sound of a cliché, but the Nambu was extremely rapid firing and its sound was a frightening rip of noise. I was sloppy and had not thought that the Japanese could have moved so close to our lines.

"At the same time this Japanese unit, probably five or six men, began lobbing knee-mortar shells at us. We used to joke that those shells would have to hit you on the head without a helmet to do any harm. The surprise of the concussive noise and the noise of the machine gun made us drop like tin soldiers. No one was hurt at that time. We were just scattered over an area of about fifty square yards. One of my squad leaders, looking for a site for his BAR, was about twenty-five yards off across a small swale.

"I had jumped into a shallow drainage ditch that ran toward the enemy line. The squad leader with the BAR and a couple of men occupied a similar ditch on the other side of the swale. We tried to fire at the enemy but the machine gun was well hidden as it searched for us with bursts of fire. I looked for the rest of the platoon and saw them running, helter-skelter across the fields, back toward their previous positions. They were, in the last rays of the sun, a mob returning 'home' with all military discipline gone. I was angry, frustrated, and very frightened.

"Waving and yelling, I tried to get the squad leader to work back to the former company position. He misunderstood and tried to come toward me. The Nambu opened up as he rose to run. He was hit, and I could see, badly. By then there were only the two of us and darkness was coming down fast. Crawling forward in my ditch, I came upon the sergeant, lying on his side, badly wounded, and crying in pain. He was a mess in his middle where the machine-gun burst had almost cut him in two. I had no idea what to do and doubted we'd get help. Every so often the Nambu or a knee mortar would fire. I got my poncho out of my pack, lay it in front of the sergeant, and, with great perseverance on his part, managed to get him onto the poncho. By dragging him a few feet at a time down the ditch I got fairly close to the company line. By this time, something had happened to silence the Nambu and knee mortars—maybe they had just pulled back—and some squads from B Company came out with a stretcher. I went back to the company perimeter, sat down and shook. All night we remained under artillery and mortar fire."

Don Dencker, with Company L of the 383d, reported a similar gradual involvement in the campaign. "Our first encounter with the Japs, except for a few sniper shots, was a heavy shelling from artillery early in the afternoon of April 5. We were still in reserve, but had moved up to about 600 yards of the front lines. Our CO, Captain Fitzpatrick, was seriously wounded trying to drag to safety a man fatally wounded by one of the first shells. This act of bravery cost us a damn good company commander. During the following days we were subjected to numerous artillery and mortar barrages. Our entrenching tools became our lifesavers."

Len Lazarick, with Company K of the 382d, had settled in that first night with the modest luxury of being in reserve. "We didn't take it for granted that we had any guarantee of safety. We did our standard two hours on guard and four hours off vigil on the company perimeter. Although the temperature during the day was comfortably warm, I found the night chilly and stood guard with a blanket draped around my shoulders. We usually dug in three men to a hole and when possible in the shape of the letter Y. The foxhole was deep enough so that from a sitting position, only our heads were exposed while on guard duty during the night. Farther south on Okinawa, we ran into hard ground and often were satisfied by piling loose rocks and coral just high enough to protect a sleeping comrade from ground-level shell or grenade fragments.

"I didn't own an OD jungle sweater until 6 April when I was able to remove one from the pack of a dead GI lying in a ditch beside the road we were marching along. The sweater was a pullover made of lightweight wool. It helped keep me warm during the chilly nights. Before I obtained it I shivered a great deal with only a single blanket. When we moved south, still in reserve, I was assigned to be the point. I don't know to this day what I did wrong to be so honored. It is not a comfortable feeling to be alone, 100 yards ahead of your column, searching for enemy snipers or stragglers."

Company K rifleman Paul Westman said, "The ground troops met very little opposition at first. We began to hope it would be a walkover. What opposition we did meet served as invaluable experience for untested replacements like myself. Later replacements wouldn't be so lucky. I remember the passwords and countersigns for the first days on Okinawa. They were glass/house; long/lane; forty/thieves; flimsy/skirt, and fair/weather. We were told that the Japanese had difficulty with the letters L and R. When I first heard the cracks of rifle bullets going past, I thought, 'Man, you can get hurt! You don't have a target pit to hide in now.' Close rounds of artillery scared me worse. My mouth would get dry, my legs would go rubbery. I found out they would still function one morning when two shells came very close. The squad leader said, 'Let's get the hell outa here!'—and we did. Two others didn't. Three more shells hit and when we came back, one of the new replacements was lying outside the hole and his clothes were smoking. The other was still in the hole with a shattered leg and other wounds. Litter-bearers took them away. I don't think either one of them got to fire his M1 even once. That was the time I learned that if I paid close attention to S. Sgt. Jeff Brooks, I'd probably last longer."

According to Dick Thom, the S-3 with the 381st Regiment, the preinvasion instructions directed that civilians on Okinawa should be treated as if they were soldiers. "But one day after we landed, we received a brand-new order that said for us to look to the welfare of the civilians we had been killing. At one point I saw fifteen people wearing tan uniforms in a rice paddy. I ordered a tank that was with us to fire on them with machine guns. They were all killed and I found out they had been in the home guard, like Boy Scouts. They had all deserted, but they didn't know enough to discard the uniforms. Nobody knew where the enemy was. Everybody seemed to be standing around and sucking their thumbs. It didn't help that we had a captain who was the CO of a rifle company and couldn't read a map."

On 8 April Bob Jackson, with B Company of the 382d, ate a noontime hot meal brought up from the company kitchens in the rear. It was for him the fourth day of the contact with the enemy. His battalion commander called for a two-platoon attack on Tombstone Ridge, so named for the mausoleum in the distance. "The ground sloped away from our positions to a ditch running across our front," recalled Jackson. "Directly in the middle was a stone bridge. The company commander, [Capt. George R. Gerrans] in textbook fashion, took me, as the leader of the two platoons, to the heights facing the front and pointed out the ditch as the jumping off point for the attack. It was almost like an exercise at Fort Benning, with the captain even giving me a regulation five-point field order.

"I collected Lt. John Fox of the other attacking platoon and our platoon sergeants for a less formal battle order. I knew Fox only slightly; he was young, from another regiment originally where he had received a battlefield commission on Leyte. Both of us had considerable battlefield experience, but neither knew our men very well. We went down to the ditch, spread out, and in good order. When we were in position there, Lieutenant Fox, with his platoon on my left, informed me he was ready to go. I raised the antenna of my SCR 536 radio, ready to inform company HQ to start the preparatory mortar barrage. It was to precede us as we moved toward Tombstone Ridge.

"I climbed up the side of the ditch, was about seven feet deep, and called the company to start the barrage. When the shiny antenna rose above the ditch, a machine gun opened up from an enfiladed position to our left. It was impossible to see where it came from. But every time I tried to use the radio, bursts of fire skimmed the top of the embankment. It would be suicide to try climbing the steep bank, get over the edge, and into a running position. I scooted down and ordered the men to dig in until I could contact the company for further instructions.

"Exposed as we were to enfilading fire, we'd lose most of our attack group if we tried to complete our move. We had no chance to take the objective. I tried to call in mortar fire by hand signals to the company commander in the position behind us. The captain was unable to read my signals in that deep ditch. I wasn't able to indicate anything but that the fire came from our left. The Japanese apparently moved the machine gun about this time. It fired directly down the ditch into our positions.

"I was wounded twice in this first burst. I had been sitting against the wall of the ditch with my feet stretched out before me, trying to figure what in hell to do. I noticed the neat hole in the middle of my combat boot, turned over and started to crawl toward the left from which direction the gun seemed to be firing. I was hit again in the upper thigh and that hurt! My runner, who was digging into the wall of the ditch right next to me, had a perfectly positioned, three-shot group through the top of his helmet.

"The men were panicking with fear; they didn't know where to fire or how to defend themselves. Neither did I, but I hauled myself under the stone bridge to Lieutenant Fox's platoon. He had taken a shot in the chest; it gurgled and he was very frightened. I have never felt so helpless! Some of my waving and motions must have gotten through to the CO because mortar fire was laid on and the machine gun was silenced. The 81mm mortars laid a heavy concentration of smoke around us.

"I figured that if we had to stay there until nightfall, I'd be able to crawl up the side of the ditch nearest the company and wiggle my way up to our positions. However, that wouldn't help those like Fox who were worse off than I. Just then several stretchers, followed by men from the company, came sliding into the ditch. I directed the evacuation and was loaded onto a litter to be carried out. Ever the pessimist, I remember looking over the side of the stretcher as I was hoisted up out of the ditch and searching for a drop place if that machine gun opened up again. I was looking out for Number

One! I didn't know that of the approximately sixty men under my command, eighteen had been wounded and two killed.

"Stupidly, after we were evacuated with the help of heavy smoke, the Gung-ho assistant battalion commander ordered me back into that trap to bring in the dead. Several were killed and wounded in this foolish and futile operation. It never made sense to me to endanger fighting troops for the sake of bringing in the dead. My last memory of Okinawa is of lying on a stretcher near the battalion aid station with smoke swirling about and much feverish activity. The battalion surgeon, a good drinking buddy, came over and congratulated me on a 'million-dollar wound.' With a broken metatarsal, infantry duty was over for me!"

In the same area, half a dozen men, including Paul Westman from Company K, sought to scout a ridgeline. "The squad leader, Willard Johnson, had the SCR 300 radio. We were spread out, moving very slow, when the first rounds cracked by. Sergeant Earl Neu hollered, 'Don't bunch up! Take cover!' About then artillery rounds started dropping down the slope, walking our way. Rifle fire seemed to let up and I recall hearing our radio operator calling the company, 'King, King, this is King One. We are receiving artillery fire. Is there friendly fire registered here?' He gave the coordinates and the answer was negative.

"By this time they were on us and Staff Sergeant Neu shouted, 'Back! Go back! Scatter!' I got blast effects from one enough to send me downhill into some coral rock. I could see others heading back and when I picked myself up, I couldn't put weight on my right foot. The leg seemed badly scraped but not broken. Why I didn't draw fire, I can't imagine. I went back, using my M1 as a crutch. It took quite a while to hobble back to the company and the aidman there and he told me to go to the hospital. On the way in an ambulance, a medical officer asked me how I felt. I told him I didn't feel so good after looking around at all those other guys, all shot and burned to hell. All of them were in far worse shape than I. He put his hand on my shoulder and said, 'Soldier, you wouldn't have been able to do your company a bit of good.'"

The 1st Battalion of the 381st, with Thom as operations officer, had continued to march south. By 9 April they faced a natural barrier for the Shuri line, Kakazu Ridge, a steep, 300-foot slope that stretched about 1,000 yards. On the western side it ran down to the sea and to the east it was separated by a cut from another escarpment, the Nishibaru Ridge. A honeycomb of pillboxes, tunnels, and caves along with an infestation of mortars on the reverse slope, covered every foot of approach with deadly fire. And before they could even attempt to climb the ridge, the troops would be forced to cross a deep gorge, well targeted by the mortar positions, which was part of the Shuri defense.

The first of the Deadeyes [nickname of the 96th division] to batter themselves against Kakazu were from the 383d Regiment, an outfit with Ellis Moore as a radio operator for 1st Battalion Headquarters. Moore admitted his first and then subsequent artillery batterings terrified him. "You just lie there in your hole while they land all around you and wonder where the next one is going to hit, and why it doesn't hit you. The whine of a shell as it passes over and the explosion as it hits are just as nerve-wracking as a shell exploding right next to you. After a while you find yourself ducking every time any shell goes over, even if it's one of ours, and we threw ten shells at them for every one they sent at us."

When the battalion moved up to a hill held by Americans, a wide-eyed Moore observed the results of a banzai charge. "About 150 of them had stormed up that hill toward our guys, and they said it was just like shooting ducks. You had to look or you'd step on them. They were scattered all over the place, so much abandoned equipment, these men with beards no heavier than mine, some with quarter-size holes in their heads; others with half their bodies blown away. A GI stooped down to one, jammed a cigarette into his mouth and muttered, 'Have a cigarette, you yellow son of a bitch. Sorry I don't have time to light it for you.'"

When the line companies of the 383d started their advance on Kakazu they could neither run nor hide. Moore, however, as a radio operator with battalion headquarters, could obtain at least temporary refuge from the terror of artillery in a tomb. "You crawled through on your knees after you removed a stone slab secured in the entrance by a putty substance. The tomb was high enough for us to stand up, with a plot of about six feet by six feet. There were stone shelves covered with iron and clay urns. They evidently died in this family at all ages. The big skulls and bones were in the larger vases and the little ones held remains of what must have been very small children.

"We hauled out the urns to let their occupants get a feel of good fresh air again. With a little further policing up we had a fairly decent and safe habitat with sleeping room for at least seven. Every tomb along the ridge was broken into sooner or later. It was an unwritten rule that if the tombs offered needed protection it was okay to open them up. But we weren't allowed to mention the raiding of the dead's resting place in our letters." So much for the Japanese belief that American reverence for the dead would preclude their use of the mausoleums.

On 8 April, just before dawn, the 383d made its initial assault on Kakazu. A fearsome downpour of artillery and mortar shells fell upon the defenders and the advance started, led by Able (A) and Charlie (C) Company with Baker (B) in reserve. "There was to be no firing," said Moore, who left the safety of the tomb to occupy a spot at the OP. "They were to get up the hill unnoticed. We just sat there while time dragged by. At about 5:30 Able radioed that they were almost to the top. It looked like it was going to work. Then all hell broke loose. The Japs must have been watching all the time. They struck at just the right moment. Machine guns from both flanks cut Able and Charlie to ribbons. Japs on the top of the ridge looked down at our guys, ten yards below, and threw everything in the book at them—rifle fire, machine-gun fire, hand grenades, satchel charges, even sticks of dynamite. Both Able and Charlie radioed for help. Since Able was farthest up the hill and catching the most hell, Erickson decided to send Baker up behind them. We got a call from Able's CO, Capt. Jack Royster. He asked if he couldn't order a retreat. Said more than half of his company was lost. Erickson replied, 'You've got to hold the ground you've got, Jack, or else all that's happened will be useless. I'm sending Baker up to help you and the two of you ought to be able to reach the top.'

"A few minutes later Royster called again. I've never heard such a pitiful voice. 'Listen, Major,' he pleaded. 'I've been hit and can't see a thing. There are only five men in my company left. There's no sign of Baker Company up here. Will you please give me permission to withdraw what's left of my company?' Erickson replied they were to hold their ground. But where the hell was Baker Company? I got them on the radio and they said they'd no sooner gotten out of their holes than they were pinned down by mortar fire and machine guns. They were trying to advance in short rushes, but the Japs had them in their sights and they were suffering heavy casualties."

All three of the units assigned to charge Kakazu experienced the same disastrous results. Remnants of the trio linked up, but they were a disorganized band desperately seeking self-preservation rather than to overcome the enemy. "Behind these men," says Moore, "was the bulk of their companies, men still pinned down in shallow shell holes, men wounded and crying for help that was to be a long time in coming, and men for whom there would never be any help."

At last convinced that the battalion had all but been destroyed, Erickson finally countenanced a withdrawal. It was about three hours after the abortive assault had begun and the enemy continued to inflict casualties. Litter parties made up mostly from headquarters personnel were shot down while on their errands of succor. Moore, with the battalion staff, had remained at the the observation post. "The Japs had kept their mortar fire out in front of us," says the former communications specialist. "But now, all of a sudden they started dropping in our sector. They were falling like raindrops in a cloudburst. You don't have any warning with these mortars, but we all dove in a trench as the first one hit. [Floyd] Gore, the battalion commander's orderly, was at one end with me, and four others beyond us. We hugged the ground and I closed my eyes. It must have lasted only five minutes, but I'd swear that 100 rounds hit within a radius of fifteen yards of our hole. The second it stopped, the three officers took off in the direction of the CP with [Lt. Col. Byron] King yelling back to me to stay at the OP.

"Then I heard a groan and became conscious of Gore next to me. He must have received a direct hit from a mortar. His whole side was ripped away and his insides were gushing out with every breath he took. The flesh on his right thigh was peeled down over his knee. While I was trying to comprehend the sight, Gore raised up on his elbows, twisted his head so he could see his body, and then fell flat. He groaned a minute or so longer and then died.

"I was shaking like a leaf as I called the CP and explained I was the only one at the OP and requested permission to return to the CP. King said for me to stay there, that I was safer up there. Another ten minutes and I asked again and this time Captain Young told me to come down. [When I got there] I told him about Gore and that finished King. He was a beat man. He hung his head in his hands and muttered over and over, 'Gore gone, Gore gone.' That night he went back to regiment and that was the last we saw of him."

Those trapped on the slope kept calling for smoke shells to cover their retreat and eventually the artillery expended all it had. The defenders continued to spray the landscape with murderous fire. A supportive strike by Navy planes missed the mark and bombs fell on the hapless GIs. Not until dark of that dreadful day could they escape, slinging makeshift litters with ponchos and shelterhalves on rifles to remove the wounded.

According to Moore, the count of able-bodied soldiers showed that of the roughly 450 involved in the attack, 128 remained. On the following day, the 383d sent its 2d Battalion into the maw and they, too, were chewed up with horrendous losses and little real estate to show for the investment of men and equipment. The division command now threw the 1st Battalion of the 381st into the battle. Its S-3, Dick Thom reported, "The 2nd Battalion was on a little knob to our right, west of us. The 3rd Battalion was to the extreme west. General Easley was there with the regimental commander and the regimental S-3. Easley said the 383d Regiment was up on the ridge. 'I want you, Cassidy [Lt. Col. John], to take your battalion in a column of twos on the double, with an attached heavy machine-gun platoon up there. Commit the 3d Battalion when you're ready.'

"The company commanders got the order and we crossed the gulch between us and Kakazu. We went up to the top of a little hill. When we got there, there was an army up there, all right, but it wasn't the 383d Regiment. All hell broke loose. Our men came tumbling down, their rifles falling. I got behind a big rock and saw a light machine gun off to my left chipping away at my rock. I was not happy. We lost half our rifle companies from the battalion. We had two company commanders either killed or wounded, along with a number of lieutenants. By the second or third day in these positions we had only one active officer per company.

"On Okinawa, each battalion had a destroyer or cruiser assigned to it. The ships would fire 5-inch gun shells for illumination—fifty-second flares that burst over the area. We endured a series of counterattacks, and after what must have been the twelfth one on a dark night we pleaded for illumination. The cruiser assigned to us said, 'There's a red alert, possible air attack.' They couldn't give fire and illumination, but, they said, 'We'll give you the baseball scores.'

"Then I got a call from one company commander who was kind of a nasty bastard. He said there are hundreds of Japs in our positions. I sent about fifty of them your way. Their artillery was also coming over. Things didn't look too bright. I thought we were done for. I couldn't think of what to do. I called for the 81mm mortars to fire almost on our positions—we were all in holes that we got into at 7:00 P.M. and never came out of until morning.

"Tech Sergeant Beauford Anderson, who was the section leader for a 60mm mortar team in A Company, had been busy with the mortar and he was down to six rounds and the mortar was no good anymore. They were swamped with Jap soldiers. I saw Anderson pull the pin on a mortar shell, bounce it on a rock to knock out the detent that keeps the shell from going off while you're handling it. Then he heaved it by hand so it would land on its nose and explode. Four out of the six went off and then, although his arm was busted, Anderson took a carbine and went up and down the gorge shooting Japs. He had seemed like just an ordinary soldier, smallish, cheerful, a guy who did his job. He just went ape that night. Later, his company commander put him in for the Medal of Honor and I was a witness. [Thom earned a Bronze Star.]

"They finally pulled us out, but there wasn't too much to pull. We left 700 dead Japs up there but we had 53 fully able enlisted men left from the three rifle companies of our battalion which had attacked Kakazu." Thom blamed much of the carnage upon General Easley. "He was too damn brave, too Gung ho. We were all going to get killed following him."

50
Ie Shima and Beyond

Well pleased by the success of the Marine campaign on the upper half of the island, even as army divisions to the south cringed under the savage response of the enemy, the brass advanced the schedule for Ie Shima, a mere three and one-half miles off the northwest coast. Its ten square miles, dominated by a large plateau, promised to provide an excellent airfield for the final assault upon Japan. The invasion was set for 16 April and the 77th Division received the assignment.

Intelligence estimated a force of 2,000 defenders, a mix of battle experienced soldiers who had fought in Manchuria and labor units. The garrison had constructed defensive positions around Mount Iegusugu, a 600-foot-high rocky tower, known as "the Pinnacle" or "the Needle," which overlooked the remainder of the largely flat terrain. From the Pinnacle, excellent fields of fire covered the gentle, southeastern beaches, nominally the prime site for invaders. Because of the strength of these emplacements, nestled in well-concealed and protected caves, the Japanese tried to seduce their foes into the belief that the southeastern beaches were more vulnerable than the steeper shores to the west. To deceive the Americans, the defenders held their fire when recon parties had approached the bait; one U.S. serviceman actually strolled a few yards surveying the area without drawing a single round. The well-disciplined Japanese soldiers hid themselves from the prying eyes of observation planes that flew as low as 100 feet over the site. On the other hand, anyone attempting to gather information about the other beaches quickly came under fire, as if these places were where the enemy could expect intense opposition.

In spite of all of the guile and camouflage, the 77th Division brass spotted the trap. The plans specified landings on the south and southwest coasts that employed the 305th and 306th Regiments supported by field artillery, including one unit set up on a sandy islet four miles off Ie. The beach choices dismayed those charged with supply because high, jagged, coral reefs limited the use of landing craft. Division commander Maj. Gen. Andrew Bruce's staff believed that a quick breakthrough would enable them to open up easier access, but the Americans committed one serious blunder, when aerial inspection was unable to find Japanese soldiers, they undercounted the size of hostile forces. Bruce advised the Tenth Army commander, Gen. Simon Bolivar. Buckner on 6 April: ". . . original estimate of enemy is considerably reduced. It is planned to take entire division to target area; secure island quickly with minimum forces, less heavy equipment."

During the three-day period prior to the debarkation of the GIs on "W day," naval guns and aircraft furiously bombarded Ie Shima. A cloud of smoke and dust soon enveloped Mount Iegusugu until it faded from sight. And when the Liberty Division soldiers headed for the beach, it seemed almost a repeat of Love Day. Bruce noted, "Our good fortune continued because we landed apparently where the Japs did not expect us. Only scattered light resistance was met during the first hour or so."

"Light resistance," while gratifying to upper echelons, still means casualties and those upon whom injury is inflicted can find little solace in the term. Buckner Creel, a company commander in the 306th Regiment, described the landing for his outfit as "rather uneventful, although the amtracs on either side of mine in the first wave hit aerial bombs planted in the ground. One was blown upside down; the other lost a track." These incidents aside, Creel and companions made swift initial progress. "We swept over the airfield with virtually no opposition."

Promoted to executive officer of Company C, in the 706th Tank Battalion, William Siegel commanded a tank that first day of the invasion. "My tank had no sooner come ashore than I was immediately ordered to rescue an infantry platoon pinned down by Jap small-arms fire on a plain about 300-400 yards from the beach. We were able to bring this unit out under extreme small-arms fire with no casualties by backing the tank up and the infantrymen using us for cover."

Larry Gerevas, a newcomer to Company K, 307th Regiment while it recovered from Leyte, now found himself on a landing boat headed for Ie Shima. "There was no enemy fire as we pulled into this small cove. The beach was surrounded on three sides by a steep, crescent-shaped slope rising about thirty feet to the island's plateau. We dug in as well as we could in the coral sand. That night, we repelled a banzai attack. An old man was killed while trying to spear one of our men. Heavy explosions shook the ground during the night, caving in foxholes dug in the coral sand slope. We thought it was Jap artillery, but it was the Navy underwater demolition team, blasting the coral reef in the cove to open the way for supply ships."

Joe Budge, a Scotland-born, Hawaiian sugar plantation technician, now a sergeant replacement in a mortar section with Company D of the 305th, boarded an amtrac for the trip to the beach. "Most impressive of all was the rocket ship, an LST with banks of rockets fired in waves from its deck, a fearsome sight and even more fearsome to hear . . . roaring and screaming of rockets and a thunderous echo from the shore, which disappeared under a gray blanket of smoke sparkling with red flashes. Someone wondered out loud if anyone could live through that and a sergeant said not to worry, there would be plenty left. 'Right now,' he said, 'they will be running around a-jibber-jabbering to themselves and a-sharpening their swords.' He asked me if I was scared and I said not yet. He said, 'Well, you better sceered [sic] and stay sceered. That way you will react quicker. Adrenaline or something.' Someone had asked him what the island looked like as an objective for infantry. He peered at it, noting that it was a flat plain, dominated by a pyramidal-like hill, militarily uninviting. He grunted and obviously with unfond memories of the South Pacific found something good to say. 'Waal, anyway, there ain't no goddamn palm trees on it.'

"At the moment, I was more worried about our mode of transport than the Japanese, so I unbuckled my ammunition belt, which meant that if it came to swimming in a hurry, I could shrug off all my equipment and retain my rifle, with which we had been trained to swim. One soldier was crossing himself and muttering prayers. Presently, the man beside the driver of our conveyance winked at me through a small hatchway and then slammed it shut. We roared down the ramp and bobbed reluctantly up to the surface, then roared across a submerged sandbar to the accompaniment of a few pillars of water that suddenly appeared near us, without apparent cause. As soon as the tractor heaved itself up on the beach, it dropped its rear ramp and we debarked to run as fast as we could through scrub bushes into the open that lay beyond. The riflemen among us pushed on while we set down the mortars and waited for further orders. A few yards away lay another amtrac, fitted with a turret like a tank, but which now lay upside down with a huge hole in its bottom. Someone asked about the crew but the rest of us just looked at the smoking, shattered hulk and said nothing.

"A certain amount of small arms fire passed overhead and we could hear our own infantry also at work. One could sometimes tell what was happening [from the sound] . . . the chatter of a Nip machine gun getting more and more erratic as the boys closed in on it, from the slow thump-thump-thump of a BAR, and a spattering of our own rifle fire. Then might come the thud and whine of a U.S. hand grenade; the whine being the flying fragments, and the Nip gun would cease forever. Sometimes there was no whine, which meant the grenade had been thrown into a pillbox.

"A jeep came down, this one fitted with brackets to hold litters. There were four litters, all occupied. It stopped by us and one of us recognized a friend and walked over to see him. There was a tremendous explosion under the jeep and the spare tire went humming over our heads. A few pieces of metal remained of the jeep and nothing of the men except for the GI who had been walking toward it. Now, he was on the ground, crawling frantically away from the site of the explosion, dragging a leg, until somebody got to him and made him lie still. 'If that was a mine, it was the damndest mine I ever saw,' said someone. We found plenty of them, large sea mines or airplane bombs, sticking up through the ground, with a rubber tubelike fuse visible above the surface."

Dick Forse was a gunner on an M8, self-propelled 75mm gun. After arriving on the beach, Forse climbed up to remove waterproof tape from around the turret. "I heard a machine gun and couldn't tell whether it was a U.S. or Japanese one. But I dropped down on my hands and knees. I tried a second time to strip off the tape and when the machine gun went off, I knew it was a Japanese one because of its rapid rate. I tried a third time to get to the tape but that machine gun opened up again and I gave up for the moment.

"We had another M8 coming in from the sea and I tried to signal them there was a machine gun firing at this beach. I saw spouts of water around the M8 but they weren't paying any attention. They were lucky, because that gunner must have run off. Lieutenant Jesse Gershberg, our platoon leader, and two others went back for orders. A machine gun opened up, hit a nearby pine tree and a piece struck Gershberg in the forehead. But he stayed with us.

"We started up again and found we were all by ourselves. There were no targets and I didn't know what we were doing. Then we came across a bunch of guys from our company and they warned us to go between the tape [put down to indicate a safe path through mined areas]. It was nerve-wracking; there were so many of them, aerial bombs buried in the ground, and the pressure of a finger could set them off. But you could see where the mines were even though they tried to camouflage the spot. They would plant grass around them but it died, turning yellow, while in the safe spots, the grass was really green.

"Gershberg learned that the road up ahead wasn't secured. We entered a field where there were a bunch of Americans moving toward a woods. I watched guys creep along, like they were reluctant to move out. Then one would get up, run, and then drop. Boom! I thought, boy these Japs are accurate with their mortars. I saw what I thought was a knapsack, but it was half a body; he must have triggered one of the mines. We settled in for the night and it was peaceful for a while and then there was an explosion. They were attacking with satchel charges and grenades. I heard a clang against the side of the tank. It must have been a grenade. In the morning I found a bone, a human knee bone. It must have come from a Jap who ran at the tank and blew himself up with one of the satchel charges."

On 17 April, the 77th welcomed Ernie Pyle, who had chafed at the relative absence of action with the Marines on Okinawa. Pyle once explained the lure of the battlefield. "The front does get into your blood and you miss it and want to be back. Life up there is very simple, very uncomplicated, devoid of all the jealousy and meanness that float around a headquarters, and time passes so fast it's unbelievable. [He tried] not to take any foolish chances but there's no way to play it completely safe and still do your job."

Pyle began his tour on Ie Shima with the 305th Regiment, led by Lt. Col. Joseph Coolidge, who wrote: "Every man in the outfit anticipated this visit with pleasure and pride and with the hopes of meeting this great little fellow who had portrayed the lot of the doughboy in Europe with such moving simplicity. Now we would have our chance to show him that fighting in the Pacific was just as rough and dirty, and a lot more unglamorous than that in civilized Europe."

The correspondent joined a group at an observation post overlooking a plain that led to a village at the foot of the Needle. According to Coolidge, two or three other reporters, "acting like general aides" accompanied Pyle. The regimental commander noted that when the other reporters stood up to get a better view, the defenders apparently noticed the activity and began dropping mortar shells. Those who had come with Pyle "had seen enough and left us. Ernie remained in his corner until the final action of the day."

On the following day, Pyle visited with General Bruce at the 305th command post. After scrawling autographs for several GIs, Pyle accepted a ride with Coolidge—bound for an observation post according to Bruce although Coolidge claimed their destination was division headquarters. Five men packed into the jeep, a driver, two members of the regimental staff plus Coolidge and Pyle. "Our route," reported Coolidge, "lay well within the area we had already 'secured'; it paralleled a coral cliff about 300 yards to our left. We fell in behind three trucks and another jeep [with military police]. Just ahead lay a road or cart trail junction. On either side, two infantry battalions had bivouacked the night before and were packing up after breakfast, getting ready to move up to the fighting. Just as we reached the road junction, a burst of machine gun fire exploded around us; our jeep with two flat tires stopped quickly, and we, in turn exploded from the jeep to the ditch on either side of the road.

"Ernie and I, on the right side of the jeep, landed in the ditch away from the line of fire; the others, we hoped, had found shelter on the left side of the road. I had seen Barnes, our driver, jumping to the left. Ernie and I were quite safe; the ditch dropped off three feet from the side of the road. The jeep fortunately had taken the brunt of the burst, two flat tires, a jagged hole in the bumper, and a hole in the radiator. Ernie reported he was safe.

"I told him to keep down while I checked the rest of the party; I raised my head and called each man in turn. They all reported that they were safe in the sheltering ditch. Then another burst from that machine gun. One shot kicked dust in my face, but ricocheted over my head. I ducked and turned to Ernie. He was lying on his back; his hands resting on his chest were holding a knitted arctic cap which he was known to carry at all times. his face was composed. It must have taken an appreciable time for me to realize that he had been hit; no blood flowed, and only after I looked at him more closely did I see the hole through each temple. His bullet had not ricocheted. A platoon was dispatched to search out the machine gunner, but hidden in the coral crevices that honeycombed the entire island, that Jap might well have escaped for another day. A tank was sent in to pick up Ernie's body.

"The ironic element to the story is that the two battalions on either side of the road knew only that machine-gun fire had hit quite close to them. The men felt no danger nor did they know the tragic loss of this fine Little Man [sic]. The machine gunner must have located himself well back in the curve so that his line of fire was limited to the road junction and he patiently awaited a vehicle carrying personnel, a far more valuable target than the lumbering two and a half ton truck that preceded our jeep."

Coolidge's account implied that the area and road seemed relatively inactive and Bruce remarked, "Many vehicles had been over [the road] and we all thought [it] was safe." But to the infantrymen near the site, danger remained a constant. Joe Budge with his mortar section recalls, "That night I kept really far down in my foxhole for two reasons. One was that a U.S. machine gun was firing protectively very close over my head. Another was that a Japanese heavy machine gun was chipping dirt off the lip of it all night." When morning came, Budge observed a jeep with an antenna—a sign of a radio and personnel of some importance—run along a road the troops knew was covered by enemy fire and clearly visible to spotters on the Pinnacle. Budge saw the occupants of the jeep fling themselves into the roadside ditch and then watched as one lifted his head for a peek at the action. "The gun fired a short burst and the man was dead." Only later did the sergeant learn that the victim was Pyle.

When Bruce learned in a series of somewhat garbled messages of Pyle's death, he immediately sent a message to Tenth Army headquarters, "Regretfully report Ernie Pyle who so materially aided in building morale for troops killed by surprise Jap mg fire while standing beside regimental commander of foot troops, 77th Division, Lt. Col. Coolidge, on outskirts Ie Shima town about 10:15 today." Later, with facts in hand, he corrected the description that placed Pyle upright when he died. When the GIs hastily erected a crude memorial, Bruce decreed an inscription, AT THIS SPOT, THE 77TH INFANTRY DIVISION LOST A BUDDY ERNIE PYLE, 18 APRIL 1945. The body was at first interred in a cemetery for Liberty Division dead on Ie Shima and later transferred to the Punchbowl military graveyard on Oahu.

Budge recalled that on the day the machine gun cut Pyle down, he moved along the shore as the troops encircled the town. A brigadier general, the assistant division commander [Edwin H. Randle], was strutting around the beach with a walking stick, a habit he had picked up from the British in Libya. He encountered a little yellow sparrow of a soldier using a mine detector on the beach, but with a bad case of the shakes.

"Son, where is your officer?" inquired Randle.

"Dead, sir" stammered the GI.

"Then where is your NCO?"

"Dead, sir."

"Where is the rest of the bomb disposal squad?"

"Sir, I *am* the bomb disposal squad."

Budge reported that the general gulped and said very gently, "Son, get on that landing barge and come back to the ship with me." According to the mortar section sergeant, booby-trapped aircraft bombs planted as mines had wiped out the disposal experts.

Larry Gerevas and Company K of the 307th left the comparatively quiet beach area and marched along a dirt road above the beach. "Within minutes machine-gun bullets were cracking all around us and we ran for cover. No one was hit and it seemed the firing came from a great distance. There were a lot of trees and brush at the sides of the road so we took advantage of this cover as we continued on our way. We all know for sure that our movements were being observed by the Japs on the Pinnacle.

"Later, as we tried to climb over a saddle on a small ridge, mortars began falling on the only path. The mortars landed every thirty seconds. As soon as one hit, the platoon leader would point to one of us and tell us, 'Go!.' The path was very slippery from the rains and when it was my turn, I started to run. About halfway there, I fell and started sliding down the slope. My rifle flew out of my hands and I knew it was only a matter of seconds before the next mortar shell exploded. There wasn't time to retrieve my rifle. I dug my fingers into the muddy path and pulled myself over the hill just before the next mortar blast.

"On the other side of the hill I expected to find the rest of my platoon, but there was nobody in sight. Here I was, without my rifle and alone. I knew that I had to find my group quickly. Nearby I found a group of tombs. I decided to hide in one for a while until I could make a plan. I decided to retrace my steps to see in which direction the others went after they came over the hill. As I was doing this, I saw some medics placing a wounded man in an ambulance. I ran over and asked for the rifle of the wounded man. They handed me the weapon and I found my platoon."

Gerevas and his companions dug in on Ie Shima. "One man in our platoon was nearly frozen with fear. He was really dangerous to everyone around him. We wouldn't let him have grenades during the night because he would throw them anywhere without thinking. Usually two shared a foxhole, but nobody wanted to be with him. That night the Japs attacked our position and we managed to kill them or drive them off. During the attack there was a lot of gunfire and grenades. When things quieted, we could hear a baby crying. We continued to throw grenades toward the sound until it stopped. The next morning we found dead Jap soldiers and women who carried spears. One of them had a baby strapped to her back. I don't think I will ever forget the sound of that crying baby.

"The really frightened guy survived the night. The following day we had to run across an open area under sniper fire to reach wooded cover. After we arrived there, grenades started falling around us. Many were duds. The scared GI was sitting with his legs spread and one of the grenades landed between his legs. He didn't move—just sat there and stared at the grenade. He was paralyzed. Thank God it was a dud. All of us were afraid, but we all felt sorry for this man who was filled with terror every moment."

On 19 April the big push for Ie Shima town and the Pinnacle started. Elements from all three regiments united in an effort to capture the town and participated in the final bloody effort to eliminate the tenacious defenders hunkered down in the deep bunkerage of Mount Iegusugu. Backed by artillery, the 305th initially gained some ground in Ie town, but a buzzsaw of machine gun and mortar fire drove the attackers back from a hill that overlooked the town. The same deadly reception met infantrymen seeking to enter the town, where defenders hid themselves in the rubble of concrete created by incessant bombardment. Tanks and self-propelled guns halted for fear of the abundant mines. Engineers could not clear these obstacles because any open space lay exposed to withering scythes of bullets.

Among those advancing on the objectives were Gerevas and his buddies. "As we reached the foot of Iegusugu Mountain, an American tank and some infantry came into an opening about 150 yards below us and immediately started firing at us, thinking we were Japs. Our squad leader frantically removed a bright orange banner from his pack and held it up. The firing from the tank and the infantry stopped. This was the closest I came to being killed by friendly fire."

On 20 April, two battalions of the 307th pressed forward in spite of intense fusillades from above them to finally occupy a major objective, the town's government house atop a hill. Their triumph proved short-lived. A battalion of the 305th that had seized a flanking hill withdrew without notifying the GIs around government house. The enemy swarmed back onto the position vacated by the men of the 305th and rained fire down upon the 307th's troops. Running low on ammunition and now highly vulnerable, the infantrymen pulled back.

The 706th Tank Battalion added its might to the battle. William Siegel in Company C remembered, "Our tank was disabled and set on fire by a satchel charge. My crew and I were forced to abandon it and wound up in a close-quarter fight with three of the enemy. Corporal Kenneth Rogers was killed in this action, but we were rescued by another unit from my platoon."

Joe Budge, as a mortar sergeant with the 305th, endured prolonged terror. "Heavy artillery or mortar fire can be seen in any war movie, but it is usually toned down because nobody would believe the size of the explosion one is expected to live through. Sometimes you can hear them coming. Usually there is too much other uproar going on, as in this case. These shells kept making great thunderous explosions in our midst, and flat on the ground—as flat as the human form can get when frightened—we felt the ground viciously kick us in the belly. Things flew around, helmets, bits of rock, bushes, branches, sometimes bits of soldiers. There was nothing to be done except to lie there and try to be ready to receive the horde of nasty men with bayonets and swords who were likely to show up the moment the barrage stopped.

"Then the rifle company we were supporting told us to pull back and we went with it. I grabbed the base plate of one of the mortars and proceeded to walk out of that hellfire spot toward a ruined building in a field. A standard Japanese reaction the moment they saw anyone retreating, was to pour on the fire. This time was no exception. Unfortunately, when we pulled back, so did another rifle company, leaving a gap at the edge of the town into which the Nips poured some infantry. Every Jap weapon in or out of range opened up, mostly mortars, machine guns, and rifles, but including one small field gun.

"The forty-pound mortar base plate jumped energetically and a bullet screamed off it. With considerable relief, and after resisting a strong temptation to run, I reached the ruins and lay down in a sunken road. I felt comparatively safe until a jerry can lying by my feet jumped up with a clang and exhibited a neat bullet hole. One forgets that bullets have a dropping trajectory. We set up the mortars to be ready for any Nip attack, which the book would have it should come at any moment. But they were too smart to charge us across a wide open field in daylight.

"Our battalion commander had been promoted to fill one of many vacancies from the slaughter of the regimental staff on the *Henrico*. We had inherited a major who carried no respect from the troops. He showed up with his radio operator. The latter squatted on the ground with his set. The major walked round and round him, actually wringing his hands and wailing out loud, 'What should I do? What should I do?' "The radio operator's head, like an owl's, swiveled about watching him in amazement. If the troops had respected the major this might have become a bad situation, the nervous collapse of a battalion commander at a bad moment. But the men had no expectations of anything better because of incidents with him on Guam.

"An old sergeant—or maybe he just looked old and tired—said, 'Oh, shit!' Then he calmly started giving orders. Other noncoms followed suit—there were no other officers around. Within minutes a call came over the radio for the major to report to the beach. Major Eugene Cook, a fine officer, took his place. We reorganized." Budge and his mates remained for the moment removed from the worst of the fray. "A few Nips came our way but they seemed to be stragglers. When we shot at them or threw grenades quite often there'd be a pause for a few seconds and then an explosion of a Nip grenade and a body would fly into the air. They were blowing themselves up, being afraid of capture and incapable of figuring out a more profitable method of committing suicide, such as taking one or more of us with them.

"Throughout the night continual heavy action continued in the town around the Pinnacle. There was one particular U.S. machine gun that seemed to be firing all night. It must have used up several barrels and thousands of rounds of ammunition. One could see the constant stream of cherry red tracer bullets encountering some target at quite close range, and disappearing or ricocheting off into the night. From the opposite direction came an equally constant stream of yellower Japanese tracers. We discovered later this fight ended in the CP of the 3d Battalion with clerks, cooks, and the battalion commander in hand-to-hand combat. The stubborn machine gunner, Pfc. Martin May, earned a posthumous Medal of Honor."

The noose around Iegusugu tightened as the American forces enveloped the base. For Buckner Creel, with G Company of the 306th, the assignment was the northern slope of the Pinnacle. At 14:30 on the afternoon of the twentieth, the troops jumped off, preceded by a concentration of shells from the 304th in addition to the rounds that tanks and self-propelled howitzers could toss onto the Pinnacle. Company C of the 306th led off, sprinting, falling, rising, and then running again across 200 yards of open, fire-swept ground. Rushing forward in the tracks of C Company and on its flanks came the others in the assault, including Creel with G Company.

Earl Miller, the replacement machine gunner with G Company, recalled the final push up Mount Iegusugu. "It was a volcanic hill with caves three stories deep. Also a field gun on tracks behind sliding doors—all of this looking right down our throats! On the morning of our assault, we charged through a mine field and barbed wire on the run, stepping in the tracks of the man in front. We all made it to the base of the hill. It was the first time I had heard bullets snap and crack around my ears. Right after we charged through the minefield, and fell behind a big rock to catch our breath, I saw my first case of battle fatigue. ——— was not hit, but he could not move. The medics gave him a shot and sent him to the rear."

While an occasional soldier flinched, as Miller saw, the assault brigades reached the steep slopes where the entrenched foe could only be routed with bayonets, flamethrowers, satchel charges, and grenades. An observer from the War Department in Washington marveled, "It was the most remarkable thing I have ever seen. The attack looked like a Fort Benning demonstration. Why, I saw troops go through enemy mortar concentrations and machine-gun fire that should have pinned them down. But instead they poured across that field and took the mountain against really tough opposition without even slowing down."

Over a period of three days, units from all three regiments fought, bled, and died on the slopes, taking ground, retreating in the face of devastating onslaughts and counterattacks, and then regrouping to climb ever higher. Even after the GIs gained the northern slopes of the 600-foot tower, groups of well-concealed, determined resisters remained. "We were 'mopping up,'" recalled Creel, "and destroying pillboxes. We made attempts with a Japanese-language interpreter to get them to come out. Rarely would they do it. On one particular occasion, we had tried to get an unknown number of Japanese soldiers to come out but to no avail. So I gave the order to blow it. An engineer demo man "capped and fused" a satchel charge, lit it, and threw it into the emplacement. We waited and nothing happened. We figured it was a dud so we threw another one in. Nothing happened; a third satchel charge followed- nothing.

"I got hold of the engineer platoon leader, 1st Lt. Charles E. Sears, who was part of my landing team. Together we figured out that the Japanese must be pulling out the flaming fuses on the charges as they came in. Sears got a satchel charge and he and his demo man rigged it up with about ten to fifteen fuses, all different lengths. The last five to be lit were capped and live. When all the fuses were lit and spurting fire, he heaved the satchel into the open door of the emplacement. We got down behind the berm and could picture the Japanese furiously pulling out the fuses, wondering which one was live. A tremendous explosion shook all of us. All the ammo in there as well as the three earlier satchel charges went up at once in a sympathetic detonation."

Company K of the 307th approached a clearing on the third day of the operation. Gerevas recalls an Okinawan woman accompanied by two small boys. "When they saw us they ran as fast as they could to escape. We caught the woman, but the little boys were too quick and got away. However, as soon as they were far enough off to feel safe, they stopped and watched to see what we were going to do with their mother. I was holding her by her arm as we walked along a dirt road. Suddenly, she tried to pull away and kick at a wire that ran across the road. Another soldier grabbed her other arm and we lifted her over the wire. We examined the wire and saw that it stretched from a stake on one side of the road to a 500-pound bomb on the other. When we continued down the road we spotted three more of these booby traps and lifted the woman over each. The small boys kept us in sight. When they saw we were not harming their mother, they came up. Later we turned all three over to a group collecting civilians. They were loaded on a truck and driven away."

A few days later, Gerevas's unit was ordered to secure a small hamlet. "The day before, a squad from another company had tried to enter the village and nearly all were killed or wounded. My squad was now picked for this attempt and I was made the scout. Up to that moment, I thought I had been very lucky, but now I felt my luck had run out. The scout leads and is at least twenty yards in front of the others. He is the bait for a sniper and usually the first to be hit. If the scout is wounded, the rest of the squad might retreat and abandon him to the enemy. I know that's not what it is like in the movies and it is what I saw happen in real combat.

"I knew someone had to do the job and it was my turn. We moved through the streets, expecting to be machine gunned at any moment. When we had walked through the entire place, we turned and came back. Not a single shot was fired. The Japs had left during the night.

"During the last week of April, we dug in as we had every night since we arrived on Ie Shima. Two of us would dig one foxhole. We would sit, facing each other. One person would sleep for an hour while the other kept watch, alternating throughout the night. About midnight we were attacked by a small group of Jap soldiers while I was sleeping. The firing of the rifles awakened me with a start. I sat up quickly. My head came up alongside the muzzle of my foxhole companion's rapidly firing automatic rifle. My head felt as if it had exploded. I thought that I had been shot. The muzzle blast caused concussion deafness in both of my ears. Still, I was able to grab my rifle and fire at the gray shadows around us. Soon they were either dead or driven off. When morning arrived, my hearing had not returned. No one knew of any aid station nearby, so I had no choice but to stay with my unit until we returned to the ship. It was especially frightening to continue in combat without being able to hear. But I had no other option."

On the third day, a small patrol of GIs with mountain climbing experience scaled the last 50-foot cliff guarding the peak. Although snipers peppered the area, one man waved an American flag from the summit, while others below tried to bring up a flagpole for a replica of the Mount Suribachi scene on Iwo Jima. Intense fire forced the GIs to abandon the project. Still, a day later, two U.S. banners waved atop the Ie Shima peak. To the troops, Bruce issued General Order 56: "Ie Shima is captured. Thank you, tough guys." Not until 27 April, when the last substantial U.S. forces boarded ships, leaving behind a small garrison, could the battle for Ie Shima be regarded as actually finished. Sandwiched between the relatively easy landing and the final few days eliminating small pockets of defenders had been six days of fierce combat that Bruce compared with other bitter battles like Iwo Jima.

The Americans estimated about 4,800 dead enemy, including as many as 1,500 civilians who put on Japanese uniforms and bore arms. As Creel's anecdote indicated, even women served the emperor on Ie Shima. The division's 239 KIA, 897 WIA, and 19 MIA nearly equaled the 1,143 casualties for Guam, a campaign that lasted three times as long. In comparison, Iwo Jima required twenty-four days to subdue, with 24,000 Marine casualties, including 1,600 classified as "combat fatigue" while the Japanese dead totaled well over 20,000. Navy losses at Iwo Jima ran around 2,700 killed, wounded, and missing.

From the Ie Shima beaches, the GIs of the 77th Division could observe war-wracked Okinawa. Joe Budge saw, "constant artillery fire and flames. One could see the shells red-hot from the guns soaring off toward the front, losing their color as they went. It did not look very inviting and from what we heard, it was turning into a World War I type of operation."

Indeed, with the 96th Division so badly battered, the Tenth Army summoned the 27th Infantry Division from its reserve status and tossed it into the fight. This was not an infusion of a full-strength, combat-ready outfit. The 27th's ranks remained badly depleted after Peleliu and the veterans were combat weary. However, initially the division achieved gains that helped bring the Americans beyond Kakazu Ridge. But then the 27th's advance bogged down to the intense frustration of General Buckner.

Across the island, the 7th Division committed itself to another natural defensive fortress, Kochi Ridge. Platoon leader Gage Rodman, preparing to send out a patrol, headed forward to deliver the orders to one of his squads. "About that time, we began receiving mortar fire. Trying to move only in the intervals between bursts, I was running forward toward an irrigation ditch. As I hurled myself forward to land lengthwise, a mortar shell exploded against the side of the ditch close to me. My eye caught a flash of black falling, which I suspect was the mortar shell. The next thing I knew, I was sitting on the ground instead of running forward. I knew I was hit but the only blood I could see was on my leg. Then I caught sight of what seemed like several yards of pink tubing on the front of my trousers."

A nearby medic, after bandaging another wounded soldier, injected Rodman with morphine while one of his squad leaders, using a first-aid dressing, covered Rodman's exposed intestines. He was evacuated and at the 102d Portable Surgical Hospital, surgeons removed the majority of the shell fragments and manufactured a colostomy to replace his severed bowel.

The 7th Division assault on Kochi Ridge stalled. Tenth Army gave up on the 27th Division and shifted it north to replace the 1st and 6th Marine Divisions in basically occupation duty. The renewed assaults slowly forced the Japanese backward but the flow of GI blood quickened.

51
Liberations and Victory

With the Rhine and then the River Main crossed the ability of the Germans to mount organized large-scale resistance collapsed. Pfc. Harry Herder Jr., an over six-foot infantry replacement, had volunteered for special assignment, and after a physical examination and an interview, was assigned to the 5th Ranger Battalion. The need for foot soldiers, which bent the color line enough for 2,500 black volunteers to serve in provisional rifle platoons, also forced the Rangers to accept recruits without the previously required credentials or training. When his new company commander spotted Herder wearing eye glasses, he almost booted him out. Ranger Harold Stover, a post–D day replacement himself, but a veteran of combat, tutored Herder in tactics with a four-day crash course. "He worked me over on the bazooka until I knew it well. He would accept nothing but complete understanding. Stover taught me that when firing at a tank to aim at the seam between the body of the tank and the turret, in order to weld the turret to the body.

"I remember once when we were working on a German pillbox, I loaded Stover up, hit him on the helmet to let him know all was ready, and he rose to one knee and fired. The round skipped in front of the bunker and into the port the machine gun was firing out of and exploded against the backside wall. Stover was mad at himself, had me load him up again quickly and fired again. The second round went right in the port. It wasn't necessary any longer, but Stover just had to know that he could do it."

The 5th Ranger Battalion reached the Rhine in time for Herder to cross the Ludendorff span in a truck. "Our outfit hooked up with a tank destroyer outfit and we were in a hurry. We blew across the landscape of eastern Germany with little opposition. We eventually drove up some gentle valley where there were trees on either side, when we made a sharp left turn, so sharp that those of us on top of the vehicles were grabbing things to keep from falling off. By the time we regained our balance, there it was; a great high barbed wire fence at least ten feet high, maybe more. Between us and the fence running parallel to the fence was a dirt road and beyond the fence two more layers of barbed wire. The barbed-wire in those fences was laced in a fine mesh, so fine, no one was going to get through it.

"Our tank destroyers slowed down, but did not stop. They blew straight at and through the barbed wire. Those of us riding the top scurried quickly to get behind the turret while those vehicles just continued to charge. At least one of those fences was hot with electricity, but they shorted out when it hit the damp ground. When we broke through the first of those fences, we got a clue, the first, as to what we had come upon, but had no real comprehension at all of what was to assault our senses for the next hours, the next days.

"I was very much on the alert. The tanker on our vehicle assigned to the machine gun was on that weapon and ready to use it. Those of us riding were ready to bail off and hit the ground on the run. As an assistant bazooka man I had a sack with ten bazooka rounds hung over my shoulder. I had an M1 Garand and some bandoliers of ammo for that; some grenades hanging one place and another; a fully loaded cartridge belt.

"I remember scouting the area in front of us. Over to the left, just inside the fence, were some major buildings and next to one of those was a monster chimney, monstrous both in diameter and in height. Now black smoke was pouring out if it, and blowing away from us, but we could still smell it. An ugly horrible smell. A vicious smell."

The tank destroyer columns performed a standard series of wheel maneuvers that enabled them to present a single front. Meanwhile the Rangers dismounted and spread out along the same line. "None of us in the lower ranks knew what it was we were up to or where we were, but we fully expected a firefight with German troops whose camp we had just stormed and I thought would be angry. It turned out there were no German troops present. Slowly, as we formed up, a ragged group of human beings started to creep out of and from between the buildings in front of us. These human beings, timidly, slowly, deliberately showing their hands, all wore a sort of uniform, or bits and pieces of a uniform, made from horribly coarse cloth, striped, the stripes running vertically, alternating a dull dark gray and a darkish blue a half inch or maybe more wide. Some of those human beings had pants made of the material, some had shirt/jackets, and some had hats. Some had only one piece of uniform. They stood there, making me feel foolish with all of that firepower hanging on me. I certainly wouldn't be needing it with these folks."

While the GIs lowered their weapons, their officers and top noncoms entered one of the buildings. The two groups outside cautiously inched toward each other. "Some of them spoke English and asked, 'Are you American?' We said we were and the reaction of the whole mass was immediate; simultaneously on their faces were relaxation, ease, joy, and they all began chattering to us in a babble of tongues. It was then that the smell of the place started to get to me. We could only rarely take a shower and our uniforms were never fresh or clean. We had been blowing around Germany for some time and we were all a little raunchy in the odor department. I was probably more than just a little gamey and would not have noticed the other guys in the company because they were in about the same state as I. Our noses, rebelling against the surroundings they were constantly subjected to, were not functioning anywhere near normally. But now there was a new odor, thick and hanging, and it assaulted the senses."

The platoon sergeant issued orders for the men to guard holes in the fencing and to allow no one to pass through. Herder and a friend, Bill Justis, at one post were instructed to inspect a nearby four-story tower. Inside they found bunks for sleeping and a platform with a table rigged to accommodate a machine gun. From their perch they could see that similar towers ringed the encampment. "None of us knew what we were encountering. We were both too young to have any meaningful way of understanding the thing going on in Germany. Our first thought was that we were at a prisoner of war camp and all the people in strange uniforms were the troops who had been captured by the German Army. That made a little sense, but where were the German guards? Why the strange uniforms? Why were we keeping them in there? Bill Justis and I, standing on top of the tower, did not know we were at Buchenwald. We had to wait another hour or so to find out that this place had the name and what a 'Buchenwald' was."

Relieved of their station, Herder and Justis piled onto the back of a truck that carried them past a string of buildings with a few barred windows and then along a well-tended road, "through a manicured area of good houses—no, better than good. We didn't know it then, but the best of them was the home of Ilse Koch. Her husband was the camp commander and from what we later heard the two of them deserved each other."

Even as the Americans were moving into some barracks for guards, they saw a long truck convoy entering, a U.S. Army field hospital. "Sergeant [Adrian] Blowers told us that some of the prisoners spoke English. Then he got even quieter, looked at the ground for a moment, raised his eyes, and looking over our heads began very softly—we could barely hear him. He told us this is what was called a 'concentration camp,' that we were about to see things we were in no way prepared for. He told us to look, to look as long as our stomachs lasted, and then to get out of there for a walk in the woods. I had never known Sergeant Blowers to be like this. The man had seen everything that I could imagine could be seen and this place was having this effect on him. I didn't understand. I didn't know what a concentration camp was or could be."

With two other Rangers, Herder began the explorations. They passed a gate with a sign the nazis hung over a number of camps, which Herder could translate into WORK WILL MAKE YOU FREE. "We were slightly apprehensive of what we might see. Our antennae were up. We had been teased by bits of information and we wanted to know more. The lane we were walking on bent to the right as we cleared the building. We had barely made the turn and there it was.

"The bodies of human beings were stacked like cordwood. All of them were dead. All of them stripped. The inspection I made of the pile was not very close, but the corpses seemed to be all male. The stack was about five feet high, maybe a little more. I could see over the top. They extended down a slight hill for fifty to seventy-five feet. Human bodies, neatly stacked, naked, ready for disposal. The arms and legs were neatly arranged, but an occasional limb dangled oddly. The bodies we could see were all face up. There was an aisle, then another stack, and another aisle, and more stacks. The Lord only knows how many there were.

"Just looking at these bodies made one believe they had been starved to death. They appeared to be skin covering bones and nothing more. The eyes on some were closed, on others open. Bill, Tim, [Daly] and I grew very quiet. I think my only comment was 'Jesus Christ.' I have since seen the movie made about Buchenwald. The stack of bodies is vividly displayed just as I saw it, but it is not the same. The black-and-white film did not depict the dirty gray-green color of those bodies, and what it could not possibly capture was the odor, the smell, the stink.

"The three of us looked and we walked down the edge of those stacks. I know I didn't count them—it wouldn't have mattered. We looked and said not a word. A group of guys from the company noticed us and said, 'Wait till you see in there.' They pointed to a long building, about two stories high and butted up tightly to the chimney. It had two barnlike doors on either end and they were open. We walked back to the building where we found others from our company, along with some of the prisoners milling around between the bodies and the building. We moved gently through those people, through the doors, and felt the warmth immediately.

"Not far from the doors and parallel to the front of the building, there was a brick wall, solid to the top of the building. In the wall were small openings fitted with iron doors. Those doors were a little more than two feet wide and about two and a half feet high. The tops had curved shapes much like the entrances to churches. Those iron doors were in sets, three high. (My memory might be wrong about the exact number but there were many.) Most of the doors were closed, but down near the middle a few stood open. Heavy metal trays had been pulled out of those openings, and on those trays were partially burned bodies. On one tray was a skull partially burned through, with a hole in the top; other trays held partially disintegrated arms and legs. It appeared that those trays could hold three bodies at a time. And the odor, my God, the odor!

"I had enough. I couldn't take it any more. I left the building with Bill and Tim close behind me. As we passed out the door, someone from the company said, 'The crematorium.' Until then I had no idea what a crematorium was. It dawned on me much later that the number of bodies which, could be burned at one time, three bodies to a tray, at least thirty trays, and the Germans still couldn't keep up. The bodies on the stacks outside were growing at a faster rate than they could be burned." Ranger leaders shut down the furnaces.

A newly freed inmate led Herder and others to the inmates' quarters, large barnlike structures packed with five- and six-tier-high cots. "The bunks were much too short even for short people," noted Herder. "Just inside the door were people on the lower bunks so close to death they didn't have the strength to rise. They were literally skeletons covered with skin. There appeared to be no substance to them. The next day when the press arrived, one of the photographers for *Life* magazine had one of the really bad ones propped up against the door frame in the daylight. He took the photograph, but out of sight, in the darkness of the building, behind the man, were the people propping him up." Most of those still alive at Buchenwald, Herder learned, were political prisoners; most of the Jews had either died or been marched away.

Blowers informed the Rangers about Ilse Koch, who favored jodhpurs, boots, and a riding crop. "He told us this story about her. Once she ordered all the Jewish prisoners stripped and lined up. She marched down the rows of them and as she saw a tattoo she liked she would touch it with her riding crop. The guards would take the man away immediately to a camp hospital where the doctors would remove the patch of skin with the tattoo, have it tanned, and with others, patched together to make lamp shades. There were three of those lamp shades."

Herder learned that the German guards had packed up and moved out several hours before the Americans arrived. "George [Patton] had assigned us to this place for four days, ostensibly to keep the now free prisoners off the roads he needed to supply his troops, who were racing through Germany. The full explanation was given to the prisoners and there was no problem. George had assigned a whole field hospital to the place along with a big kitchen unit. He eventually sent in an engineering outfit with bulldozers to dig a mass grave for those bodies. We were doing everything we possibly could for the prisoners.

"While we were sipping coffee after breakfast, a great commotion broke out down at the gate and it grabbed our attention. A bright shiny jeep came through the gate with this fellow standing in front of the passenger seat, holding onto the windshield. His helmet was gleaming and elaborately decorated, his uniform spic and span, his pistol belt highly polished and oddly shaped, and, by God, there he was; it was George himself, and he was touring this place. From time to time the jeep would stop and he would ask questions. In front of the crematorium, the jeep stopped and he alighted, walked inside, was out of sight some minutes, appearing again with a very stiff back. Into the jeep again and he was all over the place in just a few minutes. He passed us on the way out and it was obvious he was some kind of mad. Damn, he looked mad, about as mad as I had ever seen anyone look. The jeep sped back out the gate and on down the road."

A flood of visitors from other units and the press washed over the camp. "It was an exhibition, God help us," said Herder. "Those people in the stacks were dead; they were gone. Nothing could really hurt them further, but it hurt me that they were now on exhibition. Some of our guys had been disgusted by a bunch of nurses or WACs in their Class A uniforms taking pictures of the naked dead. It was not the display of genitals that shook some of us up; it was the final indignity, the exhibition." He was further appalled when he inspected a building in which physicians who experimented upon inmates stored organs harvested from their victims.

One day, a band of prisoners, with the connivance of a GI, sneaked through a hole in the fence. They returned leading an individual, a rope around his neck. While in the nearby town of Weimar, they had recognized one of their former guards. In a Buchenwald cell, they interrogated their captive. Herder observed the proceedings, saw tears roll down the man's cheeks and then left. Later he and some others returned to the scene. "The hands of the German were untied, and he held a stout piece of rope. He was being given instructions and as we watched, it wasn't long before we realized he was being told how to tie a noose. The German guard was corrected three or four times, and had to undo some of his work to redo it correctly. When he was finished, he had a very proper hangman's noose, thirteen turns of the rope and all. A table was brought to the center of the room and placed under a very strong-looking electrical fixture. The guard was assisted onto the table and instructed to fix the rope to the light fixture. Finishing that, he was to put all of his weight on the rope and lift his feet. The fixture held. The guard was told to place the noose over his head, around his neck, and to draw the noose fairly snug. Then he was told to place his hands behind his back and his wrists were tied together. The table was moved and he barely stood on its edge. He couldn't see that; his eyes were unhooded and open, but the noose kept him from looking down. He was talked to some more and then he jumped. He was caught before all of his weight was on the rope and they set him back on the table. The next time he stepped gently off the end and the table was quickly slid away from him and out of his reach and he dangled there. He slowly strangled. His face went through a variety of colors before he hung still. My stomach did not want to hold food any longer. I turned and walked away; the rest of our guys following me. The Buchenwald prisoners stayed on to view their handiwork.

"Here we were, five or six of us, fully armed with semiautomatic rifles and we did not make the Buchenwald prisoners stop. In one way, we sanctioned the event; it was murder. The prisoners never touched the rope after it was placed in the German's hands, unfastened. They did not tie the noose nor did they fix it to the ceiling. They did not place the rope around the man's neck. They did not pull the table out from under him [until after he stopped off]. In one sense they had not committed murder, rather the German had committed suicide.

"I [and his companions] had the ability and means to stop the whole thing, but did not. Ever since that day I have been convincing myself that I understood why the Buchenwald prisoners did what they did. I had witnessed their agonies. I had wondered how human beings could treat other humans beings as the prisoners at Buchenwald had been treated. I felt I knew why the prisoners did what they did—so I did not stop them. I could have stopped the whole action, and I did not. I have had that under my hat for the past [fifty-three] years. Now I have written it. I have acknowledged it. Maybe it will go away. There are so many things from that week I wish would go away, be scrubbed from my memory. When we returned to the barracks we did not tell anyone what we had witnessed." A few days later the Rangers pulled out of the camp, bearing with them images that obviously have haunted some for their entire lives.

According to Bradley, when the Third Army overran the first death camp at Ohrdruf, Patton insisted his colleagues view it. "You'll never believe how bastardly these Krauts can be," he said, "until you've seen this pesthole yourself." Subsequently, he forced townspeople to march through the installation. Afterward, the mayor of nearby Gotha and his wife hanged themselves.

Carl Ulsaker as a company commander in the 95th Division, moved into the outskirts of Dortmund. "The area through which we passed consisted of a maze of steel mills and factories that had been bombed into twisted ruins by heavy air raids. The devastation wrought by these raids had even altered the landscape so that I found it difficult to navigate. Roads had been obliterated and man-made objects so badly destroyed that they were unrecognizable."

Except for a roadblock that required a tank to discourage the Germans who manned it, the Americans met no opposition. In the stygian darkness of a rain-sodden night, they marched down a broad boulevard to the central square of the eighth-largest German city. "We moved in silence," recalled Ulsaker, "calling for no supporting fires to precede us. Somewhere in the distance off to our right, occasional volleys of artillery fired by some unknown unit lit up the horizon like summer heat lightning. We met no enemy, the Germans apparently having the good sense to seek shelter in such unpleasant weather."

On the following day the GIs marched toward the Ruhr River, again with no sign of the foe. "One of my flank guards emerged from some bushes on the right side of the road with information that just beyond a patch of woods on the other side of the bushes he had come upon a military encampment with several hundred German soldiers drawn up in parade ground formation with weapons neatly stacked. Noting that they obviously were not prepared to fight, he had approached the commander, a colonel who stood in front of his troops. The latter informed my scout he was prepared to surrender his entire command, but would do so only to an officer of his equivalent rank. Taking a squad and a machine-gun crew with me, I accompanied the flank guard to the German camp. I approached the colonel, who saluted and restated his proposition.

"'Colonel,'" I said, "'I'm the senior officer in our advance guard; no officer of your rank will be along for hours. I'm in a hurry. You can either surrender to me or take the consequences.' I pointed toward my machine gun and rifle squads, who had taken a position on the bank overlooking the scene.

"'*Ja, Herr Hauptman*, I surrender to you,'" he responded wisely. Whereupon I designated two men to escort the new POWs to the rear and two more to guard the weapons piled on the parade ground. " Ulsaker resumed the march toward the objective by the Ruhr River. Impatient to finish the mission, he joined an advance party as it entered some woods. "Suddenly a whistle blew and about a platoon of German infantrymen popped up from concealed foxholes all around us. A lieutenant walked over and said, 'I surrender my command.'

"'I accept,' I responded with relief, embarrassed at having nearly been caught in a clever ambush, then added, 'Why did you surrender? You had us surprised.'

"'I know,' he answered, 'but the Americans are there just across the river,' pointed toward the Ruhr, now visible in the distance. 'We are caught here in a vise. The situation is impossible for us.' I found this characteristic of the German. They were excellent tacticians and would fight hard until the situation became hopeless. Then they either retreated or surrendered."

Two days later, 12 April, the day President Franklin D. Roosevelt died, the battalion commander formed the outfit to announce the news and have a moment of prayer for the late commander in chief. That day also ended combat for Ulsaker and his people. With the Ruhr pocket closed, the front was now 150 miles away, where Americans in the west and Soviets in the east were closing on the Elbe River.

In the air, Cary Salter, with the 354th Fighter Group, patrolled the skies protecting the spearheads of Patton's Third Army. Ordinarily, few if any German aircraft attempted to interfere, but on 2 April, a coterie of Luftwaffe rose to challenge the Americans. "I was the wingman for Andy Ritchey and I saw four 190s below. I gave him a little space to go after them when I saw eight more. I called out, 'Watch out, Andy, the whole damn Luftwaffe is down there.' We were coming down on 'em, maybe 400 miles an hour. I got some hits on one and then he bailed out. I was coming head-on another, but I ran over him and had to pull up. Meanwhile Ritchey shot down three 190s. On the way home I came on an ME 109 and shot it down. I later heard Patton said we should have gotten a Medal of Honor for protecting his people."

On 4 April he took off from a strip at Wiesbaden for the first fighter mission to originate east of the Rhine. "This was an armed recon mission where we would search out and attack targets such as trains, motor transport, or anything supporting the war effort, while always looking for enemy aircraft. We had not gone very far when we came to an area of a good bit of ground fighting. This was not what we were looking for; this was what P-47s worked on. One of our fellows ahead was hit and killed. I don't know if he was shot down by our own forces or the Germans. About the same time, tracers were coming by me from off my left wing. I heard a loud WHAP! and hardly felt anything. One bullet went into the left side just a foot or two behind my seat. It hit my radio and put it out of commission and all of my maps had come out of place, out of reach." Salter turned around and headed in the general direction from which he took off. He eventually found his home field and when the mechanics inspected the damage, they diagnosed the pieces of the spent bullet as most likely from an American .50 caliber.

Salter said he was surprised to learn that some flyers dreaded missions and wondered whether they could strafe enemy soldiers who were caught in the open. "The enemy was the enemy and if we didn't kill him, he would kill us. We knew we were killing people when we shot down planes. I don't know any of our guys who lost sleep over it. On the other hand, we never shot at a pilot in a parachute, although three times I could have."

Bill Kunz, with the artillery for the 3d Division, crossed the Main River near Schweinfurt, the ball-bearing center where the Eighth Air Force lost so many planes early in the war, but now was in shambles. Flanked by old comrades from the 45th and 36th Divisions, the 3d advanced upon Nürnberg, still girded by numerous 88s and antiaircraft weapons now leveled as ground fire. "We entered Nürnberg April 21," said Kunz. "The city was flattened by combined Air Force and artillery action. Still, resistance was heavy. A lot of it, Hitler Youth and other civilians using individual rifle fire and *Panzerfausts*, (one-shot bazookas).

"Our section was about one-third in the city and laying wire from the OP over heaps of rubble. I needed a length of line and spotting a Kraut line I cut into it. It turned out to be electrical and live! It knocked me right off my rubble pile into the street. A few blocks away the OP was under sniper fire. It was located in a relatively high building remnant and had taken a casualty from rifle fire some distance away. One of the infantry squads had entered the building and fired into the upper floor. The 'enemy' turned out to be children—fully armed—none older than possibly twelve or fourteen. Two were girls, fanatical, ready to die for the Führer. On the other hand, many of the older men, pressed into service, were happy to surrender."

Stan Newman, a late replacement for the 162d Fighter Squadron, flew mostly recon missions. As a wingman it was his job to watch for enemy planes. "We flew in conjunction with the French who had Spitfires," said Newman. "The P-51 looked like an ME-109 and I had a friend shot down by a Spitfire. One time when some Spitfires came after us I rocked my wings up so they could see the big airscoop of a P-51. At the battle for Nürnberg, I spotted an ME-262 [German jet fighter]. I dove on him and had never flown a P-51 that fast. But just before I got within range he went—pssst, and was gone. I saw black puffs and thought it was flak. But there was another one of them up above and I'd taken the bait. Luckily, I could outturn him with a P-51.

"As we moved east, we picked up our tent city, moved to Mainz, then Wiesbaden, a German fighter strip with wrecked 109s and 190s all over the place, and finally a permanent Luftwaffe base near Nürnberg. This was luxury; flush toilets, hot water, two pilots to a room, and displaced Ukrainian girls as maids. Actually, we hardly ever saw the Luftwaffe in the air. But on one of the last days of the war, when we were flying at lower altitude than usual, we got bounced by FW 190s. Each of us shot one down. Mine put his gear down and rocked his wings to show he was going to surrender and he landed at our base. They surrounded him like he was Lindbergh at Le Bourget. I then flew another mission and came across this two-engine plane. I got him pointed west and he landed at our airfield when it was almost dark. It was a high-ranking German officer with his wife, daughter, dog, and an aide. I got a souvenir .25-caliber pistol."

Captain Charles MacDonald, wounded in mid-January with I Company of the 2d Division's 23d Infantry Regiment, returned the first week of March to a new command, G Company. He crossed the Rhine in boats uneventfully. The division was part of a combined operation of the U.S. Ninth and First Armies that snared 317,000 prisoners in the Ruhr Pocket. Said MacDonald, "As infantrymen we would have many another anxious moment in the war, but never again would we face a cohesive enemy front."

MacDonald's people pressed on against sporadic resistance, crossing the old German border with the Sudetenland, first annexed by Hitler and then Czechoslovakia proper. The stream of surrendering enemy swelled to flood stage. "As our column advanced down one side of the highway, a ragged column of Germans in horse-drawn wagons, dilapidated German Army vehicles, civilian automobiles, bicycles, and on foot met us coming down the other side. Some had their families with them. All had thrown away their weapons . . . The Germans were running from the Russians to surrender to the Americans.

"The traffic became almost a hopeless mass of milling people. Regiment would take no more POWs—division said their POW cages were overflowing and would accept no more from regiment." His colonel invited Mac-Donald to ride with him into Pilsen, amid a deliriously joyful celebration. "The news came by radio that the war was over. There was no defining our joy. Sergeant Quinn brought out the treasured keg of cognac. The next day, May 8, would be V-E Day."

Tony Vaccaro, as a member of the intelligence team with the 83d Division met up with Soviet troops. "Actually we crossed the Elbe River near Barby, north of Torgau. There were no Russians, because at that point the river turns a bit north. We had gone farther than any other American division. We were not supposed to cross, but General Macon [the division commander] was a good friend of Patton's who told him that he could continue. The Russians fired on us but most of them were drunk, they had no uniforms or helmets. They'd been told the Americans would not be on this side of the Elbe so I don't blame them. Only after about four or five days of sporadic shooting at us—we didn't return fire—did we get together, around 7 May.

"That night I went with a patrol to get information and we left at one o'clock with our faces painted black. Beyond a town called Zerf on the east side of the Elbe, we didn't meet any Germans. We could almost have walked to Berlin. The Germans were all hiding themselves. We found not much information other than some tanks knocked out by the Air Force. We came back about about 5:00 A.M., went to sleep. About eight or nine someone shook me, "Wake up, Mike, the war is over. It was 8 May."

For many of the American POWs liberation preceded V-E Day. After the Germans repulsed Task Force Baum they shut down the camp and marched the prisoners off. Alan Jones, his feet in wretched shape, remembered, "We reached Nürberg on 5 April. It had been badly bombed and the citizens spit on us and yelled epithets. We looked up and saw B-17s filling the horizon. The last ones in the group dropped a stick near us, killing the captain of our guards, wounding fifty or sixty american prisoners, including Colonel Cavender who was with us. During the march we traveled mostly at night because fighter planes patrolled the skies like police. We organized ourselves into syndicates of two and three to divide responsibilities. Just before daybreak one man would get us sleeping space in a barn, another would look for food to steal, and a third might try to pick up material that could be fashioned into weapons for use during an escape try.

"Our chance came between Nürnberg and the Danube. We were in a barnyard and the air force man and I noticed there were no guards around. We nodded to one another and then hid in a ditch. When the others moved out, we beat it, going east one day, then south and west to outguess the Germans. We became very hungry and knocked on a farmhouse door. The woman let us in, fed us bread, jam, and milk. There was a German staff sergeant, recuperating from the Russian front there. We all talked in English, and I still had on my lieutenant's bars and insignia, but nobody tried to turn us in. When we left, they gave us each half a loaf of bread.

"Still trying to reach our own lines, we heard artillery far off to the west. Late at night we reached a little town, jammed with SS troops. Before we could pass through, they caught us. We were marched about two miles and met the same column from which we escaped. The guards simply accepted us, stuck us back in line and off we went."

"On 2 May, we came to a place with signs in German that said, in effect, this is a restricted town. Any German who remains four hours must turn in his weapon to the provost. Our senior officers told us it can't be much farther. But some like me said, 'To hell with it. We're not going on.' We sat down on the curb. I wasn't there for more than a few hours when I looked up and there was a young kid, carrying an M1, chewing gum. Then I saw more and more of our kind of steel helmets. They rounded us all up. We looked more like displaced persons than officers. They threw some K rations to us and two-and-a-half-ton trucks carried us off to a regimental field hospital. I washed for the first time in months. The GIs who found us went off to a bitter fight with those SS troops who had picked us up. Seventeen days later, I was aboard a steamer, bound for the U.S."

Lyle Bouck, held in a riding stable, after being seized with the remnants of the task force, received two pieces of sausage and a chunk of bread before a brief train ride. From there he went on the road, through Nürnberg, escaping the B-17s that clobbered the column, with Alan Jones. With Matthew Reid, a captive from the 99th division he sought to escape as they approached the Danube. Caught again, Bouck was incarcerated at Moosburg with thousands of others until 29 April, when elements of the 14th Armored, which had freed Abe Baum, brought his release.

At the end of March, John Collins, captured in the Ardennes, and POW companions were laboring at a brick factory. After an air raid on the railroad next to their camp, Collins watched, "Jerries whipping some prisoners dressed in stripes and I mean whipping them! We were standing by the fence and yelled at the guards, but they ignored us. In one of the bombings, the planes dropped leaflets stating they intended to bomb the place off the map. Four of us decided we couldn't take any more of this and formed an escape plan. Very simple—wait until dark, enter the big crater by the fence, and crawl through, digging if required. Sometimes the guards walked the path between the fences, but we would take our chances. During the bombing, the smoke was so thick you could not see a damn thing."

On 1 April at 9:30 P.M. they made their break. "We made it through some small brush and into the city streets, where we separated as planned. Sergeant Vernon Hunt, who spoke four or five German dialects plus some Polish and Italian, and myself—English only, took one side of the street. Corporal Thomas Keneshea, a nice kid who could steal the Jerries blind, and T/4 Elmer George, almost deaf in one ear from concussion, but who seemed not to know what fear was went down the other side. We had almost gotten through town when we heard marching troops and ducked into a doorway. They came down the street, a light flashed, and a lot of yelling started. A German came out of the door where we were to see what the commotion was about. He and Hunt had quite a conversation. Hunt told him we were kriegies, and we were going home. The fellow did not question us and I kept my mouth shut."

Three days later, they were caught while attempting to cross a bridge. "The commander in charge asked this guard why he did not put us in the canal like they did the airman. They were Volksturm—civilian guards. They seated us against the wall, everyone returned to their posts except for seven or eight sleeping on the floor. Hunt and I stayed awake, placing lice on our knees and flipping them on the sleeping guards."

He and Hunt were taken to Stalag XI B. The guard who accompanied them gave them his food as he put them aboard the train to the camp, inhabited mostly by French and British POWs. On 11 April, Collins noted, "We were unofficially liberated. All the guards left their posts and the gates were torn off their hinges." Rather than flee, the captives waited for Allied troops.

On 13 April, the senior British officer at the stalag sent around a message stating that President Franklin Delano Roosevelt had died and that the British wanted to share in the grief of the Americans. On 16 April the "Irish army" [Irish members of the British forces] liberated Collins. "Men who have gone through hell for many months, in some case years, are like wild men. Grown men crying and giving thanks to their God." The Britons included Collins and any other Americans in the evacuation, flying them to an RAF base in England. "The English have treated us royally, feeding us one meal a day, a continuous meal from the time we arise till we leave." Collins was designated a malnutrition case, having lost just about one-third of his original 150 pounds.

Frank Raila also finally engineered his own freedom. Toward the beginning of April he was in a group of prisoners that included both Americans and Britons. Temporarily, they were held in a soccer field, surrounded by a low barbed-wire fence. Raila fell into conversation with two Welshmen and they were game for an escape try. "The guards were patrolling, but some of the Brits stopped them and offered cigarettes along with conversation. While they were distracted, it gave us time to slip away. We went separately, crawling under the wire, then running. We had planned to meet under a haystack we'd seen at dusk, but couldn't find it. We hid ourselves as best we could and when the sun came up, the haystack was only about fifty feet away. There was a large woods nearby, and we slept there the first day.

"At night we saw in the distance the glow from Leipzig being bombed. We headed in a direction that kept it on our right. Then we heard voices. They were eight to ten Russian slave laborers. At first we were scared of each other, but then they hugged us. They had made a homemade brew, a kind of vodka. Everyone was stewed, some lay on the ground puking. They shared some food with us, potatoes, and then they stole a rabbit and cooked it. I ate pieces of the head, eyeballs, tongue, even the brains. It was the first protein I had since being captured. We stayed with them several days. They told us the Germans were shooting anyone they found on the roads. Then a couple of the Russians ran into an American patrol. We approached them and they trained the .50s on the half-tracks at us. Once they realized we were escaped prisoners, I took off my overcoat and threw it to the slave laborers. The GIs also tossed them some Spam."

Shortly thereafter, Raila flew to Camp Lucky Strike. He quickly learned that overeating after a starvation diet adds complications. "One guy who stuffed himself with donuts died." He also found the interrogators suspicious of his claim of having escaped. Within a month, however, Raila shipped out for the States.

Spring brought a boost to the morale of Pfc. Phil Hannon at the stalag outside of Bad Orb. "The Germans were less strict in taking the correct count and were not insisting on our saluting them. On March 30, one of the older German guards remarked to me, 'Pretty soon' and raised his hands in the air indicating he would soon be the prisoner." Easter Sunday, 1 April, the sounds of small arms-fire and even the smells of war, said Hannon, reached Bad Orb. "We couldn't see the fighting. But none of us were in a hurry to go looking for it. We had lived this long and didn't want a stray bullet to get us. That day, most of the Germans melted away and by evening, there were no Germans around. The following morning, three American tanks rode over the gates of the camp and we were liberated!"

An outbreak of spinal meningitis early in March placed Ed Uzemack and others in a stalag near Bad Orb under quarantine. By the middle of the month, the sound of American artillery fire could be heard. "Liberation fever was mounting. Because of the quarantine, the Germans made no effort to move the prisoners to another camp. Bets were freely made the men would be free by Easter Sunday." On that holiday, Uzemack jotted in his diary, "Our boys may come up tonight. The men are all excited—now they are tearing the wire off the windows. We are sure to be liberated tomorrow—Happy Easter." Uzemach roused himself at 2:00 A.M. to work in the kitchen and see freedom arrive. An inmate MP draped a white flag on the clock towers. And at 8:12 A.M. Uzemack scrawled, "The first American recon car rolls into the camp. Holy Smokes!"

In Stalag Luft II near the Polish border, late in January 1945, Lu Cox and his fellow airmen inmates heard the heavy artillery from the advancing Soviet forces. Within a week, Cox walked at the head of a column of 1,800 officers and enlisted men marching south through a driving snowstorm to evade the oncoming Red troops. "It was so cold that our bread and margarine froze. Our clothes froze. Worst of all our shoes froze. To start up again after a ten- or fifteen-minute rest was sheer agony. I felt as though I was wearing iron shoes with loose gravel inside. My shoes had frozen so solidly that both of them broke in half at the balls of my feet." The men drew some consolation from the poor shape of the guards, some of whom had discarded helmets, packs, and rifles. A number simply deserted. It was a mini death march for the kriegies. Men collapsed from unhealed wounds, hunger, and disease. They either froze to death where they fell or else guards murdered them. Occasionally, prisoners carried a sick comrade to the door of a house and after knocking, left him, hoping for mercy from the inhabitants.

The torturous hike covered 100 miles. Cox saw a vast caravan of German refugees, old men and women, small children and babies, in farm wagons pulled by oxen or on foot, fleeing the Soviet advance. At the end of the nearly six-day journey, the prisoners entered a huge camp with 100,000 Allied soldiers and airmen. Only after pleas for help was minimal medical treatment given, but still a diet "unfit for pigs to eat" and a lack of medicine left men prone to dangerous, even fatal bouts of pneumonia, flu, dysentery, frostbite, and festering wounds. Release through the appearance of U.S. troops was too late to save many of the afflicted.

David Jones remembered that late in the war, the guards, increasingly jumpy, killed and wounded prisoners on the slightest pretext. In January 1945, as Soviet armies approached Stalag III, with twelve to eighteen inches of snow on the ground, word the prisoners would be shifted west circulated. "People had collected all kinds of junk with them. I had the money. When people came in you took everything from them and I had money buried all over the damn compound. When it came time to retrieve it, the ground was frozen. We were having people heat pots of water and I poured it in the area and maybe twenty minutes later you could dig. I recovered lots of the money and passed it out to various people." Evacuated to Moosburg in the vicinity of Munich, Jones survived a death march where prisoners and guards fell by the wayside. But the 3d Army freed him and his comrades.

Jim Mills, part of the Slaughterhouse-five contingent at Dresden, remained a prisoner until the final week of the war. The artillery noise boomed from the east, Russian forces surging ever deeper into Germany. On 7 May, the guards led them out to the road with the objective of surrendering themselves and their captives to American troops. German civilians, soldiers, and POWs clogged the highway. Suddenly, out of the sky a flight of a dozen Soviet planes peeled off and started to strafe the refugees. Mills saw one of the aircraft coming in his direction. He spotted an earthen ramp to a hayloft that might provide some protection.

"I had just gotten to the edge of it when the plane started firing its machine guns. Shells were hitting the ground all around me, then up the side of the barn. The plane banked right, hit a cow in the hind end." That threat passed and Mills started down the road again. Another plane dove and released a bomb. "The screaming and whistling noises got even louder, we knew it was coming right down on us." He crouched in a small stream, with a woman, a child, one German soldier, and two prisoners. Showered with dirt and debris from the blast, they escaped injury.

The area was overrun by Soviet troops. "We saw Russians carrying buckets of beer in each hand. The Russian soldiers indicated that if we wanted anything we should simply take it." Mills heard reports of rape and suicides. "Women would stop you on the street and want two fellows to spend the night. The Russians would not bother them if a fellow was present."

Slave laborers who picked up abandoned machine guns amused themselves with random bursts. Some British prisoners arranged for a train to haul POWs to their own forces. Mills, other prisoners, slave laborers and their female friends piled on. But the engine soon shunted off to a sidetrack. The famished prisoners stole some chickens and that aroused a mob of angry farmers. A Soviet officer quieted them, then secured some larger animals to feed the train passengers. "Our group was given a bull. One of our people had a pistol and shot the animal five times in the head. It got real mad, but finally staggered and fell. In a matter of minutes the bull was cut up and shared. The meat was still warm, when I got my piece [raw]." Mills gave up on the train and started walking. He reached Pilsen and from there was directed to American troops. It was well after the last shots had been fired.

52
Penultimate Actions

Cessation of fighting in Europe meant nothing to those embroiled in the final confrontations with the Japanese on Okinawa and in the Philippines. As platoon leader with G Company of the 1st Marine Regiment, during the first week of May, Bob Craig and his men were on a reserve status when the Japanese opened a counteroffensive. It began with a predawn seaborne expedition that sought to place Japanese soldiers behind the Marine lines. Leathernecks on G's right flank dealt with the threat. "We knew something was going on," says Craig, "because Navy star shells and land-based flares lit up that area all night long.

"The next morning, Jim Paulus, the company exec, came up from the CP to see how things were. He looked over our left flank and saw a little smoke coming up from down below. He said to me, 'I think some gook is cooking chow down there.' I replied I didn't think so; it was probably some timbers in the cave still smoldering from yesterday's burnout by the tanks, but that I'd check it out."

Craig approached the area from his ridge position. "As I looked over the edge, I saw a Jap at the entrance to the cave. At the same time he looked right up at me. I quickly pulled a hand grenade from my pocket, yanked out the safety pin, released the activator handle, counted a fast one-two, and dropped it. It had hardly left my hand before it went off. After the handle flew off, only three seconds elapsed before the grenade exploded. Of course the Jap had ducked back into the cave when he saw me, but my concern was the apparently fast fuse.

"Jim Paulus and I immediately went back to the command CP to check the supply of grenades. We found that they had sent up a new model with three-second fuses, instead of the original five-second models we had been using. No one had advised us concerning the new model and I would have been killed if I had held onto it for the time we had been trained to do with the five-second model. The reason for holding on was to avoid giving the Jap time enough to pick up the grenade and throw it back as they had done earlier in the war. I warned all my men to check the fuse model numbers on what they had and any new ones they got."

"About ten o'clock that night, I saw a smoke screen thrown up on Hill 60 [in front of Craig's position on Hill Nan]. I used the phone to call for an emergency barrage because it looked like the Japs were either going to make a night attack or were making troop movements behind the smoke screen. Within less than one minute the first of thirty rounds came over and appeared to burst right overhead, not in the draw where they were supposed to fall. I thought the FO had made a miscalculation in laying in the target because the rest of the rounds burst in similar fashion.

"No attack came and the next morning I got with the FO to find out what had happened. He explained that the shells had proximity fuses that caused them to explode so many feet above the ground, throwing shrapnel into anything or anyone below. We had suffered no injuries or death from this event, solely because howitzers fire at high-angle trajectories. The shells we thought were landing among us actually burst as they came down on the forward slope of Hill Nan. It was another near miss for my platoon." Like the shorter timed grenades, the incident illustrates the dangerous short-circuits of information and coordination that confound the vast enterprise of war.

Craig's 3d platoon jumped off around 10:00 A.M. seeking to make its way past Hill 60. "We didn't get very far before a counterattack by Jap mortars stopped us in our tracks. The 1st platoon then tried to relieve the pressure on us, but it, too, was hit by Jap mortars. Only fourteen escaped without injury. [Forty-nine officers and enlisted men ordinarily make up a Marine infantry platoon but the number available by this time was somewhat less.]"

Those in command committed the 2d platoon of G Company, but everyone was forced to fall back, and needed tank and heavy machine guns even to accomplish a successful retreat. The second day of the battle produced similar results, large numbers of casualties and a retreat back to the foxholes from which the attack was originally launched. At midnight, the Japanese tried to overrun the position. "When this battle started," says Craig, "I was off watch trying to get some badly needed sleep. My runner Lecklightner and another rifleman were on watch—we were using three men in a foxhole to avoid what had happened earlier on Hill Nan. Leck later told me he couldn't arouse me, presumably because I was so exhausted, but I didn't believe him and reamed him out. I have no recollection of that night, and, thank God, those two with the rest of the platoon stopped the counterattack.

"About 4:00 A.M., when it was over, I came to, probably because the sudden silence prodded my inner senses. I saw dead Japs all over our area, maybe eighteen or twenty. As a matter of security, Leck and I ventured out of our foxhole to check them out and make sure none were faking dead. Sure enough, one was lying on his side, still holding onto his rifle. When I kicked the bottom of his foot he flinched, then tried to rise up and shoot me. The slugs from my Tommy gun knocked him back down."

The Marines renewed their drive and the battalion with G Company advanced southeast toward Dakeshi and Wanna Ridges, natural ramparts that guarded the town of Shuri and the anchor of the defenses bearing its name. Craig became pinned down by a Nambu machine gun in a large shell hole, half full of water. With him were Leck and a wounded marine. "I concluded we were going to be there for a while because there was no cover and we would not leave the wounded man there by himself. One of our tanks appeared and I attracted his attention. The tank commander told me he would drive the tank right over our hole, open up the escape hatch in its bottom, and take the wounded man up inside. He did this and then Leck and I crawled out on the side of the tank where we were not exposed to Jap fire. We walked back to a little knoll with the tank and waited for a corpsman and stretcher-bearers. I could see bullets bouncing off the side of the tank. I hoped there was no antitank gun nearby because the tank just sat there protecting us."

After four days, the strategists determined the position of the 2d Battalion untenable and under cover of darkness the Marines retreated. "The happy surprise for us," says Craig, "was that we continued to march back to a rest area. For the next four days we got some cooked meals, daily showers, and brand-new clothing. We had been wearing the same uniforms for forty-four days and mine just about stood up by itself. We also received replacements for the three platoons, and, in addition, two new platoon leaders. But the slot of executive officer was not filled, which indicated a shortage of experienced officers."

Jim Moll, as an acting platoon sergeant in A Company of the 7th Marine Regiment, and his unit had been pinned down by artillery a day or so after they relieved the 27th Division soldiers. "I told Sgt. Vern Smith, acting as platoon guide, we were all going to be dead ducks unless we did something soon. With deadly fire coming in from behind us, the only way out would be with a few tanks to cover our rear. I told Smitty that whoever tried to get back to headquarters had a very slim chance because he had to run along the ridge we were on, run down through the draw, and climb the only footpath up to the higher ridge. I told Smitty I would go, but he insisted it would be better if I stayed with the platoon. He took off his pack to lighten the load and shook hands with me. A few minutes later, word came back to me that Smitty was killed.

"I dropped my pack and took off. When I got to the spot where Smitty was hit, they opened up on me with heavy machine guns and mortar fire. I dove into a small, shallow hole that left my feet and legs exposed. I felt two bullets hit my left shoe, but no pain. A few seconds later, a mortar exploded next to the hole. The blast knocked the stock off my weapon and me cold. When I came to, I jumped up and kept running until they tackled me. The bullets had passed right through the heel of my shoe but barely nicked me. Later, just before dusk, the Marines dropped smoke shells and got everyone off the ridge.

"That evening, we could see the Japs building up a heavy concentration of troops on a ridge about 200 to 300 yards in front of us. I had never seen such a massing of Jap troops and I was concerned because we had no protection on our right flank. I had to send a man back to bring me a telephone so I could get some artillery support. Our machine gunners wanted to open up on the Japs, but I knew then all hell would break loose. I had them hold back until I got the phone. The Japs started to blast hell out of us with their artillery and I finally contacted the 11th Marine Artillery. Unfortunately, I had no map to pinpoint our position. The Marine at the other end said they would fire three rounds and I should let him know where they landed. But with all of the Jap shells I couldn't hear anything at first. Then during a short pause in the action, I thought I heard the three more rounds they fired way off in the distance. After about a dozen more tries, shells began landing between us and the enemy. I told them to start at that point and work their way outward on a path about 400 yards wide. I never witnessed such a masterly display of artillery. They literally blew the Japs off the hill."

On 11 May, Gen. Lemuel Shepherd, CG of the 6th Marine Division, signaled for the tanks to lead the way as the 22d Marine Regiment led off the assault. Exposed to enemy artillery for a distance of 3,000 yards of level ground, the Marines slogged on through the mud until they reached the Asato River estuary, which lay in front of the city of Naha. The assault teams paid heavily; the spearhead Company C of the 22d lost 35 killed and another 68 wounded from the original 256-man contingent.

Instead of focusing upon the town, the strategists concentrated on Sugar Loaf Hill, a citadel of well-armed, well-dug-in Japanese troops who could count on additional firepower from comrades dug in on two lesser neighboring slopes. For five days, men from the 6th Marine Division battled to reach the heights of Sugar Loaf. Captain Martin "Stormy" Sexton's K Company from the 4th Marine Regiment said, "When we encountered the Japanese MLR [main line of resistance] it was vicious, hand-to-hand combat. And to aggravate the situation, the heaviest fighting coincided with the rainy season."

Harry Manion had a front-row seat to observe the butchery. "Moving forward was slow; the infantry were catching all kind of hell from the deeply dug-in enemy. The caves were a big problem. We used everything we had against them, white phosphorus, bull-dozers, flame-throwers and any other available ordnance. Throw in a smoke grenade and watch for where the smoke comes out the air openings. Pump in gasoline and bang. Some caves had many levels and complex entrances. There were no simple solutions, but we continued to underestimate the Oriental fighter. He can dig."

In the center of the American offense the 77th Division stood alongside the 1st Marine Division. While other Army units frequently expressed resentment toward the leathernecks, the Statue of Liberty Division troops believed they were respected by the Marines. Buckner Creel of the 77th notes that on Guam, they served operationally under the III Marine Amphibious corps. "We had no unforseen problems and unlike the fiasco on Saipan, things went easily. The III Phib commander, Maj. Gen. Roy Geiger was a much smoother commander than Howling Mad Smith. Furthermore, our general Andrew D. Bruce, was respected in all circles. After Guam we were known as the only division that could get along with the Marines. We did not always agree with their tactics. They seemed to use more 'frontal' assaults than we. We preferred fire and maneuver [a tactic scorned by Patton]. In their defense, many situations in the Pacific, frontal assault was the only possible thing to do."

The enemy occupied the high ground in the form of hills called Chocolate Drop and Wart. and the Japanese soldiers protected by a deep trench pumped bullets at the oncoming infantrymen. The GIs fell back more than once. Buckner Creel attempted to rally and direct his men. "While running across an open area, I would be chased by a Nambu machine gun that failed to 'lead' me correctly. The third time I crossed, he managed to shoot the heel off my combat boot." Along with Creel's G Company, E and F from the 2d Battalion had also absorbed brutal blows. "In spite of the heroics on the soldiers in G Company," says Creel, "we were now down to two officers and forty men. They formed the battalion into a 'provisional company' by consolidating E, F, and G. We had a total of only seventy-nine effectives. The World War II strength of a rifle company was 6 officers and 196 men ordinarily, more than 200 total. There should have been 600 troops. I was designated the company commander, although the COs of E and F were senior to me in rank." [The 3d Battalion of the 306th, in no better condition than the 2d also formed into a provisional unit and with Creel's group composed a single makeshift battalion.]

The ordeal reduced the effective fighting force even below the number seemingly available to fight. "I don't recall any men who broke and ran," said Creel. "But it is an axiom of combat that it is probably better to wound your enemy than kill him. Because it will take two or more people off the battlefield removing the injured soldier. We did have some problems then getting back people who had assisted the wounded to the rear. They would be gone for a day or so, sometimes because they could not physically return, but sometimes because they dawdled."

At Flattop Hill, Company K, with Larry Gerevas, was shattered by a series of futile attempts to wade through an avalanche of grenades, mortar rounds, and bullets. "I could see the squad leader and I was listening to his instructions. Suddenly, he seemed to explode. The upper part of his torso was gone.

A moment later his helmet fell from above and rolled down the hill. A mortar round had made a direct hit on him. We were all sickened to see what was left of him." When the last officer on his feet fell dead with a bullet through his forehead, Gerevas said he and his buddies felt this was an impossible mission.

"An officer from another unit came up the hill to us and ordered us to go over the top. He looked like he had just come from some rear area because he was so clean and neatly dressed. We had lost nearly our whole company in this suicidal, frontal attack and weren't about to go to a certain death for this guy. We all refused. He became very angry and demanded that we follow his orders or we would all face a court-martial. We told him to go to hell. The threat of being court-martialled didn't sound very frightening to any of us at this point. As he stood there, looking at this motley group of weary, unshaven, determined, armed men, he must have realized how hollow his threats were. He turned away, went down to the base of the hill and left the area. A short time later we were pulled off the hill and sent to the rear. It was May 17 and in two days we had lost nearly 85 percent of our company."

The torrents of blood gushing from the 77th Division prompted a distraught Sgt. Alfred Junkin, who assumed command of a unit, to write 77th division commander, Gen. Andrew Bruce. "I believe it is proper to report to you directly on my actions as 1st Platoon, C Company leader from 6 a.m. May 17 until 12 noon May 18 due to the fact that Lt. Lusk was KIA shortly after our objective was taken. Also, I understand Lt. Campbell and Sgt. Stanick since have both been KIA so I am not aware as to who is in command of C Company."

Junkin recounted some of the fight. "The Japs began to pop up on our right flank and we shot them down like ducks. Then all hell broke loose with intense mortar and MG fire punctuated by accurate sniper fire. Sergeant Chambers spotted a Nip AA gun on a knoll seventy-five yards away and blasted the crew. Sergeant Kelly was superb in encouraging thirty replacements to dig in deep and pick off Nip targets. I was one of the first to be hit, a mortar fragment punctured my cheek. . . . During the next half hour [Private first class] McCauley and Sergeant Kelly were KIA. We were getting no effective supporting artillery or mortar fire on our right flank and I dropped back to the platoon CP twenty-five yards to report to Lieutenant Lusk. I found him dead in his foxhole from a direct mortar hit."

Junkin described the slight shifts in position he directed in order to protect his diminishing forces. While he praised the mortar work of nearby E Company, he remarked that "our own artillery dropped several shells in our area" but then praised the work of some other big guns and the tanks. "I was up and down the line, trying to encourage our new men to hold fast, by pointing out troops far below who were trying to pass through us and telling them that water and ammo would be brought in at night and the wounded taken out.

"As night came, H Company withdrew their heavy machine guns, leaving our left flank exposed. By now there was no one left on the ridge except twenty men of C Company. . . . We drew a tight line, shifted the wounded so there was not more than one in each hole. Sergeant [Victor] Winschuh set up his light machine gun in the center facing the crest of the ridge. There was nothing we could do except crack down on targets as they came up within twenty or thirty yards, and pray. We did plenty of both.

"A grenade fell into the foxhole next to the CP that Del Rosso and I shared. I pulled out [Pvt. Andrew] Mezines but could not save [Pvt. Arlo] Mellberg. Our thirty replacements showed great courage, but were too new to the job. One of them saw two Japs who got Mellberg thirty feet away. His finger froze on the trigger. Another saw a Nip standing on the horizon and shouted wildly at others to shoot the man, but he had his own rifle in his hand. Another sees Nips a few yards from his hole, aims, and fires and . . . empty rifle. In the excitement he had emptied his magazine and forgotten to reload.

". . . I ask nothing for myself but I would like to see every one of my men on the line that night receive a citation. When 20 men stave off a Jap regiment, it is certainly beyond the call of duty." Junkin seized the opportunity to call for promotions for several whom he felt deserved recognition that was denied because of turnovers in commanders. The sergeant then expressed his deep misgivings over the exigencies of the war. "The record speaks for itself . . . [the victory] belongs to the 77th and especially C Company, but I deplore the necessity for taking green recruits who hardly know how to load a rifle into combat . . . I know you [Gene Bruce] have the interest of the men in our battalion at heart and believe you will agree that these teenage youngsters fight with great courage, but are just too green and inexperienced to do the job." Junkin himself received the Distinguished Service Cross. Several men earned Silver or Bronze Stars and the entire platoon was given a Presidential Unit Citation.

The flow of replacements for the GIs included OCS graduate Si Seibert, assigned to the 382d Regiment of the 96th. His initial fears of acquitting himself satisfactorily vanished with a small success in an attack. After accepting compliments from company commander Capt. Cledith Bourdeau, Seibert said he felt relieved. "My first firefight had gone better than I dared hope. It appeared that I had been accepted by the troops. In fact, I got the impression that the men were hungry for leadership, they willingly gave their loyalty and confidence to each officer placed over them until such time as he might prove himself inept, or for some other reason unacceptable. As a result, the men had accepted me with far less reserve than I had anticipated."

Much of the euphoria that gripped him earlier disappeared the following day. "Just as we were looking for a night position, there was a flurry of shots to our front. I watched in horror as one of my soldiers fell to the ground. It was obvious from the way he fell that he was dead. It was a traumatic thing for me. He was the first of my men to be killed and it was the first time that I felt responsible for the death of someone. I didn't even know his name. Suddenly, I was aware of a strange dichotomy in my thinking in combat. Killing the enemy did not bother me, though I took no pleasure or pride in it. There was no sense of responsibility for the enemy's death; it was simply the job to be done. On the other hand, the death of one of my men, although I was not directly responsible for it, placed a heavy burden on me; I could never, and have never, gotten over that feeling. I actually cried a little when that first man was killed, but soon got myself in hand. Nobody noticed.

"It is a feeling I have never ceased to have in combat [Seibert served in Korea and Vietnam]. Where had I erred that this individual was killed? Was my plan or my leadership lacking? This is probably healthy if you do not let it overwhelm you. As a result, you analyze plans, orders or leadership more carefully in order to make the best possible decision. I did not go into a deep depression or permit it to disturb me to the point that I couldn't think of anything else, but it was a difficult thing to accept."

However awful the losses inflicted on the Americans, the military resources of the Japanese eroded with each attack. The mighty waves of kamikazes that peaked during April and early May dropped off sharply as the third month of Operation Iceberg approached. But even on a lesser scale they rocked the picket ships. On 27 May, the destroyers assigned to Picket Station #5 were the *Braine* and the *Anthony*. Clyde Van Arsdall, the *Anthony* skipper, a 1934 USNA graduate, commanded a veteran, well-trained crew. "We had had our first opportunity to talk to people who had actually been under kamikaze attack right before Iwo Jima," recalled Van Arsdall. "There was no consensus as to what to do under these attacks. Everybody seemed to have their own ideas. There was a bit of an argument, whether you should go at high speeds or lower ones where you had better control of the battery [antiaircraft guns]. I was one who joined the 'speed demons.' If there was an attack imminent, we were at twenty-five knots or better. We tried to keep incoming planes on our beam to allow the maximum number of guns clear shooting. Once a fellow started in, we would then maneuver hard right or hard left to get into a turn. The idea was that when a guy made his decision to come at us in a certain way and we got into a turn, he couldn't keep up with it so we received some extra shooting time while he maneuvered either astern or on the quarter." He concluded, "Keep the guns ready and shoot like hell."

The *Anthony* had started its picket station screen duty with some success against several nighttime prowlers. When the *Braine* relieved another destroyer and became *Anthony*'s partner. about daylight, radar picked up four planes coming from the north. "It was accepted," says Van Arsdall, "that if the picket station was attacked, it was every man for himself, with number one, don't have a collision with anybody. We immediately ordered General Quarters. There was a solid overcast, my guess is 2,000-3,000 yards. Horizontal visibility was very good, there was no sea. *Braine* was clear, the LCI gunboats [accompanying them to add firepower] were out maybe 4,000 yards and we began to open up a bit on *Braine* and build up some speed.

"Combat kept reporting, 'They're coming straight in toward the picket station' followed shortly by, 'it looks like they're breaking into two groups.'" The enemy aircraft followed a course to take them directly over the pair of destroyers as the distance between the ships spread to 2,500 to 3,000 yards, as they traveled roughly in the same direction. *Anthony*'s combat intelligence now advised two planes were headed for it while the others would be on the starboard. Fire-control radar began tracking the nearest ones.

The planes passed over the picket station and then Van Arsdall received word they had turned and fire control had a solution. "I couldn't see them through the overcast," remembered Van Arsdall, "but I immediately gave the 'Commence Firing.' *Anthony* opened up with its forward guns, the main battery. I started turning to get our after guns cleared. Things started to happen very fast. I heard a report, 'we're on target' and wanting to get the planes on our broadside, turned left. About that time, a plane, on fire and smoking, came through the overcast, it went on down and splashed. A second plane headed directly toward us. I tried to keep him on the starboard beam. There was so little time left the maneuvers of the ship didn't mean anything. Our 40mms and 20mms opened up and there was really a blanket of fire going out.

"This joker came right on in. I couldn't do any more maneuvering he was so close. But he was right where we wanted him, all the guns could bear on him. Some chips flew off, but he kept coming. He actually passed over the ship, not many feet above the Number 1 stack. All of us thought he would crash into us, but he did not nose over that much. As he passed, I went to the wing of the bridge so I could watch him there. He had pulled up, just a bit to climb and turn to his left. He did a beautiful job because pieces were coming off his aircraft.

"It looked like he was in control, because he did a nice climbing left and never came out except to then put his nose down, crashing into *Braine* probably 2,500 yards from us. There was a lot of yelling and shouting, but from it I got the idea that *Braine* had been hit probably thirty seconds before this plane came down. Two kamikazes had crashed her in succession. Those who were watching said the Number 2 stack on *Braine* just disappeared. I don't know whether that was the one that came over us or the other. She was hit twice. One struck a little to the starboard of the center at the bridge, demolished the bridge, and went down into the wardroom country. A tremendous mess of the ship there and caused everyone forward of amidships on the bridge level to abandon ship.

"The second hit destroyed a fireroom, did serious damage in the engine room, and from my vantage point, the whole topside from the bridge to the afterstack was a mess. The two ships were on almost opposite courses, well clear of each other. *Braine* still was underway. What happened to the fourth plane is conjecture so far as I am concerned. I never saw it. Some on our bridge told me it had gone into the water between the two ships. We could see people from the bridge level of *Braine* jumping over the side into the water and we saw people on the ship rolling wounded off the deck, which was on fire, into the water. Many of the crew ended up in the water. Gunboats picked up some and so did we."

After a brief respite, *Anthony* returned to picket duty and on 7 June, fought off kamikazes. At dusk, a pair of Vals streaked toward the destroyer, coming in low enough to the water that they escaped interception by a combat air patrol. Pete Boyd, chief engineer for the destroyer, recalled, "When the bridge detected bogeys and sounded the GQ alarm, they also immediately rang up Flank Speed on the engine-room telegraph. This was our signal to bring up engine revolutions to maximum speed." Boyd noted that in the superheated din of the engine room in order to converse one couldn't just shout or yell. "You put your mouth close to the other guy's ear and scream. He may answer with sign language, and lip reading is almost a necessity."

Those down below could see nothing of what was happening on the surface. "In the engine control room," said Boyd, "there were two 'talkers,' ratings who wore sound-powered telephones. The first talker was on the circuit that included the topside stations. This was our only contact with the outside world. The second talker was on the circuit with all of the machinery spaces. He would repeat for them the information from the first talker. We'd get the word, 'Bogeys sighted, bearing 200 degrees, 8,000 yards.' We'd wait. Then BAM! BAM! BAM! Our main battery, the 5-inch guns would be firing. Then the report, 'He's coming our way!' and the 40s would start, FWUMP! FWUMP! FWUMP! FWUMP!. Then we'd hear the 20s— tatatatatat. By this time the first talker usually had frozen. All we could learn from him was through reading his facial expressions. The other talker would then report, 'I think he's gonna hit us,' or 'He missed us.' Only after securing from General Quarters could the machinery-space personnel emerge and learn from topside observers what had happened."

Boyd recalled the 7 June incident with the five 5-inch main battery firing and then "a good report that the first plane had been splashed at about 2,000 yards. The news on the second wasn't as good. As the ship's speed rapidly increased, the bridge was maneuvering erratically, hard left, hard right, hard left. By now the 5-inchers, the 40s, and 20s were firing everything they could. The entire ship pitched greatly as the helmsman steered an evasive pattern.

"The FWUMP FWUMP FWUMP of our 40s and the tatatatat of our 20s told us down below that the number-two Bogey was almost on us. The ship was turning hard right, then a tremendous WHAM! A very strong smell of gasoline and some smoke followed in about two seconds. The forward repair party hollered that the bow was on fire and they couldn't get pressure on the forward firemain. The vessel at very high speed turned in the other direction. As it lurched a large shower of water came down from the hatch above the chief machinist and me, dousing us completely. My immediate reaction was the firemain had been hit. I started to discuss it with the chief—screaming at him—the location of the firemain and what to relay to the repair party. Then I saw his lips and hands. He screamed back, 'Does that taste like saltwater to you?' We both screamed 'Soap!'" It was the laundry line that had ruptured."

The last week of May, Gen. Lemuel Shepherd ordered Tony Walker's Recon Company to sneak into Naha, the city on the western end of the Shuri line. Walker set up a base camp on the banks of the Asato Gawa River and a quartet of four-man teams crossed the stream to appraise the enemy strength. The interlopers bumped into Japanese patrols, exchanged a few rounds, but all of the GIs returned safely with the information that the city was not heavily defended.

On 28 May, Recon Company spearheaded an attack into Naha. "A Jap machine gun was firing through a break in one of the concrete walls surrounding most of the houses," recalled Walker. "Fuller Curtis with his squad had worked their way next to the wall. On order, each man pulled out a grenade and threw it. Then the squad all together went over the wall. When I got there, they proudly gave me a samurai sword, covered with bits and pieces of a Jap officer."

Recon settled in for what Harry Manion, one of Walker's sergeants called, "fun and a nightmare" amid the ruins. "After we cleaned out the university, bank, and other smaller buildings we found millions of yen and Japanese war bonds. Night brought in heavy artillery fire from large caves on the Oroku side of the Naha River. One time, one of our men was waving to a Marine fighter pilot coming in. The pilot shot at our man and killed him with a .50-caliber round. This was the second time Marine pilots fired at Marines on the ground. After that incident I always had a little suspicion about our air close-support Marines. We fired at him, but to no avail. Gone back to the carrier and a hot bath.

"About this time, dead at night, raining like only war can produce, we received a group of replacement Marines. Wet and miserable as Marines should be on their first night. We started switching older men with new men. The new Marines were fresh out of boot camp. Ten-day home leave and over they came. Training started in our platoon. Lessons: Don't go anywhere alone. Don't go into caves. No souvenir hunting. The next day I saw two of these Marines coming back from a souvenir search. A group of us were on a roof and I grabbed an M1 and fired three or four rounds at the feet of the Marines. They stopped, then came forward into the platoon position. Chew-out time. I believe one later shot off one of his toes." The following day, Manion spied two more recent arrivals investigating a cave. He raced after them, badly cut his head on the cave ceiling while ordering them out. Commented Manion, "It was chew out time again."

Shepherd now outwitted the defenders on the Oroku Peninsula with a seaborne assault that brought tanks and leathernecks ashore on the western point of the coast rather than striking at the base of Oroku as the Japanese commander expected. The 4th and 29th Marine Regiments began to push the foe backward. Walker's forces participated, first by seizing the island of Ono-Yama in the Kokuba estuary and then later wading out 600 yards to capture an offshore patch, Senaga Shima, disposing of a few enemy soldiers and finding many deep caves with some large artillery pieces. Meanwhile, the 22d Regiment, hitherto in reserve, entered the fray, applying pressure from the east, squeezing a dwindling pocket of resistance. With his position hopeless, his men either being cut to pieces or, in the first instance on Okinawa, surrendering in a large group (159), Admiral Ota committed suicide. By 15 June nothing remained of the Oroku defense.

Si Seibert recounted an incident in which the demands of higher echelon officers became unacceptable. "We neared a formidable escarpment made of the Yuza-Dake and Yaeju-Dake hills. The north side was steep, about 150 feet in height. The 383d fought for Yuza-Dake and was so badly mauled that our 382d was ordered to relieve two of its battalions. Our 2d Battalion took over for their 2d [Lt. Bob Muehrcke's organization] and, initially attached to the 383d, was to attack in a narrow zone to gain a foothold on the escarpment. Leading the assault was F Company, with my platoon providing the point."

At first, the advance went well and Seibert's unit gained the top of the escarpment. But as they slipped to one side to permit the remainder of the company to join them, intensive small-arms fire cracked down on them. With one soldier killed and another wounded, the platoon scrunched down behind the ridge line. Seibert peeked over the top to see a completely open field to the front, one pockmarked with bunkers, foxholes, and spider holes undoubtedly occupied by enemy soldiers prepared to spray the area with deadly results.

He consulted with his company commander, Cledith Bourdeau, who said that because of other exigencies no artillery could be brought to bear. The infantrymen would have to charge forward with only the minor aid of 60mm mortars. "The machine gun positions," said Seibert, 'seemed poorly constructed. I called for rifle grenades, but there were only three and one grenade launcher. It had been so long since the men had used them, they had gradually stopped carrying the weapon. I had failed to check this out since I assumed command and now my neglect was to be costly. None of the men left had even fired rifle grenades so I became the grenadier. Because there were no launcher sights, I used the field experience of putting my foot in the rifle sling and measuring the angle with my eye. Surprisingly, I did pretty well. The first round fell short and did no damage, but the second and third destroyed two positions.

"As I was sighting the second round, however, the platoon medic came up behind me and looked over my helmet. There was an instant report from a sniper rifle and the medic fell. he had been shot squarely between the eyes and lived only a few minutes, dying before he could be evacuated. It was obvious what the platoon was up against. I called again for supporting fire. Bourdeau told me none was available, but we had to keep moving to permit the remainder of the company and battalion to get into position. I told him it was suicide to take the platoon into that fire. I asked if there were any tanks. He said no. Finally, Bourdeau came up and looked over the situation. As I pointed out the enemy positions that permitted the Japs to cover the area in a crossfire, his radio operator looked over his shoulder. There was a characteristic report and the man fell dead. A sniper round had struck him, too, squarely between the eyes.

"Bourdeau agreed it was suicidal to continue. He went back to talk to Lieutenant Colonel Sterner, the battalion CO. He called shortly, ordering me to move out, regardless of the odds. I argued, telling him that I would not feel right if I took my platoon into certain death. Finally, he said, 'I'm giving you a direct order, Si.' 'I know you are, Cledith, but I can't obey it. We have to have some support.' There was silence on the radio. Suddenly, Bourdeau appeared, 'Dammit, Si, move out! That's a direct order. You know what it means if you fail to follow orders in the face of enemy fire.'"

Seibert acknowledged his responsibility but refused to order his platoon to advance without support. Colonel Sterner arrived and inquired of Bourdeau why the delay. The company commander explained his subordinate's reluctance. Seibert pleaded his case. "Look at those positions, Colonel. They have us in a crossfire. We have already lost three men. It is suicide to move out there until we knock out some of those positions. We need artillery or tanks." And as the lieutenant pointed out the foe's emplacements, hostile rounds whizzed overhead.

Sterner responded, "I see what you mean, but we have to get this hill and move on. Move out!" Seibert yelled to his platoon sergeant to get the GIs going and personally started to lead the advance as some of his men started to follow. But no sooner did they poke their heads over the ridge than the enemy drove them to cover with a withering slash of bullets. Seibert told the Sterner, "I can't take this platoon out there. You have to get us some support."

Grim-faced, Sterner, as Seibert remembers it, said, "You have violated a lawful order in the face of the enemy. You will have to face the consequences after this campaign is over."

"I realize that," answered Seibert. "Am I relieved of my platoon?

"No, you will continue to command. Now let's see what can be done."

As they discussed their limited options, a single tank suddenly clanked into view. Sterner and Bourdeau immediately informed the platoon leader that the tank now was attached to his platoon. Seibert explained his predicament to the tank commander, who maneuvered into a position where he could hit the enemy machine-gun positions while foot soldiers hugged his sides for protection and added their firepower.

"After he had destroyed several bunkers, he stopped. I got up on the tank deck, while drawing small-arms fire, to communicate with him. He opened a pistol port while the tank remained buttoned up. There were two more bunkers I wanted him to destroy. If they were neutralized, my platoon could take care of the foxholes and the rest of the resistance. As I was talking to him, the tank gunner spotted something and fired. My ear was about an inch from the barrel of the weapon. The concussion knocked me off the tank deck and it was five days before the ringing stopped in my ears and I could hear again. In fact, my hearing was permanently damaged, resulting in partial deafness.

"Otherwise, however, I was not hurt. The tank knocked out the two targets I had indicated. My platoon moved out, passed ahead of the tank, and swept over the area. A quick survey of the Jap defensive positions revealed it was a nest of tunnels and pillboxes completely covered by machine-gun fire on the reverse slope of the small ridge behind which we had taken cover. Had we charged over without the tank, we would have been taken in the back by those machine guns. I was glad I had stood fast to protect my platoon. They would have been wiped out if I had not refused to move out without support. But I also knew the seriousness of having disobeyed an order in combat. For the next month I lived with the dread of what would happen when the campaign ended." When the war did end, Seibert escaped with only a reprimand.

Although the enemy fought hard, the Americans squeezed the remaining defenders into ever smaller parcels of land and forced them out of their protected enclaves. George Brooks remembered a terrible scene as the last of the enemy yielded their places on the Yaeju-Dake escarpment. "There was no escape for them. We had blocked them off. The heavy-weapons company had set up their water-cooled machine guns and it seemed as if they would never stop shooting. Some of them were laughing and chortling all the while they were killing anything that moved within their field of fire. I was disgusted with their glee. It turned me off."

The 1st Division's 7th Marine Regiment was a pitiful semblance of its once-robust fighting force. Jim Moll in A Company recalls, "As we moved farther and farther south toward Kunishi Ridge, we were losing more and more men until finally we had to consolidate the rifle platoons from the entire company into a single platoon with Lt. Tom Cook as the leader and myself as platoon sergeant.

"It was about a month since I had the concussion and each day since, my physical condition was going downhill fast. I had just about run out of gas, losing my equilibrium and falling down a lot. Every bone in my body ached. I was becoming short of breath and had no more energy or endurance left. I told Cook that I thought I should turn myself in to sick bay for a few days. Maybe with some medication and a shot of something that would knock me out for a few days it would do the trick. Cook asked me to hang on a little longer and I agreed."

Don Farquhar, as a platoon leader during the march south beyond the Shuri line says, "There were no major battles, only small firefights along the way. The rains were over and we moved fast. The most interesting thing was almost all our supply had to come by air. The landscape was dotted with parachutes of different colors. But at Kunishi Ridge, as we had found earlier on Okinawa, was one more ridgeline with no room to maneuver by means of an end run."

Although his 1st Battalion of the 7th Marine Division had absorbed 125 dead and wounded in a single day at Dakeshi Ridge, Charles Owens, the kid who joined the Marines at age fourteen, says, "The battle for Kunishi Ridge was the hardest fighting I saw. The regiment took heavy casualties because of fire coming from the front and flanks while trying to go over a long open area. Colonel Edward Snedeker, the regimental commander, knew he had to do something desperate and he did. On the night of June 12, he had two companies, C and F jump off at night. This had never been done before. We thought someone had gone nuts.

"The two companies got on Kunishi Ridge okay," said Owens. "However, at daylight, the shit hit the fan. The remaining rifle companies tried to cross the open area three times to join those already on the ridge. Because of heavy losses we had to stop, although C and F needed water, ammo, and medical help."

The 1st Tank Battalion made arrangements to bring reinforcements, carry supplies, and remove wounded. Tank commander Bob Neiman explained, "The men up on Kunishi Ridge were surrounded by thousands of enemy soldiers and the Japs were mortaring, machine gunning, and grenading them. They had to have reinforcements. In the past, Marine tanks occasionally carried men into battle, but this was more significant in the outcome of the fighting than at any previous time.

"Each Sherman normally carries a crew of five, but needs only one man to drive it and a tank commander to guide it. If we removed the gunner, loader, and assistant loader, there was room for at least three men and if the ammo was removed that made room for a fourth man. On a short trip you could squeeze in a fifth Marine. Our tanks went to the designated infantry battalion where the Marine riflemen climbed in with the two-man crews and the reduced loads of ammo. The supplies for the infantry were strapped on the backs of the tanks. We began crossing the rice paddies and climbing up Kunishi Ridge, single file, like a line of ants.

"When the tanks reached the Marine positions on Kunishi, they opened the escape hatches and the riflemen crawled out through the bottom of the tank. Someone would scrape off all the ammo and other supplies from the top of the engine compartment. Marine wounded then got inside the tank or if too badly hurt they were strapped on the back along with the dead. The tanks then backed down through the valley until they could disgorge their cargo in safety. Another group of riflemen then boarded the tanks for the trip. This continued for two days."

Neiman's description fits that of the foot soldier passengers except in one respect. From their accounts, it appears that the tank commanders expected the riflemen to exit through the top of the tank. Jim Moll, the platoon sergeant in Company A of the 7th Regiment says, "I think there were only four of us with the driver and commander. We went like hell through the shellfire and as we neared our destination we heard small arms fire hitting the tank. Finally, the tank stopped and the officer said that was where we got out.

"He opened the door on the turret and as I started to climb out, machinegun bullets were hitting the door. One ricocheted off my helmet. I dropped down and asked if there were another exit. He told us about the trapdoor in the floor. Also, earlier, when I stuck my head out the turret opening, I noticed the tank was still out in the open and we'd have no kind of cover. I asked him to move in closer to the base of a vertical ridge. Reluctantly, he moved a little closer to it. One by one we stripped off our packs, canteens, etc., so we could squeeze out the trapdoor. Soon as our bodies were out of the tank, they pushed out our gear. Then we crawled out from under the tank and ran like hell to the base of this high, vertical ridge. As I was crawling out from under our tank, I saw another one nearby and the first Marine who got halfway out the turret was killed by machine-gun fire. After that, they also began to leave from the bottom."

Earl Rice received the privilege of one of these tank rides to the battlefield. "Lieutenant Cook, the other guys, and I had never been in a tank before. I could hear the bullets bouncing off the sides. I was standing beside the ladder when the tank commander ordered me to go up out the hatch. I realized the odds were against me getting out alive. Lieutenant Cook asked if there were a way out below and the tank commander said yes. Cook said that's the way we would go.

"After we left the tank, we tried to take the pinnacle of our hill. My good buddy and former squad leader, Pop Wilson, was hit in the throat by a dum dum bullet. Others were either hit or scattered back down the hill. The corpsman stayed with Pop until he passed away. I was upset, stood on the top of the hill and yelled, 'You yellow bastards! Get up here!' There was a surprised look on Lieutenant Cook's face and they all came back up. There was a Marine there, a replacement about my age who'd cracked up. Lieutenant Cook told me, 'You two take Pop back and stay there.' I protested that there wasn't anything wrong with me. I just got angry. He said, 'The less people we got up here, the more chance we'll be relieved.' We carried Wilson back and put him on a pile. The pile was over five feet, at least up to my shoulders if not higher. It was a helluva feeling to put that guy on there.

"Two Marines there told me to give them Wilson's wallet, watch, and ring. They'd see that these did not arrive before the family got the telegram about him. I found out what slimeballs they were when, a year later, someone wrote me that Wilson's family had taken out an ad in a Marine magazine asking if anyone might know where Wilson's belongings were. I did send them the rifle he took off a Jap whom he killed.

"There was a sergeant there when we brought in Wilson, a guy who looked like a poster for the Marines, but I never saw him in any bit of combat. He was giving out supplies. He says to me, 'Get back up there.' I says Lieutenant Cook told me to stay here. He says, 'You get back up there; that's an order.' He made me take the kid back with me. Cook was very angry when we came back, but he couldn't do anything about it at the time."

Charles Owens rode up onto Kunishi Ridge in the belly of a tank like the others. "The only way off was to be killed or wounded. Myself and a buddy, Jim Wolff, were put on a working party, to load the dead on trailers pulled by tanks. The bodies were wrapped in ponchos and the pile covered with a parachute. Before we finished, most of the working party had left. Wolff and

I got all of the dead on the trailers. The smell was on us for a month. It was like being on an outpost. Our supplies were dropped by parachutes from planes. We could get hit in the head because the containers would come open and cases of ammo and food fall to the ground. We just knew we were going to die on this ridge. There was no sleep. The replacements who reached us were either old or very young and not very well trained. Before you got to know them, they were dead."

Jim Moll spent nearly a week on Kunishi Ridge. "We had very little protective coverage and many casualties from grenades dropped down on us. We finally found what we thought was a way to the top and I took a squad up one morning, climbed the cliff, which I never thought I'd make in my condition. Up there, we received lots of sniper fire and our squad leader, kneeling next to me, had his whole jaw shot off. I guess they were using dum dum bullets.

"I cannot remember how the hell we got back to our platoon that night, but I know that Earl Rice carried the squad leader back to where we had climbed up that cliff. A few days later, I woke up in the field hospital. Our company was taken off the lines. I missed about two days of the whole damn battle and it bothers me even today."

Earl Rice stuck it out. "I think I became a man on Kunishi Ridge because Lieutenant Cook treated me like one. He made me a squad leader with a corporal under me. I had been the biggest shitbird in the company and he talked of me being a sergeant. I felt like I was thirty-five. I learned what discipline and responsibility were all about. When they wanted to organize petitions to leave the hill and asked me to sign, I refused.

"Later, a fellow named Birch, thirty-eight, thirty-nine years old, a replacement who had something like nine kids, because of his family, was supposed to leave the ridge. But a damn knee mortar landed in his hole. We cried for his wife and kids. There's no way an old man should have died that way.

"At this point, with all the people killed and wounded, I am only two or three men away from being platoon leader. Lieutenant Farquhar took over the company. The corporal in my squad said for us to move to the rear. As I turned around, Lieutenant Farquhar put a Tommy gun in my face and said get back. That really upset me. I may have been a screwup but I was not a coward and I thought the order to move back was his order. Subsequently, Farquhar sent me out on a few skirmishes.

"Then, June 18 Lieutenant Farquhar told us we would be relieved the next morning. That night we were pretty high up on the pinnacle with Burns and me on the flank in a hole. Arky and a new guy were in the nearest hole. I knew that during the night, the Japs would make their move. I had sixteen hand grenades around my hole plus my weapon and Burns's. After an hour or so into my watch during the night, I called over to Arky and got no answer. I called a second time. Still no answer; they were both napping. I rolled a hand grenade over, seven or eight feet from their hole and when it went off that woke them up. 'Man alive,' I yelled, 'Didn't you see them?'

"I didn't have to worry any more about them being awake during the night. Then the Japs started moving down on us. I threw about a dozen grenades all over the area. I heard some hollering and knew I hit somebody. The rest of the night there was very little sleep. The booming of the grenades kept everyone up.

"At the crack of dawn, I looked out the front for Japs, but didn't see anybody. All at once I hear someone coming over the top. It was a bunch of 2d Division Marines, in fresh uniforms. I started to prowl around, seeing what I got during the night—always the souvenir hunter. One of the 2d Marine Division guys, just coming in, got shot. I went back to my hole quick." The relieving troops belonged to the reinforced 8th Regimental Combat Team of the 2d Marine Division, in reserve from the time of a Love Day feint at the Minatoga beaches until finally capturing two small nearby islands against minimal opposition. Rice recalls his departure from Kunishi. "I wasn't moving too fast, but when I reached the place where that Marine had been hit, I did a 100-yard dash. We came off the Ridge of Death to hot food, showers—we hadn't showered from May 8 to June 18. I didn't realize until we were off the line for a few days that I had been hit, that I had shrapnel in my face. I knew I had a hole in my hand and in back; both had turned green. They put methiolate on my back, hand, and face. But the wounds stayed green."

On 18 June, as the defenders of Kunishi Ridge fell back in disarray, the Americans on the left flank of the 1st Marine leathernecks completed their mission. Bob Muehrcke and another platoon leader, Lt. Bill Frothinger, the two surviving officers of Company F, walked off the Yuza-Dake escarpment leading the handful of twenty-one GIs still on their feet. Says Muehrcke, "The men hadn't washed or shaved for the past thirty-nine days. They were exhausted, filthy dirty, their combat fatigues were coated with blood, either from their buddies or from their own bodies. All but one were wounded at least once. They were a pitiful sight, but they were alive and very proud men as they walked off the Okinawa escarpment to the reserve area. The sun was shining brightly, but they still received heavy enemy fire."

By the third week of June, the remaining defenders, their ammunition depleted, without food or water, had been squeezed into a tiny enclave. The imminent demise of the enemy resistance brought General Buckner to a forward observation post. A shell exploded nearby and drove a piece of coral into his chest, killing him. The authorities attributed the death to enemy fire, but some Americans thought it another case of friendly fire. One day after Buckner fell, Gen. Claudius Easley, the assistant commander of the

96th, known for his predilection to hang about the front lines, while pointing out the site of an enemy machine gun that had wounded his aide, took two bullets from that weapon in the forehead. Within twenty-four hours, and victory only a few days off, death in combat had claimed two general officers.

The two top Japanese generals, offered an opportunity to surrender, declined and obedient to the *Bushido* code, chose the rite of *seppuku*, self-disembowelment. For several weeks, GIs flushed holdouts from caves, but, altogether, their dead numbered 110,071 with 7,401 captured. American dead soldiers, marines, and navy personnel added up to 12,520. Wounded totaled 36,631 and nonbattle casualties were more than 26,000. The Japanese lost 7,700 planes compared to 763 American aircraft downed or destroyed. But the kamikazes sank 36 ships and damaged another 368. Few campaigns could match the savagery and destruction of Okinawa.

53
Endgame in the Philippines

Following the fall of Manila, the GIs pursued the slowly retreating enemy into a countryside hospitable to concealment, ambush, and nature-made redoubts. While the three Japanese armies of Luzon could no longer support one another or exchange men and equipment, they fought on, determined to exact as much of a blood penalty as they could before succumbing to the superior forces arrayed against them. The U.S. 6th and 43d Divisions and units from the 2d Cavalry Brigade drove the enemy soldiers concentrated to the east and northeast of Manila. Again, despite the guerrillas able to sift through the countryside, intelligence underestimated those still contesting the turf. As the commander of the 3d Battalion, Maj. Arndt Mueller of the 63d regiment, 6th division, grappled with the enemy forces along the Shimbu line in the mountainous area east of Manila. On the maps, "Hill 400" and "Hill Z" denoted the critical territory assigned to his outfit. Mueller surveyed the terrain from an observation plane, compiled data on the phases of the moon and its hours of illumination, and plotted a night attack. "The battalion, contrary to most units in the Pacific War," said Mueller, "had experience in night operations on Luzon. The troops to carry out a night attack under the circumstances possessed confidence born of experience to accomplish the mission."

Mueller commandeered as much tracer ammunition as he could for aid in directing effective fire during the dark. "We also had a standing operating procedure that on a deep operation such as this, the riflemen of units in reserve carried mortar ammunition that they dropped by platoon or company piles when they went into action. You'd be surprised how much three hundred men can carry, especially if it might mean their lives! Another item covered individual equipment. No letters, diaries, or items showing unit identification. No mess kits, which were always a source of rattles. Canteens and canteen cups muffled. Any shiny helmets dulled—mud, usually. Faces blackened, provided we could find the material. In those days camouflage grease sticks were not an item of issue. Grenades carefully secured to prevent sounds and accidental detonation. We probably issued a day's ration with the precaution they might have to make it last for two days. Usually we included one emergency ration, a large, highly concentrated chocolate-type bar. Personal items were limited to a change of underwear and socks, a poncho, a towel usually draped around the neck, shaving equipment, soap, toothbrush, and dentifrice."

The troops moved out as daylight faded into a darkness pierced only by a bright moon. "The ghostly, silent movement of those soldiers sent chills up my back. How confident they were! How calm they appeared to be! But I knew every nerve fiber in their bodies was tingling, supercharged with anticipation, alert for enemy action. Before we departed, Dwight Dickson, the regimental operations staff officer, saw us off and gave me a chew of tobacco for luck. I did not smoke or use any form of tobacco at the time, but the shot of nicotine in my unadjusted system charged up my tired body, which had not had very much sleep in the preceding thirty-six hours."

A brief firefight broke out on one flank and the troops started to turn toward the direction of the shooting and away from the path to the objective. But because Mueller with the command group was right behind the infantrymen, he was able to redirect them to the proper direction. As the columns pushed ahead, leaving behind the cries of Japanese wounded—no Americans had been hit—the radio operator informed Mueller of a code transmission that called for him to plug into the telephone line. "Bad news! The column had been broken because one of the connecting files had fallen asleep during the engagement with the Japanese outpost. Some soldiers are very adaptable to the situation. Evidently the connecting file was one who could fall asleep easily." Mueller impatiently waited for the stragglers and then the advance continued.

"The moon still shone brightly. Nervously the formation slowly crept forward. But the discipline held. No soldiers saw ghosts; none fired at phantoms. When troops are advancing in darkness across unfamiliar terrain in the presence of suspected enemy forces, it is not uncommon for them to begin firing at imaginary figures; even veterans are sometimes subject to an attack of nerves. The unforeseen, however, suddenly halted progress. The brush at the foot of Hill 400 was a tangle of undergrowth, as much as ten feet high and full of long thorns. Passage required a time-consuming labor."

The deployment of Mueller's battalion at the moment placed I and K Companies in the vanguard with L bringing up the rear. Suddenly, a group of Japanese soldiers marched along a road from the north. Machine guns from I Company scattered them. Mueller had hardly digested the news when K Company saw more enemy swarming up the slope between them and Company L. Mueller could only speculate that these defenders came from well-concealed caves in the bush or a dry stream bed. Because of concern for the whereabouts of L Company, Mueller ordered K Company to keep its fire below the crest of the slope. As the GIs poured devastating fire on the climbing interlopers, Japanese soldiers gained the top and stood upright for a few moments. Suddenly, the hitherto invisible L Company soldiers opened up. "A storm of fire swept the Japanese from the crest. They had approached within hand-grenade range and suffered a barrage of fragmentation and white-phosphorus grenades for their pains. Several unfortunates came running off the hill in flames. The K Company troops cheered when they saw the results. The action had been short, furious, and now over, we had no casualties yet reported."

But the defenders now knew of the threat from Mueller's forces. "Our time to suffer had come. A thunderstorm of mortar fire pelted K Company. I sought refuge between two K Company soldiers snuggled up against the bank of the dry stream we occupied. After what seemed like an eternity, the firing ceased. I lay quietly for a few minutes to make sure that the firing definitely had ceased. One of the oldest mortarmen tricks was to suspend firing for a few minutes to deceive their targets into believing that the firing had terminated and then blasting off again hoping to catch targets in a vulnerable posture.

"Convinced that the mortar fire had terminated, I gingerly got to my feet. Cries of 'Medic' and the groans of the wounded dominated the air. I paused, listening intently for any more sounds of mortar 'thumps' signaling the discharge of shells from their tubes. Then I spoke to my two K Company comrades, still embracing Mother Earth, advising them I thought the fire had ended. I got no response. I noticed that both were bloodied. I turned them over and checked their pulses; both dead. My God! Both dead, one on each side of me. I was shocked and unnerved."

From his command post, now shifted to another small hill, Mueller noticed that short rounds from his supporting mortar fire beat down the thorny underbrush that blocked his infantrymen. He arranged for a walking bombardment of the obstacle and a corridor up Hill 400 opened. Driven to cover by a barrage directed at the command post by the Japanese, Mueller never saw his men scale the heights of Hill 400 and establish a strong defensive position.

The enemy responded, infantrymen attacking, backed by intensive artillery and mortar fire. Mueller credits the U.S. 81mm mortarmen for preventing the enemy overrunning the GIs atop Hill 400. "Their actions were without a doubt one of the most heroic and dedicated unit actions I observed during the war. They suffered severely for their self-sacrificing devotion to duty. Among the casualties was their platoon leader, Lt. J. H. Childs. I saw him as he was carried to our location. Ugly steel shards of a 150-mm shell had penetrated his body. When the shelling ceased, the evacuation of wounded began after dark. I remember saying to my comrades there was no doubt in my mind that Childs's wounds were fatal. But he survived, although he spent the rest of his life in a wheelchair."

Mueller also observed the opposite end of the courage-cowardice spectrum. A captain in command of an independent but supporting 4.2mm mortar company pulled out with his men and weapons as soon as the enemy shelling allowed. Outraged, Mueller described to his regimental commander what had happened and wanted to prefer charges against the offending officer. He learned that because the officer was not attached to Mueller's outfit, but officially only designated as support, he had the prerogative to locate where he saw fit.

A day later when the same captain reported in for another support mission, Mueller borrowed a carbine and led the captain forward to orient him about coming operations.

"Be sure your weapon is locked and loaded because there might be some Japs lurking around," Mueller advised the mortar commander, and then escorted him through the GI positions.

They headed out for some 500 yards and then reached a point where Mueller suggested they crawl under a hut on stilts to conceal themselves while they looked over the terrain around them. "I turned to him, 'Why did you run out on us during the shelling?'

The officer answered, "I talked to the Lord and told him that I was going to pull out to save my troops from that awful shelling. I asked him to give me a sign if that was the wrong thing to do."

"What was his answer?" inquired Mueller.

"'When I ask him to give me a sign he always answers very soon. I waited for some time and then asked him again for a sign if I was doing the wrong thing. But there was no sign, so I knew that it was the right thing to do.'

"Well," said Mueller, "I also talked to the Lord. I said to him 'Lord, what shall I do to that officer who ran out on us when we needed him so urgently?' And the Lord answered, 'Take him out and show him the promised land.' I knew what the Lord meant. He meant for me to take you here and show you the land where we have never set foot. And that is the land between here and Hill Z over there, including the hill itself. Where do you think our front line is?'

"'Aren't we on our front line?' he asked

"Do you see any sign of our troops? We left our front line when we passed through those machine gunners back there. This here is Jap country. Do you know what we are going to do if the Japs attack us? We are going to fight to the death, you and I, if we have to. And you are not going to turn around and run. Do I make myself clear?'

"'Yes sir,' stammered the captain, visibly disturbed."

Mueller completed his lesson with an explanation of what he expected the captain to do on his next mission, but on his return to the American lines Mueller related his conversation to the regimental commander. He told him he did not want "this nutty officer and his unreliable outfit in support." Mueller never heard of or saw the officer again.

According to Mueller, the crest of Hill 400 resembled a moonscape. "The entire top was dug up. Because the force had been reduced to about sixty fighters [the Japanese had all but abandoned efforts to reclaim the position] there were plenty of empty foxholes, all very deep because of deadly 150mm mortar fire and some direct fire 77s from Hill Z. A very wide field of barbed wire and mines surrounded the entire position. 'We're wired in like a prison camp,' said one inhabitant. There were both light and water-cooled heavy machine guns, a couple of 60mm mortars. Ammunition of all types was stockpiled in great quantities in the extra foxholes.

"The stench of decaying flesh was unbearable, quite like that of hundreds of bodies on Lone Tree Hill, our first battle in New Guinea. There were innumerable bodies tangled in the barbed-wire barrier, the result of numerous attempts by the Japanese to retake the hill. There were probably more bodies at the bottom of the hill. Our enemy was not known to spend much time and effort to recover their dead. Eating a meal out of canned rations became a real problem because of the voracious appetite of the flies [attracted to the decomposing dead]. Because of these extremely harsh conditions, we frequently rotated troops on the hill. Morale remained surprisingly high. Soldiers seemed to regard it as a badge of honor to have served on 'Hell's Hill.'"

Grit and courage notwithstanding, Mueller also dealt with breakdowns from the stress of combat. Subsequent to the action on Hill 400, Mueller investigated a company bogged down in an attack on the town of San Isidro. At the battlefield he noticed a young enlisted man casually leaning against the bank of a ditch and then saw a lieutenant who led a platoon. "I knew him well because he was one of our old-timers who had trained with us in the States and served in all campaigns up to this point. The lieutenant did not seem to be aware of my presence. He was bent over praying a rosary. I watched him for a while because I did not want to disturb him during his prayers and maybe it would do some good. But there seemed to be no end to his prayers.

"I looked questioningly at the young soldier. He shrugged, threw up his hands and said, 'That's the way it always is. That's why we never get anything done!'" Mueller questioned the officer and unhappy with his vague responses sought out the company commander. "I instructed him to execute a left hook through the wooded area to strike San Isidro from the north. After adding some detail, I asked if he had any questions. The captain turned to the first sergeant, 'You heard the battalion commander; do you have any questions?' When the first sergeant replied in the negative, the captain said, 'See to it that the instructions are carried out.' This was most unusual; company commanders ordinarily issued orders personally to platoon leaders. I left the captain to track down the first sergeant and his party and asked, 'How long has this been going on?'

"Someone replied, 'For some time. The captain is not well.'

"I had noticed that the captain's hand was trembling and his arm twitching. He jammed his hand into his pocket and tried to keep his arm rigid. He was also one of our old-timers, in training, Stateside maneuvers, New Guinea, and the battles on Luzon. I dreaded the duty I had to perform—I hated it; but the battlefield is a harsh taskmaster, unrelenting, unforgiving. Infantry soldiers deserve the best leadership; their lives and bodies are daily on the line when they are in combat. What matters is what you do today—not what you did in the past.

"With deep regret, I had to order both those old timers, the captain and the lieutenant, to battalion headquarters, leaving the company in charge of the senior officer present. Despite the personnel changes, the company drove the Japanese intruders out of San Isidro the same day."

The 169th Regiment of the 43d Division traveled to the Ipo Dam area, which featured limestone palisades several hundred feet high and was honeycombed with caves harboring Japanese soldiers. "More replacements came in at about 2100 hours," remembered John Higgins. "Each of the rifle companies sent a guide down to the CP area to pick up its replacements, with about twelve to fifteen for each company. The next morning we had to move out two or three of the replacements through medical channels since they were killed that night during a Jap attack. At a staff meeting I strongly recommended that any time replacements came up in the dark, they remain at the battalion CP site until daylight to enable them to at least see the sergeants and officers in their new unit. Also, they would get some idea of what was happening. The CO agreed and it became SOP."

Curtis Banker, the gun crew member of Cannon Company in the 103d Regiment of the 43d Division, rode out a number of engagements in his M7, self-propelled 105mm piece. "Some of the time we did direct fire into caves and at night there were fire missions for harassment or to help stop banzai attacks. The terrain to the north, around the summer capital [Baguio], was very mountainous and easily defended. The weather there was better than New Guinea and we could get some fresh food on Luzon. I had jungle rot, malaria, and yellow jaundice. The first thirty-eight days of combat on Luzon cost the 103d 172 killed in action, 1 missing, and 551 wounded.

"I had been wounded near San Fabian; two of my fingers were severed near the first joint and sewed back on. Combat fatigue was diagnosed by the doctor after I was recuperating from yellow jaundice. I was transferred from a Manila field hospital to a unit on Leyte by air. I requested to be returned to my unit, which was advancing on Ipo Dam. Instead, I was sent to a replacement company in Manila. I threatened to go AWOL and they allowed me to rejoin my company. I traveled by train and then many miles on foot. I was not that fatigued before I went to the hospital but I sure was afterward."

Arden Kurtz, a mortarman posted to a machine-gun crew after losses near the Clark Field shootouts, recalled his company was picked for reconnaissance [43d] as the division approached the Ipo Dam area. "We went across this flat area and about 500 yards ahead of us are some cliffs. They're looking right down our throats and, boy, they started to pour it on us. Boy, everybody tried to get their whole body into that helmet. I had some shrapnel bounce off my helmet. They had the whole company pinned down. We couldn't move.

"They called in an air strike for us and there must have been thirty or forty planes. They'd come in real low, right over our heads. Boy, were they noisy. The planes hit them with rockets, napalm, bombs, machine guns, and really softened them up. Just before the planes left, we started moving up. When our regiment got through the cliffs to the other side, we stopped and dug in to consolidate our position."

Tom Howard's tank platoon from the 754th Tank Battalion, attached to the 103d Infantry Regiment, maneuvered to positions for firing at caves carved into the mountains. "The caves are all on the reverse side of the mountains," noted Howard. "You can move up, but when you pass, they open on you from your rear. The tank turrets must be traversed 180 degrees to face the rear. You have to be extremely careful when you fire back toward your own lines. Maybe there is method to their madness. Once you get in, you have to fight your way out."

Ordinarily, the tankers lived a bit more comfortably than the foot sloggers. The armor sometimes set up its perimeter at a barrio, enabling the crews to commandeer a few houses where they could maintain good observation and sleep indoors. Even when out in the field, the kitchens could advance and set up shop in the center of a circle of tanks. Occasionally, Howard and the others, granted passes, visited Manila.

"We learned to live off the land," said Howard. "We fixed fish by drying, we boiled then dried sugar cane syrup that we had squeezed and made sugar bar candy. We boiled and dried peanuts from wild plants. We gathered sweet potatoes—camotes—and fixed them by cooking into a paste, then drying it. Our mixtures could later be diluted in hot water and prepared like soup. By using bows and arrows, we killed wild chickens and cockatoo birds for meat." Obliging Filipinos even taught the Americans how to capture monkeys, turning them into useful pets. "We fed them the fruit from trees and berries from plants first. If they were poisonous the monkey would not eat them."

The Japanese slowly fell back into northern Luzon and the summer capital of Baguio in the mountains. Among those pressing the shrinking forces of Yamashita's Shobu Group were the 25th, 32d, 37th Divisions and the 1st

Cavalry Division. Emil Matula, the first sergeant of D Company for the 25th Division's 35th Infantry Regiment had remained in a field hospital for twenty days because of the sniper's bullet that penetrated his upper jawbone and sinus area. Discharged back to duty, Matula returned to his company and learned he had been awarded a field commission and transferred to Company G in the 2d Battalion as a platoon leader. The I Corps command expected the 25th in tandem with the 32d to carve a wide swatch up the middle of Luzon, exploiting the two-lane gravel road known as Route 5. Matula's 35th Regiment blessed by exceptionally heavy air, artillery, and mortar support, and confronted at first by poorly organized Japanese defenders—a rarity—stepped out faster than its brothers, the 27th and 161st Regiments of the 25th Division. But by the end of March, all three encountered ever-stiffening resistance.

While fighting toward the final redoubts of the Yamashita Shobu Group, Matula directed his platoon as it captured one of the endless hills and killed twenty of the enemy. "We received orders from battalion to turn over the defense of the hill. During the night, the Japs ran the platoon of guerrillas off, capturing a machine gun from them and used it against the 2d Battalion CP. My platoon had to take the hill back. We turned the defense over to the same guerrillas after killing another twenty Japs and recapturing our own equipment. That night the same thing happened again and I lost my platoon sergeant to a sniper. After that I refused to allow the guerrillas on the hill again."

Others held the irregulars in much higher regard. In the southern half of Luzon, the 11th Airborne counted on the guerrillas to supplement their limited numbers. The 11th's Joe Swing wrote, "The only thing that keeps my lines open and allows me to spread so thin is the fact that I have organized 5,000 guerrillas and have them attached to all the infantry, artillery, and engineer units. Even have a picked company at hdqrs. They call themselves G.S.O.G. (General Swing's Own Guerrillas). Let them wear the 11th AB shoulder patch over their left breasts. They are proud as punch and really fight. Put artillery forward observers with them, give them all the captured Jap machine guns and mortars and they keep on pushing and making the Japs like it."

On the Villa Verde Trail, Bob Teeples, a former Alamo Scout and an acting platoon leader while still first sergeant of Company L, 128th Regiment of the 32d Division, led a reconnaissance patrol. "I sent out the two scouts and I followed behind them. In turn, behind me came the BAR man, his assistant, the other members of the patrol, and a corporal known as Jim Snyder. As we moved out, the wetness of the red clay from the foxholes made our uniforms glisten against the green foliage, like walking bull's-eyes.

"We had barely started onto the plateau we were supposed to reconnoiter when we came to a mound of fresh-dug earth. It was still smoldering and

I warned the scouts to keep a sharp lookout as the Japs had undoubtedly just buried one of the victims of our artillery barrage. As the BAR man's assistant climbed onto the plateau, a shot rang out and he fell back over the edge. Almost immediately another shot and the BAR man grabbed his throat and ran forward toward me. As he ran, he began to cry, fell down on his knees, onto his face, and lay still. By this time the two scouts and I were flat on the ground as a Japanese machine gun had opened up on us from the high ground to our left. I crawled to the BAR man and felt for his pulse, but he was gone. I thought back to a couple of nights before when he had proudly showed me a pictures of his wife and their one-year-old son. Now another machine gun started to fire on us from a position on our right flank and the twigs and branches were snapping all around us. The sound of the bullets over my head reminded me of a group of wires being rattled together. The Japs started to drop occasional mortar rounds. I realized we would have to withdraw.

"I motioned for my scouts to come back, and I tried to keep firing toward the Jap position to keep the scouts covered as they made their way back past me and over the edge of the plateau. A bullet ricocheted off the helmet of the first scout, but otherwise they made it back safely. I tried to drag the BAR man's body toward the edge of the plateau, but his ammunition harness kept catching in the brush. I managed to drag him back almost to the edge, when all of a sudden it felt like someone hit me in the head with a sledgehammer. The first thing I saw when I regained consciousness was a light flashing on and off. As my mind became more clear, I realized I was in a tent, apparently the rear aid station."

Jim DeLoach, a company commander for the 32d Division from the New Guinea days, believed the division and his regiment suffered from a number of poor commanders and he was less than enthusiastic about the policies of the general staff. In particular he disparages, "the American system for leaving an outfit—particularly its troops in, until either the million-dollar wound, the ultimate, KIA, and the lucky, of which I am one." On the Ville Verde Trail, DeLoach noted, "While other divisions got to Manila and points of interest to the press, the 32d drew the losing hand, leading to nothing more than one hill after another. We were MacArthur's tactic of skipping around and leaving behind Jap forces to be cleaned up later. Worked splendidly when it came to islands, but in our case, simply set us up for small Jap groups to slip in and blow us up—charges of picric acid were their specialty.

"We were pulled out of the line for what was to be a rest and regrouping. We were at a small village and then were moved to take part in securing Balete Pass. The men expected a short rest and now faced with another assignment were, at best, pretty upset. We pulled through, but took some heavy casualties at the pass."

By the time the 32d Division finally cleared the Villa Verde Trail, over a nearly four-week period, it counted almost 3,000 combat killed and wounded with an additional 6,000 men withdrawn from the lines because of sickness or psychoneurotic problems. DeLoach himself would be fighting small pockets of the foe right up to the moment of V-J Day.

Aside from the forces directly under Yamashita on Luzon, almost all of the surviving 102,000 Japanese troops in the central and southern Philippines occupied four islands, Negros, Cebu, Panay, and Mindanao with a small detachment on Palawan. The combat-effective men, exclusive of service, navy and air force personnel, numbered about 35,000 scattered over the four sites. Whatever the makeup, the defenders could expect no help from the beleaguered Yamashita or from home and faced declining amounts of ammunition, artillery, and eventually, food. The generals understood they could not expect to defeat the Americans. Their sole duty was to delay and inflict losses that might allow a peace with honor.

The campaign beyond Luzon opened at the end of February with the 186th Regimental Combat Team from the 41st Division clearing out an area on Palawan. Lying between the South China Sea and the Sulu Sea, Palawan seemed ideal for airbases that could support assaults both on the southernmost Philippines and the former Dutch East Indies. Unfortunately, the soil composition and compaction defied the best efforts of engineers and delayed immediate exploitation of Palawan.

Mindanao, the second biggest and most southern of the Philippines, drew the next card from MacArthur's strategic deck. Under Col. Wendell Fertig, the Mindanao guerrillas operated with increasing boldness. They even controlled an airstrip at Dipolog for supply operations on the north coast of the Zamboanga Peninsula, a 145-mile-long neck of land on the western end of Mindinao. Two days before an amphibious assault, Marine fighter bombers, protected by guerrillas and troops from the 24th Division, began operations at the Dipolog site.

Fertig assured General Eichelberger and the Eighth Army that landings near Zamboanga City would be unopposed. Underwater demolition teams and guerrillas sanitized the beaches of mines without interference, but taking no chances, a preinvasion bombardment pounded sparse enemy artillery positions. When the troops of the 41st Division stepped onto the Zamboanga shores some met little or no fire while others quickly took casualties.

To conquer the eastern part of Mindanao, occupied by a mélange of 55,000 soldiers and armed civilians loyal to the Imperial Empire, the 24th and the 31st Divisions in the third week of April, landed 100 miles from the main objective, Davao, a port across the waist of the island. The Japanese apparently expected the approach to be from the Davao side and the bulk of their defenses were oriented in that direction. The Americans, aided by guerrilla intelligence and operations that ensured an absence of hostile forces, moved rapidly in the first weeks.

Han Rants, the 34th Infantry wire-section chief whose terrifying experiences during the battle for Zig Zag Pass he says converted him into a devout Christian, left Mindoro after a period of R&R for Mindanao. "We had been warned there were Moslem tribes—Moros—there and there were Huks who actually held communist-type beliefs and they hated any outsider, not just the Japanese. Fortunately for us, we found that they hated the Japanese much more."

The march to Davao took Rants and his buddies through the interior, largely uncharted section of the island. "As we crossed the center of the island and got on the Davao side, still some fifty miles away from the city, resistance got heavier and heavier. Where they had blown bridges, they would set up machine guns across streams or rivers so that as we crossed they could pick us off in the water. As we came to these streams it took a long time to send out scouts and patrols, get the area cleared, so we could ford the stream and keep on going."

Even though it must have been obvious that Imperial Japan had been defeated, a few local people still cast their lot against the Americans. Rants recounted that some Filipino traders approached the battalion and said they could lead the GIs to an enemy encampment. "My good buddy from L Company, David Flaherty, had been wounded in each campaign we had and he was one of the best line sergeants in the battalion. Flaherty was picked to lead some fifty-four men who went with these Filipinos because we felt we could trust them. But when Flaherty came out, he was one of only five left alive. Those Filipinos had led them to an area the Japanese had laced with crossfire from higher positions. Flaherty was awarded the Distinguished Service Cross because of extremely heroic action he took trying to save the group. He became a nervous wreck for life. He was in college with me some years after the war and he just couldn't stay in class. He dropped out and I lost track of him." The strategy and tactics of the Japanese failed to halt the advances but succeeded in drawing considerable blood. A number of men who had been with Rants from the beginning went down with serious wounds as his battalion struggled toward Davao.

Battalion surgeon Phil Hostetter accompanied the 19th Regiment of the 24th Division to Mindanao, and his duties covered the spectrum of medical therapy from continuing to teach first aid, sanitation, psychology, and, of course, treatment of horribly wounded men. "We received fifteen recruits fresh from the States in the medical detachment. I decided to have a class in giving blood plasma. None of the men had ever done it." Hostetter divided them into pairs, but while he would not require them to use a needle on each other, he suggested they learn by doing. "I heard, 'By God, no one is going to stick me.' I said, 'This is the way to do it, as I put a rubber band around the arm of one fellow. I inserted a hypodermic needle and drew back a little blood. Now you do it to me.' The venipuncture had not phased him, but I thought he might go into shock with that order. He may have imagined what would happen if I lost an arm or even if he messed it up. I did not expect him to be good the first time, but he did a fine job. Everyone in the group then performed the exercise with success and felt confident."

Back on the trails with the troops, Hostetter became briefly pinned down in an exchange of gunfire. When it subsided, one soldier could only drag himself on his elbows. "My legs won't work," he cried out to Hostetter, whom the soldiers recognized although he wore no insignia. The doctor recalls telling the man, "I am going to fix your legs and you will be all right." Hostetter flexed one thigh against the GI's body and then the other. Then he declared, "Now you can walk." The soldier stood up and walked back, his hysterical paralysis cured.

An epidemic of diarrhea, "the worst I had encountered," according to Hostetter, devastated the battalion. In spite of his efforts to treat the troops with sulfaguanidine tablets, they continued to weaken. "At the same time the battalion commander told me he had located some enemies, but was not able to clear them out because he didn't have enough men. Everyone knew the only honorable way a soldier could be relieved of duty was through the medical department, me in this area. I knew almost every man was affected by the epidemic, yet we were required to keep fighting. Men kept coming to me in their weakened condition believing they could never make another patrol, and I had to send them out anyway. I decided a man whose temperature was less than 101 degrees would stay on duty.

"I sent the regimental surgeon a message saying the battalion was in very bad health because of gastroenteritis, and could not carry out its mission for long. He spoke to the regimental commander and the battalion was immediately replaced by another. With no excessive demands on their strength, the men recovered within a few days."

Men rarely died of the GIs, as the disease was known, but around Hostetter, even at this late date in the war, the maiming and killing continued unabated. "'Medic!' someone shouted. I ran over to where a soldier writhed on the ground. His abdominal wall was blown away, exposing the loops of intestines. He must have been hit by a grenade or land mine." As Hostetter approached him, the injured man, "functionally decerebrated or unable to think" from extreme shock, tore at his own insides. "We put him on a litter. Someone restrained his hands while I wrapped a large towel from our medical supplies around the abdomen. I cut perforations in the ends of the towel with the pocket knife I always carried, and laced it tightly together with a roll of bandages. This served to hold in the intestines, prevent further loss of fluid, and restore blood pressure. We gave him a Syrette of morphine, started blood plasma, and moved him toward the nearest hospital. He may have lived. I never knew because I hardly ever heard what happened to such patients." At other times, Hostetter saw his patients die before they could be evacuated, or in other instances, the explosions and gunfire snuffed out the lives before he could even start treatment. And his medical unit was not immune from injury as several close associates, seeking to succor the wounded, lost their own lives.

On 1 July, Eichelberger declared the eastern Mindanao operation ended. Nevertheless, armed Japanese continued to sporadically combat elements from the 24th, 31st, 40th, and 41st Divisions, supported by the guerrillas. Rather than leave their garrisons to wither in isolation, MacArthur similarly directed operations against smaller islands like Panay, Cebu, and Negros. Each one of these wiped out the occupying Japanese forces, but liberation exacted tolls in lives and bodies.

In northern Luzon, Yamashita still counted 50,000 troops at his disposal. But they occupied an ever shrinking area of mountainous jungle, and malnutrition stalked them as fiercely as it had the defenders three years before on Bataan. Combat on land petered out. It had become a war of attrition with the last chapter the scheduled invasion of Japan itself. There were no large battles like those that occurred during the early days of the Luzon invasion and within Manila. Instead, small groups of men participated in deadly exchanges, with the defenders being forced ever deeper into the mountains, bereft of overall command and control, increasingly short of ammunition and food. After victory in Europe, the American forces could expect an influx of reinforcements. By June 1945, thousands of soldiers had begun redeployment from Germany to duty in the Pacific.

54
The Bomb and the End

Frederick L. Ashworth, who attended Dartmouth for a year before entering the U.S. Naval Academy in 1929, inspired by both Lindbergh and an elder brother, opted for flight training. As a prewar dive-bomber pilot he was advised to attend an advanced school if he hoped to make the service a career. On a whim, he chose aviation ordnance, a decision that profoundly put him on stage for the debut of the most dramatic weapon of the twentieth century.

Ashworth assumed command of Torpedo Squadron 11 after Pearl Harbor and became part of the Cactus Air Force on Guadalcanal during the height of activity around the Slot. He flew many missions, scored some hits on ships, and after a tour as an air officer on the staff of Adm. Richmond Kelly Turner, was assigned to the Naval Proving Grounds in Dahlgren, Virginia. That last post, plus his education in ordnance engineering and experience with various bombing operations, recommended him for the Manhattan Project—development of the atomic bomb under Army auspices. He took up residence at Los Alamos, New Mexico, on Thanksgiving Day 1944.

While Ashworth did not receive a crash course in nuclear physics, he had a desk in the office of Capt. William Parsons, a 1922 Annapolis graduate and chosen by the Manhattan boss, Gen. Leslie Groves, to direct the project's ordnance division. "I was able to listen in on many important technical discussions between the captain and his associates in the laboratory. I was permitted to attend the so-called colloquia that were held each week to discuss the week's technical problems and develop fixes for them. I wasn't able to absorb much of what went on, but it was fascinating to watch Oppenheimer [J. Robert, chief of the civilian scientists involved] lead these meetings. When a problem was raised and seemed to get bogged down trying to find a solution, Oppenheimer would get out of his chair, go to the blackboard. He would ask if this had been tried, and he would proceed to formulate a procedure with sketches and equations that he thought would do the trick. More often than not, the reaction would be, no, I haven't thought of that. Oppenheimer was definitely the technical leader of the laboratory. These colloquia would always be attended by the top scientific people in the lab. I recall seeing Niels Bohr, Wigner, Weisskop, Hans Bethe, Rabi—if my memory serves me, there were six Nobel laureates at the laboratory during the bomb research and development."

Ashworth brought to the table the practical experience of someone who had actually dropped bombs. He explained, "I am sure that he [General Groves] was looking ahead to the day when the bombs would be put in operation against the enemy, whether Germany or Japan. Germany was certainly contemplated as a target, but she was defeated before the bomb would be ready. Groves was certain that he would require a member of the crew on the bomb-carrying aircraft who had at least a general background on the bomb's technical characteristics, so that proper decisions could be made should they be required. Groves always wanted spares for everything. I would be Parson's spare.

"The aircraft crews that would man these aircraft in the combat operations simply did not have and never were exposed to the technical aspects that would be required for the job as he, General Groves, saw it. Up until the night of the preflight briefing for the Hiroshima operation, no one in the 509th Bomb Group had any knowledge of the ultimate mission of the group, except Paul Tibbets, a thirty-year-old Army Air Corps colonel in command of the bomb group, and he had very little if any technical knowledge of the bomb design and how it worked." (Tibbets flew the first mission of B-17s against Rouen by the Eighth Air Force in August 1942.)

The first workable design for a nuclear bomb used uranium in the form of U-235, produced from its sire, U-238. It was the fissionable material for "Little Boy," which would be exploded over Hiroshima. For the second device, "Fat Man," the scientists intended to employ plutonium. Ashworth recalled that the successful explosive system for the plutonium bomb depended upon a spherical shape, hence the nickname "Fat Man," but notoriously a poor ballistic shape. The question was how to wrap this package into an efficient ballistic form. "Some of the ancillary equipment that went into making this into a bomb-fuses, batteries, capacitors to provide the voltage to the detonators and the like-it was decided was to be mounted on opposite sides of the sphere. The elongated shape suggests that a spheroid shape was the best that could be done. Clearly some sort of a stabilizing tail structure would be required. Fins seemed to be a logical place to start. Wind-tunnel tests showed that the arrangement might work, but experimental drops from a B-29 were all unstable. Next, a large box tail was attached to the after end of the spheroid and test drops made to determine if this would improve the ballistics. Some improvement, but still not acceptable [for] uniform flight. I believe it was Parsons who suggested baffles placed in the box to create the effect of a parachute, which was adopted as the final form of the tail."

Although the role of Navy experts in the Manhattan Project is rarely mentioned, Ashworth credited his immediate boss, Captain Parsons with having contributed considerably to the technique of implosion worked out with John von Neumann."I have always believed firmly that without Parsons's drive and capability the bombs would never have been out of the laboratory in the timely fashion that they were." While Ashworth could add little expertise to the actual building of the bomb he supervised much of the in-flight testing of components carried out at Wendover Field in Utah. He also was charged with recruiting military personnel whose knowledge could contribute to the work.

After Groves gained the highest priority in the military for procurement of people and supplies, Hap Arnold, chief of staff of the Army Air Corps, created the code name "Silverplate" and directed that any time a responsible official used the code word, that person's needs would have the top priority over any programs. According to Ashworth, the Air Corps accepted the dictum, but the remainder of the Army treated it with less respect."Some of the men were the most experienced and senior enlisted ratings in the Army. Needless to say, pulling them out of the Army for this assignment became subject to a high degree of inertia. I would go to Washington to extract these people from the Army. The magic code word 'Silverplate' would help but there was a lot of foot dragging by the Army Ordnance Corps, mostly when it came to the assignment of the highly qualified men we needed. It was fun for me, a Navy commander to roams the halls of the Pentagon and try to force compliance of the orders they knew they would have to obey.

"In February 1945," said Ashworth, "I was designated to carry a top-secret letter to Guam and hand it personally to Admiral Nimitz. This letter would inform him for the first time that there was under development an atomic bomb, which would be available to him in the Pacific about the first of August 1945. This letter, although I am sure it was written by General Groves, was addressed, 'Dear Nimitz' and signed 'King' [Admiral Ernest J.]. It informed Nimitz that the explosive yield of the bomb would be about 8,000 tons of TNT equivalent, and that support of his command would be required. He was authorized to inform only one officer on his staff. If he had any questions, the bearer of the letter would be able to answer them. It directed Admiral Nimitz to give me what support I might need in selecting a site for the operation.

"I traveled from Washington direct to Guam wearing the ordinary cotton khaki uniform of that period. I carried the letter in a money belt around my waist next to my skin. When I arrived on Guam I went directly to the headquarters of Admiral Nimitz and told his aide I had an important letter to deliver to the admiral. He said okay, he would carry it in. I said that wasn't okay. I was required to hand the letter directly to the admiral. With some reluctance he went into the office to find out if the admiral would see me, coming out in a moment with word I could go in. The aide followed me. I told Admiral Nimitz that I had been ordered to hand the letter direct to him and that no one else could be present. Admiral Nimitz told the aide to leave and I proceeded to break out the letter.

"I opened my uniform jacket, unbuttoned my shirt enough to extract the money belt, all to the amusement of the admiral. After the long trip, the money belt was a bit the worse for wear and its contents a little stained and damp from sweat. However, it was in good enough shape for the admiral to open and read it. When he had finished, he rang for the chief of staff, Adm. [Charles] "Soc" MacMorris and handed him the letter to read. Then he told me to tell Admiral King he could not provide the services he knew would be required by this project without his operations officer, Capt. Tom Hill, being aware of the program as well. He pointed out to me that it was now only February and didn't they know back there that he had a lot of war to fight before August. Why couldn't he have the bomb now? I described briefly the status of the development of the weapons and told him August first was selected by General Groves as the first realistic date the bomb would be ready for delivery in his theater of operations. He turned in his chair and looked out the window for several seconds, turned, and said, 'Thank you, Commander. I guess that I was born just about twenty years too soon.' I felt he had sensed the magnitude of the thing. Perhaps he also saw that the bomb might have a possibility to end the war."

Ashworth had the responsibility to explore the area for the space to be used by the 509th Bomb Group and the Los Alamos scientists and engineers accompanying the atomic bomb when it went to war. "The selection of the island was easy," said Ashworth. "Guam was too far south, Saipan was farthest north [closest to Japan], but did not have the air operations facilities that were available on Tinian." The Air Corps commander on Tinian, Brigadier General Frederick Kimble, apprised that the project held Silverplate status, suggested the site used for B-29 operations.

Those involved at Tinian attempted to maintain strict security. When the chief engineer, Elmer E. Kirkpatrick, an Army colonel who directed a Navy SeaBee battalion to construct facilities for the A-Bomb project began to run short of concrete he informed Nimitz's operations officer Tom Hill. Immediately, Hill sent a message to an organization that possessed the materials, saying, "You will deliver to Colonel Kirkpatrick [——bags of cement]. This is a project of which you have not been informed and will not be informed."

To accommodate the nuclear devices, the engineers modified the B-29 bomb bays. Ashworth recalled that when Sheldon Dike, a young aeronautical engineer, described to Boeing experts the dimensions of Little Boy as being about eight feet in length with a twenty-two-inch diameter, and its weight of 10,000 pounds they looked at him as if he were deranged, saying it was impossible to pack that much weight in such a small package. They were unaware that the uranium, which was heavier than lead, packed around the explosive material, plus the special armor steel and the other components could add up to five tons. Standard ordnance ordinarily ranged up to 2,000 pounds maximum for a single item. However, the Air Force had experimented with larger packages.

The 509th Bomb Group under Paul Tibbets practiced for the mission both at Wendover Field and Batista Field in Cuba. George "Bob" Caron, a Brooklyn, New York, native who had attended a technical high school and then worked as a draftsman and mechanical designer, had enlisted in the Air Corps in the autumn of 1942. Eventually he was assigned to power turret school and then became an instructor on the systems. Caron met Paul Tibbets while engaged in test work with the first B-29s. When Tibbets assumed command of the 509th Bomb Group he asked Caron to join him. Caron applied for a transfer, but his commander refused to release him.

"In a telegram," said Caron, "I told Tibbets, 'I tried to get out of instructing, but I was told I was frozen.' He sent me another telegram back, saying, 'Just sit tight, we'll take care of the being frozen business. I'll have orders through for you as soon as I can.'" Apparently Silverplate again demonstrated its power for Caron soon reported to Tibbets at Wendover.

Caron recalled that Tibbets informed him, "We are on a highly secret deal, Bob, and I can't tell you a thing about it. You only need to know what you are supposed to know. We are selecting the people we think can keep their mouths shut, and security is going to be very high. I can't tell you what it's going to be, but we are going overseas and we are going to end this war. That's all I can tell you."

According to Caron, "We knew some of the men [in the 509th] weren't military people even though they were wearing khaki clothes. We knew it was highly secretive, nobody seemed to know anything, or at least they wouldn't say much. I understand the reason for a lot of the fellows just simply disappearing, stealing away in the night, was [that] they talked a little too much. They were shipped out and we didn't see anymore of them. I understand a couple of 'em had gone on a pass to Salt Lake City and got a little too talkative over a few beers. They were gone; they just packed their bedrolls, bedouin tents, and slipped away in the night.

"You didn't know whether the guy sitting next to you was an FBI man or somebody checking on security. My mother told me that within a few weeks time there were two groups of well-dressed young men who came to the house. One of them was from Brooklyn Technical Alumni Association, wanting to know how I was doing. They were coming out with a manual, and so forth. And she says, 'The Brooklyn Technical Alumni Association? Isn't that just a high school?' [there were] two well-dressed young men coming out for this interview, but she didn't say anything. Another one who came out was supposed to be an insurance investigator asking all kinds of questions. She said she was wondering what the hell was happening.

"We formed our crews and Captain [Robert] Lewis was airplane commander for ours. It was my understanding that this was Colonel Tibbets's crew, but as group commander he wasn't supposed to have a crew. Captain Lewis would be the copilot for Colonel Tibbets, who would be airplane commander for this special deal. At Wendover we did a lot of high flying, dropping a single bomb. There was a lot of flying, but there wasn't really much for me to do." Caron worked in the B-29 tail, originally equipped with a pair of .50 calibers and a 20mm cannon. The arrangement was clumsy and ineffective. The cannon disappeared.

Caron reached Tinian at the end of June 1945. "After attending some classes [in combat gunnery] we started flying a few missions with just some regular bombs. They sent us out for practice missions against Marcus Island with no opposition and some went to Truk where they had flak. Then we flew our first mission in mid-July against the empire, Kobe with one big bomb. The casing was just like Fat Man, the Nagasaki plutonium bomb. It was a great big round 10,000-pound bomb, strictly a TNT general-purpose bomb. We didn't fly out as a squadron. We went at different times, just one ship to a target. This seemed a little strange to us. One bomb and one plane to a target. On our first mission over Kobe we went back near Osaka on the way out and got a good bit of flak. I never saw a fighter over Japan, but the mission took flak."

On 16 July in the Trinity test at Alamogordo, signals relayed from a control bunker detonated the first nuclear bomb. The senior scientists conducted a betting pool on the explosive yield. The guesses ranged from Edward Teller's extravagant 45,000 tons of TNT down to Oppenheimer's modest 300 tons. Hans Bethe estimated 8,000, closest to the actual figure of roughly 12,500. Convinced the system worked, Groves and company immediately set in motion the events designed to deliver the bombs to the Japanese cities. The target material, a chunk of U-235—the active ingredient for Little Boy—traveled aboard the cruiser USS *Indianapolis*.

Ashworth himself went to a small port at the south end of Tinian to pick up the U-235 from the *Indianapolis* off shore. He commandeered an LCM landing craft for the task and the package was lowered from the cruiser to his boat. "Things progressed satisfactorily until the last moment when either the crew lost control or the LCM was lifted by a wave. The container hit the bottom of the boat with an uncomfortable crash. This was a heavy container and possibly could have gone right through the bottom of the boat. However, it and the boat appeared to have survived." The LCM tied up at a dock and a truck bore the U-235 to the airfield. A few days later, a Japanese sub torpedoed the *Indianapolis* and because, somehow, the Navy did not realize the vessel was missing, only 316 of the more than 850 who abandoned the vessel were rescued.

According to Ashworth, a major fear concerned an aborted takeoff that might result in a runway fire. "Should this occur it was recognized that the powder charge in the Little Boy bomb could 'cook off' from the heat before the firefighters could put out the fire, resulting in a low-order detonation of the bomb and partial fissioning of the uranium. This kind of accident could contaminate and place out of action the entire north end of the island. There was devised at the naval gun factory in Washington, a combination breech block that permitted part of it, just large enough to pass the powder charge into the gun, to be removed after takeoff and the powder charge inserted at that time. The original design of the breech block was too large and heavy to be handled by one man in the bomb bay after takeoff.

"The new design arrived on the island not more than a day or two prior to the upcoming operation [Hiroshima] and Captain Parsons spent many hours in the bomb bay, both in flight and on the ground, familiarizing himself with the task to be done and preparing a final check-off list to be used when the time came, an operation commonly referred to as 'arming the bomb.'

"There had to be the same worry in the case of the B-29 carrying the Fat Man bomb to Nagasaki. However, because of the design of the bomb, there was no way to remove any part of the explosive sphere. Fire in the aircraft could be disastrous as a result of the low-order detonation and partial fissioning that would undoubtedly occur. That danger was accepted and all the rescue and fire-fighting equipment on the island was arrayed along the runway to forestall an explosion in case of fire. In spite of continuing reference to 'arming' the Fat Man, there was no way to do it as was done with Little Boy."

Preparations for the first mission by the nuclear bombers were essentially completed by 1 August, but a small typhoon in the vicinity of Japan shut down operations for several days. The raid was then scheduled for 6 August. "The departure of the *Enola Gay* [named for Paul Tibbets's mother] was a relatively gala affair. There were lights and cameras, sort of a Hollywood preview, with many of the senior officers in the area present. The bomb had been loaded into the aircraft earlier in the afternoon. Captain Parsons had completed his familiarization with the new breech block by which he would 'arm the bomb.'" At 2:45 A.M., Paul Tibbets lifted the nose of the *Enola Gay*, and headed north. As Ashworth reported, Parsons, along with Lt. Morris Jeppson, the "weaponeers," the title given to the specialists, armed Little Boy once the *Enola Gay* climbed to 5,000 feet.

Caron recalled, "We knew the big one was coming up but what the big one was we didn't know for sure. We had been thinking in terms of some super TNT explosive. We had heard word of a new British explosive. We were called up outside the old man's office to get our picture taken. We had been playing softball and were kind of raggedy. I had on my Brooklyn Dodgers baseball cap, which was my rabbit's foot. About two nights before [the Hiroshima raid] we had a briefing, all ships involved in this mission, weather ships, and companion ships. There were a lot of scientists with us, civilian personnel, working in some area I never got into. I knew it existed, but it was none of my business. At this briefing we were told we were going to see some pictures. They had some movie film of a test that was just completed, but the projector broke down so they showed some slides. We saw pictures of the test explosion at the Trinity site in Alamogordo. It was just still pictures on slides, but it was just breath-taking. The only way you could think of it was, 'What the hell is this!' Tibbets gave a little talk and told us that's what we'd be taking. As soon as the weather cleared we'd be going.

"Of course we went out that afternoon to look at the bomb after they had loaded it. It looked screwy to me, with all those antennae hanging out. It wasn't like the big pumpkin shape. It was more cylindrical. This was Little Boy, the first one, the uranium bomb. We found out later that the one that was tested was the plutonium one [Fat Man] at Trinity.

"I had my nice Certo Dollina .35mm camera all loaded. They hustled us to chow and then to the airplane. I left my personal camera loaded with color film lying on my bunk. All during the Hiroshima mission, I worried about it being swiped. As it was, the photo officer, Captain Ossip, gave me a K20 which is like a big Speed Graphic. He gave it to me and I said I didn't want to take it. It was too crowded in that tail. He said, 'Take pictures. Take anything you can. It's all set. Don't touch the lens. Don't touch any speeds. We want you just to take, pictures.' I said, 'I don't know if I can even get it in there.' He answered, 'Do the best you can.'

"When we got out to the airplane, it was like a Hollywood movie set. We got out there probably about one o'clock in the morning. It was dark. Floodlights were all over the place, people by the hundreds. I always used to take off in the tail for the weight and balance and also because we had seen some crashes, a couple of ditchings off the island. The reports said the tail gunner always got out. B-29s characteristically broke by the aft-pressure bulkhead, the tail would always end up sticking out of the water last and there's never been a tail gunner lost in ditching. I always took off and landed in the tail.

"This takeoff seemed exceptionally long. I knew every inch of that runway; I had taken off so many times. I thought he was just holding the plane down, because we just came off the end of a cliff and there was the drink down below us. I was a little apprehensive about that extra-long takeoff, using every inch of the runway. Old Tibbets was a wonderful airplane driver! I think I'd fly on a carpet with him. We took off and stayed fairly low until we got to Iwo Jima." When the airplane reached Iwo Jima, a pair of B-29s rendezvoused with Tibbets. One of these ships carried instruments suspended by parachutes that would be released at the moment the *Enola Gay* emptied its bomb bay. These devices would supply information to blast gauges in the B-29. The second Iwo Jima plane held observers, including the *New York Times* correspondent William L. Lawrence, press correspondent for the Manhattan Project. To give the mission a sense of the Allied effort, an RAF pilot flew this plane. Beyond Iwo, the three bombers would start to climb.

Caron recalled, "After takeoff, I'd come out of the tail and I'd sit in the waist until time to pressurize and then I'd go back in the tail because once we were pressurized, you were there, period. A mission would run anywhere from twelve to fifteen hours and I'd be 75 to 80 percent of the time locked in the tail. I'd come back to the waist to stretch my legs. I was sitting in the waist with Bob Shumard, the assistant flight engineer and a qualified engine mechanic, and Joe Stoborik, the radar man. Tibbets came back through the tunnel and stopped to talk with us. Since the two others were relatively new to the crew he sort of addressed himself to me, because he knew me longer. 'Bob, have you figured out what we're doing today?'—his exact words. I said, 'Hell, no, Colonel, with all the security and secrecy we've been living under with this thing, I don't want to get stuck up against a stone wall and shot.'

"He said, 'How're you going to get stuck up against a stone wall and shot? We're on our way. It's too late to do that.' I got to thinking about the speculation amongst ourselves about this new British explosive and said, 'Colonel, is this a chemist's nightmare?' He shook his head a little bit and said, 'Not exactly a chemist's nightmare.' Then all of a sudden a little light lit up and I remembered an incident in the Wendover library about the Columbia University cyclotron. I said, 'Colonel, is this a physicist's nightmare?'

"He gave me a funny look and nodded his head. 'You might call it that.' After a little bit more chatting he said 'I'm going back forward. We're going to be climbing soon.' Just as his leg was sticking out of the tunnel, I reached up and yanked on one foot. He came scampering back down, thinking something was wrong. He asked, 'What's the matter?'

"I said, 'Colonel, are we splitting atoms today?' and he gave me the darndest look and said, 'Yep!' He went forward. He was going to announce it anyway on the intercom. By then I was in the tail and he announced what we were doing. He said, 'We're going to be on a wire recorder. Watch your language. We're going to make this for history, this recording, so watch your language, no cussing, and everybody talk clearly.'

"We had climbed, were pressurized, and came on over Shikoku. We had the word that the primary [target] was clear enough. Hiroshima was clear and that's where we were going. I don't remember exactly when we went on this wire recorder. I was mainly a listener back there, sort of a backseat driver. I always kept watching. You never could tell, although we never had any opposition as far as fighters.

"I don't remember any extreme apprehension, just the normal. I don't remember [worrying] whether it would work or not, or whether we'd even get away from it. We were told you just don't know. We came over the IP [Initial Point] and we went on the bomb run. Tibbets told us to put our goggles on. We had been given these dense goggles, like welders use, with side pieces completely covering the eyes. I remember looking up at the sun with these goggles on to see how bright it was. At 32,000 to 33,000 feet the sun is pretty bright, but it looked like a dim purple blob through these goggles.

"On the bomb run, we had the two wing ships, one for instrumentation. When the Japanese saw a parachute, they said [the bomb] was dropped by parachute, but that was a canister of instruments dropped by Major {Charles] Sweeney and they were off behind us, maybe five miles behind in a sort of V-formation. We were told there was going to a fifteen-second tone and at bombs away, the tone would stop. That's when everybody went into this diving turn that we had been practicing. The tone went off, and at bombs away the ship lifted up a little bit and he threw her into the damndest diving turn. I had my seat belt on; I was told to put it on. It was a 160-degree diving turn. I think he redlined the son of a gun. We had practiced and it was mainly a turn to get the biggest slant distance away from the damn thing when it went off. He had just straightened out, I think, when it went off. There was this tremendous flash of light through these goggles and so much brighter than the sun; there was no comparison. I thought, 'Oh, boy!' I understand Tibbets had thrown his goggles off because he couldn't watch his instruments in this turn. But I kept mine on, because I was facing it. Then we took the goggles off and he asked me on the intercom, 'Bob, what do you see? Do you see anything yet?' And I said, 'Outside the flash, Colonel, nothing yet. The tail turret's in the way. I don't see anything yet.' He said, 'Keep your eyes open.'

"About this time, we saw this shock wave but I didn't say anything. I thought, 'What the hell is this!' It hit the airplane. The old man yelled, 'Flak!' Up front, it felt like it was a flak hit. But in the tail, it's so bouncing and jouncing anyway, that I didn't think anything of it. Then the second one came up and this time I called it out. It was a ricochet. The second shock wave was much less severe and I said, 'Here comes another one.' I think Bob Shumard in the waist spotted it, too.

"About that time, [Tibbets] asked me again, 'Do you see anything yet?' I said, 'No, not yet,' and then 'Holy Moses, what a mess!' That's when the mushroom came into view from around the tail. He asked me to describe it. I did to the best of my ability. He had turned a little bit and I asked him to turn a few degrees one way or the other. Then I started shooting pictures. This little turn he had made allowed me to see the city. The mushroom was coming up, right to our level. It was like you see on TV, an interior core of red hot-fire and on the outside this mushroom, black, white, and purplish. What impressed me most beside the mushroom, the most spectacular thing was this turbulent mass of black purplish smoke that was flooded out like liquid mud all over the city and was flooding up into the ravines where the foothills were. Fire started up through it. I gave up counting the fires. You could see them flash up. Maybe they were explosions, maybe they were all fires. Since we knew we were away from it, Tibbets made a turn and we went alongside where everybody could take a look. We didn't hang around too long. We headed on back and the navigator told me, 'Keep you eye on the mushroom and let me know when you lose sight of it. We want to distance measure it.'

"I watched it and actually it didn't disappear over the horizon. But went behind some stratus clouds. I called in and told the navigator and he said, 'That checks out at 365 miles.' On the flight home we were all highly elated. There was that sense of relief. It was earth-shattering, wiping out a city. I don't recall talking about [the people] or thinking about it. To us it was a military target. Bob Lewis claims he said, 'Oh, my God, what have we done?' I don't recall that on the intercom. Maybe he did. I don't recall their saying they hoped it would end the war, but they might have.

"He [Tibbets] called me up and asked me how I was doing and how did I take that turn. I said, 'Hell, Colonel, that was better than a Cyclone ride down at Coney Island, a twenty-five-cent ride.' He said, 'Well, you can pay me when we land.' I said, 'You're going to have to wait until payday. I am broke.' Then I thought, this is really intelligent chatter to put down for history on the wire recorder.

"We landed and there was this reception committee. It seemed like thousands of people out there. We taxied up and piled out of the airplane. There was a lot of brass. Two MPs came up to me with the photo officer and before I could even stretch he wanted his camera to get the films developed. General Spaatz was there, General Davis, the wing commander. General Spaatz pinned the Distinguished Service Cross on Tibbets, standing there in a brace with his pipe hidden in his hand." A debriefing followed and then a celebration. "By the time the crew got to the beer and hot dog party," remembered Caron, "there was no beer left and no hot dogs left." Interviewed by newsmen, Caron, when asked what he thought about the affair, answered, "I am wondering if we are getting into God's territory with this." That question aside, Caesar rendered Silver Stars to Caron and the other participants.

Ashworth remarked that the plan for the assembly of Fat Man envisioned a five-day period to complete the job. But because of predictions of poor weather by meteorologists, the schedule was compressed with only three days of round-the-clock labor allotted for readying Fat Man. "Early in the morning of 9 August, after operations briefings, we gathered on the flight operations line where the aircraft were being preflight checked. There was no fanfare this time, no high-level officials, just us working folks getting ready to go. There were thunderstorms in the area, some rain, and an occasional flash of lightning stabbed through the darkness. Airmen don't like lightning. In many ways our mission seemed somewhat of an anticlimax, but perhaps more exciting than the operation a few days earlier.

"At this point our troubles began. {Charles] Sweeney's aircraft, *The Great Artiste*, named for Capt. Kermit Beahan, the suave bombardier in the crew, still had the yield-recording instruments installed for Hiroshima. It had been decided that the bomb would be loaded in another B-29, *Bock's Car*. In the preflight check, the flight engineer found that the transfer pump in *Bock's Car*, which would move gasoline from the after bomb bay auxiliary tank into the main fuel system to supply the engines, seemed to be inoperative. He reported it would be impossible for us to use the 600 or so gallons of fuel that had been loaded into that tank. We were confronted with our first decision, should the mission proceed with the knowledge that we would be carrying around 600 gallons of unusable fuel."

Ashworth said he wondered whether his responsibilities covered an opinion on the situation, but Sweeney and Tibbets made a decision with which he agreed, that unless something untoward occurred, the round-trip could be made with no problem. They also had the option of landing at Iwo, if necessary, to refuel. A second complication involved the now-standard meeting with companion aircraft at Iwo Jima. A storm in the area forced a new rendezvous over a small island near the Japanese coast. The primary target was the city of Kokura.

Ashworth and an Army second lieutenant, Phil Barnes, would serve as the weaponeers for this expedition. Integrated into the various electrical system of both atomic bombs were power sources including some "safe separation timers" that started to tick at the moment of bomb release. These disarmed the bomb for fifteen seconds to prevent detonation before the plane could reach safety. Any one of the nine clocks would shut down the system, and at the end of fifteen seconds the bomb would have fallen 10,000 feet. According to Ashworth, his superior, Captain Parsons, demanded a failure rate of only one in ten thousand chances.

At the same time, nine barometric switches were designed to close at an altitude of about 8,000 feet. These triggered fuses that radiated to measure the height desired for the actual explosion. The galaxy of barometric switches prevented any interference from the Japanese who might jam the radiation.

Once aloft and well clear of Tinian, Ashworth replaced green-painted plugs that isolated the arming and firing systems from other electrical components with red ones that readied the firing and fusing systems to activate after the bomb dropped. That procedure went smoothly, but at the rendezvous point, only one of the B-29s showed. Ashworth persuaded Sweeney to wait for forty-five minutes in hopes the second plane would join them. "I told Sweeney that it was particularly important that we have the plane carrying the bomb-yield measuring instruments with us before we proceeded to the primary target. I wasn't worrying much about the plane carrying the observers, but very much wanted to be able to attempt measurement of the bomb yield."

Having loitered about with no sign of the missing B-29, Ashworth said he advised Sweeney they had no choice but to continue with the mission and hope that their one associate carried the technical instruments rather than spectators. Later Ashworth said he learned that within five minutes after the second plane appeared, Sweeney knew it was the one with the measuring devices, but for some inexplicable reason this vital fact was never relayed to the Navy commander. Meanwhile in *Bock's Car* anxiety built up among the crew. Having heard of the devastation wrought upon Hiroshima, the airmen wondered how ferociously the Japanese might react when they noticed a couple of B-29s circling near their homeland.

Further complicating matters, strict guidelines dictated subsequent action. Said Ashworth, "These missions were under strict orders from Washington that under no circumstances would the bombs be dropped other than by visual bombing, using the Norden Mark XV bombsight. The weaponeer was charged with responsibility for visually certifying that this occurred." Two hours before they finally left the rendezvous point, a weather advisory from a scout B-29 reported Kokura clear and available as the target. It was also clear over Nagasaki, but there appeared to be a chance of a cloud build-up there.

Bock's Car, reached the Initial Point, then began its final bombing run. "Captain Beahan, [the bombardier], took control of maneuvering the aircraft as it approached the target, based upon the bombing solution being calculated in the Norden bombsight. The target area appeared to be hazy with some smoke in the area. The approach continued, but at the last moment as we neared the drop point, Captain Beahan reported over the plane's intercom, 'No drop.' The smoke and haze had obscured his actual aiming point so that a visual drop could not be made. We were experiencing the situation frequently found when flying at high altitudes that when at the long slant range to the ground it was difficult to see clearly through the natural haze. Then the frustrating part. As the plane reached a position more nearly above the target it became visible through the bombsight telescope, but then too late to solve the bombing problem and release the bomb."

Ashworth suggested a run from a different direction and that surface winds might clear the target area. Sweeney agreed but the visibility did not improve and Beahan again announced, 'No drop.' The Navy commander proposed a third try from still another angle but that failed for the same reason. "Fifty-five minutes of precious fuel had been expended. It was time to think about the secondary target, Nagasaki. There has been considerable criticism of these decisions," said Ashworth, "particularly in view of the fuel situation." He adamantly justified what happened. "Our job was to attack our primary target, Kokura. What might happen after that was incidental to the failure or success of the mission. Should fuel starvation later result in a ditching operation in the sea, so be it."

However, the presence of the B-29 had attracted the notice of those on the ground. Antiaircraft bursts below and behind were spotted by crewmen. More ominously, the officer monitoring Japanese radio frequencies reported conversations on fighter-director circuits that indicated interceptors might be scrambled. The inability to hit Kokura and the potential of an encounter with enemy planes convinced the crew to proceed toward the secondary target, Nagasaki.

The radar recorded the distinctive image of the long bay that led into that city. Ashworth and the others had no doubts they were in line with the new target. But as they drew nearer, the area appeared completely covered by an undercast of clouds. The flight engineer now calculated barely enough fuel to carry the bomb to the nearest friendly airfield on Okinawa. The alternative would be a ditch in the sea with the bomb aboard. On the other hand, it was also clear they could not afford the maneuvering done at Kokura. "We would have one and only one attempt at a successful drop," recalled Ashworth, "and that appeared to be impossible by visual bombsight in view of the clouds beneath us. I informed Sweeney that we would make our approach by radar and if necessary drop the bomb by use of the electronic bomb director, which would be operated by the navigator. The approach continued."

While preparing for such an execution, bombardier Beahan fed information on the position of the plane and continued to adjust his Mark XV telescope along the calculated flight path. The solid cloud coverage became patchier with the ground showing through numerous big holes. Ashworth reported, "Beahan called out, 'I have the target.' He refined the bombing solution generated by the bombsight and it was released automatically by a signal from the bombsight. We ended up actually dropping the bomb visually as he had been directed. He had about twenty seconds to synchronize and release the bomb. When you think about it, under the pressure of the shortage of fuel, picking out an aiming point through a hole in the clouds below, and knowing full well that the success of the mission depended upon this one bomb run, the skill and coolness displayed by Captain Beahan under such stressful circumstances was extraordinary."

Sweeney put *Bock's Car* into the sharp bank turn calculated by the scientists at Los Alamos, to carry the plane the maximum distance from the explosion and shock waves. "About forty-five seconds after release and the time of fall of the bomb," said Ashworth, "we were able to see through the heavy welders goggles a brilliant flash of light. When we were about eight miles away, the detonation, the first shock wave arrived, followed immediately by a second and, to my recollection, a third. The evidence of these shock waves was more one of noise than anything else. I have always characterized it as if someone had struck an empty metal trash can with a baseball bat. There was a minor movement of the plane, no worse than a sharp bump frequently experienced when flying in a commercial aircraft in clear air turbulence.

"After the shock waves had passed, we returned to the vicinity of the explosion, made one turn around the cloud, and because of our fuel situation departed immediately in a long slow glide, engines throttled back to save fuel, for Okinawa, the closest friendly airfield. By this time, the cloud had reached our altitude of about 29,000 feet. There was a tall dark column of smoke and I suppose debris from the target area, topped by a mushroom-shaped cloud, boiling and roiling as it climbed. It looked as if there was flame and fire in the cloud as it swirled around, colored a salmon pink. We learned later that the pink color was from the nitrous oxide generated in the explosion." Some crewman insisted the mushroom cloud enveloped the plane but Ashworth doubted it. "Had this actually occurred, we would have been in a very dangerous situation and would have received massive amounts of radiation from the cloud as it would be pulled into the aircraft pressurizing system."

Bock's Car barely reached the Yonton air base on Okinawa. "As usual, in the vicinity of a large active airfield," Ashworth reported, "there was a lot of chatter on the landing control radio circuits and Sweeney's request for landing instructions seemed to have been ignored. After all, we were just another aircraft wanting to land. Knowing he was low on fuel and might lose his engines at any time, Sweeney was wisely flying closer than usual to the airport on the downwind leg in order that if this should happen, he might be able to glide into the field without help from his engines. With still no response from the control tower, Sweeney announced over the radio that he was going to land. As is routine in this kind of situation, Sweeney also ordered the copilot to fire a green flare signifying he needed to land immediately. He thought this would get some response, but lacking this, he told the copilot to fire all flares we had aboard, red, green, yellow, and announced, 'This is B-29 on final. I am going to land.'

"The pyrotechnic display indicated that the plane not only had to make an immediate emergency landing, but that we had killed and wounded aboard and needed ambulance assistance on landing. This got their attention and we were met at the end of the runway by fire trucks, rescue equipment, and ambulances." The B-29 appeared to Ashworth as if it would run off the runway end, but the reversible propellers brought the plane to a roaring, safe halt. The two outboard engines shut down from fuel starvation as they taxied to the operations line and an engineer measured their remaining usable fuel at only thirty-five gallons.

On the ground, the staff at the air base, ignorant of the A-bomb mission treated Ashworth with disdain when he asked to send a message to Tinian. However, the Navy commander gained an audience with Gen. Jimmy Doolittle, who, with the war in Europe over, now bossed operations focused upon Japan. "He asked me to sit down. I spread out on his desk our target maps and proceeded to tell him about the operation and how it had happened. I indicated the point on the map where we were supposed to aim and told him where we were sure that it actually went off and related in some detail why we had apparently missed our target by about a mile and a half. General Doolittle studied the map, asked a couple of questions, and said, 'Son, I am sure that General Spaatz will be much happier that the bomb exploded where it did over the industrial area and not over the city. There will be far fewer casualties. Now I'll help you send your report."

The Soviet Union declared war on Japan two days after Hiroshima and marched into Manchuria. After the second A-bomb demolished Nagasaki, the Supreme War Guidance Council met in Tokyo. While the leading military representatives wanted to continue the war, the civilian leaders proposed to accept surrender terms. Emperor Hirohito, increasingly aware of the devastating effects of the two nuclear weapons used against his country and the threat of more, broke the stalemate. On 15 August, the emperor publicly announced defeat to his people. Prisoners like Richard Carmichael, the downed Doolittle flyers not executed, and those from the Philippines shipped to Korea, Manchuria, and Japan, soon became free men.

Peace was now temporarily restored to the world. The United States counted 290,000 military personnel dead on all fronts. Of this number the Army lost 235,000, including 52,000 in the Air Corps. Marine dead added up to nearly 19,000, and the Navy and Merchant Marine KIA totaled about 37,000. About one million earned Purple Hearts for their wounds. The price for land, sea, and in the air went well beyond the costs of all other U.S. wars combined.

55
After Action Reports

The personal accounts of the enormous number of Americans who fought, bled, and died around the globe during World War II are more than a record of what they endured. They reveal much about the essence of war, strengths and weaknesses of our society, and perhaps even touch on the universals of mankind. It was the most democratic of all American wars; there was no $300 surrogate to avoid the draft as in the Civil War; the mobilization far surpassed that of World War I. Korea, as harsh as it was, involved only a fraction of World War II, and Vietnam with its exemptions for college students and the ability to flee the country, was overwhelmingly a blue-collar war led by a professional cadre. Events such as the "liberation" of Grenada, the overthrow of Noriega in Panama, and Desert Storm against Iraq while stirring patriotic fervor hardly qualified as wars against substantial opposition.

Flagellation of succeeding generations is a popular sport for their forebears, and broadcaster Tom Brokaw, although not of the one that fought World War II, fed that zest for the game with his book *The Greatest Generation* in which he exalted the Americans who fought on land, sea, and in the air. Unlike Brokaw I am a member of that group and I demur. In the company of the veterans, those who actually endured combat, it is difficult not to be awed as they recount their experiences. And the author of *The Greatest Generation* said his inspiration came after visiting the Normandy beaches with people who had been there. But comparisons of generations and their wars is no more valid than the endless blather about whether the 1998 New York Yankees were of the equal or better than the 1927 version. Different times make for entirely unique contexts. Geography, history, politics, economics, etc. all changed. Those who shouldered weapons in Korea and Vietnam endured no less hardship than their World War II counterparts and the valor, comradeship, and selflessness as well as the less admirable qualities were no less evident.

Men and women put on uniforms to fight the Germans and Japanese more willingly than in any other American conflict because there was no way to avoid war. In Korea and Vietnam the U.S. was not directly attacked. Under the circumstances one could argue that those who battled in these conflicts were actually more dedicated to the service of their country because there was no imperative for American survival. *The Greatest Generation* also insists, apparently in contrast to those that followed, the veterans of World War II came home and immediately went to work to create a better America. The author credited them with "an extraordinary generosity of spirit." Those who were demobilized must also be charged with efforts both to preserve white supremacy and to demolish it. They formed the ranks behind the extreme right and left, exploiters like Senator Joseph McCarthy, and the forces who opposed radicals of any stripe. Along with the millions who either used the GI Bill to further their education or else went to work in private enterprise or the professions, a substantial number belonged to the "52-20 club"—veterans who elected to collect twenty dollars a week for a full year under the same benefit laws. One could cite multiple contradictions within any broad description of that generation, but above all they are the people who bred and raised their successors replete with all of their alleged faults and virtues.

Having said this is in no way a disparagement of what people did during World War II. There is a coterie of academicians that argues war is an unnatural act; a definition that makes all participants social perverts. Reviewing Barbara Ehrenreich's book *Blood Rites: Origins and History of the Passions of War,* Michael Ignatieff summed up, "Wars break out for frivolous reasons; they are sometimes pursued when almost everyone knows they are insane; they drag on when mired in stalemate; and they frequently end with both sides defeated." None of that applies to World War II. One could hardly regard the Allied cause as "frivolous." Both the Third Reich and Imperial Japan predicated their futures on armed conquest. Given their treatment of the people whose countries they occupied it is nonsense to talk about an accommodation. And there were winners as well as losers.

Confrontation with the Japanese militarists and the Third Reich was inevitable. But there was also patriotism, a sense that our way of life was better. Glen Strange, from the 27th Armored Infantry, grievously wounded near the Remagen Bridge, said, "Hitler was a no-good bastard, but he came along at a time when the German people were ripe for a change and needed a leader and this prick had the ability to take over. He had to be stopped, as he was in the process of trying to enslave all of Europe, and what he did to the Jews and to the free people of the countries they captured could not be tolerated in the free world." Undoubtedly there were many who had no ideological commitment or knowledge of world events. Still, there was a zeal that led hundreds of thousands to enlist rather than wait for the draft and then volunteer for the more dangerous duty as Rangers, Marine Raiders, Airborne, flight crews, submarine service.

The America in which these men grew up was marked by the Great Depression. Many of them spoke of hard times, families struggling to survive in a period of massive unemployment, and dust-bowl conditions that wiped out crops and an agricultural economy. Millions desperately seeking a career or to gain an education that might improve chances to earn a living had their options taken away by the obligation to enter the armed forces. Although they flocked to the colors after the Japanese attack on Pearl Harbor, for more than twenty years prevailing opinion held that the country had been inveigled into World War I and military service was not popular. Combined with the traditional American predilection for independence, as opposed to the regimented culture of the armed forces, the task of rapidly converting millions of civilians into a fighting force was not an easy one.

The outsiders, like the British, as well as the enemy, regarded the U.S. forces as lacking in discipline and the resolve to fight effectively. The naysayers were wrong and in fact the streak of independence was one of the great strengths of the American fighting man. As George Ruhlen and George S. Patton Jr. both noted, for the most part this was not a matter of massive armies contending on a grand battlefield but, instead, of a myriad of small-unit actions. While superiors exerted some command and control, in many situations those watchwords of the military text vanished and it fell to groups of men functioning on their own, perhaps without benefit of any officer or even a noncom. Whether they were Marines, paratroopers, infantrymen, naval gunners, or airmen, they built on the training and whatever discipline had been instilled to successfully carry out their missions. And in those cases where coordinated, well-regulated actions were required, aboard ships, on massive air raids, or coordinated attacks on an enemy fleet, the former free-wheeling civilians stuck to the game plan.

At the same time, it would be a mistake to think the war was prosecuted strictly by "citizen-soldiers," who once the fighting ended reverted to civilian life. Professional military people, the graduates of the service academies, some of the reservists, and those who had chosen to make a career in the armed forces, played vital roles. From this segment came both top commanders and the important ranks stretching down to the junior-officer level. Along with MacArthur, Eisenhower, Nimitz, Halsey, Patton, Vandegrift and company, the armed forces succeeded because of younger professionals. West Pointers like paratroop battalion commander Bill Boyle; platoon leader and company commander Carl Ulsaker; Naval Academy alumni like submarine skipper Slade Cutter, and pilot Jimmy Thach; reserve officer converted to regular status, infantry leader George Mabry. They went to war imbued with the motto of "Duty, Honor, Country," and that commitment ought not be discounted.

Under the circumstances World War II stirred the melting pot like no other experience in the history of the country. As navigator for the B-17 *Bad Check,* Jon Schueler, a graduate of the University of Wisconsin and an aspiring writer, said, "My pilot was a Jack Armstrong-type named Billy Southworth. Bill and I hated each other's guts. He was a cocky son of a bitch, the pampered son of the manager of the St. Louis Cards. Our backgrounds and personalities couldn't have been more different, except that we were both prima donnas of kinds." In time, however, they became the best of friends. Their crew also included waist gunner and equally alien personality Bill Fleming, a coal miner's son, and bombardier Milt Coover, a Virginia Military Academy product.

When South Carolinian George Mabry addressed a contingent of draftees from the North at Fort Benning, Georgia, he was disconcerted by their mumbling until one of his sergeants confided, "They can't understand a word you're saying." Heath Carriker, a North Carolina farm boy and Eighth Air Force pilot, remarked, "I felt pleased and happy about being part of what I considered a necessary activity, meeting new people, learning new things, a welcome change from my life to that time. Until then I had never had any contact with Jews, Italians, Polish, or Yankees." Virginia-bred Bob Slaughter, as part of his state's National Guard, said that after the outfit was federalized and added a variety of ethnic backgrounds, "They laughed at the thick-tongued drawl of the mountaineers from Appalachia. And the Southern rednecks had to strain their ears to understand them. When I went on a pass with an Italian boy, he took me to a restaurant where I had spaghetti for the first time in my life." Such encounters were replicated literally hundreds and hundreds of thousands of times. This is not to say that familiarity eliminated prejudice; many felt the sting of bias and the discrimination against blacks remained at a high level.

For all of the homogenization that occurred, war cannot be waged on the basis of democracy. Troops must be led, ships captained, and someone must make the decisions, including those that put someone else's life in jeopardy. However much the propaganda of the times and the legend-makers lionized those at the top, the upper-echelon commanders were not gods but fallible creatures. While hindsight provides a questionable lens through which to view decisions it cannot be denied that interservice rivalry, differences in combat philosophy, a certain amount of ineptitude born of ignorance, and the political cronyism that permeated much of the National Guard hurt those committed to combat. There was an appalling lack of coordination among the armed services that led to incidents of friendly fire, bombings of American troops by American airmen, lack of support when requested, territorial disputes between armies such as occurred in Sicily. Listening to the eyewitnesses, one may conclude that the Allies muddled their way to victory, overcoming the enemy not by brilliant strokes but by overwhelming them with men, materiel, and resources.

Mistakes in enterprises great and small ordinarily mean loss of money, esteem, advancement. Errors in war are paid in agony and death. All of the U.S. armed services fumbled and stumbled in the development of the tools of war. Intelligence badly underestimated the quality of enemy resources, particularly in regard to Japanese airplanes, their navy and their soldierly qualities. The entire strategic-bombing program began with a horrendous ignorance of the hazards to unaccompanied B-17s and B-24s, entailing a significant delay in the development of fighters. All along the way glitches in design and instruction hampered effectiveness. Untested torpedoes frustrated submariners; the first bazookas were too small and unreliable; as Marine platoon lieutenant Bob Craig discovered, ordnance experts changed the time interval for grenades without informing the troops. In initial encounters with the Germans, American tanks, too light, too weakly armed, and too vulnerable to enemy guns fought under severe handicaps, and while the medium weight Shermans shortened the odds, their high silhouette, flammability, and the inability of their guns to match the Panzers weakened U.S. armored units. The superficially tested floating tanks created for the Normandy beaches were another ghastly mistake. While the M1 Garand rifle was the best in the field, the .30- and .50-caliber machine guns were inferior to those of the foe. The German 88 was the best direct fire artillery piece of World War II, but the proximity fuse, developed by the U.S. after the war began, produced excellent results. The Air Corps, the Navy, and the Marines all flew second-rate planes in the beginning, but by the end of hostilities, with the possible exception of the few jets introduced in Europe, the fliers manned the best in the air.

The believers in the Eureka system that expected to guide paratroopers to their drop zone failed to take into account the navigation problems of transports blundering through the night while carrying pathfinders with the vital equipment. The pilots hauling gliders or troopers often lacked experience in the kind of flying required, and carefully plotted courses were abandoned under severe antiaircraft fire. Similarly, the strategists' faith in the accuracy of high-altitude bombing based their theories on the clear skies of the training areas of the American Southwest and neglected to consider what happened when 88s opened up or fighters attacked.

Beyond the question of manpower and weapons, in war it is not so much a matter of how one has played the game, but whether one has won or lost. War is a very messy business permeated by honest mistakes, inefficiency, foolishness, and wrong-headed obstinacy. Yet, those in command of our fighting men, whatever their faults, led the way to victory even as one may criticize their behavior. The demands of war require a hierarchical military organization, one that functions through automatic responses to orders. Getting an army, company of infantry, a bomber crew or sailors on a submarine to carry out what's necessary requires leadership. This is a subtle quality that goes beyond a matter of silver stars, bars, stripes, a loud voice, the power to discipline and punish, and that is often influenced by who the individual is and by the situation.

At the very top, leadership means something quite different from that which was employed as one moves down the ranks. Dwight Eisenhower never had an opportunity to command in the field, but his handling of the touchy, egotistical, and chauvinistic political and military figures both American and foreign, required an extraordinary combination of diplomacy and firmness. By all accounts he was a likeable man, popular with his contemporaries and with genuine ability. He could say no to Bernard Montgomery, coordinate the conflicting ideas for such a massive enterprise as the invasion of Normandy, protect Patton from self-destruction until he could serve a useful purpose, perceive the seriousness of the German penetration in the Ardennes, respond faster apparently than those around him, and restore flagging morale. According to Stephen Ambrose, when the extent of the German breakthrough became apparent, on 19 December he walked into a staff meeting of downcast generals and said, "The present situation is to be regarded as one of opportunity for us and not of disasters. There will be only cheerful faces at this conference table."

He made mistakes. He indulged Winston Churchill's politically motivated insistence on attacking through Italy, anything but a soft underbelly. He kept faith in Mark Clark, whose progress in Italy was questionable. Whatever the merits of the Anzio landings, the Fifth Army never supplied the wherewithal to make it worth the costs in men and equipment. Although Eisenhower reacted swiftly, he, too, underestimated the power of the enemy in December 1944. And the toe-to-toe slugfest that followed, rather than skilled maneuvers to outflank the German armies imperiled by their vulnerable flanks, was hardly the stuff of military brilliance.

In North Africa, George S. Patton directed an effective offense and added to his reputation with victories in Sicily, at St.-Lô, and in the relief of Bastogne. But he then compromised his achievements with a series of less than stellar decisions topped by the ill-fated raid at Hammelburg. He led with a blend of authoritarianism marked by a ferocious temper, an unswerving confidence in himself, tempered by a flair for the dramatic, that gave those of the lowest rank a sense they were part of something special. As Carl Ulsaker saw, Patton knew how to talk in a way that appealed to GIs brutalized by exposure to the miseries of a combat soldier's life. Patton was a mean son of a bitch, but there was a certain pride in being led by such an individual even as the GIs translated one of his nicknames into, "Our blood and his guts."

As a human being, Patton, was despicable—a notorious sexual predator, a behind-the-back critic, and a bigot. In his book, *War As I Knew It*, he wrote, "Individually, they [the black 761st Tank Battalion] were good soldiers but I expressed my belief at that time [when the outfit joined his Third Army] and have never found any necessity of changing it, that a colored soldier cannot think fast enough to fight in armor." And after liberating camps like Buchenwald, where he made the local people see the handiwork of their government, he could still write to his wife, "Everyone believes that the displaced person is a human being which he is not, and this applies particularly to the Jews who are lower than animals . . . Actually, the Germans are the only decent people in Europe." None of this can discount the fact that he did reenergize the American forces in North Africa after their initial defeats; he did boldly sponsor the crucial breakout at St.-Lô, and he did move to the relief of Bastogne and the flattening of the Bulge quicker than anyone thought possible. On the other hand, true strategic coups were never his forte. Patton achieved victory with blunt force, winning at considerable price.

Abe Baum, whom Patton sent on a near-suicidal mission, had mixed feelings about him. "The important thing about Patton was he believed that infantry should support tanks rather than vice versa. He had the foresight to take a stand, lose a lot of personnel in a short period of time, where in the long haul it wouldn't be as noticeable, but you would have even more casualties as the enemy built up its forces. The press ridiculed him as flamboyant and he could put Barnum and Bailey to shame. But he was ideal for the war we fought. He had a feeling for the terrain, he was the most aggressive of all of the generals. If anybody should hate him, it would be me. But I believe he shortened the war. On the other hand, I would not want him as a father."

General Terry Allen led in his own style. His rank of course brought obedience, but his 1st Division and then his 104th Division accomplished their missions without the need for Allen to kick people in the behind, as Patton was so fond of doing. There isn't any real evidence that the 1st Division, while under his leadership reputed to be careless about uniforms and saluting, performed better when Allen was replaced by a stickler for military niceties.

Douglas MacArthur represented still another form of leader at the top. MacArthur recouped from his disastrous decisions in the Philippines with a skillful, strategic island-by-island counterattack marred perhaps only by excess when he returned to the Philippines. Laudable as was liberation of the Filipinos, it was a dubious decision to pursue a cut-off, starving, but still deadly enemy on Mindanao or in the northern sectors of Luzon.

While in World War I MacArthur stayed close to the doughboys, in World War II he functioned at the utmost distance from the common soldier. He demonstrated neither Eisenhower's easy-going style nor the great-man-come-to-earth demeanor exhibited by Patton on selected occasions. Overall he worked well with Nimitz and the Marine generals. MacArthur has been credited with saving many lives by carefully plotting his advances to avoid the head-on confrontations that so often involved the Marines. Some of the brutal battles for the leathernecks were, however, unavoidable, given that the targets were small, fully fortified sites like Tarawa and Iwo Jima. On Leyte,

MacArthur's second landing at Ormoc was a master stroke—so good that he replicated it at Inchon, Korea, six years later. However, aside from the mistakes made in the Philippines, MacArthur also could not be faulted for excessive concern for the conquest of territory. That fault in Navy-controlled spheres is most evident with the attack on the unstrategic, valueless island of Peleliu, as well as the continuation of the fighting on Okinawa once the major objectives of a naval base and airfields were secured.

One of the great strengths of top leaders is their removal from the terror and the pain. Although they can be expected to declaim about the sacrifices made by those under fire, generals and admirals, unlike the common fighting men, do not personally have to charge a pillbox or seize the high ground; they rarely witness the evisceration of a close comrade, and have only a distant acquaintance with the stink of death. While Patton became genuinely emotionally distraught upon visiting the wounded, there is not much record of his having agonized over sending these same people to their graves in order to carry out his schemes. Gregory Peck may have broken down when he dispatched the bombers in *Twelve O'clock High,* but the combat fatigue more often afflicted those who flew the missions rather than those who ordered them.

There were exceptions to the insulation of the senior people from harm's way. Admirals aboard ships enjoyed no more protection from torpedoes, shells, bombs, or kamikazes or their crewmates. They paid in their own blood as well as that of shipmates for their participation, and several flag officers died or were seriously wounded. In the Air Forces, generals flew some missions, taking their chances along with the junior officers and enlisted members of the crews. Again, a number of them perished.

On the tiny beaches of coral atolls, Marine brass was exposed to enemy fire, as were those of the Army at Omaha and Utah Beaches. Indeed, the 4th Division's deputy commander, General Roosevelt, a popular figure, set an example for the troops by his demeanor and his decisive direction after their landing craft put the GIs ashore well away from their appointed site.

There can be little doubt that sharing the danger adds to the strength of a leader. Nowhere is that more apparent than in the airborne forces where the generals either jumped or landed in gliders. They became combat soldiers on the ground until an area could be secured. Into the dark maw of the Normandy night, the 82d Airborne head Matthew Ridgway dropped, a USMA graduate whose trademarks were the hand grenades hanging from his uniform and his .30-06 Springfield rifle. Maxwell Taylor, another West Pointer, made only the second jump of his life as he led the 101st Airborne. The deputy commander of the 82d Airborne, James Gavin, manned positions in Sicily, Normandy, and Holland. During the Battle of the Bulge, where he entered the battle scene by jeep, he loped about carrying an M1 rifle. Although the weapon may have kept his identity somewhat hidden from snipers looking for VIPs, Gavin in particular was favored by his men. Bill Dunfee, who jumped into combat four times and went into the Ardennes under Gavin, said, "Slim Jim Gavin was respected and loved by every man who served in his command. We of the 505 [Parachute Regiment] were very proud to have served him in his first and last combat missions."

One can argue that a general officer's presence at the front not only adds to morale but in some cases is useful. The German counterparts of the Allies had a habit of personally inspecting the terrain they defended, taking care usually to obscure their rank. The generals who flew bombing missions gained insights into the problems faced and Curtis LeMay's successful innovations in tactics could only have come after he saw firsthand what happened.

It would naturally follow that stress under fire seems to have been almost inversely proportional to rank. Whatever their backgrounds, the Air Force brass all accepted an essential aspect of combat command, a willingness to order men to kill and be killed. They may have been psychologically more prepared for the casualties of war because even in peacetime there was a much higher number of deaths due to aircraft accidents than befell those in the infantry, field artillery, or other outfits. "I won't say you get callous," said Gen. Ira Eaker, "but you get realistic." He remarked to an interviewer of the necessity to be "trained and inured" if one was to carry out his tasks. LeMay said one in his position could not "meditate on the process of death" nor "mope around about the deaths he has caused personally by deed or impersonally in the act of command."

For those caught in the thick of the bloodshed, however, it was a far different matter. As a replacement platoon leader on Okinawa, Si Seibert said his greatest concern had been whether or not he could acquit himself as a leader. He satisfied himself on that score, but was traumatized by the loss of his first GI. "The death of of one of my men, although I was not directly responsible for it, placed a heavy burden on me. I could never, and have never gotten over that feeling." Jon Schueler, the navigator, broke down: "I started to feel guilty, responsible for every death. I was not sleeping, afraid that I'd make errors and cause the death of many."

George Ruhlen remarked, "I sometimes debate whether my decision to establish an observation post removed from infantry support, which did not contribute anything to our advance, yet cost the life of a lieutenant who had served with me for two years, was the right one."

Only after the battalion surgeon informed the regimental commander that he had no 2d Battalion to deploy, were the survivors of the 34th Regiment removed from the battle in the Philippines. Paratrooper Homer Jones identified his company commander as having a kind of heroism that reflected his responsibility and leadership. "Men like Royal Taylor were so intent on what they did, and yet so conscious of the people who were with them. They knew what they were doing and that people might be killed as a consequence. They could feel the weight of these decisions and still carry them out."

Still, it was a sensible policy to keep those responsible for directing a large-size unit away from the fronts where they might be killed or wounded, depriving the organization of its leadership. Brig. Gen. Don. Pratt deputy commander of the 101st Airborne died in a glider crash the night of 6 June 1944. General Maurice Rose, Ernest Harmon's chief of staff in North Africa, who took over the 3d Armored Division in Europe, was killed in March 1945 after he drove to the front with the situation still fluid. In Okinawa, artillery fatally wounded the top U.S. commander, Gen. Simon Bolivar Buckner when he ventured into a danger zone. Losses of this nature could be critical, although in these instances capable replacements were available.

It was another matter for the smaller units, where the grand strategy depended upon specific actions by limited groups of men. Here, where decisions on tactics must be made on the spot, regimental, battalion, and group commanders could be expected to be in the thick of things. Merritt Edson and Tony Walker of the Marine Raiders, Bill Darby of the Rangers, Red Newman of the 24th Division shared the exposure of the grunts.

The mystique Bill Darby aroused in his people undeniably had something to do with his constant presence at the flash points of combat and his force of character in the worst of situations. During the American retreat in Tunisia, Darby addressed his Rangers: "Men, we are the last unit to pull out of this mess! Ahead of us lie 24 miles of flat expanse which must be crossed to reach the next American strong-point at Deria Pass. Behind us and on our flanks are enemy armored columns, looking for straggling units to cut up. We have no tanks to protect us! We have only a few bazookas and a few sticky grenades to fight tanks with. In your hands they will do the trick! Before we start I want you all to know how proud I am to command this unit. You have proved yourself well on all occasions. Onward we stagger; and if the tanks come, may God help the tanks." To some that may have the ring of a football coach's halftime exhortation, but in this instance, Darby would be in the field, facing the same extreme threats as everyone else.

George Mabry as an infantry officer insisted he learned a sound lesson while in the peacetime army. "Never ask anybody to do anything you wouldn't do willingly. Lead by doing." He practiced what he preached, getting off Utah Beach and moving inland during the early days of the invasion of France.

Bill Boyle, the intrepid leader of a parachute battalion said, ". . . the best way to imbue troops with the proper spirit [is]: Let them know you can and will do everything that you ask them to do and the best way to get that across is to let the men see you do it, not just tell it." There was a ferocity to Boyle that was not lost upon his troopers, but fear alone could not have generated the admiration and fondness for him among his troopers.

Along with the exemplars there were also battalion and regimental heads who never ventured beyond a command post and often established that as far from danger as possible. Some GIs saw as little of their regimental leader as of their division general.

Persuading the individual to follow orders is not a matter of a popularity contest. Mabry confessed that he would eavesdrop on soldier conversations during breaks to get an inkling of what his men were thinking. He concluded, "If they said, 'he's a good guy,' he probably wasn't a good noncom or officer and was too lenient or doing something they knew was wrong. If they said, 'he's firm, but a good man,' they'd probably follow him." Mabry learned he was known as "the mean little man, but okay because he was tough but fair."

Only on Omaha Beach did Felix Branham discover praiseworthy quality in his regimental commander, Col. Charles Canham, who ranged up and down the strand screaming at the GIs to get off the beach. "Canham previously had a BAR shot out of his hand. The bullet went through his right wrist and he wore a makeshift sling. His bodyguard, Private First Class Nami, followed closely behind, keeping the colonel's .45 loaded. Canham would fire a clip and hand the gun back to Nami who would inject another into the weapon. Back in training, we used to call Colonel Canham everything not fit to print. When he took command of the 116th he made life miserable for us. We thought he would be another rear-echelon commander. After seeing him in action, I sure had to eat a lot of crow."

Similarly, it was the 29th Division's assistant commander on that same blood-soaked sand, Gen. Dutch Cota, who apparently shouted "Rangers, lead the way!" And although Frank Buck Dawson claimed he never heard the order, the Ranger lieutenant did respond to the need for someone to lead.

Of tank battalion commander Creighton Abrams, who would eventually become the Army's chief of staff, Abe Baum said, "He was sincere, honest, didn't speak down to people. In eight or ten words he could put more emphasis than someone who spoke for an hour. He led his troops. He didn't have a headquarters out there in his lead tank. Instead he was another gun in the tank."

Marine Richard Wheeler, wounded on Iwo Jima spoke of his battalion commander, Lt. Col. Chandler Johnson. "He was a rigid disciplinarian and kept us apprehensive about losing his favor. But on Iwo, he quickly began to earn our esteem. He strode about unflinchingly, wearing nothing on his head but a fatigue cap and carrying no gear except a .45-caliber pistol. When he stopped to consult with one of his subordinates, he would often stand erect, gesturing and pointing authoritatively, and making no effort to keep the enemy from learning he was a senior officer.

"In view of the emphasis that combat training places on security it would seem that men like Chandler Johnson and Howard Snyder [the squad leader who did not dig in] must be regarded with disapproval. But their kind are vital to a battlefield effort. It's true that a combat team must be composed mainly of cautious men; wholesale heedlessness under fire would certainly bring the team to disaster. But there is also a need for an audacious minority. It's this minority that set the pace for an attack. If everyone were to dig in deeply and move only when it was really necessary—which is all that duty requires—the team's efforts would lack vigor. There must be a scattering of men who neglect their safety and act with a daring initiative. Most of the tough feats that win the medals are performed by men like this. Though they are called damned fools by many of their more cautious comrades, they are nonetheless greatly admired. They do much for morale, since they seem entirely unafraid, and their cool aggressiveness sets a standard that the cautious not wishing to be too far outdone, follow to the best of their ability. And that's how objectives are taken and battles are won."

The virtue of leading by doing is not an absolute, even when it comes down to the most junior officers and noncoms. Carl Ulsaker, having gone through extensive combat for five months, developed his own point of view of the question. He recalled interviewing some replacement lieutenants and while he stressed that he expected them to motivate their entire platoons to fight, he put the newcomers through a quick course in what he believed was required. Ulsaker would ask the officer what was the motto of the Infantry School. 'Follow me, sir,' was the inevitable response.

To which Ulsaker replied, "I want you to forget that 'follow me' stuff beginning right now. If you get out in front of your platoon and cry 'Follow me!' you know what your men are going to say? They'll say, 'Go right ahead, Lieutenant,' because they know from experience that the man most likely to get shot in combat is the one in front. Your job is to get the entire platoon to fight; after all twenty or thirty rifles firing at the enemy equates to a hell of a lot more firepower than one officer's carbine. I'm not looking for heroes. I want leaders. I want *pushers*. Your place is behind your men where you can control them; not too far behind but close enough where you can kick someone in the tail if he lags to the rear. Sometimes I think the Army should redefine *leadership* and call it *pushership*." Ulsaker admitted there were some who were not convinced and, "would get out in front, wave his arms, shout, 'Follow me, men!' and get shot."

In the Air Corps, John Alison explained, "The squadron commander has to lead. Even if he is not the best pilot in the outfit, he has to lead or else he is not going to have a good outfit. I led every difficult mission we ever flew. I always had more bullet holes in my airplane than anybody else. You can lead by example. You can lead by power. You can do it either way. By my own experience and particularly [for] fighter pilots, it is a hell of a lot better to lead by example."

Still, there is the question of how to generate the responses required in the face of death and destruction. The accepted practice by all military organizations for inculcating the right attitude is through the discipline that begins in training camp. Some officers, notably Patton, belong to the school that believes insistence upon a necktie, polished shoes, shaved faces, and salutes instilled the instinct to automatically obey.

Bill Boyle, who graduated from the U.S. Military Academy did not exemplify spit and polish. "I had my opinions about discipline, but my emphasis was on combat training, combat reliability, and ability to rely on one another, not spit-shined boots. I was not casual. I trained intensively and expected the same of officers and men." He did not dismiss out of hand such traditions as military courtesy. "Saluting is an exchange of greetings; the subordinate acknowledges the authority of the senior. Grooming in garrison should be neat. Close-order drill is a disciplinary exercise designed to get us in the habit of obeying orders without question. These are necessary, but they must be kept in perspective. One should hardly expect a man to look as if he is going to a dance when he is living out of a knapsack in the field."

The Rangers, fighters that even Patton praised, under Bill Darby and James Rudder, almost entirely eschewed matters of appearance and formal behavior. Paratroop leader William Yarborough described Darby's men at Anzio as looking like "cutthroats . . . the sweepings of the barrooms, stubble beards, any kind of uniform." But Yarborough admitted leadership of the sort exemplified by Darby inspired certain individuals.

There were notable cases, including one cited by Carl Ulsaker, of individuals who during training personified excellent soldierly qualities, but once under fire proved worthless. In fact, frequently soldiers who disdained the strictures on grooming, fractured rules on behavior, and ignored concerns for military courtesy, demonstrated uncommon valor, as in the case of Medal of Honor winners Private First Class Harold Moon on Leyte, or Sgt. Maynard "Snuffy" Smith, an Eighth Air Force ball-turret gunner on a B-17 who, after his ship started to burn, extinguished the fire, administered first aid to a wounded tail gunner, and manned the waist guns to fend off predatory FW 190s.

One of the great tests of command is the ability to perform in the most adverse situations. Hank Spicer not only transformed a fumbling fighter group into a high-performance unit, he continued to lead while incarcerated in a prison camp. His behavior in a stalag contrasts sharply with that of Col. Charles Cavender, a West Pointer, who not only surrendered his regiment under questionable circumstances, but also appeared willing to compromise on the issue of Jewish prisoners until others in the camp refused to follow his lead.

In his *New York Review of Books* piece, Ignatieff said, "Killing is so far from being a natural instinct that many soldiers in the First and Second World Wars either didn't fire their weapons at all or fired them over their enemies' heads. This view, angrily denied by some veterans, was first advanced by the U.S. Army historian S.L.A. Marshall in 1947. It has been defended with weighty empirical evidence in *On Killing* [by American military historian David Grossman] a study of firing rates and of the ratios of kills to ammunition . . ." John McManus reported in his book *Deadly Brotherhood* that Harold Leinbaugh, a company commander in the 84th Infantry Division who wrote a book on his experiences, spoke to many associates and could find few if any who recalled not shooting their weapons. Leinbaugh went on a personal crusade to debunk S.L.A. Marshall and found ample evidence that Marshall never asked questions about whether men fired their weapons. It is dubious that he even conducted some of the interviews upon which he supposedly based his thesis.

It is preposterous to extrapolate from the number of rounds expended how many bullets by individual GIs and leathernecks caused casualties. As anyone who was on the scene can testify, fire discipline was extremely difficult to maintain, although many commanders strove mightily to limit the shooting. Frequently any sound heard or shadow glimpsed during the night provoked volleys of gunfire. The mechanism of the basic infantry weapon, the M1 Garand enabled a man to empty eight bullets in a clip in an astonishingly short time. Furthermore, much of the fighting took place at distances measured in hundreds of yards; and with the enemy concealed in a cave, brush, house, or behind a hedgerow. No one waited until he could see the whites of the eyes before squeezing the trigger, which also explains incidentally much of the friendly fire problem. Under the circumstances in which the bodies of dead enemy were hastily buried, sometimes with mass graves dug by a bulldozer, without benefit of autopsies, it is ridiculous to believe there can have been any accounting of who died from a bullet and who from artillery, mortar rounds, or strafing from the air. That more people, soldiers and civilians, were killed by long-range artillery or air raids than by bullets from the individual soldier is irrelevant; it only makes the case that modern weapons have gone beyond the simple man-with-the-gun.

Based on personal accounts, the willingness to destroy other humans in the war was not affected by class or education. Barely literate Marines and GIs as well as the college bred carried out the necessities of combat. A hard-bitten lawyer-soldier, Dick Thom said he worried that the infusion of former members of the Army Specialized Training Program would lessen the efficiency of the 96th Infantry Division. "They turned out to be smart kids, quick to learn, good riflemen, good shooters, solid killers, and thoroughly reliable."

Ignatieff's survey of Ehrenreich's book and others delves into the alleged psychological conditioning of religious blessings, training, drilling, parades and martial speeches designed to transform humans from their "normal moral order" into ones able to destroy lives. While all of the precombat ritual and instruction may have helped condition the combat soldier, the most compelling influence was the simple imperative, "kill or be killed." During the later years of the war a film with that as its title tried to convince GIs to abandon the scruples of civil society. The testimony of the men on the line time and again is the "them or us" syndrome. It is a question of what is required to survive.

The heat of battle brought on atrocities. It is understandable for a soldier who has just lost his closest friend to gun down the enemy who only runs up the white flag after running out of ammunition. The surprise attack upon Pearl Harbor, the mutilation and murder of prisoners by both the Japanese and Germans, occasioned retaliation. But the savage slaying of prisoners because it was too much trouble to guard them or escort them to the rear speaks of a darker side of men at war. In the case of the Japanese, undoubtedly racism made slaughter easier. The shooting of airmen in parachutes after their plane has been hit was decried throughout the war. But if a pilot would be in a position to return to the war, then how much difference would killing him be than murdering a man running away from the battle? For the most part, the act of mercy to an aviator was an offshoot of the kill-or-be-killed principle—if we do this, they will do it to us.

Several eyewitnesses in this book testify to GIs harvesting gold teeth from corpses, looting bodies of valuables, even photographs. In the Air Corps there were those who scavenged in the possessions of shot-down comrades, explaining that the victims would no longer need the items. On more occasions than one wishes to remember, Americans slaughtered those who surrendered or wished to quit.

To be sure, when the action ended, many felt compassion and guilt for the dead. Ranger Bob Edlin, remembered emptying his M1 at an enemy soldier. "Afterward I rolled over the man I had shot. I see his face at night, even after almost fifty years. I wondered then and now what happened to the beautiful little boy and girl in the picture that the proud father carried to show his friends." There were numerous similar expressions of remorse from men in all theaters of combat. It was easier for artillerymen and gunners on Navy vessels who did not have to look at the faces of those they killed. Airmen like Cary Salter thought in terms of destroying machines rather than killing people. Only when shot down over Germany did fliers like Jim Goodson and Jim McCubbin become aware of the destruction done by the Air Forces.

Obviously the atomic bomb killed the most people in a single stroke. It is difficult to find a combat veteran, even today, who does not approve of the use of the weapon. Faced with the massive concrete bunker-to-bunker defenses, the availability of thousands of kamikaze planes, and an army of several million that had never deviated from the code of death before surrender, those assigned to invade Japan believe tens of thousands faced death. Infantry sergeant Don Dencker speaks for most when he declared, "God bless the atomic bomb. It probably saved my life."

Arguments against the use of A-bombs revolve around such issues as the extraordinary number killed by only two nuclear explosions at Hiroshima and Nagasaki, 210,000 in the initial blasts and another 130,000 from injuries or radiation effects within five years. Balanced against these losses by those who approved the two attacks are the estimated casualties for an invasion of Japan that run from 46,000 to 1,000,000. While the low figure hardly seems credible in light of the losses at Okinawa, Iwo Jima, and other strongholds, the projections miss the point. Once the body counts rise into the tens of thousands the debate of morality becomes pointless. The issue of whether war could be confined only to the military had been decided with the concept of strategic bombing aimed at destroying the capacity of a nation to fight.

Furthermore, the terrible deaths and disfigurements of the residents in the Japanese cities differed little from those incinerated or suffocated by flamethrowers, disemboweled by shrapnel, decapitated by mortars, who had huge portions of their faces shot away, or lost limbs from mines. Had the bomb not been used, as David Burchinal said, there were plans to firebomb every Japanese city. The incendiary raid on Tokyo killed 85,000 to 100,000, certainly as frightening as the results of the atomic bomb on Nagasaki.

The detonation of Little Boy and Fat Man in fact demonstrate the real nature of a large-scale modern war, the loss of control. The momentum that develops overwhelms the individual, even if he sits in the White House. There was never any genuine doubt that Harry Truman would authorize the use of nuclear weapons. He was the political head of a country facing an unknown amount of death and destruction should the war continue. He could hardly have risked the lives of so many countrymen in order to preserve those of an enemy nation.

Loss of control is what war is about. Bob Slaughter, who saw so many of his childhood friends killed on Omaha Beach, said, "I realized it didn't make any difference whether one was a superior soldier, was more religious, of better character. People were being killed randomly and they could not help themselves." In fact, many of the most repellant events of the war—the atrocities, the use of the nuclear bomb, the looting of bodies, the gamut from manic to depressive behavior—are products of this loss of power to govern one's fate.

Eugene Sledge, who felt "utter and absolute helplessness, said in *With the Old Breed*, "As Peleliu dragged on I feared that if I ever lost control of myself under shellfire my mind would be shattered. To be under heavy shellfire was to me by far the most terrifying of combat experiences. Each time, it left me feeling more forlorn and helpless, more fatalistic and with less confidence that I could escape the dreadful law of averages that inexorably reduced our numbers."

Theirs are common sentiments that lead to the question of why men endure and persevere at war. Writer Paul Fussell, who commanded an infantry company in Europe, attributed the dogged persistence to "inertia." He is at one with Leo Tolstoy, who while describing the Battle of Borodino in *War and Peace*, wrote, "But though towards the end of the battle the men felt all the horror of their actions, though they would have been glad to cease, some unfathomable mysterious force still led them on . . . ." Inertia may be another way of describing loss of control.

For all of the horror and the sorrow, there was also an uplifting feeling that some relished in their war. Clearly it was the best of times for Patton, although since his skin was hardly at peril, his delight is easy to understand. Hamilton Howze similarly appraised the attitude of armored division commander Ernest Harmon. "I never knew anybody of any rank who enjoyed war as much as Ernie Harmon did. His war record was fine. When he had everything in the division fighting he thought the world could give him nothing better. I recall his calling me up and saying, 'By God, I've got everything in the division shooting, including all the tankdozers.'"

Once engaged in the business of war, few lusted for the role of hero. Doolittle Raid pilot William Bower said, "I don't think there was any feeling on anybody's part that they wanted to be the first to bomb Tokyo. They just wanted to do the job and come on home. For years we couldn't understand why people would ask us to come to their town for a reunion. We thought it should have died. Now, as we see get older we see that perhaps the reason [lies in] that expression 'can do.' It gave me an association with people that I would never have had."

There were "war lovers." Many line organizations had at least one soldier who seemed to enjoy killing. Others admitted they liked blowing up things. Ben Renton, a lieutenant in the 517th Parachute Regiment, wounded six times, said he "loved" his months in combat. Renton had enjoyed his war so much that he sought to obtain a regular army commission, but his wounds left him physically unfit. His fellow trooper Ludlow Gibbons declared, "Ninety-nine percent of all the excitement I have had in my life took place during the time I spent in combat. I believe it to be the ultimate test. I have never experienced anything close to it, before or since."

Fear triggers an adrenaline rush and others, although less enthusiastic about their experiences, echoed Winston Churchill's comment, to the effect that nothing was more exhilarating than to be shot at and missed. Phil Hannon, taken prisoner during the Battle of the Bulge, recalled "a higher sense of being when under fire." But that is not the same as pleasure. Carmen Capalbo, a scout with the 99th Division, wounded in early December 1944, said, "I saw no exhilaration in anyone. I never heard any person express sentiments remotely resembling those." Frank Barron, a company commander in the 77th Infantry Division said, "I believe fighting for your country in the infantry in battle is the most purifying experience known to man. These men who trained hard together and fought for extended periods together became so completely unselfish, so absorbed with the welfare of the group that you could believe that their principal concern was for the 'other guy.' I've never wished to die before or since, nor did I wish to die in battle then. But I thought there was a good chance that I would and I thought then there was no better way to die, and no better men to be buried with."

The film *Saving Private Ryan* elicited a few carping remarks from some conservatives who felt the soldiers never voiced any comments on the cause for which they were fighting. In all of the interviews I've done for seven books on World War II I never came across a single individual who recalled foxhole discussions about religion, democracy, the Four Freedoms, the Constitution, or the horrors of totalitarianism. (Nor do they speak of Mom's apple pie, the Brooklyn Dodgers, or similar clichés.) Men under fire think and talk in terms of how to stay alive, whom they've lost, their desires for a warm, dry place and hot food, not abstractions that have nothing to do with their situations. When they pray it is for survival, not in a declaration of faith. While Barron's opening words might be attributed to an idealized recall, the essence of his remarks are close to what most men admit. It was not religion or patriotism that kept them going, but the sense of communion with their fellows.

When Bob Edlin had been treated for his wounds he began a journey to rejoin his old unit. Along the way he saw a Ranger water trailer being filled. "The driver asked me why in hell I was going back. I asked him why he was. We could both just take off over the hill. He thought about it a little and said, 'Hell, the guys up there need this water.' That's why I went back."

Said tanker Dee Paris, "I never saw a man who wasn't frightened. And I've seen cowards. The difference is PRIDE! Two kinds of pride—your personal pride in your conduct and second, you won't want others to see you are a coward."

Bill Boyle noted, "When men live, eat, train, gripe, and suffer together, they stick together. These are men I loved and protected where I could. And when I was wounded, they did the same for me." They refused to "leave him out there." It was the sense of community, the camaraderie that was the single most cited motivation for remaining in the field. A foundation for this closeness lay in the widely accepted reasons for being under fire. There was little or no dissent, in contrast to the succeeding wars. Those engaged in World War II generally spent far more time together. Many units trained for years before they went overseas and unlike Korea and Vietnam, with the exception of aircrews in Europe, there was no "tour" to complete and then return home. Until wounded or killed, for three years, Marines went from island to island and GIs fought from North Africa to the heart of Germany. Sailors prowled the seas from the date "that will live in infamy" until V-J Day, so long as they survived torpedoes, shells, and kamikazes. More than fifty years later, the ties created by shared hardships and danger remain for a huge number of survivors, now banded into alumni organizations with regular reunions, newsletters, and lifetime friendships.

At the same time, it is also true that while World War II drew together individuals from disparate backgrounds and interests, some remained aloof from their fellows and once the common cause ended, so did their association. On the other hand, society's most brutal, murderous activity, also witnessed occasions of courage, heroism, and even glory. But the supreme irony is that for all of its evil, perhaps even because of its very nature, the experience generated lifelong bonds among those who fought on land, sea, and in the air.

Roll Call

Adair, Marion. The 4th Infantry Division battalion surgeon resumed his medical practice in Georgia until retirement in 1990.

Alison, John. Air Corps lend-lease consultant, fighter pilot with the Fourteenth Air Force in the China-Burma Theater, an ace, he retired as a major general.

Allen, Brooke. Commander of the 5th Bomb Group at Hickham Field, Hawaii, on 7 December 1941, he supervised training of B-29 crews and retired in 1965 as a major general.

Allen, Terry. Commanding general of the 1st and 104th Infantry Divisions, he is deceased. His only son, who graduated from the U.S. Military Academy, was killed in Vietnam.

Altieri, James. An original Ranger, he has been active in the Rangers Association as well as the World War II Remembrance Society and makes his home in Corona Del Mar, California.

Andrusko, Ed. After thirty-three months of service, earning three Purple Hearts with the 1st Marine Division, he expressed no regrets for his experiences. "I saw our countrymen united against our enemies in a worldwide war. The men in my company were my family and friends, our senior NCOs were our parents. Item Company was my home on land or sea. We protected each other and fought for each other. After the war, I felt I could handle anything in the civilian world and took on all challenges, started college a day after my discharge. We returning veterans had pride in our accomplishments, love for our families, and ambition for our future. We assimilated into the civilian world with ease." After a career in electronics, he lives in Colorado.

Ashe, Walter. The pre-war-Navy sailor sailed on a number of ships in the Pacific theater, was aboard the first vessel to dock in Korea after the fighting began there, and in 1966 retired after thirty years of service. He lives in Asheville, North Carolina.

Ashworth, Frederick. "There's only two guys in the world who have had the experience of essentially being in tactical command of the delivery of an atom bomb in wartime, and I am one of them. You're supposed to get very emotional about it. How did it feel? I didn't feel anything in particular. I guess it is just like so many other experiences. While they are going on, you don't really feel much of anything except that this is a job that has to be done. When you get shot at, you're not scared right then. You are too busy doing what has to be done. You do get scared after it's all over. "He retired as a vice admiral and lives in New Mexico.

Austin, Gordon. An Air Corps fighter pilot, hunting deer in the Hawaiian Islands at the time of the Japanese attack, he had graduated from West Point in 1936—"I don't remember choosing anything. My father [an architect and veteran of the Spanish-American War] sent me." He retired as a major general.

Austin, Paul. Following his stint as a company commander and battalion staff officer with the 24th Infantry Division, he worked for a telephone company until retirement. "I was sick to my stomach, of all those who'd been killed or got wounded. But that's the infantry story. You take the mud, the pain, do without food, do without water, and you keep fighting." He lives in Fort Worth.

Barron, Frank Jr. Following his role as a platoon leader and company commander with the 77th Division, he became an executive in the textile industry. He makes his home in Columbia, South Carolina.

Baum, Abe. The leader of the ill-fated task force that bore his name went into the garment industry after the war. He retired to Southern California.

Behlmer, Bill. The antitank crewman with the 1st Division received a prosthesis for his amputated right leg and worked in the aircraft industry.

Bernheim, Eli. After combat in the Philippines with the 11th Airborne Division, he worked in the family business before re-entering the service to participate in the Korean War. He retired after more than twenty years to enter business and now lives in Florida.

Biddle, Melvin. The Medal of Honor awardee from the 517th Parachute Regimental Combat Team spent nearly thirty years as an employee of the Veterans Administration in his home state of Indiana.

Bluemel, Clifford. The commander of the 31st Philippine Division in 1941 survived captivity and retired as a major general. He is deceased.

Bolt, Jones E. A P-47 pilot, he recalled the depths of the Great Depression when a man with rags on his feet for shoes asked for a job and his father, a textile manufacturer, had none to offer. "Everybody elected the ROTC [at Clemson University] because we got something like twenty-five cents a day." As a prisoner of war he struggled through the infamous march from StalagLuft III to Moosburg and said "We found out that Hitler had ordered all of us shot. Goering [Hermann, the Nazi Luftwaffe chief] refused to carry out the order." He retired as a major general.

Bouck, Lyle. He became a chiropractor in St. Louis.

Bower, William. The Doolittle Raid pilot who reached China and escaped capture remained in the Air Force until he retired as a colonel.

Boyle, Bill. Commander of the 1st Battalion of the 517th Parachute Regimental Combat Team, he recovered from his wounds in the Ardennes, and served in Korea before retirement. After a few years in security he went back to school, and opened a business in accountancy. "My first company commander after I graduated from West Point told me, 'You take care of the men and they will take care of you.'" He lives in Saratoga Springs, NY.

Buckley, Pete. A glider pilot for D day in Normandy, Market Garden in Holland, and Varsity across the Rhine, he studied commercial photography under the GI Bill. "I came home ten years older than I should have been and I had enough of flying." His home is in Connecticut.

Bulkeley, John D. The 1930 United States Naval Academy graduate awarded a Medal of Honor after he helped MacArthur leave the Philippines aboard a PT boat, later commanded torpedo boats during the Normandy invasion, and then finished the war aboard the cruiser *Houston*, reborn after the original ship was sunk by the Japanese. He died a vice admiral in 1998 after sixty-four years of active duty.

Burchinal, David. A B-29 test pilot and participant in raids on Japan, he had worked in a factory and been a union leader after graduation from Brown University before the war. He remained in the Air Force, helping develop the Air University curriculum; held staff posts at upper echlons and retired as a general.

Caron, George. The tail gunner on the *Enola Gay* is deceased.

Carlton, Paul. After flying a number of B-29 missions against Japan from China and mining the Singapore Harbor as well as the enemy-controlled portions of the Yangtse River, Carlton piloted pathfinder planes from the Marianas. "We would fly upwind over the target precisely dropping our bombs. Then the follow-on force would come in and bomb on our fire, downwind. The survival rate upwind was kind of atrocious." On one such occasion, the headwind reduced the pathfinder's speed to only eighty knots; ten out of the twelve in the operation went down. The upwind approach was abandoned. He retired as a general after running the Military Airlift Command.

Carmichael, Richard. He was a 1936 graduate of the U.S. Military Academy, after joining the Texas National Guard at age fifteen. Interviewed in 1942 about a number of subjects including morale, he remarked, "The two main topics, except at the dinner table, were bombing and women. I personally believe that if there were some form of controlled prostitution around an Army camp, it would be the best solution . . . it would control the venereal rate and keep the combat crews a hell of a lot happier." He noted that as a prisoner it struck him that the Japanese "were going to fight to the bitter end . . . the military . . . and the populace went along with whatever the military decided. They put us to work digging tunnels, caves actually, inside of hills not far from where our gardens were. We presumed that this was part of their last-ditch defense system." He left the service as a major general.

Carpenter, John. As a 1939 graduate of the USMA, he transferred from the field artillery to USAF which brought him to the 19th Bomb Group in the Philippines in 1941. After he reached Australia, Carpenter flew missions in the Pacific, and following V-J Day held various staff posts before retiring as a lieutenant general. He lives in North Carolina.

Carter, Norval. The 29th Infantry Division battalion surgeon KIA in Normandy left a widow and two sons. Upon the death of Emma Ferne Lowry Carter in 1995, their son Walter discovered several caches of correspondence between her and his father. Walter Carter researched the experiences of his father and discovered in my book *June 6, 1944: The Voices of D-Day* an excerpt from Frank Wawrynovic's account that mentioned the circumstances of his father's death. Walter Carter wrote to me and very kindly allowed me to make use of portions of the collected letters of Norval Carter.

Chism, John. The medic with the 517th Parachute Regimental Combat Team left the service to attend college, where he earned a reserve commission and went on active duty as a field artillery commander during the Korean War. He remained in the Army until retirement as a colonel.

Cochran, Philip. After he completed his tour as joint leader of the 1st Air Commando unit in the Far East, he trained pilots until the war's end. Physical disabilities forced him to retire in 1947 with the rank of colonel. He provided technical expertise to Hollywood filmmakers before entering business in Pennsylvania. He died in 1979.

Conver, Milt. The bombardier with the 303d Bomb Group, coped with respiratory infections that limited his missions with the Eighth Air Force. After V-E Day he left the service, entered business in Ohio. He is deceased.

Creel, Buckner. A platoon leader with the 77th Division on Guam and in the Philippines, he commanded a company on Okinawa. He fought in Korea where he was wounded and then in Vietnam before retirement. He lives in Arlington, Virginia.

Cutter, Slade. The former submariner and 1935 USNA graduate retired as a captain and lives in Annapolis.

Darby, William O. After the disaster at Cisterna that destroyed three of his battalions, the founder of the Rangers, who previously refused offers to lead regiments, took over the 179th Regiment of the 45th Division at Anzio Subsequently named assistant commander of the 10th Mountain Division, he was killed by German artillery fire, two days before the enemy forces in Italy surrendered.

Davison, Michael. A USMC graduate, the former staff officer and battalion commander with the 45th Division earned a graduate degree at Harvard, commanded troops in Vietnam, and headed the army units in Europe before retirement as a general. He lives in Virginia.

Dawson, Frank (Buck). The 5th Ranger Battalion lieutenant who led pinned down troops off Omaha Beach on D day entered the reserves following V-E Day, but when recalled for the Korean War elected the service as a career, which culminated in 1968 after a tour in Vietnam. He is deceased.

DeHaven, Robert. The USAF ace with fourteen victories retired as a colonel and lives in southern California.

DeLoach, James. The 32d Division company officer chose to enter local government after the war and lives in Columbia, South Carolina.

Duckworth, George. The 2d Infantry Division officer stayed in uniform, retiring as a colonel, and lives in New Mexico.

Dunfee, Bill. The 82d Airborne trooper worked for a lumber business in Columbus, Ohio, and became a top executive with the organization.

Dunn, Bill. The Air Force fighter pilot began his World War II experience as an infantryman with the Canadian Seaforth Highlanders. After V-J Day he advised in China, Iran, and South America during the 1950s before he put in his papers.

Edlin, Bob. The 2d Ranger Battalion platoon leader in Normandy, the Cotentin Peninsula and in the grim winter on the German border held the job of a police chief in Indiana before moving to Corpus Christi, Texas where he operates an antique auction house.

Eller, Ernest. A USNA 1925 graduate and a gunnery officer aboard the *Lexington* at the Battle of Midway, he retired as a captain. He is deceased.

Ellis, Richard. A B-25 pilot in the South Pacific who had been drafted in 1940 before enrolling in flight training, he completed 200 missions. He left the service to practice law, but when called up for Korea he stayed on until retirement as a general.

Emmens, Robert. After the war, the Doolittle Raid pilot who spent two years as a "guest of the Kremlin" served as a military attaché and in intelligence for the Air Force before retirement as a colonel.

Engeman, Len. The 9th Armored Division tank battalion commander who directed the capture of the vital bridge at Remagen remained in the Army until retirement as a colonel. He lives in California.

Erwin, Henry. The Air Corps crewman badly burned by an incendiary and who received a Medal of Honor is deceased.

Eubank, Eugene. The commander of the B-17 19th Bomb Group in the Philippines on 7 December 1941, he earned Army wings almost thirty years earlier. He recalled that when Boeing produced the first Flying Fortress he and his associates immediately recognized it was far superior to any competitor's wares. However, while the prototype was being tested in 1935 at Wright Field, Ohio, the plane crashed. "We damned near sat down and cried when the first one was wrecked. In those days the manufacturer had to submit an article [a plane] that was tested, evaluated, and the board decided which one was going to win. If it hadn't been for that accident, Boeing would have won the competition and we would have had the B-17 two or three years ahead of what we did." He retired as a major general.

Evans, Bing. An original Ranger who was Darby's sergeant major, he received a commission before being captured at Cisterna. He noted that his experiences as a POW so scarred him that throughout his life he was subject to "black rages." He worked in private industry and now lives in Huntington, Indiana.

Gage, Tom. The Air Corps clerk captured on Bataan acts as a clearing house for information about prisoners of war from that period and lives in Tulsa, Oklahoma.

Gangel, Dick. The P-38 pilot came home from the Fifteenth Air Force in Italy to teach other flyers. After his honorable discharge he became an art director, first in advertising and then for *Sports Illustrated*. He lives in Weston, Connecticut, where he creates sculptures.

Gilliam, Tom. As an officer with the 2d Division, he recovered from wounds after a three-month hospital stay in time to participate in the final drives against the Germans. After the enemy repulsed the unit in a brutal confrontation in the vicinity of Eisenschmitt, Gilliam noted to his superior that for the third time he had wound up the senior company commander in the battalion. He added that the only other officer of that responsibility who was left from their arrival in France on 9 July was home on a forty-five-days leave. Told he was regarded as the best in the division, Gilliam said he replied, "'Colonel, I am going to be a dead company commander if this keeps up.' We retook the town the next day, but we lost 117 men up there that night. Less than three weeks later I was on orders to return home for a forty-five-day leave. But that three weeks included the second crossing of the Moselle, the closing of the Trier pocket, the crossing of the Rhine at Oppenheim, the capture of Frankfurt am Main, and the memorial service for President Roosevelt aboard ship." He lives in Lakeport, California.

Goode, John. The 36th Division officer shattered by the Rapido River experience is deceased.

Hartman, Tom. The Navy pilot recalled that while a student at Princeton, in his enthusiastic rush to enlist after the college requirements were lowered, his physical exam revealed possible problems with one eye. He was instructed to return for a second test. "A Navy corpsman was to be the examiner. His first question was, 'Are you another college boy?' I thought that I should drop through the floor. Princeton was like the kiss of death in that milieu. But I admitted my status. He said, 'Princeton! That's great.' He told me he had worked as an usher at the Chicago Opera House and the only company passing through that invited the ushers to their cast parties was the Triangle Club [the university's drama group]! He was so excited that he never gave my eye a look and signed my clearance." Hartman returned to his alma mater to complete his education and then taught at Rutgers. He lives in Princeton, New Jersey.

Hayes, Tommy. The Army fighter pilot who fought in both the Pacific and Europe retired as a colonel and lives in Pennsylvania.

Herder, Harry. The 2d Ranger Battalion replacement participated in the liberation of the Buchenwald concentration camp. "We were the last replacements taken into the battalion. Barely in my memory is the first job [that] rumor said we were scheduled to do. They were going to put us, a company at a time, in Piper Cubs and fly us over the Rhine. That was washed out when the Remagen Bridge stood. I remember a ballistic company commander. Being nearsighted made me less than perfect and unfit to be a Ranger. The way that man was mad at me was something else. With him, I did not belong. In 1947 I was accepted in jump school and allowed to be a member of the 82d Airborne for three years and they knew I wore glasses the whole time. Even jumped with them taped on once they found out. The helmet jammed them into my nose on 'opening shock.' They remained in my shirt pocket all the rest of the jumps."

Herder on his third military hitch joined the Navy and served as corpsman for the Marines in Korea. He lives in Hayward, Wisconsin.

Hill, David (Tex). The former Navy flyer who enlisted in the American Volunteer Group under Gen. Clare Chennault retired as a colonel and is a resident of San Antonio.

Hite, Robert L. The last-minute addition to the Doolittle Raiders, who endured years of captivity, remained in the service after his liberation and worked as an air attaché in North Africa. He retired as a lieutenant colonel.

Hofrichter, Joe. The rifleman from the 24th Division entered a family construction business and makes his home in Port Charlotte, Florida.

Hostetter, Philip. The battalion surgeon with the 24th Division, after mustering out, opened a practice in family medicine and lives in Manhattan, Kansas.

Howze, Hamilton. The 1930 West Point alumnus who spent World War II with armored forces in North Africa and Italy switched to airborne in the 1950s to command the 82d Airborne Division and the eighteenth Airborne Corps. He retired as a full general in 1965 and died in 1998.

Jackson, Schuyler. The 101st Airborne paratrooper worked in construction until his death in 1995.

Johnson, Fred. The former National Guardsman called up in 1940 and who fought with the 32d Division in the Pacific said, "I approved of what we did in the war then and still do. There was a sense of duty; you were scared, heck yes. But you just did what you thought you had to do. There was pride in not letting the others down. To bug out would make you ashamed. The worst food was in Buna, bully beef, and small rations, two spoons a day. I came home with malaria, having had three separate attacks." After his discharge he became a Superior, Wisconsin, policeman and then was elected sheriff ten times before retirement. He lives in Arizona.

Johnson, Leon. He was in the class of 1926 at the USMA. He led the 44th Bomb Group on the Ploesti raid, where he earned a Medal of Honor and then commanded a bomber wing with the Eighth Air Force in England. He retired in 1961 as a general and died in 1998.

Johnson, Robert. The ground crew sergeant who volunteered for the 4th Armored Division was convicted of a 1971 murder and is serving a life term in North Carolina.

Johnson, Robert. The fighter pilot with the second highest number of planes shot down in Europe, worked in the aircraft industry after the war. He died in 1998.

Jones, David M. The Doolittle Raider who parachuted into China then returned to duty was subsequently shot down in a B-26 during a raid on Bizerte. He became a prisoner of war in Germany. Following liberation he held positions in the Pentagon, with NASA, and other research projects. He retired as a major general.

Jones, Harry. The Navy pilot who helped sink the *Yamato* remarked, "I think it was a good idea to drop the atomic bomb because I think the invasion would have killed millions of Japanese. War is hell; stay the hell out of it. We had no business in Vietnam; in my opinion we should stay the hell out of Bosnia. They should have some sort of international police there." He became an FBI agent and now lives in Carlisle, Pennsylvania.

Jones, Homer. After the war ended, the paratroop platoon leader left the service but was recalled for the war in Korea. He remained on active duty until retirement and then taught Spanish in public schools. He lives in Florida.

Kelly, Walter. The Eighth Air Force pilot who flew the first B-17 raid on occupied Europe later flew missions against the Japanese in the Pacific. He continued his career in the Air Force after the end of hostilities and retired as a colonel. He worked in private industry before retiring to a home in Alexandria, Virginia.

Kidwell, Vance. The draftee from Illinois who became a replacement in a supply section of the 2d Armored Division while the outfit was in North Africa was with the outfit when it reached France on D plus 1. He lives in Donnellson, Illinois.

Kitzmann, Erich. The *Suwannee* crewman blown overboard after a Kamikaze explosion worked in aircraft maintenance until he retired to Sedona, Arizona.

Kunz, William J. The former 3d Infantry Division field artillery hand who campaigned through North Africa, Sicily, Italy, Anzio, Southern France, and Germany lives in Illinois.

Loiacano, Leonard. An artilleryman, he said "When the gun was fired it made so much noise that you had to keep your mouth open and if your hands were free you put them in your ears. We would be wet to the skin, cold and in total darkness. Most of the time we got six hours of sleep every other night. One time we went sixty hours without sleep. We were never relieved and always firing for somebody. We dug gun pits and cut down trees [to brace the artillery and cover foxholes] from Normandy to Czechoslovakia." The 105mm howitzer crewman with the 5th Infantry Division had amassed enough points to warrant discharge shortly after V-E Day. "When we were home, the two "A" bombs were dropped and the war was over. Many years later the bleeding hearts would say what a terrible thing it was to drop the bomb. For all of those people I wish them ten months of combat and then let us hear what they have to say." He makes his home in Yeadon, Pennsylvania.

Lomell, Len (Bud). The Ranger sergeant involved in the destruction of enemy big guns atop Pointe du Hoc on D day received a battlefield commission before being wounded a second time. He studied law under the GI Bill, practiced in New Jersey where he makes his home.

Long, Stanley. The first P-38 pilot to shoot down a Japanese plane in the Aleutians, he remained in the Air Force, retiring as a colonel.

Low, Martin. The fighter pilot, who was at Hickham Field on 7 December 1941 and over the Normandy beaches on 6 June 1944, came home after seventy-five missions in Europe. "I had seen enough of the Army in peacetime to know that it was not for me. I applied to the airlines but they did not think fighter pilots had the right stuff. Because of my experience of war I took up the cause of the United Nations, which I believe is a much more viable method of settling differences." As a civilian he produced commercials for TV and lives in a suburb of New York City.

Lynd, J. Q. The 90th Division platoon leader recovered from his wounds and became a research scientist and teacher at Oklahoma State University in Stillwater, Oklahoma.

Mabry, George L. Jr. The 4th Division officer finally received a regular army commission in 1944 and by the time the war ended he was the second most decorated soldier of the conflict. He subsequently graduated from the Command and General Staff College, the National War College, and held a variety of command, training, and staff positions. He led a 100-man team of officers and civilians to evaluate operations in Vietnam and later served as chief of staff and assistant deputy commanding general for the U.S. Army Forces in Vietnam. In 1975 he retired as a major general and lived in Columbia, South Carolina, until his death in 1990.

McCubbin, James. The fighter pilot now lives in Garberville, California.

Meltessen, Clarence. The 4th Ranger Battalion lieutenant captured at Cisterna survived more than a year in the stalags. He remained on active duty after the war, retiring as a colonel. He has compiled an exhaustive record of what happened to his fellow Rangers and their experiences in the prisoner of war camps. He lives in California.

Merrill, Alan. The 2d Battalion Ranger wounded and temporarily captured near Anzio recovered in a Naples hospital. During his recuperation he met a captain who offered to wangle a transfer to the Air Corps enabling Merrill to serve out his time as a limited-duty, noncombat soldier. Assigned to the 379th Bomb Group, a B-25 outfit, he learned aircraft recognition while assisting in tow-target practice. He even went along on missions that dumped aluminum foil to foul up enemy radar. But when a batch of replacement gunners failed to arrive, Merrill was pressed into service as a tail gunner beginning in October 1944. He flew twenty-four missions, occupying various positions manning a .50-caliber machine gun. Flak ripped into his airplanes on several occasions killing other members of the crew, and he survived a crash landing in the sea near Corsica. Black-outs, bleeding from his left ear and nose on his last missions grounded him after his twenty-fourth. He waited several months before orders finally sent him home via Casablanca, where he said he visited bordellos supervised by the U.S. Army with military police on duty.

"I went away a frightened boy. I returned a frightened man. The actual battle of enduring a war in the various types of combat that I participated in was not as riveting an experience as the battles my mind fought daily in the ensuing peaceful years. When the actual fighting was done I had to conquer my own personal, mental war of nerves. I found out much later that I had no control over what happened to the unprepared, mindless, loose ends of my young manhood and the residue of the code of killing or being killed. I don't believe I ever really adjusted to this code of the military survivor. Everything I was taught to do to survive was diametrically opposed to a way of life I had been raised to believe in for eighteen years.

"How does one go about 'unlearning' to kill another human being? This unlearning process comes ever so slowly or it never comes at all. It is your own individual struggle. No one can do it for you. If this cannot be done, then peace of mind eludes you all your days. In my half century, since World War II and with my battles over, I truly believe that war is like a malignant tumor on the face of mankind." He now lives in Florida.

Mott, Hugh. The platoon leader who helped preserve the Remagen Bridge over the Rhine went into politics and in 1949 was elected to the Tennessee State Legislature while remaining active in the National Guard. He retired from the Guard as a major general in 1972.

Mueller, Arndt. The 6th Infantry Division battalion commander attended the Command and General Staff College and eventually joined its faculty. He headed the ROTC program at the University of Miami, earned a law degree, and joined the Florida bar.

Newman, Stan. The P-51 pilot assigned to the fifteenth Air Force in Italy redeployed to the States after V-E Day in preparation for the finale against Japan. "I changed my mind about a regular air force career, took a reserve commission, and made it back to start my interrupted college at the University of Illinois. I was one of the first vets back and was like a fish out of water. I really missed the Air Corps life, good pay, great airplanes, and wonderful friends. But I eventually adapted." As a reserve officer, however, he was recalled during the Korean War and flew 100 missions in that conflict. During the war in Vietnam he flew cargo missions to Southeast Asia. He retired in 1983 as a major general and lives in Oklahoma.

Northrup, Jay. The replacement officer with the Rangers had been reassigned, but a bout of malaria contracted in Sicily sent him back to the States. After he left the service he entered the field of banking before retirement to Florida.

Odell, Bill. The Eighth Air Force pilot involved in the organization's first raid moved first to North Africa and then the Pacific. After he retired as a colonel he embarked on a career as a writer publishing many novels in the mystery, adventure, and Western genres. He lives in Colorado Springs.

Olson, John E. After liberation from his Philippine prison camp, the 1939 USMA graduate remained in uniform until retirement as a colonel in 1967. He has done extensive research and writing on the Bataan fighting, the Death March, and Philippine guerrilla movements. He lives in Houston, Texas.

Paris, Dee. The 9th Armored Division tank commander retained a reserve commission after the war and made barbershop quartet music his avocation while living in Maryland.

Poston, Tom. The troop carrier pilot chose the life of an actor after being mustered out. He appeared on Broadway, and in numerous roles on radio and then television. He lives in California.

Raaen, John C. Jr. One of the few West Pointers (class of 1943) to volunteer for the Rangers, his jeep accident in France ended World War II for him. In 1951 he earned a master's degree from Johns Hopkins and then held command posts with various units before retirement as a major general. He lives in Florida.

Raila, Frank. The 106th Division soldier taken prisoner in the Ardennes became a radiologist in Mississippi. The emotional outbursts, triggered by his memories of the stalag that disturbed him in the years immediately after the war, subsided.

Rants, Hanford. The wireman with the 24th Infantry Division, which fought in the Pacific theater, used the GI Bill to complete his education at Washington State University, then taught in high school before becoming a principal. He lives in Downey, California.

Robison, Noel (Eugene). As a replacement, he joined the 90th Division in November 1944, where he served as a runner until his frozen feet disabled him during the Battle of the Bulge. He lives in Claremont, California.

Rosson, William. The officer with the 3d Infantry Division, as an honor student in the ROTC program at the University of Oregon in 1940, had obtained a regular army commission. His senior captain instructed a first sergeant, "I want you to make an officer of Lieutenant Rosson." Rosson says, "The training was rather rudimentary and simply wouldn't be accepted today. It was a peacetime oriented affair with more emphasis upon spit and polish, cleanliness of barracks and whatnot rather than combat readiness. I never attended the basic course of the infantry school. I went into the war and learned on the job."

When he visited the Dachau concentration camp after its liberation, he recalled, "I was shaken—so much so that when I left I was literally unable to speak as I drove back to the division. I had never seen such depravity and inhuman treatment." Following his service in Italy and France, Rosson qualified for airborne, was involved in the Vietnam conflict before his retirement in 1975 as a general, and resides in Florida.

Ruhlen, George. The commander of the 3d Field Artillery attached to the 9th Armored Division, a 1932 graduate of the USMA, retired on a disability in 1970 as a major general. He lives in San Antonio.

Salomon, Sid. The Ranger captain who captured Pointe et Raz de la Percée at Omaha Beach entered the paper products field after the war. He makes his home in Pennsylvania.

Salter, Cary. The P-47 and P-51 fighter pilot in the Ninth Air Force said, "We were shooting down planes but we knew we were killing people, too. I don't know any of our guys who lost sleep over it. We were there to fight a war and the more we killed, the quicker it would be over and the less likely we would be killed." He became a pharmacist, then presided over a wholesale drug firm. Active in the P-40 Warhawk Pilots Association, he resides in Jackson, Mississippi.

Schueler, Jon. The B-17 navigator, invalided home for physical and emotional disabilities, became a well-known painter. His autobiography, *The Sound of Sleat* was published posthumously in 1999.

Schwarz, Otto. A prisoner of war after the sinking of the USS *Houston*, he endured years of hard labor, beatings, and lack of food in a series of camps. "We were under strict orders that, whenever a Japanese of any rank approached us, the first person seeing him had to shout in good Japanese and call the group to attention. You then all had to properly bow to the person. You had to bow from the hips down with the face tilting up and facing the person. If you deviated from this at all, you very quickly got bashed."

Schwarz recalled that the British captives treated the problem of sanitation far more casually than the Americans and as a consequence suffered a much greater incidence of dysentery. However, they insisted upon maintaining a military mode. "These guys acted as if they were on regimental maneuvers. The British held regular drills—complete uniforms, full field packs—and they would march up and down the hills, and the officers with their little 'dog-chasers,' the little sticks they carried, would be marching alongside of them." The Americans in shorts and ragged garments refused to salute and an intense dislike grew between the two allies.

Shipped to Burma, Schwarz became part of the gangs constructing a railroad much like that described in the film, *The Bridge on the River Kwai*. Along with the prisoners, the Japanese conscripted thousands of local people who, said Schwarz, "died like flies. Entire villages, the entire male populations of villages were just wiped out."

Toward the end of the war, while housed in Saigon, Schwarz and three companions escaped and sought refuge in the French quarter of the city only to be caught up in the Vietnamese effort to oust the French. Jailed by the rebels along with the French, Schwarz convinced his captors that he was an American and was allowed to return to the Japanese prison camp. A U.S. Army officer parachuted in to the camp and officially freed all of the POWs.

"My service in the Navy and World War II were years of great pride and dedication to America. I have been in the presence of men who have cried openly when hearing our National Anthem, which was picked up by a Japanese radio in Saigon. These were the kinds of men I was privileged to serve with. Despite our disadvantage of being ill prepared, outnumbered, and outgunned at the beginning of World War II, and the horrendous ordeal of three and one-half years as Japanese POWs, we never wavered in our loyalty and faith in our country."

In 1948, Schwarz entered the U.S. Postal Service and on retirement in 1980 held a senior management position. He lives in Union, New Jersey.

Shapiro, Alan. After leaving the service, the 87th Division rifleman taught school and now lives in Ridgefield, Connecticut.

Sims, Ed. The paratrooper officer with the 504th Regiment went on inactive reserve after being demobilized, but said, "I returned to active duty because good employment was hard to find and I was more oriented toward military life." He retired as a colonel in 1968, then earned a college degree and held jobs with a title company and, later, as a county probation officer. He lives in New Jersey.

Smith, Robert. The Air Force B-26 pilot in the South Pacific became intelligence director of the Strategic Air Command during the 1950s, where he pioneered in the use of computers for dealing with intelligence. He retired as a lieutenant general.

South, Frank. "The death of FDR [12 April 1945] came as a shock. There was not a dry eye that could be found. I recall leaning against a tree and bawling like an infant." After V-E Day, South's unit became part of Patton's Third Army. For a review before himself and some Soviet officers, Patton ordered clean, pressed uniforms and polished boots, which South considered reasonable. Further instruction to coat helmets with shellac and all arms and vehicles oiled on the surfaces to provide a shine struck the Ranger as foolish because of the prevalence of road dust. "Most of us had long regarded Patton as a bloody popinjay whose exhibitionist streak was witnessed by his dress and pearl-handled revolvers." The medic with the 2d Ranger Battalion used his benefits to study biophysics and physiology. He lives in Maryland.

Southworth, Billy. The B-17 pilot completed his tour in the United Kingdom but was killed on a training flight in 1945.

Stroop, Paul D. A USNA 1926 alumnus, he retired as a vice admiral and died in 1995.

Strange, Glen. The 27th Armored Infantry officer required two years of medical treatment for his wounds before he recovered enough to work in manufacturing. He later became a postmaster in Oklahoma.

Swanson, Wallace. The 101st Airborne company commander worked in the petroleum industry and lives in Alabama.

Taylor, Harold. The 3d Division GI joined the Fort Wayne police department, put in twenty years, and then operated a part-time cabinet-making shop.

Thach, John (Jimmy). The naval aviator says, "Everybody's scared, but it isn't a thing you can let prey on your mind very long because there's always something to do. And you can function just as well, maybe a little better, if you're scared." He retired as a full admiral and died in 1981.

Turner, William (Pappy). The army pilot said, "I did not shoot at anyone in a parachute although I had several chances. I figured he had his problems. Also on the ground he could be captured, some information gained. On one occasion, one of the pilots asked me for permission to strafe the Jap in the parachute. I told him to let his conscience be his guide. He broke off, made a pass at the man, but did not shoot." After the war he worked briefly in private industry before signing on with the New York State Department of Public Works and switched to the Department of Transportation. He now lives in Florida.

Ullom, Madeline. The former army nurse, taken prisoner in the Philippines, now lives in Tucson.

Ulsaker, Carl. The USMA 1942 graduate finished the war with the 90th Division. He collected a master's degree and then taught English at West Point. He retired as a colonel in 1969 and resides in Virginia.

Uzemack, Ed. The 28th Division POW returned to a career as a newspaperman and then entered public relations in Chicago.

Vaccaro, Tony. Born in the United States to Italian émigrés, the 83d Division intelligence specialist had lived in Italy for much of his childhood and early adolescence where he developed an abiding hatred of the fascist philosophy. After V-E Day he signed on as a photographer for the military newspaper *Stars and Stripes*, and then as a civilian remained in Europe several more years building a reputation for his photographs. Back in the States he worked on staff for *Look* and the short-lived but influential *Flair* before a long successful career as a free lancer. He lives in New York City.

Vogel, Walter. The 1937 enlistee in the Navy started his career in the Asiatic Fleet and served on the ill-fated *Houston* in the first months after the war began. Having survived the sinking of the destroyer *Blue* and other adventures, he was promoted to the rank of chief petty officer and assigned to the destroyer *Hyman* engaged in picket duty off Okinawa. The kamikaze hit on the *Hyman* brought a third Purple Heart to Vogel, but the full extent of his wounds only surfaced several months after V-J Day when he collapsed with ruptured lungs, apparently due to the explosion off Okinawa. He recovered after four months of hospitalization and served on a number of ships including support for the war in Korea. He taught at the USNA as well as other institutions and became a commissioned officer. He weathered an attack of blindness before retirement in 1970. He lives in Tennessee.

Walker, Anthony. The Yale graduate and Marine officer remained in the Corps. "I suppose I decided to stay on because I liked the life, was reasonably successful in the war and had nothing else to do, not being qualified or interested in other professions or business." His three sons all became leathernecks. He makes his home in Rhode Island.

Warneke, Bud. The paratrooper with the 508th Parachute Regimental Combat Team won a battlefield commission and remained in the service until 1964 when he retired and began a TV rental service. He lives in North Carolina.

Warriner, Vic. The glider pilot involved in the D day invasion, and the Market Garden and Varsity operations, completed his education at the University of Michigan and became a real estate developer in Texas. He lives in Fort Worth.

Widoff, Gerald. The interpreter with Merrill's Marauders began a career as a violinist with prominent orchestras before starting a chain of music record stores. His home is in New York City.

Yarborough, William. The USMA Class of 1936 paratrooper officer, following World War II, held top staff positions at home and abroad until his retirement in 1971 as a lieutenant general. He lives in North Carolina.

Bibliography

Adair, Charles. Oral History. Annapolis, Maryland: United States Naval Institute.

Alexander, Irvin. *Memoirs of Internment in the Philippines, 1942–45.* West Point: U.S. Military Academy.

Alison, John R. Oral Histories. Maxwell Field, Alabama: United States Air Force Historical Center, 1943, 1944, 1960, 1977, 1979.

Allen, Brooke E. Oral History. Maxwell Field, Alabama: United States Air Force Historical Center, 1965.

Altieri, James. *The Spearheaders.* Indianapolis: Bobbs-Merrill Company, Inc., 1960.

Ambrose, Stephen E. *Citizen Soldiers.* New York: Simon & Schuster, 1997.

Andrusko, Edward. Unpublished Stories. Denver, Co.

Archer, Clark, ed., *Paratroopers' Odyssey.* Hudson, Florida: 517th Parachute Regimental Combat Team Association, 1985.

Ashworth, Frederick. Oral History. Annapolis, Maryland: United States Naval Institute.

Austin, Gordon H. Oral History. Maxwell Field, Alabama: United States Air Force Historical Center, 1982.

Benitez, R.C. *Battle Stations Submerged.* Annapolis, Maryland: *Proceedings,* January 1948.

Bidwell, Sheffield. *The Chindit War.* New York: Macmillan Publishing Co., Inc., 1979.

Blair, Clay. *Ridgway's Paratroopers.* Garden City, New York: Dial Press, 1985.

Bluemel, Clifford. Private Papers: West Point: U.S. Military Academy Library.

Blumenson, Martin. *Mark Clark.* New York: Congdon & Weed, 1984.

Bolt, Jones E. Oral History. Maxwell Field, Alabama: United States Air Force Historical Center, 1984.

Bower, William. Oral History. Maxwell Field, Alabama: United States Air Force Historical Center, 1971.

Bradley, Omar. *A Soldier's Story.* New York: Henry Holt and Company, Inc., 1951.

Breuer, William. *Geronimo!* New York: St. Martin's Press, 1989.

Budge, Joseph. Unpublished Memoir. Moraga, California.

Buffington, Herman. Unpublished Memoir. Jefferson, Georgia.

Bunker, Paul D. *The Bunker Diary.* West Point: U.S. Military Academy Library.

Burchinal, David A. Oral History. Maxwell Field, Alabama: United States Air Force Historical Center, 1975.

Byers, Dick. Unpublished Memoir. Mentor-on-the Lake, Ohio.

Carlton, Paul K. Oral History. Maxwell Field, Alabama: United States Air Force Historical Center, 1979.

Carmichael, Richard. Oral Histories. Maxwell Field, Alabama: United States Air Force Historical Center, 1942, 1980.

Caron, George R. Oral History. Maxwell Field, Alabama: United States Air Force Historical Center, 1975.

Carpenter, John W. Oral History. Maxwell Field, Alabama: United States Air Force Historical Center, 1970.

Cass, Bevan, ed., *History of the 6th Marine Division.* Washington, D.C.: Infantry Journal, Inc., 1948.

Chandler, P. R. Oral History. Maxwell Field, Alabama: United States Air Force Historical Center, 1943.

Chernitsky, Dorothy. *Voices from the Foxholes.* Uniontown, Pennsylvania: Dorothy Chernitsky, 1991.

Cochran, Philip. Oral Histories. Maxwell Field, Alabama: United States Air Force Historical Center, 1943, 1975.

Cole, Hugh M. *The Ardennes: The Battle of the Bulge.* Washington, D.C.: Center of Military History, U.S. Army, 1965.

Cox, Luther C. *Always Fighting the Enemy.* Baltimore: Gateway, 1990.

Craig, Robert. Unpublished Memoir. Winter Haven, Florida.

Craven, Wesley Frank, and James Lea Cate. *The Army Air Force in World War II.* Vol. 1: vi. Chicago: U.S. Air Force History Office, University of Chicago Press, 1948.

Crosby, Harry H. *A Wing and a Prayer.* New York: Harper, 1993.

Cutter, Slade. Oral History. Annapolis, Maryland: United States Naval Institute.

Dacus, W.E. and E. Kitzmann. *As We Lived It—USS Suwannee (CVE-27).* USS *Suwannee* and its Air Groups, 27, 60, & 40. Reunion Association, 1992.

DeHaven, Robert M. Oral History. Maxwell Field, Alabama: United States Air Force Historical Center, 1977.

Dennison, Robert Lee. Oral History. Annapolis, Maryland: United States Naval Institute.

D'Este, Carlo. *Patton: A Genius for War.* New York: Harper Collins, 1995.

Duckworth, George H. Unpublished memoir. Farmington, New Mexico.

Dunn, William. Oral History. Maxwell Field, Alabama: United States Air Force Historical Center, 1973.

Edlin, Robert. Unpublished Manuscript. Corpus Christi, Texas.

Edmonds, Walter D. *They Fought with What They Had.* Washington, D.C.: Center for Air Force History, 1951.

Eisenhower, David. *Eisenhower at War 1943-45.* New York: Random House, 1986.

Eisenhower, Dwight D. *Crusade in Europe.* Garden City, New York: Doubleday & Company, Inc., 1948.

Eisenhower, John. *The Bitter Woods: The Battle of the Bulge.* New York: G.P . Putnam's Sons, 1969.

Ellington, Paul. Oral History. American Air Power Heritage Museum, Midland, Texas, 1991.

Ellis, John. *Cassino: The Hollow Victory.* New York: McGraw-Hill Book Company, 1984.

Ellis, Richard. Oral History. Maxwell Field, Alabama: United States Air Force Historical Center, 1987.

Emmens, Robert G. Oral History. Maxwell Field, Alabama: United States Air Force Historical Center, 1982.

Eubank, Eugene. Oral Histories. Maxwell Field, Alabama: United States Air Force Historical Center, 1942, 1982.

Fitzgerald, Ed. *A Penny An Inch.* New York: Atheneum, 1985.

Frank, Richard B. *Guadalcanal.* New York: Random House, 1990.

Freeman, Roger A., with Alan Crouchman and Vic Maslen. *The Mighty Eighth War Diary.* London: Motorbooks International, 1990.

Gavin, James M. *On to Berlin.* New York: Viking Press, 1978.

Gelb, Norman. *Desperate Venture: The Story of Operation Torch.* New York: William Morrow and Company, 1992.

Gerevas, Larry. Unpublished Memoir. Napa, California.

Golubock, Ralph. *Hello, Pathway: A Bomber Pilot's Memories of Love and War.* Unpublished Manuscript. St. Louis.

Goodson, James. Oral History. American Air Power Heritage Museum, Midland, Texas: 1991.

Grashio, Samuel C. and Bernard Norling. *Return to Freedom.* Spokane, Washington: University Press, 1982

Hagerman, Bart., ed. *U.S. Airborne: 50th Anniversary.* Paducah, Kentucky: Turner Publishing Company, 1990.

Hall, Leonard G. *Brother of the Fox: Company F, 172d Infantry.* Orange, Texas, 1985.

Hallden, Charles. Unpublished Memoir. Madeira Beach, Florida.

Hamilton, Tom. Unpublished Memoir. Santa Barbara, California.

Hammel, Eric. *Guadalcanal: Starvation Island.* New York, Crown, 1987.

———*Munda Trail.* New York: Orion Books, 1989.

Hannon, Philip. Unpublished Memoir. Ellicott City, Maryland.

Hanson, Robert. *Memoirs.* Unpublished manuscript.

Harmon, Ernest. Oral History. Carlisle, Pennsylvania: United States Army History Institute.

Harrington, Jasper. Oral History. Maxwell Field, Alabama: United States Air Force Historical Center, 1981.

Hastings, Max. *Overlord: D-Day and the Battle for Normandy.* New York: Simon & Schuster, 1984.

Hawkins, Ian L. *B-17s Over Berlin.* Washington, D.C.: Brassey's, 1990.

Hechler, Ken. *The Bridge at Remagen.* Missoula, Montana: Pictorial Histories Publishing Company, 1993.

Heinl, Robert Debs, Jr. *Soldiers of the Sea.* Annapolis: Naval Institute Press, 1962.

Herder, Harry J. Unpublished Memoir. Hayward, Wisconsin.

Hill, David (Tex). Oral History. Maxwell Field, Alabama: United States Air Force Historical Center, 1977.

Holloway, Bruce K. Oral History. Maxwell Field, Alabama: United States Air Force Historical Center, 1977.

Holloway, James L., III. *Historical Perspective: The Battle of Surigao Strait:* Naval Engineer's Journal, September 1994.

Hostetter, Philip H. *Doctor and Soldier in the South Pacific.* Unpublished manuscript. Manhattan, Kansas.

Howard, Thomas. *All to this End: The Road to and through the Philippines.* Unpublished Manuscript. St. Charles, Missouri.

Howze, Hamilton. Oral History. Carlisle, Pennsylvania: United States Army Military History Institute.

Hoyt, Edwin P. *Submarines at War.* Briarcliff Manor, New York: Stein and Day, 1983.

Hudson, Ed. *The History of the USS Cabot (CVL-28).* Hickory, North Carolina: 1988.

Jackson, Robert. *War Stories.* Unpublished Memoir. Anacortes, Washington.

Johnson, Robert S. Oral History. American Air Power Heritage Museum, Midland Texas: 1977.

Kunz, William J. Unpublished Memoir. Rockford, Illinois: 1996.

LaMagna, Sam. *Silent Victory: Fox Company, 169th Regimental Combat Team, 43d Infantry Division.* Unpublished Manuscript. Ocala, Florida.

Leckie, Robert. *Strong Men Armed.* New York: Random House, 1962.

Lee, Ulysses. *The Employment of Negro Troops.* Washington, D.C.: Center of Military History, 1994.

Leinbaugh, Harold P. and John D. Campbell. *The Men of Company K: The Autobiography of a World War II Rifle Company.* New York: William Morrow and Company, 1985.

Lynd, J.Q. *Château de Fontenay : Episode tragique de la libération 1944.* Unpublished Memoir. Stillwater, Oklahoma.

———*Legacy of Valor* [Video Script] South Hill, Virginia: 90th Division Association.

MacArthur, Douglas. *Reminiscences.* New York: McGraw-Hill Book Company, 1964.

MacDonald, Charles. *A Time for Trumpets.* New York: William Morrow and Company, 1985.

———*Company Commander.* New York: Bantam, 1987.

———*The Mighty Endeavor: American Armed Forces in the European Theater in World War II.* New York: Oxford University Press, 1969.

McClintock, D. H. Narrative. Washington, D.C.: U.S. Naval Historical Center, 1945.

McClure, John. Oral History. American Air Power Heritage Museum, Midland Texas, 1991.

McCubbin, James. Unpublished Memoirs. Garberville, California.

McManus, John. *The Deadly Brotherhood.* Novato, California: Presidio Press, 1998.

Mack, William. Oral History. Annapolis, Maryland: United States Naval Institute.

Manchester, William. *American Caesar.* Boston: Little, Brown & Company, 1978.

Martin, Harry. Unpublished memoir. Mt. Arlington, New Jersey

Merillat, Herbert C. *Guadalcanal Remembered.* New York: Dodd, Mead & Company, 1982.

Milkovics, Lewis. *The Devils Have Landed.* Longwood, Florida: Creative Printing and Publishing, 1993.

Miller, Thomas G., Jr. *The Cactus Air Force.* New York: Harper & Row, 1969.

Mills, James. Unpublished memoir. Vandalia, Ohio

Moore, Ellis O. *Notes on Leaving Okinawa.* Pelham, New York: Privately Published, 1988.

Morison, Samuel Eliot *The Battle of the Atlantic.* Boston: Little, Brown & Company, 1984.

———*Coral Sea, Midway and Submarine Actions.* Boston: Little, Brown & Company, 1984.

———*The Struggle for Guadalcanal.* Boston, Little, Brown & Company, 1949.

———*The Rising Sun in the Pacific.* Boston, Little, Brown & Company, 1961.

Morton, Louis. *The Fall of the Philippines, U.S. Army in World War II.* Washington, D.C.: Center of Military History, U.S. Army, 1953.

Muehrcke, Robert, ed., *Orchids in the Mud.* Chicago: Privately Published, 1985.

Mueller, Arndt. *Hill 400: The Destiny and the Agony.* Monograph.

Murphy, Robert. *Diplomat among Warriors.* Garden City, New York: Doubleday & Company, Inc. 1964.

Murray, S.S. Oral History. Annapolis, Maryland: United States Naval Institute.

Old, Archie, Jr. Oral History. Maxwell Field, Alabama: Historical Research Center, Air University, 1982.

Olson, John E. Assisted by Frank O. Anders. *Anywhere, Anytime: The History of the 57th Infantry (PS)* Houston: John Olson, 1991.

——*O'Donnell: The Andersonville of the Pacific.* Houston: John Olson, 1985.

Patton, George. *War as I Knew It.* Boston: Houghton Mifflin, 1947.

Philos, C.D. and Ernie Hayhow. *1987 History of the 83d Infantry Division.* Hillsdale, Michigan: Ferguson Communications, 1986.

Potter, E.B. *Bull Halsey.* Annapolis, Maryland: United States Naval Institute, 1985.

Potts, Ramsay. Oral History. United States Air Force Historical Center, Maxwell Field, Alabama: 1960.

Prange, Gordon W. *Dec. 7 1941.* New York: McGraw-Hill Book Company, 1988.

Pyle, Ernie. *At Dawn We Slept.* New York: McGraw-Hill Book Company, 1981.

——*Here Is Your War.* New York: Henry Holt and Company, 1943.

——*Brave Men.* New York: Henry Holt and Company, 1944.

——*Last Chapter.* New York: Henry Holt and Company, 1946.

Rants, Hanford. *My Memories of World War II.* Unpublished Manuscript. Downey, California.

Rodman, Gage. Unpublished Memoir. Hurricane, Utah.

Rooney, Andy. *My War.* New York: Random House, 1996.

Rosson, William. Oral History. Carlisle, Pennsylvania: United States Army Military History Institute.

Ryan, Cornelius. *A Bridge Too Far.* New York: Simon & Schuster, 1974.

Salomon, Sidney. *2d Ranger Infantry Battalion.* Doylestown, Pennsylvania: Birchwood Books, 1991.

Samson, Jack. *Chennault.* New York: Doubleday & Company, Inc., 1987.

Schueler, Jon. *The Sound of Sleat.* Unpublished Manuscript.

Schultz, Duane. *The Maverick War.* New York: St. Martin's Press, 1987

——*The Doolittle Raid.* New York: St. Martin's Press, 1988.

Schwarz, Otto. Unpublished Memoir.

Seibert, Donald A. Unpublished Memoir. Fort Belvoir, Virginia.

Shapiro, Alan. Unpublished Memoir. Ridgefield, Connecticut.

Sherrod, Robert. *Tarawa: The Story of a Battle,* New York: Duell, Sloan and Pearce, 1944.

Sledge, E.B. *With the Old Breed.* Novato, California: Presidio Press, 1981.

Smith, John F. *Hellcats Over the Philippine Deep.* Manhattan, Kansas: Sunflower Press, 1995.

Smith, Robert. Oral History. Maxwell Field, Alabama: United States Air Force Historical Center, 1983.

Spector, Ronald. *Eagle Against the Sun: The Amereican War with Japan*. New York: Free Press, 1985.

Stroop, Paul. Oral History. Annapolis, Maryland: United States Naval Institute.

Svihra, Albert. Transcripts of letters to his family and Diary. West Point: U.S. Military Academy Library.

Teeples, Robert. *Jackson County Veterans*, Vol. II. Black River Falls, Wisconsin, 1986.

Thach, John (Jimmy). Oral History. Annapolis, Maryland: United States Naval Institute.

Tregaskis, Richard. *Guadalcanal Diary*. New York: Random House, 1943.

Ullom, Madeline. Memoir. Washington, D.C.: U.S. Army Center for Military History.

Van der Vat, Dan. *The Pacific Campaign*. New York: Simon & Schuster, 1991.

Walker, Anthony, ed., *Memorial to the Men of C/P Company, 4th Marine Raider Battalion*. Middletown, Rhode Island, 1994.

Ward, Norvell. Oral History. Annapolis, Maryland: United States Naval Institute.

White, W.L. *They Knew They Were Expendable*. New York: Harcourt Brace and Company, 1942.

Index